Special Edition

Using

Using

Visual Basic 5

Second Edition

Special Edition

Using

Using
Visual Basic 5

Second Edition

Mike McKelvy
Brian Siler
Jeff Spotts

Special Edition Using Visual Basic 5, Second Edition

Library of Congress Catalog No.: 97-68700

ISBN: 0-7897-1288-1

99 98   6 5 4 3

Interpretation of the printing code: the rightmost double-digit number is the year of the book's printing; the rightmost single-digit number, the number of the book's printing. For example, a printing code of 97-1 shows that the first printing of the book occurred in 1997.

Screen reproductions in this book were created using Collage Plus from Inner Media, Inc., Hollis, NH.

Contents at a Glance

Table of Contents

II | Visual Basic Fundamentals

V | ActiveX Controls

VII | Object-Oriented Programming

Credits

PRESIDENT
Roland Elgey

SENIOR VICE PRESIDENT/PUBLISHING
Don Fowley

GENERAL MANAGER
Joe Muldoon

MANAGER OF PUBLISHING OPERATIONS
Linda H. Buehler

TITLE MANAGER
Bradley L. Jones

EDITORIAL SERVICES DIRECTOR
Carla Hall

MANAGING EDITOR
Caroline D. Roop

ACQUISITIONS MANAGER
Cheryl D. Willoughby

ACQUISITIONS EDITOR
Kelly Marshall

PRODUCT DIRECTOR
Chris Nelson

PRODUCTION EDITOR
Matthew B. Cox

EDITORS
Kelli M. Brooks, Patricia Kinyon,
Bill McManus, Susan Ross Moore

COORDINATOR OF EDITORIAL SERVICES
Maureen A. McDaniel

WEBMASTER
Thomas H. Bennett

PRODUCT MARKETING MANAGER
Kourtnaye Sturgeon

ASSISTANT PRODUCT MARKETING MANAGER
Gretchen Schlesinger

TECHNICAL EDITOR
Lowell Mauer

SOFTWARE SPECIALIST
Brandon K. Penticuff

ACQUISITIONS COORDINATOR
Carmen Krikorian

SOFTWARE RELATIONS COORDINATOR
Susan D. Gallagher

SOFTWARE COORDINATOR
Andrea Duvall

EDITORIAL ASSISTANTS
Travis Bartlett
Jennifer L. Chisholm

BOOK DESIGNER
Ruth Harvey

COVER DESIGNER
Sandra Schroeder

PRODUCTION TEAM
Marcia Deboy, Jenny Earhart,
Maribeth Echard, Laura A. Knox

INDEXER
Jennifer Eberhardt

Composed in *Century Old Style* and *ITC Franklin Gothic* by Que Corporation.

My work in this book is dedicated to my wife, Tina, for encouraging me to excel with her quiet devotion and unquestioned love; and to my daughter, Lauren, for her unfailing love and support. Thanks to both of you for understanding why Daddy couldn't always play outside with you this summer, and especially to Lauren for lighting up my office every time you came back in with your snaggletoothed smile!

—Jeff Spotts

To my parents, who bought me my first computer...

—Brian Siler

About the Authors

Brian Siler has spent the past two years working as a programmer analyst for a major hotel corporation, developing their executive information system in Visual Basic. Brian is a graduate of the University of Memphis with a Bachelor of Science degree in Computer Science. He has developed applications using Visual Basic, C, HTML and SQL on a variety of platforms, including PCs, AS/400, UNIX, and Vax. Brian may be contacted via e-mail at **bsiler@bigfoot.com**.

Jeff Spotts is a programmer analyst for a major express transportation company by day; by night, he teaches Visual Basic programming courses at Memphis' State Technical Institute. He also creates custom-designed software systems for individuals and businesses. His specialty is creating database applications using Visual Basic as a front-end interface to a variety of database engines. He has been involved with computer hardware and software since the late 1970s and has been programming in Visual Basic since just after its introduction. Jeff can be contacted via e-mail at **jspotts@bigfoot.com**.

Mike McKelvy is owner and president of McKelvy Software Systems, a software consulting firm in Birmingham, Alabama. He specializes in the development of database applications. Mike has been developing software for business and engineering applications for over 15 years and has written a variety of engineering and financial analysis programs for a number of businesses. Mike is also the author of *Using Visual Basic 4* and the co-author of Que's *Special Edition Using Visual Basic 4* and *Visual Basic Expert Solutions*.

Loren D. Eidahl is the president of Cornerstone Technology Systems (CTS), an Internet consulting firm specializing in providing complete Internet business solutions, ranging from Internet access to total integrated solutions. CTS has developed several successful professional business applications, including the *Gallery* point of sale application and the *NetSuite* Internet business toolkit. Currently, CTS is developing products to assist business owners who want to perform secure electronic commerce over the Internet. When not hacking code, writing computer books, or speaking about business on the Internet, he can be found somewhere in Northern Minnesota trout fishing. Loren can be reached via e-mail at **leidahl@cornerstonetech.com** or on the Web at **http://www.cornerstonetech.com**.

Bob Reselman is a Senior Software Engineer at Gateway 2000 where he is involved with designing platform architecture. He also teaches Object Oriented Programming using Visual Basic at Western Iowa Tech Community College. Bob has been programming with Visual Basic since Version 1.0. He lives in Sioux City, Iowa with his spouse Dorothy Lifka and two daughters Genvieve and Alexandra. Bob can be reached at **reselbob@pionet.net and http://www.pionet.net/~reselbob**. He likes motorcycles and reggae.

Rory Job was a contributing author of Que's *Web Development with Visual Basic 5*.

Acknowledgments

We wish to acknowledge our Acquisitions Editor, Kelly Marshall, whose amiable demeanor, expert guidance, and levelheadedness made our introduction into the world of publishing not only painless, but quite enjoyable. We will owe the longevity of our writing careers to her.

—Jeff Spotts and Brian Siler

Tell Us What You Think!

As the reader of this book, *you* are our most important critic and commentator. We value your opinion and want to know what we're doing right, what we could do better, what areas you'd like to see us publish in, and any other words of wisdom you're willing to pass our way.

As the Executive Editor for the Programming team at Macmillan Computer Publishing, I welcome your comments. You can fax, email, or write me directly to let me know what you did or didn't like about this book—as well as what we can do to make our books stronger.

Please note that I cannot help you with technical problems related to the topic of this book, and that due to the high volume of mail I receive, I might not be able to reply to every message.

When you write, please be sure to include this book's title and author as well as your name and phone or fax number. I will carefully review your comments and share them with the author and editors who worked on the book.

Fax: 317-817-7070

E-mail: adv_prog@mcp.com

Mail: Brad Jones
          Executive Editor
          Macmillan Computer Publishing
          201 West 103rd Street
          Indianapolis, IN 46290 USA

Introduction

Congratulations! You have decided to embark on learning Visual Basic.

This is an exciting time; there never has been a better time for Visual Basic programmers. While Visual Basic has always made it easy to develop Windows programs, through the years it has matured into a true professional development language and environment. You still can quickly create Windows programs with Visual Basic, but now you also can write enterprise-level client/server programs and robust database applications. While this is enough to get you hyped up about programming in Visual Basic, there's even more available in Visual Basic version 5.

If you have kept up with current events, you know that the Internet promises to revolutionize computing. You also might have seen enough of Internet programming to think that it is reserved for only a select group of programmers. In version 5, Visual Basic gives you a number of tools that let you work with the Internet. There are tools that let you easily connect your programs to the Internet and include browser capabilities in your programs. In addition, you now can create ActiveX documents and ActiveX controls from Visual Basic. Because ActiveX is the cornerstone of Microsoft's Internet strategy, this puts you right in the middle of the action. And the really good news is that all of your ActiveX pieces can be used in non-Internet programs, as well, extending the usefulness of any ActiveX components you create.

Microsoft also has integrated Visual Basic for Applications (VBA) into all the components of Office 97, Project, and other programs. Because VBA is the core language component of Visual Basic, this means that all your knowledge of Visual Basic can be applied to writing applications and macros for other products. And because Microsoft has licensed VBA 5.0 to over 40 other companies, you will soon be able to write applications and macros for those programs, as well. All this benefit comes from your Visual Basic knowledge.

Okay, so now you are excited about learning Visual Basic. Your next question is, "What will this book do for me?" ■

Fundamentals

Although this book presents a lot of material on advanced Visual Basic programming, you can't just jump into these topics and expect to understand them. You need a good foundation from which to work.

In Part I of the book, "Building Your First Application," you are introduced to what Visual Basic can do and how to work in the development environment.

Chapter 1, "Introduction to Visual Basic 5," discusses some of the new features that have been added to VB.

Chapter 2, "Introduction to the Development Environment," takes you on a tour of the newly enhanced Integrated Development Environment. Even if you are not new to VB, be sure to read this section to learn about the new IDE.

In Chapter 3, "Creating Your First Program," we instruct you step-by-step on how to build an application in Visual Basic.

Part II, "Visual Basic Fundamentals," covers the basics to get you started on your programming adventure. Chapter 4, "Working with Forms and Controls," takes you on a tour of forms and controls, which are the building blocks of every program you will create in Visual Basic. You will see how you can manipulate forms and controls by modifying their properties and how you can perform tasks with their methods.

In Chapter 5, "Adding Menus and Toolbars to Your Program," and Chapter 6, "Using Dialogs to Get Information," you look at how you can enhance your programs by using menus, toolbars, and dialog boxes. These program components give your users an interface that is familiar because of their use of other Windows programs. Properly using menus, toolbars, and dialog boxes makes your programs more intuitive to the user. You also examine the Event model, which is the cornerstone of programming in a Windows environment. Chapter 7, "Responding to the User," discusses how Visual Basic programs become interactive. You'll learn how to make your programs react to the various actions your users can initiate.

In Chapter 8, "Programming Basics," you are led into the world of programming commands, structures, and variables. Visual Basic is built upon the solid foundation of the BASIC language. This programming language is rich in features and functions that let you write programs to handle any task. You learn how to create and use variables, how to perform math and string operations, and how to control your program through the use of decisions and loops.

Chapter 9, "Displaying and Printing Reports," discusses how to output information to the screen and printer in a meaningful way. Finally, Chapter 10, "Managing Your Project," discusses how you can organize your programming environment for efficiency. You'll learn how easy it is to create forms and code that are reusable. You'll also see how you can distribute your finished program.

Creating the Face of Your Program

After you have learned some of the basics of creating programs, you are ready for more detailed material. In Part III, "Building User Interfaces," you are introduced to some of the concepts of program design. Chapter 11, "Designing User Interfaces," discusses why it is important to design your program before you start writing code. You will also see some of the things that make a bad user interface and learn how to avoid some of the common design mistakes.

In Chapter 12, "Working with Graphics," and Chapter 13, "Working with Text, Fonts, and Colors," you will learn about using text and graphics in your programs. You will see how to work with both formatted and unformatted text, and how fonts and colors affect the way that the text appears to your users. You will also see how you can use graphics to enhance your user interface, analyze data, or even create a drawing program.

Finally, in Chapter 14, "Building a Multiple Document Interface," you will learn how to create a Multiple Document Interface (MDI) program. This type of program allows your users to work with multiple windows contained within one main window. You'll see how MDI applications differ from those created with single forms.

Working with Controls

Controls are the backbone of every program that you will create in Visual Basic. Part IV, "Working with Visual Basic Controls," teaches you about most of the controls that you will encounter in Visual Basic programming.

Chapter 15, "Working with the Standard Controls," teaches you about the standard controls that have been a part of Visual Basic since the beginning. These controls are the ones that are most often used in your programs. The discussion shows you some of the basics of the controls, as well as some advanced techniques, and shows you the new features of some of these controls.

Three other chapters will teach you how to use some of the controls that are common to most Windows 95 programs and the new controls that were introduced in Visual Basic 5. Chapter 16, "Using the Windows Common Controls," shows how to create toolbars to supplement your menus, status bars, and progress bars to keep your users informed. Chapter 17, "Using Containers in Your Programs," discusses some of the new controls that Visual Basic now includes, such as the Flex Grid, a new grid control that will allow you to create spreadsheet type applications or to provide browsing capabilities for database programs. Chapter 18, "Exploring New Visual Basic 5 Controls," discusses how to group the various types of controls for better functionality.

The last chapter in this section, Chapter 19, "Advanced Control Techniques," introduces you to some advanced control concepts. You'll learn how to work with control arrays, how to add and delete controls while your program is running, as well as how to use classes to enhance your controls' capabilities.

Then we have an entire section of the book devoted to creating ActiveX controls and ActiveX documents—Part V, "ActiveX Controls." These components can be used in Visual Basic programs, Internet applications, or other ActiveX-enabled programs. Chapters 20 through 23 take you from creating your first ActiveX control through several phases, until you finally learn how to build ActiveX documents.

Database Features in Action

Database programs make up a large percentage of all programs in use in the business world today. These programs range in complexity from a simple program for managing a mailing list to a program to handle the power bills for all the customers of a major utility.

Part VI, "Databases," takes you through the process of building database applications to meet a variety of needs. Chapter 24, "Database Design and Normalization," and Chapter 25, "Using the Data Manager," discuss how to create and manipulate a database. You continue in Chapter 26, "Using Data Controls and Reports," by learning how to quickly create applications by using the Data control and data-bound controls. Chapter 27, "Doing More with Bound Controls," enhances those skills. Chapter 28, "Improving Data Access with the Data Access Objects," shows you how much programming power is available for creating database applications. In Chapter 29, "Understanding SQL," you also discover how to use the powerful commands of Structured Query Language to retrieve and modify information in a database. Ways to access databases in remote locations are covered in Chapter 30, "Using the Remote Data Objects."

While single-user, PC-based database applications are important, they are not the only database applications you will want to build. Therefore, Chapter 31, "Multi-User Databases," discusses some of the considerations required when implementing multi-user applications. You will also learn how to connect your programs to databases through ODBC. This will give you access to a wide range of PC, mini-computer, and mainframe databases.

How OLE Helps Your Programs

OLE—or ActiveX, as Microsoft is now calling it—provides a powerful means of allowing programs to work together. Using OLE techniques, you can embed Word or Excel documents in your applications; or, more importantly for many businesses, you can create your own multi-tier client/server programs. By building ActiveX DLLs and EXEs, you can have a server that handles the business rules while other programs handle the interface with the user.

Part VII, "Object-Oriented Programming," starts out in Chapter 32, "Using Classes in Visual Basic," by showing you how to build classes that can be used in OLE applications. The section continues with a discussion of the various "flavors" of Visual Basic in Chapter 33, "Visual Basic versus VBScript versus VBA." Part VII concludes this part with an interesting topic, Chapter 34, "Working with Sound and Multimedia," where you'll learn how to liven up your applications by adding multimedia elements.

Advanced Techniques

Finally, in Part VIII, "Advanced Visual Basic Programming," you'll expand on the fundamentals covered earlier in the book. You will learn how you can access Windows API functions to add even more capabilities to your programs in Chapter 35, "Accessing the Windows 32 API." You will also look at some more advanced techniques for working with forms, controls, and the Visual Basic programming language in Chapter 36, "Advanced Form Techniques," and Chapter 37, "Advanced Code Techniques."

Obtaining Materials to Complement What You Learn

Although the hard-copy book is the main part of the package, we also have supporting and supplementary materials available at the Que Web site. As you would expect, you will find complete code listings for all the projects presented in the book. You also will find some other great things:

- **Articles related to some of the chapters**—These are short discussions of programming techniques that did not quite fit into the chapters of the book.

- **Full text of chapters from other Que books**—Several chapters point you to another book for related information, such as how to create a relation in a database by using Access.

- **Microsoft white papers**—Microsoft puts out a number of reports known as *white papers* on many subjects, such as database security or using the Windows API. These papers provide a wealth of information on particular subjects. A few of these papers that should be useful to you are included.

- **Sample controls**—There are a multitude of third-party ActiveX controls out there for you to use in your Visual Basic programs. With the permission of the vendors, we included sample controls and demo programs for some of the most popular third-party products.

What's Special About the Special Edition?

This book covers a lot of material related to Visual Basic. Each topic is explained, from the most basic to the most complex, in a manner that's easy to understand. The book walks you through tasks when needed for learning now and arranges reference material for ready access when you need a quick answer or solution. Also provided is more than text about the topics; we also give you graphics to enhance your understanding, real-world examples that let you see how the concepts can be applied, and sample projects that show how we implemented the programming concepts.

Several type and font conventions are used in this book to help make reading it easier:

- *Italic type* is used to emphasize the author's points or to introduce new terms.
- Screen messages, code listings, and command samples appear in monospace typeface.
- URLs, newsgroups, Internet addresses, and anything you are asked to type appears in **boldface**.
- Keyboard hotkeys are indicated with <u>underlining</u>. For example, if you see the command <u>T</u>ools, <u>O</u>ptions, pressing Alt and T causes the Tools menu to appear.

Various code listings have been placed on the Web site for this book and can be downloaded from **www.mcp.com/info/0-7897/0-7897-1288-1**. Having access to the code will enable you to work with the entire code listing. The code listings that are available on the Web site will have the code's file name included in the listing headers in this book at the beginning of the code listing.

TIP Tips present short advice on a quick or often overlooked procedure.

NOTE Notes provide additional information that might help you avoid problems, or offer advice that relates to the topic.

CAUTION

Cautions warn you about potential problems that a procedure might cause, unexpected results, and mistakes to avoid.

▶ **See** these cross-references for more information on a particular topic.

Sidebar

Longer discussions not integral to the flow of the chapter are set aside as sidebars. Look for these sidebars to find out even more information.

TROUBLESHOOTING

What is a troubleshooting section? Troubleshooting sections anticipate common problems in the form of a question. The response provides you with practical suggestions for solving these problems.

ON THE WEB

The On the Web icon is placed next to text that contains an Internet address to Web sites relating to the topic at hand.

Building Your First Application

Introduction to Visual Basic 5

What kinds of programs can you write in Visual Basic?

Visual Basic makes it easy for you to create simple and complex Windows programs, as well as your own customized ActiveX documents, ActiveX controls, and Visual Basic add-ins.

What are the new features of Visual Basic 5?

Visual Basic 5 is full of new and improved features and controls that make it possible for you to create more powerful programs faster than ever.

What is object-oriented programming?

You learn how Visual Basic uses object-oriented techniques to create programs that are powerful, robust, and efficient.

If you have visited a local computer store lately, you've seen that there is an overwhelming number of software packages that you can purchase for your computer. In fact, there are literally thousands of programs available that run under Windows 95, not including those written by companies and individuals for their own use. Looking through the software titles, you can find game programs, productivity programs (such as word processors and spreadsheets), communications programs, databases, and many others. And if you have surfed the Internet, you've seen even more types of programs there.

In addition to all these commercial or publicly available programs, many companies need custom programs to handle their business. These programs can range from custom report writers that prepare expense statements to complex client/server programs that handle billing by using the information stored on a mainframe. Whatever the case may be, one thing these programs probably have in common is a Windows "look-and-feel." Visual Basic makes this easy.

Not content just to use available "off-the-shelf" software, you have decided to embark on the adventure of creating your own programs. Well, you've come to the right place and chosen the right programming language. Visual Basic is capable of producing almost any program that your imagination can come up with, including the following:

- Simple single-purpose applications
- Games
- Point-of-sale systems
- Internationally distributed database applications

And while another programming language might be better suited to a particular specialized situation, Visual Basic is perhaps the most versatile and easy-to-use programming language available. ■

Exploring the New Features of Visual Basic 5

As with a new version of any product, Visual Basic 5 incorporates a number of new and enhanced features that make it more powerful and easier to use than previous versions. In addition to a new and improved development environment (IDE), VB version 5.0 includes some performance enhancements. One of the most requested features for Visual Basic was the capability to compile a program to *native code*, or code that is optimized specifically for the microprocessor on which it runs. Microsoft has finally granted this wish. VB5's native code compiler allows your programs to run much faster than before. Also, a faster forms engine greatly enhances the speed of loading forms, adding to the improved performance of applications created with VB5.

In addition to these two performance features, there are a number of other major features that were added to version 5 of Visual Basic. These features are covered in functional groups in the next few sections.

- A native code compiler and improved forms engine make your programs run faster.
- The development environment has been enhanced to make entering code and designing forms easier.
- A variety of program types—other than just the standard EXE, such as DLLs and OCXs—can be created.
- A slew of new controls has been added, including several specifically designed for using the Internet.

Native Code Compiler and Other General Features

One of the key general features of Visual Basic is the capability to compile your programs to native code, much as you can do with C++. As stated previously, this gives you faster programs.

However, don't confuse native code with code that doesn't require the Visual Basic runtime library. Native-code compiled programs are optimized for the microprocessor(s) that they run on; however, the Visual Basic runtime library is still required to provide a fully functional program.

N O T E   The Visual Basic *runtime library* contains functions needed to operate your program. For example, the library includes the code for drawing a window on the screen. As a programmer you may not be aware of such functions, so distributing your program may involve including some additional files. ▓

Visual Basic also gives you some new design capabilities. As always, you can create programs that use a series of independent forms to display and handle information, or you can create Multiple Document Interface (MDI) programs (which have one main "parent" form and one or more internal "child" forms). Visual Basic 5 also has added the capability to create programs that will run inside a Web browser, either on your local machine or anywhere in the world via the Internet!

Another new feature is the capability to edit multiple projects in a single Visual Basic session. You'll find this to be a very convenient tool when you use such other new features as custom-created ActiveX controls and Dynamic Link Libraries (DLLs). These types of programs typically involve interaction among multiple VB projects. Therefore, the capability to switch between related projects or compile several projects at a time is very useful.

Development Environment Features

If you have used previous versions of Visual Basic, you will notice an entirely new interface the first time you start the program (see Figure 1.1). The interface has been redesigned to be more compatible with Microsoft's other programming languages—Visual C++, Visual J++, and so on. This makes it easier for programmers who work in multiple environments to move back and forth between them. In fact, the default installations of many of Microsoft's development products now share a common "parent" directory (usually C:\Program Files\DevStudio\).

All of the various windows that make up the Visual Basic development environment are now set up in an MDI-style interface contained within a parent Microsoft Visual Basic form (see Figure 1.2). This makes it easier to manage all the pieces of your program. Many of the windows, such as the Toolbox, Properties window, and Debug window are *dockable*, meaning that they can be placed in a fixed position that remains consistent as you work in the environment. A handy new Form Layout window shows you at a glance how all of your application's forms will be placed on the screen at runtime.

FIG. 1.1
Visual Basic version 5.0 sports a totally new user interface.

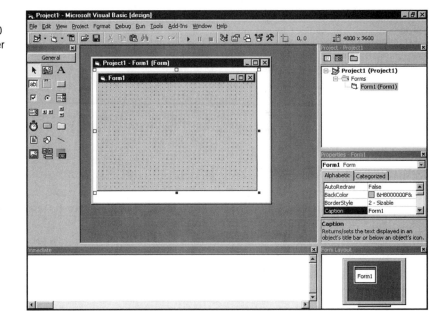

Properties
window

FIG. 1.2
In the new development environment, all windows are contained within the Visual Basic "parent" window.

Toolbox

Form Layout window

Immediate
(Debug) window

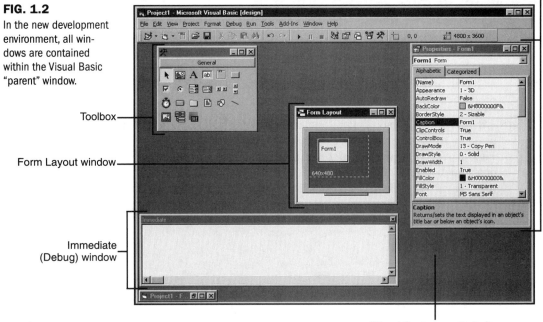

Visual Basic parent window

Other great features of the development environment include the following:

- The capability to edit multiple projects simultaneously
- Dockable toolbars and development windows
- Code editor enhancements, including a more robust, context-sensitive right-click menu
- A richer debugging environment
- Pop-up lists to help you remember the syntax of available functions, methods, and properties.

Of course, if you're resistant to change or just don't like the new development environment, Visual Basic 5 has an option to enable you to return to the "classic" Single Document Interface (SDI) environment.

▶ **See** "Understanding the Environment's Key Features," **p. 24**

Enhancements to the Code Editor

Because a great deal of the work done in creating programs takes place in the code editor, Microsoft has added some new features that make it easier to use. These features include the following:

- *Drop-down properties list*   Displays a dynamic list of the properties and methods available for an object. You can select the property or method by typing only the first couple of characters instead of having to type out the entire word. Pressing Enter or the spacebar selects the desired entry in the list. This saves time and cuts down on typographical errors.
- *Quick Info*   Provides you with the syntax of a function, statement, or method. This information appears in the form of an oversized ToolTip. Having this information appear on-screen saves you the trouble of looking it up in the Help file.
- *Parameter Info*   Displays the parameters that are required for a particular function or method. This is similar to Quick Info.
- *The Data Tips window*   While in Break mode, displays as a ToolTip the value of a variable over which the mouse pointer is placed.
- *Block Comment commands*   Allow you to comment out an entire section of code simply by selecting the code and invoking the command. Similarly, you can remove the comment character from the block of code. This makes it easier to enable and disable sections of code for debugging or other reasons.

New Database Features

Since version 3, Visual Basic has been able to access a native database—the Jet database engine that it shares with Microsoft Access. With each new version of Visual Basic, more and more powerful database features have been added. Version 5 is no exception. Also, the new ODBCDirect functionality provides a truly efficient mechanism for dealing directly with Open Database Connectivity (ODBC)-compliant database engines.

N O T E Most database features are available only in the Professional and Enterprise Editions of Visual Basic. ■

A nice new database feature is the Visual Data Manager application that is automatically installed as an add-in to the Visual Basic environment (see Figure 1.3). This add-in makes it easy for you to create and edit the structure of a database, as well as to input and edit the actual data. Additionally, the Visual Data Manager lets you create, test, and save SQL statements for use in your programs. As a bonus, the full source code for the Visual Data Manager add-in is included so you can study and utilize its data management techniques. (If you're a user of an earlier version of Visual Basic and used the old Data Manager add-in, give Visual Data Manager a try. It's a lot better!)

FIG. 1.3

The Visual Data Manager is a powerful new add-in for working with databases.

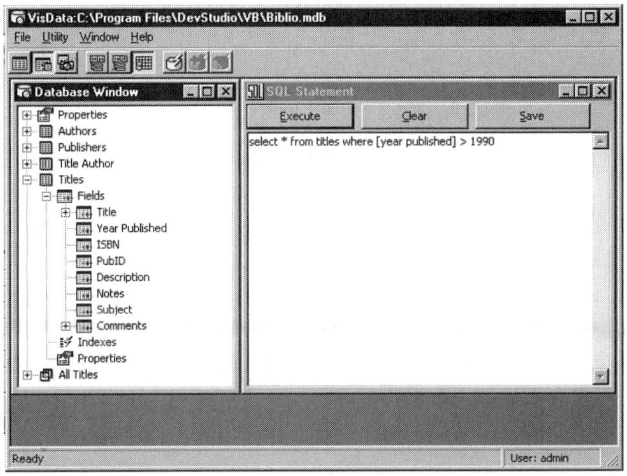

Version 3 of the Jet engine, which appeared in Visual Basic 4 and Microsoft Access 95, added the capability to replicate databases. This was a great feature for allowing multiple locations to work on the data and then combining all the changes into a central master database. Version 5 of Visual Basic takes this a step further with version 3.5 of the Jet engine. Now you can do *partial* replication of a database, meaning that you can provide copies of portions of the database instead of the entire thing. This will cut down on network traffic for updating the master database, as well as prevent people from seeing parts of the database that they don't need to see.

Internet Features

Whether you are a seasoned Internet developer or a neophyte, there are several features in Visual Basic that will help you write programs for the Internet. The first of these is the capability to create ActiveX controls, which was formerly the domain of C++ programmers. Now you can quickly write controls from within Visual Basic. You can use these controls in your Visual Basic programs (just like regular OCXs), place them on a Web page, or deploy them as part of an ActiveX document. These controls can work with any browser that supports ActiveX.

Another major feature gives you the capability to create ActiveX documents. These are applications that run inside of Internet Explorer. You can also use ActiveX documents (whether created by Visual Basic or other products) within Visual Basic. This allows you to run programs such as an icon editor or HTML editor from within Visual Basic as if it were part of the development environment.

Finally, there are new controls that make it easier for you to create Internet-enabled applications. The WebBrowser control lets you incorporate browser features into your application. With a few lines of code, you can add a fully functional Microsoft Internet Explorer Window to your program. The Winsock control makes it easier to connect your application to the Internet. Finally, the Internet Transfer control helps manage the sometimes mundane task of transferring files via two widely-used Internet transport mechanisms: HyperText Transfer Protocol (HTTP) and File Transfer Protocol (FTP).

Control Features

What new version would be complete without new controls? A couple of the Internet controls have already been mentioned, but there are a few other noteworthy additions.

The new MSChart control enables you to create many types of business charts in your programs. This control can create bar, pie, line, area, and scatter charts, just to name a few. The new MSFlexGrid control works like a regular grid but allows formatting of individual cells. The MSFlexGrid also gives you other advanced features such as sorting, cell grouping, pivoting, multiple selections, and in-cell pictures.

A couple of other new controls also deserve mentioning:

- *Animation control* This allows you to display silent AVI (Audio Video Interleaved) clips. AVI clips are a series of bitmaps that are viewed like a movie. With this control, you can add a continuous animation much like the "flying paper" displayed as Windows 95 copies files from one folder to another.

- *UpDown control* This is a pair of arrow buttons that the user can click with the mouse to modify the value of a number in a "buddy" control. For example, without writing any code you can combine a TextBox control with arrow buttons that modify its contents.

- *Internet Transfer control* This allows you to send and retrieve files on HTTP and FTP servers.

In addition to the new controls, several of the old controls have been enhanced to provide greater functionality. For example, the PictureBox and Image controls now have the capability to display GIF or JPEG files, formats that are commonly used on the Internet. Also, most controls now have a `ToolTipText` property, which allows you to specify text that appears when the mouse pointer is rested on the control.

Finally, if you haven't found what you need among the provided controls, Visual Basic gives you the capability to create your own ActiveX controls and Dynamic Link Libraries (DLLs).

Checking Out the Wizards

Visual Basic has had a Setup Wizard for a number of versions. This made it easy to create the distribution disks that you needed in order to pass your program on to your users. The Setup Wizard is still present in version 5, but with some nice enhancements. Now you can create setup programs to handle installations from floppy disks or CDs, across a network, or even from the Internet. In addition to the Setup Wizard, Visual Basic includes several other wizards to make it easier for you to develop programs. These include the following:

- *Application Wizard* Creates a fully functional application that includes a toolbar and status bar on the main form. It can include such specialized forms as a splash screen, a login screen, an options dialog, and an About box. You can then customize the code created by the wizard to meet your programming needs.

- *ActiveX Control Interface Wizard* Helps you create the public code interface of an ActiveX control.

- *ActiveX Document Migration Wizard* Helps you create an ActiveX document from your existing forms. ActiveX documents can be run in Internet Explorer and other ActiveX-enabled programs.

- *Data Form Wizard* Creates a basic data entry form based on the structure of a table in a database. This fully functional form can be used as-is or modified to handle more complex database programming.

- *PropertyPage Wizard* Helps you build property pages for the ActiveX controls you create.

Types of Programs You Can Create in Visual Basic

Visual Basic version 5 lets you create many different types of 32-bit programs for the Windows operating systems. (A few of these types of programs are listed in the Introduction.)

N O T E Programs created with Visual Basic 5.0 are 32-bit applications and can only be run on either the Windows NT or Windows 95 operating systems. They cannot be run on 16-bit Windows systems. ▓

While you will most likely create stand-alone programs that are used directly by end users, Visual Basic 5 also gives you the ability to create libraries of functions that can be compiled into DLL files. These functions can be used by other programs to handle specialized tasks. In addition, Visual Basic 5 allows you to create your own ActiveX components, which can be used by your programs, other programs, and even accessed over the Internet.

Checking Out Visual Basic's Background

Before diving into the details of Visual Basic, let's take a brief look at the history of programming and some of the basic concepts that apply to programming in any language. This understanding of program basics will make it easier for you to write better and more efficient programs.

What Is a Program?

To begin, you need to know the answer to the question, "Just what is a program?" A *computer program* is simply a set of instructions that tells the computer how to perform a specific task.

Computers need explicit instructions for every single task they perform. They even need instructions for the simplest tasks, such as how to get a keystroke, place a letter on the screen, or store information to a disk. Fortunately, many of these instructions are contained on the processor chip or are built into the operating system, so you don't have to worry about them.

Even with less advanced programming languages, you must still be concerned with mundane tasks such as drawing command buttons, repainting screens, and so on. Visual Basic takes care of much of this detail work for you. Instead, you'd rather concentrate on providing instructions for the tasks, such as calculating employee payroll, creating the mailing list for your neighborhood, or formatting text to display the information in the latest annual report. Visual Basic 5 and the Rapid Application Development (RAD) concept make this possible.

NOTE Rapid Application Development means exactly what it sounds like: an environment that lets you develop applications rapidly! Visual Basic makes it easy to spend your programming time creating a good program without having to worry about mundane "behind-the-scenes" details.

For example, if you want to use a command button in a program, all you have to do is draw one on a form (screen) as you're designing the program. You then set its properties to define how it looks and acts; you could also write small pieces of program code to tell it what to do when it's clicked. You don't have to be concerned with how the button is actually painted on the screen; for example, the button looks like it's pushed down. Visual Basic takes care of these lower-level tasks for you. ∎

A Few Definitions

Now for a few technical terms. You will hear these terms often in discussions of Visual Basic, so a general understanding of the following terms should be helpful to you:

- *Controls*   Reusable objects that provide the pieces of the visual interface of a program. Examples of controls are a text box, a label, or a command button.
- *Event*   An action initiated by the user, the operating system, or the program itself. Examples of events are a keystroke, a mouse click, the expiration of a specified amount of time, or the receipt of data from a port.
- *Methods*   Predefined actions that can be performed by an object. For example, a form has a Hide method that makes it invisible to the user.

- *Object*   A basic element of a program, which contains properties to define its character-istics, contains methods to define its tasks, and recognizes events to which it can respond. Controls and forms are examples of the objects used in Visual Basic.

- *Procedures*   Segments of code that you write to accomplish a task. Procedures are often written to respond to a specific event. Types of procedures include Sub procedures, which consist of a sequence of statements; and functions, which return a value.

- *Properties*   The characteristics of an object, such as its size, position, color, or text font. Properties determine the appearance and sometimes the behavior of an object. Proper-ties are also used to provide data to an object and to retrieve information from the object.

Event-Driven Programming

Visual Basic lets you create programs that respond to user actions and system events. This type of programming is known as *event-driven programming*. To get some insight into how event-driven programming works, let's take a look at how programs ran in the past and how things are different in the Windows environment.

▶ **See** "Handling Events in Your Programs," **p. 153**

Before the advent of Windows (back in the old days of DOS and the "prehistoric times"—before PCs), programs were written to be run in a *sequential* fashion. That is, when the pro-gram started, it proceeded, instruction by instruction, until it reached the end of the program or a fatal error occurred. The general steps for running a program that processed a data file were as follows:

1. Create an input file.
2. Start the program.
3. Wait until the program finishes—often overnight for large programs.
4. Examine the output file or printed report.
5. Check the output for errors and, if necessary, repeat the entire process.

As software matured, we saw the gradual introduction of a limited form of *interactive process-ing*, in which the user had some control over the sequence of events. Such improvements as menu systems and hot-key commands allowed a little more flexibility to the user, but the pro-gram itself still retained much control over its flow.

Even programs that most people take for granted, such as word processing packages, worked this way. For the early word processors, you would create your file with formatting codes em-bedded in the actual document (much like RTF or HTML codes today), and then run the file through a formatter to be printed. These programs got the job done, but they weren't nearly as easy to use as today's programs. They were, however, easier to write. This is because each program had a clearly defined task and little or no user interaction. The programmer had nearly complete control over the sequence of events required to complete a task.

Then came Windows. Windows programs (and many later-generation DOS programs) pro-vided the user with the ability to interact with the objects that made up the program's interface to a much greater extent. Programs would now respond to occurrences such as mouse movements and clicks, and would respond differently depending upon where the mouse pointer was located. Because this sequential programming structure would no longer work in such a wide-open environment, a new model was needed: the *event model*.

In the event model, each user interaction—such as a mouse click or a keystroke—is known as an *event*. Therefore, programs that respond to these events are known as *event-driven programs*. These programs provide almost immediate feedback to the users and give them greater control over the programs' activity. For example, an order-taking program written in a sequential processing style might ask the users for information about the items they are ordering one line at a time. They must follow the sequence of events determined by the programmer; if they were to make an error, they would have to start over. An event-driven application, on the other hand, might present the users with a visual form to fill out, as well as several processing options. Controls such as command buttons, menus, and text boxes would allow the users to determine the order in which they input the data and when the program processes the data. Correcting an error would be as simple as retyping the erroneous information. Figure 1.4 shows the interface for a typical event-driven program.

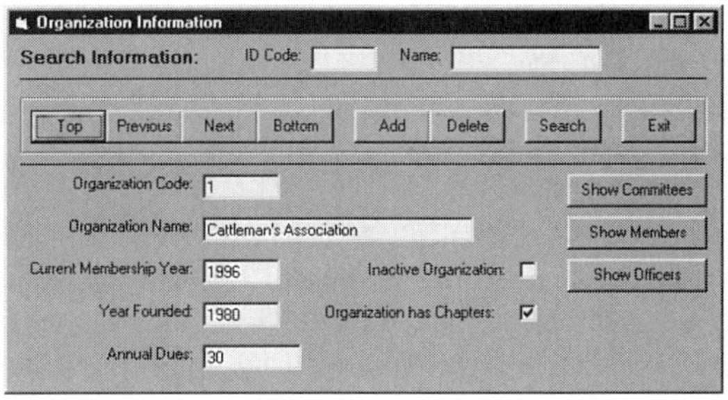

FIG. 1.4
In an event-driven program, the user might have several options governing the flow of events.

While event-driven programs are great for users, they were very difficult for developers to write until the introduction of advanced programming languages like Visual Basic. Visual Basic was designed with the event model in mind, making it much easier for people to create Windows applications.

Object-Oriented Programming

One key concept that makes it easier to create Windows programs is *object-oriented programming*, or *OOP*. This technology makes it possible to create reusable components that become the building blocks of programs.

Figure 1.5 shows the interface for a typical object-oriented program.

What Is Object-Oriented Programming?   The OOP model provides support for three basic principles—*encapsulation*, *inheritance*, and *polymorphism*. Let's take a brief look at each of these terms.

FIG. 1.5

In an object-oriented program, the user has an interactive order form.

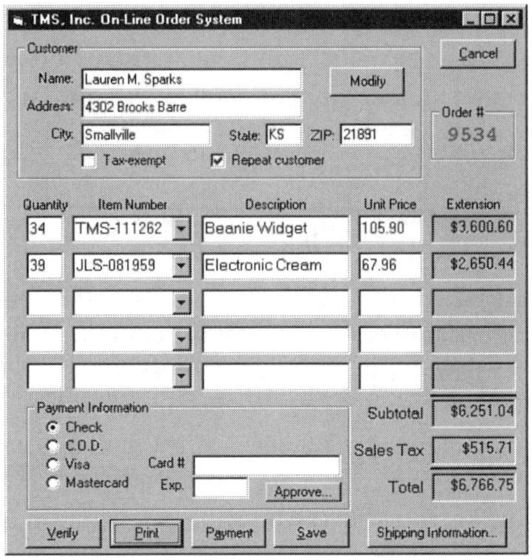

Encapsulation means that the information about an object (its *properties*) and the processes that are performed by the object (its *methods*) are all contained within the definition of the object. A real-world example of an object is a car. You describe a car by its properties, such as a red convertible or a black four-door sedan. Each characteristic—color, number of doors, convertible, or hardtop—is a property of the car. As for the methods, these are the things that a car does in response to an event. For example, you initiate an event when you turn the key to start the car. The car's "start method" takes over at that point, providing instructions such as "engage the starter gear, turn the starter, start fuel flow, initiate power to spark plugs, and disengage the starter." You don't have to tell the car *how* to start because it was taught how to start when it was designed.

Inheritance means that one object can be based upon the description of another object. Continuing with the car example, I can define a car as something that has four wheels, an engine, and passenger seats. I can then define a convertible as a car that has a retractable top. The convertible inherits the properties of the car and adds a new property, the retractable top. I don't have to redefine the car's properties for the convertible. Therefore, the convertible is said to inherit the properties of the car. In addition to properties, objects can also inherit methods and events from other objects.

N O T E This discussion of inheritance is included for the purpose of fully describing OOP. Visual Basic does not directly support inheritance in its current implementation of object-oriented programming. ■

Polymorphism means that many objects can have the same method and that the appropriate action is taken for the specific object calling the method. For example, in your programs, you display text to the screen and output text to the printer. Each of these objects (the screen and the printer) can have a print or display method that tells the object to place text in a certain location. The method knows what to do, based on the object calling the method.

What OOP Does for You   The key element of OOP with which you will be working is reusable components, known as *controls*. The controls that you will use in building your programs are objects that have properties and methods and respond to events. You control the appearance and behavior of a control through its properties. For example, you specify how the text in a TextBox control will look by setting its Font and Color properties. The controls you use have methods built into them that shield you from many of the tedious tasks of programming. Again look at the TextBox control as an example. It knows how to retrieve a keystroke and display it in the edit region of the box in the proper format. You don't have to supply the details.

Each control also recognizes specific events. Most controls know if the mouse has been moved over them or if a mouse button has been clicked. They even know which button was clicked. Components that handle text know when a key was pressed and which one it was. And, for most events, you can write code that will take specific action when the event occurs.

The Parts of a Program

As you begin to create a program, there are three basic parts of the program that you need to consider—the *user interface*, the *processing of information*, and the *storage of information*.

The user interface is the part of the program that your users see and with which they interact. This user interface is composed of the screens you design by using Visual Basic's forms and controls. A few key objectives for a good user interface are the following:

- Present information in a neat manner.
- Make instructions clear.
- Make the appropriate parts of the interface (such as menus) consistent with corresponding parts of other programs.
- Make key tasks easily accessible by providing menu shortcuts and/or toolbars.

The processing of information is handled by the code that you write to respond to events in the program. One of your objectives here is to make the code as efficient as possible, thereby providing good response time for your users. It's also important to make the code easy to maintain so that future modifications or updates to the code can be made with relative ease. Key components in making code easy to maintain include making it easy to read and using code modules to keep individual tasks small and simple. Making your code easy to read is done by properly formatting the lines of code and providing comments within the code to describe what it does.

From Here...

Now that you have been introduced to some of Visual Basic's capabilities, you are probably ready to jump right in and get started creating programs. A few chapters you might want to explore include the following:

- See Chapter 2, "Introduction to the Development Environment," to learn more about Visual Basic 5's IDE (Integrated Development Environment).

■ See Chapter 3, "Creating Your First Program," to get started creating program interfaces.

■ See Chapter 8, "Programming Basics," for more information about writing program code to have your programs perform their assigned tasks.

Introduction to the Development Environment

As old-timers will note, the development environment is completely different from the one in previous versions of Visual Basic. The environment is, however, consistent with the development environments of Microsoft's other programming languages. We'll look closely at the development environment in the section "Exploring the Visual Basic Interface," but first let's take a brief look at the key features of the new environment. ■

A completely new development environment

If you have used previous versions of Visual Basic, you will discover that almost everything about the interface has changed. I found that, after an initial adjustment period, these changes added a lot of flexibility to the development environment.

Working in multiple windows

The form and code windows are now set up as MDI child windows. The new style allows you to easily switch from one window to another, keeping your toolbar and menus available at all times.

Most windows are dockable

This means that you can have the Properties window, Project window, and toolbox docked against the edge of your screen or floating somewhere in the middle.

Toolbars for everything

Visual Basic 5 has new and improved toolbars that make it easier to accomplish many of your programming tasks, such as lining up controls precisely on a form.

Help is available

In addition to detailed help files with context-sensitive links, Visual Basic 5 includes many detailed VB articles in the Books Online.

Understanding the Environment's Key Features

A significant change in VB5 is its use of a Multiple-Document Interface (MDI). If you are unfamiliar with MDI, you can compare it to having multiple documents open in Microsoft Word. Each document is contained in a child window which is, in turn, contained within the main parent window. As with other MDI applications, such as Word or Excel, you can choose to have the child document fill the whole window or have multiple windows visible simultaneously.

 TIP If you are not already using a large monitor (17" or greater) at high resolution, get one! While the new interface is great, you need a lot of screen space to use it most effectively. I recommend a screen resolution of 800 × 600 as a minimum or 1024 × 768 if your video card (and eyes) can support it.

Next, you can edit more than one project in the same Visual Basic session. This means you don't have to close one project in order to open and make changes to another. This is very convenient if you are developing projects that interact with each other, because you can save and compile all projects in a group with a single menu option.

Another new feature is dockable toolbars and windows. This means that a window can be floating in the middle of the screen or docked along one of the edges. Dockable windows include the toolbars and windows with small title bars, such as the toolbox.

In addition to the window management enhancements, Visual Basic has some useful tools to make code entry easier. Microsoft calls them *Auto List Member* and *Auto Quick Info*; you will call them fantastic. If you have trouble remembering `MessageBox` constants, control properties, or even the parameters to your own functions, the code editor now presents the information automatically while you type! For example, as soon as you press the spacebar after a `MsgBox` function call, you are presented with the parameters in a ToolTip-like format with a drop-down box of the available constants.

TIP When you are presented with the drop-down box mentioned in the preceding paragraph, you don't have to use the mouse to select an item. Just keep typing (or use the arrow keys) until the list item you want is highlighted; then press the spacebar, comma (,), Enter, or Tab, and continue with your program!

Starting Up

When you start Visual Basic, you see the New Project dialog box, shown in Figure 2.1. This dialog box has the following three tabs:

- *New*   Lets you choose one of several types of projects to create
- *Existing*   Allows you to browse for a project that's already been created and saved
- *Recent*   Presents you with a list of projects that have been previously worked on. The most recent projects are listed first

FIG. 2.1
The New Project dialog box's New tab lets you select from several types of projects to create.

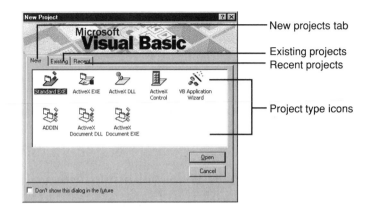

New projects tab

Existing projects
Recent projects

Project type icons

If you choose to create a new project, Visual Basic creates the appropriate project template for you based on your selection from the New Project dialog box. You can choose to create one of these project types:

- *Standard EXE*   This is the type of project you would use to create a standard Windows program (.EXE file). You will probably use this type of project most often.

- *ActiveX EXE*   This is an automation server that performs tasks as part of a multiple-tier application. The end result is a program that contains public classes that can be accessed by other programs or can run by itself. This used to be known as an *OLE automation server*.

- *ActiveX DLL*   This is a remote automation program created as a DLL. ActiveX DLLs cannot run alone; however, because an ActiveX DLL runs in-process, it is faster than an out-of-process ActiveX EXE.

- *ActiveX Control*   With this option, you can create your own custom controls (OCXs). These can be used in your Visual Basic programs or in any ActiveX-capable application.

- *VB Application Wizard*   If you want something quick and generic, this option builds the skeleton of an application (similar to a word processor template). You can then customize the application to suit your needs.

- *Addin*   This type of program is used to provide additional functionality to Visual Basic itself. An example of an add-in is the Visual Data Manager.

- *ActiveX Document DLL*   This type of project creates a DLL that can be utilized by applications running within Microsoft Internet Explorer.

- *ActiveX Document EXE*   This type of project creates an application that can run inside Microsoft Internet Explorer.

The Visual Basic Work Area

After you select the project type from the New Project dialog box, you are presented with the design environment. This is where you do the work of actually creating your masterpiece application. The basic design environment is shown in Figure 2.2.

Menu bar   Toolbar   Properties window   Project window

FIG. 2.2

The Visual Basic desktop provides an assortment of tools that you can use to create programs.

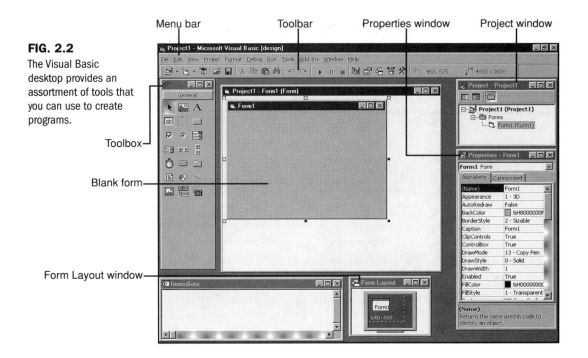

Toolbox

Blank form

Form Layout window

As you can see, Visual Basic shares a lot of elements with other Windows programs. The toolbars and menus look similar to those in Office 97. A few of the menu items are the same: File, Edit, Help, and others.

Using the Menu Bar

Many programmers want to find quick keyboard shortcuts for frequently used tasks. As with other Windows programs, the menus at the top of the Visual Basic screen can be displayed by holding down the Alt key while pressing the appropriate underlined character in the menu bar. After the initial menu is displayed, simply press the underlined character of a menu item to select it. For example, press Alt+F to open the File menu, and then press P to choose the Print command.

Visual Basic also utilizes several shortcut keys that let you bypass the menu entirely. Most of these are listed to the right of their respective menu items. For example, in the View menu you might notice F2 to the right of Object Browser. This means that you can see the Object Browser by pressing F2. Although some quick shortcuts are listed in Table 2.1, a quick perusal of the menus would definitely be worth your while.

Table 2.1 Shortcut Keys

Menu Item	Shortcut Key	Description
Edit, Cut	Ctrl+X	Removes the selected text or control from its current location and copies it to the Clipboard.
Edit, Copy	Ctrl+C	Makes a copy of the selected text or control on the Clipboard, but does not remove it from its original location.
Edit, Paste	Ctrl+V	Pastes the contents of the Clipboard to the active form or code window.
Edit, Undo	Ctrl+Z	Undoes the last change.
Edit, Find	Ctrl+F	Finds a piece of text. (You must be in an edit window to use this.)
File, Open	Ctrl+O	Opens a project.
File, Save	Ctrl+S	Saves the current file.
File, Print	Ctrl+P	Displays the Print dialog box, from which you can print the current form or module or the entire application.
View, Project	Ctrl+R	Shows the Project Explorer window Explorer (if it's not already displayed).
View, Properties Window	F4	Shows the Properties window (if it's not already displayed).

T I P Experimentation is encouraged! In addition to the preceding list, Visual Basic includes some not-so-obvious tricks such as Ctrl+Y (delete a line of code), which is apparently an homage to WordStar.

Examining the Changes in Familiar Menus   The File menu is basically the same as it was in previous versions of Visual Basic (see Figure 2.3). However, because Visual Basic 5.0 allows multiple projects on the desktop, some project management functions have been moved to the new Project menu.

The Edit menu has the standard features you would expect, such as Cut, Copy, and Paste, but also has quite a few new features that are associated with the new capabilities of the code editor (see Figure 2.4). These features give you the following capabilities:

- *Indent/Outdent*   You can indent and outdent (un-indent) selected blocks of code.
- *List Properties/Methods*   You can call up a list of properties and methods of an object.
- *List Constants*   You can list Visual Basic constants that you would use in a statement.
- *Parameter Info*   You can get information about the parameters required for a function, such as the message box.
- *Complete Word*   Visual Basic fills in the rest of partially completed code words for you, which saves you typing.

■ *Bookmarks*   You can set and use bookmarks to make it easier to move back and forth between sections of your code. (Bookmarks are indicated by blue squares in the left margin of the code window.)

FIG. 2.3
Visual Basic's File menu assists you in managing the files that make up your projects.

FIG. 2.4
The Edit menu offers quite a few commands to help you write code.

The View menu provides you with access to all the parts of the Visual Basic interface. From the View menu, you can display and hide various parts of the design environment. These can include toolbars, design windows, and windows containing program code.

The Project menu contains many of the functions you need to manage an individual project. From this menu, you can add and remove project elements—such as forms, modules, and user controls. The Project menu also provides you with access to the Components dialog box, where you select the controls to be used in the project, and to the Project Properties dialog box, where you select things like the startup form and compiler options.

The other familiar menus—Run, Tools, Add-Ins, and Help—are all similar to their counterparts in earlier versions of Visual Basic.

Checking Out the New Menus   Three new menus have been added to Visual Basic 5: Format, Debug, and Window. While the Window menu is new to Visual Basic, it should be familiar to you if you have worked with other Windows programs. This menu lets you arrange and select multiple form and code windows.

Part

Ch

The Debug menu contains tools that help you track down problems in your code (see Figure 2.5). From here, you can set breakpoints and watches, as well as control how the code is executed in debug mode. It is interesting to note that the Debug window from previous versions is now called the Immediate window and commands can be executed here even when the program is *not* running.

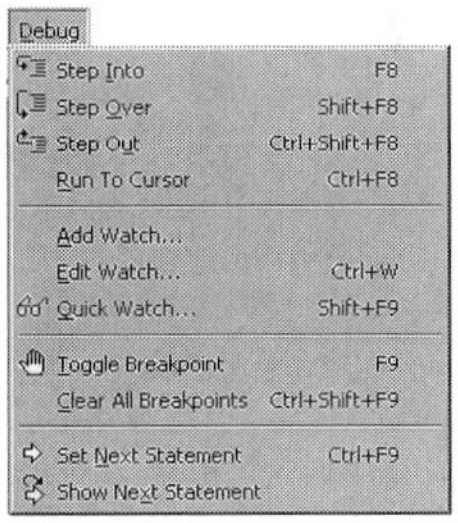

FIG. 2.5
The Debug menu provides numerous commands to aid in troubleshooting your code.

The final new menu is the Format menu, shown in Figure 2.6. This menu provides you with a number of features for working with groups of controls on your form. These features make it easy to align multiple controls, set the height or width of multiple controls to make them consistent, center a group of controls, or adjust the spacing between controls. If you have worked in previous versions of Visual Basic (and even if you haven't), you will really appreciate the power of these features.

▶ **See** "Using Controls," **p. 87**

FIG. 2.6
The Format menu helps you with the placement and sizing of controls on your forms.

Accessing Functions with the Toolbars

Visual Basic's toolbars provide you with quick access to some of the functions you will use most often. There are four toolbars available (see Figure 2.7):

- *Standard* The Standard toolbar is displayed by default and offers quick access to frequently used functions.
- *Debug* The Debug toolbar has buttons for use when you're debugging your programs.
- *Edit* The Edit toolbar's buttons are handy when you're writing code.
- *Form Editor* The Form Editor toolbar contains buttons that help you tweak the appearance of controls on your forms.

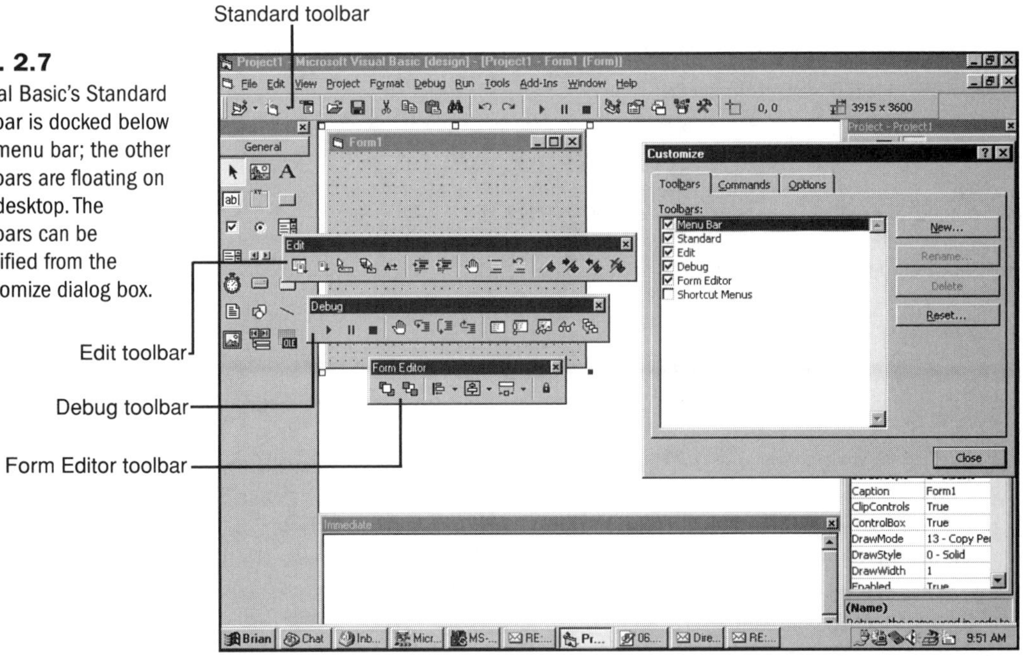

FIG. 2.7

Visual Basic's Standard toolbar is docked below the menu bar; the other toolbars are floating on the desktop. The toolbars can be modified from the Customize dialog box.

The Standard toolbar is the only one displayed the first time you start Visual Basic. You can specify which toolbars are displayed by choosing Toolbars from the View menu or by right-clicking any visible toolbar. Any of them can be free-floating or "docked" just below the menu bar; their startup positions will be the same as the last time you exited Visual Basic. Selecting View, Toolbars, Customize allows you to modify the existing toolbars or even create your own!

Visual Basic's toolbars follow the standard used by the latest generation of programs in that they provide you with ToolTips. A ToolTip is a little yellow box that pops up if you let the mouse pointer hover over a button for a few seconds; it contains a description of the underlying button's function.

TIP Starting with version 5.0, ToolTips also display the value of a variable in a code window. Use this feature by letting the mouse pointer hover over a variable name while in break mode. This is a real time-saver if you are used to setting up a watch or printing values in the Immediate window.

Display all the toolbars as explained in the preceding paragraph and move the pointer over the buttons to familiarize yourself with them. Remember that you can always use the ToolTip feature when you're unsure which button is which.

Two of these buttons require special attention. The Add Project button and the Add Form button both invoke drop-down lists of items (see Figure 2.8). If you select one of these items, the default item for the button changes to the type of item that you selected.

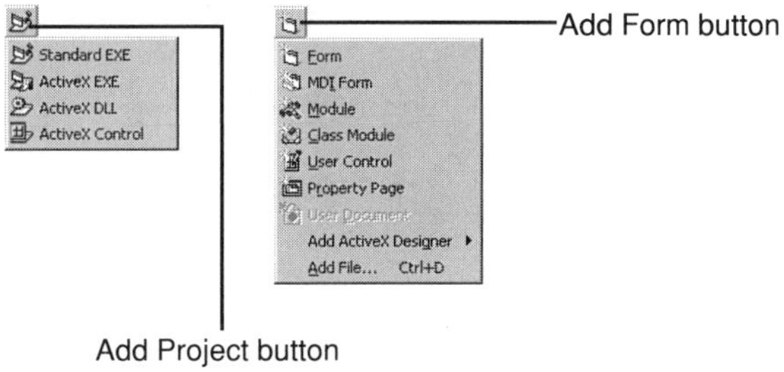

Part

I

Ch

2

FIG. 2.8

Drop-down buttons allow you to specify the type of project or file to be added.

Add Form button

Add Project button

The Add Project button allows you to add a project to the desktop. This can be one of the following four types:

- Standard EXE
- ActiveX EXE
- ActiveX DLL
- ActiveX Control

The Add Form button lets you add any of the following pieces to your current project:

- Form
- MDI form
- Module
- Class module
- User control
- Property page
- Existing files

We address most of the other buttons on the toolbar a little later. However, two special areas on the toolbar deserve mentioning. At the far right of the toolbar are two blocks with a pair of numbers in each block. These two blocks show the position and size of the form or control with which you are working. The two numbers in the first block indicate the horizontal and vertical positions, respectively, of the upper-left corner of the current object, as measured from the upper-left corner of the screen (if the current object is a form), or of the current form (if the current object is a control). The two numbers in the second block show the horizontal and vertical dimensions, respectively, of the current object. These numbers are not visible, however, when editing in a code window.

N O T E Both the position and dimension information are given in *twips*. A twip is a unit of measure that Visual Basic uses to ensure that placement and sizing of objects is consistent on different types of screens. A twip is equal to 1/20 of a printer's point; there are approximately 1,440 twips in a logical inch (the amount of screen space that would take up one inch when printed). ▪

One final note about the toolbars. If you don't like having them located at the top of the screen, you can move any of them by clicking the double bars at the left edge and dragging to a new location. You can park a toolbar against any other edge of the desktop or leave them floating in the middle as shown in Figure 2.9.

FIG. 2.9
Even the Standard toolbar can float freely on the desktop.

Standard toolbar floating——

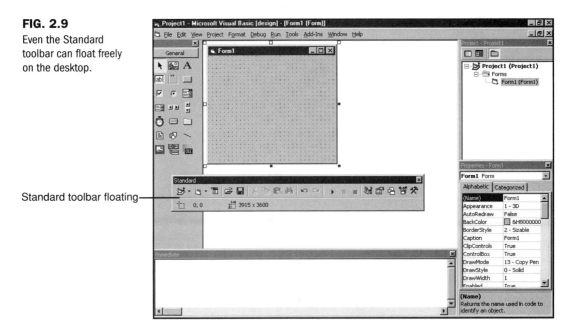

Organizing Visual Basic's Controls

The controls that are used in Visual Basic are the heart and soul of the programs that you create. The controls allow you to add functionality to your program quickly and easily. There are controls that allow you to edit text, connect to a database, retrieve file information from a user, or display and edit pictures.

Obviously, with all these controls available, you need a way to keep them organized. This is the function of the toolbox (see Figure 2.10). This toolbox contains buttons representing the controls that are available for use in your program. (A list of the basic set of Visual Basic 5 controls is contained in Table 2.2.) Clicking one of the control "tools" allows you to draw a control of that type on a form. Double-clicking a tool places a default-sized control of that type in the center of the current form. Clicking the Pointer tool in the upper-left of the toolbox cancels a pending control-drawing function and restores the mouse pointer's normal functionality.

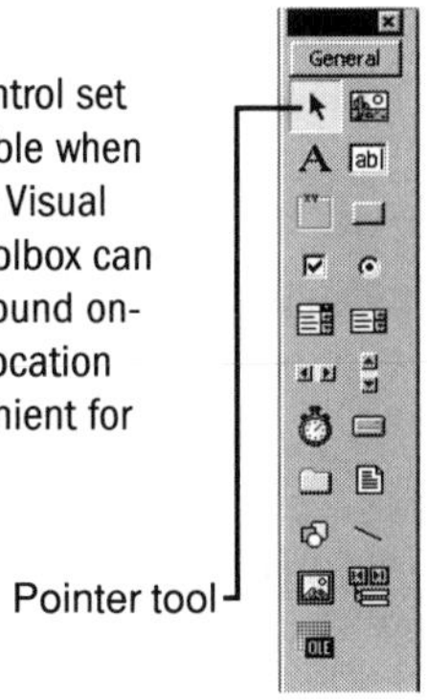

FIG. 2.10

The basic control set that is available when you first start Visual Basic. The toolbox can be moved around on-screen to a location that is convenient for you.

Pointer tool

Part

I

Ch

2

Table 2.2   Standard Visual Basic Controls

Control Button	Control Name	Function
	PictureBox	Displays a graphic image.
	Label	Displays text that the user cannot directly modify.
	TextBox	Displays text that the user can edit.
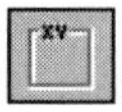	Frame	Provides a method for grouping controls. (To group controls in a frame, select the frame with a single-click first, then draw a control in it.)
	CommandButton	Allows the user to initiate a program action. Can include an icon, caption, and ToolTips.
	CheckBox	Displays or allows input of a two-part choice, such as Yes/No or True/False.
	OptionButton	Displays or allows a choice among multiple items. (Also known as a radio button.)
	ComboBox	Allows the user to select an entry from a list or enter a new value.
	ListBox	Displays a list of items from which the user can select one or more entries.
	HscrollBar (Horizontal Scroll bar)	Produces a numerical value based on the scroll bar's horizontal position.
	VscrollBar (Vertical Scroll bar)	Same as above but vertical. Note the scroll bars behave like standard Windows scroll bars.

continues

Table 2.2   Continued

Control Button	Control Name	Function
	Timer	Provides a means for an action to be taken after passage of a certain amount of time.
	DriveListBox	Displays and allows a user to choose from available disk drives on the computer.
	Dir ListBox	Displays and allows a user to choose from available subdirectories on a drive.
	FileListBox	Displays and allows a user to choose from available files in a directory.
	Shape	Displays geometric shapes on the form.
	Line	Displays lines on the form.
	Image	Displays a graphic image. Similar in appearance to the picture control but with different functionality.
	Data	Provides a link to database files.
	OLE	Provides you with a way to link to OLE servers.

You can add other controls to the toolbox by selecting the Components item from the Project menu. This brings up the Components dialog box (see Figure 2.11). This dialog box allows you to choose any additional controls (OCXs) that have been installed on your system. If you choose to add a control to the toolbox, it appears in the toolbox after you choose the OK or Apply button.

FIG. 2.11
Controls are added to the toolbox with the Components dialog box.

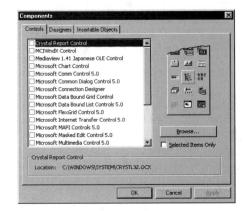

T I P You can also access the Components dialog box by right-clicking the mouse on the toolbox and then selecting the Components item from the pop-up menu.

By default, all the components for your project will appear in the toolbox in one big group. However, if you use a lot of controls, this can make it very difficult to manage all of them. To help with this problem, Visual Basic allows you to add tabs to the toolbox. (It has one tab, General, by default.) To add a tab, right-click the toolbox, select Add Tab from the pop-up menu, and give the new tab a name. You can then move controls from one tab to another and group your controls in the way that is most convenient to you. Figure 2.12 shows the toolbox with a Data Access tab added to it.

FIG. 2.12
A new feature in Visual Basic 5 gives you the ability to group control tools using custom tabs in the toolbox.

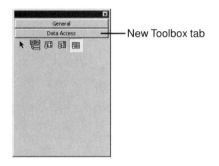

The Canvas of Your Programs

The windows you design in your Visual Basic programs are known as *forms*. The form can be thought of like an artist's canvas. You use elements in the toolbox to "draw" your user interface on a form.

The form is part of the desktop and is your primary work area for creating the user interface. If you look closely at the form in Figure 2.13, you might notice that the form has dots on it. These dots form a grid whose purpose is to help you position controls on the form; it is invisible when your program is running. You can control the spacing of the grid dots from the Tools, Options, General dialog box. You can also choose not to display the grid at all.

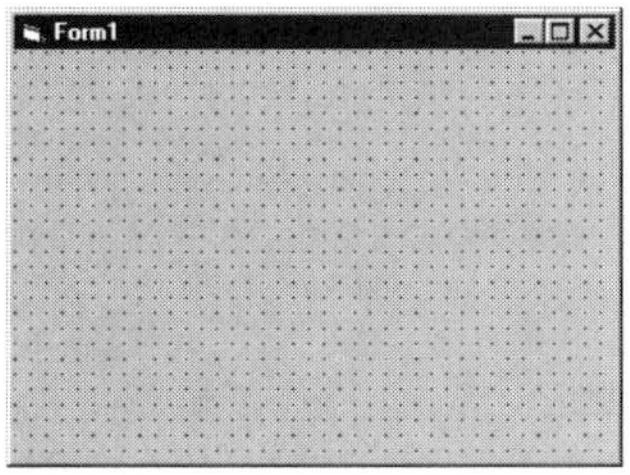

FIG. 2.13
When designing a form in Visual Basic, a grid is available to help you easily line up controls.

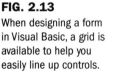

Controlling Your Forms and Controls

The Properties window is an important part of the Visual Basic desktop. It shows all the available properties for the currently selected form, control, or module (see Figure 2.14). If the Properties window isn't visible, first select the object(s) whose properties you want to view or change and then press F4. It can also be viewed by selecting Properties Windows from the View menu or by right-clicking an object and choosing Properties from the context-sensitive menu that pops up.

FIG. 2.14
The Properties window provides an easy way to change the properties that govern the appearance and behavior of controls.

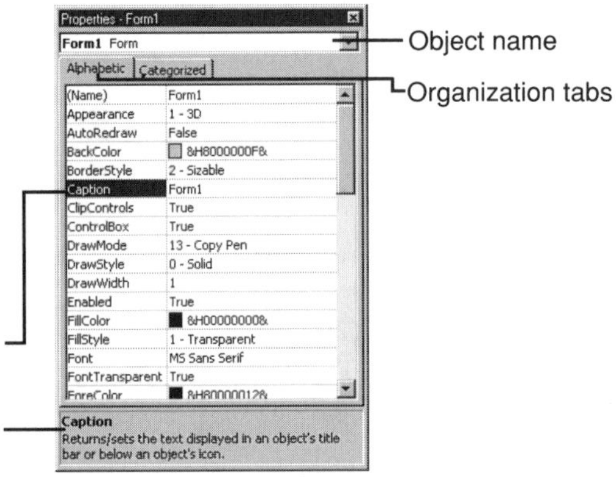

— Object name
└─Organization tabs

Selected property ┘

Property description ┐

Properties determine how a form or control looks and how it behaves in a program. The Properties window lists all of the currently selected object's properties that can be changed at *design time,* as opposed to *runtime* properties, which can be changed only during program execution. Many properties can be changed either at design time or at runtime.

An example of a property is the Caption property of a Label control. It can be changed by simply typing **Hello World** into the Caption field in the Properties window (a design-time change) or with a statement in your code like Form1.Label1.Caption = "Hello World" (a runtime change).

The Properties window has two tabs on it. These tabs allow you to group the properties either alphabetically or by logical categories. Another improvement to the Properties window is that it now includes a description of the selected property in a pane at the bottom. This avoids much of the need to look up properties in the Help system.

N O T E   In a change from previous versions of Visual Basic, the Name property of any object appears at the top of the list of properties, rather than in its proper alphabetical order.

N O T E   Many controls have an entry in the Properties window labeled (Custom). This brings up a special Property Page dialog box containing all of the design-time properties for that control in an easy-to-modify format.

Using the Project Window

Another window on the desktop is the Project window. This window shows a list of all the forms and code modules that are used in your program. Figure 2.15 shows an example of a Project window. If you want to view a form or code module, double-click it here during design time, or click it once and click the View Form or View Code button.

FIG. 2.15

The Project window shows the files that make up the open project(s).

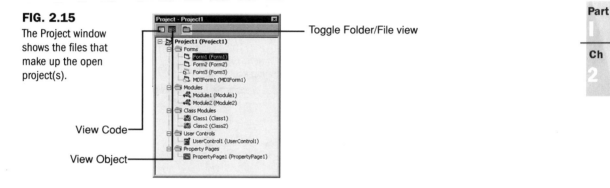

View Code
View Object
Toggle Folder/File view

N O T E One way to think of a project is as a group of related files. The Project brings together all the files needed to create your program. ▪

When you save a project, you're basically saving a list of the various files that make up a project. The project file itself is stored with a default extension of .VBP (Visual Basic Project). Several other types of files make up the components of the projects. Some of the more common types are listed in Table 2.3.

Table 2.3   Visual Basic File Types

File Type	Extension
Visual Basic Form	.FRM
Code Module	.BAS
Class Module	.CLS
User-Created Control	.CTL
ActiveX Document Form File	.DOB

The Project window uses an outline list to show you not only the Forms and Code modules in the open project(s) but also any Class modules, User-defined controls, or Property pages. There are two ways to view your project. The folder view, accessible by clicking the left button, displays the parts of your project organized by category. On the other hand, clicking the rightmost button lists the elements of your project based on their associated file names.

Where Work Gets Done

The final piece of the desktop is one or more Code windows. Code windows are where you do all the entry and editing of program code that allows your programs to actually perform tasks (see Figure 2.16). Each form has its own associated Code window. A project can also contain a couple of types of stand-alone Code windows known as *modules*. To access a Code window, you can double-click a form or one of its objects, or you can click the View Code button in the Project window while the appropriate object is highlighted.

FIG. 2.16

The Code window is where you enter and edit the instructions that perform the work of your program.

Form name

Event selection box

Object selection box

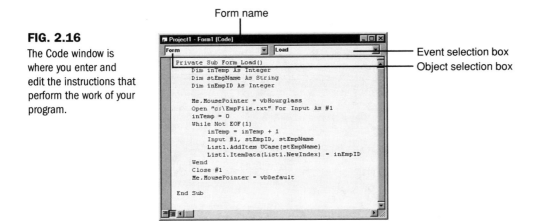

Customizing Your Environment

As we've discussed, the Visual Basic development environment is highly customizable. Most of the windows and toolbars in Visual Basic can be placed at the edges of the main program window, or they can float anywhere on the screen. You can position and resize the windows to fit your preferences; the next time you start Visual Basic, the environment will be as you left it. Figure 2.17 shows you one way the development environment can be rearranged.

FIG. 2.17
The various pieces of Visual Basic's development environment can be arranged in many ways.

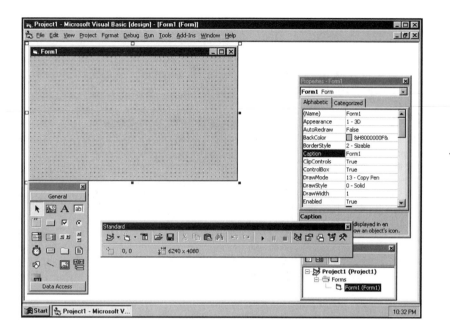

Getting Help When You Need It

As you work with the many features of Visual Basic, you may need more information about a particular command or object than is provided in this book. Fortunately, Microsoft has included a great online help system with Visual Basic 5. In addition to a searchable index, context-sensitive help is available from the development environment. This means you can highlight a word or object and press the F1 key to bring up related information.

The Basic Help System

The easiest way to access the Help system is through the Help menu. There are several choices available on the menu for Visual Basic help:

- Microsoft Visual Basic Help Topics
- Books Online
- Obtaining Technical Support
- Microsoft On the Web
- About Microsoft Visual Basic

Select Microsoft Visual Basic Help Topics to enter the main online Help system. The Contents tab you find there displays the main table of contents for the Help system, as shown in Figure 2.18. From here, you can choose topics of interest and navigate through the other parts of the Help system. You choose a topic by clicking one of the *hypertext links* (similar to those you find when browsing the World Wide Web).

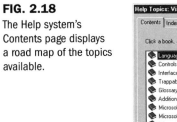

FIG. 2.18

The Help system's Contents page displays a road map of the topics available.

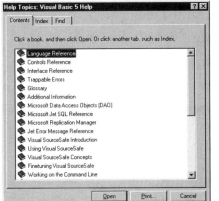

Clicking the Help system's Index tab displays an extensive listing of help topics available (see Figure 2.19). To find a specific item, type part of the name of the item in the window's text box until the desired topic appears in the list and then click the topic in the list. You can also use the scroll bar in the list box to locate a specific topic.

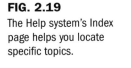

FIG. 2.19

The Help system's Index page helps you locate specific topics.

While the Index page allows a quick selection based on topic name, the Find page goes one step further. It has the additional capability of searching for a specific word or words within all of the available topics. The first time you use the Find option, a Word List will be created. Then you can type in a word or phrase and list the help topics that contain it. The Find screen is shown in Figure 2.20.

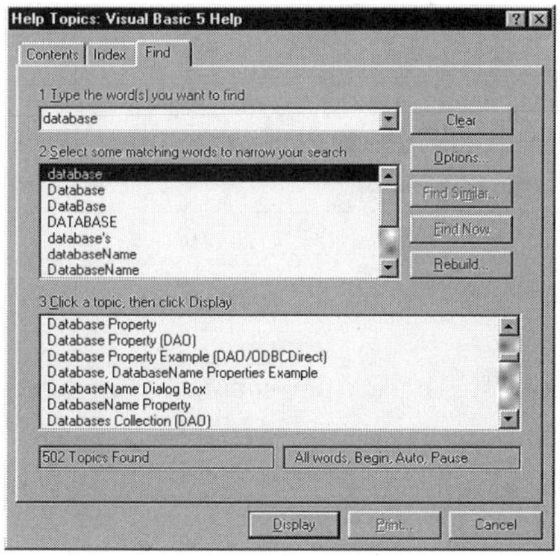

FIG. 2.20
From the online Help system's Find tab, you can search the help file for specific words.

Context-Sensitive Help

In addition to letting you look up information in the Contents, Index, and Find pages, Visual Basic provides you with context-sensitive help. This allows you to directly get the help you need for a particular control or code keyword while you're working with that object or in the Code window. To get help for any control, simply select the control on your form and then press the F1 key. The Help system displays information about the control. This help page, an example of which is shown in Figure 2.21, also provides links to detailed descriptions of the properties, methods, and events of the control.

FIG. 2.21
The Help page for a control provides a description of the control as well as links to related pages.

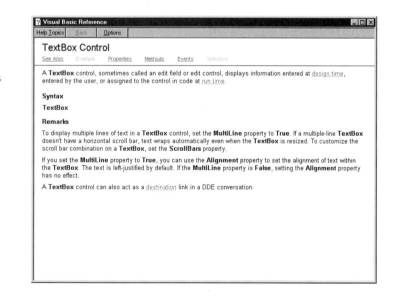

For code keywords, simply place the cursor in the word in the Code window and then press F1. The Help system goes directly to the page for that command and provides you with the syntax of the command, as well as other information about it. In addition, for most commands, a link is provided that gives you an example of how the command is used.

 TIP   When you find the help topic for a command you're working with, you can copy sample code from the help screen to the Clipboard and then paste it directly into your application's Code window. Use Ctrl+C and Ctrl+V, respectively, to copy and paste the text.

From Here...

This chapter introduced you to Visual Basic's development environment. You now know the basic methods for manipulating code and forms. As with any skill, the best way to learn is to practice! Think of some ideas for example programs and try writing them. Sample programs with varying levels of complexity are presented in this book; you can also find some in Visual Basic's Samples folder. On the other hand, if you would like to learn even more about the design environment, there are more chapters that explore it extensively. A couple of good places to go next are:

- Chapter 3, "Creating Your First Program," takes you step-by-step through creating a working VB program.
- Chapter 4, "Working with Forms and Controls," explains forms and controls.
- Chapter 8, "Programming Basics," teaches you all about the programming language of Visual Basic.

Creating Your First Program

If you're like me, the first thing you want to do with a new programming language is to jump in and start programming. Well, that's exactly what we're going to do in this chapter. You will learn some of the fundamentals of Visual Basic programming by creating a working program. The program you create will be one that should be useful—a loan payment calculator. ■

What are the basic steps in creating a program?

Learn how program creation progresses from design to implementation to distribution.

How you create the interface of a program

The interface of a Visual Basic program consists of its forms and controls (the parts that the user sees and interacts with). In this chapter, we explore how to use these tools effectively as you design your applications.

How to make the program perform tasks

Because a program must do more than just look good, you should design it to perform useful functions.

How to test a program

Obviously, as you are creating a program, you need to test it to make sure that it does what you want it to do. Read this chapter to find out about Visual Basic's extensive debugging tools.

Where and how to save your work

In order to save you hours of frustration over lost work, we will explain how to save a project and its associated files.

Designing Your Program

A college English professor of mine was once describing different types of novelists: "A traditionalist author usually orders his story beginning-middle-end, a modernist might reverse that order, and a post-modernist would only include two of the three parts."

Unfortunately, authors of computer programs do not have that luxury. Due to the structured nature of computing, designing before coding is crucial to a project's success. New programmers have a tendency to resist this, but even with small programs you need to get into the habit of planning. If you do nothing else, sit down with a blank sheet of paper and make some notes about what you want the program to accomplish, and sketch out what the interface should look like.

> **N O T E** Please keep in mind that the strategy presented in this chapter is by no means the only approach to programming, but rather one set of guidelines.

The key steps in creating a computer program are the following:

1. Design the program's tasks (how it works).
2. Design the user interface (how it looks).
3. Actually write the code (implement Steps 1 and 2).
4. Test and debug the program (beta testing).
5. Document and distribute the program (put it in use).

These steps are very generalized and definitely not all-inclusive. As we discuss the following sample program, we'll list some Visual Basic-specific steps.

> **N O T E** If you are tackling a large project, breaking it down into smaller pieces will make it much more manageable. Many of Visual Basic's features (such as custom controls) can be used for dividing up a large project in a team environment. A structured, object-oriented approach is also worth investigating.

The Importance of Design

When starting a new project, it is tempting to just sit down and start hacking out code. After all, drawing the interface and writing the program code are the most fun and creative aspects of programming. However, a good program starts with a solid design. An in-depth flowchart might not be necessary for very small-scale projects, but, on the other hand, it is never a good idea to start without a plan.

The design process should produce the following results:

- A concise list of tasks to be performed by the program
- Deadlines for when particular tasks need to be completed
- Clarification of the dependence of one part of the program on another
- The criteria for testing the program

For a program like the sample in this chapter, the design can be a simple statement of what the program should accomplish. For more complex programs, the design might include written criteria, data diagrams, flowcharts, a milestone document, and a test and acceptance plan. It is up to you and your client (the program's user) to determine the right level of documentation that is necessary for a given project. However, you should always make sure that the design is clearly spelled out, and you should always write it down.

The Sample Program Design

Now let's specify the design of the sample program. In this chapter, you create a simple program that calculates the monthly payment of a loan. The program allows the user to input values for the amount of the loan (principal), the annual interest rate, and the length (term) of the loan. The program provides the user with a way of starting the calculation. Finally, the program verifies that the necessary information was entered, performs the calculation, and then displays the results to the user.

As you can see, in one short paragraph, I specified what the program would do, what information was required to perform the task, and provided some information about how the interface should be designed. That wasn't so bad, was it?

Creating the Interface of Your Program

Now that we have specified the design of the program, it's time to get started with the actual creation of the program. (Note that I'm combining interface design and creation because our program is so simple.) Developing the user interface requires several Visual Basic controls from the Toolbox. You start out using just three controls. In the section "Enhancing Your Program," you learn how to use additional controls to make the loan calculator even better.

Starting at the Beginning

To start working on the sample program, you need to start Visual Basic; or if you are already in Visual Basic, you should start a new project by selecting File, New Project. Whichever you do, you are presented with the New Project dialog box (see Figures 3.1 and 3.2).

FIG. 3.1
The New Project dialog box that appears when you first start Visual Basic 5.

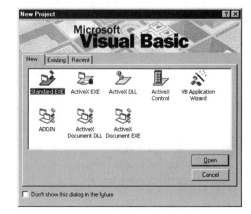

Part
I
Ch
3

FIG. 3.2

The New Project dialog box that opens when you choose File, New Project from within Visual Basic 5.

This dialog box provides you with a choice of application types that you can create. Because the first program is nothing fancy, choose to create a Standard EXE. This choice presents you with the design environment of Visual Basic, displayed in Figure 3.3.

▶ **See** "Starting Up," **p. 24**

FIG. 3.3

After starting Visual Basic's design environment, you are ready to begin creating your first program.

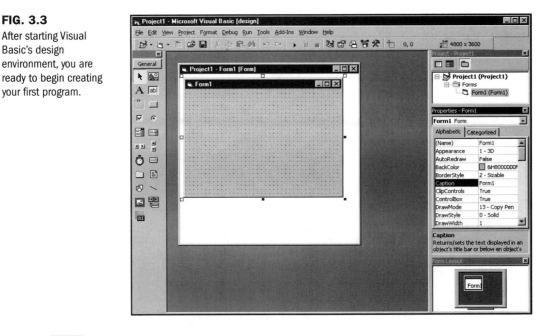

N O T E Because the design environment is customizable, your screen might not look exactly like the one shown in Figure 3.3.

Saving Your Work

As you are working on your program, you need to save it so you can use it again. In fact, you should save your work often in case of a power failure or other problem. It's a very good practice to save your projects as soon as you start working on them, and then save regularly as the work progresses. At the very least, you should save your program before the first time you run it. This way, if it causes your system to crash (yes, it happens to the best of us), you won't lose your work.

You can save your project by choosing File, Save Project from Visual Basic's menu system, or by clicking the Save Project button on the toolbar. The process of saving a project is a little more complex than you might expect; however, with a little practice you'll have no problem. In order to save a project, you must save each *component* of your project (each form, code module, and so on) into its own file and then save the *project* itself into its project file.

Look at the Project window on your Visual Basic desktop. It consists of a list of the components that make up the current project. The Forms folder under Project1 (the default name of a new project) contains exactly one entry—Form1, which is the one and only form in this application. Each form in a project is saved into its own file; the project (list) itself is saved into a separate file.

When you choose to save the project, Visual Basic first wants you to save the components (forms, for example) into their own files before saving the actual project file. The first time you save the project, you are led through a series of Save File As dialog boxes so you can specify the name and location of each file that makes up your project. Subsequent project save operations simply resave the components using the same file names as before, unless new components have been added to the project since the last save. In this case, the Save File As dialog box is presented for each new component (see Figure 3.4).

Part

I

Ch

3

TIP On my hard drive, I have created a VBCODE subdirectory. Underneath that I create a subdirectory (for example, LOANCALC) for each new Visual Basic project. This makes it easy to keep your project files organized in one place.

FIG. 3.4
The Save File As dialog box allows you to specify the name and location of your program files.

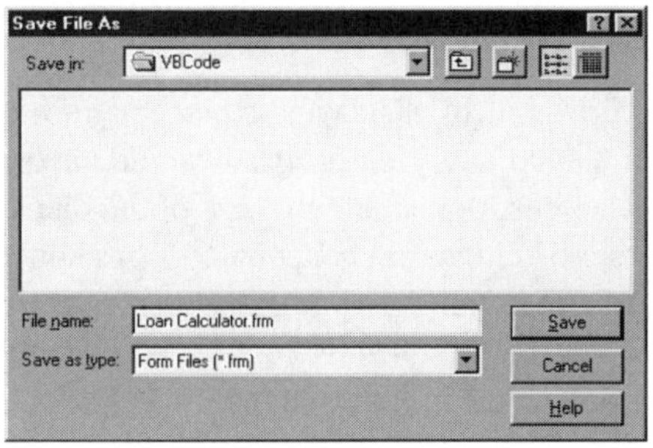

TIP You can have Visual Basic automatically save your program before you run it by setting the option in the Environment Options dialog box. You can choose to have Visual Basic save your program, prompt you to save changes, or not save the changes before running the program.

How You Get User Input

Most programs need a way for users to enter information. There are a number of Visual Basic controls that you can use for input. The first thing to do is look in the Toolbox and see which controls you need. The user interface for your loan calculator is responsible for accepting input, displaying output, and calling functions that perform the loan calculations. So, the three controls that you use initially are the TextBox, the Label, and the CommandButton. These controls are part of the basic set of controls that you find in the Toolbox when you start Visual Basic (see Figure 3.5).

FIG. 3.5
Visual Basic's controls are the building blocks of your programs.

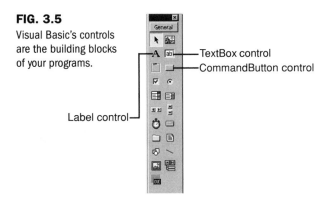

TextBox control
CommandButton control
Label control

The most commonly used control is the TextBox control, also known simply as a *text box*. The name text box is, in this case, self-explanatory (it's a *box* that accepts and displays *text*). An analogy would be boxes you see when filling out a job application or a survey. You might find a box called First Name. It can both accept user input (from a pen) and display information. This real-world box is very similar to a Visual Basic TextBox.

Without something like a TextBox control, displaying a piece of information on the screen would be quite complicated. In olden days, your program would have to determine where to position the information on the screen, determine the size of the display area, and then print the information to the desired spot. With a text box, you only are concerned with what to display, and the control takes care of the rest. If you don't like where the information is displayed, you simply reposition your text box on the form. No coding is required. Similarly, if you don't like the appearance of the text box, you can easily change the text font or the colors.

Accepting user input works the same way. Although the TextBox control sounds simple, it does a lot of work behind the scenes:

- It picks out the character that corresponds to the key pressed by the user.
- It places the character at the appropriate position in the display.
- It handles cursor movement, delete, and backspace key functions.
- It handles text insertion or overwrite functions.
- It stores the information in the computer's memory so your program can retrieve it.

Adding a Control to Your Form   To use a control in your program, you must first put it on a form. The first control we'll add for the loan calculator is a TextBox control. To do this, follow these steps:

1. Select the TextBox control in the Toolbox by clicking it.

2. Move the mouse to the form and place the cursor at one corner of the area where you want the control. Note that the mouse cursor is a cross while you are in drawing mode.

3. Click and hold the left mouse button.

4. Drag the mouse to the opposite corner of the area where you want the control. As you drag the mouse, you might notice a "rubber band" box that shows you the area that will be occupied by the control. If you stop moving the mouse, a ToolTip appears telling you the actual dimensions of the control (see Figure 3.6).

5. Release the mouse button, and the control is drawn on your form (see Figure 3.7).

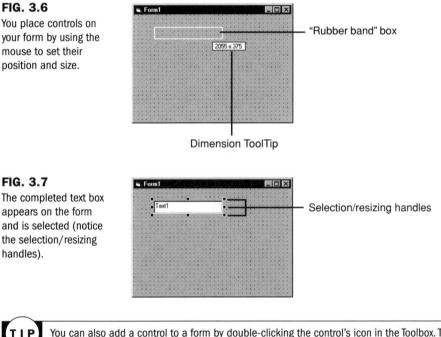

FIG. 3.6
You place controls on your form by using the mouse to set their position and size.

"Rubber band" box

2055 x 375

Dimension ToolTip

FIG. 3.7
The completed text box appears on the form and is selected (notice the selection/resizing handles).

Text1

Selection/resizing handles

T I P   You can also add a control to a form by double-clicking the control's icon in the Toolbox. This places a control of a default size in the center of the form. You can then move and resize the control to your liking with the selection/resizing handles, as described in the upcoming section, "Moving and Resizing a Text Box."

Setting the Properties of the Control   After you have added a text box to your form, you need to set some of its properties. Remember, properties control the appearance and behavior of an object. The two properties you need to set for your text box are the Name and Text properties.

The Name property is very important, because it is used in your program code to identify the control. If you don't know a control's name, you cannot write code to communicate with it. Just in case you forget to assign a name to a text box, Visual Basic initially assigns one for you. For the first text box on the form, this default name is Text1. For the second text box, the name is Text2, and so on. You could just use the default names, but that would not be a good programming practice. Remember that you will use these names to identify the text boxes in your code. A descriptive name makes it easier to maintain your program when you need to make the inevitable changes. For instance, if you have text boxes for first name, last name, and address, it is easier to remember which text box is which if they are named txtLname, txtFname, and txtAddress rather than Text1, Text2, and Text3.

N O T E   The text box names I suggested begin with the prefix *txt*. A three-character prefix is commonly used to identify the type of control, in this case a text box. Other prefixes that are often used to name controls include *lbl* for labels and *cmd* for command buttons.

▶ **See** "Referencing Forms and Controls from Your Code," **p. 73**

To change the name of your text box, go to the Name property in the Properties window and type in a new name in the edit area for the property. For the first text box in the sample program, use the name txtPrincipal (see Figure 3.8).

FIG. 3.8

Use the Properties window to set the various properties of the controls in your project.

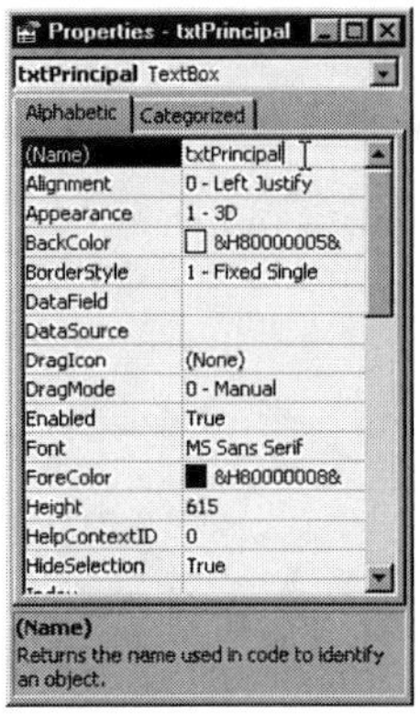

The other property that you need to set for the text box is its Text property. At any given point in time, the Text property contains the actual text (characters) that appears in the text box. You might notice that, by default, the text box displays the name *originally* assigned to the control by Visual Basic (even if you have subsequently changed the Name property). Typically, you will want different text displayed when your form is shown; and quite often, you will want the text box to appear blank. To clear the text box, go to the Text property in the Properties window, highlight the text in the edit area, and press the Delete key. If you want any other text to appear in the text box, simply type in the desired text in the edit area.

N O T E Keep in mind that right now you are in design mode; once the program is running you can only change properties with code. ▪

Adding the Remaining Text Boxes   Now that you have added one text box to the form, it should be a simple matter to add the other text boxes that are needed for the sample program. Go ahead and add three more text boxes and name them `txtTerm`, `txtInterest`, and `txtPayment`. Go ahead and remove the default value from the `Text` property of each text box, as well. When you have finished adding the text boxes, your form should look similar to the one in Figure 3.9.

FIG. 3.9
The Loan Calculator program requires four text boxes.

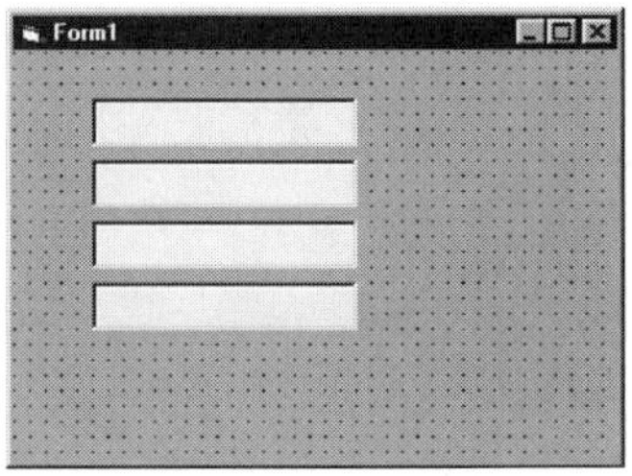

Part
I
Ch
3

T I P   To draw multiple controls of the same type, hold down the Ctrl key when you select the control in the Toolbox. This keeps the Toolbox from switching back to the mouse pointer and allows you to draw multiple instances of the control.

If your form does not look like the one in the figure, no problem. The great thing about a visual design environment is that you can easily change the appearance of an object on the form.

Moving and Resizing a Text Box   You can move the text box to a new location or change its size with just mouse movements. To move a control, simply click it with the mouse and then drag it to a new location. If you pause while you are dragging the control, a ToolTip is displayed showing you the position of the upper-left corner of the control.

To change the size of a control, select the control on the form (again by clicking it) and then click and drag one of the eight *sizing handles* (small squares positioned on each edge and each corner) on the control to make it a different size. This is similar to resizing a window in any other program. A control's sizing handles are illustrated in Figure 3.10.

Now that you have created four text boxes to accept input, you need to label them so the user knows what information to enter. To make room for the labels, let's move the four text boxes to the right side of the form. Rather than moving them one at a time, we can select all of them and move the group. To do this, first hold down the Ctrl key. Next, single-click each of the text boxes with the mouse so the selection handles are visible. Finally, while holding the mouse button down, drag the group of controls to the right side of the form. When finished, your form should look similar to Figure 3.11.

FIG. 3.10

A control's sizing handles let you use the mouse to change its size.

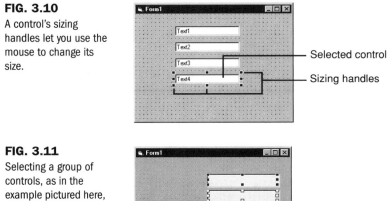

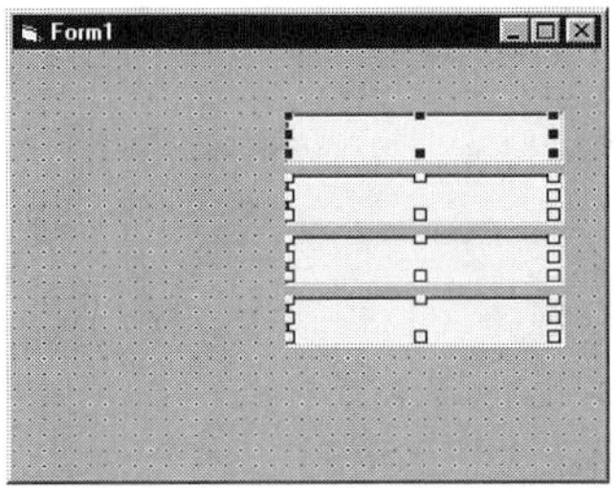

Selected control

Sizing handles

FIG. 3.11

Selecting a group of controls, as in the example pictured here, allows you to move them all at once.

Identifying the Inputs

As we mentioned earlier, you need some type of on-screen indication of what information the text boxes hold (the names that you gave the controls previously are for use within the code and are not displayed on the screen). The easiest way to do this is to place a Label control next to each text box. The label's caption can contain a description of the data to be entered.

In many respects, a label control is very similar to a text box. It can contain letters, numbers, or dates. It can contain a single word or an entire paragraph. Figure 3.12 shows several label controls that illustrate the diversity of appearances you can get. Using the earlier analogy of a job application, the labels are like the words printed on the form to tell you where to write your name or other information.

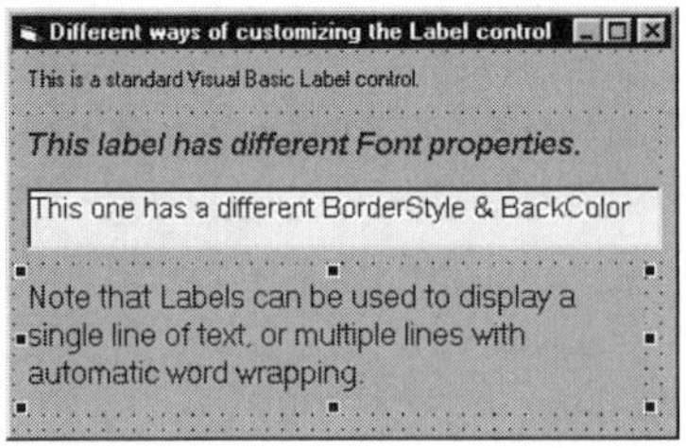

FIG. 3.12

Labels can take on many sizes and appearances.

The key difference between a label control and a text box is that *the information in a Label control can't be edited by the user.* Also, the Label control does not have a Text property. Instead, the information you see in the Label control is stored in its Caption property.

To add a label control to your program, follow these steps:

1. Select the Label control from the Toolbox.
2. Draw a Label control to the left of the topmost text box.
3. Change the label's Name property to lblPrincipal.
4. Change the label's Caption property to Principal: (be sure to include the colon at the end).

By adding this label, you have now made the program easier to use by telling the users where to enter the amount of the loan. As you did with the text boxes for the program, go ahead and create the rest of the labels. You need to create one label to go along with each of the text boxes. Table 3.1 lists the recommended Name and Caption property settings. When you have finished, your form should resemble Figure 3.13.

Table 3.1   Labels that Identify the Program's Input

Label Name	Caption
lblPrincipal	Principal:
lblTerm	Term (Years):
lblInterest	Interest Rate (%):
lblPayment	Monthly Payment:

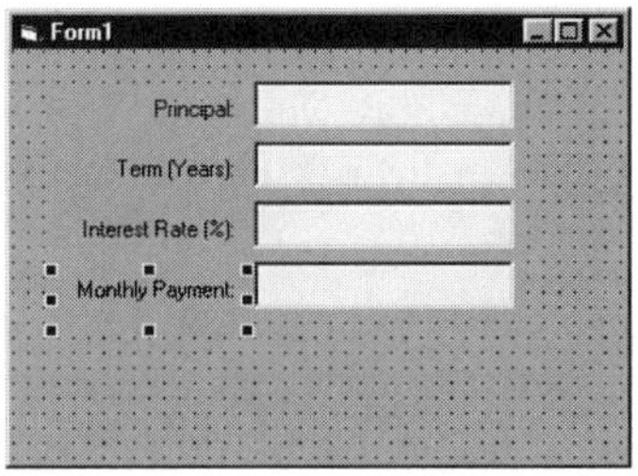

FIG. 3.13
Labels in the program tell the user what information to enter.

> **TIP** To get your labels to right-align near the text boxes like they do in Figure 3.13, select the label controls and change the Alignment property to 1 - Right Justify. The Alignment property field in the Properties window has a drop-down list of alignment choices.

Adding a Command Button

The last controls that you need for the sample program are CommandButton controls. While the TextBox and Label controls are designed for input and display, the CommandButton control is used to initiate a task, similar to a real-life pushbutton. You add a command button to your form the same way that you add the text boxes and labels—by drawing it on the form with the mouse.

First, click the CommandButton control in the Toolbox; then draw the first command button on the form and give it a unique name, just like you did for the other controls. The name used in the sample project is `cmdCalculate`. Also, command buttons, like labels, have a caption. The caption appears on the button's face and typically describes what the button does. For the sample program, change the `Caption` property to `Calculate Payment`. Draw a second command button, `cmdExit`, and set its `Caption` property to `Exit`. Your form should now look like the one in Figure 3.14.

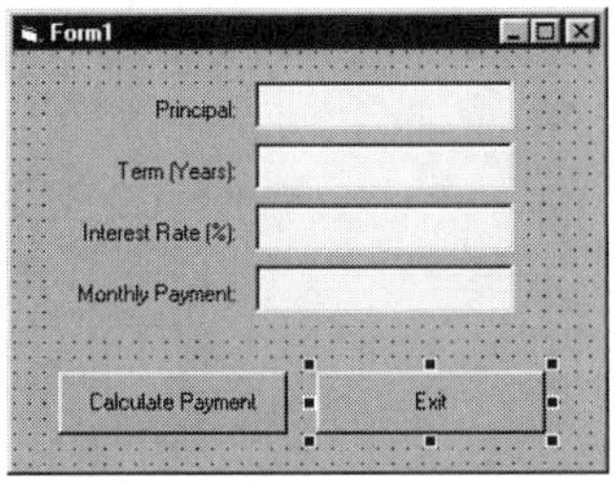

FIG. 3.14
CommandButton controls allow the user to initiate actions in the program.

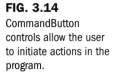

> **N O T E**   In Visual Basic 5, the CommandButton control has undergone a big improvement: You can add a graphic to it with the `Style` and `Picture` properties. In previous versions of Visual Basic, you couldn't do this with a standard CommandButton control. ▪

Performing Tasks

At this point, the interface portion of our sample program is complete. However, if you were to run the program, it wouldn't really do anything. Sure, you could type some numbers into the text boxes, but the program would not perform any calculations on them—which is why you were writing it in the first place.

In order to make your program perform a task, you need to write some code. And in order for the program to perform the task(s), you must have a way of telling the program *when* to perform *which* task. You do this by creating *event procedures*, which are segments of code that are executed when a particular event (the `Click` event, for example) occurs to a particular object (the cmdExit command button, for example). We discuss event procedures in more detail a little later.

Let's start with the easiest code, the Exit button. Double-click the button to bring up the form's Code window, and you might notice a subroutine template, which consists of two lines. These lines, illustrated in Figure 3.15, define the beginning and the end of the event procedure. The default event for command buttons is the Mouse click, so you see the `cmdExit_Click` subroutine.

Any code you place in this procedure (or sub) is executed whenever the user clicks the CommandButton control. Press Tab to indent the code (that makes it easier to read) and then type the word **End** into the subroutine so that it looks like this code:

```
Private Sub cmdExit_Click()
    End
End Sub
```

At this point, you can run the program (by clicking the Start button, by selecting Run, Start from Visual Basic's menu system, or by pressing F5); then click the Exit button to stop it.

FIG. 3.15

Visual Basic provides a skeleton procedure, or template, for each event.

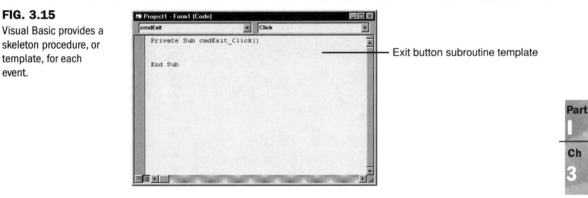

Exit button subroutine template

Activating an Event

In Visual Basic, a program typically takes actions in response to an event. In the preceding, you defined the Click event procedure for cmdExit. An *event* is something that happens to an object either as the result of a user action, an action instigated by another part of the program, or some action from the operating system. Examples of events are the user's pressing a key, the user's moving a mouse, the value of a control being changed, or a specified amount of time elapsing. Whenever the user initiates the Click event for cmdExit, the program executes cmdExit's Click event procedure, which simply consists of the End statement.

▶ **See** "Handling Events in Your Programs," **p. 153**

Each control you use in your programs has been set up to recognize certain types of events. Some controls can respond to mouse clicks, while other controls can respond to changes in their values. If you want a control in your program to respond to a specific event, you must place code in the appropriate event procedure for that control. Otherwise, your program ignores the event.

Look near the top of the Code window, and you will notice two drop-down boxes. The box on the left lists all of the objects that have been placed on the form (as well as the form itself); the one on the right lists the available events for the object that is currently selected in the leftmost box. If you browse through the list on the right-hand side, you'll see that the CommandButton control can respond to more events than just a mouse click. One helpful way to think of your form code is like a long text file, and the Code window is a navigation tool to quickly jump between different procedures.

The easiest way to begin entering code is to double-click the control that you want to have respond to an event. Double-clicking the control opens the form's Code window, automatically selecting the appropriate object, as shown in Figure 3.16.

Part

I

Ch

3

N O T E Double-clicking a control is a shortcut to the code for the control's default event, or whichever event has code in it. For example, the logical main purpose of a CommandButton control is the `Click` event. However, if there is no code in a command button's `Click` event procedure, but there is code in the `MouseMove` event, double-clicking the control would display the `MouseMove` event procedure. ▨

FIG. 3.16

Double-clicking the cmdCalculate command button opens the Code window and places the cursor in cmdCalculate's `Click` event procedure.

```
Project1 - Form1 (Code)
cmdCalculate                    Click

    Private Sub cmdCalculate_Click()

    End Sub

    Private Sub cmdExit_Click()
        End
    End Sub
```

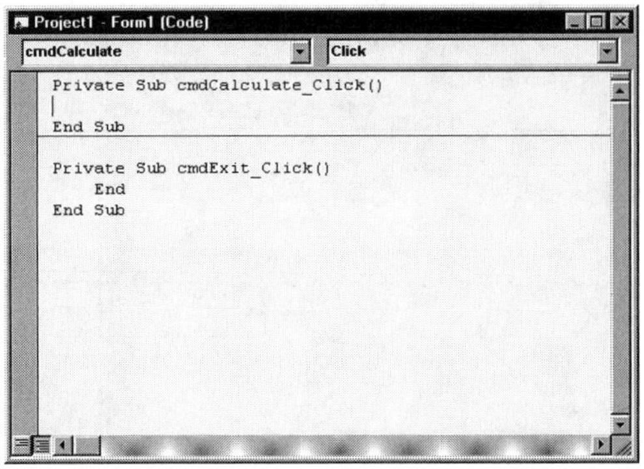

 T I P You can also open the Code window by pressing the F7 key, by clicking the View Code button in the Project window, or by selecting View, Code from the menu system.

The next event procedure code to write is for the `cmdCalculate` command button, because this is the control the user uses to start the calculation:

```
Private Sub cmdCalculate_Click()

End Sub
```

You place the code to calculate the loan payment between the two lines marking the beginning and end of the procedure. (Notice that the procedure name, `cmdCalculate_Click`, is created from the name of the control and the name of the event.)

Writing Program Code

The actual code that is used in this event procedure consists of two parts—the *variable declarations* and the *procedure code*. This section explains the code you need to enter for the Calculate Payment button.

Variable Declarations   The variable declarations area is where you tell Visual Basic the names of the variables that you will be using in the procedure and what type of information each variable will store. Although Visual Basic does not require you to declare your variables, it's good practice to do so and will save you a number of headaches.

The declarations for the sample code are shown in the following code segment. Figure 3.17 shows the variable declarations as they should appear in the subroutine for the Calculate Payment button.

```
Dim crPrincipal As Currency, sgInterest As Single
Dim crPayment As Currency, inTerm As Integer
Dim sgFctr As Single
```

FIG. 3.17
The first code entered in cmdCalculate's Click event procedure should be the variable declarations, as pictured here.

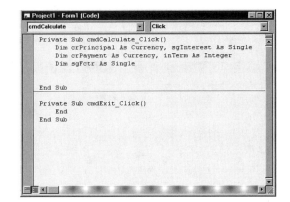

As you might notice in the preceding example, the general format for variable declarations is the word Dim, followed by a variable name of your choosing, followed by As, and the variable's type. Variables can be declared on separate lines or together on the same line.

As with object names, you should follow a naming standard. The naming standard I use for variables uses the first two characters of the variable name as a prefix designating its type; the rest of the name describes its purpose. The variable named crPrincipal, for example, is a Currency type variable that stores the principal amount; sgInterest is a Single type variable storing the interest rate. We discuss variable naming conventions more thoroughly in Chapter 8, "Programming Basics."

▶ **See** "Variable Declarations," **p. 168**

Part
I

Ch
3

Procedure Code The procedure code is the part of the subroutine that does the actual work. In the case of the sample program, the code retrieves the input values from the text boxes, performs the calculation, and inserts the monthly payment value into the appropriate text box. This code is shown in Listing 3.1. Figure 3.18 shows how the procedure code actually appears in the subroutine.

Listing 3.1 LOANCALC.FRM—Calculates the Monthly Payments Using Procedure Code

```
crPrincipal = txtPrincipal.Text
sgInterest = txtInterest.Text / 1200
inTerm = txtTerm.Text
sgFctr = (1 + sgInterest) ^ (inTerm * 12)
crPayment = sgInterest * sgFctr * crPrincipal / (sgFctr - 1)
txtPayment.Text = Format(crPayment, "Fixed")
```

FIG. 3.18

Entering the calculation code completes the Click event procedure for cmdCalculate.

Now that we have created the event procedure, let's briefly review what it does:

- The input values are retrieved from the text boxes and stored in variables.
- The actual calculation is performed using math operators.
- The value of the crPayment variable, which contains the result, is formatted and placed in a text box.

N O T E In the example code, we referred to the text boxes by specifying both the name of the control and the name of the property, separated by a dot (or period). This gives rise to the term *dot notation*. Using dot notation, you can retrieve or set the value of almost any property of a control. Both our code and descriptions of the controls we've drawn are located within the same form. If we needed our code to access one of the controls from another form or module, the form name would be added to the beginning of the dot notation, as in Form1.txtPrincipal.Text. ▓

N O T E The Text property of a text box is known as its "default" property. This means that if you do not specify a property name, the Text property is assumed for the text box; therefore, the last statement in Listing 3.1 could have been written `txtPayment = Format(crPayment, "Fixed")`. ■

▶ **See** "Referencing Forms and Controls from Your Code," **p. 73**

Running Your Program

Now let's run the program and see if it works. To run the program, click the Start button on the Visual Basic toolbar; alternatively, choose Run, Start from the menu system, or press the F5 key. Visual Basic then compiles your program to check for errors, and, if none are found, your program runs. You can now enter values for the principal, term, and interest rate of the loan. Use the following values:

Principal	**75,000**
Term	**30**
Interest	**8.5**

Then click the Calculate Payment button, and the monthly payment is displayed. The payment amount should be 576.69.

After you have finished testing the program and trying various combinations of values, you can return to the design environment by clicking the Exit button, or clicking the End button on Visual Basic's toolbar.

The loan payment calculator is contained in the file LOANCALC.VBP. You can download it from **www.mcp.com/info/0-7897/0-7897-1288-1.**

The loan payment calculator is contained in the file LOANCALC.VBP.

Sharing Your Program

If the program will be used outside of the VB design environment, you need to compile the program. You can compile your program by choosing File, Make LOANCALC.EXE. Choosing this item causes Visual Basic to check your program for errors and then create an executable file that can be used by double-clicking it from Windows Explorer or a shortcut.

▶ **See** "Compiling Your Program," **p. 263**

Enhancing Your Program

A loan payment calculator is a useful tool, but there are several things that you can do to the program to make it even more useful. Let's look at two enhancements that will help you learn a little more about Visual Basic programming techniques.

The first enhancement you will make is one that allows you to perform other types of calculations besides the loan payment. With the enhancement, the user can solve for the principal of the loan or the term of the loan, in addition to solving for the payment. The second enhancement creates an amortization schedule so that the user can see how much interest and principal is paid with each monthly payment and how much total interest was paid for a period.

Adding Loan Analysis Capabilities

Our enhancement is to allow users to choose which part of the equation to solve for, so we need a control that lists some choices and allows the user to pick one. One such control is the OptionButton control. Option buttons work like the buttons on a blender or an old car radio. Only one of the buttons can be pressed at any one time. When the user turns one option on, all the other option buttons on the form are cleared.

1. To begin, resize the form to accommodate the new controls.

2. Change the caption of cmdCalculate from Calculate Payment to Calculate.

3. Add three option buttons to the form. As you add each button, you need to set its Name property. You also need to set a value for the Caption property to identify the type of calculation to be performed. The interface will be easier to use if you place the option button for a particular calculation next to the corresponding label and text box that are already on the form. Table 3.2 shows the Name and Caption properties for each of the buttons.

Table 3.2   Option Buttons for Selecting the Calculation Type

Name	Caption
optPrincipal	Calculate Principal
optTerm	Calculate Term
optPayment	Calculate Payment

4. Set the Value property of the optPayment button to True. (Note that a dot appears inside the selected button.)

Which option has been selected is determined by the Value property of the option button. If a button's Value property is True, this button has been selected. Only one option button on a group can have a Value property of True. Because the payment calculation is the one most often used, we made this the default calculation. When you have finished setting up the option buttons, your form should look like the one in Figure 3.19.

5. Add new code to handle the option buttons. Our program will look at the Value properties of the option buttons and run the corresponding calculation. This decision is done with an old programming standby, the If statement. The If statement checks the value of an expression and then executes the code within the block if the expression is True.

▶ **See** "Programming Basics," **p. 165**

FIG. 3.19

Only one OptionButton control can be selected at a time. You can create multiple groups of Option buttons by placing them in a container control such as a frame.

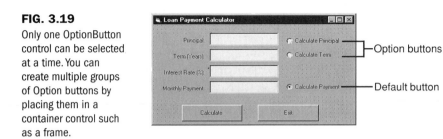

The new `Click` event code with the `If` statements added is shown in Listing 3.2.

Part

I

Ch

3

Listing 3.2   ANALYZE.FRM—By Using *If* Statements You Can Run the Calculation the User Requested

```
Dim m_Principal As Single, m_Interest As Single
Dim m_Payment As Single, m_Term As Integer
Dim m_fctr As Single, m_fctr2 As Single
m_Principal = Val(txtPrincipal.Text)
m_Interest = Val(txtInterest.Text) / 1200
m_Term = Val(txtTerm.Text)
m_Payment = Val(txtPayment.Text)
If optPayment.Value = True Then
    m_fctr = (1 + m_Interest) ^ (m_Term * 12)
    m_Payment = m_Interest * m_fctr * m_Principal / (m_fctr - 1)
    txtPayment.Text = Format(m_Payment, "Fixed")
End If
If optPrincipal.Value = True Then
    m_fctr = (1 + m_Interest) ^ (m_Term * 12)
    m_Principal = m_Payment / (m_Interest * m_fctr / (m_fctr - 1))
    txtPrincipal.Text = Format(m_Principal, "Fixed")
End If
If optTerm.Value = True Then
    m_fctr = Log(m_Payment) - Log(m_Payment - m_Interest * m_Principal)
    m_fctr2 = 12 * Log(1 + m_Interest)
    m_Term = m_fctr / m_fctr2
    txtTerm.Text = Format(m_Term, "Fixed")
End If
```

You can run this modified code to find out how large a loan you can afford for a given monthly payment.

Creating an Amortization Schedule

The final enhancement that you will make to the loan program is to add an amortization schedule to the program. For this enhancement, you need a second command button to run the amortization calculation.

1. Add the new CommandButton to the form and name it cmdAmortize. Set the caption to Amortize.

2. Make your form taller, so there is space below the command buttons for the ListBox control. We will use this control to display the payment sequence. It is like a group of label controls that allows the user to scroll back and forth through all the items.

3. Add a ListBox control to your form just like you would any other control. The modified form is shown in Figure 3.20.

4. Name the ListBox control lstAmort.

▶ **See** "Working with the Standard Controls," **p. 393**

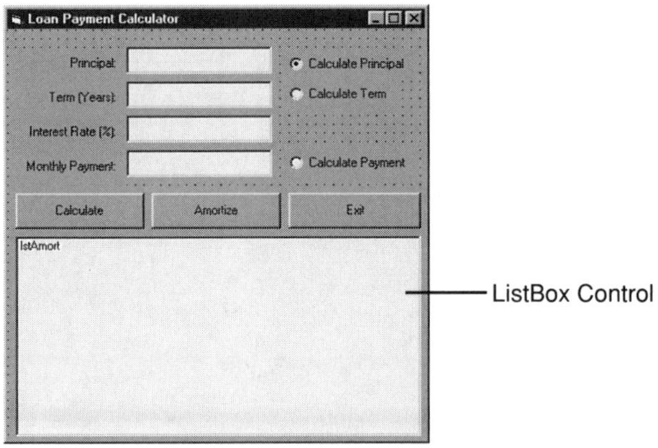

FIG. 3.20
A ListBox control holds
the results of the
amortization calculation.

ListBox Control

As with the other capabilities, you need to add code to the Click event of cmdAmortize. To do this, simply double-click cmdAmortize and enter the code in Listing 3.3.

The code in Listing 3.3 does the following:

■ Clears the list box with the Clear method

■ Adds a header line to the list box

■ Repeats the calculation in a for loop based on the term of the loan

■ Builds a formatted string that includes the calculation result

■ Adds the string with calculation results to the list box by using the control's AddItem method

Listing 3.3   AMORTIZE.FRM—Using a *For* Loop to Perform the Calculation

```
Dim I As Integer, NumPay As Integer
Dim m_int As Single, m_prin As Single, m_totint As Single
Dim AddStr As String
Dim m_Principal As Single, m_Interest As Single
Dim m_Payment As Single, m_Term As Single

m_Principal = Val(txtPrincipal.Text)
m_Interest = Val(txtInterest.Text) / 1200
```

```
m_Term = Val(txtTerm.Text)
m_Payment = Val(txtPayment.Text)
m_totint = 0
lstAmort.Clear
AddStr = "Payment        Interest        Principal      Total Int.     Balance"
lstAmort.AddItem AddStr
NumPay = m_Term * 12
lstAmort.AddItem Space(20) & CStr(m_Principal)
For I = 1 To NumPay
    m_int = m_Interest * m_Principal
    m_totint = m_totint + m_int
    m_prin = m_Payment - m_int
    If m_prin > m_Principal Then m_prin = m_Principal
    m_Principal - m_prin
    AddStr = Format(I, "###") & Space(10) & Format(m_int, "####0.00")
    AddStr = AddStr & Space(5) & Format(m_prin, "####0.00") & Space(5)
    AddStr = AddStr & Format(m_totint, "######0.00") & Space(5)
    AddStr = AddStr & Format(m_Principal, "######0.00")
    lstAmort.AddItem AddStr
Next I
```

You can now run the program to determine the payments of a loan and then run the amortization schedule to view each individual payment. Figure 3.21 shows how the program appears after an amortization calculation.

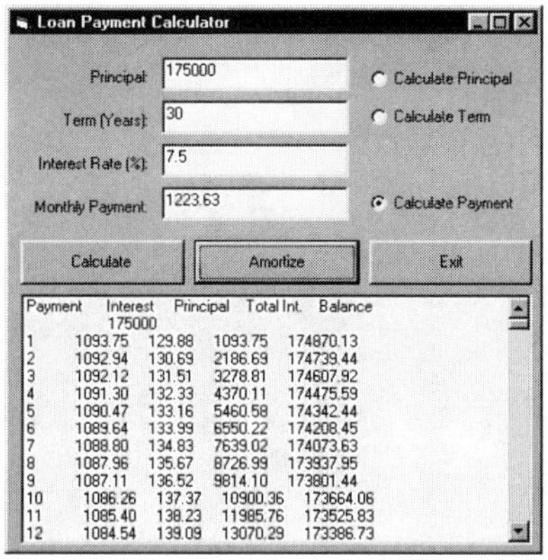

FIG. 3.21

The amortization schedule provides loan payment details.

From Here...

This chapter has introduced you to the basics of creating programs in Visual Basic. First, we discussed some concepts relating to program design and planning. Next, we created a sample program, which introduced a number of VB controls and programming concepts. This chapter was intended to get you comfortable with the Visual Basic programming environment. Other chapters in the book, such as the following, will provide you with more details about various aspects of creating programs:

- ▧ To learn more about handling forms and controls in your programs, see Chapter 4, "Working with Forms and Controls."

- ▧ To find out more about using program commands in your code, see Chapter 8, "Programming Basics."

- ▧ To learn more about option buttons, check boxes, and other controls, see Chapter 15, "Working with the Standard Controls."

Visual Basic Fundamentals

Working with Forms and Controls

A Visual Basic program can be broken up into two main components: the *visual component* and the *code component*. The code component refers to the program code that you type in, which the user never sees on-screen. The visual component, or user interface, is created by using *forms* and *controls*. The forms and controls allow you to handle user input, information display, and user decisions. The nature of Visual Basic's design also allows you to extend the program's capabilities through the use of third-party controls and add-ins. In this chapter, you'll learn the standard techniques for using forms and controls. ■

What do forms do?

Forms provide the foundation of a program's user interface. Forms act as containers for the various controls with which the user will interact.

How to use controls in your programs

Controls are the objects that the user actually interacts with. Learn how to create instances of a variety of types of controls on your forms.

How to control the appearance and behavior of forms and controls

Learn how to use properties, methods, and events of forms and controls to customize how your program looks and works.

How to work with controls as a group

Find out how to set the properties of multiple controls as a group and how to use the Form Editor toolbar to work with multiple controls.

How to use collections

See how the controls on a particular form are contained in a collection and how you can use program code to manipulate all the controls easily.

Exploring Properties

While forms and controls are typically thought of as just what the user sees on the screen, their appearance and behavior are controlled by three basic elements: *properties*, *methods*, and *events*. This section explains these elements in terms of how they define a form, but the principles discussed here apply to all controls that you might use in Visual Basic.

▶ **See** "Handling Events in Your Programs," **p. 153**

When you look at a form, you see a rectangular window on the screen, like the one shown in Figure 4.1. But in reality, this window is defined by a series of properties. For example, the position of the form on the screen is controlled by the Left and Top properties, while the form's size is controlled by its Height and Width properties. The form title that you see in the title bar displays the contents of the form's Caption property. By setting properties, you can even determine which control buttons appear on the form.

FIG. 4.1
The basic elements of a form are defined by its properties.

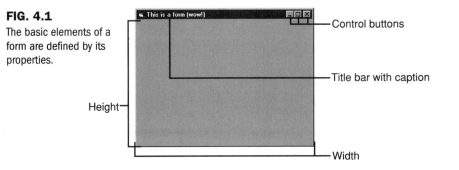

You can use a text editor such as Notepad to open the .FRM file that is created for each of your forms. This text file stores the form's property settings as well as the event code. Figure 4.2 shows a portion of an .FRM file.

> **CAUTION**
>
> For most forms, Visual Basic also creates a file with an .FRX extension. This file stores graphics and other binary elements that cannot be defined by text. It is important when moving forms to another subdirectory to copy the .FRX files as well.

You can think of the properties of a form or control as descriptions of the object's characteristics. This is similar to describing a person. For example, how would you describe yourself? You would probably cite such characteristics as height, weight, hair color, and eye color. Each element of your description could be considered a property.

FIG. 4.2

The properties of a form are stored in text format in an .FRM file.

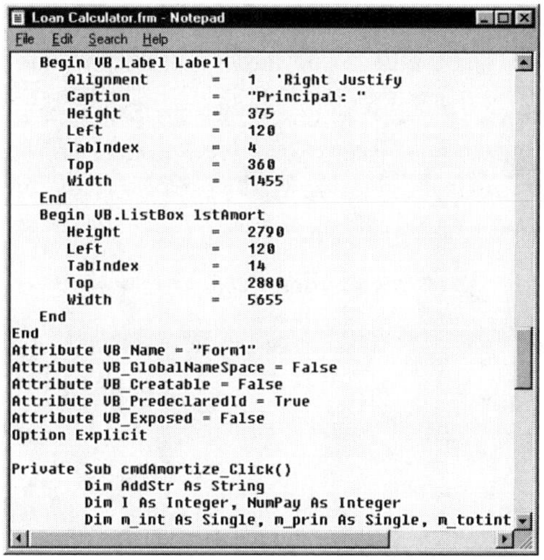

```
 Loan Calculator.frm - Notepad                              _ □ ✕
File  Edit  Search  Help
   Begin VB.Label Label1
      Alignment        =   1  'Right Justify
      Caption          =   "Principal: "
      Height           =   375
      Left             =   120
      TabIndex         =   4
      Top              =   360
      Width            =   1455
   End
   Begin VB.ListBox lstAmort
      Height           =   2790
      Left             =   120
      TabIndex         =   14
      Top              =   2880
      Width            =   5655
   End
End
Attribute VB_Name = "Form1"
Attribute VB_GlobalNameSpace = False
Attribute VB_Creatable = False
Attribute VB_PredeclaredId = True
Attribute VB_Exposed = False
Option Explicit

Private Sub cmdAmortize_Click()
      Dim AddStr As String
      Dim I As Integer, NumPay As Integer
      Dim m_int As Single, m_prin As Single, m_totint
```

N O T E The term "object" in this chapter refers to *visual* objects such as forms and custom controls. In later chapters we will further discuss objects and object-type variables, and how they relate to Visual Basic program code.

What Properties Do Most Objects Have in Common?

All objects in Visual Basic do not have the same set of properties. However, there are several properties that are common to most objects. Some important, common properties are:

- Left
- Top
- Height
- Width
- Name
- Enabled
- Visible
- Index

Controlling Form Size

You can control a form's size by selecting it and dragging its sizing handles at design time, or by changing the values of its Height and Width properties at either design time or runtime. If you do this at design time, you will see a corresponding change in the Height and Width properties in the Properties window. During program execution, you can use code to respond to or initiate a change in size. Try it now:

1. Create a new Standard EXE project and press F5 to run it.

2. Press Ctrl+Break (or click the Break button) to enter Break mode.

3. Press Ctrl+G to bring up the Immediate window.

4. In the Immediate window, type **Print Form1.Width** and press Enter. (The Immediate window, formerly known as the Debug window, allows you to type and execute program statements while in Break mode.) The current value of the `Width` property is printed (see Figure 4.3).

FIG. 4.3

You can print many properties of a form, such as the `Width` property, in the Immediate window.

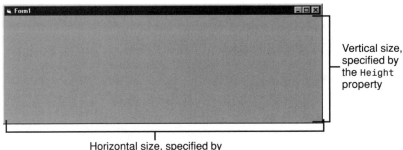

5. In the Immediate window, type **form1.Width = form1.Width * 2** and press Enter.

6. Press F5 (or click the Start button), and notice that Form1's width has doubled (see Figure 4.4).

FIG. 4.4

Setting a new value for the `Width` property in the Immediate window causes the form's width to change immediately.

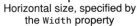

Vertical size, specified by the `Height` property

Horizontal size, specified by the `Width` property

You can see the value of the new width by returning to Break mode and again entering **Print Form1.Width** in the Immediate window.

Measurements in Visual Basic 5

By default, all distances are measured in *twips*. A twip is a unit of measure for objects. The actual physical size of a twip varies depending on screen resolution. You can specify another unit of measure for objects within a container using the container's `ScaleMode` property. However, the screen's scale mode cannot be changed, so a form's `Left`, `Top`, `Height`, and `Width` properties are always measured in twips.

Adjusting Form Position

In addition to controlling a form's size, you can control its position with the Left and Top properties (see Figure 4.5). The Left property specifies the distance of the left side of the object from the left side of the object's container. The Top property specifies the distance of the top edge of the object from the top of its container. In the case of a standard form, the container is the entire screen. If you draw a control on a form, the form is the control's container. It is also necessary to mention that some controls themselves, such as PictureBox and Frame controls, can act as containers for other controls.

FIG. 4.5
This TextBox's position is measured relative to the form.

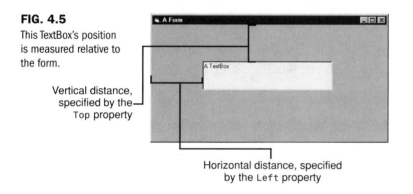

Vertical distance, specified by the Top property

Horizontal distance, specified by the Left property

N O T E   An object's Top and/or Left properties can actually have a negative value! For example, a Label control whose Left property value is -1440 would be positioned so that its left edge is approximately one inch to the left of its container; therefore, some or all of it would not be seen. ▨

While the position of most forms is measured in relation to the upper-left corner of the screen, a form that is part of a Multiple Document Interface (MDI) or browser application is positioned relative to the upper-left corner of the client area (see Figure 4.6).

Controlling User Interaction

Even if your application includes many forms and controls, you probably do not want the user to have access to all of them at the same time. For example, suppose you are writing a word processor. You might have Save File and Load File buttons, but you would not want the user to press Save File until after a file has been loaded. Two properties, the Visible property and the Enabled property, allow you to manage this process.

The Visible property determines if an object can be seen on the screen. The Enabled property determines whether the user can interact with an object. Both properties can be set to either True or False.

FIG. 4.6
MDI child forms and
ActiveX documents are
positioned relative to
the parent form.

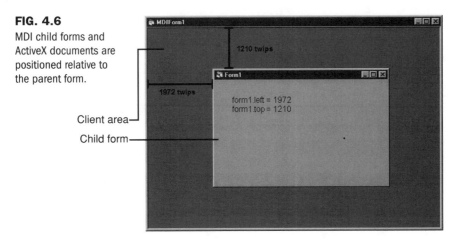

If the Visible property is set to False, the object is not shown, and the user will not know that the object is even there. If the Enabled property is set to False, the object is visible (provided that the Visible property is True), but the user cannot interact with it. Typically, if an object is disabled, it is shown on the screen in a *grayed-out*, or *dimmed*, mode. This provides a visual indication that the object is unavailable.

A good example of objects that are variably available and unavailable occurs in the wizard interface in some Windows programs. A wizard organizes a task into several logical steps, with three navigation buttons (typically labeled Back, Next, and Finish) that are used to move between steps. Depending on which step the user is currently working on, all of these buttons may not be enabled, as in Figure 4.7.

FIG. 4.7
Because the user is on
Step 1 of 4, the
Enabled property of
the Back button is set
to False, causing it to
be grayed out.

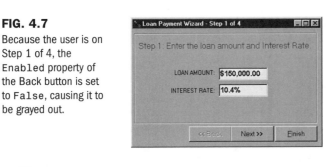

T I P If you are implementing a wizard interface in Visual Basic, one option is to draw the controls for each step in a frame. The Visual Basic Frame control acts as a container, so setting its own Visible property relevant to the user's current step affects all the controls within it. For more information, see Chapter 17, "Using Containers in Your Programs."

Referencing Forms and Controls from Your Code

One other key property of every Visual Basic object is the Name property. The Name property defines a unique identifier by which you can refer to the object in code. Each form, text box, label, and so on must have a unique name.

N O T E All forms in a project must have different names. However, control names have to be unique only for the form on which they are located. That is, you can have a "Text1" control on each form in your project, but you can't have two "Form1" forms in your project. ▨

Visual Basic provides a default name when an object is first created. For example, Form1 is the name given to the first form created for your project, and Text1 is the name given to the first text box that you place on a form. However, the first thing you should do after drawing a control or form is to provide it with a name that has some meaning. For example, I always use frmMain as the name of the main interface form in my applications.

As you are naming your objects, it's good programming practice to use the first three characters of the object's name as a prefix to identify the type of object to which the name refers. As in the frmMain form that we just discussed, the prefix frm indicates that the object is a form. Table 4.1 lists suggested prefixes for many of Visual Basic's objects (forms and controls).

Part

II

Ch

4

Table 4.1 Prefixes that Identify the Object Type

Object Type	Prefix	Object Type	Prefix
CheckBox	chk	Horizontal ScrollBar	hsb
ComboBox	cbo	Image	img
Command Button	cmd	Label	lbl
Common Dialog	cdl	Line	lin
Data Control	dat	ListBox	lst
Data Bound ComboBox	dbc	Menu	mnu
Data Bound Grid	dbg	OLE Container	ole
Data Bound ListBox	dbl	Option Button	opt
Directory ListBox	dir	Picture Box	pic
Drive ListBox	drv	Shape	shp
File ListBox	fil	TextBox	txt
Form	frm	Timer	tmr
Frame	fra	Vertical ScrollBar	vsb
Grid	grd		

Remember that the names you assign will be used in code, so avoid carpal tunnel syndrome by keeping them short!

To set the Name property for an object, select the object, view the Properties window (by clicking the Properties button, by selecting View, Properties Window, or by pressing the F4 key), and click the Name property. You can then type a new value.

FIG. 4.8

The Name property is located at the top of the list on the Alphabetic page and is the first property listed under the Misc group on the Categorized page.

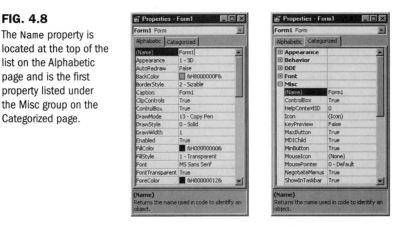

> **T I P** To quickly go to a specific property while in the Properties window, hold down the Ctrl and Shift keys
> and press the first letter of the property name. This takes you to the first property starting with that
> letter. Additional key presses take you to the next property with the same letter.

A First Look at Methods and Events

So far in this chapter, we have concentrated on properties, showing how they can control an object's appearance. However, forms and controls in Visual Basic are not just idle components that sit and look pretty. In addition to properties, an object can have *methods*, which define tasks that it can perform. The tasks can be simple, such as moving the object to another location, or they can be more complex, such as updating information in a database.

Taking Action with Methods

A method is really just a program function that is built into the object. Using its embedded methods, the object knows how to perform the task; you don't have to provide any additional instructions. For example, forms have a PrintForm method that prints them to the current printer. The statement Form1.PrintForm prints an exact duplicate of Form1. Because the low-level details for the PrintForm method are encapsulated within the form object, a Visual Basic programmer does not have to be concerned with them.

As you may have guessed, methods, like properties, use *dot notation*. When typing code, Visual Basic uses the Auto List Member feature to list an object's methods and properties when you type the object's name followed by a period.While there are different methods for different objects, many objects have the following methods in common:

- **Drag**   Handles the operation of the user's dragging and dropping the object within its container
- **Move**   Changes the position of an object
- **SetFocus**   Gives focus to the specified control
- **ZOrder**   Determines whether an object appears in front of or behind other objects in its container

N O T E   *Focus* refers to the *current* control that receives user actions, such as keystrokes. Only one control on any form can have the focus at any given time. Focus is usually indicated by the position of the edit cursor (for text boxes) or a dotted rectangle around the control (for check boxes, option buttons, and command buttons).

Responding to Actions with Events

In addition to performing tasks, the objects in your program can respond to actions, whether generated by the user or externally. These actions are handled through the use of *events*. For example, when a user clicks a command button, he causes a Click event to occur to that command button. Part of the definition of an object determines to which events it responds.

Examples of events are clicking a command button, selecting an item in a list box, or changing the contents of a text box. Events also occur when the user exits a form or switches to another form. When an event happens to an object, the object executes an *event procedure* for that specific event. To respond to events, you have to place program code in the object's event procedures. For example, in Chapter 3 you placed code in the Click event of a command button for the Loan Calculator program.

▶ **See** "Performing Tasks," **p. 54**

Chapter 7, "Responding to the User," delves into all the intricacies of events. In that chapter, you learn how to write code to handle events and how multiple events are related.

▶ **See** "Handling Events in Your Programs," **p. 153**

How Properties and Methods Are Related

By now, you know that objects have properties to define their appearance, methods that let them perform tasks, and events that let them respond to user actions. You might think that all these things happen independently of one another, but that is not always the case. Sometimes, the properties and methods of an object are related. That is, as you invoke a method of an object, the properties of the object are changed. Also, most times that you use the methods of an object or change its properties with code, you do so in response to an event.

N O T E   Some property changes can trigger events. For example, changing the `Height` or `Width` property of a form in code triggers the form's `Resize` event. ▪

You can see one example of the interdependence of methods and properties of an object when the `Move` method is used and the `Left` and `Top` properties are set. You can cause an object to change position either by using the `Move` method or by setting the `Left` and `Top` properties to new values. For example, the following two code segments accomplish the same task of changing a text box control's position to 100 twips from the left and 200 twips from the top of its container:

```
'CODE SEGMENT 1 - Move the text box by setting its properties
txtName.Left = 100
```

```
'CODE SEGMENT 2 - Move the text box using the Move method
txtName.Move 100, 200
```

You should notice two things about these code segments. First, code lines beginning with a single quote (') are considered comments; that is, Visual Basic ignores anything after the single quote. You can use comments to describe or explain your code. Second, if you type the code segments, you'll notice that the `Move` method has two additional arguments available. These optional arguments can change the size of the object. This has the same effect as setting the `Height` and `Width` properties to new values.

Similarly, the `Show` and `Hide` methods of a form have the same effect as changing the form's `Visible` property. When you invoke the form's `Hide` method, the effect is the same as setting its `Visible` property to `False`. (The effect, of course, is that the form disappears from the screen.) Likewise, the form's `Show` method produces the same effect as setting its `Visible` property to `True`.

Forms

So far, most of our examples have used the Form object. A form is a container that holds all the other controls (such as labels, text boxes, and pictures) that make up the user interface. Most of your programs will use a number of forms.

N O T E   It is possible to create a Visual Basic program that contains no forms at all! One example might be a command-line program that processes files and requires no user interface. ▪

Parts of a Form

When you start a new Standard EXE project, you are presented with the *default project*, which normally includes a single standard form (see Figure 4.9). Because this form is where you start work on your user interface, let's take a look at the different parts of it.

FIG. 4.9
A form is the starting point for building a user interface.

Minimize button   Maximize/Restore button

Caption (or title)

Close button

Form

Design grid

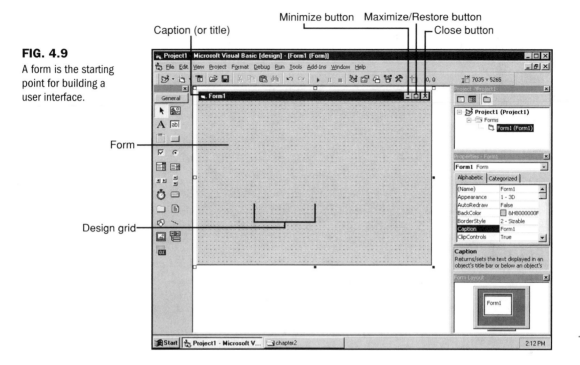

As you can see in Figure 4.9, a Visual Basic form contains all the elements you would expect to find as part of a window in a program. It contains a title bar, a control menu, and a set of Minimize, Maximize/Restore, and Close buttons. Note that many of these elements, such as the Close button, are always present at design time even if the properties are set in such a way that they are not visible at runtime.

Another design-time feature is a grid that allows you to easily line up controls as you are designing your interface. You can control the behavior of the design grid through the Options dialog box, accessible by choosing Tools, Options. In this dialog box, you can change the size of the grid or even turn it off completely. You can also choose whether or not controls are automatically aligned to the grid. If this option is on (the default setting), the upper-left corner of each control is aligned with the grid point that's closest to the corner. Using the default setting makes it easy to line up controls. In fact, I set the grid to be smaller than the default, which allows more precise control alignment.

Form Properties Revisited

Forms, like most of the objects used in Visual Basic, have a series of properties that control their behavior and appearance. In the earlier section "Controlling User Interaction," you learned about some of the properties that apply to forms. In this section, you learn about several additional key properties of forms. You also learn how these properties can be controlled

Part

Ch

during program design and execution. Table 4.2 lists several of the key properties of a form and provides a brief description of each. The table also identifies whether the value of the property can be changed while the program is running.

Table 4.2 Key Properties for Controlling a Form

Property Name	Description	Changeable at Runtime
BorderStyle	Sets the type of border that is used for the form	No
ControlBox	Determines whether the control box (containing the Move and Close menus) is visible when the program is running	No
Font	Determines the font used to display text on the form	Yes
Icon	Determines the icon that is shown in the form's title bar and that appears when the form is minimized	Yes
MaxButton	Determines whether the Maximize button is displayed on the form when the program is running	No
MDIChild	Determines whether the form is a child form for an MDI application	No
MinButton	Determines whether the Minimize button is displayed on the form when the program is running	No
StartUp Position	Determines the initial position of a form when it is first shown	Yes
WindowState	Determines whether the form is shown maximized, minimized, or in its normal state	Yes

Now let's take a closer look at some of these properties. The BorderStyle property has six possible settings that control the type of border displayed for the form (see Table 4.3). These settings control whether the form is sizable by clicking and dragging the border; they control the buttons that are shown on the form; and they even control the height of the form's title bar (see Figure 4.10).

Table 4.3   Possible *BorderStyle* Property Settings that Control the Type of Window Displayed

Setting	Effect
0 - None	No border is displayed for the form. The form also does not display the title bar or any control buttons.
1 - Fixed Single	A single-line border is used. The title bar and control buttons are displayed for the form. The form is not resizable by the user.
2 - Sizable border	The border appearance indicates that the form can be resized. The title bar and control buttons are displayed. The form can be resized by the user by clicking and dragging the border. This is the default setting.
3 - Fixed Dialog	The form shows a fixed border. The title bar, control box, and Close button are shown on the form. Minimize and Maximize buttons are not displayed. The form cannot be resized.
4 - Fixed ToolWindow	The form has a single-line border and displays only the title bar and Close button. These are shown in a reduced font size (approximately half height).
5 - Sizable ToolWindow	This is the same as the Fixed ToolWindow, except that the form has a sizable border.

FIG. 4.10

Changing the BorderStyle property can give a form many different appearances.

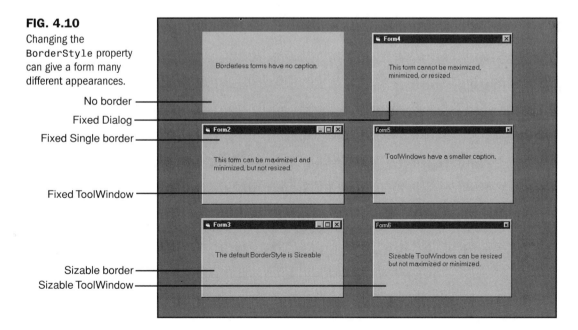

No border

Fixed Dialog

Fixed Single border

Fixed ToolWindow

Sizable border

Sizable ToolWindow

N O T E Setting the BorderStyle property to prevent resizing does not affect the form's appearance in the design environment; it affects it only at runtime. ■

The default setting provides a border that enables the user to resize the form while the program is running. This is the type of form that you find in most of the programs you use, such as Microsoft Word or Microsoft Money. However, you can change the BorderStyle setting to make the form look like almost any type of window that you would see in a program, including toolboxes and dialog boxes. You can even remove the form's border altogether.

In Table 4.3, several of the BorderStyle definitions indicate that a control box and the Close, Minimize, and Maximize buttons would be displayed in the title bar of the form. This is the default behavior. But even with these border styles, you can individually control whether these elements appear on the form. The ControlBox, MaxButton, and MinButton properties each have a True or False setting that determines whether the particular element appears on the form. The default setting for each of these properties is True. If you set a property to False, the corresponding element is not displayed on the form. These properties can be changed only at design time.

The Font property lets you set the base font and font characteristics for any text displayed directly on the form by using the form's Print method.

N O T E The Font property of a form is actually an object itself with its own properties. For example, to change the size of a form's font, you would enter **Form1.Font.Size = 10** in a Code window (or the Immediate window, for that matter) to change the size to 10 points. ■

In addition, setting the form's Font property sets the font for all controls subsequently added to the form.

TROUBLESHOOTING

I set the Font property of the form, but the font in the title of the form did not change. The Font property of the form has no effect on the form's title; it affects only its internal area. Windows itself controls the font for a window title. This can be changed in the Windows 95 Control Panel.

When I use a form's Print method, sometimes I can't see my text. If you do not set the form's AutoRedraw property to True or use the Refresh method, your text can be erased when another window is stacked on top of the form. Also, you need to look at the CurrentX and CurrentY properties to make sure that the text is displayed within the visible area of the form.

One final form property of note is the StartupPosition property. As you might guess, this property controls where the form is located when it is first displayed. There are four possible settings for the StartupPosition property. These settings are summarized in Table 4.4.

Table 4.4 Possible *StartupPosition* Property Settings that Control Where the Form Is Initially Displayed

Setting	Effect
0 - Manual	The initial position is set by the Top and Left properties of the form.
1 - CenterOwner	The form is centered in the Windows desktop unless it is an MDI child form, in which case it is centered within its parent window.
2 - CenterScreen	The form is centered in the Windows desktop.
3 - Windows Default	The form is placed in a position determined by Windows based upon the number and position of other windows open at that time.

N O T E This feature is a godsend to longtime Visual Basic programmers. In previous versions of Visual Basic, you had to write code to center the form by setting the Top and Left properties or by using the Move method. With the StartupPosition property, this is all handled for you. ▨

Although the StartupPosition property can center your form for you when the form first loads, it does not keep the form centered. For example, if you resize the form, it does not remain centered. If you want to have the form centered after it has been resized, you still need to write code to perform the task. This code (see Listing 4.1) should be placed in the form's Resize event procedure.

Listing 4.1 FORMDEMO.FRM—Using Code to Keep a Form Centered After Its Size Is Changed

```
If Me.Height >= Screen.Height Then
    Me.Top = 0
Else
    Me.Top = (Screen.Height - Me.Height) / 2
End If
If Me.Width >= Screen.Width Then
    Me.Left = 0
Else
    Me.Left = (Screen.Width - Me.Width) / 2
End If
```

Note in the preceding listing the use of the Me keyword, instead of the form name (such as Form1). When used in a form's code, Me represents the form itself without having to refer to it by name, much as a pronoun can refer to a person without having to use his or her name. This means that the same block of code could be inserted into several forms without any changes. Also, if a form is ever renamed, Me ensures that the changed name doesn't affect procedures that act upon the form.

TIP Visual Basic's new Form Layout window is useful if you are working in a higher resolution than that in which your users will be running your program. Right-click the Window and check the Resolution Guides option to see form sizes relative to standard screen resolutions.

Displaying a Form

If you write a program with just a single form, you needn't worry about displaying the form or hiding it. This is done automatically for you as the program starts and exits. This single form is known as the *Startup Object* or *Startup Form*. When you run your program, Visual Basic loads your Startup form into memory and displays it. As long as this form remains loaded, your program keeps running and responding to events. When you press the Close button on the form (or execute the End statement), the program stops.

N O T E   You can select a Startup form in the Project Properties dialog box. It is also possible to have a program start from a Sub procedure named Main in a code module rather than from a form. ■

However, if you have multiple forms—as most of your programs do—you need to understand how to manage them. The state of a form is controlled by Visual Basic's Load and Unload statements, as well as the form's Show and Hide methods.

The Load statement places a form in memory, but does not display it. The following line of code shows how the statement is used:

```
Load frmMember
```

By using this, you are *explicitly* loading the form. However, the form is loaded automatically if you access a property, method, or control on it.

Because the load operation is performed automatically, it is not really necessary to use the Load statement with a form. However, it is important to be aware when a form is being loaded, because the code in the Form_Load event will be executed at that time.

TIP There are some cases where you would want to use the Load statement (see the "Using *Load* to Enhance Performance" sidebar later in this section).

To display the form, you must use the Show method. The Show method works, whether or not the form was loaded previously into memory. If the form was not loaded, the Show method *implicitly* loads the form and then displays it. The Show method is used as follows:

```
frmMember.Show
```

The Show method also has an optional argument that determines whether the form is shown as a *modal* or *modeless* form. If a form is shown modally, then no other forms or code outside that form are executed until the modal form is closed. Think of the program code as being paused as long as a modal form is displayed. An example of a modal form is the Windows 95 Shut Down screen. You cannot put the focus on another window while the Shut Down Windows form is displayed.

If a form is shown modeless, you can move at will between the current form and other forms in the program. The preceding statement displayed a form as modeless. To create a modal form, you simply set the optional argument of the Show method to vbModal, as shown here:

```
frmMember.Show vbModal
```

N O T E A modal form is typically used when you want the user to complete the actions on the form before working on any other part of the program. For example, if a critical error occurs, you do not want the user to switch to another form and ignore it.

After a form is displayed, you have two choices for getting rid of it. The Hide method removes the form from the screen but does not remove it from memory. Use Hide when you need to temporarily remove the form from view but still need information in it, as in the following code example:

```
frmSelect.Show vbModal

frmResults.Print "The date you entered was: " & frmSelect.txtDate
```

In the preceding example, the purpose is to display a form and then retrieve a value from a text box on it. Because the form is shown modally, the second statement is not executed until the form is removed from the screen. Presumably, the user would enter the information and then press a button that executed frmSelect's Hide method.

If you are finished with a form and the information contained on it, you can remove it from both the screen and memory with the Unload statement. The Unload statement uses basically the same syntax as the Load statement, as shown here:

```
Unload frmMember
```

T I P If you are using the Unload statement from within the form you are removing, you can use the keyword Me to specify the form. This prevents errors if you later rename your form. In this case, the statement would be the following:

```
Unload Me
```

Using *Load* to Enhance Performance

Because the Show method automatically loads a form into memory, it typically is not necessary to use the Load statement in your program at all. However, some forms with a very large number of controls display slowly when they are shown. One way around this is to load the form into memory, by using the Load statement, when the program begins to run. With the form already in memory, subsequent Hide and Show methods appear to perform much more quickly. If you use this trick, be careful of two things. First, don't forget to unload the form at the end of your program. Second, be aware of possible memory limitations. If you load too many forms in memory at once, you might see a decline in the overall performance of your program.

Loading forms into memory does increase the amount of time that it takes for your program to start, but you will save time whenever the form is shown. If you show a form only once during the program, there is no net time savings by loading it at the beginning. However, if the form is shown more than once, there usually is an overall time savings. Also, users are typically more tolerant of time delays when a program loads (especially if they're busy looking at a splash screen) than later when they are performing a task.

Handling Events

In the section "Responding to Actions with Events," you learned that most objects respond to events or actions that are taken by a user, the program, or the operating system. There are five special events that occur to each form, and you can place code in the associated event procedure for any of these:

- *Load* Occurs when the form is loaded into memory
- *Activate* Occurs when the form is displayed initially or when the user returns to the form from another form
- *Deactivate* Occurs when the user moves to another form or the form is hidden
- *Unload* Occurs when the form is unloaded from memory
- *Initialize* Occurs when an instance of the form object is created

The key to understanding the purposes of these events is knowing when they occur. If you still are confused, try the simple tutorial that follows.

First, follow these steps to set up a test project:

1. Open Visual Basic and create a new Standard EXE project.
2. Double-click the center of Form1 to bring up its Code window.
3. Make sure the Load event is selected in the drop-down Event box at the upper-right of the Code window.

4. Type the statement **MsgBox "Form Load Event"** into the event procedure so that the code looks like this:

```
Private Sub Form_Load()
    MsgBox "Form Load Event"
End Sub
```

5. Repeat Steps 3–4 to place similar MsgBox statements in the Initialize and Unload events.

6. Add a second form, *Form2*, to the project by choosing Project, Add Form.

Now that you have created the project, press F5 to run it. Notice that the Initialize event comes first, followed by the Load event. Click the form's Close button, and you will notice that the Unload event occurs before the program stops.

Now start the program again and then press Ctrl+Break to pause execution. Press Ctrl+G to bring up the Immediate window. Put the cursor in the Immediate window and enter these lines (pressing Enter after each), observing the messages that appear:

```
Load Form2
Unload Form1
Load Form1
```

(The reason you load Form2 is to prevent the program from ending when you unload Form1.) You should have noticed that the Initialize event did not occur when Form1 was loaded the second time. Enter the following lines:

```
Unload Form1
set Form1 = Nothing
```

It's good practice to set an instance of a form to Nothing when you're done with it. This ensures that all resources that were allocated to the form are properly released.

Now enter this line:

```
Load Form1
```

You'll see that the Initialize event occurs again. This is because the instance of Form1 that you created before was destroyed when it was set to Nothing.

You can use program code in these events to set the properties of the form or any of its controls, set up databases or recordsets needed for the form, or run any other code that you might find necessary. The Load and Unload events each occur only once in the life of a form—when the form is loaded and unloaded from memory, respectively. On the other hand, the Activate and Deactivate events can occur many times. Therefore, you need to be careful of which code is placed in which event.

The following code segments show you a couple of simple but useful things that you can do with code in the Load event procedure. Listing 4.2 shows you how the captions of labels and command buttons can be set by using the LoadResString function to read a string from a resource file. This is useful when you want to be able to distribute your application in multiple languages, as you need only replace the resource file with one created in the appropriate language.

Listing 4.2 RESOURCE.FRM—Using *Load* to Set Captions

```
'Retrieve the captions for all controls from resource file
  'Caption range is 701 to 750
Me.Caption = LoadResString(701)
For I = 0 To 5
    cmdSearch(I).Caption = LoadResString(702 + I)
Next I
fraSearch.Caption = LoadResString(708)
For I = 0 To 4
    lblSearch(I).Caption = LoadResString(709 + I)
Next I
For I = 0 To 1
    cmdTitle(I).Caption = LoadResString(714 + I)
Next I
fraChngTitle.Caption = LoadResString(716)
For I = 0 To 1
    lblTitle(I).Caption = LoadResString(717 + I)
Next I
cmdDone.Caption = LoadResString(719)
```

Another use of the Load event is to open recordsets in a database application. This allows you to open the recordset once and then use it throughout the code in the form. This is shown in the following code:

```
Set ConvSet = MemDb.OpenRecordset("Conventions", dbOpenTable)
ConvSet.Index = "Convention"
ConvSet.MoveLast
LastRec = ConvSet("ConvID")
```

It's often also useful to maximize the form as it is displayed. This involves simply setting the WindowState property of the form when the form is loaded. This is done as follows:

```
Me.WindowState = vbMaximized
```

Another form event that you will use often is the Resize event. This event is triggered any time the size of the form is changed, either by the user or by your program. It also occurs after the form's Load event, before the Activate event occurs. Typically, you use the Resize event to change the size of one or more controls on your form. Doing this gives the user more room to work when the size of the form is increased and prevents information from being hidden when the size of the form is decreased. Listing 4.3 shows how the size of a data-bound Grid control changes when the form's size is changed. The code also checks the WindowState property of the form and does not perform the operation when the form is minimized.

> **Listing 4.3   RESIZE.FRM—Changing the Size and Position of Controls When the Form Size Changes**
>
> ```
> If Me.WindowState <> vbMinimized And AllowResize Then
>     dbgResults.Width = Me.ScaleWidth - 180
>     dbgResults.Height = Me.ScaleHeight - dbgResults.Top - 60
> End If
> ```

Using Controls

Although forms are an important part of your programs, you can't do very much without adding controls to them. Visual Basic controls let you do a wide variety of things including edit text, display pictures, and interface with a database. The liberal use of controls has always been one of Visual Basic's strongest features. Because of Visual Basic's design, you are not limited to using only the controls provided by Microsoft. The design allows easy integration of third-party controls—which has led to a thriving market for these custom controls. With this amount of third-party involvement, chances are that you can find a control to perform almost any task you want, from data acquisition to custom reporting to specialized graphics processing to game play, and everything in between. While controls have been around since the beginning of Visual Basic, the capability to create your own controls was just introduced in version 5. Visual Basic now allows you to create your own ActiveX controls for use in your programs and in any other program that adheres to ActiveX standards.

What Are Controls?

Controls are objects in Visual Basic designed to perform specific tasks. Like form objects, controls have associated properties, events, and methods. For example, if you use a Text-Box control, you can set properties to determine the size of the text box, the font for the text that it displays, and the color of the text and background. The text box correctly sizes and displays the text, based on the property values that you assign. Also, a text box has internal code that allows it to process keystrokes, so that it knows, for example, to erase a character when you press the Backspace key. If you wrote programs in earlier languages, particularly in the DOS and mainframe environments, you know that you might have had to write a significant amount of code just to accept and process keystrokes that allowed the user to enter input. Now you just drop a control on your form, and the rest is done for you.

Visual Basic 5 comes with a standard set of controls that are available in all editions and that let you perform many types of programming tasks. These controls are illustrated in the Toolbox shown in Figure 4.11 and are listed along with their functions in Table 4.5. Many of these controls are discussed in detail in the later section "Finding Out What Controls Can Do."

FIG. 4.11

The Visual Basic controls are accessible from this Toolbox.

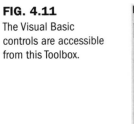

Table 4.5   Visual Basic 5 Standard Set of Controls

Control Button	Control Name	Function
	PictureBox	Displays graphics. Can also serve as a container for other controls.
A	Label	Displays text that the user cannot edit.
	TextBox	Displays text; allows the user to enter and edit the text.
	Frame	Serves as a container for other controls. Provides grouping of controls.
	CommandButton	Allows the user to initiate actions by clicking the button.
	CheckBox	Lets the user make a true/false choice.
	OptionButton	Lets the user choose one option from a group of items.
	ComboBox	Lets the user choose from a list of items or enter a new value.
	ListBox	Lets the user choose from a list of items.
	Horizontal ScrollBar	Lets the user choose a value based on the position of the button in the bar.
	Vertical ScrollBar	Same as Horizontal ScrollBar.
	Timer	Lets the program perform functions on a timed basis.
	Drive List Box	Lets the user select a disk drive.

Control Button	Control Name	Function
[icon]	Directory List Box	Lets the user select a directory or folder.
[icon]	File List Box	Lets the user select a file.
[icon]	Shape	Displays a shape on the form.
[icon]	Line	Displays a line on the form.
[icon]	Image	Similar to a PictureBox control. Uses fewer system resources, but doesn't support as many properties, events, and methods.
[icon]	Data Control	Provides an interface between the program and a data source.
[icon]	OLE	Provides a connection between the program and an OLE server.
[icon]	Common Dialog	Allows use of Windows standard dialog boxes to retrieve information such as file names, fonts, and colors.

N O T E The controls shown in the preceding figure and table are not the only ones included with Visual Basic. To add other controls, such as the Microsoft Common Dialog Control or Microsoft FlexGrid control, to your Toolbox, use the Components dialog box by choosing Components from the Project menu. ▪

Adding Controls to the Form

To be able to use any of the available controls, you must first add them to a form. To add a control, simply select the appropriate tool in the Toolbox, then draw the control on the form by clicking the form and dragging the mouse. You can also double-click the tool to add a default-sized control to the center of the current form. After the control is on the form, you can set its properties and use it in your program.

Setting and Retrieving Control Property Values

One way to set property values is by using the Properties dialog box at design time. However, for the controls to be really useful in your programs, you need to be able to set their properties in code as the program runs and, more importantly, to retrieve the values of their properties. For example, you know that a user can enter text in a TextBox control, but to be able to use the text he or she entered, you need to be able to read it from the control. For example, you may want to read a user's input and convert it to uppercase letters before further processing.

When you are using a control's property in code, you can use it just like you would a variable or constant. You can use the properties in comparison statements to make decisions, and you can use them in assignment statements to set the value of a variable. You can also use an assignment statement to set the value of a property. The following code shows how the Text property of a text box is used to retrieve a name entered by the user, convert it to all capitals, and put the modified text back in the text box:

```
Sub cmdCapitalize_Click()
  Dim sName As String
  sName = txtName.Text
  sName = Ucase$(sName)
  txtName.Text = sName
End Sub
```

To reference an object's property in code, you must specify the name of the object (the text box named txtName in the preceding code) and the name of the property (the Text property in this example), using a dot (or period) to separate them. Be aware, however, that some properties are read-only at runtime, and some only exist at runtime. An object can have more properties than those listed in the Properties window. To find a complete list, look up the control in the Help system and follow the *Properties* hyperlink.

N O T E If you are referring to a control on a form other than the current form, you also need to specify the name of the form. The form name precedes the control name and is separated from it by a dot (.). A generalized syntax for changing property values that always works is *formname.objectname.propertyname = value*. For example:

```
frmMember.txtName.Text = "Smith, John"
```

It is good programming practice to always specify the name of the property, but many controls have what is known as a *default property*. A default property can be referenced simply by specifying the name of the control. For example, the Text property is the default property of the TextBox control. Therefore, the following two statements work exactly the same:

```
'************************************
'Property name specifically referenced
'************************************
txtName.Text = "Mike"


'***************************************************
'Property name omitted, utilizing default property
'***************************************************
txtName = "Mike"
```

Table 4.6 shows the default property of a number of controls.

Table 4.6   Default Properties of Common Controls

Control Type	Value Property
Check box	Value
Combo box	Text
Directory list box	Path
Drive list box	Drive
File list box	FileName
Horizontal scroll bar	Value
Image	Picture
Label	Caption
Option button	Value
Picture box	Picture
Text box	Text
Vertical scroll bar	Value

Finding Out What Controls Can Do

In the previous sections, you learned what controls are and how to use them in your programs. You also learned a little about their properties, methods, and events. In this section, you find out more details about some of the most frequently used controls. You learn about other controls in Part IV, "Working with Visual Basic Controls."

Working with Text

One of the most common tasks in programming is working with text. Now, *text* here does not just mean paragraphs and sentences like those you handle with a word processor. When you deal with text in a program, you also might want to display or retrieve a single word, a number, or even a date. For example, in a data-entry program, you might need to handle the name, address, telephone number, date of birth, and other information about a member. Text information can easily be handled using Visual Basic's TextBox control. Figure 4.12 shows a data-entry screen for a membership application.

Visual Basic provides several controls for handling text. The major controls included with VB are the Label, TextBox, Masked Edit, and RichTextBox controls. These controls can handle most of your program's text editing and display needs.

FIG. 4.12

You can handle all types of information with text controls.

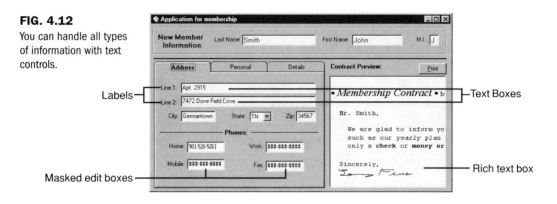

Labels

Masked edit boxes

Text Boxes

Rich text box

N O T E   In this chapter, only the Label and TextBox controls are covered. The RichTextBox and Masked Edit controls are covered in detail in Chapter 13, "Working with Text, Fonts, and Colors."

Using a Label Control to Display Text   The simplest control that displays text is the Label control. The most common use of the Label control is identifying different items on a form, such as the data-entry form shown in Figure 4.12. Each label identifies the information in the edit field next to it. Used in this way, each label typically is set up at design time, and the necessary text is assigned to the label's Caption property in the Properties dialog box.

However, you are not limited to using the Label control in this manner. In fact, you can use the Label control to display any type of information to the user. A label can display a date, a number, a single word, or even an entire paragraph of information.

While the Caption property of the Label control contains the text to be displayed, there are other properties of the control that influence *how* the text is displayed. The most obvious of these properties are the Font and ForeColor properties, which determine the typeface and text color of the control, respectively. However, if you are going to use the label to display more than a small amount of text, the AutoSize and WordWrap properties are the ones that will be most important to you.

If you know in advance what text is going to be displayed in a label's Caption property, you can set the size of the label to accommodate the text. However, if different text will be displayed in the label at different times (for instance, in a database application), it needs to be able to adjust to the length of its current contents. The AutoSize property of the Label control determines whether or not the size of the control automatically adjusts to fit the text being displayed. When AutoSize is False (the default), the label's size remains unchanged regardless of the length of its caption. If a caption is too long for the label, some of it will not be visible.

Setting AutoSize to True causes a label to automatically adjust its size to fit its caption. If the caption is longer than the label's original size allows, the method of resizing depends upon the value of the WordWrap property. If the WordWrap property is False (the default), the label expands horizontally to allow the caption to fit, even if the label grows so large that it runs past the right edge of the screen. If the WordWrap property is set to True, the label expands vertically to allow enough lines of text to accommodate the caption, even if the label runs off the bottom edge of the screen. (The *words wrap* to new lines, hence the property name WordWrap.) In either case, the Caption property contains the entire caption, even if some of the text "spills off" of the form. The effects of the different settings of the AutoSize and WordWrap properties are shown in Figure 4.13.

T I P When assigning a label's Caption property, you can force a new line by including a *carriage return* and *line feed* combination. This technique is a throwback to the ancient days of manual typewriters. When a manual typewriter user reached the end of a line, he had to manually move the paper up to the next line (a line feed) and return the carriage to the beginning of that line (a carriage return). In Visual Basic, you can insert a carriage return/line feed combination by inserting ASCII characters 13 and 10 into the caption at the point where the line should break. Visual Basic supplies a predefined constant, vbCrLf, to help you accomplish this task:

```
Label1.caption = "First Line" & vbCrLf & "Second Line"
```

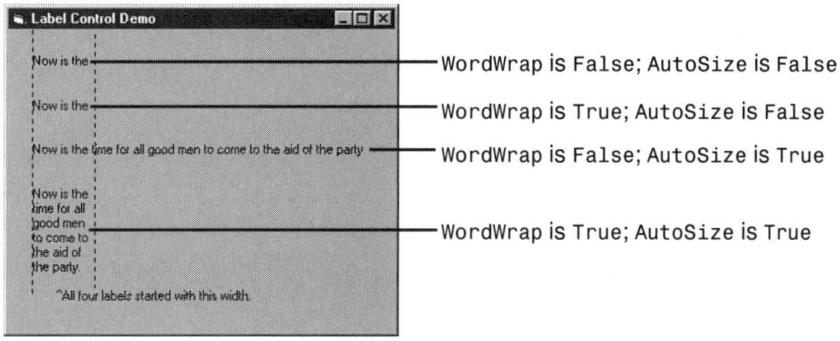

FIG. 4.13
These four labels have the same long caption; their AutoSize and WordWrap properties determine if and how they resize to fit the caption.

WordWrap is False; AutoSize is False

WordWrap is True; AutoSize is False

WordWrap is False; AutoSize is True

WordWrap is True; AutoSize is True

CAUTION
To preserve the original width of your Label control, you must set the WordWrap property to True before setting the AutoSize property. Otherwise, when you set the AutoSize property to True, the Label control adjusts horizontally to fit the current contents of the Caption property.

There are three other properties that, from time to time, you might need to use with the Label control. These are the Alignment property, the Appearance property, and the BorderStyle property. The Alignment property determines how the text is aligned within the Label control. The possible options are Left-Justified, Right-Justified, and Centered. The Appearance can be set to Flat or 3-D to govern whether the label appears raised from the form. The BorderStyle property determines whether the Label control has no border or a single-line border around the label. With BorderStyle set to Fixed Single, the Label control takes on the appearance of a noneditable text box. The effects of the Alignment, Appearance, and BorderStyle properties are shown in Figure 4.14.

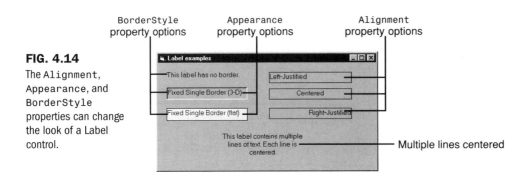

FIG. 4.14
The Alignment, Appearance, and BorderStyle properties can change the look of a Label control.

N O T E The Alignment property also affects the text when the label is used to display multiple lines. The control aligns each line according to the setting of the Alignment property (refer to Figure 4.14).

Entering Text with a Text Box Because much of what programs do is to retrieve, process, and display text, you might guess (and you would be correct) that the major workhorse of many programs is the TextBox control. The text box allows you to display text; more importantly, however, it also provides an easy way for your users to enter and edit text and for your program to retrieve the information that was entered.

In most cases, you use the text box to handle a single piece of information, such as a name or address. But the text box is capable of handling thousands of characters of text. A TextBox control's contents are stored in its Text property—the main property with which your programs will interact. You can also limit the number of characters a user can enter with the MaxLength property.

By default, the text box is set up to handle a single line of information. This is adequate for most purposes, but occasionally your program needs to handle a larger amount of text. The text box has two properties that are useful for handling larger amounts of text—the MultiLine and ScrollBar properties.

The MultiLine property determines whether the information in a text box is displayed on a single line or multiple lines. If the MultiLine property is set to True, information is displayed on multiple lines, and word-wrapping is handled automatically. The user can press Enter to force a new line. The ScrollBar property determines whether or not scroll bars are displayed in a text box, and if so, what type of scroll bars (None, Horizontal, Vertical, or Both). The scroll bars are useful if more text is stored in the Text property than fits in the text box. The ScrollBar property has an effect on the text box only if its MultiLine property is set to True. Figure 4.15 shows the effects of the MultiLine and ScrollBar properties.

FIG. 4.15
You can use a text box
to enter single lines of
text or entire para-
graphs.

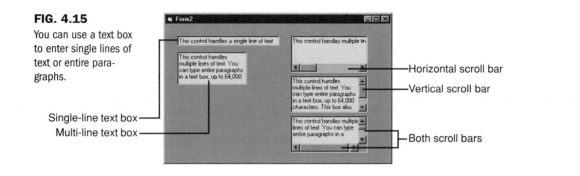

Single-line text box
Multi-line text box

Horizontal scroll bar
Vertical scroll bar

Both scroll bars

TROUBLESHOOTING

The text box in my program will handle only about 32,000 characters instead of the 64,000 specified in the documentation. When you use the default value of zero for the MaxLength property, this corresponds to a limit of 32 kilobytes (about 32,766 characters). To allow more characters, set the MaxLength property to the desired value, but don't exceed 64 kilobytes (about 65,535 characters).

T I P When a text box is activated (known as *receiving the focus*) by the user tabbing to it or clicking in it, a common practice is to select (or highlight) its contents. While there's no automatic way to accomplish this, it can be done pretty easily. One method that I recently discovered has quickly become my favorite. Enter this line of code in the text box's GotFocus event procedure:

```
SendKeys "{Home}+{End}"
```

The SendKeys statement sends a string of characters to the active form at runtime just as if the user typed them at the keyboard. In this case, we're acting as if the user pressed the Home key, then a shifted End key (the plus sign before {End} represents Shift). This causes the text to be highlighted, so the user can begin entering new text without having to delete what is already there.

Actions

Another control important to practically every application that you will develop is the CommandButton control. Typically, this control is used to let the user initiate actions by click-ing the button. Setting up a CommandButton control is quite simple. You draw the button on the form and then set the Caption property of the button to the text that you want displayed on the button's face. To activate the button, just place code in the button's Click event procedure. As any other event procedure, this code can consist of any number of valid Visual Basic pro-gramming statements.

While users most often use command buttons by clicking them, some users prefer accessing commands through the keyboard versus using the mouse. This is often the case for data-entry intensive programs. To accommodate these users, you want your program to trigger command button events when certain keys are pressed. You accomplish this by assigning an *access key* to

Part
II
Ch
4

the command button. When an access key is defined, the user holds down the Alt key and presses the access key to trigger the Click event of the CommandButton control.

You assign an access key when you set the CommandButton control's Caption property. Simply place an ampersand (&) in front of the letter of the key you want to use. For example, if you want the user to be able to press Alt+P to run a print command button, you set the Caption property to &Print. The ampersand does not show up on the button, but the letter for the access key is underlined. The caption <u>P</u>rint then appears on the command button.

N O T E   If, for some reason, you need to display an ampersand in a CommandButton caption, simply use two of them in a row in the Caption property—for example, Save && Exit. ▓

In addition to captions, your command buttons can have pictures. Simply set the Style property to Graphical, and use the Picture property to select a picture file. Figure 4.16 shows several options for creating command buttons.

FIG. 4.16
Command buttons can communicate their functions to the user in many ways.

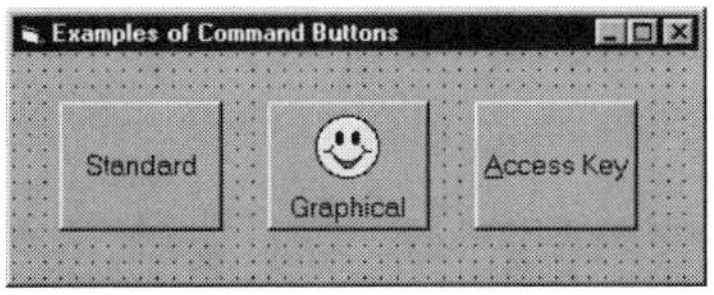

One command button on a form can be designated as the *default button*. This means the user can simply press Enter while the focus is on any control (except another command button or a text box whose MultiLine property is True) to trigger the default button. This activates the default button's Click event, just as if the user had clicked it with the mouse. To set up a button as the default button, set its Default property to True. Only one button on a form can be the default button.

You can also designate one button as the *cancel button*, which is similar to the default button but works with the Esc key. To make a command button into a cancel button, set its Cancel property to True. As with default buttons, only one button on a form can be a cancel button. As you set the value of the Default or Cancel property of one button to True, the same property of all other buttons on the form is set to False.

Working with Multiple Controls in the Design Environment

So far, you have seen how to add controls to your forms and how to set the properties of a single control at a time. But sometimes you need to be able to work with multiple controls at the same time. For example, if you have a bunch of label controls on a form and decide to change their font, you don't want to have to select and change each label control individually. That would be a real hassle. Fortunately, you don't have to handle controls one at a time; you can work with them in groups.

The first step in working with multiple controls is to select the controls you need to move or modify. You can select a group of controls by clicking the mouse on your form and dragging it. As you drag the mouse, you see a dashed-line box appear on the form as shown in Figure 4.17. Use this box to enclose the controls you want to select.

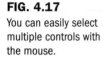

FIG. 4.17
You can easily select multiple controls with the mouse.

When you release the mouse button, any controls that are inside the box or touching it are selected. The selected controls are indicated by small boxes at each corner and in the center of each side of the control (see Figure 4.18).

FIG. 4.18
Selection points (boxes) indicate that a control is selected.

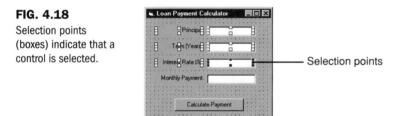

Selection points

N O T E You can also select multiple controls by holding down the Ctrl key while you click them individually. If you need to select a group of controls that are contained within a frame or picture box, you *must* Ctrl+click them because the dashed-line box technique won't work. ■

You can add controls to a group or remove them by clicking the control while holding down the Shift or Ctrl key. You can even do this after making an initial selection with a mouse drag, so you can refine your selection to exactly the group of controls you want to work with.

After the group of controls has been selected, you can move the group as a whole by clicking one of the controls in the group and dragging the group to a new location. The controls retain their relative positions within the group as you move them. You can also use editing operations such as Delete, Cut, Copy, and Paste on the group as a whole.

Using the Properties Window

In addition to the ability to move, cut, copy, paste, and delete a group of controls, you can also work with their properties as a group. For example, if you want to change the font of a group of Label controls, simply select the group of controls and access the Font property in the

Properties window. When you change the property, all the selected controls are affected. This is a great tool for making changes to many controls at once. I use this technique frequently to change the alignment of all the Label controls on my form.

While it is obvious that this works for a group of controls of the same type (such as a group of labels or a group of text boxes), you might be wondering what happens when your group includes controls of several different types. In this case, Visual Basic displays the properties that are common to all the controls in the group. These properties typically include Top, Left, Height, Width, Font, ForeColor, Visible, and Enabled. You can only edit the properties that are common to all the controls. However, this is very useful if you want to align the left or top edges of a group of controls. To do this, simply select the group and set the Left property of the group (or the Top property). Figure 4.19 shows a selected group of different controls and the Properties window containing their common properties.

FIG. 4.19

Common properties of different controls can be modified as a group.

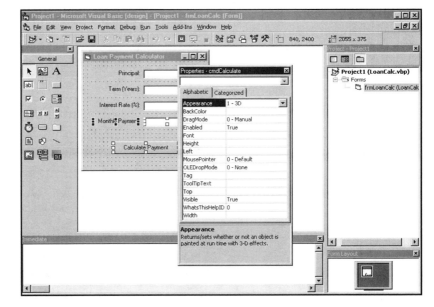

Using the Form Editor Toolbar

Editing common properties is not the only way to work with a group of controls. Visual Basic 5 adds a great tool to the development environment. This tool is the Form Editor toolbar (see Figure 4.20), which is accessible by selecting View, Toolbars, Form Editor. Table 4.7 shows and explains each of the toolbar buttons.

FIG. 4.20

The Form Editor toolbar makes it easy to align and size multiple controls.

Table 4.7   The Form Editor Toolbar Buttons

Button	Name	Function
	Bring to Front	Move selected control in front of other controls on the same part of the form.
	Send to Back	Move selected control behind other controls on the same part of the form.
	Align	Lines up a group of controls
	Center	Centers a group of controls
	Make Width Same Size	Resizes a group of controls to match
	Lock Controls Toggle	Prevents movement or resizing of controls with the mouse (however, the controls can still be modified with the Properties window)

The Form Editor toolbar allows you to manipulate the position and size of a group of controls. The Align button allows you to align the left, right, top, or bottom edges of a group of controls. While you can align the left and top edges of a group by setting the Left or Top properties directly, there is no direct way to align the right or bottom edges. The Align button also allows you to line up the vertical or horizontal centers of the controls. This cannot be done directly with the properties. To choose which type of alignment to use, click the arrow button to the right of the Align button. This displays a menu that allows you to pick the alignment. You can also choose to align all the selected controls to the grid. This causes the upper-left corner of each control to be moved so that it is touching the grid point nearest its current location.

Another task that was tedious in previous versions of Visual Basic was centering controls on the form. This has also been made easy using the Form Editor toolbar. Next to the Align button is the Center button. This button allows you to center the group of controls horizontally or vertically within the form. The entire group is centered as if it were a single control; the relative position of each control in the group remains the same. As with the alignment options, you select the type of centering you want from a pop-up menu that appears when you click the arrow button next to the Center button.

The last button on the Form Editor is the Make Same Size button. This button allows you to make the height and/or width of all the controls in the group the same. While you can do this by setting the appropriate properties, the Form Editor makes it much more convenient.

Figure 4.21 shows a group of controls that has been made the same size as well as centered horizontally within the form.

FIG. 4.21

With the Form Editor toolbar, centering and resizing controls is a snap!

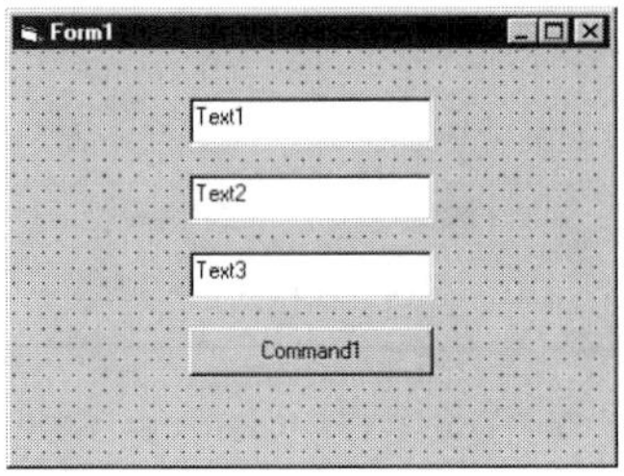

TIP If you press the wrong button on the Form Editor toolbar, you can undo the changes by clicking the toolbar's Undo button, or by pressing Ctrl+Z.

Using the Format Menu

Just when you thought you had seen every possible way to manipulate multiple controls, you find out that there is one more option available to you—Visual Basic's Format menu (see Figure 4.22). The Format menu contains all of the same functions as the Form Editor toolbar, but also has three other options for working with multiple controls—Horizontal Spacing, Vertical Spacing, and Size to Grid.

FIG. 4.22

The Format menu offers a number of tools for fine-tuning the appearance of controls on your forms.

The Horizontal Spacing option allows you to make the spacing between controls equal. This gives you a clean look for groups of controls such as command buttons. If you think the controls are too close together, you can choose to increase the spacing. The spacing is increased by one grid point. You can also choose to decrease the spacing between controls, or remove the spacing altogether. Choosing Vertical Spacing allows you to perform the same tasks in the vertical direction. Figure 4.23 shows a "before" and "after" look at a group of command buttons. The "after" portion shows the effect of setting the horizontal spacing equal.

FIG. 4.23

Equal horizontal spacing makes this group of buttons look orderly.

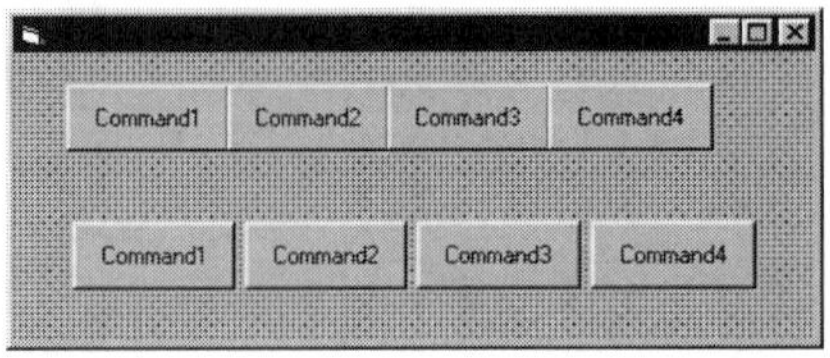

The final item on the <u>F</u>ormat menu is the Size to Gri<u>d</u> item. Selecting this option sets the `Height` and `Width` properties of each selected control so that it exactly matches the grid spacing.

Working with the Controls Collection

By now, you're probably thinking, "All this is great when I am in the design environment, but what about while my program is running?" Well, as you know, you can change the properties of any single control by specifying the control name, the property name, and the new property value. But does this mean that you have to set each control individually? No way!

Each form contains a collection called the Controls collection. This collection identifies each control that is on the form. Using this collection and a special form of the `For` loop, you can change a specific property of every control on your form.

Changing All Controls

As an example, you might want to give your users a way to select the font they want to use for the controls on the form. Trying to set each form in code would be a real pain. But, with the `For Each` loop, you can set the font of every control on the form with just three lines of code (see Listing 4.4).

On the Web

Listing 4.4   COLLECT.FRM—Collections Allow You to Set Properties for Multiple Controls in Code

```
For Each Control In Form1.Controls
    Control.Font = "Times New Roman"
Next Control
```

You can do the same thing with any other properties that are supported by all the controls on the form.

Changing Selected Controls

But what if you want to set a property that is not supported by all the form's controls? For example, if you want to change the text color of your controls, the command button doesn't have a `ForeColor` property, although other types of controls do. For this problem, you use another code statement, the `TypeOf` statement. This statement allows you to determine the type of any object. This way, you can set up a routine that changes the `ForeColor` property of all controls that are not command buttons. This is shown in Listing 4.5.

Listing 4.5   COLLECT.FRM—Using the *TypeOf* Statement to Omit Specific Controls from Processing

```
For Each Control In Form1.Controls
    If Not TypeOf Control Is CommandButton Then
        Control.ForeColor = &HFF
    End If
Next Control
```

From Here...

This chapter has introduced you to the world of forms and controls. You have seen how to control the appearance of forms and controls through their properties and how the methods of forms can be used to perform tasks. You have also seen how to work with multiple controls in both the design environment and in your programs.

The following chapters provide you with even more information about working with forms and controls:

■ Chapter 15, "Working with the Standard Controls," explores some of the other commonly used controls.

■ Chapter 18, "Exploring New Visual Basic 5 Controls," discusses some of the more complex controls that are provided with Visual Basic.

■ Chapter 19, "Advanced Control Techniques," shows you how to create control arrays, add and delete controls at runtime, and how to use classes to enhance controls.

■ Chapter 36, "Advanced Form Techniques," shows you how to extend the functionality of forms by creating your own methods and properties.

Adding Menus and Toolbars to Your Program

In Chapter 4, "Working with Forms and Controls," you learned the basics of creating programs by using the forms and controls that are provided with Visual Basic. You learned how controls such as the Label and TextBox controls are used to display and sometimes edit information. You also learned how a command button can be used to let the user initiate an action. All these controls are very powerful tools, and you can create a number of applications by using just these standard forms and controls. However, there are other tools available in Visual Basic that can make your programs even more powerful and easier to use.

For example, consider a program menu. Although it's true that a menu item provides the same functionality as a command button (a way for a user to start an action), menus are much better suited for handling large numbers of possible actions. The word processor I'm using has about a hundred menu options. Can you imagine how the program would look if it used only command buttons? There would be no room left to enter text! Fortunately, the possible actions have been arranged as choices in an organized menu system. Even better, the commands I use most often are easily accessible through one of several toolbars that I can choose to display.

Creating a menu

In this chapter, you learn how to create a menu system for your programs like the menus you would find in most Windows programs.

Modifying your menu at runtime

You see how you can hide or disable menu items to allow the user to access them only when appropriate.

Implementing pop-up menus

Many programs have context-sensitive menus that are displayed with a click of the right mouse button on a particular object. You learn how to add these to your programs.

Complementing your menus with a toolbar

Many Windows programs have one or more *toolbars* that provide the user quick access to the most commonly used menu commands. You see how the Toolbar control makes this easy to do.

In this chapter, you'll learn how you can create a sophisticated menu system for your applications. Menus in Visual Basic programs can consist of a few simple commands, or an entire repertoire of possible actions. In addition, you'll learn how to add toolbars to your programs so your users can have quick access to commonly used program functions. ■

Controlling a Program with a Menu Bar

One of the most important things in any program is providing the user with easy access to all of the program's functions. Users are accustomed to accessing most functions with a mouse click or two. And users want all the functions located conveniently in one place. You handle this in your programs by using *menus*. Visual Basic lets you quickly and easily create menus with the Menu Editor. With this editor, you create menu bars located at the top of a form, or pop-up menus that the user typically accesses by clicking the right mouse button. The menu bar from a membership program is shown in Figure 5.1.

FIG. 5.1
A menu provides a convenient location for a large number of functions.

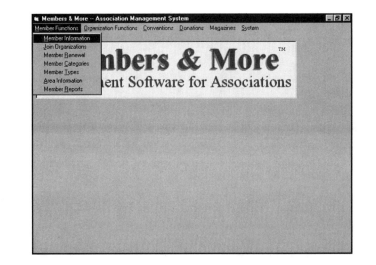

Creating a Menu Bar

The first step in creating a menu is determining what functions need to be on the menu and how these functions will be organized. Figure 5.2 shows Visual Basic's own main menu. As you can see, the functions are organized into groups of similar items (File, Edit, View, and so forth).

Common Menus   When you create your menu, you should group similar items. In fact, if possible, use groups with which your users are already familiar. This way, users have some idea where to find particular menu items, even if they've never used your program. The following list describes some standard items you will find on many menus:

■ *File*   This menu contains any functions related to the opening and closing of files used by your program. Some of the typical menu items are New, Open, Close, Save, Save As, and Print. If your program works extensively with different files, you might also want to include a quick access list of the most recently used files. If you include a File menu, the program's Exit command is usually located near the bottom of this menu.

■ *Edit*   The Edit menu contains the functions related to editing of text and using the Windows Clipboard. Some typical Edit menu items are Undo, Cut, Copy, Paste, Clear, Find, and Replace.

■ *View*   The View menu might be included if your program supports different looks for the same document. A word processor, for example, might include a normal view for editing text and a page-layout view for positioning document elements, as well as a variety of zoom options. Another use of the View menu is to allow the user to display or hide special forms in your program, like the Visual Basic View, Toolbox option.

■ *Tools*   This menu is a catch-all for your program's utilities or "helper" functions. For example, a spelling checker, grammar checker, or equation editor might be included for a word processor.

■ *Window*   This menu typically is included if your program uses a Multiple Document Interface (MDI). MDI programs, like Microsoft Word, support the simultaneous editing of different documents, databases, or files. The Window menu lets users arrange open documents or switch rapidly between them.

■ *Help*   The Help menu contains access to your program's Help system. Typically, it includes menu items for a *Help Index* (a table of contents for help), a *Search* option (to let the user quickly find a particular topic), and an *About* option (providing summary, authoring, and copyright information regarding your program).

Part

II

Ch

5

FIG. 5.2

Visual Basic's main menu, shown here with its File menu opened, provides a convenient and intuitive way for users to select the various program functions.

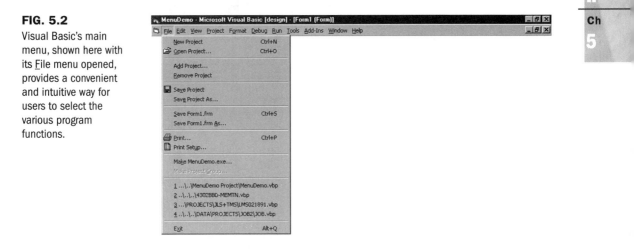

You can use these six menus as a basis for creating your own menu system. Include any or all of them as needed by your program. If you need to add other menu groups, feel free; you are not bound to use only these options. Plan well before adding a lot of new groups. Remember that your users are probably already familiar with these types of menus, so don't confuse them by going menu-happy.

Setting Up the Main Items After deciding what functions to include in your menu and how these functions will be grouped, you can build the menu. To create a menu, first open the form where you want the menu located, and then start the Menu Editor in any of three ways: click the Menu Editor button on the toolbar, choose Tools, Menu Editor, or press Ctrl+E. The Menu Editor appears, as shown in Figure 5.3.

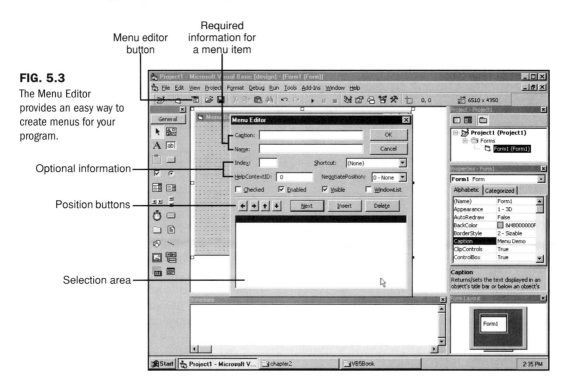

FIG. 5.3

The Menu Editor provides an easy way to create menus for your program.

Each line of text (menu item) in a menu is considered a Menu control. You can use the Menu Editor to create Menu controls, and to set these properties for each control:

- *Caption* The actual text that is displayed in the menu item. You can specify an access key, which allows the user to select the menu item with the keyboard instead of a mouse, by placing an ampersand (&) before the appropriate letter of the caption. For example, if a particular menu item's Caption property is set to F&ormat, the "o" would be underlined, and the user could select that item by pressing Ctrl+O. The Caption property is required for all menu items.

- *Name* Used to identify the menu item in code. The Name property is required for all menu items, and must be unique. Unlike other controls, Visual Basic does not give menu items a default name, so you must set the Name property of all menu items before leaving the Menu Editor.

- *Index*   If this menu item is part of an array of Menu controls, the Index property uniquely identifies the particular control array element.

- *Shortcut*   You can define shortcut key combinations that allow your users to select a menu item with one keystroke, bypassing the menu system entirely. For example, many programs use Ctrl+P as a shortcut key that eliminates the need to choose File, Print from the menu system.

- *HelpContextID*   Sets a context ID that can be used in conjunction with a custom help file to provide context-sensitive help for your application.

- *NegotiatePosition*   If your application has linked or embedded objects, this property determines if and how this menu item is displayed while the linked or embedded object is active.

- *Checked*   If True, a check mark appears to the left of the menu item's caption to indicate, for example, that the user has selected a particular option. If False, no check mark appears.

- *Enabled*   This property can be set to False if its associated action isn't appropriate at a particular time. For example, if no text is selected, an Edit menu's Copy command may be disabled by setting its Enabled property to False.

- *Visible*   Determines whether the menu item can be seen. Your application may have menu items that should not be seen at certain times; for example, you may not want the user to be able to see the Window menu item if there are no open windows.

- *WindowList*   If your application is a multiple-document interface (MDI) program, setting this property to True causes the menu item to automatically maintain a list of any open MDI child windows.

After entering the information for one menu item, click the Next button (or press the Enter key—Next is the default button). Visual Basic then accepts the property values for the item and places it in the selection area indicated in Figure 5.3. Pressing Enter also clears the property edit areas and sets them up to accept the next item. When you're finished entering items, accept the menu by clicking the OK button on the Menu Editor. Your menu appears on the form, as shown in Figure 5.4.

FIG. 5.4

This menu bar, shown at design time, was created with the Menu Editor.

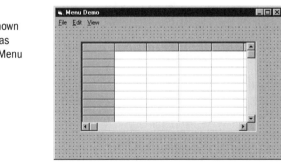

Part

II

Ch

5

TROUBLESHOOTING

When I start to exit the Menu Editor, I get the message, Menu control must have a name.
You inadvertently left out a value for the Name property of one of your menu items. Each item in a
menu must have a name, even if it is just a placeholder. Fortunately, Visual Basic helps you track down
your mistake by highlighting the offending item. Just enter a name for the item and continue working.

**After I exited the Menu Editor, I tried to click some of the menu items to see how the menu looks,
and a code window appeared.** Clicking menu items at design time brings up a code window that you
can use to define Click event procedures for the various menu items. This is the equivalent of double-
clicking the form or another control at design time. We'll learn about writing event procedures for menu
items in the section "Code for the Menu Items" a little later in this chapter. For now, just click the Close
button at the code window's upper-right corner.

Multiple-Level Menus If you entered several items in the Menu Editor and clicked OK, you
probably noticed that you created a series of items on only the main menu bar itself. You have
no items appearing below the main items. This might be acceptable for a very simple menu,
but if you place items only on the menu bar, you quickly run out of space. Obviously, you need
to use *multiple menu levels* to handle a large number of items. The first level of a menu is the
drop-down list of items appearing when you click an item on the menu bar. This is illustrated
for the File menu in Figure 5.5.

FIG. 5.5
Multiple menu levels
help organize your
program's functions.

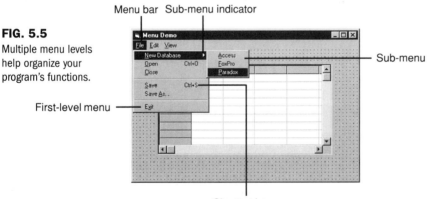

It is easy to create the items in different levels of a menu. You simply add the items to the menu
and indent them in the Menu Editor. To indent an item, select the item in the selection area of
the Menu Editor and then click the right-pointing arrow above the selection area. This indents
the item one level and indicates to Visual Basic that the item is part of a *submenu* for the
main item above it. Figure 5.6 shows the Menu Editor as it appears for the menu shown in
Figure 5.5.

FIG. 5.6
The Menu Editor makes it easy to organize your program's menu system into functional groups.

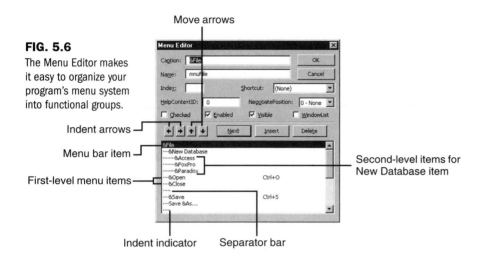

Move arrows

Indent arrows

Menu bar item

First-level menu items

Indent indicator   Separator bar

Second-level items for New Database item

N O T E When you create multiple menu levels, Visual Basic automatically provides the arrow-like indicator that lets users know a submenu exists. Any other text in the menu item is part of the `Caption` property that you must enter. ▨

If you are entering new items, each one is automatically indented to the same level as the item directly above it in the selection list. To promote an item up to a higher menu level, click the left arrow button. This promotes the item one level.

T I P Instead of clicking the arrow buttons, you can press Alt+R to indent a menu item or Alt+L to promote an item.

N O T E Visual Basic allows menus to have up to six levels. Usually, however, you should limit your program's menus to two or three levels. If you use too many levels, navigating the menu system tends to seem like more trouble than it's worth. ▨

In addition to using menu levels to organize the items in your menu, you might want to further separate items in a particular level. Placing *separator bars* in the menu breaks up a long list of items and further groups the items, without your having to create a separate level (refer to Figure 5.6). To place a separator bar in your menu, enter a hyphen (-) in the menu item's `Caption` property. This causes a bar to be placed in the menu. The bar will be the full width of the drop-down menu in which it appears. Remember, you must give the separator bar a unique value for the `Name` property, just as with any other menu item.

> **CAUTION**
> You cannot use a separator bar in the top level of the menu (the menu bar); separator bars must be part of a submenu. If you attempt to use a separator in the menu bar, Visual Basic informs you of the error as you try to save the menu.

Part

II

Ch

5

Modifying the Menu   After creating your menu, you will probably find that you need to make some changes to the menu's structure. This also is easily accomplished with the Menu Editor. Table 5.1 lists some common editing needs and how they are accomplished.

Table 5.1   Editing a Menu with a Few Mouse Clicks

Editing Function	How to Do It
Move an item	Select the item and then click one of the Move arrows to move the item up or down in the list. The indentation level of the menu does not change as you move the item.
Add an item to the middle of the list	Select the item that should appear below the new item in the list and then click the Insert button. A blank item appears; you can then enter the `Caption` and `Name` properties for the item. The new item is indented at the same level as the item below it.
Remove an item	Select the item and then click the Delete button. The item is immediately deleted, without any confirmation. (There is no Undo feature in the Menu Editor; whatever you delete is gone.)

T I P   When moving menu items, you can use the Alt+U key combination instead of the Up button, or you can use the Alt+B keys instead of the Down button.

Adding Access Keys and Shortcut Keys for Quick Access   If you have been working in Windows for a while, you have probably noticed that many menu items can be accessed by using a combination of keystrokes. You can let users access your menu items in the same way. There are two types of key combinations that can be used this way: *access keys* and *shortcut keys*.

What is the access key for a menu item? The access key (sometimes called a *mnemonic* key) is indicated by an underscore beneath the letter in the item's caption (for example, the F in File). You create an access key by placing an ampersand (&) in front of the appropriate letter in the `Caption` property. For the File menu, the `Caption` property would be `&File`. You can create an access key for any or all of the items in your menu.

N O T E   While it is typical to use the first letter of the caption as the access key, this is not a good idea if that letter is already in use. For example, Visual Basic's Format menu uses the second letter as the access key to avoid conflict with the File menu. It is possible to assign the same access key to multiple menu items. If you do that, Visual Basic just cycles through the items with each press of the access key. However, this is not standard practice because having to press an access key multiple times defeats its purpose. In addition, many users don't know that they can cycle through the items in this manner, and become frustrated when they see no apparent way to select the desired choice. ▨

When you have access keys defined for your menu, the user can select a top-level menu item (the ones in the menu bar) by holding down the Alt key and then pressing the access key. This causes the submenu for that item to drop down, showing the items for that group. The user can then start the desired task by pressing the access key defined for the menu item. For example, for the <u>N</u>ew item of the <u>F</u>ile menu, the user could press Alt+F and then press N.

N O T E Instead of holding down Alt and pressing an access key, you can just press Alt (or F10) first, and then use the arrow keys to navigate the menus. ▨

To create an effective set of access keys, you must specify a different key for each of the top-level menu items. Then specify a different key for each of the items in the submenu. Conceivably, you can have up to 36 access keys, one for each letter of the alphabet and one for each of the ten digits, but you will run out of screen space for the choices before running out of letters.

T I P If possible, use the first letter of the menu item as the access key, because typically the user expects this.

In addition to the access keys just discussed, you can assign shortcut keys to some of the more commonly used functions in your program. Shortcut keys provide direct access to a function through a single key (such as Delete) or key combination (such as Ctrl+S), without having to navigate the menu system. Users can take advantage of shortcut keys to perform tasks quickly.

To assign a shortcut key to one of your functions, enter the Menu Editor, select the menu item for which you want a shortcut key, and then select the desired key from the <u>S</u>hortcut list. The key is assigned to that function, and the shortcut-key information appears next to the menu item in the menu (see Figure 5.7). There are 79 shortcut keys that you can use.

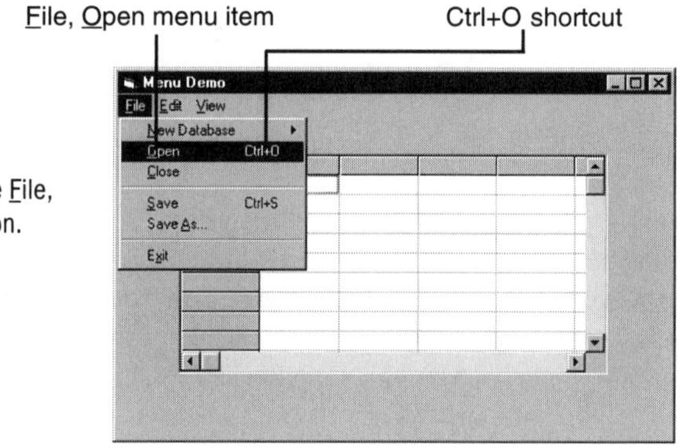

<u>F</u>ile, <u>O</u>pen menu item   Ctrl+O shortcut

FIG. 5.7
Ctrl+O has been assigned as the shortcut key for the <u>F</u>ile, <u>O</u>pen menu function.

You can assign any unused shortcut key to any menu item, but be aware that there are a few "standard" keys used in many Windows programs. Some of these keys are listed in Table 5.2. As examples, the "Description" column explains what these keys do when you're working within Visual Basic itself.

Table 5.2   Shortcut Keys Speed Access to Program Tasks

Menu Item	Shortcut Key	Description
Edit, Cut	Ctrl+X	Removes selected text or control(s) from its current location and copies it to the Clipboard.
Edit, Copy	Ctrl+C	Makes a copy of the selected text or control(s) in the Clipboard.
Edit, Paste	Ctrl+V	Pastes the contents of the Clipboard to the active form or Code window.
Edit, Undo	Ctrl+Z	Undoes the last change.
Edit, Find	Ctrl+F	Opens the Find dialog box to allow the user to search for text.
File, New	Ctrl+N	Creates a new Visual Basic project.
File, Open	Ctrl+O	Opens the Open Project dialog box to allow the user to select a project to open.
File, Save	Ctrl+S	Saves the current file.
File, Print	Ctrl+P	Opens the Print dialog box to allow selection of items to be printed.

 TIP   As with access keys, try to have the shortcut key correspond to the first letter of the item name; for example, Ctrl+P for Print. This makes it easier for users to remember the shortcuts. To avoid confusing your users, use the standard shortcut keys listed in Table 5.2 whenever possible.

TROUBLESHOOTING

When I try to save the changes to my menu, I get the error message `Shortcut key already defined`. **What happened?** If you got this message, you inadvertently gave the same shortcut key to two or more functions. You need to look through the menu-item selection area to find the duplicate definition, and then assign another key to one of your items.

Code for the Menu Items

After creating the menu's structure, you need to write code to let the menu items actually perform tasks. As with a form or other controls, you do this by writing code in an event procedure. A menu item handles only one event: the `Click` event. This event is triggered when the user clicks the menu item, or when he selects the item and presses Enter.

N O T E A menu item's `Click` event is also triggered when the user uses an access key or shortcut key to access an item. ▪

To add code to a menu item's `Click` event, first select the menu item on the form by clicking the item. This starts the Code Editor and sets up the `Event` procedure for the selected item. Then simply type in the code to handle the task. The following sample code could be used to create a new database in response to a menu selection:

```
Private Sub mnuNewDb_Click()
  Dim sFileName As String

  dlgGetFile.ShowOpen
  sFileName = dlgGetFile.FileName
  Set dbMain = DBEngine.WorkSpaces(0).CreateDatabase(sFileName,dbLangGeneral)
  MsgBox "New database created."
End Sub
```

The preceding code uses a CommonDialog control named `dlgGetFile` to obtain a file name from the user. It then uses this file name to create a new database.

▶ **See** "Using Built-In Dialog Boxes," **p. 135**

Optional Settings

In addition to the required `Caption` and `Name` properties, each menu item has several optional properties that you can set either to control the behavior of the menu or to indicate the status of a program option. Three of these properties are `Visible`, `Enabled`, and `Checked`. The menu item's `Visible` and `Enabled` properties work just like their counterparts on a form or control. When the `Visible` property is set to `True`, the menu item is visible to the user. If the `Visible` property is set to `False`, the item and any associated submenus are hidden from the user. You have probably seen the `Enabled` and `Visible` properties used in a word processing program (though you might not have been aware of how it was accomplished), where only the File and Help menus are visible until a document is selected for editing. After a document is open, the other menu items are shown. Changing the setting of the `Visible` property allows you to control what menu items are available to the user at a given point in your program. Controlling the menu this way lets you restrict the user's access to menu items that might cause errors if certain conditions are not met. (You wouldn't want the user to access edit functions if there was nothing to edit, right?)

The `Enabled` property serves a function similar to that of the `Visible` property. The key difference is that when the `Enabled` property is set to `False`, the menu item is *grayed out*. This means that the menu item still can be seen by the user but cannot be accessed. For example,

Part

Ch

5

the standard Edit, Cut and Edit, Copy functions should not be available if there is no text or object selected, but there's nothing wrong with letting the user see that they exist (see Figure 5.8).

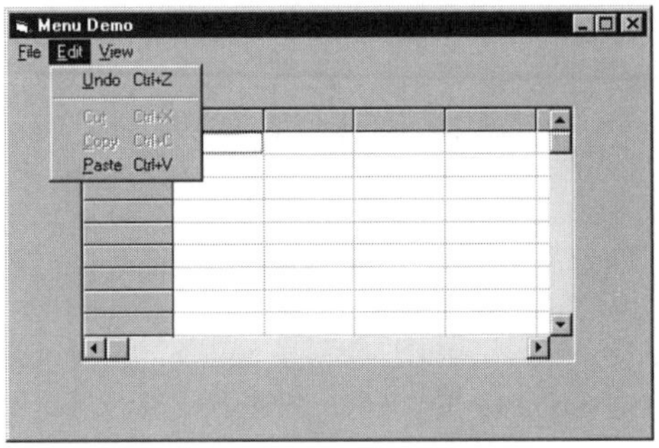

FIG. 5.8

Disabled menu items are visible to the user but are shown in gray tones, indicating that the items are unavailable at the present time.

Both the Visible and Enabled properties can be set in the Menu Editor at design time, and from your program code at runtime. In the Menu Editor, the properties are set by using check boxes. The default value of the properties is True. In code, you set the property value by specifying the name of the menu item (from the Name property), the name of the property, and the value you want to set. This is shown in the following line of code for the Edit menu:

```
Mnu_Edit.Visible = False
```

The Checked property of the menu item determines whether or not a check mark is displayed to the left of the item in the menu, as shown in Figure 5.9. The Checked property is typically used to indicate the status of a program item or option; for example, whether a toolbar or particular window is visible. The menu item is then used to toggle back and forth between two program states. The following code causes the menu's check mark to toggle on and off every time it is clicked:

```
Private Sub mnuShowSorted_Click()
  mnuShowSorted.Checked = Not(mnuShowSorted.Checked)
End Sub
```

Because the Checked property can only be True or False, the preceding code makes nice use of some Boolean logic with the Not() function. At any point in the program code, the state of the Checked property indicates whether or not the user wants something to be displayed in sorted order.

CAUTION

You cannot set the Checked property to True for an item on the menu bar (top menu level). Doing so results in an error.

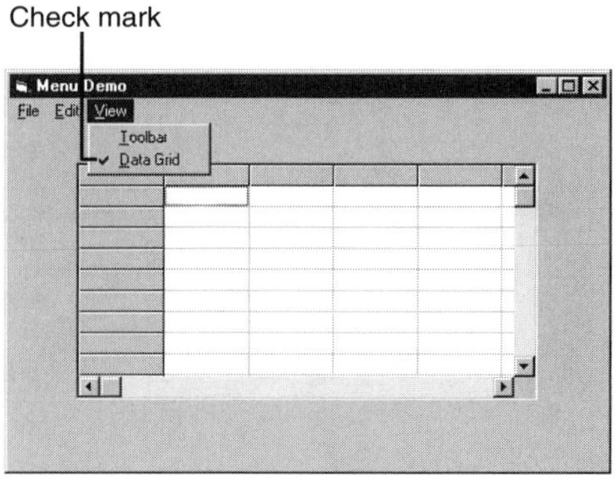

Check mark

FIG. 5.9

The Checked property controls whether or not a check mark is placed to the left of a submenu item.

You might have also noticed two other items in the Menu Editor. These items specify the value of the NegotiatePosition and WindowList properties of the menu item. The NegotiatePosition property specifies whether and where the menu item of your application is displayed when an embedded object on a form is active and its menu is shown (for example, if your application has an instance of Word embedded for modifying a document). If the NegotiatePosition property is 0, your menu is not displayed while the object is active. If the property is not 0, your menu item is displayed to the left of, in the middle of, or to the right of the object's menu (property settings of 1, 2, or 3, respectively).

The WindowList property specifies whether the current item will contain a list of MDI child forms that are open within the MDI parent. When this property is set to True, the menu automatically adds items as child forms are opened and removes the items when the corresponding child form is closed.

▶ **See** "Maintaining a Window List," **p. 376**

Part

II

Ch

5

Creating Pop-Up Menus

So far, the discussion of menus has looked at the menu bar that appears along the top of the form. Visual Basic also supports *pop-up menus* in your programs. A pop-up menu is a small menu that appears somewhere on your form in response to a program event.

Pop-up menus often are used to handle operations or options related to a specific area of the form (see Figure 5.10)—for example, a format pop-up menu for a text field that lets you change the font or font attributes of the field. You can find this menu type in many of the latest generation of Windows programs, including Visual Basic itself.

When a pop-up menu is invoked, usually with by right-clicking the mouse, it appears on-screen near the current mouse pointer location. The user then makes a selection from the menu. After the selection is processed, the menu disappears from the screen.

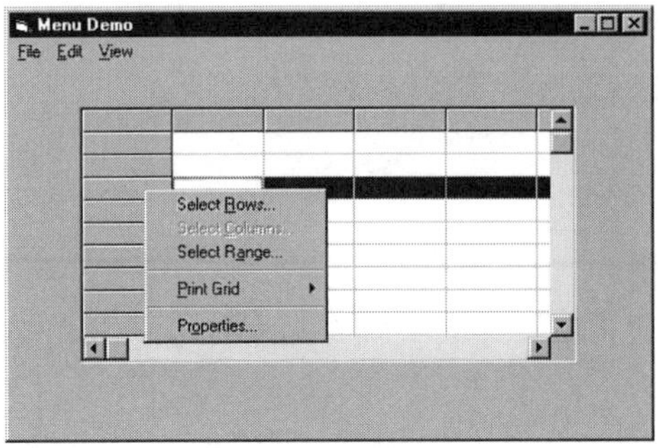

FIG. 5.10
This grid's pop-up menu provides a convenient way to initiate program functions specifically related to the grid.

Creating the Menu to Be Displayed

You create a pop-up menu in the same way that you created the main menu for your program—from the Menu Editor. There is, however, one extra step. The pop-up menu should be hidden, so that it does not appear on the menu bar. To do this, set the Visible property of the top-level menu item to False.

> **N O T E** Typically, you will hide the menu item that is used as a pop-up menu, but you can use any of the top-level items of a menu bar as a pop-up menu. That is, a particular menu can appear both as a pop-up menu and as a part of the main menu of a form. ▓

Creating a pop-up menu is easy. The following four steps tell you how to create a pop-up menu to handle text formatting:

1. Create a top-level menu item with Format as its Caption property and popFormat as its Name property.

2. Set the Visible property of the menu item to False by clearing the Visible check box in the Menu Editor.

3. Create three submenu items under popFormat, with the Caption properties Bold, Italic, and Underline and the Name properties popBold, popItalic, and popUnder, respectively.

4. Click the OK button to accept the menu changes.

Notice that the Format menu does not appear on your form's menu bar. However, the menu is present and can be modified in the Menu Editor.

The technique you must use to add code to the Click event of the items in a pop-up menu is also a little different. Because the menu is not visible on the form, you cannot just click the item to bring up the code-editing window. Instead, bring up the code-editing window by selecting the View Code button in the Project window, or double-clicking the form. Then, select the desired menu item in the Code window's Object list at the upper-left corner. This allows you to enter code for the hidden items.

Activating a Pop-Up Menu

To have the pop-up menu appear on your screen, you must invoke the form's PopUpMenu method. You do this by specifying the name of the form where the menu will be displayed, the PopUpMenu method, and the name of the menu to be shown.

While you can use this method from anywhere in your code, pop-up menus are used most often in response to mouse clicks, usually those using the right mouse button. The following code shows how the Format menu created in the last section would be called up by clicking the right mouse button anywhere on your form:

```
Private Sub Form_MouseUp(Button As Integer, Shift As Integer,  X As Single, Y As
Single)
   If Button = vbRightButton Then
      frmMain.PopUpMenu popFormat
   End If
End Sub
```

In this code segment, the MouseUp event is used to take an action whenever a mouse button is pressed. The event passes a parameter, the Button parameter, that tells you which of the mouse buttons was pressed. Because you want the menu to appear in response to only a right button click, you check for the value of the Button parameter. If it is equal to vbRightButton (an intrinsic constant for the right mouse button), the pop-up menu is displayed.

N O T E You can create multiple pop-up menus and have them displayed in response to different mouse buttons or in different areas of the screen. The X and Y parameters passed in to the MouseUp event procedure report the location of the mouse cursor at the time the event occurred.

Part

II

Ch

5

Creating a Toolbar for Your Application

You have probably noticed that many Windows programs now have one or more toolbars in addition to the menu. These toolbars provide the user with an easy way to access the most commonly used functions of the program. Some programs also use toolbars to help with specific tasks, such as the Drawing toolbar that is in Microsoft Word. Because toolbars are becoming so common, users have come to expect to find them in all programs.

Fortunately, it is easy for you to set up a toolbar in Visual Basic. To create a toolbar, you only need to use two controls—the Toolbar control and the ImageList control. The Toolbar control sets up the buttons of the actual toolbar displayed to the user and handles the user's actions. The ImageList control contains a collection of bitmaps for use by other controls. In this case, our Toolbar control will display images from the ImageList on its buttons.

Setting Up the Toolbar Control

To set up a toolbar on your form, you need to add the Toolbar and ImageList controls to the Toolbox. These two controls are part of the Windows Common Controls group. This group of controls is included with VB, but is not in the Toolbox by default. To add them to the Toolbox, use the Components dialog box, which you access by selecting Project, Components; then select the check box for Microsoft Windows Common Controls 5.0.

Getting the Images for Your Toolbar   After these controls have been added to the Toolbox, you can begin the creation of your toolbar. Follow these steps to create a toolbar:

1. Draw an ImageList control on your form and give it a unique name. Because the ImageList control is not visible to the user, its size is set by Visual Basic. No matter what size you draw it on the form, it always appears as a little box.

2. To add bitmap images to the control, open its Property Pages dialog box by either pressing the ellipsis (…) button of the Custom property in the Properties window, or by right-clicking the ImageList control and selecting Properties. From this dialog box, shown in Figure 5.11, you can add images from graphics files (icons and bitmaps) stored on your hard drive.

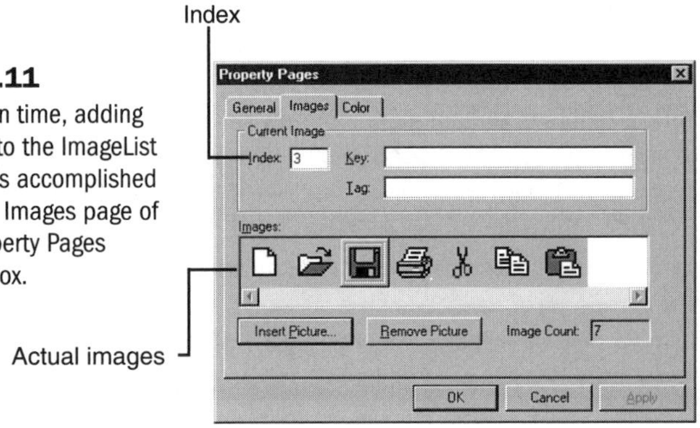

Index

FIG. 5.11

At design time, adding images to the ImageList control is accomplished with the Images page of the Property Pages dialog box.

Actual images

3. To add an image to the ImageList control, click the Insert Picture button. This presents you with the Select Picture dialog box, from which you can choose the bitmap or icon you want. As you select the picture, it is added to the control and displayed in the Images area.

4. When you have added all the pictures you might need, click the OK button to close the dialog box.

After completing these steps, your ImageList control will be ready to use for supplying images to your toolbar.

Creating the Toolbar   Next, you need to set up the toolbar itself by following these steps:

1. Select the toolbar icon in the Toolbox, and draw the Toolbar control on your form. Visual Basic positions the toolbar at the top of the form, and the control spans the width of the form.

2. A toolbar can be aligned along any of the four edges of its form. If, for example, you want to position it along the bottom of your form, set its Align property to 2 - vbAlignBottom. You can align it to the left or right edge of the form by setting the Align property to 3 - vbAlignLeft or 4 - vbAlignRight, respectively; in these cases, you should adjust

the Width property to keep it from filling the form completely. If you want a free-floating toolbar, set its align property to 0 - vbAlignNone; you can then adjust its position and size by setting the Left, Top, Width, and Height properties.

3. To continue setting up the Toolbar control, bring up its Property Pages dialog box by right-clicking the control and choosing Properties. Figure 5.12 shows the first page of the Toolbar control's Property Pages.

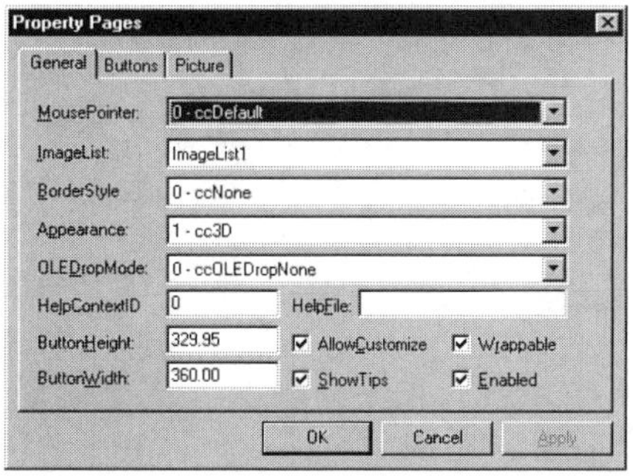

FIG. 5.12

You can assign an ImageList control to your toolbar in the General tab of the toolbar's Property Pages dialog box.

4. Next, set the Toolbar control's ImageList property to the name of the ImageList control that you already set up to provide images. Clicking the arrow to the right of the ImageList property provides you with a list of all ImageList controls on the current form.

There are several other properties on the Property Pages' General tab that control the appearance and behavior of the toolbar. These properties are summarized in Table 5.3.

Part

II

Ch

5

Table 5.3   Toolbar Properties that Control Its Appearance and Behavior

Property Name	Description
BorderStyle	Determines whether a single-line border is displayed around the toolbar or no border is used.
ButtonHeight	Specifies the height (in twips) of the buttons in the toolbar.
ButtonWidth	Specifies the width (in twips) of the buttons in the toolbar.
AllowCustomize	Determines whether the user is allowed to customize the toolbar by adding, deleting, or moving buttons.
ShowTips	Determines whether ToolTips are shown if the mouse is rested on one of the buttons.
Wrappable	Determines whether the toolbar wraps around to a second row of buttons if there are more buttons than fit on a single row.

Creating the Buttons of the Toolbar   The next step in creating your toolbar is to create the buttons that will be placed on the toolbar. For this, you move to the Buttons page of the Property Pages (see Figure 5.13).

FIG. 5.13

You assign images, captions, and identifiers to toolbar buttons in the Buttons page.

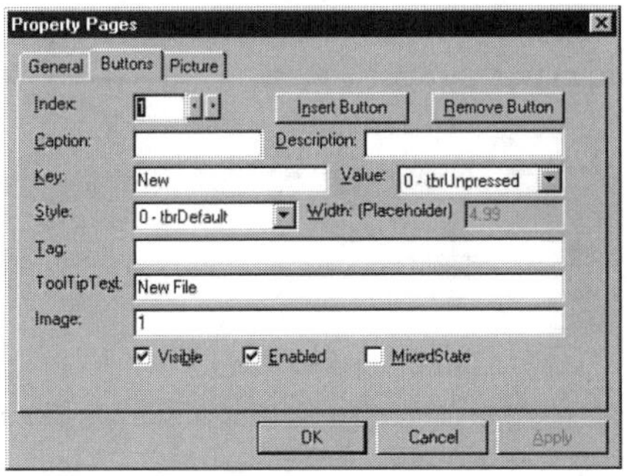

To add a button to the toolbar, click Insert Button. This adds a new button after the current button. For each button that you add, you need to specify several properties—the Key property, the Style property, and the Image property. These three are the minimum required to set up a button.

The Key property specifies a string that is used to identify the button in code. You see how this is used in the following section, "Enabling the Buttons with Code." The Key property for each button must be unique, and you should assign a string that is meaningful to you. This makes it easier to remember when you are writing your code. The Image property specifies the index of the picture that you want to appear on the face of the button. The index corresponds to the Index of the picture in the ImageList control. You can specify a value of zero for the Image property if you do not want a picture to appear on the button.

The Style property determines the type of button that you create. Table 5.4 summarizes the various settings of the Style property. Each of the button styles is shown in Figure 5.14.

Table 5.4   *Style* Property Settings that Control the Behavior of Toolbar Buttons

Setting	VB Constant	Description of Behavior	Example
0	tbrDefault	The button is a standard pushbutton.	The Save Project button in VB
1	tbrCheck	The button indicates that an option is on or off by its state.	The Bold button in Word

Setting	VB Constant	Description of Behavior	Example
2	tbrButtonGroup	The button is part of a group. Only one button of the group can be depressed at a time.	The alignment buttons in Word
3	tbrSeparator	The button is used to provide space between other buttons. The button has a width of eight pixels.	N/A
4	tbrPlaceHolder	This button is used to hold a space in the toolbar for other controls such as a combo box.	The font combo box in Word

FIG. 5.14
Examples of the different toolbar button styles. Note that the placeholder and separators are not really buttons.

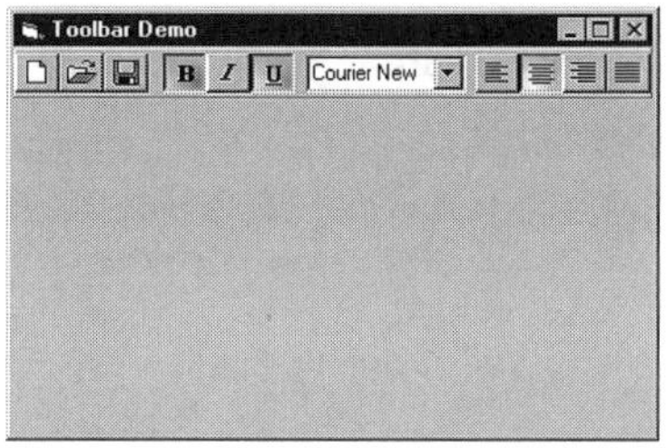

In addition to these three key properties, there are several other properties that can be set for each button on the toolbar (see Table 5.5).

Table 5.5   Optional Properties that Provide Further Control over a Button Toolbar

Property	Description
Caption	This is text that is displayed beneath the picture on a button.
Description	This is text that describes the button to the user when he invokes the Customize Toolbar dialog box.
ToolTipText	This text appears when the mouse is rested on the button. This text is only displayed if the ShowTips property of the toolbar is set to True (which is the default).
Value	Sets or returns the current state of the button. A value of 0 indicates that the button is not pressed. A value of 1 indicates that the button is pressed. You typically set the value of a single button in a button group to 1. You can then use the Value property in your code to determine which button is pressed.

TIP   Unless the images on your buttons are self-explanatory, you should make sure to include ToolTips. Otherwise, there is no way for the user to know what the button does unless he presses it. ToolTips give your program a professional appearance and are easy to add.

After setting up the buttons on the toolbar, you can exit the Property Pages dialog box by clicking the OK button. Your toolbar is now set up and ready for use—almost.

Enabling the Buttons with Code

You have seen how to set up the toolbar, but until you add code to the toolbar's events, it cannot perform any functions. The buttons of the toolbar do not have events of their own. Instead, you actually write your code for the `ButtonClick` event of the toolbar itself. This event passes a `Button` object, representing the button that was pressed, as a parameter to the event procedure. In your code, you use the value of the `Button` object's `Key` property to determine which button was actually pressed. Listing 5.1 shows a typical event procedure for taking actions based on the button pressed.

Listing 5.1   TOOLBAR.FRM—Using the _Key_ Property of the Button to Determine What Action to Take

```
Private Sub Toolbar1_ButtonClick(ByVal Button As ComctlLib.Button)

   Select Case Button.Key
      Case "New"
            mnuNew_Click
      Case "Open"
            mnuOpen_Click
      Case "Save"
            mnuSave_Click
   End Select
End Sub
```

In Listing 5.1, the procedures being called are actually the `Click` event procedures of menu items. This allows you to code an action once and then call it from either the menu or the toolbar. Doing this makes it easier to maintain your code because changes or corrections only have to be made in a single location. Also, note the introduction of the `Select Case` statement, which is more readable than a nested `If` statement. We'll discuss it in more detail in a later chapter.

The project Toolbar.vbp contains the sample program used in this chapter. The program shows a standard menu, a pop-up menu, and a toolbar. You can download this project at **www.mcp.com/info/0-7897/0-7897-1288-1.**

Allowing the User to Customize the Toolbar

One of the really great features of the Toolbar control is that you can allow your users to customize the toolbar to their liking. When the `AllowCustomize` property of the toolbar is set to `True`, the user can access the Customize Toolbar dialog box by double-clicking the toolbar. This dialog box, shown in Figure 5.15, allows the user to add buttons to the toolbar, remove buttons, or move the buttons to a different location.

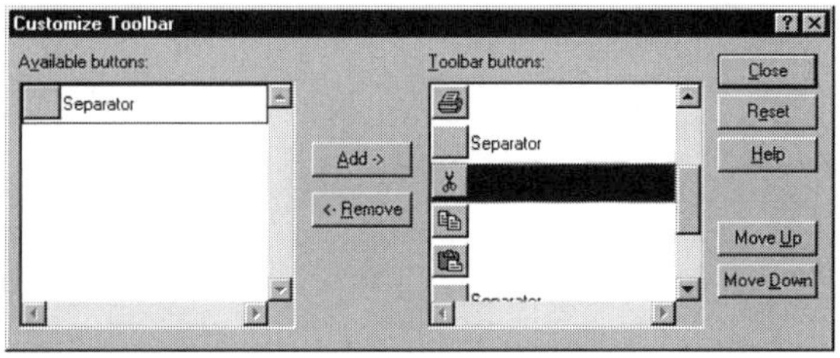

FIG. 5.15

The `AllowCustomize` property lets users customize the toolbar to their liking, without the need for additional code.

Other Methods of Creating a Toolbar

Although using the Toolbar control is the easiest method of creating a toolbar for your application, there are other ways of accomplishing the task. You can use a picture box as a container and Image controls to represent the buttons. One advantage of this method is that you can use the picture box to display other images besides the buttons. You can also use graphics methods and print methods to display other information. Another advantage is that the toolbar created with a picture box can be located anywhere on your form. You see how to create a toolbar by using a picture box in Chapter 17, "Using Containers in Your Programs."

There are also several third-party controls that allow you to create toolbars for your forms. Some of these controls even allow you to create floating toolbars like Visual Basic's Form Editor toolbar.

From Here...

This chapter has shown you the advantages of creating menus and toolbars for your programs. Hopefully, you have also seen how easy it is to create these items. You were also exposed to several other topics in this chapter. To learn more about them, refer to the following chapters:

- To learn more about MDI child forms, see Chapter 14, "Building a Multiple Document Interface."

- To learn more about the Windows common controls, including the Toolbar and ImageList controls, see Chapter 16, "Using the Windows Common Controls."

Part

II

Ch

5

Using Dialogs to Get Information

A dialog box is a small window used to display or accept information. Its name comes from the fact that it is, in essence, a *dialog* (or conversation) with the user. A dialog box is usually shown *modally*, which means the user must close it (or "answer the dialog") before continuing with any other part of the program. In this chapter, we look at two dialog boxes built in to the Visual Basic language: the message box and the input box. Next, we use the CommonDialog custom control, which allows you to place four types of standard dialog boxes in your program. Finally, we show you some guidelines for creating your own form-based dialog box. ■

Providing user information with a message box

While forms provide the main interface with your users, sometimes you just need to display a bit of information. This is where message boxes come in handy.

Getting user decisions with the message box

A message box can also be used for basic Yes/No decision making.

Using the input box

Just need one piece of information? The input box might be just the thing you are looking for.

Working with dialog boxes your users will know

With the CommonDialog control, you can use some of the same dialog boxes as other Windows programs.

What do you do if the built-in dialog boxes don't meet your needs? Build your own.

You learn how to create your own dialog boxes that provide an enhanced message box or input box.

Keeping the User Informed

A big part of any programming project is providing information to the users about the program's progress and status. While the forms and controls of your program provide the main interface to the user, they are not necessarily the best vehicles for providing bits of information that require immediate attention, such as warnings or error messages. For providing this type of information, the message box is the way to go.

The *message box* is a simple form that displays a message and at least one command button. The button is used to acknowledge the message and close the form. Because message boxes are built in to the Visual Basic language, you do not have to worry about creating or showing a form. To see a simple message box, type the following line of code into Visual Basic's Immediate window (choose <u>V</u>iew, <u>I</u>mmediate Window to open the window) and press Enter:

```
MsgBox "Hello World!"
```

Optionally, the message box can display an icon or use multiple buttons to let the user make a decision. This is done with the use of optional parameters. For example, the following code line produces the message box shown in Figure 6.1:

```
MsgBox "Delete record?", vbYesNo + vbExclamation, "Confirm Delete"
```

> **N O T E**   You can try it yourself. Just type the code in the Immediate window and press Enter. ▨

FIG. 6.1

A message box communicates with the user.

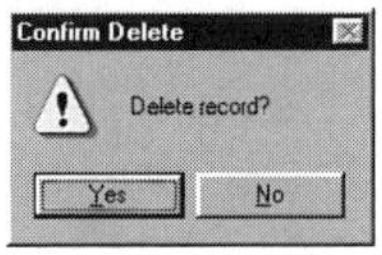

Message boxes can be used in either of two ways, depending on your needs. You can use the message box to simply display information, or you can use it to get a decision from the user. In either case, you will use some form of the MsgBox function.

> **N O T E**   Although in this chapter we refer to them interchangeably, there is a conceptual difference between using MsgBox as a function and a statement. By definition, a *function* returns a value, whereas a *statement* does not. Also, the syntax for parameters is slightly different—a function's parameters must be enclosed in parentheses. For example, if you wanted to see the return value from the MsgBox function, you could type the following line in the Immediate window:
> ```
> Print MsgBox ("Delete record?", vbYesNo + vbExclamation, "Confirm Delete")
> ```

While the message box is very useful, it does have a few limitations:

- The message box cannot accept text input from the user. It can only display information and handle the selection of a limited number of choices.

- You can use only one of four predefined icons and one of six predefined command button sets in the message box. You cannot define your own icons or buttons.

■ By design, the message box requires a user to respond to the message before the program can continue. This means that the message box cannot be used to provide continuous status monitoring of the program, since no other part of the program can be executing while the message box is waiting for the user's response.

Displaying a Message

The simplest way to create a message box in your program is to use the MsgBox function as a statement, without returning a value. Using the MsgBox function this way, you simply specify the message text that you want to appear in the message box and then call the function. For the simplest message, only the OK button is shown in the message box. This allows the user to acknowledge the message:

```
MsgBox "Please insert a disk in Drive A:"
```

When you specify the message text, you can use a *literal constant* (a string of text enclosed in quotes, as shown above) or a string *variable*, as in this example:

```
Dim stMyText as String

stMyText = "Hello," & vbCrLf & "World"
MsgBox stMyText
```

Note the use of the intrinsic (predefined) constant vbCrLf (which you learned about in Chapter 4, "Working with Forms and Controls"), representing a carriage return/line feed combination, to make "Hello" and "World" appear on separate lines.

▶ **See** "Using a Label Control to Display Text," **p. 92**

The default message box uses the project name for its caption and has only an OK button. You can dress up your messages a little bit with two optional parameters—the buttons argument and the title argument. The buttons argument is an integer number that can specify the icon to display in the message box, the command button set to display, and which of the command buttons is the default. The title argument is a text string that specifies custom text to be shown in the title bar of the message box. The full syntax of the MsgBox function is as follows:

```
MsgBox(prompt[, buttons] [, title] [, helpfile, context])
```

If you choose to display an icon in the message box, you have a choice of four icons. These icons and their purposes are summarized in Table 6.1.

Part
II

Ch
6

Table 6.1 Icons Indicate the Type of Message Being Shown

Icon	Icon Name	Purpose
⊗	Critical Message	Indicates that a severe error has occurred. Often a program is shut down after this message.
⚠	Warning Message	Indicates that a program error has occurred that requires user correction or that may lead to undesirable results.

continues

Table 6.1 Continued

Icon	Icon Name	Purpose
 (?)	Query Message	Indicates that the program requires additional information from the user before processing can continue.
 (i)	Information Message	Informs the user of the status of the program. Often used to notify the user of the completion of a task.

To tell Visual Basic that you want to use an icon in the message box, you set a value for the buttons argument of the MsgBox function. The buttons argument can be set to one of four values, as defined in the following table. You can use either the numerical value or the constant from the table:

Message Type	Argument Value	Constant
Critical	16	vbCritical
Query	32	vbQuestion
Warning	48	vbExclamation
Information	64	vbInformation

TIP Good programming practice dictates that you use the appropriate constant to represent the integer value. This makes your programs more readable and will not require any conversion should Microsoft change the integer values.

N O T E The constants listed in the preceding table not only affect the icon that is displayed, but also the sound produced by Windows when a message appears. You can set sounds for different message types in the Windows Control Panel. ▓

To illustrate how icons and titles can be used in your message boxes, the following code produces the message box that is shown in Figure 6.2:

```
MsgBox "This message box contains an icon.", vbInformation, "Icon Demo"
```

FIG. 6.2
Use titles and icons to give the user visual cues to the nature of the message.

If you are wondering how you are going to remember the syntax of the MsgBox function and the constants to be used for the options, don't worry. The new statement completion capabilities of Visual Basic's Code Editor help tremendously with this. When you type the space after the

MsgBox function name in a Code window (or the Immediate window, for that matter), a pop-up appears that shows you the syntax of the command (see Figure 6.3).

FIG. 6.3
Syntax help assists you in setting up the message box.

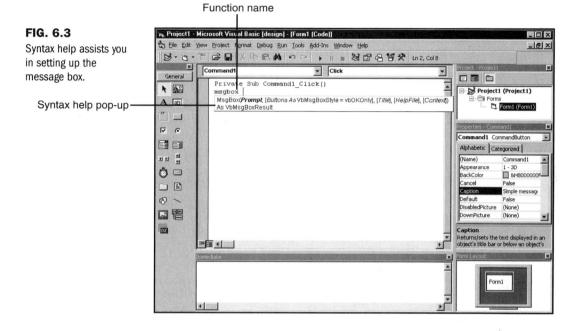

Then, after you enter the message to be displayed and enter a comma, Visual Basic pops up a list of constants that can be used to add an icon to the message box or to specify the button set to be used. You can select one of the constants from the list or type it in yourself. This is one of the really great new features in the editor. Figure 6.4 shows the constants list in action.

Returning a Value from the *MsgBox* Function

The MsgBox function, as described previously, works fine for informing users of a problem or prompting them to take an action. However, to get a decision from the user, you need to use the MsgBox function's return value. There are two key differences to using the MsgBox function this way—you (usually) assign the function's return value to a variable, and you must enclose the arguments of the function in parentheses. This value reports which command button was pressed by the user. The following line of code shows how the value returned by the function can be assigned to a variable for further processing:

```
inResult = MsgBox("The printer is not responding", vbRetryCancel,"Printer_
    Error!")
```

Additional statements after the preceding code could check the value of the variable inResult with, for example, an If statement, and take appropriate action.

Part
II

Ch
6

FIG. 6.4
You no longer have to
remember the options
constants with the pop-
ups available in the
editor.

Constants list ——

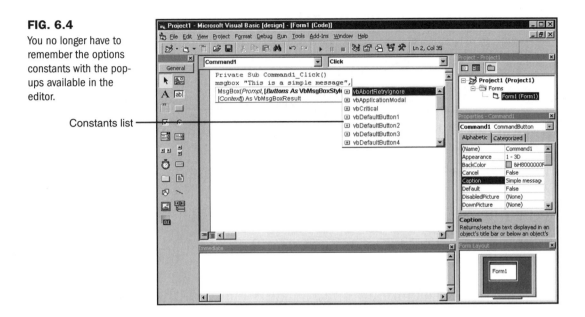

There are six sets of command buttons that can be used in the MsgBox function:

- *OK*   Displays a single button with the caption OK. This simply asks the user to acknowledge receipt of the message before continuing.

- *OK, Cancel*   Displays two buttons in the message box, letting the user choose between accepting the message and requesting a cancellation of the operation.

- *Abort, Retry, Ignore*   Displays three buttons, usually along with an error message. The user can choose to abort the operation, retry it, or ignore the error and attempt to continue with program execution.

- *Yes, No, Cancel*   Displays three buttons, typically with a question. The user can answer yes or no to the question, or choose to cancel the operation.

- *Yes, No*   Displays two buttons for a simple yes or no choice.

- *Retry, Cancel*   Displays the two buttons that allow the user to retry the operation or cancel it. A typical use is reporting that the printer is not responding. The user can either retry after fixing the printer or cancel the printout.

To specify the command buttons that will appear in the message box, you need to specify a value for the buttons argument of the MsgBox function. The values for each of the command button sets are listed in Table 6.2.

Table 6.2   Set the *buttons* Argument to One of the Following Values to Specify Which Set of Buttons to Use

Button Set	Value	Constant
OK	0	vbOKOnly
OK, Cancel	1	vbOKCancel
Abort, Retry, Ignore	2	VBAbortRetryIgnore
Yes, No, Cancel	3	vbYesNoCancel
Yes, No	4	vbYesNo
Retry, Cancel	5	vbRetryCancel

Because the buttons argument controls both the icon and the command-button set for a message box, you might wonder how you can specify both at the same time. You do this by adding the values of the constants together. The MsgBox function is designed so that any combination of the icon constant and the command-button constant creates a unique value. This value is then broken down by the function to specify the individual pieces. The following code combines an icon constant and command button constant to create a warning message that allows the user to choose an action. The results of the code are illustrated in Figure 6.5.

```
inOptVal = vbExclamation + vbAbortRetryIgnore
inRetVal = MsgBox("File does not exist.", inOptVal, "My Application")
```

TIP When you are using the pop-up constants list, you can select a second constant for the options parameter by entering a plus sign (+) after selecting the first constant.

N O T E   If you want your message box to display a Help button, add the constant vbMsgBoxHelpButton, which has a value of 16384, to whichever button set constant you choose. ▨

FIG. 6.5

The buttons argument controls both the icon and the command buttons displayed by the MsgBox function.

If you are using more than one command button in the message box, you can also specify which button is the default. The *default button* is the one that has focus when the message box is displayed. This button is the one that the user is most likely to choose so that he can just press the Enter key. For example, if you display a message box to have the user confirm the deletion of the record, you probably should set up the default button so that the record would not be deleted. This way, the user must make a conscious choice to delete the record.

Part
II

Ch
6

To specify which button is the default, you need to add another constant to the `buttons` argument of the `MsgBox` function. There are four possible default button values. These are identified in the following table:

Default Button	Value	Constant
First	0	vbDefaultButton1
Second	256	vbDefaultButton2
Third	512	vbDefaultButton3
Fourth	768	vbDefaultButton4

There are seven buttons from which a user might choose, with the selection depending on the button set used in the message box. Each of these buttons returns a different value to identify the button to your program (see Table 6.3).

Table 6.3   Return Values Indicate the User's Choice

Button	Value	Constant
OK	1	vbOK
Cancel	2	vbCancel
Abort	3	vbAbort
Retry	4	vbRetry
Ignore	5	vbIgnore
Yes	6	vbYes
No	7	vbNo

As always, it is preferable to use the constant in your code rather than the actual integer value. After you know which button the user selected, you can use that information in your program. The following code is used to confirm the deletion of a file:

```
Dim stFileName As String
Dim stMsgTitle As String
Dim stMsgText As String
Dim inReturn As Integer
Dim inOptions As Integer

stFileName = "C:\MYDIR\MYFILE.TXT"
stMsgText = "Do you really want to delete '" & stFileName & "'?"
inOptions = vbQuestion + vbYesNo + vbDefaultButton2
stMsgTitle = "Delete Confirmation"
inReturn = MsgBox(stMsgText, inOptions, stMsgTitle)

If inReturn = vbYes Then
    Kill stFileName
    MsgBox stFileName & " has been deleted.",vbInformation,"File deleted"
End If
```

For completeness, there is one final setting that can be applied to the `buttons` argument of the `MsgBox` function. You can choose to have the message box be modal for your application, or for the entire system. Remember from earlier chapters that when a *modal* window is shown, it must be closed before continuing with the program. If you specify that the message box is modal to the system, the user must respond to the message box before he can do any further work on the computer at all. The system modal option should be used with extreme care. The default behavior is application modal, which means the user could continue to work in other applications.

To use the default of application modal, you do not have to add anything to the `buttons` argument, or you can add the `vbApplicationModal` constant, which has a value of 0. To make the message box system modal, you need to add the constant `vbSystemModal`, which has a value of 4096, to the `buttons` argument.

Getting Information from the User

Many times in a program, you need to get a single piece of information from the user. You might need the user to enter a person's name, the name of a file, or a number for various purposes. Although the message box lets your users make choices, it does not allow them to enter any information in response to the message. Therefore, you have to use some other means to get the information. Visual Basic provides a built-in dialog box for exactly this purpose: the *input box*.

The input box displays a message to tell the user what to enter, a text box where the user can enter the requested information, and two command buttons—OK and Cancel—that can be used to either accept or abort the input data. A sample input box is shown in Figure 6.6.

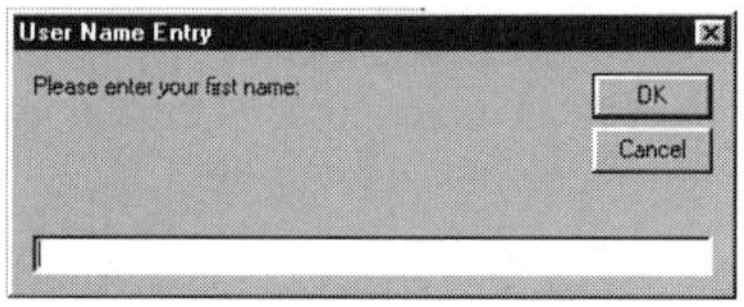

FIG. 6.6

An input box lets the user enter a single piece of data in response to a message.

Setting Up the Input Dialog Box

Programmatically, the input box works very much like the message box with a return value. You can specify a variable to receive the information returned from the input box and then supply the input box's message (prompt) and, optionally, a title and default value. An example of the InputBox function is the following:

```
Dim stMsg as String, stUserName As String
stMsg = "Please type your name below:"
stUserName = InputBox(stMsg, "Enter user name", "Anonymous")
```

In this statement, the information returned by the InputBox function will be stored in the variable `stUserName`. The first argument, the `prompt` parameter, represents the message that is displayed to the user to indicate what should be entered in the box. Like the message in the message box, the prompt can be up to 1,024 characters. Word-wrapping is automatically performed on the text in the prompt so that it fits inside the box. Also, as with the message box, you can insert a carriage return/line-feed combination (vbCrLf) to force the prompt to show multiple lines or to separate lines for emphasis.

After the prompt comes the title argument, which specifies the text in the input box's title bar. The other argument in the preceding example is the default argument. If included, it appears as an initial value in the input box. This value can be accepted by the user, modified, or it can be erased and a completely new value entered.

The minimum requirement for the InputBox function is a prompt parameter, as in the statement:

```
stReturnVal = InputBox("How's the weather?")
```

In addition to the input box's optional parameters to specify a window title and default value, other optional parameters allow you to set its initial screen position, as well as the help file to be used if the user needs assistance. Refer to the complete syntax of the InputBox function in Visual Basic's help system.

N O T E   Unlike the MsgBox function, there is no option in the InputBox function to specify any command buttons other than the defaults of OK and Cancel. ▓

Values Returned by *InputBox*

When the input box is used, the user can enter up to 254 characters of text in the input box's entry area, which resembles a text box. If he types more text than will fit in the displayed entry area, the text he's already typed will scroll to the left. Once he's done, he can choose the OK or Cancel button. If he chooses the OK button, the input box returns whatever is in the text box, whether it is new text or the default text. If the user chooses the Cancel button, the input box returns an empty string, regardless of what is in the text box.

To be able to use the information entered by the user, you must determine if the data meets your needs. First, you probably want to make sure that the user actually entered some information and chose the OK button. You can do this by using the Len function to determine the length of the returned string. If the length is zero, the user pressed the Cancel button or left the input field blank. If the length of the string is greater than zero, you know that the user entered something. To see how the Len function works, enter each of these lines in the Immediate window and note the different results:

```
Print Len("Hello")
```

```
Print Len("")
```

You may also need to check the returned value to make sure it is of the proper type. If you are expecting a number that will subsequently be compared to another number in an If statement, your program should present an error message if the user enters letters. To make sure that you have a numerical value with which to work, you can use the Val function. The Val function's purpose is to return the numerical value of a string. If the string contains or starts with numbers, the function returns the number. If the string does not start with a number, the function returns zero. To understand the Val function, enter these lines in the Immediate window to see what each returns:

```
Print Val("Hello")

Print Val("50 ways to leave your lover")

Print Val("100 and 1 make 101")
```

The following code illustrates additional processing of the returned value of the input box with Val and Len:

```
Dim stInputVal As String
stInputVal = InputBox("Enter your age")
If Len(stInputVal) = 0 Then
    MsgBox "No age was selected"
Else
    If Val(stInputVal) = 0 Then
        MsgBox "You entered an invalid age."
    Else
        MsgBox "Congratulations for surviving this long!"
    End If
End If
```

Using Built-In Dialog Boxes

In earlier sections, you learned what a dialog box is and how to use two simple dialog boxes. In this section, you learn about the Microsoft CommonDialog control, which allows you to use standard Windows dialog boxes to specify file names, select fonts and colors, and control the printer. And while the ease of setup is a great benefit, an even bigger bonus is that these dialog boxes are already familiar to the user. This is because they are the same dialog boxes used by Windows itself.

General Usage of the CommonDialog Control

Using a single CommonDialog control, you have access to the following standard Windows dialog boxes:

- *Open* Lets the user select the name and location of a file to open
- *Save As* Lets the user specify a file name and location in which to save information
- *Font* Lets the user choose a base font and set any font attributes that are desired
- *Color* Lets the user choose from a standard color or create a custom color for use in the program

■ *Print*   Lets the user select a printer and set some of the printer parameters

■ *Help*   Takes the user into the Windows Help system

Although the CommonDialog control is included with Visual Basic, it's not one of the controls included in the Toolbox by default. To access the CommonDialog control, you might first have to add it to your project (and to the Toolbox) by selecting it from the Components dialog box. This dialog box is accessible by choosing Project, Components. From there, select Microsoft Common Dialog Control 5.0 in the Controls list and click OK.

After the CommonDialog control is added to the Toolbox, you can add the control to a form by clicking the control and drawing it on the form just like any other control. The CommonDialog control appears on your form as an icon, as the control itself is not visible when your application is running.

The following sections discuss each type of dialog box that can be created with the CommonDialog control. For each of these dialog boxes, you need to set some of the control's properties. You can do this through the Properties window, or you can use the CommonDialog control's Property Pages dialog box. The Property Pages dialog box provides you easy access to the specific properties that are necessary for each of the common dialog box types (see Figure 6.7). You can access the Property Pages dialog box by clicking the ellipsis (…) button in the Custom property of the CommonDialog control, or by right-clicking the control and selecting Properties.

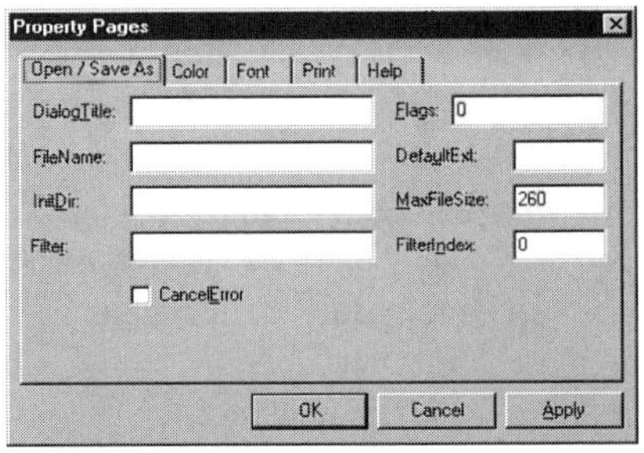

FIG. 6.7

The Property Pages dialog box makes it easy to set up the CommonDialog control.

The File Dialog Boxes

One of the key uses of the CommonDialog control is to obtain file names from the user. The CommonDialog control's File dialog box can be used in either of two modes: Open and Save As. Open mode lets the user specify the name and location of a file to be retrieved and used by your program. Save As mode lets the user specify the name and location of a file to be saved.

The dialog boxes for the Open and Save As functions are very similar. Figure 6.8 shows the Open dialog box.

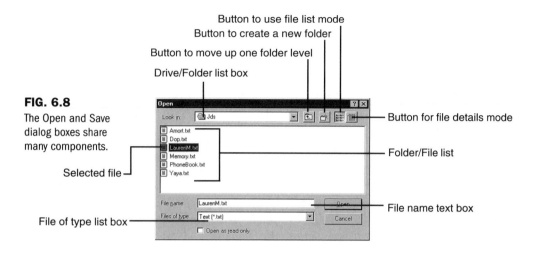

FIG. 6.8

The Open and Save dialog boxes share many components.

These are the dialog box's major components:

- *Drive/Folder list*   The current folder is listed here. If the current folder is the root (\), the current drive is listed here. You can use the combo box and navigation buttons to move up folder levels, similar to the way you would in the Windows Explorer.

- *File/Folder selection list*   The names indicated in this area are the folders and files one level beneath the item in the Drive/Folder list. An item in this area can be opened either by double-clicking it, or by highlighting it and pressing Enter. If the item you open is a folder, the display is updated to show the contents of the new current folder. If the item you open is a file, the dialog box closes.

- *File Name text box*   This text box can be used by the user for manual file name entry and folder navigation. If he enters a file name, the dialog box closes. If he enters a path like "C:\Data\Word" and presses Enter, the dialog box is updated to show that folder. Also, if a user single-clicks a file name in the file/folder selection area, it appears here.

- *File of Type list box*   Here the user selects the type of files to display. These types are determined by the extension portion of the file name; the available types are controlled by the `Filter` property of the CommonDialog control.

- *Toolbar buttons and Command buttons*   The buttons in the upper-right corner let the user move up one folder level, create a new folder, or switch the file display area between the list mode and the file details mode. The buttons at the lower-right let the user process the selection or cancel the dialog box.

Opening and Saving Files   To open an existing file, use the `ShowOpen` method of the CommonDialog control. (This method displays the dialog box in Figure 6.8.) You use this method by specifying the name of the CommonDialog control and the method name, as shown in the following lines of code:

```
cdlGetFile.ShowOpen
Msgbox "You Selected " & cdlGetFile.FileName
```

Part

II

Ch

6

After the preceding code is executed, the name of the file selected is available to your code in the control's `FileName` property.

Using the CommonDialog control for saving and opening are essentially the same operation. The name of the method used to invoke the Save As dialog box is `ShowSave`. There are a few subtle differences between the dialog boxes shown for the `Open` and `Save` functions, such as the title of the dialog box and the captions on the command buttons.

N O T E   The Open and Save As dialog boxes don't actually open or save files, they simply get information from the user as to the names and locations of the files to open or save. It's up to your program to take whatever steps are necessary to complete the operation. ▨

Specifying File Types with the *Filter* Property   When using the CommonDialog control, you might find it necessary to specify that only certain file types are listed. If your program reads Microsoft Excel (.XLS) files, for example, you would not want the user to attempt to open a batch (.BAT) file. You can restrict (or "filter") the files shown in the dialog box by using the `Filter` property.

You set the `Filter` property at design mode from either the Properties window or the Property Pages dialog box, or at runtime with an assignment statement in code. The `Filter` property is a string value that includes a file type description followed by the file extension. It requires a special format, as shown here:

```
cdlGetFile.Filter = "Word Documents¦*.DOC"
```

The vertical line in the preceding code line is known as the *pipe symbol*. This symbol must be present in the filter. Preceding the pipe symbol is a short description of the file type, in this case "Word Documents." Following the pipe symbol is the actual filter for the files. You typically express the filter as an asterisk followed by a period and the extension of the files that you want to display. Some examples are `*.txt`, `*.doc`, and `*.*`.

CAUTION

Do not include spaces before or after the pipe symbol, or you might not get the file list that you want.

If you specify the `Filter` property with an assignment statement, you must enclose the filter in double quotes, as with any string. The quotes are omitted if you specify the filter from the Properties dialog box.

You can specify multiple `description¦filter` pairs within the `Filter` property. Each pair must be separated from the other pairs by the pipe symbol, as shown in the following example:

```
cdgGetFile.Filter = "All Files¦*.*¦Text Files¦*.txt"
```

Customizing the File Dialog Boxes with the *Flags* Property   Another important property is the `Flags` property. The `Flags` property is set using a constant or combination of constants, similar to the `MsgBox` function's `Options` parameter. A complete list of constants is listed in

Visual Basic's Help system. For example, if the Open as Read Only check box doesn't make any sense in your program, you can set a flag to hide it:

```
cdlFile.Flags = cdlOFNHideReadOnly
cdlFile.InitDir = "C:\Windows"
cdlfile.ShowOpen
```

Note also the use of the `InitDir` property, which starts the dialog box in a specific folder.

N O T E Flags, filters, and properties that affect the CommonDialog box must be set *before* displaying it! ■

The Font Dialog Box

Setting up the CommonDialog control to show the Font dialog box is just as easy as setting it up for file functions. In fact, you can use the same CommonDialog control on a form to handle file, font, color, and printer functions, just by resetting the properties and invoking the appropriate method.

The first step in using the CommonDialog control to handle font selection is to set a value for the `Flags` property. Among other things, this property tells the CommonDialog control whether you want to show screen fonts, printer fonts, or both. This setting is required; the constants are listed in the following table:

Font Set	Constant	Value
Screen fonts	cdlCFScreenFonts	1
Printer fonts	cdlCFPrinterFonts	2
Both sets	cdlCFBoth	3

CAUTION

If you do not set a value for the `Flags` property, you get an error message stating that no fonts are installed.

You can set the value of the `Flags` property from the design environment—by using the Properties window or the Property Pages dialog box—or from your program, by using an assignment statement. After the `Flags` property has been set, you can invoke the Font dialog box from your code, using the CommonDialog's `ShowFont` method. After the dialog box is closed, information about the font that the user selected is contained in the CommonDialog's properties:

```
cdlFont.flags = cdlCFBoth + cdlCFEffects
cdlFont.ShowFont
txtName.Font.Name = cdlFont.FontName
txtName.Font.Size = cdlFont.FontSize
txtName.Font.Bold = cdlFont.FontBold
```

Part
II

Ch
6

Note two things in the preceding code. First, an extra flag, `cdlCFEffects`, allows the user to select additional font "effects" such as bold, color, and underline. Second, note the slight difference in syntax between the TextBox's Font properties and the CommonDialog's Font properties. The `Font` property of a text box is an object itself (a `Font` object), while the CommonDialog box stores each attribute about a Font (`Name`, `Size`, `Bold`, and so on) in a separate property. The text box has the older separate properties for compatibility, but I would avoid them. If you had to set the font for two text boxes, you could set one directly from the CommonDialog control's properties and the other one simply by assigning the first text box's Font property:

```
txtAddress.Font = txtName.Font
```

Figure 6.9 shows the Font dialog box that is presented to the user. This particular dialog box contains both screen and printer fonts.

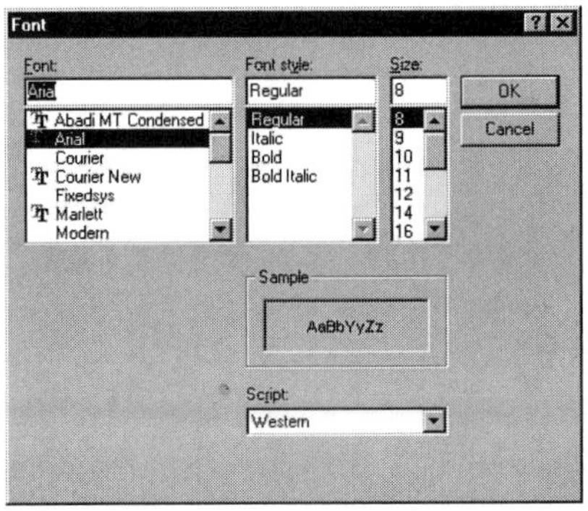

FIG. 6.9

The Font dialog box can be programmed to display screen fonts, printer fonts, or both.

Table 6.4 shows the control's properties and the font attributes that each manipulates.

Table 6.4   CommonDialog Control Properties that Store Font Attributes

Property	Attribute
FontName	The name of the base font
FontSize	The height of the font in points
FontBold	Whether boldface was selected
FontItalic	Whether italic was selected
FontUnderline	Whether the font is underlined
FontStrikethru	Whether the font has a line through it

The font information can be used to set the font of any object in your program, or even to set the font for the `Printer` object. Be sure to peruse the Help system for a complete list of `Flags` property constants.

The Color Dialog Box

The CommonDialog control's Color dialog box lets the user select colors that can be used for the foreground or background colors of your forms or controls (see Figure 6.10). The user has the option of choosing one of the standard colors or creating and selecting a custom color.

FIG. 6.10

The Color dialog box lets the user select a color graphically and then returns it to your program as a hex value.

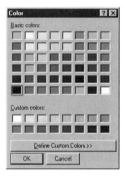

Setting up the CommonDialog control for colors is basically the same as for fonts. You set the `Flags` property to the constant `cdlCCRGBInit` and then invoke the control's `ShowColor` method.

When the user selects a color from the dialog box, a hexadecimal number representing that color is stored in the `Color` property of the control. The following code shows how to change a form's background color using the Color dialog box:

```
cdlGetColor.Flags = cdlCCRGBInit
cdlGetColor.ShowColor
frmMyForm.BackColor = cdlGetColor.Color
```

As with the other dialog boxes, you can alter the behavior of the Color dialog box with the `Flags` property. For example, if you only want default colors available, use the `cdlCCPreventFullOpen` flag so the user cannot open the Define Custom Colors window.

The Print Dialog Box

Another type of dialog box provided by the CommonDialog control is the Print dialog box. A Print dialog box is usually displayed just before your application's print process begins. It lets the user select which printer to use and specify options for the print process (see Figure 6.11). These options include specifying which pages to print and the number of copies, as well as an option of printing to a file.

To invoke the Print dialog box, just call the CommonDialog control's `ShowPrinter` method. There are no required flags to set prior to the call.

After the Print dialog box is displayed, the user can select the printer from the <u>N</u>ame list at the top of the dialog box. This list contains all the printers installed in the user's operating system. Just below the <u>N</u>ame list is the Status line, which tells you the current status of the selected printer.

FIG. 6.11

The Print dialog box provides a consistent way for your users to set printer options.

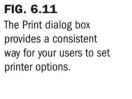

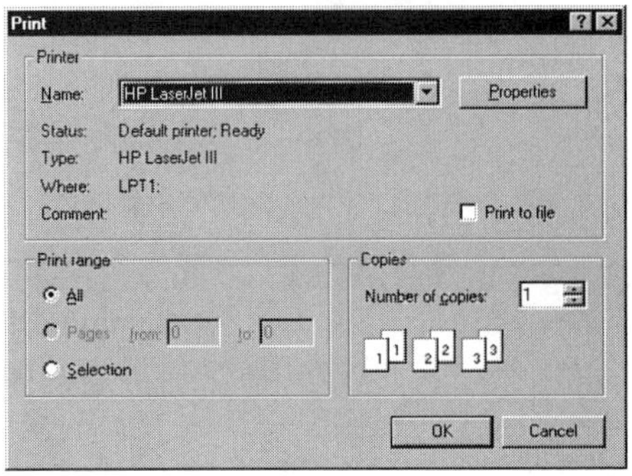

If users want to change any printer-specific parameters (such as paper size and margins), they can click the Properties button on the Print dialog box. This brings up the Properties dialog box for the selected printer, as shown in Figure 6.12. This dialog box lets you control all the settings of the printer, just as with the Windows Control Panel.

FIG. 6.12

The Properties dialog box for the printer lets you control paper size, margins, and other printer attributes.

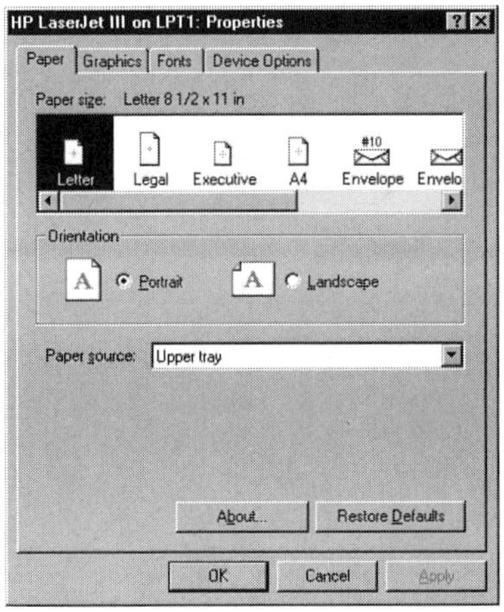

The Print dialog box returns the information provided by the user in the dialog box's properties. The FromPage and ToPage properties tell you the starting and ending pages of the printout as selected by the user. The Copies property tells you how many copies the user wants printed.

This is provided only as information. The Print dialog box does not automatically create the desired printout. As with other CommonDialogs, your program must complete the task, as in this example:

```
cdlPrint.Flags = cdlPDDisablePrintToFile
cdlPrint.Copies = 3
cdlPrint.PrinterDefault = True
cdlPrint.ShowPrinter
MsgBox "The default printer is:" & Printer.DeviceName
```

In this sample code, properties and flags are used to disable the Print to File option and set the default number of copies to 3. In addition, the `PrinterDefault` property means that the dialog box will use the control's properties to modify the default system printer.

The Help Dialog Box

This usage of the CommonDialog control invokes the Windows Help engine by running WINHLP32.EXE. To use this dialog box, you must set the CommonDialog control's `HelpFile` property to the name and location of a properly formatted Windows help (.hlp) file and set the `HelpCommand` property to tell the Help engine what type of help to offer. After setting these properties, use the CommonDialog control's `ShowHelp` method to initiate the Help system. The user can then navigate the Help system using your program's Help file.

Creating Your Own Dialog Boxes

Although the CommonDialog control provides you with a number of dialog boxes to use in your programs, sometimes there are things that just can't be accomplished with these built-in tools. For example, if you want to set your own captions for the command buttons in a dialog box, you can't do this with the message box; nor can the message box handle more than three buttons. Also, consider the built-in input box. This dialog box cannot display an icon, nor can it handle more than one input item. So what are you supposed to do? Build your own, of course.

In this section, you see how to build a simple, but flexible, dialog box to display a message and a set of custom command buttons. Your dialog box will allow you to choose to have from one to three buttons displayed and will be able to display any of four icons. From this example, you will be able to see how you can build more complex dialog boxes.

Setting Up the Dialog Box Form

The first thing you have to do in creating a dialog box is to create the form itself. To do this, follow these steps:

1. Create a new Standard EXE project.
2. Add a new form to the project (making a total of two forms).
3. Give the new (second) form a unique name, such as `frmDialog`. It will become your dialog box.
4. Set `frmDialog`'s Caption property to Custom Dialog Box.
5. Set the `BorderStyle` property to `3 - Fixed Dialog`.
6. Set the `ControlBox` property to `False`.
7. Set the `StartUpPosition` property to `2 - CenterScreen`.

With these property settings, your dialog box will start up in the center of the screen and will have a border that, like standard Windows dialog boxes, doesn't allow the user to resize it. In addition, it won't have the Control Menu icon at the left side of the title bar.

N O T E   The Project window now contains two files, one for each of the two forms. When you save the project, you need to supply file names for both form (.FRM) files, as well as a file name for the overall project (.VBP) file. ▪

Adding Controls to the Form

Now that we have created a dialog-style form, the next step is to add a Label control to display your message to the user.

Next, you will want to add Image controls that will display the icon in the dialog box. We'll be using five Image controls—the one that the user actually sees, and four other (invisible) Image controls that will hold the four icons that could possibly be displayed in the visible control. The ImageList control technique that we discussed in Chapter 5, "Adding Menus and Toolbars to Your Program," could also have been used here.

▶ **See** "Getting the Images for Your Toolbar," **p. 118**

Continue building the dialog box form as follows:

1. Place one Label control on the form. Size it to the width that you want. Name the label lblMessage so it can be referenced from code.

2. Set the label's WordWrap and AutoSize properties to True. (Note that the WordWrap property must be set first.)

3. Place one Image control near the Label control. This Image control will actually display the icon to the user. Change its name to imgShow.

4. Create four other Image controls to hold the other possible icons for display. Use the default names of Image1, Image2, Image3, and Image4.

5. For the last four Image controls, set the Picture property to the desired icon and set the Visible property to False.

6. Finally, create three command buttons on the form. Name them cmdMessage1, cmdMessage2, and cmdMessage3. The last two of these buttons need to have the Visible property set to False.

This technique allows your program to display only the requested number of buttons when the dialog box is called. Make sure that all the command buttons are the same size. When you have finished, your form should look something like the one in Figure 6.13.

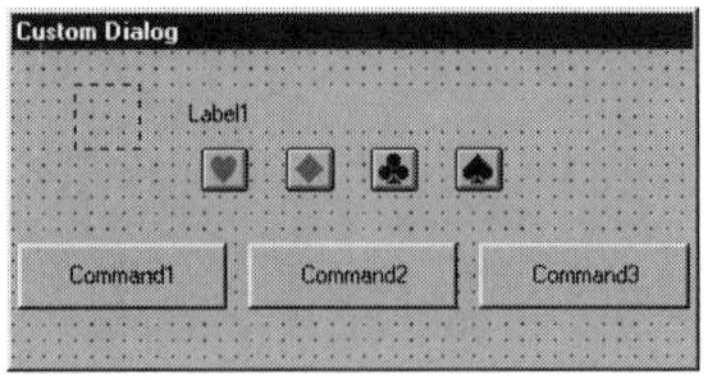

FIG. 6.13
Your custom dialog box will have several command buttons and images to allow choices.

Telling Your Dialog What to Display

While placing the controls on the form is a critical part of creating a custom dialog box, the main work of the dialog box is done with code.

First, you need to have a way for the user to set the dialog box's options before showing it. This is accomplished with *public variables*. We'll discuss public variables more fully in Chapter 8, "Programming Basics"; for now, think of a public variable as something that acts much like a property that applies to the form in which it is declared. It can be accessed from any part of our application by using the form name, a dot, and the variable name (for example, *frmMain.stFileName*).

▶ **See** "Variable Declarations," **p. 168**

You declare public variables in the form's General Declarations section:

1. Open frmDialog's Code window by double-clicking any empty part of it. (You can also select frmDialog in the Project window and click the View Code button.)

2. In the code window's upper-left drop-down box, select (General). Make sure that (Declarations) is showing in the upper-right drop-down box.

3. Enter the following code to create the public variables:

   ```
   Option Explicit
   Public inNumCmd as Integer
   Public inImageID as Integer
   Public stCmdCaption1 as String
   Public stCmdCaption2 as String
   Public stCmdCaption3 as String
   Public inBtnPressed As Integer
   ```

The main part of your code will be located in the form's `Activate` event procedure. The `Activate` event occurs when the form becomes the "active" form. Your code controls which image and command buttons are visible to the user and properly positions them on the form. The code, shown in Listing 6.1, assumes that all the command buttons are the same size. By setting the `Top`, `Left`, and `Visible` properties of the buttons, the visible command buttons are shown near the bottom of the label control that displays the message. The `Left` property of each button is set so that the button group is centered in the form. And the height of the form itself is adjusted so that there is not a lot of empty space showing.

Listing 6.1   DIALOG.FRM—Using the Form's *Activate* Event to Adjust the Position of the Controls

```
Private Sub Form_Activate()
  Dim inCtlTop As Integer
  Dim inCmdWidth As Integer

'First, select an image based
'on the ImageID public variable:
  Select Case inImageID
```

continues

Part

II

Ch

6

Listing 6.1   Continued

```
    Case 1
        imgShow.Picture = Image1.Picture
    Case 2
        imgShow.Picture = Image2.Picture
    Case 3
        imgShow.Picture = Image3.Picture
    Case 4
        imgShow.Picture = Image4.Picture
  End Select

'The tops of the controls will be
'240 twips below the message label:
  inCtlTop = lblMessage.Top + lblMessage.Height + 240
  cmdMessage1.Top = inCtlTop
  cmdMessage2.Top = inCtlTop
  cmdMessage3.Top = inCtlTop

'The form will be sized 500 twips below the buttons
  Me.Height = cmdMessage1.Top + cmdMessage1.Height + 500

'Set the CommandButton captions
  cmdMessage1.Caption = stCmdCaption1
  cmdMessage2.Caption = stCmdCaption2
  cmdMessage3.Caption = stCmdCaption3

'Set the CommandButton visible properties
  Select Case inNumCmd
     Case 2
        cmdMessage2.Visible = True
     Case 3
        cmdMessage2.Visible = True
        cmdMessage3.Visible = True
  End Select


'Finally, center the buttons on the form
  Select Case inNumCmd
   Case 1
        inCmdWidth = cmdMessage1.Width
        cmdMessage1.Left = (frmDialog.ScaleWidth - inCmdWidth) / 2
   Case 2
        inCmdWidth = 2 * cmdMessage1.Width + 105
        cmdMessage1.Left = (frmDialog.ScaleWidth - inCmdWidth) / 2
        cmdMessage2.Left = cmdMessage1.Left + cmdMessage1.Width + 105
   Case 3
        inCmdWidth = 3 * cmdMessage1.Width + 2 * 105
        cmdMessage1.Left = (frmDialog.ScaleWidth - inCmdWidth) / 2
        cmdMessage2.Left = cmdMessage1.Left + cmdMessage1.Width + 105
        cmdMessage3.Left = cmdMessage2.Left + cmdMessage2.Width + 105
  End Select
End Sub
```

Another thing that you want your dialog box to be able to do is to tell the calling program which button was pressed. You handle this by using the Public variable inBtnPressed that was declared in frmDialog's General Declarations section. The dialog box will set a different value of the variable for each command button (see Listing 6.2). You will also want to unload the form when any command button has been pressed. This ensures that the dialog box is reset when it is reloaded (causing the Load event to occur again).

Listing 6.2   DIALOG.FRM—Using the *Click* Event to Set the Variable Indicating Which Button Was Pressed

```
Private Sub cmdMessage1_Click()
  inBtnPressed = 1
  Unload Me
End Sub

Private Sub cmdMessage2_Click()
  inBtnPressed = 2
  Unload Me
End Sub

Private Sub cmdMessage3_Click()
  inBtnPressed = 3
  Unload Me
End Sub
```

Calling the Dialog from a Program

Now that you have entered all the code, you are ready to use it! This involves three basic steps:

1. Set the public variables that the dialog box is expecting.

2. Show the dialog box as a modal form.

3. After the dialog box has been unloaded, have the calling program use the returned result.

To test the dialog box, put a command button on the other form in your project and enter the sample code in Listing 6.3.

Listing 6.3   DEMO.FRM—Setting the Variables of the Dialog Box Before Showing It

```
Private Sub Command1_Click()
  Dim stMsg as string
  stMsg = "This is a dialog with a custom set of buttons. This is something that"
  stMsg = stMsg & "cannot be achieved with a normal message box."
  With frmDialog
    .lblMessage.Caption = stMsg
```

continues

Part

II

Ch

6

Listing 6.3   Continued

```
    .NumCmd = 2
    .ImageID = 4
    .CmdCaption1 = "&Discard File"
    .CmdCaption2 = "&Save File"
    .Show vbModal
    Msgbox "You pressed " & .BtnPressed
End With

End Sub
```

Notice in the listing that you can use a With...End With statement block to avoid typing frmDialog over and over. A sample of the custom dialog box is shown in Figure 6.14.

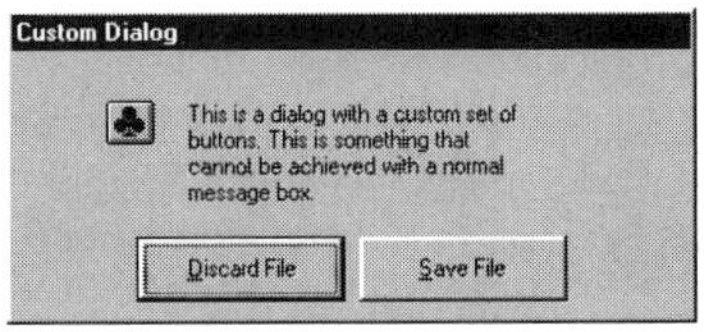

FIG. 6.14

Though there is a lot of room for improvement, our custom dialog box behaves just like a standard Windows message box.

Using Form Templates for Other Dialog Boxes

Using the procedures illustrated in this section, you can create any kind of dialog box that you want. In addition, Microsoft has included with Visual Basic 5 several form templates representing custom dialog boxes that are common to many programs. You can quickly add one of these form templates to your project by selecting the appropriate type when you add a new form; you can then customize it to suit your needs. The available templates include:

■ *About Dialog*   Used to provide the user with information about your program

■ *Log In Dialog*   Allows the user to enter a user ID and password

■ *Options Dialog*   Creates a dialog box similar to Property Pages or the Options dialog box of Visual Basic

■ *Tip Dialog*   Can provide a Tip of the Day function for your program

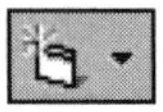

You can add these forms based on these dialog box templates to your program by choosing Project, Add Form, or by clicking the Add Form button. This presents you with the Add Form dialog box shown in Figure 6.15. You can choose the desired dialog box from the templates available, and then customize it to suit your needs.

FIG. 6.15
Several custom dialog
boxes are available as
form templates.

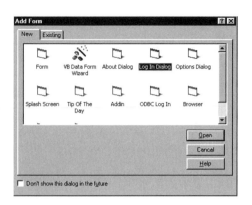

From Here...

You have seen in this chapter how dialog boxes can be used to help the user select files, printers, and fonts in your programs. You have also seen how the message box and input box are used to inform the user and to get decisions or single pieces of information. You have even seen how to create your own dialog boxes when the built-in ones are insufficient for the task. To learn more about using some of the concepts presented here, take a look at the following chapters:

- To learn more about printing, see Chapter 9, "Displaying and Printing Reports."
- To learn font and color options, see Chapter 13, "Working with Text, Fonts, and Colors."
- To learn more about control arrays that can be used in custom dialog boxes, see Chapter 19, "Advanced Control Techniques."

Part

II

Ch

6

Responding to the User

When Windows was introduced, the way that users interacted with programs was changed forever. Gone were the days when a program ran from beginning to end with few user interactions. With Windows, users gained tremendous control over what functions they performed in a program and when these functions were performed. Although this was a great benefit to users, it provided an equally great challenge to programmers. This is because the developer of a program was no longer in control of the entire program experience. As a programmer, you now have to plan for many possible user activities, and in many cases, you must protect the user from himself. ■

Programs that work the way a user thinks

Event-driven programs let your users execute tasks in almost any order. This lets them process information in the way they find most comfortable.

Common events you will encounter

Many of the elements (forms and controls) that you use in your programs have a set of common events. You see what these events are and how they are used in a program.

Responding to the events of a program

Although there are many possible events that can occur during the execution of any program, you can choose which events your programs will handle.

Multiple events from a single user action

One action taken by a user can trigger a single event or a series of events. You learn about the sequence of events and how to plan for them.

N O T E Although event-driven programs were around before Windows arrived on the scene (Macintosh programs and even a few DOS programs were event-driven), it was Windows that started the groundswell that has defined computing today. ▓

Introducing Events

The concept of an event-driven program might be fairly new to you, but the idea of responding to events should not be. Most of the world is what we would call event-driven. For example, consider your TV. You can change the channel whenever you feel like it, and with today's remote controls, you can go directly to your favorite channel instead of having to scroll through all the channels on the TV. By the same token, you can change the volume of the TV whenever you want by as much as you want. You can probably also cut out the sound altogether by pressing the mute button. This type of control over how and when things happen correlates to event-driven programming. You (the user of your TV) initiate an event (by pressing a button) that causes the TV to take an action appropriate to the event that occurred. You also control when these events happen.

If you have worked much with Windows programs, you probably have noticed that they work in a similar manner. In Microsoft Word, for example, you can easily change the font or style of a piece of text. You also can highlight a section of text and drag it to a new location. Each of these actions is made possible by the program's capability to take actions in response to user-initiated events.

As you create your own Windows programs, you will seek to model the program after the real-world tasks that the program is supposed to handle. This means that you will want to give the users command buttons or menu selections so that they can perform tasks when they want. Figure 7.1 shows an example of the interface for an event-driven program.

FIG. 7.1
Graphical user interfaces go hand in hand with event-driven programming.

Information can be entered in a text box.

Actions can be initiated by clicking a command button.

The form can be closed by clicking here.

The current record can be changed by clicking the record navigator.

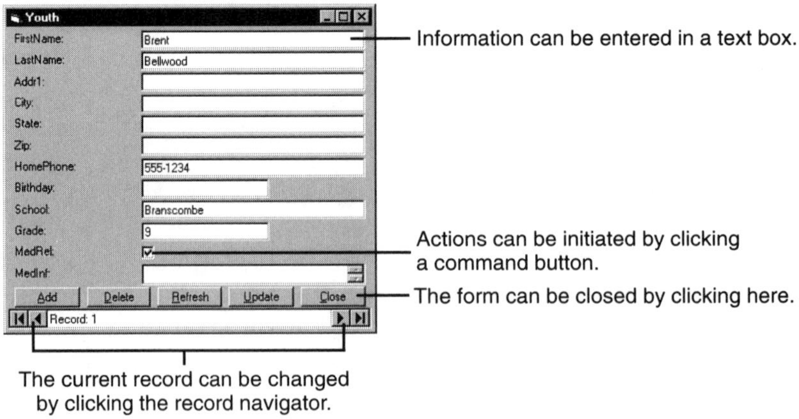

Another advantage of event-driven programming is that you can use the events to provide immediate feedback to the user. For example, you can program an event to verify a user's entry as soon as the user finishes typing. Then, if there is a problem with what the user entered, he or she knows immediately and can fix it. This type of feedback is handled by code, such as that shown in Listing 7.1, which checks the age that a user has entered.

Listing 7.1   AGECHECK.TXT—Code to Verify the Age Entered

```
Private Sub txtAge_LostFocus()
    Dim inInputAge As Integer, stMsg as String
    inInputAge = Val(txtAge.Text)
    If inInputAge <= 0 Then
        stMsg = "You must enter a numeric age greater than 0!"
        MsgBox stMsg, vbCritical, "Age Input Demo"
    End If
    If inInputAge > 120 Then
        stMsg = "Wow! That's old! Change it if it's wrong."
        MsgBox stMsg, vbExclamation, "Age Input Demo"
    End If
End Sub
```

Handling Events in Your Programs

In a typical program, there are many events that can occur and many user actions that can trigger these events. Program events can be triggered by such actions as the user pressing a key, clicking a mouse button, moving the mouse, changing the value of the information in a control, or switching to another window in the program. The program itself can cause events to occur. Windows events can also be triggered by system functions such as a timer, or even by external factors such as receiving an e-mail message. There are hundreds—if not thousands—of events that can occur in any given program. You want your program to be able to isolate these events and take action only for specific ones. Fortunately, this is not as hard as it sounds.

Determining When an Event Has Occurred

At this point, you might be wondering how in the world you are going to detect and handle all these possible events that might be occurring in your program. Well, the good news is that you don't have to do anything to detect events. This task is handled automatically by Windows.

When Windows senses an event taking place, it attempts to tell your running program about the event. Windows sends your running program a *message*. Your program must interpret that message, determine which event the message stands for, and then act accordingly. Still sounds like a lot of work, right? Well, this is where the strength of Visual Basic comes in. The messages sent by Windows are received and processed by the form(s) and controls that make up the interface of your program.

Part

II

Ch

7

With Visual Basic, each control or form in your program is capable of recognizing only a select group of events. However, the key to handling events is to write code for only the events for which you want your program to take an action. This is done by selecting the particular object and event you want to handle, and then writing some program code in the Code window. The object is selected in the Code window's upper-left drop-down list box; the appropriate event procedure is selected in the upper-right drop-down list box. If there is code written for an event, Visual Basic processes the code when the event occurs. If there is no code for an event, Visual Basic ignores the event. Figure 7.2 shows an example of an event procedure written for a specific control and event.

Object selection drop-down list box

FIG. 7.2
Visual Basic responds to an event only if you write code for it.

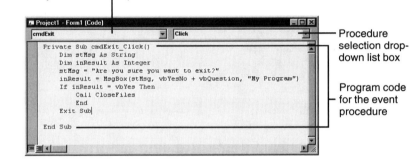

Procedure selection drop-down list box

Program code for the event procedure

Types of Events

There are two basic types of events that can occur in your Visual Basic program—*user-initiated events* and *system-initiated events*. Most often, you program for the user-initiated events. These events let your users control the direction of the program. That is, your users can take a specific action whenever they want, which gives them almost complete control over your program.

> **N O T E** You can, of course, limit the actions that a user can take by hiding or disabling controls when you don't want the user to have access to them. This technique is discussed in Chapter 4, "Working with Forms and Controls."

▶ **See** "Controlling User Interaction," **p. 71**

User-Initiated Events   User-initiated events are those that occur because of an action taken by the user. As you might guess, these events include keystrokes and mouse clicks, but there are also other events caused by the user, either directly or indirectly. For example, when the user clicks a text box to start editing the information in the box, a Click event is fired for the text box. What you might not realize is that several other events are also fired. One is the GotFocus event for the text box. This event occurs every time the user moves to the text box, either by clicking the mouse or using the Tab key. Also, if the text box gets the program's focus, another control must lose the focus. This causes a LostFocus event to fire for the other control. The GotFocus and LostFocus events are caused by the user's action, just as the Click event is. As you will see in the later section "Understanding Event Sequences," multiple events can occur for each action a user takes. The order in which the events occur can be important.

Here are some of the main user actions that trigger events in a program:

- Starting the program
- Pressing a key
- Clicking the mouse
- Moving the mouse
- Closing the program

Common Events While there are a number of events to which forms and controls can respond, there are several events that many controls have in common:

Event	Occurs When
Change	Occurs when the user modifies the text in a text box or combo box
Click	Occurs when the user clicks an object with the primary mouse button (usually, the left button)
DblClick	Occurs when the user double-clicks an object with the primary mouse button
DragDrop	Occurs when the user drags a control to another location
DragOver	Occurs when an object is dragged over a control
GotFocus	Occurs when an object receives the focus
KeyDown	Occurs when a key is pressed while an object has the focus
KeyPress	Occurs when a key is pressed and released while an object has the focus
KeyUp	Occurs when a key is released while an object has the focus
LostFocus	Occurs just before the focus leaves an object
MouseDown	Occurs when a mouse button is pressed while an object has the focus
MouseMove	Occurs when the mouse cursor is moved over an object
MouseUp	Occurs when a mouse button is released while an object has the focus

You might have noticed that several of the events seem to correspond to the same user action. For example, the Click, MouseDown, and MouseUp events all occur when the user clicks the mouse button. Although some of the differences between the events are obvious—for example, the MouseDown event occurs when you press the mouse button—there are other differences between the events. In the case of pressing a mouse button, the Click event is fired only if the left mouse button is pressed; it does not respond to the click of any other mouse button. The MouseDown and MouseUp events not only respond to any mouse button, but the event also can report which button was pressed, so your program can take appropriate action.

The KeyDown, KeyPress, and KeyUp events work in a similar manner. The KeyPress event tells you only which key was pressed, not whether a Shift or Ctrl key was held down when the key was pressed. If you need that information, you need to use the KeyDown or KeyUp events.

Writing Event Procedures

With all these events going on, how do you make your code respond to any of the events? And how do you filter out the events that you don't want? The answer to both questions is the same. To respond to any event for any object, you write program code specifically for that event happening to that object. Any object/event combination that has no code written for it is ignored. So the next question is, how do you write code for an event?

To write code, you first need to access the code-editing window. Do this by double-clicking a control on your form, by clicking the View Code button in the project window, by selecting the Code item from the View menu, or by pressing F7. Any of these actions presents you with the Code window (see Figure 7.3).

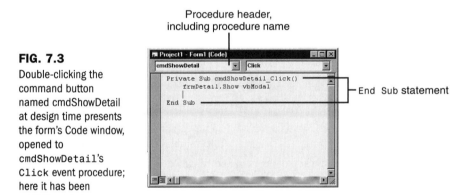

FIG. 7.3

Double-clicking the command button named cmdShowDetail at design time presents the form's Code window, opened to cmdShowDetail's Click event procedure; here it has been partially coded.

In the Code window, you select the object and event for which you want to write code. When you make a selection, Visual Basic automatically sets up the skeleton of a procedure with the procedure name and the End Sub statement. Notice that the procedure name for an Event procedure contains the name of the object and the name of the event. At this point, you can write program statements to take any actions you desire for the event. The following code shows how the program displays a second form in response to the user clicking a command button:

```
Private Sub cmdShowDetail_Click()
    frmDetail.Show vbModal
End Sub
```

N O T E   If you enter a Code window by double-clicking an object, the Code window automatically selects that object's most commonly used event procedure. For example, if you double-click a command button at design time, the Code window is opened to that command button's Click event procedure. ▨

Handling Multiple Controls with a Single Procedure

It was stated earlier that typically you would write separate procedures for each control on your form. There are times, however, when you want to write one procedure to handle the same event for multiple controls. The first step is to create a control array, as described in Chapter 19, "Advanced Control Techniques." After you have created a control array, open the Code window for one of the controls. You might notice a slight difference between the procedure declaration for the control that is part of a control array and one that is not. For a control array, the procedure declaration contains a parameter called Index, as shown in Figure 7.4. This parameter tells you which element of the control array was accessed.

▶ **See** "Creating a Control Array," **p. 497**

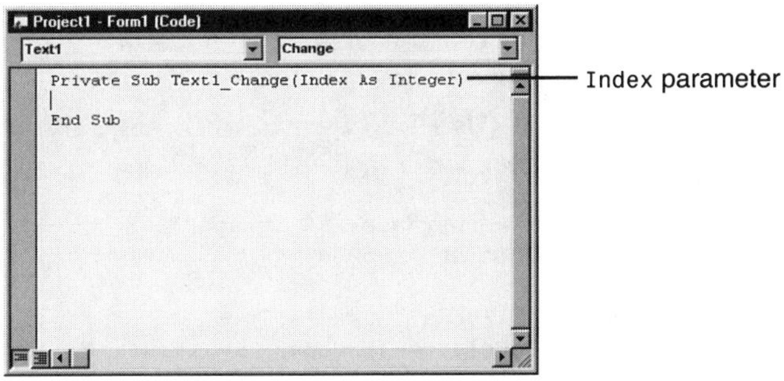

FIG. 7.4

The Index parameter identifies which specific control array element received an event.

Index parameter

If you want to write different code for each of the elements of the array, you can use a Select Case block to do so. However, the most efficient use of the control array is to handle actions for groups of elements. The following two examples from a commercial program help illustrate the point.

In the first example, an array of TextBox controls is used to display membership information from a database. The information includes a person's name, address, phone number, and so on. This information is verified on a periodic basis. When certain information is changed, the application needs to set a flag to indicate that the record needs to be reverified. By using an If statement to check the index of the control array, the program can determine whether or not to set the flag. This is illustrated in the following code:

```
Private Sub txtMember_Change(Index As Integer)
    If Index >= 6 And Index <= 11 Then blCASSChange = True
End Sub
```

In the second example, say that you want to change the foreground (text) color of all text boxes to red whenever someone makes a change to any one of them. This indicates to the user that editing is in progress. Without a control array, you would have to write code in the Change event of every text box. By using the control array, you have to write the code only once (see Listing 7.2).

Part

II

Ch

7

Listing 7.2 CTRLARAY.TXT—Write One Code Routine to Handle an Event for All the Controls in an Array

```
Private Sub txtMember_Change(Index As Integer)
    Dim I As Integer
    For I = 0 To 22
        txtMember(I).ForeColor = vbRed
    Next I
End Sub
```

You also could use a different event and change the foreground color of the text box that has the focus. You would use the GotFocus event to change the color to red while the user is editing the text box, and use the LostFocus event to return the color to normal when the user leaves the text box. Listing 7.3 shows how this could be done.

Listing 7.3 FOCUS.TXT—Use Two Events to Change the Color of Text When the User Enters and Leaves the Control

```
Private Sub txtMember_GotFocus(Index As Integer)
    txtMember(Index).ForeColor = vbRed
End Sub
Private Sub txtMember_LostFocus(Index As Integer)
    txtMember(Index).ForeColor = vbBlack
End Sub
```

Another way to handle an event for multiple controls is to use a Select Case statement to take a different action for each of the controls of the array. While you might think that doing this negates the advantage of using a control array, it does still provide you with a means to keep all the code in one place, instead of having it spread out over multiple procedures in your program. Listing 7.4 shows how this is done for the navigation buttons in a membership application. The actual form that uses this code is shown in Figure 7.5.

▶ **See** "Using *Select Case*," **p. 188**

Listing 7.4 NAVIGATE.FRM—Using a *Select Case* Statement to Handle Navigation Buttons on a Form

```
Private Sub cmdRecNav_Click(Index As Integer)
Dim stSrchStr As String, stSrchStr2 As String, lgSrchID As Long
Dim stBkMrk As String
Dim rsTXARSet As Recordset, lgTXAID As Long
Dim stTXAStr As String
'Perform navigation operation
    Select Case Index
        Case 6
            'Perform search operation
            If Val(txtSrch(0).Text) > 0 Then
```

```
                    'Search on ID code - Need Member or Contact ID switch
                    lgSrchID = Val(txtSrch(0).Text)
                    stBkMrk = MemRset.Bookmark
                    If optMemID(0).Value Then
                        MemRset.Index = "Member"
                    Else
                        MemRset.Index = "Contact"
                    End If
                    MemRset.Seek "=", LgSrchID
                    If Not MemRset.NoMatch Then
                        StBkMrk = MemRset.Bookmark
                    Else
                        MsgBox "ID not found"
                    End If
                    txtSrch(0).Text = ""
                    MemRset.Index = "Name"
                    MemRset.Bookmark = StBkMrk
                ElseIf Not txtSrch(1).Text = "" Then
                    'Search on user name
                    If Not txtSrch(2).Text = "" Then
                        StSrchStr = Trim(txtSrch(1).Text)
                        StSrchStr2 = Trim(txtSrch(2).Text)
                        MemRset.Seek ">=", StSrchStr, StSrchStr2
                    Else
                        StSrchStr = Trim(txtSrch(1).Text)
                        MemRset.Seek ">=", StSrchStr
                    End If
                    txtSrch(1).Text = ""
                    txtSrch(2).Text = ""
                Else
                    'Error message
                    MsgBox "No valid search data was entered", vbOKOnly
                End If
            Case 4
                fraNav.Visible = False
                fraSave.Visible = True
                Editing = False
                ClearMember
                EditColor
                Adding = True
            Case 5
                'Delete the current record
                RetCode = MsgBox("Are you sure you want to delete this record?", _
                    vbYesNo, "Deletion Confirmation")
                If RetCode = vbYes Then
                    MemRset.Delete
                    RecordNav 1, MemRset
                End If
            Case Else
                RecordNav Index, MemRset
                'If a record was deleted, move to the previous record
                If Index = 5 Then RecordNav 1, MemRset
        End Select
        If Not Index = 4 Then ShowMember
End Sub
```

FIG. 7.5

Navigation buttons are part of a control array.

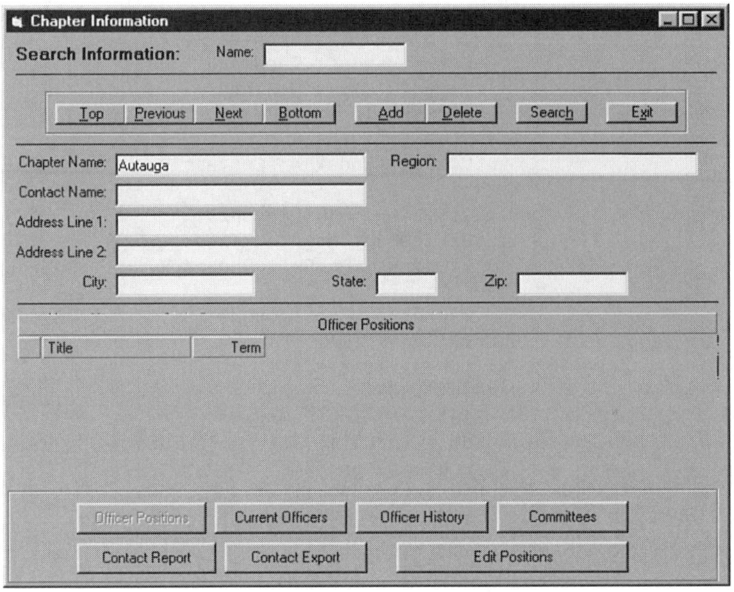

Calling an Event Procedure from Code

Although event procedures are typically run only in response to an event, you can call these procedures just like any other procedure you would write. You might do this when two different types of controls are used to perform the same function. This is the case when you have a menu and a toolbar on a form. Because both perform the same function, you need to write only one of the event procedures to handle the event; the appropriate event procedure for the other control can simply call the first control's event procedure and pass any required parameters such as the control array index. For example, the following line of code would call the Click event procedure for the command button cmdRecNav (shown in Listing 7.4), passing a parameter of 4 into the procedure's Index argument, just as if the user had clicked the Add command button (which has a control array index of 4):

```
cmdRecNav_Click 4
```

▶ **See** "Creating a Toolbar for Your Application," **p. 117**

Understanding Event Sequences

By now, you have an understanding of what events are and how Visual Basic handles them. You have seen how to write code to take action when an event occurs. But you need to dive just a little deeper into the world of events.

As stated, a user action or system event can trigger multiple events. This can be a good thing because you can use these different events to handle different situations, as in the case of the

MouseDown and Click events. However, there is a flip side. (Isn't there always?) If you write code for multiple events that can occur, these procedures can interact in ways that you don't want. In the worst case, a sequence of events—each with its own event procedure—can put your system into an infinite loop. There are several keys to avoiding these problems:

- Recognize that multiple events can occur
- Determine which events occur for a user action
- Understand the sequence in which the events occur
- Test the interactions between multiple events in your code

Multiple Events for Each Action

One of the problems of handling multiple events is that there is almost an infinite number of ways in which the user can interact with your program. For example, did the user move to the text box with a mouse or with the Tab key? Prior to the move, was the focus on another text box or was it on a command button? And what happens when you move from one form to another? As you can see, the possibilities can be almost overwhelming.

The good news, though, is that you will not write code for most control/event combinations. Therefore, even though these events might occur, your program ignores them—and they do not cause you any problems.

Even though this simplifies the task of handling multiple events, it does not eliminate it. To get a handle on this, take a look at some simple sets of events that occur when a user performs an action.

First, look at the simple keystroke. Not all controls respond to keystrokes. But for the ones that do, every time the user presses a key, three events are fired—KeyDown, KeyPress, and KeyUp (in that order). If the keystroke happens to move the focus from one control to another, two additional events are triggered—LostFocus for the current control and GotFocus for the new control.

Next, consider the innocent mouse click. This simple user action also fires three events— MouseDown, MouseUp, and Click. If the user double-clicks the mouse, two more events occur after the Click event—the DblClick event and another MouseUp event. That's five events for what would seem like a single user action. In addition, if the mouse click causes the focus to move from one control to another, the LostFocus and GotFocus events would be triggered, for a total of seven events.

Finally, there is also the problem that different actions to achieve the same purpose cause different event sequences. For example, you know that to change the value of a check box, you can either click the box with the mouse or press the spacebar while the check box has the focus. But did you know that different events occur depending on how you check the box? Using the mouse triggers the MouseDown, MouseUp, and Click events. Using the spacebar triggers the KeyDown, KeyPress, KeyUp, and then the Click events. It can be confusing, can't it?

Part

II

Ch

7

However, there are ways to determine what events will occur in your program and in what order they will occur.

Determining the Order of Events

In trying to figure out whether the interaction between events will cause a problem, the first step is to ignore every event that you don't need. If you write code for only the Click event, you don't care when or if the keystroke or mouse events occur. The only time you have to be concerned is when you are writing code for multiple related events.

N O T E The GotFocus and LostFocus events are related to just about everything else. Because these events occur whenever the focus moves from one control to another, any action that can change the focus will trigger these events. Many programmers use the LostFocus event to handle data validation. While this is the perfect place to handle this task, the event interactions can cause problems. ▪

▶ **See** "Common Events," **p. 155**

The next step in determining the event interaction is to map the order of events in a program. I've created a simple program that stores in a list box information about most of the events that can occur to a text box, a command button, and their form. Each time an event occurs to one of these objects, a line is added to the list box reporting the name of the event that just occurred. By experimenting with different actions to the form, command button, and text box, you can see the order of events. You can also see how one user action can lead to an entire sequence of events. For example, clicking the command button can cause these events to occur in this order: MouseDown, GotFocus (assuming it didn't already have the focus), Click, and MouseUp. Figure 7.6 shows how this program records the results of these actions (the "Clear and reset" button was clicked just before taking these actions):

- Clicking the "Click here" command button
- Clicking in the text box to move the focus to it
- Typing the letters **t**, **m**, and **s** in the text box
- Clicking the mouse on an empty part of the form

This program responds to common events as they happen to a text box, a command button, and a form. Each of these events has an event procedure that adds an item reporting the event procedure's name to the list box on the left side of the form.

The entire program is available as the file EVENTSEQ.VBP. You can modify this program to handle any object/event combinations you want. Download it from **mcp.com/info/0-7897/ 0-7897-1288-1**.

FIG. 7.6

The order of many different combinations of events can be recorded in this demonstration program.

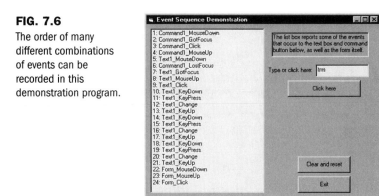

Whether you use a tool like this program, or some other method, it's critically important to understand the sequence of events. Once you realize that one user action can lead to several events, you can use that information to plan which events you want to write code for. For example, you can use a text box's KeyDown event, which is the first event that occurs when the user presses a key while the text box has the focus, to determine if the user has pressed Ctrl. That may be an indication within your program of some special action, such as opening a new record or saving initialization information. Whatever the case, you should test your applications thoroughly, using a variety of sequences of actions to your objects, to make sure that unexpected event sequences won't cause undesired results.

From Here...

This chapter focused on how Visual Basic handles events. But events are useful only in the context of forms and controls because these are the objects capable of receiving events. Also, events can cause an action in your program only if some code has been written for the event. You can learn more about these related topics in these chapters:

- Chapter 4, "Working with Forms and Controls," teaches you the basics of using controls and designing the visual interface of your programs.
- Chapter 8, "Programming Basics," teaches you about writing program code to respond to events.
- Chapter 19, "Advanced Control Techniques," and Chapter 36, "Advanced Form Techniques," explore forms and controls in more depth.

Part

II

Ch

7

Programming Basics

Although designing your program's user interface with forms and controls is important, most of its actual work is done with code. Visual Basic is a powerful programming language that is relatively easy to use. Visual Basic is a direct descendant of the BASIC programming language, which has been around for many years. BASIC was designed as a language for beginning programmers, hence the name, which is an abbreviation of *Beginner's All-purpose Symbolic Instruction Code*.

However, don't let the name fool you. Visual Basic is a much more powerful language than the BASIC you may remember from high school. With release 5.0, the language has been extended far beyond its primitive ancestry. Visual Basic has grown into a robust programming environment that can solve a wide variety of application needs.

This chapter looks at some of the basic concepts of programming in Visual Basic—starting with variables, working with information, and controlling your program with loops and conditional statements. ■

Introduction to variables

Learn how you can use variables to store and retrieve information while your programs are running.

Working with different types of data

Perform mathematical and string operations on the information your program uses.

Decision structures

Learn how you can use conditional statements to have your code make decisions that affect your program's processing flow.

Using procedures, functions, and loops

You see how procedures and functions make it easier to create, test, and reuse parts of your code. Also, discover how to use loops to make the computer run a task multiple times.

Eliminating errors in your program

Use Visual Basic's integrated debugging environment to easily track errors in your programs.

Working with Variables

Simply stated, you use variables to store information in the computer's memory while your programs are running. Three components define a variable:

- The variable's name (which correlates to its location in memory)
- The type of information being stored
- The actual information itself

Suppose you are given the assignment: "Go count all of the cars in the parking lot." As you count each car, you are storing information in a variable. Your location in memory is either a notepad or your brain. The type of information being stored is a number. And the actual information you are storing is the current number of cars.

As the name *variable* suggests, the information stored in a variable can change over time. Another way to think of a variable is that it's like a mailbox. You can perform two basic functions on a variable: get the information (remove a letter from the mailbox) and write new information (put a letter into the mailbox).

A variable has to have a name to be able to assign values to it. You might have noticed in earlier examples, statements like:

```
Dim X As Integer
```

This is a `Dim` statement, used for *dimensioning* (or *declaring)* variables. When your program declares a variable, it is, in essence, telling Visual Basic: "Set aside some memory for me and call it *X*." The last two words in the statement tell VB what type of information you will be storing, in this case integer numbers. This helps determine how much memory is to be set aside for the variable.

In naming a variable, you have a tremendous amount of flexibility. Variable names can be simple, or they can be descriptive of the information they contain. In the preceding example, *X* is a perfectly legal name, but not very descriptive to the reader. While you are allowed great latitude in naming variables, there are a few restrictions:

- The name must start with a letter, not a number or other character.
- The remainder of the name cannot contain a period. It may contain letters, numbers, and underscore characters. No spaces or punctuation characters are allowed.
- The name must be unique.
- The name can be no longer than 255 characters.
- The name cannot be one of Visual Basic's reserved words.

TIP Make your variable names descriptive of the task to make your code easy to read, but also keep the names as short as possible to make the code easy to type. Many programmers also use prefixes in their variable names to indicate the type of data stored; usually these conventions are variations of the *Hungarian Naming Convention.* These prefixes usually consist of one or two lowercase characters at the beginning of the variable; the next letter is usually capitalized.

For example, a prefix of *in*, as in `inAge`, would indicate a variable that stores an integer value. The following table lists some of the common prefixes that I use when naming variables. This convention is used for many of the original code samples in this book. You might prefer a one-character prefix or some other convention altogether.

Variable Type	Prefix	Example
String	st	stFirstName
Integer	in	inAge
Long Integer	lg	lgPopulation
Single	sg	sgAverageGrade
Double	db	dbThrustRatio
Currency	cr	crPayRate
Boolean	bl	blTaxable

Types of Variables

Okay, you know what a variable does and how to name it. But what can you store in a variable? The simple answer is: *almost anything*. A variable can hold a number; a string of text; or an instance of an object, such as a form, control, or database. This chapter looks specifically at using variables to store numbers, strings, and logical values. Use of objects and database objects is covered later in Chapters 28, "Improving Data Access with the Data Access Objects," and 32, "Using Classes in Visual Basic," respectively.

Each type of variable has its own memory requirements and is designed to work efficiently with different types of information. Therefore, you couldn't store a string like "Hello" in a variable that you declared as an integer.

Table 8.1 shows some of the standard variable types that are available in Visual Basic. The table also shows the range of values that the variable can hold and the amount of memory required. Variables with smaller memory requirements should be used wherever possible to conserve system resources.

Table 8.1 Variables Store Many Types of Information

Type	Stores	Memory Requirement	Range of Values
Integer	Whole numbers	Two bytes	–32,768 to +32,767
Long	Whole numbers	Four bytes	(approximately) +/– 2 billion
Single	Decimal numbers	Four bytes	+/– 1E-45 to 3E38

continues

Table 8.1 Continued

Type	Stores	Memory Requirement	Range of Values
Double	Decimal numbers	Eight bytes	+/– 5E-324 to 1.8E308
Currency	Numbers with up to 15 digits left of the decimal and four digits right of the decimal	Eight bytes	+/– 9E14
String	Text information	One byte per character	Up to 65,400 characters for fixed-length string and up to 2 billion characters for dynamic strings
Byte	Whole numbers	One byte	0 to 255
Boolean	Logical values	Two bytes	`True` or `False`
Date	Date and time information	Eight bytes	1/1/100 to 12/31/9999
Object	Instances of classes; OLE objects	Four bytes	N/A
Variant	Any of the preceding data types	16 bytes + 1 byte per character	N/A

In addition to the preceding variable types, there are specialized types to deal with databases (Database, Field, and Recordset). Visual Basic knows about these other data types when you add a reference to a *type library*. It is also possible to create *user-defined types* to meet your needs.

Variable Declarations

In the section "Working with Variables" earlier in this chapter, you saw an example of the `Dim` statement, which is used to tell Visual Basic the name and type of your variable. However, Visual Basic does not require you to specifically declare a variable before it is used. If a variable is not declared, Visual Basic creates the variable by using a default data type known as a *variant.* A variant can contain any type of information. Using a variant for general information has two major drawbacks—it can waste memory resources, and the variable type might be invalid for use with some data-manipulation functions that expect a specific variable type.

It is good programming practice to declare your variables before they are used, so take a look at the two ways to declare a variable in Visual Basic—explicit and implicit declaration.

Explicit Declaration   *Explicit declaration* means that you use a statement to define the type of a variable. These statements do not assign a value to the variable but merely tell Visual Basic what the variable can contain.

Each of the following statements can be used to explicitly declare a variable's type:

```
Dim varname [As vartype][, varname2 [As vartype2]]

Private varname [As vartype][, varname2 [As vartype2]]

Static varname [As vartype][, varname2 [As vartype2]]

Public varname [As vartype][, varname2 [As vartype2]]
```

`Dim`, `Private`, `Static`, and `Public` are Visual Basic keywords that define how and where the variable can be used. `varname` and `varname2` represent the names of two variables that you want to declare. As indicated in the syntax, you can specify multiple variables in the same statement as long as you separate the variables with commas. Note that the syntax shows only two variables on one line, but you can specify several. In fact, over a thousand characters will fit on one line in the Code window. From a practical standpoint, however, you should refrain from writing lines of code that are wider than the displayed Code window. This will make your code much easier to read, as you don't have to scroll left and right when looking at it.

`vartype` and `vartype2` represent the type definitions of the respective variables. The *type definition* is a keyword that tells Visual Basic what kind of information will be stored in the variable. As indicated, the variable type is an optional property. If you include the variable type, you must include the keyword `As`. If you do not include a variable type, the Variant type (which is the default) is used.

The following code shows the use of these declaration statements for actual variables:

```
Private inNumVal As Integer
Private inAvgVal As Integer, varInptVal As Variant
Static sgClcAverage As Single
Dim stInptMsg As String
```

Implicit Declaration   It is best to declare your variables using the `Dim` or other statements shown in the section "Working with Variables" earlier in this chapter, but in many cases you also can assign a type to a variable using an *implicit declaration*. With this type of declaration, a special character is used at the end of the variable name when the variable is first assigned a value. The characters for each variable type are shown in Table 8.2.

Table 8.2   Special Characters at the End of a Variable Name that Can Identify the Type of Data Stored by the Variable

Variable Type	Character
Integer	%
Long	&
Single	!
Double	#
Currency	@
String	$
Byte	None
Boolean	None
Date	None
Object	None
Variant	None

The variables that were declared using the code in the preceding section could have been used as implicitly declared variables, without having to declare their types with Dim statements, as follows:

```
inNumVal% = 0
inAvgVal% = 1
varInptVal = 5
sgClcAverage! = 10.1
stInptMsg$ = "Mike"
```

You might have noticed that the variable varInptVal didn't have a declaration character. This means that InptVal will be of the Variant type.

Fixed-Length Strings   Most strings that you use in your programs will be of the type known as *variable-length strings*. These strings can contain any amount of text, up to approximately two billion characters. As information is stored in the variable, the size of the variable adjusts to accommodate the length of the string. Both the implicit and explicit declarations shown earlier created variable-length strings. There is, however, a second type of string in Visual Basic—the *fixed-length string*.

As the name implies, a fixed-length string remains the same size, regardless of the information assigned to it. If a fixed-length string variable is assigned an expression shorter than the defined length of the variable, the remaining length of the variable is filled with the space character. If the expression is longer than the variable, only the characters that fit in the variable are stored; the rest are truncated.

A fixed-length string variable can only be declared by using an explicit declaration of the form, like the following:

```
Dim varname As String*strlength
```

Notice that this declaration is slightly different from the previous declaration of a string variable. The declaration of a fixed-length string variable contains an asterisk (*) to tell Visual Basic that the string will be of a fixed length. The final parameter, *strlength*, tells the program the maximum number of characters that the variable can contain.

Variable Arrays

All the variables you've worked with so far have been single-instance variables. Often, however, you'll find it very useful to work with *variable arrays*. An array is a group of variables of the same type, sharing the same name. This makes it easy to process groups of related areas. For example, you might want to have a group of variables that tracks the sales in each of your company's four regions. You could declare a currency variable for each region, plus one for the total sales across all regions, like this:

```
Dim crRegSales1 As Currency, crRegSales2 As Currency
Dim crRegSales3 As Currency, crRegSales4 As Currency
Dim crTotalSales As Currency
```

Then, if you wanted to calculate the total sales for all regions, you might use this code:

```
crTotalSales = crRegSales1 + crRegSales2 + crRegSales3 + crRegSales4
```

This isn't all that cumbersome. However, what if you had 20 regions? Or several hundred? You can see how working with large numbers of related variables could get messy very quickly.

You can greatly enhance this example by using a variable array. We'll create an array of variables named crRegSales; the array will contain as many elements (instances of variables) as we have regions. We could rewrite our previous example for 20 regions like this:

```
Dim crRegSales(1 To 20) As Currency
Dim crTotalSales As Currency
Dim inCounter As Integer
Dim stTemp As String

    crTotalSales = 0
    For inCounter = 1 To 20
        crTotalSales = crTotalSales + crRegSales(inCounter)
    Next inCounter
    stTemp = "Total sales for all regions = "
    stTemp = stTemp & Format(crTotalSales, "currency")
        MsgBox stTemp, vbInformation, "Sales Analysis"
```

Note this example's use of a *repetition loop*. The block of code beginning with the For instruction and ending with the Next instruction defines a group of program statements that will be repeated a certain number of times (in this case, 20). Using loops makes short work of processing variable arrays. We cover loops in the section "Working with Loops" a little later in this chapter.

As you progress through this book, you'll see several cases where variable arrays can make your coding much simpler.

Determining Where a Variable Can Be Used

In addition to telling Visual Basic what you want to be able to store in a variable, a declaration statement tells Visual Basic where the variable can be used. This area of usage is called the *scope* of the variable. This is analogous to the coverage area of a paging system. When you purchase a pager, you make a decision whether you want local service, regional service, or nationwide service. This is then programmed into your pager when you buy it. If you go outside the service area, your pager does not work. In a similar manner, you can declare variables to work in only one procedure, work in any procedure of a form, or work throughout your program.

By default, a variable that is implicitly declared is local to the procedure in which it is created. If you don't specify any kind of declaration, explicit or implicit, you create a local variable of the variant type. Therefore, to create variables that have a scope other than local, you must use a declaration statement.

N O T E   The scope of a variable is determined not only by the type of declaration, but by the location of the declaration as well. For instance, the Dim and Private keywords assume different meanings in different parts of a form's code.   ▓

Creating Variables that Are Available Everywhere   In most programs, unless you have only one form and no code modules, you will find that you need some variables that can be accessed from anywhere in the code. These are called Public variables. (Other languages, as well as earlier versions of Visual Basic, might refer to these as Global variables. In fact, Visual Basic still recognizes the Global keyword.) These variables are typically used to hold information such as the name of the program's user, or to reference a database that is used throughout the program. They might also be used as flags to indicate various conditions in the program.

To create a Public variable, you simply place a declaration statement with the Public keyword in the declarations section of a module of your program. The following line shows the Public declaration of a variable used for referencing a database:

```
Public dbMemDB As Database
```

▶ **See** "Determining the Scope of Procedures and Functions," **p. 254**

In a form or a class module, the Public keyword has a special meaning. Variables defined as Public act like a property of the form or class that is available anywhere in the program. These properties are referenced like the built-in properties of a form or control instead of like a variable. The Public properties are used to pass information between forms and other parts of your program.

▶ **See** "Creating a Public Variable," **p. 834**

Keeping a Variable Local   If you do not need to access a variable from everywhere in your program, you do not want to use the Public keyword in a declaration. Instead, you should use the Dim or Private keywords. These keywords tell Visual Basic to define the variable within the scope of the current procedure or form. With these declarations, the location of the statement determines the actual scope of the variable. If the variable is defined in the General Declarations section of a form or module, the variable is available to every procedure in that form or module. This is known as a *form-level* or *module-level variable*. If the variable is declared inside a procedure, it can be used only within that procedure. This is typically known as a *local variable*.

Using Static Variables   Most variables that are created inside a procedure are discarded by Visual Basic when the procedure is finished. There are times, however, when you might want to preserve the value of a variable even after the procedure has run. This is often the case when you call the procedure multiple times, and the value of a variable for one call to the procedure is dependent on the value left over from previous calls.

To create a variable that retains its value, you use the Static keyword in the variable declaration. This tells Visual Basic that the variable can be referenced only within the procedure, but to remember the value because it might be needed again. Here's an example of a variable declared using the Static keyword:

```
Static inPageNumber As Integer
```

N O T E   If you use the Static keyword to declare a procedure, all variables in the procedure are treated as static.

Using the *Option Explicit* Statement

You learned in the earlier section, "Variable Declarations," that it's good programming practice to declare your program's variables before they are used. You can ensure that you do this by setting one of the environment options of Visual Basic. To do this, access Visual Basic's Options dialog box by choosing Tools, Options. In this dialog box's Editor tab, you find the Require Variable Declaration option (see Figure 8.1). Selecting this box forces you to declare each variable before you use it.

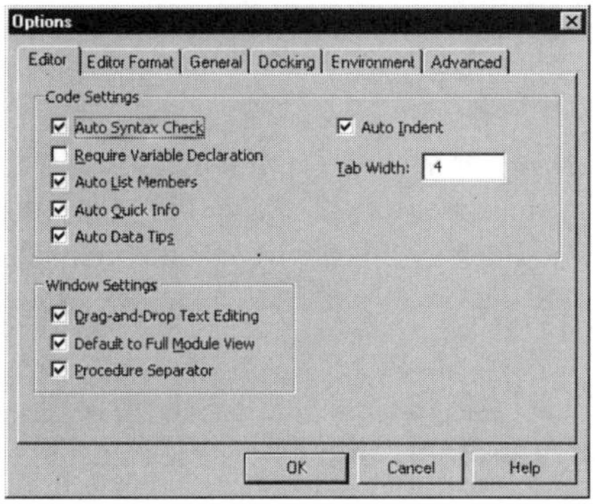

FIG. 8.1
The Require Variable Declaration option helps prevent you from mistyping variable names.

Setting the Require Variable Declaration option causes the `Option Explicit` statement to be placed in the General Declarations section of each new module or form that is added to your project, as shown in Figure 8.2.

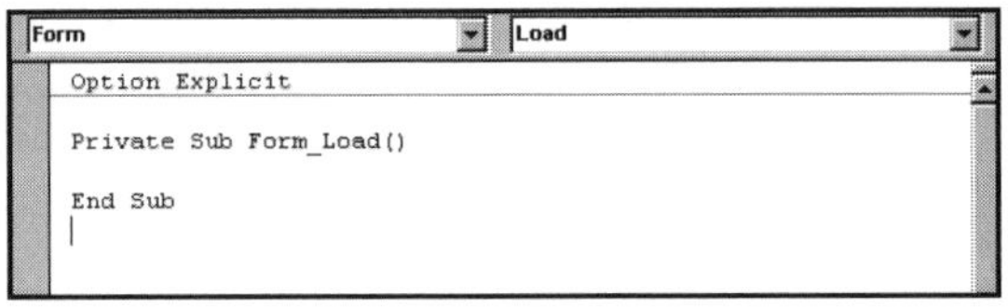

FIG. 8.2

The *Option Explicit* statement is added to your program.

```
Form                          ▼    Load                        ▼
    Option Explicit                                            ▲

    Private Sub Form_Load()

    End Sub
    |
```

If you have invoked `Option Explicit` and you fail to declare a variable, you will receive the error message `Variable not defined` when you try to run your code. The integrated debugger highlights the offending variable and pauses the execution of your program. The benefit of this is that it helps you avoid errors in your code that might be caused by typographical errors. For example, you might declare a variable using the following statement:

```
Dim stMyName As String
```

If in a later statement, you mistyped the variable name, Visual Basic would catch the error for you, rather than continue with unpredictable results. For example, the following statement would cause an error:

```
stMyNme = "Tina Marie"
```

CAUTION

If you set the Require Variable Declaration option after starting to create a program, the option has no effect on any forms or modules that have already been created. In this case, you can add the `Option Explicit` statement as the first line of code in the General Declarations section of any existing forms or modules.

TIP
If you use some capital letters in your variable declarations, then enter your code in all lowercase letters. Visual Basic automatically sets the capitalization of your variable to match the declaration. This gives you an immediate visual indication that you typed the name correctly.

What's Different About Constants

Variables are just one way of storing information in the memory of a computer. Another way is to use *constants*. Constants in a program are treated a special way. After you define them (or they are defined for you by Visual Basic), you cannot change them later in the program by using an assignment statement. If you try, Visual Basic generates an error when you run your program.

Constants are most often used to replace a value that is hard to remember, such as the color value for the Windows title bar. It is easier to remember the constant `vbActiveTitleBar` than the value 2147483646. You can also use a constant to avoid typing long strings if they are used in a number of places. For example, you could set a constant such as FileFoundError containing the string "The requested file was not found."

Constants are also used a lot for conversion factors, such as 12 inches per foot or 3.3 feet per meter. The following code example shows how constants and variables are used:

```
Const MetersToFeet = 3.3
inDistMeters = InputBox("Enter a distance in meters")
inDistFeet = inDistMeters * MetersToFeet
MsgBox "The distance in feet is: " & Str(inDistFeet)
```

Another common use for constants is to minimize changes to your code for reasons such as changing your program's name, version number, and so forth. You can define constants at the beginning of your program and use the predefined constants throughout the program. Then, when a version number changes, all you need to do is change the declaration of the constant. The following example illustrates this technique:

```
Public Const ProgTitle = "My Application Name"
Public Const ProgVersion = "3.1"
```

Note the use of the Public keyword, which makes these constants available throughout the application (assuming that their declaration is in a module).

Constants that Visual Basic Supplies   Visual Basic supplies a number of built-in constants for various activities. These are known as *intrinsic constants*. There are color-definition constants, data-access constants, keycode constants, and shape constants, among many others. Especially useful are constants correlating to a command's parameter information, such as the vbExclamation constant that we've used for a MessageBox statement in previous chapters.

The constants that you need for most functions are defined in the help topic for the function. If you want to know the value of a particular constant, you can use the Object Browser (see Figure 8.3). Access the Object Browser by clicking its icon in the Visual Basic toolbar, by selecting View, Object Browser from the menu system, or simply by pressing F7. You can use the list to find the constant that you want. When you select it, its value and function are displayed in the text area at the bottom of the dialog box.

Creating Your Own Constants   While Visual Basic defines a large number of constants for many activities, there will be times when you need to define your own constants. Constants are defined using the Const statement to give the constant a name and a value, as illustrated in the following syntax:

```
Const constantname [As constanttype] = value
```

If you think this statement looks similar to the declaration of a variable, you are right. As with declaring a variable, you provide a name for the constant and, optionally, specify the type of data it will hold. The Const keyword at the beginning of the statement tells Visual Basic that this statement defines a constant. This distinguishes the statement from one that just assigns a value to a variable. In declaring the type of a constant, you use the same types as you did for defining variables. (These types are defined in Table 8.1.) Finally, to define a constant, you must include the equal sign (=) and the value to be assigned. If you are defining a string constant or date constant, remember to enclose the value in either quotes (" ") or the pound sign (#), respectively.

FIG. 8.3
The Object Browser shows you the value and function of most of Visual Basic's internal constants.

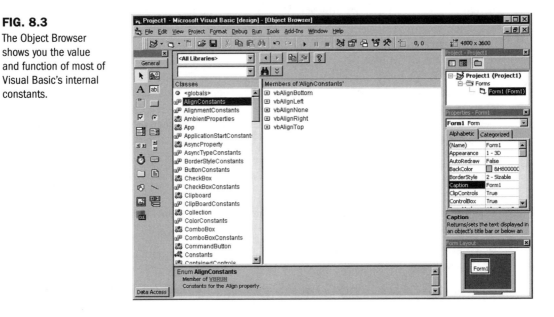

A constant's scope is also important. The same rules for the scope of variables, which were discussed in the earlier section, "Determining Where a Variable Can Be Used," apply to constants as well.

Writing Simple Statements

Now you know a little about variables and constants. You know what data they can store and how to initially set them up. But that is just the beginning of working with information in a program. You also need to be able to assign information to the variable and manipulate that information. Stay tuned—it's covered in the next section.

Using the Assignment Statement

After setting up a variable, the first thing you need to do to use the variable is to store information in the variable. This is the job of the *assignment statement*. The assignment statement is quite simple; you specify a variable whose value you want to set, place an equal sign after the variable name, and then follow this with the expression that represents the value you want stored. The expression can be a literal value, an expression or equation using some combination of other variables and constants, or even a function that returns a value. There is no limit on the complexity of the expression you can use. The only restriction is that the expression must yield a value of the same type as the variable to which it is assigned. The following statements illustrate different assignment statements:

```
inNumStudents = 25
inSumScores = 2276
sgAvgScore = SumScores / NumStudents
stTopStudent = "Janet Simon"
inISpace = InStr(TopStudent," ")
stFirstName = Left(TopStudent,ISpace)
```

You might have noticed that these statements look very similar to the ones used to set the properties of forms and controls in the section "Setting and Retrieving Property Values" in Chapter 4, "Working with Forms and Controls." Actually, they are the same. Most properties of forms and controls act like variables. They can be set at design time, but can also be changed at runtime using an assignment statement. You can also use a property on the right side of a statement to assign its value to a variable for further processing. For example, you use this assignment statement to read the top student name from a text box:

```
stTopStudent = txtTop.Text
```

Using Math Operators

Processing numerical data is one of the key activities of many computer programs. Mathematical operations are used to determine customer bills, interest due on savings or credit card balances, average scores for a class test, and many other bits of information. Visual Basic supports a number of different math operators that can be used in program statements. These operations and the Visual Basic symbol for each operation are summarized in Table 8.3. The operations are then described in detail.

Table 8.3   Math Operations and the Corresponding Visual Basic Symbol

Operation	Operator
Addition	+
Subtraction	−
Multiplication	*
Division	/
Integer division	\
Modulus	mod
Exponentiation	^

Addition and Subtraction   The two simplest math operations are addition and subtraction. You use these operations in such everyday chores as balancing your checkbook or determining how much change you should get back from a sales clerk. If you have ever used a calculator to do addition and subtraction, you already have a good idea how these operations are performed in a line of computer code.

A computer program, however, gives you greater flexibility than a calculator in the operations you can perform. Your programs are not limited to working with literal numbers (for example, 1, 15, 37.63, –105.2). Your program can add or subtract two or more literal numbers, numeric variables, or any functions that return a numeric value. Also, as with a calculator, you can perform addition and subtraction operations in any combination. Now let's take a look at exactly how you perform these operations in your program.

As indicated in Table 8.3, the operator for addition in Visual Basic is the plus sign (+). The general use of this operator is shown in the following syntax line:

```
result = number1 + number2 [+ number3]
```

result is a variable (or control property) that will contain the sum of the numbers. The equal sign indicates the assignment of a value to the variable. number1, number2, and number3 are the literal numbers, numeric variables, or functions that are to be added together. You can add as many numbers together as you like, but each number pair must be separated by a plus sign.

The operator for subtraction is the minus sign (–). The syntax is basically the same as for addition:

```
result = number1 - number2 [- number3]
```

While the order does not matter in addition, in subtraction, the number to the right of the minus sign is subtracted from the number to the left of the sign. If you have multiple numbers, the second number is subtracted from the first, then the third number is subtracted from that result, and so on, moving from left to right. For example, consider the following equation:

```
result = 15 - 6 - 3
```

The computer first subtracts 6 from 15 to yield 9. It then subtracts 3 from 9 to yield 6, which is the final answer stored in the variable result.

You can create assignment statements that consist solely of addition operators or solely of subtraction operators. You can also use the operators in combination with one another or other math operators. The following code lines show a few valid math operations:

```
val1 = 1.25 + 3.17
val2 = 3.21 - 1
val3 = val2 + val1
val4 = val3 + 3.75 - 2.1 + 12 - 3
val4 = val4 + 1
```

If you are not familiar with computer programming, the last line might look a little funny to you. In fact, that line is not allowed in some programming languages. However, in Visual Basic, you can enter a line of code that tells the program to take the current value of a variable, add another number to it, and then store the resulting value back in the same variable.

Multiplication and Division   Two other major mathematical operations with which you should be familiar are multiplication and division. Like addition and subtraction, these operations are used frequently in everyday life.

Multiplication in Visual Basic is very straightforward, just like addition and subtraction. You simply use the multiplication operator—the asterisk (*) operator—to multiply two or more numbers. The syntax of a multiplication statement is almost identical to the ones for addition and subtraction, as follows:

```
result = number1 * number2 [* number3]
```

As before, `result` is the name of a variable used to contain the product of the numbers being multiplied, and `number1`, `number2`, and `number3` are the literal numbers, numeric variables, or functions.

As a demonstration of how multiplication and division might be used in a program, consider the example of a program to determine the amount of paint needed to paint a room. Such a program could contain a form that lets the painter enter the length and width of the room, the height of the ceiling, and the coverage and cost of a single can of paint. Your program could then calculate the number of gallons of paint required and the cost of the paint. An example of the form for such a program is shown in Figure 8.4. The actual code to perform the calculations is shown in Listing 8.1.

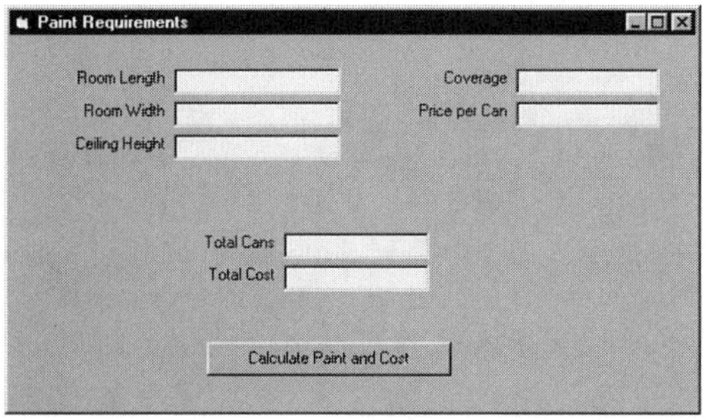

FIG. 8.4

Multiplication and division are used to determine the amount of paint needed for a room.

Listing 8.1   COSTEST.FRM—Cost Estimation Using Multiplication and Division Operators

```
sgRmLength = Val(txtLength.Text)
slRmWidth = Val(txtWidth.Text)
sgRmHeight = Val(txtHeight.Text)
sgCanCoverage = Val(txtCoverage.Text)
crCanCost = val(txtCost.Text)
sgRmPerimeter = 2 * sgRmLength + 2 * sgRmWidth
sgWallArea = sgRmPerimeter * sgRmHeight
sgNumGallons = sgWallArea / sgCanCoverage
crProjCost = sgNumGallons * crCanCost
txtGallons.Text = sgNumGallons
txtTotalCost.Text = crProjCost
```

Division in Visual Basic is a little more complicated than multiplication. In Listing 8.1, you saw one type of division used. This division is what you are most familiar with and what you will find on your calculator. This type of division returns a number with its decimal portion, if one is present.

However, Visual Basic supports three different ways to divide numbers. These are known as *floating-point division* (the normal type of division, with which you are familiar); *integer division*; and *modulus*, or *remainder*, *division*.

Floating-point division is the typical division that you learned in school. You divide one number by another, and the result is a decimal number. The floating-point division operator is the forward slash (/):

```
result = number1 / number2 [/ number3]
'The following line returns 1.333333
Print 4 / 3
```

Integer division divides one number into another and then returns only the integer portion of the result. The operator for integer division is the backward slash (\):

```
result = number1 \ number2 [\ number3]
'The following line returns 1
Print 4 \ 3
```

Modulus, or remainder, division divides one number into another and returns what is left over after you have obtained the largest integer quotient possible. The modulus operator is the word mod:

```
result = number1 mod number2 [mod number3]
'The following line returns 2, the remainder when dividing 20 by 3
Print 20 mod 3
```

As with the case of addition, subtraction, and multiplication, if you divide more than two numbers, each number pair must be separated by a division operator. Also, like the other operations, multiple operators are handled by reading the equation from left to right.

Figure 8.5 shows a simple form that is used to illustrate the differences between the various division operators. The code for the command button of the form is shown as follows:

```
inpt1 = Text1.Text
inpt2 = Text2.Text
Text3.Text = inpt1 / inpt2
Text4.Text = inpt1 \ inpt2
Text5.Text = inpt1 Mod inpt2
```

www.quebooks.com/...   The project CALCULAT.VBP contains a calculator program that demonstrates the various math operators. You can download this program from the Que Books Web site.

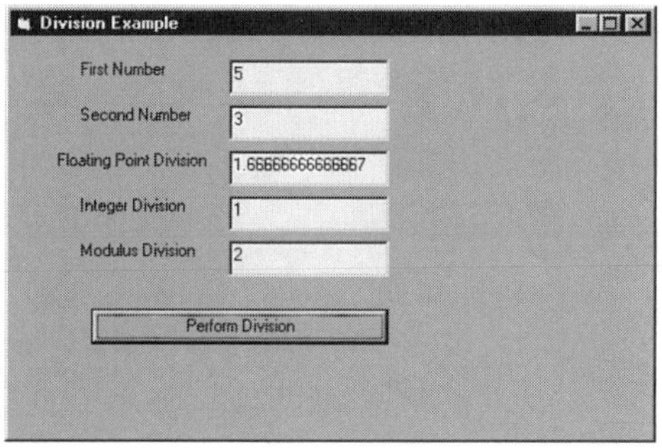

FIG. 8.5
This program demonstrates the difference between Visual Basic's three types of division operators.

After setting up the form, run the program, enter **5** in the first text box and **3** in the second text box, and then click the command button. Notice that different numbers appear in each of the text boxes used to display the results. You can try this with other number combinations as well.

Exponents   Exponents are also known as powers of a number. For example, 2 raised to the third power (2^3) is equivalent to 2×2×2, or 8. Exponents are used quite a lot in computer operations, where many things are represented as powers of two. Exponents are also used extensively in scientific and engineering work, where many things are represented as powers of ten or as natural logarithms. Simpler exponents are used in statistics, where many calculations depend on the squares and the square roots of numbers.

To raise a number to a power, you use the *exponential operator*, which is a caret (^). Exponents greater than one indicate a number raised to a power. Fractional exponents indicate a root, and negative exponents indicate a fraction. The following is the syntax for using the exponential operator:

```
answer = number1 ^ exponent
```

The equations in the following table show several common uses of exponents. The operation performed by each equation is also indicated:

Sample Exponent	Function Performed
3 ^ 2 = 9	This is the square of the number.
9 ^ 0.5 = 3	This is the square root of the number.
2 ^ –2 = 0.25	A fraction is obtained by using a negative exponent.

Operator Precedence   Many expressions contain some combination of the operators we've just discussed. In such cases, it's important to know in what order Visual Basic processes the various types of operators. For example, what's the value of the expression 4 * 3 + 6 / 2? You might think that the calculations would be performed from left to right. In this case, 4 * 3 is 12; 12 + 6 is 18; 18 / 2 is 9. However, Visual Basic doesn't necessarily process expressions straight through from left to right. It follows a distinct order of processing known as *operator precedence*.

Simply put, Visual Basic performs subsets of a complex expression according to the operators involved, in this order:

■ Exponentiation (^)

■ Negation (-)

■ Multiplication and division (*; /)

■ Integer division (\)

■ Modulus arithmetic (Mod)

■ Addition and subtraction (+, -)

Within a subset of an expression, the components are processed from left to right. When all subset groups have been calculated, the remainder of the expression is calculated from left to right.

In the previous example (4 * 3 + 6 / 2), the multiplication and division portions (4 * 3, which is 12, and 6 / 2, which is 3) would be calculated first, leaving a simpler expression of 12 + 3, for a total of 15.

An important note is that normal operator precedence can be overridden by using parentheses to group sub-expressions that you want to be evaluated first. Multiple nested levels of parentheses can be used. Visual Basic calculates sub-expressions within parentheses first, innermost set to outermost set, and then applies the normal operator precedence.

CAUTION

Understanding operator precedence is crucial to making sure your programs evaluate expressions the way that you expect. For example, if you wanted to calculate the average of two test scores, you might write this line of code:

```
sgAvgScore = inTest1 + inTest2 / 2
```

This line of code might look right, but Visual Basic's calculation won't be correct. Because the division operator has a higher precedence than the addition operator, the sub-expression inTest2 / 2 will be calculated first and then added to inTest1. This is obviously incorrect. You can avoid this problem by using parentheses to control the flow of evaluation:

```
sgAvgScore = (inTest1 + inTest2) / 2
```

This expression will be calculated properly by evaluating the sum of inTest1 + inTest2 first and then dividing the sum by 2. If inTest1's value was 97 and inTest2's value was 88, the expression would be evaluated as (97 + 88) / 2, or 185 / 2, which would store the correct result of 92.5 in sgAvgScore. Leaving out the parentheses would have resulted in an undesired answer (following the rules of operator precedence) of 97 + 88 / 2, or 97 + 44, or 141!

Visual Basic's *Operator Precedence* help screen has a very good discussion of the topic, including how the precedence extends to comparison operators and logical operators.

Working with Strings

Visual Basic supports only one string operator, the *concatenation operator.* This operator is used to combine two or more strings of text, similar to the way the addition operator is used to combine two or more numbers. The concatenation operator is the ampersand symbol (&). When you combine two strings with the concatenation operator, the second string is added directly to the end of the first string. The result is a longer string containing the full contents of both source strings.

The concatenation operator is used in an assignment statement as follows:

```
newstring = stringexpr1 & stringexpr2 [& stringexpr3]
```

In this syntax, newstring represents the variable that will contain the result of the concatenation operation. stringexpr1, stringexpr2, and stringexpr3 all represent string expressions. These can be any valid strings, including string variables, literal expressions (enclosed in quotes), or functions that return a string. The ampersand between a pair of string expressions tells Visual Basic to concatenate the two expressions. The ampersand must be preceded and followed by a space. The syntax shows an optional second ampersand and a third string expression. You can combine any number of strings with a single statement. Just remember to separate each pair of expressions with an ampersand.

N O T E   If you are working on converting programs from an older version of Visual Basic, you might find strings combined using the plus sign operator. This was prevalent in versions of Visual Basic prior to version 4, as well as in older BASIC languages. While Visual Basic still supports the plus sign operator, in case this operator is present in older code that you are modifying, I recommend that you use the ampersand for any work that you do to avoid confusion with the mathematical addition operation. ■

Listing 8.2 shows how the concatenation of strings would be used in a simple program to generate mailing labels. The fields from the different text boxes are combined to create the different lines of the mailing label. The form for this program is shown in Figure 8.6.

On the Web

Listing 8.2   Mailing.Frm—String Concatenation Used in Mailing Labels

```
stFirst$ = txtFirst.Text
stLast$ = txtLast.Text
stAddr$ = txtAddress.Text
stCity$ = txtCity.Text
stState$ = txtState.Text
stZip$ = txtZip.Text
If optTitle1.Value Then stTitle$ = "Mr. "
If optTitle2.Value Then stTitle$ = "Mrs. "
If optTitle3.Value Then stTitle$ = "Miss "
If optTitle4.Value Then stTitle$ = "Ms. "
stLine1$ = stTitle$ & stFirst$ & " " & stLast$
stLine3$ = stCity$ & ", " & stState$ & "  " & stZip$
picOutput.Print stLine1$
picOutput.Print stAddr$
picOutput.Print stLine3$
```

FIG. 8.6

The mailing label application shows how strings are combined for display or printing.

Making Decisions in Your Program

Many of the statements in your programs will be assignment statements, but there are other statements that are important for handling more complex tasks. These statements are known collectively as *control statements*. Without control statements, your program would start at the first line of code and proceed line by line until the last line was reached. At that point, the program would stop.

One type of control statement is the *decision statement*. These statements are used to control the execution of parts of your program, based on conditions that exist at the time the statement is encountered. There are two basic types of decision statements: `If` statements and `Select Case` statements. Each is covered in this section.

Using the *If* Statement

For many decisions, you will want to execute a statement (or group of statements) only if a condition is `True`. There are two forms of the `If` statement for handling `True` conditions—the *single line* `If` statement and the *multiple line* `If` statement. Each uses the `If` statement to check a condition. If the condition is `True`, the program runs the commands associated with the `If` statement. If the condition is `False`, the commands are skipped, and any `Else` portion of the `If` statement block is executed.

The Single Line *If* Statement   The single line `If` statement is used to perform a single task when the condition in the statement is `True`. The task can be a single command, or you can perform multiple commands by calling a procedure. The following is the syntax of the single line `If` statement:

`If condition Then command`

The argument `condition` represents any type of logical condition, which can be any of the following:

- Comparison of a variable to a literal, another variable, or a function
- A variable or database field that contains a `True` or `False` value
- Any function or expression that returns a `True` or `False` value

The argument *command* represents the task to be performed if the condition is True. This can be any valid Visual Basic statement, including a procedure call. The following code shows how an If statement would be used to print a person's name if his or her fortieth birthday occurred during a particular year. This code is retrieving information from a database to perform the comparison and get the names (Figure 8.7 shows the output list that might be generated):

```
inCompYear = Val(txtYear.Text) - 40
inBirthYear = Year(Members("BirthDate"))
If inBirthYear = inCompYear Then Picture1.Print Members("FullName")
```

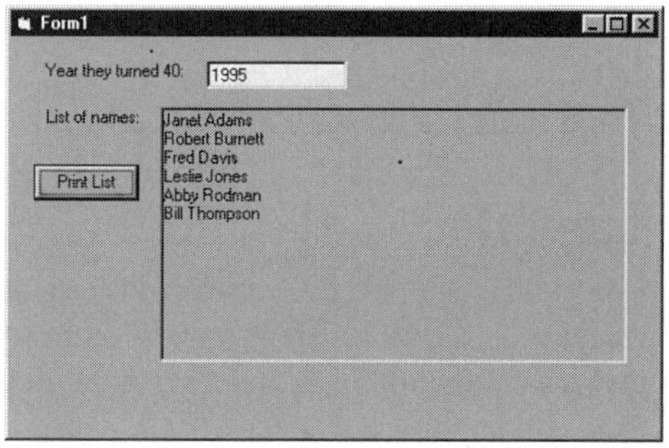

FIG. 8.7

You can use comparisons to print the names of 40-year-olds.

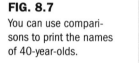

Multiple Commands for the Condition   If you need to execute more than one command in response to a condition, you can use the multiple line form of the If statement. This is also known as a *block* If statement. This form bounds a range of statements between the If statement and an End If statement. If the condition in the If statement is True, all the commands between the If and End If statements are run. If the condition is False, the program skips to the first line after the End If statement. Listing 8.3 shows how a block If statement is used to credit an invoice in a membership program. The program asks the user if a credit should be issued and executes the block of code if the user answers yes.

On the Web

Listing 8.3   CREDIT.TXT—Making Decisions in Code

```
If Retval = vbYes Then
    OrgCanc.Close
    Set OrgCanc = MemDb.OpenRecordset("Dues", dbOpenTable)
    OrgCanc.Index = "InvoiceID"
    OrgCanc.Seek "=", InvcID
    TotDues = OrgCanc("AmountDue") - TotDues
    If TotDues < 0 Then
        TotDues = 0
        OrgCanc.Edit
        OrgCanc("AmountDue") = TotDues
        OrgCanc("LastUpdate") = Date
        OrgCanc("UpdateBy") = UserID
        OrgCanc.Update
    End If
End If
```

TIP If you have a lot of commands between the If and End If statements, you might want to repeat the condition as a comment in the End If statement, as in this example:

```
If crTotalSales > crProjectedSales Then
    '
    ' A bunch of lines of code
    '
    Else
        '
        ' Another bunch of lines of code
        '
    End If 'crTotalSales > crProjectedSales
```

This makes your code easier to read.

Working with the *False* Condition

Of course, if a condition can be True, it can also be False; and there may be times when you want code to execute only on a False condition. There may be other times when you want to take one action if a condition is True and another action if the condition is False. This section looks at handling the False side of a condition.

Using the *Not* Operator   One way to execute a statement, or group of statements, for a False condition is to use the Not operator. The Not operator inverts the actual condition that follows it. If the condition is True, the Not operator makes the overall expression False, and vice versa. Listing 8.4 uses the operator to invert the value of the NoMatch property of a recordset. NoMatch is True if a record is not found in a search operation, and it is False if the search succeeds. Because the program can operate on a record only if it is found, the Not operator and NoMatch property are used as the condition of the If statement.

On the Web

Listing 8.4   FALSEIF.TXT—Handling a False Condition

```
If Not OrgCanc.NoMatch Then
    OrgCanc.Edit
    OrgCanc("Renewed") = False
    OrgCanc("LastUpdate") = Date
    OrgCanc("UpdateBy") = UserID
    OrgCanc.Update
End If
```

Handling *True* and *False* Conditions   The other way of handling False conditions allows you to process different sets of instructions for the True or False condition. You can handle this "fork in the road" in Visual Basic with the Else part of the If statement block.

To handle both the True and False conditions, you start with the block If statement and add the Else statement, as follows:

```
If condition Then
    statements to process if condition is True
Else
    statements to process if condition is False
End If
```

The If and End If statements of this block are the same as before. The condition is still any logical expression or variable that yields a True or False value. The key element of this set of statements is the Else statement. This statement is placed after the last statement to be executed if the condition is True, and before the first statement to be executed if the condition is False. For a True condition, the program processes the statements up to the Else statement and then skips to the first statement after the End If. If the condition is False, the program skips the statements prior to the Else statement and starts processing with the first statement after the Else.

N O T E If you want to execute code for only the False portion of the statement, you can just place code statements between the Else and End If statements. You are not required to place any statements between the If and Else statements. ■

Listing 8.5 shows how both parts of an If statement are used to handle different handicap calculations for men and women in a golf handicap program.

On the Web

Listing 8.5   HANDICAP.TXT—Handicap Calculation Using Conditional Statements

```
If slope = 1 Then
    avgdif! = totdif! / bstscr
    hcidx! = Int(avgdif! * 0.96 * 10) / 10
    hcp% = Int(hcidx! + 0.5)
Else
    hcidx! = 0!
    avgdif! = Int(totdif! / bstscr * 100) / 10
    hcp% = 0
    Call Hcpchrt(avgdif!, hcp%)
End If
' Get member record
Get #1, pnt, mmbr
' Set maximum handicap for gender
If mmbr.gendr = "M" Then
    If hcp% > 36 Then hcp% = 36
Else
    If hcp% > 40 Then hcp% = 40
End If
```

Working with Multiple *If* Statements

In the previous sections, you saw the simple block If statements, which evaluate one condition and can execute commands for either a True or a False condition. You can also evaluate multiple conditions with an additional statement in the block If. The ElseIf statement lets you specify another condition to evaluate whether or not the first condition is False. Using the ElseIf statement, you can evaluate any number of conditions with one If statement block. Listing 8.6 shows how a series of ElseIf conditions could be used to determine the grade distribution in a class.

On the Web

Listing 8.6 GRADESIF.TXT—Grade Distribution with Multiple *If* Statements

```
For I = 0 To numstd
    If inpGrades(I) >= 90 Then
        GradeDist(4) = GradeDist(4) + 1
    ElseIf inpGrades(I) >= 80 Then
        GradeDist(3) = GradeDist(3) + 1
    ElseIf inpGrades(I) >= 70 Then
        GradeDist(2) = GradeDist(2) + 1
    ElseIf inpGrades(I) >= 60 Then
        GradeDist(1) = GradeDist(1) + 1
    Else
        GradeDist(0) = GradeDist(0) + 1
    End If
Next I
```

The preceding code works by first evaluating the condition in the If statement. If the condition is True, the statement (or statements) immediately following the If statement is executed; and then the program skips to the first statement after the End If statement.

If the first condition is False, the program skips to the first ElseIf statement and evaluates its condition. If this condition is True, the statements following the ElseIf are executed, and control again passes to the statement after the End If. This process continues for as many ElseIf statements as are in the block.

If all the conditions are False, the program skips to the Else statement and processes the commands between the Else and the End If statements. The Else statement is not required.

Using *Select Case*

Another way to handle decisions in a program is to use the Select Case statement. This allows you to conditionally execute any of a series of statement groups based on the value of a test expression, which can be a single variable or a complex expression. The Select Case statement identifies the test expression to be evaluated. Then a series of Case statements specifies the possible values. If the value of the test expression matches the value (or values) indicated in the Case statement, the commands after the Case statement are executed. If the value does not match, the program proceeds to the next `Case` statement. The `Select Case` structure is similar to a series of `If/Then/ElseIf` statements. The following lines of code show the syntax of the `Select Case` block:

```
Select Case testvalue
    Case value1
        statement group 1
    Case value2
        statement group 2
End Select
```

The first statement of the `Select Case` block is the `Select Case` statement itself. This statement identifies the value to be tested against possible results. This value, represented by the `testvalue` argument, can be any valid numeric or string expression, including literals, variables, or functions.

Each conditional group of commands (those that are run if the condition is met) is started by a `Case` statement. The `Case` statement identifies the expression to which the `testvalue` is compared. If the `testvalue` is equal to the expression, the commands after the `Case` statement are run. The program runs the commands between the current `Case` statement and the next `Case` statement or the `End Select` statement. If the `testvalue` is not equal to the value expression, the program proceeds to the next `Case` statement.

The `End Select` statement identifies the end of the `Select Case` block.

N O T E Only one case in the `Select Case` block is executed for a given value of `testvalue`, even if more than one of the `Case` statements match the value of the test expression. ▮

CAUTION

The `testvalue` and `value` expressions must represent the same data type. For example, if the `testvalue` is a number, the values in the `Case` statements also must be numbers.

The simplest form of the `Select Case` block uses only a single value for the comparison expression. You might use this type of statement to handle a payroll calculation where you have a single pay rate for each job grade. Figure 8.8 shows a form that could be used to calculate pay for hourly employees with various job classifications. The code to perform the calculation is shown in Listing 8.7.

On the Web

Listing 8.7 PAYROLL.FRM—Payroll Calculation with the *Select Case* Statement

```
totpay = 0.0
paygrd = Val(txtGrade.Text)
payhrs = Val(txtHours.Text)
```

continues

Listing 8.7   Continued

```
Select Case paygrd
    Case 1
        totpay = payhrs * 4.35
    Case 2
        totpay = payhrs * 4.85
    Case 3
        totpay = payhrs * 5.35
    Case 4
        totpay = payhrs * 5.85
End Select
txtPay.Text = totpay
```

FIG. 8.8

A payroll calculator can use a *Select Case* structure to handle different wages for different classes of employees.

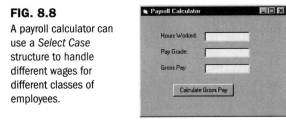

Case statements within a `Select Case` structure can also handle *lists*, *ranges*, and *comparisons* of values in addition to discrete values. Note the use of `Case Is < 0`, `Case 1 to 9`, and `Case Is > 50` in this example:

```
inQtyOrdered = Val(txtQuantity)
Select Case inQtyOrdered
    Case Is < 0 'note use of comparison
        MsgBox "Order quantity cannot be negative!", vbExclamation
        Exit Sub
    Case 1, 2, 3 'note use of list
        sgDiscount = 0
    Case 4 To 9 'note use of range
        sgDiscount = 0.03
    Case 10 To 49
        sgDiscount = 0.08
    Case Is > 50
        sgDiscount = 0.1
End  Select
```

The preceding examples work fine if your test variable matches one of the conditions in a `Case` statement. But how do you handle other values that are outside the ones for which you tested? You can have your code do something for all other possible values of the test expression by adding a `Case Else` statement to your program. The `Case Else` statement follows the last command of the last `Case` statement in the block. You then place the commands that you want executed between the `Case Else` and the `End Select` statements.

You can use the `Case Else` statement to perform calculations for values not specifically called out in the `Case` statements. Or you can use the `Case Else` statement to let users know that they entered an invalid value. Listing 8.8 shows how to add a message to let the user know that an invalid code was entered in the payroll program shown earlier.

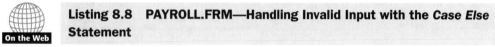

Listing 8.8   PAYROLL.FRM—Handling Invalid Input with the *Case Else* Statement

```
totpay = 0#
paygrd = Val(txtGrade.Text)
payhrs = Val(txtHours.Text)
Select Case paygrd
    Case 1
        totpay = payhrs * 4.35
    Case 2
        totpay = payhrs * 4.85
    Case 3
        totpay = payhrs * 5.35
    Case 4
        totpay = payhrs * 5.85
    Case Else
        MsgBox Str(paygrd) & " is an invalid pay code."
End Select
txtPay.Text = totpay
```

Working with Loops

The other major type of control statement is the *loop*. Loops are used to perform repetitive tasks in your program. There are two main types of loops that are supported by Visual Basic—counter loops and conditional loops. *Counter loops* are used to perform a task a set number of times. *Conditional loops* are used to perform a task while a specified condition exists or until a specified condition exists. Each of these types of loops is discussed in this section.

For Loops

A counter loop is also known as a For loop, or a For/Next loop. This is because the ends of the loop are defined by the For statement and the Next statement. At the beginning of a For loop, you define a counter variable, as well as the beginning and end points of the variable's value, and optionally the Step value, or the amount it is to be increased or decreased after each pass through the loop. The first time the loop is run, the counter variable is set to the value of the beginning point. Then after each time the program runs through the loop, the value of the counter is incremented by the Step value and checked against the value of the end point. If the counter is larger than the end point, the program skips to the first statement following the loop's Next statement.

CAUTION

If the beginning value of the loop is greater than the ending value, the loop does not execute at all. The exception to this is if you set up the loop to count backward, by setting the `Step` value to a negative number. In that case, the loop will execute until the counter variable is less than the end point.

T I P   For ease of reading your program, it is good practice to include the variable name in the `Next` statement. This is especially important in nested loops.

CAUTION

Although you can use any numeric variable for the counter, you need to be aware of the limits of variable types. For example, trying to run a loop 40,000 times using an integer variable will cause an error during execution because an integer has a maximum value of 32,767.

Listing 8.9 illustrates the use of several `For` loops to set the initial values of control arrays for a membership data-entry screen. The effect of the code is to create blank data-entry areas for a new member to be added. The form, after the code is run, is shown in Figure 8.9.

Listing 8.9   FORLOOP.TXT—Using *For* Loops to Initialize Variables

```
Dim I As Integer
'Clear the text from all text boxes
For I = 0 To 22
    txtMember(I).Text = ""
Next I
'Set each combo box to have no item selected
For I = 0 To 1
    cboMember(I).ListIndex = -1
Next I
'Clear the text from the Phone masked edit controls
For I = 0 To 3
    mskPhone(I).Text = ""
Next I
'Clear the text from the Date masked edit controls
For I = 0 To 1
    mskDate(I).Text = "  /  /  "
Next I
```

CAUTION

Never reset the value of the counter variable inside a `For` loop. Doing so can cause an infinite loop.

FIG. 8.9
A series of *For* loops is
used to initialize control
arrays.

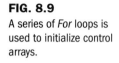

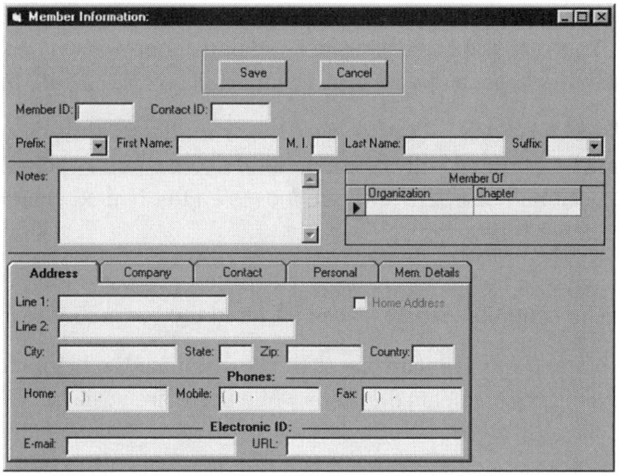

Part
II

Ch
8

Typically, you will want your For loop to run through all the values of the counter variable. However, there might be times when you want the loop to terminate early. To do this, simply place an Exit For statement at the point in your loop where you want the loop to stop. The Exit For statement is typically associated with an If statement (see Listing 8.10).

Listing 8.10   EXITFOR.TXT—Exiting a Loop Early

```
Private Sub cmdSearch_Click()
txtResults.Text = "No match was found."
For Icnt = 1 To 30
    iloc = InStr(1, NameArray(Icnt), findstr, 1)
    If iloc > 0 Then
        txtResults.Text = NameArray(Icnt)
        Exit For
    End If
Next Icnt
End Sub
```

This code is used to search an array for a particular name. When the name is found, it is not necessary to continue searching the rest of the elements of the array. Therefore, the Exit For is used to terminate the loop.

N O T E   As you have seen in this example and in others in the book, arrays and For loops are often used together. A For loop provides an easy way of looking at or processing each element of an array because the counter variable can be used as the array index. ■

Do Loops

The key feature of a conditional loop is, of course, the *condition*. The condition is any expression that can return either a True or a False value. This can be a function, such as EOF; the value of a property, such as the Value property of an Option button; or an expression, such as numval < 15. There are two basic types of conditional loops—a Do While loop, which repeats *while* the condition is True, and a Do Until loop, which repeats *until* the condition is True.

Using *Do While* Statements The keyword While in the Do While statement tells the program that the loop will be repeated while the condition expression is True. When the condition in a Do While loop becomes false, the program moves on to the next statement after the Loop statement.

There are two forms of the Do While loop. The difference between the two is the placement of the condition. The condition can be placed either at the beginning of the loop or at the end.

The first form of the Do While loop places the condition at the beginning of the loop, as shown in Listing 8.11. This code repeats the steps while there are available records in the recordset.

Listing 8.11 DOLOOP.TXT—Processing Database Records with a *Do Loop*

```
Do While Not OrgRenew.EOF
    OrgRenew.Edit
    If OrgRenew("Renew") Then
        OrgRenew("NumYears") = 0
        OrgRenew("Renew") = False
    Else
        OrgRenew("NumYears") = 1
        OrgRenew("Renew") = True
    End If
    OrgRenew.Update
    OrgRenew.MoveNext
Loop
```

By placing the While condition clause in the Do statement, you tell the program that you want to evaluate the condition *before* you run any statements inside the loop. If the condition is True, the repetitive statements between the Do statement and the Loop statement are run. Then the program returns to the Do statement to evaluate the condition again. As soon as the condition is False, the program moves to the statement following the Loop statement.

Both the Do and the Loop statements must be present.

With this form of the loop, the statements inside the loop might never be run. If the condition is False before the loop is run the first time, the program just proceeds to the statements after the loop.

To run the Do While loop at least once, the second form of the Do While loop must be used. This form of the loop places the condition in the Loop statement. This tells the program that you want the loop to run at least once and then evaluate the condition to determine whether to repeat the loop.

CAUTION

Do not put the `While` condition clause in both the `Do` and the `Loop` statements because this will cause an error when you try to run your program.

N O T E If you are working on code that was developed by someone else, you might find a loop that starts with a `While` statement and ends with a `Wend` statement. This type of loop works the same as a `Do While` loop with the `While` clause in the `Do` statement. Visual Basic still supports a `While...Wend` loop, but I recommend that you use the `Do While` type of loop because it is more flexible. ▪

Using a *Do Until* Statement The `Do Until` loop is basically the same as the `Do While` loop except that the statements inside a `Do Until` loop are run only as long as the condition is `False`. When the condition becomes `True`, the loop terminates. As with the `Do While` loop, there are two forms of the `Do Until` loop—one with the condition in the `Do` statement and one with the condition in the `Loop` statement. If you place the condition in the `Do` statement, it is evaluated before the statements in the loop are executed. If you place the condition in the `Loop` statement, the loop is run at least once before the condition is evaluated.

A frequent use of the `Do Until` statement is in reading and processing data files. A loop starts with the first record of the file and processes each record until the end of file is reached. Listing 8.12 uses a loop to load all the authors from the `BIBLIO.MDB` sample database into a list box. Figure 8.10 shows the results of the program.

On the Web

Listing 8.12   AUTHORS.FRM—Using *Do Until* to Process a Database

```
Private Sub cmdListAuthors_Click()
    Dim OldDb As Database, OldWs As Workspace, OldTbl As Recordset
    Set OldWs = Workspaces(0)
    Set OldDb = OldWs.OpenDatabase("C:\VB\BIBLIO.MDB")
    Set OldTbl = OldDb.OpenRecordset("Authors", dbOpenTable)
    OldTbl.MoveFirst
    Do Until OldTbl.EOF
        LstAuthors.AddItem OldTbl("Author")
        OldTbl.MoveNext
    Loop
    OldTbl.Close
    OldDb.Close
End Sub
```

T I P

Indenting your code inside a loop or other structure (such as an `If/Then/Else` block or `Select Case/End Select` block) makes the code easier to read. To indent a line of code, press Tab at the beginning of the line. When you press Enter at the end of the line, the indention remains at the same point. Try to match up beginning and ending points of code blocks, as has been done in many of this book's code examples.

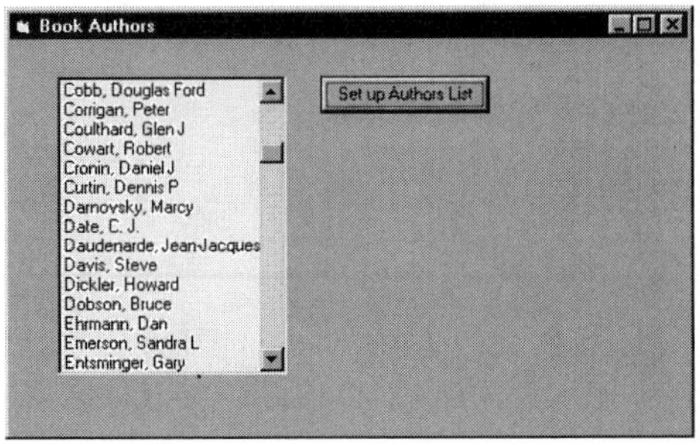

FIG. 8.10

The list was set up by using a *Do Until* loop to read through database records until the end of the data was reached.

Making Your Program Bug-Free

No matter how long you have been developing programs or how good you are at what you do, you'll still have errors crop up in your program. It's easy to make mistakes. All it takes is a simple typo to make your program refuse to run. This is called a *syntax error*. There are also *logic errors*, where your program runs but it just doesn't do what you want it to do.

Because you will make errors, one of the keys to successful program development is the ability to track down these errors, or *bugs* as they are often known, and fix them. Visual Basic provides you with a number of tools to help you find and eliminate bugs. These tools provide you with the following capabilities:

- Syntax checking, which makes sure you enter commands correctly
- Watches for variables, which let you see the changing value of variables as your program runs
- Code tracing, which lets you see which program lines are being executed
- Procedure call listing, which tells you how your program got to a certain point

How to Avoid Syntax Errors

One of the best ways to eliminate bugs is to prevent them in the first place. Visual Basic provides you with a syntax checker that checks each line of code as you enter it. If you have an error in the code, the checker alerts you to the problem as soon as you move to another line. The syntax checker looks for misspelled keywords and missing items in a statement, such as a parenthesis or a keyword. When you have a syntax error, Visual Basic shows the erroneous line in red and displays a message telling you the cause of the problem. Figure 8.11 shows how the syntax checker can alert you to a missing part of an If statement.

The syntax checker is turned on when you first install Visual Basic. However, if for some reason it has been turned off, you can activate it by checking the Auto Syntax Check box in the Editor Options dialog box (see Figure 8.12). Access this dialog box by choosing Tools, Options.

FIG. 8.11

The syntax checker is reporting an incomplete statement.

Invalid statement ———

Error message ———

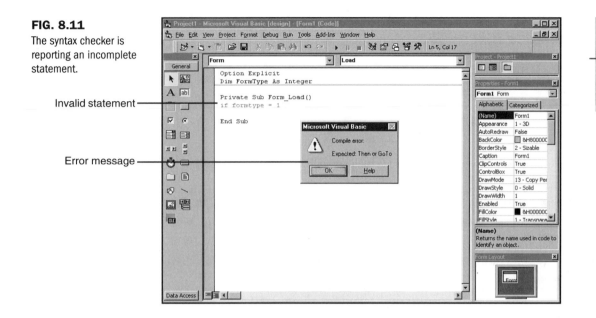

FIG. 8.12

Automatic Syntax Checking is one of many options that can be selected for Visual Basic's editor.

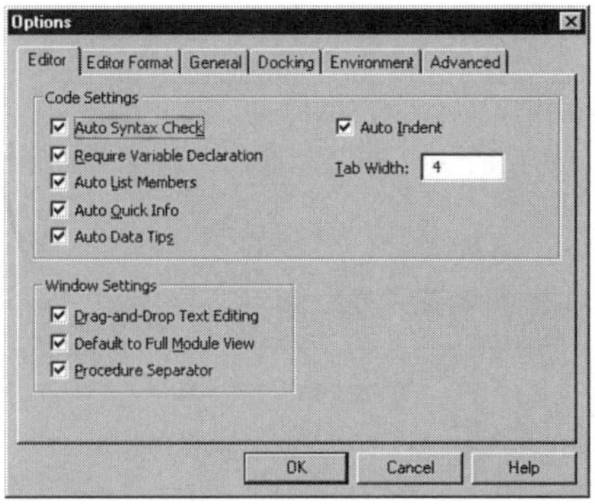

Another great feature of Visual Basic is the new Auto List Members code-completion assistant. This assistant helps you by popping up the syntax of Visual Basic functions and by providing you with property lists for any object used in the code. While this feature is designed to help speed your coding, it also helps cut down on errors. Figure 8.13 shows how a property list for a form is displayed after you enter a dot after the form's name in the code line.

Another thing that Visual Basic does for you in the Code window is properly capitalizes keywords and displays them using blue text. This gives you another visual indication that you have correctly entered a command.

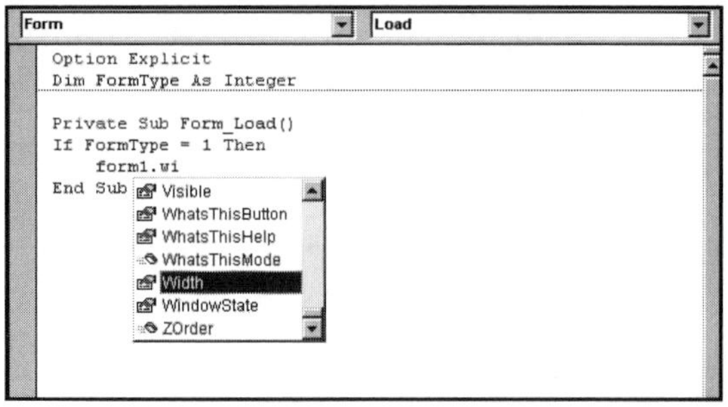

FIG. 8.13

The code-completion assistant helps eliminate programming errors.

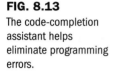

 TIP If you enter all your control names and properties in lowercase and spell them correctly, Visual Basic capitalizes them. This indicates that you didn't make any typos.

 TIP If you don't like the default colors that are used in the Code Editor, you can change them by using the Editor Format tab on the Options dialog box.

What Happens When an Error Occurs

While you are running your code from the Visual Basic development environment, you might encounter errors in your program. These errors can be the runtime errors listed in the Help files or the program manuals. When you encounter an error, you are shown an error message like the one in Figure 8.14. The error message gives you the error number and a text description of the problem.

FIG. 8.14

A missing file leads to a runtime error.

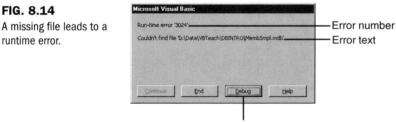

Debug button

Notice that the message box has several command buttons on it. One of these buttons, the <u>D</u>ebug button, provides you with the first line of assistance in tracking down errors in your code. If you choose the Debug button, you are shown the code-editing window with the offending line highlighted by a yellow highlight bar and arrow (see Figure 8.15).

Sometimes the error is obvious, such as mistyping a variable name or declaring a variable as the wrong type. Other times, though, you need to dig deeper to find the source of the error.

FIG. 8.15

By choosing Debug from the error message box, you can attempt to pinpoint the cause of the error.

Line causing error —

How the Debugging Environment Works

Visual Basic's debugging environment provides you with the tools you need to locate and eliminate errors in your program. These tools are easily accessible from the Debug toolbar. This toolbar, shown in Figure 8.16, provides you with quick access to all the information windows of the debug environment and all of the functions for stepping through your code. Table 8.4 describes each of the Debug toolbar buttons. The Debug toolbar is accessible by choosing View, Toolbars, Debug; or by right-clicking any visible toolbar and selecting Debug from the toolbar list.

FIG. 8.16

The Debug toolbar organizes the debug functions in a convenient location.

Table 8.4 Debug Toolbar Buttons

Button	Name	Function
 ▶	Start	Begins program execution, or continues if program has been paused.
 ❙❙	Break	Pauses program execution by placing the program in "break mode."

continues

Table 8.4 Continued

Button	Name	Function
	End	Stops a running program.
	Toggle Breakpoint	Toggles the current code line as a "breakpoint;" the program will pause and enter break mode before the line is executed.
	Step Into	When in break mode, causes the next line of code to be executed, even if it means stepping into another procedure or function.
	Step Over	When in break mode, causes the next line of code to be executed; if the next line is a procedure or function call, the entire procedure or function will be executed before the program is paused again.
	Step Out	When in break mode, causes the remainder of the current procedure or function to be executed before the program is paused again.
	Locals Window	Displays the Locals window, which lists all variables that have been defined in the active procedure, along with their current values.
	Immediate Window	Displays the Immediate window, which allow you to manually execute lines of code while in break mode.
	Watch Window	Displays the Watch window, where can add "watches" to allow you to keep an eye on how the values of your program's variables change as the program runs.
	Quick Watch	Displays the Quick Watch dialog box, which shows you the current value of the selected variable or expression. You can add the expression to the Watch window from here.
	Call Stack	Displays the Calls dialog box, which contains a list of all procedures and functions that are currently running but have not yet finished executing.

Let's take a closer look at the tools at your disposal.

How to Determine the Value of a Variable

Often when you encounter an error, it is because a variable contains a value that you did not expect. It might be that a variable had a zero value and was then used in a division operation. Or a variable that was supposed to contain the name of a file somehow had a number stored in it. You can also see how a variable changes as the program runs. Watching the change in a variable's value, or the lack of a change, is one of the major factors in finding many program errors, including infinite loops.

To debug your program, you have to be able to determine the values of the variables that are used in the program at different points in the execution. Visual Basic provides you with several basic methods of checking the values of variables, including the Watch window, the Locals window, Quick Watches, and Auto Data Tips.

Using the Watch Window   One way to view the value of variables is with the Watch window. This window shows you the expression you are watching, the value of the expression, the type of watch, and the procedure where the expression is being evaluated (see Figure 8.17). By using the Watch window, you can look at only the variables or expressions that interest you. You can access the Watch window from the Debug toolbar or by choosing View, Watch Window.

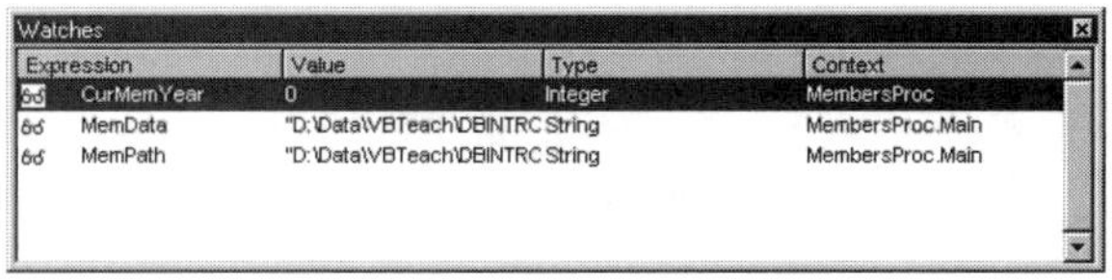

FIG. 8.17
The Watch window shows the value of variables and expressions you define.

To set up a variable or expression for viewing, you have to add it to the Watch window. To do this, choose Debug, Add Watch. This brings up the Add Watch dialog box (see Figure 8.18). This dialog box allows you to enter the name of the variable to observe in the Expression field.

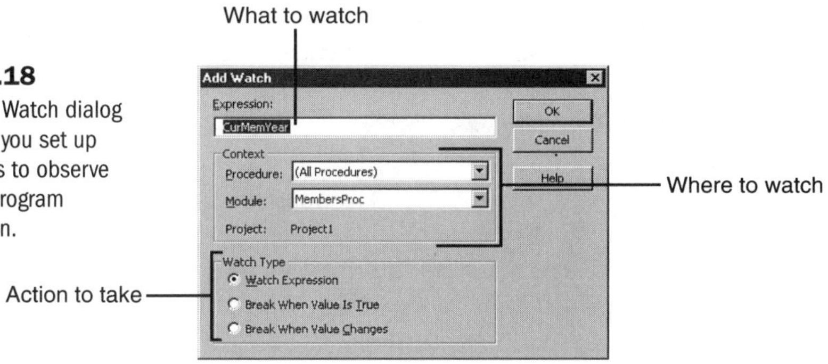

FIG. 8.18
The Add Watch dialog box lets you set up variables to observe during program execution.

What to watch

Where to watch

Action to take

The Add Watch dialog box also allows you to specify where you want to observe the variable. These context settings let you observe the value of the variable during the entire program or just during a specific procedure.

The Watch Type options let you decide whether to just look at the value of the variable or to break (pause the execution of the code) when a specific condition exists. You can choose to have the program pause every time a variable changes or when the watch expression is True. This way, you can determine when a variable reaches or exceeds a specific value. To use this type of watch, the expression must be a Boolean variable or a logical expression.

If at a later time you want to edit the watch expression, you can right-click the mouse in the Watch window and select the Edit Watch item from the pop-up window. This brings up the Edit Watch dialog box, which is basically the same as the Add Watch dialog box, but adds a command button that allows you to delete the watch.

Using the Locals Window   Sometimes it is easier to just check the values of all the variables in a procedure than it is to try to guess which variable has the problem. This is easily done with the Locals window, which is viewed by clicking the Locals Window button on the Debug toolbar, or by choosing View, Locals Window. This window, shown in Figure 8.19, lists all the variables declared in the current procedure along with their current values. Variables that are declared outside the current procedure are not shown.

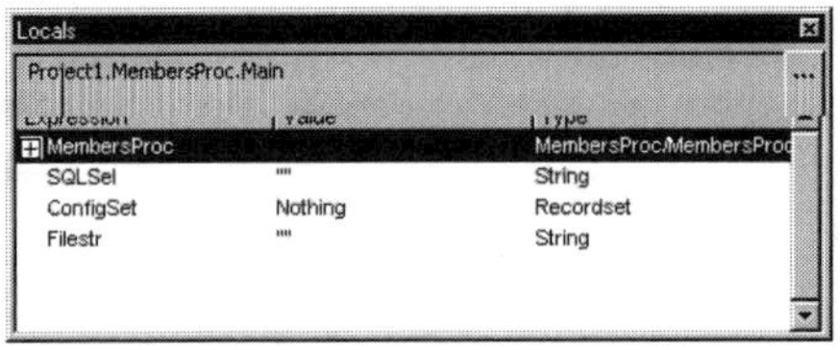

FIG. 8.19

The Locals window lets you look at all the declared variables in a procedure.

Using Quick Watches and Auto Data Tips   If you only need to find out the current value of a variable, but do not need to track its value as the program progresses, you can use a quick watch. A quick watch displays a dialog box that shows the name of the variable, its current value, and the procedure in which it is currently being used (see Figure 8.20).

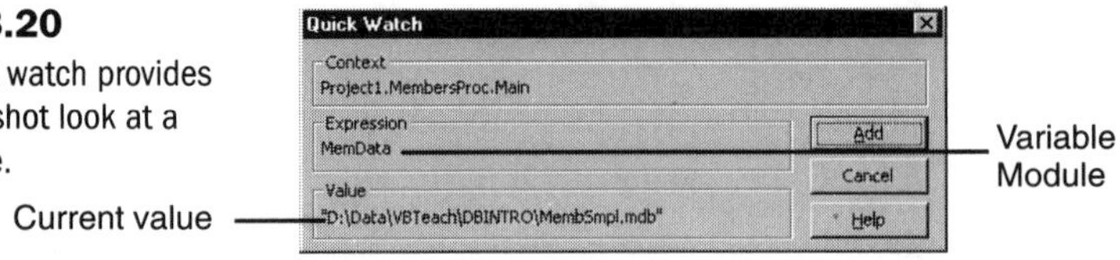

FIG. 8.20

A quick watch provides a snapshot look at a variable.

Current value ——

—— Variable
   Module

To use a quick watch, highlight a variable in the Code window while the program is paused. Then you can click the Quick Watch button on the Debug toolbar or choose Debug, Quick Watch to show the dialog box. You can also run a quick watch by pressing Shift+F9. Note that the Quick Watch dialog box has an option to add the watch to the Watch window that we described previously.

Another way to quickly view the value of a variable or an object property is to rest the mouse pointer on the variable in the Code window. After the mouse is still for a second or two, the value pops up in a little box similar to a ToolTip (see Figure 8.21). This handy tool is known as Auto Data Tips. You can also select an entire expression and rest the mouse pointer on it to see the evaluated value of the expression.

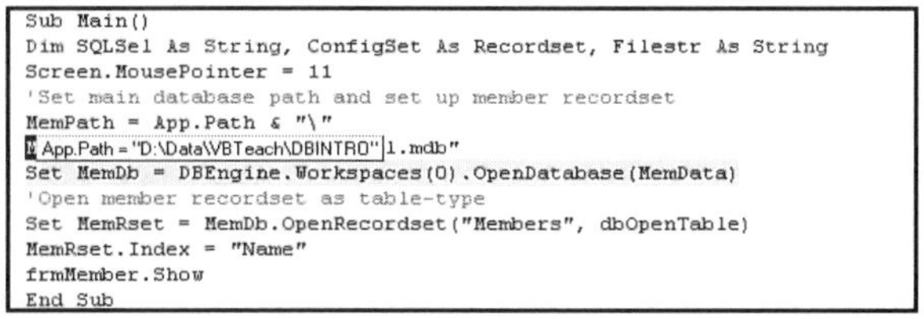

FIG. 8.21

Resting the mouse pointer on App.Path in break mode causes Auto Data Tips to display its value in a ToolTip.

```
Sub Main()
Dim SQLSel As String, ConfigSet As Recordset, Filestr As String
Screen.MousePointer = 11
'Set main database path and set up member recordset
MemPath = App.Path & "\"
App.Path = "D:\Data\VBTeach\DBINTRO" 1.mdb"
Set MemDb = DBEngine.Workspaces(0).OpenDatabase(MemData)
'Open member recordset as table-type
Set MemRset = MemDb.OpenRecordset("Members", dbOpenTable)
MemRset.Index = "Name"
frmMember.Show
End Sub
```

Running Commands

Another part of the Debug environment is the *Immediate window*. This window allows you to enter program commands, which will be executed as soon as you press Enter. From this window, you can print or even change the value of a variable using an assignment statement. You can also use commands to change the environment of your program, such as the fonts on a form or the color of text in a text box.

The Immediate window allows you to enter any single-line command. Loops and block statements (If blocks and Select Case blocks) are not allowed. If you issue the print command from the Immediate window, the results are printed on the line following the command. This provides another way to view the contents of a variable. Figure 8.22 shows how the Immediate window can be used to find the value of a variable or set a variable. If the Immediate window is not open, you can access it by clicking the Immediate Window button on the Debug toolbar, or by choosing View, Immediate Window.

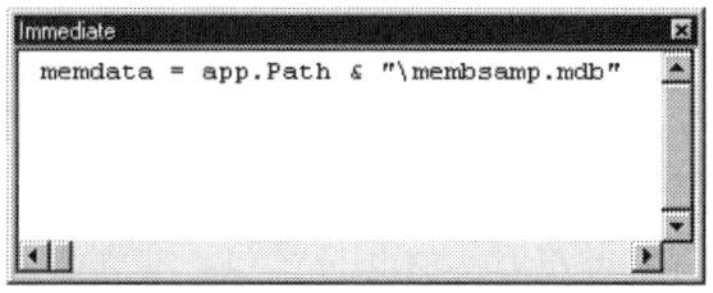

FIG. 8.22

You can execute many types of statements in the Immediate window.

```
Immediate
memdata = app.Path & "\membsamp.mdb"
```

Another Debugging Tool

One final item you might need in debugging is the *Call Stack window* (see Figure 8.23), which can be viewed by clicking the Call Stack button on the Debug toolbar, by choosing View, Call Stack, or by pressing Ctrl+L. This window tells you which procedure is currently executing. It also shows the entire string of procedure calls from the initial procedure to the current one. These calls are listed from the most recent procedure (at the top of the list) to the initial calling procedure (at the bottom of the list). This list helps you determine how you got to the current point. This way, you will know if a procedure is being accessed from an area that you don't want.

FIG. 8.23
The Call Stack shows
you the procedures that
led up to the current
procedure.

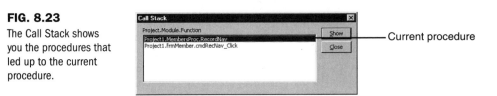

Current procedure

Pausing the Program's Execution

Whenever Visual Basic encounters an error, it automatically pauses the execution of the program by placing it in *break mode*. There also might be times that you want to pause a program when there is no error. You would do this to check the value of variables at a specific point.

There are several ways to pause a program without an error having occurred:

- Set a watch to pause the program, either when a variable changes value or when an expression is True.
- Press Ctrl+Break on the keyboard. 
- Click the Break button on either the Standard or Debug toolbar.
- Set a breakpoint in code to pause at a particular line.

Setting a watch point to pause the program was discussed previously in the "Using the Watch Window" section; clicking the Break button and pressing Ctrl+Break are self-explanatory. Therefore, let's concentrate on setting a breakpoint in the code.

A breakpoint in code is set while you are in design mode. To set the breakpoint, you must have the Code window open and be in the procedure containing the statement where you want the break to occur. At this point, you can set the breakpoint in one of these ways:

- Click the mouse in the gray margin to the left of the statement. 
- Select the statement on which to break and click the Toggle Breakpoint icon from the Debug toolbar.
- Select the statement on which to break and choose Debug, Toggle Breakpoint.
- Select the statement on which to break and press F9.
- Add the Stop statement to your code at the point where you want the program to pause.

When a breakpoint is set, the code statement is highlighted as shown in Figure 8.24.

Each of the methods for setting the breakpoint actually toggles the breakpoint status of the line. This means that if the statement is not a breakpoint, it becomes one. Conversely, if it is already a breakpoint, the breakpoint is removed.

Tracing Through Your Code

In the previous sections, you learned how to pause the code; but for debugging to be effective, you have to be able to execute program statements and watch their effects.

FIG. 8.24

A breakpoint enables you to pause the code at a specific statement.

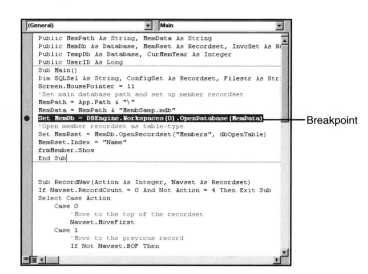

Breakpoint

After the execution of the program has stopped, you have several options for continuing the execution. You can do any of the following:

- Execute a single statement
- Execute a group of statements
- Resume normal execution of the code

 To execute a single statement or group of statements, you need to be in the code-editing window. To execute the program one statement at a time, you can press the F8 key, or click the Step Into button on the Debug toolbar. This executes the statement currently highlighted by the highlight bar and moves the box to the next statement. By repeatedly pressing the key, you move through the code a step at a time.

This method is extremely useful for determining which part of a conditional statement is being accessed. When the program encounters an If or Select Case statement, it evaluates the condition and moves immediately to the proper part of the block for the condition. For example, if the condition in an If statement is False, execution of the program immediately moves to the Else portion of the If block.

If the current statement contains a procedure call, pressing F8 or clicking the Step Into button causes you to go to the first step of the procedure. If you want to run the entire procedure and return to the next line in the current program, press Shift+F8 or click the Debug toolbar's Step Over button. Also, if you have stepped into the procedure and want to run the rest of the procedure, you can click the Debug toolbar's Step Out button or press Ctrl+Shift+F8. This runs the remaining lines of code in the procedure and pauses again at the statement after the procedure call.

If you're fairly certain that a block of statements is error-free, you might want to execute the entire block at once instead of executing each statement individually. You can accomplish this by placing the cursor on the statement where you next want to pause the program execution and pressing Ctrl+F8. This method is useful for executing an entire loop after you have determined that the loop is not part of the problem.

Finally, when you think you have resolved the problem and want to finish executing the program, you can press the F5 key to allow the program to continue running normally. You can also do this by pressing the Continue button (which is the break-mode version of the Run button) on the Standard or Debug toolbar.

From Here...

This chapter has provided you with an overview of programming in Visual Basic. You have learned how to handle mathematical operations, string manipulations, decisions, and loops in your code. You have also seen how to use the debugging environment to eliminate errors in your code. For some more material on programming, refer to the following chapters:

■ To learn how to create procedures and functions, see Chapter 10, "Managing Your Project."

■ Learn about programming with controls in Chapter 19, "Advanced Control Techniques."

■ Read about database programming in Chapter 24, "Database Design and Normalization."

■ Find out about creating classes in your programs in Chapter 32, "Using Classes in Visual Basic."

■ To learn some more advanced techniques for writing programs, see Chapter 37, "Advanced Code Techniques."

Displaying and Printing Reports

A lot of your programming effort, and a lot of the material in this book, is geared toward getting information into your program and processing it. However, all the input and processing isn't much good if you can't get the results back out to the user. In this chapter, we focus on basic reporting and information display. When we use the term "reporting" we are not only referring to printed reports, but also on-screen information. The techniques discussed in this chapter can be used to produce both types of reports. You can also write report functions that are generic enough to be used for both the screen and printer. ■

Creating on-screen reports with controls

With the right formatting, the TextBox, RichTextBox, and ListBox controls are well-suited to display large amounts of information.

Print information while you are developing a program

Print to the Immediate (or Debug) window to get values of variables and expressions.

Simple reports with the Printer Object

Send text to the printer and line up information in columns using print zones and formatting functions.

Control every aspect of your printing

Use fonts and colors to spice up your printout, add graphics, and precisely position each element of a report.

Printing to on-screen objects

Print to a form and to a picture box to display reports on the screen.

Send information to a file

Use the Print statement to send information to a file for storage or for transfer to another program.

Outputting Reports to Familiar Controls

If a paper report is not necessary, you can create fairly sophisticated-looking reports on-screen with some of Visual Basic's custom controls. In this section, we look at three controls suitable for doing this: the text box, the rich text box, and the list box.

Using the Text Box

You already know from earlier chapters that the Label and TextBox controls can display multiple lines of information in a variety of fonts and colors. If your report is mainly paragraphs of text, a TextBox control might be ideal. The `MultiLine` and `ScrollBars` properties allow the user to view more text than will fit on the screen at a time. By using the intrinsic constants `vbCrLf` to force a new line and `vbTab` to hit the tab stops, you can easily format a text box like the one in Figure 9.1.

FIG. 9.1

Simple reports can be created by using the TextBox control.

In Figure 9.1, all the formatting "logic" is in the text itself, not the text box. The way to code something like this is to fill the `Text` property incrementally:

```
Text1.Text = Text1.Text & "New Text"
```

However, rather than repeatedly accessing the `Text` property, it is more efficient to build your string in a local variable first and then assign it to the text box:

```
Dim stHeader As String

stHeader = "Gorman's Motorcycles" & vbCrLf
stHeader = stHeader & "1234 Fifth Street" & vbCrLf
stHeader = stHeader & "Anytown, MI 67321" & vbCrLf
txtRpt.Text = txtRpt.Text & stHeader & vbCrLf
```

Note in the preceding example the use of the constant `vbCrLf` to insert a special new line character. In addition, the tab character (`vbTab`) can be used to create a column effect:

```
stTemp = stTemp & " 1" & vbTab & "Carbeurator" & vbTab & "$100.00" & vbCrLf
```

If each item in a column has a different length, you might want to use spaces instead of tab characters:

```
'This code inserts one column
inPadSpaces = COLWIDTH - Len(stNewText)
```

```
If inPadSpaces < 0 then inPadSpaces = 1
txtRpt.Text = txtRpt.Text & stNewText & Space(inPadSpaces)
```

Note the use of the Space() function, which creates a string with the specified number of space characters.

Text boxes can also be assigned large strings without any formatting, like the bottom (Guarantee) section in Figure 9.1. If no special characters are included and the Multiline property is set to True, the text box simply wraps words automatically.

▶ **See** "Modifying Text with a Program," **p. 33**

See "Modifying Text with a Program," **p. 33**

TIP To make sure your columns line up properly, use a nonproportional font, such as Courier.

Part

II

Ch

9

Using the RichTextBox Control

A big drawback of using the TextBox control is that color and font options can only be applied to the entire text box. A rich text box, on the other hand, has no such limitations. It allows sections of text to be formatted individually and includes additional options such as bulleted lists and embedded objects.

The RichTextBox control is designed to work with the Rich Text File Format (RTF). RTF is a standard file format for documents, similar to DOC or HTML. Both WordPad and Microsoft Word have the capability to read and write RTF files. As a matter of fact, this feature is also built in to the RichTextBox control with the LoadFile and SaveFile methods:

```
Private Sub cmdLoad_Click()
  Rtb1.LoadFile "C:\MYFILE.RTF"
End Sub

Private Sub cmdSave_Click()
  Rtb1.SaveFile "C:\MYFILE.RTF"
End Sub
```

In addition to loading and saving files, the text in a rich text box can also be manipulated with code. You probably can already imagine some useful applications. For example, you could generate reports from a database, save them to RTF format, and e-mail them to your users—all from within a Visual Basic program.

The real strength of a RichTextBox control is in the formatting, which enables you programmatically to create sharp-looking documents like the one shown in Figure 9.2.

If you browse through the RichTextBox control's properties, you'll notice options for underlining, color, and font characteristics. The Sel prefix on many of them indicates that they affect only the selected (or highlighted) text. For example, the following code makes the selected text bold:

```
RichTextBox1.SelBold = True
```

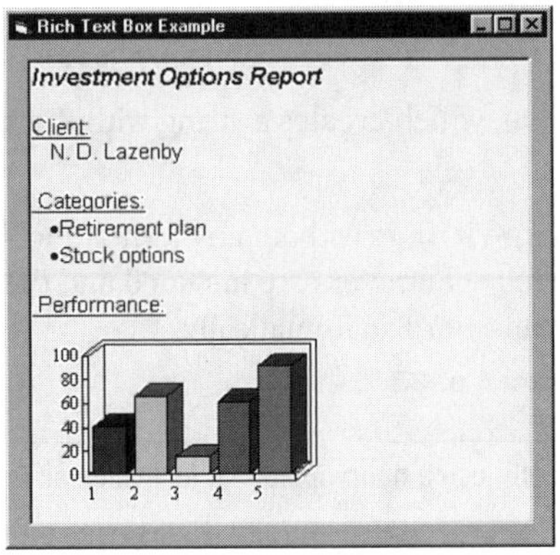

FIG. 9.2

A rich text box allows you to use multiple formatting options within the same text box.

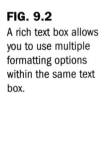

As with the text box, you can assign text using the Text property. Every time you set this property, the RichTextBox converts it to RTF format. You can view the RTF codes (similar to viewing HTML source) in the TextRTF property or by opening an RTF file with a text editor.

Let's look at the code used to create the report in Figure 9.2. First, I added all the information using the Text property:

```
Dim s As String
s = "Investment Options Report" & vbCrLf & vbCrLf
s = s & "Client" & vbCrLf & "N. D. Lazenby" & vbCrLf & vbCrLf
s = s & "Categories" & vbCrLf
s = s & "Retirement plan" & vbCrLf
s = s & "Stock options" & vbCrLf
s = s & vbCrLf & "Profits" & vbCrLf
rtb1.Text = s
```

Next, I formatted the first line, so I selected it with the SelStart and SelLength properties:

```
rtb1.SelStart = 0
rtb1.SelLength = Len("Investment Options Report")
rtb1.SelFontSize = 12
rtb1.SelItalic = True
rtb1.SelBold = True
```

A quicker way to highlight some text is the built-in Find method:

```
rtb1.Find "Client", 0
rtb1.SelUnderline = True
rtb1.SelFontSize = 11
```

When used as a function, Find returns the search string's starting position:

```
Dim nPos1 As Integer, nPos2 As Integer
nPos1 = rtb1.Find("retire", 0)
nPos2 = rtb1.Find("options", 20) + Len("options")
rtb1.SelStart = nPos1
rtb1.SelLength = nPos2 - nPos1
rtb1.SelBullet = True
rtb1.SelBold = False
rtb1.SelIndent = 200
```

Rich Text boxes also support embedded OLE objects, such as bitmaps:

```
Dim obj as OLEObject
Set obj = rtb1.OLEObjects.Add (, , "C:\graph.bmp","Paint.Picture")
```

Using the ListBox Control

Another way to present lists of information is to use the ListBox control. This control enables you to add items to a list; the user can then scroll through them. While list boxes are used primarily for presenting choices to the user and allowing him to pick one or more items, they can also be used for simple reports. Listing 9.1 shows how a list box might be used to display a list of students and grades.

Listing 9.1 LISTREPORT.FRM—Using a List Control for Simple Tables

```
'This code assumes the students and grades
'have already been stored in variable arrays

Dim I As Integer
Dim inPadSpaces As Integer
Const NUMSTUDENTS = 10
Const COLWIDTH = 20

lstGrades.Font.Name = "Courier New" 'Non-proportional font
lstGrades.Clear
For I = 1 To NUMSTUDENTS
    inPadSpaces = COLWIDTH - Len(Student(I))
    If inPadSpaces < 0 Then nPadSpaces = 1
    lstGrades.AddItem Student(I) & Space(inPadSpaces) & CStr(Grade(I))
Next I
```

Figure 9.3 shows what a list box would look like after executing the code in Listing 9.1.

> **N O T E** Although you cannot tell from looking at it, the student names in Figure 9.3 were not added in alphabetical order. Setting a list box's Sorted property to True at design time keeps your list sorted as you add items to it. ■

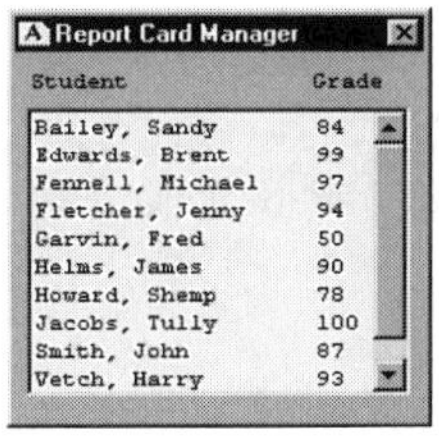

FIG. 9.3
Tabular reports can be created in a list box.

The list box has the added benefit of knowing if the user has selected an item. The items of a list box are stored in its List array, and the selected item's array index is stored in the ListIndex property. You can determine which item is selected by placing some code in the list box's Click event:

```
Private Sub lstGrades_Click()

  Dim stStudent As String
  Const COLWIDTH = 20

  stStudent = lstGrades.List(lstGrades.ListIndex)
  stStudent = left$(stStudent,COLWIDTH)
  Msgbox "You clicked on " & stStudent

End Sub
```

Instead of just using the MsgBox statement, your example could be expanded to display more information about the selected student. Note that in the preceding code you pull the student name directly from the list. The ListBox control also has a property called ItemData that can be used to store an integer value that is not displayed—for example, student ID number.

▶ **See** "Working with Lists," **p. 405**

The list box concludes the discussion of simple reports with custom controls. However, it is important to note that if you do any serious on-screen reporting, you will probably rely on a grid control more than any of the controls discussed in this chapter. There are a number of third-party grid controls available. In a later chapter, we discuss the Flex Grid, which is included with Visual Basic.

▶ **See** "Using the MSFlexGrid Control," **p. 480**

Printing Reports

For many tasks, it is convenient to display information on the screen; however, sometimes there is just no substitute for the printed page. Printed reports are simply more convenient to carry with you to read on the plane, in a meeting, or during the commercials in your favorite TV program. The reports you create can be simple, containing plain text and some columns of numbers; or the reports can be very elaborate, containing font and color effects, tables, and even graphs. You can create any type and complexity of report in Visual Basic using the techniques in this chapter. The key is in the layout and testing of the report. Unfortunately, Visual Basic does not ship with a visual report designer for general-purpose printing. Therefore, you must work with the old-fashioned method of "code and test." After you get a little experience, however, most printing tasks become relatively easy.

N O T E   Visual Basic ships with Crystal Reports, which is a visual report designer mainly used for database reports. This designer and its associated control are covered in Chapter 26, "Using Data Controls and Reports." ▪

Printable Objects

The primary means of printing text is the Print method. An object's Print method is used just like any other method. For example, place the following line of code in a form's Click event:

```
Form1.Print "Hello, World!"
```

Every time you click the form, a new line of text appears. While we will primarily discuss printing information to paper using the `Printer` object, the `Print` method works with the following four objects in Visual Basic:

- *Forms* You can print information to the background of a form. All printing will appear behind any controls that are on the form.
- *Printer* You can send information to the default printer or specify a particular printer. The information is sent to the Print Manager and then to the printer when you complete a page or document.
- *PictureBox controls* You can print to the background of a PictureBox control, superimposing text on the picture (if there is one present). This is similar to printing to a form.
- *Immediate window* During program development, you can print text to the Immediate window (formerly known as the Debug window) to help check on the progress of your program. You can also print contents of variables to help with bug hunting.

The code statements you use to create your printout work the same way no matter which of these output objects you specify. In fact, you can use a class to create a generic print routine that will work with any output object.

Printing Simple Reports

In its simplest form, the `Print` method specifies the object where you want to print, the `Print` method itself, and the information you want to have printed. For example, the following statement prints a string of text to the printer:

```
Printer.Print "This prints a single line of text."
```

Used in this way, the `Print` method prints a single piece of information and then advances to the next line of the printer. The information you print is not limited to text. You can print text, numbers, or dates by using the `Print` method. Also, as you might expect, you can specify the information to be printed using either literals or variables. The following lines show several print examples:

```
Dim stVariable As String, inVariable As Integer
stVariable = "This is text information"
inVariable = 500
Printer.Print "Print a single string"
Printer.Print stVariable
Printer.Print 25
Printer.Print inVariable
```

The `Print` method would be of limited usefulness if you could only print a single item at a time. In fact, you can send multiple pieces of information to the printer (or other object) using the `Print` method. To print more than one item, simply place multiple items in the print list, and separate each item with a comma or a semicolon. If you separate two items with a comma, the second item is printed in the next *print zone*. This usually places some space between the items, as each print zone is 14 characters wide. If you separate the items with a semicolon, the second item is printed immediately after the first item, with no intervening spaces.

Part

II

Ch

9

The following code sample (Listing 9.2) shows how separators make a difference in where information is printed. The output from this code is shown in Figure 9.4.

Listing 9.2   PRINTDEMO.FRM—Commas and Semicolons Affect the Location of a Printed Item

```
Dim s1 As String
Dim s2 As String

s1 = "String 1"
s2 = "String 2"

'Print s1 and s2 on the same line with no spaces
picTest.Print s1; s2
'Print a blank line
picTest.Print

'Print s1 and s2 separated by some spaces
picTest.Print s1;
picTest.Print "    "; s2

'Print a blank line, then s1 and s2 in separate print zones
picTest.Print vbCrLf & s1, s2
```

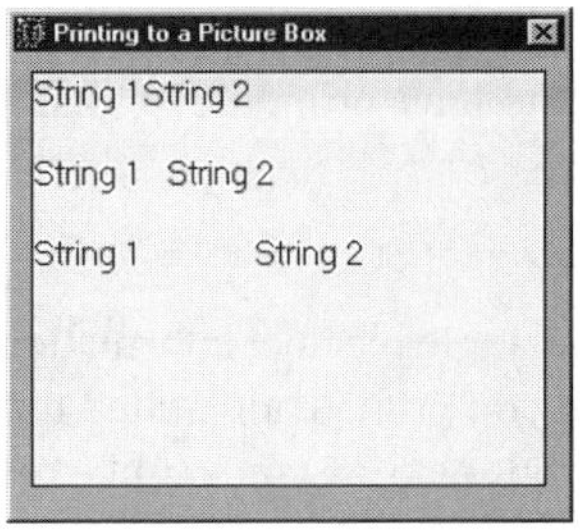

FIG. 9.4

The separators between items in a print statement determine the amount of space between them.

You can, of course, include a lot more than two or three items in the `Print` method's expression list. These items can be a mix of text and numbers, as long as each is separated by a comma or semicolon. You can even mix separators within the list.

One other item of note: The `Print` method typically starts a new line each time it is invoked. You can change this behavior by including a comma or semicolon after the last item in the expression list. This indicates to the next print statement that it should continue on the same line. Using a comma starts the next item in the next print zone, and using a semicolon starts the next item immediately after the preceding one.

> **CAUTION**
>
> Because the `Print` method does not automatically handle word wrapping, printing a lot of items or several large items can result in printing some information off the edge of the page. See the later sections "Using *TextHeight* and *TextWidth*" and "Using Word Wrapping in Your Printouts" to learn about preventing this.

Controlling Spacing in Your Reports

Specifying only a list of information to be printed leaves much to be desired in controlling the placement and appearance of any reports you are creating. Fortunately, you can position text by embedding spaces and tabs, just like the earlier examples with the TextBox control. Two special functions that are used with the `Print` method are the `Spc` and `Tab` functions.

The `Spc` function places a specified number of spaces in the printout. This is used to create a specific amount of space between two items in the expression list. You use the `Spc` function by placing it in the expression list of the `Print` method as shown in the following line of code:

```
Printer.Print "First Field"; Spc(10); "Second Field"
```

When using the `Spc` function, you should always use a semicolon as the separator. Otherwise, the spaces created by the `Spc` function will not start immediately after the preceding item, but will start in the next print zone. This will most likely give you more space than you want.

```
'Not a good way to use the Spc Function
Print "First Field", Spc(10), "Second Field"
```

The `Spc` function is most useful when you deal with information of a known length (such as five characters, ten characters, and so on) and with a fixed font. However, if you are trying to create columns in a report, the `Tab` function is usually the better choice. The `Tab` function causes subsequently printed characters to start at a specific location. You use the `Tab` function in a manner similar to the `Spc` function, but instead of specifying the number of spaces, you specify the character position where you want the printing to start. The following line of code causes the second item to be printed in column 30 of the printout:

```
Printer.Print "First Field"; Tab(30); "Second Field"
```

Figure 9.5 shows the effects of using the `Spc` and `Tab` functions to create columns in a report. Notice that the report using the `Tab` function produces more consistent results than the `Spc` function.

FIG. 9.5

The `Spc` function inserts a specified number of spaces, while the `Tab` function moves to a specific position.

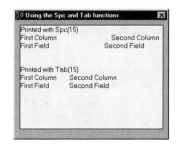

> **CAUTION**
>
> If the position specified by the Tab function is further to the left on the page than the end of the last printed item, the Tab function causes the printout to move to that character position on the next line on the page.

Using Functions to Control the Appearance of Your Text

In addition to using the Spc and Tab functions to handle the spacing of your reports, there are other functions that are extremely useful in creating reports for your programs. The String function works like the Spc function, except that you can specify any character you want to fill the spaces. The Format function lets you apply special formatting to strings, numbers, and dates to make them more readable for your users.

Using the *String* Function   You have probably seen the Table of Contents of a book where a series of dots (a *dot leader*) separates the title of a chapter from the page number where it starts. If you want to do this in your reports, use the String function. The String function requires two arguments—the character to use and the number of times to repeat the character. For example, the following line of code would place a series of 20 periods on the printout after the first data item:

```
Printer.Print "Chapter 1"; String(20, "."); "15"
```

In the String function, you can either specify the literal character to use or the ASCII code of the character. The following code has the same effect as the preceding line:

```
Printer.Print "Chapter 1"; String(20, 46); "15"
```

Figure 9.6 shows an example of dot leaders embedded by using the String function.

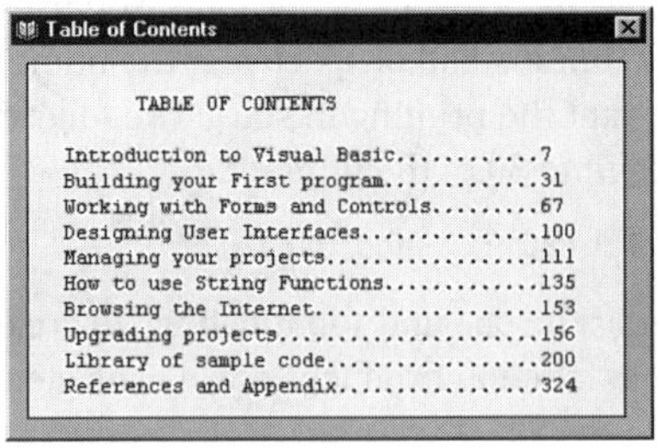

FIG. 9.6

Use the String function to embed characters in your printout.

Another use of the String function would be in printing checks, where you want to be sure that the amount line of the check is filled to avoid tampering. In this case, the typical character to use is the asterisk (*).

Using the *Format* Function   There are several types of information that require special handling. Two, in particular, are numbers and dates. When you tell the Print method to print a number, it prints it using the least number of digits possible. There are two problems with this. First, users might be accustomed to seeing numbers in a particular format, such as two decimal places for currency numbers. Second, if all your numbers are not the same size, it makes it difficult to line them up in columns. Similar problems apply to printed dates. For example, you may want only two digits in the year or to print the full name of the month instead of an abbreviation.

The Format function makes it easy for you to apply custom formatting to any text that you want to print. You can choose from some of the built-in formats or create your own by specifying format strings.

Formatting Numbers The most common use of the Format function is to place numbers in a particular format to make them easier for the users to read. To use the Format function, you specify the input value and the format as shown in the following line of code:

```
Printer.Print Format(crGrossSales, "Currency")
```

For working with numbers, there are several named formats that you can use. Table 9.1 shows the named formats for numbers that are available with the Format function. Figure 9.7 shows the various format types for a group of numbers. In all cases, you must enclose the name of the format in double quotes.

Table 9.1 Named Formats Make It Easy to Display Numbers

Named Format	Description
General Number	Displays the number with no special formatting.
Currency	Displays the number with a thousands separator, and two digits to the right of the decimal.
Fixed	Displays at least one digit to the left and two digits to the right of the decimal.
Standard	Displays the number with the thousands separator, and at least one digit to the left and two digits to the right of the decimal.
Percent	Multiplies the number by 100 and displays the number followed by the percent (%) sign.
Scientific	Displays the number in standard scientific notation.
Yes/No	Displays Yes for a non-zero value and No for zero.
True/False	Displays True for a non-zero value and False for zero.
On/Off	Displays On for a non-zero value and Off for zero.

If the named formats in Visual Basic don't meet your needs, you can define your own formats. (See Table 9.2 for the codes needed to define formats.) You specify a format by creating a "template" string indicating where the digits of the number will be placed, if thousands and decimal separators will be used, and any special characters that you want printed. For example, the following line of code prints a number with four decimal places and a thousands separator:

```
Printer.Print Format(TotalDistance, "##,##0.0000")
```

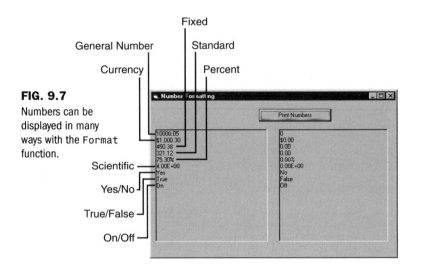

FIG. 9.7
Numbers can be
displayed in many
ways with the Format
function.

Table 9.2   Codes for Defining Numeric Formats

Symbol	Purpose	Meaning
0	Digit placeholder	Displays the digit or displays 0 if there is no digit in that location.
#	Digit placeholder	Displays the digit or displays nothing if there is no digit in that location. This causes leading and trailing zeros to be omitted.
.	Decimal Separator	Indicates where the decimal point will be displayed.
,	Thousands Separator	Indicates where the separators will be displayed.
%	Percentage Indicator	Indicates where a percent sign will be displayed. Also causes the number to be multiplied by 100.
E-, E+, e-, e+	Scientific Notation	Using E- or e- displays a minus sign next to negative exponents, but displays no sign for positive exponents. Using E+ or e+ displays a sign for any exponent.

Formatting Dates   Another form of data that is often a chore to print is dates. If you specify
the Print method with a date, it is displayed in the default format for your system—typically
something like 2/18/98. If you want to display the date in another manner (for example,
February 18, 1998), you need to use the Format function. Table 9.3 lists some predefined date
and time formats (see Figure 9.8). If they do not suit your needs, you can create a custom
format. The codes for creating user-defined date and time formats are listed in Visual Basic's
Help system.

To include the current date and/or time on your report, you can use the Now function:

```
Form1.Print Format(Now,"mm/dd/yyyy")
```

Table 9.3   Named Date Formats

Named Format	Description
General Date	Shows the date and time if the expression contains both portions. Otherwise, displays either the date or the time.
Long Date	Prints the day of the week, the day of the month, the month, and the year.
Medium Date	Prints the day of the month, a three letter abbreviation for the month, and the year.
Short Date	Prints the day, month, and year as 3/5/97.
Long Time	Prints hours, minutes, and seconds along with the a.m./p.m. indication.
Medium Time	Prints hours and minutes along with A.M. or P.M.
Short Time	Prints hours and minutes in military time.

FIG. 9.8
By using named formats, you can enhance the appearance of date information.

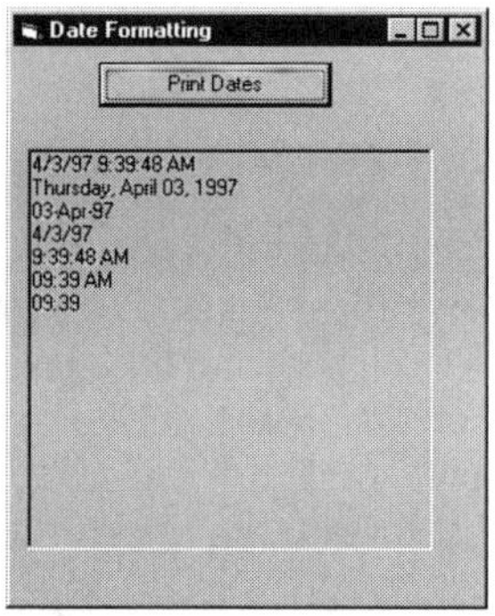

Date Formatting

```
Print Dates

4/3/97 9:39:48 AM
Thursday, April 03, 1997
03-Apr-97
4/3/97
9:39:48 AM
09:39 AM
09:39
```

 User-defined formats can be useful for making decisions in your program. The expression

```
Format(stMyDate,"w")
```

returns a number representing the day of the week. You could use the result of the expression to skip printing reports on the weekend, for example.

Creating Special Effects in Your Reports

The Print method is fine for displaying text, but used by itself is not enough to make your reports visually pleasing. If you have used a Windows word processor, you are probably already aware of several ways to alter the appearance of printed text. For example, you can make report headings larger, bold-faced, or in a different font altogether. You may also wish to change the color of certain information to draw the reader's attention to it. In addition, you can add lines, boxes, and other graphical elements to separate different sections of the report.

All of these options are available in Visual Basic. When combined with the Print method they can turn your otherwise dull printouts into sharp-looking reports. Although there are custom reporting tools available, a careful programmer can create professional-looking output using the functions described in this section.

Working with Fonts

The first step in making reports more exciting is to use different font effects to highlight information. The Print method always uses the object's current font and font characteristics when it prints information to the printer or the screen. Therefore, to use a different font or font attribute, you must make the change to the Font object before you issue the Print method. For example, place the following code in a command button:

```
Private Sub Command1_Click()
  Form1.Font.Bold = True
  Form1.Print "This is one font style,"
  Form1.Font.Bold = False
  Form1.Font.Size = 14
  Form1.Print "and this is another."
End Sub
```

Note how the Font properties act differently here than with controls such as labels or text boxes. When used with the Print method, Font properties act in a "toggle" mode. One way to think of this is that the Print method draws text on the form based on the current Font object settings, whatever they might be. A text box, on the other hand, applies any changes to the Font object to *all* of the text in its Text property.

The three main output objects—the printer, the form, and the picture box—all allow you to use the various attributes of the Font object, and the attributes are controlled the same way for each object.

We cover fonts in detail in Chapter 13, "Working with Text, Fonts, and Color," but the following list shows you the available font attributes that you can use to control the appearance of text in your printouts:

- *Name*   Determines which typeface is to be used.
- *Size*   Determines the height, in points, of the font.
- *Bold*   Determines whether characters are displayed with **heavy, dark strokes**.
- *Italic*   Determines whether characters are displayed in *italic*.

■ *Underline*   Determines whether a solid line is drawn under the text.

■ *StrikeThrough*   Determines whether a solid line is drawn through the text.

▶ **See** "Controlling the Appearance of Your Text," **p. 348**

These properties are changed using assignment statements in your code. For forms and picture boxes, you can change the initial font settings using the Properties dialog box while you are in design mode. For the Printer, the initial font settings are determined by the Windows Print Manager.

As an example of using different font attributes in your program, consider a report that lists gross sales per salesperson for a company. As the program is printing out the columns of names and sales figures, you could use a bold font for the salespeople who made more than a specified amount in sales and use an italic font to highlight those who were below a specified minimum. This would make the information stand out and make the report more useful. The code in Listing 9.3 shows how this would work. The results of the printout are shown in Figure 9.9.

Listing 9.3   PRINTEFFECT.FRM—Using Bold and Italic to Highlight Sales Figures

```
Dim I As Integer
Dim GrossSales(1 To 10) As Currency
Dim SalesPerson(1 To 10) As String

'Note: the code for filling arrays has been omitted

picOutput.Font.Name = "Times New Roman"
picOutput.Font.Size = 14
picOutput.Font.Bold = False
picOutput.Font.Italic = False

For I = 1 To 10
    If GrossSales(I) > 150000 Then picOutput.Font.Bold = True
    If GrossSales(I) < 50000 Then picOutput.Font.Italic = True
    picOutput.Print SalesPerson(I); Tab(40);
    picOutput.Print Format(GrossSales(I), "$##0,000.00")
    picOutput.Font.Bold = False
    picOutput.Font.Italic = False
Next I
```

Note that you are not limited to specifying a font or attribute for an entire line. You can change fonts in the middle of a line as well. To do this, use the Print method to print part of the line, followed by a semicolon. Then change the font attributes and use the Print method a second time to print the next part of the line. For example, you could modify Listing 9.3 to highlight only the number portion and not the salesperson's name, as in the following code lines:

```
For I = 1 To 10
   picOutput.Print SalesPerson(I); Tab(40);
   If GrossSales(I) > 150000 Then picOutput.Font.Bold = True
```

```
      If GrossSales(I) < 50000 Then picOutput.Font.Italic = True
      PicOutput.Print Format(GrossSales(I), "$##0,000.00")
      picOutput.Font.Bold = False
      picOutput.Font.Italic = False
   Next I
```

FIG. 9.9

Font attributes are an
effective way to make
your data come alive.

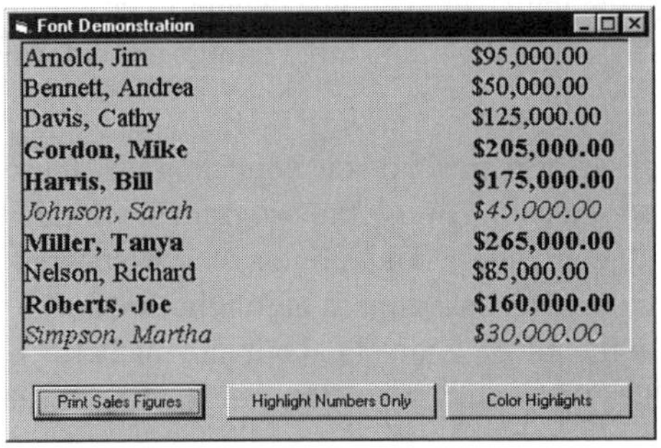

Arnold, Jim	$95,000.00
Bennett, Andrea	$50,000.00
Davis, Cathy	$125,000.00
Gordon, Mike	**$205,000.00**
Harris, Bill	**$175,000.00**
Johnson, Sarah	*$45,000.00*
Miller, Tanya	**$265,000.00**
Nelson, Richard	$85,000.00
Roberts, Joe	**$160,000.00**
Simpson, Martha	*$30,000.00*

Print Sales Figures   Highlight Numbers Only   Color Highlights

Adding a Splash of Color

Using fonts is one way to add emphasis to various parts of a report. Color is another way. If you are printing to a form or picture box, or if you are working with a color printer, you can change the color of the text that is being printed. To change the color of the text, you specify a value for the `ForeColor` property of the Printer or screen object to which you are printing. Values for the `ForeColor` property can be intrinsic constants like `vbBlue`, or numeric values. Unlike TextBox or Label controls, changing the `ForeColor` property affects only the text that is printed after the property change. Any text already printed remains in its original color.

If you are working with a color printer, you need to change one other property—the `ColorMode` property. This property determines whether the printer prints in color or monochrome. There are only two possible settings of the `ColorMode` property, both represented by Visual Basic constants—monochrome printing (`vbPRCMMonochrome`) and color (`vbPRCMColor`). A monochrome printer ignores the setting of the `ColorMode` property.

To illustrate the use of color in your printouts, let's look once again at the sales figures illustrated in Listing 9.3. This time, instead of using bold and italic font properties, we will change the text color to green for the top salespeople and red for the poor performers. This change is shown in Listing 9.4.

Listing 9.4   PRINTEFFECTS.FRM—Using Color to Enhance Your Reports on the Screen and Color Printers

```
Dim I As Integer
Dim CurColor As Long

picOutput.Font.Name = "Times New Roman"
picOutput.Font.Size = 14
CurColor = picOutput.ForeColor
```

```
For I = 1 To 10
    picOutput.Print SalesPerson(I); Tab(40);
    If GrossSales(I) > 150000 Then picOutput.ForeColor = vbGreen
    If GrossSales(I) < 50000 Then picOutput.ForeColor = vbRed
    picOutput.Print Format(GrossSales(I), "$##0,000.00")
    picOutput.ForeColor = CurColor
Next I
```

Part
II

Ch
9

We do not show a figure with the color highlights because it would not show up well in black and white. However, you can download the PrintDemo.Vbp project from the Que Web site at **www.mcp.com/info/0-7897/0-7897-1288-1** and see how the color highlighting works.

When you are printing on a form or picture box, you can also set the BackColor property to provide a background for your text. However, you need to set the property before you start printing any text on the screen. If you try to set the BackColor property after you have started printing, you will wipe out all the text that has already been printed.

> **CAUTION**
>
> The BackColor property is not supported by the Printer object; you will get an error if you try to set it. In the chapter entitled "Working With Graphics," you learn how to use the PaintPicture method, which could be used to move a section of a picture box (including background color) to the printer.
>
> ▶ **See** "Using the Color Palette," **p. 359**

Displaying Graphics

This chapter's primary focus is printing text. However, you can also include graphics in your reports. These graphics can be simple lines that set off various areas of the report, charts that complement the text that is in the report, or even graphics images such as bitmaps or JPEG and GIF pictures.

There are several graphics methods to draw on an object. For example, the following statement would draw a diagonal red line on your form:

```
frmTest.Line (0,0)-(200,200),vbred
```

The following are the three main methods used in printing graphics on a form or the printer:

- Line—Draws a line or a box on the object.
- Circle—Draws a circle, ellipse, arc, or pie on the object.
- PaintPicture—Draws a graphic image from a picture box to a form, the printer, or another picture box.

NOTE These drawing functions are discussed in detail later in the book. There is a section about each of them in Chapter 12, "Working with Graphics." ▓

Positioning the Parts of Your Report

So far, we have only looked at printing information in the print zones established by the `Print` method itself. For many situations, you will want even more control over the placement of text and graphical objects on the screen and the printed page.

Naturally, there are properties that allow you to set the absolute position of a piece of information anywhere in your print area. Using these properties allows you great flexibility in the layout of your reports. However, with the added flexibility comes added work. You have to determine the size of the object you are printing on and the size of the elements you want to print. Then you need to make sure all the pieces fit properly on the page or screen. If you have ever arranged furniture in a room, you have some idea of the process.

Visual Basic has several functions that help you determine the size of your space and the various pieces with which you are working. Printable objects also have properties to help you specify exact placement text.

Finding an Object's Printable Area

In most instances, you probably think of the printed page as a sheet of 8.5 × 11 inch paper. However, Visual Basic doesn't typically work with dimensions in terms of inches. Instead, Visual Basic works with units of measure called *twips*. (Recall from Chapter 2 that there are 1440 twips in an inch.) This makes measurement of spacing a little more difficult, but much more accurate. Also, when you are determining the available space on a printed page, you must consider whether the printer is working in portrait or landscape mode, and whether the paper is some size other than the standard 8.5 × 11. (For example, many legal papers are 8.5 × 14 inches.)

▶ **See** "Accessing Functions with the Toolbar," **p. 30**

If you are working with the Printer object, the dimensions of the printable space are controlled primarily by the Windows Print Manager and the printer itself. (We look at how to make changes to the printer settings in the section "Controlling the Printer" later in this chapter.) For forms and picture boxes, the printable area is controlled by the initial design of the object and any resizing that has been done by the user. Because the user can resize the form (and in some cases, other objects), you cannot assume that the initial dimensions that you set will be the ones available when your printing process starts.

The best way to determine the available space in an object is to use the `ScaleHeight` and `ScaleWidth` properties of the object. These properties determine the *interior* dimensions of the object to which you will be printing. These properties are illustrated for a form and picture box in Figure 9.10. (Also see the "What Is the Difference Between *ScaleHeight* and *Height*?" sidebar.)

FIG. 9.10
You can determine the interior dimensions of an object with its `ScaleHeight` and `ScaleWidth` properties.

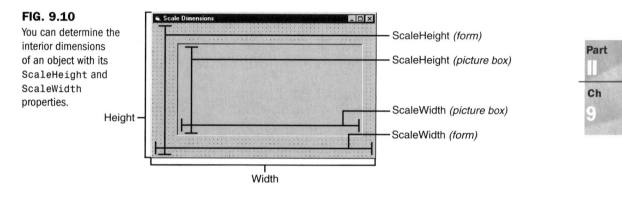

What Is the Difference Between *ScaleHeight* and *Height*?

You might be wondering why we just don't use the `Height` and `Width` properties of the object to determine its size. The reason is that the `Height` and `Width` properties specify the external dimensions of an object. For example, on a form, the `Height` property would include the size of the title bar, the borders on the form, and any menu bar that you might place on the form. For some forms, the `Height` property can be as much as 690 twips larger than the `ScaleHeight` property, or almost half an inch larger. You can see how this could cause problems when determining the printable area of a form. The relation of the `Width` and `ScaleWidth` properties is the same. `Width` specifies the external dimensions of the object while `ScaleWidth` specifies the internal dimensions.

To use the `ScaleHeight` and `ScaleWidth` properties in your program, you need to retrieve their values. The easiest way to do this is to store the values of the properties in a pair of variables just before your report generation routine. This is shown in the following two lines of code:

```
inPicWid = picOutput.ScaleWidth
inPicHgt = picOutput.ScaleHeight
```

After you have established the dimensions of the object, you can use them to establish relative positions on the object. For example, the following code sample starts printing some text in the middle of the object:

```
picOutput.CurrentX = inPicWid *.5
picOutput.CurrentY = inPicHgt *.5
picOutput.Print "Hello!"
```

Note the use of the `CurrentX` and `CurrentY` properties, used to set coordinates on the picture box before printing.

Using *TextHeight* and *TextWidth*

Now that you can determine the size of an object's printable area, you need to determine the size of the text you are placing on that object. The Print method is very simple-minded. It does not check to see whether the text is wider than the area where it is to be printed. Therefore, if the text is too wide, it simply disappears off the right edge of the print area, as shown in Figure 9.11.

▶ **See** "Using Word Wrapping in Your Printouts," **p. 239**

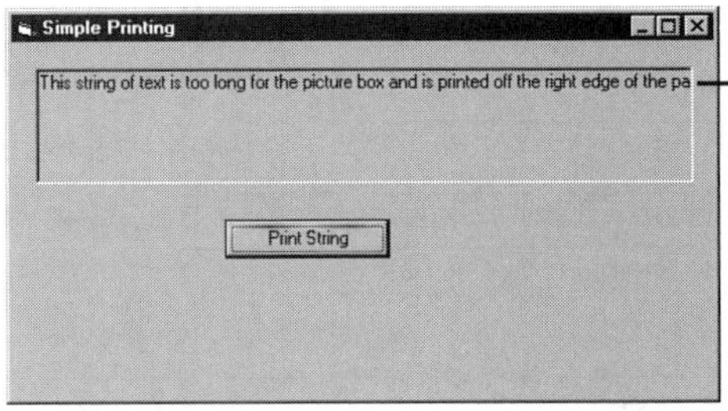

FIG. 9.11
Word wrapping would be useful here.

Runover text

Each of the objects that support the Print method also has two other methods that allow you to determine the size of the text to be printed. These methods are the TextHeight and TextWidth methods. As you can probably guess, the TextHeight method tells you the vertical dimensions (in twips) of a piece of text, and the TextWidth method tells you how much of an area the text will cover horizontally. The following lines of code demonstrate the use of the two methods:

```
Dim sgHeight As Single
Dim sgWidth As Single
Dim stUserName As String

stUserName = "STEVE BAKER"

sgHeight = Printer.TextHeight(stUsername)
sgWidth = Printer.TextWidth(stUsername)
```

When using the TextHeight and TextWidth methods, you must supply a string in the form of a literal string, a string variable, or a string function. If you try to use a number or numeric variable, you get an error. Therefore, if you need to print a number, use the Str, CStr, or Format functions to convert the number to a string. You should also remember that literal strings must be enclosed within quotation marks.

▶ **See** "Working with Strings and Numbers," **p. 347**

When determining the size of a piece of text, the TextHeight and TextWidth methods take into account the font used by the target of the output, as well as the font attributes such as size, bold, and italic. One use of the value returned is to adjust the font size to be sure that a piece of text fits in a specified area or to make sure the maximum possible font size is used. Listing 9.5

shows how you would check the size of the text and then reduce the font if necessary to make it fit in the available space. The results are shown in Figure 9.12.

Listing 9.5 PRINTSIZE.FRM—Using *TextHeight* and *TextWidth* to Determine Whether the Font Size Needs to Be Changed

```
Private Sub CmdSizetext_Click()

    Const MINIMUM_SIZE = 8
    Dim stInput As String
    Dim inWidth As Integer
    Dim inHeight As Integer
    Dim inFontSize As Integer
    Dim blTooBig As Boolean

    picOutput.Cls
    stInput = InputBox$("Enter some text")
    If Len(stInput) = 0 Then Exit Sub
    inFontSize = Val(InputBox$("Enter initial font size", , "12"))
    lblInitial = "Initial Size: " & inFontSize
    inWidth = picOutput.ScaleWidth
    inHeight = picOutput.ScaleHeight
    picOutput.Font.Size = inFontSize
    blTooBig = True

    Do While blTooBig And inFontSize > MINIMUM_SIZE
        If picOutput.TextWidth(stInput) < inWidth And _
                picOutput.TextHeight(stInput) < inHeight Then
            blTooBig = False
        Else
            inFontSize = inFontSize - 1
            picOutput.Font.Size = inFontSize
        End If
    Loop
    picOutput.Print stInput
    lblActual = "Actual size: " & inFontSize
End Sub
```

FIG. 9.12

The text had to be resized because it would not have fit at the requested font size.

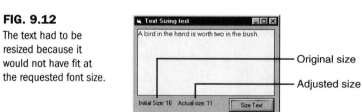

Placing the Elements of the Report

In our examples so far, we have controlled the position of printed text by adding spaces or tabs. However, there are two properties that can set the position of a piece of text within the print area. These properties are the CurrentX and CurrentY properties. Setting these properties is like positioning your drawing pencil on the form. For text, the CurrentX and CurrentY properties define the upper-left corner of the print position. When the Print method is issued, the text is printed down and to the right of this position. In other words, if the text you are about to print had a box around it, the coordinates (CurrentX, CurrentY) would represent the upper-left corner of the box, as measured from the upper-left corner of the screen.

▶ **See** "Controlling Form Size," **p. 69** and "Adjusting Form Position," **p. 71**

The primary use of these two properties is to set the current position before printing the next piece of text in your report. If you do not modify the values of these properties, each time the Print method is invoked, the printout will start at the far left of the next available line (unless the previous Print method ended with a semicolon or comma). You can use the CurrentX and CurrentY properties to create indented areas on your report, or to handle centering and right-justifying the text. To see how the CurrentX and CurrentY properties are used, take a look at Listing 9.6 and its resulting output in Figure 9.13.

Listing 9.6   PRINTSIZE.FRM—Using *CurrentX* and *CurrentY* to Position Text on a Page

```
Private Sub cmd_Center_Click()
    Dim stTest As String
    Dim inWidth As Integer
    Dim inHeight As Integer

    stTest = "This text is centered"
    With picOutput
        inWidth = .ScaleWidth
        inHeight = .ScaleHeight
        .Font.Name = "Times New Roman"
        .Font.Size = 14
        .Font.Bold = True
        .CurrentX = (inWidth - .TextWidth(stTest)) / 2
        .CurrentY = (inHeight - .TextHeight(stTest)) / 2
    End With
    picOutput.Print stTest

End Sub
```

FIG. 9.13

Center text by using CurrentX and CurrentY.

You look at more ways to handle text positioning later in the chapter in "Exploring Printer Functions You Can Create."

Controlling the Printer

In our discussions so far, we have assumed that the printer was set up and ready to print, and that it would just print whatever we sent to it. For the most part, this is correct. However, there are a number of properties and methods that are used to set up the printer and then control it while your report is being created. Some of the things you can do include the following:

- Set the orientation of the printer.
- Set the number of copies to be printed.
- Start a new page.
- End a print job in progress.

This section shows you how to set up the printer and how to control it.

Setting the Properties of the Printer

Although the default settings of the printer are usually sufficient for most jobs, you do have quite a bit of control over the way the printer is set up. As with most everything else in Visual Basic, you control the printer by setting properties. These properties are part of the `Printer` object and can be set with simple assignment statements. Table 9.4 summarizes these properties and the effects that they have on your printouts. Keep in mind that some of the properties listed in the table (such as `Duplex`) do not apply to every printer.

Table 9.4   Properties that Control a Printer

Property Name	Description
Copies	Tells the printer how many copies of each page to make.
DeviceName	Returns the name of the printer—for example, HP DeskJet 660C.
DriverName	Returns the name of the printer driver—for example, HPFDJC04.
Duplex	Determines whether the printout will be on one side of a page or both sides. If the printout is on both sides of the page, this property also determines whether the second side assumes a horizontal or vertical flip of the page.
FontTransparent	Determines whether background text and graphics will show through text printed on the page.
Orientation	Determines whether the page is in portrait or landscape mode.
Page	Tells your program the current page number.

continues

Table 9.4 Continued

Property Name	Description
PaperBin	Determines which paper bin of a printer will be used. This property is also used to tell the printer to wait for manual insertion of each page to be printed. This is very useful for handling pre-printed forms.
PaperSize	Sets the size of paper to be used for the printout. This property can be set to one of a number of default paper sizes. The property can also be set to allow a user-defined paper size, in which case you must define the Height and Width properties of the page.
Port	Returns the name of the printer port. Can be a local or mapped port like LPT1: or a network path like \\myserver\myprinter.
PrintQuality	Sets the printer resolution to draft, low, medium, or high quality.
Zoom	Sets a percentage by which the size of the printout is scaled up or down. Setting the Zoom property to 50 would cause the report to be printed half-size.

You might be wondering how you can give the user choices of how to control the printer. Fortunately, this is a relatively easy task. Most of the properties of the printer can be set using the Printer Setup dialog box of the CommonDialog control. The properties of the CommonDialog control's Print dialog box match the properties of the Printer object. The common dialog box provides an easy way for the user to select various printer properties. The Print dialog box is shown in Figure 9.14.

▶ **See** "Using Built-In Dialog Boxes," **p. 135**

FIG. 9.14

The Print dialog box lets your users select and set up a printer, as well as select options such as number of copies.

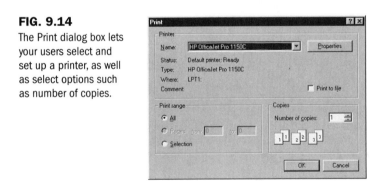

Starting a New Page

As you are sending information to the printer, at some point you will print more information than will fit on a single sheet of paper. For most printers, this is not a problem as they will automatically print multiple pages as needed. However, if you are including header information on your reports, such as the report name, date, or page number, this header information will not be automatically printed at the top of the next page. This is something that you have to control from your program.

Unfortunately, the `Printer` object does not have any events associated with it. Therefore, it cannot tell you when you have reached the end of a page or when a new page has started. The only way for you to determine this is by keeping up with the value of the `CurrentY` property of the printer. When the printer moves to a new page, the values of the `CurrentX` and `CurrentY` properties are reset to 0. However, you want to be able to determine when a page break is about to occur and handle the transition to the new page yourself.

To actually force the printer to start a new page is very easy. You simply issue the `NewPage` method as shown in the following line of code:

```
Printer.NewPage
```

The trick in creating proper page breaks in your report is to know when the current page is full. This is accomplished using a combination of the `CurrentY` and `ScaleHeight` properties and the `TextHeight` method of the printer. Take a look at Listing 9.7 to see how this is accomplished.

Listing 9.7   PRINTPAGE.FRM—Using the *NewPage* Method to Force Page Breaks

```
If Printer.CurrentY + Printer.TextHeight(stOutput) > _
    Printer.ScaleHeight Then
    Printer.NewPage
    PrintHeader '(PrintHeader is programmer-defined)
End If
Printer.Print stOutput
```

This code sums up the value of the `CurrentY` property and the height of the next line to be printed. If the sum of these numbers exceeds the `ScaleHeight` of the printer, the code forces a page break and then calls the `PrintHeader` to print the headers at the top of the next page. This code could easily be modified to handle printing a footer at the bottom of the current page before moving to the next page. This is shown in Listing 9.8.

Listing 9.8   PRINTPAGE.FRM—Handle Footers by Triggering Page Breaks Before the End of the Page

```
inPageHt = Printer.ScaleHeight - inFooterHt
If Printer.CurrentY + Printer.TextHeight(stOutput) > inPageHt Then
    PrintFooter
    Printer.NewPage
    PrintHeader
End If
Printer.Print stOutput
```

Of course, you are not limited to starting new pages only when the current page is full. You might also want to start a new page when a condition of the report changes. For example, if you are printing employee summary information, you might want to start a new page for each employee. Again, you start a new page by issuing the NewPage method.

Sending the Document to the Printer

As you are sending information to the printer, what you are really doing is sending information to the buffer of the Windows Print Manager. The information is not actually sent to the printer until you tell Windows to do so. Your printout is automatically sent to the printer when you shut down your application, but this does not provide sufficient control to be useful. In fact, while the Print Manager is waiting to print your report, it might be holding up printouts from other programs.

To tell Windows to send the report to the printer, you use the printer's EndDoc method. This method has no additional arguments, and simply tells Windows that your printout is finished. You run the EndDoc method by specifying the Printer object and the method name as shown in the following line:

```
Printer.EndDoc
```

Aborting the Printout

Finally, you will from time to time need to abort a printout before it is finished or prevent it from going to the printer at all. This need might arise for several reasons, including user decisions or runtime errors in the program. In any case, the method to use for aborting a printout is the KillDoc method, which is shown in the following code line:

```
Printer.KillDoc
```

One way to implement a cancel button for a printing operation is to use a form-level Boolean variable. Create a Cancel button whose Click event procedure sets the variable to True:

```
Private Sub cmdCancel_Click()
    blCancel = True

End Sub
```

While printing, check the variable with an If statement to see if you need to use the Killdoc method.

```
Dim inCounter As Integer

    blCancel = False

    For inCounter = 1 To 1000
        frmStatus.Caption = "Printing Line " & inCounter
        Printer.Print "This is line number " & inCounter
        DoEvents
        If blCancel = True Then
            Printer.KillDoc
            Exit For
```

```
        End If
    Next inCounter

    If blCancel = False Then Printer.EndDoc
```

In the preceding example, the DoEvents statement is used to temporarily give control back to the Windows event handler. The reason we need to do this is to make sure that the system is handling other events, specifically cmdCancel's Click event.

Typically, when this method is invoked, the Print Manager is handling the printout in the background, and the method kills the entire printout. However, there are several print-spooling options available, so using the KillDoc method does not guarantee that no information will be sent to the printer. Even if some pages have already been printed, however, the KillDoc method can still terminate the remainder of the printout, and the printer driver will reset the printer.

Part

II

Ch

9

Printing to a Form

While the bulk of this chapter has been aimed at creating reports on the printer, you have probably gathered that most of the methods and techniques demonstrated will also work for printing information to a form or a picture box. In fact, all the figures in the chapter have used a form or picture box to represent the printer, because it is easier to show you screen shots than to create a printer page and scan it back in for a figure.

Printing to a form is basically the same as printing to the printer. You can print text, create graphics, control the fonts of the printout, handle text centering, and anything else that you can do with the printer. The only things that we have covered for the printer that are not applicable to forms and picture boxes are the printer setup properties and the NewPage, EndDoc, and KillDoc methods covered in the previous section, "Controlling the Printer."

Clearing the Form

The key difference between printing to the printer and printing to a form is that a form has a limited amount of space and cannot create multiple pages. Although this does not prevent you from creating long reports on the screen, it does force you to use different techniques to handle more than a single page of information.

If you will be printing multi-page reports to a form or a picture box, you need to do two things. First, you need functions to allow the user to navigate within the pages of data you are printing. Second, you need to clear the object before you print (display) the next page.

For the sake of this example, our data will be a string array filled by the following code (this probably should occur during the form Load event):

```
Const NUM_RECORDS = 100
Dim stData(1 To NUM_RECORDS) As String
Dim inCount As Integer

For inCount = 1 To NUM_RECORDS
    stData(inCount) = "This is line " & inCount & " of a 100 line report."
Next inCount
```

Before starting the printout, you need to establish how much information will fit on a page (the variables should have been declared in the General Declarations section of the form):

```
'Calculate Line height of a line of text
inLineHeight = picOutput.TextHeight("X")

'Leave 2 lines for a footer
inPageHeight = picOutput.ScaleHeight - inLineHeight * 2

'Determine lines per page
inLinesPerPage = inPageHeight / inLineHeight
```

With this information, you can write a procedure to print a given page:

```
Sub DisplayPage(inPage As Integer)

    Dim inStartRecord As Integer
    Dim inLastRecord As Integer
    Dim inCounter As Integer

    If inPage <= 1 Then
        inStartRecord = 1
    Else
        inStartRecord = 1 + (inLinesPerPage * inPage) - inLinesPerPage
    End If

    If inStartRecord > NUM_RECORDS Then inStartRecord = NUM_RECORDS

    inLastRecord = inLinesPerPage * inPage
    If inLastRecord > NUM_RECORDS Then inLastRecord = NUM_RECORDS

    picOutput.Cls

    inCounter = inStartRecord

    While inCounter <= inLastRecord
        picOutput.Print stData(inCounter)
        inCounter = inCounter + 1
    Wend

    picOutput.CurrentY = picOutput.ScaleHeight - inLineHeight * 2
    picOutput.Print "Footer Line 1"
    picOutput.Print "Footer Line 2"

End Sub
```

The output of the sample code is seen in Figure 9.15. It is left as an exercise to the reader to write code for the Previous and Next buttons, which simply change a counter variable and call the DisplayPage procedure.

The earlier sample also showed you the form's Cls method (see the picOutput.Cls line), which is used to clear the form before printing the next page of information. It clears the form (or picture box) and resets the CurrentX and CurrentY properties to 0. This is the form's equivalent of the NewPage method.

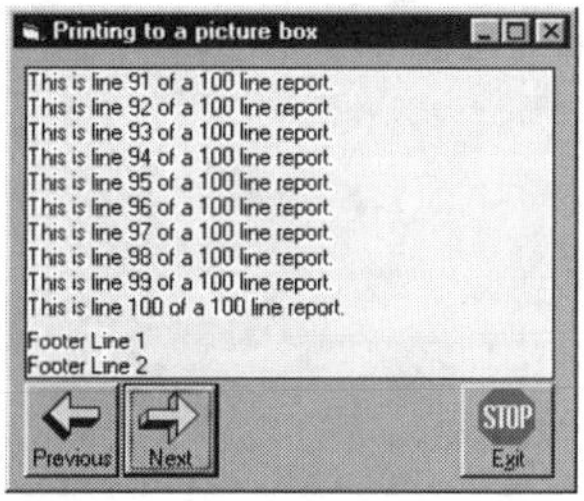

FIG. 9.15
This sample program
uses the dimensions of
the picture box to
determine where a
page begins and ends.

Using the *PrintForm* Method

In addition to the reporting techniques we've discussed, you can also print the entire viewable area of the form to a printer. The viewable area is all parts of the form displayed on the screen, excluding the border, the title bar, and the menu. Printing the entire form is a very simple way to generate a report from whatever is on the form. This is accomplished with the form's `PrintForm` method. To invoke this method, you simply specify the form to be printed as shown in the following line of code:

```
frmPrintPage.PrintForm
```

> **CAUTION**
> For information printed to the form to show up on the printed page, the `AutoRedraw` property of the form must be set to `True`.

If you omit the name of the form, the current form is assumed. Figure 9.16 shows how a form would appear on the screen and how the printed form would look.

> **CAUTION**
> On rare occasions, a video driver conflict will not allow the `PrintForm` method to work. On one occasion we had the CEO's laptop disassembled to the circuit-board level before figuring this out. Based upon this personal experience, I would suggest that you should use this method of printing information sparingly.

Exploring Printer Functions You Can Create

At this point, you have seen most of the properties and methods that are used to create printouts on the screen and the printer. This section shows you how to use those methods to create procedures that handle a number of text effects for you. The procedures presented in this section are designed to be as generic as possible, to give them the widest possible range of usefulness. For example, while it would be fairly easy to create a routine to center a piece of text horizontally on a printed page, the routine presented here allows you to center the text within any region on either a printed page or screen object (form or picture box). This allows you to use the procedures almost anywhere in your code.

FIG. 9.16
The form on the left shows what you see on-screen, and the one on the right shows which parts of a form are omitted by the PrintForm method.

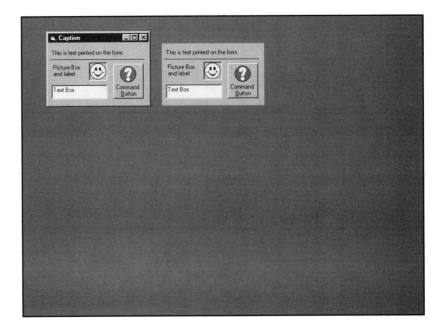

Aligning the Text on a Page

One of the most commonly used techniques is to align the text on the page. If you use word processors, you are probably familiar with the concept of text justification. The three main types of justification are left-justified, right-justified, and centered. These all refer to the horizontal position of the text within the line. In addition, we will look at aligning text vertically with the top or bottom of the page and at centering the text vertically in the page.

Moving to the Left   Left-justifying text is the simplest way to align text. If left alone, the Print method will start at the left edge of the output object and print from left to right. The routine shown in Listing 9.9 shows the function for left-justifying text and the routine that calls the function. The call to the procedure specifies the output object, the starting CurrentX and CurrentY properties for the printout, the size of the print region, and the text to be printed.

Listing 9.9   TEXTFUNC.FRM—Setting the *CurrentX* Property to Left-Justify Text

```
Dim txStr As String
Dim objWid As Integer
Dim  objHgt As Integer

txStr = Text1.Text
objWid = Picture1.ScaleWidth
objHgt = Picture1.ScaleHeight
Picture1.Cls
LeftJustify Picture1, 5, 5, objWid, objHgt, txStr
```

```
Private Sub LeftJustify(objOut As Object, LMarg, TMarg, RgWid, RgHgt _
        As Integer, InptStr As String)

    objOut.CurrentX = LMarg
    objOut.CurrentY = TMarg
    objOut.Print InptStr
End Sub
```

This same routine could be used to align text at the top of the specified region.

Moving to the Right   Right-justifying text is a little trickier than handling left-justified text. To align text with the right edge of a region, you must know the size of the text and the size of the region. As with the procedure for left-justifying text, the size and position of the region are passed to the procedure to right-justify the text. Therefore, the key task involved is to determine the size of the text to be printed. As you know, this can be accomplished with the TextWidth method. Listing 9.10 shows how the right-justification is accomplished. The results of the procedure are displayed in Figure 9.17.

Listing 9.10   TEXTFUNC.FRM—Using the *TextWidth* Function to Determine Where to Print Right-Justified Text

```
Private Sub RightJustify(objOut As Object, LMarg, TMarg, RgWid, RgHgt _
        As Integer, InptStr As String)

    Dim txMarg As Integer

    txMarg = RgWid - objOut.TextWidth(InptStr) - 10
    If txMarg < 0 Then txMarg = 0
    objOut.CurrentX = LMarg + txMarg
    objOut.CurrentY = TMarg
    objOut.Print InptStr

End Sub
```

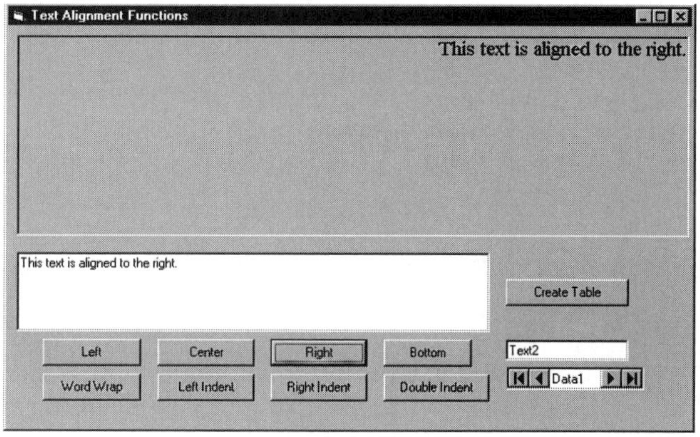

FIG. 9.17

A sample program demonstrates a technique for right-justification of text.

Text can be aligned along the bottom of the object as well. This is handled by the routine in Listing 9.11, which uses the TextHeight method to determine the position of the text.

Listing 9.11   TEXTFUNC.FRM—Using *TextHeight* to Handle Alignment Along the Bottom of the Object

```
Private Sub BottomAlign(objOut As Object, LMarg, TMarg, RgWid, RgHgt _
        As Integer, InptStr As String)

    Dim txMarg As Integer

    txMarg = RgHgt - objOut.TextHeight(InptStr) - 10
    If txMarg < 0 Then txMarg = 0
    objOut.CurrentX = LMarg
    objOut.CurrentY = TMarg + txMarg
    objOut.Print InptStr
End Sub
```

Staying in the Middle   The final alignment function is centering. Centering is accomplished by determining the blank space available on the line and placing an equal amount of the space on both sides of the text to be printed. This is again accomplished using the CurrentX property and the TextWidth method. Listing 9.12 shows the procedure for centering text horizontally on the page. A similar method can be used to center the text vertically on the page, or to center the text in both directions. Figure 9.18 shows the results of the centering operation.

Only horizontal centering is shown in the listing, but all three routines are included in the sample project TextFunc.Vbp. You can download this project from the Que Web site at **www.mcp.com/info/0-7897/0-7897-1288-1**.

Listing 9.12   TEXTFUNC.FRM—The Custom *CenterText* Function

```
Private Sub CenterText(objOut As Object, LMarg, TMarg, RgWid, RgHgt _
        As Integer, InptStr As String)

    Dim txMarg As Integer

    txMarg = (RgWid - objOut.TextWidth(InptStr)) / 2
    If txMarg < 0 Then txMarg = 0
    objOut.CurrentX = LMarg + txMarg
    objOut.CurrentY = TMarg
    objOut.Print InptStr

End Sub
```

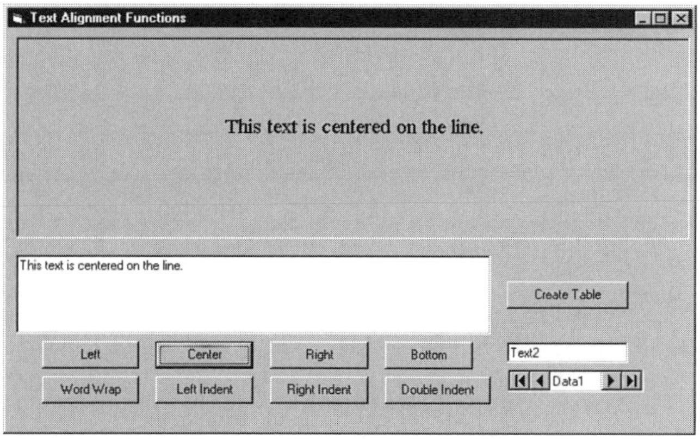

FIG. 9.18
Center text on the page either horizontally, vertically, or both.

Part
II

Ch

9

Using Word Wrapping in Your Printouts

One of the most useful functions that you can create is word wrapping. Word wrapping breaks up a line of text (usually at a space) and places additional text on the following lines of the printout. This prevents the information in the report from being printed off the edge of the page. To handle its task, the word wrapping function performs the following steps:

1. Finds the first/next word in the text using the InStr function to look for a space
2. Adds the word to a variable containing the line to be printed
3. Determines whether the text in the variable will fit on the current line
4. Repeats Steps 1 through 3 until the maximum number of words are included for the line
5. Prints the line of text
6. Removes the printed text from the input string
7. Repeats these steps until the entire input string has been printed

The procedure to handle word wrapping is shown in Listing 9.13. Figure 9.19 shows the input text in the text box and the word wrapped text in the picture box.

Listing 9.13 TEXTFUNC.FRM—Word Wrapping Ensures that Information Is Not Printed Past the End of the Line

```
Private Sub WordWrap(objOut As Object, LMarg, TMarg, RgWid, RgHgt _
        As Integer, InptStr As String)

    Dim StrtPos As Integer
    Dim EndPos As Integer
    Dim TxtLen As Integer
    Dim PrntLn As String
    Dim PrntIn As String
```

continues

Listing 9.13 Continued

```
PrntIn = InptStr
objOut.CurrentY = TMarg

Do
    EndPos = 0
    TxtLen = 0
    PrntLn = ""
    Do
        StrtPos = EndPos + 1
        EndPos = InStr(StrtPos, PrntIn, " ")
        PrntLn = Left(PrntIn, EndPos)
        TxtLen = objOut.TextWidth(PrntLn)
    Loop Until TxtLen > RgWid - 10 Or EndPos = 0
    If EndPos = 0 Then
        PrntLn = PrntIn
        PrntIn = ""
    Else
        PrntLn = Left(PrntIn, StrtPos - 1)
        PrntIn = LTrim(Mid(PrntIn, StrtPos))
    End If
    objOut.CurrentX = LMarg
    objOut.Print PrntLn
Loop While Len(PrntIn) > 0

End Sub
```

FIG. 9.19

Word wrapping makes your report look more professional.

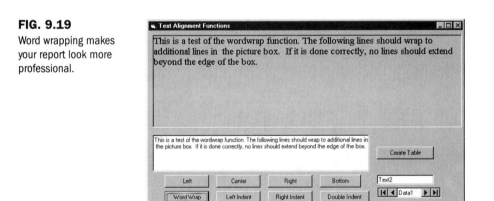

As with the other procedures, the WordWrap procedure allows you to specify the starting position and print region size for the output. This gives you much greater flexibility in what you can accomplish with the procedure. By varying the starting position and region size, you can handle left, right, and double indents for your paragraphs. The results of these techniques are shown in Figures 9.20 through 9.22. The actual code is contained in the sample project.

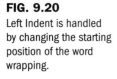

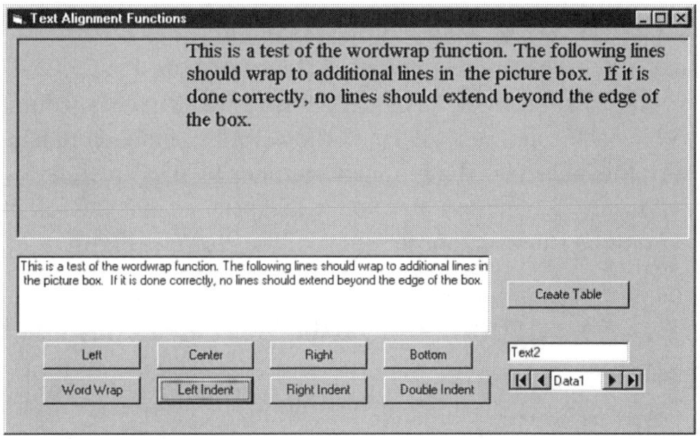

FIG. 9.20
Left Indent is handled by changing the starting position of the word wrapping.

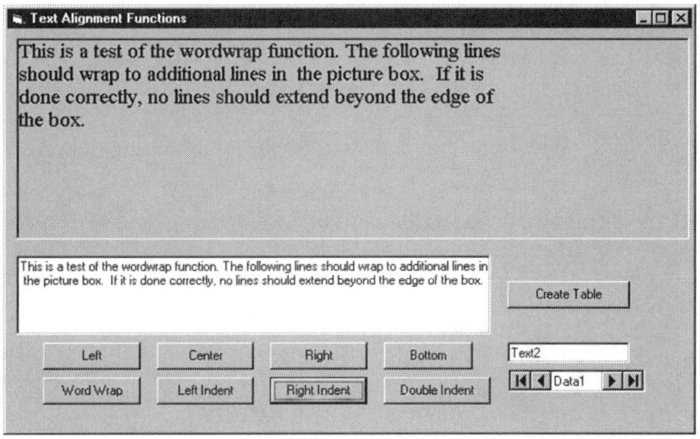

FIG. 9.21
Right Indent is handled by changing the print region width for the word wrapping.

FIG. 9.22
Double Indent is handled by changing both the starting position and the region width.

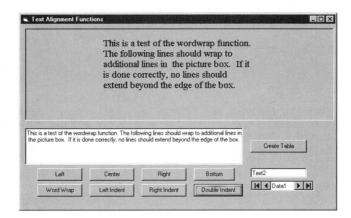

Creating a Table with a Display Grid

The final technique we want to show you is how to create a table. The table uses several of the functions that we just created. Specifically, it uses the CenterText function to center the table headers within each column. It also uses the WordWrap function to handle word wrapping within a cell. Finally, the table uses the graphics methods to draw the lines of the table. The example presented in Listing 9.14 shows how you would print a table of book titles, ISBN numbers, and comments from the Biblio database. The table is shown in Figure 9.23.

Listing 9.14 TEXTFUNC.FRM—Using Text Functions and Line Methods to Create a Table

```
Dim txStr As String
Dim LineY As Integer
Dim  I As Integer
Dim  objWid As Integer
Dim  objHgt As Integer
Dim ColLft(1 To 3) As Integer, ColWid(1 To 3) As
Intege

Printer.Font.Name = "Times New Roman"
Printer.Font.Size = 14
Printer.Orientation = vbPRORLandscape
objWid = Printer.ScaleWidth - 20
objHgt = Printer.ScaleHeight - 10
ColLft(1) = 10
ColWid(1) = objWid / 3
ColLft(2) = ColLft(1) + ColWid(1)
ColWid(2) = objWid / 3
ColLft(3) = ColLft(2) + ColWid(2)
ColWid(3) = objWid - ColWid(1) - ColWid(2)
LineY = 10
Printer.Line (ColLft(1), LineY)-(ColLft(1) + objWid, LineY)
CenterText Printer, ColLft(1), LineY + 5, ColWid(1), objHgt, "Title"
CenterText Printer, ColLft(2), LineY + 5, ColWid(2), objHgt, "ISBN"
CenterText Printer, ColLft(3), LineY + 5, ColWid(3), objHgt, "Comments"
Printer.Font.Size = 10

For I = 1 To 2
    LineY = Printer.CurrentY + 10
    Printer.Line (ColLft(1), LineY)-(ColLft(1) + objWid, LineY)
    txStr = Data1.Recordset!Title & ""
    LeftJustify Printer, ColLft(1), LineY + 5, ColWid(1), objHgt, txStr
    t xStr = Data1.Recordset!ISBN & ""
    LeftJustify Printer, ColLft(2), LineY + 5, ColWid(2), objHgt, txStr
    txStr = Data1.Recordset!Comments & ""
    WordWrap Printer, ColLft(3), LineY + 5, ColWid(3), objHgt, txStr
    Data1.Recordset.MoveNext
Next I

LineY = Printer.CurrentY + 10
Printer.Line (ColLft(1), LineY)-(ColLft(1) + objWid, LineY)
Printer.Line (ColLft(1), 10)-(ColLft(1), LineY)
Printer.Line (ColLft(2), 10)-(ColLft(2), LineY)
```

```
Printer.Line (ColLft(3), 10)-(ColLft(3), LineY)
Printer.Line (ColLft(1) + objWid, 10)-(ColLft(1) + objWid, LineY)

Printer.EndDoc
```

FIG. 9.23

You can create tables using text functions.

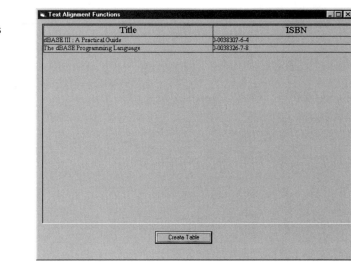

From Here...

In this chapter, you have seen how you can display reports on the screen and print them on paper. You also saw that while the `Print` method is fairly simple, you can use code to create a number of text effects in your printouts. You even saw how graphics could be used to enhance your reports. To learn more about some of the topics covered in this chapter, refer to the following:

- To learn more about the Picturebox and drawing functions, see Chapter 12, "Working with Graphics."

- To learn more about the options available for displaying text and fonts, see Chapter 13, "Working with Text, Fonts, and Colors."

CHAPTER 10

Managing Your Project

In Chapter 8, "Programming Basics," you learned a little about writing code to make your computer programs accomplish various tasks. You saw how you can manipulate data and how control statements allow you to execute repetitive tasks and to selectively execute statements. However, there is more to creating a good, maintainable program than just writing code.

One of the things you need to be able to do is create reusable pieces of code and reusable program pieces so you are not constantly reinventing the wheel (or the program, in this case). Another important skill is the ability to manage those various pieces of code and forms effectively. This chapter deals with both of these aspects of project management. First, we discuss how you can use *procedures* to eliminate repetitive code in your programs. Then you learn how those procedures and other program components are added to your project. Finally, this chapter gives you a brief look at compiling and distributing your programs for others to use. ■

Using the same code in multiple parts of your program

You often find that several parts of your program perform the same function. It is easier to maintain your program if you only have the code for the function in one place.

Reusing forms that were created for other programs

You can use the same form in multiple programs, or you can create a form template to make it easier to create similar forms.

Managing custom controls in the program

As you work more with Visual Basic, you will probably add third-party controls to your set of tools. You will see how to add these controls to your project.

Keeping up with all the pieces

Your programs will typically consist of a number of forms, some code modules, class modules, and possibly some user-defined controls. Visual Basic provides you with a set of tools to manage all these pieces.

Getting your program to the users

After you create your program, you need to distribute it to your users. You see how to compile your program and use the Setup Wizard to create distribution sets.

Using Procedures and Functions

As you create more and larger programs, you will often find yourself using the same block of code over and over in several places throughout your program and in multiple programs. Surely there must be a better way to handle repetitive code than to just place it in multiple locations in your program. The solution is the use of functions and procedures. Functions and procedures are segments of code that perform a particular task and then return processing to the area of the code from which they were called. This means that a procedure can be called from multiple places in your code and, if set up properly, can be used with multiple programs.

You have already been exposed to working with procedures even if you didn't know it. Each time you entered code to be executed by a command button (or other control) in response to an event, you were building an event procedure. These procedures are called by the program when an event is triggered. As you might already know, you can also create your own procedures and call them when you need them. The procedures that you build are referred to as Sub procedures (or subroutines) to distinguish them from event procedures. Although the code in earlier examples was mostly in the event procedures, it is quite possible that a "real" program will contain more code in user-defined subprocedures.

Working with Procedures

The key idea behind working with procedures is to break your program down into a series of smaller tasks. Each of these tasks can then be encapsulated in a procedure, function, or possibly a class. (Classes are discussed in Chapter 2, "Introduction to the Development Environment.") There are several advantages to programming in this manner:

- You can test each task individually. The smaller amount of code in a procedure makes it easier to debug, and easier to work on the same project with other developers.

- You can eliminate redundant code by calling a procedure each time a task needs to be performed, instead of repeating the program code.

- You can create a library of procedures that can be used in more than one program, saving yourself development time in new projects.

- Program maintenance is easier for a couple of reasons. First, if code is not repeated, you have to edit it only once. In addition, separating key components (for example, the user interface and the database functions) allows you to make major changes in one part of the program without recoding the whole thing.

> **TIP** To make your code reusable, use comments often. This allows another programmer (or yourself after a long period of time) to quickly see the purpose of each procedure.

Creating the Procedure   As with your program as a whole, creating a procedure starts with design. You need to determine the task to be performed and the inputs and outputs of the procedure. After this is done, you can start the actual coding of the procedure. There are two ways to start building a procedure in Visual Basic—starting from scratch or using the Add

Procedure dialog box. Both methods are relatively easy, and the one you use is a matter of personal preference. Also, both methods require you to be in the Code window before you can build a procedure.

To create a procedure from scratch, place your cursor in the Code window in a location that is not within a currently defined function or procedure. This would be after the End Sub statement of a procedure, before the Sub statement of another procedure, or at the top of the Code window. Figure 10.1 shows where you can start.

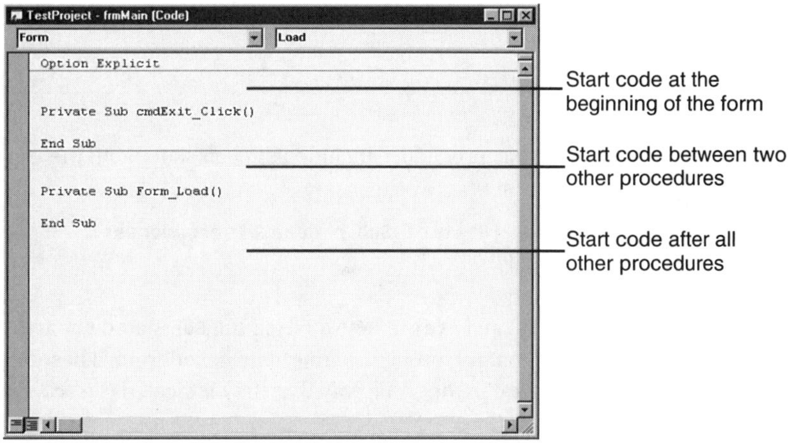

FIG. 10.1
Start a procedure in the Code window by using a Sub statement.

Start code at the beginning of the form

Start code between two other procedures

Start code after all other procedures

Part
II
Ch
10

TIP Placing your procedures in alphabetical order makes it easier to find them when you page through the Code window. However, they will always be in alphabetical order in the Code window's drop-down Procedure box.

You can create a new procedure in the Code window with the following steps:

1. Open the code for Form1 by clicking the View Code button.
2. Type the keyword **Sub,** followed by a space.
3. Type the name of your new procedure—**FirstProc** in this example.
4. Press the Enter key to create the procedure.

When you press Enter, three things happen—a set of parentheses is added at the end of the Sub statement, an End Sub statement is placed in the Code window, and the current object in the Procedure drop-down list of the code editing window becomes your new procedure name. This is shown in Figure 10.2 for a procedure named FirstProc.

You are now ready to enter any commands that you want to run when the procedure is called.

FIG. 10.2

The End Sub statement is automatically added when you define a new procedure.

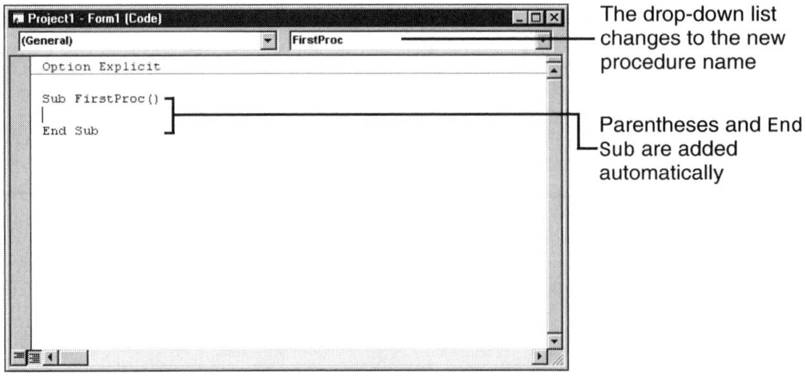

The drop-down list changes to the new procedure name

Parentheses and End Sub are added automatically

The full syntax of a Sub procedure includes the Sub statement, the End Sub statement, and the procedure commands:

```
[Public ¦ Private] [Static] Sub procname([arguments])
statements_to_be_run
End Sub
```

The Public, Private, and Static keywords in the Sub statement are optional parameters that affect the locations that the procedure might be called from. These keywords indicate the scope of the procedure in the same way that they indicated the scope of a variable.

▶ **See** " Determining Where a Variable Can Be Used," **p. 172**

The other method of creating a procedure is to use the Add Procedure dialog box (see Figure 10.3). You access this dialog box by choosing Tools, Add Procedure.

FIG. 10.3

Although typing it in by hand is faster, you can also create a new procedure in the current module or form by using the Add Procedure dialog box.

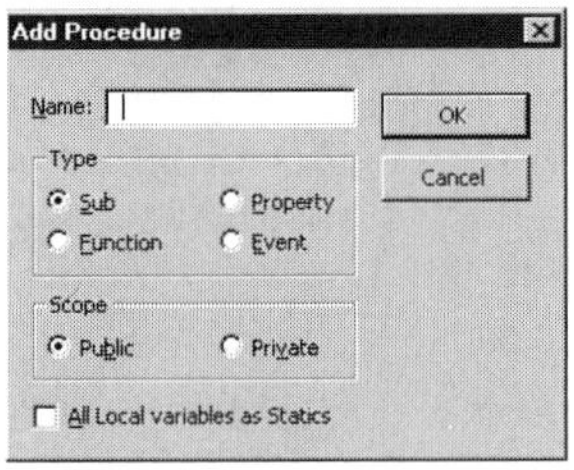

After you are in the dialog box, perform the following steps to create the shell of your procedure:

1. Enter the name of the procedure in the Name text box.
2. Choose the type of procedure (Sub, Function, Property, or Event).
3. Choose the scope of the procedure (Public or Private).
4. Choose whether to treat All Local Variables as Statics.

To create a procedure, you need to choose the Sub procedure type. This is the same as the procedures that are used in handling events in your code. A *function type of procedure* is one that returns a specific value. These procedures are covered later in this chapter. A *property procedure* is one used to set or retrieve the value of a property in a form or class module. An *event procedure* is one that is used to respond to an event in a form or class module. The Property and Event procedures are described in Chapter 32, "Using Classes in Visual Basic."

▶ **See** "Property Procedures," **p. 835**

After you have entered the necessary information, choose OK. Visual Basic then creates the framework of a procedure in the Code window.

Running the Procedure   After a procedure has been developed, you need a way to run it from other parts of your program. There are two methods for running a procedure—use the Call statement or use just the procedure name. With either method, you simply specify the procedure name and any arguments that are required by the procedure. (The arguments are the ones specified in the Sub statement when you defined the procedure.)

The syntax for running a procedure is as follows:

```
Call procname([arguments])
```

or

```
procname arguments
```

In either syntax, *procname* refers to the name of the procedure. This is the name that is specified in the Sub statement that defined the procedure. *Arguments* refers to the parameters passed to the procedure. In the calling statement, the arguments can be literal values, variables, or functions that return the proper data type. This is different from the Sub statement where all the arguments have to be variable names. All parameters must be separated by commas.

Let's look at a brief example of a procedure that uses parameters. Suppose your program needs to log all of its operations and errors to a text file. A procedure that handled writing messages to the log file, along with a date and time, could be very useful:

```
Sub LogPrint(stMessage As String)
Dim inFileNum As Integer
    inFileNum = FreeFile
    Open "C:\EVENTLOG.TXT" for append as #inFileNum
    Print #inFileNum, Now & " - " & stMessage
    Close #inFileNum
End Sub
```

The following line of code calls the procedure. When calling a procedure, you can supply values for its arguments using either a variable, a literal string, or a combination of the two:

```
LogPrint "Error Opening the file " & stUserFile
```

The LogPrint procedure is very simple, yet it saves a lot of time in the long run. It makes the calling code shorter and more readable. In addition, if you ever to want change the output of the log file from a text file to a database, printer, or pager, you only have to change the LogPrint function itself.

Part
II

Ch
10

> **CAUTION**
>
> Typically, you must include the same number of parameters in the calling statement as are present in the definition of the procedure. Also, the values supplied by the calling statement must match the data types expected by the procedure. Violating either of these conditions results in an error when you run your program.

N O T E You can use optional parameters in a procedure. This is discussed in Chapter 37, "Advanced Code Techniques."

At the start of this section, I listed two methods of calling a procedure. The following line of code calls the LogPrint procedure using the other syntax:

```
Call LogPrint ("The server was rebooted")
```

As you can see, the Call keyword can either be included or omitted in running the procedure. However, the Call keyword and parentheses go together. If you use the Call keyword, you must include the parameters in a set of parentheses. I recommend using the syntax that does not use Call. As you will see after looking at the examples in the next section, this makes it easier to distinguish between procedure calls and function calls.

Passing Data to the Procedure   There are two ways to get information into a procedure for processing—you can define the variables as public variables that are available everywhere in your program, or you can pass the variables directly to the procedure in the calling statement.

For example, you could add a second argument to the LogPrint procedure that allows it to work with multiple files:

```
Sub LogPrint(stLogFile As String, stMessage As String)
Dim inFileNum As Integer
    inFileNum = FreeFile
    Open stLogFile for append as #inFileNum
    Print #inFileNum, Now & " - " & stMessage
    Close #inFileNum
End Sub
```

However, this means that if you only wanted to use one log file, you still would have to pass the file name to the procedure each time you called it:

```
LogPrint "C:\LOGFILE.TXT", "Error Opening the file " & stUserFile
```

For this particular procedure, the stLogFile argument probably does not change much throughout the program. However, hard-coding it into the LogPrint procedure does not make much sense either, so a public variable would be the logical choice:

```
Public stLogFileName As String
Sub LogPrint(stMessage As String)
    Dim inFileNum As Integer
```

```
      inFileNum = FreeFile
      Open stLogFileName for append as #inFileNum
      Print #inFileNum, Now & " - " & stMessage
      Close #inFileNum
End Sub
```

Before calling the procedure, your program would need to set the value of stLogFileName. The Public keyword makes it visible to all the other procedures in your program. The variable inFileNum, on the other hand, can only be used within the LogPrint procedure, as it should be.

If you are going to use the variables in a number of procedures and the procedure is specific to the current program, it is better to set up the variables as public variables. However, for the sake of reusability among projects, it is a good idea to keep procedures as independent as possible. To do this, you should define all the necessary parameters to be passed to the procedure in the Sub statement and pass the parameters in the calling statement.

The parameters used by a procedure can provide two-way communication between the procedure and the calling program. The procedure can use information in the parameters to perform a calculation and then pass the results back to the calling program in another parameter.

Part
II
Ch
10

For example, the following procedure gets the height and width of a rectangle from the parameters list and then calculates the area and perimeter of the rectangle. These values are returned through the parameters list:

```
Sub CalcRectangle(rcWidth as Integer, rcHeight as Integer,_
    rcArea as Integer, rcPerimeter as Integer)
    rcArea = rcWidth * rcHeight
    rcPerimeter = 2 * (rcWidth + rcHeight)
End Sub
```

The procedure can be called by either of the following code segments in Listing 10.1.

Listing 10.1   PROCCALL.TXT—Two Ways of Calling a Procedure

```
'********************************
'This code can call the procedure
'********************************

sqWid = 5
sqHgt = 5
sqArea = 0
sqPerm = 0
Call CalcRectangle(sqWid, sqHgt, sqArea, sqPerm)

'************************************
'This code can also call the procedure
'************************************

newArea = 0
newPerm = 0
CalcRectangle 4, 10, newArea, newPerm
```

T I P

This example has a single output value, which makes it more suited to a function than a sub, but we discuss that shortly in the section entitled "Working with Functions."

Passing parameters to a procedure this way is known as *passing by reference*. In this case, the variable name passed to the procedure and the variable name used in the procedure both refer to (reference) the same location in memory. This is what enables the procedure to modify the value that is then passed back to the calling code. You can also pass a parameter to a procedure *by value*. This causes the procedure to use a *copy* of the information that was passed to it, which prevents the procedure code from modifying the value used by the calling program.

By default, when you declare a parameter for a procedure, passing by reference is used. To modify this behavior, you must explicitly tell Visual Basic to pass the parameter by value. Do this by placing the ByVal keyword in the parameter list before each variable that is to be passed by value. This is illustrated in the following line of code:

```
Sub CalcRectangle(ByVal rcWidth As Integer, ByVal rcHeight As Integer,_
    _rcArea, rcPerimeter As Integer)
```

CAUTION

If you are passing parameters by reference, you need to explicitly declare the variable in the calling program and in the procedure, and you need to be sure that the variable types are the same.

Exiting a Procedure Early   As your programs, and therefore procedures, grow in complexity, there might be times when you don't need to execute all the commands in the procedure. If you need to exit the procedure before all the commands have been executed, you can use the Exit Sub statement.

One way that we often use the Exit Sub statement is in the beginning of the procedure in a routine that checks parameters for proper values. If any of the parameters passed to procedure are the wrong type or have values that could cause a problem for the procedure, we use Exit Sub to terminate the procedure before the error occurs. This is a type of *data validation*. The following code modifies the previous area calculation code to perform this check:

```
Sub CalcRectangle(rcWidth as Integer, rcHeight as Integer, rcArea as Integer,
rcPerimeter as Integer)
If rcWidth <= 0 Or rcHeight <= 0 Then
    Exit Sub
   End If
   rcArea = rcWidth * rcHeight
   rcPerimeter = 2 * (rcWidth + rcHeight)
End Sub
```

Working with Functions

Functions are very similar to procedures, with one key difference—they return a value. This value can be assigned to a variable or used in expressions. Visual Basic has a variety of built-in functions that you can use, such as Abs which returns the absolute value of a number, or Left which returns a specified number of characters from the left end of a string. You can build your own functions, as well.

To build a function, you have the same two choices you had in building a procedure—start from scratch or use the Add Procedure dialog box. To start from scratch, select the point in the Code window where you want the function to start and then enter the keyword Function followed by the name of the function. The naming conventions for functions are the same as those for procedures. To use the Add Procedure dialog box, just select the Function Type on the dialog box. Either method will create the shell of the function just as it did for a procedure. This shell is shown in the following lines of code:

```
Public Function NumAverage()

End Function
```

Although the first line is an acceptable function declaration, most of the time you will define the type of value that will be returned by the function. You define this function type like you define variable types in a Dim statement—by using the As keyword followed by the variable type. This function type declaration follows the parentheses that enclose the parameter declaration. In addition, you will typically declare the parameters that are passed to the function in the declaration statement. A more complete declaration statement is shown in the following line:

```
Public Function NumAverage(inpt1 As Single, inpt2 As Single) As Single
```

The other key difference between building a function and a procedure is that you will assign a value to the function somewhere within the code of the function. This value must be of the same type as specified in the function declaration. This is shown in the second line of the following code:

```
Public Function NumAverage(inpt1 As Single, inpt2 As Single) As Single
    NumAverage = (inpt1 + inpt2) / 2
End Function
```

N O T E Although your function code can assign a value to the function multiple times, only the last value assigned before the end (or exit) of the function is returned. ■

When you call a function, you typically assign its return value to a variable in your program, or use the value in a conditional statement as shown here:

```
'Assigning a function to a variable
AvgNum = NumAverage(25, 15)

'Using a function in a conditional expression
If NumAverage(num1, num2) > 20 Then Msgbox "What an average!"
```

N O T E If you need your function to simply perform a task (opening a database, for example), you can call the function the same way that you would call a procedure, throwing away the return value. ■

Part
II

Ch
10

There are a number of functions built and demonstrated in the FUNCDEMO.VBP project, which you can download from **www.mcp.com/info/0-7897/0-7897-1288-1.**

Determining the Scope of Procedures and Functions

When you create a procedure (or function), you might want to limit where it can be used, and how resources are allocated to make its code available to other parts of your program. Where a procedure can be called from is referred to as the *scope* of the procedure.

Procedures can be defined in either of two ways: *public procedures* or *private procedures.* Which of these keywords you use in the Sub statement determines which other procedures or programs have access to your procedure.

N O T E   The scope of procedures and functions is related to the scope of variables, which is discussed in the section entitled "Determining Where a Variable Can Be Used" in Chapter 8, "Programming Basics."

▶ **See** "Determining Where a Variable Can Be Used," **p. 172**

Going Public   If you want to have your procedure or function available throughout your program, you need to use the Public keyword when you define the procedure. Using the Public keyword allows a procedure defined in one form or module to be called from another form or module. However, you have to be more careful with the names of public procedures because each public procedure must have a unique name.

If you omit the keywords Public and Private from the Sub statement, the procedure is set up by default as a public procedure.

Keeping It Private   Using the Private keyword in the Sub statement lets the procedure be accessed from only the form or module in which it is defined. There are, of course, advantages and disadvantages to this approach. The advantage is that you can have private procedures of the same name in separate modules. The disadvantage is that the procedure is not accessible from other modules.

One thing you might have noticed in working with event procedures in other chapters is that they are, by default, private procedures. This is because, typically, controls are not accessed outside of the form on which they reside. This is an example of *information hiding,* or *encapsulation,* a technique used in object-oriented programming. If you are sharing a module with a team of developers, you could define the functions they call as public, while the internal procedures they don't need to know about remain private.

Preserving Variables   Typically, when a procedure is executed, the variables it uses are created, used in the procedure, and then destroyed when the procedure is terminated. However, there might be times when you want to preserve the value of the variables for future calls to the procedure. You can handle this by using the Static keyword. This keyword can be applied to the declaration of the variables in the procedure or in the declaration of the procedure itself.

When `Static` is used in a variable declaration, only the variables included in the `Static` statement are preserved. If you use the `Static` keyword in the procedure declaration, all the variables in the procedure are preserved. In the following example, `inCurrentCount` is a static variable:

```
Public Function AddItUp(inNew As Integer) As Integer

    Static inCurrentCount As Integer
    inCurrentCount = inCurrentCount + inNew
    AddItUp = inCurrentCount

End Function
```

TIP For efficiency's sake, it's important to place your procedures in the appropriate scope. Giving a procedure too broad of a scope (for example, making a procedure public when it only needs to be private) wastes valuable system resources. If you create a public procedure, Visual Basic must allocate appropriate resources to make it available to all parts of your program. Using the `Static` keyword to force a procedure to "remember" its local variables causes an extra allocation of resources as well. In general, you should make procedures private if possible, and avoid the use of static variables as well. This allows Visual Basic to manage memory more efficiently, since it is free to unload the various sections of code as needed.

Part
II

Ch
10

Reusing Functions and Procedures

You can create a procedure in either of two places—a form or a module. Where you place the procedure depends upon where you need to use it and what its purpose is. If the procedure is specific to a form or modifies the properties of the form or its associated controls, you should probably place the procedure in the form itself.

If, on the other hand, you are using the procedure with multiple forms in your program or have a generic procedure used by multiple programs, you should place it in a module. The storage location of your procedure is determined by where you create it. If you want, you can move a procedure from a form to a module or vice versa by using cut-and-paste editing.

Storing a Procedure in a Form File   To create a procedure in a form file, you just need to choose the form from the Project window and then access the code for the form. This is done by either double-clicking the form itself (or any control) or choosing the View Code button in the project window (see Figure 10.4). After the Code window appears, you create a procedure as described in the earlier section "Creating a Procedure."

Using a Module File for Procedures   A module file contains only code, no form elements or events. If you already have a module file in your project, you can create a new procedure by selecting the file, opening the Code window, and then using the previous steps to build the procedure.

TIP Double-clicking the module name in the Project window automatically opens the Code window for the module.

FIG. 10.4

You can select a form for your procedure from the Project window.

Button used to open the Code window

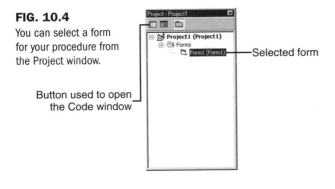

Selected form

If you don't have a module file in your project, or if you want to use a new module, you can create a module by selecting Project, Add Module. You can also create a new module by clicking the arrow on the Add Form button in the toolbar and then choosing Module from the drop-down menu. Either way, a new module is created and the Code window appears for you to begin editing. When you save your project or exit Visual Basic, you are asked for a file name for the module file.

N O T E The toolbar button for adding new forms and modules is a drop-down button, which means clicking the arrow will give you a list of items. Once an item has been selected, the icon on the button changes. ▨

Working with Multiple Forms

Although some programs you write will be simple enough that you can use a single form, most will be made up of multiple forms. One reason for this is the limitation of the amount of space on a single form. Another more important reason is that you will want to use multiple forms in your program to logically separate program tasks. For example, if you have a task in your program that is not performed often, it makes more sense to put it ont a separate form than try to squeeze it onto a single form with everything else. Also, loading and unloading forms as you need them saves system resources. In other words, your program takes up as little space as possible while running.

Adding New Forms to Your Program

When Visual Basic first starts a new project, typically it loads one blank form, as shown in Figure 10.5. As you design your program, you add controls to this form and write code to handle events that occur on the form.

At some point in your design, you will decide that you need one or more additional forms to handle a new task or provide space to relieve the crowding on the initial form. Adding a new form is simple. You can either click the Add Form button or select Project, Add Form. This places a new blank form on the screen. This form looks just like your first form initially did.

If you did not rename your first form from the default of Form1, the new form is named Form2 (or Form3, Form4, and so on). Otherwise, the new form is named Form1.

FIG. 10.5

Visual Basic starts a new project with a single blank form.

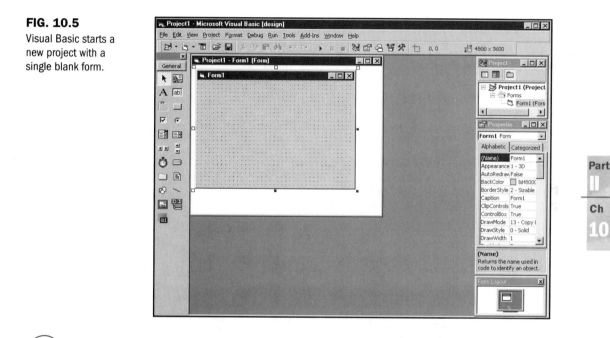

TIP You can add files, forms, or modules from a pop-up menu by right-clicking within the Project window.

After you have added a new form, you can place controls on it and write code for its events, just like for the initial form. You also need to be able to access the new form from other forms in your program. This is handled through the Load and Unload statements and the Show and Hide methods of the form object.

▶ **See** "Displaying a Form," **p. 82**

Adding Code Modules to a Project

As you write more code to handle more events and more tasks, you will often find that you need to access the same procedure from a number of different places on a form or from multiple forms. If this is the case, it makes sense to store the procedure in a module file.

TIP If you have a library of common functions, such as printing routines, keep them in a separate module file so you can easily add the library to different projects.

A module file contains only Visual Basic code. It does not contain any controls, pictures, or other visual information. When the time comes to add a module file to hold your procedures, you can do this either by clicking the arrow on the Add Form button and choosing Module from the drop-down menu, or by choosing <u>P</u>roject, Add <u>M</u>odule. Either of these actions adds a new module to your project and places you in the Code window for the module (see Figure 10.6).

Module name

FIG. 10.6
You can open the Code window by double-clicking the module name in the Project window.

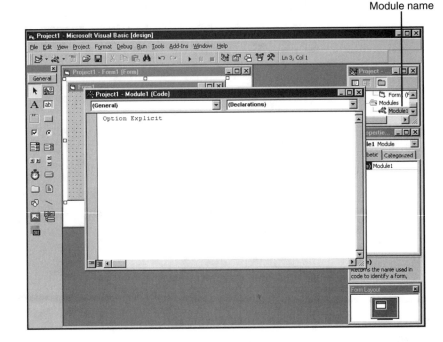

When you first open a new module, Visual Basic gives it the default name of `Module1` (or `Module2` for a second module, and so on). Like your forms and controls, it is a good idea to give the module a unique name. The module has a `Name` property, just as a form does. To change the name of the module, simply change the value of the `Name` property in the Property window.

Accessing the Forms and Modules of a Project

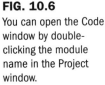As you add forms and modules to your program, they are added to the Project window. This window allows you to easily access any of the pieces of your program (see Figure 10.7). You simply select a form or module by clicking its name in the Project window. For a form, you can then click the View Object button to work on the design of the form, or click the View Code button to edit the code associated with the form. For a module, only the View Code button is enabled because a module has no visual elements. Double-clicking the name of a form has the same effect as clicking the View Object button. Double-clicking a module name has the same effect as clicking the View Code button.

FIG. 10.7
The Project window gives you easy access to all your forms and modules.

View Code button—

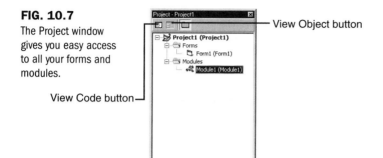

—— View Object button

Managing Components in Your Project

Forms and modules are just two of the types of components that you can add to your project. In addition, you can also add *custom controls* and *class modules*. Some of these components, such as forms and modules, are editable code. Others, such as third-party controls and DLLs, are usually already compiled. While these types of items are part of your project, they do not show up in the Project window and are added by means of some special dialog boxes.

Managing Program References

One of the things that you have to manage is your program's *references*. The references point to different library routines that enable your code to perform specific tasks. For example, if you will be accessing databases with your programs, you need to specify the Data Access Object library as one that is used by your code. Controlling references is quite easy in Visual Basic. The References dialog box lets you select the references required by your program by marking the check box to the side of the reference (see Figure 10.8). Mark the ones you need and unmark the ones you don't need. You access the References dialog box by selecting Project, References.

FIG. 10.8
The References dialog box lets you choose which libraries are used by your program.

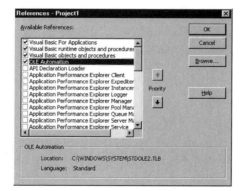

Part
II

Ch
10

TIP   After adding a reference to your project, its public constants and functions can be viewed in the Object Browser, which is displayed by clicking the Object Browser button or by pressing F2.

Controlling Your Controls

In a manner similar to library references, you can add and remove custom controls from your project. When you loaded Visual Basic, a number of custom controls were loaded into the Toolbox window automatically. However, you will usually need controls designed to perform specific tasks that are beyond the capabilities of the standard controls. You manage the custom controls in your project by using the Components dialog box (see Figure 10.9). Select Project, Components to access this dialog box. As with the References dialog box, you choose the custom controls to add to your program by marking the check box next to the control name. After you exit the dialog box, your control toolbox is modified to display the new controls.

FIG. 10.9
The Components dialog box lets you add controls to your project.

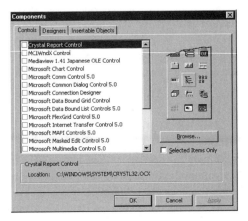

Adding Forms, Modules, and Classes to the Project

As you develop more programs, you might find that you have standard procedures or forms that can be used in many of your projects. You also might have developed custom procedures for getting the names and passwords of users, for opening files, or for any number of other tasks that are used in almost every program.

You could rebuild the form or rewrite the procedure for each program, but that would be a very inefficient way to do your program development. A better way is to reuse modules and forms that have been previously developed and fully tested.

Getting these modules and forms into your current project is a simple process. By selecting Project, Add File, you bring up the Add File dialog box (see Figure 10.10). This dialog box lets you locate and select files to be added to your current project. Unfortunately, the Add File dialog box lets you add only a single file at a time. Therefore, if you have multiple files to add, you must repeat the operation several times.

CAUTION

If you add the same form or module to separate projects, remember that changing functions in the module will affect all projects that use it. If you are about to radically change a shared module, use the Save *modulename* As option in the File menu or copy the module to another subdirectory first.

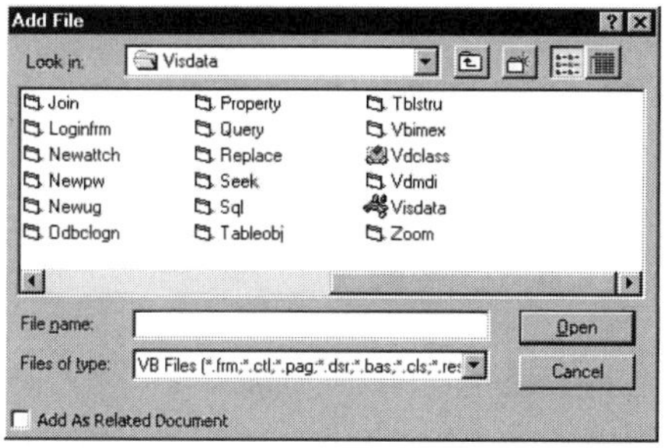

FIG. 10.10

The Add File dialog box can be accessed from the menu system, standard toolbar, by right-clicking in the Project window, or by pressing Ctrl+D.

NOTE Files with the .FRM and .FRX extensions are form files. Files with the .BAS extension are module files.

You also might want to use one of Visual Basic's form templates in your project. These templates are predefined forms that are set up for a specific function, such as an About Box, a Splash Screen, a DataGrid form, or a Tip of the Day form. The advantage of using these templates is that the skeleton of the form is already created for you. You simply add your own graphics, label captions, and minimal code to customize the form to your needs. As an example, Figure 10.11 shows the About Box form template.

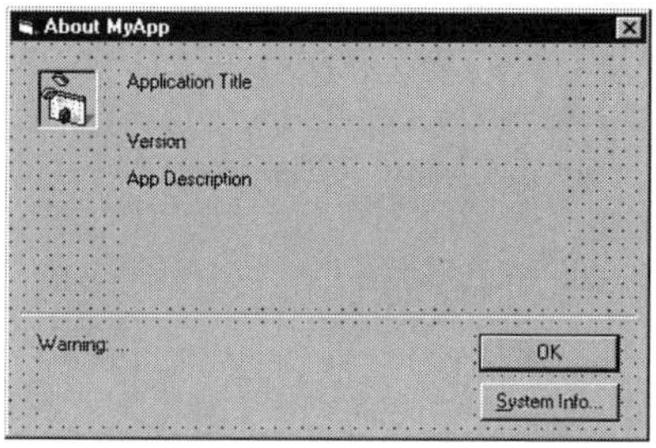

FIG. 10.11

Form templates make it easy to develop common pieces of a program.

To access one of the form templates, bring up the Add Form dialog box by clicking the Add Form button on the toolbar or selecting Project, Add Form (see Figure 10.12). You can then choose one of the form types from the New tab of the dialog box.

If you create a form that you think you will use in a number of programs, you can make a template out of it as well. Simply save the form in the form template folder of Visual Basic. Then the next time you want to add a new form, your template will appear in the Add Form dialog box as well.

FIG. 10.12
Form templates are "canned" templates that can be quickly customized and used in your project.

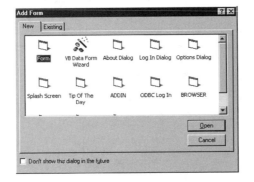

N O T E If you let Visual Basic install to the default directory, the forms templates are stored in the `\Program Files\DevStudio\Vb\Template\Forms` folder. This folder might be different on your machine, depending on where you installed Visual Basic.

Removing Pieces

To remove a module or form from your project, simply select the form or module in the Project window and choose Project, Remove *file name*. Visual Basic asks you to confirm that you want to remove the file and then removes it from your project.

Controlling How Your Program Starts

When you first start a programming project, Visual Basic assumes that the first form created is the one that will be displayed as soon as the program starts. Although this will be the case for many programs, for others you will want to start with one of the forms you create later in the development process. For some programs, you might not want to start with a form at all.

Setting the Startup Form

If the first form is not the one you want to use to start your program, Visual Basic lets you choose which of your forms is shown initially by the program. This selection is made in the *Projectname* – Project Properties dialog box, as shown in Figure 10.13. You access this dialog box by selecting Project, Project Properties.

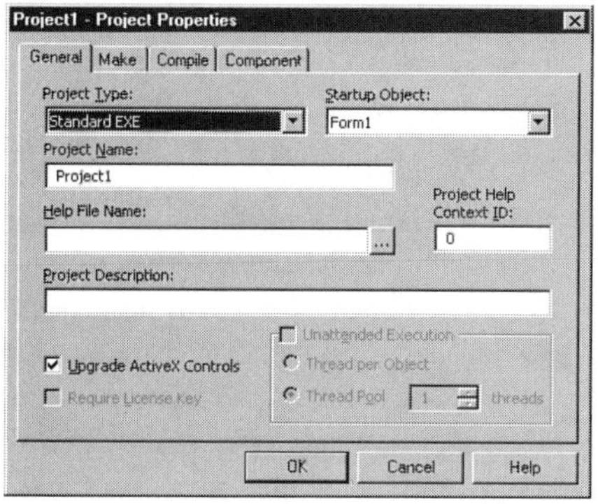

FIG. 10.13
The Startup Object list
lets you choose which
form is loaded when
your program starts.

Using *Sub Main*

You might have noticed that, in addition to listing all the forms contained in your project, the Startup Object list includes the entry Sub Main. This is a reserved procedure name that lets your program start without an initial form. If you choose this option, one of your module files must include a procedure called Main.

One reason to start your program with the Sub Main option might be that you need to perform some initialization routines before loading any forms. Another reason might be if you are developing a command-line utility that requires no user interaction.

Creating Distributable Programs

When you complete your program, it is time to move it out of the VB development environment so others can use it. The first step is to compile the source code. The objective here is to create an .EXE file (or .DLL, depending upon the project type) that can be distributed to other machines. After compiling, you create installation files for the program by using the Application Setup Wizard. The purpose of the Setup Wizard is to package your program and all necessary support files, so it will run on a machine that does not have Visual Basic installed.

Compiling Your Program

When you are ready to compile your program, all you have to do is select File, Make. This menu item lists the project name and the proper file extension for the type of program you are creating. For a Standard EXE or ActiveX EXE, the file extension is .EXE. For an ActiveX DLL, the file extension is .DLL, and for the ActiveX Control, the file extension is .OCX. After selecting the Ma_k_e item, you are shown the Make Project dialog box, which allows you to specify the name and location of the executable file. Visual Basic then does the rest of the work.

While Visual Basic handles the actual compilation with no intervention, there are a few decisions you need to make in the Compile tab of the *projectname* – Project Properties dialog box. The first choice to make is whether to compile to P-code or native code. P-code is the way Visual Basic programs have been compiled since version 1, while compiling to native code is a new option to Visual Basic 5.0. Native code is optimized for the processor chip and runs faster than P-code, but produces a significantly larger executable file. If you choose to compile to native code, you also need to make a decision about compiler optimization. You can choose to have the compiler try to create the smallest possible code, the fastest possible code, or not perform any optimization. You also have the option of compiling your program specifically for the Pentium Pro processor.

To choose the compiler options, you need to click the Compile tab of the Project Properties dialog box (see Figure 10.14). To squeeze every last bit of speed out of VB, you might want to also look at the Advanced Optimizations dialog box, also shown in Figure 10.14. As you can see, Microsoft put these options in here with a "use at your own risk" warning. However, I usually check Remove Array _B_ounds Checks, because the program code itself should do this, and _R_emove Safe Pentium™ FDIV Checks, which turns off software correction for the infamous Pentium chip bug. If you want to play it safe, the Advanced Options dialog box should probably be the last thing you do.

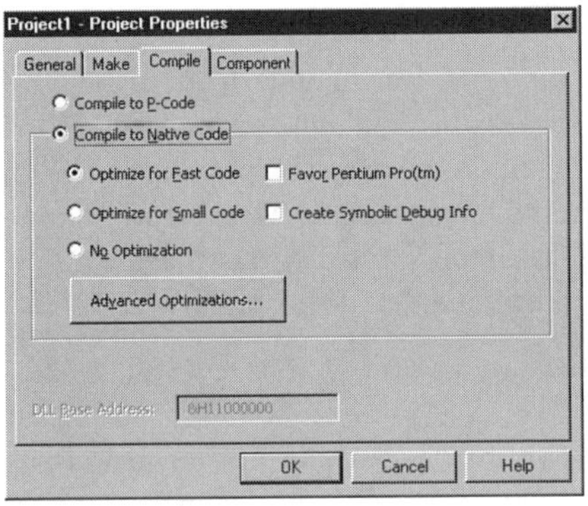

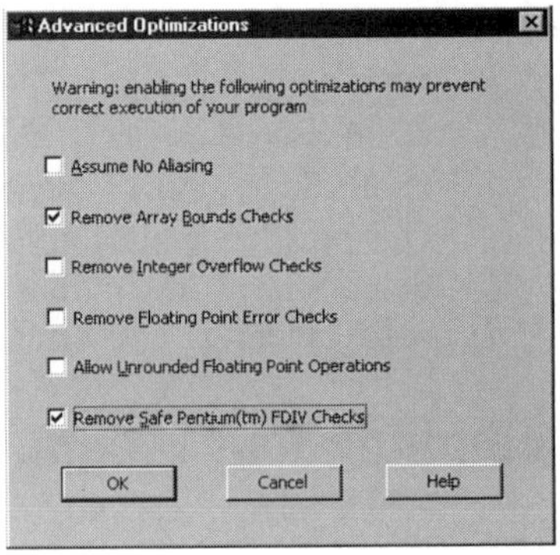

FIG. 10.14
In Visual Basic 5, there are several options for optimizing the compiled program.

Using the Setup Wizard

Even though you might have just compiled your code into an executable file, that executable file cannot run on its own. Users of your program must have some Visual Basic runtime files (that is, DLLs) properly installed first. I would be lying if I said that each new release of Visual Basic has made it simpler to distribute your application to other PCs; on the contrary, just the opposite has occurred. In the days of Visual Basic 3.0, sometimes copying the 400K file

VBRUN300.DLL and your EXE were the only steps required. Today, the equivalent Visual Basic 5.0 DLL file is over 1 megabyte in size. Additionally, the mere presence of a required DLL file is usually not enough; more often than not it must also be *registered* in the Windows Registry. On the bright side, the Application Setup Wizard included with Visual Basic 5.0 is much better than previous versions. The Application Setup Wizard is used to "package" your program with the required support files, so that it can be installed from a disk, directory, or the Internet—just like any off-the-shelf program. In this section, we focus on the setup steps for a Standard EXE project.

Using the Setup Wizard with a Standard EXE Project A shortcut to the Application Setup Wizard should have been installed with VB. If you run the Setup Wizard, after you get past the introductory message you see a screen like the one in Figure 10.15.

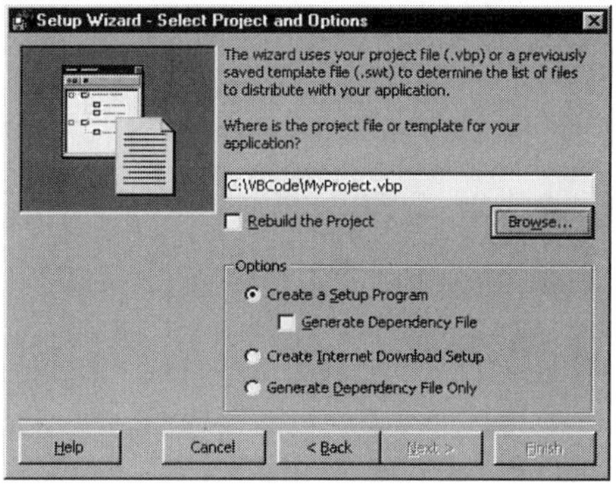

FIG. 10.15
The first step in the Application Setup Wizard is to choose a project and select the type of installation.

The purpose of this screen is to tell the Setup Wizard which project you want to work with, as well as what kind of installation to create. As you might guess, the Internet Download option is for distribution over the Internet. For a Standard EXE project, you should choose the default Create a Setup Program option. If you check Rebuild the Project, the Setup Wizard attempts to launch VB and compiles your EXE before adding it to the installation. I usually do not do this, because it adds an extra step. Note that you can choose Generate a Dependency File either as part of the standard setup or by itself. A dependency file holds information about all the files required by your program, for the purpose of combining the installation of your project with another one. After you press Next, you are presented with the Distribution Method screen, shown in Figure 10.16.

The screen in Figure 10.16 lets you select how to group the installation files. Unless you are distributing your application on floppy disks (which is becoming less and less common these days), you will probably want to choose one of the directory options. Single Directory means all the setup files will be placed in a single subdirectory on your hard drive. Disk Directories divides the files into floppy-size subdirectories, should you ever need to manually copy them to disk. If you know your application will always be installed from a network server or CD-ROM, Single Directory is the best choice. Depending on your choice, the next screen (not pictured here) asks you to select an installation directory or floppy disk size.

FIG. 10.16

The Application Setup Wizard can create install files on disks, a single subdirectory, or multiple subdirectories.

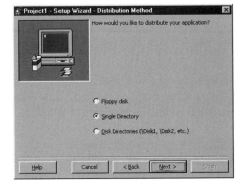

Now that you have told the Application Setup Wizard where to create the install files, it presents a series of screens as it determines what files are necessary. The first screen, ActiveX Server Components, is shown in Figure 10.17. (ActiveX server components are ActiveX DLLs or EXEs that your main project uses.) Although the setup wizard automatically scans your project's references for these items, you still have the option of adding and removing them here.

FIG. 10.17

The check box indicates an item (and its dependent files, if known) will be included in the installation package.

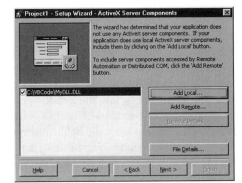

When you move on from the screen in Figure 10.17, the Setup Wizard scans your project and displays the File Summary, as shown in Figure 10.18. The File Summary lists all the files that the Setup Wizard thinks your application needs. If you have additional files to distribute, such as .INI or .BMP files used by your program, you can add them with the Add... button. You can also find out more information about individual files (such as the destination directory) by pressing the File Details... button.

Suppose you want to add another EXE, DLL, or OCX file to your project. One reason might be because you have separated your application into multiple projects; for example, you might have created an "Administration module" for managing login IDs. If you have not already run the Setup Wizard for the other project, you might see the warning shown in Figure 10.19. Do not panic, however, as this simply means that the dependency information for the new file is not available.

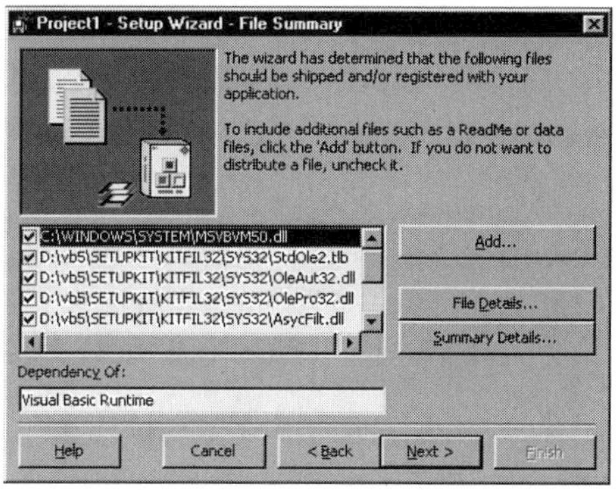

FIG. 10.18
The File Summary screen allows you to add or remove files from the installation.

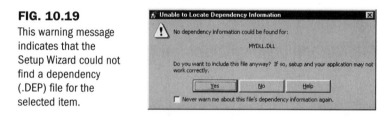

FIG. 10.19
This warning message indicates that the Setup Wizard could not find a dependency (.DEP) file for the selected item.

The reason for this message is to make sure your installation works. For example, if you decide to include additional EXEs, you also need the DLLs and OCXs required by those EXEs. You can either generate the dependency information with the Setup Wizard or skip this step if you know that no special files are required. After the File Summary screen, you are given the option to save your setup template so that you can create an install for this project without answering all these questions again.

Finally, now that the Setup Wizard has all the information it needs, your installation files will be copied to the location specified earlier. After this is complete, you should be able to test your install by running SETUP.EXE.

N O T E The setup wizard compresses installation files to save space. Compressed files are indicated by an underscore (_) in the last character of the file name, as in MYPROGRAM.EX_. If you need to compress files manually, the utility COMPRESS.EXE is included with Visual Basic. ▮

When creating a setup for a bunch of different users, test your installation thoroughly to make sure all the necessary components are included. Testing on your own PC is not sufficient, because you already have the required DLLs and OCXs.

T I P   A method of ensuring that your installation includes all the right parts is to try it on a test machine that contains nothing but the operating system. This can be a tricky situation, because each test of the install changes the test machine. I suggest getting software that allows you to restore a PC from an image file, so that you can test with a variety of software configurations.

A Closer Look at the Setup Process   You've just seen what goes into creating a set of setup files. It is probably a safe bet to assume that most computer users are already familiar with the concept of installing, or setting up, an application. Who hasn't spent 30 minutes feeding their PCs floppy disks to install some new software? From the user's viewpoint, the setup program performs a very simple function. However, for troubleshooting purposes, the developer needs to realize that there is a lot more going on than just copying files to the destination PC. One of the files created by the setup wizard, SETUP.LST, is the controlling "script" for the entire setup process. You can view SETUP.LST in a text editor, as shown in Figure 10.20.

FIG. 10.20

A typical SETUP.LST created by the Setup Wizard.

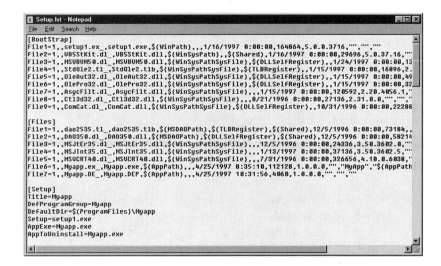

Don't let the cryptic lines of text intimidate you; the structure of the file is actually fairly straightforward. It contains all the information necessary to control the entire installation. Let's take a brief step-by-step look at how SETUP.LST is used:

1. When SETUP.EXE is executed, the files in the [BootStrap] section of SETUP.LST are copied, uncompressed, and registered on the destination machine. Because the Visual Basic runtime files might not be present, SETUP.EXE must be written in a language capable of running without them (such as C).

   The files in the [BootStrap] section are necessary to run a Visual Basic 5.0 program, specifically SETUP1.EXE, which does most of the work in setting up your application. This is the main purpose for SETUP.EXE, basically a "wrapper" for SETUP1.EXE.

2. SETUP1.EXE displays a welcome screen and asks the user to choose a destination directory for the application, as seen in Figure 10.21.

FIG. 10.21
Installations created by the Setup Wizard default to the Program Files directory.

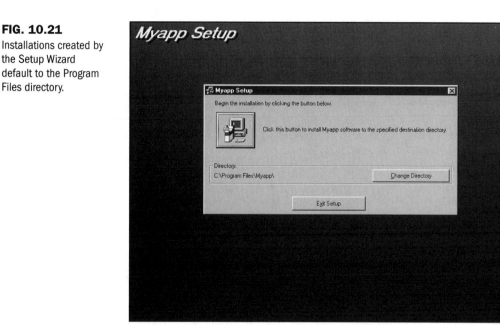

3. If you choose to continue, the program creates the application directory and begins copying files. The files to be copied are listed in the [Files] section of SETUP.LST. You might notice that for each file in the [Files] section there is a long list of parameters. Parameters 3, 4, and 5 represent the compressed file name, destination file name, and destination directory, respectively.

4. When SETUP1.EXE finishes copying files, it attempts to register some of them. Typically, a message like Updating your system is displayed during this process. Whether a file needs to be registered or not is determined by the 6th parameter, typically $(DLLSelfRegister) or $(EXESelfRegister).

N O T E If you need to manually register a file, use the REGSVR32 utility included with Visual Basic. ActiveX EXEs can be registered with Windows by running them with the command line parameter /REGSERVER.

5. Finally, SETUP1.EXE creates the shortcut icons for your program. The last two file parameters determine the icon's description and command line. The default program group name is listed in the [Setup] section.

Customizing Setup   Now that you are familiar with what the installation process actually does, you can modify it to meet your needs. Although tampering with an "official" SETUP.LST files is probably not a supported activity, I have had success with the customizations listed in Table 10.1.

Part
II
Ch
10

Table 10.1   Editing the SETUP.LST File

Customization	How To
Adding Files	Copy an existing `Filexx=` line and increment the number. Make sure to supply the copy and registration parameters mentioned in the last section, as well as the file date, size, and version number, all of which can be obtained from the Windows Explorer.
Default directory	The suggested install directory is usually a subdirectory of the \Program Files directory on the user's PC. To specify a different default directory, change the `DefaultDir` line in the `[Setup]` section—for example, `DefaultDir=C:\MYAPPDIR`.
Forcing a directory	If you want to take away a user's option to choose the destination directory, set the `DefaultDir` option as previously described. Then add the line `ForceUseDefDir=1` to the `[Setup]` section.
Background description	By default, the message displayed on the screen will be the project name. You can modify the `Title=` line in the `[Setup]` section to make it a bit more descriptive, as in `Title="On-Line Reporting System"`.
The setup program itself	If you want to run a setup program other than SETUP1.EXE, you can still use Microsoft's SETUP.EXE to install the VB5 runtime DLLs. To do this, change the Setup line in the `[Setup]` section to point to your program—for example, `Setup=MySetup.exe`. You can also remove the `[Files]` section entirely if your setup program doesn't need it.
Annoying messages	Although it is not the intended purpose, setting the 7th file parameter to `$(Shared)` removes two warning messages regarding replacing an existing file. The messages are contradictory, like `Cancel Setup?` followed by `Continue Setup?`, and probably would confuse some users. By marking the file as a Shared component, you are telling the setup program that the user does not need to be prompted before overwriting it.

N O T E   Microsoft includes the source code for SETUP1.EXE with Visual Basic. If you want to make changes to it, open the project SETUP1.VBP in the \kitfiles\setup1 directory.

Even though you can customize SETUP.LST to a great extent, a standard Setup Wizard install still might not be suitable for your needs. For example, you might want to create your own "wrapper" program around SETUP.EXE. This program could be very useful in a corporate environment. For example, you could temporarily map a network drive to the install server, run SETUP.EXE, and then disconnect the drive after installation. If you e-mailed this program to the users, they would not have to worry about connecting to the right network drive. Another possibility would be storing each user's date of installation in a database. As with SETUP.EXE, you might have to write this program so it would run without the VB5 runtime files.

> **CAUTION**
>
> When using the Setup Wizard, the version number of your program is very important. If you do not increment the version number in the Project Properties dialog box, SETUP assumes a previous user already has the correct version; therefore, it does not need to copy over it. After an install is complete, view the ST5UNST.LOG file to see which files the Setup Wizard actually copied.

From Here...

This chapter has given you a look at how you manage the various parts of your programs. You've seen several techniques for making your programming more efficient. You've also been exposed to many of the assorted components that comprise a complete program. For more information on creating and using the various parts, see the following chapters:

■ To learn more about how forms work with controls to enhance your Visual Basic programs, see Chapter 4, "Working with Forms and Controls."

■ To learn more about specific controls, see Chapter 16, "Using the Windows Common Controls," and Chapter 18, "Exploring New Visual Basic 5 Controls."

Building User Interfaces

CHAPTER 11

Designing User Interfaces

Visual Basic was created to allow programmers to write real applications, real fast. Prior to the release of Visual Basic 1, writing a Windows application was hard work, requiring a lot of very low-level programming knowledge just to get a simple window to appear. Visual Basic removed this level of "under-the-hood" complexity by automating a good deal of the difficult nuts-and-bolts programming that was required to be able to write even the simplest of Windows applications. Procedures such as creating and placing windows, selecting fonts by which to output text to a control, or defining an event such as a button click— though very difficult things to do in a low-level language such as C—are relatively simple in Visual Basic. However, although VB frees the programmer from the more mundane chores of Windows programming, it does not relieve the programmer from the responsibility to follow good software design and programming practices. ■

A good computer program should be designed to work the way a user does

You will learn what a user-centered design process is and how to implement it.

Graphical user interfaces should be intuitive for the user

Learn how to create consistent and effective interfaces. Also discover how to incorporate standard Graphical User Interface (GUI) design without stifling your creativity.

Perception is reality

You will see how to improve the user's perception of your programs.

While there are easy design traps to fall into, they can be avoided

Learn how to avoid some common programming pitfalls.

Implementing a User-Centered Software Development Process

An analogy can be drawn here: A programmer is to Visual Basic as a cabinetmaker is to power tools. While a power tool can make the labor of cabinetmaking easier, mere use of the tool does not guarantee that the cabinetmaker will make a good cabinet. The use of the tool is only as good as the cabinetmaker's ability to make and follow a schematic, select the appropriate materials, and execute the fundamental skills of cabinetmaking.

The same can be said of writing programs in Visual Basic. Although Visual Basic is a very powerful and easy-to-learn tool, programs created with Visual Basic are only as good as the design and implementation skills of the programmer. Visual Basic makes programming easier, but it does not necessarily make programmers better. Being an effective software developer means having a clear idea of *what* program you want to write, *whom* you want to write it for, and *how* you want to do it. Many times, paying attention to the needs, expectations, and habits of the user of your software is a trivial afterthought in the software development process. This tendency is self-defeating because, in most cases, intrinsic ease of use determines the long-term success of your code.

The process of software development can be broken up into three phases (see Table 11.1).

Table 11.1   The Three Phases of Software Development

Phase	Activities
Pre-production	Identify your users. Analyze their needs and skills. Determine the features they require. Prioritize features. Create a program specification. Create a schematic of the program.
Production	Divide the work among developers. Write code and build objects. Debug and test your code. Perform usability tests. Correct bugs and address usability issues.
Post-production	Prepare online help and end user manuals. Document program for future maintenance. Prepare program for deployment. Evaluate program and process for future versions.

Understanding the activities and dynamics of each of these phases is important to the overall efficiency of your development effort and the quality of your end product.

The Pre-Production Phase

The pre-production phase of developing a Windows application is where your product is defined and specified. In pre-production, you draw up the blueprint upon which your product will be built. In this phase, you decide what is the purpose of the product, what are its features, and—of those determined features—which version of your product will implement a given feature set.

In pre-production, you create a *user profile*. The purpose here is to gather as much information as possible about the users of your program. For instance, you determine whether your intended users are comfortable with Windows, thus requiring little elementary support. If your users have never used a computer before, your program will require a good deal of on-screen instruction.

Localization issues are also identified during this phase. Will your product be released only in the U.S. version of English? Will it eventually require other languages? Additionally, consider where and when the customer will run your program. Will it be a point-of-sale system that handles thousands of daily transactions, or will it be used only once a month?

For example, suppose you are writing an Internet application with a Login page. If you are expecting a large number of hits (or hackers), loading your entire program into memory for every login attempt is probably not a good idea. One solution would be to design a fast and small Login object, so you don't bog down the server. It is best to address issues like these at the beginning of the development process where change is cheap, rather than at the end of the process where change is very, very expensive.

Part

III

Ch

11

TIP It is always most cost effective to correct a mistake or make a change to a program feature in the pre-production phase. Making a change at a later point in the development process is costly in terms of time and money. This is because the program must be respecified, recoded, retested, and re-documented.

The Production Phase

The production phase of the development process is where you take the product specification prepared in pre-production and turn it into code. In addition, you create media and other resources that your code might require. In this phase, you determine the optimal language in which to code. (Since this is a book on Visual Basic, for all intents and purposes the optimal language *is* Visual Basic. However, keep in mind that this might not always be the case. Even VB has its limitations and misapplications.)

If you are working within a group of programmers, production is where you divide up the work and do *build* (or version) *control*. A *build* is the process of taking all the pieces of code that each developer is working on and compiling the software. Depending on the testing requirements of your project, you might want to have a daily build scheduled. Because there can be several builds during the development process, there must be a system in place so that each programmer can submit the latest version of his or her code. There is a variety of version control software available to do this, including Microsoft Visual SourceSafe, which is included with the Enterprise Edition of Visual Basic 5.0.

System testing is the process of testing code for bugs, usability, and compliance to specifications. The testing process is also done within the Production phase. There are two major schools of thought concerning testing methods, and both are worth mentioning here.

One method of testing is called *waterfall testing* (see Figure 11.1). In the waterfall method, the testing process is considered to be separate from the programming part of the software development process. Waterfall testing requires that, prior to testing, all the code is written to specifications. Then that code is sent to the tester for testing. After the testing is completed, the results are sent back to the developers to make the necessary code corrections and modifications.

FIG. 11.1

Waterfall testing requires that most testing take place at the end of the production phase.

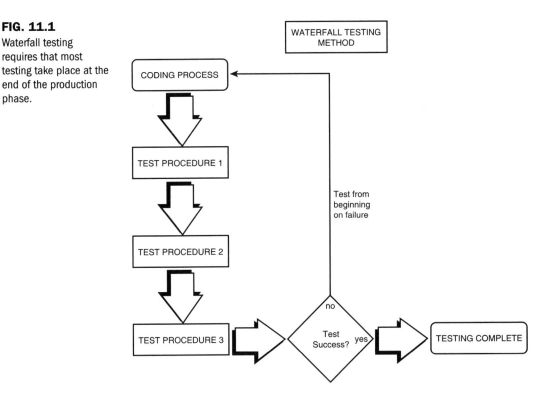

Another testing method is called *iterative testing* (see Figure 11.2). In this method, testing is considered to be part of the programming process. As the programmer completes a discrete set of procedures, he is continually sending his completed work to the tester for inspection and response. While the iterative method might seem like nothing more then a lot of little waterfall tests, it is not. In the iterative testing method, the tester is included in and consulted about the development process from as early as the pre-production phase. In the waterfall method, the tester is brought in well toward the end of the production phase.

Both methods work, and both have their virtues and shortcomings. The waterfall method allows programmers to quickly move from task to task, concentrating on code. However, bugs that the developer overlooks can create their own waterfall of problems when testing finally occurs, especially if the bug happens to be at an early point of the program. And although an iterative approach can provide quicker feedback, requiring the developer to spend a lot of time testing can slow the entire process. One important thing to remember is that any given testing method does not excuse the programmer from testing his own procedures and functions.

FIG. 11.2
Iterative testing requires that testing take place throughout the production phase.

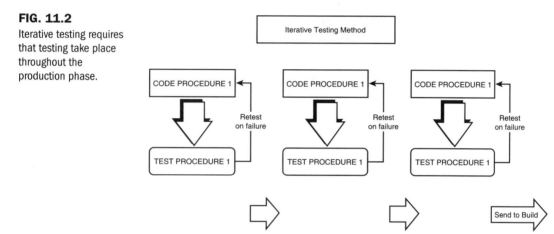

Part III

Ch 11

The Post-Production Phase

The post-production phase of software development is where built software is documented, prepared for deployment, and evaluated for future version releases. This process involves all the steps necessary before releasing the software to the public. In the post-production phase, you create both user and programmer documentation, as well as installation media. Beta testing and user feedback can occur during and after this process.

Documentation   After your code is acceptably bug-free and compliant to specifications, you must write the documentation for it. The scope of the documentation includes not only the online help and manuals for the end user, but also the blood-and-guts manuals for the people who will be maintaining your code in following versions. The section "Avoiding Programming Pitfalls" later in this chapter discusses some techniques that you can use to make your code easier to document.

> **CAUTION**
>
> Unfortunately, documentation is one area that people often skimp on. This is never a good idea. Just remember, it might be you who has to maintain the code—and your memory might not be as reliable as you think!

Deployment As your program is being documented, you can also prepare it for deployment. *Deployment* is the act of distributing your program to others. Whether you use a modest floppy disk in an envelope or a more extravagant shrink-wrapped CD-ROM release, you want to put as much effort into your deployment as you did with programming.

N O T E Visual Basic programs can be deployed several ways, including CD-ROM, floppy disks, or a network. Distribution via the Internet is now a reality as well. See Chapter 10, "Managing Your Project," for a detailed discussion on creating Setup programs. ▪

▶ **See** "Using the Setup Wizard," **p. 264**

First, you need to use the Setup Wizard or another setup utility to create an installation process for your program. After you have created this installation process, you must thoroughly test it on as many different systems as possible. You might write the most sophisticated piece of software in the world, but if its setup program doesn't install your program properly, your labor is lost.

If you are shipping your program on floppy disks, you should label each disk clearly, avoiding handwritten labels in favor of ones printed on a laser printer or by a professional printer. Using Disk X of Y tagging on the labels is a good practice to follow. For an end user, there are few things more frustrating than trying to install a piece of software only to find out that you are missing a disk.

However, due to the increasing size of Windows applications, it would not be too bold a prediction to say floppy disk installations are going the way of the dinosaur. Program setup can be an incredibly time-consuming process if the install files must be broken into a large number of 1.44M disk-sized chunks. On the other hand, a blank CD can hold about 650 megabytes of data, and the cost of CD recorders and media has decreased considerably in recent years.

Whatever media you use, label it with clear and brief instructions. If your application is built around components that require their own setup (such as ODBC), try to integrate the setup programs as much as possible. Users will appreciate setups that are simple, with a single icon or command. If distributing via CD-ROM, you might want to include an AUTORUN.INF file, which allows your setup program to start automatically. Also, offer a clear, noticeable message in the deployment package informing the user what to do in the event of difficulty. These things are important and have definite impact on how the quality of your work is perceived.

CAUTION

Files copied from CD-ROM to hard disk have the default file attribute of read-only. You cannot write to them. This can cause problems if your program is deployed with files to which it must write—for example, .INI files or database files. When testing your deployment, check to make sure that your setup program removes the read-only file attribute from the files it copies from CD-ROM.

Evaluation and Future Versions At the end of every software development process is a period where you look over what you have done to determine how to do it better on the next version. Next version? That's right, because most software gets revised, no matter how small the project. As an example, take the Internet browser market, which releases new browser versions with an almost nauseating frequency. As you were developing your project, without a doubt you came across problems. And, as you solved these problems, you probably said to yourself that the next time you did this, you would do so and so, in such and such a way. Mistakes are things from which we learn, and you would do well to anticipate applying what you have learned from your errors to a future version. Make sure to document your thoughts as you get them, for easy "memory retrieval" later.

Most software is developed under strict time constraints. No person or enterprise can afford to take forever to produce a functional piece of code. As a result, it is often not possible to implement every specified feature in a given release. Therefore, planning to implement features over progressive versions is a viable development strategy.

TIP

As you program, keep notes of ideas you have for future versions. Remember also (although it might make you snarl) that part of a programmer's job is being a salesperson. The decision to upgrade to a new version of Visual Basic is a perfect example. While the developer sees a cool and exciting programming tool, his boss might just see an expense. Do not be afraid to write small prototype programs or mocked-up forms to show others what is possible. This is sometimes known as a *proof-of-concept.*

The evaluation of real-life use of your code happens in the post-production period. The true test of a software product's effectiveness and usability is the test of time. No laboratory condition can ever adequately anticipate every nuance of user interaction. It is only by deploying your program, supporting your program, and eliciting the end users' responses that you can accurately evaluate what works and what doesn't.

Creating Consistent and Effective Graphical Interfaces

Software programs are like cars: The more predictable and sensible they are to use, the easier it is to get where you want to go.

Although the Windows operating system has set some standards regarding graphical user interface design—and VB has made programming for Windows a whole lot simpler—there is still a good deal of unpredictable and improper use of Windows components (menus, buttons, list boxes, combo boxes, and so on). This inconsistency defeats the fundamental purpose of the graphical user interface idea—to make operating a computer a more productive, enjoyable, and less frustrating experience for the user.

Do not think that providing a consistent, predictable graphical interface for your program requires you to forego creativity in any way. Take the active toolbar (or coolbar) used first in Microsoft Internet Explorer. Although it broke standards regarding the look of Windows toolbar buttons, it was a great idea and set the standard for the Office 97 toolbars.

Making a Well-Designed Form

Although designing a form in Visual Basic is a simple thing to do, doing it *well* is not that easy. Good form design involves more than just inserting controls and programming events. To make a well-designed form, you should understand the form's purpose, how it is going to be used, when it is going to be used, and its relationship with the rest of the program.

Let's take a look at the form frmSettings (FRMESET.FRM) in Figure 11.3. The purpose of this form is to set the display attributes for another form. This form suffers from a number of poor design choices that prevent it from effectively achieving its full functionality.

On the Web

You can find the FRMESET.FRM form in the EVILJOT.VBP project, which is downloadable from **www.mcp.com/info/0-7897/0-7897-1288-1**.

FIG. 11.3

The code behind the pictured form might work flawlessly, but it leaves much to be desired in terms of layout.

Lack of descriptive labeling for this box

Dialog box functionality, yet sizable

Form has too much extra space for the number of controls it holds

Disrupted button grouping

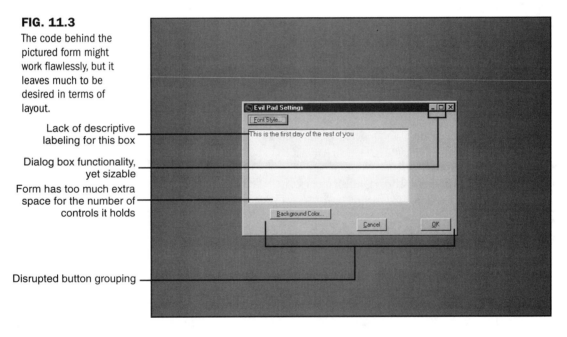

The first item for correction is the choice of setting the form's BorderStyle property to Sizable. Should the user resize the form either by intention or mistake (double-clicking the title bar is not an uncommon accident), the form does not resize or reposition the controls to accommodate the new form size (see Figure 11.4). Forms that are sizable are generally used in instances where the user needs a window of varying size to accomplish something—for example, Word's document windows or Paint's drawing window. To correct this problem, set the form's BorderStyle property to Fixed Single or Fixed Dialog.

▶ **See** "Form Properties Revisited," **p. 77**

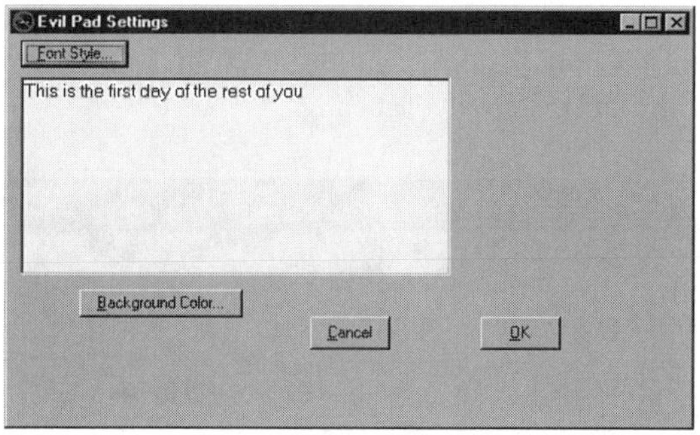

FIG. 11.4

The controls are not resized or repositioned when the form is resized. The form's BorderStyle property should be set to Fixed Single or Fixed Dialog.

> **T I P** To provide basic resizing capabilities, you can place code to move controls around on a form and alter their dimensions in the form's Resize event. For example, the line
>
> ```
> If frmMain.Width > 300 Then lstUserList.Width = frmMain.Width - 300
> ```
>
> could be used to always keep a list box sized to 300 twips less than the form width, as long as it doesn't result in a negative width.

Another mistake is the initial size and location of the form. It completely covers the form whose attributes are to be set (refer to Figure 11.3, in which the primary form is completely hidden behind the settings form). An analogy would be if Microsoft Word's Find window covered up your entire document. To remedy this flaw, the form should be repositioned so that when it appears, at least a portion of the form to be affected is still showing.

Notice, too, that the form suffers from poor labeling. The designer is assuming that the user intuitively knows what this form is about, what the function of the label control is, and how each button affects the overall program.

Probably the biggest cause for concern with regard to this form's design is the almost arbitrary use of space and the inconsistent placement of buttons and labels on the form. When it comes to the size of a fixed size form (a.k.a. a dialog box), the rule of thumb is "less is best." You want to allow the form to take up no more real estate than it needs, but not to make it so small that controls are congested and text is illegible.

▶ **See** "Setting up the Dialog Box Form," **p. 143**

You should also organize the placement of controls according to functionality. In the frmSettings form, separating the Font Style button from the Background Color button is confusing and causes a lot of unnecessary mouse movement activity. Positioning the Font Style and Background Color buttons together in one group and the OK and Cancel buttons in another would create distinct areas of functionality that the user would find more organized and memorable.

Taking into account the pitfalls discussed here, look at Figure 11.5. This is an illustration of the improved form, frmSettngs (FRMSET.FRM), which is part of the Visual Basic project

GOODJOT.VBP. Notice the reduced size of the form, the change of the form's `BorderStyle` property, the reorganization of the form's buttons, and the inclusion of a frame to provide a sense of functional unity and descriptive labeling.

FIG. 11.5

Notice that in the improved form pictured here, controls have been grouped according to their functionality.

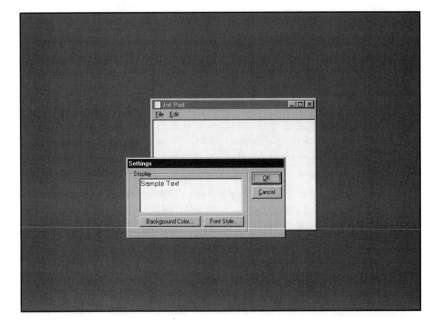

Designing Menus

Another important part of form design is creating consistent, effective menus. This means following some straightforward design guidelines and organizing your menus consistently and concisely. Here are a few guidelines and suggestions that enable you to make professional looking menus that meet the users' expectations:

- Follow standard Windows menu conventions: File, Edit, View, and so on.
- Group menu items logically and concisely.
- Use separator bars to group related items in a drop-down menu.
- Avoid redundant menu entries.
- Avoid menu bar items without drop-down menus.
- Don't forget to use the ellipses (...) to denote menu entries that activate dialog boxes.

Follow Standard Windows Menu Conventions   Windows has been around for a long enough period of time that its users have developed certain expectations about how Windows applications should work and look. One of the areas where user expectations are fairly specific is the layout of the menu bar.

Take a look at Figure 11.6. In this example, the designer of this menu has chosen to breach the standard Windows menu bar layout convention. Users expect that the menu bar item File comes first, followed by Edit. This design changes the menu bar item order to be Edit, followed by File. The unconventional reordering of the menu bar will probably cause the user to experience initial confusion. In this case, reordering the menu really adds no value to the program, so it is better to stick with the *de facto* Windows convention.

FIG. 11.6

There is no reason to re-order the standard Windows menu bar; it will only confuse users.

Group Menu Items Logically and Concisely   Figure 11.7 shows another problem with the example menus. Notice that the illustrated Settings menu has only two submenus, Show Settings and Always on Top. These two submenus should be moved to the File menu. Doing this condenses the menu bar without affecting the functionality or accessibility of the moved items.

Part

III

Ch

11

FIG. 11.7

Since there are only two items in the Settings menu, a better choice would be to move them to the File menu.

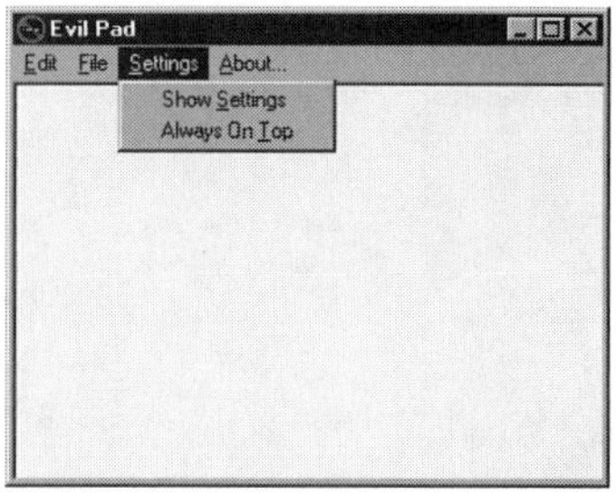

Use Separator Bars to Group Related Items in a Drop-Down Menu   Separator bars provide a level of grouping within a top-level menu. Take Visual Basic's Edit menu for example—related functions such as Copy and Paste are set apart from other items because they logically go together. The separator bars create a visual break in a long menu, allowing the user to quickly know if he or she is looking at the right area. In your example, after the Show Settings and Always on Top drop-down menu items have been moved to the File menu, they can be grouped together by putting a separator bar before and after the items (see Figure 11.8).

▶ **See** "Controlling a Program with a Menu Bar," **p. 104**

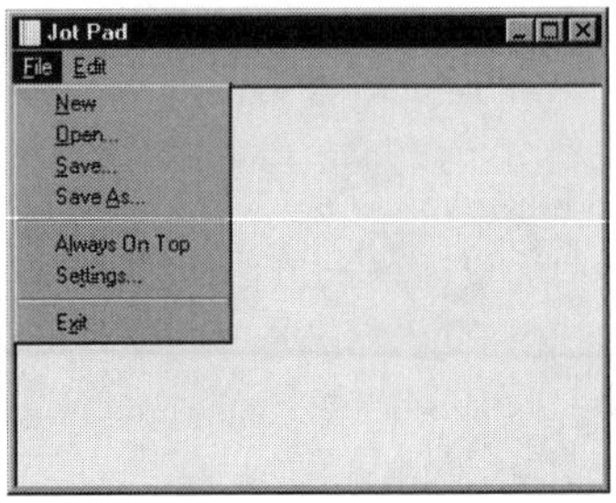

FIG. 11.8
This menu system has been simplified by grouping similar functions.

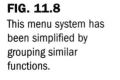

Avoid Redundant Menu Entries Although it is always a good idea to offer the user multiple ways of performing the same tasks within your program—for example, selecting Edit, Copy or pressing Ctrl+C to copy selected data to the Clipboard—it is not good practice to have a given functionality appear in more than one place within your program's menu system. Nor is it a good idea to have the same menu caption appear in more than one place in your program and perform two entirely different actions.

In Figure 11.9, notice that the caption Settings appears both in the File menu and as a menu item. When you select File, Settings, the Settings dialog box appears. However, when you click the Settings menu bar item, the Settings drop-down menu appears. This is poor practice. Not only will having this caption in two different areas of the program's menu confuse the user, having two different behaviors attached to each caption will absolutely confound him.

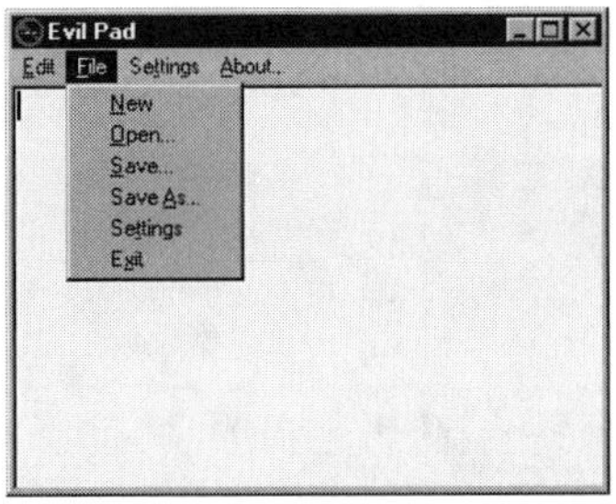

FIG. 11.9
In this example, the Settings menu item appears in two places: in the File drop-down menu and the menu bar. This is a confusing design choice. Avoid redundant menu items.

Avoid Menu Bar Items Without Drop-Down Menus Avoid the situation in which you have a menu bar item that does not have a drop-down menu of selections. In Figure 11.10, you see the About dialog box that appears when you choose About, which has no menu items under it. A lone top-level item, or *orphan*, has the same behavior as a command button or drop-down menu item. If that sort of behavior is what you want, a CommandButton control could be used to achieve the same effect. The better solution, however, is to move the orphan menu bar item to another menu with a similar set of functions. This is the same principle discussed earlier in "Group Menu Items Logically and Concisely."

FIG. 11.10
A menu bar item that doesn't invoke drop-down menus might confuse users.

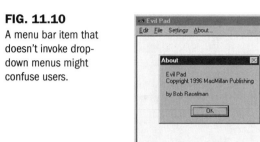

Use the Ellipsis to Denote Menu Entries that Activate Dialog Boxes   When ellipses (...) appear next to an item in a drop-down menu, they let users know that selecting this item does not have any immediate results, but rather brings up a dialog box with more options (as you saw with the About... item in the preceding section). Many people unfamiliar with designing Windows applications frequently forget to use them. Using the ellipses when the situation warrants adds to the professionalism of your application.

Offering Choices

When it comes time for a user to make a decision within your program, it is usually more efficient to provide a set of choices from which to select (see Figure 11.11) than requiring typed input. Providing the user with choices reduces the risk of error due to typing mistakes. It also makes input validation much easier, as well as shows the user the range of possible choices in many cases.

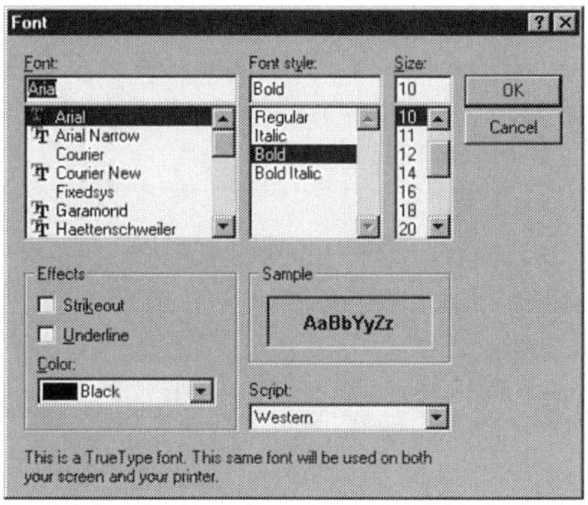

Part
III

Ch
11

FIG. 11.11
Selecting a typeface from a list of available fonts is easier for the user than typing in a selection.

See "Working with User Choices," **p. 396**

List Boxes versus Combo Boxes   Two useful controls for offering choices to the user are the list box and the combo box. The ListBox control allows the user to view a list of all available choices before, during, and after a selection is made. The ListBox control allows no typed input; the user can select one (or sometimes more) item from the list. This can be a drawback should the user need to input data that the program does not provide. Another drawback of the list box is that it requires a good deal of window space to be useful. A list box that shows only two or three items can appear cramped and awkward.

N O T E Windows standards dictate that when you use a list box, you let the user select an item in
one of two ways: selecting it and pressing a button or double-clicking. An example of this
behavior (which uses the ListView control) is a File dialog box. ▦

When window space is at a premium, using the ComboBox control might be a better design
choice than a list box. The ComboBox control has three styles (see Figure 11.12):

- DropDown Combo – Displays a drop-down list of selections and also permits users to
  type input
- Simple Combo – Shows an input box above a list, just like a list box with a text box
  above it
- DropDown List – Similar to the Simple Combo but does not allow typed input

The drawback of using the Simple Combo style is that, like the ListBox control, it requires a
good deal of window space to be effective.

FIG. 11.12

Depending on the style
setting of a combo box,
typed user input may or
may not be allowed.

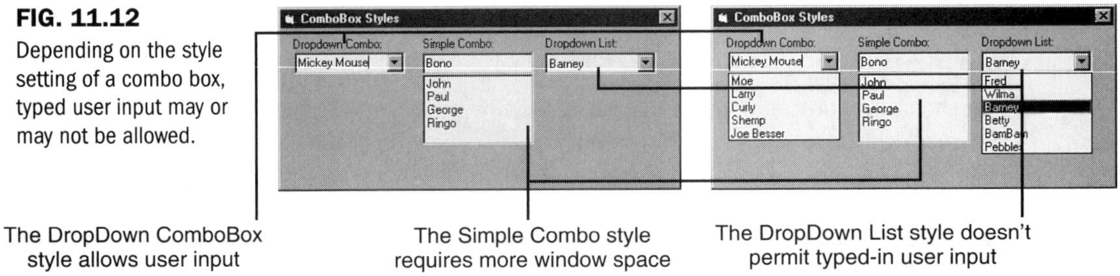

The DropDown ComboBox
style allows user input

The Simple Combo style
requires more window space

The DropDown List style doesn't
permit typed-in user input

T I P A DropDown List style combo box is a useful control for online report viewing. It allows the user to both
select a report parameter (for example, Month-to-date versus Quarter-to-date) and, at the same time,
shows the currently selected item.

Overusing list boxes and combo boxes can also harm an application's performance. If a list box
or combo box lists too many items, the control can increase the form's load time. You can
reduce the number of items in a list by finding out what the actual limits are. Does a user need
all the states in the United States or only the ten with which the company normally does business?

Option Buttons versus Check Boxes To present a fixed number of choices, use the
CheckBox and OptionButton controls. A check box gives the user two choices only: on or off.
For example, the Windows Explorer Options dialog box (accessed through the View menu)
uses a check box to indicate whether to Display the Full MS-DOS Path in the title bar or not
(see Figure 11.13). Selecting or deselecting a check box has no effect on any other check
boxes on a form.

Option buttons present the user with a fixed list of mutually exclusive choices. Option buttons
are usually grouped by placing related buttons in a frame. Only one option button in a group
can be selected at any time; selecting one button in a group automatically deselects the other

buttons in that group. The Background tab in Windows' Display Properties dialog box uses option buttons to set the background wallpaper to the exclusive states of Tile or Center (see Figure 11.14).

FIG. 11.13
A good use of check boxes is shown in the lower section of the Windows Explorer dialog box, which uses two check boxes to present the user with independent on/off options.

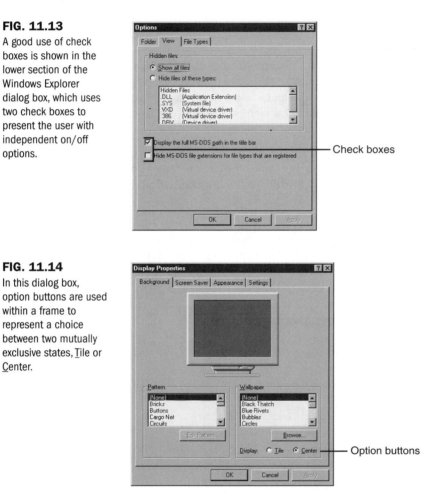

Check boxes

FIG. 11.14
In this dialog box, option buttons are used within a frame to represent a choice between two mutually exclusive states, Tile or Center.

Option buttons

Part III
Ch
11

Improving User Perceptions of Your Programs

Perception is reality. No, I'm not having flashback to the 1960s, I am merely referring to how users' *observations* can influence their like or dislike of your program, regardless of its actual functionality. Application speed is a prime example. You might have written the fastest Visual Basic code ever, but it matters little if the user thinks it runs slow. Visual Basic programmers tend to get defensive when users complain about speed, because "the users don't know what the program is doing." However, there are a few tricks you can use to make your program *seem* to run faster.

The key to a program's perceived speed is the fact that when a user clicks an icon, *something needs to happen* right away. Users are more willing to wait if they think the computer is working as fast as it can. Booting Windows 95 is a good example; it usually takes quite a long time. However, all the graphics, beeps, and hard drive noise keep you distracted enough to make it an acceptable wait. The techniques discussed in this section give you suggestions for creating "faster" Visual Basic applications.

Load Time   If you load all of a program's forms at startup, they all appear quickly when the application needs to show them. Although this slows the application's performance at program startup, overall runtime performance is much faster. Simply load all the forms that belong to an application by using the Load method. This method places the forms in memory, but they are invisible to the user until the Show method is executed.

This technique works well for applications with a small number of forms (2–5). For applications with more forms, you might use this technique for similar groupings of forms. For example, an accounting payroll application might load all the forms associated with displaying employee information during an employee data-entry session.

The *Sub Main* Subroutine   The General tab of the Project Properties dialog box (which you display by choosing *projectname* Properties from the Project menu) allows you to choose a startup form or Sub Main (see Figure 11.15). To take advantage of this setting, you need a module with a subroutine named Main. This frees you from having to keep any startup routines within a form's Load event.

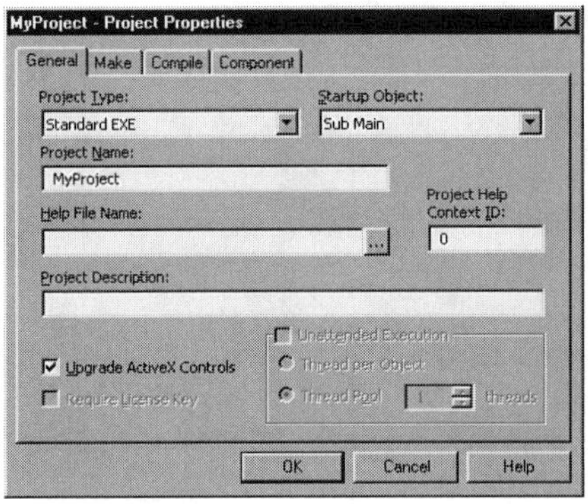

FIG. 11.15

After setting your startup object to *Sub Main*, you can consolidate your program's initialization tasks into a single procedure.

The Sub Main subroutine is an excellent place for all the initialization code required at startup time. For example, the Sub Main subroutine might contain code for opening configuration files, checking the application's path, and connecting to a networked database. If your initialization procedures are very long, you might want to display a splash screen during this process.

Splash Screens   One way to deal with lengthy program startups is to display a *splash screen* during load time. A splash screen is a form that displays information about the application and its designer (see Figure 11.16). Many commercial applications, including Microsoft Word, Excel, and Visual Basic itself, display splash screens at program startup. A splash screen with a status bar provides the user with visible proof that something is happening.

FIG. 11.16
This splash screen appears when the application first loads to give the user something to look at while program initialization takes place.

You can also update information in a splash screen to keep the user informed of the tasks being done in setting up the program. A similar technique can be used during a long process, such as modifying a large number of database records.

Avoiding Programming Pitfalls

Regardless of whether you are a member of a large development team or you are a one-coder shop, your code will have to be maintained by someone. Just because you have spent hours of coding and debugging to get a function working just right does not mean that there won't come a time to improve and enhance it. Even maintaining your own code can be a daunting task if you have not seen it in six months (or, in my case, six hours). However, the task doesn't have to be horrendous. If you take certain precautions and use a little foresight, you can make the time needed to maintain your code reasonable and relatively painless.

Programming Readable Code

The most important thing that you can do toward making your code easy to maintain is to make it readable, not only to yourself but to others. If another programmer cannot read your code, he or she must waste precious time figuring out exactly what the program does and how. Readable code gives others a quick, intuitive feel for how your program works. Also, readability has a definite impact as to how your code is perceived within the professional community. Depending on how you write code, others who have to follow your work will either curse your name or admire your skill.

Using Visual Basic Constants

Many Visual Basic code statements utilize numeric parameter values to specify how an object should behave. This capability makes writing code easier, but makes reading the code afterwards difficult. The solution is to use global constants that represent these numeric values. Code that uses constants is much easier to read.

To use built-in constants, you no longer have to add a text file to your project as you did with versions of Visual Basic prior to version 4. Visual Basic now includes *intrinsic* (built-in) constants in the language. By using these intrinsic constants, you make your code more readable to all programmers, even those who have not memorized the constant values. Using constants can also help you, especially if you tend to forget what you have done and why. For example, which of the following code lines is more readily understandable?

```
MsgBox "This is a warning", 64
```

```
MsgBox "This is a warning", vbExclamation
```

When you read code that uses the intrinsic constants, you do not have to remember what each value means.

Commented Code

Writing commented code is a pain, but reading uncommented code—even code that you wrote just yesterday—can be an even greater pain. Trying to figure out the logic of a code segment can be time-consuming. Taking the time on the front end to put in comments, on the other hand, saves you time in the long run. There's an old saying among programmers, "You can never comment too much!" Imagine trying to read and understand the meaning and use of the code in Listing 11.1 without the comments.

Listing 11.1   11LIST01.TXTS—Searching the *Tag* Property of Each Control and Displaying the Appropriate Database Field Information in Each Control

```
' The following routine searches through all the controls
' on a form and checks each control's TAG property.
' If the tag property is a field name, this routine loads
' the current field's value into that control

Sub LoadFormData (WndName As Form, dyn As Dynaset)
Dim Cntl%, FieldName$, Result$, N%, i%

Screen.MousePointer = vbHOURGLASS

'Search through all the controls on the indicated form
For Cntl% = 0 To WndName.Controls.Count - 1
  FieldName$ = WndName.Controls(Cntl%).Tag
  If TypeOf WndName.Controls(Cntl%) Is OptionButton Then

    ' Find the value of this field and store in the appropriate
    ' option button control
    N% = Abs(dyn(FieldName$))
    If WndName.Controls(Cntl%).Caption = "YES" Then
        WndName.Controls(Cntl%).Value = N%
    ElseIf WndName.Controls(Cntl%).Caption = "NO" Then
        WndName.Controls(Cntl%).Value = Abs(N% - 1)
    End If

  ElseIf TypeOf WndName.Controls(Cntl%) Is ComboBox Then

    If dyn(FieldName$) <> Null Then
```

```
        ' Format the current field's value
        Result$ = dyn.Fields(FieldName$)
        ' Find the field's value in the current combo box
        For N% = 0 To (WndName.Controls(Cntl%).ListCount - 1)
          i% = WndName.Controls(Cntl%).ListIndex + 1
          WndName.Controls(Cntl%).ListIndex = i%
          If Len(WndName.Controls(Cntl%).Text) <> 0 Then
            Exit For
          End If
        Next N%
      End If

    ' If the control is a text box
    ElseIf TypeOf WndName.Controls(Cntl%) Is TextBox Then

      ' If the current field's value is blank then skip
      If dyn(FieldName$) <> Null Then

        ' Store the formatted value in the text box
        WndName.Controls(Cntl%).Text = dyn.Fields(FieldName$)
      End If
    End If
  Next Cntl%

  Screen.MousePointer = vbDEFAULT

  End Sub
```

Listing 11.1 contains the subroutine LoadFormData. You could reference this subroutine in the Load event of any form. Simply provide the name of the recordset containing the data, position, and the table at the appropriate record; place the names of the fields that you want in the appropriate control's Tag property; and run this routine. In instances where you cannot use Bound controls, this routine works amazingly well. Notice that the use of vbHourGlass and vbDefault makes it clear what the program is doing to MousePointer.

Use Descriptive Naming

Visual Basic allows you to use up to 255 characters to name a variable, sub, or function; it allows 40 characters for a control name. You can take advantage of this feature by giving your variables, functions, and controls names that reflect their identity, purpose, or position. In addition, as discussed in Chapter 8, it's a good idea to use a naming convention for your objects and variables that helps you determine their type at a glance.

Listing 11.2 shows an example of using descriptive object naming to make your code more readable.

Listing 11.2 11LIST02.TXT—Using Descriptive Naming for Variables and Controls

```
Private Sub cmdChoices_MouseDown(Index As Integer, Button As Integer,
Shift As Integer, X As Single, Y As Single)
    Dim i%
    '"The pressed button typeface will be set according to the option,
opFontFace
    'value set

    'Set the old font (the gf prefix denotes global to form) so it can
    'reset on MouseUp
    gfOldFontFace$ = cmdChoices(Index).Font
    'Adjust for the new font setting
    If opFontFace(0) = True Then
        cmdChoices(Index).Font = opFontFace(0).Caption
    Else
        cmdChoices(Index).Font = opFontFace(1).Caption
    End If

    'Query to option buttons and set the caption case for the button depressed
    For i% = 0 To 2
        Select Case i%
        Case 0
            If optFontCase(i%).Value = True Then cmdChoices(Index).Caption =
UCase(cmdChoices(Index).Caption)
        Case 1
            If optFontCase(i%).Value = True Then cmdChoices(Index).Caption =
LCase(cmdChoices(Index).Caption)
        Case 2
            If optFontCase(i%).Value = True Then cmdChoices(Index).Caption =
gfOldFontCase$(Index)
        End Select
    Next i%
End Sub
```

Notice in the example that you do not even need to look at the form to know optFontCase is an option button used to select upper- or lowercase. This would have been a little harder to determine if its default name of Option1 had been kept.

From Here...

Designing an effective Windows application requires a bit more understanding and planning than just putting controls on a form. Implementing a user-centered software development process helps you design cost-effective, user-friendly applications that work well and are easy to deploy and revise.

An application's appearance is as important as what the application does. A poorly thought-out application interface detracts from the application's usefulness because users focus on the bad interface rather than what it does. Be careful how you organize controls and menus. Also be careful to ensure that your program complies with and responds to the user's expectations.

To find information on related topics, see the following chapters:

- For more information on using the toolbar in Visual Basic, see Chapter 5, "Adding Menus and Toolbars to Your Program."

- To see more on making your interface esthetically pleasing, see Chapter 13, "Working with Text, Fonts, and Colors."

- To find out more about the use of common Windows components in your programs, see Chapter 16, "Using the Windows Common Controls."

- For a treasure trove of styles for different kinds of screens and designs, see *Look for the Windows Interface* (Microsoft Press, 1992). Use this book in conjunction with the *Visual Design Guide*.

Part

III

Ch

11

CHAPTER 12

Working with Graphics

What do you think of when someone mentions graphics? Do you envision the artistic creations of a graphic designer? Do you conjure up images of the last sales presentation that you attended? Maybe you think of computer-aided design (CAD) or intricate data charts. The point is that the *graphics* topic encompasses a very wide range of images and applications.

Defined in the simplest terms, graphics (in the computer world) is the placement of lines, circles, points, and text in a specific pattern on a screen. These objects can be different sizes, shapes, and colors. The purpose of this chapter is to illustrate how to control the placement and characteristics of these objects.

The design and use of graphics is a large and complex subject. This single chapter cannot cover all the bases. However, it provides you with enough information and techniques to get you well on your way to creating great graphics programs. ■

Enhance the user interface

Use the Line and Shape controls to highlight areas of your forms, making your user interface more visually pleasing.

Want to show a picture?

The form itself, as well as several controls, enables you to display almost any type of picture. You can even display pictures that are stored in a database.

Change your pictures

With some of Visual Basic's methods you can even modify the pictures that you display.

Create your own pictures

Visual Basic's graphics methods enable you to create many types of graphics-related programs.

Analyze data with graphics

You can even use the graphics methods to create charts and other data analysis tools.

Enhancing the User Interface

A typical user interface for an application consists of one or more forms containing a menu, labels, text boxes, command buttons, and perhaps a few other controls for specific pieces of data. However, without graphics, an otherwise functional interface can be quite boring and unintuitive. You can use graphics to enhance the user interface in the following ways:

■ Highlighting specific information on the screen

■ Providing a different view of the information

■ Providing a more intuitive link to the application's functions

These enhancements can be accomplished through the use of the Line and Shape controls, color, pictures, and drawing methods.

Using the Line and Shape Controls

The Line and Shape controls provide the easiest means to add a graphic element to a form. The controls are drawn on the form at design time and placed where you need them. During the program's execution, these controls can be hidden or moved. Their colors can be changed by setting the appropriate property values in your code.

As you would guess by its name, the Line control places a line on the form. You can control the width of the line, the line style, the color, and the position of the terminal points of the line by setting the control's properties. Figure 12.1 shows several Line controls drawn on a form using the various styles and the `BorderStyle` property options for the Line control.

FIG. 12.1

The Line control enables you to place lines of different styles on a form. You assign the style by selecting the appropriate `Border-Style` property.

CAUTION

If you set the `BorderWidth` property of the Line control greater than one, the `BorderStyle` property has no effect.

The Line control can be used on a form to separate areas of the form from one another. For instance, you might want to separate the data display portion of a form from the command buttons, as shown in Figure 12.2. Or you may want to separate the information on the form into distinct groups. If you are presenting a lot of information on a form, the use of a line is a good way to enable the user to focus on one group of information at a time.

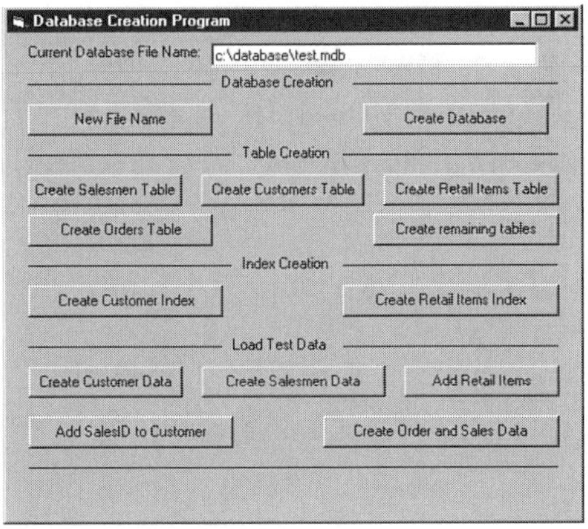

FIG. 12.2

The Line control is used to provide a visual separator between different areas on the form.

The Shape control provides another simple means of placing graphics elements on a form. You could use the Shape control to create any of six shapes. Simply change the control's Shape property (see Figure 12.3).

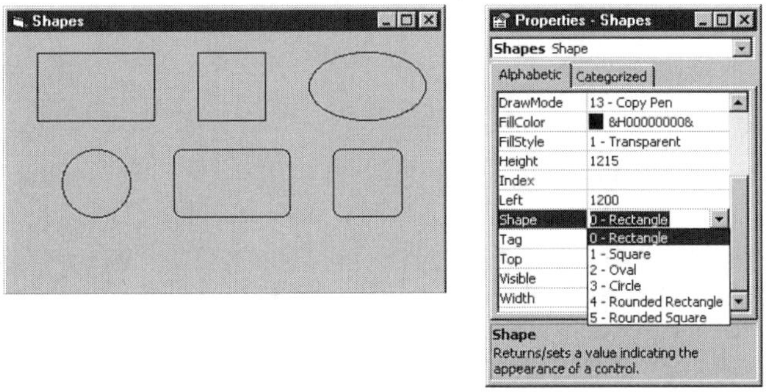

FIG. 12.3

You can change the Shape property of the Shape control to create any of the shapes pictured.

You can set the BorderStyle property of these shapes to any of the six line styles shown in Figure 12.1. You can also select patterns and colors for the shapes by setting the FillStyle and FillColor properties. The Shape control can be used to enclose various areas of a form and other controls, as shown in Figure 12.4.

N O T E Although a Shape control can visually enclose other controls, it cannot be used as a *container* for other controls, as the Frame and PictureBox controls can. If a frame is placed on a form, then other controls can be placed within the frame's borders. The frame and the controls contained within it then act as one unit. When the frame is moved, the other controls are moved with it, maintaining their relative position within the frame. If a frame is hidden, all controls in the frame are

Part

III

Ch

12

also hidden. These characteristics are also true of a picture box. Not so with a Shape control. Any controls placed within the border of a Shape control are independent of the shape. If the shape is moved or hidden, the other controls remain unaffected.

▶ **See** "Exploring the Use of Containers," **p. 460**

FIG. 12.4
The Shape control can be used to provide a border or other visual effects.

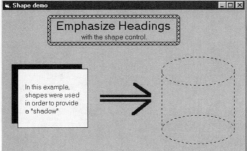

The Shape control can also be used to highlight information in a different manner. Suppose you want to draw your user's attention to the fact that he or she entered an incorrect value in a field. One way to do this is to draw a shape around the text box where the data was entered and to set its Visible property to False. Then place code to either show or hide the shape (depending on the value of the text) in the Change event procedure of the text box. The following code shows a shape when the text box's value is less than zero and hides the shape otherwise:

```
If Text1.Text < 0 Then
    Shape1.Visible = True
Else
    Shape1.Visible = False
End If
```

The Change event is triggered whenever the user starts typing in the text box. Therefore, if he or she starts to enter an incorrect value, the shape immediately appears. When an acceptable value is entered, the shape disappears. A good shape for this function is an oval with a BorderWidth of three and a red BorderColor.

Pictures on the Form

Another way to enhance your screens with graphics is to place pictures on the form. A *picture* is a bitmap file that can contain art, flow diagrams, or photos. The picture can be purely decorative, or it can be used to communicate specific information. You have probably seen pictures used for information in the setup screens of many programs. These pictures tell you about the features and benefits of the program while the installation is running. Visual Basic is capable of displaying many types of graphics files, which are summarized in Table 12.1.

Table 12.1 Graphics Files Compatible with Visual Basic

File Extension	Type of File
.BMP	Windows bitmap
.DIB	Bitmap file
.ICO	Windows icon
.WMF	Windows metafile
.EMF	Enhanced Windows metafile
.GIF	Graphics Interchange Format; a file format originally developed by CompuServe as a way to store raster (as opposed to vector) graphics images; commonly used to store graphics on the Internet
.JPG	JPEG images, named after the Joint Photographic Experts Group, developer of the format; similar to GIF images, but use compression algorithms to reduce file size; these are also used extensively on the Internet

There are several ways to add a picture to a form. The picture can be placed on the form itself, or it can be placed in a PictureBox or Image control on the form. The advantages and disadvantages of each of these methods are addressed in the following paragraphs.

Loading a Picture on the Form   The simplest way to add a picture to your screen is to add it to the form itself. You can do this at design time by setting the form's `Picture` property from the Properties window. To load a picture, select the `Picture` property, and then press the ellipsis (...) button at the far right of the line. This will call up the Load Picture dialog box shown in Figure 12.5. From this box, you can select the file containing the desired picture.

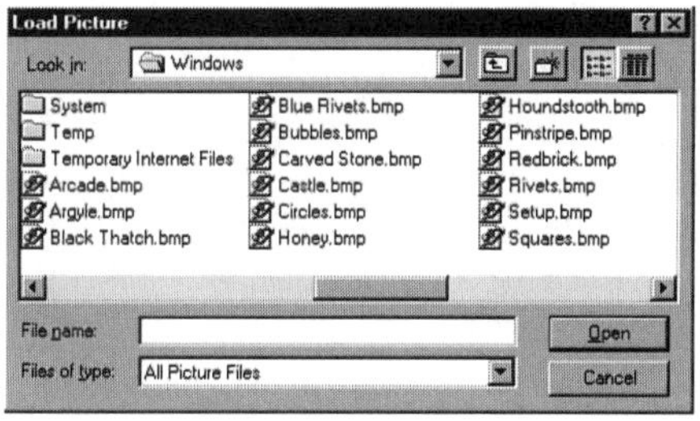

FIG. 12.5
To place a picture on a form at design time, the Properties window invokes the Load Picture dialog box. Pictures can also be loaded during program execution.

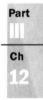

When a picture is loaded on the form, the entire picture is placed on the form, starting in the upper-left corner. If the picture is smaller than the form, space is left below or to the right of the picture. If the picture is larger than the form, the entire picture is still loaded, but only part of it is visible. As the form is re-sized, the amount of the picture shown changes.

N O T E   The picture is always placed starting in the upper-left corner. It cannot be placed anywhere else on the form. If you want a small picture in another area of the form, you must use either a Picture or Image control, as explained in the next two sections. ▨

When a picture is loaded on the form, it provides a background for the form. Any other controls added to the form appear on top of the picture. With the exception of the Label and Shape controls, the picture does not show through the background of the control. The Label and Shape controls allow the picture to show through if the `BackStyle` property of the control is set to `Transparent`. Figure 12.6 illustrates controls placed on a form containing a picture. Note the background of the controls.

FIG. 12.6

Some controls placed on a form do not allow the picture to show through.

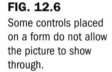

You can also add a picture to a form at runtime. This is done by setting the `Picture` property of the form with the `LoadPicture` function as shown in the following code:

```
Form1.Picture = LoadPicture("C:\MYPICT.BMP")
```

You can also remove the picture from the form by specifying a null argument for the `LoadPicture` function:

```
Form1.Picture = LoadPicture("")
```

The key advantage to placing your picture directly on the form is that this method uses fewer system resources than placing the picture in a Picture or Image control. Another benefit of placing the picture on the form is that you can use drawing methods to annotate the picture. For example, you could display a product's picture and then, by using the `Print` method, overlay the price or other database information on top of the picture. This capability is available with the PictureBox control as well, but is not available with the Image control.

Placing the picture directly on the form does, however, have several drawbacks:

- ▨ You cannot hide the picture; it can only be loaded or unloaded.
- ▨ You cannot control the placement of the picture on the form.
- ▨ You can only place one picture on the form at a time.

These drawbacks can be overcome with the use of the PictureBox or Image control. However, the added flexibility comes at the expense of system resources.

Using the Image Control A second way of placing pictures on a form is to use an Image control. The Image control provides a frame for a bitmap or other picture on a form. The control can be placed anywhere on the form and drawn to any desired size. You assign a picture to the Image control by setting the `Picture` property of the control. This can be done either at design time using the Properties window or at runtime using an assignment statement:

```
Image1.picture = LoadPicture("C:\mypic.bmp")
Image2.picture = Image1.Picture
```

One other property of the Image control greatly affects the appearance of any pictures you may use. This is the `Stretch` property. The `Stretch` property determines whether the Image control is sized to fit the picture, or the picture is sized to fit the control as drawn. If the `Stretch` property is set to `False` (the default), the Image control is automatically re-sized to fit the picture you assign to it. If the `Stretch` property is set to `True`, the picture is automatically re-sized so that the entire picture fits within the current boundaries of the Image control. This setting causes the overall size of the picture to change and can change the aspect ratio of the picture (the ratio of vertical to horizontal size). Figure 12.7 shows the same picture in several Image controls. The one with the `Stretch` property set to `False` shows the image at its original size, while the others show some possible effects of re-sizing the Image controls that have their `Stretch` properties set to `True`.

FIG. 12.7
The `Stretch` property of the Image control enables you to re-size the picture to the size of the control or vice versa.

Part
III

Ch
12

T I P If you are showing pictures of different sizes in your application, you should probably set the `Stretch` property to `True`. Otherwise, the size of the Image control will change with each picture and may cause the Image control to overlap other controls on the form. The Image control is anchored at its top-left corner, so only objects to the right and below the control would be affected. If the appearance of the pictures is unsuitable due to stretching, you may want to use the PictureBox control instead of the Image control.

The advantages of using the Image control instead of placing a picture directly on the form include the following:

- You can control the size of the picture's display area.
- You can place the picture anywhere on the form.
- You can place multiple Image controls on a form and use code to move them around.
- You can easily hide the picture using the Visible property of the Image control.

Using the Image control does have a few drawbacks, however:

- The Image control uses more resources than placing the picture directly on the form.
- You cannot use drawing methods to modify the picture in the Image control, as you can with a picture placed directly on the form or one in a PictureBox control.
- The Image control cannot serve as a container for other controls the way the PictureBox control can.

Using the PictureBox Control   The third way to place a picture on a form is with the PictureBox control. As with the Image control, multiple picture boxes can be placed on a form. The PictureBox control uses the most resources of the three methods. Loading a picture in a PictureBox control is accomplished the same way as loading a picture on a form or into an Image control. The picture can either be loaded at design time or at runtime.

Like the Image control, the PictureBox control enables you to place a picture anywhere on a form and to size the control. However, re-sizing the PictureBox control does not have the same effect on the picture as re-sizing an Image control. The default behavior of the PictureBox control is to show only as much of a picture as will fit in its current boundaries. If the picture is larger than the PictureBox control, the upper-left corner of the picture is shown. If the picture is smaller than the PictureBox control, space is shown around the edges of the picture. In either case, the entire picture, displayed or not, is loaded in the PictureBox control and available if the control is re-sized. Setting the PictureBox's AutoSize property to True changes this default behavior, causing the PictureBox control to re-size itself to fit the current picture. As with the Image control, the top-left corner of the control is anchored in place, and re-sizing of the control occurs to the right and down. However, don't confuse the AutoSize property with the Image control's Stretch property. The PictureBox control always preserves the aspect ratio of the picture being shown. Figure 12.8 shows the same picture in each of two PictureBox controls—one with the AutoSize property set to False, and the other with the AutoSize property set to True.

The PictureBox control also provides you with other capabilities that help you work with pictures. You can use the drawing methods to make changes to the picture, just as you can with the picture on a form. You can hide the picture or move it on the screen, just as you can with the Image control. But the PictureBox control also has some added benefits. Like the Frame control, the PictureBox control can be used as a container for other controls, so that any controls placed on the PictureBox control are treated as a unit with the PictureBox control itself. If the PictureBox control is hidden or moved, the other controls on it are also hidden or moved.

This feature allows the PictureBox control to be used to display multiple views or portions of data on a single form. For more detail on this feature, see "Exploring the Uses of Containers" in Chapter 16, "Using the Windows Common Controls."

▶ **See** "Exploring the Uses of Containers," **p. 460**

FIG. 12.8
The AutoSize property determines whether the PictureBox control will change size to fit the picture being displayed. Note that the size of the picture itself does not change.

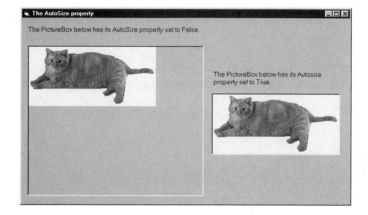

Invisible Buttons

As useful as it is to be able to display a picture on a form, you probably would like to be able to do more with pictures. One way to take advantage of the visual information displayed in a picture is to use it to control part of your application's interface.

For example, consider a flowchart displayed on a form that shows the various input files and calculations in a complex application (see Figure 12.9).

FIG. 12.9
A flowchart can be used to display information about an application.

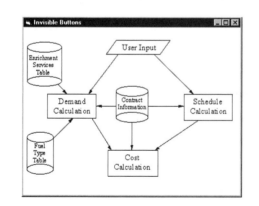

The flowchart helps the user understand how the information in the application is related. But suppose you could set up your application so that the user could access an input file merely by clicking the file name in the flowchart. This can be done by superimposing Image controls over the flowchart to create invisible buttons.

Load a picture onto the form or into a PictureBox control. Wherever you want an invisible button, place an Image control over the region that you want to activate. Finally, place code in the Click event of each Image control to accomplish the task you want performed. The Image control is invisible because it has no border; and with no picture assigned to it, the background of the control is transparent. Figure 12.10 shows the flowchart from Figure 12.9 in design mode so that you can see the invisible buttons. During program execution, these controls would not be seen because their BorderStyle property is set to None (which is the default). Image controls are needed because the Shapes have no events of their own.

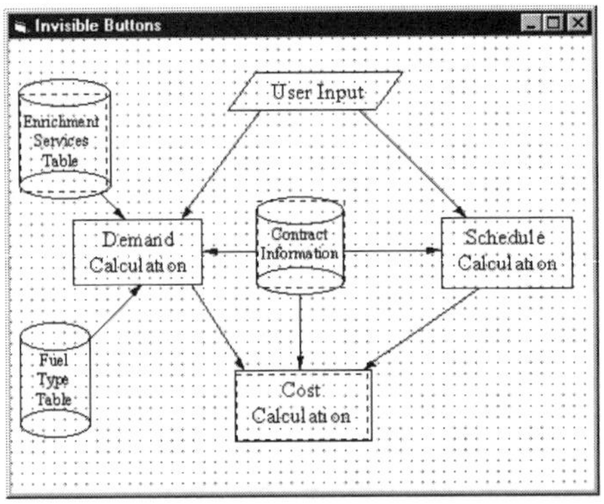

FIG. 12.10

Invisible buttons can make a picture part of your user interface.

This flowchart and invisible button application are contained in the file INVISBTN.VBP, which you can download from **www.mcp.com/info/0-7897/0-7897-1288-1**.

NOTE   When the buttons are clicked, a message box appears to tell you which button or area you pressed. ▨

Okay, since the buttons are invisible, how do you let the user know where they are and that he can click them? You can use a characteristic of the mouse pointer and the MouseMove event of the Image controls to change the mouse pointer when it is over one of the invisible buttons. Set the mouse pointer to an icon as shown in the following code:

```
Image1.MousePointer = vbCustom
Image1.MouseIcon =  LoadPicture("C:\myicon.ico")
```

This code changes the mouse pointer to an icon of your choosing for as long as the mouse is over the Image control. When the mouse is moved off of the control, the mouse pointer reverts to its original style. Figure 12.11 shows the invisible button with the changed mouse pointer over it.

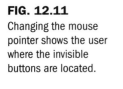

FIG. 12.11

Changing the mouse pointer shows the user where the invisible buttons are located.

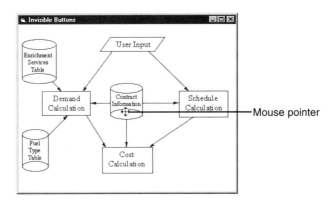

This invisible button concept can be used with all types of applications. For example, you can create a demonstration application for a new car. By placing invisible buttons on a picture of the car, you can enable the user to click the parts of the car to obtain information about its features—for example, the application can describe the car's engine capabilities if the user clicks the hood. The invisible buttons can be made any size you want them.

Creating and Managing Graphics

Earlier sections of this chapter have shown how you can use graphics to enhance the user interface through displayed pictures, invisible buttons, and other devices. To obtain the graphics used in these display elements, you can either use a graphics image from a library or create your own with a package such as Paintbrush.

But what if your application needs to be able to create graphics on its own? For example, certain data analysis programs create charts and programs for which the user might need a sketchpad for note taking. The following section discusses how you can create graphics images from within your application and how to store and manage the created graphics.

Creating Graphics

Visual Basic provides several tools that you can use to create graphics. The drawing methods can work on a form or in a PictureBox control. They can also be used with Visual Basic's `Printer` object to send the output to the printer. If no object is specified with the method, the form that is currently the focus will receive the output of the methods.

Visual Basic provides seven basic methods for creating graphics. These methods can be used to create many types of graphics images:

- `Line` method, which draws a line or a box on the target object
- `Circle` method, which draws a circle or oval on the target object
- `PSet` method, which places a single point on the target object

Part
III

Ch
12

■ `Point` method, which returns the color of a specific point

■ `PaintPicture` method, which draws an image from another control onto the target object

■ `Cls` method, which clears the output area of the target object

■ `Print` method, which places text on the target object

N O T E   In the following sections, we discuss these various graphics methods. For simplicity, code samples are given with the assumption that the target object is the form itself; therefore, the form name is left out of the syntax for invoking the method. For example, the first code sample below, `Line (1500, 750)-(2000, 750)`, draws a line on the form itself. However, the `Line` method can also apply to a PictureBox control. If you want to use one of these graphics methods on another object to which it applies, you can add the appropriate object name to the method syntax. To invoke the sample above on a PictureBox control named *Picture1*, you could use `Picture1.Line (1500, 750)-(2000, 750)`. ■

Using the *Line* Method   You use the `Line` method to draw lines and boxes on the form. To draw a line, you need to provide the `Line` method with the starting and ending points of the line. If you omit the starting point, the method draws a line from the current position to the ending point. The following code draws a triangle on a form:

```
Line (1500, 750)-(2000, 750)
Line -(2000, 1250)
Line -(1500, 750)
```

As with a form's `Left` and `Top` properties, the coordinate system's origin is at the upper-left corner. The `Line` method enables you to specify the color used to draw the line. You can also use the `Line` method to draw a box on the form by including the optional `B` argument. In this case, the coordinates passed to the `Line` method specify the top-left and bottom-right corners of the box. This example shows how to draw a red box from the upper-left coordinate (2000, 2000) to the lower-right coordinate (2500, 2500):

```
Line (2000, 2000)-(2500, 2500), vbRed, B
```

When drawing a box, you can see the form behind it if the `FillStyle` property of the form is set to transparent. If you want the box to be filled, you can also specify the optional `F` argument, which fills the box with the same color used to draw the border. In the following example, you get a filled blue box:

```
Line -(3000, 3000), vbBlue, BF
```

In the preceding example, the starting point is omitted; therefore, the box is drawn from the current position to the ending point.

As you can see, the commands to draw lines and boxes are quite simple. The key to controlling the appearance of lines and boxes is setting the drawing properties of the form (or other object that is receiving the graphics). The graphics methods use the object's current settings when drawing. The properties that affect the graphics methods are summarized in Table 12.2. The effects of some of these properties are shown in Figure 12.12.

Table 12.2   Drawing Properties that Affect the Appearance of Graphics Drawn with the Graphics Methods

Property Name	Purpose
DrawMode	Determines how the color used to draw the border of the object interacts with objects already on the screen
DrawStyle	Determines the pattern used to draw the border of the object
DrawWidth	Determines the width of the line used to draw the border of the object
FillColor	Determines the color used to fill an object
FillStyle	Determines the fill pattern used to fill an object
ForeColor	Determines the primary color used in drawing the border of an object

The values of these properties are explained in Visual Basic's Help system. All of these properties can be set for a form or PictureBox control at design time. However, they are most useful when they are set at runtime, when they can be set for a single drawing operation. The following code segment stores the form's drawing properties in variables, draws a series of boxes, and then returns the properties to their original settings:

```
frmset1 = Form1.DrawStyle
frmset2 = Form1.DrawWidth
frmset3 = Form1.FillColor
frmset4 = Form1.FillStyle
frmset5 = Form1.ForeColor
Line (1000, 1000)-(1500, 1500), , B
Form1.DrawStyle = 2
Form1.FillStyle = 2
Line -(2000, 2000), , B
Form1.FillColor = &hff
Line -(2500, 2500), , B
Form1.DrawWidth = 3
Form1.ForeColor = &hff0000
Line -(3000, 3000)
Form1.DrawStyle = frmset1
Form1.DrawWidth = frmset2
Form1.FillColor = frmset3
Form1.FillStyle = frmset4
Form1.ForeColor = frmset5
Line (100, 100)-(500, 500), , B
```

Figure 12.12 displays the appearance of the form after executing this code sample.

Using the *Circle* Method   The Circle method allows you to draw circles, ellipses, arcs, and pies on the form. The simplest form of the method is the following:

```
Circle (X, Y), R
```

FIG. 12.12

The Line method can be used to draw lines and boxes on an object such as a form or printer.

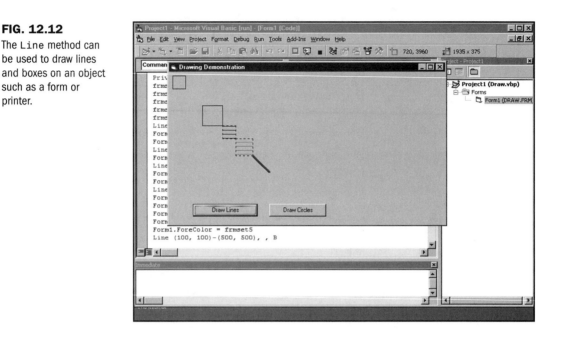

This command draws a circle of radius R with a center at the position specified by X and Y. As with the Line method, the pattern and color of the circle's border and fill are determined by the settings of the drawing properties. The full syntax of the Circle method is as follows:

```
object.Circle [Step] (x, y), radius, [color, start, end, aspect]
```

Several optional arguments can be used with the Circle method. See the Visual Basic help system for the complete syntax. You use the start and end arguments of the method to draw an arc rather than a full circle. The values of start and end are the angles from horizontal expressed in radians. (The value of an angle in radians is determined by multiplying the angle in degrees by $\pi/180$.) The values of start and end can range from zero to 2π, or zero to -2π. If the values of both the start and end arguments are negative, the method draws a pie (an arc with lines extending to the center of the circle). If both values are positive, a simple arc is drawn. If one of the values is negative, a line is drawn from that end of the arc to the center.

Another argument that can be specified is the *aspect* argument. This argument is used to draw an ellipse or an oval. The aspect is the ratio of the vertical size of the ellipse to the horizontal size. An aspect of one draws a circle. If the aspect is greater than one, the ellipse is taller than it is wide. If the aspect is less than one, the ellipse is wider than it is tall. In all cases, the radius specified in the method sets the size of the longer dimension. The code for drawing several shapes with the Circle method is the following. (The results of this code are shown in Figure 12.13.)

```
'Circle
Circle (500, 500), 500
'Arc
```

```
Circle (1500, 1500), 500, , 1.57, 0
'Piece of pie
Circle (2500, 2500), 500, , -4.7, -6.2
'Ellipse
Circle (3500, 3500), 500, , , , 1.5
'Another piece of pie
Circle (4500, 4500), 500, , -0.01, -1.57, 1.5
```

N O T E In the previous code, there's a "missing" argument, which is after the radius but before the start and end arguments. This place is reserved for the optional `color` argument. If this argument is not present, the color used to draw the circle is the `ForeColor` property of the object on which it's drawn. Notice also that even though the color argument is left out, its place is "saved" by an extra comma. ▓

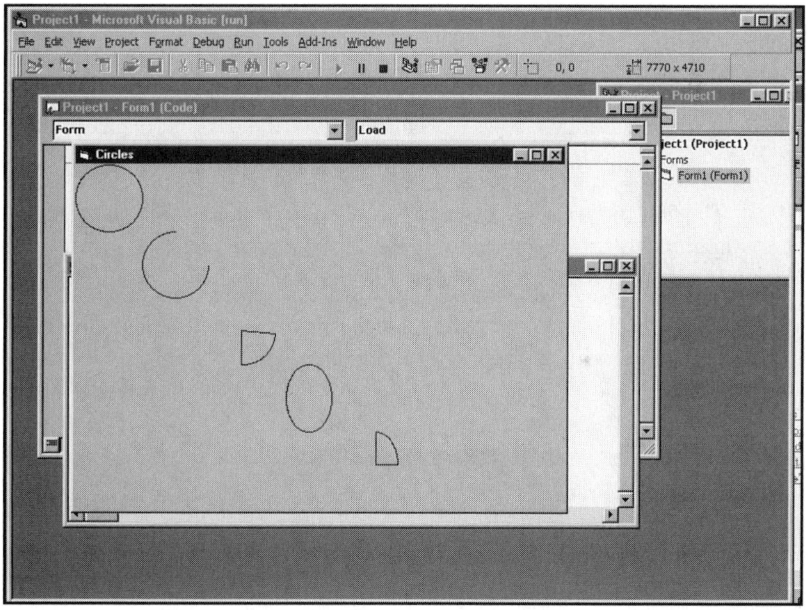

FIG. 12.13

The `Circle` method has several optional para-meters that allow it to draw ellipses, arcs, and pies.

Part

III

Ch

12

Using the *PSet* Method The `PSet` method is used to draw a single point on the form using the color specified by the `ForeColor` property. The size of the point drawn is dependent on the setting of the `DrawWidth` property. A larger `DrawWidth` setting produces a larger point. The `PSet` method draws the point at the coordinates specified in the argument of the method. The following code will draw a point at position 100, 100:

```
PSet (100, 100)
```

One use of the `PSet` method is to provide a freehand drawing capability for the users of your application. This use is covered in the later section "Creating a Sketchpad Application."

Using the *PaintPicture* Method The `PaintPicture` method enables you to place all or part of a picture from one object into a specific location in another object. Also, by carefully setting the height and width of the source and target objects, you can enlarge or reduce the size of the source picture. The following code paints part of a picture from a PictureBox control named *picSource* onto the base form:

```
frmdest.PaintPicture picSource.Picture, 50, 50, 750, 750, 0, 0, 500, 500
```

As you can see from the line of code, the `PaintPicture` method contains several arguments:

- *Source picture*   All or part of this source picture is drawn in a "target region" on the destination object.
- *Target X and Y*   These two numerical arguments specify the coordinates of the upper-left corner of the target region. Therefore, in the previous example, drawing occurs on frmDest 50 twips from the left edge and 50 twips from the top edge.
- *Target Size*   Specifies the horizontal and vertical size of the target region. If this size is different from the size of the source picture or region, the picture is stretched or compressed to fit the target region.
- *Source X and Y*   The third pair of numbers in the command specifies the upper-left corner of the source region—that is, the part of the picture being copied.
- *Source Size*   Specifies the height and width of the source region.

The first three arguments are the only ones required for the `PaintPicture` method. All other arguments are optional. If only the three required arguments are specified, the entire source picture is copied to the target at full size.

The code shown in this listing takes a piece of a picture from the PictureBox control, enlarges it by 50 percent, and places it on the form. The results of this command are shown in Figure 12.14.

FIG. 12.14

The `PaintPicture` method can copy all or part of a picture from one object to another and enlarge or reduce the picture.

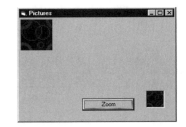

Some uses of the `PaintPicture` method in creating graphics would be the following:

- To provide a zoom feature for looking more closely at specific regions of a picture. This feature would be useful for implementing print preview in your application.
- To make multiple copies of a picture (or a portion of one) on a target object.
- To clear a specified region of a picture or combine several pictures.
- To print the contents of a PictureBox control—for example, to put a company logo on your report.
- To be able to create data point markers for a chart.

Using the *Print* Method   Although the `Print` method is not usually thought of as a graphics method, it works the same way. Its primary use is to place text on a form, PictureBox control, or the `Printer` object. The `Print` method can be used in conjunction with the graphics methods to create charts or drawings or to annotate existing bit maps. The `Print` method itself is quite simple. The following code displays a single line of text at the current position on the form:

```
Print "This is a one-line test."
```

Remember, these code examples assume that the graphics methods are directed to the current form. To print the line of text in the previous sample to the printer, you could invoke the `Printer` object's `Print` method:

```
Printer.Print "This is a one-line test."
```

The output of the `Print` method is controlled by the settings of five properties of the object being printed on. These properties are as follows:

- `CurrentX`—This sets the horizontal position for the starting point of the text.
- `CurrentY`—This sets the vertical position for the starting point of the text.
- `Font`—This determines the font type and size used for the text.
- `ForeColor`—This determines the color of the text.
- `FontTransparent`—On a form or picture, this determines whether or not the background behind the text will show through the spaces in the text.

Other Methods   The other two graphics methods mentioned at the beginning of this section are the `Point` method and the `Cls` method. These two methods each perform a single function. The `Point` method returns the RGB color setting of a single specified point. The `Cls` method, which stands for "Clear Screen" (a carryover from DOS-based programming languages that needed to clear the entire screen before writing more information), clears all graphics drawn with the graphics methods from a form, PictureBox control, or Image control. The `Cls` method has no effect on any *controls* that are on the object. It only clears *graphics* that were drawn at runtime.

Creating a Sketchpad Application

To further illustrate how the different graphics methods work, this section discusses how to create a sketchpad application. This application is similar to the familiar Windows Paintbrush application. The starting form for the application is shown in Figure 12.15.

This sketchpad application only creates bit map (.BMP) drawings. After being created, any object placed on the screen is handled simply as a series of points. The objects cannot be selected later to be re-sized or moved. In contrast to this application, programs like Microsoft PowerPoint save information about the size, type, location, and other characteristics of an object. This feature allows the object to be re-selected and those characteristics to be modified in order to change the object's appearance at a later time.

Setting Up the Toolbar   The sketchpad application uses Image controls to create a toolbar, which enables the user to select which type of object to draw. The toolbar is set up by placing three arrays of Image controls on the form. Two of the arrays are used to store the image of the "up" button and the "down" position for each tool. The third image array acts as the actual toolbar. When the button for a tool is pressed, two results occur. First, the down image of the button is displayed to indicate which tool was selected. Second, a variable is set to tell the program which drawing tool to use. The sketchpad application provides the user with the capability to draw the following six objects:

- Line
- Open Box
- Filled Box
- Open Circle
- Filled Circle
- Freehand Sketch

FIG. 12.15

You can create a Paintbrush-style application by using the drawing methods.

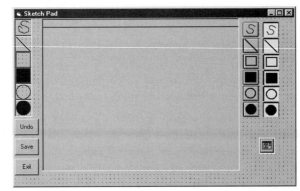

You use the Image control array to make programming simpler. The index of the control array defines the tool used to draw on the PictureBox control. An example of the code for setting the Image control pictures and the tool type is shown here. The variable inToolNum is declared in the declarations section of the form and is initially set to zero, the number for the Freehand tool:

```
Private Sub imgToolBar_Click(Index As Integer)
    'Reset the button for the previously used tool to the Up position
    imgToolbar(inToolNum).Picture = imgUp(inToolNum).Picture

    'Set the button for the newly selected tool to the Down position
    imgToolBar(Index).Picture = imgDown(Index).Picture

    'Set the inToolNum variable to the new tool
    inToolNum = Index
End Sub
```

Using the Various Drawing Tools The sketchpad enables the user to press the mouse button and then drag the mouse to draw an object, just like VB controls or any Windows drawing program. The sketchpad application provides a PictureBox control on which the user may draw.

▶ **See** "Common Events," **p. 155**

To implement the various drawing tools, you need to work with three events: MouseDown, MouseMove, and MouseUp. These events correspond with the user's actions as he or she is drawing an object.

The MouseDown event is responsible for telling the program that the user is drawing on the PictureBox control and for setting the initial position of the object. The purpose of this initial point depends on the type of object being drawn. Table 12.3 shows the purpose of the initial point for each of the objects in the sketchpad application.

Table 12.3   Initial Point of a Drawing Operation Has Different Meanings for Each Object

Object	Use of Initial Point
Line	One of two points defining the line
Box (open or filled)	One of the corners of the box
Circle (open or filled)	One corner of a box which would bound the circle
Freehand	The first point drawn

A variable has been defined to tell the program whether to draw objects while the mouse is in motion. This variable, DrawNow, has a value of either True or False. The MouseDown event sets this variable to True. The following code is placed in the MouseDown event to enable the drawing methods. In the code, the variables curX and curY are the coordinates of the initial point. The variables oldX and oldY are the coordinates of the last mouse position. These variables are important in the MouseMove event, as you will see:

```
Private Sub PicMain_MouseDown(Button As Integer, Shift As Integer, _
    X As Single, Y As Single)
  DrawNow = True
  curX = X
  curY = Y
  oldX = X
  oldY = Y
End Sub
```

The MouseMove event is the main workhorse of the sketchpad application. If the mouse button is down (DrawNow is set to True), the code in the MouseMove event draws the selected object between the initial point of the drawing and the current mouse position. The event contains a set of cases to handle the various types of objects that might be drawn. You might notice that the open and filled boxes and the open and filled circles use the same code. This is because in the MouseMove event, it is only necessary to show the outline of a filled object while the drawing is in progress.

You might also notice that the Line method is used for the Freehand drawing instead of the PSet method. The reason for this is that the MouseMove event is triggered at certain intervals, not as a continuous event. Rapid movements of the mouse leave gaps in the lines drawn with the PSet method. When the Line method is used, a line is drawn between the last position of the mouse and the current position, thereby providing a continuous line. The code for the MouseMove event is shown in Listing 12.1.

Listing 12.1   The *MouseMove* Event Draws the Outline of the Object as the Mouse Is Dragged

```
Private Sub PicMain_MouseMove(Button As Integer, Shift As Integer, _
        X As Single, Y As Single)
If DrawNow Then
    Select Case inToolNum
        Case 0 'Freehand drawing tool
            PicMain.Line (oldX, oldY)-(X, Y)
            oldX = X
            oldY = Y
        Case 1 'Lines
            PicMain.Line (curX, curY)-(oldX, oldY), PicMain.BackColor
            PicMain.Line (curX, curY)-(X, Y)
            oldX = X
            oldY = Y
        Case 2,3 'Open and filled boxes
            PicMain.Line (curX, curY)-(oldX, oldY), PicMain.BackColor, B
            PicMain.Line (curX, curY)-(X, Y), , B
            oldX = X
            oldY = Y
        Case 4,5 'Open and filled circles
            cntX = curX + Int((X - curX) / 2)
            cntY = curY + Int((Y - curY) / 2)
            radX = Abs(curX - X)
            radY = Abs(curY - Y)
            radcir = IIf(radX > radY, radX, radY) / 2
            If radX = 0 Then
                aspcir = 1
            Else
                aspcir = radY / radX
            End If
            PicMain.Circle (oldX, oldY), oldrad, PicMain.BackColor, , , _
                oldasp
            PicMain.Circle (cntX, cntY), radcir, , , , aspcir
            oldX = cntX
            oldY = cntY
            oldasp = aspcir
            oldrad = radcir
    End Select
End If
End Sub
```

When the user is finished drawing and releases the mouse button, the MouseUp event creates the final drawing for the object and turns off the drawing mode (see Listing 12.2). Much of the same code is used in the MouseUp event as in the MouseMove event, but separate cases have been added for the filled boxes and circles.

Listing 12.2   The *MouseUp* Event Renders the Final Drawing and Turns Off the Drawing Mode

```
Private Sub PicMain_MouseUp(Button As Integer, Shift As Integer, _
    X As Single, Y As Single)
If DrawNow Then
    Select Case inToolNum
        Case 1   'Line
            PicMain.Line (curX, curY)-(oldX, oldY), PicMain.BackColor
            PicMain.Line (curX, curY)-(X, Y)
        Case 2   'Open Box
            PicMain.FillStyle = vbFSTransparent
            PicMain.Line (curX, curY)-(oldX, oldY), PicMain.BackColor, B
            PicMain.Line (curX, curY)-(X, Y), , B
        Case 3   'Filled Box
            PicMain.FillStyle = vbFSSolid
            PicMain.Line (curX, curY)-(oldX, oldY), PicMain.BackColor, B
            PicMain.Line (curX, curY)-(X, Y), , B
            PicMain.FillStyle = vbFSTransparent
        Case 4   'Open Elipse
            cntX = curX + Int((X - curX) / 2)
            cntY = curY + Int((Y - curY) / 2)
            radX = Abs(curX - X)
            radY = Abs(curY - Y)
            radcir = IIf(radX > radY, radX, radY) / 2
            If radX = 0 Then
                aspcir = 1
            Else
                aspcir = radY / radX
            End If
            PicMain.FillStyle = vbFSTransparent
            PicMain.Circle (oldX, oldY), oldrad, PicMain.BackColor, , , _
                oldasp
            PicMain.Circle (cntX, cntY), radcir, , , , aspcir
        Case 5   'Filled elipse
            cntX = curX + Int((X - curX) / 2)
            cntY = curY + Int((Y - curY) / 2)
            radX = Abs(curX - X)
            radY = Abs(curY - Y)
            radcir = IIf(radX > radY, radX, radY) / 2
            If radX = 0 Then
                aspcir = 1
            Else
                aspcir = radY / radX
            End If
```

Part

III

Ch

12

continues

Listing 12.2   Continued

```
        PicMain.FillStyle = vbFSSolid
        PicMain.Circle (oldX, oldY), oldrad, PicMain.BackColor, , , _
            oldasp
        PicMain.Circle (cntX, cntY), radcir, , , , aspcir
        PicMain.FillStyle = vbFSTransparent
    End Select
End If
DrawNow = 0
End Sub
```

Creating an Undo Feature   Most applications that perform drawing functions have an Undo feature that allows the user to restore the picture to its state prior to the last drawing operation. An Undo function can be implemented in the sketchpad application by adding a second PictureBox control to the form, placing some additional code in the MouseDown event, and adding an Undo button. The second PictureBox control contains a copy of the image in the PictureBox control that contains the "primary" drawing. This second PictureBox control has its Visible property set to False so that it is not visible when the application is running. The second picture is updated each time a new drawing operation is started. This update is performed in the MouseDown event as shown in the following code:

```
picUndo.Picture = picMain.Image
```

N O T E   In the previous code, a picture was copied to a picture box's Picture property by assigning to the property another picture box's Image property. The Image property was used because it not only contains the loaded picture, but also the results of any drawing operations. ▨

To undo an operation, the code simply copies the picture in the second PictureBox control back to the main PictureBox control, returning the drawing area back to the way it was before the last drawing operation. This code is shown in the following line:

```
picMain.Picture = picUndo.Picture
```

Saving the Picture   Finally, you should give your users the capability of saving the pictures they create. The drawings on a PictureBox control can be saved as a bit map file using the SavePicture function. This function requires the name of the source picture and the name of the output file. You probably want to use the CommonDialog control to enable the user to specify a name for the output file. For a drawing, the source of the picture is the Image property of the PictureBox control or the form on which the drawing was made. The following code gets a file name using the CommonDialog control (named GetFile) and stores the drawing created by the sketchpad application:

```
GetFile.Filter = "Bitmap Files (*.BMP)¦*.bmp"
GetFile.DefaultExt = "BMP"
GetFile.ShowSave
DataName = GetFile.FileName
SavePicture PicMain.Image, DataName
```

Bit Map Annotation

The sketchpad application showed how you can create graphics with the graphics methods and how to store the graphics in files. Because the PictureBox control is also capable of displaying an existing graphics file, you can use the sketchpad program to modify graphics from other sources. You might want to use this program to annotate fax images before sending them on to another person. You can also use the sketchpad to make changes to bit maps created by others.

To annotate bit maps, you need to add a `LoadPicture` function to the sketchpad application so that you can import the picture into the editing area. The code for this operation is shown here. This code again uses the CommonDialog control to obtain the name of the file to be edited:

```
stTemp = "Bitmap Files (*.BMP)¦*.bmp¦Icon Files ¦ *.ico ¦All Files¦*.*"
GetFile.Filter = stTemp
GetFile.DefaultExt = "BMP"
GetFile.ShowOpen
DataName = GetFile.FileName
PicMain.Picture = LoadPicture(DataName)
```

Using a Database to Store Pictures

There are two ways to use pictures with databases. The most obvious is to store a *pointer* to the name of the picture file in the database. However, an Access database created in Visual Basic can store pictures in the database itself. The field type to use for pictures is a *long binary* field. If the database is bound to a Data control, the field containing the pictures can be bound to either a PictureBox control or an Image control. If a PictureBox control is used, the drawing methods discussed in this section can be used to create or edit the pictures in the database.

It is important to know how to save the changes to the pictures back into the database. A problem arises in saving these changes because the data field containing the picture is bound to the `Picture` property of the PictureBox control. The drawings that are made with the graphics methods are not part of the `Picture` property, but rather part of the `Image` property. It is therefore necessary to copy the `Image` property to the `Picture` property prior to the update of the database, which you can do with the following line of code:

```
PicMain.Picture = PicMain.Image
```

Once the drawing or annotations have been copied to the `Picture` property, the drawing is stored in the database. An application that requires a number of sketches can benefit from using this technique to store the drawings. When you use the database, all the drawings are stored in one file rather than a series of bitmap files. It is also possible to add other fields to the database that contain a description of the drawing and possibly supporting information or notes.

Part

III

Ch

12

> **CAUTION**
>
> If you use a great number of pictures in a database, it may grow to an unmanageable size!

Analyzing Data with Graphics

This final topic in the chapter deals with analyzing data or information with the use of graphics or charts. Often charts are very useful in giving users a better feel for the information than numbers alone can give. The percentage of your household budget devoted to debt reduction is presented far more dramatically by a pie chart than by the mere presentation of dollar amounts. Charts can also help a user spot trends in the data that would not be possible from viewing only the numeric data.

Generating charts with the graphics methods is much more difficult than using the Chart control, but there are some advantages to the effort:

■ You can create multiple charts on the same PictureBox control (such as a bar chart for regional sales by month and a pie chart for total sales by region).

■ You can place multiple axes on the same chart, enabling you to plot multiple variables (for example, a chart of engine temperature and coolant pressure versus speed).

■ You can create charts that change with time.

■ Graphics methods do not have the overhead of distributing a custom control.

■ You can superimpose the chart on another graphic for special effects.

This section discusses the general programming aspects of creating your own charts and then looks in detail at some of the advantages mentioned in the list.

Creating a Simple Chart

To begin the discussion, consider the pie chart shown in Figure 12.16. To create this chart in a program, you follow these steps:

1. Calculate the total value of all the points.
2. Convert the value of each point to a fraction of the total.
3. Convert the fractional value to the radian values of a circle.
4. Set the `FillColor` property for each point.
5. Draw the pie shape for each of the points.

FIG. 12.16
By using the `Circle` method to draw arcs, you can create a pie chart.

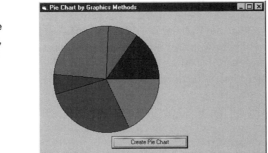

Listing 12.3 demonstrates how you can perform these steps for the graph illustrated in Figure 12.16.

Listing 12.3   Creating a Pie Chart

```
Sub CreatePieChart()
    Const SLICES = 6
    Const PIEX = 2000
    Const PIEY = 2000
    Const PIERADIUS = 1500
    Dim inData(1 To SLICES) As Integer
    Dim inCounter As Integer
    Dim inTotal As Integer
    Dim lgStartPoint As Single
    Dim lgEndPoint As Single
    Dim lgPercent As Single
    Dim lgSliceSize As Single


    'First, we create sample data points
    'with random numbers from 1 to 20
    For inCounter = 1 To SLICES
        inData(inCounter) = Int(20 * Rnd + 1)
    Next inCounter

    'Next, we'll add all the data points
    'together to get a total value.
    For inCounter = 1 To SLICES
        inTotal = inTotal + inData(inCounter)
    Next inCounter

    'Finally, we calculate each data point's
    'percent of the total value and plot it.
    frmMain.FillStyle = vbFSSolid
    lgStartPoint = -0.001
    For inCounter = 1 To SLICES
        lgPercent = inData(inCounter) / inTotal
        lgSliceSize = lgPercent * 2 * 3.14159
        lgEndPoint = lgStartPoint - lgSliceSize
        lgEndPoint = IIf(lgEndPoint < -6.2831, -6.2831, lgEndPoint)
        frmMain.FillColor = QBColor(inCounter)
        frmMain.Circle (PIEX, PIEY), PIERADIUS, , lgStartPoint, lgEndPoint
        lgStartPoint = lgEndPoint
    Next inCounter

End Sub
```

Part

III

Ch

12

This is a somewhat generic routine for creating a pie chart. In a real program, of course, the data would not be generated randomly. Notice also, the QBColor function is used to assign a color to a particular data point. QBColor (QB stands for "QuickBasic," which was Visual

Basic's granddaddy) converts integer color codes used by older versions of BASIC into an equivalent hexadecimal color code that can be used by Visual Basic. I just used it here because the data is random and the color doesn't matter anyway.

What Methods to Use for Different Chart Types

As you saw previously, a pie chart can be created using the `Circle` method. Most of the chart types described for the graphic control can be easily ("easy" being a relative term) created with the graphics methods. Each graphic type uses one or more of the graphics methods to create the charts. Table 12.4 shows several of the most common chart types and the methods used to create them.

Table 12.4 Different Graphics Methods Are Used to Create Different Types of Charts

Chart Type	Graphics Method
Pie	`Circle` method
Bar	`Line` method (drawing boxes)
Gantt	`Line` method (drawing lines or boxes)
Line	`Line` method
Scatter	`PSet` method, `PaintPicture` method, `Print` method
High-Low-Close	`Line` method

Symbols can be drawn on any of the chart types using the `PaintPicture` method; or, if the symbols are simple characters, the `Print` method can be used to place the character on the chart. You may also notice that the chart indicates that the `Print` method can produce scatter charts. This process works the same way as placing symbols on the chart. You establish the necessary position of the symbol using the `CurrentX` and `CurrentY` properties and then print the symbol.

Determining Where to Place Points on the Chart

The previous section, "Creating a Simple Chart," showed how to use the `Circle` method to create a pie chart. The code used to produce the chart assumed that the size of the form and the position of the chart were predetermined. This may not always be the case. If you are drawing a chart on a form whose size can change, you need to calculate the position of the chart on the form. In addition, for many chart types (such as line or bar), you need to establish the range of the horizontal and vertical coordinates that are available for showing data.

This section walks you through this process using a line chart containing 50 data points with a random value of 0 to 1,000 as an example. (The program code for the chart is shown in Listing 12.3.) The actual chart is shown in Figure 12.17.

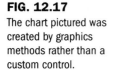

FIG. 12.17
The chart pictured was created by graphics methods rather than a custom control.

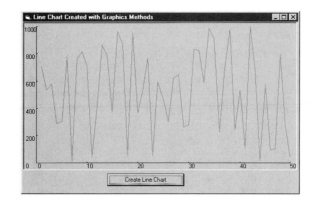

The first step in determining where the data for the chart should be placed is to find the size of the form or PictureBox control that can contain the chart. Horizontal and vertical size are determined using the ScaleWidth and ScaleHeight properties, respectively. These properties determine the maximum space available for the output of the chart.

Next, you determine the amount of space needed for labels on the two axes. This space is handled by the TextHeight and TextWidth methods. You will want the maximum length of all the labels on the chart. For this sample, the Y-axis ranges from 0 to 1,000 in increments of 200. Therefore, the maximum TextWidth would be for 1,000. Along the X-axis, the values range from 1 to 50 in increments of 10, but all the values should have the same text height. The TextWidth determines the margin between the edge of the output object (form or picture box) and the Y-axis. Similarly, the TextHeight gives the margin between the bottom of the output object and the X-axis. If you also want a margin at the top and right of the chart, you have to establish values for these as well. The code for the sample chart uses half the TextWidth and TextHeight margins for the right and top margins, respectively.

Subtracting the margin sizes from the total size of the object gives you the size of the area where you will draw the line graph. The size of this area determines the scaling factor that you need to use to place data points. For the Y-axis values, this is the height of the drawing area divided by the maximum value. For the X-axis value, the scaling factor is the width of the drawing area divided by the maximum X value. To obtain the drawing position of any point you need to perform the following steps:

1. Multiply the X value by the horizontal scaling factor to determine the distance from the Y-axis.

2. Add the distance obtained in Step 1 to the width of the left margin to obtain the actual X position on the output object.

3. Multiply the Y value by the vertical scaling factor to determine the distance from the X-axis.

4. Subtract the distance obtained in Step 3 from the position of the X-axis to obtain the actual Y position on the output object.

Part

Ch

You might notice that the last step instructs you to subtract the value obtained in Step 3 from the position of the X-axis. The reason for this step is that the vertical position coordinates of an object increase from top to bottom. Therefore, a point above the X-axis has a smaller number for the vertical position than the axis itself (see Listing 12.4).

Listing 12.4   Creating a Chart with Graphics Methods

```
Sub CreateLineChart()
    Dim inCounter As Integer
    Dim inMaxX As Integer
    Dim inMaxY As Integer
    Dim inLmarg As Integer
    Dim inRmarg As Integer
    Dim inBmarg As Integer
    Dim inTmarg As Integer
    Dim inScaleX As Integer
    Dim inScaleY As Integer
    Dim inYPos As Integer
    Dim inXPos As Integer

    picChart.ForeColor = vbBlack
    picChart.Cls

    'Determine maximum size of chart
    inMaxX = picChart.ScaleWidth
    inMaxY = picChart.ScaleHeight

    'Determine chart margins, including
    'width for the axis labels
    inLmarg = picChart.TextWidth("1000")
    inBmarg = picChart.TextHeight("50")
    inRmarg = inMaxX - 0.5 * inLmarg
    inTmarg = 0.5 * inBmarg
    inBmarg = inMaxY - inBmarg

    'Determine scale factors for each axis
    inScaleX = (inRmarg - inLmarg) / 50
    inScaleY = (inBmarg - inTmarg) / 1000

    'Draw axes
    picChart.Line (inLmarg, inTmarg)-(inLmarg, inBmarg)
    picChart.Line -(inRmarg, inBmarg)

    'Draw labels and tic marks for vertical axis
    For inCounter = 1 To 6
        picChart.CurrentX = 5
        inYPos = inBmarg - ((inCounter - 1) * 200 * inScaleY)
        picChart.CurrentY = inYPos
        picChart.Print Right(Str((inCounter - 1) * 200), 4)
        picChart.Line (inLmarg, inYPos)-(inLmarg + 40, inYPos)
    Next inCounter

    'Draw labels and tic marks for horizontal axis
    For inCounter = 1 To 6
```

```
            inXPos = inLmarg + ((inCounter - 1) * 10 * inScaleX)
            picChart.CurrentX = inXPos
            picChart.CurrentY = inBmarg + 5
            picChart.Print Right(Str((inCounter - 1) * 10), 2)
            picChart.Line (inXPos, inBmarg)-(inXPos, inBmarg - 40)
        Next inCounter

        'Draw Random Points
        picChart.ForeColor = vbRed
        For inCounter = 1 To 50
            inXPos = inLmarg + (inCounter * inScaleX)
            inYPos = inBmarg - (1000 * Rnd * inScaleY)
            If inCounter = 1 Then
                picChart.CurrentX = inXPos
                picChart.CurrentY = inYPos
            Else
                picChart.Line -(inXPos, inYPos)
            End If
        Next inCounter

    End Sub
```

Dynamic, or Time-Dependent, Graphs

One of the advantages of creating your own data analysis charts is that you can create a chart that changes with time. To create this *dynamic*, or *time-dependent*, *chart*, you need a way to add points to the chart at specified intervals. An example you may have seen is the Windows NT Performance monitor, which can be used to provide a timed graph of CPU usage. There are two ways to handle plotting time-dependent information. You can track all the information—adding new points but never removing old points—or you can track some number of points representing the most recent measurements (for instance, the last 100 points).

Part

III

Ch

12

Tracking a number of recent points is usually the preferable method of developing a dynamic chart. The advantages of this method are that you have a limited number of points that keep system resource requirements down, and you do not have to constantly recalculate the scale factors to account for additional points.

The following sample code segments build a dynamic chart based on our previous example. The same code is used to draw the axes and set up the chart. First, move the code from Listing 12.3 to a separate procedure called SetupChart. Next, remove the last For loop, which draws all the points. Add the lines

```
SetupChart
inCounter = 1
```

to the form's Load event. Finally, move all the variable declarations from SetupChart to the form's general declarations section so that they are visible to other procedures.

The new code needed is a function that draws one segment of the line graph at a time. This function can then be placed in a Timer control's Timer event to fill the chart gradually:

```
Private Sub Timer1_Timer()

    inXPos = inLmarg + (inCounter * inScaleX)
    inYPos = Int(inBmarg - (1000 * Rnd * inScaleY))

    If inCounter = 1 Then
        picChart.CurrentX = inXPos
        picChart.CurrentY = inYPos
    Else
        picChart.Line -(inXPos, inYPos)
    End If

    inCounter = inCounter + 1

    If inCounter > 50 Then SetupChart

End Sub
```

Notice in the code above that when the 50th data point is reached, the graph simply starts over from the left. Figure 12.18 illustrates the chart created by this code.

FIG. 12.18
You can create a
dynamic chart that
changes as new points
are added.

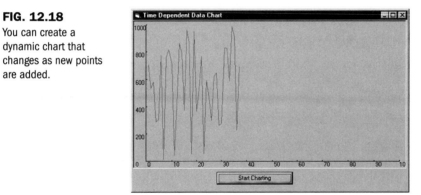

From Here...

In this chapter, you learned about which controls and objects can be used to add pictures to a program. You also learned how to use some low-level graphics to draw on the screen or printer. These methods can be used for creating visual effects or informational displays, such as charts.

■ To learn more ways to add visual appeal to your forms, see Chapter 11, "Designing User Interfaces."

■ To learn more about the Print method, see Chapter 12, "Working with Graphics."

■ For a more detailed discussion of the PictureBox control's capabilities, Chapter 16, "Using the Windows Common Controls."

■ To find out how to use these enhancements in a manner that is useful to the end user, see Chapter 21, "Extending ActiveX Controls."

CHAPTER 13

Working with Text, Fonts, and Colors

The vast majority of your programs will use text as the primary means of communicating information to the users. "Text" refers not only to text displayed on-screen in controls, but also to text that is stored and created in your program code. To write almost any program in Visual Basic, you need to know how to work with text. In earlier chapters, you learned about displaying text in labels and text boxes. This chapter expands on that knowledge by showing you how properties and functions are used to manipulate text. You also see how to change the appearance of your text by using fonts and colors in your programs. ■

Using controls to work with text

You will see how to display text on-screen through the use of the TextBox and Masked Edit controls.

Manipulating text in Visual Basic

You will learn about some of the many functions available in Visual Basic for working with text.

Controlling the appearance of your text with fonts

You will explore the use of the Font object's properties in your programs.

Letting users control text formatting

You will see how to use the RichTextBox control to create a simple word processor that allows your users to control the appearance of the text that they enter.

Using colors to enhance your interface

You can use a variety of colors to display text and other objects on-screen and on color printers. You will see how the color of the text is controlled.

Getting and Displaying Text

Two of the primary tasks of any program are to retrieve information from the user and to display information to the user. This information is often in the form of text and can be something as simple as the names in a membership list, or something as complex as developing a specialized word processor for a particular industry. Visual Basic provides a number of ways to input and display information. For input, the primary control is the text box, but there are several other controls covered in this chapter. For output, you can display information on-screen by using the TextBox and Label controls, or you can print information directly on a Form object or to the Printer object. This chapter sticks with using the controls; printing is covered in Chapter 9, "Displaying and Printing Reports."

Reviewing the Basic Controls

In Chapter 4, "Working with Forms and Controls," you were introduced to the TextBox and Label controls. As you probably remember, the label can display text to the user, whether the text was entered into the label at design time or assigned with code to the label's Caption property at runtime. The Label control can display a single line of text or multiple lines easily, but it does not allow the user to input text or scroll through the text if there is more than would fit in the control.

The text box, on the other hand, can do everything a label can do—and it allows editing and scrolling. Using a text box, users can enter anything they want, and your program can retrieve this information through the Text property. Your program can also set the Text property to display information back to the user.

Using Other Features of the TextBox Control

In addition to the text box's standard properties, there are several other properties and features of the text box that make it even more versatile. Some key additional properties are the following:

- Locked—This prevents the user from entering information in the text box.
- MaxLength—This limits the number of characters that the text box can display.
- PasswordChar—This causes the textbox to hide the information typed by the user.
- SelLength, SelStart, and SelText—These enable the user to manipulate only the selected (highlighted) part of the text in the text box.

Locking Out the User   First, take a look at the Locked property. Its purpose is to enable you to use the TextBox control for display only. When this property is set to True, no editing can be performed in the text box. One example of using the Locked property is the display of a large amount of text in a text box with scroll bars. This permits users to scroll through the information, but prevents them from changing it. Even when a text box is locked, however, the user can select text and copy it to the Windows Clipboard by right-clicking it and selecting Copy from the context menu that appears.

N O T E Do not confuse the Locked property with the Enabled property. Setting the Locked
property to True does not create the "grayed-out" effect. It prevents users from modifying
your text, but it still allows them to select and copy text from the text box to the Windows Clipboard.
Text in text boxes whose Enabled property is set to False cannot be selected; therefore, it cannot be
copied to the Windows Clipboard. ▪

There is nothing special involved in using the Locked property; it can be set to True or False in
code, as follows:

```
txtTest.Locked = True
txtTest.Text = "You can't edit this!"
```

One obvious use of the Locked property is to prevent a user from accidentally changing the
information in a text box. In this case, you could place a command button on the form that the
user must click to be allowed to edit the information on the screen. For example, suppose your
Personnel department frequently needs to look up information on employees. A locked text
box will prevent accidental editing of this information. This example is shown in Figure 13.1.

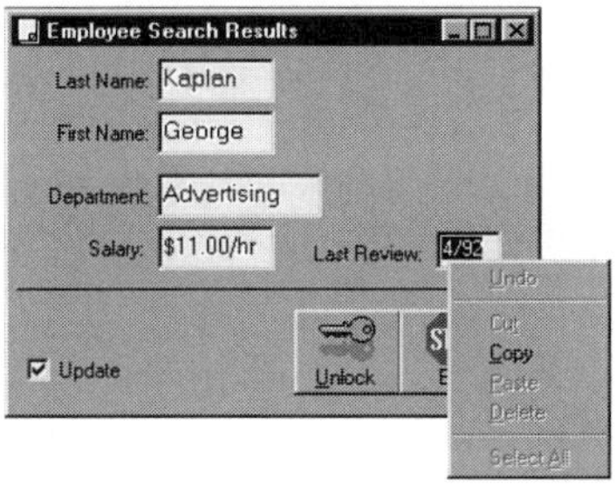

FIG. 13.1

Using the Locked
property prevents
inadvertent editing of
text. Notice in the pop-
up menu (automatically
implemented by
Windows), only the
Copy option is available
for a locked text box.

One way to process a bunch of text boxes as a group is to use a control array, which enables
you to use a For loop rather than list each text box individually. In this case, code could be
written in the command button's Click event procedure to change the Locked property from
True to False as follows:

```
Private Sub cmdEdit_Click()

  Dim I As Integer
  For I = 0 To 5
   txtInfo(I).Locked = False
  Next I

End Sub
```

▶ **See** "Using Control Arrays," **p. 496**

Another way to change the Locked property on a bunch of text boxes is to use a For Each loop.
This works even when your text boxes are not in a control array:

Part
III

Ch

13

```
Private Sub cmdEdit_Click()

    Dim objControl As Control

    For Each objControl In Me.Controls
        If TypeOf objControl Is TextBox Then objControl.Locked = True
    Next objControl

End Sub
```

Notice that the For Each structure in this code works with any property or control, not just the Locked property. Also notice that a real-life version of the program probably would check the security level of the user before allowing the edit.

The form in Figure 13.1 and the code are contained in the LOCKED.VBP project, which you can download from this book's Web site at **www.mcp.com/info/0-7897/0-7897-1288-1**.

Placing a Limit on Characters   Although typically you think of the text box as handling any amount of text, there are times when you will want to limit the amount of text that a user can enter. You can handle this by using the MaxLength property of the text box control. The purpose of this property is to restrict the number of characters that the user can enter.

There are a number of reasons that you might want to limit the number of characters a user can enter. In many programs, you will be dealing with IDs that are a fixed length. For example, an inventory program might use numbers that are 10 characters long for their parts, or a personnel information system might use Social Security numbers, which are, by definition, nine digits long.

Another need to limit the length of a text field occurs when working with database files. Most fields in a database file have a specific length. If you allow your user to enter more characters than can be stored in the field, information may be lost, or an error may be generated.

Setting the maximum number of characters is quite easy. Just select the MaxLength property of the text box and type in a number. If you want to permit the user to enter an unlimited number of characters, then enter 0 (the default setting) for the value.

N O T E   The amount of text that the user can enter is not really unlimited. A text box whose MultiLine property is set to True can handle a maximum of about 32,000 characters; single-line text boxes are limited by system memory constraints. ▓

So what happens when the user is entering data and gets to the maximum number of characters? At that point, the text box stops accepting additional characters and beeps each time another character is typed. You can try this for yourself. Place a text box on a form and set the MaxLength property to 10. Then, run the program and start typing in the letters of the alphabet. You will see that A–J are accepted, but when you try to type in the k, the text box does not accept it. This occurs even if you have sized the control so that there is plenty of additional space to the right of the text you entered.

Hiding the Contents If you are using a text box as part of a login form, you will want the capability to hide the password that is entered by the user. To do this, simply enter a character in the `PasswordChar` property of the text box. This changes the text box's display behavior so that the password character is substituted for each character in the `Text` property. You may have seen this effect many times when logging in to Windows or to your company's network.

Note that the contents of the `Text` property still reflect what is actually typed by the user, and your code always sees the "real" text. Although you can enter any character, it is customary to use the asterisk (*) character for hiding text (see Figure 13.2).

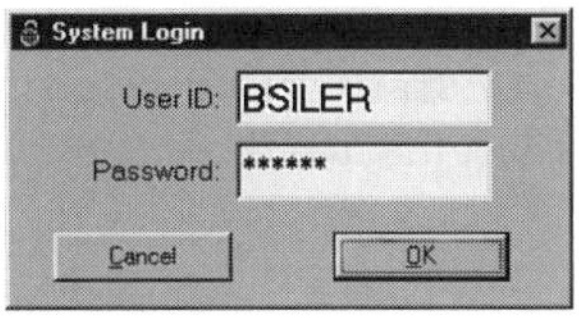

FIG. 13.2
Avoid prying eyes by using the `PasswordChar` property.

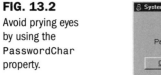

Editing Text in a Text Box Thus far, you have looked at how to create various types of text boxes, but how can users edit what they've entered? Are they limited just to typing information? Fortunately, no.

If you have used any Windows word processor, you are already familiar with how to edit the text in a text box. Just as with a word processor, users can use ordinary keys, such as Delete and Backspace, and they can highlight text with the mouse or by using Shift with the cursor keys. They then can cut (Ctrl+X), copy (Ctrl+C), or paste (Ctrl+V) text and even undo their last change by pressing Ctrl+Z. Using these techniques, they can remove or change text and move text around within a text box or between text boxes (see Figure 13.3).

FIG. 13.3
Your users can copy text from one text box and paste it into another.

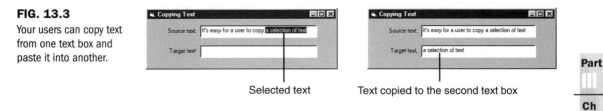

Selected text   Text copied to the second text box

TIP To select a single word in a text box, double-click the word. You can also use a combination of Shift, Ctrl, and the arrow keys to highlight a word at a time.

Windows also provides a pop-up menu for editing use. The user can simply highlight some text in a text box and right-click the text box. A pop-up menu opens containing the Cut, Copy, Paste, and Delete commands, as well as a Select All option. This menu also has an Undo command users can employ to reverse a change, though it's active only when no text is selected.

You already know that the `Text` property contains all the text in a text box. Suppose a user has selected some text in a text box, and you want to manipulate only that text. The selected text is identified by three properties:

Part
III

Ch
13

- SelStart—Identifies the starting position of the selected text.
- SelLength—Identifies the length of the selected text.
- SelText—Contains the contents of the selection.

You can use these properties to work with a selected piece of text in your program. Look at the example in Figure 13.3. In this case, the SelText property would contain just the phrase "a selection of text." The SelLength property would contain the integer value 19, which is the length of that string. And the SelStart property would contain the integer value 29, which means the selected phrase starts with the 29th character in the text box.

In addition to determining what has been selected, you can also set the properties from code to alter the selection. Every time you set the SelStart property, you must set the SelLength property to highlight some characters. To select the first three characters, you could use this code:

```
txtTest.SelStart = 0
txtTest.SelLength = 3
```

The SelLength property can be changed multiple times. This will cause the selection to increase or decrease in size, automatically updating the SelText property. Setting the SelText property from code causes the currently selected text to be replaced with a new string, for example:

```
txtTest.SelText = "jumped into oncoming traffic."
```

One use of these properties is to highlight the entire contents of a text box. Suppose, for example, that you have populated some text boxes for a user to edit. When the user presses the Tab key to move to a text box, you might want to highlight whatever is in the text box automatically (this is a Windows standard). This way, the user can start typing immediately, automatically deleting the existing text. This is illustrated in the following code for a text box's GotFocus event:

```
Private Sub txtSelect_GotFocus()
  With txtSelect
    .SelStart = 0
    .SelLength = Len(.Text)
  End With
End Sub
```

N O T E The first character in a text box has an index value of 0.

Although the text box is great, you can't perform the drag-and-drop editing that you find in some newer word processors. You are also limited to one font and one color of text within each text box. If you require formatting capabilities that are more advanced, you'll probably find what you're looking for in the Masked Edit control described in the next section.

Limiting Text with the Masked Edit Control

Although limiting the number of characters that a user can enter is one way of controlling the input, it often is also necessary to control the type of characters that can be entered (such as letters, digits, or punctuation marks). In addition, there may be times when you want to change the appearance of the text box to include familiar placeholders for data entry, such as parentheses in a phone number or hyphens in a Social Security number. You could use a standard text box and program code to accomplish this, but there is an easier way.

Visual Basic provides a number of custom controls that are not among the standard set present when you start Visual Basic. Among these is the Masked Edit control. This control enables you to specify the number, type, and position of characters in the data entry field. It also enables you to use placeholder characters within the field. Figure 13.4 illustrates two examples of the Masked Edit control after the user has entered text. Note that they look like ordinary text boxes; however, the masked edit capability of the controls have helped ensure that the data entered conforms to the program's needs.

FIG. 13.4

The Masked Edit control provides considerable control over the number, type, and position of characters in a text field, although it looks to the user just like a normal text box.

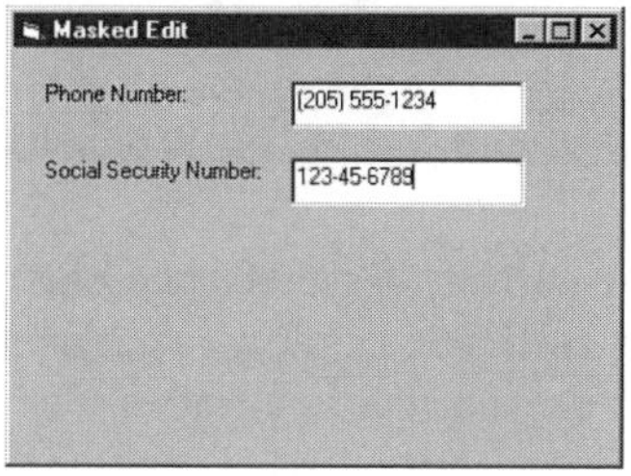

Adding the Masked Edit Control to Your Project   Because the Masked Edit control is not part of the standard control Toolbox, the first step in using the control is to instruct Visual Basic to make the control available to you. Choose Project, Components to open the Components dialog box. After you are in the dialog box, click the box next to Microsoft Masked Edit Control 5.0 and click Apply or OK to add the control to the Toolbox (see Figure 13.5).

T I P   You can also access the Components dialog box by pressing Ctrl+T or by right-clicking the Toolbox.

Now that you have added the Masked Edit control to the Toolbox, you are ready to work with it in your program. As with any other control, to add a Masked Edit control to your form, you select its tool in the Toolbox and then draw it on the form where you want it to appear. A Masked Edit control supports only one line of input, so you need to draw it wide enough to contain all the characters to be entered.

N O T E   The Masked Edit control is capable of handling a maximum of 64 characters. Although this is quite sufficient for most needs, if your program requires a larger field, you have to use a standard text box and control the formatting with code. ▧

FIG. 13.5

Any control that displays a check mark next to its name will appear in the Toolbox.

The Masked Edit control added to the Toolbox

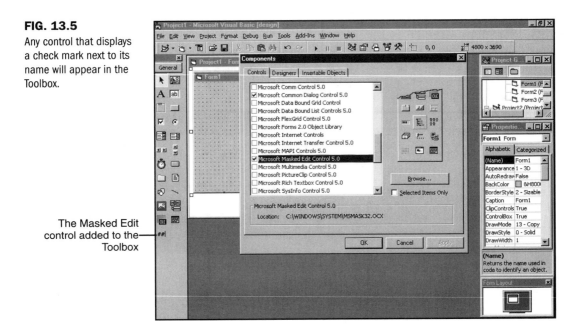

Allowing Only Certain Characters   The purpose of the Masked Edit control is to make sure data is entered in a specific format. Suppose, for example, you put a text box on a form and ask the user to enter a date. One user might use a date format with slashes—12/7/41, for example—whereas another might spell it out—Dec. 7, 1941. The same type of inconsistent input could occur with phone numbers or dollar amounts, among others. You could handle this in code by validating the information before processing it. However, using the Masked Edit control is a cleaner way to do this because it requires no code. With this control, you can specify which characters are allowable and where they are placed in a field.

The Masked Edit control has a Mask property that allows you to tell the control where you want specific characters placed. The Mask property is a string that represents a template of what the text input should look like; for example, ###-#### represents seven numbers with a dash after the third number. The # is a special *character code*, which means only an integer (0–9) can be entered at this location.

The character codes also specify how many characters can be entered in the field. If you put only five character codes in the mask, then no more than five characters can be entered by the user. Table 13.1 shows some of the different character codes that can be used in the Masked Edit control.

Table 13.1   Specify the Characters to Be Entered Using the Mask Property

Mask Code	Allowable Characters
#	Any digit 0–9, space, plus or minus (+ or –) signs
?	Any letter a–z or A–Z
A	Any letter or digit
&	Any character or space

If the Mask property is blank (which is the default setting), then the Masked Edit control behaves like a simple text box.

N O T E   A complete list of allowable character codes is listed in Visual Basic's help system under "Mask property." Take a moment to go over this list, which includes number placeholders and optional masks. ▪

By using the Mask property, you can develop input masks for almost any type of data. For example, the mask for a five-digit ZIP code would be #####, or a ZIP+4 code would be entered as #####-####. If you wanted a mask for two-letter state abbreviations, you would use ??. The great thing about this control is that it relieves the developer from some extra coding.

If the user "violates" the mask rules, then the Masked Edit box beeps; the user cannot continue entering text unless it is correct. For example, if the mask is ####, no characters will be displayed until a number is entered. Optional masks, such as 9 for optional numbers, produce a different effect. For example, the mask ?9? would accept either two letters in a row or a number surrounded by two letters.

Several input masks are set up in the MASK.VBP project, which you can download from this book's Web site at **www.mcp.com/info/0-7897/0-7897-1288-1**. Run this project and check out how these work.

Keeping Your Place in the Field   Character codes are not the only things that you can enter in the Mask property. You can also place any other characters in the mask for use as placeholders. These characters include (but are not limited to) asterisks (*), dollar signs ($), parentheses, hyphens, and commas. For example, the typical notation for a phone number is (212) 555-1234. Within this notation, the parentheses, space, and hyphen are all placeholders. To represent this in an input mask, you would set the Mask property to (###) ###-####. As a user types a phone number, the first three numbers are entered between the parentheses; then the input skips to the third location in front of the hyphen. In other words, the masked input control automatically skips the placeholders.

By using the character codes and placeholders, you can create many kinds of custom input fields. A few examples are shown in Table 13.2.

Part
III

Ch
13

Table 13.2 Create Many Types of Input Masks with Character Codes and Placeholders

Desired Input	Mask	Example
ZIP Code	#####	35242
Phone Number	(###) ###-####	(205) 555-7575
Social Security Number	###-##-####	123-45-6789
Month-Day-Year	AAA ##, ####	Feb 18, 1998
Date	##/##/##	02/18/98
Time	##:## AA	02:31 pm

Figure 13.6 shows how the Masked Edit control appears before the user types any text in it. Notice that there are underscore (_) characters in every location in which you had entered a character code in the Mask property. This tells you, or the user, what locations are available for typing. The character used to indicate these input positions is contained in the PromptChar property. The default value of this property is the underscore, but you can change it to any other character you want, for example, # for a phone number.

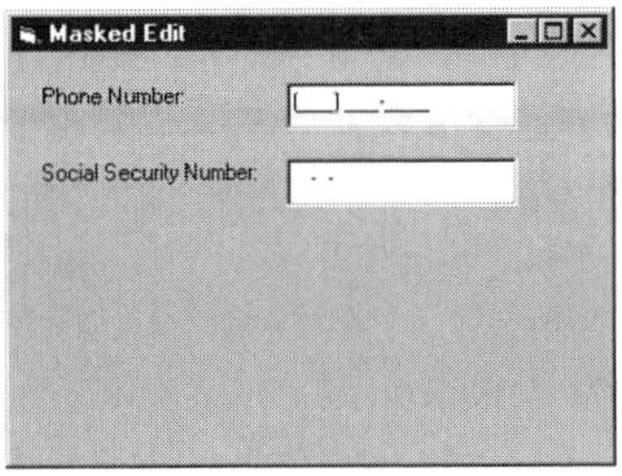

FIG. 13.6

Use the PromptChar property to specify which character to use to indicate input positions.

Getting the Information from the Masked Edit Control   Like the text box, the Masked Edit control supports both the Text and SelText properties. This lets you access the entire contents of the field, or just a selected portion.

There are a few differences in the behavior of these properties of which you should be aware. The Text property contains all the information that the user entered, plus any placeholder characters that were in the Mask property. For example, the phone number mask that was used earlier contained parentheses, a space, and a hyphen ((###) ###-####). When a user enters a phone number, only the digits are entered, but the Text property contains all the digits and the placeholders. That is, if the user entered 2055550770, the Text property would contain (205) 555-0770.

There is also another property that can be used to reference the information in the Masked Edit control. This property is the ClipText property. This property, in conjunction with the ClipMode property, enables you to retrieve only the information that the user typed, with or without the placeholder characters. The `ClipMode` property has two settings, 0—`mskIncludeLiterals` and 1—`mskExcludeLiterals`. By setting this property to `mskExcludeLiterals`, you can retrieve just the user information, with no placeholder characters. Figure 13.7 shows the difference between the information retrieved with the `Text` and `ClipText` properties.

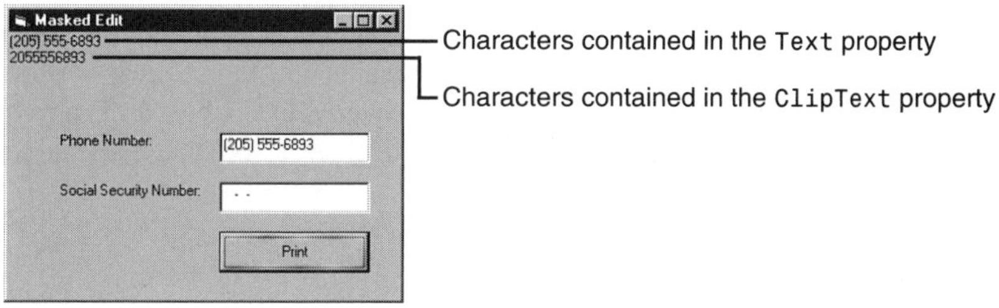

FIG. 13.7
The `Text` and `ClipText` properties return different parts of the entered information.

— Characters contained in the `Text` property

— Characters contained in the `ClipText` property

Why is the `ClipText` property important? Because with many types of numerical entries, such as dates, times, and phone numbers, you want to provide the placeholders for easy data entry by users, but you do not want to store the numbers with all the placeholders. Also, the `Mask` property can display numbers with commas separating the thousands, millions, and other groups (such as 1,000,000). When the number is used for calculations, you cannot have the commas present.

T I P The Masked Edit box's beep may not be informative enough for users to correct invalid keystrokes, in which case you might want to use the control's `ValidationError` event. For example, if the mask is ## and the user types an A, then the `ValidationError` event occurs. You could add code to this event to inform the user of the proper formatting.

Modifying Text with a Program

Although the text box allows the user to enter and edit text, you will also have many occasions in which you need to modify text strings within your program. Visual Basic provides a number of functions that are useful in modifying text. These functions are as follows:

- `UCase` and `LCase`—Changes the case of text to all uppercase or all lowercase, respectively
- `InStr`—Finds the location of one string contained within another
- `Left` and `Right`—Retrieves a selected number of characters from one end of a string
- `Mid`—Retrieves or replaces a selected number of characters in a string
- `LTrim`, `RTrim`, and `Trim`—Removes spaces from one or both end(s) of a string
- `Len`—Returns the length of a string

N O T E All of the functions in this list (except Len) return a Variant data type. For each of them, there is an identical function with a dollar sign ($) at the end of the function's name to indicate a String type return value. I recommend using the $ versions (such as Left$) whenever possible because they are more efficient. For the sake of readability, the Variant versions are used in this chapter. ▪

In addition, Visual Basic has the concatenation operator and the ampersand (&), which enables you to combine strings. This section explains how to use these various functions in your program. The concatenation operator was covered in Chapter 8, "Programming Basics." If you need to refresh your memory about its use, please refer to that chapter.

▶ **See** "Working with Strings," **p. 183**

Changing the Case of Letters

There are two functions that can modify the case of letters in a string: UCase and LCase. The UCase function returns a string with all the letters converted to uppercase (capital) letters. The LCase function does just the opposite, converting the entire string to lowercase letters.

Although these may appear to be somewhat trivial functions, they actually are quite useful for a number of tasks. First, you can use the functions to properly capitalize names or other words that a user may enter. The code in Listing 13.1 capitalizes the first letter of a word and makes the rest of the word lowercase.

Listing 13.1 CASES.FRM—Using *UCase* and *LCase* to Properly Capitalize a Word

```
Dim lcWord, as String, ProperWord as String, WordLen As Integer
lcWord = LCase(lcWord)
WordLen = Len(lcWord)
ProperWord = UCase(Left(lcWord, 1)) & Right(lcWord, WordLen - 1)
```

These functions are useful, for example, when comparing user input to a predefined value or a range of values. If we convert the user's input to uppercase, we can compare it to an uppercase test string, as in the following example:

```
Select Case UCase(txtOperation.Text)

    Case "WASH"
      ' Do Something
    Case "RINSE"
      ' Do Something Else
    Case "SPIN"
      ' Do Something Else Yet
    Case Else
       MsgBox "Invalid Entry!"

End Select
```

In the preceding code, if the UCase function had not been used, then the user would receive the Invalid Entry message even if he had entered a "correct" choice in lowercase or mixed case ("Rinse," for example).

Another Visual Basic function, StrConv, performs special conversions of strings. Most of the conversions it can perform are either redundant (converting to all uppercase or all lowercase, for example) or beyond the scope of this book (converting between different types of Japanese characters), but one of its conversion types is worth mentioning here. StrConv can convert a string to *proper case*, where the first letter of each word is capitalized. The following code sample demonstrates this technique:

```
lblHeadline = StrConv(stHeadline, vbProperCase)
```

Examples of using UCase and LCase, as well as StrConv, are illustrated in Figure 13.8.

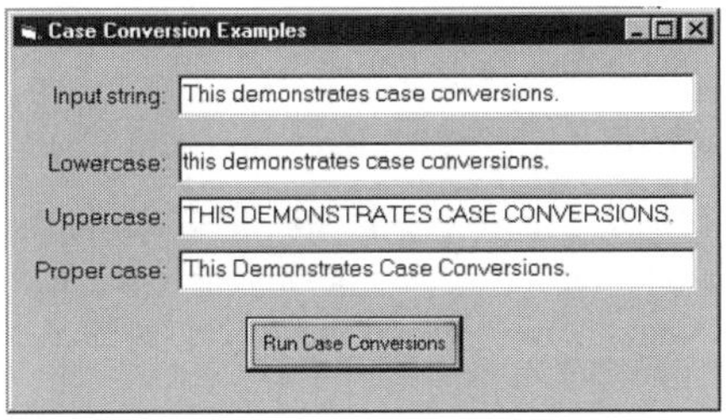

FIG. 13.8

LCase, UCase, and StrConv can be used to modify the case of the letters in a string of text.

Case Conversion Examples

Input string:	This demonstrates case conversions.
Lowercase:	this demonstrates case conversions.
Uppercase:	THIS DEMONSTRATES CASE CONVERSIONS.
Proper case:	This Demonstrates Case Conversions.

Run Case Conversions

Chapter 10, "Managing Your Project," provides more information on functions and their uses.

▶ **See** "Using Procedures and Functions," **p. 246**

Getting Pieces of a String

Look at the following code from Listing 13.1 again. In addition to using just the UCase and LCase functions, it also uses several functions to extract pieces of text from the original string. This illustrates one of the more important tasks involved in manipulating strings—the capability to add, remove, or change single characters, words, or sections of a string.

```
Dim lcWord, as String, ProperWord as String, WordLen As Integer
lcWord = LCase(lcWord)
WordLen = Len(lcWord)
ProperWord = UCase(Left(lcWord, 1)) & Right(lcWord, WordLen - 1)
```

Visual Basic provides a number of functions that are designed for string manipulations. There are functions that add and remove spaces, a function for determining the length of a string, a function for performing a search, and a function for exchanging one piece of a string for another string.

Determining What Is in the String For many string-related tasks, the first programming requirement is to determine if a word, phrase, or other group of characters exists in a string, and if so, where. The capability to find one string within another enables you to perform word searches within text. This can be used to perform a global replacement of a string, such as replacing the word "text" with the word "string" throughout a word-processing document.

Part
III

Ch
13

Another, more common, reason for searching within a string is *parsing* the string. For example, suppose you have an input string that contains a person's name in this format: "Dr. Stirling P. Williams, Jr." If you have a file of a hundred such strings, putting this information into a database with separate first and last name fields would be a little difficult. However, you could use a string search function along with a little program logic to parse the string into smaller pieces. The function that enables you to search a string for a character or group of characters is the InStr function. This function has two required and two optional parameters. The required parameters are the string to be searched and the text to search for. If the search text appears in the string being searched, InStr returns the index of the character where the search string starts. If the search text is not present, InStr returns 0. The simple syntax of the InStr function is shown here:

```
chrpos = InStr(sourcestr, searchstr)
```

For example, the function call

```
Print Instr("I'll see you next Tuesday.","you")
```

would print a result of 10 because that is the position where the word "you" begins.

The first optional parameter of the InStr function tells the function the character position from which to start the search. This position must be a positive integer. If the starting position is greater than the length of the string, InStr will return 0. This syntax of the InStr function is as follows:

```
chrpos = InStr(StartPos, sourcestr, searchstr)
```

For example, the function call

```
Print Instr(7,"Pride cometh before a fall","e")
```

would return the value of 10, even though the first "e" in the string is at position 5, because the search starts from position 7.

The other optional parameter determines whether the search to be performed is case-sensitive (uppercase and lowercase letters do not match) or case-insensitive. Setting the value of the comparison parameter to 0, its default value, performs a case-sensitive search. Setting the value to 1 performs a case-insensitive search. This syntax is shown here:

```
chrpos = InStr(StartPos, sourcestr, searchstr, 1)
```

Note that with the optional parameters, you can write code that will find each successive search string in your text. The code in Listing 13.2 will print the words in a string that are separated by spaces. It works by taking the result of the Instr function and passing it back in to the StartPos parameter.

Listing 13.2 PARSESTR.FRM—Using the *InStr* Function to Divide a String into Words

```
Sub PrintWords(stInput As String)
    Dim inCounter As Integer
    Dim inFoundPos As Integer

    Const PARSECHAR = " " 'Space

    'If string is blank then do nothing
    If Len(stInput) = 0 Then Exit Sub

    'Start at the first character
    inCounter = 1

    'Search for a space
    inFoundPos = InStr(inCounter, stInput, PARSECHAR)

    'If a space is found print the word and keep searching
    While inFoundPos <> 0
      Debug.Print Mid$(stInput, inCounter, inFoundPos - inCounter)
      inCounter = inFoundPos + 1
      inFoundPos = InStr(inCounter, stInput, PARSECHAR)
    Wend

    'Print the remainder of the string
    If inCounter < Len(stInput) Then
        Debug.Print Mid$(stInput, inCounter)
    End If
End Sub
```

The input and results of this code appear in Figure 13.9.

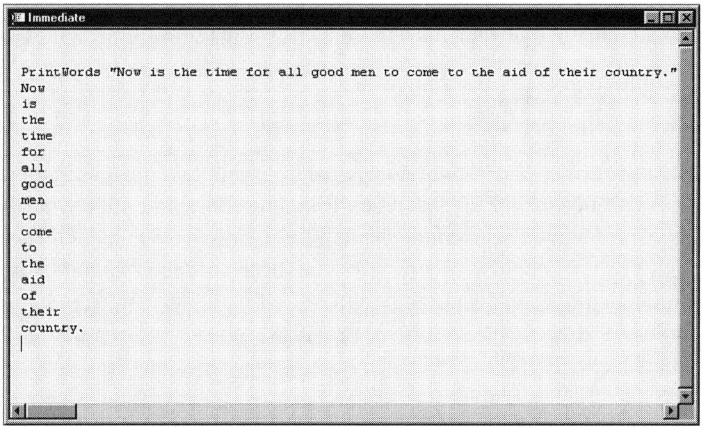

FIG. 13.9
Use InStr to find all the spaces in a string.

```
PrintWords "Now is the time for all good men to come to the aid of their country."
Now
is
the
time
for
all
good
men
to
come
to
the
aid
of
their
country.
```

Determining the Length of the String   For many operations, you may need to know how many characters are in a string. You might need this information to know whether the string with which you are working will fit in a fixed-length database field. Or, if you are working with big strings, you may want to make sure that the combined size of the two strings does not exceed the capacity of the string variable. In any case, to determine the length of any string, the Len function is used, as illustrated in the following code line:

```
result = Len(inputstr)
```

You can use the Len function in a number of applications. In many cases, it is used to determine whether there are any characters in a string. If there are no characters, you may want to issue an error message, or at least bypass any further processing. In Listing 13.1, you saw how the Len function was used to find the number of characters so that you could use the Right function to get the remainder of a string.

> **CAUTION**
>
> The Len function reports only the number of characters that are present in a string. It does not report whether a string will fit within a control or on a line of a printout. For these purposes, you need to use the TextWidth and TextHeight methods of the object to which the string is being written. These methods are discussed in Chapter 9, "Displaying and Printing Reports."
>
> ▶ **See** "Using *TextHeight* and *TextWidth*," **p. 226**

Getting Rid of Spaces   Long strings typically contain spaces in the middle of the string, which are necessary for proper spacing of words, paragraphs, and so on. However, you also may end up with spaces at the beginning or end of your strings, which often are unwanted spaces. These spaces typically occur when the user accidentally types a space at the beginning or end of a text field. They also show up when you are using a fixed-length string and the number of characters in the string do not fill the available space.

For example, the following calls to the Len() function would each return a different number:

```
Print Len("Hello, world!")
Print Len("  Hello, world!")
Print Len("Hello, world!   ")
```

Most of the time, spaces don't do any harm except take up a little memory. However, when you combine strings, or try to take action based on their content, unwanted spaces can cause all kinds of problems. For example, suppose you had two 30-character text boxes for first and last names. The user could inadvertently type three characters of text and then a bunch of spaces. If you needed to concatenate the first and last name for a mailing label, the extra spaces would be included. However, Visual Basic provides some string "trimming" functions to eliminate the trailing spaces.

To get rid of the spaces at the end of a string, you can use one of these Visual Basic functions:

- **LTrim**—Removes the spaces from the beginning of a string
- **RTrim**—Removes the spaces from the end of string
- **Trim**—Removes the spaces from both the beginning and end of a string

Each of these functions use a similar syntax. The code in the following lines shows how the Trim function would be used to remove the spaces in the mailing label example (the results of these trimmed strings are shown in Figure 13.10):

```
picMail.Print Trim(FirstName) & " " & Trim(LastName)
picMail.Print Trim(Address)
picMail.Print Trim(City) & ", " & Trim(State) & "  " & Trim(Zip)
```

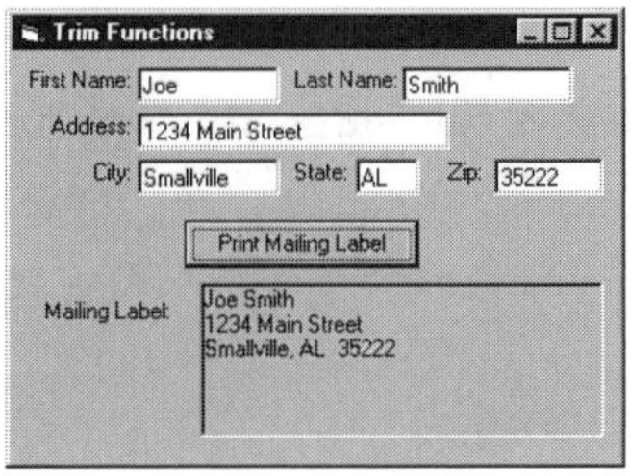

FIG. 13.10

This user typed extraneous spaces (that we can't see) after the words "Joe" and "Smallville," but Visual Basic's Trim function removed them.

Extracting Pieces of a String   Okay, you have the capitalization of the string right and you have removed all the spaces that you don't need at the ends of the string, but now you find you need to work with only a part of the string. Can Visual Basic help with this problem too? Of course, it can.

You will find many situations in which you need to work with only part of a string. Perhaps you'll need to extract the first name of a person from her full name, or maybe you'll need to make sure that the information with which you are working will fit in the database field in which it needs to be stored. This is easy to accomplish by using one of the following Visual Basic functions:

- **Left**—Retrieves a specified number of characters from the left end of a string
- **Right**—Retrieves a specified number of characters from the right end of a string
- **Mid**—Retrieves characters from the middle of a string

First, look at the Left and Right functions, as these are slightly easier to use. (By the way, none of these functions is hard to use.) To use these functions, you specify the input string and the number of characters to be retrieved. The syntax of these two statements is shown in the following lines:

```
OutStr = Left(InptStr, NumChars)
OutStr = Right(InptStr, NumChars)
```

Part
III

Ch
13

When you use these functions, the number of characters specified must be a number greater than or equal to 0. If you enter **0**, a 0 length string is returned. If the number of characters is greater than the length of the input string, the entire string is returned. You will find, as you write programs that manipulate strings, that the Left and Right functions are often used in conjunction with the other string functions.

This is illustrated in Listing 13.3, which retrieves the first name of a person from the full name. This function is used to print name tags for an organization's events. Figure 13.11 shows how this code is used. The function assumes that the person's first and last names will be separated by a space. The function then looks for a space in the input text and, upon finding the space, it extracts the characters preceding the space and supplies those characters as the first name. If there are not any spaces in the input string, the function assumes that only a first name was entered.

Listing 13.3   NAMETAG.FRM—Using the *InStr* and *Left* Functions to Extract a Person's First Name

```
BasString = Trim(txtName.Text)
I = InStr(BasString, " ")
If I > 0 Then
    ScndString = Trim(Left(BasString, I))
Else
    ScndString = BasString
End If
PrtLine1 = ScndString
PrtLine2 = BasString
```

FIG. 13.11

Print name tags using the Left and InStr functions.

Mid is another function that is used to retrieve a substring from a string, and it works in a similar manner to the Left and Right functions, but it has one additional argument. The Mid function is used to retrieve a letter, word, or phrase from the middle of a string.

The Mid function contains two required arguments and one optional argument, as shown in the following syntax:

```
newstr = Mid(sourcestr, startpos[, numchars])
```

`Startpos` represents the character position at which the retrieved string will begin. If `startpos` is greater than the length of the string, an empty string is returned. The optional argument `numchars` represents the number of characters that will be returned from the `sourcestr`. If `numchars` is omitted, the function will return all characters in the source string, from the starting position, on to the end. The following are some examples of the `Mid` function:

```
Print Mid("Robert Allen",8)    'Returns "Allen"
Print Mid("Robert Allen",8,2)  'Returns "Al"
```

Replacing Characters in a String   Now to add a little confusion to your life. You just saw how the `Mid` function retrieves a piece of a string from the middle of a source string. The same keyword, `Mid`, is used to replace a part of a string. However, the syntax is quite different, in that we're using the function on the left side of an assignment statement in this case. When used to replace characters in a string, it is referred to as the `Mid` statement.

The `Mid` statement replaces part of one string with another string by using the following syntax:

```
Mid(sourcestr, startpos[, numchars]) = replstr
```

The `sourcestr` in this case is the string that will receive the replacement characters. `Sourcestr` must be a string variable; it cannot be a literal string or string function. `Startpos` is the character position at which the replacement will start. This must be an integer number greater than zero. `Numchars` is an optional argument that specifies the number of characters from the replacement string being used by the function. `Replstr` represents the string containing the replacement characters. This string can be a string variable, a literal string, or a string function.

The `Mid` statement preserves the original length of the string. In other words, if the space remaining between the starting position and the end of the string is less than the length of the replacement string, only the leftmost characters will be used from the replacement string.

There are a number of uses for the `Mid` statement in your programs. Remember the capitalization example in Listing 13.1? Using the `Mid` statement, you can perform the same function with the following code:

```
inptstr = Trim(txtInput.Text)
frstLtr = UCase(Left(inptstr,1))
Mid(inptstr, 1) = frstLtr
txtOutput.Text = inptstr
```

In another program, I needed to eliminate any carriage return or line feed characters that were embedded in a string to keep them from causing printing problems. I used the `Mid` statement to replace these characters with a space. This is shown in Listing 13.4.

Part
III

Ch
13

Listing 13.4   NAMETAG.FRM—Using the *Mid* Statement to Eliminate Specific Characters in a String

```
'Replace Line feeds with spaces
   nFindPos = 0
   Do
     nFindPos = InStr(sInput, Chr$(10))
     If nFindPos > 0 Then Mid(sInput, nFindPos) = " "
   Loop Until nFindPos = 0

'Replace Carriage returns with spaces
   nFindPos = 0
   Do
     nFindPos = InStr(sInput, Chr$(13))
     If nFindPos > 0 Then Mid(sInput, nFindPos) = " "
   Loop Until nFindPos = 0
```

Working with Specific Characters

Listing 13.4 shows the use of a function that you have not seen before—the Chr function. This function is used to return a character that corresponds to a specific ASCII code. For example, the following two statements both print "HELLO":

```
Print "HELLO"
Print Chr$(65) & Chr$(69) & Chr$(76) & Chr$(76) & chr$(79)
```

N O T E   As with other functions mentioned earlier in this chapter, Chr has two forms: Chr() returns a Variant; Chr$() returns a string. ▪

In the previous example, typing **HELLO** is a lot simpler. However, there are some characters you can't type, such as line feeds and carriage returns, so you have to use the Chr function:

```
Print "Line 1" & Chr$(13) & Chr$(10) & "Line 2"
```

The carriage return/line feed combination deserves special mention. Frequently, you will find yourself using this combination to force a new line in a string, text box, or message box. For this purpose, Visual Basic has included an intrinsic constant, vbCrlf, so that the preceding line of code could be rewritten as follows:

```
Print "Line 1" & vbCrLf & "Line 2"
```

The Chr function can also be used to include quotes:

```
Print Chr$(34) & "This will be printed with quotes" & Chr$(34)
Print "this will not have quotes"
```

You can also use the Chr function to return any letter or number character. Table 13.3 lists some commonly used ASCII character codes.

Table 13.3 ASCII Codes for Some Commonly Used Characters

Code	Represents
8	Backspace
9	Tab
10	Line feed
13	Carriage return
32	Space
34	Double quote (")
48	0 (the character for zero)
65	A
97	a

Asc is the companion function to the Chr function. Asc returns the ASCII code of the input character. The following code shows how Asc is used:

```
Print Asc("A") 'Returns 65
```

Working with Strings and Numbers

Another thing to consider is the relationship between strings and numbers. You may already know that some numbers are often treated as character strings. ZIP Codes and phone numbers are two such examples. However, there are times when you need to convert a number to a string variable to use it in a string function, or to print it in combination with another string. Likewise, there are times when you need to use numbers contained in a string variable in a mathematical equation or a numeric function.

Visual Basic provides the Str function to convert a number to a string, and the Val function to convert a string to a number. To convert a number to a string, you can do the following:

```
numstr = Str(inptnum)
```

numstr represents a string variable that contains the output of the function. inptnum represents the number to be converted. This can be a number, a numeric variable, or a numeric function. If inptnum is a positive number, Str will return a space in front of the number because Str reserves one character to contain a negative sign, if necessary.

To convert a string to a number, the Val function is used, as follows:

```
numvar = Val(inptstr)
```

numvar represents a numeric variable that stores the output of the function. inptstr can be a literal string, a string variable, or a string function. The Val function first strips out any spaces from the string and then starts reading the numbers in the string. If the first character in the

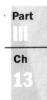

string is not a number (or minus sign), Val returns 0. Otherwise, Val reads the string until it encounters a non-numeric character. At this point, it stops reading and converts the digits it has read into a number.

A Closing Note on Working with Strings

In the preceding few sections, you have read a lot of information about string functions. Make sure, before continuing, that you have learned the concept of what each function is doing. More importantly, understand that string functions return values, but they *do not* modify the input. Consider the following example with the UCase function:

```
Dim s1 As String
Dim s2 As String
s1 = "which case am i"
s2 = UCase$(s1)
```

After this code is executed, the variable s2 will appear in all uppercase letters, whereas s1 will remain unchanged.

Also note that it is common practice to nest string functions within statements rather than using an extra variable. For example, consider the following Select Case statement, which uses a bunch of nested string functions to help with input validation. Users can come up with any capitalization they want to, but it will be handled by the code.

```
stUserInput = InputBox$("Type Yes or No, please!")
Select Case Left$(Trim$(Ucase$(stUserInput)),1)
   Case "Y"
     MsgBox "Yes"
   Case "N"
     MsgBox "No"
   Case Else
     MsgBox "type YES or NO please!"
End Select
```

Controlling the Appearance of Your Text

Being able to manipulate the text in a string is only part of working with text. After manipulating the text within your program, you probably will also want the capacity to control how the text appears to the user. This is the function of *fonts*. If you have worked with a word processor at all, you probably have done some work with fonts. A font describes how the letters and numbers that you use will look. Figure 13.12 shows several different fonts in different sizes. Fonts are like different styles of handwriting—some people print in block capital letters, other people write in script, and some people produce beautiful calligraphy.

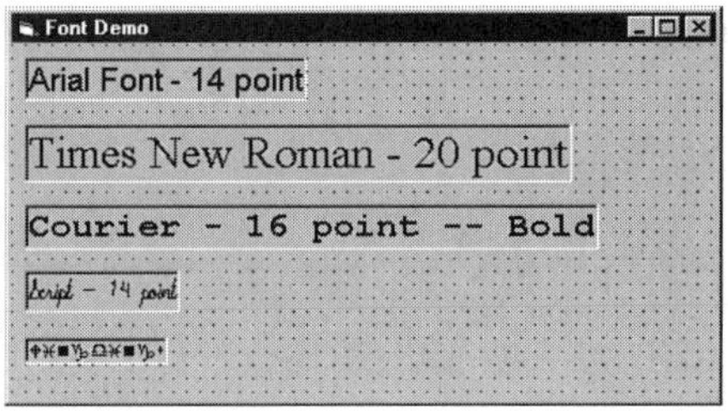

FIG. 13.12

Fonts control the appearance of the text on-screen.

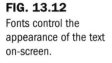

Properties of the *Font* Object

You may remember from earlier chapters that the Font property is actually an object that has its own properties. The following font object properties control the appearance of the fonts in your program:

- Name—Identifies one of the fonts installed on your system. This is a descriptive name in the form of a string, such as "Arial" or "Times New Roman."

- Bold—Determines whether or not the font is presented in boldface. Boldface increases the thickness of the lines used to draw the letter, making the letters appear darker and heavier than non-bold characters.

- Italic—Controls whether letters are italicized. An italicized character is slanted, with the top of the letter more to the right than the bottom of the letter.

- Underline—Controls whether the text is displayed with a thin line under each letter that is printed.

- Size—Controls the point size of the font. A font's size is measured in the traditional printer's measure of points. One point is 1/72 of an inch; therefore, capital letters in a 72-point font would be approximately one inch high.

- Strikethrough—Controls whether the text is displayed with a thin line through the middle of each letter.

- Weight—Controls the width of the line that is used to draw each letter. There are two settings for Weight—400 or 700. These correspond to normal and bold text, respectively.

Recall that the Font property can be accessed in code with dot notation:

```
TxtName.Font.Name="Arial"
TxtName.Font.Size = 10
```

The Font property that you probably will use most often is the Size property. Typically, the default font size is in the range of 8 to 12 points. If desired, though, you can set the font size anywhere from 1 to over 2,000 points, though I wouldn't recommend either extreme. A point size below 8 becomes difficult to read, and a point size of 250 will cause just a few characters to fill the entire screen. Figure 13.13 gives you an idea of the different point sizes.

Part

III

Ch

13

FIG. 13.13

Fonts can range in size
from tiny to jumbo.

4-point font —

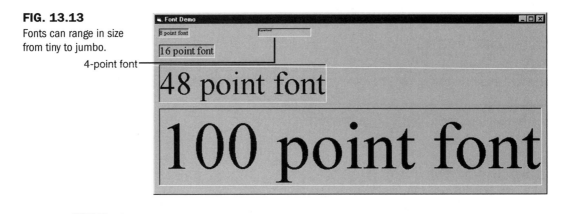

NOTE   A *point* defines the height of the character cell used to draw a character. It is equivalent to
1/72 of an inch. Therefore, when using a 12-point font, approximately six lines of text fit in
a vertical inch. ▪

The idea behind using different fonts and font attributes is to increase the readability of the
information on the screen or to add emphasis to a particular piece of information. The proper
use of fonts can greatly enhance the programs you create.

CAUTION

It is easy to get carried away using different fonts, and this can cause some problems. Too many different
fonts on a single screen can make it look disorganized and confusing. It is best to choose one or two fonts
and then use the fonts' attributes to achieve effects. This will give your programs a cleaner look. However, try
not to get carried away with the other attributes!

Making Life Easier for Portable Computer Users

One big advantage of being able to control font size is that you can make text more readable on
portable computers by increasing the font size. Portable (laptop) PC users probably already know this
well. The 10- or 12-point font that looks great on a 17-inch desktop monitor can be difficult to read
on the 10-inch screen of a portable computer. Therefore, keep in mind the users' screen resolution.
While developers and other "techies" might have 1024×768 or higher screen resolution, the general
public usually uses a much lower resolution, such as 800×600, or even 640×480.

As you may have noticed already, to set a particular font, you have to know its name. It's important to account for the fact that not all systems have the same fonts installed. The Screen and
Printer objects have properties that let you determine the available fonts for display and printing, as demonstrated in the following code:

```
Dim inCount As Integer
For inCount = 0 To Screen.FontCount - 1
  Print Screen.Fonts(inCount)
Next inCount
```

Of course, you also could use a Font dialog box (from the Common Dialog control) to let the user select from a list of available fonts.

▶ **See** "Form Properties Revisited," **p. 77**
▶ **See** "The Font Dialog Box," **p. 139**

Controlling Fonts in Your Program

Visual Basic lets you control all the attributes of the fonts in your programs. You can specify a font for an entire form or for individual controls. You can even control the fonts used by the printer. Visual Basic allows you to set up fonts during the design phase of your program. It also gives you the ability to actually change them while the program is running. This means that you can allow your user to select fonts for certain parts of the program. Or, you can set up the program so that the fonts change in response to some event in the program, such as a change in the value of a text box.

Setting an Initial Font   The default font for Visual Basic programs is called *MS Sans Serif.* This is the font used in the title bars of most Windows programs. Unless you change the font for a control, this font will be used in every control that you add to your program.

If you want to use a single font for all the components on a form, you can set that font as the form's *base font* before you place any controls on the form. When you change a form's font before adding any controls, all its controls will use that same font (assuming you don't change it for any subsequent controls).

To set the base font for your form, click the form, and then open the Properties window by pressing F4 or clicking the Properties Window button. Click the ellipsis button next to the Font property to open the Font dialog box. This dialog box, shown in Figure 13.14, enables you to choose the base font, as well as any other attributes you want to set for the form's Font object. Once you have set a particular font, it will be used for all controls added to the form.

N O T E   Changing the font used for the form will not affect any controls already on the form, only new controls that are added to the form. Also, the font setting does not affect the font used for the form's caption (the text in the title bar). This font is controlled from the Windows Control Panel setting. ■

Part

III

Ch

13

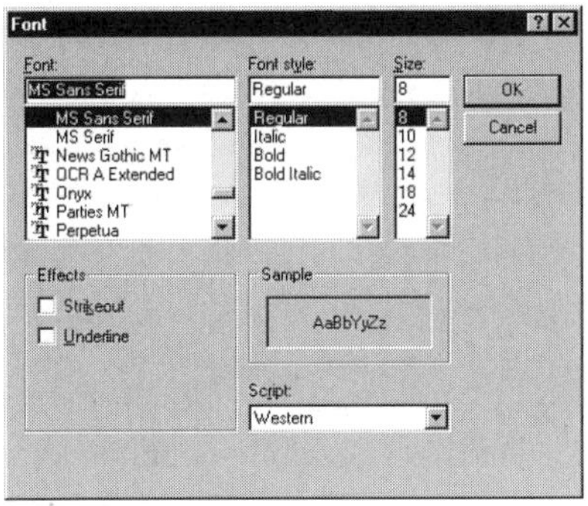

FIG. 13.14

You can change the font for a form by using the Font dialog box.

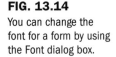

> **CAUTION**
>
> If you are creating programs for others to use on their machines, be careful choosing fonts. Others using your program may not have the same fonts as you do. Windows will attempt to substitute a similar font on the user's machine, but the resulting display may be unacceptable.

Setting the Font for Individual Controls   In addition to setting the font for the form, you may want to set a different font, or different attributes, for a single control or group of controls. For example, you may want to give all of your labels one font and all your text boxes a different font. Or, you may decide to use one font for controls containing numbers and another font for those containing letters. (For more information about working with multiple controls, see Chapter 4, "Working with Forms and Controls.")

▶ **See** "Working with Multiple Controls in the Design Environment," **p. 96**

Fonts for individual controls can be changed the same way they are changed for the form. This is done in the design environment by using the Font dialog box. Each control has a Font property. In fact, you could use a different font for each control on your form, though this would lead to a very confusing form.

Changing Fonts While the Program Is Running   Changing fonts in the design environment is great, but if you want your users to be able to set the fonts in your program, you have to provide a way to change your fonts in code. Fortunately, this is easy to do with assignment statements. Each of the properties of the font object can be set from code, as well as from the design environment. Take a brief look at how each property is handled in code; Figure 13.15 shows a program that illustrates the different font properties.

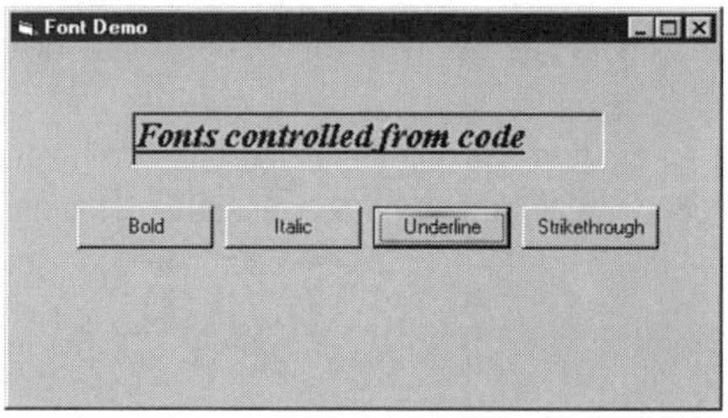

FIG. 13.15
Fonts can be controlled from code.

The program FONTDEMO.VBP illustrates the use of the different Font properties. You can download the program from this book's Web site at **www.mcp.com/info/0-7897/0-7897-1288-1**.

Changing the Base Font   To change the base font of an object, you use an assignment statement that specifies the Name property of the object's Font property. While you can specify the name of a font in a variable or constant, typically you will use the Font dialog box of the CommonDialog control to ask the user for the desired base font. This makes it easy for your users to choose a font. (For more information about the Font dialog box, see Chapter 6, "Using Dialogs to Get Information.")

▶ **See** "The Font Dialog Box," **p. 139**

The following line of code shows how you would change the base font of an object:

```
txtFontDemo.Font.Name = "Times New Roman"
```

Changing the Size of a Font   To set the size of a font, you specify an integer value for the `Size` property of the `Font` object. As stated earlier, this value can range from 1 to over 2,000, although values of 8 to 48 are the ones most often used. The following line shows how a font's size is set:

```
txtFontDemo.Font.Size = 16
```

> **CAUTION**
>
> When changing the font size in code, the control using the font may not be able to adjust to accommodate the new size. Therefore, part of the text in the control may not be visible to the user.

Recall from earlier chapters that setting `Font` properties of a text box causes all existing text to change, whereas setting `Font` properties of a form or printer does not.

Setting the Other Properties of the Font Object   The other four key properties of the `Font` object (`Bold`, `Italic`, `Underline`, and `StrikeThrough`) all have possible values of either `True` or `False`. To turn on a property, set its value to `True`; to turn off a property, set its value to `False`. The following lines of code illustrate this:

```
txtFontDemo.Font.Bold = True
txtFontDemo.Font.Italic = True
txtFontDemo.Font.StrikeThrough = True
txtFontDemo.Font.Underline = True
```

Working with Formatted Text

Thus far, you have learned how the user can enter text and how you can display text by using the TextBox and Label controls. You also have learned how to manipulate text in your program. Finally, you have seen how fonts can be used to change the appearance of text. But, even with all these capabilities, you haven't learned how to give your users the capability to format text like they can do with a word processor.

Starting with version 4, Visual Basic includes the RichTextBox control. This control enables the user to apply different fonts, font attributes, and colors to different sections of the text being edited. The user can also control the justification of text and create such effects as indention and bulleted lists. The RichTextBox control accomplishes all these functions by providing support for the Rich Text Format (RTF) language. The control interprets RTF codes and applies the proper formatting to the text. The control also has the capability of importing and exporting RTF files. Figure 13.16 shows how text appears in a RichTextBox control and which RTF codes are used to create the effects.

Part
III

Ch
13

FIG. 13.16
RTF codes allow formatting information to be stored in a text file.

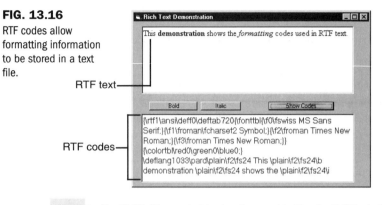

NOTE   The RichTextBox control is also discussed in Chapter 9, "Displaying and Printing Reports." ▨

▶ **See** "Using the RichTextBox Control," **p. 209**

RTF versus HTML

You might think that because both RTF and HTML use codes to store formatting information in a text file, they can be used together, or interchangeably. Unfortunately, that is not true. RTF codes originally were designed as a means for different word processors to exchange information through the use of text files. This means that you can work in one word processor, save the information to an RTF file, and then send the information to another person with a different word processor. The other person can then see the formatting of the text when the file is opened. HTML, on the other hand, is designed to pass formatting information across the Internet so that it can be interpreted and displayed by a browser. While both formats use the same concept of tags to embed formatting information, the tags used are not the same.

Using the RichTextBox Control

In many ways, the RichTextBox control works the same way as the standard text box. It shares many properties with the TextBox control, including the Text property, which works in the same way. In fact, the rich text box supports all properties that are supported by the text box. This makes it easy to substitute rich text boxes for any text boxes in your program. Simply delete a text box and insert a rich text box with the same name in its place. You do not need to change any of your program code to accomplish this. You will, however, want to add new code to take advantage of the additional capabilities of the rich text box.

Like the TextBox control, the RichTextBox control supports single- and multiple-line display and editing of text. Both controls can be locked (by setting the Locked property to True) to provide a read-only display of information. Both controls support cut, copy, and paste operations for editing. And finally, both can be bound to a Data control for use in database applications.

The discussion in this section focuses on the unique capabilities of the RichTextBox control. To learn about the basic capabilities that it shares with the text box, refer to the section "Getting and Displaying Text," earlier in this chapter.

Understanding Text Formatting The RichTextBox control enables the user to select a portion of the text in the control and apply special formatting to it. The user can change the font of the selection, make the selection bold or italic, or underline the selection. When the user applies any or all of these formats to the selection, the new formatting is shown on-screen. In addition, formatting codes (which are not shown on the screen) are placed in the text of the control. These codes allow the formatting information to be stored and then used by other programs that support RTF format codes. This means that you can export your formatted text to a word processor or other program and retain the formatting.

Setting Up the RichTextBox Control The RichTextBox control is one of the custom controls that comes with Visual Basic. You must add it to the Toolbox by using the Components dialog box, which is accessible by choosing the Components item from the Project menu.

 Once you have added the control to the Toolbox, you can use it just like any other control. Simply select it from the Toolbox and draw it on your form. As you can see in Figure 13.17, a rich text box looks just like a standard text box on the form. But remember—looks can be deceiving.

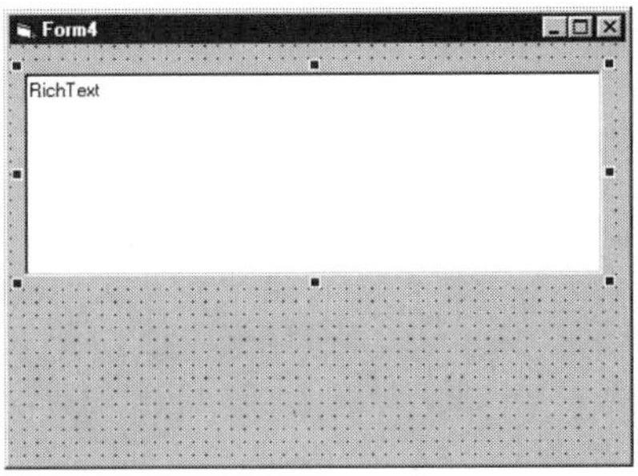

FIG. 13.17
The RichTextBox control looks like a standard text box when drawn on the form.

Working with the Font Options

The rich text box is a very powerful tool for creating programs that edit text because it provides tremendous control over the formatting of the text it contains. This section will cover many of the effects that are possible with the rich text box.

A common denominator of all the formatting options is the manner in which they affect the text that is displayed in the control. If you set a format property while some text is selected, only the selected text is affected by the new property value. However, if you set a new format value with no text selected, the property affects all text typed from the point at which it is inserted, until the property value is again changed. This works exactly like the formatting options in a word-processing program.

Part
III

Ch
13

Setting the Initial Font   After placing a rich text box on your form, probably the first thing you will want to do is set the properties of the Font object. You do this by following the guidelines described earlier in this chapter in the section "Controlling Fonts in Your Program." Setting the font in the design environment does two things—it sets the initial font the user sees and it sets the initial values of the SelFontName, SelFontSize, SelBold, SelItalic, SelUnderline, and SelStrikeThru properties. These properties control the appearance of selected text.

N O T E   If you change the value of the Font property or any of its attributes, it will affect all text that has not had any special formatting applied. ■

In a similar manner, setting the ForeColor property of the RichTextBox control sets the initial value of the SelColor property.

Changing the Appearance of Words   After the font has been set and the user begins entering text, formatting individual words and phrases can be accomplished by setting one or more of the following properties:

- SelFontName—Changes the font of the selection
- SelBold—Makes the selection bold
- SelItalic—Makes the selection italic
- SelFontSize—Changes the size of the selection's type
- SelUnderline—Underlines the selection
- SelStrikethru—Shows the selection in strikethrough mode

Each of these properties can be set by using an assignment statement. Some of these properties can be applied through the use of buttons in a toolbar that will set the properties. Figure 13.18 shows the main form of an example project. This project contains a RichTextBox control and a toolbar that enables the user to turn on the SelBold, SelItalic, SelUnderline, and SelStrikethru properties of the selected text. The form also contains drop-down lists that enable users to change the font and font size of the selection.

▶ **See** "Creating a Toolbar for Your Application," **p. 117**

Figure 13.19 shows the form after modifying the font for portions of the text.

FIG. 13.18

You can set the font properties of text by using a toolbar and the proper code.

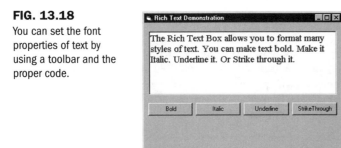

FIG. 13.19

You can change the appearance of a single word or a phrase with the RichTextBox control.

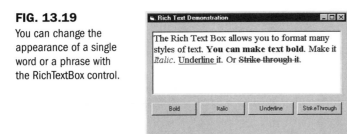

Working with Paragraphs

With the RichTextBox control, you also can change the alignment of individual paragraphs in your text. You can align paragraphs along the left edge of the RichTextBox (the default), or along the right edge, or centered in the box. The SelAlignment property controls the alignment of the paragraph and can have one of three values, which are set forth in Table 13.4. Figure 13.20 shows three RichTextBox controls that contain the same paragraph but with different alignment settings.

Table 13.4   The *SelAlignment* Property Values and Their Effects

Property Value	Effect
rtfLeft (0)	Sets the beginning of each line flush with the left side of the box
rtfRight (1)	Sets the end of each line flush with the right side of the box
rtfCenter (2)	Centers each line between the edges of the box

FIG. 13.20

Setting the SelAlignment property controls how the selected paragraphs appear in the control.

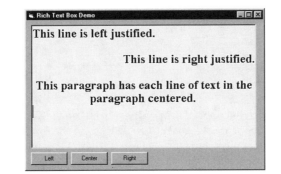

Part
III

Ch
13

Searching the Text

Another feature of the RichTextBox control is that you can search its contents for a string of text. You can choose to have the search confined to the selected text or to a specific section of the text. You can also have the search look through the entire contents of the rich text box.

Another available search option is the choice of whether to match the case of the search string. If case matching is not required, the strings "The" and "the" are considered a match. If case matching is required, the strings do not match because one contains a capital letter and the other does not.

This sounds very similar to the Instr function; as a matter of fact, you could use the Instr function with the RichTextBox control's Text property. However, the RichTextBox control has a special function of its own: the Find Method. This method specifies the string for which to search, the starting and ending points of the search, and any optional parameters. An advantage to using this instead of Instr is that Find causes the text it finds to be selected, so that font properties can be applied. The Find method uses the following syntax:

```
rtbname.Find(searchstr, start, end, options)
```

In this method, the searchstr parameter identifies the string that you want to find. This can be a literal string, a variable, or a string function. Start and end specify the scope of the search. If both parameters are included, the search is performed on all text between the two points. If end is omitted, the entire contents of the RichTextBox are searched. If both parameters are omitted, only the selected text is searched.

Adding a Splash of Color

Using different fonts is one way to change the appearance of information in your programs. Another method is to use color, which can grab a user's attention, convey important information, or simply make an application more visually appealing.

Setting the Color of Controls at Design Time

As with fonts, you can set color properties for your form and for individual controls at design time. In fact, most controls allow you to set two colors. You can set the background color by using the BackColor property and you can set the foreground or text color by using the ForeColor property.

N O T E Unlike font settings, the color settings for a form do not carry forward to controls placed on the form.

The default setting for each of the color properties is based on the Windows system color settings. The default setting of the BackColor property is the window background color, usually white. The default setting of the ForeColor property is the color of the text in Windows menus, usually black.

N O T E If you use the default color settings, changing the Windows system colors will make the colors in your program change, too. This is an important point to consider when distributing programs.

There are two ways to set the colors of your form and controls at design time. You can either use the color palette or select colors from a list from the Properties window. You can also, of course, set color properties by using code.

Using the Color Palette   The color palette is one of the tools available to you at design time. The color palette is accessed by choosing Color Palette from the View menu. The color palette is shown in Figure 13.21.

FIG. 13.21
The color palette enables you to easily choose the foreground and background colors of your controls.

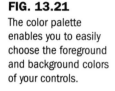
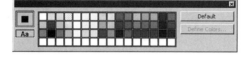

The color palette consists of a property selection area (two concentric squares), a series of color indicators, and two command buttons. To change the color properties of one of your controls, first select the control with a single-click. Then, using the mouse, choose either the foreground (click the inner box) or background (click the outer box). Next, click the color that you want in the color indicator boxes. As you choose the colors, you immediately will see the results both in the color palette and in your control. If you want to return your control's colors to their default values, just click the default button.

Using the Color List   The other way to set the colors of a control at design time is to modify the individual properties from the Properties window. To set a color, select the property (ForeColor, BackColor, or one of the other color properties); then click the arrow button at the right of the property value. This opens the color list (see Figure 13.22). This color list contains two tabs. The first tab shows the system colors for Window Text, Desktop, Window Background, and so on. You can choose to use one of these colors by clicking the appropriate color block. The other tab contains a series of color squares from the color palette. On this tab, you can choose the color you want by clicking the appropriate square.

FIG. 13.22
You can set the color of the ForeColor or BackColor property from the color list.

Part

III

Ch

13

Changing Colors with Code

As with most everything else, the `ForeColor` and `BackColor` properties can be changed with code in your program. You can do this with an assignment statement in which you tell the program what control and property to change, and what the new value is for the property. But what are the values? Can you just say, "Make this red"? Well, almost.

In the computer world, every color is a combination of some amount of red, green, and blue; the color number used as the property setting represents the amounts of blue, green, and red, respectively, in the desired color. The number is often represented in hexadecimal format; for example, blue is represented by `&H00FF0000&`.

If you are a glutton for punishment, you can figure out how much red, green, and blue go into a particular shade and then convert that information into the right numerical value. Fortunately, it is much easier than that. Visual Basic provides a set of constants for several common colors. These constants represent the numerical value needed for the color. Table 13.5 shows the names of the constants and the color they represent.

Table 13.5   Color Constants Provide the Numerical Values for Many Common Colors

Color	Constant	Numerical Value (Decimal)
Black	vbBlack	0
Red	vbRed	255
Green	vbGreen	65280
Yellow	vbYellow	65535
Blue	vbBlue	16711680
Magenta	vbMagenta	16711935
Cyan	vbCyan	16776960
White	vbWhite	16777215

To use one of these color constants, simply enter its name in the assignment statement. The following code displays yellow text on a blue background:

```
ColorDemo.ForeColor = vbYellow
ColorDemo.BackColor = vbBlue
```

In addition to the predefined color constants, you can use Visual Basic's RGB function, which accepts parameters for the amounts of red, green, and blue (each expressed in the range of 0–255) and returns the appropriate color number. For example,

```
frmTestForm.BackColor = RGB(0, 255, 0)
```

sets a form's background color to green.

T I P If you want to use a color that does not have a constant, the Common Dialog control's Color dialog box can be used to find out the numeric value.

Remember, the colors you select may be affected by the color scheme on an individual PC. This means selecting colors that change with the system will make your application better suited for an individual's color preferences. On the other hand, it is not unusual for the user to "mess up" his color scheme. For example, he might pick the right color combination so that highlighted text looks the same as other text. Therefore, in some instances, it might be beneficial for a program to choose a specific color. The determining factor should be how important colors are to the usefulness of your program.

From Here...

In this chapter, you learned about manipulating text—both from code and in the design environment. You saw how the Masked Edit control can make input validation easier, and how the RichTextBox control can be the foundation of a simple word processor. The code examples in the chapter also provided some examples of what you can do with string functions. Finally, some additional properties of the font object were introduced and you learned how to set colors in an application.

- To learn more about using the RichTextBox in code, see Chapter 9, "Displaying and Printing Reports."
- To apply what you have learned to interface design, see Chapter 11, "Designing User Interfaces."
- To find out about other controls you can use to display text information, see Chapter 16, "Using the Windows Common Controls."

Part

III

Ch

CHAPTER 14

Building a Multiple Document Interface

As you begin to write more advanced Visual Basic applications, at some point you will probably want to use Windows' Multiple Document Interface (MDI). The MDI allows your programs to work with multiple forms contained within a parent form. This makes your interface cleaner than one that has forms scattered about the screen.

The MDI standard can enhance your programs in two ways. First, you can have one container form that acts as the background for your overall application. If the user moves the container form, the child forms contained inside move as well. This helps keep your application's interface organized and self-contained. Second, and perhaps even more powerful, your users can work on multiple documents at one time. MDI applications allow the use of multiple instances of the same form, which can add much power and flexibility to your programs. ■

MDI applications provide a different user interface than standard forms

You will see how to create a Multiple Document Interface (MDI) application and manage all the child forms of the application.

Object variables let you create a number of similar forms

You will see how to create instances of forms on-the-fly. This will allow you to create applications similar to Word that handle multiple files at the same time.

Both MDI parent and MDI child forms can have menus

You will learn how the menus interact and how to control the behavior of the child menus.

MDI applications provide the user with easy access to all the forms of the application

In an MDI application, you can automatically arrange all the open windows and keep a list of the windows in the menu. You will see how to apply these techniques to your MDI programs.

Introducing MDI Applications

Many of the applications that you create in Visual Basic will consist of a series of independent forms, like the ones shown in Figure 14.1. Each of these forms is displayed separately on the screen and is moved, maximized, or minimized separately from any other form. With this type of interface, there is no easy way to organize the forms or to deal with them as a group. Even with this limitation, this is a good interface to use for many programs and is probably the most prevalent interface design.

FIG. 14.1

This program's user interface consists of two forms that appear to have no visual relationship to each other.

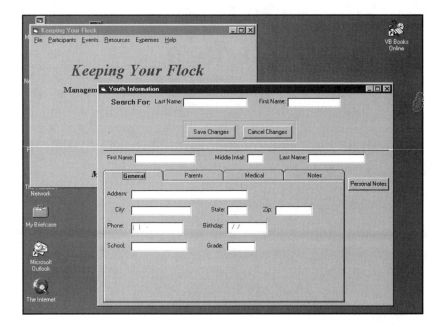

An alternative to this standard interface is the Multiple Document Interface, or MDI. This type of application has one *parent form* that contains most of the other forms in the program. Other forms can be *child forms*, which are contained within the parent, or *standard forms*, which are not. With an MDI application, you can easily organize all the child forms, or minimize the entire group of forms just by minimizing the parent form. Programs such as Microsoft Word and Excel are examples of MDI applications. If you have worked with these programs, you know that you can open multiple windows in the program, access them easily from the menu, and minimize the whole thing with a single click of the mouse. In version 5, even Visual Basic has gone to a true MDI interface style. Figure 14.2 shows three blank workbooks opened simultaneously in Excel as an example of a typical MDI application.

FIG. 14.2
MDI applications let
you manage multiple
document windows with
ease.

Parent window —

Child windows —

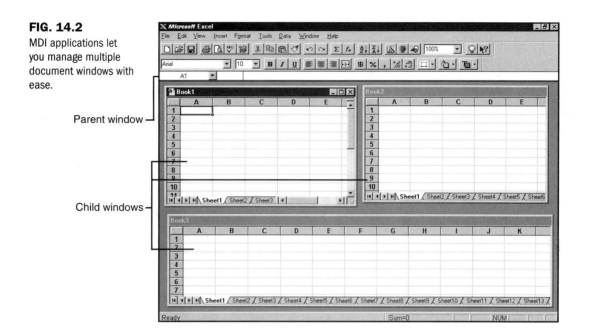

Characteristics of MDI Parent Forms

The MDI form, also known as the parent form, is the container for all the child forms of the application. The MDI form has a number of characteristics that define its behavior. These are:

- An application can only have one MDI form.

- The only controls that the MDI form can contain are those that support the Align property, such as the PictureBox or Toolbar controls. You cannot place other controls on the MDI form.

- You cannot use the Print method or any of the graphics methods to display information on the MDI form.

- When the MDI parent form is minimized, the parent window and all child windows are represented by a single icon on the Windows taskbar. When the parent form is restored, all the child forms are returned to the same layout as they had before the application was minimized.

- If a menu is defined for a child form, the menu will be displayed in the *parent form's* menu bar. If a menu is defined for the parent form, it is not shown at all unless there are no child forms present.

Characteristics of MDI Child Forms

Just as the MDI form has characteristics of its behavior, the MDI child forms also behave in a certain way. The characteristics of an MDI child form are:

Part
III

Ch
14

■ Each child form is displayed within the confines of the parent form. A child form cannot be moved outside the boundaries of the MDI parent form.

■ When a child window is minimized, its icon is displayed in the parent window, not on the taskbar.

■ When a child form is maximized, it fills the entire work area of the parent form. Also, the parent form's title bar will contain both the name of the parent form and the name of the child form.

■ When one child form is maximized, all other child forms are maximized as well.

Creating a Simple MDI Program

As with many programming concepts, the best way to understand how MDI applications work is to create a simple MDI program. This section walks you through the process of setting up a "shell" of an MDI program. It will contain an MDI form and a single child form. You can then use this program as the basis for a fully functional MDI application.

The first step is to start a new project in Visual Basic by choosing the New Project item from the File menu.

Setting Up the Parent Form

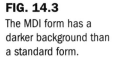

After you have started the new project, the next step is to create the MDI parent form. To create the MDI form for your project, select the Add MDI Form item from the Project menu, or choose MDI Form from the Add Object button's drop-down menu. Then, from the Add MDI Form dialog box, select the MDI Form icon and click Open. When the MDI Form is added to your project, it will look like the one in Figure 14.3.

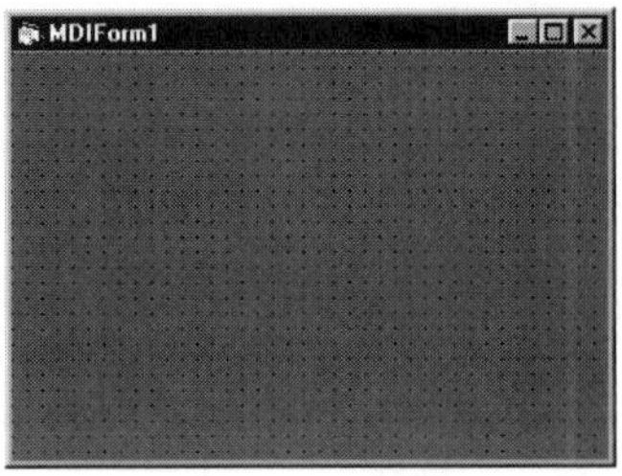

FIG. 14.3
The MDI form has a darker background than a standard form.

You might also notice that the MDI Form is added to the Forms folder of your project. However, if you look closely, you might notice that the MDI form is displayed in the Project window with a different icon than a standard form. The icons help you to easily identify the type of form that you have. Figure 14.4 illustrates the difference between normal and MDI form icons.

After you have added the form to your project, you should specify a descriptive name for the form and set any of the other properties that you need. Most of the properties of the MDI form are the same ones that you set to control the appearance of a standard form.

FIG. 14.4

Icons show the form type in the Project window.

Standard form icon

MDI (Parent) form icon

▶ **See** "Parts of a Form," **p. 76**

There are, however, two properties that are unique to the MDI form and deserve special note—the AutoShowChildren property and the ScrollBars property. The AutoShowChildren property determines whether child forms are shown automatically as they are loaded. If the AutoShowChildren property is set to True (the default value), then child forms are shown as soon as they are loaded. This means that the Load statement and the Show method have the same effect on the form.

The ScrollBars property determines whether the MDI form shows scroll bars when necessary. When this property is set to True (the default value), scroll bars are shown on the MDI form if one or more of the child forms extend beyond the boundary of the MDI form, as shown in Figure 14.5. If the property is set to False, scroll bars are not shown under any conditions.

One other property of note is the Picture property. While the MDI form does not support the Print method and graphics methods like a standard form, you can still include a picture as the background of the form.

FIG. 14.5

Scroll bars let you view portions of child forms that extend beyond the boundary of the parent form.

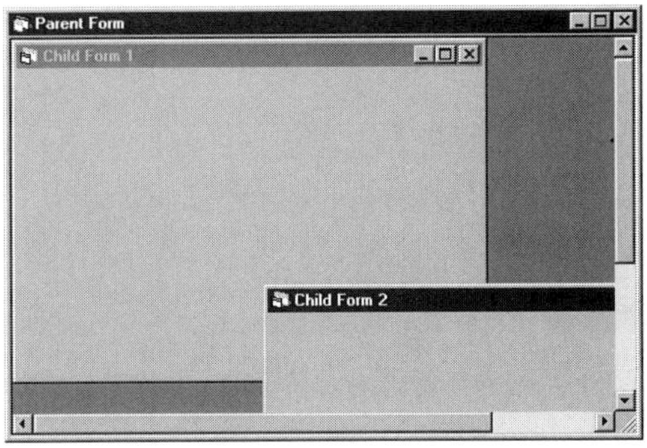

Setting Up a Child Form

Setting up a child form in an MDI application is even easier than setting up the parent form. A child form is basically a standard form that has the MDIChild property set to True. Therefore, everything you know about creating standard forms applies to creating the child forms of an MDI application.

For the sample application, all you need to do is set the MDIChild property of the form that was first created for the project. To do this, select the form in the Project window, select the MDIChild property in the Properties window, and change its value to True. You might notice that the icon for the form in the Project window changes from a standard icon to an MDI child icon. This is the only change that you will notice in the form while you are in the design window (see Figure 14.6).

FIG. 14.6

Notice how the two child forms' icons differ from those for standard and parent forms.

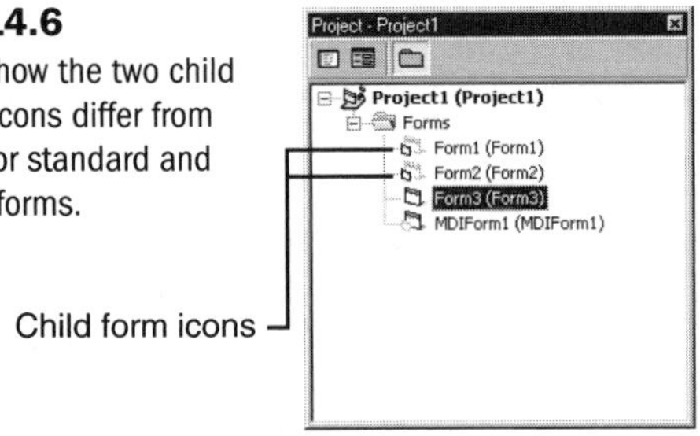

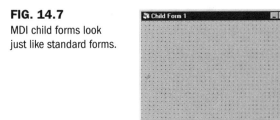

Child form icons

T I P As with other properties with predefined values, you can double-click the MDIChild property in the Properties window to toggle back and forth between the True and False values.

After setting the MDIChild property, all that is left to complete the form is to add the controls you need for your program. You can, of course, design the form first and change the MDIChild property later. The order of the operation has no effect on the behavior of the form. A typical MDI child form is shown in Figure 14.7.

FIG. 14.7

MDI child forms look just like standard forms.

Running the Program

After you have finished setting up both the parent and child forms, you are ready to run the program to see how a child form behaves inside the parent form. First, as always, you should save your work. Then click the Start button on the toolbar or press F5 to run the program. When the program runs, the form layout should resemble Figure 14.8.

There are several things that you should try so that you fully understand the behavior of the parent and child forms. Try the following tasks:

- Minimize the child form and note the location of its icon.
- Move the child form around. It does not move beyond the parent form's boundaries.
- Maximize the child form.
- Minimize and maximize the parent form.

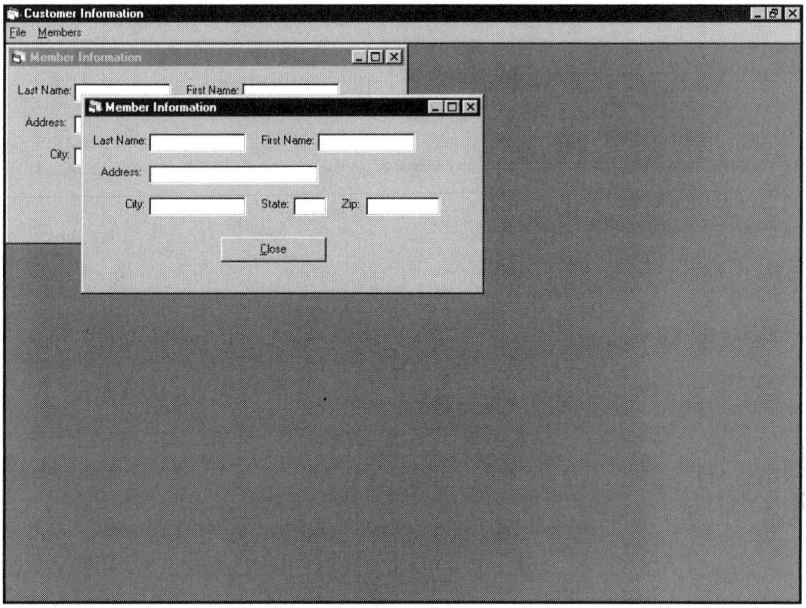

FIG. 14.8
This simple MDI application shows a parent form and two child forms. Note that the child forms are two instances of the same form.

One thing that you might have noticed when you started the program was that the child form was shown automatically when the program started. In the simple example, this is because the child form (the one first created when you started the project) was designated as the startup form. If you would like to have the empty MDI parent form shown when you start the program, you need to change the Startup Object setting in the Project Properties dialog box as shown in Figure 14.9. You access the project properties by choosing the Project Properties item from the Project menu.

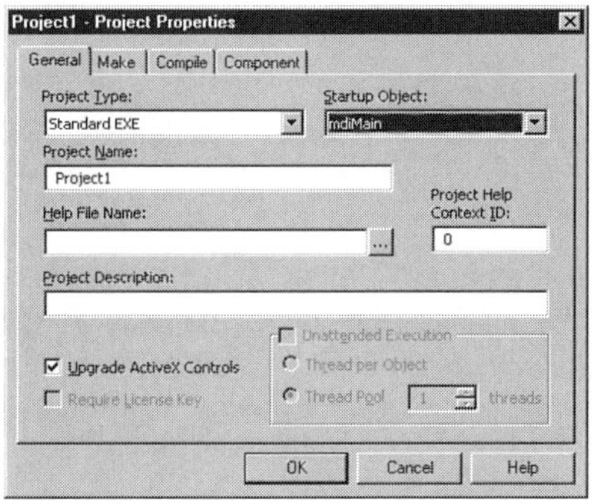

FIG. 14.9
Set the startup form and other properties of the project from this dialog box.

Creating Multiple Instances of a Form

You can use the MDI form just to make your application neater and its forms easier to manage. However, if that's all you use MDI forms for, you're missing out on the real power of MDI applications. The most powerful feature of an MDI application is its capability to create and handle *multiple instances of a form* at the same time. For example, if you are working in Microsoft Word, each document you open or each new document that you create is a new instance of the same basic form. In fact, many MDI applications are made up of only two forms: the MDI parent form and the template form for all the child forms in the application.

> **N O T E**   You can have more than one type of template child form in your application. For example, Visual Basic has two basic types of MDI child forms: the Form design child form and the Code child form. You can create as many of each of these types of forms as you need, within the constraints of your system. ▪

Creating an MDI application of this type requires a little more work than was required in the sample application. You first have to define the basic MDI child form at design time and then use object variables to create instances of the form at run time.

To start the process of creating an MDI application with multiple instances of a form, you need to start a new project and then add an MDI form to the project as described in the section "Creating a Simple MDI Program." Next, be sure to set up the MDI form as the startup object using the Project Properties dialog box.

Setting Up the Basic Form

As was the case in "Creating a Simple MDI Program," creating the form template is the same as creating a standard form. You add all the controls to the form that you need for the user interface. Also, you need to write any necessary code for the controls to perform their intended functions. You also need to set the MDIChild property of the form to True.

> **N O T E**   To optimize your application, you might need to write some code for the form in the MDI parent form or a separate module. See the section "Optimizing Your MDI Application" for more details on this subject. ▪

One thing you might notice as you first create an MDI application is that the child form, when first shown at run time, is probably sized differently than it was when you created it. This is illustrated in Figure 14.10. The reason is because an MDI application, by default, assigns a certain size and position to each child form that is shown.

If the default size and position are not acceptable to you, you need to place code in the Load event procedure of the child form to position and size it the way you want. To determine the desired size of the child form, check the Height and Width properties of the form while you are in design mode, and then add code to the form's Load event procedure to set the Height and Width properties to their original values. The same concept applies to the position of the form.

You can set the Top and Left properties of the child form to set its position. The code in Listing 14.1 shows how to set the size of a child form and center it within the parent form. Figure 14.11 shows the effect of this code.

FIG. 14.10

MDI applications automatically size and position their child forms.

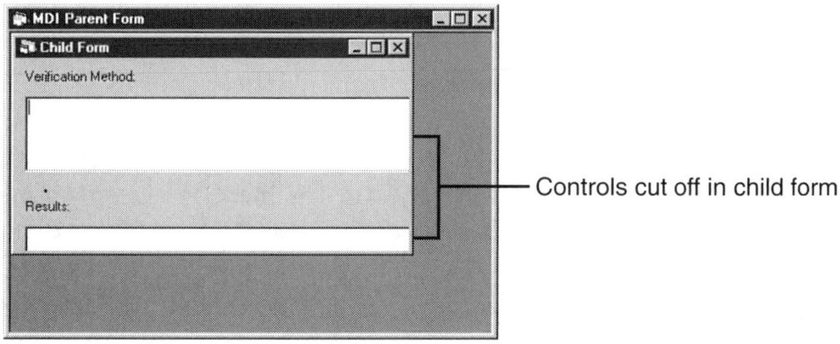

Controls cut off in child form

> **N O T E**   If a child window's size becomes too large for its parent, whether by user action or through code, the parent's size is not changed automatically. The parent does, however, automatically show scroll bars when needed, as mentioned in the section "Setting Up the Parent Form" earlier in this chapter. ▓

Listing 14.1   MDIDEMO2.FRM—Use Code to Size and Position the Child Form

```
Private Sub Form_Load()
    Me.Height = 4545
    Me.Width = 6810
    Me.Top = (mdiMain.ScaleHeight - Me.Height) / 2
    Me.Left = (mdiMain.ScaleWidth - Me.Width) / 2
End Sub
```

FIG. 14.11

You can use code to override the default size and position of an MDI child form.

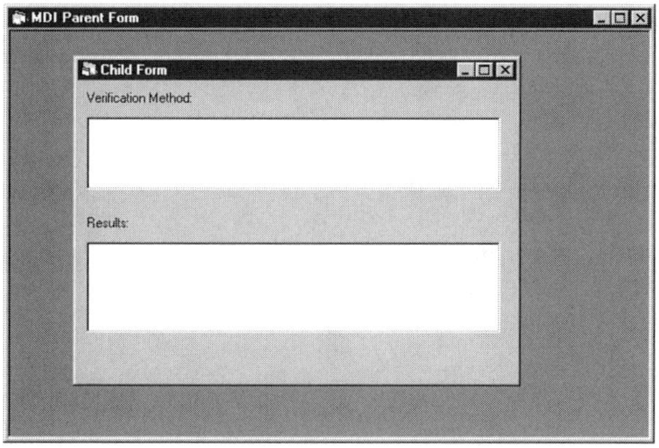

Part
III

Ch
14

NOTE You cannot use the StartUpPosition property to set the initial position of a child form in an MDI window. In fact, you cannot change the setting of the property from its default value of 0 - Manual. ▨

Creating Forms Using Object Variables

After you have created the basic child form, you need a means to create an instance of the form (at run time) and display it in the MDI application. Doing this requires all of two code lines. First, you use a Dim statement to create an *object variable* (a variable of Object type) that will contain an instance of the form. In the Dim statement, you need to use the New keyword to tell Visual Basic to create a *new instance* of the form. Otherwise, the statement just creates a new handle to the existing form. After you create the object variable, you use the Show method to display the form. However, *instead of using the form name, you specify the name of the variable.* The two required lines of code are shown here:

```
Dim NewFrm As New frmText
NewFrm.Show
```

To see how this code works, place the lines of code in the Click event procedure of the MDI form, and then run the program. Each time you click the MDI form, a new instance of the child form is displayed.

Using the Keywords *Me* and *ActiveForm*

Because all the child forms are the same and you use the same variable to create each of them, how can you know which form to specify when running code? Especially code that is generic and can work with any of the forms?

There are two particular keywords that you will use extensively in working with MDI applications: Me and ActiveForm. These two keywords let you create generic code routines that will work with any child form that you create.

Me is a keyword that can be used in any form to refer to itself, just as you can use the word *me* to refer to yourself without having to use your name. You saw how this keyword was used in Listing 14.1 to size and position the child form on startup. If you write all code in the child form using Me to refer to the form name, your code will work for whichever instance of the form is active at the time.

ActiveForm is actually a property of the MDI form. Its purpose is similar to the Me keyword. ActiveForm refers to whichever MDI child form is currently active. By using the ActiveForm property in all code that resides in the MDI form, the code operates only on the active form and on no other. The following line of code provides a simple example of the ActiveForm property:

```
mdiMain.ActiveForm.Print "This form is currently active."
```

NOTE Notice, here and in Listing 14.1, the use of the prefix mdi that was used when naming the MDI parent form. ▨

Using the `ActiveForm` property, you can reference any property, method, or event of the currently active child form without having to know its name.

Working with Menus

In Chapter 5, "Adding Menus and Toolbars to Your Program," you saw how to create a menu for your application. You also found out that you can have a different menu for each form in your program, if you so desire. MDI forms can also have menus. You create a menu for your MDI form the same way that you create a menu for a standard form, using the Menu Editor. The menu for the MDI form is usually the primary means by which you access the capabilities of an MDI application.

▶ **See** "Creating a Menu Bar," **p. 104**

In an MDI application, the child forms can also have menus. Like the menu for the MDI form itself, you create child form menus using the Menu Editor. However, when a child form is displayed, its menu is not displayed as part of the child form but on the menu bar of the MDI form. This behavior presents a problem in your MDI applications, because the MDI child form's menu actually *replaces* the MDI parent form's menu when the child is active. This problem is that you cannot access the functions of the parent form while the child is active.

There are two solutions to the problems associated with the replacement of menus. First, you can duplicate all the necessary parent form functions on each child form. Unfortunately, this can lead to a bloated and hard-to-maintain program if you have several child forms with menus.

An alternative solution is to include in the parent window's menu all the menus that are necessary for all child windows. Then you can place code in the `Activate` and `Deactivate` events of the child form to show the parent's menus that are applicable to that child form. For example, in a word processing program, you want the File and Help menus to be available all the time, but you only want the Edit and Format menus available when you are working on a document. You could use code similar to Listing 14.2 to show the menus when a document is active and to hide the menus when the document is inactive. As an alternative, you could show and hide the menus as the form opens and closes using the `Load` and `Unload` events.

Listing 14.2   MDIDEMO.FRM—Use Code to Show and Hide Child Menus

```
Private Sub Form_Activate()
    mnuEdit.Visible = True
    mnuFormat.Visible = True
End Sub

Private Sub Form_Deactivate()
    mnuEdit.Visible = False
    mnuFormat.Visible = False
End Sub
```

Part

III

Ch

14

To make sure that any menu code in the parent form acts upon the proper child form, use the parent form's `ActiveForm` property as described in the preceding section.

Managing the Children

One of the other benefits of working with MDI applications is that it is easy to manage all the child forms of the application. Visual Basic has a number of tools that make it easy for your users to access the multiple forms that are open inside the MDI form. Your program can provide the user with the means to automatically arrange the child windows. You can even provide a menu item that keeps up with all the open child windows and lets the user access one of them by selecting it from the menu. These capabilities are particularly useful if the user will be switching back and forth between multiple tasks or multiple files in the application.

Using Automatic Organization

One way the user can access multiple forms is by displaying each form on the screen in a particular organizational style. This provides the user with access to each form with just a click of a mouse button. The key to this functionality is the `Arrange` method of the MDI form. The `Arrange` method organizes all the child forms of the application in a particular pattern. Each of these patterns results in at least a portion of each form's being visible to the user, and they are commonly used by MDI-compliant Windows applications. To use the `Arrange` method, you specify the name of the MDI form, the method itself, and a constant representing the pattern that you want to use for the arrangement of the forms. The following line of code illustrates the use of the method:

```
mdiMain.Arrange vbCascade
```

There are four possible window arrangement patterns that you can create with the `Arrange` method. Each of these patterns is represented by an intrinsic constant. Table 14.1 summarizes the patterns. The four patterns are illustrated in Figures 14.12 through 14.15.

Table 14.1 Arrangements of MDI Child Windows

Constant	Description
vbCascade	Arranges the non-minimized forms in a pattern where each form is offset slightly from the others.
vbTileHorizontal	Each non-minimized child form occupies the full width of the parent form and the child forms are displayed on top of one another. If there are many child forms, they can occupy multiple columns when tiled.
vbTileVertical	Each non-minimized child form occupies the full height of the parent form and the child forms are displayed side-by-side. If there are many child forms, they can occupy multiple rows when tiled.
vbArrangeIcons	Arranges the icons of all minimized child forms near the bottom of the parent.

FIG. 14.12
These child forms have
been arranged in a
cascade pattern.

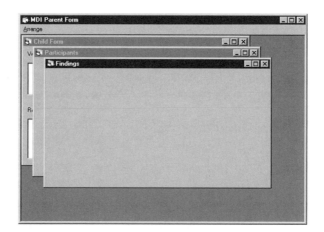

FIG. 14.13
These child forms have
been arranged in a
vertically tiled pattern.

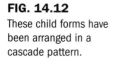

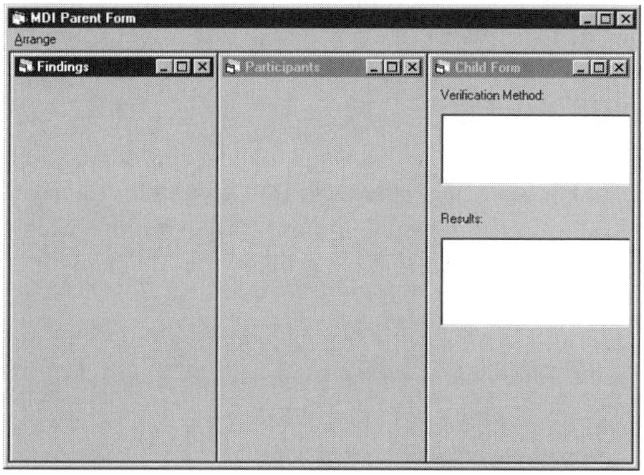

FIG. 14.14
These child forms have
been arranged in a
horizontally tiled
pattern.

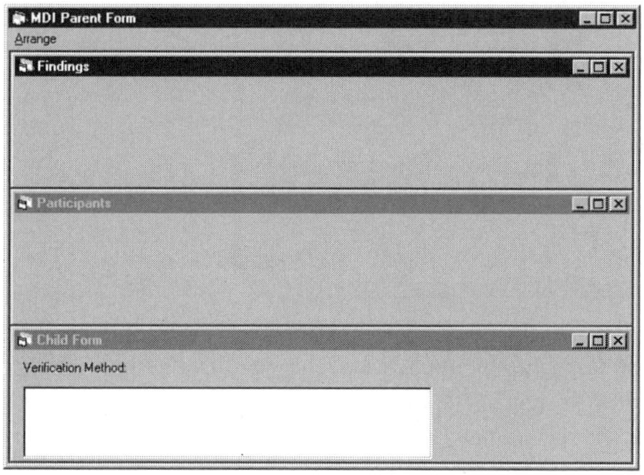

FIG. 14.15
Minimized child forms
are represented by icons
arranged at the bottom
of the MDI form.

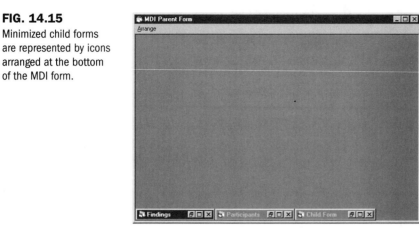

Typically, you place the arrangement options in a Window menu on the MDI form. Each arrangement option that you want to support is a separate menu item.

Maintaining a Window List

The other way of providing easy access to the child forms of your application is to maintain a list of the open child forms. Fortunately, this is an easy task. You create a window list while you are creating the menu for the MDI parent form. You determine which menu will contain the list and then set that menu item's WindowList property to True in the Menu Editor, as shown in Figure 14.16.

N O T E   You can also change the setting of the WindowList property from code. ▨

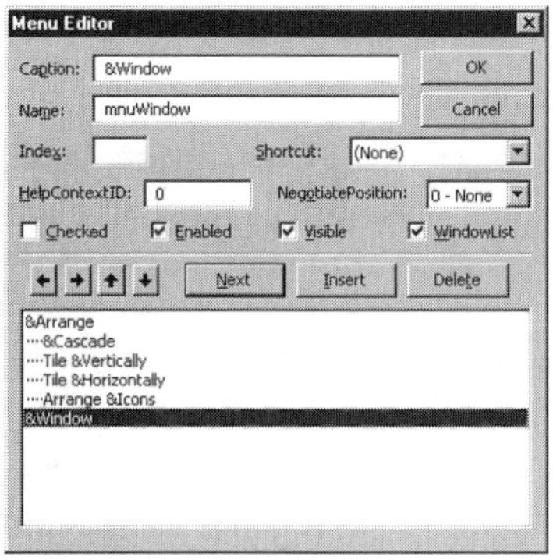

FIG. 14.16
Check the WindowList
box to create a list of
open child windows in
your MDI menu.

As you add child forms to the application, the window list menu item is automatically updated to include the new form. The caption of the menu item is the caption that is given to the form that you create. The active form in the window list is indicated by a check mark. Figure 14.17 shows a window list for an MDI application.

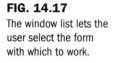
FIG. 14.17
The window list lets the user select the form with which to work.

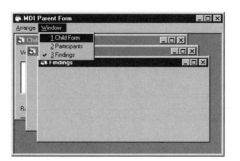

Creating a Sample Application—an MDI Contact Manager

Obviously, the best way to demonstrate the techniques of MDI applications is to build an application that you might actually use. This program uses multiple instances of a template form to become an MDI application.

If part of your job is keeping up with customer contacts, you probably use some kind of contact manager. These programs let you keep up with information about each of your customers, such as their name, address, phone numbers, the date you last contacted them, and so forth. One of the disadvantages of some contact managers is that you can only work with a single contact at a time. This can be very inconvenient if you are working on an order for one customer and another customer telephones to discuss a new service. In this case, you have to close the client information for the current customer and open the information for the second customer. Wouldn't it be great if you could just open the information for the second customer in a new window? Well, with an MDI contact manager, you can.

This section shows you how to build a very simple MDI contact manager. The program displays only name and address information for a client and is basically an illustration of the concept. To create a full-fledged contact manager, you have to add additional database code. The program uses a Microsoft Access database and the Jet engine to retrieve the data.

▶ **See** "Using Tables," on **p. 722**

Creating the MDI Form

The setup of the MDI form is the same as you have seen in previous sections. You first need to add an MDI form to your project and then set the `AutoShowChildren` property to `False`. You also should set the `Name` and `Caption` properties of the MDI form to something other than the defaults.

After setting the properties of the form, you need to create a menu that displays the customer information in the appropriate child form. The menu items that you need to add are shown in Figure 14.18.

▶ **See** "Creating a Menu Bar," **p. 104**

Part

III

Ch

14

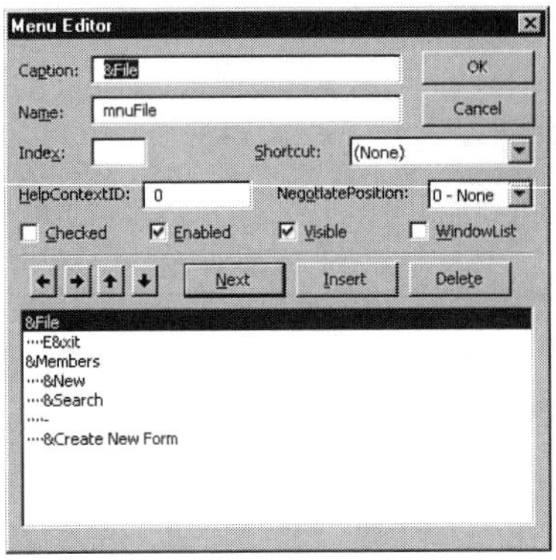

FIG. 14.18

Our sample MDI
Contact Manager
application has these
menu items.

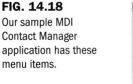

One menu item of note is the Create New Form item. The user can use this option to tell the
program whether to display a selected customer in the existing child form or to create a new
form for each new customer. The Checked property of the item is set to show the status of the
user choice.

Of course, after you create the menu, you need to add code to make the menu options work.
Listing 14.3 shows the code for the menu items shown in Figure 14.18.

**Listing 14.3   MAINMDI.FRM—Use Menu Code to Handle the Tasks of the
Contact Manager**

```
Private Sub filExit_Click()
    Unload Me
End Sub


Private Sub MDIForm_Load()
    Me.WindowState = vbMaximized
End Sub


Private Sub MDIForm_Unload(Cancel As Integer)
    CustDb.Close
End Sub


Private Sub memCreate_Click()
Dim CheckSet As Boolean
    CheckSet = Not memCreate.Checked
    memCreate.Checked = CheckSet
    CreateForm = CheckSet
End Sub


Private Sub memNew_Click()
    If CreateForm Then
        Dim frmMem As New frmMember
        frmMem.Show
    End If
    ClearCust
End Sub
```

```
Private Sub memSearch_Click()
    frmSearch.Show vbModal
    If CreateForm Then
        Dim frmMem As New frmMember
        frmMem.Show
    End If
    ShowCust
End Sub
```

Setting Up the Customer Child Form

The next step in creating the contact manager is setting up the child form that will display a customer's information. To set up the customer form, add a form to your project (or use the initial form that was created) and then set its MDIChild property to True. You probably also need to change the Name and Caption properties of the form. (Set the name of the form to frmMember to match the code in the menu items.) After setting the properties of the form, you need to add controls to the form to display the data. The completed form is shown in Figure 14.19.

FIG. 14.19

Customer information is displayed in a child form.

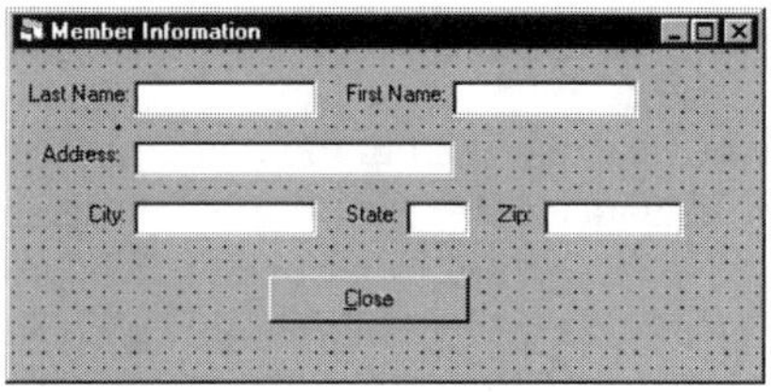

Creating the Search Form

As you look up customer records, you need a search form to allow the user to enter a name to find. The search form can be very simple, consisting of a label, a text box to enter the name, and two command buttons to perform or cancel the search. The code for the form is also very simple; if you proceed with the search, the code uses the FindFirst method of the recordset that contains the contact information to locate the first name corresponding to the desired search information. The complete search form is shown in Figure 14.20, and the code for the form is shown in Listing 14.4.

N O T E A *recordset* is a special type of object that acts as a link between a Visual Basic program and information stored in a database. You learn about recordsets in Chapter 28. ▪

▶ **See** "Deciding Which Recordset Type to Use," **p. 722**

Part
III

Ch
14

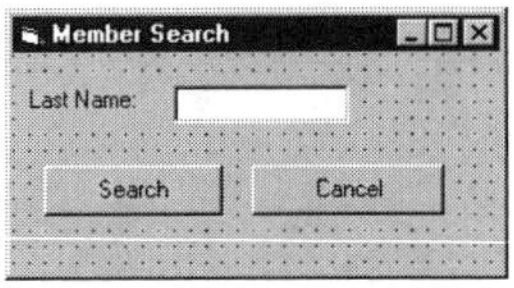

FIG. 14.20
You can make the
search form more
complex by adding a
First Name search as
well.

Listing 14.4   SEARCH.FRM—Use the *FindFirst* Method to Locate the Desired Customer

```
Private Sub cmdCancel_Click()
    Unload Me
End Sub

Private Sub cmdSearch_Click()
Dim SrchStr As String
    SrchStr = txtSearch.Text
    CustRset.FindFirst "LastName = '" & SrchStr & "'"
    Unload Me
End Sub
```

Creating the Heart of the Program

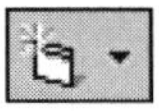

The forms provide the interface of the program, but the real heart of the program is a group of procedures that actually display the data and set the program up. To create the procedures, you first need to add a module to your program. You can do this by selecting the Add Module item from the Project menu, or by selecting Module from the Add Object button's drop-down menu.

▶ **See** "Determining the Scope of Procedures and Functions," **p. 254**

After the module is added to the project, you need to define a couple of Public variables and create the procedure that sets up the program. The public variables are used to provide your entire program with access to the database object. After you define the variables, you need to create a Sub Main procedure to set up the database information and display the MDI parent form. The Public variable declarations and the Sub Main procedure are shown in Listing 14.5.

Listing 14.5   MDIPROCS.BAS—Use *Sub Main* to Set Up the Database and Load the Main Form

```
Public CustDb As Database, CustRset As Recordset
Public CreateForm As Boolean

Sub Main()
    Set CustDb = DBEngine.Workspaces(0).OpenDatabase("D:\VB5Book\NewDb.mdb")
    Set CustRset = CustDb.OpenRecordset("Customers", dbOpenDynaset)
```

```
    mdiMain.Show
    CreateForm = True
End Sub
```

After you create the Sub Main procedure, you need to change the project options to make Sub Main the startup object of the program.

The next two procedures are the ones which either display information about a current customer or set up the information form for you to enter a new customer. These procedures are called by the appropriate menu items of the MDI form. The key feature to note in these procedures is that the ActiveForm property of the MDI form is used to designate which child form will receive the data being sent. The ClearCust and ShowCust procedures are shown in Listing 14.6.

Listing 14.6 MDIPROCS.BAS—Use the *ActiveForm* Property to Send the Output of the Procedure to the Proper Location

```
Public Sub ClearCust()
Dim I As Integer
    For I = 0 To 5
        mdiMain.ActiveForm.txtMember(I).Text = ""
    Next I
End Sub

Public Sub ShowCust()
    With mdiMain.ActiveForm
        .txtMember(0).Text = CustRset!LastName & ""
        .txtMember(1).Text = CustRset!FirstName & ""
        .txtMember(2).Text = CustRset!Address1 & ""
        .txtMember(3).Text = CustRset!City & ""
        .txtMember(4).Text = CustRset!State & ""
        .txtMember(5).Text = CustRset!Zip & ""
    End With
End Sub
```

Running the Program

As you run the program, you can create new windows for each customer that you add, or change the status of the Create New Form menu item to display each customer in the same window. Try it out. As stated before, this example is merely an illustration of the concept, so feel free to add your own enhancements to the program. The MDI contact manager is shown in Figure 14.21.

Part
III

Ch
14

FIG. 14.21
You can display multiple clients at the same time.

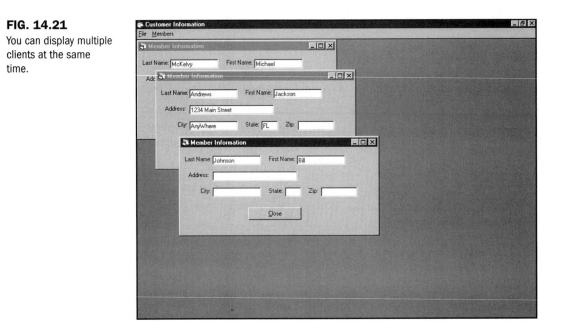

Optimizing Your MDI Application

This chapter has demonstrated a number of techniques that you can use to create MDI applications. As you can see, the MDI form can be a powerful tool for creating programs. However, there are several considerations to keep in mind to optimize your MDI applications. These considerations help keep the performance of your programs as crisp as possible and help keep your users from running into problems. The considerations are:

- Each new child window that is loaded consumes memory. Having memory-intensive child windows causes your application to drain memory quickly, so keep the amount of code and the number of controls in your child windows to a minimum.

- If your child and parent windows have the same menu commands (such as File Open or File Exit), keep the code in the parent. This means your child form's menu Click event procedures should simply call the parent menu's Click event procedure for all shared code.

- Change all of your menu Click event procedures from Private to Public so your child and parent windows can share these events.

- Avoid using the Name property of your child form. Instead, your child forms should use Me (or nothing at all), and your parent form should use ActiveForm.

- Put *all* invisible controls (such as a common dialog control or image list) on the MDI parent form. This allows all of your child windows to share these controls, without consuming extra memory.

Adhering to these concepts both simplifies your code and improves the performance of your MDI application.

Creating an MDI Application Framework

The code shown in this section is designed to provide a basic skeleton for any MDI applications that you create. The skeleton code can be modified to suit your specific needs. Then you can use the skeleton project as a template for your other MDI applications. The completed application is shown in Figure 14.22.

FIG. 14.22
Creating a template project can simplify your future MDI work.

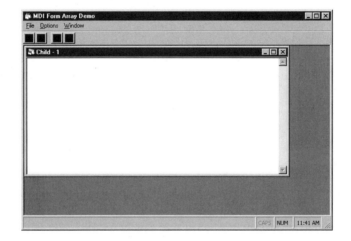

Creating the MDI Parent Template

The MDI parent form is the keeper (or container) of the child windows, so it is responsible for creating new children. With this duty, it is common for the parent to also keep track of the number of child windows it has created. In addition, the parent usually holds shared user interface elements like a toolbar, status bar, and so on.

The following code in Listing 14.7 shows the code used to maintain and expose the window count. `WindowCreate` and `WindowDestroyed` are called by the child windows in their `Form_Load` and `Form_Unload` event procedures, respectively. `ChildWindowCount` is a `Public` property that allows the child windows to find out how many children are loaded.

Part
III

Ch
14

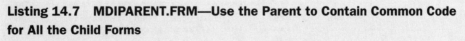

Listing 14.7   MDIPARENT.FRM—Use the Parent to Contain Common Code for All the Child Forms

```
'*********************************************************************
' MDIParent.frm - Demonstrates some basic concepts on how a MDI parent
'    form should behave in an MDI application.
'*********************************************************************
```

continues

Listing 14.7   Continued

```
Option Explicit
Private mintChildWinCount As Integer
'*********************************************************************
' Returns how many child windows have been created
'*********************************************************************
Public Property Get ChildWindowCount() As Integer
    ChildWindowCount = mintChildWinCount
End Property
'*********************************************************************
' Called when a window is created to increment the window counter
'*********************************************************************
Public Sub WindowCreated()
    mintChildWinCount = mintChildWinCount + 1
    UpdateButtons True
End Sub
'*********************************************************************
' Called when a window is created to decrement the window counter
'*********************************************************************
Public Sub WindowDestroyed()
    mintChildWinCount = mintChildWinCount - 1
    UpdateButtons mintChildWinCount
End Sub
```

You also might notice a call to UpdateButtons in Listing 14.7. This private helper routine enables and disables toolbar buttons. If children exist, then the toolbar buttons are enabled. When the last child is unloaded, WindowDestroyed decrements the variable mintChildWinCount to 0, which causes UpdateButtons to disable the toolbar buttons.

The most important code in MDIPARENT.FRM is the File menu's Click event procedure. This code is responsible for creating windows, opening files, and terminating the application. Because all of these actions on the MDI parent file menu are also on the child form's file menu, you make this event public as shown in Listing 14.8.

Listing 14.8   MDIPARENT.FRM—Handling Menu *Click* Events

```
'*********************************************************************
' File menu handler for the MDI form when no windows are displayed.
' In this demo the child windows will have a menu just like this,
' so we will make this Public so the children can call this event.
'*********************************************************************
Public Sub mnuFileItems_Click(Index As Integer)
    Select Case Index
        '*********************************************************************
        ' File New - Create a new child form, then display it.
        '*********************************************************************
        Case 1
            Dim frmNew As New frmChild
            frmNew.Visible = True
        '*********************************************************************
```

```
' File Open - Prompt the user for a filename, then load
'    it into the child window (in OpenFile) if the user didn't
'    press cancel in the dialog.
'****************************************************************
Case 2
    On Error Resume Next
    With cdlg
        .Flags = cdlOFNFileMustExist
        .Filter = "Text Files (*.txt)¦*.txt¦All Files (*.*)¦*.*"
        .ShowOpen
    End With
    If Err <> cdlg.cdlCancel Then OpenFile cdlg.filename
'****************************************************************
' Index 3 is the separator, so don't do anything.
'****************************************************************
'Case 3
'****************************************************************
' File Exit - Terminate the application
'****************************************************************
Case 4
    Unload Me
    End Select
End Sub
```

When the File New menu is clicked (Index = 1), the `Dim frmNew As New frmChild` line creates a new instance of your child form. However, this doesn't really create the new form. The form is actually created as soon as you access one if its properties or methods. This means that the `frmNew.Visible = True` line is the line of code that creates the form. After the form is created, the `Visible` property is set to `True`, which displays your form.

T I P Forms created using New are hidden by default, so remember to display them by setting
`Visible = True`.

The File Open (Index = 2) code in Listing 14.8 simply displays an Open dialog box so the user can supply a file name. If the user doesn't click Cancel, then the file is opened using the `OpenFile` routine, as presented in Listing 14.9. The last item in the select statement is `Index 4`, which represents the File Exit case. This is an easy one because the proper way to terminate an MDI application is to unload the MDI form.

As mentioned earlier, the `OpenFile` code is responsible for opening a text file and loading it into a text box on your child form. This code is very simplistic and includes no basic error handling for such cases as testing for files greater than 44k under Windows 95. However, it does provide a basic example of how to load a file into a text box, which is sufficient for this example.

Part
III

Ch
14

CAUTION

Avoid using the End statement to terminate your applications. End terminates your application immediately, which prevents your Form_Unload events from being executed. The best way to end an MDI application is to unload the MDI form.

Listing 14.9   MDIPARENT.FRM—Shared Code

```
'*********************************************************************
' Code shared among the child windows should be put in either a
' module or the MDI parent form.  This OpenFile code will be used
' by all of the children, so we will keep it in the MDI parent form.
'*********************************************************************
Public Sub OpenFile(strFileName As String)
    Dim strFileContents As String
    Dim intFileNum As Integer
    '*************************************************************
    ' Get a free file handle
    '*************************************************************
    intFileNum = FreeFile
    '*************************************************************
    ' Open the file
    '*************************************************************
    Open strFileName For Input As intFileNum
        '*********************************************************
        ' Put the contents of the file into the txtData control of
        ' the child form. This code will fail if the file is too
        ' large to fit in the textbox, so you should include
        ' additional error handling in your own code.
        '*********************************************************
        With ActiveForm
            .txtData.Text = Input$(LOF(intFileNum), intFileNum)
            '*****************************************************
            ' Set the caption of the child form to the filename
            '*****************************************************
            .Caption = strFileName
        End With
    '*************************************************************
    ' Always close files you open as soon as you are done with them
    '*************************************************************
    Close intFileNum
End Sub
```

You might notice that the OpenFile routine simply loads the file into the text box on the active window by referencing the ActiveForm property. This is a valid assumption to make, because the active menu will always refer to the active form. Because the user can open a file via the menu (even if he is using the toolbar), you can always assume that any actions you perform in your menu event handlers should be applied to the active form.

The MDI Child

Now that you have had a chance to understand what your MDI parent form is responsible for, let's take a look at how the child should behave in this parent/child relationship.

As mentioned earlier, child forms are responsible for calling the WindowCreated and WindowDestroyed methods of the MDI parent form. Listing 14.10 demonstrates how this is done from the `Form_Load` and `Form_Unload` events. In addition, your child window sets its initial caption based on the MDI parent `ChildWindowCount` property. Although this technique is good for this sample, you might want to make your algorithm for setting your initial caption a little more complex. What do you think would happen if you had three windows, closed the second window, and then created a new window? How could you avoid this problem?

Listing 14.10   MDICHILD.FRM—Use the Child Form for Code Specific to Each Child

```
'*********************************************************************
' MDIChild.frm - Demonstrates some basic techniques on how a MDI child
'    window should behave.
'*********************************************************************
Option Explicit
'*********************************************************************
' When a new form is created it should call the WindowCreated function
' in the MDI parent form (which increments the window count in this
' case). It should also set its caption to distinguish it from other
' child windows.
'*********************************************************************
Private Sub Form_Load()
    MDIParent.WindowCreated
    '*********************************************************************
    ' This works, but it has a fatal flaw.
    '*********************************************************************
    Caption = Caption & " - " & MDIParent.ChildWindowCount
End Sub
'*********************************************************************
' Make sure txtData always fills the client area of the form.
'*********************************************************************
Private Sub Form_Resize()
    txtData.Move 0, 0, ScaleWidth, ScaleHeight
End Sub
'*********************************************************************
' Let the MDI parent know that this window is being destroyed.
'*********************************************************************
Private Sub Form_Unload(Cancel As Integer)
    MDIParent.WindowDestroyed
End Sub
```

One other minor detail you might have noticed in this code is the `Form_Resize` event. This code makes sure your TextBox control always covers the entire client area of the form. This code works with any control, so keep this in mind for your own applications.

Another important concept mentioned previously is that your child forms should use event handlers of the parent menu whenever possible (and vice versa). Listing 14.11 contains the event handlers for all of the menus used by MDICHILD.FRM.

Part
III

Ch
14

Listing 14.11   MDICHILD.FRM—Handling the Menu Code for the Application

```
'*********************************************************************
' Since the child File menu is identical to the MDI parent File menu,
' we should avoid duplicate code by calling the parent's mnuFileItems
' click event.
'*********************************************************************
Private Sub mnuFileItems_Click(Index As Integer)
    MDIParent.mnuFileItems_Click Index
End Sub
'*********************************************************************
' The options menu is unique to the child forms, so the code should
' be in the child form or separate BAS module.
'*********************************************************************
Public Sub mnuOptionsItems_Click(Index As Integer)
    '*************************************************************
    ' Don't stop for errors
    '*************************************************************
    On Error Resume Next
    '*************************************************************
    ' Show the color dialog (since all menu items here need it)
    '*************************************************************
    MDIParent.cdlg.ShowColor
    '*************************************************************
    ' If the use selected cancel, then exit
    '*************************************************************
    If Err = cdlCancel Then Exit Sub
    '*************************************************************
    ' Otherwise set the color based on the value returned from the dlg
    '*************************************************************
    Select Case Index
        Case 1 'Backcolor...
            txtData.BackColor = MDIParent.cdlg.Color
        Case 2 'Forecolor...
            txtData.ForeColor = MDIParent.cdlg.Color
    End Select
End Sub
'*********************************************************************
' If you set your indexes of your Window menu properly, you can save
' yourself some code. I was careful to make sure my Window menu items
' indices were equivalent to the possible values for the Arrange
' method.
'*********************************************************************
Private Sub mnuWindowItems_Click(Index As Integer)
    MDIParent.Arrange Index
End Sub
```

The first menu is the File menu, which is identical to the parent form, so you simply call the mnuFileItems_Click event in the parent for default processing. The second menu is the Options menu, which only appears in the child form, so you write your implementation code here. However, you make this event handler public so it could be accessed by your Toolbar control, which resides on the parent form. In addition, you use the CommonDialog control on the parent for your code, which displays the color dialog box.

T I P If any menu item on your child form requires greater than 12 lines or so of code (excluding `Dims`, comments, and white space), you should move that code to a shared module or into the parent form. That prevents this code from consuming too much free memory every time a new form is added.

Finally, you have your <u>W</u>indow menu that only applies to child forms (although it is the parent form that is responsible for this menu). By carefully creating your menu control array indexes, you are able to write the implementation code for this menu using only one line of code.

From Here...

This chapter has provided you with an introduction to creating MDI applications using Visual Basic. For more information about some of the related topics covered in this chapter, see the following chapters:

- To learn more about setting up forms, see Chapter 4, "Working with Forms and Controls."

- To learn more about creating menus and toolbars, see Chapter 5, "Adding Menus and Toolbars to Your Program."

- To learn more about creating database programs, see Chapter 28, "Improving Data Access with the Data Access Objects."

- To learn more about property procedures, see Chapter 32, "Using Classes in Visual Basic."

Part
III

Ch
14

Working with Visual Basic Controls

Working with the Standard Controls

In the first two parts of the book, you learned some of the fundamentals of writing programs in Visual Basic. Along the way, you were exposed to some of the basics of working with controls. Part IV of the book takes you deeper into the world of Visual Basic controls. In this first chapter, you will look at some of the standard controls, most of which have been a part of Visual Basic since version 1. You will see some of the basic operations of these controls, as well as see some of the new features that have been incorporated into Visual Basic 5. ■

Most of your programs will require users to make choices

You will see how option buttons and check boxes enable you to control with ease the choices available to the user.

For many applications, you will have a large number of available choices

You will see how the ListBox and ComboBox controls make quick work out of creating and managing lists of choices.

Scroll bar—another way to enter numbers

While you will use a text box for many types of numeric input, you will often find that a scroll bar is easier for the user to work with and for you to handle in your program.

Keeping time with a control

If you need to have certain activities occur at specific intervals, the Timer control is the right tool for the job.

Recapping the Basics

Because several of the standard controls have been covered earlier in the book, they will not be covered in this chapter. These controls and the chapters that cover them are summarized in Table 15.1.

Table 15.1   Controls Covered in Previous Chapters

Control Name	Chapter
TextBox	Chapter 13, "Working with Text, Fonts, and Colors"
Label	Chapter 13, "Working with Text, Fonts, and Colors"
Command Button	Chapter 4, "Working with Forms and Controls"
PictureBox	Chapter 12, "Working with Graphics"
Image	Chapter 12, "Working with Graphics"
Shape	Chapter 12, "Working with Graphics"
Line	Chapter 12, "Working with Graphics"

Recall from these previous chapters that there are several properties, methods, and events that are common to almost all controls. Most controls have Name, Top, Left, Height, Width, Enabled, and Visible properties. There are also several other common properties that have yet to be discussed—until now.

Maintaining Order

The first of these properties is the TabIndex property. This property determines the order in which controls are accessed as the user presses the Tab key while the form on which the controls reside is active. The TabIndex property starts with zero for the first control you add to a form. As you add more controls, each control is given a TabIndex property that is one greater than the last control. If you design your form perfectly the first time, your controls will be accessed in the proper order and you will never have to worry about this property. However, changes to your form are inevitable and the order can get messed up. When this happens, you will have to reset the Tab order of the controls by setting the TabIndex properties.

Figure 15.1 shows a typical form used in a program. Since it is not possible to show the effects of good and bad tab orders in print, two programs are included on the companion CD to illustrate the concept. The form in Figure 15.1 is used in both programs. The two programs are BadTab.Vbp and GoodTab.Vbp. A user reasonably might expect to move from field to field in a logical order, which, in this case, would be First Name, Middle Initial, Last Name, Address, and so on. You should make sure the TabIndex property of your forms' controls causes the focus to flow correctly.

Since it is not possible to show the effects of good and bad tab orders in print, two programs are available on the Que Web site to illustrate the concept. The form in Figure 15.1 is used in both programs. The two programs are BadTab.Vbp and GoodTab.Vbp, and you can download them from **www.mcp.com/info/0-7897/0-7897-1288-1**.

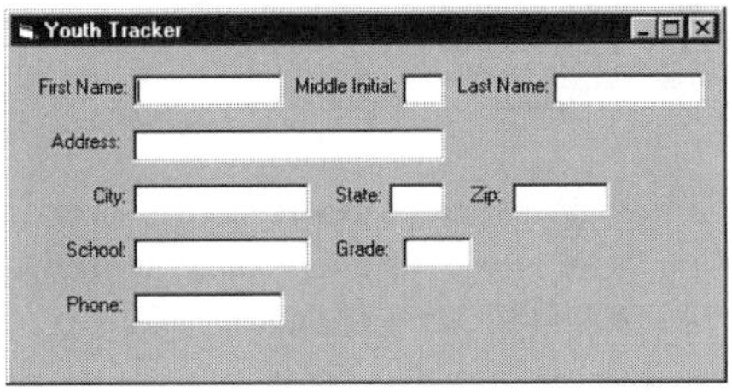

FIG. 15.1

Users expect a form's
focus to flow logically.

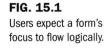

The only way to change the tab order of the controls on your form is to set the TabIndex property of each control that you need to shift. As you set a new value for the TabIndex property of a control, Visual Basic automatically adjusts the property values for all controls that have higher TabIndex property values than the new value.

> **N O T E** Even though Label controls can't receive the focus, they still have a TabIndex property. This is to aid in creating keyboard-friendly programs. TabIndex comes into play if a Label control's Caption property includes an access key; for example, a Label control whose Caption property is &Name will show the "N" to be an access key (<u>N</u>ame). If the user presses the access key (in this case, Alt+N), the focus moves to the control with the next-higher TabIndex (assuming that it's a control that can receive the focus). If our Label control has a TabIndex property of 9, for example, you might have an associated TextBox control whose TabIndex property is 10. Then, when the user presses Alt+N, the focus moves to the "Name" TextBox, which is probably positioned next to the label. This technique, in effect, lets a Label control act as a caption for a text box. ■

Another property related to the TabIndex property is the TabStop property. TabStop is a property of any control that can receive the focus in a program. The value of the TabStop property determines whether the user can move the focus to the control by pressing the Tab key. The default value of True allows the user to use the Tab key. Setting the TabStop property to False means that the control won't receive the focus as the user presses Tab; however, it can still be accessed with the mouse.

Exploring Other Common Properties

Another useful property of many controls is the ToolTipText property, which enables you to display text in a ToolTip when the user pauses the mouse pointer over a control. ToolTips are used to help the user determine which controls will perform a desired action. A ToolTip is enabled if any text is entered for the ToolTip property. Figure 15.2 shows a ToolTip at work.

FIG. 15.2

ToolTips provide a clue to the function of a control.

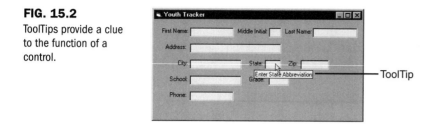

Another common property of note is the `Index` property. If this property has a value (0 or greater), this indicates that the control is part of a control array. You will find a discussion of control arrays in Chapter 19, "Advanced Control Techniques."

▶ **See** "Using Control Arrays," **p. 496**

Working with User Choices

Previously, you have seen how to acquire input from a user through the use of a text box. This works well for a number of data-gathering needs. But what if you just want a simple piece of information, such as "Do you own a car?" or "What is your marital status?" In these cases, the choice of answers you want to provide is limited to two or, at most, a few choices.

Although a text box works for getting this information, what is the user supposed to enter? For a "yes" or "no" choice, do you want the user to type out the entire word or just use the first letter? Or would you prefer *true* or *false* responses? By the same token, what should a person enter for marital status? Are you looking just for married or single, or do you want to include divorced and widowed?

These differences may not seem like much on the surface, but they can have a critical difference in how you write a program. If you set up a program to handle only the words *yes* and *no*, your program will have a problem if users type in "Maybe," or if they mistype a word.

You can eliminate this problem and provide the user with more direction to the responses you seek by giving them a specific set of choices from which to select. This can be accomplished through the use of check boxes and option buttons.

Check boxes and option buttons are great for small numbers of options, but sometimes you need the capability to handle a large number of options. For example, you might want to allow your users to pick the state in which they live instead of having to type it in a text box. Trying to cram 50 option buttons onto a form would be difficult and would make for a poorly designed form. Fortunately, there is another solution to the problem: lists.

Visual Basic provides two basic types of lists to handle large numbers of choices—list boxes and combo boxes. Lists can support a single choice or multiple choices. Some lists even allow the user to enter values that are not on the list.

Each of these controls used for obtaining user input will be discussed in the remainder of this chapter. We'll also look at scroll bars, which give the user an easy way to specify a value within a controlled range.

Checking for Yes or No

Visual Basic's CheckBox control is used to get an answer of either "yes" or "no" from the user. It works like a light switch. Either it is on or it is off; there is no in between. When a check box is on, a check mark ( ) is displayed in the box. This indicates that the answer to the check box's corresponding question is "Yes." When the check box is off, or unchecked, the box is empty, indicating an answer of "No." Figure 15.3 shows a selected (on) and deselected (off) box.

N O T E   The check mark or empty box format is characteristic of the standard-form check box. If you set the check box's Style property to 1-Graphical, pictures are used to indicate checked and unchecked.

FIG. 15.3

A check box can indicate a "Yes" or "No" response to a question.

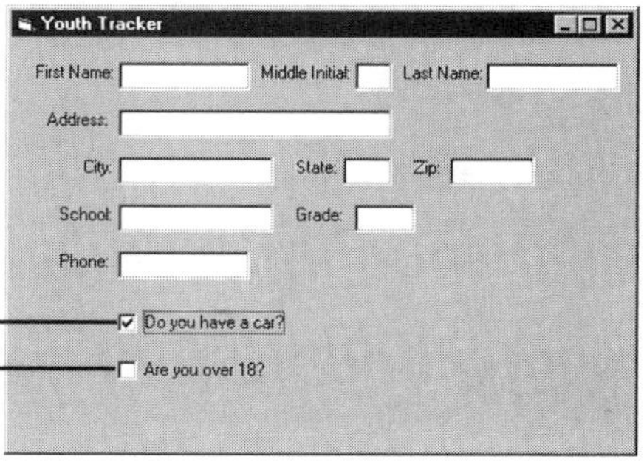

Selected (on)

Deselected (off)

The prompts used in a check box do not necessarily have to be in the form of a question. If you have looked at some of the option dialog boxes used for programs, you have seen check boxes used to specify which options should be turned on. The prompt for the check box is simply the option name, instead of a question. Figure 15.4 shows the Environment Options dialog box for Visual Basic, which shows this type of use.

FIG. 15.4

In the Environment tab of Visual Basic's Options dialog box, users can choose the templates they want to be shown by selecting check boxes.

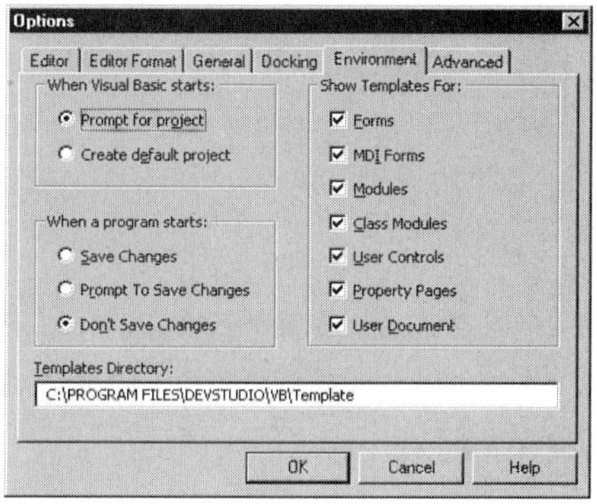

Creating a Check Box

Although the check box has been around for a while, Visual Basic 5 has added a new twist to the old standard. When a check box's Style property is set to 1-Standard or 2-Graphical, your check box will appear in one of the following ways:

- *Standard* check boxes use the familiar box that either is empty or contains a check mark.

- Graphical check boxes look like command buttons. When the check box is "unchecked," it appears in the up position. When it is "checked," it appears in the down position.

The appearance of each of these check box styles is shown in Figure 15.5.

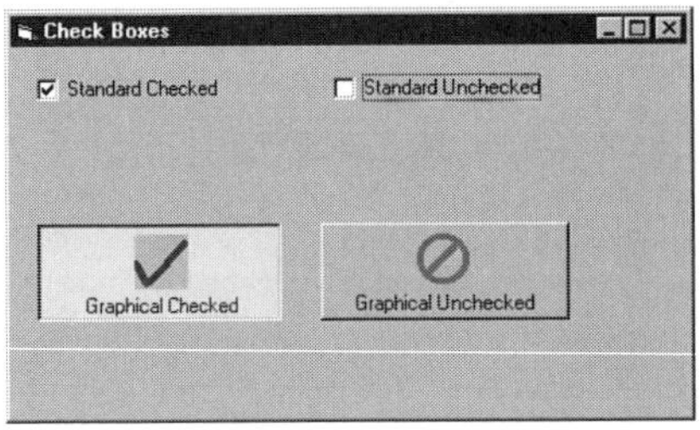

FIG. 15.5

Graphical-style check boxes can give a new appearance to your programs.

To create a check box, select CheckBox control from the Toolbox and draw one (or more) on your form. When you first draw the check box, it has the default caption (prompt) of Check1. Since this will have absolutely no meaning to a user, you need to change the caption to something more descriptive. Select the Caption property from the Properties window and change it to something meaningful. At this point, what you do to control the appearance of the check box depends on the style of check box you select.

Controlling the Appearance of a Standard Check Box   If you are creating a standard check box, leave the Style property in its default setting of 0-Standard. After you have selected the standard style, there are several things you can do to change the appearance of the check box:

- Change the font used for the control's prompt.
- Modify the ForeColor and BackColor properties to change the control's colors.
- Change the Appearance property to create either a Flat or 3-D appearance.
- Change the Alignment property to determine on which side of the box the prompt is placed.

The effects of the Appearance and Alignment properties are shown in Figure 15.6. The default value of the Appearance property is 3-D and the default value of the Alignment property is left-justified. Both the Alignment and the Appearance properties are read-only at runtime; this means that they can only be set while you are in the design environment. You cannot change these properties with program code.

FIG. 15.6

By modifying properties of your check boxes, you can produce a wide variety of visual effects.

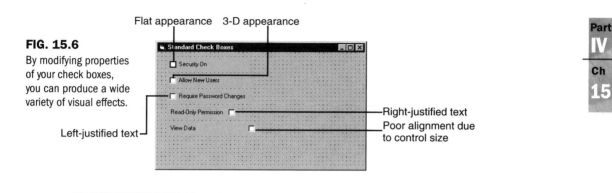

Flat appearance   3-D appearance

Left-justified text

Right-justified text
Poor alignment due to control size

> **CAUTION**
>
> If you use right justification for the check box, make sure that the control is sized so that the box is next to the prompt. Otherwise, a misalignment (like the one in Figure 15.6) can cause confusion for the user.

Controlling the Appearance of a Graphical Check Box   If you are creating a graphical check box, set the Style property to 1–Graphical. Several of the properties that you can set for the Standard check box also can influence the appearance of the graphical check box. Specifically, you can set the font used for the prompt, and you can set the colors of the check box. Also, the Appearance property can be used to give the control a flat or 3-D appearance. The Alignment property has no effect on the graphical check box.

However, these properties are not the really great feature of the graphical check box—the greatest feature is that you can include pictures on the check box. In fact, you can assign three different pictures to the check box, one for each of the three different states. The properties used to set the pictures, and the check box states they represent, are summarized in Table 15.2.

Table 15.2   Picture Used to Indicate the State of the Check Box

Property	State	Description
DisabledPicture	Disabled	The Enabled property of the check box has been set to False. This indicates that the user cannot access this check box.
DownPicture	Checked	This indicates that the user has selected the option represented by the check box.
Picture	Unchecked	The user has not selected this check box.

To set any one of these picture properties, you can enter the file name (including path) of a bitmap or other graphics file. You also can use the Load Picture dialog box to select a picture to be loaded. This is the easier of the two methods for selecting a picture. Figure 15.7 shows the various states of a graphical check box.

FIG. 15.7

Pictures can represent the different states of the check box.

Setting the Initial Value   No matter which style of check box you choose to create, one final thing that you need to do is set the initial state for the control, either checked or unchecked. Whether the check box is checked or not is controlled by the Value property. If you want the check box to be checked when the program starts, set the Value property to 1–Checked, otherwise leave the property with a setting of 0–Unchecked, which is the default value.

N O T E   There is a third setting possible for the check box's Value property. The setting is 2–Grayed. When set to this value, the check box will show a gray check mark in the box. This usually indicates that the choice represented by the check box *must* be True, and, thus, the user cannot change it. The user cannot set the check box to this value. ▪

Determining the User's Choice

When a check box is shown on a form, the user can change the value of the check box by clicking it (unless it's gray). The user also can use the Tab key to move the focus to the check box and then press the spacebar to change its value. One click of the mouse or one press of the spacebar toggles (changes) the value from checked to unchecked, or *vice versa*. A second click returns the check box to its original setting.

For most programs, you will want to determine in your code whether the check box is checked. You do this by looking at the Value property. The code in Listing 15.1 shows how you would set the global options in a program using an Options dialog box comprised of check boxes. Note the use of the intrinsic constant vbChecked, which represents a Value property setting of 1. The intrinsic constants vbUnchecked and vbGrayed also are available to represent the other possible values. The form used for this dialog box is shown in Figure 15.8.

Listing 15.1   OPTIONS.FRM—Setting Global Options Using a Series of Check Boxes

```
glbSecurity = False
glbAddUser = False
glbPassChange = False
If chkSecurity.Value = vbChecked Then glbSecurity = True
If chkAddUser.Value = vbChecked Then glbAddUser = True
If chkPassChange.Value = vbChecked Then glbPassChange = True
```

```
'************************
' Alternate coding
'************************
If chkSecurity = vbChecked Then glbSecurity = True
If chkAddUser = vbChecked Then glbAddUser = True
If chkPassChange = vbChecked Then glbPassChange = True
```

N O T E While specifying the Value property makes reading the code easier, Value is the default property of the check box. Therefore, the code could be written the way it is shown in the last three lines of Listing 15.1. ▪

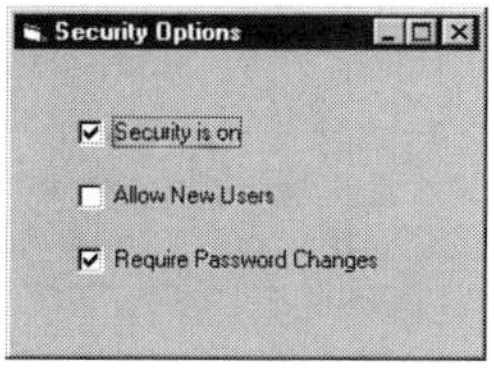

FIG. 15.8

A user may select any number of check boxes, such as those contained in a typical Options dialog box.

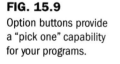

N O T E You can provide an access key for check boxes by specifying an ampersand (&) in the Caption property immediately before the desired access key character. For example, if a check box's Caption property is &Registered Voter, the user can check or uncheck it by pressing Alt+R, rather than clicking the mouse. The same concept applies to option buttons, which are discussed in the following section. ▪

Picking One Option Out of Many

Another way to allow users to make choices is through the use of option buttons. Option buttons let the user select a single item out of a group of items. This is the equivalent of a multiple-choice test. You can choose one, and only one, option button from a group. A typical option button group is shown in Figure 15.9.

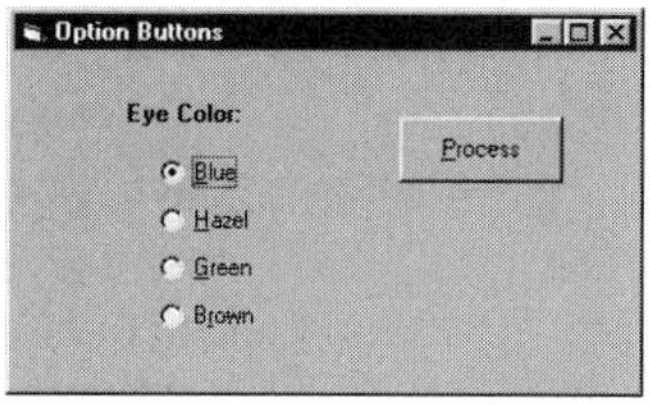

FIG. 15.9

Option buttons provide a "pick one" capability for your programs.

Option buttons work like the speed selection buttons on a blender. If you press down one button, all the other buttons come up. The option buttons work the same way insofar as that, when you select one button, whichever other button was currently selected becomes deselected.

Creating a Set of Buttons

To use option buttons, you need to create a button for each possible choice the user can select. For instance, you might have the user select eye color from the choices blue, hazel, green, or brown. For this, you would need four option buttons.

Placing the Buttons on the Form   To create the set of option buttons, you draw each button on the form and set its properties. Like the check box, the prompt for the option button is contained in the Caption property. To create the form shown in Figure 15.9, draw four buttons on the form and set the Caption of each button to one of the four eye color choices—blue, hazel, green, and brown. For other programs, you might have more or fewer options than four. You can create as many option buttons as are needed to allow for all the choices you want to present to your user.

> **T I P** If you need to include the possibility of an option other than the ones you have presented, you can use an option button labeled "Other" and have a text box next to it to accept the user's entry. The text box would be enabled only when the user selected the "Other" button.

Setting the Appearance of the Buttons   Option buttons have the same capabilities for controlling the appearance of an individual button as a check box. You can, of course, choose different fonts for the prompts, and different colors, too. As with the check box, you also can change the Alignment property of the option buttons to place the circle to the right or left of the prompt; however, if you use right-justification, make sure that the control isn't so large that the caption is too far from the button.

The arrangement of individual buttons within the group is an additional factor in the appearance of option buttons. You can arrange buttons either horizontally or vertically, as shown in Figure 15.10. My personal preference is to use vertical groups when using standard-style buttons so that all the circles in the buttons are aligned. If you are using Graphical-style buttons, the arrangement is less important.

FIG. 15.10

Option buttons may be arranged in either horizontal or vertical groups, depending on your preference.

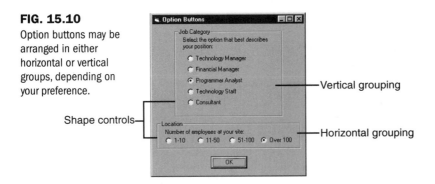

Like the check box, option buttons in Visual Basic 5 can be created in either of two styles—standard or graphical. To choose the type of button, you set the `Style` property of the button. For the graphical-style button, you then set the pictures that will be displayed for each of the button states. The different styles of option buttons are shown in Figure 15.11.

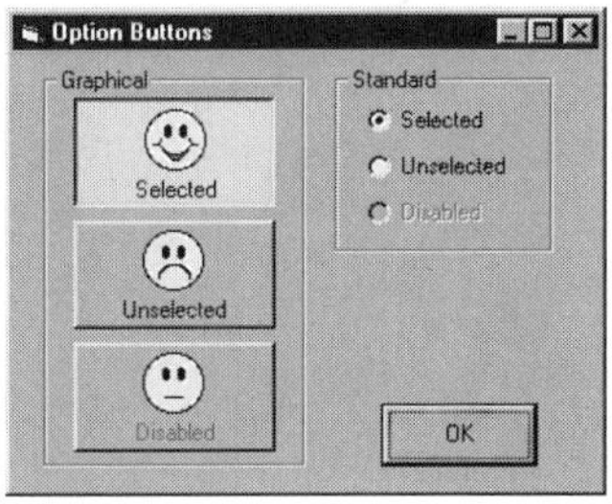

FIG. 15.11

Your choice of standard or graphical option buttons can profoundly affect your program's appearance.

N O T E   Although it isn't required that you use the same style for all the option buttons on your form, it is a good idea to use a consistent style to avoid confusing the user. This will also help prevent forms that look too cluttered with unnecessary graphics. ▩

Choosing the Initial Button   Once you have placed all the required buttons on the form, you probably will want to designate one of the buttons as the initial choice. To do this, select the button you want to be the initial choice and set its `Value` property to `True`. The circle associated with this button becomes a filled circle (or the graphical button displays the picture in the `DownPicture` property). All the other buttons on the form change to empty circles, or display the picture in the `Picture` property. (Remember, only one button can be selected at a time.)

Determining the User's Selection

When the option buttons are displayed in your program, the user can choose one by clicking it. A button also may be selected by using the cursor keys. Whichever option button has the focus is the one that has the filled circle. The filled circle indicates the choice on-screen.

Since your program can't see the screen to tell which option button is selected, it needs another means to ascertain which button the user picked. The `Value` property of each option button tells your program whether that particular button is selected. The property is set to `True` for the selected option button and `False` for all others. Therefore, you need to examine the `Value` property of each option button to find the one that is `True`.

Looking at the eye color example, the code in Listing 15.2 examines the `Value` property of the option buttons and prints out the appropriate eye color on the form. To be able to run this code, we added a command button (which we named `cmdColorChoice`) to the form. The code is contained in the `Click` event procedure for the command button.

Listing 15.2 EYECOLOR.FRM—Checking for the Selected Button Using a Series of If Statements

```
Private Sub cmdColorChoice_Click()
    Form1.Cls
    If BlueEyes.Value Then
        Form1.Print "Your eyes are blue"
    ElseIf GreenEyes.Value Then
        Form1.Print "Your eyes are green"
    ElseIf HazelEyes.Value Then
        Form1.Print "Your eyes are hazel"
    ElseIf BrownEyes.Value Then
        Form1.Print "Your eyes are brown"
    End If
End Sub
```

Creating Multiple Groups of Option Buttons

Although only one option button placed *directly* on a form can be selected at a time, there is a way to give your users choices from several groups of buttons at the same time. Grouping your buttons allows users to select items cafeteria-style, like one entree, one vegetable, one dessert, and one drink. When the buttons are grouped properly, the user can select one, but only one, button from each group of buttons. The cafeteria example is shown in Figure 15.12.

FIG. 15.12

You can create multiple option-button groups that enable the user to select one button from each group.

The secret to creating button groups is the use of a *container* control, which is a control that can hold other controls within its borders. There are several controls that can be used for this purpose, including the Frame control, the Picture control, the SSTab control, and the Shape control (refer to Figure 15.10). Each of these controls can hold other controls within its borders. Any controls placed within a container control are treated as a part of the container. This means that when a container is moved, all the controls within it move, too. Likewise, if a container is disabled, none of the controls in it are accessible.

The purpose of using a container with option buttons is to segregate the buttons within the container from buttons that are on the form or in another container. This means that the user can select one button from each container, in addition to one button that is on the form itself.

You can create as many containers as you need. Refer to Chapter 17, "Using Containers in Your Programs," for more detailed information about working with containers.

▶ **See** "Creating Groups of Option Buttons," **p. 461**

Because your users now can select a button from each group, you need a set of statements, such as the ones in Listing 15.2, for each group of buttons.

N O T E While check boxes and option buttons may appear to be very similar, the fact that only one option button (within a group) may be selected makes them quite different functionally. For example, if you offer the user a group of check boxes, you can obtain multiple on/off responses at once that you couldn't get with option buttons. This is handy when a question you ask the user might have more than one valid response (the responses aren't mutually exclusive). Also, if you have a group of option buttons, the user can't deselect all options if one option has been selected. The user can select and deselect check boxes at will. This is an important consideration if you want your user to be able to select none of your choices. ▓

Working with Lists

Often, you may want to give your user a greater number of choices than might be feasible with check boxes and option buttons. Visual Basic supplies two controls that allow you to present your user with a list of choices. Each of these controls has the capability of presenting your user with a list that can get rather lengthy if necessary.

The most straightforward control of this type is the ListBox control. We'll discuss the other one, the ComboBox control, a little later in the section "Using Combo Boxes to Handle Choices."

Making a List

The simplest control that can be used to present a list of choices is the ListBox control. Figure 15.13 shows a simple list used to pick a state abbreviation for use on a mailing label. This simple list shows all the components that make up the list box.

FIG. 15.13

A simple list box contains a series of choices for the user.

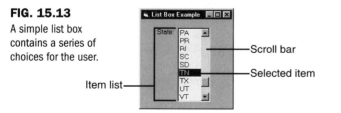

The key parts of the list box are the following:

- **Item list**   This is the list of items from which the user can select. These items are added to the list in the design environment or by your program as it is running.

- **Selected item**   This is the item that is chosen by the user. Depending on the style of list you choose, a selected item is indicated by a highlight bar or by a check in the box next to the item.

- **Scroll bar**   This indicates that there are more items on the list than fit in the box and provides the user with an easy way to view the additional items.

To the user, the simple list box is similar to choosing channels on their TV. The cable company decides which channels to put on the selection list. The customer then can pick any of these channels, but can't add one to the list if they don't like any of the choices provided. With the list box, the choices are set up by you, the programmer; the user can select only from the items you decide should be available.

Setting Up the List Box   When you first draw a list box on the form, it shows only the border of the box and the text List1 (for the first list box). There is no scroll bar present and, of course, there are no list items. A vertical scroll bar is added to the list box when you have listed more items than fit in the box. This is done automatically by the control.

After you draw the list box, the next step in setting it up is to add items to the list. These will be the choices available to the user. The list items are stored in a string array in the List property of the list box. Each list item is an element in this array. To add items to the list at design time, select the List property from the Properties dialog box. You will see the text (List) and a down arrow in the property field. Click the down arrow to access the list item input area, as shown in Figure 15.14.

FIG. 15.14

You add items to a list box by using the item input area of the *List* property.

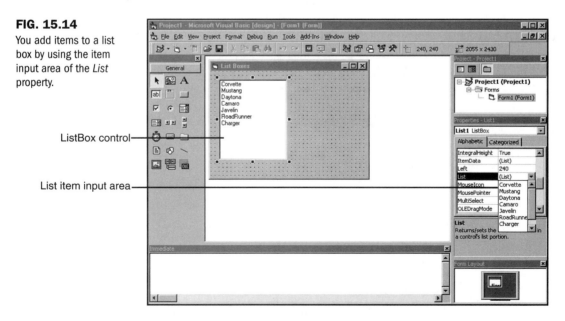

ListBox control

List item input area

You add items to the list by typing in the text that you want to appear in the list box. Each line in the List property corresponds to a selection that is presented to the user. After you add an item to the list, press Ctrl+Enter to move to the next line of the list.

After you have added all the items you need, press Enter to accept the list. At this point, the list box displays all the items you have entered and, if necessary, includes a vertical scroll bar at the right of the list. Note that the list box doesn't have a horizontal scroll bar if the choices are too wide for the control, so you should make sure that the list box is wide enough to display all of its entries. It's also a good idea to keep the items' textual names as short as possible to help avoid this problem.

Modifying the Item List from Your Program   There may be situations at runtime where you want to modify the list of items displayed in the list. For example, if you are using a list box to display food items, you might want to set up the list so that meat items are not displayed for a vegetarian user.

To accommodate these types of situations, the list box allows you to use code to add items to or remove items from the list box as the program is running. If you want, you even can place code in the Load event procedure of your form to set up the initial list, instead of typing the entries in through the Properties window. To manipulate items in the list, use the AddItem and RemoveItem methods.

Using the AddItem method is very straightforward. You simply specify the name of the ListBox control, the name of the method, and specify a string that you want added to the list. This is shown in the following line of code:

```
lstAvailable.AddItem "Corvette"
```

The list item can be a string of text or a number (though numbers are not typically handled by lists), and can be in the form of a literal value or a variable. Remember, if you are using a literal string, you need to enclose it within double quotes. There is an optional parameter, Index, that may be used with the AddItem method. This parameter specifies the location within the list where you want the new item to appear. You will specify the index value of the item in front of which you want to add your item. For example, if there are five items in the list and you want your item to appear ahead of the third item, you use code like the following:

```
lstAvailable.AddItem "Corvette", 2
```

N O T E   The Index of the list items is zero-based. This means that the first item on the list has an index of 0, the second item has an index of 1, and so on.

If you include an index value, it must be separated from the list item by a comma. Including the index causes the item to be placed exactly where you want it. If you omit the index, the item is placed at the end of the list, or in alphabetic order if the Sorted property is set to True.

CAUTION

If you specify an index value that is outside the range of indexes in the list box, an error will be generated. You can avoid this by checking the `ListCount` property, which reports the number of items currently in the list, to make sure this doesn't occur. Also, specifying an index less than 0 will cause an error.

Deleting an item from the list is a little trickier than adding an item because you need to know the index of the item to be deleted. If you know in advance what the index is, you can simply delete the item by using the `RemoveItem` method. For example, the following code deletes the first item in the list:

```
lstAvailable.RemoveItem 0
```

In a more typical situation, you will want to delete an item that the user has selected. You will learn about determining the user's selection in the section "Determining the User's Choice" a little later in the chapter. For now, you can look at the code in Listing 15.3 to see how to delete the selected item.

Listing 15.3   LISTDEMO.FRM—Removing a Selected Item by Using the
RemoveItem Method

```
Dim LstIdx As Integer
LstIdx = lstAvailable.ListIndex
If LstIdx >= 0 Then lstAvailable.RemoveItem LstIdx
```

In another situation, you might want to remove a specific item based on the item's text. This involves searching the list to find the item and then using the `RemoveItem` method to delete the item (see Listing 15.4).

Listing 15.4   LISTDEMO.FRM—Searching the Items to Find the One to Be
Deleted

```
Dim I, LstIdx As Integer
LstIdx = -1
For I = 0 To lstAvailable.ListCount - 1
    If lstAvailable.List(I) = "Mustang" Then
        LstIdx = I
        Exit For
    End If
Next I
If LstIdx >= 0 Then lstAvailable.RemoveItem LstIdx
```

T I P If you want to remove all the items in a list, use the `Clear` method (for example, `lstAvailable.Clear`). Essentially, this method throws away your entire list.

Sorting the List   In the preceding section, you saw how to modify the list by adding and removing items. You also saw that you can add an item to a specific location by specifying an index. But what do you do if you want your entire list sorted in alphabetic order?

Fortunately, this is a very simple task. To sort the list, you simply set the Sorted property to True. Then, no matter in which order you enter your items, they appear to the user in alphabetic order. The indexes of the list items are adjusted as they are added so that they remain in proper order.

Setting the Appearance of the List   In previous versions of Visual Basic, lists like the one shown in Figure 15.13 were the only available styles—In Visual Basic 5, you now have a choice. You can use a standard list, or you can make your list look like a series of check boxes. You handle the selection of the list type by setting the Style property. The two settings of the property are 0–Standard and 1–Checkbox (see Figure 15.15). This property also can be changed at run time by setting its value to one of the intrinsic constants vbListBoxStandard or vbListBoxCheckBox, respectively.

FIG. 15.15
Checkbox-style list boxes provide the user with an intuitive way to select multiple items.

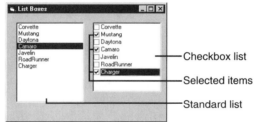

Checkbox list
Selected items
Standard list

Another way to change the list's appearance is to use the Columns property. The default value of the property is 0. This results in the standard list box previously discussed. Setting the property to 1 causes the list to be presented one column at a time, but to scroll horizontally instead of vertically. Setting the property to greater than 1 causes the list to display in the number of columns specified by the property (for example, a value of 2 displays the list in two columns). When the list is displayed in multiple columns, the list scrolls horizontally. The Columns property can be used with either the Standard or Checkbox styles of lists. These styles are shown in Figure 15.16.

FIG. 15.16
You also can create multicolumn lists.

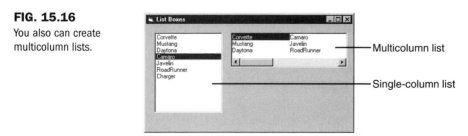

Multicolumn list
Single-column list

The list works the same way no matter how many columns you use.

Determining the User's Choice

For most programs, you will want to retrieve the user's selection and do something with it. To find out what the user selected, you need to work with two properties of the list box: the ListIndex and List properties.

The ListIndex property reports the index number of the item that was selected. You then can retrieve the actual item from the List property by using the index number. The following code displays the selected item in a text box:

```
idx = Fruits.ListIndex
ChosenFruit.Text = Fruits.List(idx)
```

Handling Multiple Choices   There are occasions when you need to let the user select more than one item from a list. The list box supports this with the MultiSelect property. This property has three possible settings: 0–None, 1–Simple, and 2–Extended.

A setting of 0–None means that multiple selections are not permitted, and the list box can accept only one selection at a time. This is the default setting. The other two settings both permit multiple selections; the difference is in how they let the user make selections. This will be explained through the example that follows.

One great use of multiple item selections is in an order-entry system. When a person places an order with a company, they usually are buying more than one item. A multiple-selection list allows the salesperson to select all the items for the order and then to process the entire order at once.

With a setting of 1–Simple, users can click an item with the mouse to select it, or click a selected item to deselect it. If they is use the keyboard to make the selection, they can use the cursor keys to move the focus (the dotted line border) to an item, then press the spacebar to select or deselect it. Figure 15.17 shows a list with multiple items selected.

FIG. 15.17

You can select multiple items from a list with the proper setting of the MultiSelect property.

The other setting of the MultiSelect property, 2—Extended, is more complex. In this mode, users quickly can select a range of items by clicking the first item in the range and then, while holding down the Shift key, click the last item in the range—All items in between the first and last item are selected. To add or delete a single item to or from this selection, the user holds down the Ctrl key while clicking the item.

Getting All the Selections Getting the selections from a multiple-selection list box is a little different than getting them for a single selection. Since the `ListIndex` works only for a single selection, you can't use it. Instead, you have to examine each item in the list to determine whether it is selected.

Whether an item is selected or not is indicated by the list box's `Selected` property. This property is an array that has an element for each item in the list. The value of the `Selected` property for each item is either `True` (the item is selected) or `False` (the item is not selected).

You also need to know how many items are in the list so that you can set up the loop to check all the selections. This information is contained in the `ListCount` property. The following code prints onto the form the name of each list item that is selected:

```
numitm = Fruits.ListCount
For I = 0 to numitm - 1
    If Fruits.Selected(I) Then Form1.Print Fruits.List(I)
Next I
```

Keeping Other Data in the List

What if you want the user to see a meaningful list, such as a list of names, but you also want to have the list remember a number that's associated with each name? The `ItemData` property of a list box is, in essence, an array of long integers, one for each item that has been added to the list box. No matter what position an item occupies in the list box, the `ItemData` array remembers the number associated with that particular element. This happens even if the list box's `Sorted` property is `True`, meaning that items won't necessarily be listed in the order that they're added. For example, the `ItemData` array element associated with the first item in a list box named List1 can be accessed as `List1.ItemData(0)`. The array element for the currently selected list box entry can be accessed with `List1.ItemData(List1.ListIndex)` (recall that the `ListIndex` property reports which item is currently selected).

As items are added to a list box, an associated element is created in the `ItemData` array. Of course, it's your job to place the appropriate value into the proper position of the `ItemData` array. So how can your program know into which list box position a newly added item went, especially if the list box is sorted? Visual Basic makes this easy. A list box's `NewIndex` property contains the index number of the most recently added item in the list. The following code adds a new customer to a sorted list box and then adds that customer's account number to the correct element of the associated `ItemData` array:

```
lstCustomers.AddItem "Thomas, June"
lstCustomers.ItemData(lstCustomers.NewIndex) = "21472301"
```

Now, our program can allow the user to select from a list box containing meaningful elements (names), but the background processing can be done with an associated number, which is easier for the computer. This is illustrated in the `Click` event procedure of the list box:

```
Private Sub lstCustomers_Click()
    Dim lgThisCust As Long
    lgThisCust = lstCustomers.ItemData(lstCustomers.ListIndex)
    Call LookUpAccount(lgThisCust)
End Sub
```

Creating a Two-Column Pick List

One of the best ways to demonstrate the use of the methods for modifying a list is to create what is known as a two-column pick list. You probably have seen these pick lists used in a number of applications. A form contains two lists; one list contains the available choices and the other list contains the user's selections. As the user selects an item from the available list, the item is removed from that list and is added to the selected list. If the user removes a selection, the process is reversed. These lists also give the user the capability to select all items, or remove all items. Figure 15.18 shows the list created by the following example.

FIG. 15.18

Two-column pick lists clearly show the user's choices.

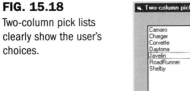

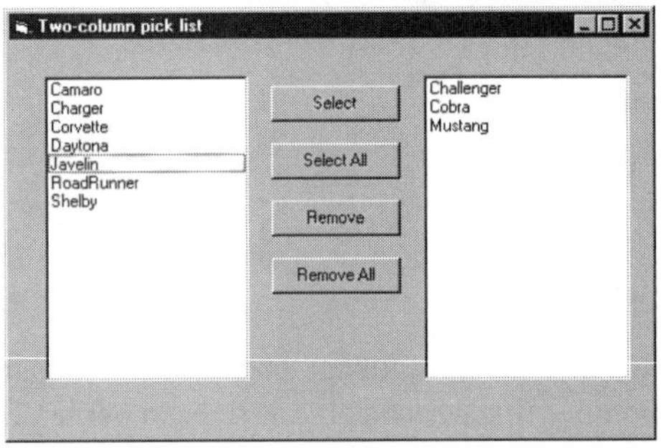

To start creating the list, follow these steps:

1. Place two ListBox controls on your form. For aesthetic purposes, these two controls should be the same size and should be lined up vertically with each other.

2. To match the sample code, name one of the ListBox controls `lstAvailable` and the other `lstSelected`.

3. Set the `Sorted` property of each ListBox control to `True`. This makes it easier for your users to find individual items.

4. Next, create an array of four control buttons in between the lists. These buttons will handle the user options of Select, Select All, Remove, and Remove All.

   ▶ **See** "Using Control Arrays," **p. 496**

5. The key to the pick list is the code for the command buttons:

   - For the buttons that remove or add a single selection, you need to determine the index of the selection, remove it from one list, and add it to the other.

   - For the buttons that process all items, you need a loop that runs through all the items on the list, adding them to the other list and then clearing the source list.

   The code for all this is shown in Listing 15.5.

Listing 15.5   TWOCOLUMN.FRM—Two-Column Pick Lists Make Use of the
***AddItem*, *RemoveItem*, and *Clear* Methods**

```
Private Sub cmdSelect_Click(Index As Integer)
Dim I, LstIdx As Integer, MovItm As String
Select Case Index
    Case 0
        'Single selection
        LstIdx = lstAvailable.ListIndex
        If LstIdx < 0 Then Exit Sub
        MovItm = lstAvailable.List(LstIdx)
        lstSelected.AddItem MovItm
        lstAvailable.RemoveItem LstIdx
    Case 1
        'Select all
        If lstAvailable.ListCount = 0 Then Exit Sub
        For I = 0 To lstAvailable.ListCount - 1
            MovItm = lstAvailable.List(I)
            lstSelected.AddItem MovItm
        Next I
        lstAvailable.Clear
    Case 2
        'Single removal
        LstIdx = lstSelected.ListIndex
        If LstIdx < 0 Then Exit Sub
        MovItm = lstSelected.List(LstIdx)
        lstAvailable.AddItem MovItm
        lstSelected.RemoveItem LstIdx
    Case 3
        'Remove all
        If lstSelected.ListCount = 0 Then Exit Sub
        For I = 0 To lstSelected.ListCount - 1
            MovItm = lstSelected.List(I)
            lstAvailable.AddItem MovItm
        Next I
        lstSelected.Clear
End Select
End Sub
```

As shown in Listing 15.5, the code works only when the user clicks the command button. You would probably also want your users to be able to select items directly from the list. You can do this by placing code to call the command button procedure in the DblClick event procedure of each list (see Listing 15.6).

**Listing 15.6   TWOCOLUMN.FRM—Using the *DblClick* Event to Allow the User
to Pick with the Mouse**

```
Private Sub lstAvailable_DblClick()
cmdSelect_Click 0
End Sub

Private Sub lstSelected_DblClick()
cmdSelect_Click 2
End Sub
```

The complete project for this example is available as TWOCOLM.VBP, which you can
download from this book's Web site:

www.mcp.com/info/0-7897/0-7897-1288-1

As an exercise, you can modify this pick list to handle multiple selections by the user in
each list.

Using Combo Boxes to Handle Choices

Another control that enables you to present lists to the user is the ComboBox control. The
combo box can be used in three different forms.

- **The drop-down combo box**. Presents the user with a text box combined with a drop-
  down list. The user can either select an item from the list portion or type an item in the
  text box portion.

- **The simple combo box**. Displays a text box and a list that doesn't drop down. As with
  the drop-down combo box, the user can either select an item from the list portion or type
  an item in the text box portion.

- **The drop-down list**. Displays a drop-down list box from which the user can make a
  choice. He cannot enter an item that is not in the list.

The combo box has many things in common with the list box. Both use the AddItem,
RemoveItem, and Clear methods to modify the contents of the list. Both can present a sorted or
an unsorted list. Both support the ItemData array and NewIndex property, mentioned earlier.
However, there are some things that one box can do but the other cannot.

The main thing the combo box lacks is support for multiple selections. The key advantage of
the combo box, though, is that it allows the user to enter a choice that is not on the list. This
works like an election ballot, where you can choose a candidate from the list of those running,
or write in your own.

N O T E   The drop-down list does not support the user entering choices that are not on the list.   ■

FIG. 15.19
Each of the three styles of combo boxes behaves differently when the user selects his choice.

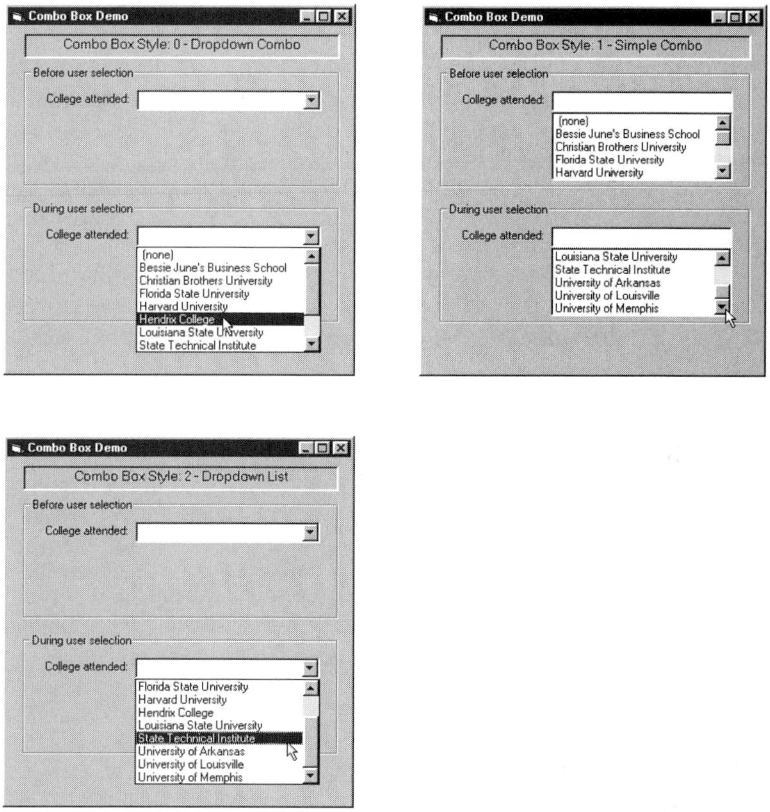

This section explains how to use the different forms of the combo box. The drop-down list is examined first because it is the simplest of the combo box styles.

Creating a Drop-Down List

A drop-down list functions exactly like a list box. The key difference is that the drop-down list takes up less room on your form. When users want to select an item from the list, they click the down arrow, located to the right of the box, to extend the list. After the drop-down list appears, they then make a selection by clicking the item they want to choose. After the selection is made, the list retracts like a window shade, and the selection appears in the box.

 You create a drop-down list by drawing a combo box on the form, and then setting the Style property to 2–Dropdown List. You then can begin adding items to the list by using the List property, just like you did for the list box. However, keep in mind that the user can't add an item that's not in the list.

Working with Choices that Are Not on the List

The drop-down list is very useful for presenting a number of choices in a small amount of space. However, the real power of the combo box is its capability to allow users to enter choices other than those on the list. This capability is available with the other two styles of combo box—the simple combo box and the drop-down combo box. Both styles provide a list of items from which you can select and both allow you to enter other values. The difference between the two styles is the way in which you access items already in the list.

A simple combo box is set up by drawing the control on the form, and then setting the Style property to 1—Simple Combo. With the simple combo box, the user can access the items in the list using the mouse or the arrow keys. If the user doesn't find what he wants on the list, he can type in a new choice.

The drop-down combo box works like a combination of the drop-down list and the simple combo box. You select an item from the list the same way you would for a drop-down list, but you also can enter a value that is not on the list. The drop-down combo box is created by setting the Style property to 0—Dropdown Combo. The drop-down combo box is the default setting of the Style property.

As with the list box and the drop-down list, you can use the List property to add items to the list of selections. You also can modify the list for any of the combo box styles while your program is running. As with the list box control, you modify the list by using the AddItem, RemoveItem, and Clear methods.

Setting the Initial Choice

Depending on your application, you might want to set the initial item for a combo box. An example of setting the choice is in a program that needs to know your citizenship. You can provide a list of choices, but set the initial value to "U.S. citizen" because that would be the selection of most people in this country.

You set the initial value by using the ListIndex property, as shown in the following code:

```
Fruits.ListIndex = 3
```

This statement causes the fourth item in the list to be displayed when the combo box is first shown. (Remember, the list indexes start at 0.) Setting the initial choice will work with any of the three combo box styles. You also can set the initial choice of the combo box by setting the Text property to the desired value. If you do not set an initial choice by setting the index, the text contained in the Text property will be displayed.

> **CAUTION**
>
> The initial value of the Text property is the name of the combo box. If you do not want this to appear in your combo box on start up, set either the ListIndex property or the Text property in code.

TIP If you want your combo box to be blank when the form is first shown, simply delete the contents of the `Text` property while you are in the design environment.

Retrieving the User's Choice

Getting the user's choice from a combo box is different than getting it from a list box. With a combo box, you need the capability to handle users entering a value that is not on the list. You can retrieve the user's choice with the `Text` property of the combo box. The `Text` property holds any value that is typed in by the user, or holds the item selected from the list. The following line of code prints the user's selection:

```
Form1.Print cboFruits.Text
```

Adding a User-Created Item to the List

If you include a combo box as part of a data entry form, you may want the capability to take any new items entered by the user and add them to the list of choices. That way, when the user enters another record, they won't have to type the same choice again.

The combo box does not have a specific method to handle this function, nor does the addition of a new item trigger a particular event. However, you can take advantage of the fact that there will be more than one control on the form into which the user must enter data. A typical data entry form for a personnel application is shown in Figure 15.20. The combo box to which you want to add choices is the one for College Attended. As users enter colleges not on the list, those colleges are added to the list so that they only have to be entered one time.

FIG. 15.20
This typical application uses a combo box to obtain college information.

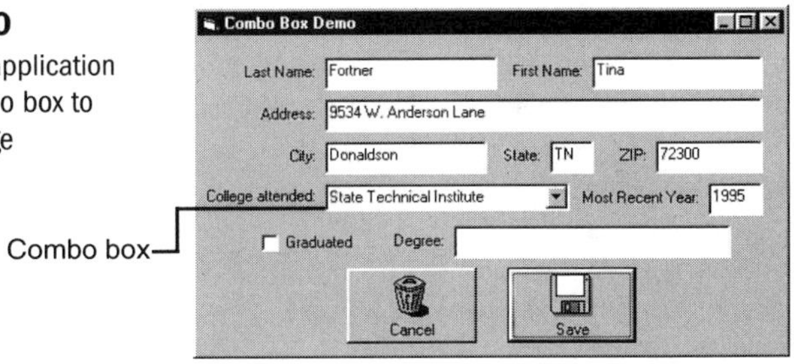

Combo box ⌐

Handling this enhancement makes one assumption—in almost all cases, after users enter the college name, they will move to the next field to enter more information, or click a command button to execute a task. Either way, the focus moves from the combo box to another control. This triggers the `LostFocus` event. Therefore, you can use this event as the trigger to add new items to the list. When the user moves the focus, your code first needs to retrieve the value of the `Text` property as the new item. Next, you need to scan the list of items to make sure that the item does not exist already. Then, if the item is, in fact, new, you can add the item to the list. Listing 15.7 illustrates how this can be accomplished.

Listing 15.7   COMBODEMO.FRM—Adding User Entries to the List

```
Dim NewItm As String, I As Integer, AddNewItm As Boolean
AddNewItm = True
With cboCountry
    NewItm = cboCountry.Text
    For I = 0 To .ListCount - 1
        If .List(I) = NewItm Then
            AddNewItm = False
            Exit For
        End If
    Next I
    If AddNewItm Then
        .AddItem NewItm
    End If
End With
```

Inputting Data with the Scroll Bars

You have seen scroll bars used in a text box for multiple line editing and in lists to access long lists of items. While they look basically the same, these scroll bars are different from the scroll bar controls in Visual Basic.

Scroll bars work like the volume control on your stereo system. Your stereo has minimum and maximum volume settings. The volume knob, or slider bar, enables you to set any volume in between the minimum and maximum ranges. Scroll bars also have minimum and maximum settings and let you use a slider to set a value anywhere within the range.

Visual Basic provides two types of scroll bars for entering numerical data: the vertical scroll bar and the horizontal scroll bar. These two controls are shown in Figure 15.21. The two scroll bars are referred to in the documentation as the VScrollBar and HscrollBar controls, respectively.

FIG. 15.21

The VScrollBar and HScrollBar controls can be used to enter or display numerical data.

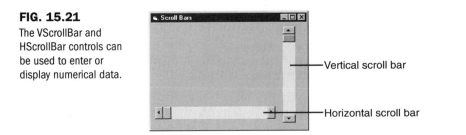

Vertical scroll bar

Horizontal scroll bar

The only difference between these two controls is the orientation of the bar on the form. All the methods, events, and properties of the controls are the same. The following discussion examines the HScrollBar control, but it applies equally to the VScrollBar.

Setting Up the Bar

The scroll bar is capable of accepting whole numbers (integers) anywhere in the range of -32,768 to 32,767. One typical range is from 0 to 100, where the user enters a number as a percentage. Another possible use of scroll bars is to control the speaker volumes in a multimedia application. Also, if you have experimented with the colors in Windows, you have seen the scroll bars that enable you to enter the relative amounts of red, green, and blue that will appear in a color. These bars have a range of 0 to 255, the possible values of the color settings.

Setting the Upper and Lower Boundaries   The range of values that can be entered with the scroll bars is determined by the settings of the Min and Max properties. The Min property sets the lower boundary of the value range and has a default setting of 0. The Max property sets the upper boundary of the range and has a default value of 32,767. You can change the settings of these properties from the Properties window, or through the use of code statements, as shown in the following example. For this example, use the Properties window to set the Min property to 0 and the Max property to 100.

```
hsbPercent.Min = 0
hsbPercent.Max = 100
```

Controlling the Size of the Value Changes   If you have used a scroll bar in a word processor or other program, you know that clicking the arrow at either end of the bar moves you only a short distance, but clicking in between an arrow and the position button moves you a greater distance. The scroll bar controls work the same way, and you get to set how much the numbers will change with each kind of move. The number entered in a scroll bar is contained in the Value property. This property changes every time the user clicks the scroll bar or drags the position button, as indicated in Figure 15.22.

FIG. 15.22

Clicking various parts of the scroll bar changes its value by different amounts.

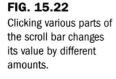
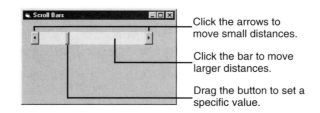

Click the arrows to move small distances.

Click the bar to move larger distances.

Drag the button to set a specific value.

The amount that the Value property increases or decreases when an arrow is clicked is controlled by the SmallChange property, which gives you very fine control over the numbers being entered. Its default value is 1, which probably is a good number to use for most purposes.

When you click between the arrow and the position button, the Value property can change by a different amount than if you click an arrow. The amount of this change is set by the LargeChange property. The default setting of the LargeChange property is 1. The setting you use depends on your application. For example, a value of 10 is a good number if you are setting percentages.

T I P   A good rule of thumb is to set the LargeChange property to a number about 5 to 10 percent of the total range (for example, a value of 50 for a 0 to 1000 range).

How to Show the User the Numbers

A scroll bar, by itself, is not all that useful. The user cannot determine the range of numbers. Without knowing the number range, making a guess at the actual value of the scroll bar is fruitless. There are several ways to display additional information about the scroll bar value that will make them easier for the user to work with. These options are discussed next.

First, you can tell the user the minimum and maximum values. You can do this by adding label controls above (or beside) each end of the scroll bar. Although these labels help users to see what is the approximate value, they still cannot see the exact value. The only way to know the actual value of the scroll bar is to display it in another control, such as a text box or label. Figure 15.23 shows these enhancements.

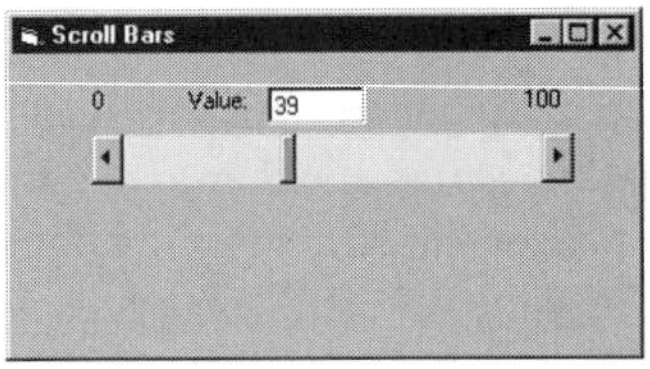

FIG. 15.23

Associating labels or text boxes with the scroll bar shows users the range and actual value.

Assigning the value of the scroll bar to a text box is easy. You use a code statement like the following:

```
txtActValue.Text = hsbPercent.Value
```

The statement itself is the easy part. What's tricky is knowing where to put the statement. To show the value at all times, you actually have to place this statement in three events:

- Load—The first event is the Load event for your form. Placing the assignment statement in this event displays the initial value of the scroll bar.

- Change—The second location for the statement is the Change event of the scroll bar. This event is triggered each time the user clicks one of the arrows or clicks the bar. The Change event is triggered also when you release the mouse button after dragging the position button to a new location.

- Scroll—Unfortunately, the Change event is not triggered while the position button is being dragged. If you want the user to be able to see the changes in the Value property while dragging the button, you need to place the code statement in a third location, the Scroll event of the scroll bar.

If you use a text box to display the actual value of the scroll bar, you can let the user enter a value directly in the text box. Then, using the Change event of the text box, you can update the value of the scroll bar accordingly. The code for this process is shown in Listing 15.8.

Listing 15.8 SCROLLDEMO.FRM—Updating the Scroll Bar from a Text Box

```
Dim ValSet As Integer
ValSet = Val(txtValue.Text)
If ValSet > hsbPercentage.Max Then ValSet = hsbPercentage.Max
If ValSet < hsbPercentage.Min Then ValSet = hsbPercentage.Min
hsbPercentage.Value = ValSet
```

Counting Time

Another control that comes in handy on occasion is the Timer control. This control works like the cooking timer on your microwave oven. It counts down a specified amount of time and then fires the Timer event. You can specify the action that should occur by writing code for the Timer control's Timer event procedure.

The timer works by counting the number of milliseconds (thousandths of a second) that have elapsed since the form containing the control was loaded, or since the Timer event was last fired. When the count reaches the amount set by the Interval property, the control triggers the Timer event and runs whatever code is present.

Setting Up the Timer

You set up a Timer control by first drawing it on the form. At design time, the Timer control shows up as an icon on the form, no matter how large you draw it to begin with (see Figure 15.24). The Timer control is not visible on the form when your program is running.

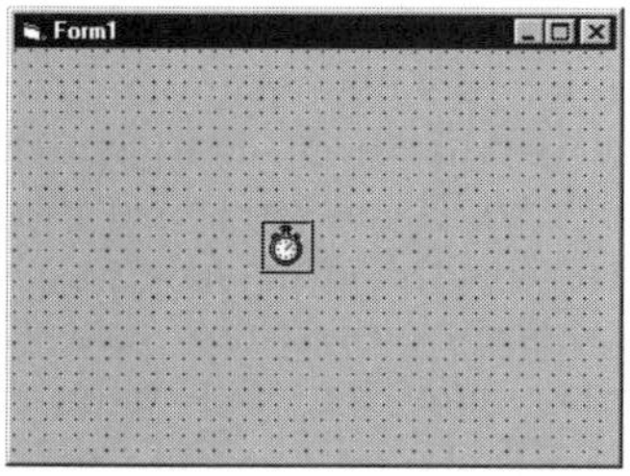

FIG. 15.24

The Timer control is visible only at design time.

To make the control work, the Interval property is the only property that you need to set. You can set the Interval property for any value between 0 and 65,535. A setting of 0 disables the Timer control. Any other setting specifies the number of milliseconds that should elapse before the Timer event is triggered. The minimum setting, 1, is shorter than the blink of an eye. The maximum setting is just a little longer than a minute. If you want 10 seconds to elapse, set the Interval property to a value of 10,000.

Since the maximum value of the Interval property corresponds to about a minute, how can you set up longer time intervals? You set up code within the Timer event that tracks how many times the Interval has elapsed, as shown in Listing 15.9.

Listing 15.9 TIMERDEMO.FRM—Using a *Static* Variable to Track Multiple Minutes Elapsing

```
Private Sub tmr_Timer()
    Static ElTime
    If ElTime >= 20 Then
        MsgBox "Time's Up!"
        ElTime = 0
    Else
        ElTime = ElTime + 1
    End If
End Sub
```

The first line of the code defines the variable that tracks the number of times the interval has elapsed. The keyword Static means that the value of the variable is maintained even after the event procedure is ended, so it will be intact the next time the event procedure is executed. (For more information about Static variables, see Chapter 8, "Programming Basics.")

▶ **See** "Determining Where a Variable Can Be Used," **p. 172**

The conditional statement determines whether the timer has elapsed 20 or more times. If so, a message box displays, informing the user. The number of times then is reset to 0 to start the cycle over again. If the number of times is less than 20, one is added to the ElTime variable and the procedure is exited.

By adjusting the Interval property of the timer and the number of times it elapses, you can make the Timer control count any amount of time.

Creating a Screen Blanker

A useful function for the Timer control is to blank the screen after a specified period of time. Screen-blanking routines were originally used to prevent damage to the screen from having the same image displayed for long periods of time. The more current usage is for security reasons. Many times, people are in the middle of an application and have to leave their desk for a few minutes to attend to other tasks. If the users are not careful, sensitive information can be left on-screen for anyone to see. Screen blankers provide a way to hide this information if there is no program activity for a specified period of time. Of course, this security measure would reasonably need to be enhanced with some type of password protection before the original screen is restored.

 The Timer control can be used to create a simple screen blanker for use with your programs. To start, add a Timer control to your main form. Set the Interval property of the timer to the desired amount of time. (For demonstration purposes, set the timer to 10 seconds, or an Interval value of 10,000.)

Next, add a second form to your program. You now need to change the `BackColor` property of the new form to black and change the `BorderStyle` property to `0–None`. This will give you a black form with no borders, captions, or buttons when the program is run. You then need to add the following line of code to the form's `Load` event:

```
frmScreenBlank.WindowState = vbMaximized
```

This code causes the form to be maximized as it is loaded, covering the entire screen.

Now all you need is code to activate the blank form and to deactivate it. The code to activate the form is placed in the `Timer` event of the Timer control on the first form. The code is as follows:

```
frmScreenBlank.Show
```

This causes the form to be loaded and displayed when the Timer event is triggered. Finally, to deactivate the blank form, place the following line in both the `Click` and `KeyPress` events of `frmScreenBlank`:

```
frmScreenBlank.Hide
```

This code causes the blank form to be hidden when a key is pressed or the mouse is clicked while the blank form is displayed. When the form is hidden, the original form and the rest of the screen once again displays. Now, run the code and try it for yourself.

To add to the security of the screen blanker, you can add a password routine to the code that hides the form. This way, the user has to enter a password before the screen displays again. You also might want to have the application terminate after a set period of time instead of just having the screen go blank.

From Here…

This chapter discussed the use of a number of standard controls that are included with Visual Basic. You have seen examples of how to use each one. You can enhance your understanding of these controls by practicing! Try using them in a variety of applications to see how they behave in different situations. For more information about using these controls and others with which they may interact, refer to the following chapters:

- To learn about using the Windows controls that can be accessed from a Visual Basic program, see Chapter 16, "Using the Windows Common Controls."
- To see how to arrange these and other controls in functional groups, see Chapter 17, "Using Containers in Your Programs."
- For a discussion of the controls that have been recently added to Visual Basic, see Chapter 18, "Exploring New Visual Basic 5 Controls."
- To learn more advanced ways to use these and other controls, see Chapter 19, "Advanced Control Techniques."

CHAPTER 16

Using the Windows Common Controls

Visual Basic includes a group of common controls that enable you to develop programs with many of the same features as programs from Microsoft and other vendors. These controls let you create toolbars to supplement your menus, status bars to keep your users informed, progress bars to indicate the completion level of a task, and other neat controls. This chapter continues the in-depth discussion of controls that began in Chapter 15, "Working with the Standard Controls," by covering the capabilities of the Windows Common Controls. ■

Adding Toolbars to your program

With a little bit of programming, you can make your toolbars respond to changes in your program.

Keeping the user informed

A status bar allows you to inform users of program operations in a manner with which they are familiar.

Following a program's progress

When users run a task, they want to see action. A progress bar lets users know that a task is running and gives them an approximation of the time remaining until completion.

Making input easier for the user

Make numerical input simple with the Slider control.

Working with lists of objects

The TreeView and ListView controls provide the capability to implement Windows Explorer-style interfaces for working with lists.

Giving your application pages

The TabStrip control enables you to create multiple pages and allows your user to navigate among them.

Working with the Windows Common Controls

In order to use the controls described in this chapter, you must first make them available in your Toolbox. From the Visual Basic menu, choose Project, Components. When the Components dialog box appears, place a check mark next to Microsoft Windows Common Controls 5.0 and click OK. Your Toolbox will then be updated with the new controls.

Creating Toolbars

Toolbars, such as the one shown in Figure 16.1, are an integral part of Windows interface standards, so much so that Microsoft has packaged them into the COMCTL32.OCX custom control. Applications that don't have toolbars are becoming the exception to the rule for an obvious reason: Toolbars provide a convenient place on-screen for users to look for frequently used functions. Because the toolbar is normally near the top of the window, it provides a familiar place for the user to look in almost any application.

FIG. 16.1
A Visual Basic program can include the Toolbar control.

Toolbar—

The Toolbar control works with an ImageList control, which holds all the button images. Visual Basic includes a number of images in the Graphics subdirectory. Icon and bitmap files can be stored in an ImageList control; the size of these pictures will influence the size of the toolbar buttons. Before you can design an effective toolbar, you need to pick out your images and add them to an image list.

Reviewing the Basics

Toolbars were first discussed in Chapter 5, "Adding Menus and Toolbars to Your Program," in which you saw how toolbars were used to supplement the menus of a program by placing commonly used functions where the user could get to them easily.

The Toolbar control enables you to create five different types of buttons:

- Push buttons that work like command buttons
- Check buttons that work in an on-off mode, like a check box
- Button groups that work like option buttons
- Separator buttons that create spaces in the toolbar
- Placeholder buttons that create empty space, allowing you to place other controls, such as combo boxes, on the toolbar

The ImageList control was used to hold the images that were placed on the toolbar buttons. The Toolbar and the ImageList controls can be set up through the Properties window and through the Property Pages of the controls.

▶ **See** "Creating a Toolbar for Your Application," **p. 117**

Creating a Toolbar with Code

Part

IV

Ch

16

Although you can set up a toolbar in the design environment, you can also set up and change a toolbar at runtime with program code. To use the Toolbar and other common controls successfully, you need to understand the concept of collections.

Understanding Collections   A *collection* is a group of objects. In the case of the ImageList control, there is a collection called ListImages. The objects stored in this particular collection are the images in the ImageList control. By manipulating the ListImages collection from code, you can add, remove, and change images.

Think of a collection as being similar to, but not exactly like, an array. You can access it like an array, as in the following line of code, which sets a form's picture to the first image in an ImageList control:

```
Set form1.Picture = ImageList1.ListImages(1).Picture
```

Notice that a specific object is referred to with its *index*, in this case 1. Remember, a collection stores objects, unlike an array, which stores values. These objects have their own set of properties.

One special property that objects in a collection have is the Key property. An object's key is a text string that can be used in the same manner as an index:

```
Set form1.Picture = ImageList1.ListImages("Smiley Face").Picture
```

Of course, you have to set the key first, usually when an object is added to a collection. Each type of collection has Add and Remove methods defined that include Key and Index as parameters. If omitted, the index is supplied by Visual Basic. The key, however, is optional.

Setting Up the Toolbar   To set up a Toolbar control in code, you have to first set up an ImageList control (either in design mode or with code.) Then, you can assign ImageList to the toolbar with the following statement:

```
Set ToolBar.ImageList = ImageList1
```

Next, you manipulate the toolbar's Buttons collection to create toolbar buttons. In the example below, a separator and standard button are added to a toolbar control, tbrMain:

```
tbrMain.Buttons.Add 1, "Sep1",, tbrSeparator, 0
tbrMain.Buttons.Add 2, "open","Open File" , tbrDefault, 1
```

In the example above, two additional Button objects are created in the Buttons collection by using the Add method. The first two parameters are the button's index and key, each of which must be unique. The third parameter is the button caption. The fourth parameter (tbrSeparator and tbrDefault) is a constant representing the type of button. Finally, an index value from the associated image list tells the toolbar which picture to use.

The Add method can also work as a function. If used in this manner, it returns a pointer to the Button object just created. The code above could be rewritten like this:

```
Dim btn As Button

Set btn = tbrMain.Buttons.Add(, "Sep1", , tbrSeparator, 0)

Set btn = tbrMain.Buttons.Add(,"open", , tbrDefault)
btn.ToolTipText = "Click to open a file"
btn.Caption = "Open File"
btn.Image = 1
```

Note that the ToolTipText property must be defined from a Button object because it is not in the Add method's parameters. Also, in the preceding example, the Index properties will be defined automatically because they were not specified. This is generally the preferred way of doing things because, as objects are added and deleted from a collection, the index of a particular object will change. The Key, however, will always be associated with a specific object.

Your code can use the Key to determine which button was pressed. For example, consider the following code in the toolbar's ButtonClick event:

```
Private Sub Toolbar1_ButtonClick(ByVal Button As ComctlLib.Button)

    Select Case Button.Key
        Case "open"
            'Insert open file code here
        Case "save"
            'Insert save file code here
        Case "exit"
            'Insert code to end the program
    End Select

End Sub
```

The preceding code works great for buttons of type tbrDefault. However, if you have any tbrCheck buttons, you should have your code also check the Value property to see what the state of the button is:

```
        Case "boldface"
            If Button.value = tbrUnpressed then
                'Button is "Up" - Turn bold off
            Else
                'Button is "down" - Turn bold on
            End If
```

If you set the MixedState property of a button to True, it will always look grayed out—no matter what the value.

Monitoring the Status of Your Program

One of the most important aspects of any program is keeping the user informed about what is going on in the program at any given time. Users like to know whether a database is open, how many records there are in a set, and how many records have been processed so far in the current task. For a program such as a word processor, the users like to know what's the current page and what's the current position on that page. This type of information is called *status information*, which is usually displayed on-screen all the time, rather than in a message box.

Before the StatusBar control, Visual Basic programmers often used "fake" status bars made from panels and Label controls. These worked quite well (and still do today). However, the StatusBar control introduced in Visual Basic 4 provides a much better alternative. You don't have to worry about extra overhead, because it is likely that you probably already are using one of the other Common Controls in the same OCX.

Figure 16.2 shows a typical status bar from a Visual Basic program.

FIG. 16.2
Status bars display current information about a program.

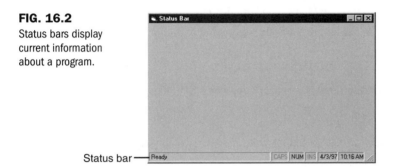

Status bar

Creating a Status Bar

You start the creation of the status bar by selecting the control and drawing it on your form. When it is first drawn, the status bar will span the width of its parent form and will contain a single panel, as shown in Figure 16.3. You will also notice that no matter where on your form you draw the status bar, it moves to the bottom of the form automatically. This is the typical location for a program's status bar.

FIG. 16.3
When you place a status bar on a form, it is configured automatically.

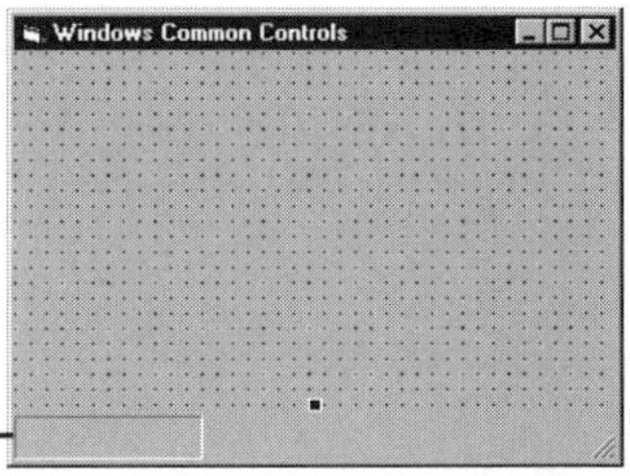

Beginning status bar panel

After you have drawn the status bar, you are ready to start setting the properties to control its appearance and to create any additional panels that you will need for to display information. As you saw when you first drew the status bar control, it sizes itself to fit across the entire form. This is an automatic action, and you have no control over it. You can, however, control the height of the status bar either by setting its Height property or by clicking and dragging one of its sizing handles. There are two other properties that control the basic appearance of the entire status bar: the `Align` property and the `Style` property.

The `Align` property of the status bar controls which edge of the form, if any, the status bar is "docked" against. The `Align` property has five possible settings:

- `vbAlignNone`—Allows the status bar to be positioned anywhere on your form
- `vbAlignTop`—Positions the status bar at the top of the form
- `vbAlignBottom`—Positions the status bar at the bottom of the form. This is the default setting of the property and the position where users probably expect to find the status bar
- `vbAlignLeft`—Places the status bar at the left edge of the form
- `vbAlignRight`—Places the status bar at the right edge of the form

> **CAUTION**
>
> If you change the `Align` property of a status bar after placing it on a form, it may resize itself to fill the entire form. If this happens, you must change the `Height` or `Width` property from the Properties window.

Figure 16.3 showed how the status bar looked aligned at the bottom of the form. Top alignment and no alignment have a similar appearance.

Figure 16.4 shows how the status bar looks aligned at an edge of the form. Unless you have a specific reason for using a different alignment, it is best to stick with the default, bottom alignment. Although another alignment might be a novel approach, it would probably confuse users who are accustomed to the standard alignment.

FIG. 16.4

You can align a status bar at one of the edges of the form.

Side-aligned status bar

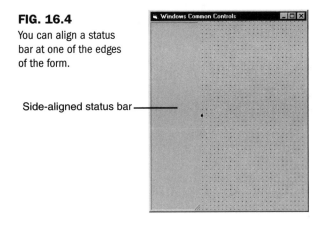

The other property that controls the overall appearance of the status bar is the `Style` property. This property has two settings that determine whether the status bar will display a single panel or multiple panels. The two settings are:

- `sbrNormal`—Allows multiple panels to be displayed
- `sbrSimple`—Allows only a single panel to be displayed

The effect of these two settings are shown in Figure 16.5.

FIG. 16.5
You can create either a
single-panel or a
multiple-panel status
bar.

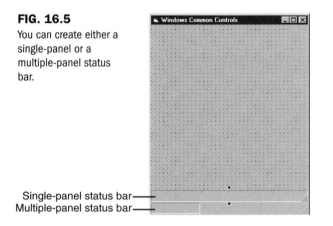

Single-panel status bar———
Multiple-panel status bar———

Working with the Panels of the Status Bar

The real work of the status bar is handled by its panels. Each panel is a separate object with its own properties that control its appearance and behavior. Each panel is part of the status bar's `Panels` collection. After you draw the status bar on your form and set its basic properties, you can begin adding panels to the bar. You do this through the Property Pages of the status bar. This dialog box, shown in Figure 16.6, is accessible by clicking the ellipsis button to the right of the `Custom` property in the Properties window.

FIG. 16.6
Property Pages let you
manage the panels of
your status bar.

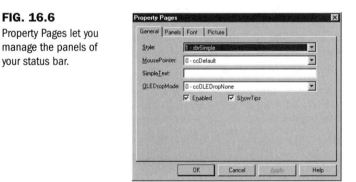

T I P You can also access the Property Pages by right-clicking the status bar to access the pop-up menu and then by choosing Properties from the menu.

Setting Up a Panel To set up an individual panel, you simply set the properties of the panel by using the Property Pages. There are eight main properties that control the appearance and behavior of the panel:

- Text—Determines the text that will be displayed in a text style panel
- ToolTipText—Sets the text that is displayed when the user rests the mouse over the panel
- Alignment—Determines whether the text in the panel is left-justified, right-justified, or centered in the panel
- Style—Determines the type of panel created
- Bevel—Sets the type of shadowing used for the 3-D look of the panel
- AutoSize—Determines how the size of the panel is handled by the program
- MinWidth—Sets the minimum size of the panel
- Picture—Determines what, if any, picture is displayed in the panel

While most of these properties are self-explanatory, the Style and AutoSize properties merit further attention.

There are seven different styles of panels that you can create for your status bar. While one of the styles is designed for you to display text, most styles are predefined status items. These styles display the settings of the lock keys, (such as Caps Lock, Num Lock, and so on) or the system date and time. These styles are handled by the control itself, so you can set them up in design mode and then you don't have to do anything while the program is running. The styles of panels are summarized in Table 16.1 and are displayed in Figure 16.7.

Table 16.1 Panel Styles Are Available to Your Programs

Setting	Description
sbrText	Displays text or a bitmap. The text displayed is contained in the Text property of the panel, whereas the bitmap would be contained in the Picture property.
sbrCaps	Handles the status of the Caps Lock key. This panel will display CAPS in bold letters when the key is on, and will display the letters dimmed when the key is off.
sbrNum	Handles the status of the Num Lock key. This panel will display NUM in bold letters when the key is on, and will display the letters dimmed when the key is off.

Setting	Description
sbrIns	Handles the status of the Insert key. This panel will display INS in bold letters when the key is on, and will display the letters dimmed when the key is off.
sbrScrl	Handles the status of the Scroll Lock key. This panel will display SCRL in bold letters when the key is on, and will display the letters dimmed when the key is off.
sbrTime	Displays the current time.
sbrDate	Displays the current date.

Part

IV

Ch

16

N O T E An eighth setting, sbrKana, is also associated with the Scroll Lock key. It displays KANA in bold letters when the key is on, and dimmed letters when the key is off. The KANA indicator is a special setting for Katakana characters used in Japanese programs. ▨

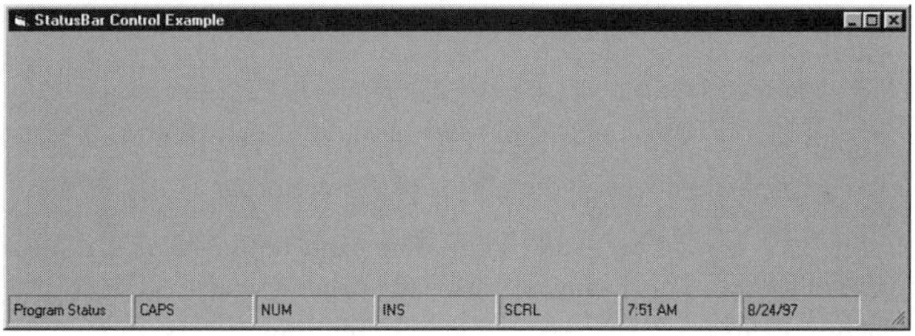

FIG. 16.7
Most panel styles automatically keep track of status information.

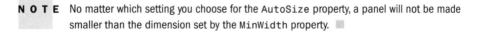

The AutoSize property has three settings that help determine the size of the panel in your program. The default setting, NoAutoSize, sets the size of the panel to the dimension specified in the MinWidth property, and this size will not change as other panels are added and removed. The sbrContents setting sets the size of the panel to fit the text that the panel contains, whether this is text entered by you or the text used for the key status and date/time panels. The final setting, sbrSpring, allows panels to stretch to fit the width of the status bar. This prevents any empty space from being present in the bar.

N O T E No matter which setting you choose for the AutoSize property, a panel will not be made smaller than the dimension set by the MinWidth property. ▨

One final property of note is the Bevel property. As stated above, this property determines whether and how the 3-D effects of the panel are displayed. There are three settings for the Bevel property—sbrNoBevel, which produces a flat panel, sbrInset (the default), which produces a panel that looks embedded in the status bar, and sbrRaised, which produces a raised panel. These three bevel styles are shown in Figure 16.8.

FIG. 16.8

You can create flat,
inset, or raised panels.

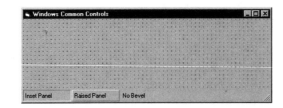

Managing Your Panels   You have seen how to set the properties of an individual panel, but
you also need to know how to add and remove panels. Within the Property Pages, this is very
easy. To add a new panel, you simply click the Insert Panel button on the Panel page. This sets
up a blank set of properties for the new panel. To remove a panel, click the Remove Panel
button. This instantly removes the panel from the status bar, without requesting verification.
Finally, if you want to move from panel to panel, click the arrow buttons on the Panel page.

The status bar also gives you the capability to add and remove panels from code. This is
handled by the methods of the Panels collection. There are three methods of the Panels collection:

- Add—Creates a new panel for the status bar
- Remove—Deletes a specific panel from the status bar
- Clear—Removes all the panels of the status bar

Listing 16.1 shows how to add a new date panel to the status bar and how to delete the first
panel in the bar. This listing also uses the Count property of the Panels collection, which tells
you how many panels are present in the status bar.

**Listing 16.1   STATUS.FRM—Use the Methods of the *Panels* Collection to
Manage Panels in Code**

```
Dim NewIdx
StatusBar1.Panels.Add
NewIdx = StatusBar1.Panels.Count
With StatusBar1.Panels(NewIdx)
    .Style = sbrDate
    .Bevel = sbrRaised
    .ToolTipText = Format(Date, "Long Date")
End With
StatusBar1.Panels.Remove 1
```

N O T E   Unlike most other collections, the Panels collection starts with an index of 1 and the
index values run up to the Count property. ▨

Running the Status Bar from Code

Now that you know how to set up the status bar, you are ready to see how it is used in code. You have seen that the key status and date/time panels handle their tasks automatically. These things are great, but the real power of the status bar is its capability to change the text that appears in the text-style panel(s) as your program is running. These text panels tell the user the actual status of operations in your program.

Part

IV

Ch

16

To update the status of an item in your program, you assign a text string to the Text property of the Panel object, as shown in the following line of code:

```
StatusBar1.Panels(1).Text = "Viewing record 1 of 10"
```

You can, of course, set other properties of the panels the same way. You can even set up your entire status bar from code by using the methods of the Panels collection and the properties of the Panel objects. As an example, Listing 16.2 shows how to set up the status bar shown in Figure 16.9.

Listing 16.2   STATUS.FRM—You Can Set Up Your Entire Status Bar from Code

```
Private Sub Form_Load()
With StatusBar1
    .Panels(1).AutoSize = sbrSpring
    .Panels(1).Text = "Ready"
    .Panels.Add
    .Panels(2).Style = sbrCaps
    .Panels(2).AutoSize = sbrContents
    .Panels(2).MinWidth = 100
End With
End Sub
```

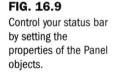

T I P   As with the Toolbar control, you also can reference a specific panel with its key:

```
sbrMain.Panels("page").Text = "Page 1 of 14"
```

FIG. 16.9

Control your status bar by setting the properties of the Panel objects.

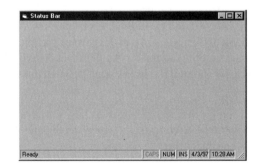

For some of the status messages in your program, you will need more space than is available in one of the text panels. In this case, you can switch the style of the status bar from normal to simple. This gives you the full width of the status bar in which to display the message. To show the message, you will need to set the `SimpleText` property. After the user has responded to the message, or moved the mouse to another area, you can change the status bar back to normal style. This technique is shown in Listing 16.3.

Listing 16.3   STATUS.FRM—Change the Style of the Status Bar to Display Long Messages

```
Dim StatText As String
StatusBar1.Style = sbrSimple
StatText = "No database is open yet. You cannot access "
StatText = StatText & "any records at this point."
StatusBar1.SimpleText = StatText

'To return the status bar to normal -
StatusBar1.Style = sbrNormal
```

Keeping Tabs on Your Progress

Although the status bar is the primary means for you to keep users informed about what is going on in your program, it is not the only control that you can use to monitor progress in your program. Many programs have some tasks that take a relatively long time and you'll want the capability to provide users with a dynamic indication of the operation's progress. The ProgressBar control is ideal for this situation. For example, Microsoft Internet Explorer uses a progress bar to indicate the percentage completed of a file transfer operation. In this case, the progress bar lets you know two things: First, as long as the bar is changing, you know that the file transfer is progressing. Second, by looking at the progress bar, you have some idea how much time is left in the transfer operation.

Setting Up the Progress Bar

The ProgressBar control is very easy to set up and use. As with other controls, you first draw the bar on your form. Then you will need to set the bar's properties. Among the several properties that can influence the look of the progress bar, `Height` and `Width` are the key properties. A progress bar typically is many times wider than it is tall. In fact, Microsoft recommends (in the Help system) that you make the width of the bar at least 12 times the height. Figure 16.10 shows a typical progress bar.

The `Value` property of the progress bar sets or retrieves how much of the progress bar appears filled in. If you compare a ProgressBar control to a thermometer, the Value property is like the temperature. Everything below the current temperature is filled with mercury, while the remaining area is blank.

FIG. 16.10

Progress bars let the user know how much of an operation has been performed.

Progress bar

Max and Min are the other properties that you need to set for the progress bar. These represent the maximum and minimum values allowed for the Value property. In the case of the thermometer, they represent the top and bottom of the temperature scale. For example, if you set the Min property to 0 and the Max property to 100, setting the Value property to 50 causes the progress bar to look half-full.

The setting of the Max and Min properties can be any valid integer, though the Max property must always be greater than the Min property. You can set these properties to any values that make sense for your applications. Some examples might be

- In processing a database, set Min to 0 and Max to the number of records to be processed. As each record is processed, incrementing the Value property will inform the user of the processing progress.

- For a file download operation, you might set Max to the number of kilobytes or number of blocks in the file. One typical setting is a Min of 0 and a Max of 100 to represent the percentage of the file that has been transferred.

Updating the Progress Bar as Your Code Runs

The key to displaying the progress of an operation in the progress bar is setting the Value property. As your code runs through an operation, you periodically update the setting of the Value property. As you might expect, you often do this in a loop that is performing a repetitive operation. Listing 16.4 shows how this is done for a long database operation.

Listing 16.4 Setting the *Value* Property to Show Actual Progress

```
'In the following code, "rsMain" is a recordset
'that has already been opened and populated.
'"pbr" is the ProgressBar control.

pbr.Min = 0rsMain.MoveLast
pbr.Max = rsMain.RecordCount
rsMain.MoveFirst

inCounter = 0

While Not rsMain.EOF
'Insert code to process record here
      inCounter = inCounter + 1
      pbr.Value = inCounter
      rsMain.MoveNext
Wend
```

Part

IV

Ch

16

Sliding into Numbers

Another of the Windows Common Controls is the Slider control. The Slider control provides another means for the user to enter numeric data into a program. The slider works like the slider switches you might find on your stereo system's graphic equalizer or in a manner similar to the scroll bars that you have in the standard control set of Visual Basic. However, the slider has one advantage over the scroll bars. With the slider, you can also select a range of values, not just a single value by specifying minimum and maximum desired values.

Setting Up the Slider Control

You start creating the slider by drawing it on your form. There then are four main properties that control the appearance of the slider. These properties are summarized in Table 16.2. The effects of these properties are shown in Figure 16.11.

Table 16.2   Properties of the Slider Control

Property	Settings
BorderStyle	Set to 0 for no border or 1 for a single line border.
Orientation	Set this property to 0 for a horizontal slider or 1 for a vertical slider.
TickStyle	This property controls the placement of the tick marks on the slider. Set this to 0 to display tick marks below or to the right of the slider, set it to 1 to place tick marks above or to the left of the slider, set it to 2 to place tick marks on both sides, or set it to 3 to show no tick marks.
TickFrequency	Determines how many tick marks are displayed. This can be set to any positive number.

FIG. 16.11

The slider lets you select numeric information.

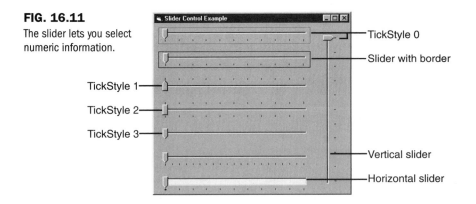

After you have set up the appearance of the slider, you will need to set several properties that control its operation. The first two properties are the Min and Max properties, which control the range of values that can be handled by the slider control. The other two properties are the LargeChange and SmallChange properties. The LargeChange property controls how much the value of the slider will change if the user presses the PageUp or PageDown keys or clicks the mouse to either side of the slide bar. The SmallChange property controls how much the value of the slider will change if the user presses the right or left arrow keys. SelectRange is the final property affecting the operation of the slider. This property determines whether the slider can select only a single value or possibly select a range of values.

Using the Slider Control

When your users encounter the Slider control in your program, they can click the slide bar and drag it to set a value. They can also use the PageUp, PageDown, and right and left arrow keys to change the value. The information entered by the user is contained in the Value property of the slider.

N O T E The keyboard keys only work on a Slider control if it has the focus. ▪

If the SelectRange property is set to True, the user also can select a range of values by holding down Shift while clicking and dragging the slider bar. Unfortunately, this technique is not automatic; it must be managed by your code. You'll need to add code to the slider's MouseDown event procedure to determine whether the user has held down Shift while dragging the slider. If so, your code can set the slider's SelStart property, which defines the starting value of the range, and the SelLength property, which defines the extent of the range. Visual Basic's help system contains a very good example under the topic "SelLength, SelStart Properties (Slider control)."

Creating a Project with the Slider Control

To really demonstrate the use of the Slider control, you now will build a "color blender" project that uses an array of Slider controls to set the BackColor property of a form.

Setting Up the Interface of the Project   To create the color blender, start a new project in Visual Basic and save it as **ColorBld.Vbp**. Next, rename the form to **frmBlend** and save it as **frmBlend.Frm**.

N O T E At this point, you need to add the Windows Common Controls to the Toolbox, if they are not already present (refer to "Working with the Windows Common Controls," earlier in this chapter). Now you can start creating the interface of the program by adding controls. ▪

Follow these steps to add the controls for the color blender project:

1. Place a check box on the form and name it **ckGray**. Set the Caption property of the check box to Only Shades Of Gray.

2. Place a Slider control on the form and name it **sldColor**.

3. Place a label on the form to the left of the slider and name it **lblColor**.

4. Make a set of control arrays for lblColor and sldColor. To do this, hold down the Ctrl key and click both lblColor and sldColor. Go to the <u>E</u>dit menu and click <u>C</u>opy. <u>P</u>aste the copied controls onto the form. You will be presented with a dialog box asking if you want to create a control array. Click <u>Y</u>es.

5. Add a third element to each control array by choosing <u>P</u>aste again.

6. Using the Properties window, set the caption of lblColor(0) to Red:, the caption of lblColor(1) to Green:, and lblColor(2) to Blue:.

7. Place the lblColor() and sldColor() control arrays as shown in Figure 16.12.

FIG. 16.12
The main form of the color blender project contains an array of Slider controls.

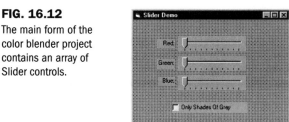

Setting Up the Code of the Project   After you have set up the interface of the program, you will need to add some code to a couple of events to make the program work. The first event is the Load event of the form. This event sets the initial condition of the program. The code for the Load event is shown in Listing 16.5.

Listing 16.5   COLORBLD.VBP—Initialize the Program in the *Load* Event of the Form

```
Private Sub Form_Load()

    Dim nCount As Integer
    Dim lRed As Long, lGreen As Long, lBlue As Long

'Set up the sliders
    For  nCount = 0 To 2
        sldColor(nCount ).Min = 0
        sldColor(nCount ).Max = 255

        sldColor(nCount ).TickFrequency = 4
```

```
Next  nCount

'Initialize the color of the form
'control. (This will set the color to black. RGB(0,0,0))
frmBlend.BackColor = RGB(lRed, lGreen, lBlue)

End Sub
```

Next, you will need to add the code that actually changes the colors in response to movements of the Slider control. This code will be placed in the Scroll event of the Slider controls. The code is shown in Listing 16.6.

Listing 16.6   COLORBLD.VBP—Moving the Slider Changes the Color in the Color Blender

```
Private Sub sldColor_Scroll(Index As Integer)
    Dim nCount As Integer
    Dim lRed As Long, lGreen As Long, lBlue As Long


    'Gray is equal values of Red, Green and Blue
    If ckGray Then
        'move all the sliders


        For nCount = 0 to 2
            sldColor(nCount).Value = sldColor(Index).Value
        Next nCount
    End If

    'Set the RGB value
    lRed = sldColor(0).Value
    lGreen = sldColor(1).Value
    lBlue = sldColor(2).Value

    'Assign the resultant RGB value to the backcolor

    frmBlend.BackColor = RGB(lRed, lGreen, lBlue)

End Sub
```

 Running the Project   After you have entered the code, you are ready to run the program. Click the Start button or press F5 to compile and run the program. Then try setting different combinations of the color sliders to see the effect on the color blender.

The ColorBld.Vbp project works like this: After an initialization process in the Form_Load event, most of the work takes place in the sldColor_Scroll event. As the user moves a slider from the array of Slider controls, the moved slider's index is passed into the sldColor_Scroll event. The application checks the value of the ckGray check box. If it is checked (True), the value of the moved slider is assigned to all the controls in the slider control array. This causes all the sliders to move to the same position before any other code is executed.

The application then assigns the value from the Value property of each Slider in the sldColor control array to their respective color variables, lRed&, lGreen&, lBlue&. The color variables are then passed as parameters to the RGB() function. The return of the RGB() function is used to set the BackColor property of the form.

Viewing Data with ListView and TreeView

The ListView and TreeView controls are two of the Windows Common Controls. These controls allow you to organize data for viewing in a manner similar to that used by the Windows Explorer (see Figure 16.13). You now will be guided through the creation of sample ListView and TreeView projects, but these are tricky controls to master. You might want to spend a little time going over the online help files that accompany your version of Visual Basic to get a good grounding in their use. It will be time well spent.

FIG. 16.13

The Windows 95 Explorer uses both the TreeView and ListView Win32 Common Controls. The left pane uses the TreeView, the right pane uses the ListView.

TreeView control——

ListView control——

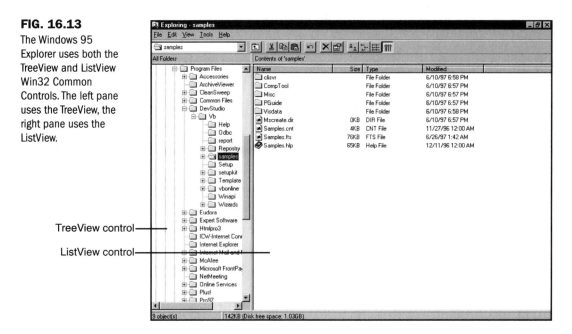

Using the ListView Control

The ListView control is similar to the ListBox but is enhanced in a number of ways. It enables you to display a list with large icons, small icons, as a list, or as a report. These options correspond to the options in the Windows Explorer's View menu (Large Icons, Small Icons, List, or Details). In fact, the most common use of the ListView control is the right pane of the Explorer window (refer to Figure 16.13).

The ListView control can display information in one of a variety of modes—icon lists that are arranged from left to right, a columnar list, or a "report" view. Once the items are stored in the ListItems collection, it is simply a matter of setting the View property to switch to any of the desired modes.

The report-style list is special because it shows more information than the other modes. When using the Windows Explorer, you may have noticed that the Details option displays more information than just the file name. In this case, the file name is the main item, and the size, type, and date modified are "sub-items" associated with each file name.

In your programs, you control sub-items with the SubItems property, which is an array of strings associated with each item in the list. There is also a ColumnHeaders collection used to supply the headings at the top of the report.

Recall from earlier in this chapter that your toolbar needs an associated ImageList control to supply the button pictures. The ListView control needs two ImageLists because it can display both large and small icons. These ImageLists can be set from the Property Pages dialog box or from code, as follows:

```
lViewMain.Icons = ImageList1
lViewMain.SmallIcons = ImageList2
```

If you don't set the SmallIcons and Icons properties of the ListView control, the associated list images will not appear. Also, it's a good idea to use the smaller ImageList dimension (16×16) when filling the image list that you are going to use for small icons.

N O T E As with many of the other controls in the Common Controls group, ListView makes extensive use of collections. If you are unfamiliar with this concept, you may want to re-read the earlier section "Understanding Collections" for a quick introduction. ▪

Recall that the ListBox control's items were stored in an array. All the items in a ListView control are in a collection called ListItems, which is necessary because each item in a list view has several properties, including an index to the icon images and a caption. As with the Toolbar's Buttons collection, the ListItems collection has an Add method defined as follows:

```
listview1.ListItems.Add ,"mykey","My Item",1,1
```

Starting the Project   To illustrate the concepts of using the ListView control, a project will be created next that displays a list of baseball team standings in a ListView control.

For your convenience, the complete project is available from this Que Web site at **www.mcp. com/info/0-7897/0-7897-1288-1**

To begin the creation of the project, start a new project in Visual Basic and save it as **LISTVIEW.VBP**. Next, change the name of the default form to frmListV and save the form as **FRMLISTV.FRM**.

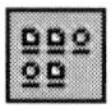

Next, add a ListView control to the form. For simplicity, make the ListView's name short, lvMain. Finally, you need to add two ImageList controls to the form. Again, make the names short, ilNormal and ilSmall.

N O T E The ImageList and ListView controls must be added to your Toolbox before you can use them. See the earlier section entitled "Working with the Windows Common Controls" for an explanation.

Setting the Properties of the ListView Control As with most controls, there are two ways that you can set up the ListView control—by using the Properties window and Property Pages or by using code. If you want to set up the ListView while you are in the design environment, you can use the Property Pages, shown in Figure 16.14. There are three key properties that you will need to set: View, Icons, and SmallIcons.

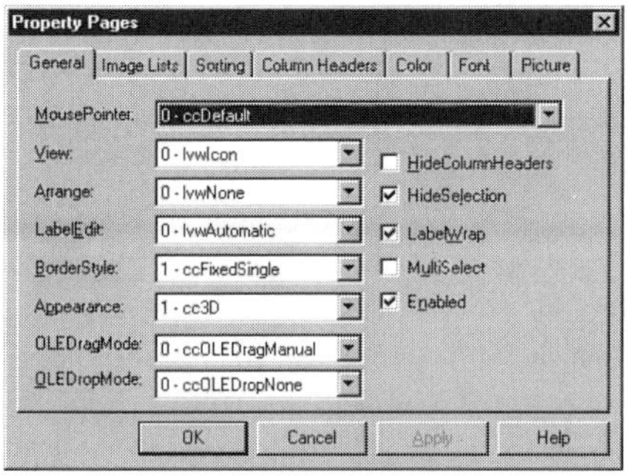

FIG. 16.14

Property Pages let you set the ListView control properties.

First, you need to set the View property, which determines how the list will present information to the user. The View property has four possible values:

- lvwIcon—Displays each item in the list using a large icon and a simple text description

- lvwSmallIcon—Displays each item in the list using a small icon and a simple text description. The items are ordered horizontally

- lvwList—Similar to the small icon view, except that items are arranged in a single vertical column

- lvwReport—Displays each item with a small icon, a text description, and detailed information, if it is provided. As with the list view, items are arranged in vertical columns

The names of the ImageList controls that contain the normal and small icons that are shown in the list are the other things that need to be set for the ListView control. If you are using the Property Pages, you can select the ImageList controls from drop-down lists on the Image List page. These lists contain the names of all the ImageList controls on your form.

As stated previously, you can also set the properties of the ListView control from your code. This is done in the sample project. The code in Listing 16.7 is placed in the Load event of the frmListV form.

Listing 16.7   FRMLISTV.FRM—Use the *Load* Event to Set Up the ListView Control

```
Private Sub Form_Load()


    'Set up the icons from the image List
    lvMain.Icons = ilNormal
    lvMain.SmallIcons = ilSmall


    ' Add ColumnHeaders.  The width of the columns is the width
    ' of the control divided by the number of ColumnHeader objects.
    Dim clmX As ColumnHeader
    Set clmX = lvMain.ColumnHeaders.Add(, , "Team")
    Set clmX = lvMain.ColumnHeaders.Add(, , "Wins")
    Set clmX = lvMain.ColumnHeaders.Add(, , "Losses")

    'Create a ListItem object.
    Dim itmX As ListItem

    'Add some data setting to the ListItem
    'The Red Sox
    Set itmX = lvMain.ListItems.Add(, , "Red Sox", 1, 1)  'Team
    itmX.SubItems(1) = "64"    ' Wins
    itmX.SubItems(2) = "65"    ' Losses

    ' You can duplicate the above 3 lines of code
    ' to add information for more teams…


    lvMain.View = lvwReport ' Set View property to Report.

End Sub
```

Figure 16.15 shows the results of the code.

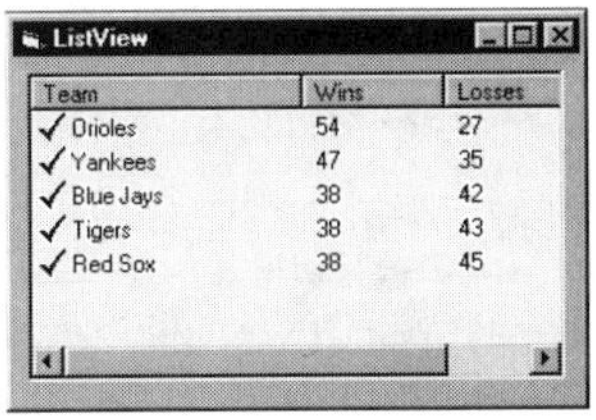

FIG. 16.15

This is how the ListView control looks after being set up by your code.

Notice in the preceding code that temporary object variables were used. For the code that set up the column headings, this was not really necessary. However, when the team was added, a key was not supplied. Therefore, the object itmX was needed to set the two sub-items. If a key had not been supplied, the code also could have been written as follows:

```
lvMain.ListItems.Add , "RSox", "Red Sox", 1, 1
lvMain.ListItems("RSox").SubItems(1) = "64"
lvMain.ListItems("RSox").SubItems(2) = "65"
```

Adding a *ListItem* Object to a ListView Control

In the examples in this section, the ListItems collection was introduced. The ListItems collection stores ListItem objects that are created using the Add method.

The syntax for a ListItem's Add method is as follows:

```
object.Add(index, key, text, icon, smallIcon)
```

Here's what the different pieces are and what they do:

- object   For all intents and purposes, you can use "*ListViewName*.ListItems". This is required.

- index   You can use this number to position the ListItem object within the ListItems collection. If you don't assign a number to this argument, the ListItem is added to the end of the collection. This is optional. Remember that the index of an item can change as other items are added or deleted.

- key   You can use a string to give a unique, friendly name to the ListItem. This is optional.

- text   This is the string that you want the ListItem to display in the ListView window. It is optional. However, for novice users of this control, it is recommended that you use it. This argument should not be confused with the "key" argument.

- icon   This is the index number of the image within the ImageList that has been assigned to the Icons property of the ListView control. Use this number to select the image you want. This argument is optional. Be careful—if you forget to fill in a value, no large icon will appear in the ListView lvwIcons view.

- smallIcon   Similar to the previous argument, icon, it is the index number of the image within the ImageList that has been assigned to the SmallIcons property of the ListView control. It is optional. If you do not fill in a value, no small icon will appear in the ListView's lvwSmallIcons, lvwList, or lvwReport views.

If you want to add additional information, such as the file creation date or file size, to the created ListItem object, MyListItem, you manipulate the object's SubItems(Index) property. See your online Visual Basic documentation for additional information on the SubItems property.

Setting Up the ImageList Controls   To provide the icons for the ListView control, you will need to have ImageList controls on your form as well. If you followed the earlier instructions for the baseball example, you already have two ImageList controls on the form. All that remains is to set the images in the list:

1. To begin, right-click the ImageList control, ilNormal. A context menu will appear.

2. Left-click the Properties menu item at the bottom of the context menu. The Property Pages dialog box for ilNormal will appear.

3. Select the Image tab and click the Insert Picture button.

4. Choose a bitmap or icon file (for example, a picture of a baseball). The bitmap is now inserted as the first image, as shown in Figure 16.16.

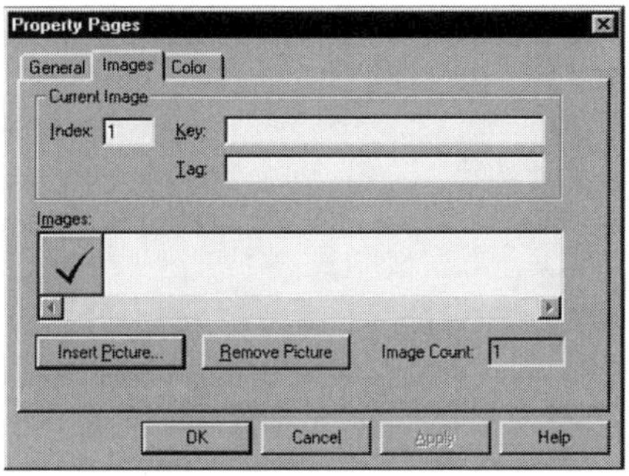

FIG. 16.16

Insert an icon or bitmap as the first image in ilNormal.

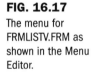

You then will need to repeat the process for ilSmall. Because this ImageList is for the SmallIcons property, first set the dimensions to 16×16 in the General tab.

▶ **See** "Creating Toolbars," **p. 426**

 Creating the Menu for the Project   To make it easy for you to run different parts of the sample program, you will need to create a menu. Using the Menu Editor (Menu Editor button, or Tools, Menu Editor), create the menu items, as shown in Figure 16.17.

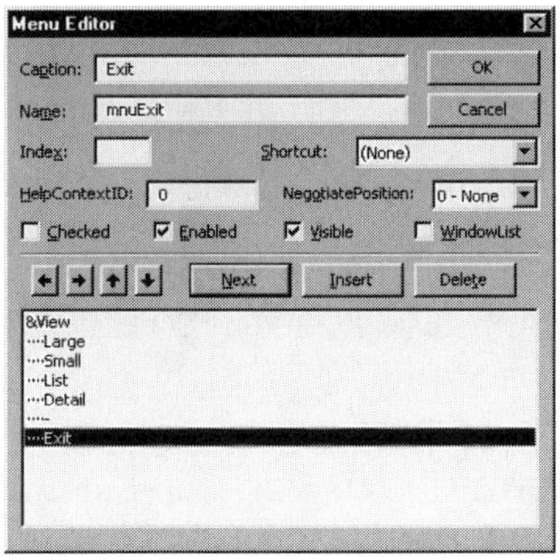

FIG. 16.17

The menu for FRMLISTV.FRM as shown in the Menu Editor.

After exiting the Menu Editor, you will need to add code to each menu item to make it perform a task. The code for each of these items is contained in Listing 16.8.

Listing 16.8 FRMLISTV.FRM—The Menu *click* Events for *FRMLISTV.FRM*

```
Private Sub mnuLarge_Click()
    lvMain.View = lvwIcon
End Sub

Private Sub mnuSmall_Click()
     lvMain.View = lvwSmallIcon
End Sub

Private Sub mnuList_Click()
     lvMain.View = lvwList
End Sub

Private Sub mnuDetail_Click()
     lvMain.View = lvwReport
End Sub

Private Sub mnuExit_Click()
    End
End Sub
```

▶ **See** "Creating a Menu Bar," **p. 104**

 Running the Program   You now can run the program by clicking the Start button or by pressing F5. Figure 16.18 shows two different views of the same list.

FIG. 16.18

While the report view displays detailed information with column headings, the large icons view simply shows a picture above the item text.

In the Form_Load event, the ListItem objects (baseball teams) for the ListView's ListItem collection are created and added. As each ListItem is added to the ListItems collection, values are assigned to SubItems(1), (the "Win" column) and SubItems(2) (the "Loss" column) of the ListItem, itmX.

The menu has six menu items with the captions Large Icons, Small Icons, List, Details, a separator bar, and Exit. The Click event handlers of the first four menu items set the View property of the ListView control. The views are lvwIcons, lvwSmallIcons, lvwList, and lvwReport, respectively. The itmExit_Click event terminates the application.

You have just seen a sample project that demonstrates the ListView's ability to display items. Like the ListBox, however, the ListView control has many events and properties, such as the ItemClick event discussed below, designed to select and manipulate item(s).

The `ItemClick` event passes an object to your program, so you can take appropriate action:

```
Private Sub ListView1_ItemClick(ByVal Item As ComctlLib.ListItem)
    If Item.Text = "Magic Item" Then MsgBox "You clicked the magic item!"
End Sub
```

The ListView control has properties to sort the report view based on a column header. By using the `ColumnClick` event, it would be very easy to change the sort order to the selected column:

```
Private Sub lvMain_ColumnClick(ByVal ColumnHeader As ComctlLib.ColumnHeader)
    lvMain.SortKey = ColumnHeader.Index - 1
    lvMain.Sorted = True
End Sub
```

As you may have noticed, items in a ListView can be renamed by single clicking the text. Two events, `BeforeLabelEdit` and `AfterLabelEdit`, let your program know which item the user is changing.

As stated at the beginning of the chapter, the ListView and TreeView are fairly complex controls. To discover all the features, I suggest creating several sample programs to test all the properties and methods.

Using the TreeView Control

The TreeView control is similar to a ListView in that it can display items with a combination of text and graphics. However, the TreeView does so by showing items within a tree hierarchy. If you have taken a math or computer science class, you already may have discussed the "tree hierarchy." An example of a tree you might have seen in math class is shown in Figure 16.19.

FIG. 16.19
In the tree structure pictured here, each node of the tree is represented by a circle.

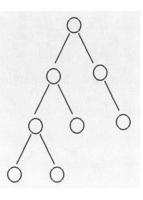

If you are unfamiliar with tree hierarchies, study the next few sections carefully as this concept will make understanding the TreeView control a lot easier.

> **N O T E** If you have used the OutLine control in previous versions of Visual Basic, you'll find that the TreeView control is a more robust alternative. ▪

Given the hierarchical nature of the TreeView control, *root, parent,* and *child* are fundamental concepts that must be understood for you to work effectively with the control. Also, the TreeView uses the `Node` object extensively. This being the case, mastery of the `Node` object is also a requirement for effective use of the TreeView. The most common example of the TreeView is the left pane of the Windows Explorer (refer to Figure 16.13).

Understanding Nodes   A *hierarchy* is an organization in which each part has a defined relationship with the other parts. For example, take your family tree. Your parents and their parents are "above" you in the hierarchy; your children and their children are "below" you.

In the family tree example, each person is considered to be a *node* on the tree. Relationships between nodes are indicated by *branches.* A node's branches can connect it to other nodes (for example, lines on the family tree connecting you to your parents), or it can simply exist by itself (if you don't have any children).

Like the family tree or a real-life tree, all TreeView controls have nodes. `Nodes` is (notice the use of the singular verb) both a property of a TreeView control and an object in itself. If you have followed the discussion up to now regarding collections, this concept probably makes some sense to you. (If you're unclear about collections, review the "Understanding Collections" section, earlier in this chapter.) Like the Toolbar control's `Buttons` collection, the TreeView's `Nodes` collection has properties and methods, including an `Add` method used to create new nodes:

```
tv1.Nodes.Add , , "mykey", "Test Node", 1, 2
```

And, like the other `Add` methods discussed so far, it can return a reference to the object just created:

```
Dim tempNode As Node
Set tempNode = tv1.Nodes.Add(, , "mykey", "Test Node")
tempNode.Image = 1
tempNode.SelectedImage = 2
tempNode.ExpandedImage = 3
```

The TreeView control presents a "collapsible" view of the tree structure, as seen in Figure 16.20.

FIG. 16.20
A simple tree structure created in a TreeView control.

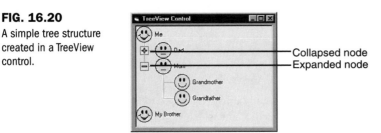

Collapsed node
Expanded node

In this figure, notice the use of plus, minus, lines, and images to indicate which parts of the tree are "expanded" and which are "collapsed."

Understanding the *Root* Property   At the very top (or bottom, depending on how you look at it) of a tree structure is its root. A root is the node from which all other nodes descend. A tree has only one root node. In the tree pictured in Figure 16.20, the node called "Me" is the root node, simply because it was the first one added to the TreeView control.

Part of what defines a node is its root. Therefore, each node in the Nodes collection has a Root property that refers to the tree's root node. For the tree pictured in Figure 16.20, the following code would verify that "Me" is the root of every node:

Part
IV

Ch
16

```
Dim tempNode As Node
For Each tempNode in tv1.Nodes
        Print tempNode.Text & "'s root is " & tempnode.Root.Text
Next tempNode
```

Note that Root is both a property of a node and a node itself.

Working with the *Parent* Property   You have just seen that every node in the Nodes collection can access the root. However, just knowing the root of a node is not enough to define a position in the tree hierarchy. Look at, for example, Figure 16.21, which is a company organizational chart.

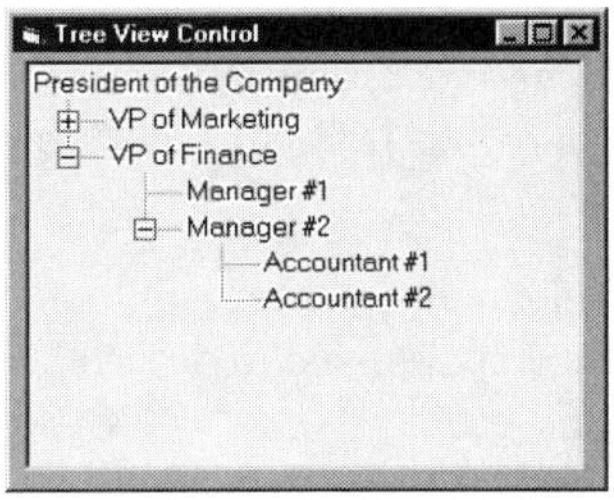

FIG. 16.21

Note in this particular TreeView control that the images for each node have been disabled.

If you want to know where you are in this structure, you need to know more than just where the root (President) is. This brings us to the first of several tree relationships, the *Parent relationship*. To be a parent, a node must have children. In Figure 16.21, the president of the company is a parent to both of the vice president nodes. Both managers shown in the figure also have the same parent, VP of Finance.

Suppose you were an ambitious little node trying to climb the corporate ladder. You could use this code to check your progress:

```
Dim MyNode As Node

Set MyNode = tv1.Nodes("Me")

If MyNode = MyNode.Root Then
    MsgBox "You're the boss!"
Else
    MsgBox "Try getting promoted to " & MyNode.Parent.Text
End If
```

As you can see from the example, each node object has a `Parent` property that refers to its parent node. The only exception is the root node, whose `Parent` property does not refer to anything.

Working with the *Children* Property To be a parent, a node must have children. To find out if a node is a parent, you query the `Children` property by using code like this:

```
Private Sub TreeView1_NodeClick(ByVal MyNode As Node)
    If MyNode.Children = 0 Then
        MsgBox "I am not a parent"
    End If
End Sub
```

As you can see, the `Children` property returns an integer value that represents the number of children a given node has. To be considered a child, a node has to have a direct connection. In other words, as shown in Figure 16.21, the president of the company has two children—the two VPs.

Working with the *Child* Property Whereas the `Children` property simply returns the count of child nodes, the `Child` property returns an actual node (just like the `Root` and `Parent` properties). However, even if a parent has multiple children, the `Child` property returns only the first of the given parent node's descendants. If a given node doesn't have a child, then its `Child` property will contain an invalid reference. Therefore, you should not try to access it if the `Children` property is `0`. In the example, Figure 16.21, Manager #2's `Child` property is Accountant #1.

The immediate question that comes to mind is how to access child nodes other than the first one. Well, each node has several properties that are used to determine who its "brothers and sisters" are, as demonstrated in the following code:

```
Sub PrintAllChildren()

    Dim anyNode As Node
    Dim kidNode As Node
    Dim inCounter As Integer

    For Each anyNode In tv1.Nodes

        If anyNode.Children <> 0 Then 'this node is a parent

            Print anyNode.Text & "'s children are: "
            Set kidNode = anyNode.child
            Print kidNode.Text

            inCounter = kidNode.FirstSibling.Index
            While inCounter <> kidNode.LastSibling.Index
                Print tv1.Nodes(inCounter).Next.Text
                inCounter = tv1.Nodes(inCounter).Next.Index
            Wend

        End If

    Next anyNode
End Sub
```

Remember, for a given node, there is only one child. All the other nodes that share the child's parent are considered Next or Previous nodes. However, among all the nodes that share the same value for the Parent property, there is a FirstSibling and a LastSibling.

N O T E Nodes are tricky; there's no question about it. One of the best ways to get a grasp of nodes is to see the node code (no poetry intended) in action. The online help file examples that Microsoft provides with your version of VB are pretty good once you get a basic understanding of the hierarchy concepts. It is suggested that you create several test programs until you are comfortable using the TreeView control. ■

To learn more about the TreeView control, keep reading. This section focused on accessing nodes already in the TreeView control. The next section will add nodes to a TreeView control as part of a sample project.

Using the TabStrip Control

The last control that will be covered is the TabStrip control. The TabStrip, shown in Figure 16.22, adds a whole new dimension to form organization and information presentation. Of all the controls in the Common Controls group, it probably has attained the most prominence in the Windows interface arsenal.

N O T E The TabStrip control is different from the tabbed dialog box. Aside from the visual differ-ence, the most important distinction is that the TabStrip is not a container. Containers are discussed in Chapter 17, "Using Containers in Your Programs." ■

▶ **See** "Using the Tabbed Dialog," **p. 469**

FIG. 16.22
A Property Pages dialog box is an example of using a TabStrip control.

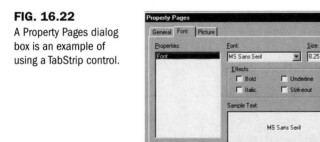

Next, a sample project will be created to illustrate the capabilities of the TabStrip. In this sample project, the purpose of the TabStrip control will be to switch between two lists of information. The lists will be baseball teams displayed in a TreeView control. The TabStrip will enable you to select which league to display.

Starting the Project

To begin the TreeTab project, start a new project in Visual Basic. Next, rename the default form "Form1" to **frmTreTb**. Then follow these steps:

1. Add a TabStrip control and name it something short and meaningful, like tsMain.

2. Next, add a TreeView control to the form and name it tv1. Now you are ready to start setting the properties of the controls.

> **CAUTION**
>
> The TabStrip control is *not* a container. This means that controls placed in a TabStrip control do not assume the Visible, Enabled, and relative Top and Left properties of the TabStrip, as they would if you were to draw a control into a selected Frame control. Thus, clicking a TabStrip will bring it to the front, covering other controls that are before it.
>
> To manipulate how controls appear in relation to a TabStrip, pay particular attention to the ZOrder method of the TabStrip and the affected controls. During design mode, you can right-click the TabStrip control and choose Send to Back.

Setting Up the TabStrip

The next step in creating the project is to create the tabs in the TabStrip. Because there are two leagues that need to be shown, two tabs are needed in the TabStrip. To set up the TabStrip control, follow these steps:

1. Start by right-clicking tsMain. This will bring up the TabStrip context menu.

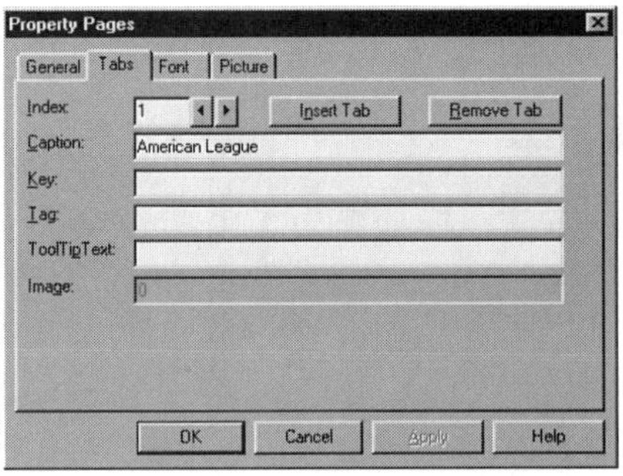

FIG. 16.23

The Property Pages dialog box makes it easy to insert tabs into a TabStrip control.

2. Click the Properties menu item at the bottom of the context menu to display the Property Pages dialog box for tsMain.

3. Click the Tabs tab and type **American League** in the Caption field (see Figure 16.23).

4. Click the Insert Tab button. A tab will be added.

5. In the Caption field, type **National League**.

6. Click OK. You will see that the captions have appeared in the TabStrip control.

Creating the Code to Set Up the TreeView Control

As was the case in the ListView project, the setup of the TreeView control is easier to accomplish through code. In the case of your sample project, you want to display a hierarchical organization of a selected baseball league. Each league has three divisions: East, West, and Central. The divisions have five, five, and four teams, respectively.

FIG. 16.24

In our sample program, the TreeView will be filed with items from the two text files pictured here.

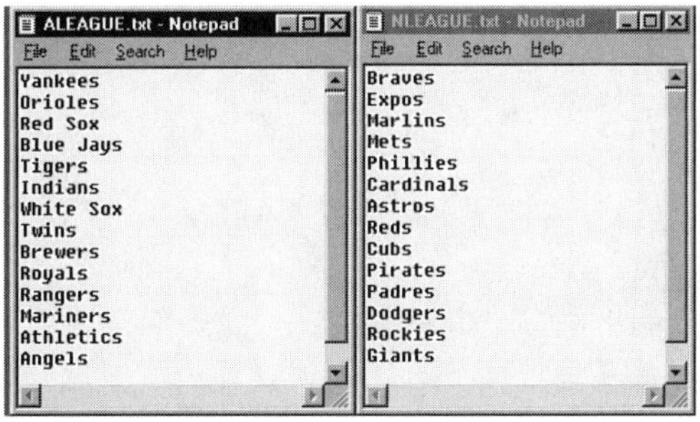

We'll take advantage of this common structure by putting the data into two text files, ALEAGUE.TXT and NLEAGUE.TXT. These files will contain a list of the 14 teams in each league. They can be created in Notepad or any other text editor, as shown in Figure 16.24.

Create the subroutine shown in Listing 16.9 to load information from the text files into the TreeView control.

Listing 16.9 FRMTRETB.FRM—*DisplayLeague* Procedure Displays League Information in the TreeView Control

```
Public Sub DisplayLeague(sLeague As String)

    Dim tempNode As Node
    Dim nCounter As Integer
    Dim sTemp As String

    tv1.Nodes.Clear

    'Add the League
    Set tempNode = tv1.Nodes.Add(, , "R", sLeague)

    'Add the Divisions
    Set tempNode = tv1.Nodes.Add("R", tvwChild, "E", "East Division")
    Set tempNode = tv1.Nodes.Add("R", tvwChild, "C", "Central Division")
    Set tempNode = tv1.Nodes.Add("R", tvwChild, "W", "West Division")
```

continues

Listing 16.9   Continued

```
'Open the text file with team names
If sLeague = "National League" Then
Open "C:\NLEAGUE.TXT" For Input As #1
Else
Open "C:\ALEAGUE.TXT" For Input As #1
End If

'Add the 5 EAST teams
For nCounter = 1 To 5
    Line Input #1, sTemp
    Set tempNode = tv1.Nodes.Add("E", tvwChild, "E" & nCounter, sTemp)
Next nCounter
tempNode.EnsureVisible

'Add the 5 CENTRAL teams
For nCounter = 1 To 5
    Line Input #1, sTemp
    Set tempNode = tv1.Nodes.Add("C", tvwChild, "C" & nCounter, sTemp)
Next nCounter
tempNode.EnsureVisible

'Add the 4 WEST teams
For nCounter = 1 To 4
    Line Input #1, sTemp
    Set tempNode = tv1.Nodes.Add("W", tvwChild, "W" & nCounter, sTemp)
Next nCounter
tempNode.EnsureVisible

'Close the Input file
Close #1

'Set the Desired style
tv1.Style = tvwTreelinesText
tv1.BorderStyle = vbFixedSingle

'Set the TreeView control on top
tv1.ZOrder 0

End Sub
```

Notice that the relationships in the tree view are defined as a node is added. The Add method's first parameter lists a "relative" node and the second parameter lists the relationship to that relative. The constant tvwChild indicates the new node is a child of the relative node.

Taking Action in the Program

Now, return to the topic of the TabStrip control and set up the form's Load event. When the form first appears, you probably want it to show something, so call the DisplayLeague procedure to display the American League teams. The code for the Load event is shown in Listing 16.10.

Listing 16.10   FRMTRETB.FRM—Use the *Load* Event to Initialize the Program

```
Private Sub Form_Load()

    'Put the tree view on top of the tab
    tv1.ZOrder 0

    'Call our procedure
    DisplayLeague "American League"
End Sub
```

At this point, you can run your program and the American League teams will be displayed. However, clicking the TabStrip will have no effect on the TreeView. This is because you have not yet added the necessary code to the TabStrip's Click event. This code, shown in Listing 16.11, calls the DisplayLeague procedure with the name of the desired league.

Listing 16.11   FRMTRETB.FRM—Switch Leagues by Clicking the Appropriate Tab

```
Private Sub tsMain_Click()
    Dim nTemp As Integer

    nTemp = tsMain.SelectedItem.Index
    DisplayLeague tsMain.Tabs(nTemp).Caption

End Sub
```

Now your sample program is done. Figure 16.25 shows how the program looks.

FIG. 16.25
The sample application displays a list of baseball teams when a tab is clicked.

Understanding How the Application Works

The crux of the project is the DisplayLeague procedure. First, this procedure creates a node for the League divisions:

```
Set tempNode = tv1.Nodes.Add("R", tvwChild, "E", "East Division")
```

The constant tvwChild tells the application to make this new node a child of the node, "R".

Then, to each Division node, several team nodes are added:

```
Set tempNode = tv1.Nodes.Add("E", tvwChild, "E" & nCounter, sTemp)
```

Notice that the first argument in the Add method is now "E", which is the unique key of the Node of the Eastern Division. This is how the "E1" node (which displays Yankees) knows that it is a child of the Eastern Division.

Next, the entire Division node and its children are told to remain expanded (TreeView nodes can be expanded and collapsed) in the line:

```
MyNode.EnsureVisible
```

(We also could have set each Division node's Expanded property to True.)

The last thing that deserves attention is the way the TabStrip reports back which tab has been clicked.

In the TabStrip control, tabs are an array of, well, tabs. So, when you click a tab, you are actually selecting a tab, like selecting a ListIndex in a ListBox control. In light of this, to find out which tab is being clicked, the following line makes a bit more sense:

```
nTemp = tsMain.SelectedItem.Index
```

From Here...

The Windows Common Controls covered in this chapter can enhance your programs in many ways. Each has its own special capabilities that can improve the interface of your applications. The best way to learn about them is to put them in your programs and try them out. Some of the topics mentioned here are covered in more detail in other chapters:

- ■ To learn more about creating toolbars and menus for your programs, see Chapter 5, "Adding Menus and Toolbars to Your Programs."

- ■ For a discussion of some additional new controls, see Chapter 18, "Exploring New Visual Basic 5 Controls."

- ■ To learn more about control arrays, see Chapter 19, "Advanced Control Techniques."

CHAPTER 17

Using Containers in Your Programs

So far, we've learned a good bit about designing programs. You know by now that your programs must not only function properly, they must look good as well. No matter how hard you work to make your program perform its assigned tasks as efficiently as possible, a bland or poorly-designed interface can cause your users to have the perception, however unfounded, that your program is junk.

In Chapter 11, "Designing User Interfaces," we discussed several techniques for enhancing the part of your program that your user sees. We've also seen several different types of controls that you can use in your programs. In this chapter, you're going to take this knowledge a step further. You will see how to use containers to organize the controls that your application uses. Proper use of containers to group your programs' controls often means the difference between a "functional" program and a really nice one. ■

Using frames to create button groups

By placing option buttons in different containers, you can create multiple groups and allow multiple selections.

Increase your available screen space

The amount of space on a form is limited. By using containers to hold other controls, you can create multiple pages on a single form.

Control the functions accessible to the user

By placing command buttons or toolbars in containers, you can show only the buttons that a user needs at any given time. This can help the user work with the program and make the programming easier.

Create professional-looking dialog boxes

You can use containers, including the tabbed dialog box control, to create dialog boxes that strengthen your program's user interface.

Create wizards for your programs

Many programs today contain wizards to help users with difficult tasks. By using containers, you can create your own wizard to help users with your program.

Exploring the Uses of Containers

Containers are a special type of control that is available in Visual Basic. The primary function of containers is to help you organize other controls on your forms. Containers can help you show or hide controls as a group, to respond to changes in the program or to respond to user actions. Containers are also used to create functional groups of option buttons so that you can select more than one button at a time on a form. This extends what you can do with option buttons in your programs.

Creating Multiple Pages on a Form

When you develop a simple program, one form might provide sufficient space for your entire application. But as you develop more complex programs, you will find that the available space on a form is one of the most limiting factors in program design. You can only place so many controls on a single form before you either run out of room or, more often, before your form starts looking very cluttered. A cluttered form looks unprofessional and is hard to use. Figure 17.1 shows a membership information form that tries to handle too much information.

FIG. 17.1

Cluttered forms are a poor design choice.

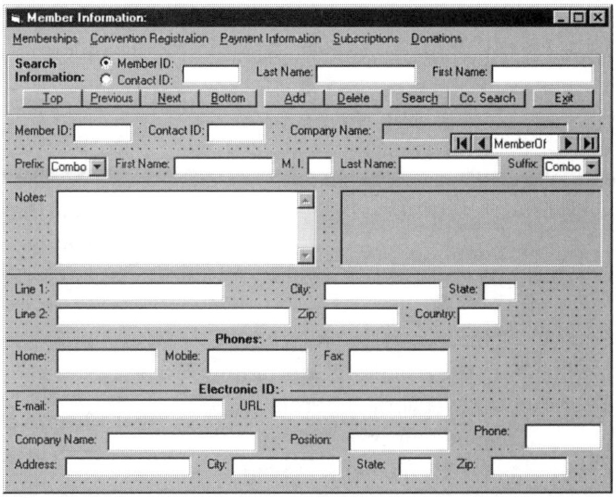

You could solve the problem by using multiple forms. This way you can place some of the controls on a second or third form and only show the supplemental forms when necessary. For many applications, this is the best solution to the problem, especially if the data on the different forms is not closely related.

However, many applications (like the membership program shown in Figure 17.1) contain a large amount of related data. For these types of applications, moving between multiple forms to enter data is very inconvenient. Another solution is to go ahead and add all the controls you need to the form, but selectively hide and show certain controls by using their `Visible` properties. However, this method requires an unwieldy amount of code if you have more than a few controls, and it makes positioning them in design mode almost impossible.

Fortunately, there is an alternative. There are several container controls in Visual Basic that allow you to show, hide, and position groups of controls. They are known as *container controls* because you can draw other controls inside of them. For example, you could draw a TextBox on a PictureBox similar to the way you draw it on a form. The PictureBox then "contains" the TextBox.

N O T E   Container controls create a different visual relationship between the form and the controls they contain. The code events and scope of variables on the form remain unaffected. ■

Containers enable you to place all the controls on one form, but display only the ones that you need to work with at the moment. You can use command buttons, toolbar buttons, or the container's own tabs to switch back and forth between groups of controls. There are three container controls that come with Visual Basic:

- ■ Frame control
- ■ PictureBox control
- ■ Tabbed Dialog control

N O T E   The Tabbed Dialog is one of the Custom Controls in Visual Basic. To use it, you must first add it to the Toolbox from the Components dialog box (choose Project, Components). ■

CAUTION
Even when using containers, you should still limit the number of controls that you place on a single form. Remember, they are still on the form even if they are not currently visible. Too many controls use a lot of memory and make your forms load much slower. A good limit is 200 controls on a single form.

Creating Groups of Option Buttons

In addition to using containers to place more controls on a single form, you will find that containers are useful for creating groups of option buttons. In Chapter 15, "Working with the Standard Controls," you saw that you could only select a single option button on a form. Let's now revise that rule to read "you can only select a single option button within a container." Being able to place container controls on the form allows you to create multiple groups of option buttons. This lets you create applications with groups of multiple choice questions, such as the survey form shown in Figure 17.2.

Using Frames

The Frame control is the simplest of all the container controls. The only function of the Frame control is to hold other controls. In contrast, the PictureBox control is capable of displaying graphics in addition to holding other controls, and the Tabbed Dialog control has built-in page navigation features.

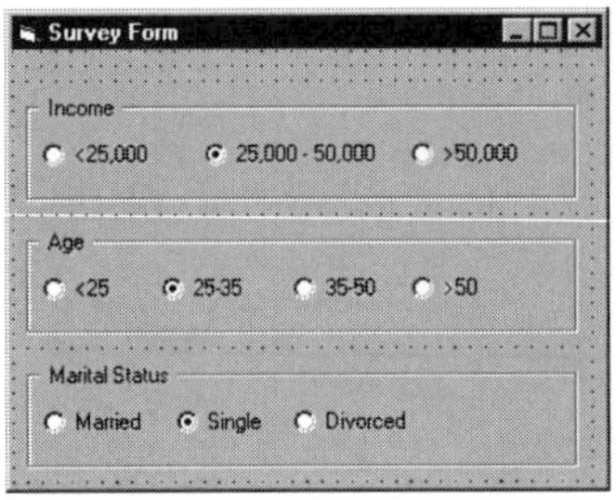

FIG. 17.2

Survey forms use containers to create multiple button groups.

The Frame control is quite simple, and it performs its job very well. In fact, it has one key advantage over the other container controls: It uses fewer of your system's resources than the other controls. Therefore, if you do not need to display pictures in the background of your container and do not need the built-in navigation features, the Frame control is the best choice for the job. You will almost always use the frame for creating button groups.

Setting Up a Frame

As with all other controls, the first step in setting up the Frame control is to draw it on your form in the size that you want. Then, of course, you need to set the Name property to a unique name. At this point, there are several properties you can set that control the appearance of the frame: Caption, Appearance, and BorderStyle. Figure 17.3 shows a variety of frames that display different effects of these properties.

▶ **See** "Controlling User Interaction," **p. 71**

FIG. 17.3

You control the frame's appearance through the Appearance, BorderStyle, and Caption properties.

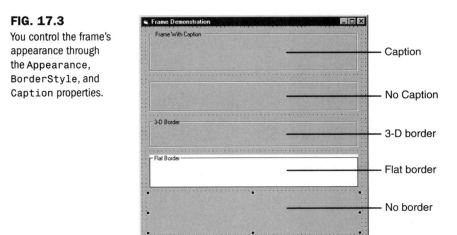

The first property of note is the Caption property. If you enter a value in the Caption property, the text you enter appears in the upper-left corner of the frame. This caption can be used to identify the contents of the frame or provide other descriptive information. If you don't want a caption and simply want an unbroken border around the frame, delete the text in the Caption property.

T I P To avoid having the lines of the border touch the text of the caption, insert a space before and after the text when you set the Caption property.

The second property is the Appearance property. This property controls whether the border of the frame is shown as a single-line, single-color border, which gives the control a flat look, or is shown using lines, which give the control a 3-D effect.

The final property is the BorderStyle property. This property determines whether the border around the frame is displayed. If the BorderStyle property is set to None (using a value of 0), no border is displayed, and the caption is not displayed because it is also part of the border.

T I P If you want the frame to appear without a border, leave the border turned on while you are in design mode, but then set the BorderStyle property to 0 when your form loads. Having the border displayed in the design environment makes it easier to see the boundaries of the frame.

Working with Controls in a Frame

After you have set the properties of the frame, you are ready to start placing controls in the frame. You can place any controls you like in the frame (or any other container). You can even place containers within containers.

To place controls in a frame, first highlight the frame with a single click (It's important that the frame is selected before drawing the control). Then draw controls in the frame just like you would draw them on the form. You need to make sure that the cursor is inside the frame when you start drawing the control. Otherwise, the control will not be contained by the frame. Figure 17.4 shows several controls for a personnel application drawn in a frame.

▶ **See** "Adding Controls to the Form," **p. 89**

FIG. 17.4

Make sure your cursor is inside the frame before you start to draw a control.

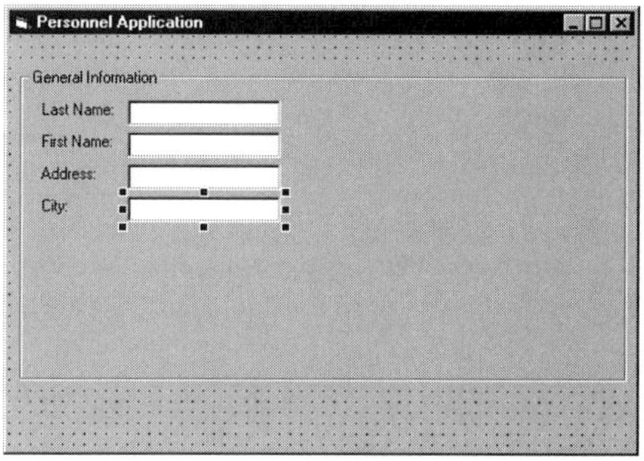

Here are a couple of points about controls and frames. First, if you already have controls on the form, these will not be contained by the frame, even if you draw the frame over the control. Second, unlike moving controls around on the form, you cannot move a control into or out of a frame by dragging and dropping the control. You can drag a control over the frame and the control will look like it is contained within the frame, but it really isn't. The only way to move a control from other parts of the form into the frame is to use cut and paste. You first cut the control from the form by selecting the control and then pressing Ctrl+X or choosing Edit, Cut. The next step is to paste the control into the frame by selecting the frame and then pressing Ctrl+V or choosing Edit, Paste. The control is initially placed in the upper-left corner of the frame, but after the control is in the frame, you can use drag and drop to move the control. You can use the same technique to move a control out of the frame. You can, of course, move multiple controls at the same time.

 If you want to make sure a control is in the frame, try moving the frame. If the control moves with it, the control is part of the frame. If the control does not move with the frame, you can use cut and paste to move it into the frame.

In Chapter 4, "Working with Forms and Controls," you saw how you could select multiple controls on a form to work with their common properties or to handle alignment and sizing tasks. You can do the same thing with controls inside a frame. The only difference is in the way that you select the controls. To select a group of controls, you need to first click the form so that no controls are selected. Then hold down the Shift or Ctrl key while you click and drag the mouse around the controls in the frame. This selects the group of controls as shown in Figure 17.5. You can still select or deselect other controls by holding down the Ctrl key while you click the controls.

FIG. 17.5
You can work with multiple controls inside a container.

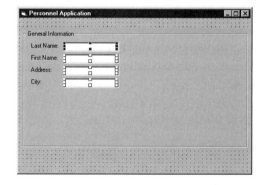

N O T E When selecting a group of controls, the selected controls must either be all inside or all outside a container. Also, control selection cannot span containers. ▪

After the multiple controls are selected, you can work with their common properties or use the Format menu's commands to position and size the controls.

CAUTION

The Format menu's Center in Form command centers the selected controls in the form, not within the frame or other container control that they might reside in. This, in effect, renders the Center in Form command useless for controls that are placed inside a container.

Swapping Pages on a Form

In the section "Creating Multiple Pages on a Form" earlier in this chapter, you read that one of the uses of frames and other containers is to create multiple "pages" on a form. This technique refers to alternately showing different controls in the same location, much like turning the pages in a book. Now you get to see how this is done. The first step of the process is to determine what data will be placed in each frame to create the pages of the form. After you have determined what data will fit into each frame, you can start creating the frames themselves. You create the first frame in the manner that was discussed in the last two sections—that is, draw the frame on the form and then add the controls to the frame. Figure 17.6 shows the frame used to create the first page of a personnel application.

FIG. 17.6
The first page of a sample personnel application contains general information.

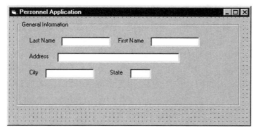

> **TIP** If you're going to use a series of "pages" on a form, including several frames, frames within frames, and so forth, it's a good idea to create a "storyboard" to help stay organized. This involves sketching out each frame and the controls it will contain, as well as tracking the navigation order between the various frames, much like a story editor might sketch out the various scenes of a cartoon to keep track of how it flows.

Creating the second page of the form is only slightly trickier than the first page. The key thing that you have to watch is that you start drawing the second frame outside the bounds of the first frame. If you don't do this, the second frame will be contained within the first frame, and this defeats the purpose of multiple frames. The easiest way to handle this is to start the second frame below and to the right of the bottom right corner of the first frame. After you draw the second frame, you can add the control of the "page" to the frame. Figure 17.7 shows the second page of the personnel application.

You will probably want to have both frames sized the same. The easiest way to do this is to set the Height and Width properties of the frames to the same value. You might notice in Figure 17.7 that the first frame is hidden by the second frame. If you need to work with the first frame again, select it and press Ctrl+J to bring it to the front of the form. (Ctrl+K moves it to the back of the display order.)

> **TIP** Use code at the beginning of your program to align and size frames. This makes them easier to select in the design environment, and it means you don't have to re-align them before running the program.

FIG. 17.7

The second page of the sample application contains education information.

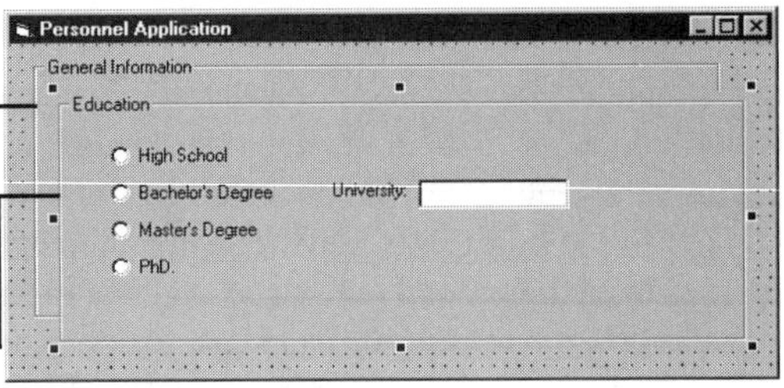

First frame ⏋

Second frame ⏌

Now that the frames are set up, you need a way to switch back and forth between them in your program. You switch between the frames by setting the Visible property of one to True while setting the Visible property of the other to False. When the Visible property of a container is set to False, the container and all its associated controls disappear from view. When the Visible property is set to True, the container and controls reappear.

The actual switch takes place in code that you write for the program. You can place the code in any event you want. However, the most typical location is in the Click event of command buttons. The code in Listing 17.1 shows how the second frame would be hidden and the first frame displayed.

Listing 17.1   FRAMES.FRM—Use a Command Button to Switch Between Frames

```
fraEducation.Visible = False
fraGeneral.Visible = True
fraGeneral.Top = 240
fraGeneral.Left = 240
```

Similar code would be used to display the second form and hide the first form. You would also want to place the code from Listing 17.1 in the Load event of the form to set up the initial page of the application. Figure 17.8 shows how the form would look with the first frame displayed.

FIG. 17.8

You can use one command button for each page of the application.

Another approach to handling two pages is to use the same command button for both pages and to change the Caption property of the command button to identify which frame it will display. Listing 17.2 shows how to accomplish this.

Listing 17.2   FRAMES.FRM—Use a Single Button to Switch Between Two Frames

```
If fraGeneral.Visible Then
    fraGeneral.Visible = False
    fraEducation.Visible = True
    fraEducation.Top = 240
    fraEducation.Left = 240
    cmdGeneral.Caption = "General Information"
Else
    fraEducation.Visible = False
    fraGeneral.Visible = True
    fraGeneral.Top = 240
    fraGeneral.Left = 240
    cmdGeneral.Caption = "Education Information"
End If
```

Part
IV
Ch
17

You can obviously extend this discussion of using two frames to handle more frames or other containers. In fact, you'll do this when you look at creating a wizard in the section "Creating Your Own Wizard" later in this chapter.

Using Picture Boxes

Like the Frame control, the PictureBox control can also be used as a container for other controls. When used as a container, the picture box holds other controls and allows you to hide and display the controls as a group. Setting up the picture box is very similar to setting up a frame. Simply draw the picture box on your form and then add the controls that you want the picture box to contain.

The PictureBox control has two key advantages over the Frame control: The picture box can display a picture as the background for the other controls, and you can use the Print method and graphics methods to display information directly in the picture box. The only drawback to using the picture box is that it requires more resources than the frame does. Figure 17.9 shows a children's software sign-in screen in which a picture box with a background is used as a container for other controls.

Picture boxes are extremely versatile and can greatly enhance your application's interface. You can, for example, use one or more picture boxes within other containers to precisely place graphic images or to have multiple graphics within one frame. You can also print text to picture boxes instead of a printer, in effect creating a "print preview" for your reports.

▶ **See** "Outputting Reports to Familiar Controls," **p. 208**

▶ **See** "Using the PictureBox Control," **p. 304**, for more information about setting up a picture box.

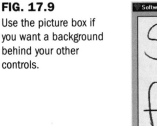

FIG. 17.9
Use the picture box if you want a background behind your other controls.

Using Tabbed Dialogs

Another way to display large amounts of information on a single form is to use a tabbed dialog, also known as an SSTab control. Tabbed dialogs are used in many of the programs with which you are already familiar. For example, the Options dialog box of Visual Basic (shown in Figure 17.10) and the Options dialog box of Word both use tabbed dialogs to organize and present the various program options.

FIG. 17.10
Tabs enable you to place a lot of informa-tion on a form and allow your users easy access to the information.

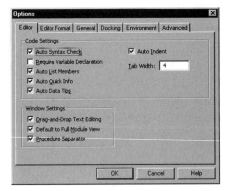

The tabbed dialog can best be compared to the use of file tabs or index tabs in a notebook. Each tab can have a label on it to indicate its contents. Each of the tab pages functions like a Frame control to separate the controls on the current page from the controls on other pages. The tabbed dialog is one of the custom controls that comes with Visual Basic. To be able to use it, you must first select Microsoft Tabbed Dialog Control 5.0 from the Components dialog box (choose Project, Components). After you have selected it, the SSTab control is added to the Toolbox.

> **N O T E** There are two minor differences between the functionality of a tab in the tabbed dialog and a frame. First, you cannot create groups of option buttons directly on a tab. (If you need to place separate groups of option buttons on a tab, you need to place them within a frame on the tab.) Second, tabs have hiding, showing, and alignment built in, while frames must be controlled more with code. ▪

Creating the Tabbed Dialog

Setting up the tabbed dialog begins like the setup of any other control—you draw it on the form. When you first draw the control, it is displayed with three tabs in a single row as shown in Figure 17.11. You can change the total number of tabs and the number of tabs on each row by setting the Tabs and TabsPerRow properties. Changing the setting of the Tabs property increases or decreases the number of tabs from the initial value of three. The TabsPerRow property tells the control how many tabs to display on each row of the SSTab control. If the number of tabs is greater than the number per row, additional rows are added to accommodate all the requested tabs.

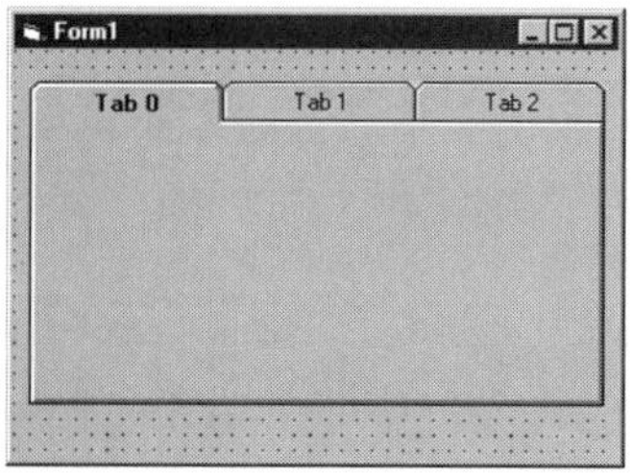

FIG. 17.11
The tabbed dialog is initially drawn with three tabs.

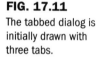

After you have created the tabbed dialog on your form, you can begin adding controls to the tabs. To do this, select the tab where you want the controls to be, and begin drawing controls directly on the tab. To work with another tab, simply select it by clicking the tab with the mouse. As with the frame or picture box, you can place any controls you want on each tab of the tabbed dialog. (See the note earlier in this section about grouping option buttons.) Figure 17.12 shows a completed tabbed dialog.

> **N O T E** Unless you set the Tab property in your startup code, the initial tab displayed will be the last one selected in the design environment. ▪

Customizing the Dialog

In addition to controlling the number of tabs in the tabbed dialog, there are a number of properties that allow you to control its overall appearance. There are also two properties that are available for each tab that allow you to customize the individual tabs.

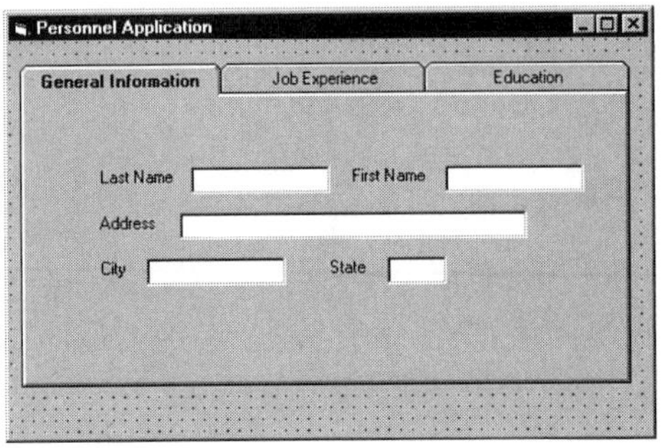

FIG. 17.12

Place controls on each page of the tabbed dialog to create multiple pages of an application.

Changing the Appearance of the Dialog   There are five key properties of the tabbed dialog that control its overall appearance: Style, TabHeight, TabMaxWidth, TabOrientation, and WordWrap.

The Style property controls whether the tabs look like those in Microsoft Office for Windows 3.1 or the property page tabs of Windows 95 applications. The Office-style tabs are the default setting of the property. With the Office-style tabs, each tab is the same width, and the width is set by the TabMaxWidth property. If you choose Windows 95-style tabs, the TabMaxWidth property is ignored, and the tabs are sized to fit the caption of the tab. Figure 17.13 shows both styles of tabs.

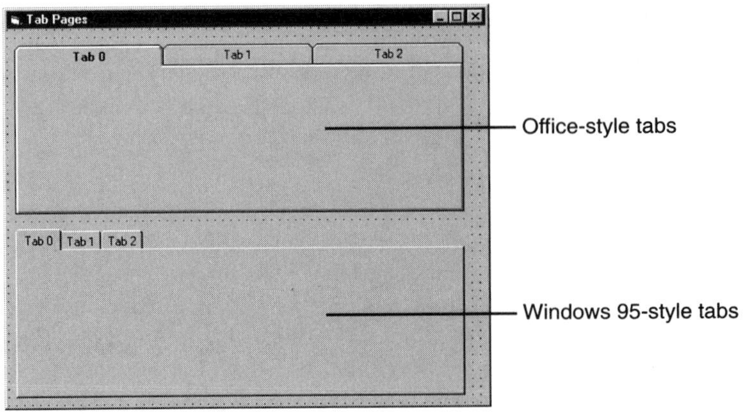

FIG. 17.13

The two styles of SSTab controls illustrate how different-length tab captions are treated.

The TabHeight property controls the height (in twips) of the tab portion of each page. The TabMaxWidth property sets the maximum width (in twips) of each tab. Setting this property to 0 causes the tabs to be sized to fit all the way across the control. Remember, the TabMaxWidth property has no effect on Windows 95-style tabs.

The TabOrientation property controls the placement of the tabs in relation to the body of the control. You can choose to have the tabs placed at the top of the control (the default setting), the bottom of the control, or on the right or left side of the control. Figure 17.14 shows the placement of tabs at the top and right of the control.

FIG. 17.14

You can choose where to position the tabs on the control.

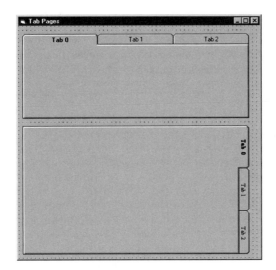

T I P If you are placing the tabs at the side of the control, be sure to use a TrueType font that can be rotated to be displayed vertically.

The final property we're going to look at is the WordWrap property. This property controls whether multiple lines of text will be printed in the tab. If WordWrap is set to True, the text of the Caption property will be placed on multiple lines if necessary. If there are more lines than will fit within the height of the tab, some of the caption will be lost. If the WordWrap property is set to False, only one line will be shown in the tab. If the Caption is larger than the tab can accommodate, only the center portion of the caption will be visible.

Customizing the Individual Tabs   While the previous section dealt with the appearance of the tabbed dialog as a whole, you can also customize the individual tabs of the control. There are two properties for customizing each tab: the TabCaption property and the TabPicture property. These properties allow you to specify a custom caption and a picture for each tab in the control. While you are working with the tabbed dialog in the design mode, you do not see these properties listed in the Properties window. Instead, you see the Caption and Picture properties. As you work with each tab, the TabCaption and TabPicture properties for that tab are displayed in the Caption and Picture properties.

Setting the Caption property has the same effect on a tab as it does on a label or command button. The contents of the Caption property are displayed on the tab. Unless you are using long captions, each caption will probably appear as a single line of text on the tab. If the caption is long, its appearance will be controlled by the setting of the WordWrap property.

If you want to include a picture on the tab, you simply set the Picture property of the tab to the image that you want displayed. If a picture is used, the SSTab control places as much of the picture on the tab as possible. The picture is centered vertically and horizontally on the tab. If the picture is taller than the tab height, both the top and bottom of the picture are cropped.

From side to side, the picture and the caption are centered together. This means that the caption text appears to the right of the picture, and the total width of the picture and the caption are centered. The picture is not cropped on the sides unless the picture is wider than the width of the tab. For pictures smaller than the width of the tab, the full width of the picture is shown and the caption is given the remaining space. Figure 17.15 shows a SSTab control with pictures and captions set for each tab.

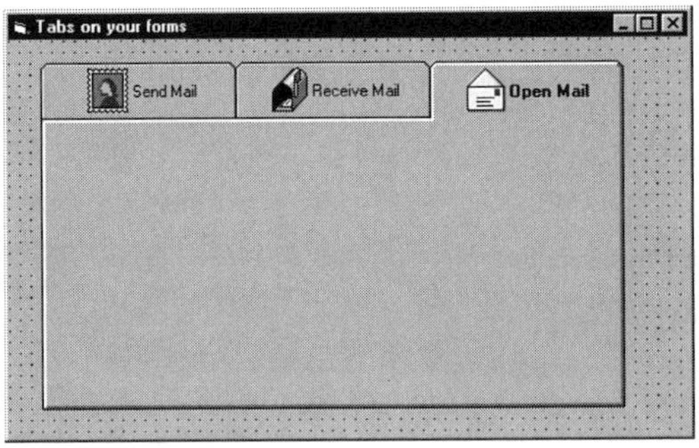

FIG. 17.15

Pictures on the tabs can indicate the information they contain.

Using the Property Pages   Although you can set all the properties of the Tabbed Dialog control from the Properties window, you might find it easier to use the Property Pages. You access the Property Pages by clicking the ellipsis (...) button next to the Custom property in the Properties window. The Property Pages give you access to all the properties of the tabbed dialog and make it easy for you to set the caption and picture of the individual tabs. Figure 17.16 shows the Property Pages for the tabbed dialog.

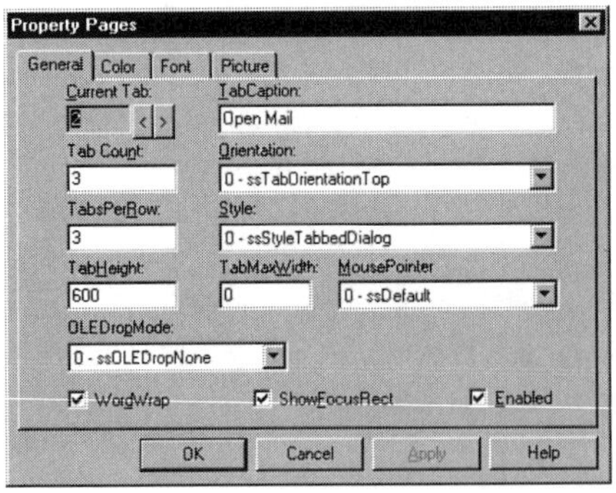

FIG. 17.16

Access all properties of the tabbed dialog by using the Property Pages.

Controlling the Dialog from Code

You can set up all the pages of the tabbed dialog from the design mode, but there might be times when you want to change some parts of the dialog while your program is running. The most common thing to do in code is to disable or hide particular tabs in the control. You might do this for a personnel application where you would want only managers to have access to information about employee compensation or evaluations. Most of the properties of the tabbed dialog are handled through the use of simple assignment statements. However, changing the properties of individual tabs requires special treatment.

Previously you saw that the caption and picture displayed on each tab were contained in the `TabCaption` and `TabPicture` properties, respectively. These properties are actually property arrays, with one element for each tab in the control. The index of the array runs from 0 to one less than the total number of tabs in the control. For example, if you want to change the caption of the first tab in the tabbed dialog, you would use the following code:

```
tbdPersonnel.TabCaption(0) = "Employee"
```

In a similar manner, you could change the picture displayed on the tab by setting the `TabPicture` property. In this case, you would use the `LoadPicture` statement to get a picture from a file, or you could use a picture contained in the `Picture` property of another control.

To handle the personnel application, you would want to either disable or hide any tabs that contained confidential information. To disable a tab, you would set its `TabEnabled` property to `False`. When the tab is disabled, its caption is grayed to indicate that the tab cannot be accessed. This is shown in Figure 17.17. If you want to hide the tab altogether, you can set the `TabVisible` property to `False`. This keeps the user from even knowing that the tab exists.

Part
IV
Ch
17

FIG. 17.17
Disabled tabs cannot be accessed by the user.

One other thing that you might want to do in your application is to show a specific tab in response to a user action. You might want to have a data validation routine that checks the value of all entered data before saving it to a database. If the user failed to enter a value or entered an improper value, you will want to display the tab that contains the control with the invalid data. To show a specific tab, you simply set the `Tab` property of the tabbed dialog. For example, the following code displays the second tab of a dialog:

```
tbdPersonnel.Tab = 1
```

Putting Containers to Work

Now that you have seen how to create the various types of containers for your programs, let's take a look at how you might use a few of these in real-life situations. We take a look at several relatively simple situations and then move on to creating a wizard that you could use in your applications.

Displaying the Proper Buttons

You saw that one use of frames was to create multiple pages of information on a single form. However, you can also use frames to provide the user with only the command buttons that are appropriate to a specific task. I have used several variations of this method in my own programs.

The first use of this technique is in data-entry applications. In a typical application, you have buttons that allow you to move from record to record within a table. This lets the user display data and search for a particular record. Figure 17.18 shows a typical set of buttons.

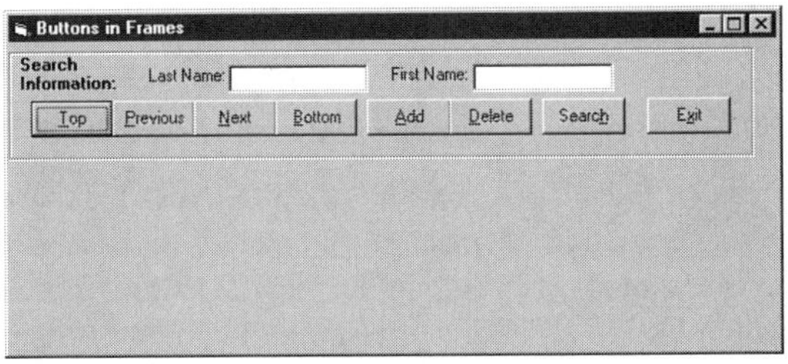

FIG. 17.18

One set of buttons shown is for record navigation.

However, as soon as the user starts editing the record, you would want to display buttons that allow her to either save the changes or cancel the changes and return the original values to the display. Also, it is a good idea to avoid any problems that might be associated with moving to other records while editing is in progress. How can you handle this? Frames to the rescue!

By placing the record navigation buttons in one frame and the Save and Cancel buttons in another frame, you can easily switch between the two buttons sets. To make the switch, you simply set the `Visible` property of one frame to `True` and set the other one to `False`. This is handled by code similar to that shown in Listing 17.3. The code also changes the `ForeColor` property of the controls to give a visual indication to the user that she is in edit mode. You can call this code from the `Change` event of your text boxes so that it is invoked whenever the user makes a change. Figure 17.19 shows the same form after the button switch.

Listing 17.3   SWITCH.FRM—Use Multiple Frames to Handle Command Button Sets

```
Dim I As Integer

' For the sake of this example, we have an array of 8 text boxes
For I = 0 To 8
    txtOrg(I).ForeColor = vbRed
Next I

'Here we hide one frame and then show another
fraRecNav.Visible = False
fraSave.Visible = True
```

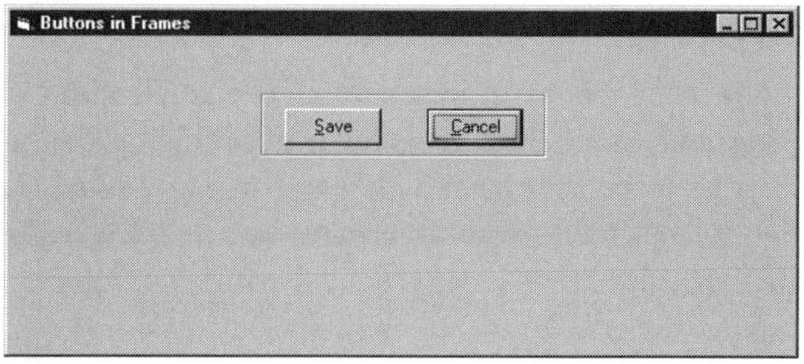

FIG. 17.19

A second set of buttons is used to handle Save and Cancel functions.

A second use of frames for containing buttons is to display only the functions that a user is allowed to see. In one of my applications, different sets of command buttons were available to users with different security levels. By grouping the buttons in frames, it was easy to show only those buttons that corresponded to the user's security level.

Creating Browse and Detail Pages

One use of the two-page form is to create a browse and detail page for information in a database. The browse page would use a grid control to display selected information from a number of records. The detail page would then display all the information for the record currently selected in the grid. A single command button could be used to make the switch between the two pages. Figures 17.20 and 17.21 show the two views of the data.

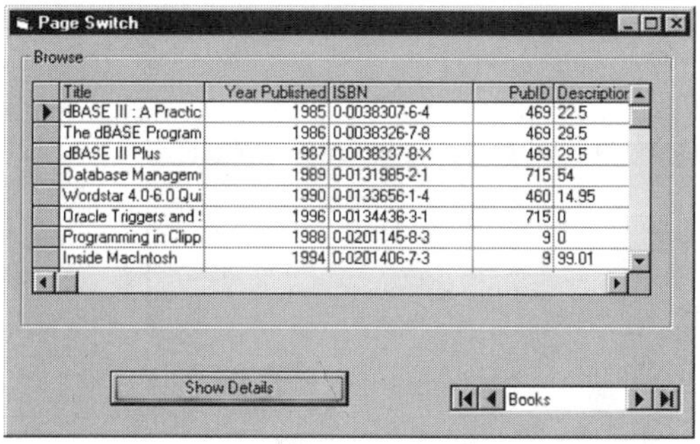

FIG. 17.20

Browse multiple records to get an overall view of data.

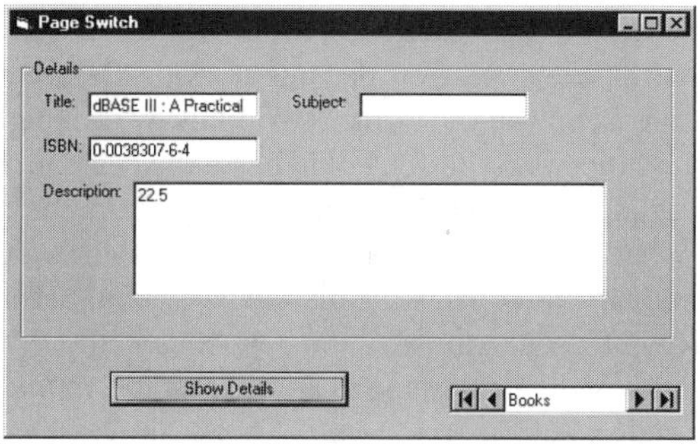

FIG. 17.21

Switch to detail view to get more information or to edit the data.

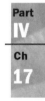
Part
IV
Ch
17

Creating Your Own Wizard

You have probably come across *wizards* in several of the applications that you use. Wizards are actually miniature programs that help you perform a specific task step-by-step. For example, Word has a wizard that helps you perform a mail merge, and Visual Basic has a wizard that helps you set up a data access form. You can create your own wizard by using a series of frame controls. To make the wizard that we create really flexible, we will use control arrays for the frames and the command buttons. This makes the wizard easier to set up and easier to program.

▶ **See** "Advanced Control Techniques," **p. 495**

The first step in creating a wizard is to set up a frame template. To do this, start with a clean form and draw a frame that is the size you need for all the pages of your wizard. Next, check the Height and Width properties of the form and place code in the Load event of the form to set these properties to their initial values. You will see why this is necessary in a moment. After drawing the frame, set its Name property to a unique name. Next, delete the text in the Caption property so that you have an unbroken border on the frame. Finally, create the first element of the frame array by setting the Index property to 0.

After you have set up the frame, you need to set up three command button arrays. Within each frame we will place command buttons with captions set to Exit, Previous, and Next. To create a command button array, draw a command button on the frame and set its Name and Caption properties. Then set its Index property to 0. As with the frame array, this creates the first element of each button array. After you have added the command buttons, your form should look like Figure 17.22.

FIG. 17.22

Start the wizard by creating a template frame as the first element of a control array.

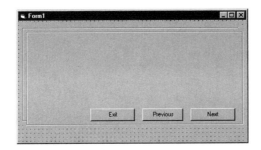

The reason for using control arrays will now become obvious. Before you place any other control on the frame, make a copy on the form. You do this by clicking the frame, pressing Ctrl+C to make a copy, and then pressing Ctrl+V to paste the copy on the form. As you make the copy of the frame, you also create copies of all the controls in the frame. This makes it easy to create multiple pages that have the same basic look. Also, by using command button arrays, you only have to enter code in one place to handle the navigation between pages. Listing 17.4 shows the code that would be used to move to the next page in the wizard. This code also sets the Top and Left properties of the next frame to assure that it is in the same position as the previous frame. Similar code would be used to move to the previous page. Also, if you had processing that needed to occur between pages, you could use a `Select` statement and check the `Index` argument to determine which page you are on.

Listing 17.4 WIZARD.FRM—Use a Control Array to Facilitate the Programming of the Wizard

```
Private Sub cmdNext_Click(Index As Integer)
 fraWizard(Index).Visible = False
 fraWizard(Index + 1).Visible = True
 fraWizard(Index + 1).Top = 240
 fraWizard(Index + 1).Left = 240

 Select Case Index + 1
    Case 1
         'Code to process first page goes here
    Case 2
         'Code to process second page goes here
 End Select
End Sub
```

Part
IV

Ch
17

After you have created all the pages you need, you need to place a Finish button on the last page. Also, on the last page, you need to disable or hide the Next button because there is no next page. Similarly, you should disable the Previous button on the first page of the wizard. At this point, the shell of your wizard has been created and you can begin setting up the other controls for the individual pages.

From Here...

Containers provide a number of useful functions in your programs. They allow you to place more information on your forms, create groups of options, and even create your own wizards. To learn more about some of the other topics mentioned in this chapter, take a look at the following chapters:

- To learn more about using picture boxes, see Chapter 12, "Working with Graphics."
- To learn more about option buttons, see Chapter 15, "Working with the Standard Controls."
- To learn more about control arrays, see Chapter 19, "Advanced Control Techniques."

CHAPTER 18

Exploring New Visual Basic 5 Controls

Displaying information in a grid

Learn how to present data to your users in a grid format with the MSFlexGrid control.

Playing video clips

Add AVI animations to your programs with the Animation control.

Making data entry easier

The UpDown Control can be used with a TextBox or other control to aid in entering numeric values.

In some of the previous chapters, you learned about many of the controls that you can use in Visual Basic. These controls are the heart and soul of most programs that you create. In Chapter 15, "Working with the Standard Controls," you learned about many of the controls that have been a part of Visual Basic since its inception. These controls let you work with text, handle choices, work with lists, and initiate program actions. In Chapter 16, "Using the Windows Common Controls," you learned about the controls that are used in many Windows 95/Windows NT programs. ■

If you have followed the progress of Visual Basic, you know that each new version brings with it new and enhanced controls. In version 5 of Visual Basic, Microsoft did not disappoint us. Visual Basic 5 contains some new controls that give you greater capabilities in your programs. Three of these controls are the subject of this chapter:

- *MSFlexGrid* Displays information in a tabular form like a spreadsheet or the grid display of a database program

- *Animation* Enables you to display animation sequences with no sound

- *UpDown* Works with other controls to enable you to increment the value of a control such as a text box or label

N O T E The controls discussed in this chapter are available only in the Professional and Enterprise Editions of Visual Basic. If you are using the Learning Edition, you won't be able to re-create the examples. ▪

Using the MSFlexGrid Control

Much of the information that computer programs deal with is presented in the form of columns and rows. The most common example of a program which deals with this type of information display is a spreadsheet. Since spreadsheets were among the first successful commercial PC programs, and spreadsheet software is one of the two most widely used program categories in the world (word processors being the other), it is safe to assume that people have become very comfortable seeing data displayed in rows and columns. In fact, for many people, and many types of data, this is the preferred method of viewing information.

Figure 18.1 shows a typical table view of data.

FIG. 18.1

A table view allows users to quickly view and process a large amount of data.

Visual Basic has two separate controls for working with rows and columns of information: the DBGrid control for displaying and editing the contents of a database, and the new MSFlexGrid control for handling many other grid display needs. The DBGrid control is covered in Chapter 27, "Doing More with Bound Controls."

N O T E The MSFlexGrid control can be bound to a data control to display information from a database. However, the information is displayed as read-only and therefore cannot be modified as it can with the DBGrid control. ■

The MSFlexGrid control is capable of displaying text or pictures in any of its cells. Moreover, you can use the grid to sort information in the tables and format the information for easier viewing. The FlexGrid, as it's also known, is capable of fixing (or freezing) rows and columns along the top and left edges of the grid. This lets you provide labels for the items that are always displayed to the user. Sounds great, right? Then let's take a look at how this grid works.

Setting Up the MSFlexGrid Control

The first step to using the MSFlexGrid control is to add it to the Toolbox. You do this by choosing Project, Components. This brings up the Components dialog box, which allows you to add and remove controls and other components from your project. To add the MSFlexGrid, select the check box next to the control name and click OK. The control is listed as *Microsoft FlexGrid Control 5.0* and is contained in the Msflxrd.ocx file, usually in your \Windows\System directory. When you close the Components dialog box, the FlexGrid is added to the Toolbox. It appears as a yellow grid with a cylinder attached.

After adding the control to the Toolbox, you are ready to add a FlexGrid to your form. Do this by clicking the control and then drawing it on the form. The FlexGrid is initially drawn with two rows and two columns as shown in Figure 18.2.

FIG. 18.2
Resizing the FlexGrid in the design environment does not change the number of rows or columns.

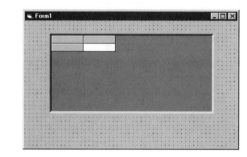

After drawing the control on the form, you first want to specify a unique name for the control. Then you are ready to begin setting the properties that will control its appearance and behavior.

Controlling the FlexGrid's Appearance   There are several properties that affect the appearance of the FlexGrid control. The FlexGrid control is much more customizable than the standard grid included with previous versions of Visual Basic. Properties can be used to control the headers of the grid, the colors that are used to indicate the various states of cells, and, of course, the fonts used to display information.

The Rows and Cols properties of the FlexGrid determine how many total rows and columns display in the grid. If the number of rows and columns is greater than can fit on-screen, the FlexGrid automatically provides scroll bars. Some of the displayed rows and columns can set as *fixed* (non-scrolling), which creates Excel-style headers. The headers are controlled by the FixedRows and FixedCols properties. The default value of these properties is 1, but you can set them to anything from 0 up to the value of the Rows and Cols properties, respectively. These four properties are illustrated in Figure 18.3.

FIG. 18.3
Use fixed rows and columns for the headers of the grid.

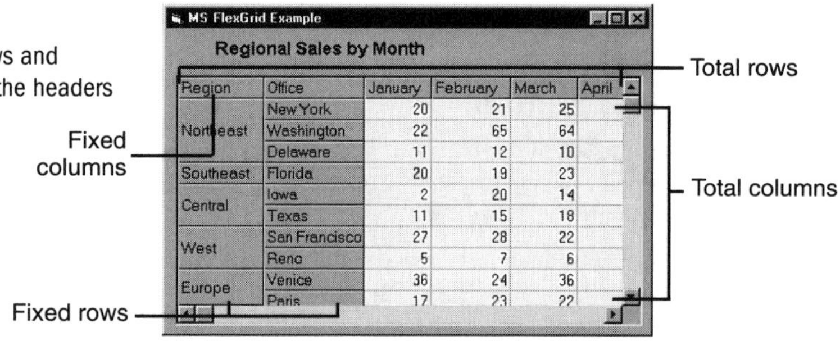

To control the colors displayed, the FlexGrid control has five major sets of color properties. These properties are summarized in Table 18.1.

Table 18.1   Color Properties

Background Color Property	Foreground Color Property	Color Use
BackColor	ForeColor	Controls the colors of any standard cells in the grid. A standard cell is one that is not part of the fixed rows or columns and is not selected.
BackColorFixed	ForeColorFixed	Controls the colors of the "header" cells in the fixed rows and columns.
BackColorSel	ForeColorSel	Controls the colors in cells that are selected.
BackColorBkg	N/A	Controls the color of the "empty space" in the FlexGrid control that is not occupied by any cells.
CellBackColor	CellForeColor	Controls the color of an individual cell. Can only be used during runtime.

The font information for most cells in the grid is controlled by the Font property of the grid itself. This property has the same effect as the Font property in other controls. However, you can format individual cells with different fonts using the properties listed as follows:

- `CellFontName` Specifies the name of the font for the given cell
- `CellFontSize` Specifies the size of the font for the cell
- `CellFontBold` Determines whether the font appears in boldface
- `CellFontItalic` Determines whether italic fonts are used
- `CellFontUnderline` Determines whether text in the cell appears underlined

When the settings of the `CellFont` properties are changed, the properties will affect only the current cell, unless a group of cells is selected. If multiple cells are selected, the property change affects all the selected cells.

To change the appearance of an individual cell, you can use the `Color` and `Font` properties in conjunction with the `Row` and `Col` properties. For example, the following code selects the cell in row 3, column 4, and then changes it to a bold red font:

```
fgMain.Row = 3
fgMain.Col = 4
fgMain.Text = "Bold Font"
fgMain.CellFontBold = True
fgMain.CellForeColor = vbRed
```

In addition to handling the cells' colors, the FlexGrid control gives you control over the lines that make up the grid. These lines are controlled by the following properties:

- `GridColor` Sets the color of the grid lines in all standard cells
- `GridColorFixed` Sets the color of the grid lines in the fixed cells
- `GridLines` Sets the appearance of the grid lines for the standard cells. This property can have one of these settings:

  0 - `flexGridNone` (no grid lines)

  1 - `flexGridFlat` (flat grid lines)

  2 - `flexGridInset` (inset grid lines)

  3 - `flexGridRaised` (raised grid lines)

- `GridLinesFixed` Sets the appearance of the grid lines in the fixed cells. This property has the same possible settings as the `GridLines` property
- `GridLineWidth` Sets the width of the lines use to make up the grid

Controlling the FlexGrid's Behavior As you know, the properties of a control affect not only its appearance, but its behavior as well. The FlexGrid is no exception. The FlexGrid has several unique properties that control how it behaves while running in your program. These properties include:

- `AllowBigSelection` Determines whether the user can select a row or column by clicking the header (fixed cell) of the row or column. The default value of this property is `True`.
- `AllowUserResizing` Determines whether the user can change the size of the rows or columns in the grid. The property has four possible settings:

     0 - `flexResizeNone` (no resizing allowed, the default)

     1 - `flexResizeColumns` (the user can resize columns only)

     2 - `flexResizeRows` (the user can resize rows only)

     3 - `flexResizeBoth` (the user can resize rows and columns)

When allowed, the user can resize a row or column by clicking the mouse on the grid line to the right or below a cell and then dragging the mouse to set the new size.

- `FillStyle`   Determines whether setting the value of a cell property will affect only the current cell or all selected cells. The default value (0 - `flexFillSingle`) allows only the current cell's properties to be set. Changing the `FillStyle` property's value to 1 - `flexFillRepeat` causes setting a cell property (such as `CellFontName` or `Text`) to set the value for all selected cells.

- `MergeCells`   Determines whether adjacent cells with the same contents will be merged to be shown in the grid as a single cell. This feature is useful in presenting information such as sales data where you might have multiple sales people in the same region. The property's default value is 0 for no merging. You can change the value to 1 to allow merging of anywhere in the grid, 2 to allow merging across columns but not across rows, or 3 to allow merging across rows but not across columns. Figures 18.4 through 18.6 show the effects of the `MergeCells` property.

- `SelectionMode`   Determines how the user can select cells in the grid. The default value (0) allows the user to select cells individually, just like you would in a spreadsheet. Setting the `SelectionMode` property to 1 forces selections to cover entire rows, while setting the property to 2 forces the selections to cover entire columns.

- `WordWrap`   Determines whether the text in a cell will wrap to multiple lines (property set to True) or will only show the text that will fit on a single line in a cell (False).

FIG. 18.4

No merging keeps all cells separate regardless of their contents.

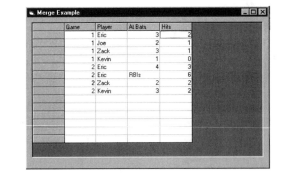

FIG. 18.5

Free merging allows cells to automatically combine if their contents are the same.

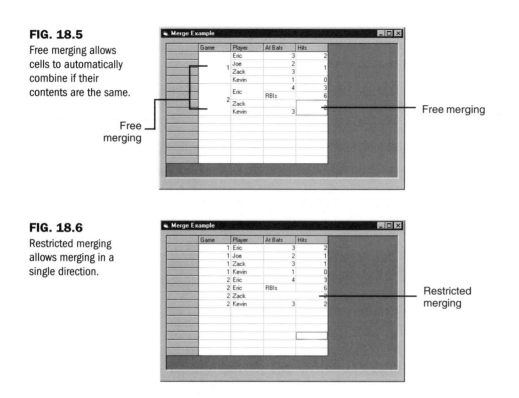

Free merging

Free merging

FIG. 18.6

Restricted merging allows merging in a single direction.

Restricted merging

Binding the FlexGrid to Data

One use of the FlexGrid is to display the contents of a database table or the results of a query. The FlexGrid is can be bound to a data source, but can only display the data from the source; you cannot update via the attached Data control.

To use the FlexGrid to display data, follow these steps:

1. Start a new project and add the FlexGrid to your Toolbox (refer to "Setting Up the MSFlexGrid Control" earlier in the FlexGrid coverage).

2. Place a Data control on your form.

3. Set the DatabaseName property of the Data control to the database containing the desired information.

4. Set the RecordSource property to the name of the table or query that you want displayed. You can also set the property to a valid SQL statement.

5. Add a FlexGrid control to your form.

6. Set the DataSource property of the FlexGrid to the name of the data control you just created.

N O T E   Chapter 26, "Using Data Controls and Reports," contains detailed coverage of setting up
and using data controls. ▮

▶ **See** "Understanding the Data Control," **p. 678**

Figure 18.7 shows a FlexGrid being used to display information from biblio.mdb, a sample
database included with Visual Basic. The RecordSource property of the data control has been
set to the following SQL statement:

```
Select PubID, Name, [Company Name] from Publishers
```

As you can see, the column headings default to the field names in the query results.

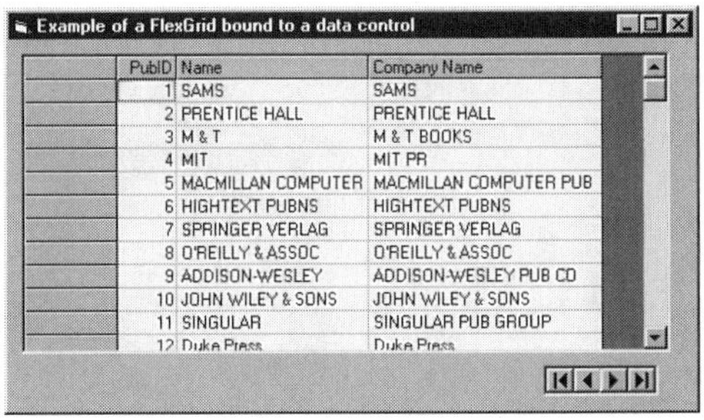

FIG. 18.7

You can display
information from a
database in the FlexGrid
control.

Working with the MSFlexGrid Control in Code

Obviously, the FlexGrid would be of limited value if you could only make changes to it at design time or use it only to display database information. You can, of course, work with the grid
and its contents from your program code. Most of the properties that you can set at design
time can also be set from program code. In addition, there are other properties that enable you
to set and retrieve the contents of individual cells. There are also several methods and events
that are specific to the FlexGrid control. You take a look at these features in this section.

Working with Cells   The most common task that you will perform in working with a grid is
setting or retrieving the value of a cell. In the FlexGrid, the contents of all cells are treated as
text strings. This means that you have to perform the appropriate checks and conversions if
you need to retrieve numerical values or dates from the cells.

There are three properties that you can use to set or retrieve the value of a cell in the FlexGrid:
Text, TextArray, and TextMatrix. You can use each of these properties to retrieve or set the
value of a single cell.

When used to retrieve a value, the Text property returns the value of the current cell. This cell
is defined by the settings of the Row and Col properties. The following code shows how you
would retrieve the value of the cell in the second row and second column of the grid:

```
fgMain.Row = 1
fgMain.Col = 1
txtReturn = fgMain.Text
```

N O T E The row and column numbers are zero-based, meaning that the first row is row 0, the second row is row 1, and so forth. ▮

When using the Text property to set a value, the cell(s) that are affected depend on the setting of the FillStyle property and the current user selection. If only a single cell is selected, the Text property only sets the value of the selected cell. If multiple cells are selected, the Text property will set the value of the current cell if the FillStyle property is set to 0, or will set the value of all the selected cells if the FillStyle property is set to 1. The Text property has one disadvantage in its use: You can only retrieve or set the value of the current cell. This means if you want to process multiple cells, you will have to set the Row and Col properties for each cell's value you want to retrieve:

```
fgMain.Row = 1
fgMain.Col = 1
fgMain.Text = "One Cell"
fgMain.Col = 2
fgMain.Text = "Another Cell"
```

The TextArray property provides another means of setting and retrieving the value of a cell. The TextArray property can be used to retrieve the value of any cell, not just the current cell. This makes it a little easier to use than the Text property for working with multiple cells. The TextArray property uses a single index to specify the cell to be retrieved. This index is determined by multiplying the desired row number by the number of columns in the grid and then adding the desired column number. This index numbering system is shown in Figure 18.8. The following code shows how to retrieve the value from the cell in the third column of the second row:

```
inDesiredCol = 2
inDesiredRow = 1
txtRet = fgMain.TextArray(inDesiredRow * fgMain.Cols + inDesiredCol)
```

FIG. 18.8

TextArray indexes go across each row sequentially.

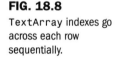

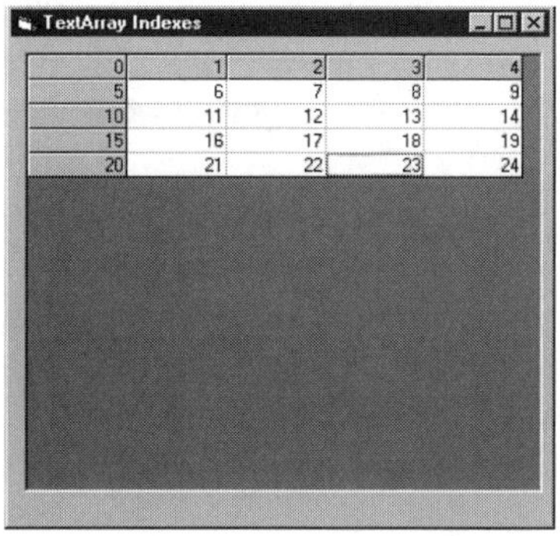

The final property for setting and retrieving the value of a cell is the TextMatrix property, which requires two arguments: the index of the row and the index of the column to be retrieved. This is probably the easiest of the value properties to use. The following code shows how the TextMatrix property would be used to retrieve the value from the cell in the third column of the second row:

```
txtReturn = fgMain.TextMatrix(1,2)
```

Notice in Figure 18.8 that the row and column numbers start with 0. Therefore, code example row 1 is actually the second row in the grid, and column 2 is the third column.

Adding and Deleting Rows There are two ways that you can change the number of rows that are contained in the FlexGrid: You can change the Rows property of the grid, or you can use the AddItem and RemoveItem methods. Whereas changing the Rows property adds or removes items from the bottom of the grid, the FlexGrid's methods let you control the insertion and deletion points.

N O T E The only way to change the number of columns is by setting the Cols property of the grid. ▨

The AddItem method enables you to add a new row to the FlexGrid control. By default, the row is added to the bottom of the grid. You can, however, specify an index value for the method to insert the row somewhere else in the grid. This method works the same way as a list box's AddItem method. When using the AddItem method, you must specify the text to insert in at least the first column of the grid. The following lines of code show how the AddItem method can be used:

```
fgMain.AddItem "NewRow"
fgMain.AddItem "NewRow",2
fgMain.AddItem "NewRow" & Chr(9) & "NewRow"
```

N O T E To specify the values for multiple cells, create a text string containing the values of all the input cells, in column order. Between each pair of values, insert the Tab character by using the Chr(9) function. ▨

To delete a specific row from the grid, you use the RemoveItem method, which requires you to specify the row number of the row to be removed. This method works in a similar manner to the RemoveItem method of the ListBox control. The following code shows you how to remove the second row of the grid. (Remember that row numbers are zero-based.)

```
fgMain.RemoveItem 1
```

N O T E The AddItem and RemoveItem methods do not work with fixed rows. ▨

To clear the entire grid, you use the Clear method, as shown in the following line:

```
MSFlexGrid1.Clear
```

Understanding the Unique Events of the FlexGrid The FlexGrid control responds to many of the same events as other controls. There are, however, several unique events that you will find useful as you program the grid:

- **EnterCell**   Fires each time the focus moves into a cell. This is similar to a control's **GotFocus** event. The event procedure does not pass the index of the cell as a parameter. Therefore, you have to use the **Row** and **Col** properties of the grid to determine the cell.

- **LeaveCell**   Fires when the focus moves out of a cell. This is similar to the **LostFocus** event of a control.

- **RowColChange**   Fires when the focus is moved from one cell to another.

- **SelChange**   Occurs when the selection of cells changes to a different cell or range of cells.

A possible use of these events is updating another control when a user chooses a new cell. For example, you could have report detail information displayed when a user clicks a particular cell.

Using Video in Your Programs

The Animation control provides you an easy way to get animation in your programs. You use the Animation control to play silent AVI (Audio Video Interleaved) clips. The AVI file format is basically aseries of bitmaps that are shown in sequence to create the animation effect, similar to the individual drawings in a cartoon. You would typically use the Animation control to indicate that a task is in progress, such as the File Copy routine of Windows 95, shown in Figure 18.9. These animations run in the background while other tasks are performed.

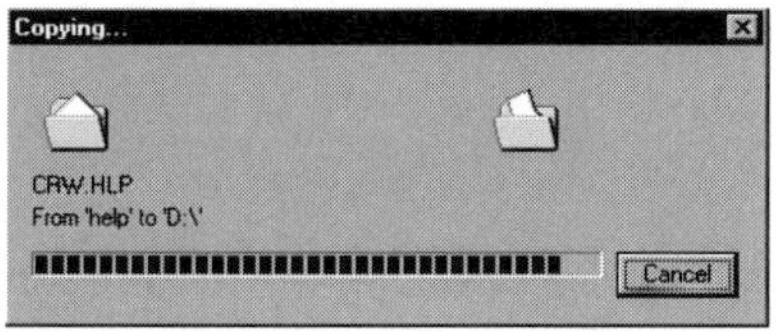

FIG. 18.9
A copy in progress is indicated by a simple animation.

Part
IV

Ch
18

N O T E   Another way to create simple animation effects might be to use a Timer control to change the position of an Image control at a specified interval. Although this method requires a little more coding than is necessary with the Animation control, you do not need to have your animation already saved in an AVI file. The Timer control is covered in Chapter 15, "Working with the Standard Controls."

You can find additional information about creating your own animation in Chapter 34, "Working with Sound and Multimedia."

▶ **See** "Counting Time," **p. 421**

▶ **See** "Using Animation in Your Programs," **p. 881**

Setting Up the Animation Control

The Animation control is one of the two controls contained in the Windows Common Controls 2 set. The other control is the UpDown control discussed in the later section called "Using the UpDown Control." These controls are contained in the file Comct232.ocx. To use the Animation control, you have to first add "Microsoft Windows Common Controls-2 5.0" to your

Toolbox by using the Components dialog box. Choose <u>P</u>roject, <u>C</u>omponents to access this dialog box.

 After you have added the Animation control to your Toolbox, you can add an instance of the control to your form by drawing it on the form. Figure 18.10 shows the initial appearance of the Animation control.

FIG. 18.10
The Animation control initially looks like a picture box with a reel of film in the middle.

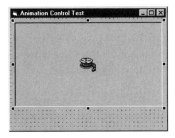

Running the Animation Control

Drawing the Animation control on the form provides the container for the animation sequence. However, to run an animation, you need to open a file and start playback.

To open a file, use the Open method of the Animation control. (Several AVI videos are included in the \Graphics\AVIs subdirectory of Visual Basic, if you chose to install them.) After opening an AVI file, execute the Play method to start the animation. The sample code in Listing 18.1 is used to play an AVI file.

Listing 18.1   ANIMATE.FRM—Using *Open* and *Play* to Start Running an Animation

```
Private Sub cmdPlayAvi_Click()

 anmAVIPlayer.Open  "D:\VB5\Graphics\AVIs\filenuke.avi"
 anmAVIPlayer.Play

 End Sub
```

T I P   You can set the Animation control's AutoPlay property to True to start the video automatically, without executing the Play method.

To stop the animation, simply use the Stop method of the control as shown in the following line of code:

```
anmAVIPlayer.Stop
```

Figure 18.11 shows the setup of the Animation control with a CommonDialog control and command buttons to start and stop the playback of the video. Figure 18.12 shows the program in use.

FIG. 18.11

The complete setup of the Animate project includes buttons to control playback.

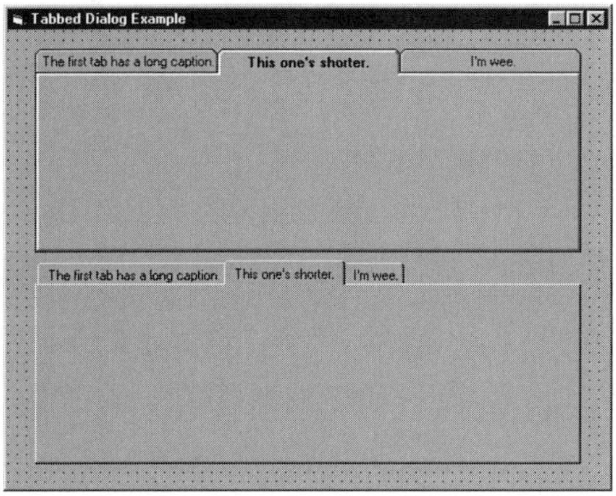

FIG. 18.12

Running the Animate project and pressing the Play Animation button causes the video to play repeatedly.

The project shown in Figures 18.11 and 18.12 is available in the file Animate.Vbp, which you can download from **www.mcp.com/info/0-7897/0-7897-1288-1.**

Working with Optional Parameters

The code shown in Listing 18.1 "loops" the video's playback. In other words, the animation will be played over and over from start to finish until the Stop method executes. There are, however, three optional parameters to the Play method which allow you to change this behavior:

- Repeat—Specifies the number of times to play the video segment.
- Start—Specifies the frame where playback should begin.
- Stop—Specifies the frame where playback should end. You can use the Windows 95 Media Player (mplayer.exe) to find out frame numbers.

Part

IV

Ch

18

These optional parameters are used in the following line of code, which repeats frames 5 through 15 of an animation two times:

```
anmAviPlayer.Play 2, 5, 15
```

You can specify any or all of the optional parameters. Any parameters that are omitted will use their default values. The parameters must be specified in the order `Repeat`, `Start`, and `Stop`. If you omit one of the earlier parameters, you must use a comma as a placeholder.

Using the UpDown Control

The UpDown control is unique in that it is not designed to be a stand-alone control. Instead, it is designed to work with another "buddy" control to allow the user to easily modify its numeric values. The UpDown control, shown in Figure 18.13 with a text box, consists of a pair of arrow buttons. These buttons let the user increment or decrement the value of a numeric control. The UpDown control can be used with any other control that can handle numbers, including text boxes, labels, scroll bars, and sliders.

FIG. 18.13
The UpDown Control allows the user to adjust the value of a number.

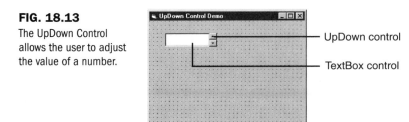

UpDown control

TextBox control

Setting Up the UpDown Control

To use the UpDown control in your program, you must first add it to the Toolbox by using the Components dialog box. The control is part of the group `Microsoft Windows Common Controls - 2`. After you have added the control to your Toolbox by choosing Project, Components, you can add an instance of the control to the form. To set up the UpDown control, follow these steps:

1. On your form, draw a control which is capable of handling numbers, such as the TextBox control.

2. Draw the UpDown control on your form.

3. Set the `BuddyControl` property of the UpDown control to the name of the control which will display the numeric values. Note that you have to type the name of the control (such as **Text1**) or use the `AutoBuddy` property.

4. Set the `BuddyProperty` of the UpDown control to `Default`. This causes the UpDown control to update the default property of its buddy control, such as the `Text` property of a text box.

After completing the basic setup of the UpDown control, you can set other properties to control its appearance and behavior. For controlling the appearance of the UpDown control, the two key properties are:

- Alignment—Controls whether the UpDown control appear to the left or the right of the buddy control

- Orientation—Controls whether the UpDown control's buttons are oriented horizontally or vertically

The effects of the Alignment and Orientation properties are shown in Figure 18.14.

FIG. 18.14
The UpDown control can appear in several forms.

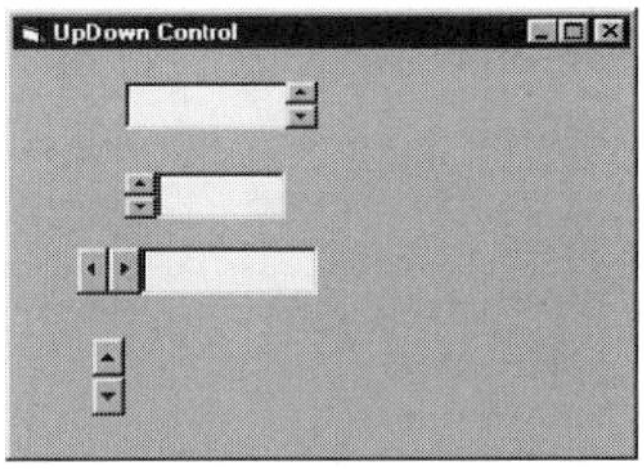

Probably of greater importance to the programmer and user are the properties that determine the behavior of the UpDown control. These properties are:

- Increment — Sets the amount that a value will change each time a button is pressed

- Max—Sets the maximum value the control can contain

- Min—Sets the minimum value the control can contain

- SyncBuddy—Causes the UpDown control to update the buddy control. The only time when you would want this property set to False is if you were using the UpDown control without a buddy control. For example, you might use the UpDown control by itself to allow the user to move between pages in a report.

- Wrap—Determines whether the control starts over with the minimum value if the user presses the up button after the maximum value is reached (or vice versa)

Retrieving the Control's Value

When you use the UpDown control, there are two ways of obtaining the number selected by the user: retrieving the Value property of the UpDown control or retrieving the appropriate property of the buddy control. For almost all cases, you will use the Value property of the UpDown control. The only time you would want to use the property of the buddy control is if the user were allowed to enter a value that is outside the range of the UpDown control.

Part
IV

Ch
18

> **CAUTION**
>
> Keep in mind that the SyncBuddy property previously mentioned updates the buddy control with its values, not the other way around. In the example figures, if a user were to type a number in the text box, the UpDown control's Value property would not be updated. One way to remedy this would be to assign the Value property in the text box's Change event.

Working with the UpDown Control's Events

In addition to the usual events that are present for most controls, the UpDown control has three key events of interest:

■ Change—Occurs any time the Value property of the control is changed

■ DownClick—Occurs when the user presses the down arrow of the control

■ UpClick—Occurs when the user presses the up arrow of the control

From Here...

This chapter introduced you to some of the new controls that were added to Visual Basic 5. The first control, the FlexGrid, allows you to display data in a spreadsheet format. The Animation control lets you add videos to your forms. The UpDown control lets the user change numeric values by using the mouse. To learn more about other controls, refer to the following chapters:

■ To learn about the Visual Basic standard controls, see Chapter 15, "Working with the Standard Controls."

■ To learn about the other group of common controls, see Chapter 16, "Using the Windows Common Controls."

■ To learn about control arrays, see Chapter 19, "Advanced Control Techniques."

■ To learn to create your own controls, see Chapter 20, "Creating ActiveX Controls."

Advanced Control Techniques

By now, you've learned how to use controls to allow your programs to interact with your users. The controls you've added to forms so far have been independent controls, with no particular relationship to other controls on your forms. As you design more complex user interfaces, however, you will often find it convenient to work with controls as a group.

In Chapter 4, "Working with Forms and Controls," you saw how you could select multiple controls in the design environment and manipulate their properties as a group. Although this type of manipulation is convenient at design time, it does nothing to allow you to work with groups of controls while your program is running. Using control arrays can make runtime manipulation of multiple controls easy. ■

Why use control arrays?

You will learn the advantages that control arrays can provide to your programs.

Creating control arrays

You will learn the three different ways to create a control array. You will also see the key property that identifies elements of an array.

Using control arrays

You will see how control arrays can simplify the processing of multiple controls at one time.

Adding controls at runtime

You will see how you can add controls to a form while your program is running, and how this technique can be used to enhance data-driven programming.

Using classes to enhance a control

You will see how you can add capabilities to a control by combining it with a class module.

Using Control Arrays

A control array is a group of controls, all of the same type, that have the same name and are identified by an index. If you are familiar with variable arrays, control arrays are very similar. Each individual control in the array is referred to as an *element* of the array. There are several criteria that each element of a control array must meet:

- Each control must be of the same type. For example, a control array can contain either labels or text boxes, but cannot contain both.
- Each control must have the same value for the Name property.
- Each control is identified by a unique value of the Index property. The Index property is an Integer type; therefore, its maximum possible value is 32767.

Often, a control array's elements will share the same values for appearance-related properties such as Font and BorderStyle, but only the Name property is required to be the same. All other properties can be different for each element of the array.

Understanding the Advantages of Control Arrays

There are a number of advantages to working with control arrays instead of a group of individual controls; these will help you in designing the interface of your program and in handling the program code. Some of the advantages of control arrays are:

- Adding an element to a control array requires fewer resources than adding an individual control of the same type. For example, three independent text boxes (txt1, txt2, and txt3) use more resources than a three-element text box array.
- In the design environment, you can set key properties of the first control in the array and then have these properties carried forward to the other elements of the array as you add them. For example, you could set the DatabaseName property of a data control and then make multiple copies of the control. Each additional copy would reference the same database.
- The elements of a control array share a common set of event procedures. This means you only have to write program code in one place to handle the same event for all controls in the array.
- Control arrays provide the only means of adding controls to a form while your program is running.
- Using control arrays, you can avoid hitting the limit of 254 control names per form. Because a control array uses only one name, you can have as many elements of the array as you need. This allows you to place more controls on a form.

> **CAUTION**
> Placing too many controls on a form will make your forms load slowly and can exhaust your system resources.

Creating a Control Array

All control arrays must be created while you are in the design environment. Although you can add elements to a control array while your program is running, at least the first element of the array must be created at design time. There are three ways to create a control array:

- Add a control to a form and then use copy and paste to duplicate the control on the form.
- Add individual controls to a form and then change the Name properties of all the controls to the same value.
- After adding a control to your form, set its Index property to a number between 0 and 32767.

Let's work through the steps of creating a control array by using the first method described. If you follow along, you will create an array of text boxes that will be used for a membership application. Create the control array following these steps:

1. Create a new TextBox control on a form, as shown in Figure 19.1.

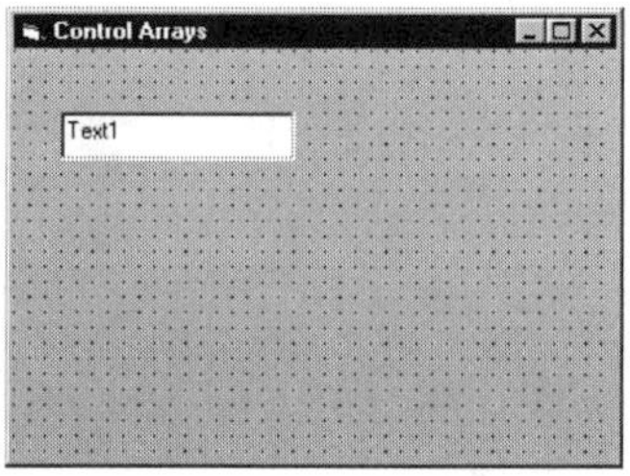

FIG. 19.1

Although this text box will be part of a control array, it is initially created by normal means.

2. Set the Name property of the text box to txtArray (or any other valid name) and clear its Text property.

3. Press Ctrl+C or choose <u>C</u>opy from the <u>E</u>dit menu to copy the control to the Clipboard.

4. Press Ctrl+V or choose <u>P</u>aste from the <u>E</u>dit menu to place the copy of the control on the form.

   At this point, a confirmation box opens that allows you to create a control array (see Figure 19.2).

FIG. 19.2

Choose <u>Y</u>es to create a control array.

Microsoft Visual Basic

You already have a control named 'txtArray'. Do you want to create a control array?

Yes   No   Help

5. Create any additional elements of the control array by repeatedly pasting copies of the control on the form (the original text box that you copied is still on the Clipboard, so you don't have to copy it again).

You don't see the control array confirmation box again, as it appears only when you attempt to make the first copy of the control. As each control is added to the control array, its Index property is assigned a value that is one greater than the Index of the previous element. The indexes of a control array start at 0.

Figure 19.3 shows a completed data entry form that uses three control arrays: one for labels, one for text boxes, and one for command buttons. The figure also points out the Index property of a control. The non-null value of the Index property indicates that the control is part of a control array.

FIG. 19.3

This data entry form was created by using three control arrays.

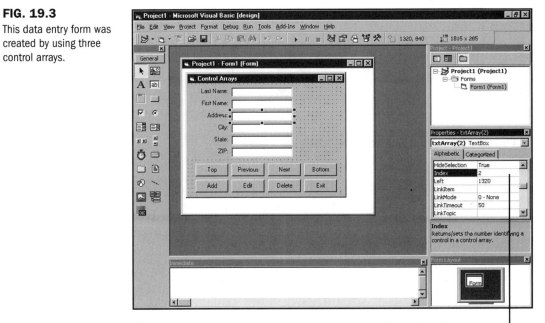

Non-null Index property

Removing Elements from a Control Array

While you are in the design environment, you can remove control array elements from a form by selecting the control element and pressing the Delete key; by choosing Edit, Delete from the menu system; or by right-clicking it and selecting Delete from the context menu. This clears the control from the form and reduces the number of elements of the control array. If, for some reason, you want to return the elements of the control array to individual controls that are not part of the array, you need to specify new Name property values for all but one of the controls and then delete the Index property values of the controls to return them to null values.

CAUTION

When you remove a control from a control array, the rest of the controls are not automatically renumbered. Therefore, deleting controls can leave gaps in the `Index` values of the array's remaining elements. This can cause problems if, for example, you have code that uses a `For` loop to work with the elements of the control array. In this particular case, an error will occur when the loop tries to access a control array element via an `Index` property value that has been deleted.

Writing Code for a Control Array

After you create a control array, you can write a single piece of code to handle an event for all the controls in the array. For each event, Visual Basic passes the index of the control that triggered the event to the event procedure as an argument. This is shown in Figure 19.4.

FIG. 19.4

Control array event procedures can use the `Index` parameter to act according to which element caused the event to occur.

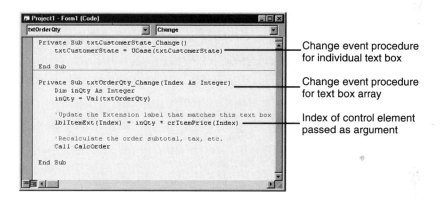

Change event procedure for individual text box

Change event procedure for text box array

Index of control element passed as argument

Part
IV
Ch
19

Handling the Events of the Control Array   If you want to use the same code for each of the elements of the control array, you simply write the code in the event procedure just like you would for a standard control. Then, whenever the event is fired by any of the controls in the array, the code is executed. If you need to execute separate code for one or more specific member(s) of the array, your code can use the `Index` argument to determine which element fired the event. Then you can, for example, place the necessary code within an `If` block or `Select Case` block. An example of this is shown in Listing 19.1.

Listing 19.1   ARRAYSAMPLE.TXT—Using an Event Procedure's *Index* Parameter to Allow Your Code to Determine Which Element Caused the Event to Occur

```
Private Sub cmdSave_Click(Index As Integer)
    If Index = 0 Then
        ChngMember
    End If
    fraNav.Visible = True
```

continues

Listing 19.1   Continued

```
    fraSave.Visible = False
    ResetColor
    Editing = True
    ShowMember
End Sub
```

Manipulating Multiple Controls in Code   The other benefit of using a control array is that you can set properties for each element in an array by using a For loop. This makes it easy for your program to work with all the controls in a control array. For example, in a number of my applications, I change the foreground color of text boxes to red while the user is editing the information on the screen. If the foreground color is black, the user knows that no changes have been made. Changing the colors back and forth is very easy with a control array. Listing 19.2 shows how the colors are changed to red and back to black.

Listing 19.2   ARRAYSAMPLE.TXT—Changing Properties with a Control Array

```
'Changes control color to red to indicate editing
Dim I As Integer
For I = 0 To 22
    txtMember(I).ForeColor = vbRed
Next I

'Changes control color back to default
For I = 0 To 22
    txtMember(I).ForeColor = vbBlack
Next I
```

Using a Control Array in Your Programs

There are a number of uses for control arrays in your programs. The example of changing the text color of text boxes is one. Another example is using Image control arrays to create a toolbar for a program.

To create a toolbar, you need to place three arrays of Image controls on your form. The first array will be the controls actually displayed to the user to create the buttons. The other two arrays contain the Up button and Down button images for each button you want to create. The Visible properties of the controls in these arrays should be set to False. The three arrays of Image controls are shown in Figure 19.5.

After you have created the arrays of images, you can use code to place the Up button images in the displayed buttons when the form loads. Then to simulate the clicking of the button, you place code in the MouseDown event of the imgButton control to display the Down button picture and place code in the MouseUp event to redisplay the original Up button. An example of this code is shown in Listing 19.3.

FIG. 19.5

Three Image control arrays have been added to a form in preparation for creating a toolbar.

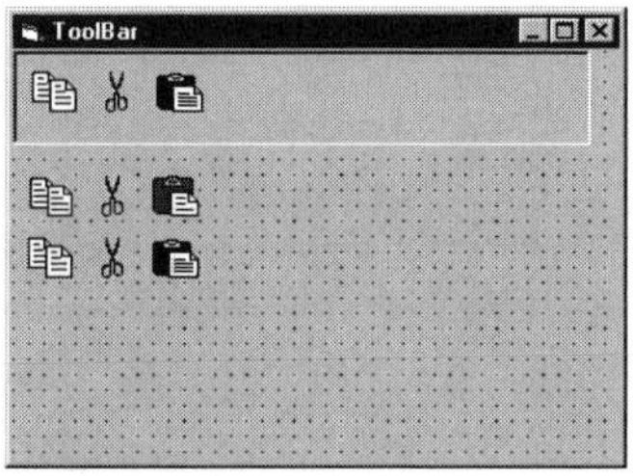

Listing 19.3   ARRAYSAMPLE.TXT—Using Mouse Events to Simulate the Clicking of a Button in Image Control Arrays

```
Private Sub Form_Load()
Dim I As Integer
For I = 0 To 2
    imgButton(I).Picture = imgUpButton(I).Picture
Next I
End Sub

Private Sub imgButton_MouseDown(Index As Integer, Button As Integer,_
    Shift As Integer, X As Single, Y As Single)
imgButton(Index).Picture = imgDownButton(Index).Picture
End Sub

Private Sub imgButton_MouseUp(Index As Integer, Button As Integer,_
    Shift As Integer, X As Single, Y As Single)
imgButton(Index).Picture = imgUpButton(Index).Picture
End Sub
```

You can also use control array processing to find which option button in an array is selected. Because only one option button in a group can be selected at any one time, you can use a For loop to determine the value. This is shown in Listing 19.4.

Listing 19.4   OPTIONARRAY.TXT—Using *LBound* and *UBound* to Determine the Range of the Array

```
Dim I As Integer, optChosen As Integer
For I = optArray.LBound To optArray.UBound
    If optArray(I).Value Then
        optChosen = I
        Exit Sub
    End If
Next I
```

You might notice in Listing 19.4 that, instead of specifying exact values for the ends of the loop, the code used the LBound and UBound properties. These properties return the lower and upper boundaries of the control array indexes, respectively. Using these properties allows your code to automatically handle additions or deletions in the control array. The LBound and UBound properties are only valid for control arrays and cannot be used with an individual control.

Creating a Menu Item Array

In addition to arrays of controls, you can also create an array of menu items. Like control arrays, menu item arrays provide the only means to add items to the menu at runtime. You might use a menu item array to keep a list of the files most recently used by your program. This feature is found in many commercial programs.

 To create a menu item array, you need to be in the Menu Editor (click the Menu Editor button or choose Tools, Menu Editor). You then create menu items by entering the Caption and Name properties of each item. When you create the menu item array, you also specify a value for the Index property of the item. Figure 19.6 shows the Menu Editor with these properties set.

FIG. 19.6

You can set a Menu control's Index property in the Menu Editor to create an array of Menu controls.

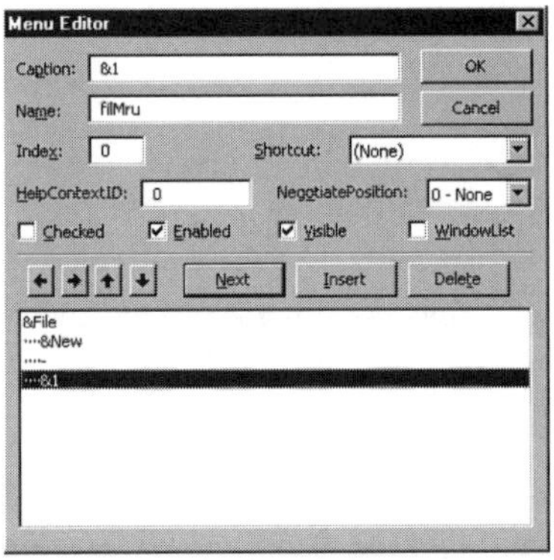

Like control arrays, the elements of a menu item array must meet certain requirements:

- All elements must have the same value for the Name property.
- All elements must be at the same indentation level in the menu.
- All elements must be contiguous in the menu. If you need a separator bar in the menu, it must also be part of the array.
- Each element of the menu array must have a unique index number.

TIP If you plan on adding items at runtime, place the menu item array at the bottom of a menu.

Manipulating Controls at Runtime

In a number of other chapters, you have seen how you can add different controls to forms while you are in the design environment. In the previous section, you even saw how you can create control arrays to handle processing of multiple controls easily in code. However, nothing you have seen yet shows you how to add and remove controls at runtime.

N O T E You can hide and show controls at runtime by setting the `Visible` property appropriately. However, these controls must have been created before they can be used. This is not the same as adding new controls.

The only way to add controls at runtime is to add elements of a control array. You cannot add a new individual control, because there would be no event code to handle any events triggered by the user. Because event code is already defined for a control array, new elements of the array are automatically handled.

CAUTION

If you use `If` or `Select` statements to process code for different index values, you should make sure that your code works for all array elements, even new ones that might have been added at runtime.

Creating the First Element of a Control Array

Because any new control that you add at runtime must be part of a control array, you must create the array, or at least the first element, while you are in design mode. For many arrays, you will want only a single element to be created at design time. This gives you the maximum flexibility to add and remove controls during program execution. To create the first element of a control array, follow these steps:

1. Draw the control on your form.
2. Set the `Name` property of the control.
3. Set the `Index` property of the control to `0`.

This process is illustrated in Figure 19.7 for a text box array.

Adding Controls

After you have created the first element of the array, you can use code to add other elements in response to events. For many applications, you add the controls during form load. One application of this technique would be to create a generic data entry form. By using control arrays, you could pass a recordset to the form and then create the number of controls you need to handle all the fields in the recordset.

Part

IV

Ch

19

FIG. 19.7
Setting a control's
Index property to a
non-null value creates a
control array.

Control

Control name

Index value of 0

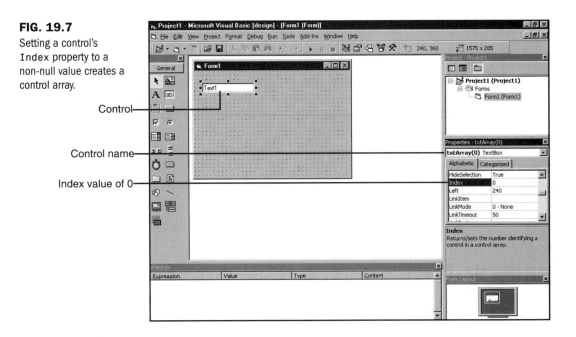

To add a control, you need to use the Load statement. This is the same statement that you can use to bring a form into memory. With the Load statement, you must specify the name of the control to be loaded and its index. To avoid an error, you must also make sure that the index is unique. Note that the new control's Visible property is set to False. The complete process for adding a new control is detailed in the following list:

1. Use the Load statement to create the new control and bring it into memory.
2. Set the new control's Visible property to True to display it on the form.
3. The new control is shown in the same position as the original control because it inherits the properties of the original control. Therefore, you need to move the new control by using the Move method or by setting its Top and Left properties.
4. Set any other necessary properties of the new control.

TIP Setting the index of the new element to one greater than the UBound property of the array ensures that you will have a unique index.

Listing 19.5 shows how the preceding steps are implemented for adding a new text box and displaying it appropriately.

Listing 19.5 Adding a New Element to a Control Array

```
Dim I As Integer
I = txtArray.UBound
Load txtArray(I + 1)
txtArray(I + 1).Visible = True
txtArray(I + 1).Top = txtArray(I).Top + txtArray(I).Height + 120
txtArray(I + 1).Left = txtArray(I).Left
```

The preceding code uses the position of the last control in the array to set the position of the new element. Placing the code in the Click event procedure of a form allows you to add controls each time you click the form. Figure 19.8 shows how the form looks after several clicks.

FIG. 19.8

Control array elements can be added by code.

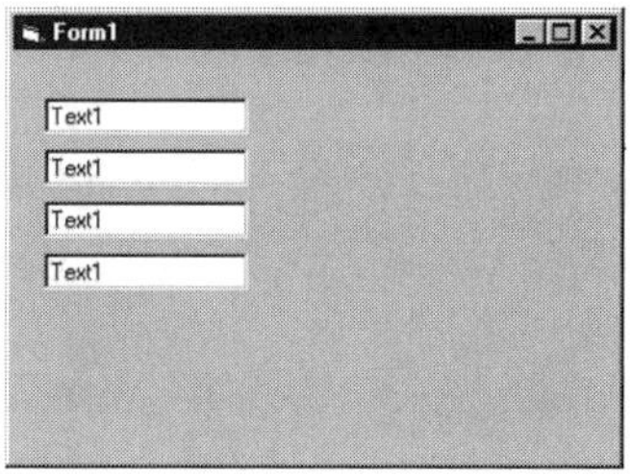

Removing Controls

Just as you may need to add one or more controls at runtime, you might also need to remove one or more controls at runtime as well. To remove a control, you use the Unload statement. Like the Load statement, you need to specify the name of the control and its index. This is shown in the following line of code:

```
Unload txtArray(5)
```

> **CAUTION**
> You cannot unload any control array elements that were created in the design environment.

Part
IV

Ch
19

Creating a Generic Data Entry Form with Control Arrays

We mentioned earlier that you could use control arrays to create a generic data entry form. This form would examine the structure of a recordset and then create controls to handle all the fields in the recordset. In this section, you see how such a form would work.

To keep it simple, the form will have two arrays: one for the labels describing the fields and one for text boxes to hold the field values. To start the setup of the form, you need to add a label array and a text box array to a form, as shown in Figure 19.9. You also need to add a Data control to the form to provide the recordset for the form to use. You will learn about the Data control and related data bound controls in Chapter 26, "Using Data Controls and Reports," and Chapter 27, "Doing More with Bound Controls," a little later in this book.

FIG. 19.9

At design time, the generic data entry form contains the beginnings of two control arrays.

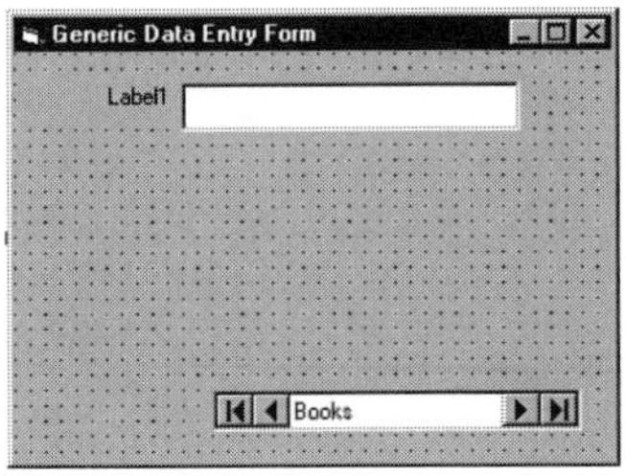

For the Data control, you need to set the DatabaseName and RecordSource properties of the control to access a recordset. After setting up the Data control, assign the control to the DataSource property of the text box. This property is inherited by each of the text boxes you add to the form. Next place the code in Listing 19.6 in the form's Activate event procedure.

Listing 19.6   GENDATA.FRM—Using the *Fields* Collection to Drive the Code for Creating Controls

```
Dim FrstLoad As Boolean

Private Sub Form_Activate()
Dim I As Integer, FieldCnt As Integer
Dim FldName As String
If Not FrstLoad Then Exit Sub
With datBooks.Recordset
    FieldCnt = .Fields.Count
    For I = 0 To FieldCnt - 1
        FldName = .Fields(I).Name
        If I > 0 Then
            Load lblArray(I)
            Load txtArray(I)
            txtArray(I).Top = txtArray(I - 1).Top + txtArray(I - 1).Height + 120
            txtArray(I).Left = txtArray(I - 1).Left
            lblArray(I).Top = txtArray(I).Top
            lblArray(I).Left = lblArray(I - 1).Left
            txtArray(I).Visible = True
            lblArray(I).Visible = True
        End If
        lblArray(I).Caption = FldName
        txtArray(I).DataField = FldName
    Next I
End With
I = txtArray.UBound
datBooks.Top = txtArray(I).Top + txtArray(I).Height + 120
Me.Height = datBooks.Top + datBooks.Height + 525
FrstLoad = False
End Sub

Private Sub Form_Load()
FrstLoad = True
End Sub
```

This code adds a new label and text box for each field after the first one. New controls are positioned directly below the last set of controls. Then the code assigns the Caption property of the Label control and the DataField property of the TextBox control. After all the fields have been added, the code positions the Data control below the other controls and resizes the form to accommodate all the controls. A runtime example of the form is shown in Figure 19.10.

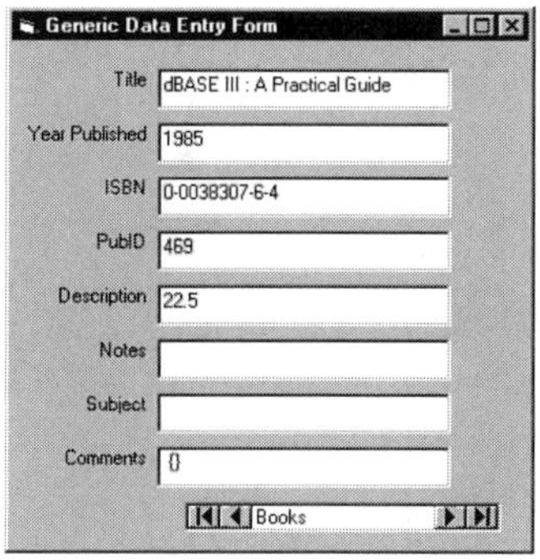

FIG. 19.10

The generic data form can handle almost any recordset.

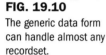

Enhancing a Control with a Class

In Chapter 21, "Extending ActiveX Controls," you see how you can create a new ActiveX control by enhancing the capabilities of an existing control. This is not, however, the only way to improve a control. You can also enhance a control by using code to control how it responds to user actions. For example, if you want to limit a text box to accepting only numbers, you can place the following code in the KeyPress event of the control:

```
If (KeyAscii <> 8) And (KeyAscii < 48 Or KeyAscii > 57) Then
    KeyAscii = 0
    Beep
End If
```

This is great for occasional use with small amounts of code. But suppose your code is fairly complex and needs to be used by a number of controls in your program. You could copy the code to the event procedures of every control that needs it, but this would take up a lot of space in your program and would be a maintenance nightmare.

There is, of course, a better way to handle the code for enhancing a control—use a *class module* to encapsulate the code. In this way, the code is located in one place but is accessible from anywhere in your program, as well as from other programs. This cuts down on the size of your code and greatly simplifies maintenance.

To demonstrate the principles of using a class to enhance a control, let's look at adding typeahead capability to a data bound combo box. With this capability, as you type characters in the edit portion of the combo box, the class locates the first occurrence of the characters in the recordset. It then places this information in the Text property of the combo box with the

Part

IV

Ch

19

remainder of the text highlighted. If the entry it finds is the one for which you are looking, you can quit typing. If it is not the right entry, enter the next character. This type of capability is great for data entry applications where users will be using the keyboard more than the mouse to enter data.

Setting Up the Basic Control

The basic control for the typeahead combo is the data bound combo box (DBCombo control) that comes with Visual Basic. This combo box can be bound to a Data control to handle the list of items that is presented to the user. To make the control work, you need to add both a Data control and a data bound combo to a form, as shown in Figure 19.11.

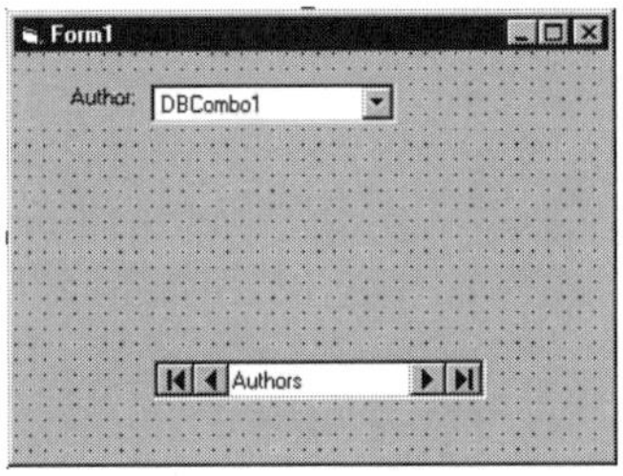

FIG. 19.11

Two controls are needed for the typeahead combo box.

> **N O T E**   For more information about working with data controls and bound controls, see Chapter 26, "Using Data Controls and Reports," and Chapter 27, "Doing More with Bound Controls." ▪

After you add the controls to your form, you need to set a few properties. First, set up the properties of the Data control. For the example, use the Biblio.Mdb database that comes with Visual Basic. Set the `DatabaseName` property of the Data control to this database. (It is typically located in the same directory as Visual Basic's executable.) Next, you need to set the `RecordSource` property of the Data control. You can set this property to the name of a table or query in the database, or you can specify your own query. For the example, you only need to access the names of the authors in the database, and you will want to have them listed in order. Therefore, you need to use a query to create the recordset. Enter the following text in the `RecordSource` property of the data control:

```
Select Author From Authors Order By Author
```

▶ **See** "Using *SELECT* Statements," **p. 758**

You might also want to set the `Name` and `Caption` properties (possibly `datListSource` and `Authors`, respectively) of the Data control. Also, because the control is used only as the source for a list, you need to set its `Visible` property to `False`.

After you have set up the Data control, you are ready to set the properties of the data bound combo box. First, set the Name property of the combo box (for example, dbcAuthors). Then to link the list portion of the combo box to the Data control, you first need to set the RowSource property to the name of the Data control containing the list. In the Properties window, you can select the Data control from a list of those that are on the form. Next, you need to set the ListField property to the name of the field you want displayed (in this case, *Author*). Again, you can select the name from a list of available fields.

That's it! You have now set up the basic controls necessary for the program.

Creating the Class

After you have set up the controls, you need to create the class that will perform the work of finding the entries in the recordset. You start creating a class by adding a Class module to your project. You can do this by selecting the Add Class Module item from the Project menu. When the Class module is added to your program, the Code window for the class opens. Notice that the module has been added to the Project window. You can specify a name for the class by entering a value for the Name property in the Properties window. (The sample project uses EnhCombo.)

▶ **See** "Building a Class in Visual Basic," **p. 832**

Defining the Properties of the Class   The class uses two properties to interface with the data bound combo and Data control. We will call these properties DBCList, which allows you to tell the class the name of the data bound combo, and ListSource, which specifies the Data control that the class is to associate with. Because these properties need to be available as part of the Public interface of the class, you define the properties using Property Set and Property Get procedures.

N O T E   The Property Set procedure is equivalent to the Property Get procedure but is used for objects instead of variables. Because the Data control and data bound combo are objects being passed to the class, the Set procedure must be used. ■

Listing 19.7 shows the procedures used to pass these objects to and from the class module. Notice in the Set procedure that a check is made of the object type to assure that the object will work with the class.

Part
IV

Ch
19

Listing 19.7   ENHCOMBO.CLS—Using *Property Set* Procedures to Pass Objects to a Class Module

```
Public Property Set DBCList(DBCbo As Object)
    '
    ' Make sure object is a DBCombo box and, if so, initialize.
    '
    If TypeOf DBCbo Is DBCombo Then
        Set m_DBCList = DBCbo
        Set m_Edit = DBCbo
```

continues

Listing 19.7   Continued

```
        m_field = m_DBCList.ListField
    Else
        MsgBox "DBCList is not a valid DBCombo."
    End If
End Property

Public Property Get DBCList() As Object
    Set DBCList = m_DBCList
End Property

Public Property Set ListSource(LstSrc As Object)
    '
    ' Make sure object is a Data control and, if so, initialize.
    '
    If TypeOf LstSrc Is Data Then
        Set m_ListSource = LstSrc
    Else
        MsgBox "ListSource is not a valid Data control."
    End If
End Property

Public Property Get ListSource() As Object
    '
    ' Return the current Data control to the caller.
    '
    Set ListSource = m_ListSource
End Property
```

Notice that the Property procedures set the values of internal private variables for the class module to use. Notice also that when setting the property for the data bound combo box, the field containing the actual data field to be searched is set. By linking the search field to the field defined as the ListField of the combo box, you make the class independent of any one recordset.

Defining the Methods of the Class   The search of the recordset and the display of the data are handled by methods of the class. Methods defined in a class are just Sub or Function procedures that use the Public keyword in their declaration. This gives these procedures the capability to be called from outside the class module. For other programs, you might also need to define Private procedures that can only be called from within the class module.

The typeahead combo box uses three such methods to do its work:

- The ShowText method displays the search results to the combo box.
- The ShowSel method highlights the part of the text that was not keyed in.
- The TextSearch method performs the actual search of the data control's recordset.

These three methods are shown in Listing 19.8.

Listing 19.8 ENHCOMBO.CLS—Using Methods to Perform the Data Search

```
Public Sub ShowText(InpText As String)
    m_Edit.Text = InpText
    Call ShowSel
End Sub

Public Sub ShowSel()
    m_Edit.SelStart = 0
    m_Edit.SelLength = Len(m_Edit.Text)
End Sub

Public Sub TextSearch(Kascii As Integer)
    '
    ' Preserve keystrokes
    '
    If m_Edit.SelLength = Len(m_Edit.Text) Then m_Keyed = ""
    '
    ' Process backspace key if pressed or add keystroke to search
    '
    If Kascii = vbKeyBack And Len(m_Keyed) > 0 Then
        m_Keyed = Left(m_Keyed, Len(m_Keyed) - 1)
    Else
        m_Keyed = m_Keyed & Chr(Kascii)
    End If
    '
    ' Look for first entry beginning with the characters
    ' saved. If none found, restore the controls to the previous
    ' state.
    '
    m_ListSource.Recordset.FindFirst m_field & " Like """ _
                                        & m_Keyed & "*"""
    If m_ListSource.Recordset.NoMatch Then
        m_Keyed = Left(m_Keyed, Len(m_Keyed) - 1)
        m_ListSource.Recordset.FindFirst m_field & " Like """ _
                                        & m_Keyed & "*"""
        Beep
    End If
    '
    ' Display the record found
    '
    m_DBCList.Text = m_ListSource.Recordset(m_field)
    m_Edit.Text = m_DBCList.Text
    m_Edit.SelStart = Len(m_Keyed)
    m_Edit.SelLength = Len(m_Edit.Text) - (Len(m_Keyed))
End Sub
```

Linking the Class and the Control

After you have created both the controls for the interface and the class to handle the processing, you are ready to link the two together to let them work their magic. To link the class and the control, you must follow these simple steps:

1. Create a new instance of the class in your form by placing a statement in the Declarations section of the form.

2. Set the DBCList property of the class to the data bound combo you will be using.

3. Set the ListSource property of the class to the Data control containing the list.

4. Call the TextSearch method from the KeyPress event of the data bound combo.

The entire code for linking the data bound combo with the class is shown in Listing 19.9.

Listing 19.9   ENHTEST.FRM—Linking the Class and the Control by Setting Properties

```
Dim EnhCbo As New EnhCombo

Private Sub dbcAuthors_KeyPress(KeyAscii As Integer)
EnhCbo.TextSearch KeyAscii
KeyAscii = 0
End Sub


Private Sub Form_Load()
Set EnhCbo.DBCList = dbcAuthors
Set EnhCbo.ListSource = datListSource
End Sub
```

Testing the Enhanced Control

To test the capabilities of the control, run your program and then begin typing a name in the combo box. As you type, notice that the text changes to match the first name that contains the letters you have entered. Figure 19.12 shows how this would look.

FIG. 19.12

Text search capabilities are added by the class module.

CAUTION

Because the Author table is large, this function might work slowly on some less powerful PCs. It is best to use this with small recordsets.

Now that you have created the class, you can use it any time the need arises. In one of my programs, I used a similar function for four different data bound combo boxes. I only needed to define one instance of the class and then used the GotFocus event of each combo box to set the properties of the class appropriately.

From Here...

This chapter has shown you some of the techniques you can use to make your programs do more with your controls. You've learned how to use control arrays to enhance your ability to work with similar controls as a group. You've also seen how to add controls dynamically while your program is running.

For more information on some of the topics presented here, see the following chapters:

- To learn the basics of controls, see Chapter 4, "Working with Forms and Controls."
- To learn how to create your own controls, see Chapter 20, "Creating ActiveX Controls," Chapter 21, "Extending ActiveX Controls," and Chapter 22, "Creating a User-Drawn Control."
- To learn more about working with the data control, see Chapter 26, "Using Data Controls and Reports," and Chapter 27, "Doing More with Bound Controls."
- To learn more about classes, see Chapter 32, "Using Classes in Visual Basic."

Part

IV

Ch

19

ActiveX Controls

CHAPTER 20

Creating ActiveX Controls

One of the most exciting features of Visual Basic 5 is the ability to create your own ActiveX controls. No longer are you limited to using the controls created by C/C++ programmers; if you can dream up a great control, you can build it yourself by using Visual Basic. What's even better is that you are not limited to using the controls you create only in Visual Basic. You can use your controls in any application or development tool that can use ActiveX controls. This means that you can turn the tables and begin building ActiveX controls in Visual Basic that C++ programmers will be using in their applications. It's a brave new world for the Visual Basic developer.

This chapter discusses building your own controls by using the latest version of Visual Basic. It covers the various approaches that you can take and some of the issues that you need to take into consideration. The information contained in this chapter is then built upon in later sections, as you learn how to build your own ActiveX controls by enhancing an existing control that "almost" does what you need your control to do. ■

ActiveX control evolution

ActiveX controls have gone through quite an evolution over the past few years; see how ActiveX controls have grown and changed from their earliest incarnation as Visual Basic controls.

Options for building ActiveX controls

There are two basic approaches to building ActiveX controls by using Visual Basic 5. Take a look at what each approach involves, and some of the issues you need to consider when choosing between the two approaches.

Building an ActiveX control

You build a simple ActiveX control, learning how to expose the control's properties, methods, and events.

Enhancing ActiveX controls

Learn how you can take an existing control that almost does what you want and transform it into your own special creation.

ActiveX Basics

ActiveX is a technology that was introduced by the Microsoft Corporation in March 1996. It was not really a new technology, but a renaming of Microsoft's existing OLE technologies. These technologies include the OLE Controls that were introduced with Visual Basic 4 during the previous year. It was the OLE/ActiveX controls that introduced a way to build component objects that can be placed in various applications, including Web pages. This enhanced the ability of programmers to build robust applications quickly with pre-built components.

N O T E ActiveX isn't just a new name slapped on an old technology. Along with the new name, Microsoft significantly re-engineered its OLE technologies to make them more "network-friendly." In part, Microsoft removed from the OLE Control (OCX) specification most of the implementation requirements that had added unnecessary overhead to the controls by making them larger and slower than necessary. Along with these changes, Microsoft introduced several new technologies that were aimed specifically for use on the Web, including its Authenticode technology for signing controls and applications. In short, Microsoft put a lot of work into making the evolution of OLE into ActiveX a lot more than just a new name on an old technology.

ActiveX controls can be used in Web pages to add functionality and to greatly improve appearance. As HTML and scripting languages are fairly limited, ActiveX controls have no limitations. Web page designers can interact with the ActiveX controls on their pages with scripting languages such as VBScript.

ActiveX is the next step of the Visual Basic component technology. Visual Basic component technology was started with VBXs, which were used in 16-bit implementations, and were followed by OCXs, which were used in both 16- and 32-bit implementations.

With Visual Basic 5, you can create an ActiveX control as an ActiveX control project. These controls can be used with any container application that supports ActiveX controls. To use an ActiveX control on a Web page, the user's browser must support ActiveX. Microsoft Internet Explorer 3.0 and 4.0 support ActiveX controls. A typical ActiveX control as viewed by IE 3.0 is shown in Figure 20.21.

N O T E Netscape Communicator, the latest version of Netscape's popular Web browser, now supports ActiveX controls. Previous versions of Netscape's browser still require special plug-ins to accept ActiveX controls.

Building and Implementing an ActiveX Control: An Overview

The basic process of building an ActiveX control is simply a matter of following these steps:

1. Determine what you want your ActiveX control to do.
2. Determine what you want your ActiveX control to look like, if you want it to have any appearance at all.
3. Determine what properties, methods, and events your control will provide.

FIG. 20.1

The ActiveX control on this page allows users to select a specific html page based upon contents of the combo box.

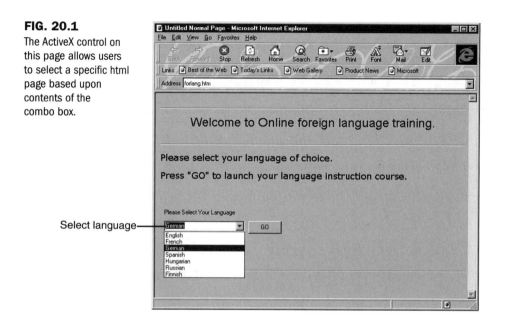

Select language—

4. Determine whether you want to build your control by using the constituent (built-in) controls or by using other controls as building blocks for your control. When considering other controls, consider licensing and distribution issues.

5. Start a Visual Basic ActiveX control project and draw your control.

6. Add code to enable all the properties, methods, and events you want your control to have. Consider whether your control will still be safe for initialization and scripting with the enabling of properties and methods.

7. Create a storage location for your control and all of its supporting files. If you are using a project management system, such as Visual SourceSafe, register your project in it.

8. Build a test project and test your control. Make sure to use all the properties, methods, and events that you gave your control.

9. Compile your control into an OCX.

10. Use the Setup Wizard to build a distributable version, including all the supporting files.

11. If you plan on a Web-based control, test your control on an HTML form. Use the one the Setup Wizard made as a starting point. Test all properties, methods, and events from scripting code.

Two Ways to Build an ActiveX Control

Building a Visual Basic ActiveX control can be as easy or as difficult as you choose. It all depends on whether you can use existing controls in your design, how sophisticated your control's user interface will be, and of course, how much program code you have to write to implement the control's functionality. In any case, there are two basic ways to go about building a control:

    ■ *Assemble the control from existing controls*   This is also know as using *Constituent Controls*. This is the easiest of the two choices, requiring only that you have ActiveX controls.

    ■ *Enhance an existing control*   You can use an existing control as a starting point for your own creative efforts by modifying properties. This is a good way to get the exact functionality that you need in your control.

These two methods of building a control are listed in the order of general difficulty, although, again, how difficult a control is to create depends on several other factors, as well.

This chapter looks at how to create ActiveX controls from existing controls. The next chapter, "Extending ActiveX Controls," explains how you can add additional functionality to your ActiveX controls.

N O T E   Before you begin building an ActiveX control, you need to decide what type of control it will be. Will your control perform all of its functions without using any non-constituent controls? Does the control need another control? Will the control be a visual or non-visual control? These decisions all have to be made before beginning your ActiveX control project. ■

Advantages of Using Constituent Controls

There are many advantages to assembling an ActiveX control from existing controls. The first is obvious: Because your control's user interface consists of existing controls, you don't have to draw the interface yourself. Another advantage is that your control's users will probably already be familiar with the controls that make up your new control. This familiarity makes your new control easier to use.

Still another advantage is that, when you add an existing control to your new custom control, you get the existing control's complete functionality, too; an important consideration when you consider how many event procedures, methods, and properties are supported by a standard control.

You can often use third-party controls as constituent controls, but usually you'll use Visual Basic's standard controls or intrinsic controls. The Visual Basic *intrinsic controls* include the following:

Icon	Name	Description
☑	CheckBox	A small button-like control that the user can check or uncheck.
▤	ComboBox	A control that is comprised of a scrollable list containing valid selections and an edit box into which the user can type selections. The user can also use the mouse to choose selections from the list.

Icon	Name	Description
	CommandButton	A typical push-button type of control.
	Data	A control that you can link to database fields.
	DirListBox	A control that displays the directories on the current drive.
	DriveListBox	A control that displays the drives on the system.
	FileListBox	A FileListBox displays the files in the current directory.
	Frame	A control that enables you to place controls into a group, by providing an outline to enclose the group and a caption to identify the group.
	HScrollBar	A control that represents a horizontal scroll bar.
	Image	A control that displays an image.
	Label	A control that holds a static (unchangeable) line of text.
	Line	A control that enables you to draw lines on a form or control.
	ListBox	A control that features a scrollable list from which the user can make a selection. Similar to a ComboBox, but without the edit box.
	OptionButton	A small, circular, button-like control that the user can use to toggle options on or off.
	PictureBox	A control that's similar to an Image control, but which features more methods.
	Shape	A control you can use to draw various types of shapes on a form or control.
	TextBox	A control that represents an editable line of text.
	Timer	A control that's used in Visual Basic projects to access and control Windows timers.
	VScrollBar	A control that represents a vertical scroll bar.

Part

V

Ch

20

A big advantage of using the intrinsic controls as constituent controls is that you don't need to acquire additional licenses to distribute the controls with your programs. The intrinsic controls are built in to the Visual Basic run-time files that you always need to distribute. If you use third-party controls, you almost certainly have to pay licensing fees. (For more information on licensing, see Chapter 21, "Extending ActiveX Controls.")

Using Constituent Controls

The following sections take a look at how you can use constituent controls to build an entirely new control. The address control that you create can itself become a constituent control for future ActiveX controls; in this way, a complete library of controls can be built up quite rapidly and without a lot of coding.

Creating the Address Control

Now that you have some background information on using constituent controls, you can get started creating your first full-fledged ActiveX control. The control that you'll build in the following sections enables users to enter their name and address into a pre-defined form. To create the control, you'll use Visual Basic Label and TextBox controls as constituent controls. To build this control, follow these steps:

1. Start Visual Basic 5. If it is already running, choose File, New Project.
2. In the New Project dialog box, select ActiveX Control Project. A new project should start with a UserControl object named UserControl1, as shown in Figure 20.2.

FIG. 20.2
ActiveX controls can contain all of the controls that a regular application has.

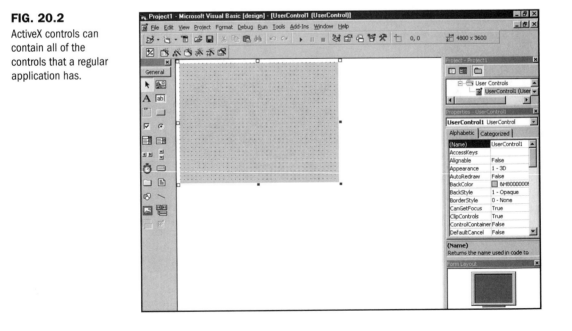

3. Change the `Name` property of the `UserControl` to `AddressPrj`. If the Properties window is not visible, select <u>V</u>iew, Properties <u>W</u>indow or click the Properties Window button. Find the `Name` property and change it by typing **Address.**

4. Add five Labels to the form and give them the following properties:

Name	`lblName`
Caption	`"Name:"`
Name	`lblStreet`
Caption	`"Street:"`
Name	`lblCity`
Caption	`"City:"`
Name	`lblState`
Caption	`"State:"`
Name	`lblZip`
Caption	`"Zip:"`

5. Add five Text boxes to the form with the following properties.

Name	`txtName`
Name	`txtStreet`
Name	`txtCity`
Name	`txtState`
Name	`txtZip`

6. Click the `UserControl` object and resize it so that the constituent controls fit neatly inside. You can resize the control by using the sizing handles or by changing the `Height` and `Width` properties in the Properties window to 3090 and 3810, respectively. The completed form will now look like that shown in Figure 20.3.

FIG. 20.3
The full set of
constituent controls
should look like this.

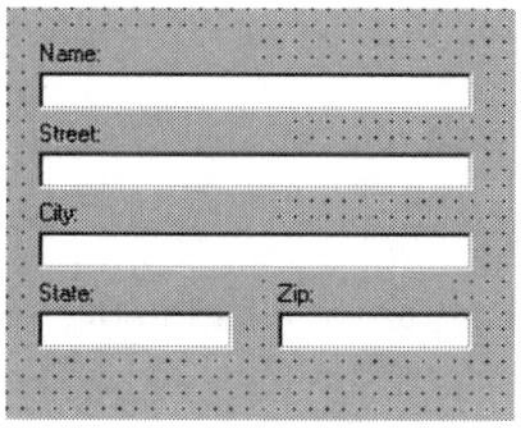

7. Save your project to its own folder, which you should name **..\Samples\Address**. Save the `UserControl` with the name **Address.ctl**. Save the project with the name **Address.vbp**.

Adding Program Code to the Control

The next step is to add code that responds to the `Resize` event, which occurs whenever a control is created or resized.

To add program code for the Resize event, first double-click the UserControl object to display the control's code window. When the window pops up, it'll display the UserControl_Initialize() event procedure. In the Procedures box, select Resize, and the UserControl_Resize() event procedure appears in the code window. Add the lines shown in Listing 20.1 to the UserControl_Resize() event procedure.

Listing 20.1   LSTz_01.TXT—Code for the *UserControl_Resize()* Event Procedure

```
' Don't let the developer make the
' height of the control too small.
If UserControl.Height < 3090 _
    Then UserControl.Height = 3090

' Don't let the developer make the
' width of the control too small.
If UserControl.Width < 1500 _
    Then UserControl.Width = 1500

' Change the width of the controls
' to fit into the resized UserControl.
txtName.Width = ScaleWidth - 500
txtStreet.Width = ScaleWidth - 500
txtCity.Width = ScaleWidth - 500
txtState.Width = ScaleWidth / 2 - 400
txtZip.Width = ScaleWidth / 2 - 400

' Reposition the Zip Code controls.
lblZip.Move ScaleWidth / 2 + 160
txtZip.Move ScaleWidth / 2 + 160
```

After adding the previous lines to the UserControl_Resize() event procedure, be sure to save your changes by clicking the Save Project Group button on VB5's toolbar or by choosing File, Save Project Group.

Understanding *UserControl_Resize()*

When a developer (who uses the control to create an application or Web page) resizes the Address control, be sure that the control's interface still looks okay. For this reason, you don't want the height of the Address control to get smaller because then there won't be room for all the Label and TextBox constituent controls. (Okay, if you really want to, you can use smaller fonts, but who wants to go to all that trouble?) So, the first thing UserControl_Resize() does is make sure that the control's height doesn't get set to less than 3090:

```
If UserControl.Height < 3090 _
    Then UserControl.Height = 3090
```

N O T E   The height of 3090 is an arbitrary number. For the sake of this example, a height of 3090 was chosen. Your control height may be less than or greater than this size. ▪

Now, if the developer tries to make the control too small, UserControl_Resize() will set the height back to where it belongs. The developer can make the control taller, but he can't make it shorter.

N O T E Notice how you can change the value of a property with a line of code such as *Object.Property = Value*, where *Object* is the object whose property you want to change, *Property* is the name of the property to change, and *Value* is the value to which you set the property. Notice also that you separate the object and property names with a period. ▪

Although you have to be careful about how the developer changes the control's height, the control's width has a little more flexibility. Because TextBox controls can scroll text, the TextBox doesn't necessarily have to be wide enough to hold the entire line that the user types in. So, your new control can allow the developer to change the width of the Address control. Still, you want to limit the width to a sensible amount. In Listing 20.1, that limit is 1500, which is enforced like this:

```
If UserControl.Width < 1500 _
    Then UserControl.Width = 1500
```

N O T E As with the height, the width of 1500 is an arbitrary number. For the sake of this example. a width of 1500 was chosen. Your control width may be less than or greater than this size. ▪

Because you can never know how the developer has set the Address control's size, you need to size and position the constituent controls every time a Resize event occurs. The first step in this task is to set the constituent controls' widths, like this:

```
txtName.Width = ScaleWidth - 500
txtStreet.Width = ScaleWidth - 500
txtCity.Width = ScaleWidth - 500
txtState.Width = ScaleWidth / 2 - 400
txtZip.Width = ScaleWidth / 2 - 400
```

ScaleWidth and ScaleHeight hold the width and height of the UserControl object's visible area. In the first three lines of the previous code segment, the code sets the width of the constituent controls to 500 twips less than the width of the UserControl object's visible width. The width of the txtState and txtZip controls is a little trickier to set because these controls are on the same line. To fit these TextBoxes properly, the code first divides ScaleWidth by 2, giving the total amount of space each TextBox can have. Then the code subtracts 400 twips to put a little space between the controls.

Because the controls for the State and Zip fields are on the same line, when the UserControl object changes width, the Zip controls (lblZip and txtZip) have to be repositioned. The UserControl_Resize() event procedure takes care of that little detail like this:

```
lblZip.Move ScaleWidth / 2 + 160
txtZip.Move ScaleWidth / 2 + 160
```

N O T E   You can use an object's Move() method to reposition the object. A call to Move() looks like *object*.Move *left*, *top*, *width*, *height*, where *object* is the object to move, *left* is the position of the object's left edge, *top* is the position of the top edge, *width* is the object's new width, and *height* is the new height. Only the *left* argument is required; that is, *top*, *width*, and *height* are optional arguments. ■

Testing the Address Control

You've created your control's interface and added code to handle one important event. You're now ready to see Address in action, by opening the test application's designer window and adding an instance of the Address control. At this point, you'll be playing the role of an application or Web page developer. In this role, you want to see how the control will act when another developer gets his hands on it.

After you have entered all the code for the control, you are ready to test the control. A good way to test your ActiveX control is in a control project. To test the Address control, follow these steps:

1. Remember to save your code.
2. Add a Standard EXE project to the project group.
3. Close the design and Code windows for the User Control. Notice an icon for your control appears in the Toolbox.
4. Add an instance of the Address control to Form1.
5. Set the properties of the control.
6. Run the test program and try out the control.

If you have problems with the control, you can use the same debugging techniques to find problems in controls that you used to find problems in standard programs. You can set break points and step through the code line by line, whether in the ActiveX Control project or in the Standard EXE project. (See Chapter 21, "Extending your ActiveX Controls," for more information on debugging your code.)

As you can see, the Address control looks exactly as you designed it. That's because the first time the instance appears in the test application's form, it uses the width and height of the control as you set it when you designed the control. The sizes and positions of the constituent controls are handled in the UserControl_Resize() event procedure, based on the current size of the Address control.

To really see UserControl_Resize() in action, reduce the width of the Address control. When you do, the constituent controls automatically resize themselves according to the new Address size. If you try to reduce the height of the Address control, the control springs back to its minimum size. You can, however, enlarge the control as much as you like. If you reduce the width of the control as far as it'll go, you end up with something like Figure 20.4. No matter how narrow you try to make the control, it'll always stay at least at its minimum size.

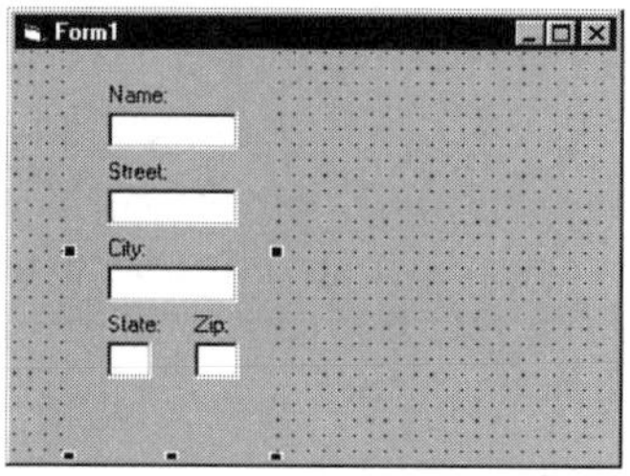

FIG. 20.4

This is the test application when the Address control is at its minimum width.

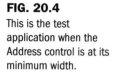

Compiling the Address Control

After you've created and tested your control, you need to compile it into an .OCX file, which is the standalone binary version of the control that you can distribute. When you compile your control into an .OCX file, developers can install the control on their systems and then use the control in their own projects, regardless of whether they're working with a programming language, a Web-page authoring application, or some other development tool.

To create a standalone .OCX file for the Address control, perform the following steps:

1. Double-click Address in the Project Group window. The control's designer window appears.

2. Choose File, Make ADDRESS.OCX. The Make Project dialog box appears.

3. Change the control's file name to **Address.ocx** (you may also need to set the directory to where you want the file to be saved), and click OK. VB5 compiles the new control and writes the .OCX file out to your disk.

4. Choose File, Remove Project. When Visual Basic asks whether you want to remove the project, click Yes. (If you're asked to save files, also choose Yes.)

After completing the previous steps, your project group will contain only the test application, AddressTestApp. However, if you look at Visual Basic's Toolbox, you'll see that the Address control is again available. Now, however, Visual Basic will use the compiled control rather than the version that was originally part of your project group.

N O T E If you need to, you can easily add the Address control project back to the control group from which you deleted it. Just select the File, Add Project command from VB5's menu bar, and then select the project from the Existing page of the Add Project property sheet. ■

The Address control is one of those controls that can easily be used as the basis for other ActiveX controls. One possible use for the Address control is to provide a consistent look and feel to all of your applications that require user data entry. Another possible use is in a Web page to collect data in a guest book control.

The Address control is by no means a complete and robust control. The next few sections will examine how methods and events can be added to your control. Chapter 21, "Extending ActiveX Controls," provides some ways to make your control more robust and bulletproof.

▶ **See** "Extending ActiveX Controls," "Control Error Handling" **p. 581**

Part

V

Ch

20

A Quick Example: Build the AXYesNo

In the previous example, you built an ActiveX control out of constituent controls. You added some code to one of the events and successfully tested the control in a test project. However, you did not add any additional methods or events. You used only those methods and events that were supported by your constituent controls. In the present example, you build an ActiveX control and provide some methods and events.

This ActiveX control has three constituent controls: two command buttons and one label. In this example, you toggle the caption of the label by clicking the two command buttons. To build this control, follow these steps:

1. Start Visual Basic 5. If it is already running, choose File, New Project.

2. In the New Project dialog box, select ActiveX Control Project. A new project should start with a UserControl object named UserControl1.

3. Change the Name property of the UserControl to **AXYesNo.** If the Properties window is not visible, choose View, Properties Window or click the Properties Window button. Find the Name property and change it by typing **AXYesNo.**

4. Add two command buttons to your UserControl. To add controls to the UserControl, click the CommandButton control in the Toolbox, and then draw the buttons, as in Figure 20.5.

FIG. 20.5
Draw two command buttons on the control drawing area by selecting the CommandButton icon and then clicking and dragging on the drawing area.

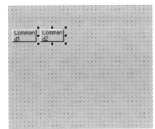

5. Position the two CommandButtons so that you can see both of them. To move a CommandButton, click and drag it across your UserControl. You can also resize it by dragging the sizing blocks located on each of its corners.

6. Name one of the command buttons **cmdYes** and the other **cmdNo.**

7. Set the caption of cmdYes to Yes and the caption of cmdNo to No.

8. Add a Label control to the UserControl object and name it **lblDisplay**.

9. Add code to the Click event of cmdYes to have lblDisplay's Caption property say Yes. To go to the Code window, click cmdYes twice or click the View Code button. The cursor should be set in the Private Sub cmdYes_Click() event. Add the code shown in Listing 20.2.

Listing 20.2 AXYESNO\AXYESNO.CTL—cmdYes Code

```
Private Sub cmdYes_Click()
    lblDisplay.Caption = "Yes"
End Sub
```

10. Add code to the `Click` event of the cmdNo button to have it change lblDisplay's `Caption` property to `No`. To navigate between object events inside of the code window, go to the object list and select the `cmdNo` object. Verify that the event you are looking at in the procedure list is the `Click` event. Add the code shown in Listing 20.3.

Listing 20.3 AXYESNO\AXYESNO.CTL—cmdNo Code

```
Private Sub cmdNo_Click()
    lblDisplay.Caption = "No"
End Sub
```

11. Choose Project, Project1 Properties to open the Project Properties dialog box, and then name the project **AXEYesNo** and provide a project description.

12. Build your control by selecting the File, Make AXYesNo.ocx menu entries.

13. Save your project to its own folder, which you should name **..\Samples\AXYesNo**. Save the `UserControl` with the name **AXYesNo.ctl**. Save the project with the name **AXYesNo.vbp**.

14. Test the control in a test project. Choose File, Add Project. From the Add Project dialog box, select Standard EXE. Inside Visual Basic, close the `UserControl` object window. Notice that the user control object you made `AXYesNo` is now available in the Toolbox. Add a `AXYesNo` to Form1, as in Figure 20.6. Now, test your control by selecting Run, Start, or by clicking the Start button. Click each of the command buttons and verify that they work correctly, as in Figure 20.7. Stop the project by choosing Run, End, or by clicking the End button.

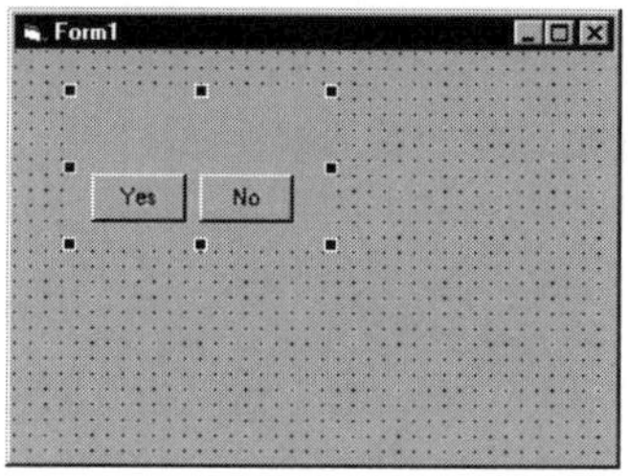

FIG. 20.6

Once you close the window containing the control you are developing, it becomes available in the Toolbox for use in any other Visual Basic application.

Part
V

Ch
20

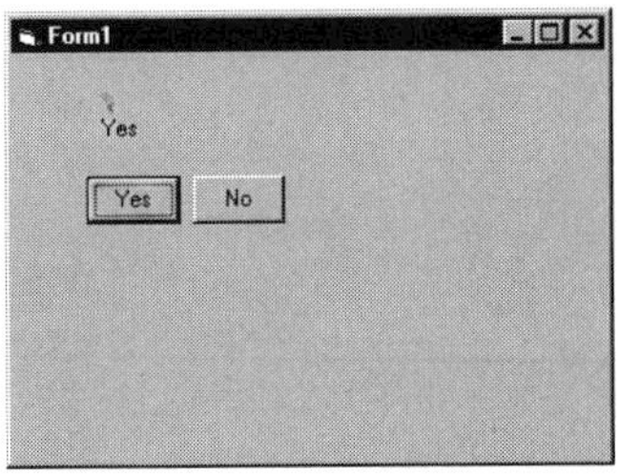

FIG. 20.7

When you run the standard Visual Basic project, you can verify that your control works correctly.

15. Test your ActiveX control from an HTML container by using the Setup Wizard. Close Visual Basic. From the Visual Basic program group on the Start menu, select Application Setup Wizard. On the Select Project dialog box, select ...\AXYesNo\AXYesNo.vbp and check Create Internet Download Setup, as in Figure 20.8.

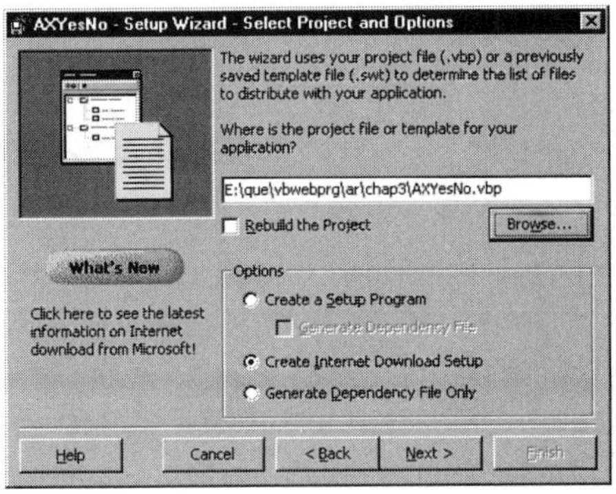

FIG. 20.8

To build the necessary files for use in an HTML document, you need to use the Application Setup Wizard to create an Internet Download Setup.

16. On the Internet Distribution Location dialog box, pick a location where you want your distribution files to become available.

17. On the Internet Package dialog box, pick Use Alternate Location for runtime components, but do not give a location, as in Figure 20.9. A blank location will put the files with the other runtime files.

FIG. 20.9

You can specify whether the Visual Basic runtime files (and other necessary files) will be downloaded from the Microsoft Web site, the same Web site as your control, or a third Web site.

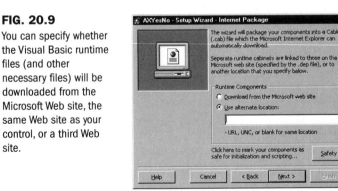

18. On the Internet Package dialog box, click the Safety button. On the Safety dialog box, specify that your control is Safe for Initialization and Safe for Scripting (these settings will be discussed in greater detail in Chapter 21, "Extending ActiveX Controls"), as in Figure 20.10.

FIG. 20.10
By marking your control as safe for initialization and scripting, you place your guarantee that your control can't harm the user's computer, even if used in HTML documents that you didn't build.

19. Move forward through the ActiveX Server Components dialog box. In the File Summary dialog box, the Setup Wizard shows you a summary of the files that will be included in the package, as in Figure 20.11.

FIG. 20.11
The File Summary dialog box shows which files will be included in the Internet download files that will be packaged for inclusion on a Web site.

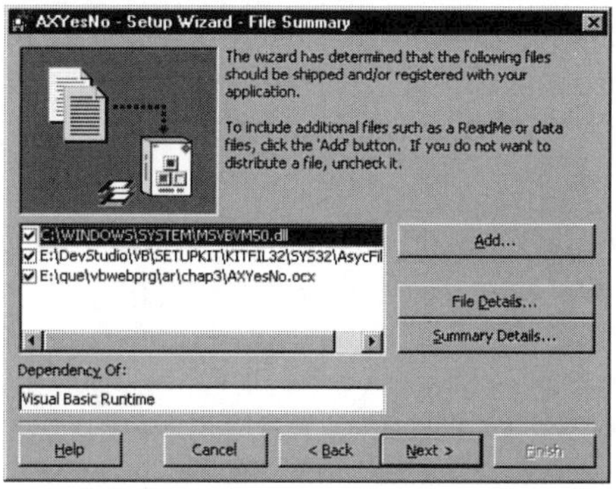

20. After the Setup Wizard has completed building the Internet Download files, open the AXYesNo.HTM document in Internet Explorer to test your control in a Web browser, as in Figure 20.12.

Exposing Properties, Methods, and Events

You can make properties, methods, and events of your ActiveX controls available to Web designers to increase your controls' flexibility. After properties, methods, and events are exposed, they are available to be manipulated from script code on an HTML page, such as VBScript. You can make the native properties, methods, and events of your constituent controls available, or you can make up your own properties, methods, and events for the special functionality that you are trying to achieve with your control. You need to be careful in what you enable, as it might make your control unsafe.

▶ **See** "Marking Your Controls Safe for Scripting and Initialization," **p. 589**

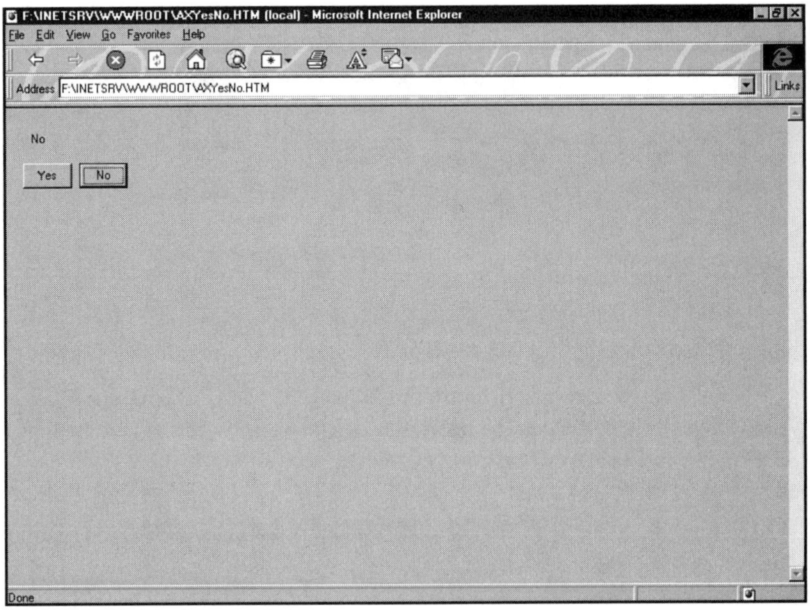

FIG. 20.12
After the Setup Wizard has completed building the download files, it creates a simple HTML file you can open in Internet Explorer to test your control.

Exposing Properties of ActiveX Controls

Properties are characteristics of your controls. By changing properties, you can change the appearance and behavior of ActiveX controls. By exposing your ActiveX control's properties, you allow Web developers to manipulate your control. The availability of your ActiveX control's properties is controlled by property procedures. A property procedure is a public procedure that makes your property available to the outside world. Property procedures allow you to make properties read, write, or read *and* write.

You need to implement two property procedures for all properties that you want to make available to the user of your control. These two property procedures are the Get and Let procedures. The property Get procedure allows the current value of the property to be read by programming code or script, whereas the property Let procedure allows the current value of the property to be changed by the code. These methods also allow the property to appear in the Properties window when using the control in a Visual Basic application.

In the following example, you are going to make the UserControl object that you made in the first example have a public property named BackColor, which will be available for read and write.

To make a property of your control available to be read from script, make a property Get procedure. The name of the procedure is BackColor, and it is of type OLE_Color. It returns the value of the UserControl, as seen in Listing 20.4.

Listing 20.4   AXYESNO\AXYESNO.CTL—Reading the *BackColor* Property

```
Public Property Get BackColor() As OLE_COLOR
    BackColor = UserControl.BackColor
End Property
```

To make a property available to be changed from script, use a property Let statement, as in Listing 20.5.

Listing 20.5   AXYESNO\AXYESNO.CTL—Setting the *BackColor* Property

```
Public Property Let BackColor(ByVal New_BackColor As OLE_COLOR)
    UserControl.BackColor() = New_BackColor
    PropertyChanged "BackColor"
End Property
```

To the Web designer, your ActiveX control should look like one object, although it might be made of many constituent controls. For that reason, a Web designer should have to change only one property to change one attribute—for example, there should be only one BackColor property. You can change multiple objects on your control's properties with one property procedure. For example, if you want the BackColor of the UserControl and the label to have the same BackColor, use one property procedure and have it modify two properties, as in Listing 20.6. This enables you to change both BackColor properties with the single property.

Listing 20.6   AXYESNO\AXYESNO.CTL—Setting the *BackColor* Property of Both the *UserControl* and the Label

```
Public Property Let BackColor(ByVal New_BackColor As OLE_COLOR)
    UserControl.BackColor() = New_BackColor
    lblDisplay.BackColor() = New_BackColor
    PropertyChanged "BackColor"
End Property
```

Exposing Methods of ActiveX Controls

Methods give Web designers the ability to perform actions on the objects of their ActiveX controls. A method is just a function or sub that is declared as public. The function or sub's name associates with the name of a method of an object. For instance, you can use the code in Listing 20.7 to add a method to the AXYesNo control, which can then be used to set the label.

Listing 20.7 AXYESNO\AXYESNO.CTL—*SetText* Method

```
Public Sub SetText(Item As String)
  lblDisplay.Caption = Item
End Sub
```

Exposing Events of ActiveX Controls

By exposing events, you give Web designers the ability to call the code that is associated with those events.

To expose an event, you first declare the event's name in the General Declarations section of your UserControl object. Use the keyword Event and then the events name, followed by parentheses—for example, Event Click() declares there will be a Click event.

Second, create a procedure that uses your new event by using the code in Listing 20.8.

Listing 20.8 AXYESNO\AXYESNO.CTL—Exposing the cmdNo's *Click* Event

```
Private Sub cmdNo_Click()
    'Change the caption
    lblDisplay.Caption = "No"
    'Raise the Click event
    RaiseEvent Click
End Sub
```

Enhancing ActiveX Controls

The previous sections introduced the concepts involved in creating ActiveX controls, including how to place controls on a User Control window, and how to create an entirely new control by adding properties, methods, and events. However, you can also create "new" controls simply by adding capabilities to an existing control. This means you will be working with a single base control, but adding properties, methods, and events to provide additional capabilities to the user. For example, you might want a text box that accepts only certain characters, or perhaps a scroll bar that works with a range of letters rather than numbers. Placing the code that performs these tasks into an ActiveX control makes it easier to use the code in future programs. For example, rather than adding special code to every TextBox control in your program, you simply use your "enhanced" control in place of the text box.

To create these enhanced controls, you use many of the same techniques that you have already learned. However, you also can use a Visual Basic Wizard to make quicker work out of the process, which is explained later in the chapter.

Adding Capabilities to a Control

To create an enhanced control, follow these five basic steps:

1. Start a new ActiveX control project.
2. Add the base control to the User Control Window.
3. Add the properties and methods to the control.
4. Test the control in a test application.
5. Compile your control so that others can use it.

The following sections walk you through these steps, using a text box as the base control. Your "enhanced" text box will have a property that allows the programmer to choose a set of acceptable characters that the user can enter. This control will be called TxtCharLimit (short for "Limited Character TextBox"). It will be just like the standard TextBox but with one additional property, CharAccept, which will allow the user to choose either all characters, just letters, or just numbers.

Creating the Basic Control

The steps to create the enhanced text control are very similar to the steps you used to create the Address and AXYesNo controls. For the enhanced text control, these steps are as follows:

1. Start a new ActiveX control project.
2. Add a text box to the User Control Window with the upper-left corner of the text box in position 0, 0.
3. Name the text box **txtCharSet** and clear its Text property
4. Set the properties of the ActiveX project and the User Control to the values specified in Table 20.1.

    To set the first three values in the table, use the *projectname* Properties dialog box. To set the remaining values, highlight the UserControl object and press F4 to show the Properties window.

Part

V

Ch

20

Table 20.1   Project and Property Settings for the Enhanced Text Custom Control

Item	Setting
Project Type	ActiveX Control
Project Name	TextLimited
Project Description	Text Box for Limited Character Set
User control Name property	TxtCharLimit
User control Public property	True

When you have completed setting up the user interface of the enhanced text control, it should look like the one in Figure 20.13.

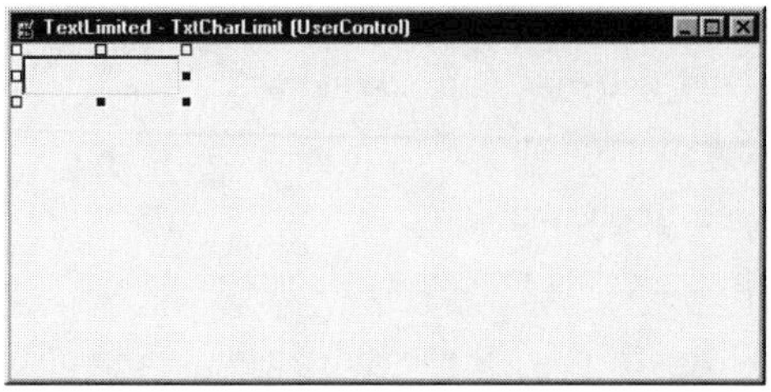

FIG. 20.13

A simple text control can be enhanced with other capabilities.

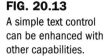

You also need to set up the `Resize` event procedure of the User Control to make the text box fit the space that is drawn by the developer when using your control. This `Resize` event procedure is shown in Listing 20.9

Listing 20.9   TXTCHARLIMIT.CTL—Using the *Resize* Event to Make Sure the Text Control Fills the Space

```
Private Sub UserControl_Resize()
  txtCharSet.Height = UserControl.ScaleHeight
  txtCharSet.Width = UserControl.ScaleWidth
End Sub
```

The simple two-line `Resize` event procedure is all the code necessary for the user interface of your sample control. Its purpose is to keep the text box the same size as the `UserControl` object. Before moving on, test it by performing the following steps:

1. Save your project.
2. Close the UserControl window. If you have the Toolbox open, you will notice a new icon appear for your control.
3. Choose File, Add Project. Add a Standard EXE project.
4. Draw your control on Form1 and try resizing it.

The purpose of jumping the gun like that is to get you used to the idea that the code in your ActiveX control does not have to be explicitly executed. Remember, when developing an ActiveX control, the code you write is used at design time in the host program.

For now, remove the Standard EXE project by right-clicking it in the Project Explorer window and then choosing Remove Project1. Now it is time to work on the enhancements to the control.

Creating the Additional Capabilities

The enhancement you are going to make to the TextBox control is to tell it whether it should accept any characters, just letters, or just numbers. You accomplish this by adding your own property, called CharAccept, which can have one of the following three values:

- 0—Accept any character
- 1—Accept only numbers
- 2—Accept only letters

The first thing you need is a private variable to store the property value internally. To do this, create the variable in the General Declarations section of the UserControl object:

```
Private mCharAccept As Integer
```

Next, you need to create the new property, called CharAccept. You can do this either by typing in the Let and Get procedures by hand, or by choosing Add Procedure, Property from the Tools menu. The code for the CharAccept property is fairly easy to understand. When the developer needs the value of the CharAccept property, the Property Get procedure simply passes what is stored in the private variable. When the value of the CharAccept property is set, the Property Let procedure assigns one of the valid values to the private variable. The following is the code for both Property procedures:

```
Public Property Get CharAccept() As Integer
    CharAccept = mCharAccept
End Property

Public Property Let CharAccept(ByVal nNewValue As Integer)

    Select Case nNewValue
    Case 1 To 2
        mCharAccept = nNewValue
    Case Else
        mCharAccept = 0
    End Select

    PropertyChanged "CharAccept"

End Property
```

Notice the use of the PropertyChanged method. This method works in conjunction with the ReadProperties and WriteProperties events, which we'll discuss in the next few paragraphs.

You now need to use the InitProperties event of the user control to specify an initial value of the property, as follows:

```
Private Sub UserControl_InitProperties()
    mCharAccept = 0
End Sub
```

This code makes sure that a value is set, even if the developer does not set it.

Part
V

Ch
20

You also need to create the code for the WriteProperties and ReadProperties events to pre-serve the design time settings of CharAccept. These two events use the PropertyBag object to save and retrieve the value of the CharAccept property. The PropertyBag object enables you to maintain the design environment value of CharAccept. The code for these two events, shown in Listing 20.10, is not hard to understand. What is important, however, is why you need the code.

Listing 20.10   TXTCHARLIMIT.CTL—Holding the Property Value

```
Private Sub UserControl_ReadProperties(PropBag As PropertyBag)
   mCharAccept = PropBag.ReadProperty("CharAccept", 0)
End Sub

Private Sub UserControl_WriteProperties(PropBag As PropertyBag)
   PropBag.WriteProperty "CharAccept", mCharAccept, 0
End Sub
```

Remember that an ActiveX control's code starts executing the moment you draw it on a form. Suppose you set the value of a property during design time. In your sample control, assume you set the value of CharAccept to 1. You also may change it several times while your program is running. The normal behavior for a control is to revert to its original design-time values when the program ends, thus adding the requirement of maintaining two separate *states* of the property.

More simply put, if you change a property at design time, the control has to know to get this new value rather than use the default. Conversely, if the property's value is changed during program execution, the control has to retrieve the value when it returns to the design state.

The PropertyBag object allows your ActiveX control to store properties about itself, making this behavior possible. The PropertyChanged method provides notification that the user has changed a property. By knowing the state of the program and whether the PropertyChange method has been invoked, VB can fire the WriteProperties and ReadProperties events.

The next step in your sample project is to create the code that makes it do something different than a normal text box. In this case, you'll use the text box's KeyPress event to scan each char-acter as it is entered. Visual Basic will pass the ASCII code of the characters through the event's KeyAscii parameter. Depending on the ASCII code and setting of CharAccept property, you will either accept the character or set KeyAscii to 0, which causes the text box to not dis-play the character.

In addition to not displaying the character, you want to inform the host program that the user has entered an invalid character. You do this by creating an event called UserError. To create this event, add the following line of code to the General Declarations section of the UserControl object:

```
Public Event UserError()
```

This event works like an event in any other control; someone using your control can place code in it. The only thing you have to do is fire the event by using the `RaiseEvent` method.

Because there are three sets of acceptable characters, you can use a `Select` statement to handle the choices. One other item of note—you need to enable the backspace key (ASCII code 8) in any of the character sets that you use. Otherwise, the user won't be able to delete the previous character. The code for the `KeyPress` event is shown in Listing 20.11.

Listing 20.11   TXTCHARLIMIT.CTL—Using the *KeyPress* Event to Handle Screening the Keys Entered by the User

```
Private Sub txtCharSet_KeyPress(KeyAscii As Integer)
    If KeyAscii = 8 Then Exit Sub

    Select Case mCharAccept
        Case 0 'Any character is acceptable
            Exit Sub
        Case 1 'Only numbers may be entered
            If KeyAscii >= 48 And KeyAscii <= 57 Then
                Exit Sub
            Else
                KeyAscii = 0
                Beep
                RaiseEvent UserError
            End If
        Case 2 'Only letters may be entered
            If KeyAscii >= 65 And KeyAscii <= 90 Then
                Exit Sub
            ElseIf KeyAscii >= 97 And KeyAscii <= 122 Then
                Exit Sub
            Else
                KeyAscii = 0
                Beep
                RaiseEvent UserError
            End If
    End Select

End Sub
```

The code in this listing is fairly simple. `KeyAscii` represents the typed character, which is checked for validity by `Select Case` and `If` statements. If the character falls outside an acceptable range, the control beeps and raises the `UserError` event.

Testing the Capabilities

After you have entered all of the code for the control, you are ready to test the control. To test the TxtCharLimit control, follow these steps:

1. Remember to save your code.
2. Add a Standard EXE project to the project group.

3. Close the design and Code windows for the User Control.

   Notice that an icon for your control appears in the Toolbox.

4. Add an instance of the TxtCharLimit control to the form in the test application.

5. Set the properties of the control.

6. Run the test program and try out the control. Try setting the `CharAccept` property to different values to verify that it accepts only the keystrokes you want.

If you have problems with the control, you can use the same debugging techniques to find problems in a control as you do for finding problems in standard programs. You can set break points and step through the code line by line, whether in the ActiveX Control project or in the Standard EXE project. (See Chapter 8, "Programming Basics," for more information on debugging your code.)

Choosing a Toolbox Icon

One thing you may have noticed by now is that all the custom controls you create have the same symbol in the Toolbox. This can cause a lot of confusion if you are working with multiple controls. Although the ToolTips provide a description of the control, it is better to have a custom icon to identify each control. You can do this by setting the value of the `ToolboxBitmap` property of the user control. This property determines what is displayed in the Toolbox for your control. If the property is set to `None`, the default icon is used. You can set the property to any bitmap, but be aware that the Toolbox icon is only 16×15 pixels. Therefore, you should use custom bitmaps that are created in that size.

Using the ActiveX Control Interface Wizard

When you created the `CharAccept` property of the enhanced text box, you created one piece of the public interface of the control. However, your users probably will also want to be able to access most of the standard properties, methods, and events of the text box. For example, you may have noticed that the `Text` property was not accessible from your custom control. This makes sense because you did not add any code for it. The section "Exposing Properties of ActiveX Controls" exposed properties with the same name as the component property to allow the user to access these properties. Because there were only a few properties, each property was created by hand. However, you can imagine that handling this for the dozens of properties of a control could get very tedious.

Fortunately, Visual Basic provides a tool to make this process much easier—the ActiveX Control Interface Wizard. First you tell the Wizard the names of all the properties that you want to have for your control. It then enables you to "bind" the properties of your control to the properties of a component of your control. The end result is that the Wizard generates the appropriate code for you.

Adding the Wizard to Visual Basic

The first step to using the VB ActiveX Control Interface Wizard is adding it to your design environment. For this purpose, Visual Basic includes the Add-In Manager. To start the Add-In Manager, choose Add-Ins, Add-In Manager. This opens the Add-In Manager dialog box.

To add the VB ActiveX Control Interface Wizard, click the box next to the name of the Wizard. This places a check mark in the box, indicating that the Wizard will be part of your desktop. Next, click the OK button to exit the Add-In Manager and add the Wizard to Visual Basic.

Next, you need to re-create the Limited text control by using the Wizard. To begin, start a new ActiveX Control project and draw a text box on the UserControl window. Set up the names and sizes the same way you did in the previous example. Next, start the Wizard by choosing the ActiveX Control Interface Wizard item from the Add-Ins menu. The Wizard will start by displaying the initial screen, shown in Figure 20.14. You then click the Next button to start the actual work of setting up your properties.

FIG. 20.14

The ActiveX Control Interface Wizard simplifies the process of creating properties by creating much of the code for you.

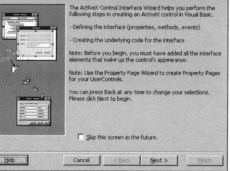

N O T E For the Wizard to work most effectively, you must add all the required components to the user control before starting the Wizard. ▪

Selecting and Creating Properties

The next step in using the Wizard is to select the properties, methods, and events that you want to make available to your control. Collectively, properties, methods, and events are referred to as *members*. On page two, shown in Figure 20.15, the Wizard contains a list of the names of just about every item that you could find in any control in Visual Basic. To select a property or method to create, highlight the name of the item in the Available names list, and then click the right arrow button to select the item. For your sample control, highlight the Text property on the left and click the right arrow button.

Part

V

Ch

20

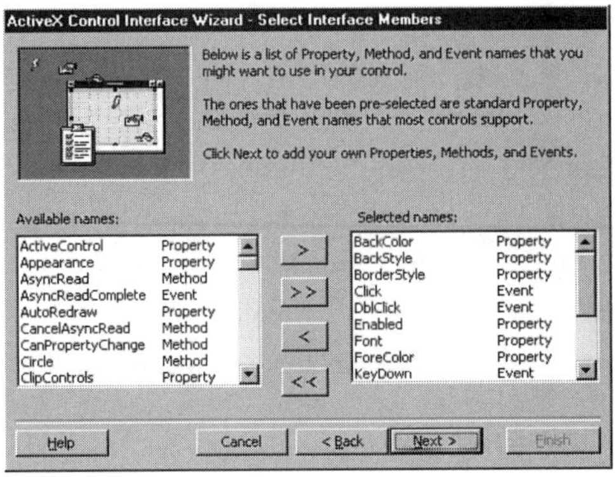

FIG. 20.15

Select properties, methods, and events for your control from the Available names list.

After adding the Text property to the Selected Names list, click the Next button to move to the next page of the Wizard.

> **T I P** You can also select an item by double-clicking it in the list.

After selecting the pre-defined properties, methods, and events for your control, you are taken to the page of the Wizard where you can enter the new custom items for your control. The Create Custom Interface Members page of the Wizard contains a list of all the custom members that will be created for your control.

If you have previously defined public properties or other members, they will appear in this list when you first access the page. From this page of the Wizard, you can add new members, or edit or delete existing ones. To add a new member, click the New button of the Wizard. This opens the Add Custom Member dialog box. In this dialog box, specify the name of the member and its type. Create the CharAccept property by typing **CharAccept** in the Name field, and then click OK.

While you are on this step, create the UserError event. Then click the Next button to move on.

CAUTION

It is advisable not to edit members of the control that you previously defined with code alone. This is because the Wizard works by analyzing comments it places in the code. The Wizard may or may not be able to correctly interpret your hand-typed code.

Assigning Properties

The next step in the Wizard is to assign the public members of the custom control to members of the constituent controls. This process is referred to as *mapping the members*. For example, rather than creating your own Text property, you can simply *map* the Text property of your custom control to the Text property of txtCharSet. The Set Mapping page of the Wizard, shown in Figure 20.16, contains a list of all the properties, methods, and events, that you identified as being part of the public interface of the custom control.

FIG. 20.16

Mapping the public members of the control gives you a direct link to items in the constituent controls.

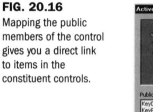

The Set Mapping page contains two combo boxes for identifying the control and the control's member to which a public member should be mapped. To map a single public member of the custom control, first select the member in the Public Name list. Go ahead and highlight the Text property on the left. Next, select txtCharSet from the Control drop-down list. (This list contains the names of all the components in your custom control.) After selecting the component, you can select the member of the component from the Member drop-down list. In this case, the Text property will be selected automatically for you. This process is illustrated in Figure 20.17 for the Text property of the TxtCharLimit control.

FIG. 20.17

Select all the public members for the TxtCharLimit control and let the mapping occur automatically.

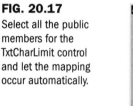

Note that with this screen, you can map more than one public member at a time. The list of public names supports multiple selections. You can select multiple members from the list, then select a component to which to map the members. Each public member will be mapped to the property or method of the component that bears the same name. For example, the Text property of the custom control would automatically map to the Text property of a text or combo box.

After you have mapped the Text property, click the Next button to proceed to the final page of the Wizard. This final page, shown in Figure 20.18, lets you set the attributes of each public member that is not mapped to a constituent control.

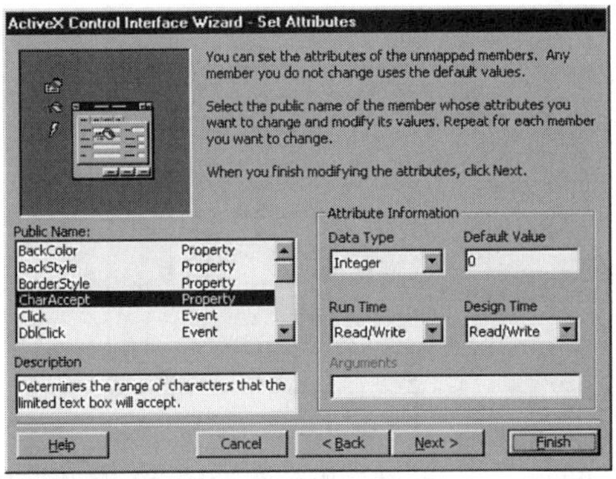

FIG. 20.18

Set the attributes for properties and methods before completing the code for the control.

Depending on the type of member you are creating, the Wizard allows you to specify different attributes. For a property, you can specify the type of data the property will hold, the default value of the property, and what type of access the user has to the property at design time and runtime. The access type determines if a Property Let, Property Get, or both procedures are created for the property. For Runtime access, you can choose Read/Write, Read Only, Write Only, or none. For Design Time access, you can choose Read/Write, Read Only, or none.

For your sample control, set the Data Type of the CharAccept property to Integer and set the default value to 0. You can also type an optional description in the Description box. Property descriptions appear at the bottom of the Properties window during design time. Because this is the final step of the Wizard, you now are ready to click the Finish button.

Finishing the Code

After you click the Finish button, the ActiveX Control Interface Wizard creates a number of code modules in your control. The Wizard also displays a summary page, providing you with details of the steps remaining to finish your control.

After reviewing the information on the summary page, you can take a look at the code that was generated by the Wizard. You can view the code by clicking the user control in the Project window and then clicking the View Code button. This opens the Code window containing the code that the Wizard created for you.

Take a look at some of the pieces of the code that is generated. First, in the General Declarations section, you will find that the Wizard has created constants for the default values of any unmapped properties. The CharAccept property has been given a default value of 0. In addition, the Wizard has automatically created the private property variable CharAccept. This is followed by the declaration of any events that you requested to be included in the control. A sample of this code is shown in Listing 20.12. If you mapped any events, you will notice that the Wizard places comments in the code that indicate how events are mapped to component events.

Listing 20.12   TEXTLIMITED.CTL—Declarations Code Generated by the Wizard

```
Option Explicit

'Default Property Values:
Const m_def_BackColor = 0
Const m_def_ForeColor = 0
Const m_def_CharAccept = 0

'Property Variables:
Dim m_BackColor As Long
Dim m_ForeColor As Long
Dim m_CharAccept As Integer

'Event Declarations:
Event Click() 'MappingInfo=txtCharset,txtCharset,-1,Click
Event DblClick()
Event UserError()
Event KeyPress(KeyAscii As Integer)
```

The declarations of variables and events are followed by the property procedures. These procedures are created for properties that are mapped to a component property and those that are custom properties. As seen in Listing 20.13, the code for the Text property is complete, whereas the CharAccept property has a skeleton function ready for you to finish.

Listing 20.13   TEXTLIMITED.CTL—Property Procedures Provide the Means to Set and Retrieve Property Values

```
'WARNING! DO NOT REMOVE OR MODIFY THE FOLLOWING COMMENTED LINES!
'MappingInfo=txtCharset,txtCharset,-1,Text
Public Property Get Text() As String
    Text = txtCharset.Text
End Property

Public Property Let Text(ByVal New_Text As String)
    txtCharset.Text() = New_Text
    PropertyChanged "Text"
End Property
```

Part

V

Ch

20

continues

> **Listing 20.13   Continued**
>
> ```
> Public Property Get CharAccept() As Integer
>     CharAccept = m_CharAccept
> End Property
>
> Public Property Let CharAccept(ByVal New_CharAccept As Integer)
>     m_CharAccept = New_CharAccept
>     PropertyChanged "CharAccept"
> End Property
> ```

Note that if you had requested any methods, the Wizard would create them as Functions, instead of Sub procedures.

Finally, the code to read and write property values to the PropertyBag object is generated automatically. This code is illustrated in Listing 20.14.

> **Listing 20.14   TEXTLIMITED.CTL—*UserControl* Events Set Up the Control as Changes Are Made and Saved**
>
> ```
> 'Load property values from storage
> Private Sub UserControl_ReadProperties(PropBag As PropertyBag)
>
>     m_BackColor = PropBag.ReadProperty("BackColor", m_def_BackColor)
>     m_ForeColor = PropBag.ReadProperty("ForeColor", m_def_ForeColor)
>     txtCharset.Text = PropBag.ReadProperty("Text", "")
>     m_CharAccept = PropBag.ReadProperty("CharAccept", m_def_CharAccept)
> End Sub
>
> 'Write property values to storage
> Private Sub UserControl_WriteProperties(PropBag As PropertyBag)
>
>     Call PropBag.WriteProperty("BackColor", m_BackColor, m_def_BackColor)
>     Call PropBag.WriteProperty("ForeColor", m_ForeColor, m_def_ForeColor)
>     Call PropBag.WriteProperty("Text", txtCharset.Text, "")
>     Call PropBag.WriteProperty("CharAccept", m_CharAccept, m_def_CharAccept)
> End Sub
> ```

To complete the coding of your control, you need to add the custom code that is required for the CharAccept property and KeyPress event because the Wizard created only a "skeleton" for these items. After all, if the Wizard could do everything, then you would be out of a job!

Using the Property Page Wizard

You have seen Property Pages used for some of the controls that come with Visual Basic. These dialog boxes make it easy for you to set the properties of a control by organizing them into groups. You can create property pages for your own custom controls by using the Property Page Wizard. Like the ActiveX Control Interface Wizard, you have to add the Property Page Wizard to the desktop by using the Add-In Manager. After this is done, you can access the Wizard from the Add-Ins menu of Visual Basic. As you start the Property Page Wizard, you are shown an introductory screen that explains the purpose of the Wizard. Clicking the Next button on this page takes you to the first page, where the real work is done.

Creating the Pages

The first page of the Wizard lets you define the pages of the Property Pages dialog box (see Figure 20.19). If you have included Font and Color properties in your control, the Wizard starts out with two default pages—StandardColor and StandardFont. If you do not need these pages, just click the box next to the name to remove them from your Property Pages.

FIG. 20.19
Create new pages or rename old ones in the Property Page Wizard.

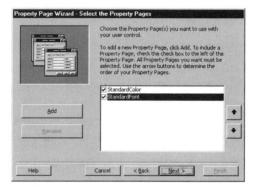

In addition to the default pages, you can add new pages to the dialog box. Clicking the Add button brings up the Property Page Name dialog box, which is an input box where you can enter the name of the page to create. As you add a page name, it is placed in the list of available pages and is automatically checked. The order of the page names in the list is the order in which the tabs will appear in your Property Pages dialog box. You can change the order by selecting a page and using the arrow keys to move it within the list.

When you have finished adding pages to the dialog box, click the Next button to move to the next page of the Wizard.

Adding Properties to the Pages

The next step in creating your Property Pages is to add the appropriate properties to each page of the dialog box. The Add Properties page of the Property Page Wizard is shown in Figure 20.20.

To add a property to a page, click the tab corresponding to the page where you want the property placed, and then select the property from the Available Properties list and click the right arrow button. Notice in Figure 20.20 the addition of a General property page and the inclusion of the CharAccept property. In addition, if you have the default pages of StandardColor and StandardFont, you will notice that the appropriate properties have already been added to these pages.

Part
V
Ch
20

FIG. 20.20
The Add Properties page displays a list of available properties and shows the defined pages of the dialog box.

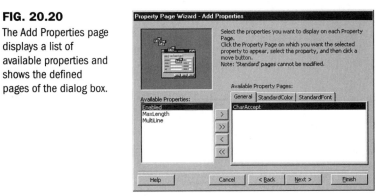

> **TIP** You can drag and drop a property onto a tab to place it on the corresponding page of the Property Pages.

When you have finished adding properties to the pages, click the Finish button to complete the creation of your Property Pages. As with the ActiveX Control Interface Wizard, the Property Page Wizard shows you a summary page that provides additional information to complete your custom control.

Using the Property Pages in Your Applications

To use the Property Pages you created, you need to add an instance of your custom control to a project. Then, in the Properties window, click the ellipsis button next to the Custom property. Then, just like the Property Pages of other controls, your Property Pages dialog box appears to allow the user to customize the control. A sample of a custom control's Property Pages is shown in Figure 20.21.

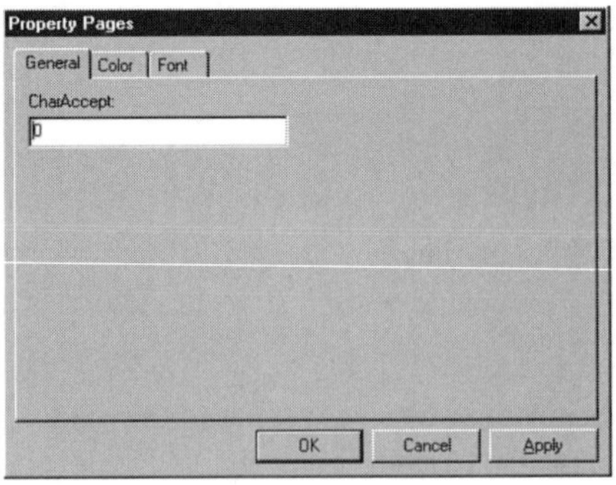

FIG. 20.21
Your Property Pages help users set up your custom control.

> **TIP** You can also access the Property Pages by right-clicking the control and then selecting the Properties item from the context menu.

Creating Other Enhanced Controls

Now that you have seen the general concepts for enhancing controls, you are ready to begin creating your own enhanced controls. One idea to get you started is a scroll bar that lets you select letters rather than numbers. This scroll bar lets the user set the upper and lower range of letters for the bar, and to set whether the letters returned by the Value property are upper-case or lowercase. Figure 20.22 shows the use of the scroll bar in a program, and Listing 20.15 shows the code required to make the scroll bar work.

FIG. 20.22

Use a scroll bar to enter letters.

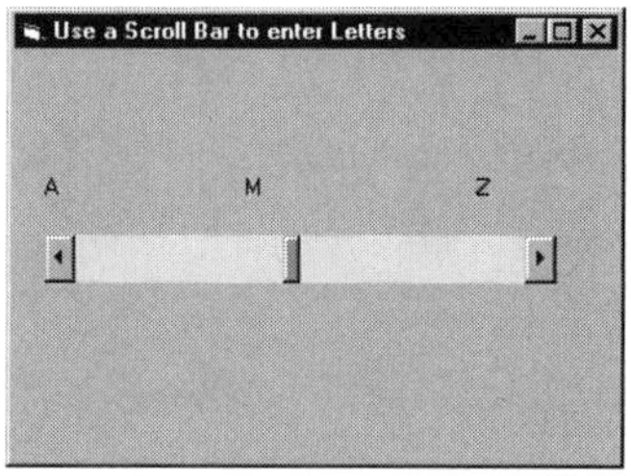

Listing 20.15   LTRSCROLL.CTL—Code to Make the LtrScroll Control Work

```
'Default Property Values:
Const m_def_Max = 26
Const m_def_Min = 1
Const m_def_Value = 0
Const m_def_ReturnCase = 0

'Property Variables:
Dim m_Max As Integer
Dim m_Min As Integer
Dim m_Value As Integer
Dim m_ReturnCase As Integer

Private Sub hsbLetter_Change()
    RaiseEvent Change
End Sub

Public Property Get Max() As String
    m_Max = hsbLetter.Max
    Max = Chr(m_Max + 64)
End Property

Public Property Let Max(ByVal New_Max As String)
    m_Max = Asc(UCase(New_Max)) - 64
    hsbLetter.Max = m_Max
    PropertyChanged "Max"
End Property

Public Property Get Min() As String
    m_Min = hsbLetter.Min
    Min = Chr(m_Min + 64)
```

Part

V

Ch

20

continues

Listing 20.15 Continued

```
End Property

Public Property Let Min(ByVal New_Min As String)
    m_Min = Asc(UCase(New_Min)) - 64
    hsbLetter.Min = m_Min
    PropertyChanged "Min"
End Property

Private Sub hsbLetter_Scroll()
    RaiseEvent Scroll
End Sub

Public Property Get Value() As String
    m_Value = hsbLetter.Value
    If m_ReturnCase = 0 Then
        Value = Chr(m_Value + 64)
    Else
        Value = Chr(m_Value + 96)
    End If
End Property

Public Property Let Value(ByVal New_Value As String)
    m_Value = New_Value
    m_Value = Asc(UCase(New_Value)) - 64
    hsbLetter.Value = m_Value
    PropertyChanged "Value"
End Property

Public Property Get ReturnCase() As Integer
    ReturnCase = m_ReturnCase
End Property

Public Property Let ReturnCase(ByVal New_ReturnCase As Integer)
    If New_ReturnCase > 1 Then New_ReturnCase = 1
    If New_ReturnCase < 0 Then New_ReturnCase = 0
    m_ReturnCase = New_ReturnCase
    PropertyChanged "ReturnCase"
End Property

'Initialize Properties for User Control
Private Sub UserControl_InitProperties()
    m_Max = m_def_Max
    m_Min = m_def_Min
    m_Value = m_def_Value
    m_ReturnCase = m_def_ReturnCase
End Sub
```

Another idea for an enhanced control is a type-ahead combo box. This type of combo box keeps the items in the drop-down list sorted and then perform a search on the item as the user types letters in the edit portion of the box. This type of feature makes the combo box easier to use for data entry.

From Here...

This chapter has shown you how to enhance existing controls to create new controls, and how to use the ActiveX Control Interface Wizard and Property Page Wizard to make your control-creation work easier. To learn more about other topics covered in this chapter, see the following:

- To learn more about creating robust ActiveX controls, see Chapter 21, "Extending ActiveX Controls."
- To learn more about creating ActiveX controls, refer to Chapter 22, "Creating a User-Drawn Control."
- To learn more about creating ActiveX documents, see Chapter 23, "Building ActiveX Documents."

Part

V

Ch

20

Extending ActiveX Controls

In the previous chapter, you received an introduction to the creation of Visual Basic ActiveX controls. In this chapter, you learn how to enhance already existing controls in order to create a new version of the control. In addition, you will learn how to create a control that is able to function without risk of failure. ■

Learn how to use the Extender objects

There's a special relationship between a control and its container. Specifically, a Visual Basic ActiveX control provides Extender and Ambient objects through which the control can communicate with its container.

Learn how to create property pages for your control

You can use standard coding techniques to create property sheets that provide you the greatest flexibility at design time.

Discover how to trap for errors and handle exceptions in your control

Properly debugging and handling errors and exceptions can mean the difference between a usable control and one that is a major security risk to the users of the control.

Package the control for Web use

Using the Application Setup Wizard, you can package your ActiveX control for use in Web pages. Learn how to prepare your control so that it can be used in Web pages and automatically downloaded by users of Microsoft's Internet Explorer Web browser.

Introducing the *Extender* Object

A Visual Basic control's Extender object provides a number of properties, called *extender properties*, that at first glance may appear to be a part of a control instance. Extender properties, though, are in reality part of the Extender object. You can see extender properties when you place an instance of a control on a Visual Basic form.

For example, start a new ActiveX Control project. Then, in the Project Group window, double-click UserControl1 to open the control's designer window, and display the control's properties in the Property window. Reduce the size of the control by setting its Height property to 1275 and setting its Width property to 1800.

Take a look at the properties listed in the Properties window. These are your control's properties. What's special about these properties is that only you, the control programmer, can change them. The only way a developer can manipulate the properties currently displayed in the Properties window is if you expose the properties in your control's code.

When you used the ActiveX Control Interface Wizard in the previous chapter, you saw one way to expose control properties to the developer. Figure 21.1 shows the Wizard's Select Interface Members dialog box. The control members in the right box are the properties, events, and methods that the Wizard is exposing to developers. That is, only the members in the Selected Names box can be accessed by a developer after you've completed the control.

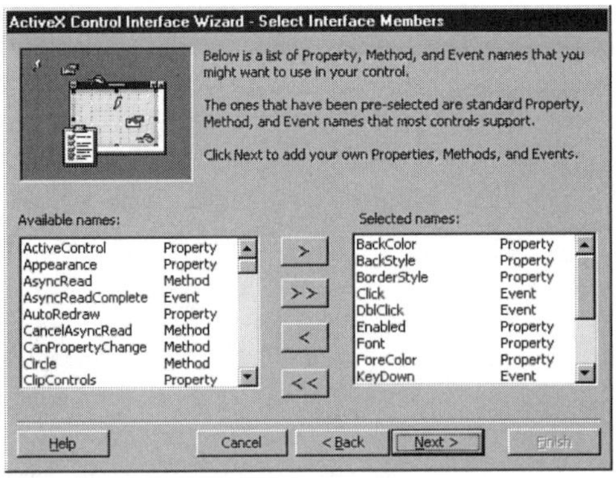

FIG. 21.1

The ActiveX Control Interface Wizard's Select Interface Members dialog box is one place you can expose properties, events, and methods to a developer.

Close the designer window so that the control is available on VB5's Toolbox. Now, double-click Form1 in the Project Group window. The test application's designer window appears. Double-click the control's icon in the toolbox to add an instance of the control to the test application's form. When the control instance appears, its properties appear in the Properties window. Because you haven't exposed any of the control's own properties yet, the properties in the Properties window are all extender properties, supplied by the Extender object.

Although you can manipulate extender properties from your control, you usually won't want to, because extender properties are meant to be used by a developer. The developer is the person who will decide things such as where the control is located in its container (determined by the

Left and Top extender properties), and how big the control will be (determined by the Height and Width extender properties).

If you do want to manipulate extender properties, you can do so through the control's Extender object. For example, suppose, for some reason, that you want your control to always start off set to a specific size. You could write the control's InitProperties() event procedure, as shown in Listing 21.1. Now, whenever an instance of the control is first created (not when it's re-created), it'll be set to a height of 300 twips and a width of 4000 twips.

Listing 21.1   LSTAA_01.TXT—Setting the Starting Size of a Control

```
Private Sub UserControl_InitProperties()
    Extender.Height = 300
    Extender.Width = 4000
End Sub
```

N O T E   Because the InitProperties() event procedure is called only when a control instance is first created, the developer can easily resize the control however they like. When the developer reloads the control instance, InitProperties() is not called, so the Height and Width properties don't get reset to their default values. Of course, you can set the starting height and width of a control simply by resizing the control in its designer window. There's no need to write code for setting the Height and Width extender properties. ■

N O T E   A control's Extender object is not available until the control has been sited on its container. This makes sense because the extender properties are based on the container's properties. Until the control is placed on the container, there is no way to determine what the container is or what properties it'll support. For this reason, you can't access the Extender object in a control's Initialize() event procedure, which is called before the control is completely sited on its container. You can, however, access the Extender object in InitProperties() and ReadProperties(). ■

The *Ambient* Object

Of greater interest to a control programmer is the control's Ambient object, which enables a control to respond to changes in the container. The capability of the control to respond to its container provides for the seamless integration of a control. This also increases the control's inherent value through its capability to dynamically adjust itself, in some cases, to the environment of the container.

The Ambient object features many properties, but only a few are especially important to a control programmer. These important ambient properties are listed in Table 21.1 along with their descriptions.

Table 21.1 Important Ambient Properties

Property	Description
BackColor	Holds the container's background color
DisplayAsDefault	Indicates whether a user-drawn control is the default control in the container
DisplayName	Holds the control instance's name. You can use DisplayName to identify the control in messages presented to the developer at design time
Font	Represents the container's currently selected font
ForeColor	Represents the container's foreground color
LocaleID	Indicates the locale in which the control is being used. You use this property to set things such as the language of the text and the formats of dates and times for different parts of the world
TextAlign	Represents the container's text-alignment setting
UserMode	Indicates whether the control is running at design time or runtime. A UserMode value of False indicates design time, and a value of True indicates runtime

One important reason to use your control's Ambient object is to ensure that the control's colors match those of its container. Imagine what it would look like if your control's background was gray and it was placed into a white spreadsheet. Most likely, the control would work properly, but the color difference would be a distraction to the users and would present an unprofessional appearance. To adjust the colors of your control to match that of its container, you use the BackColor and ForeColor properties. To see how this works, you'll create the AmbientDemo control in the next few sections.

AmbientDemo Control, Example 1

Now that you have the basic control project created, you can experiment to see why ambient properties are so important. To do this, first set the control's Height property to 1125, and set its Width property to 1950. Close the control's designer window so that the control's icon becomes available on VB5's toolbox. Now, in the Project Group window, double-click frmAmbientDemoTestApp. When you do so, the test application's form designer window appears. In the form's Properties window, change the background color to purple.

When you select the new background color, the form's background immediately changes to the selected color. Now, double-click the AmbientDemo control's icon on the toolbox. An instance of the control appears on the form. However, because the control doesn't pay attention to ambient properties, the control's background color is different from the form's background color, as shown in Figure 21.2.

FIG. 21.2
The control's and form's background colors don't match.

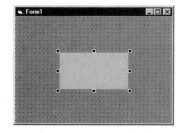

AmbientDemo Control, Example 2

To fix this problem with the AmbientDemo control, you have to set the control's colors to match those of its container. This is where the `Ambient` object enters. First, press your keyboard's Delete key to remove the control instance from the test application's designer window. Then, close the designer window. Double-click AmbientDemo in the Project Group window to open the control's designer window. Double-click the control to display its code window. Next, use the Properties box to find and display the `InitProperties()` event procedure. Finally, add the following two program lines to the procedure:

```
BackColor = Ambient.BackColor
ForeColor = Ambient.ForeColor
```

Your control can now match itself to the container's colors. To prove this, close the control's designer window so that it becomes available in the toolbox. Then, double-click `frmAmbientDemoTestApp` in the Project Group window to reopen the test application's designer window. Finally, double-click the control's icon in the toolbox. *Presto!* When the new control instance appears, it's the same color as the container (see Figure 21.3).

FIG. 21.3
Now the control is the same color as the container.

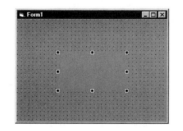

AmbientDemo Control, Example 3

What happens, though, if the designer now changes the form's background color again? Go ahead and try it. Set the form's `BackColor` property to another color. When you do, the form in the designer window immediately changes color to match your selection. The control, however, remains purple. That's because the control doesn't respond to the all-important `AmbientChanged` event.

You can fix that little problem now. First, double-click `AmbientDemo` in the Project Group window to open the control's designer window, and double-click the control to open its code window. In the Properties box, select the `AmbientChanged` event. The `AmbientChanged()` event procedure appears in the code window. Add the following two lines to the procedure:

```
BackColor = Ambient.BackColor
ForeColor = Ambient.ForeColor
```

Close the control's designer window so that the control is again available on VB5's toolbox. Reselect the test application's form, and again change its `BackColor` property. This time, the control keeps up by also changing its background color to match. As you have probably guessed, the `AmbientChanged()` event procedure is called whenever the developer changes an ambient property. The procedure's single parameter is the name of the property that changed.

Building the Calculator Control

The Calculator control is designed to build upon what you have already learned. As a result, the Calculator control will be used as the basis for the majority of the topics presented in this chapter.

The Calculator control enables the user to enter two values that are either summed or multiplied, depending on the setting of a control property, when the user clicks the control's button (see Figure 21.4).

FIG. 21.4
Here's the Calculator control with its constituent controls in place.

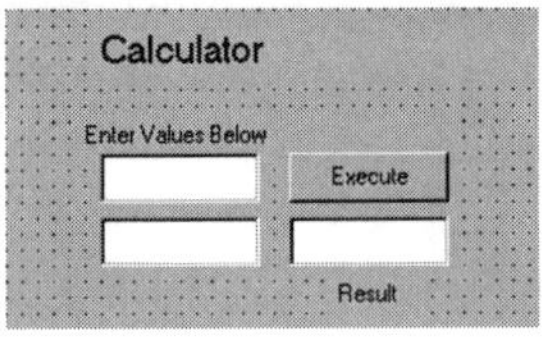

Creating the Interface

The next step, after all the controls are in place, is to create the control interface. As you might recall from the previous chapter, the ActiveX Control Interface Wizard enables you to expose properties, methods, and events of your control. The Calculator control that you are using has a number of properties that can be exposed through this wizard.

Briefly, the Calculator control enables the developer to set the control's main caption, as well as the label shown on the CommandButton control. The `Caption` property, which handles the main caption, will be delegated to the constituent lblCaption control, whereas the new

ButtonCaption property will be delegated to the constituent btnExecute control. In addition, the control will need a MultValues property that, when set to True, indicates that the calculator should multiply the entries rather than add them. Finally, the control will need a ValidateEntries() method, which validates user input, and a BadEntries event, which is triggered when ValidateEntries() returns False. Figure 21.5 show the Create Custom Interface Members dialog box with the new members.

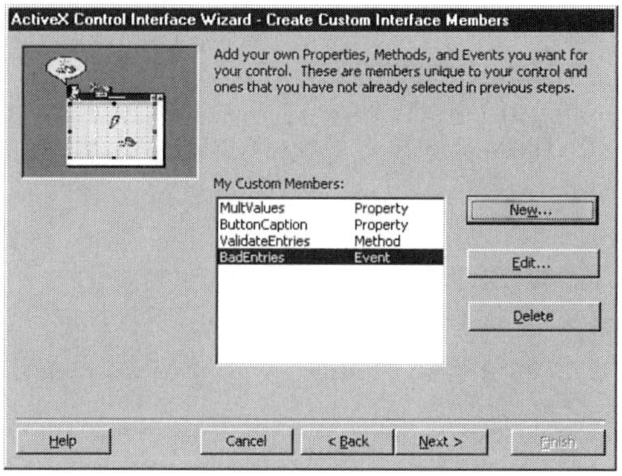

FIG. 21.5

The Calculator control needs four new control members.

After using the ActiveX Control Interface Wizard on the Calculator control, the Wizard creates additional source code for your control. Listing 21.2 shows the source code created for the Calculator control. As you can see, the code includes not only all the needed constant, variable, and event declarations, but also all of the property procedures, as well as ready-to-go InitProperties(), ReadProperties(), and WriteProperties() events. Now all you have to do is write the program code that completes the control. You do that in the next section.

Listing 21.2   LSTV_02.TXT—Code Created by ActiveX Control Interface Wizard

```
'Default Property Values:
Const m_def_BackColor = 0
Const m_def_ForeColor = 0
Const m_def_Enabled = 0
Const m_def_BackStyle = 0
Const m_def_BorderStyle = 0
Const m_def_MultValues = False
'Property Variables:
Dim m_BackColor As Long
Dim m_ForeColor As Long
Dim m_Enabled As Boolean
Dim m_Font As Font
Dim m_BackStyle As Integer
Dim m_BorderStyle As Integer
Dim m_MultValues As Boolean
```

Part
V

Ch
21

continues

560 | Chapter 21 Extending ActiveX Controls

Listing 21.2   Continued

```
'Event Declarations:
Event Click()
Event DblClick()
Event KeyDown(KeyCode As Integer, Shift As Integer)
Event KeyPress(KeyAscii As Integer)
Event KeyUp(KeyCode As Integer, Shift As Integer)
Event MouseDown(Button As Integer, Shift As Integer, _
    X As Single, Y As Single)
Event MouseMove(Button As Integer, Shift As Integer, _
    X As Single, Y As Single)
Event MouseUp(Button As Integer, Shift As Integer, _
    X As Single, Y As Single)
Event BadEntries()

Public Property Get BackColor() As Long
    BackColor = m_BackColor
End Property

Public Property Let BackColor(ByVal New_BackColor As Long)
    m_BackColor = New_BackColor
    PropertyChanged "BackColor"
End Property

Public Property Get ForeColor() As Long
    ForeColor = m_ForeColor
End Property

Public Property Let ForeColor(ByVal New_ForeColor As Long)
    m_ForeColor = New_ForeColor
    PropertyChanged "ForeColor"
End Property

Public Property Get Enabled() As Boolean
    Enabled = m_Enabled
End Property

Public Property Let Enabled(ByVal New_Enabled As Boolean)
    m_Enabled = New_Enabled
    PropertyChanged "Enabled"
End Property

Public Property Get Font() As Font
    Set Font = m_Font
End Property

Public Property Set Font(ByVal New_Font As Font)
    Set m_Font = New_Font
    PropertyChanged "Font"
End Property

Public Property Get BackStyle() As Integer
    BackStyle = m_BackStyle
End Property
```

```
Public Property Let BackStyle(ByVal New_BackStyle As Integer)
    m_BackStyle = New_BackStyle
    PropertyChanged "BackStyle"
End Property

Public Property Get BorderStyle() As Integer
    BorderStyle = m_BorderStyle
End Property

Public Property Let BorderStyle(ByVal New_BorderStyle As Integer)
    m_BorderStyle = New_BorderStyle
    PropertyChanged "BorderStyle"
End Property

Public Sub Refresh()

End Sub

'WARNING! DO NOT REMOVE OR MODIFY THE FOLLOWING COMMENTED LINES!
'MappingInfo=lblCaption,lblCaption,-1,Caption
Public Property Get Caption() As String
    Caption = lblCaption.Caption
End Property

Public Property Let Caption(ByVal New_Caption As String)
    lblCaption.Caption() = New_Caption
    PropertyChanged "Caption"
End Property

Public Property Get MultValues() As Boolean
    MultValues = m_MultValues
End Property

Public Property Let MultValues(ByVal New_MultValues As Boolean)
    m_MultValues = New_MultValues
    PropertyChanged "MultValues"
End Property

'WARNING! DO NOT REMOVE OR MODIFY THE FOLLOWING COMMENTED LINES!
'MappingInfo=btnExecute,btnExecute,-1,Caption
Public Property Get ButtonCaption() As String
    ButtonCaption = btnExecute.Caption
End Property

Public Property Let ButtonCaption(ByVal New_ButtonCaption As String)
    btnExecute.Caption() = New_ButtonCaption
    PropertyChanged "ButtonCaption"
End Property

Public Function ValidateEntries() As Boolean

End Function
```

Part

V

Ch

21

continues

Listing 21.2   Continued

```
'Initialize Properties for User Control
Private Sub UserControl_InitProperties()
    m_BackColor = m_def_BackColor
    m_ForeColor = m_def_ForeColor
    m_Enabled = m_def_Enabled
    Set m_Font = Ambient.Font
    m_BackStyle = m_def_BackStyle
    m_BorderStyle = m_def_BorderStyle
    m_MultValues = m_def_MultValues
End Sub

'Load property values from storage
Private Sub UserControl_ReadProperties(PropBag As PropertyBag)

    m_BackColor = PropBag.ReadProperty("BackColor", m_def_BackColor)
    m_ForeColor = PropBag.ReadProperty("ForeColor", m_def_ForeColor)
    m_Enabled = PropBag.ReadProperty("Enabled", m_def_Enabled)
    Set Font = PropBag.ReadProperty("Font", Ambient.Font)
    m_BackStyle = PropBag.ReadProperty("BackStyle", m_def_BackStyle)
    m_BorderStyle = PropBag.ReadProperty("BorderStyle", _
        m_def_BorderStyle)
    lblCaption.Caption = PropBag.ReadProperty("Caption", "Calculator")
    m_MultValues = PropBag.ReadProperty("MultValues", _
        m_def_MultValues)
    btnExecute.Caption = PropBag.ReadProperty("ButtonCaption", _
        "Execute")
End Sub

'Write property values to storage
Private Sub UserControl_WriteProperties(PropBag As PropertyBag)

    Call PropBag.WriteProperty("BackColor", m_BackColor, _
        m_def_BackColor)
    Call PropBag.WriteProperty("ForeColor", m_ForeColor, _
        m_def_ForeColor)
    Call PropBag.WriteProperty("Enabled", m_Enabled, m_def_Enabled)
    Call PropBag.WriteProperty("Font", Font, Ambient.Font)
    Call PropBag.WriteProperty("BackStyle", m_BackStyle, _
        m_def_BackStyle)
    Call PropBag.WriteProperty("BorderStyle", m_BorderStyle, _
        m_def_BorderStyle)
    Call PropBag.WriteProperty("Caption", lblCaption.Caption, _
        "Calculator")
    Call PropBag.WriteProperty("MultValues", m_MultValues, _
        m_def_MultValues)
    Call PropBag.WriteProperty("ButtonCaption", btnExecute.Caption, _
        "Execute")
End Sub
```

Testing the Interface

To see the interface in action, close the new control's design window by clicking its close box in the window's upper-right corner. After you close the design window, the control's icon becomes available in VB5's toolbox. Now, double-click frmCalculatorTestApp in the Project Group window. The test application's form designer window appears. Double-click the new control's icon in the toolbox. An instance of the control appears on the test application's form.

To test the control from the developer's point of view, click the control instance to display its properties in the Properties window. You see that the ButtonCaption, Caption, and MultValues properties are now available in this window (see Figure 21.6).

FIG. 21.6
Your control's custom properties appear in the same window as the default properties.

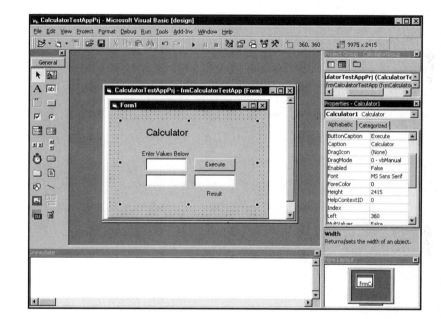

You're now going to use the Calculator control instance to create a simple adding machine. In the Properties window, change the ButtonCaption property to **Add**, change the Caption property to **Adding Machine**, and leave the MultValues property set to False.

Now, close the test application's designer window, and save your files. When you do, the WriteProperties() event procedure saves your new property settings to the form's source code. Listing 21.3 shows the newly updated source code. About three quarters of the way down the listing, you can see the settings for the Calculator control instance's properties. Notice that the MultValues property is not listed in the source code. This is because that particular property is still set to its default value. WriteProperties() saves only modified properties, assuming that you've supplied the correct default value to the PropBag.WriteProperty() method. In this case, the ActiveX Control Interface Wizard supplies the code for you.

Listing 21.3   frmCalculatorTestApp.frm—Source Code Containing the Control's Saved Properties

```
Object = "*\ACalculatorPrj.vbp"
Begin VB.Form frmCalculatorTestApp
   Caption         =   "Form1"
   ClientHeight    =   3195
   ClientLeft      =   60
   ClientTop       =   345
   ClientWidth     =   4680
   LinkTopic       =   "Form1"
   ScaleHeight     =   3195
   ScaleWidth      =   4680
   StartUpPosition =   3  'Windows Default
   Begin CalculatorPrj.Calculator Calculator1
      Height       =   2415
      Left         =   360
      TabIndex     =   0
      Top          =   360
      Width        =   3975
      _ExtentX     =   7011
      _ExtentY     =   4260
      Caption      =   "Adding Machine"
      ButtonCaption =  "Add"
   End
End
Attribute VB_Name = "frmCalculatorTestApp"
Attribute VB_GlobalNameSpace = False
Attribute VB_Creatable = False
Attribute VB_PredeclaredId = True
Attribute VB_Exposed = False
Private Sub Calculator1_Click()

End Sub
```

Go ahead and reopen the test application. Visual Basic now loads the source code and calls the ReadProperties() event procedure to read the property settings back in to the control. As a result, the test application's form reappears exactly as you left it.

Now run the test application. When you do so, the application's window appears. Type two numbers into the left text boxes and then click the Add button. The result of the addition appears in the Result text box.

What happens, though, if you enter an invalid value or leave one of the text boxes blank, and then click the Add button? As the application stands now, the result box will show the word "Undefined."

The developer can, however, add more error handling to the program by responding to the BadEntries event that you defined when you programmed the control. Whenever the user tries to perform a calculation with invalid entries, the control generates the BadEntries event. To see how the developer can supply additional error handling, close the test application. Then, double-click the control in the test application's form designer window. The code window appears. In the Procedures box, select `BadEntries`. The `Calculator1_BadEntries()` event procedure appears in the code window. Add the following line to that event procedure:

```
MsgBox "Please enter valid numerical values."
```

Now, rerun the application and enter invalid values into the text boxes. When you click the Add button, not only does the "Undefined" result appear, but a message box also appears, telling the user how to fix the problem (see Figure 21.7).

FIG. 21.7
By responding to the
`BadEntries` event, the
control can display error
messages.

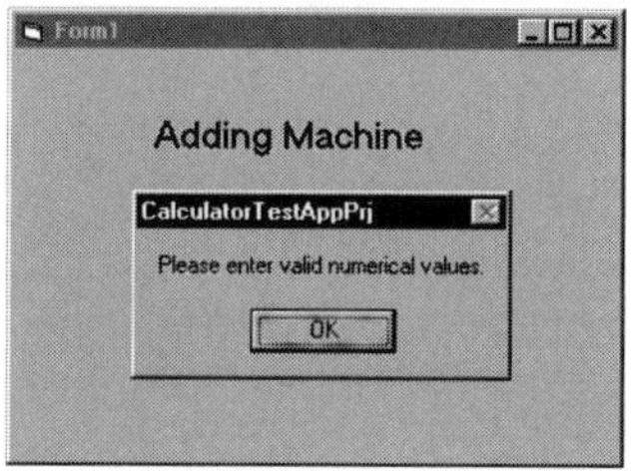

As a final experiment, close the test application and then click the control in the test application's form designer window. In the Properties window, change `ButtonCaption` to **Multiply**, set `Caption` to **Multiplying Machine**, and set `MultValues` to `True`. Now, when you run the application, the Calculator will multiply the given values, rather than add them.

Understanding the *btnExecute_Click()* Procedure

When the user clicks the `btnExecute` CommandButton control, Calculator must perform the requested operation, whether it be addition or multiplication. The program lines that handle this task are found in the `btnExecute_Click()` event procedure, which responds to the button click. That procedure first declares the local variables it'll use, as shown in Listing 21.4.

Listing 21.4   LSTV_04.TXT—Declaring Local Variables

```
Dim EntriesOK As Boolean
Dim s As String
Dim value1 As Integer
Dim value2 As Integer
Dim result As Integer
```

The procedure then calls the `ValidateEntries()` method to ensure that the text boxes contain numeric values:

```
EntriesOK = ValidateEntries
```

If `EntriesOK` gets set to `False`, there are invalid values in the text boxes. In this case, the procedure triggers the `BadEntries` event and sets the Result text box to `"Undefined"`:

Part

V

Ch

21

```
If Not EntriesOK Then
    RaiseEvent BadEntries
    txtResult.Text = "Undefined"
```

If the text boxes do contain valid values, the procedure can do the requested processing. In this case, the procedure first extracts the strings from the text boxes and converts the strings to integers, as shown in Listing 21.5:

Listing 21.5   LSTV_05.TXT—Converting Strings to Integers

```
s = txtValue(0).Text
value1 = Val(s)
s = txtValue(1).Text
value2 = Val(s)
```

After converting the strings, the procedure can perform the requested operation, which is controlled by the MultValues property, as shown in Listing 21.6:

Listing 21.6   LSTV_06.TXT—Performing the Requested Operation

```
If MultValues Then
    result = value1 * value2
Else
    result = value1 + value2
```

Finally, the procedure converts the result to a string and displays the string in the Result text box:

```
s = str(result)
txtResult.Text = s
```

Understanding the *ValidateEntries()* Method

As you just saw, before the btnExecute_Click() event procedure can perform its addition or multiplication, it must be sure that the given values are valid. It does this by calling the ValidateEntries() method, which returns True if the entered values are valid, and returns False if they're not valid. This method first declares the local variables it uses, as shown in Listing 21.7.

Listing 21.7   LSTAA_07.TXT—Declaring *ValidateEntries()*'s Local Variables

```
Dim str As String
Dim asciiValue As Integer
Dim x As Integer
Dim EntriesOK As Boolean
```

The Boolean value EntriesOK will hold the result of the validation. The method initializes this value to True:

```
EntriesOK = True
```

The method then starts a For loop that will iterate through the control array:

```
For x = 0 To 1
```

In this case, there are only two controls in the control array, so the loop goes from 0 to 1.

Inside the loop, the method first extracts the string from the indexed text box:

```
str = txtValue(x).Text
```

If it's not an empty string (the text box isn't empty), the method gets the ASCII code for the first character in the string. Otherwise, if the text box is empty, the method sets the ASCII value to 0, as shown in Listing 21.8.

Listing 21.8   LSTV_08.TXT—Getting the ASCII Value of the First Character in the String

```
If str <> "" Then
    asciiValue = Asc(str)
Else
    asciiValue = 0
End If
```

The method then compares the returned ASCII code with the ASCII codes for the digits 0 and 9. To be valid, the value being tested must lie within that range. If it doesn't, the method sets EntriesOK to False:

```
If (asciiValue < 48) Or (asciiValue > 57) Then _
    EntriesOK = False
```

After the For loop completes, the method returns the value of EntriesOK:

```
    ValidateEntries = EntriesOK
```

In the next section, you take the newly created Calculator control and create property pages.

Using Property Pages

While using Visual Basic, you may have noticed that when you select a Windows 95 control in a project, the Properties window displays not only all the control's properties but also a selection called Custom. This custom selection contains an ellipsis button that, when clicked, displays a property sheet for the control. The property sheet contains all the control's custom properties, and a developer can use the property sheet to set properties even when not working under Visual Basic.

For example, suppose you add a property sheet to the Calculator control that you created earlier in this chapter. After you've added the property sheet, Visual Basic displays the Custom ellipsis button in the properties section for the control. When you click the ellipsis button, the control's property sheet pops up. When working in Visual Basic on a project containing the

Part
V

Ch
21

control, you can set the control's custom properties from Visual Basic's Property window or from the control's property pages. Figure 21.8 shows what such a property sheet might look like.

FIG. 21.8

A control's property sheet often contains several pages of properties.

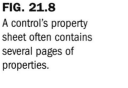

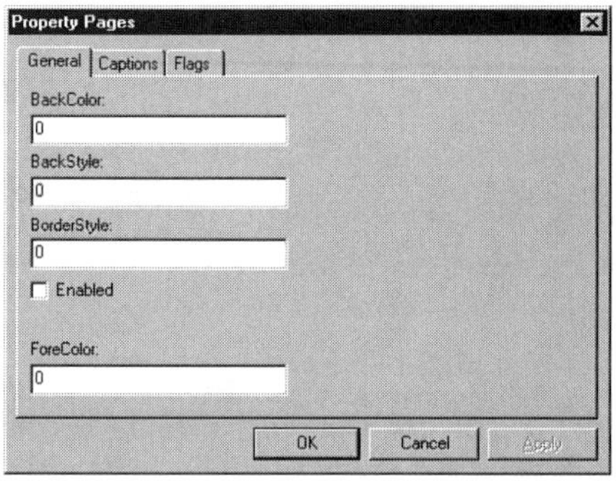

Creating Property Page Objects

The previous chapter taught how to create property pages by using the Property Page Wizard. The property sheet created with the Wizard in that chapter was easy to construct and required very little additional code to be functional. The Property Page Wizard is designed to provide you with a quick way of completing a property sheet; however, the Wizard does not provide many options from which to choose for your own modifications. In this section, you will create property sheets the old-fashioned way, with code. The advantage to this method is that you are able to make design and feature choices that otherwise would be unavailable through the Property Page Wizard.

The first step in creating your custom control's property sheet is to create property page objects for each group of properties. How you organize your properties into groups is up to you, although you'll want to use common sense. If your control has only a few properties, you can probably get away with representing them on a single property page. If the control has many properties, though, you should group related properties onto their own property pages. The typical steps involved in creating a property page for a control are as follows:

1. Create property page objects for each page you want in the property sheet.
2. On the property pages, place controls that the developer will use to edit each of the properties. (For example, you might use a TextBox control to represent a control's `Caption` property.)
3. Implement the `SelectionChanged()` event procedure for each property page. This event procedure is called when a developer opens the property page or selects one or more controls in the current project. The `SelectionChanged()` event procedure is responsible for reading in the current values of each controls' properties.
4. Implement the `Change()` event procedure (or sometimes `Click()`) for each control in each property page. This event procedure is called whenever the developer changes the contents of one of a property page's controls. The `Change()` event procedure notifies

Visual Basic of the change, so that Visual Basic can enable the property sheet's Apply button.

5. Implement the ApplyChanges() event procedure for each property page. This event procedure is called when the developer closes a property page or when the developer clicks the property sheet's Apply button. Its task is to copy the new property values from the property page's controls to the custom control's properties.

6. Connect the property pages to the custom control.

For the calculator project, you'll create three property pages called General, Captions, and Flags. Follow these steps to create these property page objects:

1. Choose File, Open Project to load the Calculator project into VB5.

2. Select Calculator in the Project Group Window.

3. Choose Project, Add Property Page from the menu bar. The Add Property Page property sheet appears.

4. On the Add Property Page property sheet's New page, double-click the Property Page icon to add a property page object to the project. The property page's designer window appears on the screen.

5. Double-click the Name property in the property page's Properties window and type **CalculatorGeneral**.

6. Also in the Properties window, double-click the Caption property and type **General**.

   A property page's tab uses the Caption property as its label. Because the page's tab is provided by the property sheet that contains the pages, the caption doesn't appear in the designer window.

7. Create two more property sheet objects named **CalculatorCaptions** and **CalculatorFlags**, with Caption properties of **Captions** and **Flags**, respectively.

Placing Controls on the Property Pages

Now that you have created the property page objects, you can add the control you need to represent the properties of the custom control to which the property sheet will be attached. The types of controls to use are up to you. Usually, though, you'll use TextBoxes to represent text properties, CheckBoxes to represent *Boolean properties* (properties that can be set to True or False), ListBoxes to represent properties with multiple settings, and so on. Follow these steps to add controls to the property pages you created in the previous section:

1. Double-click CalculatorGeneral in the Project Group window. The CalculatorGeneral property page's designer window appears.

2. Add four Label controls to the property pages by using the following properties:

Name	Caption
lblBackColor	Backcolor
lblBackStyle	BackStyle
lblBorderStyle	BorderStyle
lblForeColor	ForeColor

3. Add four TextBox controls to the property page, using the following properties:

Name	Height	Left	Top	Width
txtBackColor	330	90	370	3700
txtBackStyle	330	90	1020	2700
txtBorderStyle	330	90	1670	2700
txtForeColor	330	90	2970	2700

4. Add a CheckBox control to the property page, using the following properties. When complete, the `CalculatorGeneral` property page should look like Figure 21.9.

Name   chkEnabled
Caption   "Enabled"

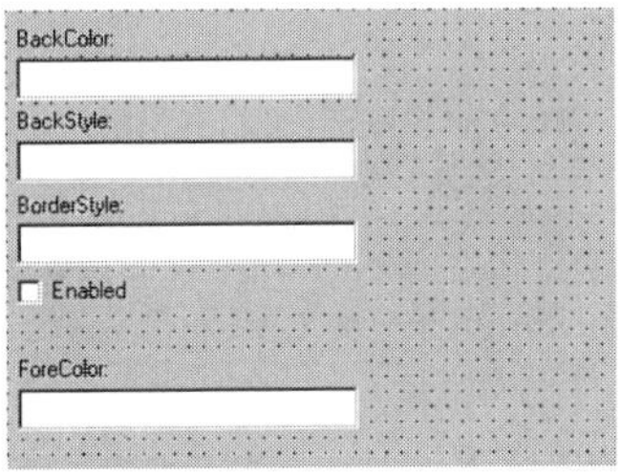

FIG. 21.9

Here's the `CalculatorGeneral` property page with all its controls.

5. Double-click `CalculatorCaptions` in the Project Group window. The `CalculatorCaptions` property page's designer window appears.

6. Add two Label controls to the property pages, using the following properties:

Name	Caption
lblButtonCaption	**"ButtonCaption:"**
lblCaption	"Caption:"

7. Add two TextBox controls to the property page, using the following properties. When complete, the `CalculatorCaptions` property page should look like Figure 21.10.

Name   txtButtonCaption
Name   txtCaption

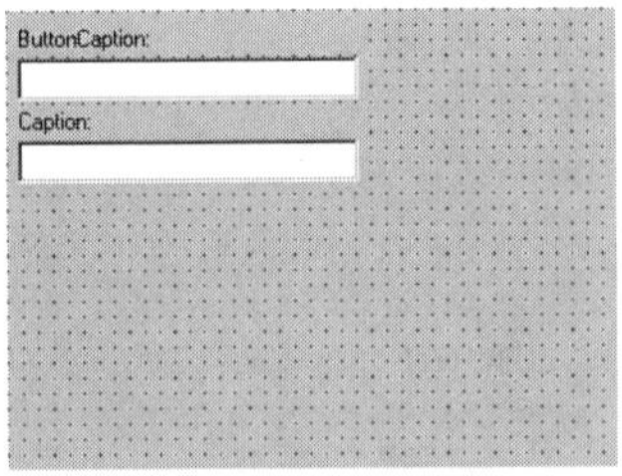

FIG. 21.10

Here's the `CalculatorCaptions` property page with all its controls.

8. Double-click `CalculatorFlags` in the Project Group window. The `CalculatorFlags` property page's designer window appears.

9. Add a CheckBox control to the property page (see Figure 21.11), using the following properties:

> Name`chkMultValues`
> Caption   `"MultValues"`

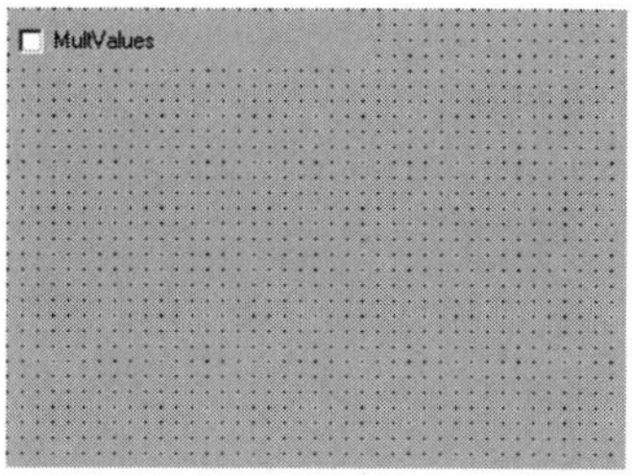

FIG. 21.11
Place the CheckBox control as shown here.

Implementing the *SelectionChanged()* Event Procedure
==

Imagine for a moment that a developer is using the Calculator control as part of an application. The developer has placed two Calculator controls in the application's window. One Calculator control will perform addition and the other will perform multiplication. Now the developer wants to set the controls' properties and therefore calls up the controls' property sheet. When this happens, each property page's `SelectionChanged()` event procedure gets called, so that each controls' current property settings can be loaded into the property pages' controls, where the developer can change them.

Of course, at this point, all you've done is create the property page objects and position Label, TextBox, and CheckBox controls on them. Now you need to write the code for the `SelectionChanged()` event procedure. To do that, follow these steps:

1. Double-click `CalculatorGeneral` in the Project Group window to display the `CalculatorGeneral` property page's designer window.

2. Double-click the property page to display its code window. The window appears, showing the `SelectionChanged()` event procedure.

3. Add the program lines shown in Listing 21.9 to the `SelectionChanged()` event procedure.

Part

V

Ch

21

Listing 21.9   LSTV_9.TXT—Program Lines for the *SelectionChanged()*
Event Procedure

```
txtForeColor.Text = SelectedControls(0).ForeColor
chkEnabled.Value = (SelectedControls(0).Enabled And vbChecked)
txtBorderStyle.Text = SelectedControls(0).BorderStyle
txtBackStyle.Text = SelectedControls(0).BackStyle
txtBackColor.Text = SelectedControls(0).BackColor
```

4. Double-click `CalculatorCaptions` in the Project Group window to display the `CalculatorCaptions` property page's designer window.

5. Double-click the property page to display its code window. The window appears, showing the `SelectionChanged()` event procedure.

6. Add the following program lines to the `SelectionChanged()` event procedure:

```
txtButtonCaption.Text = SelectedControls(0).ButtonCaption
txtCaption.Text = SelectedControls(0).Caption
```

7. Double-click `CalculatorFlags` in the Project Group window to display the `CalculatorFlags` property page's designer window.

8. Double-click the property page to display its code window. The window appears, showing the `SelectionChanged()` event procedure.

9. Add the following program line to the `SelectionChanged()` event procedure:

```
chkMultValues.Value = (SelectedControls(0).MultValues And vbChecked)
```

If you examine the program lines you added to the `SelectionChanged()` event procedures, you'll see that each control in each property page copies a value from the control into the property page's control. For example, the Calculator control's `Caption` property is represented in `SelectionChanged()` by the following program line:

```
txtCaption.Text = SelectedControls(0).Caption
```

Recall from the previous section that the developer placed two Calculator controls on the application's window. If the developer selects both controls before displaying the controls' property sheet, the property sheet represents a multiple selection. In the previous code line, you can see that the `SelectedControls` collection object represents the selected controls. `SelectedControls(0)` is the first selected control and `SelectedControls(1)` is the second.

Currently, the property page can handle only single control selections because it processes only `SelectedControls(0)`, copying the selected control's Caption property into the property page's `txtCaption` TextBox control. You'll learn about multiply selected controls later in this chapter in the section titled "Handling Multiple Control Selections."

Understand that when the property page first appears, its `SelectionChanged()` event procedure copies the current property values into the property page's controls. This enables the property page to display the current settings to the developer. Each control in each property page must be represented by a line in `SelectionChanged()`.

Implementing the *Change()* Event Procedure

When the developer changes the contents of a TextBox (or other similar Visual Basic controls), the control's `Change()` event procedure is called. In the case of a property page, this gives you a chance to notify Visual Basic that the contents of a property have changed, allowing Visual Basic to enable the property sheet's Apply button. All you have to do to tell Visual Basic about this change is to set the control's Changed property to `True`.

N O T E   Some controls, such as CheckBoxes, use their `Click()` event procedure instead of `Change()` to handle the change notification. ▣

To handle this important event in the `CalculatorGeneral` property page, bring up the property page's code window and add the lines shown in Listing 21.10 to the window, outside of any other methods or event procedures. Add the procedures shown in Listing 21.11 to the `CalculatorCaptions` property page's code window. Finally, add the following procedure to the `CalculatorFlags` property page's code window.

```
Private Sub chkMultValues_Click()
    Changed = True
End Sub
```

Listing 21.10   LSTV_10.TXT—New Event Procedures for the *CalculatorGeneral* Property Page

```
Private Sub txtForeColor_Change()
    Changed = True
End Sub

Private Sub chkEnabled_Click()
    Changed = True
End Sub

Private Sub txtBorderStyle_Change()
    Changed = True
End Sub

Private Sub txtBackStyle_Change()
    Changed = True
End Sub

Private Sub txtBackColor_Change()
    Changed = True
End Sub
```

Listing 26.11   LSTV_11.TXT—New Procedures for the *CalculatorCaptions* Property Page

```
Private Sub txtCaption_Change()
    Changed = True
End Sub

Private Sub txtButtonCaption_Change()
    Changed = True
End Sub
```

Part

V

Ch

21

Implementing the *ApplyChanges()* Event Procedure

The `ApplyChanges()` event procedure is the opposite of `SelectionChanged()`. Whereas `SelectionChanged()` copies the custom control's current properties into the property page, the `ApplyChanges()` event procedure copies the property page's contents back into the custom control's properties. This happens when the developer clicks the property sheet's Apply button or when the developer closes a property page.

To add program code for the `ApplyChanges` event, add the procedure shown in Listing 21.12 to the CalculatorGeneral property page's code window. Then, add the procedure shown in Listing 21.13 to the `CalculatorCaptions` property page's code window. Finally, add the following procedure to the CalculatorFlags property page's code window.

```
Private Sub PropertyPage_ApplyChanges()
    SelectedControls(0).MultValues = (chkMultValues.Value = vbChecked)
End Sub
```

Listing 21.12   LSTV_12.TXT—The *ApplyChanges()* Event Procedure for the *CalculatorGeneral* Property Page

```
Private Sub PropertyPage_ApplyChanges()
    SelectedControls(0).ForeColor = txtForeColor.Text
    SelectedControls(0).Enabled = (chkEnabled.Value = vbChecked)
    SelectedControls(0).BorderStyle = txtBorderStyle.Text
    SelectedControls(0).BackStyle = txtBackStyle.Text
    SelectedControls(0).BackColor = txtBackColor.Text
End Sub
```

Listing 21.13   LSTV_13.TXT—The *ApplyChanges()* Event Procedure for the *CalculatorCaptions* Property Page

```
Private Sub PropertyPage_ApplyChanges()
    SelectedControls(0).ButtonCaption = txtButtonCaption.Text
    SelectedControls(0).Caption = txtCaption.Text
End Sub
```

Connecting the Property Pages to the Control

The property pages you've been building are now complete. All you have to do now is connect the property pages to the control whose properties they represent. To perform that task, follow these steps:

1. Double-click `Calculator` in the Project Group window. The control's designer window appears.

2. In the control's Properties window, double-click the `PropertyPages` property. The Connect Property Pages dialog box appears.

3. Place check marks in the `CalculatorGeneral`, `CalculatorCaptions`, and `CalculatorFlags` check boxes (see Figure 21.12).

FIG. 21.12
The checked property
pages will be attached
to the control.

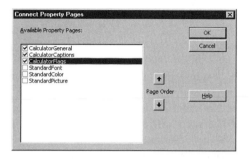

4. Click OK in the Connect Property Pages dialog box to associate the selected property
   pages with the Calculator control.

Using the Property Sheet

You've completed the creation of your Calculator control's property sheet. When you're working on an application that contains the control, you can set the control's properties from Visual
Basic's Properties window or from the control's property sheet. To see this in action, first make
sure that you have closed all of your control's design forms. After you have done this, double-
click frmCalculatorTestApp in the Project Group window. When the test application's designer
window appears, click the Calculator control to select it. When you do, the control's properties
appear in the Properties window. If you look closely, you'll see a new property entry called
Custom.

This new Custom property entry is your gateway (under Visual Basic) to the control's property
sheet. To see the property sheet, double-click the Custom entry. You can also display the property sheet by clicking Custom and then clicking the ellipsis button. When you do, the property
sheet appears. Using this property sheet, you can set the properties of the selected control
(see Figure 21.13). Notice that, as soon as you start typing in one of the TextBoxes, or when
you click on a CheckBox, the property sheet's Apply button becomes enabled.

FIG. 21.13
Here's your finished
property sheet showing
the Caption page.

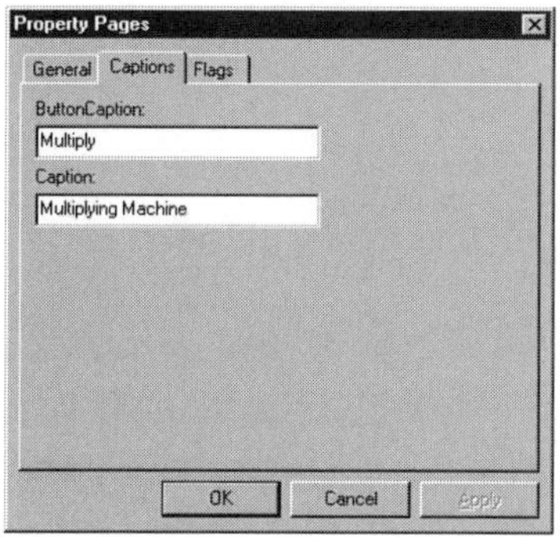

N O T E Remember to save the changes you've made to the Calculator project. Notice that when
you do save the changes, the property page files are stored with .PAG file extensions.

Handling Multiple Control Selections

You may recall that the `SelectedControls` collection object represents all the controls that a developer has selected when he calls up the property sheet. You use the `SelectedControls` object in the `SelectionChanged()` and `ApplyChanges()` event procedures to access the selected controls' properties. For example, suppose the developer has two Calculator controls selected. Then, in the appropriate property page, `SelectedControls(0).ButtonCaption` represents the `ButtonCaption` property of the first control and `SelectedControls(1).ButtonCaption` represents the `ButtonCaption` property of the second control. The developer can set both controls' button captions to the same value by selecting both controls and then setting the `ButtonCaption` property in the property page that displays that property.

This brings up an important point. Not all properties should be set the same in multiple controls. Suppose that the developer selects two `Calculator` controls and uses the property sheet to change `ButtonCaption` to "Add." In this case, both instances of the control will have a button labeled "Add," which may be what the developer wants. However, it's not likely that two `Calculator` controls will have the same `Caption` property because it is the caption that labels the control for the user. So, when dealing with multiple control selections, you have two types of properties:

- Properties that may be set to the same value for multiple controls.
- Properties that should be unique in each control of a multiple control selection.

You can tell how many controls are selected by examining the `SelectedControls` object's `Count` property. If `Count` is greater than 1, you're dealing with a multiple selection. You can also simply code `ApplyChanges()` such that only the properties of the first control in the control collection get assigned properties that should be unique, whereas all controls get assigned properties that can logically be the same from one control to another. Listing 21.14 shows a version of `ApplyChanges()` that takes this latter approach.

Listing 21.14   LSTV_14.TXT—An *ApplyChanges()* Event Procedure that Can Handle Multiple Controls

```
Private Sub PropertyPage_ApplyChanges()
    Dim control As Calculator

    ' Set only the first control's caption.
    SelectedControls(0).ButtonCaption = txtButtonCaption.Text

    ' Set every control's button caption.
    For Each control In SelectedControls
        control.Caption = txtCaption.Text
    Next control
End Sub
```

The special For Each loop enables the program to iterate through the control collection, without dealing with indexes and without needing to know how many controls the collection contains.

Visual Basic's Debugger

As the developer changes property settings, Visual Basic calls the properties' Get and Let property procedures. Event procedures may also be called if the developer does something such as resize the control instance. The important thing to notice is that none of the control's methods or procedures that implement its runtime functionality are called at design time. Therefore, you have to test the control's design time and runtime features separately.

To test design time features, you must act as a developer, placing the control on a test application's form and manipulating it as a developer would, changing property values and resizing the control. To test your control's runtime features, you must run the test application and manipulate the control as the user would.

One very effective way to fully test a control is to create a test project. The test project should call out to all the properties, methods, and events that your control uses. The test project should also test the validation routines that you have in place by providing values outside of the accepted range. The test project should be an .exe program; this way, it can be fully compiled into a standalone program.

The Calculator control that we just completed is a good example of a control that needs a test project to fully test its functionality. The test project should try to invoke the Add method when there is no data or the multiply method when the value is a negative number. What you learn from your test application will help to produce better exception and error handling routines for your control.

Your test project should be capable of locating most of the errors that could occur in your control. It is especially important to test out any error handling that you have in your control. This will verify that your control will not cause damage to the user's machine and that you have properly handled the error.

N O T E The test project can detect a lot of potential problems; however, it can't trap all of the errors that may occur. This can be done only through the use of good code design and solid unit-level testing of each component of the control. ▪

To make the testing and debugging task a little easier, Visual Basic includes a built-in debugger. You can use the debugger to set breakpoints in a control's code or to step through program code one line at a time. As you're stepping through program lines, you can watch how the values of variables change. Visual Basic 5 provides you with the debugging commands shown in Table 21.2.

Part
V

Ch
21

Table 21.2   Visual Basic Debugger Commands

Command	Description
Step Into	Steps into the procedure being called
Step Over	Executes the procedure being called without stepping into the procedure
Step Out	Executes the remaining lines in a procedure
Run to Cursor	Executes all lines up to the current position of the cursor
Add Watch	Adds a variable to the Watch window
Edit Watch	Edits an entry in the Watch window
Quick Watch	Displays the value of the expression at the mouse cursor position
Toggle Breakpoints	Turns a breakpoint on or off
Clear All Breakpoints	Removes all breakpoints that were set
Set Next Statement	Sets the next statement to execute
Show Next Statement	Shows the next statement to execute

To get some practice with Visual Basic's 5 debugger, first create a folder called Calculator2 and copy all the files from the section exercise to the new Calculator2 folder. Then, follow these steps to see Visual Basic's debugger in action:

1. Load the CalculatorGroup.vbg project group from the new Calculator2 folder.

2. In the Project Group window, double-click Calculator. The Calculator control's designer window appears.

3. Double-click the designer window. The Calculator control's code window appears, showing the InitProperties() event procedure.

4. Click the gray bar to the left of the text cursor. Visual Basic sets a breakpoint on the selected line. This line is marked as a red bar in the code window. You can also turn on the breakpoint by selecting Debug, Toggle Breakpoint from the menu bar or by pressing F9 on your keyboard.

   When the control's code is running, Visual Basic stops program execution when it reaches a breakpoint. This enables you to examine a procedure more carefully, as you'll soon see.

5. Close the code and designer windows. The Calculator control becomes available on VB5's toolbox.

6. In the Project Group window, double-click frmCalculatorTestApp. The test application's designer window appears.

7. In the designer window, click the instance of the Calculator control to select it. Then, press your keyboard's delete key to remove the instance from the test application.

8. Double-click the Calculator control's icon in VB5's toolbox. Visual Basic creates an instance of the control, but stops the control's initialization on the first line of the InitProperties() event procedure. The line is marked with a red and yellow bar.

   Visual Basic stopped execution on this line because that's where you set the breakpoint in Step 4. Now that the control's code execution has stopped, you can use other debugger commands to examine the event procedure line by line. The red part of the bar tells you that there's a breakpoint set on this line. The yellow portion of the bar indicates that this is the next line that will execute.

9. Place the mouse cursor over m_BackColor in the code window. The value of the m_BackColor variable appears in a small tip box (see Figure 21.14).

FIG. 21.14
You can examine the contents of variables just by placing the mouse cursor over the variable's name in the code window.

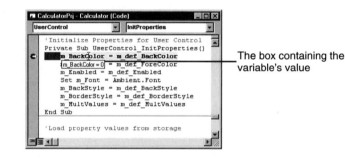

The box containing the variable's value

10. Press F8 (Step Into) a few times. Each time you do, Visual Basic executes the current program line and moves the yellow bar to the next line (see Figure 21.15). This line-by-line execution enables you to examine variables that may have been set or how the program flow is progressing. This knowledge can help you to determine if certain code is being executed, or if your variables have the expected values.

FIG. 21.15
The yellow bar moves to always indicate the next line to execute.

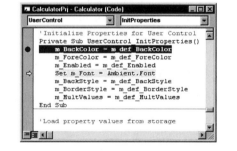

11. Scroll the code window up until you can see the Get Caption() property procedure. Set a breakpoint on the Caption = lblCaption.Caption line.

12. Press F5 (Start) to continue the program execution. When you do so, the program runs until it hits the breakpoint you set in the Get Caption() property procedure.

Part
V

Ch
21

13. Select Debug, Add Watch from VB5's menu bar. The Add Watch dialog box appears (see Figure 21.16).

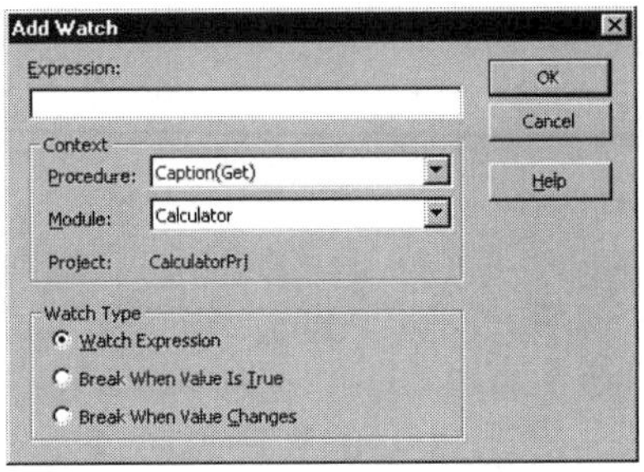

FIG. 21.16
You use the Add Watch dialog box to add expressions to the Watch window.

14. Type **Caption** in the Expression box, and click OK. The Watch Window appears at the bottom of VB5's main window, showing the variable's name, current value, data type, and the context in which you're viewing the expression.

15. Press F8 to execute the current program line. Visual Basic assigns a new value to the Caption variable.

   Many program bugs can be traced to bad values being assigned to variables. Using the Watch Window, you can quickly locate these kinds of problems.

16. Select Debug, Clear All Breakpoints from the menu bar. Visual Basic removes all the breakpoints you set.

17. Select Run, End to end the debugging session. Then, close the open code window, and delete the Calculator control instance from the test application's designer window.

The VB5 debugging tools can be a powerful way to look inside your code while it is executing. The previous example enabled you to walk through the process of debugging your code. If you used the code contained on the Web site for the book at **www.mcp.com/info/0-7897/0-7897-1288-1**, you probably found that there were no errors in the source code. To fully experience the power of the debugger, you need to use it on code that has bugs in it. To help you, Listings 21.15 and 21.16, which have typical programming bugs included in them, provide sample code segments from the Calculator.ctl project.

Listing 21.15   LSTV.15—The Entry Validation Function

```
Public Function ValidateEntries() As Boolean
    Dim str As String
    Dim asciiValue As Integer
    Dim x As Integer

    EntriesOK = True
    For x = 0 To I
        str = txtValue(x)Text
        If str <> "" Then
            asciiValue = Asc(str)
        Else
            asciiValue = 0
```

```
        End If
        If (asciiValue < 48) Or (asciiValue > 57) Then
            Entries = False
    Next x

    ValidateEntries = EntriesOK
End Function
```

Listing 21.16   LSTV.16—Read Properties Subroutine

```
'Load property values from storage
Private Sub UserControl_ReadProperties(PropBag As PropertyBag)

    m_BackColor = PropBag.ReadProperty("BackColor", m_def_BackColor)
    m_ForeColor = PropBag.ReadProperty("ForeColor", m_def_ForeColor)
    m_Enabled = PropBag.ReadProperty("Enabled", m_def_Enabled)
    Set Font = PropBag.ReadProperty("Font" Ambient.Font)
    m_BackStyle = PropBag.ReadProperty("BackStyle", m_def_BackStyle)
    m_BorderStyle = PropBag.ReadProperty("BorderStyle", m_def_BorderStyle)
    lblCaption.Caption = PropBag.Property("Caption", "Calculator")
    m_MultValues = PropBag.ReadProperty("MultValues", m_def_MultValues)
    btnExecute.Caption = PropBag.writeProperty("ButtonCaption", "Execute")
End Sub
```

Control Error Handling

The importance of controls running correctly cannot be overstated. Developers and users are depending on you to create a product that they can use with confidence. If a developer incorporates your control into an application and the application then fails for the user because of your control, it's the developer who'll take the blame. It'll appear to the user that the developer's application is at fault. (Of course, in this situation, both you and the developer would have to share the blame. The developer is responsible for testing that his application runs correctly with your control.) There are a few things you should do, and a few things you should not do, to help ensure that your controls won't present developers and users with nasty surprises.

First, use plenty of error handling, especially in event procedures. If an error occurs in an event procedure, and your program code doesn't handle it, the control will crash—bringing down the container in which the control is sited. Notice that you are advised to provide plenty of error handling. Do not *raise* your own errors in event procedures. If you do, your application will surely crash and take everything down with it.

N O T E   One way of generating errors is through the `Raise` method. You can use this method if you want more information than generally is available using the Error statement. One of the bits of information that the `Raise` method provides is the source of the error. Additional help related information can also be provided The information that the `Raise` method provides can be useful during the creation of classes in VB.

Any `Raise` methods that are executed within your ActiveX during runtime will cause your control to escape beyond the boundaries of the control. ■

Typically, all events that have any code attached to them should be error handled. There are some key areas that need special attention:

- File handling
- Input/Output Connectivity
- Screen Control
- User Resource checks
- Interaction with other controls
- Boundary conditions

CAUTION

Do not be tempted into taking the easy way out of error handling with the "on error resume next" method. This method allows your program or ActiveX control to continue working even if there was a error, serious or otherwise. This method of error handling does not provide any method of gracefully handling errors.

Properly error handling your procedures and functions takes only a few lines that can easily be cut and pasted where they are needed. In Listing 21.17 you see one example of how to trap for the "No Current Record" error during database activity.

Listing 21.17   Errordemo.bas—Proper Error Handling

```
on error goto errhandler

'Write property values to storage
Private Sub UserControl_WriteProperties(PropBag As PropertyBag)

    Call PropBag.WriteProperty("BackColor", m_BackColor, m_def_BackColor)
    Call PropBag.WriteProperty("ForeColor", m_ForeColor, _
        m_def_ForeColor)
    Call PropBag.WriteProperty("Enabled", m_Enabled, _
        m_def_Enabled)
    Call PropBag.WriteProperty("Font", Font, Ambient.Font)
    Call PropBag.WriteProperty("BackStyle", m_BackStyle, _
        m_def_BackStyle)
    Call PropBag.WriteProperty("BorderStyle", m_BorderStyle, _
        m_def_BorderStyle)
    Call PropBag.WriteProperty("Caption", lblCaption.Caption, _
        "Calculator")
    Call PropBag.WriteProperty("MultValues", m_MultValues, _
        m_def_MultValues)
    Call PropBag.WriteProperty("ButtonCaption", btnExecute.Caption, _
        "Execute")

exit sub
errhandler:

' Here is where you would put your error handling routines
```

```
' such as this:
' if err = 3021 then
'   msgbox("There are no records in the database")
' endif

' Note: You may find it more appropriate to use a CASE
' construct rather than a If..Then..Else.

End Sub
```

In Listing 26.17 you saw how to trap for a specific type of error in a procedure. Notice that the first line of code:

```
on error goto errhandler
```

refers to the errhandler routine. This routine, located at the end to the parent procedure, actually looks for and traps the error as shown in the following lines of code:

```
errhandler:

' Here is where you would put your error handling
' routines such as this:
' if err = 3021 then
'   msgbox("There are no records in the database")
' endif
```

Although these lines only trap one error, they could easily be modified to trap more than one or to call out to a global error handling procedure. The following code examples shown how a global error handling procedure might be constructed. They are meant to illustrate a point only, your actual code will need to be tailored to the specific needs of the application.

The following code segment would be placed the procedures that you want to trap for errors. The `errortrap()` function is passed the value contained in `err object`.

```
Errhandler:
errortrap(err)
```

The following code segment would be placed in a .BAS file or a .CLS file. The purpose is to assign a message to a global variable based upon the error number passed to it.

```
Function errortrap(err as integer)

Select Case err
    Case 3021
        gError_Msg = "A problem has occurred with your database."
    Case 13
        gError_Msg = "A System error has occurred"

...( more error handling code)

    Case Else
        gError_Msg = "An unexplained error has occurred"
```

Part

V

Ch

21

```
End Select
... (any additional code)
```

Another tip is to always use Get and Let property procedures for a control's properties. Don't create properties by adding public variables to a control. If you use the Get and Let mechanism, you can validate a property's value once, in the property's Let procedure. The property is then guaranteed to be valid in the rest of the program.

If you use public variables for properties, the developer has complete access to the properties' values and can change them behind your program's back. This means that you must check the properties' values every time they're used. Not only is such a practice a pain, it's also a good way to crash a program. You can't raise errors in event procedures, should that be where you discover that a property has been assigned an invalid value.

In general, wherever the developer can change values of data in your control, be sure that the changes are valid. Any such values should be implemented as properties, giving your control the capability to verify the values in the property's Let procedure. Similarly, at runtime, be sure that any values that the control accepts from the user are valid. A good example is the Calculator control you worked with in this chapter. When the user enters values into the control's test boxes, you want to be sure that those values can be added or multiplied. The ValidateEntries() method of the Calculator control handles that little detail as described in the "Understanding the *ValidateEntries()* Method" section.

Distributing ActiveX Controls by Using Setup Wizard

The Setup Wizard is a tool used with the Visual Basic Setup Toolkit that aids you in the creation of application setup and distribution. The Setup Wizard sets up distribution of your application across the Internet using automatic code download from Microsoft Internet Explorer, Version 3.0 and Version 4.0. The Setup Wizard enables automatic downloading of your object with the initialization of the page that contains it with cabinet (.CAB) files. Also, the Setup Wizard analyzes your project and determines what supporting files need to be included with your control.

N O T E Cabinet files are specially formatted files that contain ActiveX controls along with all of the necessary support files. These files contain information about the control and the necessary support files that tell the Web browser what files need to be downloaded. The Web browser takes the information from the cabinet file and compares it to the files already on the computer to determine whether any of the files need to be downloaded. This enables the Web browser to avoid downloading any unnecessary files.

You can start the Setup Wizard by choosing Application Setup Wizard from your Start menu or Setupwiz.exe from the \Setupkit\Kitfil32 directory where you installed Visual Basic.

Then you choose to build an Internet Download package with the Application Setup Wizard, and you'll be presented with a series of dialog boxes.

Introduction Dialog Box The Introduction dialog box makes you aware of the capabilities of the Setup Wizard. The first time you run the Setup Wizard, read the description and then select the Skip the Screen in the Future check box, shown in Figure 21.17. Choose Next to go to the next dialog box.

FIG. 21.17
The Setup Wizard
Introduction dialog
box provides you with
some basic information
about using the Wizard
to build application
distribution files.

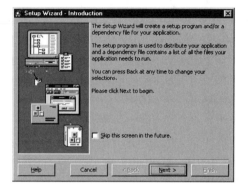

Select Project and Options Dialog Box Type the name of the project file or use the Browse button to find the project file. For the distribution options, select Create Internet Download Setup, as seen in Figure 21.18. Choose Next to go to the next dialog box.

FIG. 21.18
To build the necessary
files for use in an HTML
document, you need to
use the Application
Setup Wizard to
create an Internet
Download Setup.

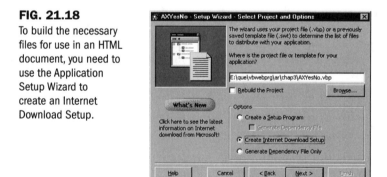

Internet Distribution Location Dialog Box Use the file browser to specify where you want your ActiveX control to be placed for Internet download, as shown in Figure 21.19. Choose Next to go to the next dialog box.

Part
V

Ch
21

FIG. 21.19

You need to specify a location for the Setup Wizard to build the Internet Download files.

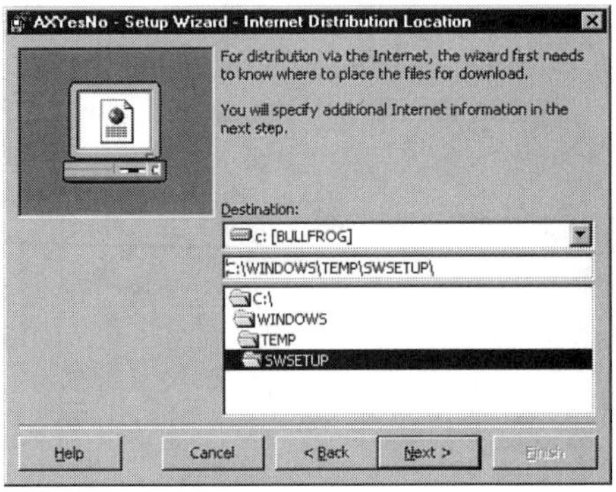

Internet Package Dialog Box   You must decide where you want to locate the runtime components of your applications. You can either select your own location on one of your own servers or download runtime components from the Microsoft Web site. Specifying a location on an internal server might be better if you don't have a fast connection to the Internet. On the other hand, by specifying the Microsoft Web site at **http://www.microsoft.com/vbasic/ icompdown,** you guarantee that your users always get the latest copies of the runtime components.

Click the Safety command button to set safety levels for each ActiveX control in your project. If your control is safe for initialization, check Safe for Initialization. If your control is safe for scripting, check Safe for Scripting, as in Figure 21.20. (See the later section "Marking Your Controls Safe for Scripting and Initialization" for more information.) Choose OK on the Safety dialog box, and Next on the Internet Package dialog box to go to the next dialog box.

FIG. 21.20

By marking your control as safe for initialization and scripting, you are placing your guarantee in your control that it cannot harm the user's computer, even if being used in HTML documents that you did not build.

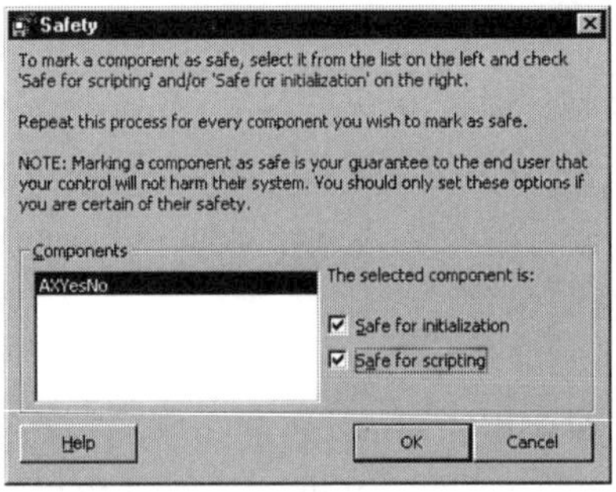

ActiveX Server Components Dialog Box   The Setup Wizard analyzes your project and looks for any ActiveX controls that you might be using as server-side controls. If your control uses any server-side components, either as local or remote components, add them with this dialog box. Choose Next to go to the next dialog box.

If your control will be distributed to other developers for use in building Web pages, you need to include the Property Page DLL with your file distribution. This provides developers with the ability to specify property settings for the control in other, non-Visual Basic development environments. The Setup Wizard stops and asks you if you want to include this DLL with the setup files, as seen in Figure 21.21.

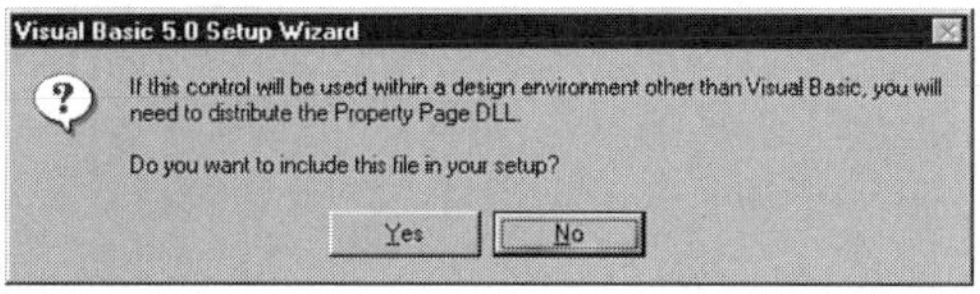

FIG. 21.21
The Setup Wizard asks you if you want to include the Property Pages DLL with your file distribution package.

File Summary Dialog Box   The File Summary dialog box lists all of the files that are distributed with your ActiveX control, as shown in Figure 21.22. If there are any other files you want to include with your file distribution, including readme and licensing files, this is where you add them. Use the Add button to add additional files. Choose Next to complete the Setup Wizard.

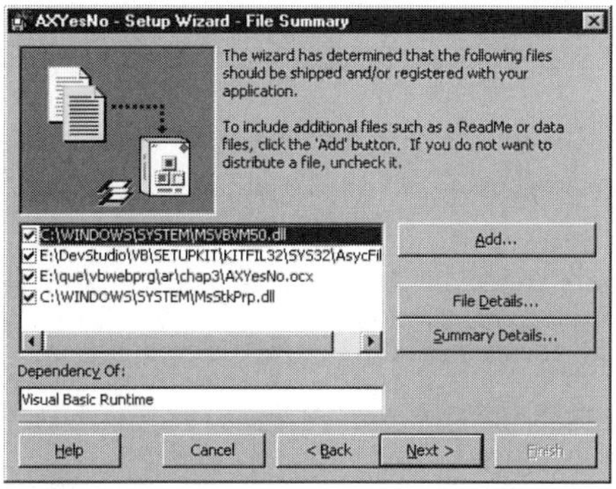

FIG. 21.22
The File Summary dialog box shows you what files will be included in the Internet download files that will be packaged for including on a Web site.

Finally, the Setup Wizard provides you with the opportunity to save the information you have specified as a template to be used every time you run the Setup Wizard on this same project. Click the Finish button to build your distribution package.

Viewing Your ActiveX Control in a Web Browser

The Setup Wizard creates a default Web page that has your ActiveX control inserted on it. This Web page is located where you decide to place your ActiveX control. Open this page with a Web browser that supports ActiveX, such as Internet Explorer 3.0, as seen in Figure 21.23. If you view the source code of the page, you see a simple HTML document that contains the `<OBJECT>` element, specifying the Class ID of your control, as seen in Listing 21.18.

Part
V

Ch
21

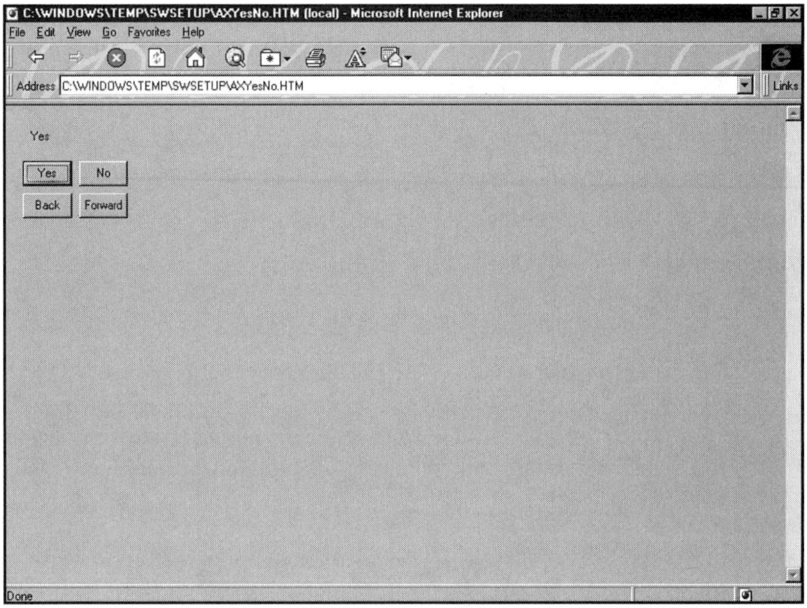

FIG. 21.23

Once you have finished building your Internet distribution files, you can open the HTML file that was generated by the Setup Wizard in Internet Explorer to test your control.

Listing 21.18   AXYESNO.HTM—Source of AXYesNo.HTM

```
<HTML>
<!--     If any of the controls on this page require licensing,
 you must create a license package file.
     Run LPK_TOOL.EXE in the tools directory to create the
required LPK file.
<OBJECT CLASSID="clsid:5220cb21-c88d-11cf-b347-00aa00a28331">
     <PARAM NAME="LPKPath" VALUE="LPKfilename.LPK">
</OBJECT>
-->
<OBJECT
     classid="clsid:B7C523AE-6500-11D0-AB01-444553540000"
     id=AXYesNo
     codebase="AXYesNo.CAB#version=1,0,0,0">
</OBJECT>
</HTML>
```

N O T E   The Class ID included in the HTML in Listing 21.18 will be different from the Class ID generated in your HTML document. This Class ID is a globally unique identifier automatically generated by Visual Basic when you build your control. You will never generate two matching Class IDs, and the Class IDs generated by Visual Basic to identify your controls will never be the same as any other Class IDs generated by anyone else to identify anyone else's control. This Class ID is automatically registered with your system Registry database and is used by the operating system to determine whether the control needs to be downloaded from the Web site, or whether you already have the control on your system. ■

All object information is defined between the <Object> and the </Object> tags. The following lists some important tags you should be familiar with:

ClassID	The unique ID for this object
ID	The name that you use to specify this control in script
Codebase	Location of distribution files for your ActiveX control

Responsible ActiveX Creation and Distribution

ActiveX controls give the control programmer a new tool that can be used responsibly or otherwise. We as ActiveX programmers have a obligation to provide controls that are safe to use and instill a high level confidence in the developers use our controls. This type of responsible creation encompasses the following ideas which you look at in detail in this section.

- Marking controls safe for initialization and scripting
- Licensing issues
- Versioning of controls

Marking Your Controls Safe for Scripting and Initialization

Safe for Scripting means that there is no way to harm a user's computer or obtain information about the user's computer without permission, no matter what commands are scripted to the control. *Safe for Initialization* means that there is no way to harm a user's computer or obtain information about a user's computer by just executing the control.

If you have not marked your control as *Safe for Scripting* and *Safe for Initialization*, then the user's Web browser warns the user that the control is not safe and does not load the control. Only if the user has set the security level on his or her browser to its lowest and least safe setting does the browser download and run your control.

Marking Your ActiveX Controls Safe for Initialization

By marking your control safe for initialization, you guarantee users that there is no way to harm their computer or steal information about their computer by loading your control, regardless of the initialization parameters specified in the HTML file. If a user can specify parameters in the <PARAM> tags that accompany the <OBJECT> element that could cause your control to damage or alter the user's system in any way, you should not mark your control as *Safe for Initialization*.

An ActiveX control's initial state is defined by the PARAM statement on the HTML page that calls the object. If your control is safe for initialization, you must verify all properties given in PARAM statements in the controls InitProperties and ReadProperites events.

Part

V

Ch

21

To mark your control safe for initialization, select the Safe for Initialization check box on the Setup Wizard Safety dialog box. Keep in mind that you are specifying that your control is *Safe for Initialization* by using the honor system. If you have not thoroughly tested your control by using all sorts of corrupt and malicious initialization settings, then you may be dishonestly stating to your users that your control is safe, when it really may not be safe.

Marking Your ActiveX Control Safe for Scripting

By marking your control safe for scripting, you guarantee your control's users that there is no way to harm their computer or steal information about their computer no matter what scripting commands are given to your control.

Following are things that are not safe:

- Reading or writing a file from the user's hard drive with a name supplied by script
- Reading or writing into the Windows Registry by using a key supplied by the script. Using a fixed key in the Windows Registry would be okay, especially if it was a key associated with the control itself.
- Calling certain Windows API functions
- Sending commands to other applications

Be careful when using constituent controls. Many have methods that can be used maliciously. Choose cautiously what properties and methods you make available.

To mark your control safe for initialization, select the Safe for Initialization check box on the Setup Wizard Safety dialog box. Once again, you are specifying this on your honor. You are giving your users your word that your control is safe for their use.

Control Certification

Users of your control might never have heard of your company and might be skeptical of downloading objects from you. Unlike when you buy a program from the store, there is no accountability when you distribute controls over the Internet; your controls are not shrink-wrapped with your company logo on the package. A programmer who is malicious, or at least not careful, can cause bad things to happen to a user's computer. A poorly written ActiveX control can do the following among other things:

- Delete important files, such as a configuration file
- Find out information about the user's computer and distribute this information without the user's permission
- Make system configuration changes without the user's permission

Digital signatures through third parties give a path back to you in case something unethical is performed with your control. By signing your control with a digital certificate, you are essentially placing your control into an electronic shrink-wrap and placing your company logo on the package, providing your customers with some degree of comfort that they know who built the controls.

Licensing Issues

When you build ActiveX controls with Visual Basic and use Visual Basic intrinsic constituent controls to aid in your product development, you do not need to include any additional support files with your distribution files, other than the VB run-time DLL. Also, by using the Visual Basic constituent controls, you do not need to worry about any licensing issues.

In most cases, but not all, the authors of programmable objects VBXs, OCXs, and ActiveX controls give you the right to distribute them with your finished project without royalties. However, when you build ActiveX controls that you plan to distribute, you are giving a developer, the Web designer, the ability to create new things with your ActiveX control. Most licensing agreements that come with custom controls do not give you the right to distribute any part of the author's control in a non-finished product form. Also, if the author uses Standard Registry Licensing Scheme, you cannot distribute the author's controls on a Web server.

Versioning of Controls

After you have created and distributed some of your ActiveX controls, you will most likely need to address the question of version control. When you enhance an existing version of a ActiveX control, you run the risk of adding or removing code that will cause the previous version of your control to fail for the user. Consider the Calculator control: If you created a new version that added a division function, existing users may not be affected. However, if you created a new version that changed the way the add function worked, you would run the risk of control failure for your installed user base. Versioning of ActiveX controls is not hard, but it does take a little forethought and planning.

A complete discussion of versioning of ActiveX controls can be found in the Books Online menu option under the Help menu. You can also visit Microsoft's Site Developer Network located at **www.microsoft.com/msdn/** for more information about versioning of ActiveX controls.

From Here...

In this chapter you looked at how to enhance existing controls. You looked at the advantages of using existing controls and how they can be used in our application. You also looked at how to extend ActiveX controls by creating property sheets for your controls. Finally, you looked at how to responsibly create and distribute controls.

The following chapters provide additional coverage on creating ActiveX controls:

- Chapter 22, "Creating a User-Drawn Control" shows you how to create a control using by using a code driven approach.
- Chapter 23, "Building ActiveX Documents," shows you how to create ActiveX documents and how they can be used in your applications.

Creating a User-Drawn Control

The previous two chapters have demonstrated how to create ActiveX controls from other controls. In Chapter 20, "Creating ActiveX Controls," you saw how to combine standard controls to create a new control that could be used in your programs. In Chapter 21, "Extending ActiveX Controls," you learned how to add properties, methods, and events to existing controls to give them greater functionality than they had before.

In the two previous chapters, the focus was on using existing pieces to create a new control. This chapter will demonstrate how to create a control totally from scratch by drawing the interface with graphics methods and by creating the properties, methods, and events of the control.

Creating a user-drawn control is the hardest method for creating your own ActiveX controls. However, it is also the most flexible because you are in control of everything. You can also do things with user-drawn controls that you cannot do with standard controls. For example, the control you create in this chapter is a command button that enables you to set the foreground and background colors of the button, something you simply cannot do with a regular command button.

If you intend to create controls for use by other developers, here are a couple of general things to keep in mind:

- If your control is similar to another control, such as a command button, keep your control's appearance and functionality as close as possible to the existing control. This will help users understand how to use the control.

- If your control is completely different from any others, try to make the control as intuitive as possible. Try to think of how a user would work with the control and make it easy to use.

Building the User-Drawn Command Button

Although a command button is a fairly simple example of creating a user-drawn control, it illustrates the main concepts for creating this type of control. The first major step you have to take is to determine the design of the control. To make sure your control works like a normal CommandButton control, you should examine a standard command button to note the behavior of the properties, methods, and events. For example, when you click a standard command button, the button's appearance changes so that it looks as if it has been pressed or pushed in. These lower-level procedures are the types of things you need to include in user-drawn controls.

The initial design of the button will be kept simple. This button control, named ColorBtn (short for "Color Button"), will have four key properties: BackColor, Caption, Font, and ForeColor. In addition, the button will respond to a minimal number of events: Click, GotFocus, LostFocus, MouseDown, and MouseUp.

Starting the Project

As with all other custom controls you create, you need to start a new ActiveX control project. After creating the project, set the properties of the project and the User Control, as shown in Table 22.1.

Table 22.1   Properties of the Project and Control

Item	Setting
Project Type	ActiveX Control
Project Name	ColorButton
Project Description	Color Enhanced Command Button
User control Name property	ColorBtn
User control Public property	True

Creating the User Interface

Since the user interface is drawn completely by you, you will create it in the code of the control. The code needs to be placed in the Paint event of the control. The Paint event is fired whenever the container (such as a form) that holds your control is redrawn. You can also force the Paint event by issuing the Refresh method. Keep in mind that your command button is really just a picture. You will be using graphics methods, such as the Line method, to control what the user sees. For example, when the user clicks your control, you will use lines to re-draw the button so that it looks like it has been pressed. (For more information about graphics methods, refer to Chapter 12, "Working with Graphics.")

▶ **See** "Using the Line and Shape Controls," **p. 298**

To draw a rectangular command button, you need only the Line and Print methods. In this case, the button will fill the entire space of the User Control area. Therefore, use the Height and Width of the control as parameters in the Line method. Drawing a colored button involves three steps:

1. Draw a filled rectangular box the full size of the control, using the selected background color.

2. Draw a white line along the top and left edges of the control, and draw a black line along the bottom and right edges of the control. These lines give the button the standard "raised" appearance. (When the button is "pressed," you'll reverse the appearance by swapping the white and black lines.)

3. Using the Print method, draw a caption on the button.

The code for creating the body of the button is shown in Listing 22.1.

Listing 22.1   COLORBTN.CTL—Using the *Line* Method to Draw the Body of the Button

```
Dim inHeight As Integer
Dim inWidth  As Integer

With UserControl
    'leave some room  for the border
    inHeight = .Height - 10
    inWidth = .Width - 10

    'Set backcolor, draw a colored box
    .DrawWidth = 1
    .FillColor = mBackColor
    .FillStyle = 0
    UserControl.Line (0, 0)-(inWidth, inHeight), , B

    'Draw lower right lines
    .DrawWidth = 3
    If bMouseDn = False Then .ForeColor = vbBlack Else .ForeColor = vbWhite
    UserControl.Line (0, inHeight)-(inWidth, inHeight)
    UserControl.Line (inWidth, 0)-(inWidth, inHeight)
```

continues

Listing 22.1   Continued

```
'Draw upper-left lines
If bMouseDn = False Then .ForeColor = vbWhite Else .ForeColor = vbBlack
UserControl.Line (0, 0)-(inWidth, 0)
UserControl.Line (0, 0)-(0, inHeight)

End With
```

This code should be fairly easy to follow. It simply draws a box and some lines to represent the command button. Note that the button's color is determined by a variable, mBackcolor, which will hold the contents of the BackColor property. This variable should be declared in the General Declarations section so that it can be set from another procedure. You also have to declare a Boolean variable, bMouseDn, to control whether the button is drawn "raised" or "pressed."

N O T E   Buttons like those in Office 97 and Internet Explorer are very similar to the button you are creating in this chapter. Although a free ActiveX control called the "Soft Button" exists on the Microsoft Web site (**www.microsoft.com**), it will not be very hard to create an Explorer-like button by using the techniques described here.

Figure 22.1 shows how this basic button would look on the form of a test project.

FIG. 22.1
The custom button is a working control with a unique appearance.

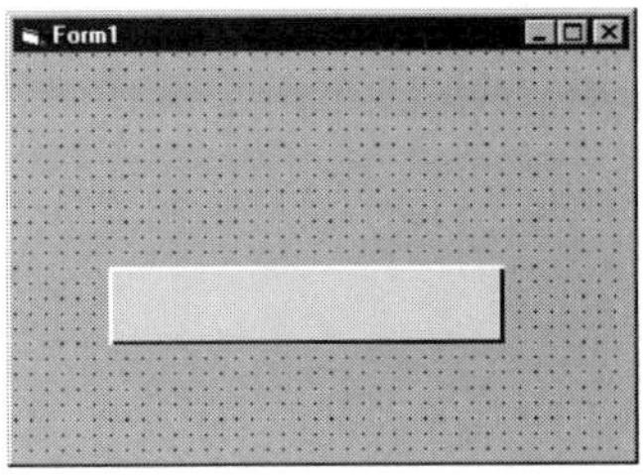

After you have drawn the body of the button, you need to draw the caption on the button. To draw the caption, you need to use the Print method. So that your button is similar to a standard command button, you need to add code to center the caption in the button. To do this, follow these steps:

1. Use the TextHeight and TextWidth methods of the user control to determine the size of the caption.

2. Use the size of the caption and the size of the control to determine the coordinates for starting the printing.

3. Set the print color by setting the ForeColor property of the user control.

4. Use the Print method to display the caption.

The steps defined previously are illustrated in Listing 22.2.

Listing 22.2   COLORBTN.CTL—Using the *Print* Method to Write the Caption on the Button

```
With UserControl
    .ForeColor = mForeColor

    .CurrentX = (.Width - .TextWidth(m_Caption)) / 2
    If .CurrentX < 5 Then .CurrentX = 5

    .CurrentY = (.Height - .TextHeight(m_Caption)) / 2
    If .CurrentY < 5 Then .CurrentY = 5

    UserControl.Print m_Caption

End With
```

This code, along with the previous listing, should be placed in the Paint event. Whenever you need to redraw the button in a different state, you can call the UserControl_Paint event procedure.

The final appearance of the ColorBtn control is shown in Figure 22.2.

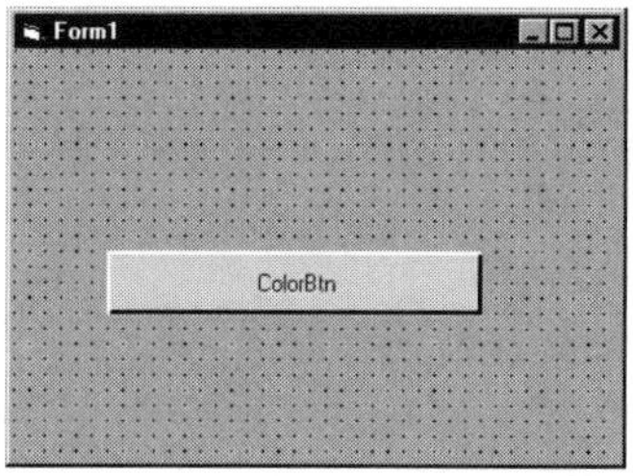

FIG. 22.2

The caption is centered on the button and is printed in the requested foreground color.

You should *always* remember to initialize the variables that are used in the control for this; you need to place the code in Listing 22.3 in the Initialize event of the user control.

Listing 22.3   COLORBTN.CTL—Initializing the Variables of Your Control

```
Private Sub UserControl_Initialize()
    mBackColor = vbCyan
    mForeColor = vbBlue
    UserControl.BackColor = mBackColor
    UserControl.ForeColor = mForeColor
End Sub
```

Creating the Properties of the Button

As stated previously, the design of the command button will be kept simple. The four key properties of the button are the BackColor, Caption, Font, and ForeColor properties. Three of these properties—BackColor, Font, and ForeColor—will be tied to the corresponding properties of the user control. In addition, the `BackColor` and `ForeColor` properties will be stored as variables for use in the code.

By using the ActiveX Control Interface Wizard, it is easy to create the properties that you need. Just make sure to map all the properties, except `Caption`, to those in the `UserControl` object. The Wizard creates the `Property Let` and `Property Get` procedures for the four properties. Take, for example, the `Property Get` procedure for the control's `BackColor` property:

```
Public Property Get BackColor() As OLE_COLOR
    BackColor = UserControl.BackColor
End Property
```

This procedure simply returns the background color of the user control and can be used as is. However, you will need to add an extra line to the `Property Let` procedure:

```
Public Property Let BackColor(ByVal New_BackColor As OLE_COLOR)
    UserControl.BackColor() = New_BackColor
    mBackColor = UserControl.BackColor
    PropertyChanged "BackColor"
End Property
```

Notice that in this code, a line was added to store the color in the variable `mBackColor`. This variable, declared in the General Declarations section, is used by code in the `Paint` event. The other properties, shown in Listing 22.4, are coded in a similar fashion.

Listing 22.4 COLORBTN.CTL—Most of the Property Procedures Were Created by the Wizard

```
Public Property Get Font() As Font
    Set Font = UserControl.Font
End Property

Public Property Set Font(ByVal New_Font As Font)
    Set UserControl.Font = New_Font
    PropertyChanged "Font"
End Property

Public Property Get ForeColor() As OLE_COLOR
    ForeColor = UserControl.ForeColor
End Property

Public Property Let ForeColor(ByVal New_ForeColor As OLE_COLOR)
    UserControl.ForeColor() = New_ForeColor
    mForeColor = UserControl.ForeColor
    PropertyChanged "ForeColor"
End Property

Public Property Get Caption() As Variant
    Caption = m_Caption
End Property

Public Property Let Caption(ByVal New_Caption As Variant)
    m_Caption = New_Caption
    UserControl_Paint
```

```
    PropertyChanged "Caption"
End Property
```

N O T E   Although you need to declare the variables mForeColor and mBackColor, the wizard declares m_Caption for you automatically. The reason for this difference is that the Caption property is not mapped to the UserControl object. You also might want to set the constant for the default caption name, m_def_Caption, to something other than 0. "ColorBtn" would be an appropriate choice. ■

The wizard also creates the code for the WriteProperties and ReadProperties events so that the property values can be saved in the PropertyBag object.

Setting Up the Button's Events

The wizard also will be used to create the events for the control. This can be done at the same time as when you create the properties, or you can simply run the wizard again. Remember that only the Click, GotFocus, LostFocus, MouseDown, and MouseUp events are needed for the control. As it turns out, the GotFocus and LostFocus events are included in the custom control automatically, so you only need to be concerned with the other three. After you select the needed events, you can map them to the corresponding events in the user control. The wizard then will create the basic code to define and raise the events.

After the wizard creates the skeleton code, make an addition to the code for the MouseDown and MouseUp events. Since you want your custom button to behave similarly to a standard command button, change the appearance of the button as it is pressed. You do this by drawing black lines along the top and left edges of the button when the MouseDown event is fired and by redrawing the white lines along those edges when the MouseUp event is fired. This will be coded by setting the Boolean variable bMouseDn and then running the code in the UserControl's Paint event. After you have made the additions to these two events, the event code for the ColorBtn control will look like the code in Listing 22.5.

Listing 22.5   COLORBTN.CTL—Event Code Defined by the Wizard and Enhanced by You

```
Private Sub UserControl_MouseDown(Button As Integer, _
    Shift As Integer, X As Single, Y As Single)
    bMouseDn = True
    UserControl_Paint
    RaiseEvent MouseDown(Button, Shift, X, Y)
End Sub

Private Sub UserControl_MouseUp(Button As Integer, _
    Shift As Integer, X As Single, Y As Single)
    bMouseDn = False
    UserControl_Paint
    RaiseEvent MouseUp(Button, Shift, X, Y)
End Sub
```

N O T E   It is important that you do not confuse the events discussed here with the events of the
ColorBtn control, as seen from the user's perspective. The previous code executes when the
UserControl object receives mouse events. The last statement, RaiseEvent, fires the correspond-
ing event in the ColorBtn control, executing any code the user may have placed there. ▓

Figure 22.3 shows the pressed state of the ColorBtn control.

FIG. 22.3
Black lines give the
indication of a pressed
button.

Creating Property Pages for the Button

The final thing you will do for the design of your ColorBtn control is to create the Property
Pages so that the user can set the properties of the control easily. Use the Property Page
Wizard to create the pages and follow these steps:

1. Add a General page to the pages.
2. Place the Caption property on the General page.
3. Verify that the BackColor and ForeColor properties are on the StandardColor page.
4. Verify that the Font property is on the StandardFont page.

Using the Button in a Program

At this point, the design of the ColorBtn control is complete. You now are ready to test it in a
program. You first need to add a Standard EXE project to the project group containing the
ColorBtn. You then need to close the ColorBtn design window to make the control available
to your project.

Drawing the Button

Once the button is available for use, you can draw the control on your form just like any other
control. As you draw the button, you will see the typical rubber band box indicating the size of
the control. When you release the mouse button, the control will be drawn using the default
colors and caption. This is shown in Figure 22.4.

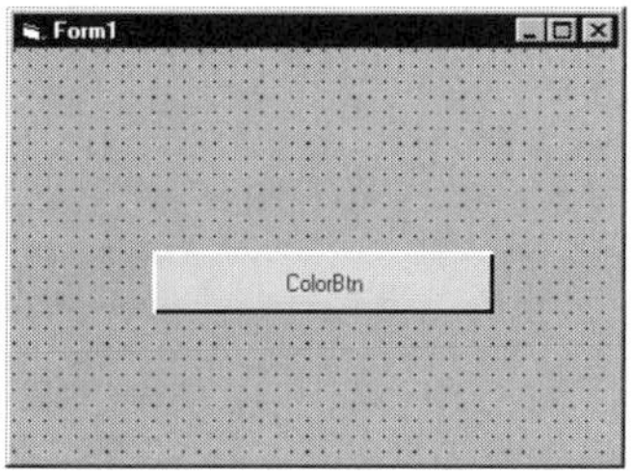

FIG. 22.4
A new instance of
the ColorBtn control
on a form.

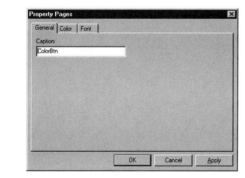

After the control is drawn, you can move and resize it like you would any standard control. Try it and see how it works.

Setting the Button's Properties

After the button is placed on the form, set the values of the properties. You can, of course, set the properties from the Properties window. One thing to notice is that if you placed a description in the `Caption` property when you defined it in the Wizard, this description shows up in the area below the properties list when the `Caption` property is selected. This description is another way to help your users work with your custom control.

Another way to set the properties of your control is to use the Property Pages you created. The dialog box, shown in Figure 22.5, enables you to set the `Caption`, `BackColor` and `ForeColor`, and `Font` properties of the control. The `Paint` event is fired whenever you close the Property Pages. At this time, the effects of the new properties are shown.

FIG. 22.5
Property Pages provide
an organized way for
users to set properties
of a control.

Writing Code for the Events

Writing code for the events of the custom control is like writing any other event code. You can double-click the control to access the Code window and then begin writing code. Just to make sure the `Click` event of the ColorBtn control works, place a message box in the event procedure that announces the button has been clicked. This code is shown in the following line:

```
MsgBox "You clicked the ColorBtn control."
```

Testing the Button

You now can test your control by pressing F5 to run the test program. Try clicking the ColorBtn to be sure the events work correctly. If things are not working right, use the normal debugging techniques to find the errors in the control. After you have finished testing and debugging the control, you are ready to compile your control and make it available for use in other projects.

▶ **See** "Making Your Program Bug-Free," **p. 196**

Trying Other Button Styles

After you have created a rectangular button, you may want to try your hand at creating other shapes. For example, you could draw a button that looks like a circle or ellipse. Or, you could draw a triangular button. In fact, you can use any shape that you can create with the graphics methods. The code in Listing 22.6 could be the basis for a circular button. Figure 22.6 shows you how this button would look on a form.

Listing 22.6   CIRCBTN.CTL—Other Button Shapes Can Be Achieved with the Appropriate Code

```
Dim inHeight As Integer
    Dim inWidth As Integer
    Dim CircDim As Integer

    With UserControl
        inHeight = .Height - 10
        inWidth = .Width - 10
        If inHeight > inWidth Then
            CircDim = inWidth / 2
        Else
            CircDim = inHeight / 2
        End If

        .FillColor = mBackColor
        .FillStyle = 0
        UserControl.Circle (CircDim, CircDim), CircDim

        'Print caption
        .ForeColor = mForeColor

        .CurrentX = CircDim - .TextWidth(m_Caption) / 2
        If .CurrentX < 5 Then .CurrentX = 5

        .CurrentY = CircDim - .TextHeight(m_Caption) / 2
        If .CurrentY < 5 Then .CurrentY = 5

        UserControl.Print m_Caption

    End With
```

FIG. 22.6
You can draw other
button shapes such
as a circle.

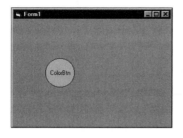

From Here...

This chapter has shown you the basics of creating a user-drawn control. While user-drawn controls involve a lot of work, they are very flexible because the programmer is in charge of everything. This chapter demonstrated how to use a programmer-defined Paint event to change the appearance of your control. You also learned that modifying the output from the ActiveX Control Interface Wizard is an easy way to produce the effects desired. To find out more about the other aspects of creating controls, see the following chapters:

- ■ To learn more about creating properties, methods, and events, see Chapter 20, "Creating ActiveX Controls."

- ■ To learn more about using the wizards, see Chapter 21, "Extending ActiveX Controls."

- ■ To learn more about graphics methods, see Chapter 12, "Working with Graphics."

CHAPTER 23

Building ActiveX Documents

You probably are aware that there are a lot of things happening with the Internet these days. In particular, the World Wide Web has gained enormous popularity. It seems that everywhere you turn, everyone has a Web site—from car manufacturers to charitable organizations to the guy next door. Internet stuff is everywhere. And although it used to be acceptable to just have a static Web page, more and more people and organizations are providing dynamic content on their pages. These interactive Web pages do a lot more than just display fixed information. It is commonplace to see Web pages that act like applications, and a variety of tools are available to let you create such pages.

When you first take a look at creating interactive content, it can appear very daunting—I know it did for me. More often than not, the concern I hear is not "Can I do this?" but "What's the best way to do this?" When you try to think of ways to program for the Web, dozens of terms may come to mind: PERL, CGI, Active Server Pages, VBScript, and Java, to name a few. The ActiveX documents discussed in this chapter are not necessarily the best choice for all occasions, but they do make Internet programming very accessible to VB programmers. ∎

What is an ActiveX document?

You will learn the differences and similarities between ActiveX documents and standard Visual Basic applications.

Creating an ActiveX document

You will see how to use the Visual Basic design environment to create ActiveX documents.

What is a UserDocument object?

You will see how a UserDocument object compares with a standard form and how it differs. You also will see how to add properties to a UserDocument.

Working with multiple documents

You will see how to use the Hyperlink object to move back and forth between the multiple documents of a project.

Testing and running a document-based application

You will see that, although you have to use a second program such as Internet Explorer to test your documents, all of Visual Basic's debugging tools are available to you.

Understanding ActiveX Documents

Since ActiveX documents are perfect for use on the World Wide Web, this chapter will begin with a quick refresher course. You probably have become familiar enough with Web pages to know that they are basically just document files. Web files are very similar to Word documents except they are written in a special format: HTML (which stands for Hypertext Markup Language). Just as Word is the viewer for .doc files, a Web browser (such as Netscape or Internet Explorer) is used to view HTML files. HTML files on the Internet have an address, or *URL* (Uniform Resource Locator), that is used to locate a specific document.

That's how the Web began, just a bunch of linked documents. But a static document cannot produce the level of interactivity we see today. Two things about the Web have made this possible:

- The way in which Web pages are retrieved
- Browser enhancements

The Hypertext Transfer Protocol, or HTTP, is the means by which your browser and the Web server communicate. The browser simply requests an URL, and then displays the returned HTML stream.

Notice that I use the word "requests"—this is an important concept. Requesting a file is very different from opening one on your hard drive; hence the need to have a protocol. Think of this process as being similar to you asking a friend to send you a document via e-mail. Unlike opening a document on your hard drive, your friend could edit the document before sending it, or send you a completely different document. In a similar manner, logic can be placed on the Web server to modify the returned document based on any number of things.

On the browser side, the returned HTML stream has evolved quite a bit since the Web's first days. In addition to formatted text and graphics, Web pages can include script code and Java applets. These advances were made possible by the increasing complexity of the Internet browser, which has evolved to support all of these embedded objects. ActiveX documents, discussed in this chapter, take browser enhancements to a new level.

What Is an ActiveX Document?

Put in simplest terms, an ActiveX document is an application that runs inside a container, such as Internet Explorer, instead of running as a stand-alone program. An example of such an application is shown in Figure 23.1.

The "document" portion of the name comes from the analogy to word processing documents or spreadsheets. These files contain data, but must be accessed by a program in order to be viewed or edited. For example, you can create a document in Word and store it in a file. If you pass the file along to another user, that user can't do anything with it unless they have a copy of Word. An ActiveX document works much the same way. You can create an ActiveX document and store it in a file. If you pass the file to someone else, they must have a program capable of supporting ActiveX documents before they can use the file.

FIG. 23.1
A simple ActiveX document running in Internet Explorer.

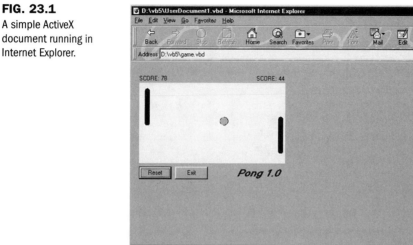

Fortunately, there are many containers that support ActiveX documents, including Internet Explorer, Microsoft Office 97 binders, and the Visual Basic IDE. Your users will run your program inside one of these container applications.

What Are the Advantages of ActiveX Documents?

The primary reason to use ActiveX documents in Visual Basic is to create Internet-enabled applications. Creating ActiveX documents provides a number of advantages over creating Internet applications by other means. Some of these advantages include:

- You do not have to learn another programming language to create the documents. All of your Visual Basic expertise can be applied to ActiveX documents.

- You can design your Internet application by using the Visual Basic design environment. This is a much simpler process than the code-and-test method that you have to use with some other languages.

- You also have access to Visual Basic's rich debugging environment for testing your code and fixing any problems that arise.

- Use of the Hyperlink object makes it easy to navigate to other pages from the browser. These pages can be other ActiveX documents, or any Web address.

So, Visual Basic makes it easy to create an ActiveX document, but why would you want to create one in the first place? Why not just create a standard application? The answer, in a word, is "Internet." ActiveX frees you of the complications involved with the older means of distributing an application. If your program is a standard EXE, then you must send install disks to all of the users. ActiveX documents, on the other hand, can be set up on a Web server so that they are downloaded automatically when a user opens the Web page. Codes embedded in the Web page tell Internet Explorer to download a cabinet (CAB) file containing your application and all necessary components. This Web-based approach makes it simpler to maintain your code and to keep everyone running the same version.

Creating Your First ActiveX Document

Creating an ActiveX document is very similar to creating standard applications in Visual Basic. In this chapter, we re-create the loan payment calculator example from Chapter 3, "Creating Your First Program," but this time as an ActiveX document. To create a document, we will follow this basic sequence of events:

1. Start a new ActiveX document project.
2. Create the user interface of the application.
3. Write the code to perform the application's tasks.
4. Test and debug the application.
5. Use the Setup Wizard to create an Internet download setup.

Obviously, there are a number of details involved in each of these steps, but you can see that the process is something with which you are familiar. To walk through the process of creating an ActiveX document, you will create a mortgage calculator like the one you created in Chapter 3. Using this same application will illustrate the similarities between creating an ActiveX document and a standard Visual Basic program.

N O T E The preceding steps refer to creating an *application*. Since an ActiveX document is an interactive application, as opposed to a static file, such as word processing documents, the term *application* will often be used to refer to an ActiveX document. ▪

Starting an ActiveX Document Project

The first step toward creating an ActiveX document is to start your project. You do this by selecting the New Project item from the File menu. This opens the New Project dialog box (see Figure 23.2). From this dialog box, select the option to create an ActiveX Document EXE by double-clicking the icon. This starts the new project and displays a blank UserDocument form on the screen, as shown in Figure 23.3.

FIG. 23.2

Select the project type to create from the New Project dialog box.

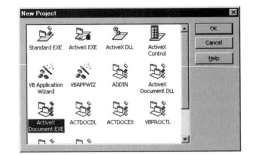

N O T E If the UserDocument is not displayed automatically, double-click the UserDocument object in the Project window to display it. ▪

FIG. 23.3
A UserDocument object
looks very much like a
form.

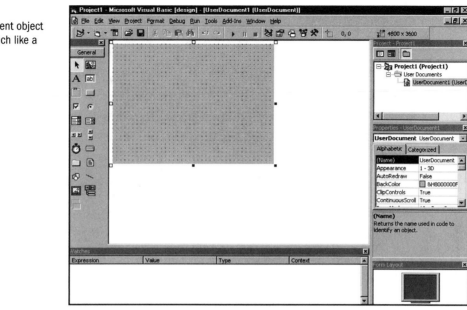

Notice that the UserDocument looks a lot like a form without a border. As a matter of fact, it is exactly like the UserControl object that you will use to create ActiveX controls. You will create the user interface for the ActiveX document here, just like with a form. (For more information about creating ActiveX controls, see Chapter 20, "Creating ActiveX Controls.")

After you have created the project, change the properties of the project and the UserDocument to descriptive names, as listed in Table 23.1. To access the properties of the project, choose *projectname* Properties from the Project menu. The properties of the UserDocument are accessible from the Properties window (View, Properties Window). After setting the properties, save the files of the project by clicking the Save button on the toolbar. You then specify names for each of the new files.

Table 23.1   Project and UserDocument Properties

Property	Setting
Project Type	ActiveX EXE
Project Name	ActXCalc
Project Description	ActiveX Document Loan Calculator
UserDocument Name	CalcDoc

Part

V

Ch

23

Document File Names

The source code of ActiveX documents is saved in a text file, much the same way a form is saved. The description of the UserDocument object and any controls is stored along with the code of the document in a file with the extension .dob. This is similar to the .frm file of a form. If there are any graphical components of the interface, these are stored in a .dox file, similar to the .frx file for forms. When you compile your ActiveX document, you create either an .exe or .dll file, along with a .vbd file. The .vbd file is the one accessed by Internet Explorer. This .vbd file is the "document" part of the file, similar to a .doc file from Microsoft Word.

Creating the Interface of the Document

The interface of your ActiveX document is created by drawing controls on the UserDocument object, just as you would draw them on the form of a standard program. You can use almost any Visual Basic control in the creation of your document. The only exception to this statement is that you cannot use the OLE Container control as part of an ActiveX document. Another restriction is that an ActiveX document cannot contain embedded objects, such as Word or Excel documents.

> **CAUTION**
>
> If you use custom controls in your document, you need to check licensing and royalty requirements before distributing the controls.

To create the interface of the sample application, you need to add four Label controls, four TextBox controls, and one CommandButton to the UserDocument.

The Label controls should have the following settings for the Name and Caption properties:

Name	Caption
lblPrincipal	Principal:
lblTerm	Term (Years):
lblInterest	Interest Rate (%):
lblPayment	Monthly Payment:

 All four text boxes should have their Text properties deleted so that the text boxes appear empty when the document is first shown. The text boxes should be named txtInterest, txtPayment, txtPrincipal, and txtTerm.

The command button of the document should have the Name property set to cmdCalculate and the Caption property set to Calculate Payment.

When you have completed adding the controls to the document, your UserDocument should look like the one in Figure 23.4.

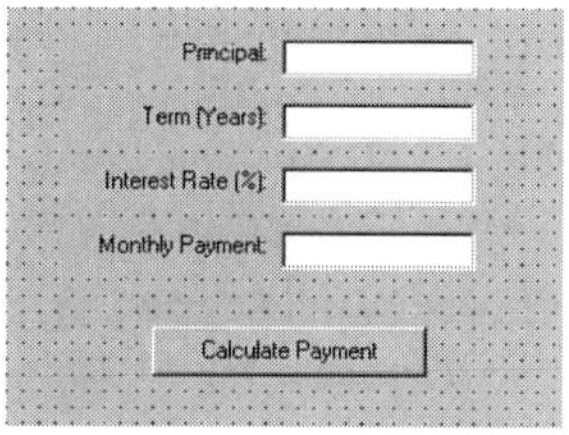

FIG. 23.4
The Document calculator looks similar to the LoanCalc program created earlier.

Principal	
Term (Years):	
Interest Rate (%):	
Monthly Payment:	

Calculate Payment

Adding Code to the Document

After you create the interface of the document by using Visual Basic controls, you are ready to write the code that makes the document perform a task. As with the forms in a standard program, you will write code for events of the controls in the document. All code work is done in the Code window. You can access the Code window by double-clicking a control or by clicking the View Code button in the Project window. For the sample application, you need to enter the code from Listing 23.1 in the Click event of the command button.

Listing 23.1   CALCDOC.DOB—Placing Code in the *Click* Event to Run the Calculation

```
Private Sub cmdCalculate_Click()

    Dim m_Principal As Single, m_Interest As Single
    Dim m_Payment As Single, m_Term As Integer
    Dim m_fctr As Single

    m_Principal = txtPrincipal.Text
    m_Interest = txtInterest.Text / 1200
    m_Term = txtTerm.Text
    m_fctr = (1 + m_Interest) ^ (m_Term * 12)
    m_Payment = m_Interest * m_fctr * m_Principal / (m_fctr - 1)
    txtPayment.Text = Format(m_Payment, "Fixed")

End Sub
```

Testing Your ActiveX Document

After entering the code and saving your document, you are ready to test the code. Testing an ActiveX document is a little different than testing a standard program because the document must run inside another application. To test your code, follow these steps:

1. Run your document by pressing F5 or clicking the Start button on the toolbar. (Note that Visual Basic will not display the user interface of your program.)

2. Minimize Visual Basic and start Internet Explorer.

3. From IE's File menu, choose the Open item. This will present an Open dialog box in which you can enter the name of the file to be opened by IE.

4. Specify the path and name of your ActiveX document and the name. The name will be the value of the Name property of the UserDocument object, followed by a .vbd extension. If you are running your document within VB, the file is located in the same folder as Visual Basic. For a typical installation, this is C:\Program Files\DevStudio\VB.

5. Click the OK button in the Open dialog box to load your document. The CalcDoc document is shown running in Internet Explorer in Figure 23.5.

N O T E If you click the Browse button of the Open dialog box to find the file, remember to change the Files of Type selection from HTML files to All Files. ▪

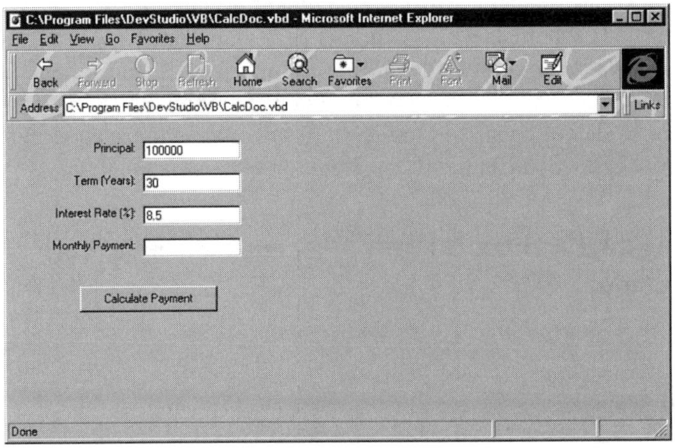

FIG. 23.5
Internet Explorer can host an ActiveX document.

If your code doesn't perform like it should, you can use all of Visual Basic's debugging tools to track down and eliminate errors. (Debugging is discussed in detail in Chapter 8, "Programming Basics.") You can set breakpoints in your code, set "watches" to observe the values of variables, and step through the code line by line to locate an error. Figure 23.6 shows a typical debugging session.

▶ **See** "Making Your Program Bug-Free," **p. 196**

CAUTION
Terminating your program without closing Internet Explorer may cause errors in IE. Therefore, you should close and restart IE each time you run your document.

Compiling Your Document

After you have finished testing and debugging your document, you are ready to compile the document for distribution. To start the compilation process, select the Make item from the File menu of Visual Basic. This opens the Make dialog box, in which you specify the name and location of the EXE or DLL file. The name of the .vbd file is based on the Name property of the UserDocument object. This file is placed in the same folder that you specified for the EXE file.

FIG. 23.6

Debugging tools make it easy to find and correct errors.

Breakpoint——

Line causing error——

Variable being watched——

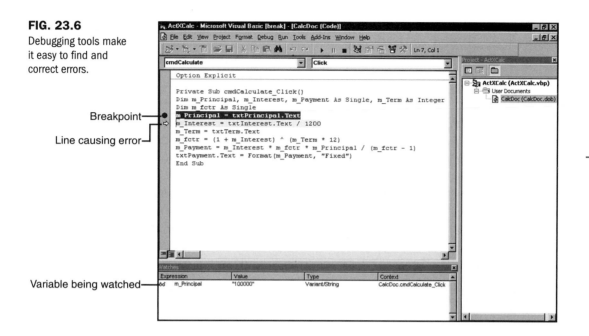

After compilation, your document can be used in any of the programs that handle ActiveX documents. As you learned previously, Internet Explorer is one such program. The Office 97 Binder is another. To access an ActiveX document with the Binder, start the Binder and then select the Add from File item in the Section menu. This opens a dialog box that enables you to specify the file to be loaded. You specify the name and location of your .vbd file and then click the OK button to load the document. Figure 23.7 shows the CalcDoc document running inside the Office 97 binder.

FIG. 23.7

The Office 97 Binder provides another means with which to run your ActiveX documents.

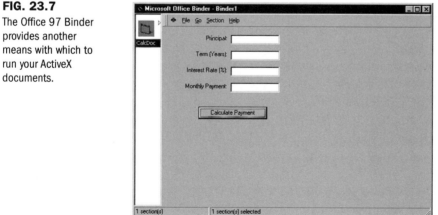

If you want to put your ActiveX document on the Internet, you first need to run the Setup Wizard with the Internet Download Setup option. The Wizard will create a CAB file that contains the required components, as well as sample HTML that shows you how to include your document on a Web page. It also creates a SUPPORT directory with the components in the CAB file, should you need to modify anything.

▶ **See** "Distributing ActiveX Controls by Using Setup Wizard," **p. 584**

Exploring the UserDocument Object

Just as a form is the main part of a standard program, the UserDocument object is the key part of an ActiveX document. The UserDocument provides the container for all the controls that make up the user interface of the document. Like a form, you can place controls on the UserDocument or you can use graphics methods and the Print method to display other information directly on the document. This provides great flexibility in the design of your documents and the manner in which you present information to the user.

Understanding the Key Events of a UserDocument

Although the UserDocument is similar to a form in many respects, there are also some key differences. For example, there are several key properties, methods, and events that are supported by a UserDocument but are not supported by a form, and vice versa.

The main events of a form that are not supported by the UserDocument object are the Activate, Deactivate, Load, and Unload events. The UserDocument, on the other hand, supports the following events that are not supported by a form:

- ▪ AsycReadComplete   Occurs when the container holding the document has finished an asynchronous read request.
- ▪ EnterFocus   Occurs when the ActiveX document receives focus.
- ▪ ExitFocus   Occurs when the ActiveX document loses focus.
- ▪ Hide   Occurs when the user navigates from the current ActiveX document to another document.
- ▪ InitProperties   Occurs when the document is first loaded. However, if any properties have been saved by using the PropertyBag object, the ReadProperties event will occur instead.
- ▪ ReadProperties   Occurs in place of the InitProperties event if items are stored in a PropertyBag object. This event also occurs as the document is first loaded.
- ▪ Scroll   Occurs when the user uses the scrollbar of the container in which the ActiveX document is running.
- ▪ Show   Occurs when the user navigates from another document to the ActiveX document.
- ▪ WriteProperties   Occurs as the program is about to be terminated. This event happens right before the Terminate event, but occurs only if the PropertyChanged statement has been used to indicate that a change has occurred in a property's value.

Creating and Storing Properties for a UserDocument

Despite the similarities between the UserDocument and a form, there are some ways in which the UserDocument is much more similar to a UserControl than a form. All three objects—the form, the UserControl, and the UserDocument—enable you to create properties and methods to extend their capabilities. However, only the UserControl and the UserDocument have the capability to use the PropertyBag object. The PropertyBag object, along with some special events, is used to store values of public properties so that settings are preserved between sessions.

Part

V

Ch

23

Since the process for creating and saving properties was discussed in detail in the coverage of ActiveX controls, the details won't be repeated here (see Chapter 20, "Creating ActiveX Controls" and Chapter 22, "Creating a User-Drawn Control"). However, a quick recap will help you remember the steps involved. To create and store properties for the UserDocument, you need to do the following:

1. Create a property by using the Property Let and Property Get procedures. You can create the shell of the property by using the Add Procedure dialog box, accessible from the Tools menu of Visual Basic.

2. To indicate that the value of a property has changed, place the PropertyChanged statement in the Property Let procedure of each property whose value you want to store.

3. To store the values of the property, use the WriteProperty method of the PropertyBag object to output the values of the changed properties. The code for this is placed in the WriteProperties event of the UserDocument.

4. To retrieve the values of the property, use the ReadProperty method of the PropertyBag object to output the values of the changed properties. The code for this is placed in the ReadProperties event of the UserDocument.

   ▶ **See** "Creating the Properties of the Button," **p. 597**

The result of the code for handling these tasks in a sample document is shown in Figure 23.8.

FIG. 23.8

Use the ReadProperty and WriteProperty methods to retrieve and store public properties of the UserDocument.

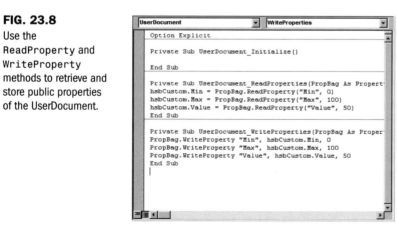

Working with the Methods of the UserDocument

In addition to the different events that are supported by the UserDocument, there are also two key methods that the UserDocument supports but a form does not: AsyncRead and CancelAsyncRead. The AsyncRead method enables the document to request that its container read in data from a file or URL. As the name implies, the read is performed asynchronously. The AsyncRead method requires that you specify the file (or information) to be read and the type of information that is being read. There are three supported data types, as summarized in Table 23.2. The following line of code shows how the method can be used:

```
AsyncRead "C:\Vb\Default.Htm", vbAsyncTypeFile
```

As you can imagine, reading a file asynchronously comes in very handy when working with the Internet. For example, you might write a data viewer application that retrieves information from a server.

Table 23.2   Types of Data Supported by the *AsyncRead* Method

Constant	Description
vbAsyncTypeFile	The data is contained in a file created by Visual Basic.
vbAsyncTypeByteArray	The data is a byte array containing retrieved data.
vbAsyncTypePicture	The data is stored in a picture object.

The CancelAsyncRead method is used to terminate an asynchronous read prior to its completion.

Using the Hyperlink Object in Your Document

One object of extreme importance in ActiveX documents is the Hyperlink object. This object has no properties and only three methods. However, the Hyperlink object is what enables an ActiveX document to call another ActiveX document, or to navigate to a Web site. The three methods of the Hyperlink object are the following:

- ■ NavigateTo   This method causes the container that holds the ActiveX document to jump to a file or URL specified in the method. This is the method to use to move from one ActiveX document to another.
- ■ GoBack   This method performs a hyperlink jump to the previous document in the history list of a container. If the container does not support hyperlinking or there are no items in the history list, an error occurs.
- ■ GoForward   This method is the counterpart of the GoBack method. GoForward causes the container to move to the next document in the history list. If there is no next document, an error occurs.

N O T E A container such as Internet Explorer, which supports hyperlinking, will execute on its own the jump specified in a `NavigateTo` method. A container such as Office 97 Binder, which does not support hyperlinking, will start a hyperlink-capable program to process the jump. ▇

Using the ActiveX Document Migration Wizard

Part

V

Ch

23

So far, you have learned how to create an ActiveX document from scratch. But, if you are like me, you have a lot of time and effort invested in creating standard Visual Basic applications. Is there any way that you can capitalize on the work you have already done, short of using cut and paste to bring in pieces of a program?

Fortunately, the answer is yes! Visual Basic provides a tool called the ActiveX Document Migration Wizard that can *help* you convert forms from an existing application to UserDocument objects for an ActiveX document. The key word here is "Help." The Wizard does not create a complete ActiveX document directly from your standard application. Instead, the Wizard does the following:

■ Copies the properties of the form to a new user document.

■ Copies menu items from the source form to the new user document.

■ Copies all controls from the source form and retains their relative positions on the form. All control properties are retained. Note that OLE container controls and embedded OLE objects are not copied.

■ Copies the code from the form event procedures to the corresponding procedures in the user document. This includes all event procedures associated with the component controls.

■ Comments out code statements that are not supported by ActiveX documents, such as `Load`, `Unload`, and `End`.

Although the ActiveX Document Migration Wizard can do a lot of the work of converting a document for you, there are some things that it cannot handle. Therefore, you have to do some coding work before you can compile and distribute your document.

First, you need to remove unsupported events, such as `Load` and `Unload`. Although the Wizard will comment out the `Load` and `Unload` statements, it will not do anything with the event procedures code. If you use these events to initialize the properties of a form or its controls, you may want to move some of the code from the `Load` event to the `Initialize` event of the UserDocument. Likewise, you may want to move some of the code from the `Unload` event to the `Terminate` event of the UserDocument.

You also need to make sure that you do not reference any non-existent objects. For example, if you migrate a form to a UserDocument, any references to the form by name (for example, "Form1") would be invalid.

Running the ActiveX Document Migration Wizard

To run the ActiveX Document Migration Wizard, you need to make sure that it is available in Visual Basic. You make the Wizard available by selecting it from the Add-In Manager dialog box, which is accessible by choosing the Add-In Manager item from the Add-Ins menu. After you have added the Wizard to your desktop, you can run it by choosing the ActiveX Document Migration Wizard item from the Add-Ins menu.

To begin converting the forms of a project into ActiveX documents, you first must open the project's forms that you want to convert. The Wizard will work correctly only from within the project. Next, start the ActiveX Document Migration Wizard. This presents the introductory screen, which explains a little of what the Wizard will and will not do for you. Click the Next button on the Wizard to proceed to the second screen—where the work begins.

The second screen of the Wizard, shown in Figure 23.9, enables you to select the forms from the current project that you want to convert to ActiveX documents. All the forms of the current project are shown in the forms list. You can select any form by clicking the check box next to the form name. Multiple selections are allowed. After you have made your selections, click the Next button to proceed to the next step of the process.

FIG. 23.9

Select your forms from the list in the Wizard.

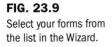

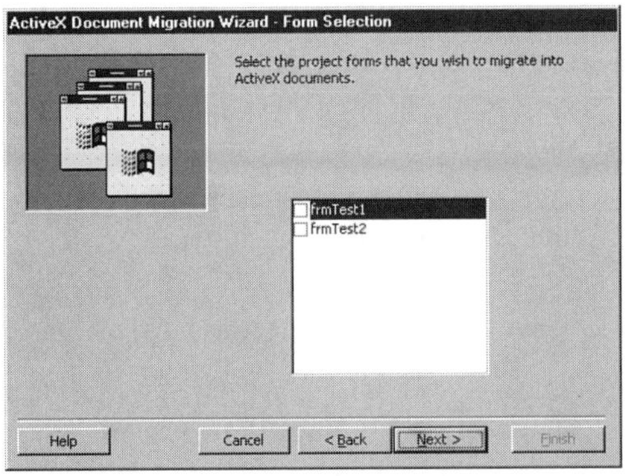

The Options page of the ActiveX Document Migration Wizard, shown in Figure 23.10, lets you control how the Wizard will process the forms you have selected. The three options enable you to do the following:

- Choose to comment out invalid code. This option will comment out statements such as Load, Unload, and End that are not supported by ActiveX documents.

- Remove original forms after conversion. This option will remove the forms from the current project after the conversion is made. Typically, you will *not* want to check this option because you will want your original project intact.

- Choose whether to convert your project to an ActiveX EXE or ActiveX DLL project. The option defaults to ActiveX EXE. (ActiveX DLLs are used for creating shared components rather than applications.)

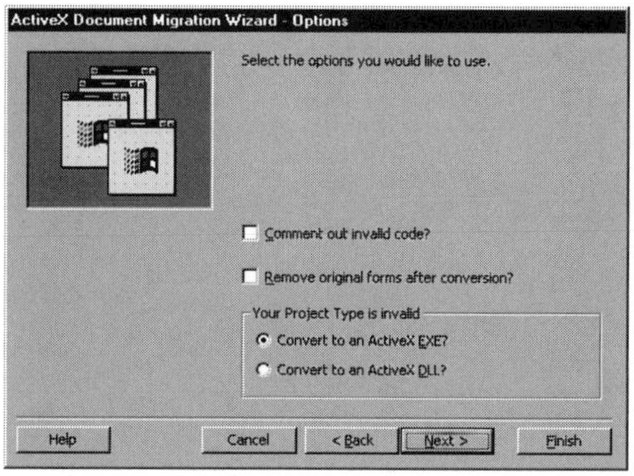

FIG. 23.10

Select the options that are appropriate to your needs.

After making your choices, click the Next button to proceed. The final page of the Wizard asks if you would like to see a summary report after the Wizard's part in the conversion has been completed. After making your selection, click the Finish button to begin the conversion. The summary report, shown in Figure 23.11, describes which additional activities you need to perform to complete the conversion process.

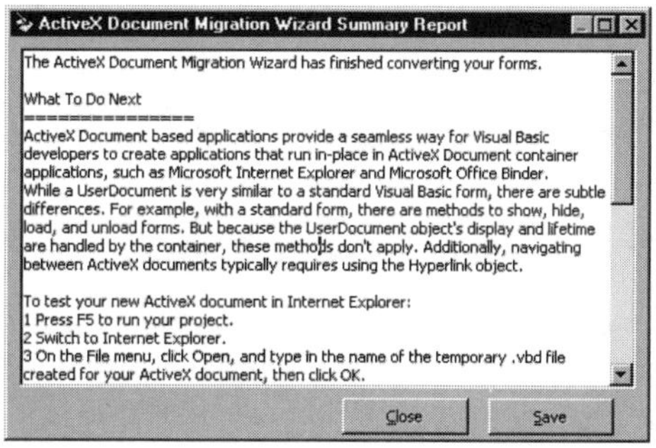

FIG. 23.11

The ActiveX Document Migration Wizard uses a summary report to guide you through the rest of the conversion process.

Looking at the Results of the Wizard's Work

When the ActiveX Document Migration Wizard has finished its work, it places the newly created UserDocument objects in the same project as the original forms. The document source files are stored in the same folder as the original form files and are given similar names, with the appropriate extension. For example, a form stored in the file frmTest1.frm would create a UserDocument stored in the file docTest1.dob. As previously stated, the controls of the form are copied to the UserDocument and their relative positions are preserved. Figure 23.12 shows both the original form and the resulting UserDocument.

Also, as stated previously, most of the code from your original form is copied over to the UserDocument. Invalid code is commented out and identified by the ActiveX Document Migration Wizard. (This assumes that you chose to comment out invalid code on the Options page of the Wizard.) Figure 23.13 shows an example of this process.

FIG. 23.12
The UserDocument and the original form have the same user interface.

FIG. 23.13
Invalid code is identified by the [AXDW] mark in a comment statement.

Invalid code line

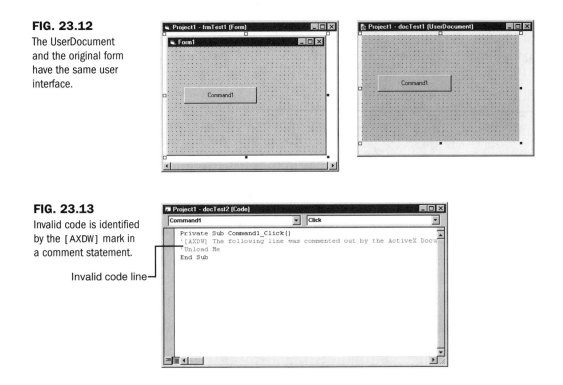

Creating a More Complex Document

Obviously, there is only so much room available on a UserDocument object. Therefore, you are limited in the amount of information that can be displayed in a single document. In this regard, a single document is like an application with a single form. However, you can create additional documents as part of your project and then navigate between the various documents. You can also include standard forms in the applications that you create with ActiveX documents. This section takes a look at what is involved in using multiple documents and forms in your ActiveX document-based application.

Programming Additional Documents

To use additional documents in your ActiveX application, you need to create the additional documents and then provide a mechanism for moving back and forth between the documents. This is a little different than moving between forms in a standard program because the UserDocument object does not support the Load and Unload statements, or the Show and Hide methods that are available to forms.

The first step necessary to add another document to your project is to add another UserDocument object to the project. You do this by choosing the Add User Document item from the Project menu. This places a second (or third, fourth, and so on) document in your project, under the UserDocuments folder. As with the first document you created, you need to specify a name for the document.

The next step required is to draw the interface of the additional document and add the code that enables it to do its tasks. This process is the same as the one you used to create the original document.

Now for the tricky part! Since you cannot use the Show method to display a document (as you can with forms), how do you get back and forth between the various documents in your application? The answer is to use the NavigateTo method of the HyperLink object. The NavigateTo method instructs a container application to go to a particular file or URL and load the page. If the file is an ActiveX document, it gets processed just like your original page.

Part
V
Ch
23

To move from your first document to your second, you need to run the NavigateTo method as shown in the following line of code:

```
HyperLink.NavigateTo App.Path & "\docnav2.vbd"
```

The App.Path property specifies the path to the current document. By using this as the basis for locating the second document, the document can be loaded without incident, provided that the documents are stored in the same directory. Figures 23.14 and 23.15 show the two pages of a sample document loaded in Internet Explorer. To get from the second document back to the first, you use the NavigateTo method again. For both documents, the method is used in code that responds to an event. The event is typically the Click event of a command button.

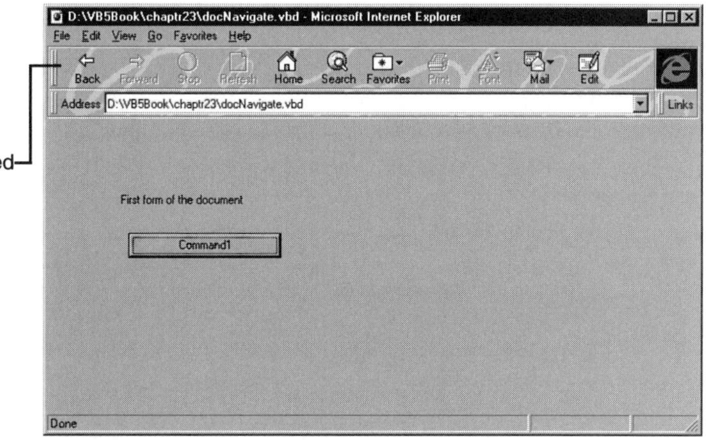

FIG. 23.14

The first document of a multiple document application.

Back button is enabled—

When you moved to the second document of the application, you may have noticed that the Back button of Internet Explorer was enabled. You can use this button to move back to the first document. However, you should provide a direct link using the NavigateTo method because the first document may not always be the previous document in the history list. Also, if the first document has scrolled out of the history list, the NavigateTo method is the only way to get to the document again.

Using and Displaying Forms from the Document

In addition to working with more than one document, you can work with standard forms in
your ActiveX document applications. To use a form in a project, you create it the same way you
would create a form for a standard project—draw the interface of the form and write the code
to perform tasks. To display the form from your document, use the Show method. Then, to
remove the form, use the Unload statement.

N O T E For more information about creating forms, see Chapter 4, "Working with Forms and
Controls." ▪

Although forms can be part of your application, they are not handled the same way as documents. Forms are not contained within the application that contains the ActiveX document.
Forms are independent of the container, as shown in Figure 23.16.

From Here...

This chapter introduced you to the world of ActiveX documents. You have seen how these documents make it easy to create applications that can run inside Internet Explorer or other ActiveX-enabled container applications. You also have seen the similarity between the UserDocument object and the forms of a standard application.

This chapter also touched on some other topics related to the creation of ActiveX documents that are covered in more detail in other chapters. To learn more about these topics, see the following chapters:

- To learn more about designing and creating forms, see Chapter 4, "Working with Forms and Controls."

- To learn more about debugging your programs, see Chapter 8, "Programming Basics."

- To learn more about creating ActiveX controls, see Chapter 20, "Creating ActiveX Controls," and Chapter 22, "Creating a User-Drawn Control."

PART

VI

Databases

CHAPTER 24

Database Design and Normalization

It's probably fair to say that most business-oriented computer applications work with data in one form or another. This data often is stored in one or more databases. Visual Basic can create powerful data-management programs with a little planning and effort. The most fundamental part of that planning is in how the data is structured. A poorly designed database can doom even the most well-intentioned program from the start. On the other hand, a well-designed database can make a programmer's life much easier.

Creating an organized data structure requires you to learn about two separate tasks. First, you must learn about how to design a database. In the design, you decide what data goes in the database and how it will be organized. Second, you must learn how to translate the design into the actual database. You can do so in a variety of ways. In this chapter, I walk you through the process of designing and creating a sample database that contains information about parents and their children. The database you create here will mirror a portion of the database used in one of my commercial applications that tracks the members of youth groups. ■

How do you determine the data required for a database?

Learn how to find out which information should be stored in the database.

How do you organize the data in the database?

Data in a database should be stored in a way that makes the information easy to retrieve and maintain.

How can you create a database with a program?

The methods of the data access objects allow you to write programs to create or modify a database.

What can the Visual Data Manager do?

The Visual Data Manager provides an easy way to create and modify databases for your programs.

Can you use Microsoft Access?

If you have Access, you have the best tool for working with database structures.

How are queries used in creating databases?

You can create, delete, and modify tables in a database with SQL queries.

Designing a Database

Like most tasks, building a database starts with a design. After all, you wouldn't try to build a house without a blueprint, and most people wouldn't attempt to prepare a new dish without a recipe. Like these other tasks, having a good design for your database is a major first step to a successful project.

In designing a database application, you must set up not only the program's routines for maximum performance, but you must pay attention also to the physical and logical layout of the data storage. A good database design does the following:

- Provides minimum search times when locating specific records
- Stores data in the most efficient manner possible to keep the database from growing too large
- Makes data updates as easy as possible
- Is flexible enough to allow inclusion of new functions required of the program

Design Objectives

When you're creating the design for your database, you must keep several objectives in mind. Although meeting all these design objectives is desirable, sometimes they are mutually exclusive. The primary design objectives are:

- Eliminate redundant data
- Be able to locate individual records quickly
- Make enhancements to the database easy to implement
- Keep the database easy to maintain

Key Activities in Designing Your Database

Creating a good database design involves the following seven key activities:

- Modeling the application
- Determining the data required for the application
- Organizing the data into tables
- Establishing the relationships between tables
- Setting index and validation requirements for the data
- Creating and storing any necessary queries for the application
- Reviewing the design

Now, look briefly at the initial two activities in the list. First, take a look at modeling the application. When you model an application, you first should determine the tasks that the application is to perform. For example, if you're maintaining a membership list, you know that you want to create phone directories and mailing lists of the members. As you're determining the tasks to be performed by the application, you are creating what is called the *functional specification*. For a project that you are creating, you probably know all the tasks that you want to perform, but writing down these tasks in a specification document is a good idea. This document can help you keep focused on what you want your program to do. If you're creating the program for another person, a functional specification becomes an agreement of what the application will contain. This specification also can show milestones that need to be achieved on a set schedule.

When you're creating the program for other people, the best way to learn what task must be performed is to talk to the people requesting the work. As a first step, you can determine if they already have a system that they are looking to replace, or if they have reports that they want to produce. Then, ask a lot of questions until you understand the users' objectives for the program.

After you determine the functional specifications for the program, you can start determining what data the program needs. In the case of a membership application, knowing that you have to produce directories and mailing lists tells you that the database needs to contain the address and phone number of each of the members. Taking this situation a little further, you know that, by presorting mail by ZIP Code, you can take advantage of reduced rate postage. Therefore, you need an index or query that places the mailing list information in ZIP Code order. So, you can see that the model not only tells you the data needed but also defines other components of the database, as well.

Part
VI
Ch
24

Organizing the Data

One of the key aspects of good database design is determining how the data will be organized in the database. To have a good design, you should organize the data in a way that makes the information easy to retrieve and makes maintenance of the database easy. Within a database, data is stored in one or more *tables*. For many database applications, you can accomplish efficient data management by storing data in multiple tables and by establishing relationships between these tables. In the following sections, you learn how to determine what data belongs in each table of your database.

Tables as Topics   A *table* is a collection of information related to a particular topic. By thinking of a key topic for the table, you can determine whether a particular piece of data fits into the table. For example, if a country club wants to track information about members and employees, the club management might be tempted to put both in the same table (because both groups refer to people). However, look at the data required for each group. Although both groups require information about a person's name, address, and phone number, the employee group also requires information about the person's Social Security number, job category, payroll, and tax status. If you were to create just one table, many of the entries would be blank for the members. You also would have to add a field to distinguish between a member and an employee. Clearly, this technique would result in a lot of wasted space. It also could result in slower processing of employee transactions or member transactions because the program would have to skip a number of records in the table. Figure 24.1 shows a database table with the two groups combined. Figure 24.2 shows the reduction in the number of fields in a member-only database table.

FIG. 24.1

Combining the employee and member tables wastes a lot of space.

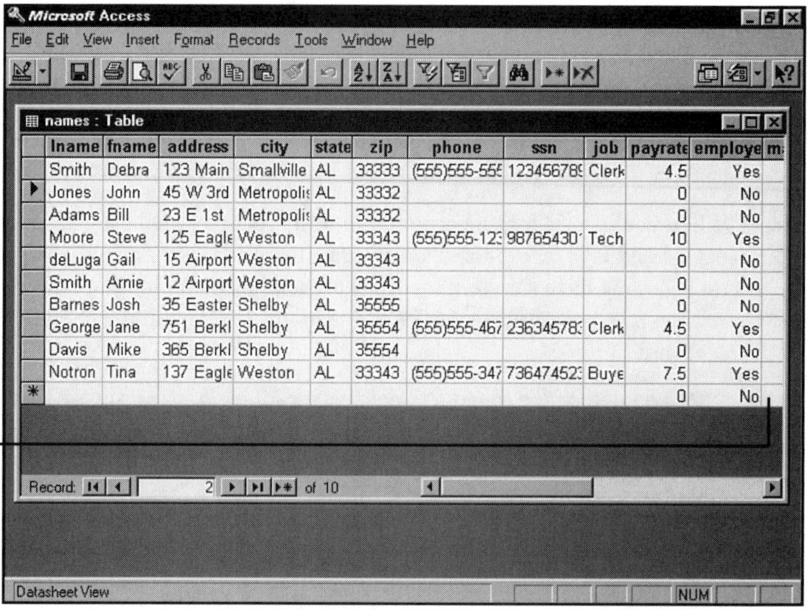

Note the blank fields in the member records

FIG. 24.2

A separate database table for members has only the relevant fields and is more efficient.

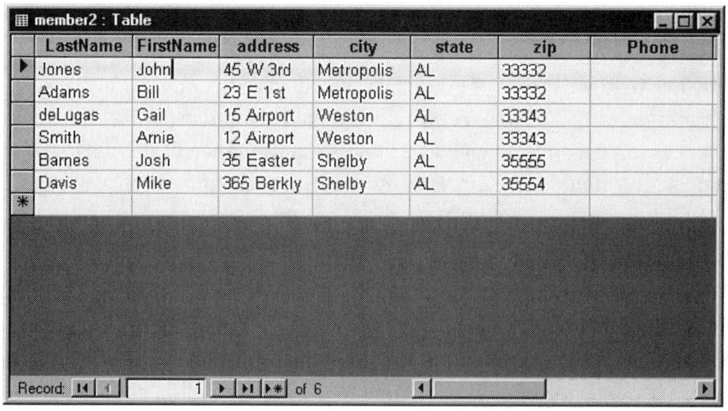

By thinking of the topic to which a table relates, you can determine more easily whether a particular piece of information belongs in the table. If the information results in wasted space for many records, the data belongs in a different table.

Data Normalization *Data normalization* is the process of eliminating redundant data within a database. Taking data normalization to its fullest extent results in each piece of information in a database appearing only once, although that's not always practical.

Consider the example of order processing. For each item a person orders, you need the item's number, description, price, order number, and order date, as well as the customer's name, address, and phone number. If you place all this information in one table, the result looks like the table shown in Figure 24.3.

FIG. 24.3
Non-normalized data produces a large, inefficient data table.

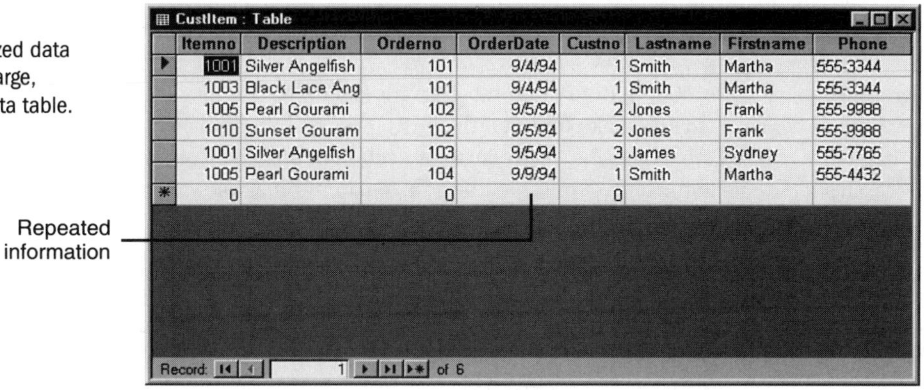

Itemno	Description	Orderno	OrderDate	Custno	Lastname	Firstname	Phone
1001	Silver Angelfish	101	9/4/94	1	Smith	Martha	555-3344
1003	Black Lace Ang	101	9/4/94	1	Smith	Martha	555-3344
1005	Pearl Gourami	102	9/5/94	2	Jones	Frank	555-9988
1010	Sunset Gouram	102	9/5/94	2	Jones	Frank	555-9988
1001	Silver Angelfish	103	9/5/94	3	James	Sydney	555-7765
1005	Pearl Gourami	104	9/9/94	1	Smith	Martha	555-4432
0		0		0			

CustItem : Table — Record: 1 of 6

Repeated information

As you can see, much of the data in the table is repeated. This repetition introduces two problems. The first problem is wasted space, because you repeat information. The second problem is one of data accuracy or currency. If, for example, a customer changes his or her phone number, you have to change it for all the records that apply to that customer—with the possibility that you will miss one of the entries. In the table in Figure 24.3, notice that Martha Smith's phone number was changed in the latest entry but not in the two earlier entries. If an employee looks up Martha Smith and uses an earlier entry, that employee would not find Martha's updated phone number.

A better solution for handling the data is to put the customer information in one table and the sales order information in another table. You can assign each customer a unique ID and include that ID in the sales order table to identify the customer. This arrangement yields two tables with the data structure shown in Figure 24.4.

FIG. 24.4
Normalized Customer and Order tables eliminate data redundancy.

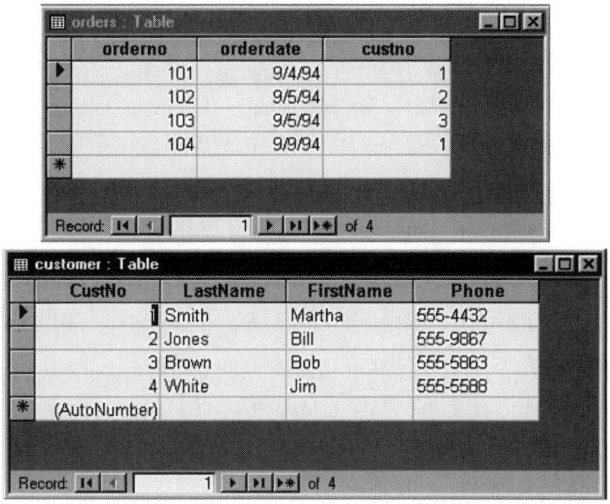

orders : Table

orderno	orderdate	custno
101	9/4/94	1
102	9/5/94	2
103	9/5/94	3
104	9/9/94	1

Record: 1 of 4

customer : Table

CustNo	LastName	FirstName	Phone
1	Smith	Martha	555-4432
2	Jones	Bill	555-9867
3	Brown	Bob	555-5863
4	White	Jim	555-5588
(AutoNumber)			

Record: 1 of 4

Part VI
Ch 24

With this type of arrangement, the customer information appears in only one place. Now, if a customer changes his or her phone number, you have to change only one record.

You can do the same thing to the items sold and order information. This leads to the development of four tables, but the organization of the tables is much more efficient. You can be sure that when information must be changed, it will change in only one place. This arrangement is shown in Figure 24.5. With the four-table arrangement, the Orders table and the Items Ordered table provide the links between the customers and the retail items they purchased. The Items Ordered table contains one record for each item of a given order. The Orders table relates the items to the date of purchase and the customer making the purchase.

FIG. 24.5
Complete normalization of the tables provides the greatest efficiency.

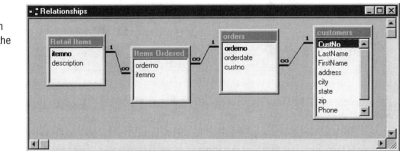

When information is moved out of one table and into another, you must have a way of keeping track of the *relationships* between the tables. You can do so through the use of data keys. For example, your Customers table has a field called CustNo. The Orders table also has a field called CustNo. These tables are said to be linked through that field. If a program needs to obtain information about the customer who made a particular order, that customer's record can be located quickly in the Customers table via the common CustNo field.

Child and Lookup Tables   Another way to handle data normalization is to create what is known as a child table. A *child table* is a table in which all the entries share common information that is stored in another table. A simple example is a membership directory; the family shares a common last name, address, and phone number, but each family member has a different first name. The table containing the common information is called the *parent table,* and the table containing the members' first names is the *child table.* You use this data structure in the Youth system that is created later in the chapter. Figure 24.6 shows a parent table and its related child table.

A *lookup table* is another way to store information to prevent data redundancy and to increase the accuracy of data entry functions. Typically, a lookup table is used to store valid data entries (for example, a state abbreviations table). When a person enters the state code in an application, the program looks in the abbreviations table to make sure that the code exists.

You also can use a lookup table in data normalization. If you have a large mailing list, many of the entries use the same city and state information. In this case, you can use a ZIP Code table as a related table to store the city and state by ZIP Code (remember that each ZIP Code corresponds to a single city and state combination). Using the ZIP Code table requires that the mailing list use only the ZIP Code of the address, and not the city and state. During data entry, you can have the program check an entered ZIP Code against the valid entries.

Rules for Organizing Tables   Although no absolute rules exist for defining what data goes into which tables, here are some general guidelines to follow for efficient database design:

- Determine a topic for each table, and make sure that all data in the table relates to the topic.
- If a number of the records in a table have fields intentionally left blank, split the table into two similar tables. (Remember the example of the Employee and Member tables.)
- If information is repeated in a number of records, move that information to another table and set up a relationship between the tables.
- Repeated fields indicate the need for a child table. For example, if you have Item1, Item2, Item3, and so on in a table, move the items to a child table that relates back to the parent table.
- Use lookup tables to reduce data volume and to increase the accuracy of data entry.
- Do not store information in a table if it can be calculated from data in other tables.

N O T E   As stated previously, the guidelines for defining tables are not hard-and-fast rules. Sometimes it makes sense for you to deviate from the guidelines. ■

Performance Considerations

One of the most frequent reasons for deviating from the guidelines just given is to improve performance. If obtaining a total sales figure for a given salesperson requires summing several thousand records, for example, you might find it worthwhile to include a Total Sales field in the Salesperson table that is updated each time a sale is made. This way, when reports are generated, the application doesn't have to do large numbers of calculations and the report process is dramatically faster.

Another reason to deviate from the guidelines is to avoid opening a large number of tables at the same time. Because each open table uses precious resources and takes up memory, having too many open tables can slow down your application.

Deviating from the guidelines results in two major consequences. The first is increasing the size of the database because of redundant data. The second is the possibility of having incorrect data in some of the records because a piece of data was changed and not all the affected records were updated.

There are tradeoffs between application performance and data storage efficiency. For each design, you must look at the tradeoffs and decide on the optimum design.

Using Indexes

When information is entered into a table, records usually are stored in the order in which they are added. This is the *physical order* of the data. However, you usually want to view or process data in an order different from the order of entry; that is, you want to define a *logical order*. You also frequently need to find a specific record in a table. Doing so by scanning the table in its physical order can be quite time-consuming.

An index provides a method of showing a table in a specific order. An *index* is a special table that contains a key value (usually derived from the values of one or more fields) for each record in the data table; the index itself is stored in a specific logical order. The index also contains pointers that tell the database engine where the actual record is located. This type of index is similar to the index in the back of this book. By using the book's index, you easily can look up key words or topics, because it contains pointers (page numbers) to tell you where to find the information.

Why Use an Index?   The structure of an index allows for rapid data search and retrieval. If you have a table of names indexed alphabetically, you rapidly can retrieve the record for a specific name by searching the index. To get an idea of the value of such an index, imagine a phone book that lists the customer names in the order in which they signed up for phone service. If you live in a large city, finding a person's number could take forever, because you have to look at each line until you find the one you want.

A table can have a number of different indexes associated with it to provide different organizations of the data. For example, an Employee table can have indexes on last name, date of birth, date of hire, and pay scale. Each index shows the same data in a different order, for a different purpose.

> **CAUTION**
>
> Although having many different views of the data may be desirable, keeping multiple indexes can take a toll on performance, since all indexes must be updated each time data changes. Once again, you must consider the tradeoffs in the database design.

N O T E   You also can create different views of the information in a table by sorting the records or by specifying an order using the ORDER BY clause of a Structured Query Language (SQL) statement. Even though indexes aren't used directly by the SQL engine, their presence speeds up the sorting process when an ORDER BY clause is present. You learn about this topic in detail in Chapter 29, "Understanding SQL."

▶ **See** "Setting the Sort Conditions," **p. 772**

Single-Key Expressions   The most common type of index is the *single-key index,* which is based on the value of a single field in a table. Examples of this type of index are Social Security number, ZIP Code, employee ID, and last name. If multiple records exist with the same index key, those records are presented in physical order within the sort order imposed by the single-key index. Figure 24.7 shows the physical order of a Names table and how the table appears after being indexed on the last name field.

FIG. 24.7

The physical and logical order of a table can be different. Logical order depends on an index.

Physical order

Logical order with single-key index

First names out of order

Multiple-Key Expressions   Although single-key expressions are valuable in presenting data in a specific order, imposing an even more detailed order on the table is often necessary. You can do so by using multiple-key indexes. As you can infer from the name, a *multiple-key index* is based on the values of two or more fields in a table. A prime example is to use last name and first name when indexing a membership list. Figure 24.8 updates the view of the table shown in Figure 24.7 to show how using the first name field to help sort the records changes the order of the table. As with single-key indexes, if the key values of several records are the same, the records are presented in physical order within the index order.

FIG. 24.8

Multiple-key indexes further refine the logical order of a table.

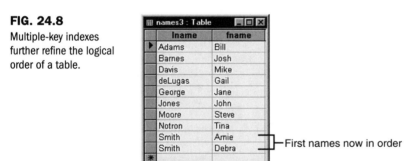

First names now in order

CAUTION

Although this point might be obvious, I must stress that the order of the fields in the index expression has a dramatic impact on the order of the records in the table. Indexing on first name and then last name produces different results than indexing on last name and then first name. Figure 24.9 shows the undesirable results of using a first name/last name index on the table used in Figure 24.7.

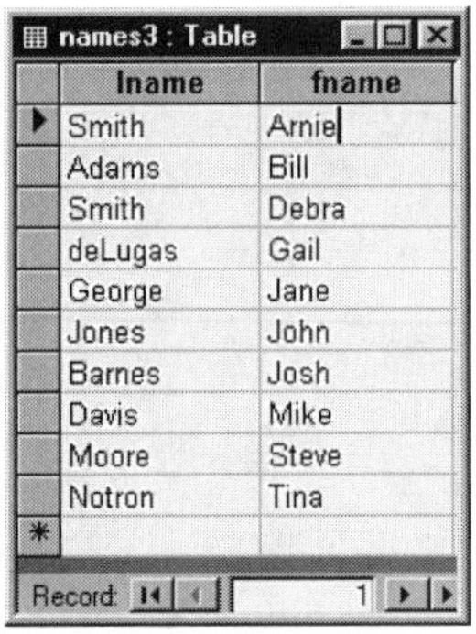

FIG. 24.9
An improper index field order yields undesirable results.

lname	fname
Smith	Arnie
Adams	Bill
Smith	Debra
deLugas	Gail
George	Jane
Jones	John
Barnes	Josh
Davis	Mike
Moore	Steve
Notron	Tina

Using Queries

When you normalize data, you typically are placing related information in multiple tables. However, when you need to access the data, you want to see the information from all the tables in one place. To do so, you need to create recordsets that consolidate the related information from the multiple tables. You create a recordset from multiple tables by using a SQL statement that specifies the desired fields, the location of the fields, and the relation between the tables. One way of using a SQL statement is to place it in the OpenRecordset method, which you use to create the recordset. However, you also can store the SQL statement as a query in the database.

Using stored queries presents several advantages:

- You can use the SQL statement more easily in multiple locations in your program or in multiple programs.
- Making changes to the SQL statement in a single location is easier.
- Stored queries run faster than those that are handled by parsing the statement from code.
- Moving your application up to a client/server environment is easier.

Implementing Your Design

The first step in implementing the database design is to create the database itself. There are three main methods of creating an Access database for use with Visual Basic. You can use the following:

- Data access objects within a program
- The Visual Data Manager application provided with Visual Basic
- Microsoft Access

Creating the Database

You can use Visual Basic's database commands to write a program that creates a database for use in your design work or to write a program that creates a new database while the program is running. Using the database creation commands is the only way you can make a new database at runtime. Using the program to create the database is particularly useful in creating and distributing commercial applications, because you don't have to worry about including and installing the database files with the application. If the code is included in your program, the database can be created the first time the user runs your application. Also, if future releases of the program require modifications of the database structure, you can use program commands to update the database on-the-fly, without requiring the user to handle conversions from the old format to the new.

Creating files at runtime also is useful if the user is expected to create different database files with the same structure but different user-defined names. Each time the user wants to create a new file, the program asks for the file name and then creates the database accordingly. As an example, a user might create a different database to hold data for each calendar year.

Part

VI

Ch

24

N O T E In order to do any work with databases in your program, you must add a reference to the appropriate DAO object library (typically the Microsoft DAO 3.5 Object Library). This is done in the References dialog box, which is accessible by choosing Project, References.

To create a new database, follow these eight steps:

1. Create a new database object variable with the `Dim` statement.
2. Use the `CreateDatabase` method to create the new database.
3. Create `TableDef` objects with the `Dim` statement and `CreateTableDef` method.
4. Set the properties for the new tables.
5. Create `Field` and `Index` objects with the `Dim` statement and `CreateField` and `CreateIndex` methods.
6. Set the properties for the fields and indexes.
7. Use the `Append` method to add fields and indexes to the tables.
8. Use the `Append` method to add the table to the database.

The heart of Visual Basic's data access object structure is the `DBEngine` object, which represents the database engine that Visual Basic programs use to interface with physical databases. All data access objects are contained within the `DBEngine` object. Programs interface with the `DBEngine` object through `Workspace` objects, which represent sessions with the `DBEngine` object and are members of the `DBEngine`'s `Workspaces` collection. Visual Basic creates a default `Workspace` object, `Workspaces(0)`, that is used unless the program explicitly creates another one. When a program references the various data access objects, Visual Basic assumes that the objects are contained in this default `Workspace` object unless another one is named.

You will be using the `CreateDatabase` method, which is a method of a `Workspace` object, to create a database. Listing 24.1 shows the statements you will use in this example to define `Database` and `Workspace` objects, and then actually create a database using the `Workspace` object's `CreateDatabase` method.

Listing 24.1   Defining a Database Object and Creating a Database

```
'**************************************
'Full syntax of CreateDatabase method
'**************************************
Dim NewDb As Database, NewWs As Workspace
Set NewWs = DBEngine.Workspaces(0)
Set NewDb = NewWs.CreateDatabase("C:\YOUTH\YOUTHTRK.MDB",dbLangGeneral)
```

You can define any valid variable name as a database object by using the `Dim` statement. Although a literal file name (`"C:\YOUTH\YOUTHTRK.MDB"`) is specified explicitly in the argument of the `CreateDatabase` method, you can use a string variable to hold the name of the database to be created. This arrangement gives the user the flexibility of specifying a database name meaningful to him or her, or it enables you to create multiple databases with the same structure.

T I P   If your program allows the user to create a database, you might want to use the `CommonDialog` control's File Open dialog box to retrieve the file name and path for the new database.

The constant `dbLangGeneral` represents the required *Locale* argument of the `CreateDatabase` method. It specifies the database's collating order (how strings are sorted and compared), which may be different depending upon the language and culture in which the program will be utilized. The constant `dbLangGeneral` that you used specifies that the database engine should use English sorting rules. The Visual Basic help screen "Data Access Objects (DAO) Constants" lists the constants that you can use for different languages in the CollatingOrder section.

Another (optional) argument, the *options* argument, is available for the `CreateDatabase` method that enables you to specify which version of the Jet database engine to use to create the database, and to specify whether the database should be encrypted. The default Jet engine for both Windows 95 and Windows NT is version 3.5.

To specify the options argument, supply the sum of the Visual Basic constants that define the options you want. The following lines show how you can change the code in Listing 24.1 to create a Jet 2.5 database and encrypt it (if, for instance, your program needed to share data with 16-bit applications):

```
Dim NewDb As Database, NewWs As Workspace
Dim DbOpts As Long, DbName As String
Set NewWs = DBEngine.Workspaces(0)
DbName = "C:\YOUTH\YOUTHTRK.MDB"
DbOpts = dbVersion25 + dbEncrypt
Set NewDb = NewWs.CreateDatabase(DbName, dbLangGeneral, DbOpts)
```

CAUTION

When you use the `CreateDatabase` method, a trappable error occurs if the file name to be created already exists. Include a trap for this error in your error-handling routine or, better yet, check for the existence of the file name before invoking the function, while you're still got a chance to specify a different name.

Creating a Table

Creating a database using the code in Listing 24.1 creates only a file on a disk. You can't do anything with that file until you create the tables and add them to the database (refer to Steps 3 through 8 in "Creating the Database," earlier in this chapter). You can think of the `CreateDatabase` method as simply building the shell of a warehouse. To store items, you still have to lay out the aisles and build the shelves. You do just that when you create the tables.

Defining the *TableDef* Object　　The first step in creating a new table is to create a new `TableDef` object. `TableDef` is short for "Table Definition." When you create a `TableDef`, you define what type of information will be stored in a table and some optional properties of that table. Using the `TableDef` object, you can set the properties for the new table. The following lines of code show how to create a `TableDef` object and give the table a name:

```
Dim NewTbl As TableDef
Set NewTbl = NewDb.CreateTableDef("Youth")
```

The `Name` property of the table is only one of several properties for the `TableDef` object, but it is typically the only one required for the creation of a Jet table. You can use some of the other properties (`Attributes`, `Connect`, and `SourceTableName`) when attaching an external table to the database; these can be set in successive arguments of the `CreateTableDef` method. You also can specify other properties by setting them equal to a value after the `TableDef` object has been created, as you do if you want to set the validation rule and validation error message for a table (as shown in the following section). These statements follow the `CreateTableDef` method:

```
NewTbl.ValidationRule = "Age > 0"
NewTbl.ValidationText = _
    "You cannot enter an age of 0 or less."
```

Defining the Fields　　After defining the `TableDef` object for the new table, you must define one or more `Field` objects. For each field, you must define its name and type. Depending on the type of field, you might be required to define other properties, or you might want to set some optional properties.

For text fields, you must set the `Size` property to specify how long a string the field can contain. The valid entries for the `Size` property of the text field are 1 to 255. If you want to allow longer strings, you can set the field type to `Memo`, which allows over a gigabyte of text!

Listing 24.2 shows how field objects are created and field properties set for the Youth table of the sample application. You can specify the field name, type, and size as optional arguments of the `CreateField` method, or you could use the `CreateField` method without any arguments and then set all the field properties with assignment statements. Listing 24.2 shows both techniques. You must use an assignment statement to set any other properties. As an example of an assignment statement, the listing sets a validation rule for the age field.

Listing 24.2 Creating Field Objects and Setting Properties

```
Dim F1 As Field, F2 As Field, F3 As Field, F4 As Field
Dim F5 As Field, F6 As Field, F7 As Field
'**************************************************************
'Specify field name, type, and size as CreateField arguments
'**************************************************************
Set F1 = NewTbl.CreateField("LastName", dbText, 20)
Set F2 = NewTbl.CreateField("FirstName", dbText, 20)
Set F3 = NewTbl.CreateField()
'******************************
'Explicitly set field properties
'******************************
F3.Name = "Address"
F3.Type = dbText
F3.Size = 30
Set F4 = NewTbl.CreateField("Age", dbInteger)
'**************************************
'Set validation properties for a field
'**************************************
F4.ValidationRule = "Age > 0"
F4.ValidationText = "A person's age must be greater than 0."
Set F5 = NewTbl.CreateField("City", dbText, 20)
Set F6 = NewTbl.CreateField("State", dbText, 2)
Set F7 = NewTbl.CreateField()
F7.Name = "Birthdate"
F7.Type = dbDate
```

After you define each of the fields to include in the table, use the Append method of the TableDef object to add the fields to the table definition, as shown in Listing 24.3.

Listing 24.3 Adding Fields to the Table Definition

```
NewTbl.Fields.Append F1
NewTbl.Fields.Append F2
NewTbl.Fields.Append F3
NewTbl.Fields.Append F4
NewTbl.Fields.Append F5
NewTbl.Fields.Append F6
NewTbl.Fields.Append F7
```

N O T E If you have a large number of fields, or if you want to create a generic routine for adding fields to a table, consider using an *array* to define your fields. By using arrays, you can write a simple FOR loop to add all the fields to the table (as shown in the following code statements). Depending on the structure of the table, you might be able to use a loop to set the type properties of several fields, although you must still define each field you intend to add to the table:

```
ReDim Fld(1 To 7) As Field
'************************************************
'Field definition statements go here for each
'array element.
'************************************************
FOR I = 1 To 7
  NewTbl.Fields.Append Fld(I)
NEXT I
```

Setting Optional Field Properties   In the preceding section, you learned how to specify the name of a field, the type of data it can store, and, for some fields, the size of the field. These elements are the minimum requirements for defining a field. However, you can set several other properties of a field to further define its behavior.

The first of these properties is the `Attributes` property. Two key settings of this property are applicable to creating fields in a table. The first is the auto-increment setting, which tells the database to increment the value of a numeric field each time a new record is added. This setting can provide a record counter; you can use it to ensure a unique value in that field for each record. You then can use the auto-increment field as a primary key field. The auto-increment setting is valid only for fields with the Long data type. Another optional setting is the updatable setting, which enables you to specify whether a field can be changed. This setting is not typically used in initial table creation but can be useful in limiting access to information, particularly in a multi-user environment.

You set the `Attributes` property by assigning it a value in a code statement. For example, the following code segment creates a field and then specifies that it be used as a counter field by setting the `Attributes` property to auto-increment:

```
Set F1 = NewTbl.CreateField("YouthID", dbLong)
F1.Attributes = dbAutoIncrField
```

Note that `dbAutoIncrField` is a predefined constant that can be used to specify an auto-increment field. The other constants that you can use in the `Attributes` property are listed in Table 24.1. You can apply multiple settings to the `Attributes` property by combining the values of the constants and then setting the property to the sum of the values.

Table 24.1   The Attributes Settings to Control the Behavior of a Field

Constant	Function
dbFixedField	The length of the field is fixed.
dbVariableField	The field size can change. (Text fields only.)
dbAutoIncrField	The value of the field is incremented automatically by the database engine.
dbUpdatableField	The value of the field can be changed.

In addition to the `Attributes` property, you can set several other optional properties for individual fields. As with the `Attributes` property, these optional properties are set using assignment statements; they cannot be set as part of the `CreateField` method. Table 24.2 lists optional field properties, their functions, and their default settings, if applicable.

Table 24.2   Optional Properties that Provide You Further Control over the Behavior of a Field

Property	Function
AllowZeroLength	Specifies whether the value of a `Text` or `Memo` field can be a zero-length (empty) string. The default is False; setting this option to True allows zero-length strings.
DefaultValue	Allows you to specify a default value for the field.
Required	Determines whether a value for the field must be entered. The default value is False.
ValidationRule	Specifies criteria that must be met for the field before the record can be updated. The default value is no rule (an empty string).
ValidationText	Specifies the error message that is displayed when the validation rule is not met. The default value is an empty string.

CAUTION

As mentioned, the default setting for the `AllowZeroLength` property is False. A zero-length string, therefore, cannot be used in the field. You might want to change this value for many of the fields you create, as your program might not need values for these fields. For example, you might have a field for a work phone but need to allow a zero-length string for people who don't work or don't provide the information.

Adding the Table to the Database   The final step in creating a database is adding the table or tables to the database. Use the `Append` method of the `Database` object to accomplish this by appending the `TableDef` object you just created to the database's `TableDefs` collection (see the following code). The `TableDefs` collection contains one `TableDef` object for each table in the database. The code also shows the `Close` method, which closes the database file and releases the system resources associated with the `Database` object:

```
NewDb.TableDefs.Append NewTbl
NewDb.Close
```

Using a Query to Create a Table   In the preceding sections, you learned how to use data access objects to create a table in a database. However, you also could use the SQL `CREATE TABLE` statement in a query to accomplish the same goal with less effort. In this query, you specify the table name, followed by the names, types, and, optionally, sizes of the fields to include in the table. The list of fields is enclosed in parentheses. The query is run using the Database object's Execute method. The following code shows how to create the Youth table containing the LastName, FirstName, Age, and Birthdate fields using a query:

```
Dim SQLSel As String
SQLSel = "Create Table Youth (LastName TEXT(20),FirstName TEXT(20),"
SQLSel = SQLSel & "Age INTEGER,Birthdate DATETIME);"
NewDb.Execute SQLSel
```

The main drawback of using a CREATE TABLE query is that you cannot use it to set optional properties of the fields. You can set these properties only with the data access objects and the CreateField method.

Creating Indexes

Defining indexes for a table is another key aspect of developing your database. The method for creating an index is closely related to the method for creating the table itself. For each index, you must assign a name, define the fields to include in the index, and determine whether the index is a primary index and whether duplicate values are allowed in the fields that comprise the index key.

To create an index, follow these six steps:

1. Use the CreateIndex method of the TableDef object to create the Index object.
2. Set any optional properties of the index (such as primary or unique).
3. Use the CreateField method of the Index object to create the Field objects.
4. Set any optional properties of the Field objects.
5. Append the Field object(s) to the Fields collection of the Index object.
6. Append the Index object to the Indexes collection of the TableDef object.

Two commonly used optional properties of the Index object are the Primary property and the Unique property. A *primary index* is one that is typically used for finding a specific record in a table. To make an index primary, set the Primary property to True. Making an index primary ensures that the value of the index key for each record is unique and that no null values exist.

> **CAUTION**
>
> If you create a primary index, you must include logic in your program to ensure that any records added have unique, non-null values for the fields in the primary index. If you attempt to add a record with a non-unique or null value, an error is generated.

Use the Unique property on a non-primary index to make sure that the values of fields other than the primary index field are unique (for example, to make sure that you enter a unique Social Security number for each employee in a table).

N O T E   You can specify only one primary index per table.

For the `Field` objects that will be part of the `Fields` collection of an `Index` object, the only property of concern for creating indexes is the `Attributes` property. This property determines whether the sort order of the field is ascending (from A to Z) or descending (from Z to A). The default value is ascending. If you want to sort the field in descending order, set the `Attributes` property to the constant `dbDescending`.

You can create a multiple-field index (for example, an index on the first and last names of a customer). To create such an index, simply set up multiple fields using the `CreateField` method, and then append these fields one-by-one to the `Index` object's `Fields` collection. Remember that the order of the fields can have a dramatic impact on the order of your records. The order of the fields in an index is determined by the order in which the fields are appended to the index, not the order in which the field objects are created.

As I described in the preceding section, after you create the fields and set the properties of the fields and index, use the `Append` method to add the fields to the index and the index to the table definition.

N O T E   You can create a maximum of 32 indexes per table.

For the sample case, create a primary index on the `YouthID` field and an index on the `LastName` and `FirstName` fields. You also might want to create an index on the `Birthdate` field in descending order. Listing 24.4 shows how you accomplish this task.

Listing 24.4   Creating Index Objects, Assigning Properties, and Adding Indexes to the Table

```
'********************************
'Dimension the data access objects
'********************************
Dim Idx1, Idx2, Idx3 As Index
Dim Fld1, Fld2, Fld3 As Field
'********************************
'Create the primary YouthID index
'********************************
Set Idx1 = NewTbl.CreateIndex("YouthID")
Idx1.Primary = True
Set Fld1 = Idx1.CreateField("YouthID")
Idx1.Fields.Append Fld1
NewTbl.Indexes.Append Idx1
'*********************
'Create the name index
'*********************
Set Idx2 = NewTbl.CreateIndex("Name")
Idx2.Unique = False
Set Fld1 = Idx2.CreateField("LastName")
Set Fld2 = Idx2.CreateField("FirstName")
```

```
Idx2.Fields.Append Fld1
Idx2.Fields.Append Fld2
NewTbl.Indexes.Append Idx2
'************************************************
'Create the birthdate index in descending order
'************************************************
Set Idx3 = NewTbl.CreateIndex("Born")
Set Fld1 = Idx2.CreateField("Birthdate")
Fld1.Attributes = dbDescending
Idx3.Fields.Append Fld1
NewTbl.Indexes.Append Idx3
```

Creating Relations

Earlier in this chapter, I described normalizing data and the need to relate normalized tables. The Jet engine relates tables through the use of a `Relation` object stored in the database. The `Relation` object tells the database which two tables are related, which table is the parent, which is the child, and the key fields used to specify the relationship.

Follow these seven steps to create a relationship between two tables:

1. Use the `Dim` statement to define a `Relation` object variable.
2. Create the `Relation` object by using the `CreateRelation` method of the `Database` object.
3. Set the primary table and the foreign table properties of the relationship.
4. Create the relation field for the primary table by using the `CreateField` method of the `Relation` object.
5. Set the foreign field property of the `Field` object.
6. Append the field to the `Relation` object.
7. Append the `Relation` object to the database.

Listing 24.5 demonstrates the creation of a relationship, showing how to create a relation between the Family (primary) table and the Youth (foreign) table of the sample database.

Listing 24.5   Specifying a Relationship Between Two Tables Using the
***Relation* Object**

```
Dim NewRel As Relation
Dim Fld1 As Field
'**************************
'Create the Relation object
'**************************
Set NewRel = NewDb.CreateRelation("Parents")
'**********************************
'Set the properties of the relation
'**********************************
NewRel.Table = "Family"
```

continues

Listing 24.5 Continued

```
NewRel.ForeignTable = "Youth"
'**************************************************
'Create the relating field and set the properties
'**************************************************
Set Fld1 = NewRel.CreateField("ParentID")
Fld1.ForeignName = "ParentID"
'*********************************************************************
'Append the field to the relation and the relation to the database
'*********************************************************************
NewRel.Fields.Append Fld1
NewDb.Relations.Append NewRel
```

TROUBLESHOOTING

When I try to create a relation in the database, I get the error message `Parents is not an`
`index in this table`. You get this message if you do not have a primary index on the key field in
the primary table. In the preceding case, the primary index must be on the `ParentID` field in the
Family table. Although the documentation does make this point, you must have a primary key field in
your primary table. This field identifies the records to the relationship.

Creating Queries

Using queries is a powerful way of gathering information from more than one table or of selecting information from a table that matches specific criteria (for example, customer records for
people who live in Alabama). As you learn in Chapter 28, "Improving Data Access with Data
Access Objects," an object called a *recordset* can store this type of information for use in your
programs. In fact, using a query is one method of creating a dynaset- or snapshot-type
recordset. The advantage of creating a query is that the information about it is saved in the
database itself, making it convenient to test and store information needed to create recordsets
that are used often. You learn a lot more about SQL Chapter 29, "Understanding SQL."

Setting Up the Query   To create a query, you define a `QueryDef` object, and then use the
`CreateQueryDef` method of the database. When calling the function, you must specify the name
of the query. You can specify the SQL syntax of the query, or you can define the SQL statement
in a separate program line. The following code shows two methods of creating a query:

```
Dim OldDb As Database, NewQry As QueryDef
Set OldDb = OldWs.OpenDatabase("C:\YOUTH\YOUTHTRK.MDB")
Set NewQry = OldDb.CreateQueryDef("Local")
NewQry.SQL = "SELECT * FROM Youth Where State = 'AL';"
'**************************************************
'Alternative form of query creation statement.
'**************************************************
Set NewQry = OldDb.CreateQueryDef("Local", "SELECT * FROM _
    Youth Where State = 'AL';")
```

The heart of defining queries is the SQL statement. This statement defines the fields to be included, the source of the fields, record filters, and the sort order of the resulting recordset.

N O T E The Jet engine can store queries only for Access (Jet) databases. It can, however, use queries to retrieve the data in many database types, such as FoxPro, Paradox, dBASE, SQL Server, and others. ▪

Deleting a Query   As with most other objects in the database, if you create a query, you might, at some time, need to delete it. If you have a query that you no longer need in your database, you can remove it by using the following command:

```
OldDb.DeleteQueryDef "Local"
```

CAUTION

When you use a query, you open the query by creating a data access object. Therefore, before deleting a query that has been used, you should close the associated query object. This way, you can ensure that the query is not in use and that no error occurs during deletion. The syntax for closing a query is `NewQry.Close`.

Part

VI

Ch

24

Creating a Database with Other Tools

Although the data access objects provide you with a way to create a database by using program code, this approach is not the only way to create a Jet database. Several other methods are available to you:

- ▪ *Visual Data Manager*—Using this Visual Basic add-in, you can create databases, as well as create, modify, and delete tables, indexes, and relations within a database. VisData, as it's also known, represents a major improvement over its predecessor, Data Manager.

- ▪ *Microsoft Access*—Using this application, you can create Jet databases. It provides the added advantage of enabling you to create relations by using a visual drag-and-drop interface.

- ▪ *Third-party programs*—A number of other programs, both commercial and shareware, are available to manage Jet (and other) databases. Some are highly specialized, while others are general-purpose utilities much like Visual Data Manager.

Using Visual Data Manager

The Visual Data Manager application that comes with Visual Basic provides you with an interactive way of creating and modifying databases. You can run this application by selecting the <u>V</u>isual Data Manager item from Visual Basic's <u>A</u>dd-Ins menu.

N O T E Visual Data Manager can work with Access (Jet), dBASE, FoxPro, Paradox, and ODBC databases, as well as text files. Typically, in Visual Basic applications, you will use it to manipulate Access databases.

continues

continued

> Visual Data Manager is also one of the sample applications that can be found in the Visual Basic
> folder when you installed Visual Basic. Examining this project can provide a tremendous education into
> creating database applications in Visual Basic. ■

The first step in creating a new database is to create the database file itself. This provides a physical location for the rest of your work. To do this in Visual Data Manager, first choose File, New. This brings up a submenu that allows you to specify the type of database to create. For the purpose of this discussion, you will create an Access (Jet) database by choosing the Microsoft Access item. This brings up another submenu from which you can choose the version of Access database to create. If you will be sharing data with users on a Windows 3.1 system, you should choose the 2.0 version; otherwise, choose the 7.0 version. Figure 24.10 shows the different menu levels for creating a database. After you have chosen the type of database, you are presented with the Select Microsoft Access Database to Create dialog box. This dialog box allows you to choose a name and folder for your database. After entering a name, click the Save button on the dialog box. This takes you to the design mode shown in Figure 24.11.

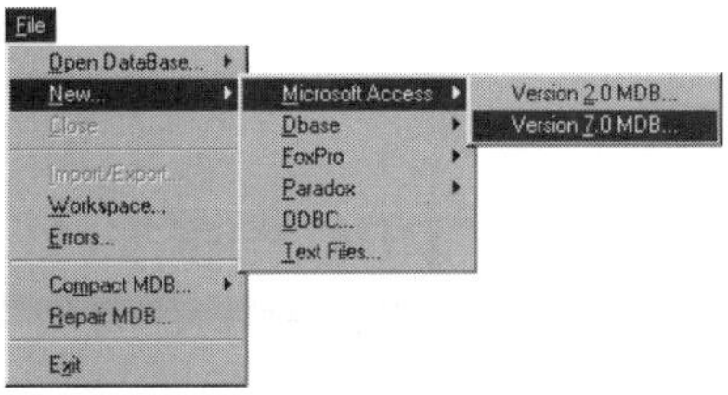

FIG. 24.10

The menus allow you to choose the type and version of database to create.

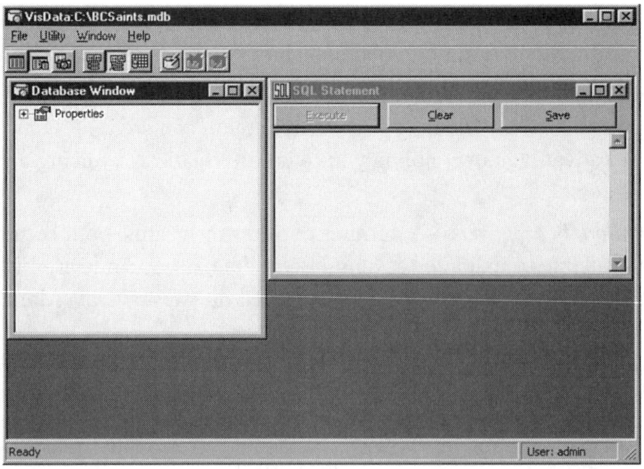

FIG. 24.11

The Visual Data Manager Database window provides access to the design functions for tables, fields, and indexes.

The Visual Data Manager presents the database information in a tree-like view. This type of view allows you quickly to see the tables and queries in the database. It also allows you to open the view further to see the fields and indexes of a table as well as its properties. Finally, you can open the view all the way up to see the properties of the individual fields.

Adding a New Table   After creating the database, the next thing you will want to do is create tables. To create a new table, right-click anywhere in Database Window. Select the New Table item. This brings up the Table Structure dialog box, as shown in Figure 24.12. This dialog box shows you information about the table itself, as well as a list of fields and indexes in the table. There are also buttons in the dialog box to add and remove fields and indexes. To add fields to the table, click the Add Field button to bring up the Add Field dialog box, as shown in Figure 24.13.

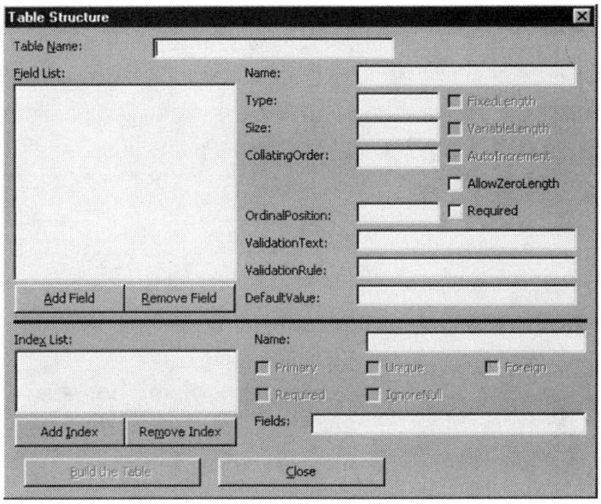

FIG. 24.12

In the Table Structure dialog box, you can specify a table name.

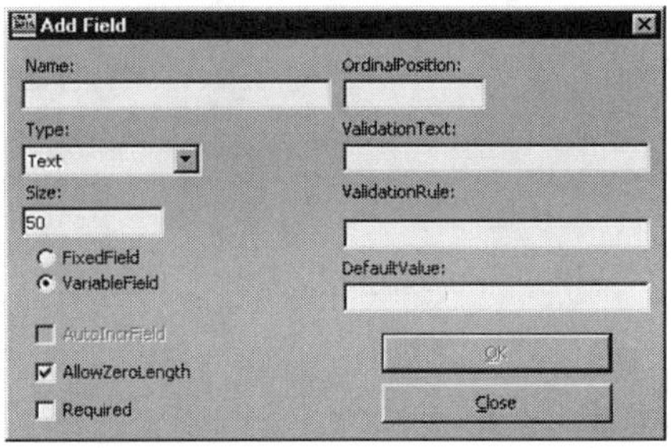

FIG. 24.13

In the Add Field dialog box, you can specify the properties of the fields for a table.

After you are in the Add Field dialog box, you need to follow these steps for each field you want to add:

1. Enter the name of the field.
2. Select the field type from the Type drop-down list.
3. Enter the size of the field (if necessary).
4. Enter any optional parameters, such as validation rules.
5. Click the OK button to add the field to the table.

After you have entered all the fields for your table, click the Close button in the Add Field dialog box. This returns you to the Table Structure dialog box.

If you want to remove a field from the table, select the field name in the dialog box's field list, and then click the Remove Field button. When you are satisfied with the fields in the table, click the Build the Table button to create the table.

Making Changes to the Fields in Your Table
After you have created the fields in the table, you can set or change a number of the field properties from the Table Structure dialog box. To modify the properties, select the field name in the Field List. The properties of the field that can be modified appear in the dialog box as enabled text or check boxes. All other properties appear as disabled controls.

> **TIP** You also can edit the properties of a field from the Database window of the Visual Data Manager. Simply expand the database view to show field properties and right-click the property to be edited. You then can select Edit from the pop-up menu to change the property.

> **NOTE** In Visual Basic, you cannot edit or delete any field that is part of an index expression or a relation. If you need to delete such a field, you must delete the index or relation containing the field and then make the changes to the field. ■

Adding an Index to the Table
The Table Structure dialog box also allows you to add, modify, or remove indexes in the table. Any indexes currently in the table appear in the Index List at the bottom of the dialog box, as shown in Figure 24.14.

FIG. 24.14

You can add, edit, or delete indexes for a table from the Table Structure dialog box.

To add a new index, click the Add Index button; the Add Index dialog box then appears, as shown in Figure 24.15. In this dialog box, first enter an index name. Next, select the fields to be included in the index by clicking the fields in the Available Fields list. As you select each field, it is added to the Indexed Fields list in the order in which it was selected. By default, all fields are indexed in ascending order. To change the order to descending, precede the field name in the Indexed Fields list with a minus sign (-).

FIG. 24.15
The Add Index dialog box provides a visual means of creating the indexes for a table.

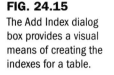

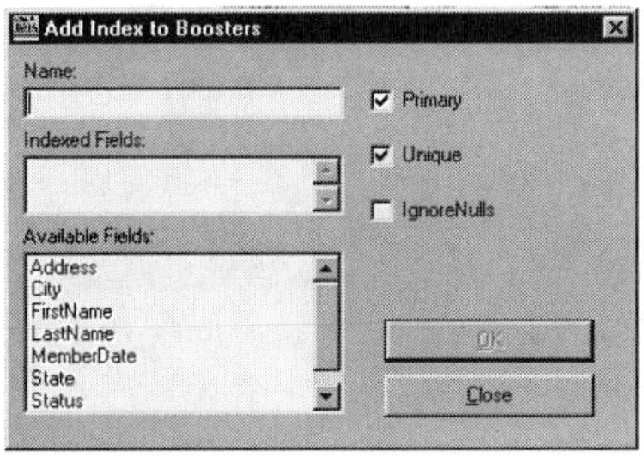

After you define the fields for the index, you can choose to require the index to be unique or to be the primary index (assuming there's not already a primary index) by selecting the appropriate check box in the window. When the index is completed to your liking, save it by clicking OK. The index you have just created is added to the index list on the Table Structure dialog box. To delete an index, simply select it in the list box and click Remove Index.

Returning to the Visual Basic Design Window   Closing the Visual Data Manager window or selecting Exit from the File menu takes you back to Visual Basic's main design window. (You also can switch back and forth between the Data Manager and the Visual Basic design environment.) To manipulate databases without having to start Visual Basic every time, make the Data Manager application a program item in your Visual Basic group.

Using Microsoft Access

Another option for creating a Jet database for use with a Visual Basic application is to use Microsoft Access. Access has a good visual design interface for setting up tables, indexes, queries, and table relationships. Obviously, this option is available only if you own a copy of Access. Note that Visual Basic can work with databases created with any version of Access; however, in order to exploit the power of 32-bit databases, Access 95 or later must be used.

Third-Party Database Designers

In addition to Visual Data Manager and Access, a number of third-party programs enable you to create and maintain Jet databases. Some of them provide you with advanced data modeling capabilities. These modeling capabilities make it easy for you to determine what information goes in which table and to set up the relations easily between the tables. Then, after your data model is complete, the program automatically can generate the database for you.

Modifying the Database Structure

Even if you create the perfect database for an application, sooner or later someone will come along and say, "Well, I really need this program to handle other data, too." At this point, you must modify the structure of your database and tables. Modifications can take the form of new tables, new fields or indexes in tables, or changes in the properties of tables, fields, or indexes. On occasion, you also might have to delete a table, field, or index.

Part
VI

Ch
24

In the following sections, you learn about the modification of a database through the use of Visual Basic code. As with the creation of a database, you also can use Visual Data Manager application or Microsoft Access to perform the modifications.

Adding and Deleting Tables

To add a table, follow the same steps that you took to create tables in a new database:

1. Define the table, field, and index objects by using the `Dim` statement and appropriate create methods.
2. Define the properties of the table, fields, and indexes.
3. Append the fields and indexes to the table.
4. Append the table to the database.

To delete a table from a database, you need to delete its `TableDef` object from the database's `TableDefs` collection, as shown in this statement:

```
OldDb.TableDefs.Delete "Members"
```

> **CAUTION**
>
> Use the `Delete` method with extreme caution. When you delete a table, all fields, indexes, and—most importantly—data are deleted along with it. And when it's gone, it's gone. The only way to get the data back is to create the table again from scratch and reload all your data.

Adding, Deleting, and Editing Indexes

Adding a new index involves the same steps as creating an index for a new table. You must define an `Index` object, set its properties, and append it to the `Indexes` collection of the appropriate `TableDef` object. An example of these steps was shown earlier in Listing 24.4.

To delete an index, simply use the `Delete` method as shown in the following line of code. This code deletes the Born index from the Youth table:

```
OldDb.TableDefs("Youth").Indexes.Delete "Born"
```

You cannot modify the properties of an existing `Index` object. Therefore, if a change to an index is required, you must delete the old index from the table and create a new index with the new properties. You do so by using the methods shown in the section "Creating Indexes," earlier in this chapter.

N O T E You cannot delete an index that is required by a relation. To delete such an index, you first must delete the relation. ▨

Adding, Deleting, and Editing Fields

As you learned when creating a new database, you add a field to a table by defining the field object, setting its properties, and appending it to the table. These commands were presented earlier in Listings 24.2 and 24.3.

To delete a field, use the `Delete` method to remove the `Field` object from the appropriate `TableDef` object's `TableDefs` collection, as shown here. This example deletes the `Address` field from the Youth table:

```
NewDb.TableDefs("Youth").Fields.Delete "Address"
```

Unfortunately, you cannot change a field's properties directly. You can, however, accomplish this task in two indirect ways. If the table contains no data, or if you don't care about losing the data in the field, you can delete the field from the table and then re-create it with the new properties. If you have a table that contains data, and you want to preserve the data, you must create a whole new table (making the appropriate changes to the `Field` object), copy the data to the new table, and then delete the old table. The difficulty of this process of making changes to fields dramatically underscores the importance of a good initial design.

Part
VI

Ch
24

To move data from one table to another existing table, follow these steps:

1. Open both tables.
2. Set up a loop to process each record in the table currently containing the data.
3. Then, for each record in the old table, follow these steps:
   a. Retrieve the value of each field to be transferred from the old table.
   b. Add a record to the new table.
   c. Set the values of the field in the new table.
   d. Update the new table.

N O T E If you have Microsoft Access, you can change the properties of a table's fields while preserving the fields' contents.

Remember that you cannot delete a field that is part of an index or relation.

Deleting a Relation

If you need to delete a relation, you can use the `Delete` method of the `Database` object to remove the `Relation` object from the database's `Relations` collection. The following statement shows how to delete the relation created earlier in Listing 24.5:

```
NewDb.Relations.Delete "Parents"
```

Using SQL to Modify the Database

Just as you can create a table with SQL statements, you also can modify or even delete a table by using SQL. To modify a table, you can use an ALTER TABLE query. By using this type of query, you can add a new field to the table or delete a field from the table. The following code segment shows how you can use an ALTER TABLE query to add an Address field and delete the Birthdate field from the Youth table created earlier:

```
'*********************************
'Add an address field to the table
'*********************************
NewDb.Execute "ALTER TABLE Youth ADD COLUMN Address TEXT(30);"
'*********************************************
'Delete the birthdate field from the table
'*********************************************
NewDb.Execute "ALTER TABLE Youth DROP COLUMN Birthdate;"
```

If you want, you also can delete an entire table by using a DROP TABLE query. The following statement deletes the entire Youth table:

```
NewDb.Execute "DROP TABLE Youth;"
```

Why Use a Program Instead of Visual Data Manager?

In this chapter, you have learned that the Visual Data Manager application and Microsoft Access can create, modify, and load data into a database. So the question you might be asking is: "Why do I ever need to bother with the Visual Basic program commands for these functions?" The answer is that, in many cases, you don't. If you have direct control over the database (that is, you are the only user or you can access the database at any time), you may never need to use program commands to create or change a database.

If, however, you have an application with many users—either throughout your company or across the country—using a program for data management offers several benefits. One benefit is in initial installation. If the database creation routines are in the program itself, you don't have to include empty database files on your setup disks. This can reduce the number of disks required, and it certainly reduces the possibility that a key file is left out. Along the same lines, a user accidentally may delete a database file, leading to the necessity to create a new one.

Another benefit occurs when you distribute updates to the program. With changes embedded in a program, your user merely can run the update program to change the file structure. He or she doesn't need to reload data into a new, blank file. Also, by modifying the file in place, you can preserve most structure changes in the database made by the end user.

Another reason for putting database creation and maintenance commands in a program is for performance considerations. Sometimes it is desirable, from a performance standpoint, to create a temporary table to speed up a program or to store intermediate results, and then delete the table at the completion of the program. You also might want to create a temporary index that creates a specific order or speeds up a search.

From Here...

In this chapter, you learned how to design and create a database for use in an application. To use the database, however, you must write a database access application. This topic is covered in other chapters of the book. For further information, refer to the following chapters:

- To learn how to quickly create a database application, see Chapter 26, "Using Data Controls and Reports."
- To see how to use bound controls to easily display database information in your programs, see Chapter 27, "Doing More with Bound Controls."
- Creating an application with the data access objects is covered in Chapter 28, "Improving Data Access with the Data Access Objects."
- If you want to create and use SQL statements, see Chapter 29, "Understanding SQL."

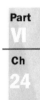

Part

VI

Ch

24

CHAPTER 25

Using the Data Manager

If you are using Visual Basic to create database applications, you will, at some point, have to create or modify the actual database that your program will be using. The process of creating a database for an application generally involves the following tasks:

Create a database for your program

You will see how to create a database and all its associated tables and queries with Visual Data Manager.

Enter and modify data

After you create a database, you will need to be able to enter the actual data into the tables. You can do this using a data entry form or grid.

Create and test SQL queries

You will see how to create a SQL query and test it in Visual Data Manager. You will also see how the Query Builder makes it easier for you to create queries.

Handle database security

Visual Data Manager also lets you define users and groups for your database. These elements are part of the security system of a Jet database.

- Creating the actual database file
- Creating the data tables, which includes defining fields and indexes
- Defining the relationships between tables
- Entering the actual data into the tables
- Creating queries to retrieve selected data
- Setting up database security, if it is required

If you have a copy of Microsoft Access, this is the best tool for working with Jet databases. (Jet is the name of the database engine that is shared by Visual Basic and Microsoft Access.) However, if you do not have Access available or simply prefer working strictly from the Visual Basic design environment, Visual Data Manager (VisData) is an excellent tool for handling database functions. ■

N O T E   Visual Data Manager can't create and manage relationships between tables. If you need to work with this capability, you need to use Microsoft Access. ■

Getting Started

The first step in working with Visual Data Manager is to start the program. You can access Visual Data Manager by choosing the Visual Data Manager item from the <u>A</u>dd-Ins menu of Visual Basic. When the program first starts, you see the screen shown in Figure 25.1.

FIG. 25.1
Visual Data Manager
helps you create and
modify databases.

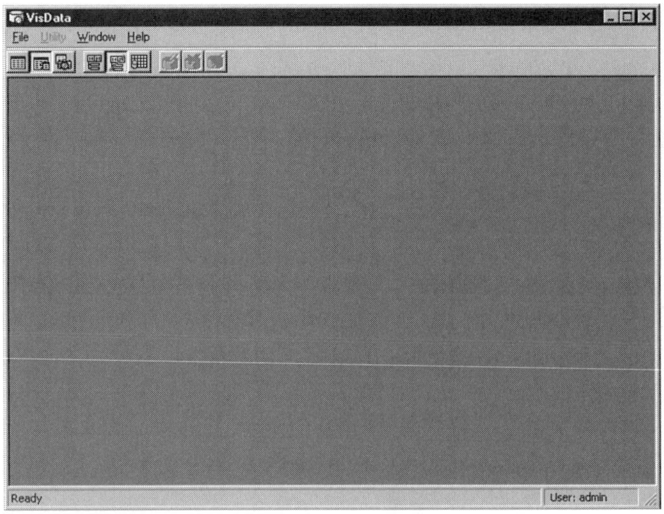

At this point, you can create a new database or open an existing one. In this chapter, we concentrate on creating a new database, but the techniques shown apply equally to working with an existing database. To illustrate the creation of a database, we create a sample Jet database that contains information about customers and products for a retail business.

Creating a New Database

The first step in creating a new database is to determine the type of database that you want to create. When you choose the New item from the File menu (shown in Figure 25.1), you might notice that you can create databases for several popular database programs: Access, dBASE, FoxPro, Paradox, and even ODBC or text file databases. For several of these formats, you can even choose from among several versions of the database.

FIG. 25.2

You have many choices of database types to create.

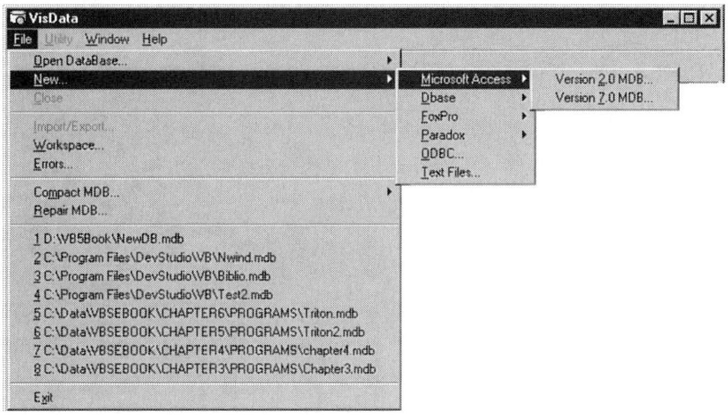

For the example in this chapter, choose the Microsoft Access option for creating a new file. When you choose this, you then can choose a Version 2.0 MDB or Version 7.0 MDB. The 2.0 database format corresponds to the 16-bit Jet 2.0/2.5 database engine that was used with Visual Basic 3.0 and Access 2.0. The 7.0 database format corresponds to the 32-bit Jet 3.0/3.5 database engine that is used with Visual Basic 4.0/5.0 and Microsoft Access 95/97. For the sample database, choose the version 7.0 database.

> **N O T E** For your own work, if your database needs to be backward compatible with Microsoft Access 2.0, choose the 2.0 format. Otherwise, choose the 7.0 format, as there are significant enhancements in the capabilities of the database engine. ▪

After choosing the database format, a dialog box opens that allows you to specify the name and location of the database you are creating. You can choose the folder for the database and then specify the name you want. You do not need to specify a file extension as this is handled automatically, based on the database type you chose.

> **TIP** If you are creating a database to be compatible with 16-bit operating systems, remember to limit the file name to eight characters.

After you choose the file name, you see the main database screen of Visual Data Manager, as shown in Figure 25.3. As you can see, Visual Data Manager is an MDI application that presents the database information and other tools in a series of child windows. The Database window uses a tree view to display all the objects and properties of the database. When you first create the database, only the properties of the database itself are shown.

Part

VI

Ch

25

FIG. 25.3

Click the box next to the Properties caption to see the properties of the database.

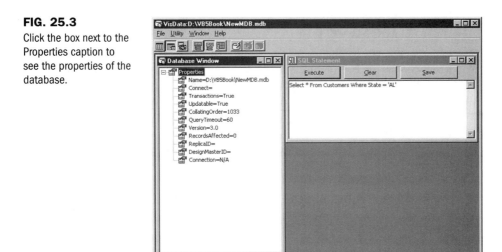

Creating a Table for the Database

After the database file is created, the next step in setting up the database is creating tables for it. Tables are the structures that actually contain the information that you store in the database. You typically design each table to hold a set of related information. As you create multiple tables, you can create links between them using key fields to identify specific records. (For more information about designing database tables, refer to Chapter 24, "Database Design and Normalization.")

▶ **See** "Creating a Table," **p. 639**

To create a table in Visual Data Manager, right-click anywhere in the Database window. This opens a context menu. Choose New Table to open the Table Structure dialog box where you will create your table (see Figure 25.4).

N O T E   When there are no tables in the database, there are only two items in the context menu. When there are tables to work with, the context menu contains a number of other choices. ▨

After you are in the Table Structure dialog box, you can set up the fields and indexes that make up the table structure. However, the first thing you should do is enter a name for your table. You can name a table almost anything you want. The name can include letters, numbers, spaces, and the underscore character. You should make the table name long enough to be descriptive but short enough to be easy to type. You enter the name of the table in the Table Name field at the top of the dialog box. For the first table of the sample database, enter the name **Customers**.

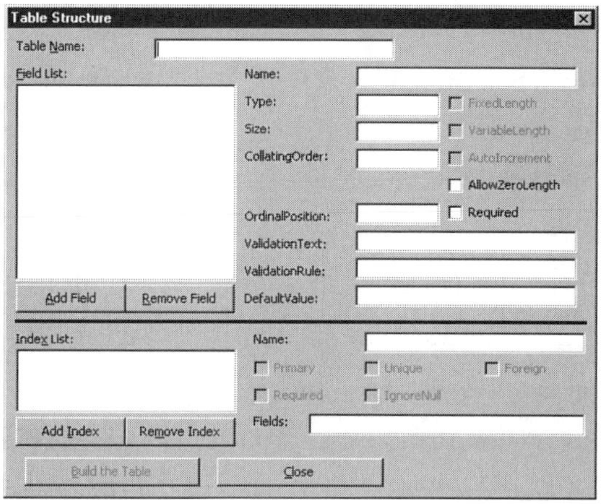

FIG. 25.4

The Table Structure dialog box lets you set the properties of the table and manage the fields and indexes.

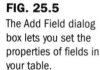

Creating Fields for the Table   The next step in creating the table is to create the fields that will be included in the table. Each field contains one piece of information. For example, if you were creating a customer phone book table, two of your fields would contain the first and last names of a person, and another field would contain the corresponding phone numbers. All of the information (fields) for a single person is a *record*.

To add a field to the table in Visual Data Manager, click the Add Field button in the Table Structure dialog box. This opens the Add Field dialog box shown in Figure 25.5.

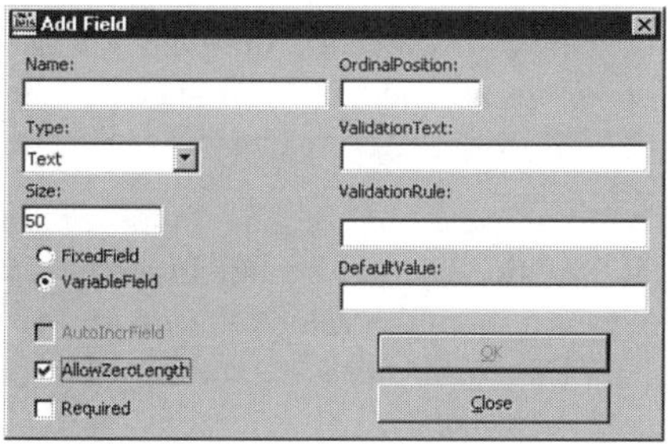

FIG. 25.5

The Add Field dialog box lets you set the properties of fields in your table.

You are required to enter at least two properties for each field that you create: the Name of the field and the Type. The Name property contains the name by which the field will be referenced when you use it in your programs. Like the table name, the name of a field can contain letters, numbers, spaces, or underscores. Each field in a table must have a unique name.

The Type property determines the type of information that can be stored in the field. There are 11 different field types that you can use. These types are summarized in Table 25.1.

Part

VI

Ch

25

Table 25.1   Data Types Available for Database Fields

Name	Information Stored	Range or Size
Text	Character strings	255 characters maximum
Memo	Long character strings	Up to 1.2G (gigabytes)
Byte	Integer (numeric data)	0 to 255
Integer	Integer (numeric data)	–32,768 to 32,767
Long	Integer (numeric data)	–2,147,483,648 to 2,147,483,647
Single	Real (numeric data)	-3.4×10^{38} to 3.4×10^{38}
Double	Real (numeric data)	-1.8×10^{308} to 1.8×10^{308}
Currency	Real (numeric data)	-9.0×10^{14} to 9.0×10^{14}
Boolean	Contains a value of True or False	
Date	Date and time values	Dates from 1/1/100 to 12/31/9999
Binary	Binary data	Up to 1.2G
OLE	OLE objects	Up to 1.2G

You can select the field type from the drop-down list in the Add Field dialog box. If you decide to create a Text field, you also need to specify the number of characters that the field can contain. This value is entered in the Size property of the dialog box.

After entering the required information for the field, there are several optional properties that you can enter. Some of these properties are valid only for specific data types. These optional properties are summarized in the following:

- AutoIncrField—This is valid only for the Long field type. Setting this property to True causes the Jet engine to automatically enter a value in the field when a new record is created. The value is one greater than the value entered for the last new record. Setting up a field with the AutoIncrField property is a good way to create a unique key for each record.

- AllowZeroLength—This is valid only for Text and Memo field types. If this property is True, the user can enter a zero length text string for the field value. If the property is False, entering a zero length string causes an error which can be trapped by your program.

- Required—This property determines whether the field must have a value entered. If no value is entered in a required field, an error occurs when you try to save the record.

- ValidationRule—This specifies a criterion that the value of the field must meet before the record can be saved. If the validation rule is not met, an error is generated and the text of the ValidationText property is displayed as the error message.

- ▣ ValidationText—This specifies the error message that will be displayed if the validation rule is not met.

- ▣ DefaultValue—This specifies the value that is used for the field if no other value is set.

For the first field of the Customers table, enter CustomerID for the Name, Long for the field Type, and check the box next to the AutoIncrField property. This sets up a unique customer ID for each person entered in the table. When you have entered the information for the field, click the OK button on the Add Field dialog box to add the field to the table. After you add the field, notice that it is displayed in the Field List of the Table Structure dialog box as shown in Figure 25.6.

FIG. 25.6

You need to click Close to return to the Structure Table dialog box, but wait until you've added the rest of the fields.

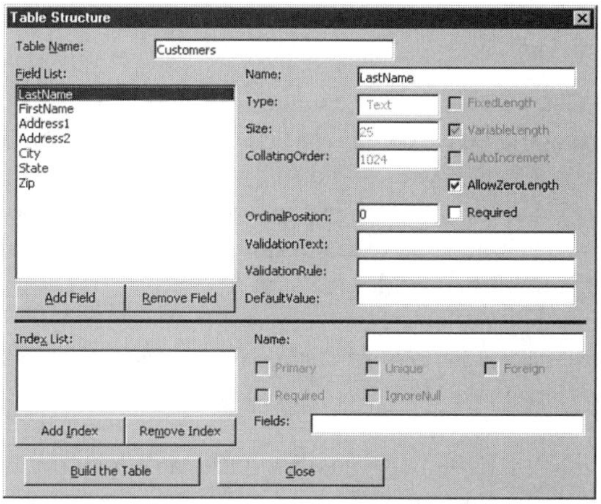

Now that you have gone step-by-step through the process of adding one field, you can add the rest of the fields yourself. Table 25.2 lists the names, types, sizes, and optional properties of the rest of the fields in the Customer table.

Table 25.2 The Fields of the Customer Table

Name	Type	Size	Optional Properties
LastName	Text	25	AllowZeroLength=True
FirstName	Text	25	AllowZeroLength=True
Address1	Text	40	AllowZeroLength=True
Address2	Text	40	AllowZeroLength=True
City	Text	25	AllowZeroLength=True
State	Text	2	AllowZeroLength=True
Zip	Text	10	AllowZeroLength=True

continues

Part

VI

Ch

25

Table 25.2   Continued

Name	Type	Size	Optional Properties
HomePhone	Text	14	AllowZeroLength=True
WorkPhone	Text	14	AllowZeroLength=True
LastContact	Date/Time	N/A	None

The complete sample database, including the Customer table, is available on the Que Web site. Download it from **www.mcp.com/info/0-7897/0-7897-1288-1**.

After you have finished entering all the fields for the table, click the Close button to return to the Table Structure dialog box.

Modifying the Field List   In the Table Structure dialog box, you can examine the properties of a field by highlighting the field in the Field List. If you want to change the Name of the field or one of the optional properties, you can do so by making the changes in the edit fields to the right of the Field List. Unfortunately, you cannot change the data type of the field or the size of a text field. Therefore, it is important to make sure you design your table correctly and enter the proper values the first time around.

N O T E   Microsoft Access allows you to make changes such as field size or field type, often without losing the underlying data. ■

If you decide that you need to remove a field from the table, you can highlight the field in the Field List and then click the Remove Field button. Visual Data Manager confirms that you want to remove the field before doing so.

CAUTION

You cannot remove a field that is part of an index.

Creating Indexes for the Table   Most tables that you create will also need an index. Indexes are used to set the presentation order of the information in the table and to make data searches much faster. Most tables will have a primary index that handles the unique key for each record. The index is what actually forces you to enter a unique key as each record is added. In addition to the primary index, you might have other indexes in your database, depending on how you want to view and search data in the table. In general, it is a good idea to have an index for each type of search that you will perform. For example, in the customer table, you need a primary index to assure the uniqueness of the key field, and you need a name index that will show the information in name order and allow you to quickly search on a customer's name.

▶ **See** "Creating Indexes," **p. 643**

▶ **See** "Positioning the Record Pointer," **p. 730**

To create an index for a table, click the Add Index button in the Table Structure dialog box. This opens the Add Index dialog box shown in Figure 25.7. The first step to creating an index is to give it a name. You can name an index the same way you name a field or table, *except* that the name of an index cannot contain a space.

FIG. 25.7

Set the properties of an index using the Add Index dialog box.

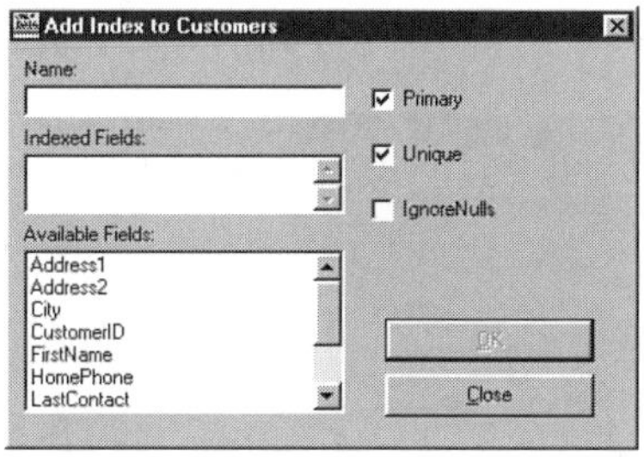

After you have specified a name for the index, you can begin adding the fields for the index and setting the optional properties. For illustration, we will create both the PrimaryKey and Name indexes for the Customers table. To create the PrimaryKey index, follow these steps:

1. Enter the text **PrimaryKey** in the Name field.
2. Select the CustomerID field from the Available Fields list by clicking it. You might notice that the field name is added to the Indexed Fields list.
3. Make sure that the Primary and Unique check boxes are both checked.
4. Click the OK button to add the index to the table.

N O T E You can have a Unique index that is not a Primary index, but any Primary index must be Unique. Also, you can have only one Primary index per table. ▪

The second index is the Name index, which allows you to display the customers in alphabetical order. To create this index, follow these steps:

1. Enter the text **Name** in the Name field.
2. Add the LastName field to the index by clicking the field name in the Available Fields list.
3. Add the FirstName field to the index the same way.
4. Because there can be duplicate names, clear the Primary and Unique check boxes.
5. Click the OK button to add the index to the table.

Notice in the last set of instructions that you had to add the LastName field to the index before adding the FirstName field. For an index, the order of the fields is important. If you had entered the FirstName field first, your customers would be sorted alphabetically by their first names when you displayed the table.

If you accidentally enter a field in the index, you can highlight the field name in the Indexed Fields list and press the Delete key to remove it.

On your own, create one more index. The name of the index should be Contact, the indexed field should be LastContact, and the Primary and Unique properties should both be false. After adding this index to the table, click the Close button to return to the Table Structure dialog box. At this point, the dialog box should look something like Figure 25.8. You can view the properties of an index by highlighting it in the Index List. You can also change the name of the index and its fields from here.

FIG. 25.8

The Customers table is ready to be built.

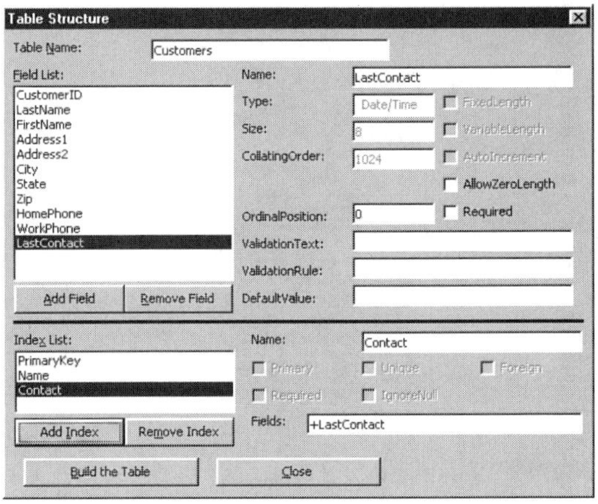

There is one thing you should notice about the fields of an index: a + sign is in front of each field name. This implies that the index sorts the field in ascending order. There might be times when you want to sort a field in descending order. In this case, simply change the + sign to a × sign.

Building the Table and Setting Optional Properties   After you have finished entering the information about the fields and indexes of the table, you can build the actual table in the database. To do this, just click the Build the Table button in the Table Structure dialog box. When the table is built and you have exited the Table Structure dialog box, you can view the fields, indexes, and properties of the table in the tree view of the Database window, as shown in Figure 25.9.

If you look at the properties of the table, there are two that are of particular interest: the ValidationRule and ValidationText properties. The ValidationRule property of the table is similar to the property of the field, except that a table validation rule can work with multiple fields within the table. A field validation rule applies only to the contents of the field for which it is defined. One use of a validation rule would be in a price list for a retail store. You could set the ValidationRule property to assure that the retail price entered for an item is greater than the wholesale price. The ValidationText property specifies the message that is issued if the validation rule is violated.

To edit the ValidationRule and ValidationText properties (or any other editable property), right-click the property name to open the context menu. Then choose the Edit item from the menu. If the property is one that you can edit, an input box (as shown in Figure 25.10) is displayed to allow you to enter the new value of the property. If the property is not editable, you see a message that indicates that the property is read-only. When you enter a new value for a property, Visual Data Manager does check the validity of the information you enter.

FIG. 25.9
All elements of a table are viewable from the Database window.

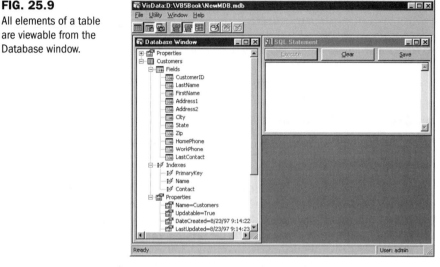

FIG. 25.10
You can change property values using this Edit input box.

Creating a Simple Query

Tables are one key element of a database. Queries are another. Queries allow you to retrieve selected information from a table or multiple tables. For example, you can select only certain fields from a table, or you can select only the records that meet a specific criteria, such as all the customers in a particular state.

Visual Data Manager provides you with two means to create a query in your database—using the SQL Statement window and using the Query Builder. You will examine the Query Builder in detail in the section, "Building Queries with the Query Builder." For the moment, take a look at the SQL Statement window. This window allows you to enter, test, and save queries for the database. To create a query, enter a SQL statement in the input area of the window. To test the query, click the Execute button in the window. Visual Data Manager attempts to run the query and display the results in a DBGrid or data form. If the query is successful, you see the results of the query. If the query is unsuccessful, an error message is displayed that will help you locate the problem. After you have gotten the query to perform the task you want, you can click the Save button to store the query in the database. At this point, you are prompted for a name for the query. Query names follow the same rules as table names. Figure 25.11 shows the SQL Statement window with a query for selecting all customers in the state of Alabama.

FIG. 25.11
Test queries in the SQL
Statement window.

If you want to start a new query after completing the current one, click the Clear button in the
SQL Statement window.

▶ **See** "The Parts of the SQL Statement," **p. 756**

Displaying the Structure of Tables

From time to time, you will need to examine the structure of one of the tables that you have
created. Or you might need a printout of the structure for documentation of your program.
Visual Data Manager provides you with a utility that will print out the structure of a table, including field names and data types and the indexes of the table. To access the Table Structure
utility, right-click the table you want to examine and choose Design from the context menu.
This takes you back to the Table Structure dialog box, except that now the dialog box contains
a Print Structure button. Clicking this button starts the printout of the table structure. You can
also, of course, edit the structure of the table from this dialog box.

The Que Web site contains a utility program that will print out the structure of the entire database for you. The utility is contained in the project DBAnalyz.Vbp, and you can download it
from **www.mcp.com/info/0-7897/0-7897-1288-1**.

Adding Data to the Database

Tables and queries are of no use if there is no data in the database. Therefore, after you create
the tables, you need to add data to them. Visual Data Manager provides you with several
means of doing this: a DBGrid form, a data entry form with a data control, and a data entry
form with navigation buttons. Any of these forms will allow you to enter or edit data in your
tables. You select which form to use by clicking the appropriate button on the toolbar as called
out in Figure 25.12. After you have selected the type of form to use, you access a table by right-
clicking the table name and choosing Open from the context menu. The same method applies
to running a defined query and displaying the results.

T I P   Double-clicking a table or query name also opens the recordset using the selected form type.

FIG. 25.12
Choose the type of data
entry form you want
from the toolbar.

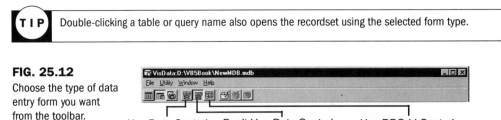

Using a DBGrid Control to Add and Modify Data

The DBGrid is one of the data bound controls that comes with Visual Basic. Using this grid, you can display the entire contents of a table or the results of a query. The grid displays the information in a manner similar to a spreadsheet. The fields are the columns of the grid, and the records are the rows of the grid (see Figure 25.13).

FIG. 25.13
A DBGrid displays multiple records at a time.

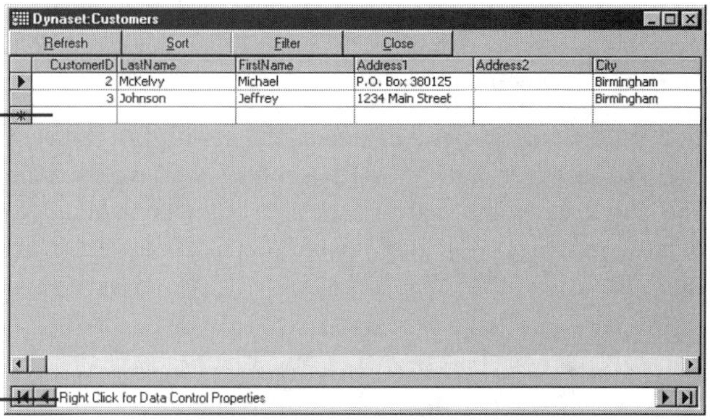

Enter new data here

Data control

To add information to a table using the DBGrid, move the cursor to the first column of the last row of the grid. This row contains a * in the far left column. At this point, you just start entering the information. You can use the Tab key to move from column to column in the grid. After entering the information for the last column, pressing the Tab key moves you to the first column of a new record. You can also edit any piece of information in an existing record by clicking the cell containing the information and entering a new value.

The DBGrid is connected to the information in a table by the Data control. This control is also visible on the form. If you want to change the properties of the Data control, you can right-click it to open the Data Control Properties dialog box shown in Figure 25.14.

▶ **See** "Getting Acquainted with Bound Control Basics," **p. 682**

FIG. 25.14
Change the source of your data or other properties through this dialog box.

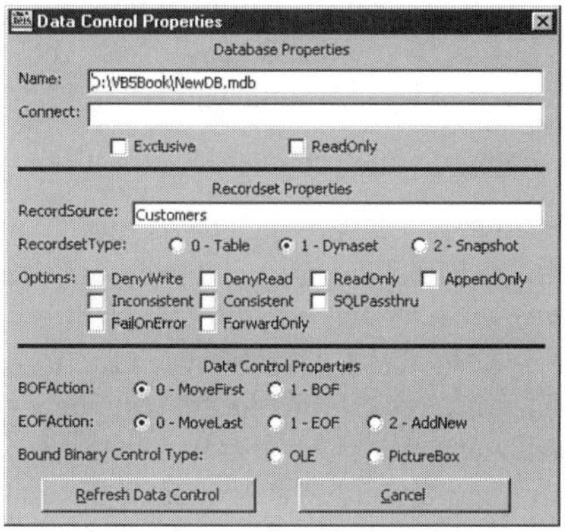

Using Data Entry Forms

The other choice for entering data into your tables is the data entry form. This form allows you to edit one record at a time. If you are entering data for a number of fields or for fields that are large, this form is often easier to use than the DBGrid form. In both data entry forms, the information from the fields in a table is displayed in text boxes or, if the data is Boolean, in check boxes on the form. For both types of data entry forms, you enter the information for a new record or edit the information in an existing record, then click the Update button to send the addition or changes to the database. The difference between the two types of data entry forms is the manner in which you navigate through the table.

Working with a Data Control   The data entry form with the Data control (shown in Figure 25.15) uses the VCR-like buttons on the Data control to move back and forth through the recordset. The single arrow buttons on each side of the control move you one record forward or backward in the recordset. Clicking the buttons marked with an arrow and bar move you to the beginning or the end of the recordset.

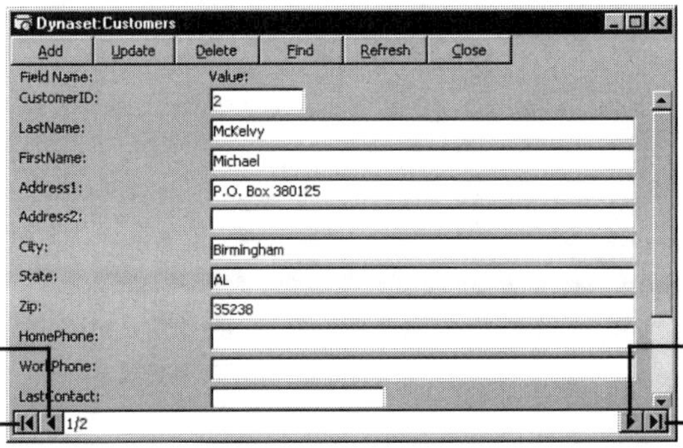

FIG. 25.15
Use the Data control to move from one record to another.

When you open an empty table, you are presented with a set of blank data entry fields. After you enter the information for these fields, you click the Update button on the form. To add a new record after the first one, click the Add button on the form. This clears the data entry fields for you to enter new information. As you are editing information for a record, the Add button is replaced by the Cancel button. If you decide not to save the changes you make, click the Cancel button to restore the fields to their original values.

As with the DBGrid form, you can change the properties of the Data control by right-clicking the Data control.

Working Without the Data Control   The data entry form without the Data control (also known as an *unbound data entry form*) is shown in Figure 25.16. It is very similar to the form with the Data control. There are two key differences between the forms. First, with the unbound form, you move back and forth through the recordset using a scroll bar at the bottom of the form. Second, to edit a record, you cannot just start typing the new information. You must explicitly start the edit by clicking the Edit button at the top of the form. This unlocks all the controls and replaces the buttons at the top of the form with Update and Cancel buttons, which let you save or discard any changes you make.

FIG. 25.16

Without the Data control, the data fields are not bound directly to the table.

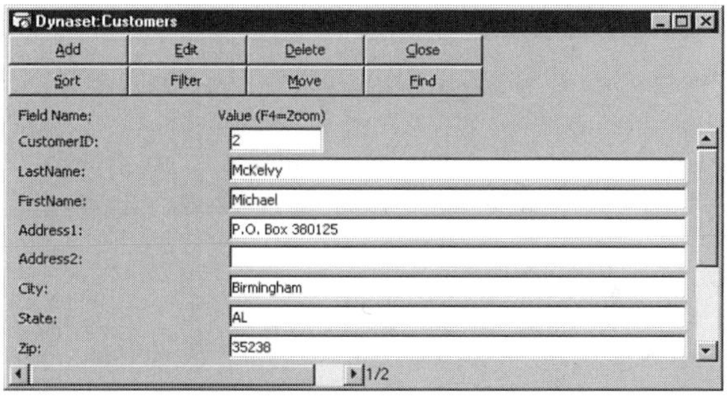

Importing and Exporting Data

Keying in information is one way to get data into your database. Another way is to import the data from an existing file. Visual Data Manager has the capability of importing tables from other PC databases, ODBC data sources, Excel spreadsheets, or text files. Using the import function can bring an entire table into your database. You cannot use the import function to populate an existing table, nor can you limit the records brought in from the source data.

To import one or more tables from an external source, choose the Import/Export item from the File menu. This opens the Import/Export dialog box shown in Figure 25.17. To import a table, click the Import button. You are prompted to specify the type of external data you will be accessing and then to specify the file name. You are then presented with a list of tables in the external data source. You can choose one of these tables and start the import process. The import function makes a copy of the structure and data in the table in your current database.

FIG. 25.17

You can exchange data with external files using the Import/Export dialog box.

If you want to export information from your database to an external source, you again start from the Import/Export dialog box. In this case, you choose the table(s) that you want to export from the list of tables in the database and then click the Export Table(s) button. You are then prompted for the type of database to which to export the data and then for the name of the actual database. As with the import function, the external database can be a PC database, an Excel spreadsheet, or a text file. After you specify the name of the database, you are prompted to confirm the export. After you have confirmed, the export function sends a copy of the table in your database to the external database you specified.

Attaching External Tables

The final way of accessing information through your database is to attach a table from another database. This process creates a link from your database to the external database but does not make a copy of the information in the external database. This method is used most often for external tables that are updated by other programs. To attach an external table, follow these steps:

1. Select the Attachments item from the Utility menu.
2. Click the New button on the Attachments dialog box. This opens the New Attached Table dialog box shown in Figure 25.18.
3. Enter the name by which you want to refer to the table in the Attachment Name field.
4. Enter the name of the source database in the Database Name field.
5. Select the database type in the Connect String drop-down list.
6. Select the specific table to attach from the drop-down list.
7. Click the Attach button.

FIG. 25.18

External tables can be accessed by attaching to them instead of importing them.

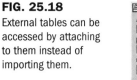

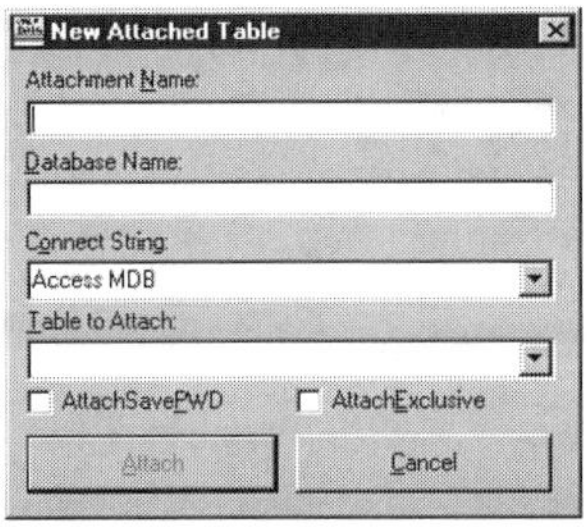

Building Queries with the Query Builder

Earlier in the chapter, we took a brief look at creating queries using the SQL Statement window. This capability is great for anyone who understands how to write SQL statements, but if you are just starting out with database programming, you need an easier way to create queries. Visual Data Manager has the answer for you in the form of the Query Builder. The Query Builder (shown in Figure 25.19) lets you set up queries by selecting the tables, fields, and conditions that you need for the query from a series of lists. The Query Builder then creates the proper SQL statement and shows you the results of your query. After the query is built to your liking, you can save it to the database.

N O T E   The Query Builder only supports queries that select records from tables. If you want to create queries that update the information in a table, you must create them with the SQL Statement window or with Microsoft Access. ▪

You start the Query Builder by right-clicking in the Database window and choosing New Query from the context menu.

FIG. 25.19
Create SQL statements
by using the Query
Builder.

Table selection
Field selection
Filter condition
Action buttons

Data groupings
Sort order
Join conditions

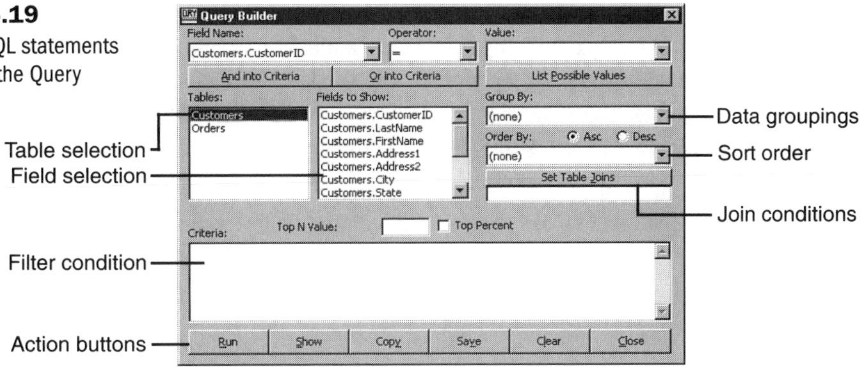

Selecting Tables and Fields

The first step in creating a query is to select the tables that are the source of the information you want to include in your query. The Tables list of the Query Builder shows you all the tables available in the current database. You can select and deselect the tables by clicking the table names. As a table is selected, the fields from that table are added to the list marked Fields to Show.

> **N O T E** The Jet engine supports queries that are based on other queries, but you cannot create this type of query using the Query Builder. ▪

After you have selected the tables to include in the query, you need to select the individual fields. As with selecting tables, you select fields from the fields list by clicking them. You must select each field individually; you cannot select groups of fields. After you have selected the tables and fields for the query, you can click the Show button to display the created SQL statement in a message box. If you want to see the results of the query, you can click the Run button. This displays the query results in a data entry or DBGrid form, depending on which form type is selected.

> **CAUTION**
> The Query Builder is not perfect. It helps you build queries, but you can still create a query that does not run or, more often, returns incorrect results. Therefore, it is important to have some understanding of the basics of SQL.

Setting Filter and Sort Conditions

If you want to view all the information in a recordset and don't mind viewing records in the order in which they were entered, then your query is finished after you select the tables and fields. However, in most cases, you only want to see records that meet a specific selection criterion, and you want them presented in a convenient order such as alphabetical or chronological. For this, you need to set filter and sort conditions.

A filter condition allows you to limit the number of records returned in a recordset. You can limit records based on the content of any field in the table. For example, you might want to show a list of clients who have not been contacted in the last 60 days, or possibly look only at those clients in a specific geographical area. These tasks can be handled by a filter condition. To set a filter in the Query Builder, you need to follow these steps:

1. Select the field that will be the basis of the comparison. You select the field from the Field Name drop-down list. This list contains all the fields from all the tables that are included in the query.

2. Select the type of comparison that you want to perform from the Operator drop-down list.

3. Enter the value to which the field will be compared.

4. Click either the <u>A</u>nd into Criteria or <u>O</u>r into Criteria button to add the condition to the filter. When combining two conditions, "And" means that the record must meet both criteria to be included in the recordset. "Or" means the record must meet at least one of the criteria.

After you add the criteria to the filter, it shows up in the Criteria list at the bottom of the Query Builder. The filter shows up as a Where clause in the SQL statement.

▶ **See** "Setting the Filter Criteria," **p. 768**

The sort condition determines the order in which records in the recordset are presented. To set a sort condition, select the field from the Order By drop-down list and check the appropriate option button to specify an ascending or descending sort. This condition appears in the SQL statement as an Order By clause.

N O T E   Although you can only enter a single field in the Order By clause in the Query Builder, you can use multiple fields in SQL statements. ▪

Setting Join Conditions

If you are working with multiple tables to create your query, you must relate the information in the tables through common fields. Specifying the relation between the tables is the function of a join condition. To specify the join conditions for tables, you need to click the Set Table <u>J</u>oins button in the Query Builder. This opens the Join Tables dialog box shown in Figure 25.20.

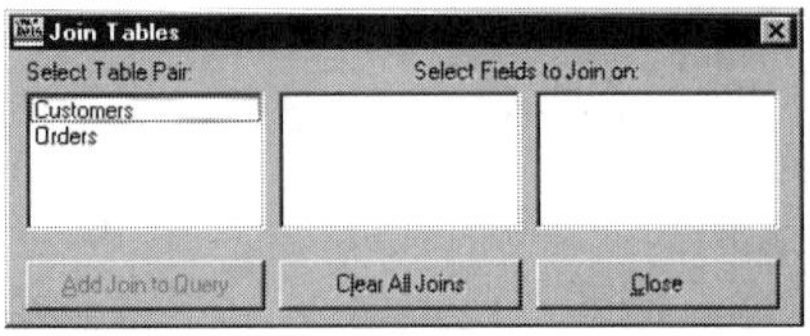

FIG. 25.20

Join conditions specify how two tables are related.

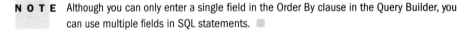

For each pair of tables that you need to relate, follow these steps:

1. Select the two tables to be related from the Select Table Pair list. This displays a list of all field names from the two tables in the Select Fields lists.

2. Select the key field from the first table using the first Fields list.

3. Select the related field from the second table using the second Fields list.

4. Add the condition to the query by clicking the Add Join to Query button.

N O T E SQL syntax supports several types of Join conditions: Inner, Left, and Right. The Query Builder only supports Inner joins, emulating them with a Where clause. ■

CAUTION
Recordsets created using the Where clause to handle the relationship between tables cannot be updated.

Saving the Query

After you have created and tested your query using the Query Builder, you can save the query to the database. To do this, click the Save button in the Query Builder. You are prompted for the name of the query and are asked if the query is a SQL Passthrough query. A passthrough query is one that is handled by a database server instead of the Jet engine. Most of your queries will not be passthrough queries.

After you have added the query, you will see that it appears in the Database window along with the other objects of your database.

Using Database Utilities

There are two database utilities available in Visual Data Manager that you might need to use from time to time: the Compact utility and the Repair utility.

The Compact utility is used to remove unused space from your database. As you add records to a database, the database gets larger. However, as you delete records from the database, the space they occupied is not automatically recovered. If you have been performing a lot of deletions, there might be a significant amount of unused space in the database. This causes the file to be larger than it needs to be, which takes up space on your disk and increases the time it takes to load the database. Running the Compact utility removes all the unused space.

To run the Compact utility, you need to select the Compact MDB item from the File menu and then select the type of MDB that you want the compacted database to be. You are then prompted for the name of the source database, followed by the target database. You also are asked if you want to encrypt the target database. After you answer the prompts, the utility runs itself.

The Repair utility is used to fix problems that keep you from being able to open a database. Typically, the problem occurs when a user is disconnected from the database in the middle of an update activity. This can cause the database to become corrupted. When this happens, you get an error as you try to open the database. To repair a database, select the Repair MDB item from the File menu. You then are prompted to enter the name of the database. Then the Repair utility takes care of the rest. Hopefully, you will not need this utility, but it is nice to have if you do need it.

From Here...

Although this chapter has shown you the mechanics of creating a database and SQL queries, you still need an understanding of the basic database design theories and the basics of SQL. You can refer to the following chapters for more information:

■ To learn more about database design, see Chapter 24, "Database Design and Normalization."

■ To learn more about SQL, see Chapter 29, "Understanding SQL."

CHAPTER 26

Using Data Controls and Reports

Visual Basic is designed to enable you, the developer, to create applications for the Windows environment quickly and easily. This ease-of-use extends to the creation of database programs as well. If you have an existing database that you want to access, Visual Basic makes it easy for you to write a complete data management and reporting application with almost no programming. You just drop a few controls on a form and set the properties. In fact, Visual Basic makes the task so easy that it can even create the data entry forms for you.

The components that make all these capabilities possible are the Data control and the data-bound controls for data entry forms and Crystal Reports for report generation. With just these few tools, you can create a wide variety of applications. Of course, as you progress to more complex applications, you need to do more of the programming yourself. But even for more complex applications, these tools provide a good first step in the programming process and enable you to create application prototypes rapidly. ▪

Navigating a recordset with the Data control

The Data control provides several buttons that allow you to move from one record to another in a recordset.

Displaying data from a recordset

We examine how the bound controls make it easy to get information from a database to the user's screen.

Adding and deleting records

You will see how to use code to add record management features to your applications.

Using automatic data entry forms

If you want the easiest way to create a data entry form, Visual Basic can create it for you. You'll see how to use a wizard to make this happen.

Running reports from your program

You'll also see how to use Crystal Reports forms from within your program.

Understanding the Data Control

The centerpiece of easy database applications is the Data control. The Data control is one of the controls available in Visual Basic's Toolbox, as shown in Figure 26.1. Setting up the Data control requires only four simple steps:

1. Select the control from the Toolbox.
2. Draw the control on your form.
3. Set the DatabaseName property of the control.
4. Set the RecordSource property of the control.

> **N O T E**   Following these four steps is the minimum required to set up the Data control. If you want to access non-Jet databases or use any of the control's other capabilities, you need to set additional properties. These properties are covered in Chapter 27, "Doing More with Bound Controls." ▨

▶ **See** "Using the Data Control," **p. 813**

FIG. 26.1
The Data control is one of the standard components of the Visual Basic Toolbox.

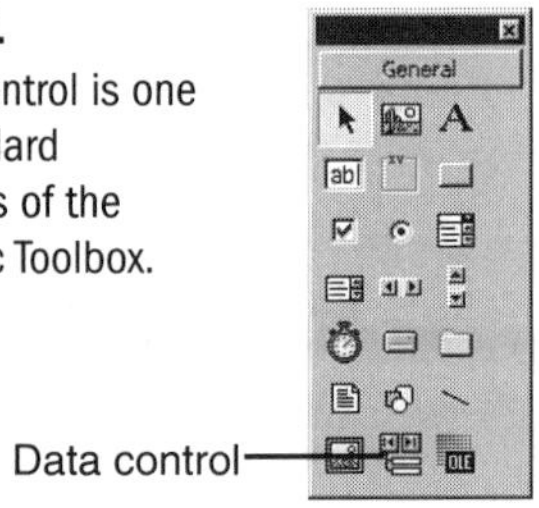

Data control

What Is the Data Control?

Basically, the Data control is a link between information in your database and the bound controls that you use to display the information. As you set the properties of the Data control, you tell it which database and what part of the database to access. By default, the Data control creates a dynaset-type recordset from one or more of the tables in your database.

The Data control also provides the record navigation functions that your application needs. With these buttons, indicated in Figure 26.2, the user can move to the first or last record in the recordset or to a record prior to or following the current record. The design of the buttons makes their use intuitive; they are similar to the buttons you would find on a VCR or a CD player.

The recordset created by the Data control is determined by the settings of the DatabaseName and RecordSource properties. The recordset is created as the form containing the Data control loads and is activated. This recordset is active until the form is unloaded, at which time the recordset is released.

FIG. 26.2
The VCR-like buttons on the Data control indicate their function to the user.

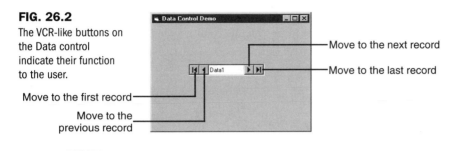

Move to the next record

Move to the last record

Move to the first record

Move to the previous record

> **N O T E** A *recordset* is an object that represents the data in a physical database. Even after a recordset is released or closed, the data in the underlying table(s) is still in the database. ■

Adding a Data Control to Your Form

The first step in using a Data control is to add the control to your application's form. Select the Data control object from the Visual Basic Toolbox (refer to Figure 26.1). Next, place and size the Data control just as you do any other design object. After you set the desired size and placement of the Data control on your form, you can set its Name and Caption properties.

The Name property sets the control name, which identifies the control and its associated data to the bound controls. The default name for the first Data control added to a form is Data1. Additional Data controls added to a form are sequentially numbered as Data2, Data3, and so on. To change the name of a Data control, select its Name property from the Properties window and type the name you want (see Figure 26.3).

The Caption property specifies the text that appears on the Data control. You usually want the caption to be descriptive of the data the control accesses. The default for the Caption property is the initial setting of the Name property (for example, Data1 for the first Data control). You can change the Caption property the same way you change the Name property (see Figure 26.3).

Part
VI

Ch
26

FIG. 26.3
The Data control's Caption property has been set to a more meaningful value.

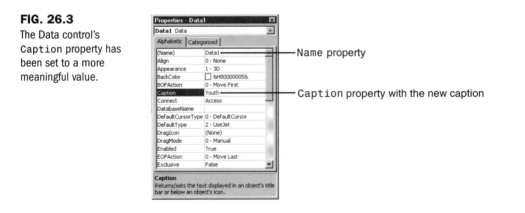

Name property

Caption property with the new caption

For the example you're creating in this chapter, add a Data control with the name datYouth and the caption Youth. Figure 26.4 shows the form with this control added.

> **T I P** You also can add code to your program to change the Data control's caption to reflect information in the current record, such as a person's name.

FIG. 26.4
Draw the Data control on your form and set its caption appropriately.

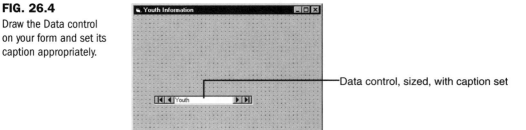

Data control, sized, with caption set

Two Properties Are All You Need to Set

After you place the Data control on your form, you need to make the connection between the Data control and information stored in a database. You do so by setting the Data control's properties. Although several properties can affect the way a Data control interacts with the database, only two properties are required to establish the link to a Jet database: the DatabaseName and RecordSource properties. Specifying these two properties tells the Data control what information to retrieve from the database and causes the Data control to create a recordset that allows nonexclusive, read/write access to the data.

> **N O T E** The DatabaseName property is not the same as the Name property mentioned earlier. The Name property specifies the name of the Data control object. This name references the object in code. The DatabaseName property specifies the name of the database file that the Data control is accessing.

What's in a Name?   For Jet databases, the DatabaseName property is the name of the database file. To enter the name, select the DatabaseName property from the Properties window and type the database's file name.

If you'd like to locate the database by browsing, click the ellipsis button (...) at the right of the property input line to display the DatabaseName dialog box, as shown in Figure 26.6. Browse to the appropriate database file and click OK. The selected file name and path are automatically entered into the DatabaseName property.

FIG. 26.5

Use the Properties window to set the database name for the control.

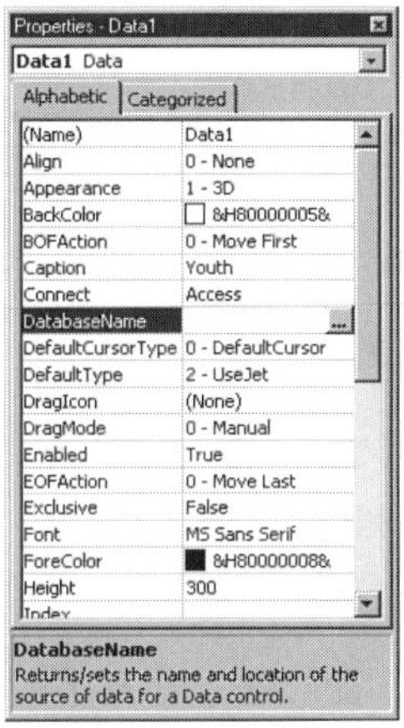

FIG. 26.6

You can enter a database name or choose it from the DatabaseName dialog box.

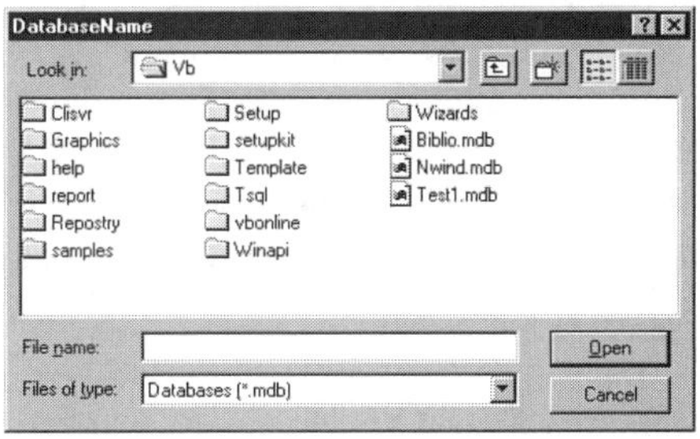

CAUTION

If you browse to the DatabaseName property at design time using the dialog box, the property will include a fully qualified path to the database's file name, for example, C:\MyData\LMS\TMS1112.MDB. This may be dangerous since the database will be expected to be in the same exact location at runtime. It would be better to allow some flexibility in the location of the database: set the DatabaseName property using no path (that is, use TMS1112.MDB), in which case your program would expect to find it in the program's current directory; use a relative path from the current directory (that is, use LMS\TMS1112.MDB); or set the property from code based on user input or some type of program initialization parameters (that is, use Data1.DatabaseName = stDataLocation).

Straight from the Source   After you've set the DatabaseName property, specify the information you want from that database with the RecordSource property. If you are working with a single table as your recordset, you can enter the table name or select it from the list of tables, as shown in Figure 26.7.

FIG. 26.7
You can select the RecordSource property from a list of tables available in the database.

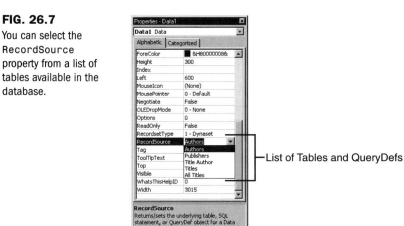

—List of Tables and QueryDefs

If you want to use only selected information from a table or use information from multiple tables, you can use a SQL statement in the RecordSource property. To do this, you can either set the RecordSource property to the name of a QueryDef in the database that contains a SQL statement or enter a valid SQL statement as the value of the RecordSource property. You can use any SQL statement that creates a recordset. (You can also include functions in your SQL statement.) If you're using a QueryDef, it must be a QueryDef that has already been defined and stored in the database.

TIP To make sure that your SQL statements work correctly, you can test them in Visual Data Manager. Then copy and paste to place the statements in the RecordSource property.

Getting Acquainted with Bound Control Basics

Bound controls in Visual Basic are controls that are set up to work with a Data control to create database applications; hence, the controls are "bound" to information in the database. Most of the bound controls in Visual Basic are simply standard controls that have additional properties allowing them to perform data access functions. A few custom controls are designed specifically to work with the Data controls. These controls are covered in Chapter 27, "Doing More with Bound Controls."

▶ **See** "Other Bound Controls," **p. 711**

The controls that you use as bound controls are ones with which you are already familiar:

- TextBox
- Label
- CheckBox
- PictureBox
- Image

These controls are highlighted in the Toolbox shown in Figure 26.8.

PictureBox Control

FIG. 26.8
Several familiar controls also have properties that let them access data.

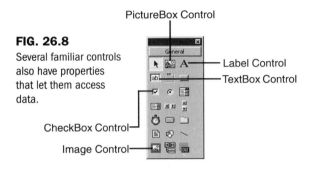

Label Control
TextBox Control
CheckBox Control
Image Control

What Do These Controls Do?

Each bound control is tied to a Data control and, more specifically, to a particular field in the recordset attached to the Data control. The bound control automatically displays the information in the specified field for the current record. As the user moves from one record to another using the navigation buttons of the Data control, the information in bound controls is updated to reflect the current record.

The bound controls are not limited, however, to just displaying the information in the record. Most also can be used to modify the information. To do so, the user just needs to edit the contents of the control. Then, when the current record is changed or the form is closed, the information in the database is automatically updated to reflect the changed values.

N O T E Because the Label control has no editable portion, the data displayed in the Label cannot be changed. Also, if a control is locked or editing is otherwise prevented, the user cannot change the value of the information. ■

You use each of the basic bound controls to edit and display different types of data. With the bound controls, you can handle strings, numbers, dates, logical values, and even pictures and memos. Table 26.1 lists the five basic bound controls and the types of database fields that they can handle. The table also lists the property of the control that contains the data.

Table 26.1 Different Controls Used to Handle Different Types of Data

Control Name	Data Type	Control Property
Label	Text, Numeric, Date	Caption
TextBox	Text, Memo, Numeric, Date	Text
CheckBox	Logical, True/False	Value
PictureBox	Long Binary	Picture
Image	Long Binary	Picture

Part
VI

Ch
26

Adding Controls to Your Forms

To add a bound control to your form, select the control from the Toolbox and draw it on the form. Figure 26.9 shows a text box added to the form that contains the Data control.

FIG. 26.9
You draw bound controls on your form just as you draw any other control.

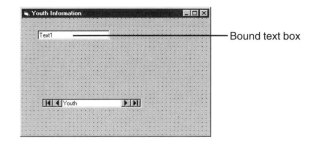

Bound text box

T I P Hold down the Ctrl key when you click a control in the Toolbox, and you can add multiple controls of that type to your form. This way, you don't have to click the control's Toolbox button repeatedly. When you're done, click the mouse pointer button in the Toolbox.

Data Display in Two Easy Properties

For a bound control to work with the data from a recordset, you must first tie the bound control to the Data control representing the recordset (recall that we've already discussed how to bind the Data control to physical data). You do this by setting the bound control's DataSource property. Depending on the specific control used, you might have to set other properties. By working on the sample Retail Items data entry screen throughout the remainder of this chapter, you will learn several of the bound controls, which properties you must set, and how to set them.

Setting the *DataSource* Property   To set the DataSource property, select it from the Properties window for your control. Click the arrow to the right of the input area to see a list of all the Data controls on the current form. To set the DataSource property, select one of the controls from the list. Figure 26.10 shows this procedure.

T I P Double-click the DataSource property to scroll through the available Data controls.

Setting the *DataField* Property   Although the DataSource property tells the bound control from which Data control to retrieve data, you still need to tell the bound control what specific data to retrieve. You do so by setting the DataField property. This property tells the control which field of the recordset will be handled by this bound control.

To set the DataField property of the control, select the DataField property from the Properties window, click the arrow to the right of the input area, and select one of the fields from the displayed list. The list includes all available fields from the recordset defined in the specified DataSource (see Figure 26.11).

FIG. 26.10
Select the
DataSource property
for the bound control
from a list of the form's
Data controls.

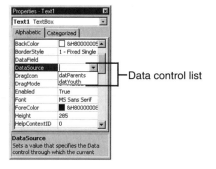

Data control list

FIG. 26.11
Select the DataField
property for the bound
control from the list of
fields in the selected
Data control.

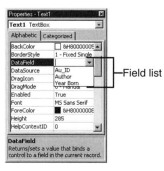

Field list

> **T I P** Double-click the DataField property to scroll through the available fields.

Part
VI

Ch
26

> **CAUTION**
> You cannot select a field for the DataField property from a list until the DataSource property has been set.

Creating a Simple Application

To help further illustrate the concepts of creating a data access application, let's walk through the process of creating a data entry form using the biblio database, which is included with Visual Basic.

Setting Up the Form

The first step in setting up the data access form is to start a new project. Add a Data control to the default form. Change the Data control's Name property to dtaMain and its Caption property to Author Info. Next, set the DatabaseName and RecordSource properties of the Data control.

First, set the DatabaseName property to the path to biblio.mdb on your hard drive. After you set the database name, you can set the RecordSource property. From the property's selection list, select the Authors table. The Data control is now ready for use.

The next step in creating the data access form is to add the bound controls. To make the example easy, just use text boxes for each of the fields. Also, for each field, place a label control on the form to identify the information in the text box. For the sample case, you need three text boxes and three corresponding labels. The DataSource property of all the text boxes is dtaMain, which is the name of the Data control you just created. For each text box, you also need to specify a DataField property. Remember that the DataField property ties the control to a specific field in the database. Table 26.2 lists the DataField settings for each text box and the suggested captions for the corresponding label controls. The table uses the default names for the text boxes.

Table 26.2   *DataField* and *Caption* Settings for the Data Access Form

TextBox Name	DataField	Caption for Corresponding Label
Text1	Au_ID	Author ID:
Text2	Author	Name:
Text3	Year Born	Year Born:

After you add the bound controls and set their properties, your form should look like the one shown in Figure 26.12.

FIG. 26.12
You can create a simple data entry form by using just the Data control and bound text boxes.

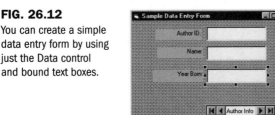

Navigating the Database

Now that you have created the data entry form, try it out by running the program. As the program first starts, you should see the form load, and the information for the first record should appear in the text boxes. Now you can see how the Data control is used to navigate through the records of the database. You can move to the first record, the previous record, the next record, or the last record by clicking the appropriate button on the Data control.

With this simple program you can even update and edit the database. Try typing a year in the Year Born text box and moving to another record. This enters new information into the database.

◆

TROUBLESHOOTING

The records of the database seem to be in random order, not alphabetical order. You have not created an error or done anything wrong in setting up the form. You are seeing the records presented in the physical order of the table, the order in which the records were entered. If you want to see the records in alphabetical order, place the following string in the RecordSource property of the Data control:

Select * from Authors Order by Author

Then run the program again. You can also set the RecordSource property from code:

frmMain.dtaMain.RecordSource = "Select * from Authors Order by Author"
frmMain.dtaMain.Refresh

Essential Functions the Data Control Forgot

As you can see, the Data control is quite flexible, but it lacks a few functions that are necessary for most data entry applications—specifically, adding and deleting records. To overcome these shortcomings, you can add the functions to the data entry screen using program commands assigned to a command button.

To add these functions to the sample application, add two command buttons named Add and Delete to the form. To make the buttons functional, add the code segments shown in Listing 26.1 to the Click event of the appropriate button.

> **Listing 26.1 ProgramName.ext—Program Statements Placed in the *Click*
> Event of Command Buttons to Add Capabilities to the Data Entry Screen**

```
'Command to add a new record,
'place in click event of Add button
dtaMain.Recordset.AddNew

'Commands to delete a record,
'placed in click event of Delete button
dtaMain.Recordset.Delete
If Not dtaMain.EOF Then
   dtaMain.Recordset.MoveNext
Else
   dtaMain.Recordset.MoveLast
  End If
```

As you can see, this listing does not enter a command to invoke the Update method. (Updates are done automatically by the Data control whenever you move to a new record or close the form.)

N O T E   You add the MoveNext and MoveLast commands to the Delete button to force a move to a new record. After a record is deleted, it is no longer accessible but still shows on-screen until a move is executed. If you do not force a move and try to access the deleted record, an error occurs. ▨

Your data entry form should now look like the one shown in Figure 26.13.

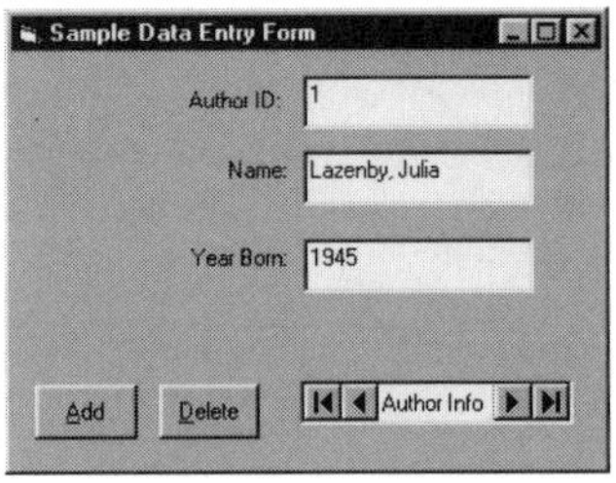

FIG. 26.13
You can add new capabilities to the data entry screen by assigning program commands to command buttons.

Creating Forms Automatically

The bound controls make it easy for you to create data entry forms with a minimum of effort. You just draw the controls on your form, set a few properties, and you're done. What could be easier?

Well, actually you can create data entry forms in an even easier way—by using the Data Form Wizard (DFW). The DFW is one of the add-ins that comes with Visual Basic. Using this add-in, you can select a database and a record source; then it creates your data entry form automatically. Of course, the form might not be exactly like you want it, but you can easily change the default design and then save the changes. Using the DFW is a great way to create a series of data entry forms rapidly for a prototype or for a simple application.

Setting Up the Data Form Wizard

As you learned in the preceding section, the DFW is one of the add-ins that comes with Visual Basic. If, however, you look at the Add-Ins menu in Visual Basic, you don't see this option initially. You have to first tell Visual Basic that you want access to the form designer. You do so by choosing Add-Ins, Add-In Manager. The dialog box shown in Figure 26.14 then appears.

To access the DFW, click the box next to the text in the Add-In Manager. A check mark then appears in the box. Next, click the OK button and you're set. Now, when you select the Add-Ins menu, you see the DFW as one of the items. Selecting the DFW opens the first dialog box of the wizard, which you can see in Figure 26.15. This screen tells you a little about the DFW. You can choose not to have this form presented on subsequent uses of the DFW.

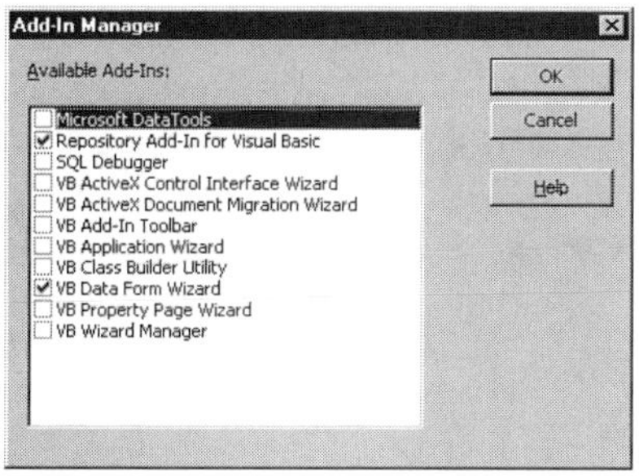

FIG. 26.14

By using the Add-In Manager, you can add capabilities to your Visual Basic design environment.

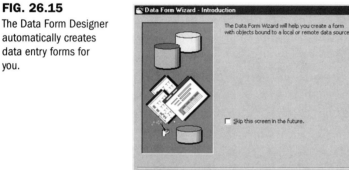

FIG. 26.15

The Data Form Designer automatically creates data entry forms for you.

Clicking the <u>N</u>ext button on the initial form takes you to the second screen of the DFW. This screen, shown in Figure 26.16, enables you to choose the type of database that your form will be accessing. To choose a database type, simply click the type name in the list and then click the <u>N</u>ext button to continue creating your form.

FIG. 26.16

You can choose to create a form from many common desktop databases.

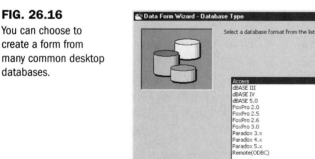

Getting to the Source of Your Data

After you have chosen the type of database to use, you need to choose the actual database and record source with which you will be working. The screen shown in Figure 26.17 allows you either to enter the name of the database or to select the database from a dialog box. Clicking the Browse button on the dialog box presents you with a database dialog box that allows you to choose the database to open. After selecting the database, you are returned to the Database screen of the DFW. You might notice at this point that the file name of the selected database, including the full path, has been entered in the text box on the form.

FIG. 26.17

The Database screen allows you to specify the database and the types of record sources to use.

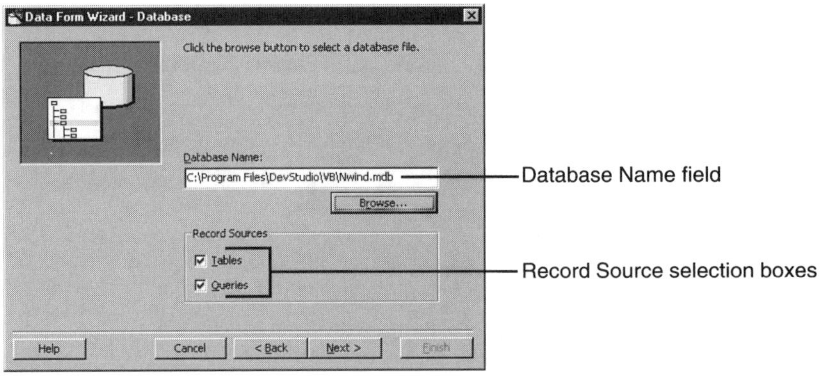

Database Name field

Record Source selection boxes

In addition to specifying the database name, you can also specify the types of record sources that will be displayed for selection in a later screen. You can choose to have tables, queries, or both displayed. You make your selection by clicking the appropriate check boxes. When you have finished, you need to click the Next button to proceed.

The next screen allows you to select the type of data entry form that you want the DFW to create. There are three types of data entry forms that can be created:

- *Single Record*   Allows you to edit the information in the recordset one record at a time. This is the classic data entry type of form.
- *Grid*   Allows you to edit multiple records at a time. This screen is similar to the recordset view in Access or the Browse window in FoxPro.
- *Master/Detail*   Allows you to edit the information of a single parent record along with its associated child records. This type of form might be used to show information about an order along with all the items ordered.

Choosing the type of form to create not only affects the appearance of the form but also determines what recordset(s) must be selected for the form. For a single record or grid form, you only need to select a single record source. For the Master/Detail form, you need to select two record sources. You really don't have to worry too much about this because the wizard guides you through it. That's what wizards are for, right?

CAUTION

If you are creating a Master/Detail form, you need to have established a relation between the tables you select. The relation information is what is used to keep the information synchronized.

Choosing Fields with the Data Form Wizard

After you have selected the database and the type of form, you need to select the table or query to use for the form and the actual fields that you want to have included on the form. This is done on the Record Source screen of the wizard, as shown in Figure 26.18.

FIG. 26.18
You choose the record source and fields using simple combo boxes and lists.

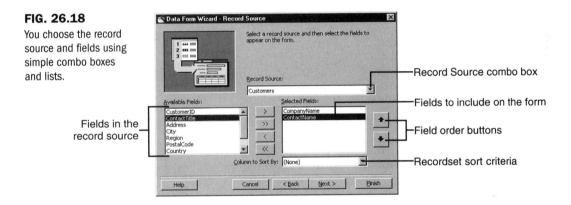

To set up the fields for the form, you need to follow these steps:

1. Select a record source from the combo box.
2. Select the fields to include by clicking the field names in the Available Fields list. You can double-click a field to select it or highlight the field and click the selection button (>).
3. Place the fields in the desired order by moving them in the Selected Fields list. You move a field by highlighting it and then clicking the up or down buttons. (This step is optional.)
4. Select the column on which to sort the recordset by choosing it from the Column to Sort By combo box. (This step is optional.)
5. Click the Next button to move to the next screen.

What Does This Button Do?

After selecting all of the fields that you want on the form, you have one final set of choices to make—the buttons that you want to appear on your form. You make this selection in the Control Selection screen of the DFW, shown in Figure 26.19.

Part
VI
Ch
26

FIG. 26.19

You can choose a number of command buttons to appear on your form.

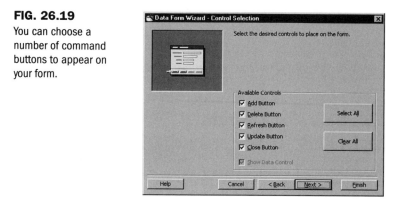

Table 26.3 lists the buttons that you can elect to have appear on your data form.

Table 26.3 Command Button Controls and Their Functions

Available Controls	Function
Add	Adds a new record to the recordset and clears the data entry fields
Delete	Deletes the current record
Refresh	Causes the Data control to re-execute the query used to create it. This process is necessary only in a multi-user environment
Update	Stores any changes made to the data entry fields to the database for the current record
Close	Closes and unloads the data entry form

You are now ready for the final step of the DFW—actually creating your form. In the last screen of the DFW, you specify the name of the form (the DFW gives you a default name) and then click the Finish button. This starts the creation process. At this point, you sit back and relax for a minute while the DFW does the work. When it is finished, your program has a new data form, and all you did was answer a few questions and make a few selections. Figures 26.20 through 26.22 show you the various types of data forms that can be created with the DFW.

FIG. 26.20

A Single Record data form created by the Data Form Wizard.

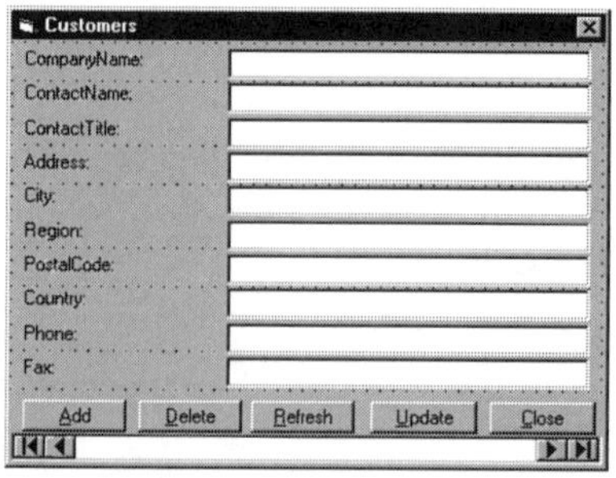

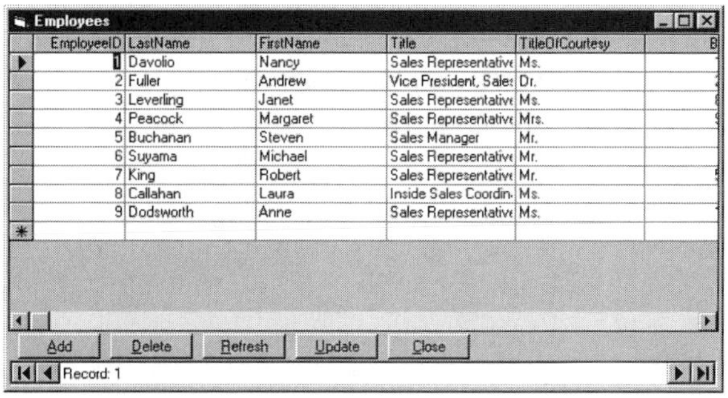

FIG. 26.21
A Grid data form created by the Data Form Wizard.

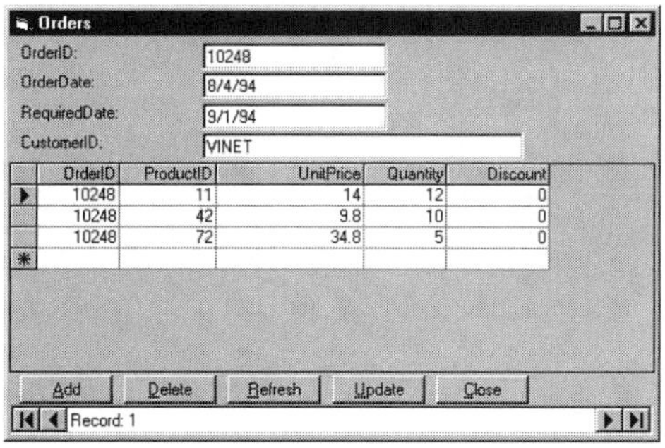

FIG. 26.22
A Master/Detail data form created by the Data Form Wizard.

Using Crystal Reports with Visual Basic 5

Although the Data control and bound controls do a great job of enabling you to create forms to enter and display data, they don't have any reporting capabilities. As a result, if you want to display and print reports, you need some additional capabilities. Visual Basic does have a Printer object with which you can send information to the printer. However, trying to set up a custom database report with the Printer object requires a lot of programming and a lot of trial and error.

Fortunately, you can accomplish database reporting in an easier way. Visual Basic comes with a reporting product—Crystal Reports. The Crystal Reports custom control that comes with Visual Basic allows you to access reports from within your Visual Basic program. The Crystal Reports control provides a link between the Crystal Reports engine and the reports you create with the report designer.

Crystal Reports Control

The first step in accessing Crystal Reports is to make the control available to your program. First, you need to add the Crystal Reports control to your Visual Basic Toolbox. To do so, choose Components from the Project menu of Visual Basic. The Components dialog box, shown in Figure 26.23, then appears. In this dialog box, you can specify which custom controls are available in your project.

Selected controls

FIG. 26.23
You must make the
Crystal Reports control
available to your project
by selecting it in the
Components dialog box.

Crystal Reports control

Controls not used

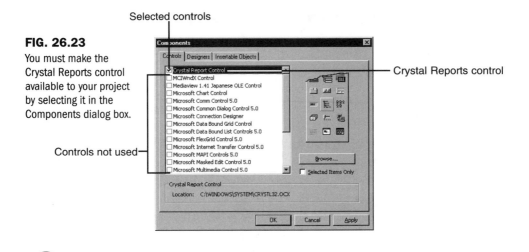

T I P   You also can access the Components dialog box by right-clicking the Toolbox and choosing Components from the pop-up menu or by pressing Ctrl+T.

TROUBLESHOOTING

The Crystal Reports control does not show up in the Custom Controls dialog box. If you elected to
perform a custom setup of Visual Basic, you might have left Crystal Reports out of the setup process.
You need to rerun the Visual Basic setup program and add Crystal Reports.

Check Your Version of Crystal Reports!

If you have a version of Crystal Reports on your machine that is later than version 4.6.1 (the version
that comes standard with VB5), you will need to uninstall it first before you can install the version
that comes with Visual Basic 5. After you have uninstalled your existing version of Crystal Reports,
you can then install the version that comes with Visual Basic 5. If you want to use the newer version
that you previously had, you can reinstall it at this time.

Certain releases of the newest Crystal Reports (version 5.108) DLLs and OCXs may not be completely replaced or overwritten when you install an earlier version of Crystal Reports. This can produce
reports that work fine on the development machine but produce inconsistent results on the user's
machine.

Setting Up the Control

After the Crystal Reports control is available in your Toolbox, you can use it in your program.
To gain access to the control, simply select it from the Toolbox, and place it on the form from

which you plan to access reports. Because the Crystal Reports control is not visible at runtime, it appears only as an icon on your form. After the control is on the form, you can set the properties that access the reports you create with the report designer.

Specifying the Report to Run   The key property that you need to specify is the ReportFileName property. This property specifies the actual report that you will run from your program. You can easily set this property by clicking the ellipsis button that appears to the right of the property in the Properties window. The Crystal Reports Property page, shown in Figure 26.24, then appears. From this page, you can specify the name of the report and whether the report should go to the printer, a preview window, a file, or a message through the MAPI interface.

FIG. 26.24

Select the report name and destination from the Property page of Crystal Reports.

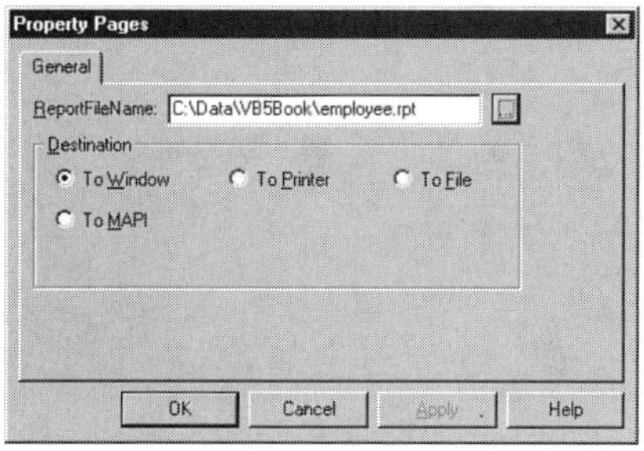

On the Property page, you can either type the name of the report into the field for the ReportFileName property or select the report from a file dialog box by clicking the ellipsis button on the Property page.

Selecting the ReportFileName is the minimum setup for Crystal Reports. At this point, you can write the line of code necessary to run the report and test it by running your program.

Setting Optional Properties   Although only the ReportFileName is required for a report, you might want to use several optional properties with the report. The first of these properties is the SelectionFormula property. This property enables you to limit the number of records that are included in the report. The SelectionFormula property is similar to the Where clause of a SQL statement but uses its own particular format to enter the information. To specify the SelectionFormula, you must specify the name of the recordset and the field to be compared. You must express this recordset/field combination in dot notation and enclose it in curly brackets. After specifying the recordset and field, you must specify the comparison operator and the value to be compared. The final result is an expression like the following:

```
{MemberShipList.OrgCode}=1
```

You also can use multiple expressions by including the And or Or operators.

Part

VI

Ch

26

> **CAUTION**
> If you enter a SelectionFormula when you're designing your report, any formula you enter in the SelectionFormula property of the Crystal Reports control provides an additional filter on the records.

Another optional property is the CopiesToPrinter property. This property enables you to print multiple copies of your report easily at one time. You can set this property to any integer value.

Taking Action

After you add the Crystal Reports control to your form and set its properties, you are ready to start printing, right? Well, not quite. You still have to tell Crystal Reports when to print the report. To do so, you write a line of code to initiate the report. The line of code sets the Action property of the Crystal Reports control to 1. The report then prints using the report file and other properties that you set. If you have your report set up to preview on the screen, it looks like the one shown in Figure 26.25. The following is the code to run this report (rptMember is the name of the Crystal Reports control):

```
rptMember.action = 1
```

FIG. 26.25
Printing the desired report to the screen.

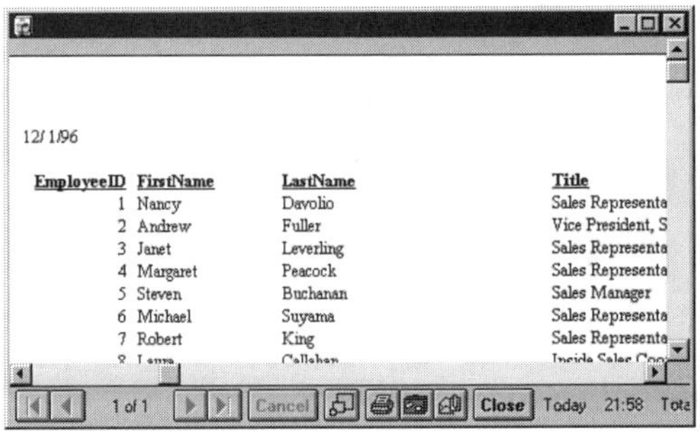

12/1/96			
EmployeeID	**FirstName**	**LastName**	**Title**
1	Nancy	Davolio	Sales Representa
2	Andrew	Fuller	Vice President, S
3	Janet	Leverling	Sales Representa
4	Margaret	Peacock	Sales Representa
5	Steven	Buchanan	Sales Manager
6	Michael	Suyama	Sales Representa
7	Robert	King	Sales Representa
8	Laura	Callahan	Inside Sales Coo

Setting Properties at Runtime

Because you will probably have a number of reports that you need to print, you need to be able to change the Crystal Reports control's properties at runtime; otherwise, you would need a separate report control for each of your reports. All the major properties of the Crystal Reports control, such as ReportFileName and SelectionFormula, are available at runtime. You set these properties, like any other properties, to new values using an assignment statement. The following code sets up the Crystal Reports control for a new report and specifies a selection criteria based on user input:

```
rptMember.ReportFileName = "CntyMbr.rpt"
rptMember.SelectionFormula = "{MemberShipList.OrgCode}=" & OrgID
rptMember.action = 1
```

The other property you might need to set at runtime is the DataFiles property. This property is not available at design time. The property specifies the name of the database file to be used with the report. Now you might be thinking, "I told the report what file to use when I created it." That is true, but when you created the report, the database file was stored with a path based on your directory structure, and your path might not be the same as the directory structure of your users.

The DataFiles property is actually an array with the first element number of 0. If you're using more than one database in your report, you need to set the value of each DataFiles array element. For most of your reports, however, you will be using only a single database. The following line of code shows you how to set the value of the DataFiles property for the database; this line assumes that the database file is in the same folder as your application:

```
rptMember.DataFiles(0) = App.Path & "\Members.mdb"
```

From Here...

In this chapter, you learned how to set up a database application quickly for an existing database. If you would like to learn more about related topics, check out the following:

■ If you want to create your own database, see Chapter 24, "Database Design and Normalization."

■ To learn more about the Data control and bound controls, see Chapter 27, "Doing More with Bound Controls."

■ To learn about more advanced ways to work with databases, see Chapter 28, "Improving Data Access with the Data Access Objects."

Part
VI

Ch
26

Doing More with Bound Controls

In Chapter 26, "Using Data Controls and Reports," you got a first look at the Data control and some of the bound controls that are available in Visual Basic. You saw how the controls can work together to create a good data access application. What you might not have realized is that the Data control and bound controls have a wider range of functionality than that presented in Chapter 26.

In this chapter, we'll learn how to use the Data control in conjunction with the data bound controls to make our data-aware applications extremely powerful and easy to create. ■

Working with other databases using the Data control

While Microsoft Jet (Access) is Visual Basic's database format of choice, the Data control can work with several other types of databases.

Programming the Data control to do more

Some properties of the Data control allow it to perform additional tasks in specific situations.

Changing the recordset of the Data control with code

You are not limited to the recordset that was created when you set the `DatabaseName` and `RecordSource` properties at design time.

Bound lists and combo boxes

You can bind list boxes and combo boxes to a Data control. There are also special versions of these controls that automatically can populate themselves from a Data control's recordset.

Windows 95 bound controls

Several of the new Windows 95 controls also can be bound to a Data control.

Working with multiple Data controls on a form

In many situations, you need more than one Data control on your form.

Exploring the Data Control In-Depth

One of the Data control's additional features is the capability to access a number of other database types beside the Jet database. It also can work with all types of recordsets, not just dynaset-type recordsets. In addition to this flexibility, you can use program code to change the properties of the Data control and enhance its capabilities. You get a brief look at this when program code is used to enable you to add and delete records in the data entry application in Chapter 28, "Improving Data Access with the Data Access Objects."

What Are Its Advantages and Limitations?

While the Data control does have a lot of capabilities, there are also some things that only can be done with program code. As Chapter 28, "Improving Data Access with the Data Access Objects," shows you, you can create a database application without using the Data control at all. In order to help you determine whether to create your program with the Data control, with just the data access objects, or with a combination of the two, you need to have an understanding of the advantages and limitations of the Data control.

▶ **See** "Creating the Database," **p. 637**

Advantages of the Data Control   The key advantage to using the Data control is that you don't have to do much, if any, programming to develop a data access application. You don't have to provide program code to open a database or recordset, to move through the records, to edit existing records, or to add new records. The Data control makes initial application development quicker and code maintenance easier.

When using the Data control, you also have the advantage of specifying data objects (database and recordset) at design time, and you can select these options from dialog boxes and lists. Selecting options from lists cuts down on typographical errors that you can introduce into the application.

Another advantage of the Data control is that it provides a direct link to the data. You don't have to specifically invoke the Edit and Update methods to modify the data in the database. Consequently, your users' changes show up in the database as soon as they enter them.

In addition to these advantages of using the Data control, there are several bound controls, which provide an easy way to accomplish tasks that are difficult to duplicate with just the data access objects and program commands. These bound controls are the data bound list box, data bound combo box, and data bound grid. (See the sections on these controls in this chapter: "Data Bound Lists and Combos," and "Data Bound Grids.")

Limitations of the Data Control   As useful as the Data control is, it also has a few limitations. These limitations include the following:

■ No Add or Delete functions are built in to the Data control.

■ Because the Edit and Update functions are automatic, implementing transaction processing in the Data control is more difficult.

■ You can't use the Data control to create a database or a table; it will only work with existing data.

In the section "Programming the Data Control's Events" later in this chapter, you see how to overcome some of these limitations by combining the Data control with program code.

Using Other Databases

The Data control is designed to work best with Jet (Access) databases, but you can work just as easily with other database formats. These formats include some traditional database formats like dBASE, FoxPro, and Paradox, as well as data that is not typically thought of as a database—for example, Excel spreadsheets or text files.

For any of the database formats, you still need to set the `DatabaseName` and `RecordSource` properties of the Data control. You also need to set the control's `Connect` property to identify the type of database being used. In addition, the `DatabaseName` property is treated differently for some database formats than for Jet databases. For example, with dBASE files, the `DatabaseName` property refers to a directory instead of a single file.

Setting the *Connect* Property The `Connect` property tells the Jet engine what kind of database you are using. A listing of `Connect` property settings for various database types can be found in the *Connect Property (DAO)* topic of Visual Basic's help system.

The Data control makes it easy for you to set the `Connect` property. To change its value, you select the desired database format from a drop-down list in the Properties window, as shown in Figure 27.1.

FIG. 27.1

The `Connect` property lets you use the Data control with many types of databases.

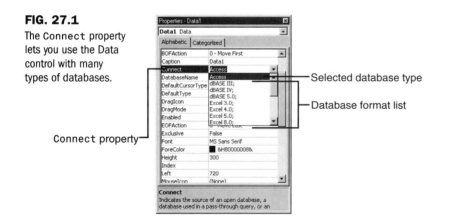

Connect property

Selected database type

Database format list

Part
VI

Ch
27

Considerations for the *DatabaseName* Property Some database formats, like Jet, store all the tables of the database along with other database information in one database file. Other formats, like FoxPro and dBase, store each table in a separate file, and may even have other files for such things as indexes and Memo field contents. Depending on the database format you select, the information you specify in the `DatabaseName` property may represent something different. For Jet databases, you just specify the name of the database file. For dBase databases, the `DatabaseName` property must be set to the name of the folder containing the database files. If you need to use a database type other than Jet, refer to Visual Basic's help system for specific `DatabaseName` property requirements.

Working Directly with Tables and Snapshots

The Data control, by default, creates a dynaset-type recordset when you specify the `RecordSource` property. However, you can have the Data control create a snapshot-type recordset or even a table-type recordset to access a table directly. To handle this, you just need to change the setting of the `RecordsetType` property. You do this by selecting the desired type from a drop-down list in the Properties dialog box (see Figure 27.2).

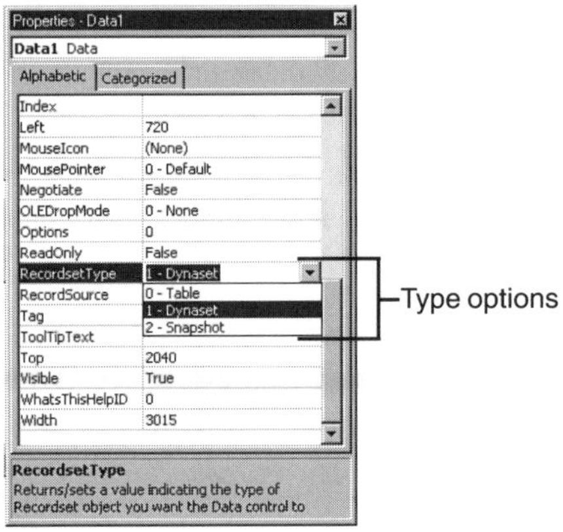

FIG. 27.2

Use the `RecordsetType` property to determine the type of recordset created by the Data control.

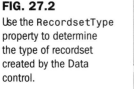

Type options

One reason you might want to change the `RecordsetType` is for performance. For example, if you do not need to be able to edit the contents of the recordset, you might want to use a snapshot-type recordset because it provides faster access than a dynaset-type. In another case, you might want to use a table-type so that you can change the presentation order of the recordset by changing the controlling index of the table, since indexes are supported only by table-type recordsets.

> **CAUTION**
>
> If you specify a `RecordsetType` that cannot be created in a particular situation, you will get an error when you try to run your program. This is most likely to occur when you set the `RecordsetType` to `Table` and use a SQL statement or query in the `RecordSource` property.

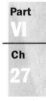

TROUBLESHOOTING

I tried to set an index for my recordset using the `Index` **property of the Data control, but was unable to do so.** The `Index` property does not refer to a database index, but to the index position in an array. A Data control, like any other Visual Basic control object, can be part of a control array. If you have such an array, the `Index` property specifies the position of the current control in that array. Remember that a Data control, by default, creates a dynaset-type recordset, and you cannot apply an index to this type of recordset. You can use an index if you specify that the Data control should create a table-type recordset, but you must set the `Index` property of the `Recordset` object associated with the Data control, as in this example:

```
datYouth.Recordset.Index = "Name"
```

You can set an index only for the Data control's `Recordset` object if you have set the `RecordsetType` property to `0` - `Table`.

▶ **See** "Using Control Arrays," **p. 496**

Tracking the Current Record

A recordset has a *record pointer* that keeps track of the current record. There cannot be more than one current record at any given time.

You may think of the beginning and end of a file as the first and last record, respectively, of a recordset. However, this is not actually the case. A recordset has a special position called beginning-of-file (BOF) that is located *before* the first record. Similarly, the special end-of-file (EOF) position is located *after* the last record. This can create problems in some data access programs because there is no current record when the record pointer is positioned at the beginning or the end of the file.

By default, the Data control avoids this problem by setting the record pointer to the first record when the beginning-of-file is reached and setting the pointer to the last record when the end-of-file is reached. This assures that there is always a current record for viewing or editing. However, there may be times when you want to know when you have actually reached the BOF or EOF positions even while using the Data control. You can control what the Data control does at the beginning or end of the file by setting the `BOFAction` and `EOFAction` properties of the Data control.

The `BOFAction` property, which tells the Data control what to do when the beginning of file is reached, has two possible settings:

- Execute the `MoveFirst` method of the Data control's recordset to set the record pointer at the first record and the BOF flag to False (property value of `0` - `Move First`). This is the default setting.
- Set the BOF flag to True (property value of `1` - `BOF`).

Part

VI

Ch

27

The EOFAction property, which tells the Data control what to do when the end-of-file is reached, has three possible settings:

■ Execute the MoveLast method to set the record pointer at the last record and the EOF flag to False (property value of 0 - Move Last). This is the default setting.

■ Set the EOF flag to True (property value of 1 - EOF).

■ Execute the AddNew method to set up the recordset for the addition of a new record (property value of 2 - Add New).

You can choose the values of each of these properties from a drop-down list in the Properties dialog box. The 2 - Add New setting of the EOFAction property can be useful if you have an application that needs to add new records. As with most other properties of the Data control, you can reset these properties at runtime.

N O T E   These BOF and EOF actions are triggered only when the user reaches the beginning or end of the file by using the Data control's navigation buttons. They have no effect if the beginning- or end-of-file is reached by using data access methods (such as MoveNext) in code. ■

Other Optional Properties

In addition to the properties already covered, there are three other key properties for the Data control that you can set:

Exclusive   Determines whether others can access the database while your application is using it. You can set the property to True (your application is the only one that can access the database) or False (others can access the database). The default value is False.

ReadOnly   Determines whether your application can modify the data in your defined recordset. You can set the property to True (your application can't modify data) or False (your application can modify data). The default value is False. Setting this property to True is not the same as using a snapshot. Because a snapshot-type recordset is a copy of the data in memory, it is faster than a read-only dynaset-type recordset.

Options   Allows you to specify other properties for the recordset created by the Data control. Chapter 32, "Using Classes in Visual Basic," and Chapter 28, "Improving Data Access with the Data Access Objects."

▶ **See** "Opening an Existing Database," **p. 721**

Programming the Data Control

There are several ways that you can use program code to work with the Data control and the bound controls. By using program code, you can make your program more flexible than with the Data control alone. The following list gives you a few of the ways that you can have program code work with the Data control:

- Change the properties of the Data control and bound controls in code.
- Place code in the `Validate` event of the Data control to handle user actions.
- Use the methods of the recordset to provide capabilities that the Data control does not have on its own.

Changing Properties On-the-Fly

Like any other control that you have on a form, you can change the properties of the Data control and bound controls at runtime. Most of the properties of the Data control and the bound controls are changeable. Only a few, like the `Name` property, are read-only at runtime.

Properties of the Data Control   You can choose to set (or reset) the `DatabaseName`, `RecordSource`, and `RecordsetType` properties of the Data control at runtime. The following list outlines some of the reasons why you might want to do this:

- To enable the user to select a specific database file from a group of related files. For example, a central office application keeps a separate database for each store of a chain; your application must enable the user to select the store with which he or she wants to work.

- To enable users to set specific conditions on the data they want to see. These conditions can take the form of filters or sort orders (for example, show only salespeople with over $10,000 in sales in order of total sales). Alternatively, your application might have to set the filters as part of an access control scheme, such as allowing a department manager to see data about only the people in his or her department. If the application sets the filters, it incorporates the information into code at runtime instead of at design time. Remember that the initial values of the Data control properties are set at design time.

- You can enable the user to specify the directory in an initialization file (or have your setup program do it for them) and then use the information from the initialization file to set your Data control properties. If you're developing a commercial application, there is no guarantee that the user has the same directory structure as you do. Many users are annoyed if you impose a specific directory structure or drive designation as a requirement for your program.

> **TIP**   If you distribute your application, you will often need to change the `DatabaseName` property of the Data control to handle differences between your directory structure and that of the user.

Part
VI
Ch
27

If you need to set the parameters at runtime, simply set the properties with code statements like those shown in Listing 27.1. Note that you must specify the name of your Data control, the property name, and the desired property value.

After you set the properties, use the Data control's `Refresh` method to implement the changes, as shown in the last line of Listing 27.1. The changes to the Data control (that is, the creation of the new recordset) take effect *after* the `Refresh` method is invoked.

Listing 27.1   Setting or Changing the *DatabaseName* and *RecordSource* Properties of a Data Control at Runtime

```
'***********************************************
'Set the value of the DatabaseName property
'***********************************************
datMembers.DatabaseName = "C:\YOUTH\YOUTHTRK.MDB"
'*********************************************
'Set the value of the RecordSource property
'*********************************************
datMembers.RecordSource = "Family"
'**************************************************************
'Set the value of the RecordsetType property to table (0)
'**************************************************************
datMembers.RecordsetType = vbRsTypeTable
'***************************************************
'Use the Refresh method to implement the changes
'***************************************************
datMembers.Refresh
```

Properties of the Bound Control   In a similar manner, you can set the properties of the bound controls at runtime. You can change the `DataSource` of a bound control to access a different Data control on the form. You also can change the setting of the `DataField` property to have the control display the contents of a different field in the recordset.

CAUTION

Be careful when you change the `DataSource` or `DataField` properties in code. If you enter an invalid Data control name or field name, an error will occur.

Recordsets and the Data Control (*Set* Command)

One particularly useful feature of the Data control is the capability to create a recordset with the data access objects and then assign the recordset to the Data control. This gives you increased flexibility in the recordsets that can be used. Because you also can assign the recordset of the Data control to a recordset object, this means you can pass the recordset to other procedures or to class modules for processing. This feature is something that was not available in Visual Basic prior to version 4.

The `Set` statement is the key statement to use when you want to allow recordsets to be moved back and forth between a recordset object and the Data control. Use the `Set` statement any time you want to assign a value to an object. You will also see the `Set` statement used in Chapter 28, "Improving Data Access with Data Access Objects," when you open databases and recordsets with the data access objects.

The following code shows you how to use the OpenRecordset method to create a recordset:

```
'Create the recordset
SQLSel = "Select LastName, FirstName From Members "
SQLSel = SQLSel & "Where Member Order By LastName, FirstName"
Set datRec = OldDb.OpenRecordset(SQLSel, dbOpenDynaset)
```

After the recordset has been created, this code will assign it to a Data control:

```
'Assign the recordset to the Data control
Set datNames.Recordset = datRec
```

You can use this capability to enable your users to specify sort or filter criteria for a recordset. Then, with the user-defined criteria you can create a recordset using a SQL statement. This recordset then can be assigned to an existing Data control to display the results of the query in a grid or a series of bound controls.

Being able to pass the contents of a Data control to a recordset object enables you to do things like write a generic routine for handling deletions. This way, you can write one procedure or class to query the user for verification of the deletion and then perform the deletion if the user agrees. The code in Listing 27.2 shows you how such a procedure works.

Listing 27.2 Procedures Let You Reuse Code Easily

```
'Define the procedure
Sub DelRecord(Navset As Recordset)
Dim MsgStr As String
'Delete the current record
MsgStr = "Are you sure you want to delete this record"
RetCode = MsgBox(MsgStr, vbYesNo, "Deletion Confirmation")
If RetCode = vbYes Then
        Navset.Delete
End If
End Sub
'*********************************************************
'Call the procedure with the recordset of a Data control
'*********************************************************
DelRecord datNames.Recordset
```

CAUTION

A recordset object and the Data control recordset are identical immediately after the Set statement, and at this time, they both point to the same record. However, after a record movement function is performed on either recordset, they are out of synchronization. Therefore, be careful when you are using both a recordset object and a Data control to manipulate the same data.

Programming the Data Control's Events

The Data control has three key events for which you can write program code: the Validate event, the Reposition event, and the Error event. While most of the actions of the Data control are handled automatically, programming for these events can help you add capabilities to your program and help you handle errors.

Using the *Validate* Event   When you create a Jet database, you can specify validation rules to be checked before each record is saved. However, you might have situations where the validation rules for your program are more complex than the Jet engine can handle. In this case, you need to perform the data validation in program code. How can you do this when the Data control saves data automatically?

The Data control has an event, the Validate event, that is triggered whenever the record pointer is *about to be moved*. This event occurs when the user presses one of the navigation buttons on the Data control or when the form containing the Data control is unloaded.

When the Validate event is triggered, the Data control examines all controls that are bound to it to determine if any data in any of the controls has changed. Two parameters then are set for the Validate event: the Save parameter, which tells you whether any data has been changed, and the Action parameter, which tells you what caused the Validate event to fire. The Save parameter can be either True or False. The Action parameter can have one of 12 values, as defined in Table 27.1.

Table 27.1   The Value of the *Action* Parameter Tells You Why the *Validate* Event Fired

Constant	Value	Description
vbDataActionCancel	0	Cancels any Data control actions
vbDataActionMoveFirst	1	MoveFirst
vbDataActionMovePrevious	2	MovePrevious
vbDataActionMoveNext	3	MoveNext
vbDataActionMoveLast	4	MoveLast
vbDataActionAddNew	5	AddNew
vbDataActionUpdate	6	Update
vbDataActionDelete	7	Delete
vbDataActionFind	8	Find
vbDataActionBookmark	9	Sets a bookmark
vbDataActionClose	10	Uses the Close method of the Data control
vbDataActionUnload	11	Unloads the form

Listing 27.3 shows how you can use the Validate event to perform data checking.

Listing 27.3 Data Checking in the *Validate* Event

```
Private Sub datMembers_Validate(Action As Integer, Save As Integer)
    Dim CompStr As String
    If Save = True Then
        CompStr = Trim(txtYouth(0).Text)
        If Len(CompStr) = 0 Then
            MsgBox "First Name cannot be blank"
            Action = vbDataActionCancel
        End If
    End If
End Sub
```

This code checks the Save parameter to see if any of the data in the bound controls has been changed. If it has, the code proceeds to perform the data checking. In this case, the code is checking to make sure a non-null string was entered in one of the text boxes. If the string is zero-length, a message is displayed to the user, and the action that was being processed is canceled by setting the Action parameter to vbDataActionCancel.

N O T E This particular data verification can be handled by the database engine when you set a validation rule or set the AllowZeroLength property of the field to True. However, many programmers prefer to handle data validation from within the program, rather than relying upon the Jet engine's validation rules.

Using the *Reposition* Event The Reposition event occurs *after* the Data control's current record has changed, as opposed to the Validate event, which occurs *before* the current record changes. This allows you to perform some type of processing once the new record becomes current. For example, you may want to modify the form's caption to reflect the record that is being displayed, or recalculate information such as an invoice total based on data from the new record. This code sample demonstrates how to accomplish both of these tasks:

```
Private Sub Data1_Reposition()
    Dim crTemp As Currency
    Me.Caption = "Invoice Number " & txtInvNumber.Text
    crTemp = Val(txtInvGross) - Val(InvSalesTax)
    lblInvTotal.Caption = Format(crTemp, "currency")
End Sub
```

Handling Errors with the *Error* Event The other event of note for the Data control is the Error event. The Error event also has two parameters associated with it: the DataErr and the Response parameters. The Error event is triggered when a data access error occurs when no program code is running, such as when the Data control is loaded or the user clicks one of its buttons, but the database specified in the DatabaseName property cannot be found or has been corrupted. When the event is triggered, the error number is reported via the procedure's DataErr parameter. You then can write code in the event procedure to handle the different data access errors.

The Response parameter determines the action to be taken by your program. If the parameter is set to vbDataErrContinue (0), your program attempts to continue with the next line of code. If the parameter is set to vbDataErrDisplay (1), the default value, an error message is displayed. When you write your error handling for the Error event, you can set the Response parameter to vbDataErrContinue for those errors that are corrected by your code and set it to vbDataErrDisplay for all other errors.

Data Control Methods

In addition to being able to respond to events, the Data control also has several methods that you probably will want to use in your programming. We'll discuss these three:

- Refresh
- UpdateControls
- UpdateRecord

The Refresh method causes the Data control to rerun the query that created the recordset and access all data that is currently in the recordset. There are several occasions when you need to use the Refresh method:

- When you change the Data control's RecordSource property.
- When you assign a recordset created with data access objects to the Data control.
- When other users have been accessing simultaneously the same database and tables. Refreshing the Data control shows any additions, modifications, or deletions made by the other users.

The UpdateRecord method forces the Data control to save the information in the bound controls to the recordset. Typically, you will want to place a Save or Update button on any data entry form you create. (This is done automatically if you use the data form designer.) The reason for this is to enable the user to save his work on the current record without having to move to another record. The Data control only saves changes when the record pointer is moved or when the form containing the Data control is unloaded. The following line of code shows how you can force a Data control to update the current record:

```
datYouth.UpdateRecord
```

The companion method to the UpdateRecord method is the UpdateControls method. This method retrieves information from the current record and redisplays it in the bound controls. This has the effect of canceling any changes made by the user. By placing the following line of code in the Click event procedure of a command button, you can implement a cancellation feature:

```
datYouth.UpdateControls
```

Other Bound Controls

In Chapter 26, "Using Data Controls and Reports," you were introduced to five bound controls: the TextBox, Label, CheckBox, PictureBox, and Image controls. Visual Basic actually has quite a few bound controls that you can use in your programs:

- TextBox
- Label
- CheckBox
- PictureBox
- Image
- ListBox
- ComboBox
- Data bound ListBox
- Data bound ComboBox
- Data bound Grid
- RichTextBox
- MaskedEdit

Lists and Combo Boxes

The ListBox and ComboBox controls enable the user to choose one item from a list of items; the ComboBox control also allows the user to enter an item that's not in the list. You can bind either of these controls to a data field to store the user's choices in a field. You do this by setting the DataSource and DataField properties of the control. To give your user a list of items from which to select, use the control's AddItem method. For this sample case, use a combo box to enable users to select the title for the member they are editing (see Figure 27.3). Listing 27.4 shows how to populate the list of choices.

Listing 27.4   Populating the List with the *AddItem* Method

```
Combo1.AddItem "Mr."
Combo1.AddItem "Mrs."
Combo1.AddItem "Ms."
Combo1.AddItem "Miss"
Combo1.AddItem "Dr."
```

TIP You also can enter the list items at design time by using the List property.

Part
VI

Ch
27

FIG. 27.3

Use a list or combo box to present your user with a list of choices.

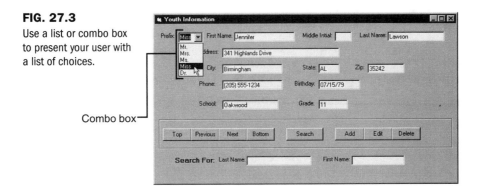

Combo box

Data Bound Lists and Combos

The data bound list box (DBList control) and data bound combo box (DBCombo control) are similar in function to their standard counterparts. They are designed to present the user with a list of choices. The key difference is that the data bound list and combo box controls get their list information from a recordset rather than from a series of AddItem statements.

> **TIP**   In order to use the DBList or DBCombo controls, you must add them to the Toolbox. Choose Project, Components. In the Controls tab of the Components dialog box, make sure Microsoft Data Bound List Controls 5.0 is selected.

Consider an example from the sample case. As your users enter data about a member, you want the user to be able to enter easily the county and state names of the member. One of the tables in the database contains county information. You can use the data bound list box to let your users select a county from those contained in the county table. The data bound list takes the county ID selected from the County table and stores it in the appropriate field of the Members table. You might think it would be hard to select the appropriate county if all you can see is the ID. However, the data bound list and combo boxes let you select a second field from the source table to serve as the display in the list. This means that you can display the name of the county in the list box but store only the county ID in the Members table. Figure 27.4 shows this concept graphically.

You set up the data bound list or combo box by specifying five properties. Table 27.2 describes these properties.

Table 27.2 Properties for Data Bound List Box or Combo Box

Property	Sample Case Setting	Description
RowSource	datCounty	The name of the Data control containing the information used to populate the list
BoundColumn	CountyID	The name of the field containing the value to be copied to the other table
ListField	CountyName	The name of the field to be displayed in the list
DataSource	datYouth	The name of the Data control containing the recordset that is the destination of the information
DataField	CountyID	The name of the destination field

FIG. 27.4
The data bound list and combo boxes let you pick an item from one table for inclusion in another table.

You can set each of these properties by selecting the property from the Properties dialog box and choosing the setting from a drop-down list. When setting the properties of the data bound list and combo boxes, keep in mind the following points:

- The Data controls you specify for the RowSource and DataSource properties can be the same control, or they can be different controls.
- The fields for the BoundColumn and DataField properties must be of the same type.
- You can set the ListField property to the same field as the BoundColumn property.

Part
V

Ch
27

Figure 27.5 shows the data bound combo box added to a sample data entry form.

FIG. 27.5

A data bound combo box lets the user select from a list of counties.

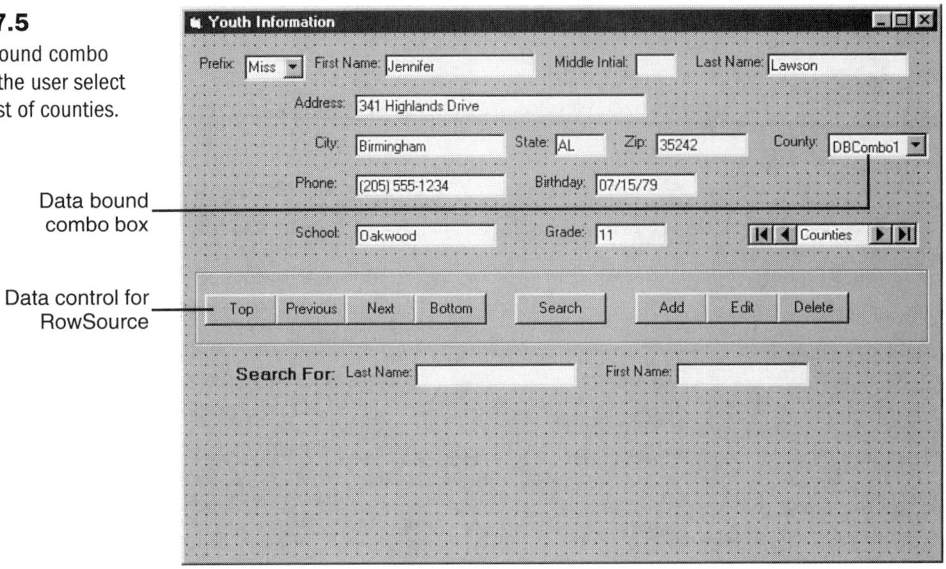

Data bound combo box

Data control for RowSource

Data Bound Grids

The data bound grid (DBGrid control) provides a means to view the fields of multiple records at the same time. The data bound grid is similar to the table view used in Access or the Browse command used in FoxPro. It displays information in a spreadsheet style of rows and columns. You can use it to display any alphanumeric information.

To set up the data bound grid, you need only to specify the DataSource property to identify the Data control containing the data. The grid then displays all fields of all records in the recordset. If the information is larger than the area of the grid you defined, scroll bars are presented to let you view the remaining data.

TIP To conserve application resources, use a QueryDef or SQL statement in the grid Data control's RecordSource property. This way, you can keep the number of records and fields that the grid handles to a minimum.

Your user can select a grid cell to edit by clicking the cell with the mouse. To add a new record, the user positions the pointer in the last row of the grid indicated by an asterisk (*) and enters the desired data. These capabilities are governed by the AllowUpdate and AllowAddNew properties, respectively. The default value of the AllowUpdate property is True; the default value of the AllowAddNew property is False. You can set these properties appropriately either at design time or runtime.

For the sample case, use the data bound grid to display the Members information in a browse mode. Allow the user to switch between the browse mode and single-record mode by using the command button at the lower-right corner of the screen. This saves screen real estate. Figure 27.6 shows the data bound grid for the sample case.

FIG. 27.6
You can use the data bound grid to display information from many records at once.

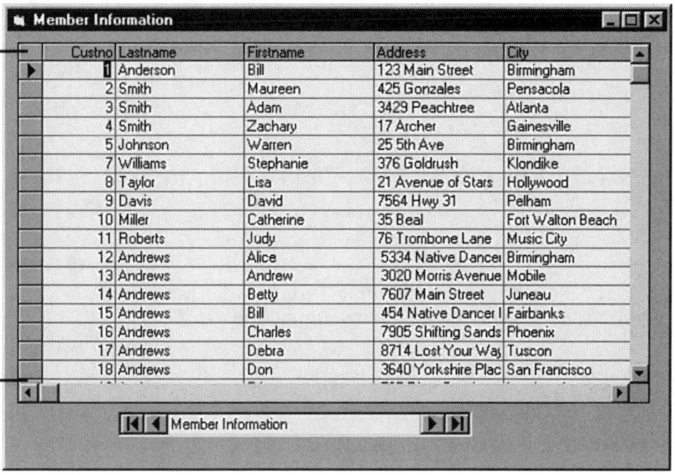

Data bound grid —

Custno	Lastname	Firstname	Address	City
1	Anderson	Bill	123 Main Street	Birmingham
2	Smith	Maureen	425 Gonzales	Pensacola
3	Smith	Adam	3429 Peachtree	Atlanta
4	Smith	Zachary	17 Archer	Gainesville
5	Johnson	Warren	25 5th Ave	Birmingham
7	Williams	Stephanie	376 Goldrush	Klondike
8	Taylor	Lisa	21 Avenue of Stars	Hollywood
9	Davis	David	7564 Hwy 31	Pelham
10	Miller	Catherine	35 Beal	Fort Walton Beach
11	Roberts	Judy	76 Trombone Lane	Music City
12	Andrews	Alice	5334 Native Dancer	Birmingham
13	Andrews	Andrew	3020 Morris Avenue	Mobile
14	Andrews	Betty	7607 Main Street	Juneau
15	Andrews	Bill	454 Native Dancer	Fairbanks
16	Andrews	Charles	7905 Shifting Sands	Phoenix
17	Andrews	Debra	8714 Lost Your Way	Tuscon
18	Andrews	Don	3640 Yorkshire Plac	San Francisco

Member Information

Other Visual Basic Controls

The other bound controls are set up the same way you would set up a text box or check box. Specifically, you set the `DataSource` property to the name of the Data control containing the data to be displayed and then set the `DataField` property to the specific field in the recordset.

Third-Party Controls

One of the greatest features about Visual Basic is the capability to extend its functionality through the use of third-party controls. This functionality also extends to bound controls. Many third-party vendors have controls that can be bound to a Data control, and some vendors even market enhanced Data controls. For example, Apex Software Corporation, which developed the DBGrid control included with Visual Basic, sells an enhanced version called True DBGrid Pro, which adds many features to the standard control.

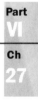
Part
VI
Ch
27

Further Enhancements

In Chapter 26, "Using Data Controls and Reports," you saw how you needed to use code to implement some features that were not available with the Data control alone. Specifically, an `Add` and `Delete` function were added to the capabilities of the data entry form with some simple coding. There are a few other enhancements that can be implemented with just a little bit of code and some ingenuity.

▶ **See** "Essential Functions the Data Control Forgot," **p. 687**

Find and Seek Operations

Another enhancement to the features provided by the Data control is the capability to search for a specific record. To add this feature, you must use either the `Find` method or the `Seek` method of the Data control's `Recordset` object, depending upon the recordset type. For a table-type recordset, use the `Seek` method; for the others, use the `Find` method. To implement the search in our example, add a command button to the form. This command button invokes a dialog box that requests the ID to be found and then uses the appropriate method to perform the search (see Listing 27.5).

Listing 27.5   Use the *Seek* or *Find* Method to Search for a Specific Record

```
'*****************************************************************
'The variable SrchCond contains the value of the search criteria
'*****************************************************************
If dayYouth.RecordsetType = vbRSTypeTable Then
  datYouth.Recordset.Seek ">=", SrchCond
Else
    datYouth.Recordset.FindFirst "datYouth.Recordset([LastName]) >= " _
        & SrchCond
End If
```

What About Options? (Option Buttons)

Another very useful control is the option button. Unfortunately, it is not a bound control that can be used directly with the Data control. However, this does not have to stop you from using the control. Option buttons come in handy for letting the user select between a number of mutually exclusive choices. A typical use is for selecting gender in a membership application, as shown in Figure 27.7.

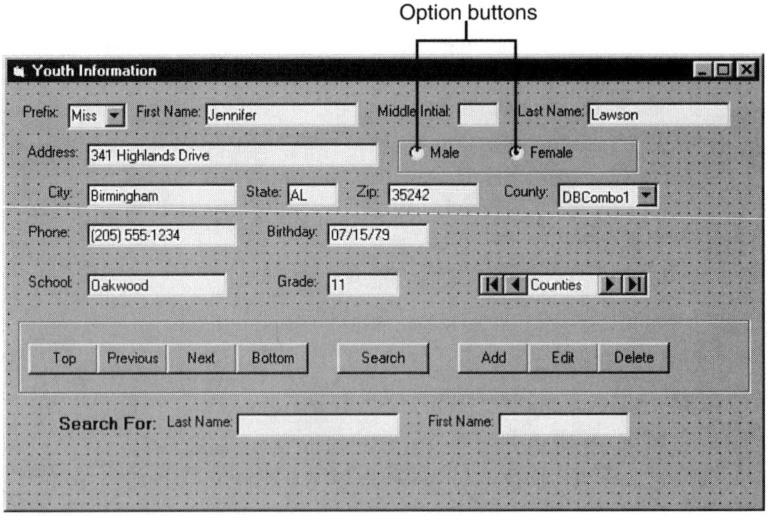

FIG. 27.7
Option buttons can be used to present the user with choices.

In code, you determine which option button was chosen by checking the Value property of each one. If the value of a button is True, then this was the selected button. Only one option button of a group can be selected. Option buttons can be grouped on a form, in a picture box, or in a frame. It is good practice to set up each group of option buttons in a picture box or frame to avoid conflicts with other groups.

After you have determined which option button was selected, you can assign the desired value for your data field based on the selection. For the membership case, either an M (male) or an F (female) is stored, depending on the option button selected.

TIP If you have more than two option buttons, you might want to put them in a control array. Then, you can use a loop to look for the selected option, as shown in this code example:

```
isel = 0
'Loop through five option buttons
For I = 0 To 4
   If Option(I).Value Then
      isel = I
      'Exit the loop when the selection is found
      Exit For
   End If
Next I
```

The option buttons are not bound controls, but you can still use them in an application with the Data control. You can place code in the Validate event of the Data control to store the desired value from the option buttons. However, there is a method that I find easier to use. (It's a sneaky way to trick the Data control.) For the field that you are modifying, create a text box and bind it to the field. Then set the Visible property of the text box to False. This keeps the box from being seen by the user. Then, in the Click event of each option button, place a line of code that changes the contents of the text box to the value represented by the option button. Then, when the Data control is invoked to move the record pointer, the field bound to the hidden box is updated along with all other bound fields. For the membership case, the following code would be used:

```
Sub Male_Click()
   txtGender.Text = 'M'
End Sub
Sub Female_Click()
   txtGender.Text = 'F'
End Sub
```

Using this hidden box method has an additional benefit. You can use the Change event of the box to mark the proper option box for each record that is accessed. The code for this follows:

```
If txtGender.Text = 'M' Then
   Male.Value = True
Else
   Female.Value = True
End If
```

Part

VI

Ch

27

While this discussion has focused on how to use the option buttons with the Data control, you also can use them when you program with just the data access objects. In this case, you use an assignment statement to set the value of your field just like you do any other field. For the membership case (assuming the field is named Gender), you would use the following code:

```
OldTbl.Edit
If Male.Value Then
   OldTbl("Gender") = 'M'
Else
   OldTbl("Gender") = 'F'
End If
OldTbl.Update
```

From Here...

This chapter has shown you how to use some additional features of the Data control, what other bound controls are available to you, and how you can add features to enhance your data entry forms. There are other chapters that address other aspects of database applications:

- To see how to create a database, see Chapter 24, "Database Design and Normalization."

- To learn how to quickly set up a data entry form, see Chapter 26, "Using Data Controls and Reports."

- To learn how to create a database application without the Data control, see Chapter 28, "Improving Data Access with the Data Access Objects."

Improving Data Access with the Data Access Objects

Use different recordset types

Depending on your application, you might have different data access needs. There are different recordset types to support these needs.

Move from one record to another in a recordset

Recordset navigation is one of the key functions of any database application.

Find a specific record

Most applications also need to be able to find a specific record. The technique you use depends on the type of recordset you open.

Working with multiple records

While data access objects normally work with one record at a time, often you'll want to manipulate records as a group. We'll discuss how this can be accomplished.

Modifying your recordset

You can use filters to narrow down the number of records that you work with, based on specific criteria.

Add, edit, and delete records in a database

What database application would be complete without the capability to add new records and modify old ones.

In Chapters 26, "Using Data Controls and Reports," and 27, "Doing More with Bound Controls," you saw how you could write a database application very quickly by using the Data control and bound controls that come with Visual Basic. These chapters showed you that, by setting a few properties, you can create a nearly complete data-entry screen. I say *nearly* complete because, in Chapter 27, you also saw that you needed to write some program code to handle some additional functions of a database application—for example, adding or deleting records or finding a specific record.

These additional functions introduced you to some of the programming that you can do in a database application. However, you can write an entire database application with just program commands and not use the Data control at all. When you use just the program commands, you work with Visual Basic's *data access objects* (DAO).

In this chapter, we'll learn how Visual Basic's data access objects can be used to create complete, robust data-management applications. Data access objects act as a Visual Basic program's internal representation of *physical data*—data stored in some type of database or data-management engine. Think of the data access objects as special types of variables. These "variables," however, represent data stored *outside* the program rather than information stored in the computer's memory while the program is running. ■

Introduction to DAO

Using the data access objects and their associated program commands is more complex than using the Data control and bound controls, but does offer greater programming flexibility for some applications. The data access objects and programming commands also provide the basis for many of the actions of the Data control and the bound controls. Therefore, they help you understand the concepts behind the controls. As you saw in Chapter 26, even if you use the Data control, you may also need to write some programming code to augment its capabilities.

▶ **See** "Essential Functions the Data Control Forgot," **p. 687**

To demonstrate the similarities and differences between data access objects and the Data control, this chapter instructs you on how to build a data entry screen similar to the ones you created in the previous chapters. This way, you can compare how the programming commands work to how the Data control implements the commands. Figure 28.1 shows the data entry screen that you will build in this chapter.

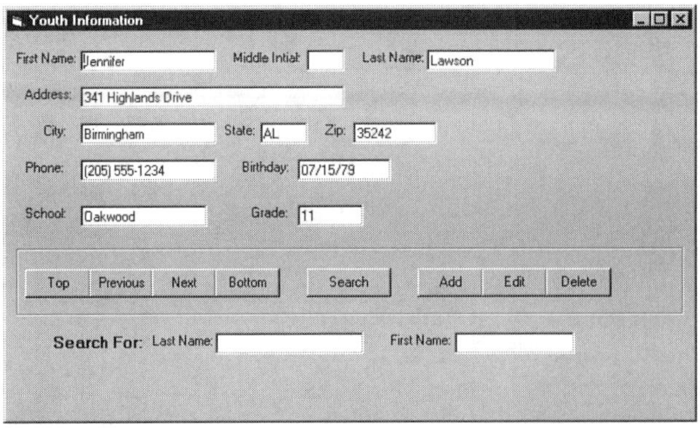

FIG. 28.1

You can create this data entry screen by following this chapter's instructions.

A key reason for using program commands is the flexibility they give you beyond what is available with the Data control. You can perform more detailed input validation than is possible with just data engine rules because program commands do not directly access the database. You also can cancel changes to your edited data without using transactions. The use of program commands also provides an efficient way to handle data input and searches that do not require user interaction. Examples of this are receiving data from lab equipment or across a modem, or looking up the price of an item in a table. Program commands enable you to do transaction processing as well.

Opening an Existing Database

The first step in writing many data access programs is to set up a link to the database with which you want to work. If your application will be working with a database that already exists, you'll need to create a Database object within the program, then use that object to create a link to the existing database. In effect, you are "opening the database" for use in your program. Most of the other data access objects will flow from that Database object.

▶ **See** "Implementing Your Design," **p. 636**

As we discussed in Chapter 24, a database is opened as part of a session with the database engine. The database engine is represented in a program by the DBEngine object; we define sessions by creating Workspace objects within the DBEngine object. You can then open a database with the Workspace object's OpenDatabase method. To use the OpenDatabase method, create a database object and call the method, as shown in this bit of code:

```
Dim OldDb As Database, OldWs As Workspace
Set OldWs = DBEngine.Workspaces(0)
Set OldDb = OldWs.OpenDatabase("C:\YOUTH\YOUTHTRK.MDB")
```

▶ For a detailed discussion of the DBEngine and Workspace objects, **see** "Creating the Database," **p. 637**

TROUBLESHOOTING

When I try to run the preceding commands, I get the error User-defined type not defined. What's happening? In order to use any database capabilities (beyond the Data control and bound controls) in your program, you must have one of the Data Access Object libraries specified in your program references. To set the program references, select the <u>R</u>eferences command from the <u>P</u>roject menu and select one of the DAO libraries from the "References – (projectname)" dialog box.

> **N O T E** There are two basic Jet DAO libraries that Visual Basic can include in an application. These external libraries are the "Microsoft DAO 3.5 Object Library" and the "Microsoft DAO 2.5/3.5 Compatibility Library." If you will be programming for 32-bit clients only, and using 32-bit Jet (Access 95/97) databases, you should select the 3.5 library. If you have a need to exchange data with 16-bit systems or Access 2.0 applications, you will have to use the 2.5/3.5 compatibility library. ▪

These commands open a Jet database with the default options of read/write data access and shared access. The full syntax of the OpenDatabase method lets you specify that the database should be opened exclusively (no other users or programs can access it at the same time), that it be opened in read-only mode (no updates are allowed), or, if you are connecting to a non-Access database, you can specify the database type. The use of exclusive access and read-only access are usually only required for multi-user applications (as discussed in Chapter 31, "Multi-User Databases").

▶ **See** "Denying Table Access to Others," **p. 809**

Part
VI

Ch
28

However, you might want to use the read-only mode even in a single-user application for a lookup database (for example, a ZIP Code database or a state abbreviations database that you include with your application but do not want the user to be able to modify). To open the database as read-only, change the Set statement to the form shown in the following code. The first parameter after the database name indicates whether the database is opened for exclusive access; the second parameter indicates whether read-only mode is to be used:

```
Set OldDb = OldWs.OpenDatabase("C:\ZIPCODE.MDB",False,True)
```

After you open the database, you have only created a link from your program to the database file itself. You still do not have access to the information in the database. To gain access to the information, you must create and open a Recordset object that links to data stored in one or more of the tables in the database.

Deciding Which Recordset Type to Use

When you create a Recordset object to open a recordset in your program, you can access any entire table, specific fields and records from the table, or a combination of records and fields from multiple tables. There are three types of recordsets available in Visual Basic:

Recordset Type	Definition
Table	Directly represents all records in an entire physical table in a database.
Dynaset	Sets of pointers that provide access to fields and records in one or more tables of a database.
Snapshot	Read-only copies of data from one or more tables. They are stored in memory.

N O T E This chapter refers to tables, dynasets, and snapshots, but it is important to remember that they are all recordsets and can only be accessed by using the Recordset object. Specifically, all mentions of tables, dynasets, and snapshots actually refer to table-type recordsets, dynaset-type recordsets, and snapshot-type recordsets, respectively. Previous versions of Visual Basic-supported objects that are now outdated: Table objects, Dynaset objects, and Snapshot objects. ▩

The following sections describe each type of recordset, point out some of the advantages and disadvantages of each, and demonstrate the commands used to access the recordset.

Using Tables

A *table* (table-type recordset) is a direct link to one of the physical tables stored in the database. Because all data in a database is stored in tables, using this type of recordset provides the most direct link to the data. Tables are also the only form of recordset that supports indexes; therefore, searching a table for a specific record can be quicker than searching a dynaset or snapshot.

When using tables, data is addressed or modified one table at a time, one record at a time. This arrangement provides very fine control over the manipulation of data. However, it does not give you the convenience of changing records in multiple tables with a single command, such as an action query.

Advantages of Using Tables   Using tables in your programs gives you several advantages:

- You can use or create indexes to change the presentation order of the data in the table during program execution.
- You can perform rapid searches for an individual record by using an appropriate index and the Seek command.
- Changes made to the table by other concurrent users or programs are immediately available. It is not necessary to "refresh" the table to gain access to these records.

Disadvantages of Using Tables   Of course, using tables in your programs also has disadvantages:

- You can't set filters on a table to limit the records being processed to those that meet a certain criteria.
- You can't use the Find commands on a table; the Seek command finds only the first record that meets its criteria. This implies that, to process a series of records in a range, you, the programmer, must provide a means to find the additional records.

You can usually overcome these disadvantages with programming, but the solutions are often less than elegant. This chapter discusses some of the workarounds in its coverage of the various methods for moving through a recordset and for finding specific records. These topics are covered later in this chapter.

▶ **See** "Positioning the Record Pointer," **p. 730**

Opening a Table for Use   To open a table for the program to use, define a Recordset object and then use the OpenRecordset method to access the table. To identify the type of recordset to create, specify the dbOpenTable constant in the parameters of the method, as shown in the following segment of code. This code assumes that you have already opened the database by using the OldDb object and that the database contains a table called "Youth":

```
Dim OldTbl As Recordset
Set OldTbl = OldDb.OpenRecordset("Youth",dbOpenTable)
```

These commands open a table in a Jet database, with the default parameters of shared use and read/write mode. You can include optional parameters in the OpenRecordset method to open the table for exclusive use or to open the table in read-only mode. These options are summarized in Table 28.1.

Part
VI

Ch
28

Table 28.1   Some Options Used to Modify the Access Mode of Tables

Option	Action
dbDenyWrite	Prevents others in a multi-user environment from writing to the table while you have it open
dbDenyRead	Prevents others in a multi-user environment from reading the table while you have it open
dbReadOnly	Prevents you from making changes to the table

Using Dynasets

A *dynaset* is a grouping of information from one or more tables in a database. This information is comprised of selected fields from the tables, often presented in a specific order and filtered by a specific condition. Dynasets address the records present in the base tables at the time the dynaset was created. Dynasets are an updatable recordset, so any changes made by the user are stored in the database. However, dynasets do not automatically reflect additions or deletions of records made by other users or programs after the dynaset was created. This makes dynasets less useful for some types of multi-user applications.

A dynaset is actually a set of record pointers that point to the specified data as it existed when the dynaset was created. Changes made to information in the dynaset are reflected in the base tables from which the information was derived as well as in the dynaset itself. These changes include additions, edits, and deletions of records.

Advantages of Using Dynasets   Some of the advantages provided by dynasets are as follows:

- Dynasets give you the ability to join information from multiple tables.
- You can use Find methods to locate or process every record meeting specified criteria.
- Dynasets enable you to limit the number of fields or records that you retrieve into the recordset.
- Dynasets make use of filters and sort order properties to change the view of data.

Disadvantages of Using Dynasets   Dynasets do have some limitations:

- You can't use indexes with dynasets; therefore, you can't change the presentation order of a dynaset by changing the index or by creating a new one.
- A dynaset does not automatically reflect additions or deletions made to the data by other users or other programs. A dynaset must be explicitly refreshed or re-created to show the changes.

Setting Up a Dynaset   To set up a dynaset for use within a program, you must define the Recordset object with the Dim statement and then generate the dynaset by using the OpenRecordset method with the dbOpenDynaset parameter. For creating a dynaset, the key part of the OpenRecordset method is the SQL statement that defines the records to be included, the filter condition, the sort condition, and any join conditions for linking data from multiple tables.

The code shown in Listing 28.1 shows the simplest form of creating a dynaset, in which all records and fields are selected from a single table with no sort or filter conditions specified. This is the type of dynaset created by default when using a Data control (though you can use a table or snapshot with the Data control). The statements in Listing 28.1 provide you access to the same information as you had by accessing the table directly with the previous code. The only difference is the type of recordset that was created.

Listing 28.1   How to Create a Simple Dynaset

```
Dim OldDb As Database, NewDyn As Recordset,OldWs As Workspace
Set OldWs = DBEngine.Workspaces(0)
Set OldDb = OldWs.OpenDatabase("C:\YOUTH\YOUTHTRK.MDB")
Set NewDyn = OldDb.OpenRecordset("SELECT * FROM Youth", _
     dbOpenDynaset)
```

N O T E   If you want to include all records from one table in a dynaset in no particular order, you can omit the SQL statement and simply use the table name (`Set OldDb = OldWs.OpenDatabase("Youth")`). However, it's a good idea to go ahead and use a SQL statement in case you want to modify it later. ▨

When you create a dynaset, you can use any valid SQL statement that selects records. You can also specify options that affect the dynaset's behavior. Table 28.2 lists these options.

Table 28.2   Some Options Used to Modify the Access Mode of a Dynaset

Option	Action
dbDenyWrite	Prevents others in a multi-user environment from writing to the dynaset while you have it open
dbReadOnly	Prevents you from making changes to the dynaset
dbAppendOnly	Enables you to add new records, but prevents you from reading or modifying existing records
dbSQLPassThrough	Passes the SQL statement used to create the dynaset to an ODBC database server to be processed

The following code shows how to create a dynaset-type recordset that only allows the user to read the information in the database:

```
Set NewDyn = OldDb.OpenRecordset("Youth", dbOpenDynaset, dbReadOnly)
```

N O T E An *ODBC server* is a database engine, such as Microsoft SQL Server or Oracle, that conforms to the Open Database Connectivity (ODBC) standards. The purpose of a server is to handle query processing at the server level and return to the client machine only the results of the query. ODBC drivers, which are usually written by the vendor of the database engine, handle the connection between Visual Basic and the database server. An advantage of using ODBC is that you can connect to the information on the database servers without having to know the inner workings of the engine. ▪

You can also create a dynaset from another dynaset28., as illustrated in Listing 28.2. The reason for creating a second dynaset from an initial dynaset is that you can use the `filter` and `sort` properties of the first dynaset to specify the scope of records and the presentation order of the second dynaset. Creating a second dynaset enables you to create a subset of your initial data. The second dynaset is usually much smaller than the first, which allows faster processing of the desired records. In Listing 28.2, a dynaset was created from the Customer table to result in a national mailing list. A second dynaset was then created, which includes only the customers living in Alabama and sorts them by city name for further processing. Figures 28.2 and 28.3 show the records returned by these two dynasets.

Listing 28.2 How to Set the *filter* and *sort* Properties of a Dynaset and Create a Second Dynaset from the First

```
Dim OldDb As Database, NewDyn As Recordset, ScnDyn As Dynaset
Dim OldWs As Workspace
Set OldWs = DBEngine.Workspaces(0)
Set OldDb = OldWs.OpenDatabase("C:\YOUTH\YOUTHTRK.MDB")
Set NewDyn = OldDb.OpenRecordset("SELECT * FROM Youth", _
    dbOpenDynaset)
NewDyn.Filter = "State = 'AL'"
NewDyn.Sort = "City"
Set ScnDyn = NewDyn.OpenRecordset(dbOpenDynaset)
```

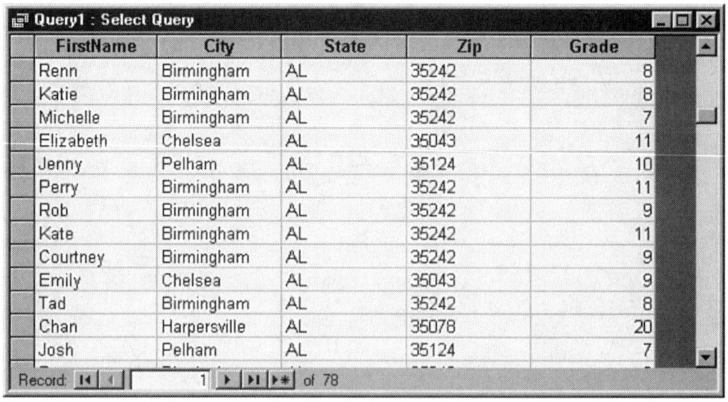

FIG. 28.2

The results of the creation of a dynaset from base tables.

FirstName	City	State	Zip	Grade
Renn	Birmingham	AL	35242	8
Katie	Birmingham	AL	35242	8
Michelle	Birmingham	AL	35242	7
Elizabeth	Chelsea	AL	35043	11
Jenny	Pelham	AL	35124	10
Perry	Birmingham	AL	35242	11
Rob	Birmingham	AL	35242	9
Kate	Birmingham	AL	35242	11
Courtney	Birmingham	AL	35242	9
Emily	Chelsea	AL	35043	9
Tad	Birmingham	AL	35242	8
Chan	Harpersville	AL	35078	20
Josh	Pelham	AL	35124	7

Query1 : Select Query

Record: 1 of 78

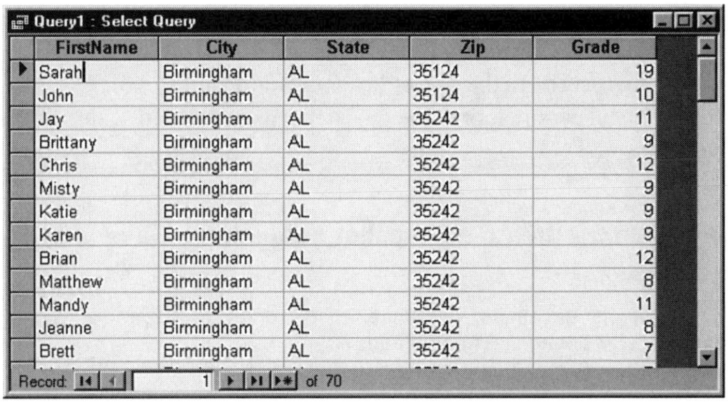

FIG. 28.3

The results of creating one dynaset from another dynaset after `filter` and `sort` conditions have been set.

You might wonder why, if you need the results in the second dynaset, you can't just create it from the base tables in the first place. The answer is that you can do so if your application needs *only* the second table. However, consider a member tracking system in which you want access to all your members (the creation of the first dynaset), and one of the functions of the system is to generate a mailing list for a particular region (the creation of the second dynaset). Because the pointers to all the required information are already present in the first dynaset, the creation of the second dynaset is faster than if it were created from scratch.

Using Snapshots

A *snapshot,* as the name implies, is a "picture," or copy, of the data in a recordset at a particular point in time. A snapshot is very similar to a dynaset in that it is created from base tables, using a SQL statement, or from a `QueryDef`, dynaset, or another snapshot. A snapshot differs from a dynaset in that it is not updatable. As a general rule, use a snapshot whenever you want a set of data that isn't time-sensitive; that is, it doesn't matter if records in the underlying database are modified after the snapshot is created. The most frequent use of snapshots in a program is to generate reports or informational screens in which the data is static.

Advantages of Using Snapshots   Snapshots provide you with the following advantages:

- You can join information from multiple tables.
- You can use the `Find` methods to locate records.
- Record navigation and recordset creation can be faster for a snapshot than for a read-only dynaset because a snapshot is a copy of the data, not a set of pointers to the data.

Disadvantages of Using Snapshots   The primary disadvantage of using a snapshot is that it is not an updatable recordset. In addition, you can't use an index with a snapshot to help set the order of the data or locate specific records.

Part
VI

Ch
28

> **CAUTION**
>
> To avoid memory constraints, make sure that a snapshot returns only a small set of records.

Setting Up a Snapshot   You can create a snapshot by defining a `Recordset` object with the `Dim` statement and then using the `OpenRecordset` method with the `dbOpenSnapshot` parameter to assign the records to the object (as shown in Listing 28.3). As with a dynaset, you can specify optional parameters in the `OpenRecordset` method. Table 28.3 summarizes these parameters.

Listing 28.3   Create a Snapshot in Much the Same Way You Create a Dynaset

```
Dim OldDb As Database, NewSnap As Recordset, OldWs As Workspace
Set OldWs = DBEngine.Workspaces(0)
Set OldDb = OldWs.OpenDatabase("C:\YOUTH\YOUTHTRK.MDB")
Set NewSnap = OldDb.OpenRecordset("Youth",dbOpenSnapshot)
```

Table 28.3   Some Options Used to Modify the Access Mode of a Snapshot

Option	Action
dbDenyWrite	Prevents others in a multi-user environment from writing to the snapshot while you have it open.
dbForwardOnly	Enables only forward scrolling through the snapshot.
dbSQLPassThrough	Passes the SQL statement used to create the snapshot to an ODBC database to be processed.

Using a Forward-Only Recordset

A forward-only recordset is a special type of snapshot that allows only forward scrolling through its records. This means that the `MoveFirst`, `MovePrevious`, and `Find` methods will not work on the recordset. The advantage of using this type of recordset is that it is faster than a snapshot. However, the forward-only recordset should be used only in situations where a single pass through the recordset is needed, such as in report generation routines.

To set up a forward-only recordset, you use the `OpenRecordset` method and specify the `dbOpenForwardOnly` constant as shown in the following line of code:

```
Set NewRSet= OldDb.OpenRecordset("Youth",dbOpenForwardOnly)
```

Placing Information On-Screen

Suppose that you have written a data entry screen using the Data control and bound controls. To display information on-screen, you simply draw bound controls and then set the appropriate data fields for the controls. The display of the information is automatic. Using the data access objects, the process is only slightly more involved. You still use control objects (text boxes, labels, check boxes, and so on) to display the information, but you have to assign the data fields to the correct control properties with each record displayed. When used in this manner, the control objects are typically referred to as *unbound controls*. One advantage of using un-bound controls is that you can use any control to display data, not just the bound controls specifically designated for use with the Data control.

Information in fields can be accessed through a recordset's `Fields` collection in one of several ways. For example, any of these techniques would suffice for retrieving the contents of a field named `ThisField` in a recordset named `MyRS` and placing it into a text box named `Text1`:

- Use the field's ordinal position in the `Fields` collection: `Text1.Text = MyRS.Fields(0)` (assuming `ThisField` is the first field in the recordset).
- Use the field's name to retrieve it from the `Fields` collection: `Text1.Text = MyRS.Fields("ThisField")`.
- Take advantage of the fact that the `Fields` collection is the default collection of a recordset: `Text1.Text = MyRS("ThisField")`.
- Use the shorthand method of the previous technique: `Text1.Text = MyRS!ThisField`.

N O T E If a field's name contains spaces, you can enclose the entire name in square braces, as in `Text1.Text = MyRS![longer field name]`. ■

For an example, we'll detail how to build a member data entry screen based on the Youth table of the sample database we've discussed. You can apply these concepts to any existing database. To begin building this screen, start a new project in Visual Basic. Then, on the default form, add the data labels and text boxes to hold the data from the table. Figure 28.4 shows the form with these controls added.

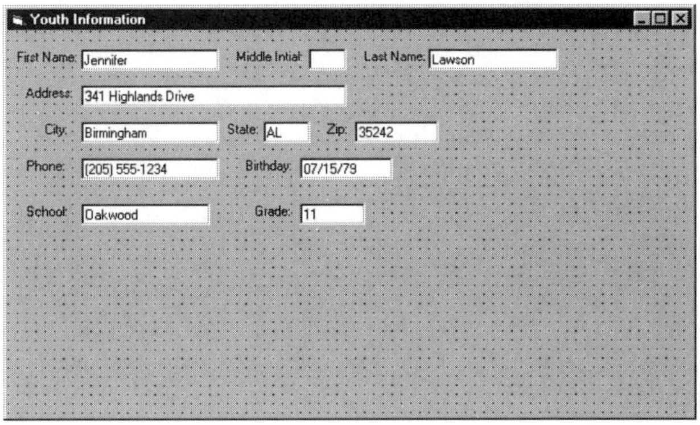

FIG. 28.4

Use unbound controls to display data from the data access objects.

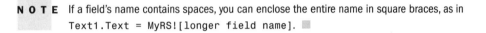

To set up the table for use, you must open the table by using the `OpenRecordset` method. For this case, place the `Dim` statements that define the data access objects (like the ones in Listing 28.3) in the General Declarations section of the form so that the objects are available throughout all the code in the form. You then open the database and table in the `Form_Load` event (see Listing 28.4). At this point, the table is open and you are positioned at the first record in the table.

Listing 28.4 Placing the *OpenDatabase* and *OpenRecordset* in the *Form_Load* Event

```
Set OldWs = DBEngine.Workspaces(0)
'********************************
'Open database and Customer table
'********************************
Set OldDb = OldWs.OpenDatabase("C:\YOUTH\YOUTHTRK.MDB")
Set RcSet = OldDb.OpenRecordset("Youth",dbOpenTable)
'********************************************
'Move to first record and display information
'********************************************
RcSet.MoveFirst
Call ShowFields
```

To display the data, assign the value of the desired data fields to the display properties of the controls (captions for labels, text for text boxes, and so on) that contain the data. Listing 28.5 shows this process. Notice that the listing defines the text boxes as a control array; you can use a loop to quickly modify certain properties of the controls such as foreground color or visibility. Also notice that the assignments are placed in a subroutine; you can call the same routine from a number of command button events rather than repeat the code in each event. This arrangement makes the code more efficient and easier to maintain.

Listing 28.5 Assigning Data Fields to the Display Properties of the Form's Controls

```
Private Sub ShowFields()
Text1(0).Text = RcSet("Lastname")
Text1(1).Text = RcSet("Firstname")
Text1(2).Text = RcSet("Address")
Text1(3).Text = RcSet("City")
Text1(4).Text = RcSet("State")
Text1(5).Text = RcSet("Zip")
Text1(6).Text = RcSet("Phone")
End Sub
```

N O T E   Because the Text property is the default property of a text box, you do not have to include the property name in the assignment statement. My personal preference is to include the name for readability. ▨

Positioning the Record Pointer

Because a database with only one record is fairly useless, a database engine must provide ways to move from one record to another within recordsets. Visual Basic provides six such techniques:

Technique	Description
Move methods	Changes the position of the record pointer from the current record to another record
Find methods	Locates the next record that meets the find condition. Find methods work on dynasets and snapshots
Seek method	Finds the first record in a table that meets the requested condition
Bookmark property	Identifies the location of a specific record
AbsolutePosition	Moves the record pointer to a specific record position in the recordset
PercentPosition	Moves the record pointer to the record property nearest the indicated percentage position in the recordset

Each of these has benefits and limitations, as described in the following sections.

Using the *Move* Methods

You can use the Move methods on any recordsets available in Visual Basic. There are five different Move methods:

Move Method	Action
MoveFirst	Moves the record pointer from the current record to the first record in the opened recordset
MoveNext	Moves the record pointer from the current record to the next record (the record following the current record) in the opened recordset. If there is no next record (that is, if you are already at the last record), the end-of-file (EOF) flag is set.
MovePrevious	Moves the record pointer from the current record to the preceding record in the opened recordset. If there is no previous record (that is, if you are at the first record), the beginning-of-file (BOF) flag is set.
MoveLast	Moves the record pointer from the current record to the last record in the opened recordset
Move n	Moves the record pointer from the current record n records down (if n is positive) or up (if n is negative) in the opened recordset. If the move would place the record pointer beyond the end of the recordset (either BOF or EOF), an error occurs.

Part
VI

Ch
28

These commands move the record pointer to the record indicated based on the current order of the recordset. The current order of the recordset is the physical order, unless an index was set for a table, or a dynaset or snapshot was created with a specific order specified. To show the use of the MoveFirst, MovePrevious, MoveNext, and MoveLast methods, add command buttons to the data entry screen so that the user can move through the recordset (see Figure 28.5). To activate these buttons, add the code shown in Listing 28.6. The code for each button is preceded by an identifying comment line.

FIG. 28.5

Add command buttons to enable the user to navigate through the recordset.

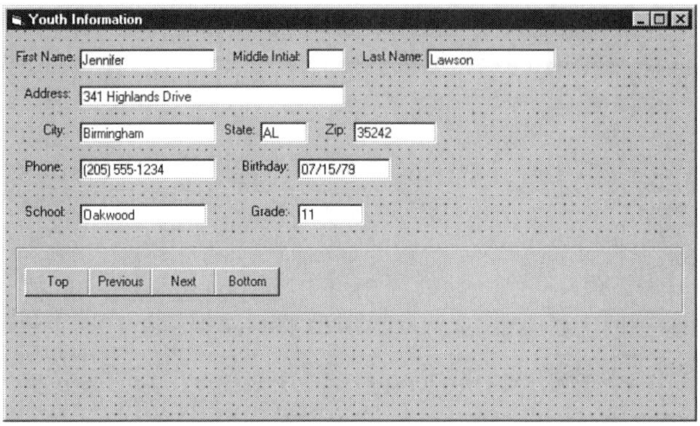

Listing 28.6 Assigning *Move* Methods to Navigation Command Buttons to Make Them Work

```
'*************************************************
'The MoveFirst method activates the "Top" button.
'*************************************************
RcSet.MoveFirst
Call ShowFields
'*********************************************************
'The MovePrevious method activates the "Previous" button.
'*********************************************************
RcSet.MovePrevious
Call ShowFields
'*************************************************
'The MoveNext method activates the "Next" button.
'*************************************************
RcSet.MoveNext
Call ShowFields
'***************************************************
'The MoveLast method activates the "Bottom" button.
'***************************************************
RcSet.MoveLast
Call ShowFields
```

The Move *n* method lets you move more than one record from the current position. The value of *n* is the number of records to move in the recordset. This value can be either positive or negative to indicate movement either forward or backward in the recordset. The following piece of code shows the use of this method to move two records forward from the current record:

```
RcSet.Move 2
```

The Move *n* method also has an optional parameter that enables you to move a specified number of records from a bookmark. You must set the bookmark prior to using this form of the Move method. The following line of code shows how this method is used:

```
RcSet.Move 2, bkmrk
```

Using the *Find* Methods

You can use the Find methods on dynasets and snapshots only. You can't use Find methods on table objects. (Because the data entry screen was created with a table, you can't use the Find methods in the example.) The Find methods are used to locate records that meet specified criteria. You express the criteria in the same way that you specify the Where clause of a SQL command—except without the Where keyword. There are four Find methods:

Find Method	Action
FindFirst	Starting at the top of the database, finds the first record in the recordset with the specified criteria
FindNext	Starting at the current location in the recordset, finds the next record down with the specified criteria
FindPrevious	Starting at the current location in the recordset, finds the next record up with the specified criteria
FindLast	Starting at the bottom of the recordset, finds the last record in the database with the specified criteria

After the Find method is run, check the status of the NoMatch property of the recordset. If NoMatch is True, the method failed to find a record that matched the requested criteria. If NoMatch is False, the record pointer is positioned at the found record.

Listing 28.7 shows the use of the Find methods to move through a dynaset.

Listing 28.7   How to Move Through Selected Records in a Dynaset Using
***Find* Methods**

```
'*****************************************
'Set up the database and Dynaset objects
'*****************************************
Dim OldDb As Database, NewDyn As Recordset, FindCrit As String
Dim OldWs As Workspace
Set OldWs = DBEngine.Workspaces(0)
Set OldDb = OldWs.OpenDatabase("C:\YOUTH\YOUTHTRK.MDB")
Set NewDyn = OldDb.OpenRecordset("SELECT * FROM Youth", _
    dbOpenDynaset)
'*************************************************
'Set the search criteria for the find methods
'*************************************************
FindCrit = "State = 'AL'"
'*************************************************
'Find the first record matching the criteria
```

Part

VI

Ch

28

continues

Listing 28.7   Continued

```
'********************************************
NewDyn.FindFirst FindCrit
Do While Not NewDyn.NoMatch
'*********************************************************
'Loop forward through all records matching the criteria
'*********************************************************
    NewDyn.FindNext FindCrit
Loop
'********************************************
'Find the last record matching the criteria
'********************************************
NewDyn.FindLast FindCrit
Do While Not NewDyn.NoMatch
'*********************************************************
'Loop backward through all records matching the criteria
'*********************************************************
    NewDyn.FindPrevious FindCrit
Loop
```

> **TIP**
>
> You might want to set a bookmark prior to invoking one of the Find methods. Then, if a matching record is not found, you can return to the record that was current before the Find was attempted.

The Find methods work by scanning each record, starting with the current record, to locate the appropriate record that matches the specified criteria. Depending on the size of the recordset and the criteria specified, this search operation can be somewhat lengthy. The Jet engine can optimize searches if an index is available for the search expression. If you are going to do many searches, consider creating an index for the field or fields in the base table.

> **TIP**
>
> In many cases, it is faster to re-create a dynaset by using the search criteria than it is to use the Find methods to process all matching records. You can also create a second filtered dynaset from the first dynaset by using the search criteria as the Filter condition. The best technique depends upon the amount of data, size of each record, as well as other factors. Try different approaches with your data to see what's best for a given situation. Listing 28.8 shows the comparison of these two approaches.

Listing 28.8   Creating a Dynaset with a *Filter* Condition in the SQL Statement or Creating a Second Dynaset After Setting the *Filter* Property of the First Dynaset

```
'**********************
'Create Initial Dynaset
'**********************
Dim OldDb As Database, NewDyn As Recordset, ScnDyn As Recordset
Dim OldWs As WorkSpace
Set OldWs = DBEngine.Workspaces(0)
Set OldDb = OpenDatabase("C:\YOUTH\YOUTHTRK.MDB")
```

```
Set NewDyn = OldDb.OpenRecordset("SELECT * FROM Youth", _
    dbOpenDynaset)
'********************************
'Use Find method to search records
'********************************
NewDyn.FindFirst "State = 'FL'"
Do Until NewDyn.NoMatch
    NewDyn.FindNext "State = 'FL'"
Loop
'*****************************************************************
'Create second dynaset and use Move methods to process records
'*****************************************************************
NewDyn.Filter = "State = 'FL'"
Set ScnDyn = NewDyn.OpenRecordset()
ScnDyn.MoveFirst
Do Until ScnDyn.EOF
    ScnDyn.MoveNext
Loop
'*******************************************************
'Create initial dynaset with "Where" clause and use Move
'*******************************************************
Set NewDyn = OldDb.OpenRecordset _
    ("SELECT * FROM Youth WHERE State = 'FL'", dbOpenDynaset)
NewDyn.MoveFirst
Do Until NewDyn.EOF
    NewDyn.MoveNext
Loop
```

◆ TROUBLESHOOTING

When you use variables as the value to be compared to, you might encounter the error `Cannot bind name` *item* **when you run the program.** When the field and the variable you are comparing are string (or text) variables, surround the variable name by single quotes ('), as shown in the following sample code:

```
Dim FindCrit As String, FindStr As String
FindStr = "Smith"
FindCrit = "Lastname = '" & FindStr & "'"
NewDyn.FindFirst FindCrit
```

For the sake of readability, you can also assign the single quote to a constant and use that constant in your code.

In the same manner, surround a date variable with the pound symbol (#) to compare it to a date field. You don't need to include any additional symbols when comparing numbers.

When a `Find` method is successful, the record pointer moves to the new record. If a `Find` method is not successful, the recordset's `NoMatch` property is set to `True` and the record pointer does not move. One way to use the `NoMatch` property is to write an `If` condition that checks the value, as shown in the following code:

```
If NewDyn.NoMatch Then
    'Notify user of event
    MsgBox "Record not found"
Else
    'Process found record.
    command
End If
```

Using the *Seek* Method

The Seek method is the fastest way to locate an individual record in a table; however, it is also the most limiting of the record-positioning methods. The following list outlines the limitations of the Seek method:

- Can be performed only on a table; you can't use it with a dynaset or snapshot
- Can be used only with an active index; the parameters of the Seek method must match the fields of the index in use
- Finds only the first record that matches the specified index values; subsequent uses do not find additional matching records

The Seek method, as shown in Listing 28.9, consists of the method call, the comparison operator, and the values of the key fields. The comparison operator can be <, <=, =, >=, >, or <>. The key values being compared must be of the same data type as the fields in the controlling index. Although you are not required to include the same number of key values as there are fields in the index, you *do* have to include a key value for each field you want to search. These values must appear in the same order as the fields in the index and be separated by commas, as shown in the second part of Listing 28.9.

Listing 28.9 Using the *Seek* Method to Find a Specific Record in a Table

```
Dim OldDb As Database, OldTbl As Recordset
Dim OldWs As WorkSpace
Set OldWs = DBEngine.Workspaces(0)
Set OldDb = OldWs.OpenDatabase("C:\YOUTH\YOUTHTRK.MDB")
Set OldTbl = OldDb.OpenRecordset("Youth",dbOpenTable)
'**********************************
'Set the index property for the table
'**********************************
OldTbl.Index = "Name"
'******************************************
'Execute the seek for the desired condition
'******************************************
OldTbl.Seek ">", "Smith"
'********************************************************
'Display information or "Not Found" message as appropriate
'********************************************************
If OldTbl.NoMatch Then
    MsgBox "Not Found"
Else
    MsgBox OldTbl("Lastname") & ", " & OldTbl("Firstname")
End If
```

```
'***********************************************************
'Seek method with first and last name information supplied
'***********************************************************
OldTbl.Seek ">=", "Smith", "M"
```

You must carefully plan for one behavior of the `Seek` method. When the `Seek` method uses the comparison operators =, >=, >, or <>, `Seek` starts with the first record for the current index and scans forward through the index to find the first matching occurrence. If the comparison operator is < or <=, `Seek` starts with the last record in the table and scans backward through the table. If the index has unique values for each record, this presents no problem. However, if there are duplicate index values for the key fields being specified, the record found depends on the comparison operator and the sort order of the index. Figure 28.6 shows a table of first and last names indexed on last name and then first name. The table on the top is indexed in ascending order; the table on the bottom is indexed in descending order. Listing 28.10 shows four possible combinations of controlling index and comparison operator for finding a record for the last name of *Smith*. Each of these combinations is labeled in the comments of the code. Note that the comparison operator is a string value that is to be enclosed in quotes, as is the data that is to be compared (if it's in a Text field). Table 28.4 shows the results of each of these `Seek` operations.

FIG. 28.6
These tables show the difference between using ascending and descending order in an index.

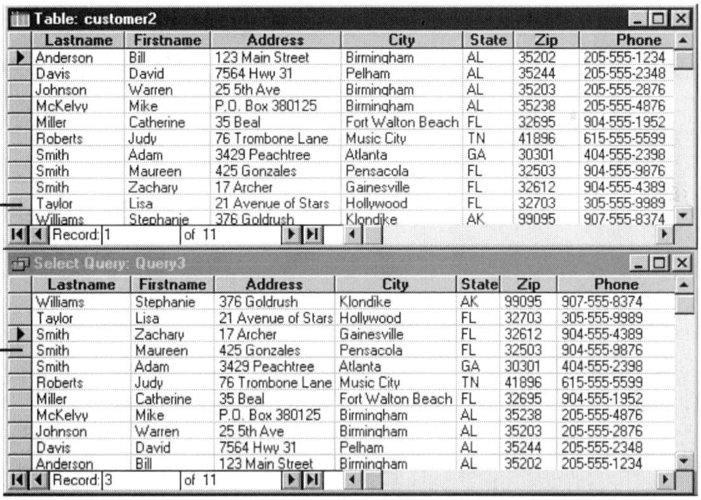

Table: customer2

Lastname	Firstname	Address	City	State	Zip	Phone
Anderson	Bill	123 Main Street	Birmingham	AL	35202	205-555-1234
Davis	David	7564 Hwy 31	Pelham	AL	35244	205-555-2348
Johnson	Warren	25 5th Ave	Birmingham	AL	35203	205-555-2876
McKelvy	Mike	P.O. Box 380125	Birmingham	AL	35238	205-555-4876
Miller	Catherine	35 Beal	Fort Walton Beach	FL	32695	904-555-1952
Roberts	Judy	76 Trombone Lane	Music City	TN	41896	615-555-5599
Smith	Adam	3429 Peachtree	Atlanta	GA	30301	404-555-2398
Smith	Maureen	425 Gonzales	Pensacola	FL	32503	904-555-9876
Smith	Zachary	17 Archer	Gainesville	FL	32612	904-555-4389
Taylor	Lisa	21 Avenue of Stars	Hollywood	FL	32703	305-555-9989
Williams	Stephanie	376 Goldrush	Klondike	AK	99095	907-555-8374

Record: 1 of 11

Select Query: Query3

Lastname	Firstname	Address	City	State	Zip	Phone
Williams	Stephanie	376 Goldrush	Klondike	AK	99095	907-555-8374
Taylor	Lisa	21 Avenue of Stars	Hollywood	FL	32703	305-555-9989
Smith	Zachary	17 Archer	Gainesville	FL	32612	904-555-4389
Smith	Maureen	425 Gonzales	Pensacola	FL	32503	904-555-9876
Smith	Adam	3429 Peachtree	Atlanta	GA	30301	404-555-2398
Roberts	Judy	76 Trombone Lane	Music City	TN	41896	615-555-5599
Miller	Catherine	35 Beal	Fort Walton Beach	FL	32695	904-555-1952
McKelvy	Mike	P.O. Box 380125	Birmingham	AL	35238	205-555-4876
Johnson	Warren	25 5th Ave	Birmingham	AL	35203	205-555-2876
Davis	David	7564 Hwy 31	Pelham	AL	35244	205-555-2348
Anderson	Bill	123 Main Street	Birmingham	AL	35202	205-555-1234

Record: 3 of 11

Ascending index order

Descending index order

Part VI

Ch 28

Listing 28.10 Varying Results Are Obtained Using Different *Seek* Operators and *Index* Orders on a Table

```
Dim OldDb As Database, OldTbl As Recordset
Dim OldWs As WorkSpace
Set OldWs = DBEngine.Workspaces(0)
Set OldDb = OldWs.OpenDatabase("C:\YOUTH\YOUTHTRK.MDB")
Set OldTbl = OldDb.OpenTable("Youth", dbOpenTable)
```

continues

Listing 28.10 Continued

```
'*************************
'Set ascending order index
'*************************
OldTbl.Index = "Name"
OldTbl.Seek ">=", "Smith", "A"
printer.Print OldTbl("Lastname") & ", " & OldTbl("Firstname")
OldTbl.Seek "<=", "Smith", "Z"
printer.Print OldTbl("Lastname") & ", " & OldTbl("Firstname")
'*************************
'Set descending order index
'*************************
OldTbl.Index = "Name2"
OldTbl.Seek ">=", "Smith", "A"
printer.Print OldTbl("Lastname") & ", " & OldTbl("Firstname")
OldTbl.Seek "<=", "Smith", "Z"
printer.Print OldTbl("Lastname") & ", " & OldTbl("Firstname")
```

Table 28.4 Different *Seek* Comparison Operators and *Index* Sort Orders Yield Different Results

Seek Comparison Operator	*Index* Order	Resulting Record
">=", "Smith, A"	Ascending	Smith, Adam
"<=", "Smith, Z"	Ascending	Smith, Maureen
">=", "Smith, A"	Descending	Roberts, Judy
"<=", "Smith, Z"	Descending	Smith, Zachary

Notice that you must also be careful when using the > ,< , >=, or <= operator on a descending index. The > (and >=)operator is interpreted as finding the record that occurs later in the index than the specified key value. That is why the ">=", "Smith" search on a descending index returns the record Roberts, Judy. Similar behavior is exhibited by the < and <= operators. As you can see from the preceding example, you must use care when choosing both the index sort order and the comparison operator with the Seek method to ensure that the desired results are achieved.

As with the Find methods, if a Seek is successful, the record pointer moves. Otherwise, the recordset's NoMatch property is set to True and the record pointer does not change. Figure 28.7 shows the Seek Name button and dialog box added to the sample case.

Using the *Bookmark* Property

It is often desirable to be able to return to a specific record after the record pointer moves or new records are added. You can do so by using the Bookmark property of the recordset. The bookmark is a system-assigned variable that is correlated to the record and is unique for each record in a recordset. Listing 28.11 shows how to obtain the value of the bookmark for the current record, move to another record, and then return to the original record by using the bookmark previously obtained.

FIG. 28.7
The Seek button presents the user with an opportunity to enter search conditions.

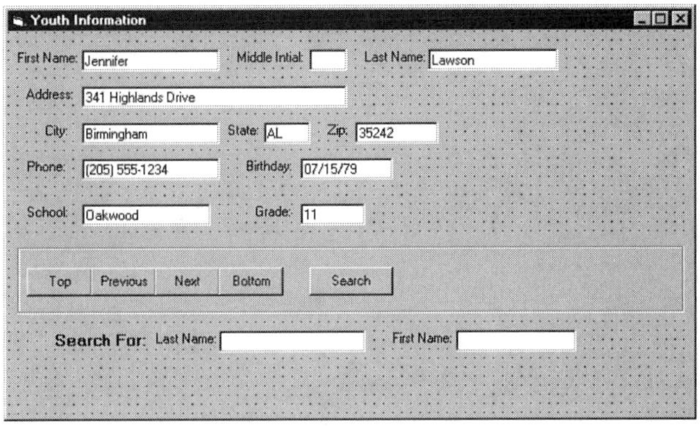

Listing 28.11 Using a Bookmark to Return to a Specific Record in a Recordset

```
Dim OldDb As Database, NewDyn As Recordset
Dim OldWs As WorkSpace
Set OldWs = DBEngine.Workspaces(0)
Set OldDb = OldWs.OpenDatabase("C:\YOUTH\YOUTHTRK.MDB")
Set NewDyn = OldDb.OpenRecordset _
    ("SELECT * FROM Youth", dbOpenDynaset)
'*******************************************************
'Set a variable to the bookmark of the current record
'*******************************************************
CrntRec = NewDyn.Bookmark
'**********************
'Move to another record
'**********************
NewDyn.MoveNext
'**************************************************************
'Return to the desired record by setting the bookmark property
'   to the previously defined value.
'**************************************************************
NewDyn.Bookmark = CrntRec
```

Part

VI

Ch

28

CAUTION
If you're working with a database type other than Jet, check the Bookmarkable property of the recordset you are using to see whether bookmarks are supported before you execute any methods that depend on the bookmarks.

If you must store multiple bookmark values, consider storing them in an array for faster processing. Listing 28.12 shows code that, while processing a mailing list, uses a bookmark array to identify customers whose birthdays are coming up.

Listing 28.12 Storing Multiple Bookmarks in an Array

```
ReDim BkMrk(1)
nmbkmk = 0
NewDyn.MoveFirst
Do Until NewDyn.EOF
'***************************
'Check for birthday in month
'***************************
   If birthday Then
'********************
'Add bookmark to array
'********************
      nmbkmk = nmbkmk + 1
      If nmbkmk > 1 Then
         ReDim Preserve BkMrk(1 To nmbkmk)
      End If
      BkMrk(nmbkmk) = NewDyn.Bookmark
   End If
   NewDyn.MoveNext
Loop
'*****************
'Process bookmarks
'*****************
For I = 1 To nmbkmk
   NewDyn.Bookmark = BkMrk(I)
   Debug.Print Lastname, Birthday
Next I
```

Using the *PercentPosition* and *AbsolutePosition* Properties

In addition to the Bookmark property, the Recordset object has two other properties that you can set to establish the position of the record pointer. These properties are AbsolutePosition and PercentPosition.

The PercentPosition property specifies the approximate position in a recordset where a record is located. By setting this property to a value between 0 and 100, you cause the pointer to move to the record closest to that location. Setting the property to a value outside the range causes an error to occur. You can use the PercentPosition property with all three types of recordsets.

The AbsolutePosition property enables you to tell the recordset to move to a specific record. The value of the property can range from 0 for the first record in the recordset to 1 less than the number of records. Setting a value outside of that range causes an error. Therefore, it is a good idea to include error checking in the code used to set the AbsolutePosition property. The AbsolutePosition property can be used only with dynasets and snapshots.

Listing 28.13 shows how you can use the `AbsolutePosition` and `PercentPosition` properties. Note the validation of the requested position; this is used to prevent errors.

Listing 28.13   *AbsolutePosition* and Percent*Position* Are Other Ways to Move in a Recordset

```
'Move to the percent position specified
If rcpct > 100 Then rcpct = 100
If rcpct < 0 Then rcpct = 0
NewDyn.PercentPosition = rcpct
  'Move to the absolute position specified
If rcabs > NewDyn.RecordCount Then rcabs = NewDyn.RecordCount
If rcabs < 0 Then rcabs = 0
NewDyn.AbsolutePosition = rcabs
```

Using Filters, Indexes, and Sorts

Filters, sorts, and indexes are properties of the `Recordset` object. You can set these properties by using an assignment statement such as:

```
NewDyn.Filter = "Lastname = 'Smith'"
```

Filters, indexes, and sorts enable you to control the scope of records being processed and the order in which records are processed. *Filters* (which are available only for dynasets and snapshots) limit the scope of records by specifying that they meet certain criteria, such as "last name starts with *M*." *Indexes* (available only for tables) and *sorts* (available only for dynasets and snapshots) specify the order of a recordset based on the value of one or more fields in the recordset. For sorts and indexes, you can also specify ascending or descending sort order.

Setting the *Filter* Property

The `Filter` property is available only for dynasets and snapshots. Although the following discussion refers only to dynasets, the same statements hold true for snapshots. When set, the `Filter` property does not affect the current dynaset, but filters records that are copied to a second dynaset or snapshot created from the first.

You can specify the `Filter` property of a dynaset the same way you specify the `Where` clause of a SQL statement, but without the `Where` keyword. The filter can be a simple statement, such as `State = 'AL'`, or one that uses multiple conditions, such as `State = 'FL' AND Lastname = 'Smith'`. You can also use an expression, such as `Lastname LIKE 'M*'`, to find people whose last names begin with *M*. The following sample code shows how these `Filter` properties are set for a dynaset created from the Youth information table:

```
Dim NewDyn As Recordset, ScnDyn As Recordset
Set NewDyn = OldDb.OpenRecordset("Youth",dbOpenDynaset)
NewDyn.Filter = "State = 'FL' AND Lastname = 'Smith'"
'Second recordset contains only "filtered" records.
Set ScnDyn = OldDb.OpenRecordset(dbOpenDynaset)
```

Part

VI

Ch

28

You can include added flexibility in your `Filter` conditions by using functions in the condition. For example, if you want to filter a dynaset of all states with the second letter of the state code equal to *L,* use the `Mid` function, as shown here:

```
NewDyn.Filter = "Mid(State,2,1) = 'L'"
```

Using functions does work, but it is an inefficient way to filter a dynaset. A better approach is to include the condition in the query used to create the dynaset.

More About Filters

The `Filter` condition of the dynaset has no effect on the current dynaset—only on secondary dynasets created from the current one. The only way to "filter" the existing recordset is to move through the recordset with the `Find` methods. By setting the `Find` condition to your `Filter` condition, you only process the desired records.

If you work with only the filtered dynaset, it is more efficient to create the required dynaset by using the appropriate SQL clause in the `OpenRecordset` method. This method is shown here:

```
Fltr = "State = 'FL' AND Lastname = 'Smith'"
Set NewDyn = OldDb.OpenRecordset("SELECT * FROM Youth WHERE" & Fltr)
```

Setting the *Sort* Property

As with the `Filter` property, the `Sort` property is available only for dynasets and snapshots. Although the following discussion refers only to dynasets, the same statements apply to snapshots. You can specify the `Sort` property by providing the field names and order (ascending or descending) for the fields on which the dynaset is to be sorted. You can specify any field or combination of fields in the current dynaset. The `Sort` condition is similar to the `Order By` clause of a SQL statement. Listing 28.14 shows the syntax for setting the `Sort` property.

Listing 28.14   Two Techniques for Creating a Sorted Dynaset

```
Dim OldDb As Database, NewDyn As Recordset, ScnDyn As Recordset
Dim OldWs As WorkSpace
Set OldWs = DBEngine.Workspaces(0)
Set OldDb = OldWs.OpenDatabase("C:\YOUTH\YOUTHTRK.MDB")
'*****************************************************************
'The first method sets the sort property of one dynaset then
'    creates a second dynaset from the first.
'*****************************************************************
Set NewDyn = OldDb.OpenRecordset("SELECT * FROM Youth")
NewDyn.Sort = "Lastname,Firstname"
Set ScnDyn = NewDyn.OpenRecordset()
'********************************************************
'The second method creates the sorted Dynaset directly
'********************************************************
Set ScnDyn = OldDb.OpenRecordset _
    ("SELECT * FROM Youth ORDER BY Lastname,Firstname")
```

> **CAUTION**
>
> When specifying a multiple field sort, the order of the fields is important. A sort on first name and then last name yields different results than a sort on last name and then first name.

As was the case for the `Filter` property, the `Sort` property has no effect on the current dynaset; it specifies the order of any dynaset created from the current one. You can also achieve the same results of a sorted dynaset by specifying the `Order By` clause of the SQL statement used to create the dynaset. This alternate technique is shown in Listing 28.14.

Setting the Current Index in a Table

You can use an index with a table to establish a specific order for the records or to work with the `Seek` method to find specific records quickly. For an index to be in effect, the `Index` property of the table must be set to the name of an existing index for the table. An example of how to use a program command to set the current index follows:

```
OldTbl.Index = "NameIndex"
```

The index specified for the table must be one that has already been created and is part of the indexes collection for the given table. If the index does not exist, an error occurs. The index is not created for you!

Creating an Index for a New Situation

If the index you want does not exist, create it as described in Chapter 26 and then set the `Index` property of the table to the newly created index. The example shown in Listing 28.15 creates a ZIP Code index for the Youth table by creating a new `Index` object, appending a `Field` object to the `Index` object's `Fields` collection, then appending the `Index` object to the `Recordset` object's `Indexes` collection.

▶ **See** "Creating Indexes," **p. 643**

Listing 28.15 Creating a New Index and Setting the *Index* Property

```
Dim Idx1 As Index, Fld1 As Field
Set Idx1 = NewTbl.CreateIndex("Zip_Code")
Set Fld1 = Idx1.CreateField("Zip")
Idx1.Fields.Append Fld1
NewTbl.Indexes.Append Idx1
NewTbl.Index = "Zip_Code"
```

If your program needs an index, why not just create it at design time so you don't have to worry about creating it at runtime? There are several reasons why it may be more beneficial to create an index at runtime:

- It takes time for the data engine to update indexes after records are added, deleted, or changed. If there are a large number of indexes, this process can be quite

Part
VI

Ch
28

time-consuming. It might be better to create the index only when it is needed. Also, indexes take up additional disk resources; therefore, many indexes on a large table can cause your application to exceed available resources.

■ You are limited to 32 indexes for a table. Although this is a fairly large number, if you need more than 32, you must create some indexes as they are needed and then delete them.

■ You cannot anticipate all the ways a user of your application wants to view data. By providing a method for creating indexes, specified by the user at runtime, you add flexibility to your application.

Of these reasons, the performance issue of updating multiple indexes is the one most often considered. To determine whether it is better to add the index at design time or to create it only when you need it, set up the application both ways and test the performance of each.

N O T E   Although it is desirable to limit the number of indexes your table has to keep current, it is advisable to have an index for each field that is commonly used in SQL queries. This is because the Jet engine (starting with version 2.0) employs query optimization that uses any available indexes to speed up queries. ▨

Considering Programs that Modify Multiple Records

Some programs, or program functions, are meant to find one specific piece of information in a database. However, the vast majority of programs and functions work with multiple records as a group. There are two basic methods of working with multiple records:

Method	Definition
Program loops	Groups of commands contained inside a DO...WHILE, DO...UNTIL, or FOR...NEXT programming structure. The commands are repeated until the exit condition of the loop is met.
SQL statements	Commands written in Structured Query Language that tell the database engine to process records. SQL is covered in detail in Chapter 29, "Understanding SQL."

Using Loops

Most programmers are familiar with the use of Do...While and For...Next loops. In working with recordsets, all the programming principles for loops still apply. That is, you can perform a loop *while* a specific condition exists or *for* a specific number of records. Loops of this type were shown earlier in this chapter (refer to Listings 28.4 and 28.5).

Another way of working with multiple records forms an *implied loop*. Most data entry or data viewing programs include command buttons on the form to move to the next record or previous record. When a user repeatedly presses these buttons, he or she executes a type of program loop by repeating the move events. A special consideration for this type of loop is what to do when you are at the first record, the last record, or if you have an empty recordset. The problem is that if you move backward from the first record, forward from the last record, or try to move anywhere in an empty recordset, an error occurs. Fortunately, the Jet database engine provides some help in this area. There are properties of the recordset that can tell you when these conditions exist, as described in the following section.

You can use four main recordset properties to control the processing of multiple records in a recordset. Table 28.5 gives the definitions of these properties.

Table 28.5 Properties Used to Control Loop Processing

Property	Indicates
BOF	Beginning of `File` flag, indicates whether the record pointer is positioned before the first record (BOF = True) or not (BOF = False).
EOF	End of `File` flag, indicates whether the record pointer is positioned past the last record (EOF = True) or not (EOF = False).
RecordCount	Indicates the number of records in the recordset that have been accessed. This gives a count of the total records in the recordset only after the last record has been accessed (for example, by using `MoveLast`), unless the recordset in question is a table-type recordset.
NoMatch	Indicates that the last `Find` method or `Seek` method was unsuccessful in locating a record that matched the desired criteria.

You can use these properties to terminate loops or prevent errors. Consider the data entry form in Figure 28.5. To prevent an error from occurring when the user presses the Next button, use code that allows the move only if the recordset is not at the end of the file. The following code takes this possibility into account:

```
If NOT OldDyn.EOF Then
    OldDyn.MoveNext
    If OldDyn.EOF Then DolDyn.MoveLast
End If
```

Alternatively, you can disable the Next button when you reach the end of file. You can apply the same principle to the Previous button and the BOF condition. You might also want to check the RecordCount property of a recordset and enable only the Add Record button if the count is zero.

N O T E After the `MoveNext` method has been executed, it is possible that the pointer is now at the end of the file (EOF). This would mean that there is no current record. Therefore, if the end of the file is encountered, a `MoveLast` method is used to make sure the record pointer is positioned at the last record in the recordset.

Part

VI

Ch

28

Using SQL Statements

In addition to processing records with a program loop, you can use SQL statements to handle a number of functions that apply to multiple records. The following sections discuss two main types of functions:

- Calculation queries provide cumulative information about the requested group of records.

- Action queries insert, delete, or modify groups of records in a recordset.

Calculation Queries   *Calculation queries* allow you to determine cumulative information about a group of records such as the total; average, minimum, and maximum values; and the number of records. Calculation queries also enable you to specify the filter criteria for the records. For example, you can extract total sales for all salesmen in the Southeast region or the maximum price of a stock on a given day (assuming, of course, that the base data is in your tables). Figure 28.8 shows a table of purchasing data for the fish inventory in an example database. The code in Listing 28.16 shows how to determine the total purchase costs for one type of fish and the minimum, maximum, and average unit cost of all the fish. Figure 28.9 shows the table that results from the SQL query.

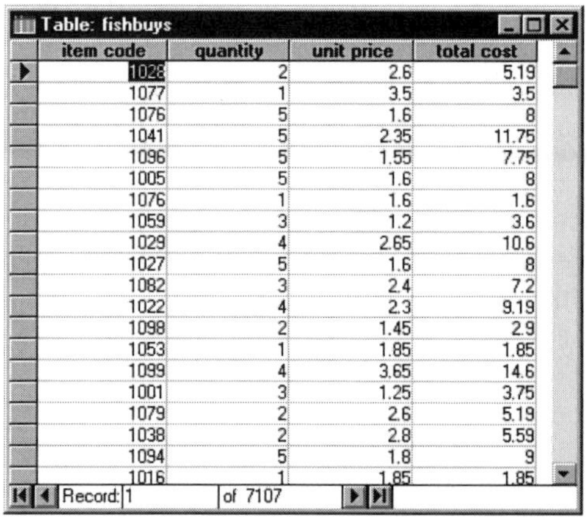

FIG. 28.8

You can process purchasing data shown here with calculation queries or action queries.

item code	quantity	unit price	total cost
1028	2	2.6	5.19
1077	1	3.5	3.5
1076	5	1.6	8
1041	5	2.35	11.75
1096	5	1.55	7.75
1005	5	1.6	8
1076	1	1.6	1.6
1059	3	1.2	3.6
1029	4	2.65	10.6
1027	5	1.6	8
1082	3	2.4	7.2
1022	4	2.3	9.19
1098	2	1.45	2.9
1053	1	1.85	1.85
1099	4	3.65	14.6
1001	3	1.25	3.75
1079	2	2.6	5.19
1038	2	2.8	5.59
1094	5	1.8	9
1016	1	1.85	1.85

Table: fishbuys

Record: 1 of 7107

Listing 28.16   Using Calculation Queries to Determine Information About Data in the Recordset

```
Dim OldDb As Database, NewDyn As Recordset, _
    NewDyn2 As Recordset, SQL As String
Dim OldWs As WorkSpace
Set OldWs = dbEngine.Workspaces(0)
Set OldDb = OldWs.OpenDatabase("C:\FISH\TRITON.MDB")
'*********************************************
'Use the SUM function to get the total cost.
'*********************************************
SQL = "SELECT SUM([Total Cost]) As Grand FROM Fishbuys _
```

```
         WHERE Fishcode = 1001"
Set NewDyn = OldDb.OpenRecordset(SQL)
Print NewDyn("Grand")
NewDyn.Close
'******************************************************************
'Use the MIN, AVG, and MAX functions to get unit price statistics.
'******************************************************************
SQL = "SELECT MIN([Unit Price]) As Mincst, _
       AVG([Unit Price]) As Avgcst, "
SQL = SQL + _
   " MAX([Unit Price]) As Maxcst FROM Fishbuys WHERE Fishcode > 0"
Set NewDyn2 = OldDb.OpenRecordset(SQL)
Print NewDyn2("Mincst"), NewDyn2("Avgcst"), NewDyn2("Maxcst")
NewDyn2.Close
OldDb.Close
```

FIG. 28.9

A calculation query produces a dynaset with a single record containing the results.

Using a calculation query can replace many lines of program code that would be required to produce the same results. In addition, a query is usually faster than the equivalent program code.

Action Queries   *Action queries* operate directly on a recordset to insert, delete, or modify groups of records based on specific criteria. As with calculation queries, action queries perform the same work that would require many lines of program code. Listing 28.17 shows examples of several action queries.

Listing 28.17   Using Action Queries to Perform Operations on Multiple Records

```
Dim OldDb As Database, NewDyn As Recordset, NewQry As QueryDef
Dim OldWs As WorkSpace
Set OldWs = DBEngine.Workspaces(0)
Set OldDb = OldWs.OpenDatabase("C:\FISH\TRITON.MDB")
'*****************************************
'Calculate the total cost of each purchase.
'*****************************************
SQL = _
    "Update Fishbuys Set [Total Cost] = [Quantity] * [Unit Price]"
Set NewQry = OldDb.CreateQueryDef("Calc Total", SQL)
NewQry.Execute
NewQry.Close
'*************************************
'Delete all records for Fishcode = 1003
'*************************************
SQL = "Delete From Fishbuys WHERE Fishcode = 1003"
```

Part
VI

Ch
28

continues

Listing 28.17 Continued

```
Set NewQry = OldDb.CreateQueryDef("Del Fish", SQL)
NewQry.Execute
NewQry.Close
OldDb.DeleteQueryDef ("Calc Total")
OldDb.DeleteQueryDef ("Del Fish")
OldDb.Close
```

> **CAUTION**
>
> When using action queries to modify groups of records, be very careful when specifying the WHERE clause of the query that defines the records to be modified. Improperly setting this clause can produce disastrous results, such as the deletion of all records in a recordset.

Understanding Other Programming Commands

In this chapter, you have learned how to find specific records and how to move through a group of records. However, in most programs, you also must add, modify, and delete records. The commands covered in the following sections apply only to tables and dynasets (remember that snapshots are not updatable).

Adding Records

To add a new record to a recordset, use the AddNew method. AddNew does not actually add the record to the recordset; it clears the copy buffer to allow information for the new record to be input. To physically add the record after you've put data into the record's fields, use the Update method. Listing 28.18 shows how to add a new record to the recordset.

Listing 28.18 Using *AddNew* and *Update* to Add a Record to the Recordset

```
'********************************
'Use AddNew to set up a new record
'********************************
NewDyn.AddNew
'*********************************************************
'Place the necessary information in the recordset fields
'*********************************************************
NewDyn("Lastname") = "McKelvy"
NewDyn("Firstname") = "Mike"
NewDyn("Address") = "6995 Bay Road"
NewDyn("City") = "Pensacola"
NewDyn("State") = "FL"
NewDyn("Zip") = "32561"
'*********************************************************
'Use the update method to add the new record to the recordset
'*********************************************************
NewDyn.Update
```

CAUTION

Because AddNew places information only in the copy buffer, reusing the AddNew method or moving the record pointer with any Move or Find method (before using the Update method) clears the copy buffer. Any information entered in the record is therefore lost.

Editing Records

In a manner similar to adding a record, you use the Edit method to make changes to a record. The Edit method places a copy of the current record's contents into the copy buffer so that information can be changed. As with AddNew, the changes take effect only when the Update method is executed. Listing 28.19 shows the use of the Edit method.

Listing 28.19   Using *Edit* and *Update* to Change the Data in a Record

```
'***************************************************
'Use the find method to locate the record to be changed.
'***************************************************
NewDyn.FindFirst "Lastname = 'McKelvy'"
'***********************************************
'Check the NoMatch Property to avoid an error
'***********************************************
If NewDyn.NoMatch Then
   MsgBox "Not Found"
Else
'***************************************************
'Use the edit method to set up the record for changes
'***************************************************
   NewDyn.Edit
'***************************************************
'Change the necessary information in the copy buffer
'***************************************************
   NewDyn("Address") = "P. O. Box 380125"
   NewDyn("City") = "Birmingham"
   NewDyn("State") = "AL"
   NewDyn("Zip") = "35238"
'*****************************************************
'Use the update method to write the changes to the recordset
'*****************************************************
   NewDyn.Update
End If
```

Part

VI

Ch

28

CAUTION

Because Edit only places information in the copy buffer, reusing the Edit method or moving the record pointer with any Move or Find method (before using the Update method) clears the copy buffer. Any information entered in the record is therefore lost.

Updating Records

The Update method is used in conjunction with the AddNew and Edit methods to make changes to the recordsets. The Update method writes the information from the copy buffer to the recordset. In the case of AddNew, Update also creates a blank record in the recordset to which the information is written. In a multi-user environment, the Update method also clears the record locks associated with the pending Add or Edit method. (Listings 28.17 and 28.18 show the use of the Update method.)

N O T E If you use Data controls to work with recordsets, the use of the Update method is not required. An update is automatically performed when a move is executed by the Data control. ■

Deleting Records

Deleting a record requires the use of the Delete method, as shown in Listing 28.20. This method removes the record from the recordset and sets the record pointer to a null value.

Listing 28.20   Using *Delete* to Remove a Record from the Recordset

```
'*******************************************************
'Use the find method to locate the record to be deleted
'*******************************************************
NewDyn.FindFirst "Lastname = 'McKelvy'"
'*******************************************
'Check the NoMatch property to avoid an error
'*******************************************
If NewDyn.NoMatch Then
   MsgBox "Not Found"
Else
'*******************************************
'Use the delete method to remove the record
'*******************************************
   NewDyn.Delete
End If
```

CAUTION

After you delete a record, it is gone. You can recover the record only if you issued a BeginTrans command before you deleted the record, in which case you can RollBack the transaction. Otherwise, the only way to get the information back into the database is to re-create the record with the AddNew method.

Incorporating *Add*, *Edit*, and *Delete* Functions in the Sample Case

Figure 28.10 shows some command buttons added to the data entry screen for the sample case. These buttons make use of the add, edit, and delete capabilities described in the preceding sections. The Delete Record button deletes the current record. The Add New Record button blanks out the text boxes to prepare them for new input. The Edit Record button prepares the recordset for editing. As a visual indication of editing, the foreground color of the text boxes also changes. Both the Edit Record and Add New Record buttons cause the normal command buttons (the Top, Previous, Next, Bottom, and Seek Name buttons) to be hidden and two new buttons to be displayed. The new buttons are Save and Cancel. The Save button stores the values displayed in the text boxes to the appropriate fields in the recordset and issues the Update method. The Cancel button terminates the Edit or Add process and restores the original information for the current record. After either Save or Cancel is selected, both buttons disappear and the eight main buttons are again shown.

N O T E I stated previously that deletions and changes to the database are made without confirmation by the user. If you want your program to have confirmation built in, you have to provide it in your code. The easiest way to do this is through the MsgBox function. With this function, you can provide a warning to the user and ask for confirmation. ▨

FIG. 28.10

Add, Edit, and Delete functions are added to the data entry screen with new command buttons.

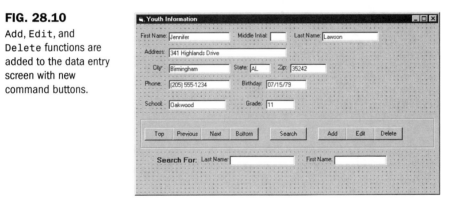

Introducing Transaction Processing

Transaction processing enables you to treat a group of changes, additions, or deletions to a database as a single entity. This is useful when one change to a database depends on another change, and you want to make sure that all changes are made before any of the changes become permanent. For example, you have a point-of-sale application that updates inventory levels as sales are made. As each item is entered for the sales transaction, a change is made to the inventory database. However, you only want to keep the inventory changes if the sale is completed. If the sale is aborted, you want to return the inventory database to its initial state before the sale was started. Transaction processing is a function of the Workspace object and, therefore, affects all databases open in a particular workspace.

Visual Basic provides three methods for transaction processing. These methods perform the following functions:

Part

VI

Ch

28

Transaction Method	Function
BeginTrans	Starts a transaction and sets the initial state of the database.
RollBack	Returns the database to its initial state before the BeginTrans statement was issued. When RollBack is executed, all changes made after the last BeginTrans statement are discarded.
CommitTrans	Permanently saves all changes to the database made since the last BeginTrans statement. After the CommitTrans statement has been issued, the transactions cannot be undone.

Listing 28.21 shows the BeginTrans, RollBack, and CommitTrans methods as they are used in an order entry application. The transactions are used in case the customer cancels the order prior to the completion of the order processing.

Listing 28.21   Using Transaction Processing to Handle Multiple Changes to a Database as One Group

```
OldWs.BeginTrans
'************************************************
'Perform loop until user ends sales transaction
'************************************************
Do While Sales
'************************************************
'Get item number and sales quantity from form
' Input Itemno,SalesQty
' Find item number in inventory
'************************************************
   Inv.FindFirst "ItemNum = " & Itemno
'*************************
'Update inventory quantity
'*************************
   Inv.Edit
   Inv("Quantity") = Inv("Quantity") - SalesQty
   Inv.Update
Loop
'*****************************************
'User either completes or cancels the sale
'*****************************************
If SaleComp Then
   OldWs.CommitTrans
Else
   OldWs.Rollback
End If
```

From Here...

Some of the topics mentioned in this chapter are covered in greater detail in other portions of the book:

- Chapter 26, "Using Data Controls and Reports," explains how to quickly write data access programs by using the Data control.
- Chapter 27, "Doing More with Bound Controls," shows you how to make applications using the Data control do more.
- Chapter 29, "Understanding SQL," explains more about the SQL statements used in creating dynasets, snapshots, and queries.

Understanding SQL

In several of the earlier chapters on working with databases, you saw how SQL statements were used to determine what information would be available in a recordset. This chapter explains how to create those SQL statements and how to do much more with SQL. The examples in this chapter all use an Access database, but the techniques of using SQL are applicable to many database formats. In fact, SQL statements are the cornerstone of working with many database servers, such as Oracle or SQL Server.

There are two basic types of SQL statements that are covered in this chapter: *data-manipulation language* (DML) and *data-definition language* (DDL). Most of the chapter deals with DML statements, and, unless a statement is identified otherwise, you should assume that it is a DML statement. ■

What is SQL?

SQL allows you to quickly retrieve or modify groups of records in your database.

Retrieve selected records

By setting the appropriate clauses, you can work with only a portion of a table instead of having to work with the entire table.

Get information from multiple tables

Using SQL statements allows you to easily combine information from two or more tables.

Calculate summary information

You can find out how many records are in a recordset, or determine the total or average values of specific fields.

Use SQL to modify the information in tables

With a single SQL statement, you can change the values of multiple records in a database. To do the same thing with a program would require a number of statements.

Use SQL to change the structure of the database

SQL statements can even be set up to create a table, modify the structure of a table, or delete a table.

Defining SQL

Structured Query Language (SQL) is a specialized set of programming commands that enable the developer (or end user) to do the following kinds of tasks:

- Retrieve data from one or more tables in one or more databases.
- Manipulate data in tables by inserting, deleting, or updating records.
- Obtain summary information about the data in tables, such as totals; record counts; and minimum, maximum, and average values.
- Create, modify, or delete tables in a database (Access databases only).
- Create or delete indexes for a table (Access databases only).

SQL statements enable the developer to perform functions in one line or a few lines of code that would take 50 or 100 lines of standard BASIC code to perform.

What SQL Does

As the name implies, Structured Query Language statements create a query that is processed by the database engine. The query defines the fields to be processed, the tables containing the fields, the range of records to be included, and, for record retrieval, the order in which the returned records are to be presented.

When retrieving records, a SQL statement usually returns the requested records in a *dynaset*. Recall that a dynaset is an updatable recordset that actually contains a collection of pointers to the base data. Dynasets are temporary and are no longer accessible after they are closed. SQL does have a provision for the times when permanent storage of retrieved records is required.

N O T E   The Microsoft SQL syntax used in this chapter is designed to work with the Jet database engine and is compatible with ANSI SQL (there are, however, some minor differences between Microsoft SQL and ANSI SQL). In addition, if you use SQL commands to query an external database server such as SQL Server or Oracle, read the documentation that comes with the server to verify that the SQL features you want to use are supported and that the syntax of the statements is the same. ■

The Parts of the SQL Statement

A SQL statement consists of three parts:

- **Parameter declarations**—These are optional parameters that are passed to the SQL statement by the program.
- **The manipulative statement**—This part of the statement tells the Query engine what kind of action to take, such as SELECT or DELETE.
- **Options declarations**—These declarations tell the Query engine about any filter conditions, data groupings, or sorts that apply to the data being processed. These include the WHERE, GROUP BY, and ORDER BY clauses.

These parts are arranged as follows:

```
[Parameters declarations] Manipulative statement [options]
```

The parameters declaration section is where you define any parameters used in the SQL statement. Any values defined in the parameters declaration section are assigned before the SQL statement is executed.

▶ For more detailed discussion of the parameters declaration, **see** "Using Parameters," **p. 777**

Most of this chapter uses only the manipulative statement and the options declarations. Using these two parts of the SQL statement, you can create queries to perform a wide variety of tasks. Table 29.1 lists four of the manipulative clauses and their purposes.

Table 29.1   Parts of the Manipulative Statement

Statement	Function
DELETE FROM	Removes records from a table
INSERT INTO	Adds a group of records to a table
SELECT	Retrieves a group of records and places the records in a dynaset or table
UPDATE	Sets the values of fields in a table

Although manipulative statements tell the database engine what to do, the options declarations tell it what fields and records to process. The discussion of the optional parameters makes up the bulk of this chapter. In this chapter, you first look at how the parameters are used with the SELECT statement and then you apply the parameters to the other manipulative statements. Many of the examples in this chapter are based on the sales-transaction table of a sample database that might be used to manage an aquarium business.

The following discussions of the different SQL statements show just the SQL statement syntax. Be aware that these statements can't be used alone in Visual Basic. The SQL statement is always used to create a QueryDef, to create a dynaset or snapshot using the Execute method, or as the RecordSource property of a data control. This section explains the part of a SQL statement. Later in the chapter, the "Using SQL" section explains how these statements are actually used in code. For other examples of using SQL statements, look back through Chapters 26, "Using Data Controls and Reports," 27, "Doing More with Bound Controls," and 28, "Improving Data Access with the Data Access Objects."

N O T E   A QueryDef is a part of the database that stores the query definition. This definition is the SQL statement that you create. ▪

Using *SELECT* Statements

The SELECT statement retrieves records (or specified fields from records) and places the information in a dynaset or table for further processing by a program. The SELECT statement follows this general form:

```
SELECT [predicate] fieldlist FROM tablelist [table relations]
    [range options] [sort options] [group options]
```

N O T E   In my demonstrations of code statements, words in all caps are SQL keywords, and italicized words or phrases are used to indicate terms that a programmer would replace in an actual statement—for example, *fieldlist* would be replaced with Lastname, Firstname. Phrases or words inside square brackets are optional terms.

The various components of the preceding statement are explained in this chapter. Although a SQL statement can be greatly complex, it also can be fairly simple. The simplest form of the SELECT statement is shown here:

```
SELECT * FROM Sales
```

Defining the Desired Fields

The fieldlist part of the SELECT statement is used to define the fields to be included in the output recordset. You can include all fields in a table, selected fields from the table, or even calculated fields based on other fields in the table. You can also choose the fields to be included from a single table or from multiple tables.

The fieldlist portion of the SELECT statement takes the following form:

```
[tablename.]field1 [AS alt1][,[tablename.]field2 [AS alt2]]
```

Selecting All Fields from a Table   The *, or wild-card parameter, is used to indicate that you want to select all the fields in the specified table. The wild card is used in the fieldlist portion of the statement. The statement SELECT * FROM Sales, when used with the sample database you are developing, produces the output recordset shown in Figure 29.1.

Selecting Individual Fields from a Table   Frequently, you need only a few fields from a table. You can specify the desired fields by including a field list in the SELECT statement. Within the field list, the individual fields are separated by commas. In addition, if the desired field has a space in the name, as in Order Quantity, the field name must be enclosed within square brackets, [].The recordset that results from the following SELECT statement is shown in Figure 29.2. A recordset created with fields specified is more efficient than one created with the wild card (*), both in terms of the size of the recordset and speed of creation. As a general rule, you should limit your queries to the smallest number of fields that can accomplish your purpose.

```
SELECT [Item Code], Quantity FROM Sales
```

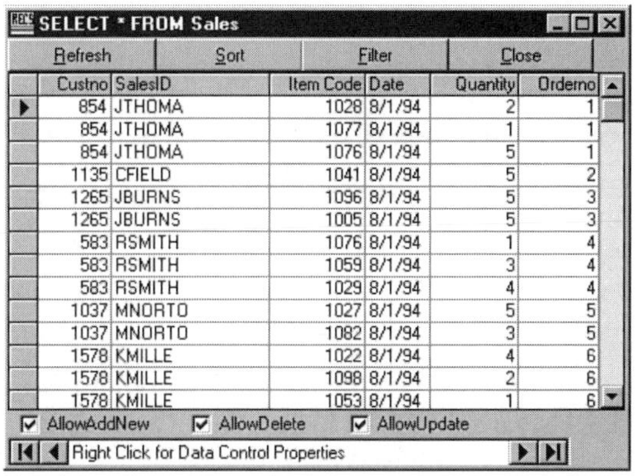

Custno	SalesID	Item Code	Date	Quantity	Orderno
854	JTHOMA	1028	8/1/94	2	1
854	JTHOMA	1077	8/1/94	1	1
854	JTHOMA	1076	8/1/94	5	1
1135	CFIELD	1041	8/1/94	5	2
1265	JBURNS	1096	8/1/94	5	3
1265	JBURNS	1005	8/1/94	5	3
583	RSMITH	1076	8/1/94	1	4
583	RSMITH	1059	8/1/94	3	4
583	RSMITH	1029	8/1/94	4	4
1037	MNORTO	1027	8/1/94	5	5
1037	MNORTO	1082	8/1/94	3	5
1578	KMILLE	1022	8/1/94	4	6
1578	KMILLE	1098	8/1/94	2	6
1578	KMILLE	1053	8/1/94	1	6

FIG. 29.1
Using * in the `fieldlist` parameter selects all fields from the source table.

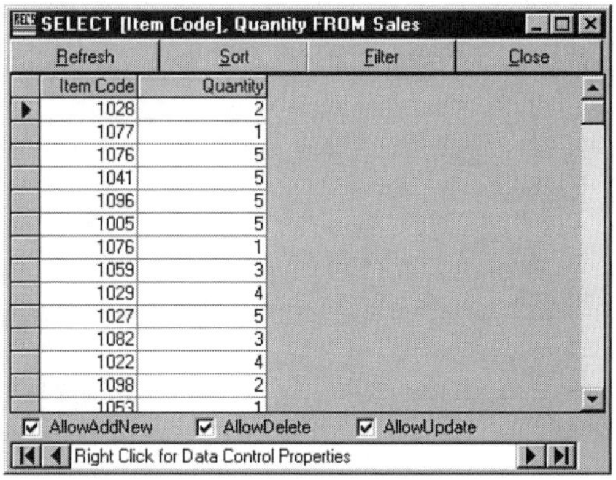

Item Code	Quantity
1028	2
1077	1
1076	5
1041	5
1096	5
1005	5
1076	1
1059	3
1029	4
1027	5
1082	3
1022	4
1098	2
1053	1

FIG. 29.2
This recordset results from specifying individual fields in the `SELECT` statement.

Selecting Fields from Multiple Tables As you might remember from the discussions on database design in Chapter 24, "Database Design and Normalization," you normalize data by placing it in different tables to eliminate data redundancy. When you retrieve this data for viewing or modification, you want to see all the information from the related tables. SQL lets you combine information from various tables into a single recordset.

▶ **See** "Designing a Database," **p. 628**

To select data from multiple tables, you specify three things:

- The table from which each field is selected
- The fields from which you are selecting the data
- The relationship between the tables

Specify the table for each field by placing the table name and a period in front of the field name (for example, `Sales.[Item Code]` or `Sales.Quantity`). (Remember, square brackets must enclose a field name that has a space in it.) You also can use the wild-card identifier (*) after the table name to indicate that you want all the fields from that table.

To specify the tables you're using, place multiple table names (separated by commas) in the `FROM` clause of the `SELECT` statement.

The relationship between the tables is specified either by a `WHERE` clause or by a `JOIN` condition. These elements are discussed later in this chapter.

The statement in Listing 29.1 is used to retrieve all fields from the Sales table and the Item Description and Retail fields from the Retail Items table. These tables are related by the Item Code field. Figure 29.3 shows the results of the statement.

FIG. 29.3
Selecting fields from multiple tables produces a combined recordset.

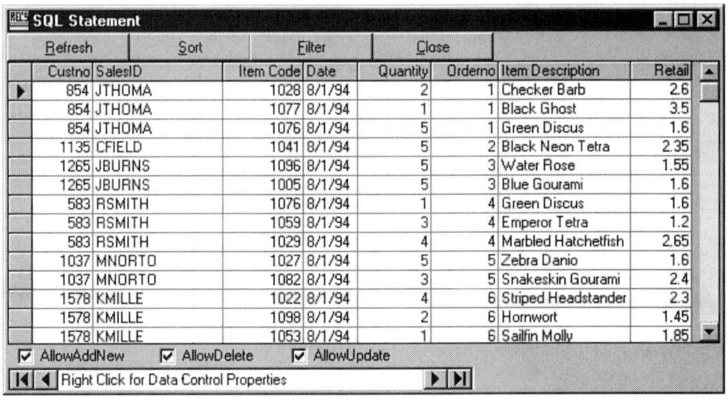

Custno	SalesID	Item Code	Date	Quantity	Orderno	Item Description	Retail
854	JTHOMA	1028	8/1/94	2	1	Checker Barb	2.6
854	JTHOMA	1077	8/1/94	1	1	Black Ghost	3.5
854	JTHOMA	1076	8/1/94	5	1	Green Discus	1.6
1135	CFIELD	1041	8/1/94	5	2	Black Neon Tetra	2.35
1265	JBURNS	1096	8/1/94	5	3	Water Rose	1.55
1265	JBURNS	1005	8/1/94	5	3	Blue Gourami	1.6
583	RSMITH	1076	8/1/94	1	4	Green Discus	1.6
583	RSMITH	1059	8/1/94	3	4	Emperor Tetra	1.2
583	RSMITH	1029	8/1/94	4	4	Marbled Hatchetfish	2.65
1037	MNORTO	1027	8/1/94	5	5	Zebra Danio	1.6
1037	MNORTO	1082	8/1/94	3	5	Snakeskin Gourami	2.4
1578	KMILLE	1022	8/1/94	4	6	Striped Headstander	2.3
1578	KMILLE	1098	8/1/94	2	6	Hornwort	1.45
1578	KMILLE	1053	8/1/94	1	6	Sailfin Molly	1.85

NOTE The listing shows an underscore character at the end of each of the first three lines. This is used to break the lines for the purpose of page-width in the book. When you enter the expressions, they need to be on a single line.

Listing 29.1 Sales.txt—Selecting Fields from Multiple Tables in a SQL Statement

```
SELECT Sales.*, [Retail Items].[Item Description], _
    [Retail Items].Retail  _
    FROM Sales, [Retail Items]  _
    WHERE Sales.[Item Code]=[Retail Items].[Item Code]
```

NOTE You can leave out the table name when specifying fields as long as the requested field is present only in one table in the list. However, it is very good programming practice to include the table name, both for reducing the potential for errors and for readability of your code.

Creating Calculated Fields   The example in Listing 29.1 has customer-order information consisting of the item ordered, quantity of the item, and the retail price. Suppose that you also want to access the total cost of the items. You can achieve this by using a *calculated field* in the SELECT statement. A calculated field can be the result of an arithmetic operation on numeric fields (for example, Price * Quantity) or the result of string operations on text fields (for example, Lastname & Firstname). For numeric fields, you can use any standard arithmetic operation (+, -, *, /, ^). For strings, you can use the concatenation operator (&). In addition, you can use Visual Basic functions to perform operations on the data in the fields (for example, you can use the MID$ function to extract a substring from a text field, the UCASE$ function to place text in uppercase letters, or the SQR function to calculate the square root of a number). Listing 29.2 shows how some of these functions can be used in the SELECT statement.

Listing 29.2   Totprice.txt—Creating a Variety of Calculated Fields with the *SELECT* Statement

```
'****************************************
'Calculate the total price for the items
'****************************************
SELECT [Retail Items].Retail * Sales.Quantity FROM _
      [Retail Items],Sales _
      WHERE Sales.[Item Code]=[Retail Items].[Item Code]
'******************************************************************
'Create a name field by concatenating the Lastname and
'Firstname fields
'******************************************************************
SELECT Lastname & ', ' & Firstname FROM Customers
'******************************************************************
'Create a customer ID using the first 3 letters of the Lastname
' and Firstname fields and make all letters uppercase.
'******************************************************************
SELECT UCASE$(MID$(Lastname,1,3)) & UCASE$(MID$(Firstname,1,3)) _
    FROM Customers
'******************************************************************
'Determine the square root of a number for use in a data report.
'******************************************************************
SELECT Datapoint, SQR(Datapoint) FROM Labdata
```

In the listing, no field name is specified for the calculated field. The Query engine automatically assigns a name such as Expr1001 for the first calculated field. The next section, "Specifying Alternative Field Names," describes how you can specify a name for the field.

Calculated fields are placed in the recordset as read-only fields—they can't be updated. In addition, if you update the base data used to create the field, the changes are not reflected in the calculated field.

N O T E If you use a calculated field with a data control, it is best to use a label control to show the contents of the field. This prevents the user from attempting to update the field and causing an error. You could also use a text box with the locked property set to `True`. (You can learn more about the Data control and bound controls by reviewing Chapter 26, "Using Data Controls and Reports," and Chapter 27, "Doing More with Bound Controls.") If you use a text box, you might want to change the background color to indicate to the user that the data cannot be edited. █

Specifying Alternative Field Names Listing 29.2 created calculated fields to include in a recordset. For many applications, you will want to use a name for the field other than the one automatically created by the query engine.

You can change the syntax of the SELECT statement to give the calculated field a name. You assign a name by including the AS clause and the desired name after the definition of the field (refer to the second part of Listing 29.3). If you want, you can also use this technique to assign a different name to a standard field.

Listing 29.3   Custname.txt—Accessing a Calculated Field's Value and Naming the Field

```
'***********************************************
'Set up the SELECT statement without the name
'***********************************************
Dim NewDyn As RecordSet
SQL = "SELECT Lastname & ', ' & Firstname FROM Customers"
'*****************************************
'Create a dynaset from the SQL statement
'*****************************************
NewDyn = OldDb.OpenRecordset(SQL)
'*********************************
'Get the value of the created field
'*********************************
Person = NewDyn.Recordset(0)
'*****************************************************************
'Set up the SELECT statement and assign a name to the field
'*****************************************************************
SQL = "SELECT Lastname & ', ' & Firstname As Name FROM Customers"
'*****************************************
'Create a dynaset from the SQL statement
'*****************************************
NewDyn = OldDb.OpenRecordset(SQL)
'*********************************
'Get the value of the created field
'*********************************
Person = NewDyn.Recordset("Name")
```

Specifying the Data Sources

In addition to telling the database engine what information you want, you must tell it in which table to find the information. This is done with the FROM clause of the SELECT statement. Here is the general form of the FROM clause:

```
FROM table1 [IN data1] [AS alias1][,table2 [IN data2] [AS alias2]]
```

Various options of the FROM clause are discussed in the following sections.

Specifying the Table Names   The simplest form of the FROM clause is used to specify a single table. This is the form of the clause used in this statement:

```
SELECT * FROM Sales
```

The FROM clause can also be used to specify multiple tables (refer to Listing 29.1). When specifying multiple tables, separate the table names with commas. Also, if a table name has an embedded space, the table name must be enclosed in square brackets, [] (refer to Listing 29.1).

Using Tables in Other Databases   As you develop more applications, you might have to pull data together from tables in different databases. For example, you might have a ZIP Code database that contains the city, state, and ZIP Code for every postal code in the United States. You do not want to have to duplicate this information in a table for each of your database applications that requires it. The SELECT statement lets you store that information once in its own database and then pull it in as needed. To retrieve the information from a database other than the current one, you use the IN portion of the FROM clause. The SELECT statement for retrieving the ZIP Code information along with the customer data is shown in Listing 29.4.

Listing 29.4   Getcust.txt—Retrieving Information from More than One Database

```
'****************************************************************
'We are working from the TRITON database which is already open.
'****************************************************************
SELECT Customers.Lastname, Customers.Firstname, Zipcode.City, _
    Zipcode.State  FROM Customers, Zipcode IN USZIPS  _
    WHERE Customers.Zip = Zipcode.Zip
```

Assigning an Alias Name to a Table   Notice the way the table name for each of the desired fields was listed in Listing 29.4. Because these table names are long and there are a number of fields, the SELECT statement is fairly long. The statement gets much more complex with each field and table you add. In addition, typing long names each time increases the chances of making a typo.

To alleviate this problem, you can assign the table an alias by using the AS portion of the FROM clause. Using AS, you can assign a unique, shorter name to each table. This alias can be used in all the other clauses in which the table name is needed. Listing 29.5 is a rewrite of the code from Listing 29.4, using the alias CS for the Customers table and ZP for the Zipcode table.

Listing 29.5   Alias.txt—Using a Table Alias to Cut Down on Typing

```
'*******************************************************
'We use aliases to make the statement easier to enter.
'*******************************************************
SELECT CS.Lastname, CS.Firstname, ZP.City, ZP.State  _
    FROM Customers AS CS, Zipcode IN USZIPS AS ZP    _
    WHERE CS.Zip = ZP.Zip
```

Using *ALL*, *DISTINCT*, or *DISTINCTROW* Predicates

In most applications, you select all records that meet specified criteria. You can do this by specifying the ALL predicate in front of your field names or by leaving out any predicate specification (ALL is the default behavior). Therefore, the following two statements are equivalent:

```
SELECT * FROM Customers
SELECT ALL * FROM Customers
```

There might be times, however, when you want to determine the unique values of fields. For these times, use the DISTINCT or DISTINCTROW predicate. The DISTINCT predicate causes the database engine to retrieve only one record with a specific set of field values—no matter how many duplicates exist. For a record to be rejected by the DISTINCT predicate, its values for all the selected fields must match those of another record. For example, if you are selecting first and last names, you can retrieve several people with the last name Smith, but you can't retrieve multiple occurrences of Adam Smith.

If you want to eliminate records that are completely duplicated, use the DISTINCTROW predicate. DISTINCTROW compares the values of all fields in the table, whether or not they are among the selected fields. For the sample database, you can use DISTINCTROW to determine which products have been ordered at least once. DISTINCTROW has no effect if the query is on only a single table.

Listing 29.6 shows the uses of DISTINCT and DISTINCTROW.

Listing 29.6   Distinct.txt—Obtaining Unique Records with the *DISTINCT* or *DISTINCTROW* Predicates

```
'*****************************
'Use of the DISTINCT predicate
'*****************************
SELECT DISTINCT [Item Code] FROM Sales
```

```
'********************************
'Use of the DISTINCTROW predicate
'********************************
SELECT DISTINCTROW [Item Code] FROM [Retail Items], Sales _
    [Retail Items] INNER JOIN Sales _
    ON [Retail Items].[Item Code]=Sales.[Item Code]
```

Setting Table Relationships

When you design a database structure, you use key fields so that you can relate the tables in the database. For example, you use a salesperson ID in the Customers table to relate to the salesperson in the Salesperson table. You do this so that you don't have to include all the salesperson data with every customer record. You use these same key fields in the SELECT statement to set the table relationships so that you can display and manipulate the related data. That is, when you view customer information, you want to see the salesperson's name, not his or her ID.

You can use two clauses to specify the relationships between tables:

- ■ JOIN—This combines two tables, based on the contents of specified fields in each table and the type of JOIN.

- ■ WHERE—This usually is used to filter the records returned by a query, but it can be used to emulate an INNER JOIN. You will take a look at the INNER JOIN in the following section.

N O T E Using the WHERE clause to join tables creates a read-only recordset. To create a modifiable recordset, you must use the JOIN clause. ■

Using a *JOIN* Clause   The basic format of the JOIN clause is as follows:

```
table1 {INNER¦LEFT¦RIGHT} JOIN table2 ON table1.key1 = table2.key2
```

The Query engine used by Visual Basic (also used by Access, Excel, and other Microsoft products) supports three JOIN clauses: INNER, LEFT, and RIGHT. Each of these clauses returns records that meet the JOIN condition, but each behaves differently in returning records that do not meet that condition. Table 29.2 shows the records returned from each table for the three JOIN conditions. For this discussion, *table1* is the left table and *table2* is the right table. In general, the left table is the first one specified (on the left side of the JOIN keyword) and the right table is the second table specified (on the right side of the JOIN keyword).

N O T E You can use any comparison operator (<, <=, =, >=, >, or <>) in the JOIN clause to relate the two tables. ■

Table 29.2   Records Returned Based on the Type of *JOIN* Used

JOIN Type Table	Records from Left Table	Records from Right Table
INNER	Only records with corresponding record in right table	Only records with corresponding record in left table
LEFT	All records	Only records with corresponding record in left table
RIGHT	Only records with corresponding record in right table	All records

To further understand these concepts, consider the sample database with its Customers and Salesperson tables. In that database, you created a small information set in the tables consisting of ten customers and four salespeople. Two of the customers have no salesperson listed, and one of the salespeople has no customers (he's a new guy!). You select the same fields with each JOIN but specify an INNER JOIN, LEFT JOIN, and RIGHT JOIN (refer to Listing 29.7). Figure 29.4 shows the two base-data tables from which this listing is working. Figure 29.5 shows the resulting recordsets for each of the JOIN operations.

FIG. 29.4

The Customers and Salesmen tables are RIGHT JOINED to match salesmen to their customers.

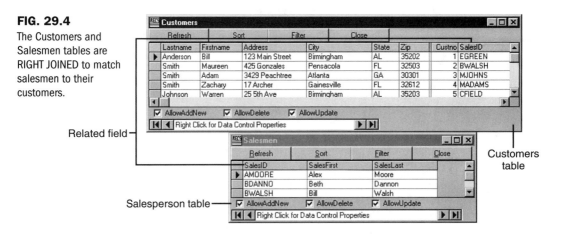

Listing 29.7   Join.txt—Examples of the Three *JOIN* Types

```
'***************************
'Select using an INNER JOIN
'***************************
SELECT CS.Lastname, CS.Firstname, SL.Saleslast, SL.Salesfirst  _
    FROM Customers AS CS, Salesmen AS SL,  _
```

```
        CS INNER JOIN SL ON CS.SalesID=SL.SalesID
'*************************
'Select using an LEFT JOIN
'*************************
SELECT CS.Lastname, CS.Firstname, SL.Saleslast, SL.Salesfirst _
    FROM Customers AS CS, Salesmen AS SL, _
    CS LEFT JOIN SL ON CS.SalesID=SL.SalesID
'*************************
'Select using an RIGHT JOIN
'*************************
SELECT CS.Lastname, CS.Firstname, SL.Saleslast, SL.Salesfirst _
    FROM Customers AS CS, Salesmen AS SL, _
    CS RIGHT JOIN SL ON CS.SalesID=SL.SalesID
```

FIG. 29.5
Different records are
returned with the
different JOIN types.

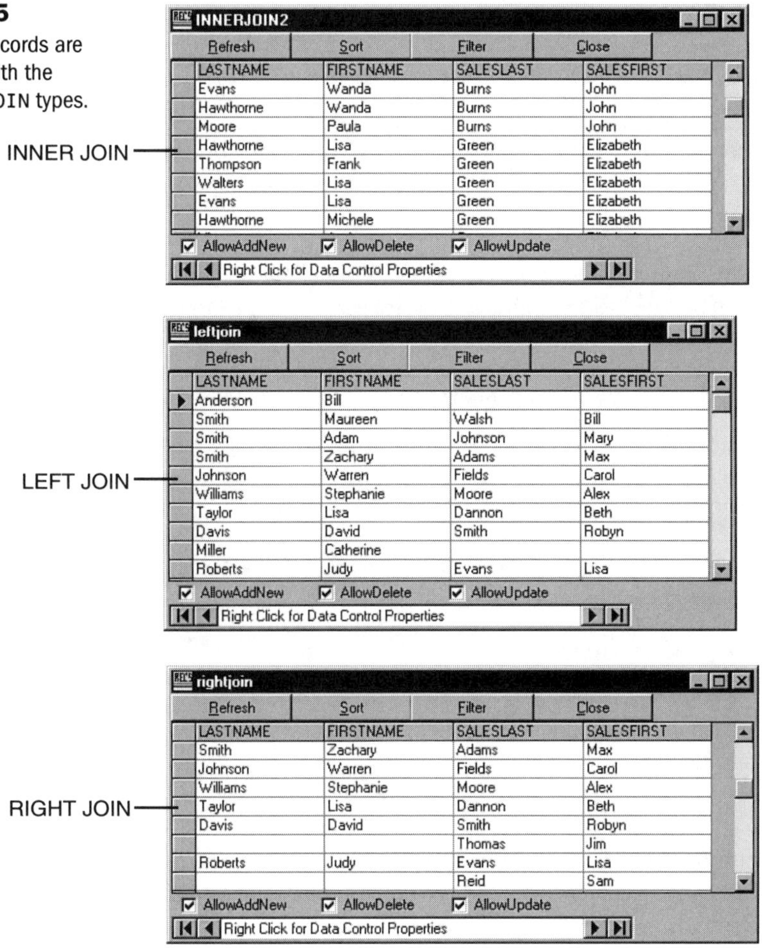

INNER JOIN

INNERJOIN2

LASTNAME	FIRSTNAME	SALESLAST	SALESFIRST
Evans	Wanda	Burns	John
Hawthorne	Wanda	Burns	John
Moore	Paula	Burns	John
Hawthorne	Lisa	Green	Elizabeth
Thompson	Frank	Green	Elizabeth
Walters	Lisa	Green	Elizabeth
Evans	Lisa	Green	Elizabeth
Hawthorne	Michele	Green	Elizabeth

☑ AllowAddNew   ☑ AllowDelete   ☑ AllowUpdate
◀◀ ◀ Right Click for Data Control Properties   ▶ ▶▶

LEFT JOIN

leftjoin

LASTNAME	FIRSTNAME	SALESLAST	SALESFIRST
▶ Anderson	Bill		
Smith	Maureen	Walsh	Bill
Smith	Adam	Johnson	Mary
Smith	Zachary	Adams	Max
Johnson	Warren	Fields	Carol
Williams	Stephanie	Moore	Alex
Taylor	Lisa	Dannon	Beth
Davis	David	Smith	Robyn
Miller	Catherine		
Roberts	Judy	Evans	Lisa

☑ AllowAddNew   ☑ AllowDelete   ☑ AllowUpdate
◀◀ ◀ Right Click for Data Control Properties   ▶ ▶▶

RIGHT JOIN

rightjoin

LASTNAME	FIRSTNAME	SALESLAST	SALESFIRST
Smith	Zachary	Adams	Max
Johnson	Warren	Fields	Carol
Williams	Stephanie	Moore	Alex
Taylor	Lisa	Dannon	Beth
Davis	David	Smith	Robyn
		Thomas	Jim
Roberts	Judy	Evans	Lisa
		Reid	Sam

☑ AllowAddNew   ☑ AllowDelete   ☑ AllowUpdate
◀◀ ◀ Right Click for Data Control Properties   ▶ ▶▶

Note that, in addition to returning the salesperson with no customers, the RIGHT JOIN returned all customer records for each of the other salespeople, not just a single record. This is because a RIGHT JOIN is designed to return all the records from the right table, even if they have no corresponding record in the left table.

Using the *WHERE* Clause   You can use the WHERE clause to relate two tables. The WHERE clause has the same effect as an INNER JOIN. Listing 29.8 shows the same INNER JOIN as Listing 29.7, this time using the WHERE clause instead of the INNER JOIN.

Listing 29.8   Where.txt—A *WHERE* Clause Performing the Same Function as an *INNER JOIN*

```
'****************************************
'Select using WHERE to relate two tables
'****************************************
SELECT CS.Lastname, CS.Firstname, SL.Saleslast, SL.Salesfirst  _
    FROM Customers AS CS, Salesmen AS SL,  _
    WHERE CS.SalesID=SL.SalesID
```

Setting the Filter Criteria

One of the most powerful features of SQL commands is that you can control the range of records to be processed by specifying a filter condition. You can use many types of filters, such as Lastname = "Smith", Price < 1, or birthday between 5/1/94 and 5/31/94. Although the current discussion is specific to the use of filters in the SELECT command, the principles shown here also work with other SQL commands, such as DELETE and UPDATE.

Filter conditions in a SQL command are specified using the WHERE clause. The general format of the WHERE clause is as follows:

WHERE *logical-expression*

There are four types of *predicates* (logical statements that define the condition) that you can use with the WHERE clause. These are shown in the following table:

Predicate	Action
Comparison	Compares a field to a given value
LIKE	Compares a field to a pattern (for example, A*)
IN	Compares a field to a list of acceptable values
BETWEEN	Compares a field to a range of values

Using the Comparison Predicate   As its name suggests, the *comparison predicate* is used to compare the values of two expressions. There are six comparison operators (the symbols that describe the comparison type) that you can use; the operators and their definitions are summarized in Table 29.3.

Table 29.3   Comparison Operators Used in the *WHERE* Clause

Operator	Definition
<	Less than
<=	Less than or equal to
=	Equal to
>=	Greater than or equal to
>	Greater than
<>	Not equal to

Here is the generic format of the comparison predicate:

```
expression1 comparison-operator expression2
```

For all comparisons, both expressions must be of the same type (for example, both must be numbers or both must be text strings). Several comparisons of different types are shown in Listing 29.9. The comparison values for strings and dates require special formatting. Any strings used in a comparison must be enclosed in single quotes (for example, 'Smith' or 'AL'). Likewise, dates must be enclosed between pound signs (for example, #5/15/94#). The quotes and the pound signs tell the Query engine the type of data that is being passed. Note that numbers do not need to be enclosed within special characters.

Listing 29.9   Compare.txt—Comparison Operators Used with Many Types of Data

```
'*********************************************************
'Comparison of text data using customer table as source
'*********************************************************
SELECT * FROM Customers WHERE Lastname='Smith'
'****************************************************
'Comparison of numeric data using Retail Items table
'****************************************************
SELECT * FROM [Retail Items] WHERE Retail<2
'*****************************************
'Comparison of date data using Sales table
'*****************************************
SELECT * FROM Sales WHERE Date>#8/15/94#
```

Using the *LIKE* Predicate   With the LIKE predicate, you can compare an *expression* (that is, a field value) to a pattern. The LIKE predicate lets you make comparisons such as last names starts with *S*, titles containing *SQL*, or five-letter words starting with *M* and ending with *H*. You use the wild cards * and ? to create the patterns. The actual predicates for these comparisons would be Lastname LIKE 'S*', Titles LIKE '*SQL*', and Word LIKE 'M???H', respectively.

The LIKE predicate is used exclusively for string comparisons. The format of the LIKE predicate is as follows:

```
expression LIKE pattern
```

The patterns defined for the LIKE predicate make use of wild-card matching and character-range lists. When you create a pattern, you can combine some of the wild cards and character lists to allow greater flexibility in the pattern definition. When used, character lists must meet three criteria:

- The list must be enclosed within square brackets.
- The first and last characters must be separated by a hyphen.
- The range of the characters must be defined in ascending order (for example, a z, and not z a).

In addition to using a character list to match a character in the list, you can precede the list with an exclamation point to indicate that you want to exclude the characters in the list. Table 29.4 shows the type of pattern matching you can perform with the LIKE predicate. Listing 29.10 shows the use of the LIKE predicate in several SELECT statements.

Table 29.4 The *LIKE* Predicate Using a Variety of Pattern Matching

Wild Card	Used to Match	Example Pattern	Example Results
*	Multiple characters	S*	Smith, Sims, sheep
?	Single character	an?	and, ant, any
#	Single digit	3524#	35242, 35243
[list]	Single character in list	[c-f]	d, e, f
[!list]	Single character not in list	[!c-f]	a, b, g, h
combination	Specific to pattern	a?t*	art, antique, artist

Listing 29.10 Like.txt—Use the *LIKE* Predicate for Pattern-Matching

```
'***************************
'Multiple character wild card
'***************************
SELECT * FROM Customers WHERE Lastname LIKE 'S*'
'**************************
'Single character wild card
'************************
SELECT * FROM Customers WHERE State LIKE '?L'
'***********************
```

```
'Character list matching
'***********************
SELECT * FROM Customers WHERE MID$(Lastname,1,1) LIKE '[a-f]'
```

Using the *IN* Predicate The IN predicate lets you determine whether the expression is one of several values. Using the IN predicate, you can check state codes for customers to determine whether the customer's state matches a sales region. This example is shown in the following sample code:

```
SELECT * FROM Customers WHERE State IN ('AL', 'FL', 'GA')
```

Using the *BETWEEN* Predicate The BETWEEN predicate lets you search for expressions with values within a range of values. You can use the BETWEEN predicate for string, numeric, or date expressions. The BETWEEN predicate performs an *inclusive search*, meaning that if the value is equal to one of the endpoints of the range, the record is included. You can also use the NOT operator to return records outside the range. The form of the BETWEEN predicate is as follows:

```
expression [NOT] BETWEEN value1 AND value2
```

Listing 29.11 shows the use of the BETWEEN predicate in several scenarios.

Listing 29.11   Between.txt—Using the *BETWEEN* Predicate to Check an Expression Against a Range of Values

```
'*****************
'String comparison
'*****************
SELECT * FROM Customers WHERE Lastname BETWEEN 'M' AND 'W'
'******************
'Numeric comparison
'******************
SELECT * FROM [Retail Items] WHERE Retail BETWEEN 1 AND 2.5
'***************
'Date comparison
'***************
SELECT * FROM Sales WHERE Date BETWEEN #8/01/94# AND #8/10/94#
'**********************
'Use of the NOT operator
'**********************
SELECT * FROM Customers WHERE Lastname NOT BETWEEN 'M' AND 'W'
```

Combining Multiple Conditions The WHERE clause can also accept multiple conditions so that you can specify filtering criteria on more than one field. Each individual condition of the multiple conditions is in the form of the conditions described in the preceding sections on using predicates. These individual conditions are then combined using the logical operators AND and OR. By using multiple-condition statements, you can find all the Smiths in the Southeast, or you can find anyone whose first or last name is Scott. Listing 29.12 shows the statements for these examples. Figure 29.6 shows the recordset resulting from a query search for Scott.

> **Listing 29.12 Andor.txt—Combining Multiple *WHERE* Conditions with**
> ***AND* or *OR***
>
> ```
> '*******************************
> 'Find all Smiths in the Southeast
> '*******************************
> SELECT * FROM Customers WHERE Lastname = 'Smith' AND   _
>     State IN ('AL', 'FL', 'GA')
> '**************************************************
> 'Find all occurrences of Scott in first or last name
> '**************************************************
> SELECT * FROM Customers WHERE Lastname = 'Scott'  _
>     OR Firstname = 'Scott'
> ```

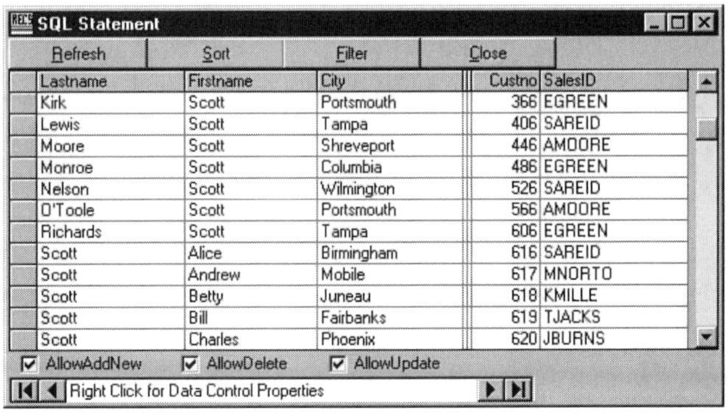

FIG. 29.6

You can use multiple conditions to enhance a WHERE clause.

Setting the Sort Conditions

In addition to specifying the range of records to process, you can also use the SELECT statement to specify the order in which you want the records to appear in the output dynaset. The SELECT statement controls the order in which the records are processed or viewed. Sorting the records is done by using the ORDER BY clause of the SELECT statement.

You can specify the sort order with a single field or with multiple fields. If you use multiple fields, the individual fields must be separated by commas.

The default sort order for all fields is ascending (that is, A Z, 0 9). You can change the sort order for any individual field by specifying the DESC keyword after the field name (the DESC keyword affects only the one field, not any other fields in the ORDER BY clause). Listing 29.13 shows several uses of the ORDER BY clause. Figure 29.7 shows the results of these SELECT statements.

N O T E When you're sorting records, the presence of an index for the sort field can significantly speed up the SQL query. ■

FIG. 29.7
The ORDER BY clause specifies the sort order of the dynaset.

Note that first names are out of order.

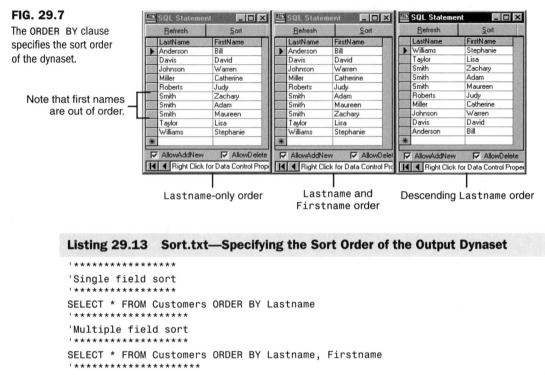

Lastname-only order   Lastname and   Descending Lastname order
                           Firstname order

Listing 29.13   Sort.txt—Specifying the Sort Order of the Output Dynaset

```
'*****************
'Single field sort
'*****************
SELECT * FROM Customers ORDER BY Lastname
'*******************
'Multiple field sort
'*******************
SELECT * FROM Customers ORDER BY Lastname, Firstname
'**********************
'Descending order sort
'**********************
SELECT * FROM Customers ORDER BY Lastname DESC, Firstname
```

Using Aggregate Functions

You can use the SELECT statement to perform calculations on the information in your tables by using the SQL *aggregate functions*. To perform the calculations, define them as a field in your SELECT statement, using the following syntax:

`function(expression)`

The expression can be a single field or a calculation based on one or more fields, such as Quantity * Price or SQR(Datapoint). The Count function can also use the wild card * as the expression, because Count returns only the number of records. Table 29.5 shows the 11 aggregate functions available in Microsoft SQL.

Table 29.5   Aggregate Functions Provide Summary Information About Data in the Database

Function	Returns
Avg	The arithmetic average of the field for the records that meet the WHERE clause
Count	The number of records that meet the WHERE clause
Min	The minimum value of the field for the records that meet the WHERE clause
Max	The maximum value of the field for the records that meet the WHERE clause
Sum	The total value of the field for the records that meet the WHERE clause
First	The value of the field for the first record in the recordset
Last	The value of the field for the last record in the recordset
StDev	The standard deviation of the values of the field for the records that meet the WHERE clause
StDevP	The standard deviation of the values of the field for the records that meet the WHERE clause
Var	The variance of the values of the field for the records that meet the WHERE clause
VarP	The variance of the values of the field for the records that meet the WHERE clause

N O T E   In Table 29.5, StDev and StDevP seem to perform the same function. The same is true of Var and VarP. The difference between the functions is that the StDevP and VarP evaluate populations where StDev and Var evaluate samples of populations.

As with other SQL functions, these aggregate functions operate only on the records that meet the filter criteria specified in the WHERE clause. Aggregate functions are unaffected by sort order. Aggregate functions return a single value for the entire recordset unless the GROUP BY clause (described in the following section) is used. If GROUP BY is used, a value is returned for each record group. Listing 29.14 shows the SELECT statement used to calculate the minimum, maximum, average, and total sales amounts, as well as the total item volume from the Sales table in the sample case. Figure 29.8 shows the output from this query.

FIG. 29.8

The table shows the summary information from aggregate functions.

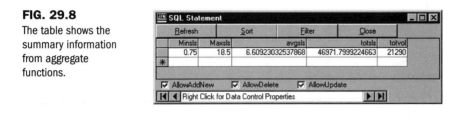

Listing 29.14   Summary.txt—Using Aggregate Functions to Provide Summary Information

```
SELECT Min(SL.Quantity * RT.Retail) AS Minsls,  _
    Max(SL.Quantity * RT.Retail) AS Maxsls,  _
    Avg(SL.Quantity * RT.Retail) AS Avgsls,  _
    Sum(SL.Quantity * RT.Retail) AS Totsls,  _
    Sum(SL.Quantity) AS Totvol  _
    FROM Sales AS SL, [Retail Items] AS RT  _
    WHERE SL.[Item Code]=RT.[Item Code]
```

Creating Record Groups

Creating record groups lets you create a recordset that has only one record for each occurrence of the specified field. For example, if your group the Customers table by state, you have one output record for each state. This arrangement is especially useful when combined with the calculation functions described in the preceding sections. When groups are used in conjunction with aggregate functions, you can easily obtain summary data by state, salesperson, item code, or any other desired field.

Most of the time, you want to create groups based on a single field. You can, however, specify multiple fields in the GROUP BY clause. If you do, a record is returned for each unique combination of field values. You can use this technique to get sales data by salesperson and item code. Separate multiple fields in a GROUP BY clause with commas. Listing 29.15 shows an update of Listing 29.14, adding groups based on the salesperson ID. Figure 29.9 shows the results of the query.

Listing 29.15   Group.txt—Using the *GROUP BY* Clause to Obtain Summary Information for Record Groups

```
SELECT SL.SalesID, Min(SL.Quantity * RT.Retail) AS Minsls,  _
    Max(SL.Quantity * RT.Retail) AS Maxsls,  _
    Avg(SL.Quantity * RT.Retail) AS Avgsls,  _
    Sum(SL.Quantity * RT.Retail) AS Totsls,  _
    Sum(SL.Quantity) AS Totvol  _
    FROM Sales AS SL, [Retail Items] AS RT  _
    WHERE SL.[Item Code]=RT.[Item Code]  _
    GROUP BY SL.SalesID
```

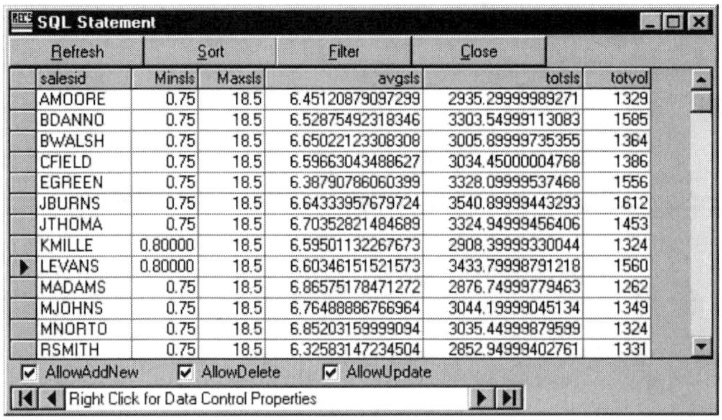

salesid	Minsls	Maxsls	avgsls	totsls	totvol
AMOORE	0.75	18.5	6.45120879097299	2935.29999989271	1329
BDANNO	0.75	18.5	6.52875492318346	3303.54999113083	1585
BWALSH	0.75	18.5	6.65022123308308	3005.89999735355	1364
CFIELD	0.75	18.5	6.59663043488627	3034.45000004768	1386
EGREEN	0.75	18.5	6.38790786060399	3328.09999537468	1556
JBURNS	0.75	18.5	6.64333957679724	3540.89999443293	1612
JTHOMA	0.75	18.5	6.70352821484689	3324.94999456406	1453
KMILLE	0.80000	18.5	6.59501132267673	2908.39999330044	1324
LEVANS	0.80000	18.5	6.60346151521573	3433.79998791218	1560
MADAMS	0.75	18.5	6.86575178471272	2876.74999779463	1262
MJOHNS	0.75	18.5	6.76488886766964	3044.19999045134	1349
MNORTO	0.75	18.5	6.85203159999094	3035.44999879599	1324
RSMITH	0.75	18.5	6.32583147234504	2852.94999402761	1331

FIG. 29.9
Using GROUP BY creates a summary record for each defined group.

The GROUP BY clause can also include an optional HAVING clause. The HAVING clause works similarly to a WHERE clause but examines only the field values of the returned records. The HAVING clause determines which of the selected records to display; the WHERE clause determines which records to select from the base tables. You can use the HAVING clause to display only those salespeople with total sales exceeding $3,000 for the month. Listing 29.16 shows this example; Figure 29.10 shows the output from this listing.

Listing 29.16 Having.txt—The *HAVING* Clause Filters the Display of the Selected Group Records

```
SELECT SL.SalesID, Min(SL.Quantity * RT.Retail) AS Minsls,  _
     Max(SL.Quantity * RT.Retail) AS Maxsls,  _
     Avg(SL.Quantity * RT.Retail) AS Avgsls,  _
     Sum(SL.Quantity * RT.Retail) AS Totsls,  _
     Sum(SL.Quantity) AS Totvol  _
     FROM Sales AS SL, [Retail Items] AS RT  _
     SL INNER JOIN RT ON SL.[Item Code]=RT.[Item Code]  _
     GROUP BY SL.SalesID  _
     HAVING Sum(SL.Quantity * RT.Retail) > 3000
```

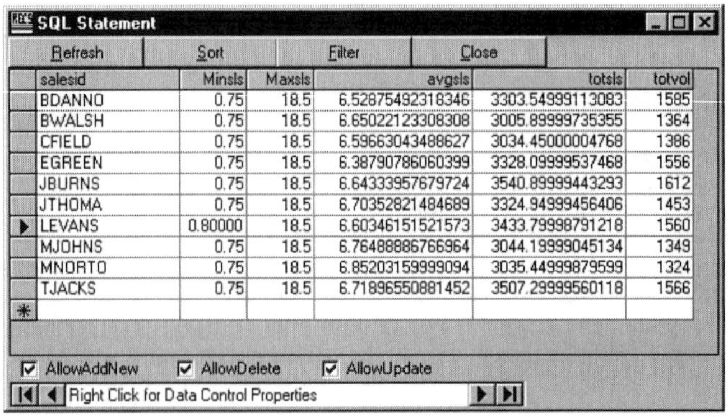

salesid	Minsls	Maxsls	avgsls	totsls	totvol
BDANNO	0.75	18.5	6.52875492318346	3303.54999113083	1585
BWALSH	0.75	18.5	6.65022123308308	3005.89999735355	1364
CFIELD	0.75	18.5	6.59663043488627	3034.45000004768	1386
EGREEN	0.75	18.5	6.38790786060399	3328.09999537468	1556
JBURNS	0.75	18.5	6.64333957679724	3540.89999443293	1612
JTHOMA	0.75	18.5	6.70352821484689	3324.94999456406	1453
LEVANS	0.80000	18.5	6.60346151521573	3433.79998791218	1560
MJOHNS	0.75	18.5	6.76488886766964	3044.19999045134	1349
MNORTO	0.75	18.5	6.85203159999094	3035.44999879599	1324
TJACKS	0.75	18.5	6.71896550881452	3507.29999560118	1566

FIG. 29.10
The HAVING clause limits the display of group records.

Creating a Table

In all the examples of the SELECT statement used earlier in this chapter, the results of the query were output to a dynaset or a snapshot. Because these recordsets are only temporary, their contents exist only as long as the recordset is open. After a close method is used or the application is terminated, the recordset disappears (although any changes made to the underlying tables are permanent).

Sometimes, however, you might want to permanently store the information in the recordset for later use. Do so with the INTO clause of the SELECT statement. With the INTO clause, you specify the name of an output table (and, optionally, the database for the table) in which to store the results. You might want to do this to generate a mailing-list table from your customer list. This mailing-list table can then be accessed by your word processor to perform a mail-merge function or to print mailing labels. Listing 29.4, earlier in this chapter, generated such a list in a dynaset. Listing 29.17 shows the same basic SELECT statement as was used in Listing 29.4, but the new listing uses the INTO clause to store the information in a table.

Listing 29.17   Into.txt—Using the *INTO* Clause to Save Information to a New Table

```
SELECT CS.Firstname & ' ' & CS.Lastname, CS.Address, ZP.City, _
    ZP.State, CS.ZIP INTO Mailings FROM Customers AS CS, _
    Zipcode IN USZIPS AS ZP WHERE CS.Zip = ZP.Zip
```

CAUTION

The table name you specify should be that of a new table. If you specify the name of a table that already exists, that table is overwritten with the output of the SELECT statement.

Using Parameters

So far in all of the clauses, you have seen specific values specified. For example, you specified 'AL' for a state of 1.25 for a price. But what if you don't know in advance what value you want to use in comparison? Well, this is precisely what parameters are used for in a SQL statement. The parameter is to the SQL statement what a variable is to a program statement. The parameter is a placeholder whose value is assigned by your program before the SQL statement is executed.

To use a parameter in your SQL statement, you first have to specify the parameter in the PARAMETERS declaration part of the statement. The PARAMETERS declaration comes before the SELECT or other manipulative clause in the SQL statement. The declaration specifies both the name of the parameter and its data type. The PARAMETERS clause is separated from the rest of the SQL statement by a semicolon.

After you have declared the parameters, you simply place them in the manipulative part of the statement where you want to be able to substitute a value. The following code line shows how a parameter would be used in place of a state ID in a SQL statement:

```
PARAMETERS StateName String; SELECT * FROM Customers
    WHERE State = StateName
```

When you go to run the SQL statement in your program, each parameter is treated like a property of the QueryDef. Therefore, you need to assign a value to each parameter before you use the Execute method. The following code shows you how to set the property value for the preceding SQL statement and open a recordset:

```
Dim OldDb As Database, Qry As QueryDef, Rset As Recordset
Set OldDb = DBEngine.Workspaces(0).OpenDatabase("C:\Triton.Mdb")
Set Qry = OldDb.QueryDefs("StateSelect")
Qry!StateName = "AL"
Set Rset = Qry.OpenRecordset()
```

As you can see, using parameters makes it easy to store your queries in the database and still maintain the flexibility of being able to specify comparison values at runtime.

SQL Action Statements

In the previous section, you saw how the SELECT statement can be used to retrieve records and place the information in a dynaset or table for further processing by a program. This was just one of the four manipulative statements that you defined earlier in this chapter. The three remaining statements are as follows:

- ■ DELETE FROM—An action query that removes records from a table
- ■ INSERT INTO—An action query that adds a group of records to a table
- ■ UPDATE—An action query that sets the values of fields in a table

In the following sections, you take a look at how to use these statements to further refine that data that you are manipulating in a database via a SQL function.

Using the *DELETE* Statement

The DELETE statement is used to create an *action query.* The DELETE statement's purpose is to delete specific records from a table. An action query does not return a group of records into a dynaset as SELECT queries do. Instead, action queries work like program *subroutines.* That is, an action query performs its functions and returns to the next statement in the calling program.

The syntax of the DELETE statement is as follows:

```
DELETE FROM tablename [WHERE clause]
```

The WHERE clause is an optional parameter. If it is omitted, all the records in the target table are deleted. You can use the WHERE clause to limit the deletions to only those records that meet specified criteria. In the WHERE clause, you can use any of the comparison predicates defined in the earlier section "Using the Comparison Predicate." Following is an example of the DELETE statement used to eliminate all customers who live in Florida:

```
DELETE FROM Customers WHERE State='FL'
```

> **CAUTION**
>
> After the DELETE statement is executed, the records are gone and can't be recovered. The only exception is if transaction processing is used. If you're using transaction processing, you can use a ROLLBACK statement to recover any deletions made since the last BEGINTRANS statement was issued.

Using the *INSERT* Statement

Like the DELETE statement, the INSERT statement is another action query. The INSERT statement is used in conjunction with the SELECT statement to add a group of records to a table. The syntax of the statement is as follows:

```
INSERT INTO tablename SELECT rest-of-select-statement
```

You build the SELECT portion of the statement exactly as explained in the first part of this chapter in the section "Using *SELECT* Statements." The purpose of the SELECT portion of the statement is to define the records to be added to the table. The INSERT statement defines the action of adding the records and specifies the table that is to receive the records.

One use of the INSERT statement is to update tables created with the SELECT INTO statement. Suppose that you're keeping a church directory. When you first create the directory, you create a mailing list for the current member list. Each month, as new members are added, you either can rerun the SELECT INTO query and re-create the table, or you can run the INSERT INTO query and add only the new members to the existing mailing list. Listing 29.18 shows the creation of the original mailing list and the use of the INSERT INTO query to update the list.

Listing 29.18 Insert.txt—Using the *INSERT INTO* Statement to Add a Group of Records to a Table

```
'*******************************
'Create a new mailing list table
'*******************************
SELECT CS.Firstname & ' ' & CS.Lastname, CS.Address, ZP.City, _
    ZP.State, CS.ZIP INTO Mailings FROM Members AS CS, _
    Zipcode IN USZIPS AS ZP WHERE CS.Zip = ZP.Zip
'*********************************
'Update the mailing list each month
'*********************************
INSERT INTO Mailings SELECT CS.Firstname & ' ' & CS.Lastname, _
    CS.Address, ZP.City, ZP.State, CS.ZIP _
    FROM Customers AS CS, Zipcode IN USZIPS AS ZP _
    WHERE CS.Zip = ZP.Zip AND CS.Memdate>Lastmonth
```

Using the *UPDATE* Statement

The UPDATE statement is another action query. It is used to change the values of specific fields in a table. The syntax of the UPDATE statement is as follows:

```
UPDATE tablename SET field = newvalue [WHERE clause]
```

You can update multiple fields in a table at one time by listing multiple *field = newvalue* clauses, separated by commas. The inclusion of the WHERE clause is optional. If it is excluded, all records in the table are changed.

Listing 29.19 shows two examples of the UPDATE statement. The first example changes the salesperson ID for a group of customers, as happens when a salesperson leaves the company and his or her accounts are transferred to someone else. The second example changes the retail price of all retail sales items, as can be necessary to cover increased operating costs.

Listing 29.19   Update.txt—Using the *UPDATE* Statement to Change Field Values for Many Records at Once

```
'**********************************************
'Change the SalesID for a group of customers
'**********************************************
UPDATE Customers SET SalesID = 'EGREEN' WHERE SalesID='JBURNS'
'*********************************************************
'Increase the retail price of all items by five percent
'*********************************************************
UPDATE [Retail Items] SET Retail = Retail * 1.05
```

Using Data-Definition-Language Statements

Data-definition-language statements (DDLs) let you create, modify, and delete tables and indexes in a database with a single statement. For many situations, these statements take the place of the data-access-object methods described in Chapter 24, "Database Design and Normalization." However, there are some limitations to using the DDL statements. The main limitation is that these statements are supported only for Jet databases (remember that data-access objects can be used for any database accessed with the Jet engine). The other limitation of DDL statements is that they support only a small subset of the properties of the table, field, and index objects. If you need to specify properties outside of this subset, you must use the methods described in Chapter 24.

Defining Tables with DDL Statements

Three DDL statements are used to define tables in a database:

- CREATE TABLE—Defines a new table in a database
- ALTER TABLE—Changes a table's structure
- DROP TABLE—Deletes a table from the database

Creating a Table with DDL Statements To create a table with the DDL statements, you create a SQL statement containing the name of the table and the names, types, and sizes of each field in the table. The following code shows how to create the Orders table of the sample case:

```
CREATE TABLE Orders (Orderno LONG, Custno LONG, SalesID TEXT (6), _
    OrderDate DATE, Totcost SINGLE)
```

Notice that when you specify the table name and field names, you do not have to enclose the names in quotation marks. However, if you want to specify a name with a space in it, you must enclose the name in square brackets (for example, [Last name]).

When you create a table, you can specify only the field names, types, and sizes. You can't specify optional parameters such as default values, validation rules, or validation error messages. Even with this limitation, the DDL CREATE TABLE statement is a powerful tool that you can use to create many of the tables in a database.

Modifying a Table By using the ALTER TABLE statement, you can add a field to an existing table or delete a field from the table. When adding a field, you must specify the name, type, and (when applicable) the size of the field. You add a field using the ADD COLUMN clause of the ALTER TABLE statement. To delete a field, you only need to specify the field name and use the DROP COLUMN clause of the statement. As with other database-modification methods, you can't delete a field used in an index or a relation. Listing 29.20 shows how to add and then delete a field from the Orders table created in the preceding section.

Listing 29.20   Altertab.txt—Using the *ALTER TABLE* Statement to Add or Delete a Field from a Table

```
'***************************************************
'Add a shipping charges field to the "Orders" table
'***************************************************
ALTER TABLE Orders ADD COLUMN Shipping SINGLE
'*********************************
'Delete the shipping charges field
'*********************************
ALTER TABLE Orders DROP COLUMN Shipping
```

Deleting a Table You can delete a table from a database using the DROP TABLE statement. The following simple piece of code shows how to get rid of the Orders table. Use caution when deleting a table; the table and all its data are gone forever after the command has been executed.

```
DROP TABLE Orders
```

Defining Indexes with DDL Statements

Two DDL statements are designed especially for use with indexes:

■ CREATE INDEX—Defines a new index for a table

■ DROP INDEX—Deletes an index from a table

Creating an Index   You can create a single-field or multi-field index with the CREATE INDEX statement. To create the index, you must give the name of the index, the name of the table for the index, and at least one field to be included in the index. You can specify ascending or descending order for each field. You can also specify that the index is a primary index for the table. Listing 29.21 shows how to create a primary index on customer number and a two-field index with the sort orders specified. These indexes are set up for the Customers table of the sample case.

> **Listing 29.21   Createind.txt—Create Several Types of Indexes with the *CREATE INDEX* Statement**
>
> ```
> '*******************************************
> 'Create a primary index on customer number
> '*******************************************
> CREATE INDEX Custno ON Customers (Custno) WITH PRIMARY
> '*************************************************************
> 'Create a two field index with ascending order on Lastname and
> '   descending order on Firstname.
> '*************************************************************
> CREATE INDEX Name2 ON Customers (Lastname ASC, Firstname DESC)
> ```

Deleting an Index   Getting rid of an index is just as easy as creating one. To delete an index from a table, use the DROP INDEX statement as shown in the following example. These statements delete the two indexes created in Listing 29.21. Notice that you must specify the table name for the index that you want to delete:

```
DROP INDEX Custno ON Customers
DROP INDEX Name2 ON Customers
```

Using SQL

As stated at the beginning of the chapter, you can't place a SQL statement by itself in a program. It must be part of another function. This part of the chapter describes the various methods used to implement the SQL statements.

Executing an Action Query

The Jet engine provides an execute method as part of the database object. The execute method tells the engine to process the SQL query against the database. An action query can be executed by specifying the SQL statement as part of the execute method for a database. An action query can also be used to create a QueryDef. Then the query can be executed on its own. Listing 29.22 shows how both of these methods are used to execute the same SQL statement.

Listing 29.22   Execute.txt—Run SQL Statements with the *DatabaseExecute* or *QueryExecute* Method

```
Dim OldDb AS Database, NewQry AS QueryDef
'*******************************************************
'Define the SQL statement and assign it to a variable
'*******************************************************
SQLstate = "UPDATE Customers SET SalesID = 'EGREEN'"
SQLstate = SQLstate + " WHERE SalesID='JBURNS'"
'*****************************************
'Use the database execute to run the query
'*****************************************
OldDb.Execute SQLstate
'*****************************************
'Create a QueryDef from the SQL statement
'*****************************************
Set NewQry = OldDb.CreateQueryDef("Change Sales", SQLstate)
'*****************************************
'Use the query execute to run the query
'*****************************************
NewQry.Execute
'*******************************************************
'Run the named query with the database execute method
'*******************************************************
OldDb.Execute "Change Sales"
```

Creating a *QueryDef*

Creating a QueryDef lets you name your query and store it in the database with your tables. You can create either an action query or a *retrieval query* (one that uses the SELECT statement). After the query is created, you can call it by name for execution (shown in a listing in the previous section "Executing an Action Query") or for creation of a dynaset (as described in the following section). Listing 29.22 showed how to create a QueryDef called Change Sales that is used to update the salesperson ID for a group of customers.

Creating Dynasets and Snapshots

To use the SELECT statement to retrieve records and store them in a dynaset or snapshot, you must use the SELECT statement in conjunction with the OpenRecordset method. Using the OpenRecordset method, you specify the type of recordset with the options parameter. With this method, you either can use the SELECT statement directly or use the name of a retrieval query that you have previously defined. Listing 29.23 shows these two methods of retrieving records.

Listing 29.23 Createmeth.txt—Using the Create Methods to Retrieve the Records Defined by a *SELECT* Statement

```
Dim OldDb As Database, NewQry As QueryDef, NewDyn As Recordset
Dim NewSnap As Recordset
'********************************************************
'Define the SELECT statement and store it to a variable
'********************************************************
SQLstate = "SELECT RI.[Item Description], SL.Quantity,"
SQLstate = SQLstate & " RI.Retail, _
    SL.Quantity * RI.Retail AS Subtot"
SQLstate = SQLstate & "FROM [Retail Items] AS RI, Sales AS SL"
SQLstate = SQLstate & "WHERE SL.[Item Code]=RI.[Item Code]"
'***********************
'Create dynaset directly
'***********************
Set NewDyn = OldDb.OpenRecordset(SQLstate, dbOpenDynaset)
'***************
'Create QueryDef
'***************
Set NewQry = OldDb.CreateQueryDef("Get Subtotals", SQLstate)
NewQry.Close
'*****************************
'Create snapshot from querydef
'*****************************
Set NewSnap = OldDb.OpenRecordset("Get Subtotals", dbOpenSnapshot)
```

You have seen how SELECT statements are used to create dynasets and snapshots. But, the comparison part of a WHERE clause and the sort list of an ORDER BY clause can also be used to set dynaset properties. The filter property of a dynaset is a WHERE statement without the WHERE keyword. When setting the filter property, you can use all the predicates described in the section "Using the *WHERE* Clause," earlier in this chapter. In a like manner, the sort property of a dynaset is an ORDER BY clause without the ORDER BY keywords.

Using SQL Statements with the Data Control

The data control uses the RecordSource property to create a recordset when the control is loaded. The RecordSource can be a table, a SELECT statement, or a predefined query. Therefore, the entire discussion on the SELECT statement (in the section "Using *SELECT* statements") applies to the creation of the recordset used with a data control.

N O T E When you specify a table name for the RecordSource property, Visual Basic uses the name to create a SELECT statement such as this:

```
SELECT * FROM table
```

Creating SQL Statements

When you create and test your SQL statements, you can program them directly into your code and run the code to see whether they work. This process can be very time-consuming and frustrating, especially for complex statements. There are, however, three easier ways of developing SQL statements that might be available to you:

- The Visual Data Manager Add-in that comes with Visual Basic
- Microsoft Access (if you have a copy)
- Microsoft Query

N O T E Users of Microsoft Excel or Microsoft Office also have access to Microsoft Query, the tool in Access. ▓

The Visual Data Manager and Access both have query builders that can help you create SQL queries. They provide dialog boxes for selecting the fields to include, and they help you with the various clauses. When you have finished testing a query with either application, you can store the query as a QueryDef in the database. This query can then be executed by name from your program. As an alternative, you can copy the code from the query builder into your program, using standard cut-and-paste operations.

Using the Visual Data Manager

The Visual Data Manager is a Visual Basic add-in that allows you to create and modify databases for your Visual Basic programs. The Visual Data Manager also has a window that allows you to enter and debug SQL queries. And if you don't want to try to create the query yourself, VDM has a query builder that makes it easy for you to create queries by making choices in the builder.

N O T E If you want to learn about the inner workings of the Visual Data Manager, it is one of the sample projects installed with Visual Basic. The project file is VISDATA.VBP and is found in the VISDATA folder of the Samples folder. ▓

To start the Visual Data Manager, simply select the Visual Data Manager item from the Add-Ins menu of Visual Basic. After starting the program, open the File menu and select the Open Database item; then select the type of database to open from the submenu. You are presented with a dialog box that allows you to open a database. After the database is opened, a list of the tables and queries in the database appears in the left window of the application. The Visual Data Manager with the Triton.Mdb database open is shown in Figure 29.11.

FIG. 29.11

You can use the Visual Data Manager Add-In to develop SQL queries.

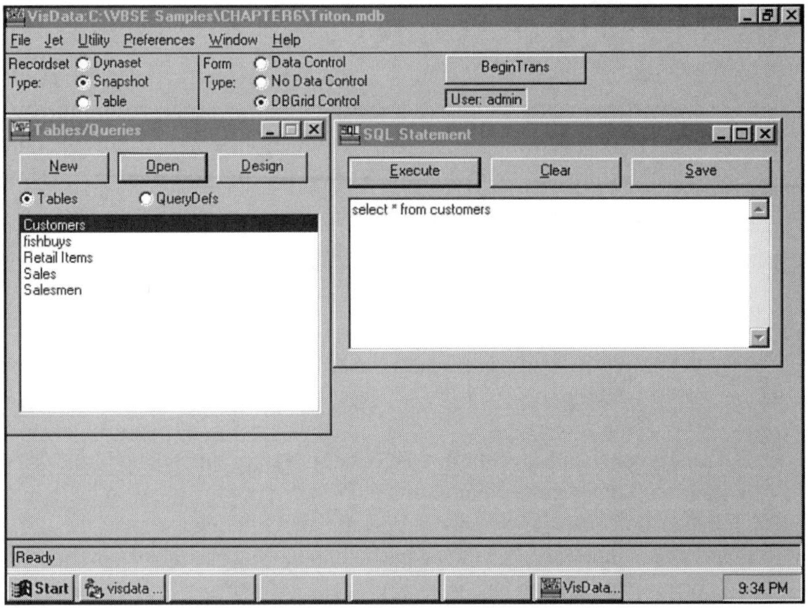

To develop and test SQL statements, first enter the statement in the text box of the SQL dialog box (the one on the right of Figure 29.11). When you're ready to test the statement, click the Execute SQL button. If you're developing a retrieval query, a dynaset is created and the results are displayed in a data entry form (or a grid) if the statement has no errors. If you're developing an action query, a message box appears, telling you that the execution of the query is complete (again, assuming that the statement is correct). If you have an error in your statement, a message box appears informing you of the error.

The Visual Data Manager Add-In also includes a Query Builder. You can access the Query Builder (shown in Figure 29.12) by choosing Query Builder from the Utilities menu of the Visual Data Manager. To create a query with the Query Builder, follow these steps:

1. Select the tables to include from the Tables list.

2. Select the fields to include from the Fields to Show list.

3. Set the WHERE clause (if any) using the Field Name, Operator, and Value drop-down lists at the top of the dialog box.

4. Set the table JOIN conditions (if any) by clicking the Set Table Joins command button.

5. Set a single-field ORDER BY clause (if any) by selecting the field from the Order By Field drop-down box and selecting either the Asc or Desc option.

6. Set a single GROUP BY field (if any) by selecting the field from the Group By Field drop-down box.

FIG. 29.12
The Query Builder
makes it easy to build
SQL statements.

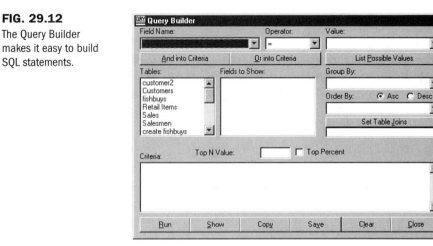

After you have set the Query Builder parameters, you can run the query, display the SQL statement, or copy the query to the SQL statement window. The Query Builder provides an easy way to become familiar with constructing SELECT queries.

When you have developed the query to your satisfaction (either with the Query Builder or by typing the statement directly), you can save the query as a QueryDef in your database. In your Visual Basic code, you can then reference the name of the query you created. Alternatively, you can copy the query from Visual Data Manager and paste it into your application code.

Using Microsoft Access

If you have a copy of Microsoft Access, you can use its query builder to graphically construct queries. You can then save the query as a QueryDef in the database and reference the query name in your Visual Basic code.

One of more creative uses for Access is to reverse-engineer a QueryDef. Microsoft Access allows you to build a graphical representation of the tables and databases for a particular QueryDef entered in SQL format. This reverse-engineering process gives you a unique way to debug or make modifications graphically to an existing query.

Optimizing SQL Performance

Developers always want to get the best possible performance from every aspect of their applications. Wanting high performance out of SQL queries is no exception. Fortunately, there are several methods you can use to optimize the performance of your SQL queries.

Using Indexes

The Microsoft Jet database engine uses an optimization technology called Rushmore. Under certain conditions, Rushmore uses available indexes to try to speed up queries. To take maximum advantage of this arrangement, you can create an index on each of the fields you typically use in a WHERE clause or a JOIN condition. This is particularly true of key fields used to relate tables (for example, the Custno and SalesID fields in the sample database). An index also works better with comparison operators than with the other types of WHERE conditions, such as LIKE or IN.

> **N O T E**   Only certain types of queries are optimizable by Rushmore. For a query to use Rushmore optimization, the WHERE condition must use an indexed field. In addition, if you use the LIKE operator, the expression should begin with a character, not a wild card. Rushmore works with Jet databases and FoxPro and dBase tables. Rushmore does not work with ODBC databases. ■

Compiling Queries

Compiling a query refers to creating a QueryDef and storing it in the database. If the query already exists in the database, the command parser does not have to generate the query each time it is run, and this increases execution speed. If you have a query that is frequently used, create a QueryDef for it.

Keeping Queries Simple

When you're working with a lot of data from a large number of tables, the SQL statements can become quite complex. Complex statements are much slower to execute than simple ones. Also, if you have a number of conditions in WHERE clauses, this increases complexity and slows execution time.

Keep statements as simple as possible. If you have a complex statement, consider breaking it into multiple smaller operations. For example, if you have a complex JOIN of three tables, you might be able to use the SELECT INTO statement to create a temporary table from two of the three and then use a second SELECT statement to perform the final JOIN. There are no hard-and-fast rules for how many tables are too many or how many conditions make a statement too complex. If you're having performance problems, try some different ideas and find the one that works best.

Another way to keep things simple is to try to avoid pattern-matching in a WHERE clause. Because pattern-matching does not deal with discrete values, pattern-matching is hard to optimize. In addition, patterns that use wild cards for the first character are much slower than those that specifically define that character. For example, if you're looking for books about SQL, finding ones with *SQL* anywhere in the title (pattern = "*SQL*") requires looking at every title in the table. On the other hand, looking for titles that start with *SQL* (pattern = "SQL*") lets you skip over most records. If you had a Title index, the search would go directly to the first book on SQL.

Passing SQL Statements to Other Database Engines

Visual Basic has the capability of passing a SQL statement through to an ODBC database server such as SQL Server. When you pass a statement through, the Jet engine does not try to do any processing of the query, but it sends the query to the server to be processed. Remember, however, that the SQL statement must conform to the SQL syntax of the host database.

To use the pass-through capability, set the options parameter in the OpenRecordset or the execute methods to the value of the dbSQLPassThrough constant.

On the Web The project file, SQLDEMO.VBP, available from the Que Web site, contains many of the listings used in this chapter. Each listing is assigned to a command button. Choosing the command button creates a dynaset by using the SQL statement in the listing; the results are displayed in a data-bound grid. The form containing the grid also has a text box that shows the SQL statement. Download the file from **www.mcp.com/info/0-7897/0-7897-1288-1**.

From Here...

This chapter has taught you the basics of using SQL in your database program. You have seen how to select records and how to limit the selection using the WHERE clause. You have also seen how SQL statements can be used to modify the structure of a database and how to use aggregate functions to obtain summary information.

To see how SQL statements are used in programs and with the data control, refer to the following chapters:

- Chapter 24, "Database Design and Normalization," explains how to write data-access programs.
- Chapter 25, "Using the Data Manager," explains how to create databases and queries without the need for Access 95 loaded on your machine.
- Chapter 26, "Using Data Controls and Reports," and Chapter 27, "Doing More with Bound Controls," explain how to use the Data control.

CHAPTER 30

Using the Remote Data Objects

What is client/server computing?

Client/server computing uses a database server to handle many of the data processing tasks. The client works with only a small amount of data returned by the server.

What does ODBC do?

ODBC is a specification that allows your program to communicate with a variety of databases, whether on your local PC or on a mainframe server.

Is there an easy way to work with ODBC databases?

The Remote Data Objects and Remote Data control provide a rich object model that makes working with ODBC databases relatively easy.

How does RDO compare with DAO?

The object model of the Remote Data Objects is very similar to that of the data access objects.

So far in the discussions of accessing databases, the focus has been on using PC-based databases. These types of databases include Access, FoxPro, dBASE, and Paradox. However, Visual Basic is also a great tool for creating front ends for client/server applications. These types of applications are used to access data stored in database servers such as SQL Server and Oracle. Most of your front-end work—such as designing forms and writing code to process information—will be the same whether you are writing an application for a PC database or a client/server database. The key difference is in how you make the connection to the data.

In this chapter, we'll discuss how your Visual Basic programs can easily access data stored in a variety of remote locations through the use of Remote Data Objects (RDO). You'll see how the recent addition of RDO to Visual Basic's repertoire makes short work of writing applications that need to work with remote data. ∎

Database Access Philosophies

Before delving further into actually setting up applications that access client/server databases, you'll take a look at the difference in the philosophy of the two types of database access. In the PC-database world, the information is accessed through the database engine, which is part of the application. For Visual Basic, the Jet engine is a part of your database applications. As you issue commands to retrieve information from the database, the commands are interpreted by the Jet engine and the processing of the commands is done locally on your PC. Whether the database file actually resides on your PC or is located on a file server, the database engine remains on your PC. The application itself contains the logic to directly access the database file. In the client/server world, this is not the case. Your application issues a request for information, usually in the form of a SQL statement. This request is passed to the database server which processes the request and returns the results. This is true client/server computing, in which a database server does the actual processing of the request.

Client/server systems have a number of advantages over just sharing a database file. First, database logic is removed to a central, more maintainable location. For example, suppose you have a program that calculates sales tax based on your company's rules. In a client/server environment, the logic for this calculation process would be located on the database server. This means you can make changes to it in one place, without having to rewrite the client application. Other advantages include being able to distribute processing and separating the user interface design from the business logic.

Introducing ODBC

One method used by Visual Basic to communicate with client/server databases is called *Open Database Connectivity*, or ODBC. ODBC is a component of Microsoft's *Windows Open System Architecture* (WOSA). ODBC provides a set of *application program interface* (API) functions, which makes it easier for a developer to connect to a wide range of database formats. Because of the use of ODBC standards, you can use the same set of functions and commands to access information in a SQL Server, Oracle, or Interbase, even though the actual data-storage systems are quite different. You can even access a number of PC databases using ODBC functions.

Understanding ODBC Drivers

ODBC drivers are the DLLs containing the functions that let you connect to various databases. There are separate drivers for each database type. For many standard formats, such as PC databases and SQL Servers, these drivers are provided with Visual Basic. For other databases, the ODBC driver is provided by the server manufacturer.

> **N O T E**   If you use ODBC in your application, make sure the appropriate drivers are distributed with your application. If you selected the Redistributable ODBC option when installing VB, an ODBC subdirectory should have been created in the Visual Basic program directory. Running Setup.exe will install ODBC drivers, although you will still have to set up your data sources. ▪

ODBC drivers can be one of two types: *single-tier* or *multiple-tier.* A single-tier driver is used to connect to PC-based database systems that may reside on either the local machine or a file server. Multiple-tier drivers are used to connect to client/server databases where the SQL statement is processed by the server, not the local machine.

Each ODBC driver you encounter must contain a basic set of functions, known as the *core-level capabilities.* These basic functions are:

- Providing database connections
- Preparing and execute SQL statements
- Processing transactions
- Returning result sets
- Informing the application of errors

Setting Up an ODBC Data Source

Before you can use ODBC to connect to a database, you must make sure of two things:

- The ODBC drivers are installed on your system.
- You have set up the ODBC data source.

Both of these functions can be accomplished by using the ODBC Manager application. Also, the second function can be accomplished from code, by using the data access objects. Remember, an ODBC driver is used to connect to a *type* of database, for example, SQL Server. An ODBC Data Source is a configuration of an ODBC driver used to connect to a *specific database,* that is, "Accounting Department Database."

N O T E On Microsoft Windows 95 systems, you will find the ODBC manager in the Control Panel, under the Settings item on the Start menu. The icon you are looking for is labeled "32-bit ODBC." You might also have an icon called "ODBC" if you have some older 16-bit programs.

N O T E To ensure that all readers can use the information presented here, the Access ODBC driver is used in all examples. While this is a PC database, the methods used can also be applied to server databases. It is important to remember that connecting to an Access MDB file via ODBC is different than connecting directly through the Jet engine.

Gaining Access to ODBC Drivers   To set up the ODBC Data Sources on your system, you need to use Windows 95's ODBC Data Source Administrator. You will find this in the Control Panel, which is accessible by choosing the Control Panel item from the Settings submenu on the Start menu. The Control Panel is illustrated in Figure 30.1.

FIG. 30.1

The ODBC Data Source Administrator is accessed by selecting the "32-bit ODBC" icon on the Control Panel.

ODBC Data Source Administrator

The ODBC Administrator Dialog Box

If you see different dialog boxes than the ones pictured here when you click the 32-bit ODBC icon, don't panic. As with any product, Microsoft has produced several versions of ODBC. ODBC is included with many of their products, including Office and Visual Basic. Depending on the installation options you chose, you may or may not have the latest version. Older versions of ODBC do not have the "tabbed" dialog style. Fortunately, ODBC is included with VB so you can install it during setup.

When you open the ODBC Manager, you see the ODBC Data Source Administrator dialog box, as shown in Figure 30.2. The Data Source administrator includes several tabs used to add data sources as well as new ODBC drivers.

FIG. 30.2

The Data Sources Administrator dialog box allows you to configure ODBC data sources.

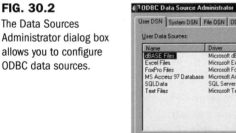

As you'll notice, the titles of the first three tabs in the dialog box end in the letters *DSN*. DSN is an abbreviation for *Data Source Name*. The DSN is the key that your program uses to identify an ODBC Data Source. ODBC takes care of mapping the DSN to the actual driver, server, and database file.

The ODBC Data Sources are divided into three types: user, system, and file. Although the purpose of all DSNs is essentially the same—to provide information about a specific data source—there are differences where and when you can use each type:

- A System DSN, more applicable in Windows NT than Windows 95, is not associated with a particular user profile. This means that once the DSN has been set up, all programs and services running on the machine can access it. For example, if you are using Internet Information Server to connect to a database, you will probably be setting up a System DSN for the database.

- A File DSN stores DSN information in a text file. The text file is an INI file containing information about the database driver and location. It is not associated with a particular machine, so it can be on a network drive.

- A User DSN is the type you will probably use most often. User DSN information is stored in the Registry of the local machine. In Windows NT, each User DSN is associated with a specific user profile and invisible outside of it.

The remaining three tabs in the ODBC Data Source Administrator dialog box are used for informational and debugging purposes. The ODBC Drivers tab, shown in Figure 30.3, displays a list of the ODBC drivers installed on your machine.

Part

VI

Ch

30

FIG. 30.3
The ODBC Drivers tab tells you which drivers are installed on your system.

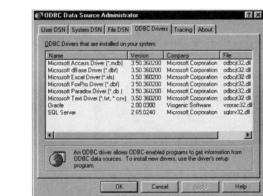

The last tab, the About tab, is very similar to the ODBC Drivers tab. It lists the versions and files used by ODBC itself. You may find these two screens helpful in determining whether or not your users have the correct drivers installed.

Before moving on, note the Tracing tab, pictured in Figure 30.4. This tab allows you to trace each call made by the ODBC Manager to the ODBC Drivers. Remember that ODBC is a means to connect to various databases via some common API functions. The Tracing options allow you to view those API calls. This is something you probably won't do very often, but it is nice to know about.

Creating an ODBC Source with the ODBC Manager To set up a data source for use in your application, you need to know which driver to use and how to configure it. For example, you will need to know the name of the SQL Server or Access MDB file the data resides in. You also will need to come up with a unique name to identify the data source.

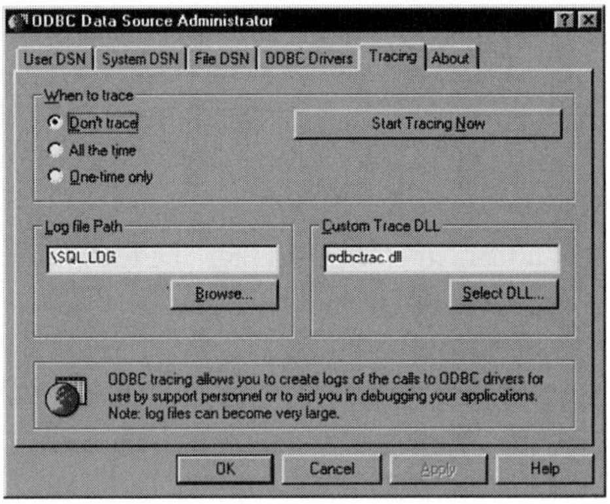

FIG. 30.4

The Tracing tab of the ODBC Administrator is a low-level debugging aid.

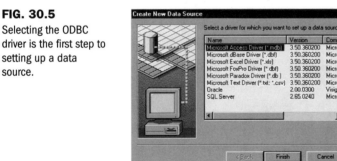

Set up a sample data source now. Go to the User DSN screen and click the Add button to create a new data source. This presents you with the Create New Data Source dialog box, shown in Figure 30.5. In this first dialog box, you choose the ODBC driver that will be used to access the data.

FIG. 30.5

Selecting the ODBC driver is the first step to setting up a data source.

After choosing the driver and clicking the OK button, you are presented with the Setup dialog box for the particular database type associated with the driver. Choose the Microsoft Access Driver and press the Finish button. You will be presented with a dialog box like that in Figure 30.6.

In this dialog box, you provide a name in the Data Source Name box. This is the name you will use in your applications to refer to the data source. You can also choose to include a Description of the data source.

After setting the name, you need to choose the actual database file or server you want to use with your program. For the Access driver, this is done by clicking the Select button of the dialog box. You are then presented with a Select Database dialog box (which is basically an open-file dialog box). Try opening a file by choosing an MDB file on your PC. Figure 30.7 shows a data source called MyDSN linked to the biblio database that comes with Visual Basic.

FIG. 30.6

A Setup dialog box lets you specify the information necessary to connect to an ODBC data source.

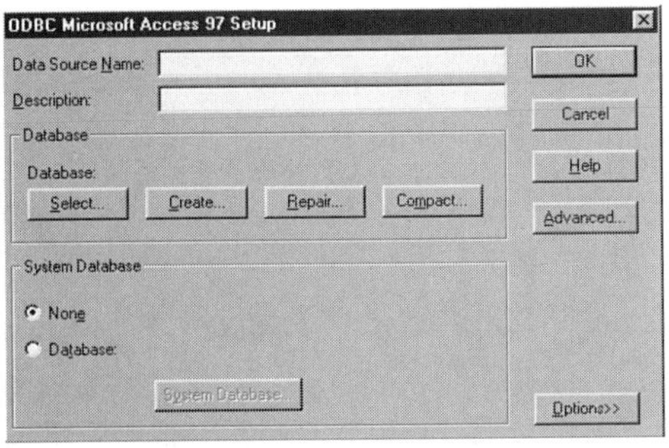

FIG. 30.7

The Access dialog box allows you to select which MDB file you are going to be working with.

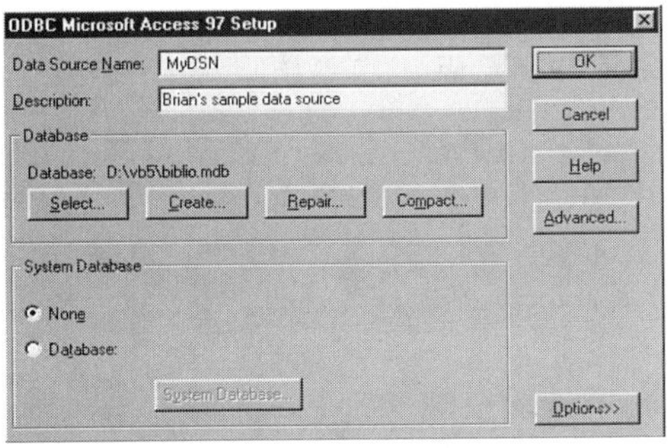

Keep in mind that the setup dialog boxes are driver dependent. In each case, however, you specify both a data-source name and the location of the data. Figure 30.8 shows the dialog box for Microsoft SQL Server.

FIG. 30.8

The SQL Server dialog box requires you to specify the server where the information is located.

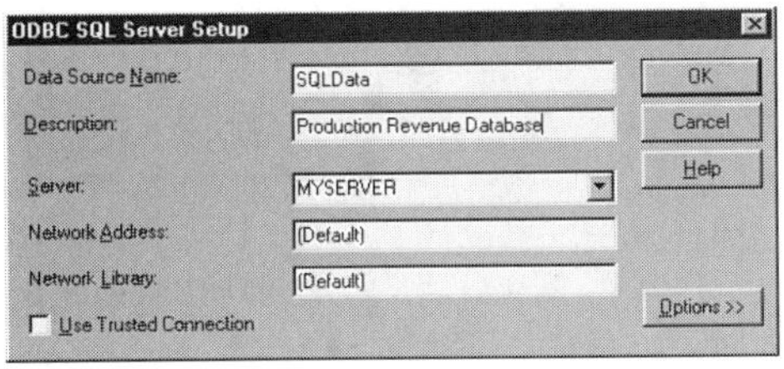

The DSN screens also give you the capability to Configure or Remove ODBC data sources. To modify a data source, select the data source and then click the Configure button. This presents you with the same dialog box that you used initially to set up the data source. To delete a data source, select it and then click the Remove button.

Using the DAOs to Create an ODBC Source   You are not limited to setting up data sources interactively. There are times, such as application installation, where you might want to add a data source with code. For this purpose, you can use the `RegisterDatabase` method of the `DBEngine` object.

Here is the syntax of the `RegisterDatabase` method:

`DBEngine.RegisterDatabase` *dbname, driver, silent, attributes*

Table 30.1·defines the parameters used in the `RegisterDatabase` method.

Table 30.1   Parameters of the *RegisterDatabase* Method

Parameter	Definition
dbName	A user-definable string expression that specifies the data source name (for example, `"MyDatabase"`).
driver	A string expression that indicates the installed driver's name (for example, `ORACLE`) as listed in the ODBC Drivers tab of the ODBC Administrator. *silent* `True` specifies that the next parameter (*attributes*) indicates all connection information. `False` specifies to display the Driver Setup dialog box and ignore the contents of the *attributes* parameter.
attributes	All connection information for using the ODBC driver. This parameter is ignored if *silent* is set to False.

The following code sample illustrates how the `RegisterDatabase` method is used to create a link to an Access database. Before attempting to use the data access objects, remember to add the appropriate reference.

```
Dim sAttrib As String
Dim sDriver As String

sAttrib = "DBQ=D:\VB5\BIBLIO.mdb"
sDriver = "Microsoft Access Driver (*.mdb)"
DBEngine.RegisterDatabase "MyDSN", sDriver, True, sAttrib
```

After executing the above code, you can go back to the Data Source Administrator window and verify that a new User DSN has been added.

N O T E   You can also use the `rdoRegisterDataSource` method of the `rdoEngine` to perform the registration task for Remote Data Objects. ▨

Notice that for the Access driver the `"DBQ"` parameter indicates the name of the database file. To determine all the parameters required for a particular ODBC driver, you should create a connection with the ODBC Manager and then examine the settings in the Registry. You will find these under HKEY_USERS\Default\Software\ODBC\ODBC.INI. (To view the Registry, use the REGEDIT application included with Windows 95.) To specify multiple parameters with the `RegisterDatabase` method, separate them with a semicolon.

Using the Remote Data Objects

Data access objects (DAO) are a layer on top of the ODBC API. Before the advent of *Remote Data Objects* in Visual Basic, programmers would sometimes skip this layer by calling the ODBC API directly. The reason, of course, was to make their applications run faster. However, the ODBC API calls are much harder to use than the data access objects. Remote data objects changed this by providing an interface to the ODBC API that uses the familiar operations of setting properties and calling methods. Because properties and methods are used in all Visual Basic programs, this made the access of ODBC databases much easier for developers to understand and accomplish.

Part

VI

Ch

30

Comparison of RDO to DAO

The remote data objects, or RDO, are very similar to the data access objects (DAO), which were covered in Chapter 28, "Improving Data Access with Data Access Objects." This similarity not only makes RDO easier to understand, but it also makes the conversion of programs from PC databases to client/server databases much easier. In fact, once the connection to the data source is made, the same code statements can be used to access the data by using RDO as were used for DAO.

To give you a feel for the similarities between the RDO and DAO models, Table 30.2 lists a number of RDO objects and their corresponding DAO objects.

Table 30.2 Some RDO Objects and Their DAO Counterparts

RDO Object	DAO Object
rdoEngine	DBEngine
rdoEnvironment	Workspace
rdoConnection	Database
rdoTable	TableDef
rdoResultset	Recordset
rdoColumn	Field
rdoQuery	QueryDef
rdoParameter	Parameter

In addition, the rdoResultset object supports several types of returned sets of records, similar to the recordset types of the Recordset object. Table 30.3 summarizes these similarities.

Table 30.3 *rdoResultset* Types and the Corresponding *Recordset* Types

rdoResultset Types	*Recordset* Types	Definition
Keyset	Dynaset	Updatable set of records in which movement is unrestricted.
Static	Snapshot	Non-updatable set of records that were present when the set was created. Updates by other users are not reflected.
Dynamic	N/A	Similar to a keyset.
Forward-only	Forward-only	Similar to a static resultset or snapshot, but you can move forward only through the set of records. This is the default Resultset type.

Notice that the Remote Data Objects do not support any rdoResultset type that returns a table. This is because the Remote Data Objects are geared to using SQL statements to retrieve subsets of information from one or more tables. You must set the order of the rdoResultset with the Order By clause of the SQL statement used to create the set. Also, because there is no table equivalent, RDO does not support indexes.

As you might expect with the similarity of the objects, there are methods of the RDO that are similar to the methods of the DAO. These methods and their respective objects are summarized in Table 30.4.

Table 30.4 RDO Objects Methods and Related DAO Methods

RDO Method	RDO Object	DAO Method	DAO Object
rdoCreateEnvironment	rdoEngine	CreateWorkspace	DBEngine
BeginTrans	rdoConnection	BeginTrans	Workspace
CommitTrans	rdoConnection	CommitTrans	Workspace
OpenConnection	rdoEnvironment	OpenDatabase	Workspace
RollbackTrans	rdoConnection	Rollback	Workspace
CreateQuery	rdoConnection	CreateQueryDef	Database
Execute	rdoConnection	Execute	Database
OpenResultset	rdoConnection	OpenRecordset	Database

And finally, the rdoResultset object and the Recordset object have the following methods in common:

- ■ AddNew—Adds a new row (record) to the set
- ■ Delete—Removes the current row (record) from the set
- ■ Edit—Prepares the current row for changing the information in the row
- ■ MoveFirst—Moves to the first row of the set
- ■ MoveLast—Moves to the last row in the set
- ■ MoveNext—Moves to the next row in the set
- ■ MovePrevious—Moves to the previous row in the set
- ■ Update—Commits the changes made to the copy buffer to the actual record. The copy buffer is a memory location that contains the values of the record with which the user is working

Accessing a Database with RDO

To further illustrate the similarities between the RDO and DAO models, the code in Listings 30.1 and 30.2 perform the same function on the "biblio" database. The difference between the two listings is simply the objects and methods used to create returned records. Once the recordset or resultset is established, the remaining statements simply print each entry in the first field. In the RDO example, the ODBC data source "MyDSN" was created previously with the ODBC Manager.

N O T E In order to use the Remote Data Objects, you need to add a reference to the "Microsoft Remote Data Object" from the Project, References menu. ■

Listing 30.1 RDOSampl.txt—Access Information in an ODBC Data Source Using the RDO Methods

```
Dim db As rdoConnection
Dim rs As rdoResultset
Dim sSQL As String

Set db = rdoEngine.rdoEnvironments(0).OpenConnection("MyDSN")

sSQL = "Select * From Titles"
Set rs = db.OpenResultset(sSQL, rdOpenKeyset)

rs.MoveFirst
While Not rs.EOF
    Print rs.rdoColumns(0)
    rs.MoveNext
Wend

rs.Close
db.Close
```

Listing 30.2   DAOSampl.txt—Access the Same Information Using the DAO Methods

```
Dim db As Database
Dim rs As Recordset
Dim sSQL As String

Set db = DBEngine.Workspaces(0).OpenDatabase("D:\VB5\BIBLIO.MDB")

sSQL = "Select * From Titles"
Set rs = db.OpenRecordset(sSQL, dbOpenDynaset)

rs.MoveFirst
While Not rs.EOF
    Print rs.Fields(0)
    rs.MoveNext
Wend

rs.Close
db.Close
```

Another thing you will want to explore with RDO is asynchronous execution of database operations. This means control is returned to your program *before* the database operation completes, as in the example below:

```
Set db = rdoEngine.rdoEnvironments(0)._
    OpenConnection("MyDSN", , , , rdAsyncEnable)
While db.StillConnecting = True
    Print "Connecting..."
Wend
```

The constant `rdAsyncEnable` indicates asynchronous operation. The `while` loop keeps running until the connection is made and the `StillConnecting` property becomes False.

Using the Remote Data Control

If you want a faster way to create applications by using ODBC data sources, you can use the *Remote Data control* (RDC). The RDC lets you set a few properties of the control, and then the RDC handles all the tasks of making the connections to the ODBC data source for you. In this way, the RDC automates the methods of the remote data objects in the same way that the data control automates the methods of the data access objects.

After setting up the Remote Data control, you can use the bound controls to display and edit information that is in the resultset created by the data control. The bound controls are set up the same way they would be for use with the Data control that was discussed in Chapter 26, "Using Data Controls and Reports," except that now, the `DataSource` property of the bound controls points to a Remote Data control. Once set up, the bound controls are updated with new information each time a new row is accessed by the Remote Data control.

Comparing the RDC and the Data Control

The Remote Data Objects were compared to the data access objects in the earlier "Using the Remote Data Objects" section; now take a look at the similarities of the Data control and the RDC. As you might expect, many of the properties of the RDC have counterparts in the Data control. These properties and their functions are summarized in Table 30.5.

Table 30.5   Remote Data Control Properties Compared to Data Control Properties

RDC Property	Data Control Property	Purpose
BOFAction	BOFAction	Determines whether the beginning of file flag is set when the user invokes the MovePrevious method while on the first record.
DataSourceName	DatabaseName	Specifies the database containing the desired information.
EOFAction	EOFAction	Determines whether the end of file flag is set or if a new row (record) is added when the user invokes the MoveNext method while on the last record.
ResultsetType	RecordsetType	Determines the type of dataset created by the control.
SQL	RecordSource	The SQL statement that identifies the specific information to be retrieved.

Setting Up the RDC

Setting up the RDC for use in your program is also very similar to setting up the Data control. Before you can use the RDC, you must first add it to your project. You do this by using the Components dialog box, which you access by choosing the Components item from the Project menu. After you close the dialog box, the remote data control is added to your toolbox.

TROUBLESHOOTING

The Remote Data control does not appear as one of the available controls in the Custom Controls dialog box.

You may have chosen not to install the remote data control when you first set up Visual Basic. You need to reinstall that portion of Visual Basic. Also, if you do not have the Enterprise Edition of Visual Basic, the remote data control is not available to you at all.

To set up the remote data control, follow these steps:

1. Draw the remote data control on your form.

2. Set the `Name` and `Caption` properties of the RDC to values that have meaning to you.

3. Set the `DataSourceName` property. You may enter a value or choose one from the drop-down list.

4. Set the `SQL` property to a valid SQL statement that specifies the information you need.

As stated in Step 3, you can choose the `DataSourceName` value from a drop-down list. This list contains every registered ODBC data source on your system. An example of this list is shown in Figure 30.8.

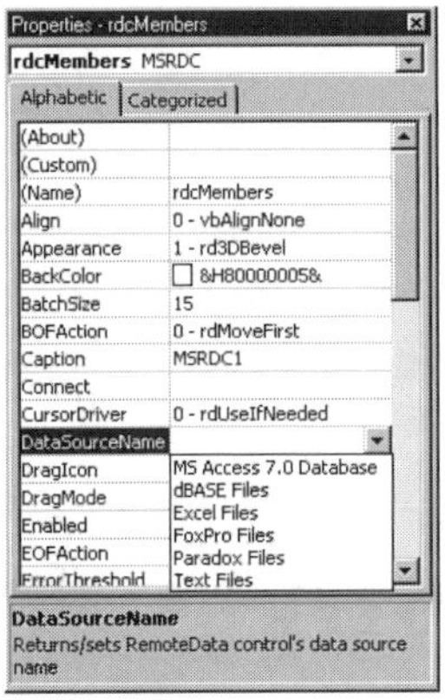

FIG. 30.9

You can choose from a list of available ODBC data sources when setting the `DataSourceName`.

After you have set up the remote data control, you then can attach bound controls to it by setting the `DataSource` property. As shown in Figure 30.10, a drop-down list in the `DataSource` property contains the names of any remote data controls or data controls on the current form. After the `DataSource` property has been set, you can select the `DataField` property from a list, just as you did for the controls bound to a data control.

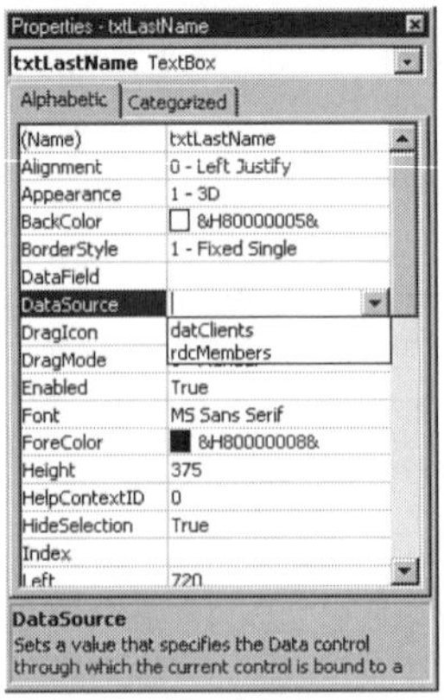

FIG. 30.10

The `DataSource` property list contains all available data controls, remote or not.

From Here...

This chapter has given you a basic understanding of client/server applications. The chapter has also shown you how the Remote Data Objects and Remote Data control make it easier to access the ODBC databases that are part of many client/server programs.

■ To learn more about working with the data control, see Chapter 26, "Using Data Controls and Reports," and Chapter 27, "Doing More with Bound Controls."

■ To learn more about the data access objects, see Chapter 28, "Improving Data Access with the Data Access Objects."

■ To learn more about creating SQL statements, see Chapter 29, "Understanding SQL."

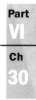

Part

VI

Ch

30

CHAPTER 31

Multi-User Databases

In preceding chapters, you learned several aspects of database programming, particularly how to develop an application that would be used by a single user on a stand-alone PC. However, many of today's database applications must be written for a network environment, where multiple users will be reading, modifying, deleting, and adding to the data in the database. This type of application presents an additional set of challenges for you as a database developer.

Controlling users' access to the database

For many programs, you want users to be able to access only certain parts of the database.

Using Jet engine security features

Jet has built-in security that you can use to prevent users from accessing sensitive information.

Using locking to keep one user from changing a record while another user is using it

Record-locking schemes keep multiple users from changing the same record at the same time.

Maintaining application performance with multiple users

Many applications slow down when they are distributed across a network, but there are ways you can enhance performance.

Dealing with some common database errors

Because database errors can occur, you need to know what they are so you can deal with them.

Replicating the database and synchronizing multiple database copies

Using replication places the burden of keeping multiple copies of the data on the database engine.

N O T E   The examples in this chapter are tailored to a PC-level database, specifically the Jet database engine. A client/server environment, such as SQL Server, would handle all of these issues in a different (and usually better) manner. ▓

In addition to multiple users accessing a single database, we will also look at how the multi-user concept works if each user has a separate copy of the database. The Jet engine has special database replication features designed to handle this.

The main considerations involved in multi-user program development are the following:

- Database access
- Database security
- Data currency
- Record-locking to prevent simultaneous update attempts
- Application performance

Even if you don't develop applications for a network environment, you still need to be aware of some multi-user considerations. In Windows or any other multi-tasking environment, two programs on the same machine can try to access the same data. As an example, consider a PC monitoring a manufacturing process. One program can receive the process data from instruments and store the data in a database. Another program can then generate reports on the data or modify erroneous or abnormal data points. Although the same user can run both programs on the same machine, the two programs appear to the database to be multiple users of the data.

Determining the multi-user needs of the application is part of the design process. And, as with other aspects of programming, a good design helps tremendously in producing a good and efficient application. ▓

Controlling Data Access

Controlling data access involves placing restrictions on part or all of a database. Data access restrictions can be put in place as either user restrictions or function restrictions.

You need user restrictions when you want to prevent certain people (or, as a corollary, to allow only certain people) from looking at sensitive information. An example is a payroll system, in which most people can view the names of employees, but only a select few can see or modify the actual pay information. These restrictions are usually handled through user IDs and passwords and are the basis of data security.

Function restrictions, on the other hand, place limits on specific parts of a program, regardless of who the user is. An example is opening a price table in read-only mode in an order-entry system. You add function restrictions so that a user cannot inadvertently change the price of an item while processing an order.

You can handle the restrictions in an application in two ways: using *programmatic controls* or using *database engine controls*. A programmatic control is one that you put into the application itself. Engine-level controls restrict any program trying to access the information in the database.

Using a Database Exclusively

The most restrictive limit that you can place on a database is to open it exclusively. This limit prevents any other user or program from gaining access to any information in the database while it is in use. Because this method is so restrictive, you should use it only for operations that affect the entire database. These operations include the following:

- Compacting a database
- Updating entire tables (for example, using the UPDATE query)
- Changing the structure of the database by adding or deleting tables, fields, or indexes
- Handling special user needs, such as posting accounting information

Within a program, you can open a database exclusively using the options portion of the Data Access Object OpenDatabase method, as shown in the following code:

```
Dim db  As Database
Set db = DBEngine.Workspaces(0).OpenDatabase("D:\VB5\BIBLIO.MDB", True, False)
```

If the database is not in use, it opens and no one else can access it until it is closed again. If the database is in use, an error is returned. (Handling errors is discussed later in this chapter in the section "Handling Errors and Conflicts.")

Denying Table Access to Others

In addition to opening the database exclusively, you can also open recordsets exclusively. This is a less restrictive way to lock part of a database. When you create a recordset, you can deny other users or programs access to the table being used by your program function. You can do so by using the options of the OpenRecordset method to deny read or write access to the information with which you will be working. Similarly, you can deny write access to the information in a dynaset-type recordset by using the options of the OpenRecordset method.

> **CAUTION**
>
> When you use the Deny options on a recordset created from multiple tables, other users are restricted from the base tables used to create the recordset.

You should use these options, as with exclusive access, only for administrative functions, when you don't want others viewing or updating any of the table's information during the process.

Using the Deny Read Option (*dbDenyRead*)   The dbDenyRead option for the OpenRecordset method prevents other users from looking at the data in the affected table until you close the table. You use this option if you need to update information in the entire table, such as a global price increase. The following code shows the use of this option:

```
Dim tblMain As Recordset
Set tblMain = db.OpenRecordset("Titles", dbOpenTable, dbDenyRead)
```

N O T E   The dbDenyRead option is available only for table type recordsets. You cannot use it with dynasets or snapshots. ▪

Using the Deny Write Option (*dbDenyWrite*)   The dbDenyWrite option used in the OpenRecordset method also restricts other users' access to information. In this case, however, the users can view but not update information in the affected table or tables. Again, other users' access is restricted only until you close the recordset. You might use the dbDenyWrite option if you're inserting new records into a table but not making changes to existing records. The dbDenyWrite option is available for both table- and dynaset-type recordsets. Listing 31.1 shows the use of the dbDenyWrite option for the two functions.

Listing 31.1   Use *dbDenyWrite* to Prevent Others from Updating Tables While You Are Working with Them

```
Dim tblTitles As Recordset
Dim rsAuthors As Recordset
Dim sSQL As String

' Open a table with the dbDenyWrite option.
Set tblTitles = db.OpenRecordset("Titles", dbOpenTable, dbDenyWrite)

' Create a Recordset with the dbDenyWrite option.
sSQL = "Select * From Authors"
Set rsAuthors = db.OpenRecordset(sSQL, dbOpenDynaset, dbDenyWrite)
```

Using the deny options does not restrict other users' access to information in the database all the time. They are denied access only if they attempt to open a table while you are using it with one of the options in effect. In other words, this is not really a security feature but a way to manage multiple updates to the database.

Using Read-Only Tables

Often you might have functions in your applications that have data you don't want the users to be able to modify at any time. You might also have some tables that you want only certain people to modify. In these cases, you can open a table or recordset in read-only mode, or you can use a snapshot-type recordset.

Using Lookup Tables   One example of a read-only table is a lookup table. A *lookup table* contains reference information that is necessary for the users to see but that the users do not need to change. For instance, your application might use a ZIP Code table for a mailing list application or a price table for an order-entry system. In either of these cases, you open the table in read-only mode using the options shown in Listing 31.2. Unlike the deny options, the read-only option does not restrict other users' access to the information.

Listing 31.2 Use the Read-Only Option to Prevent Users from Modifying Data

```
Dim rsPubs As Recordset
Set rsPubs = db.OpenRecordset("Publishers", dbOpenTable, dbReadOnly)
```

N O T E You can open an entire database in read-only mode by setting the ReadOnly parameter of the OpenDatabase method to True. ▨

Using Snapshots Another way to restrict a program function to read-only is to use a snapshot-type recordset. Jet engine snapshots are always read-only. You can use a snapshot when data in the base tables is not being changed frequently by others or when a point-in-time look at the data is sufficient. Snapshots are usually used for reporting functions. An advantage to using snapshots is that they are stored in memory. Therefore, some operations using snapshots are faster than the same operations using tables or dynasets. However, because of the memory requirements for a snapshot and the time that it takes to load the data into memory, snapshots are best used for queries that return fewer than 200 records.

Restricting Specific Users Finally, you might have occasion to want to restrict certain users to read-only access, no matter what program functions they are performing. You can do so only through the Jet security system. These security features are described later in this chapter in the section "Exploring Jet Security Features."

Understanding Record-Locking Schemes

The features described in the preceding section place restrictions on an entire table or even the entire database. In this section, we discuss locking the database at the record level. One of the main considerations in multi-user programming is assuring that a record is not in use by another user at the same time that you are trying to update it. You do so through the use of record locks. A *record lock* temporarily limits the access of other users to a specific record or group of records.

In a typical application, a record lock is set while a user updates the data in the record and then is released after the update is completed. As the developer, you must take into account the following considerations in the use of record locks:

- What to do if the record cannot be locked (for example, if another user is already accessing the record)
- How to prevent a user from keeping a record locked for too long
- Whether to lock the record when the user first accesses it or only when the changes are being written to the database

How you handle these considerations has an impact on many aspects of the application development. Therefore, you should address these issues as much as possible in the design phase of the application.

Part
VI
Ch
31

Page-Locking versus Record-Locking

The Jet engine does not support true record-locking. In record-locking, only the individual record currently being accessed by the user is locked. Instead, Jet uses a page-locking scheme. Jet reads data in pages of 2K (2,048 bytes). When it places a lock on a record, it locks the entire page containing the record.

In this locking scheme, multiple records are locked each time a lock is issued. The number of records locked depends on the size of each record. For example, suppose each record in a sample table is 230 bytes long. Nine records therefore are locked each time. On the other hand, if the table has records that are only 30 bytes long, each record lock affects 68 records.

When a page is locked by one user, another user cannot modify any records on that page (although the second user can read the records). This is true even if the first user is working with only one of the records. This aspect of page-locking requires you to be even more careful in the application of record locks, because it increases the chances of a conflict between users.

Visual Basic has no commands to specifically request a record lock. Instead, the record locks are automatically created and released when the Add, Edit, and Update methods are used. Visual Basic supports two locking schemes: pessimistic and optimistic.

Pessimistic Locking

Pessimistic locking locks the page containing a record as soon as the Edit method is used on that record. The lock on the page is released when the Update method is used and the data is written to the file. The advantage of this approach is that it prevents other users from changing the data in a record while one user is editing it. The disadvantage is that it keeps the record locked for a longer period of time. In the worst case, a user could open a record for editing, place a lock on it, and then head out to lunch. This lock would keep other users from editing that record, or any others on the same page, for a long time.

N O T E To prevent locks from being held too long, you can put a timer in your code that releases the record after a specified period of inactivity. You would do this by placing code in the Timer event of the Timer control. This code would use the Idle method of the database engine as shown in the following line of code:

```
DBEngine.Idle dbFreeLocks
```

Optimistic Locking

Optimistic locking locks the page containing a record only when the Update method is invoked. The lock on the page is immediately released when the update operation is completed. The advantage of optimistic locking is that the lock is on the page for only a short period of time, reducing the chance that another user might try to access the same data page while the lock is in place. The disadvantage is that another user can change the data in the record between the time the Edit and Update methods are used. If the data has changed in that time period, VB issues an error message.

Which Locking Method to Use and When

For most database applications, optimistic locking is the better choice of the two methods. The probability that someone else will change or delete the record you are working on is less than the probability that someone will try to access a record on the page that you have locked. If, however, you have an application in which many users are accessing and editing records simultaneously, you might want to use pessimistic locking to ensure that the record is not changed while you are performing your edits. In this case, you should put some method in place to limit the time that the record is locked.

Pessimistic locking is the default record-locking scheme used by Visual Basic. To set the method of record-locking, you must set the LockEdits property of the table or dynaset with which you are working. Setting the property to True gives you pessimistic locking. Setting the property to False yields optimistic locking. Listing 31.3 shows how to set the LockEdits property for pessimistic and optimistic locking, respectively.

Part

VI

Ch

31

Listing 31.3   Set the Recordset's *LockEdits* Property to Choose How Record-Locking Works

```
Dim rsTemp As Recordset

'Set the locking method to pessimistic
rsTemp.LockEdits = True

'Set the locking method to optimistic
rsTemp.LockEdits = False
```

Releasing Locks

As I stated previously, the record locks are released automatically when the Update method has completed. However, releasing record locks is a background process, and sometimes other activities are occurring so rapidly that the database does not have time to catch up. If you are developing a data-entry-intensive program, you might need to pause the processing in the application momentarily. You can do so by using the Idle method of the database engine.

The Idle method pauses the application and allows the database engine to catch up on its housekeeping work. The following line shows the syntax of the Idle method:

```
DBEngine.Idle dbFreeLocks
```

Using the Data Control

Because the data control uses tables or dynasets (the default) as its record source, the same locking schemes mentioned previously are used with the data control. Pessimistic locking is the default; therefore, as each record is accessed, the data control automatically performs the Edit method, which in turn automatically locks the record's page. When you move from one record to another, the lock on the current record is released by the Update method, and a lock is placed on the next record by the Edit method. In a multi-user system in which you want to use optimistic locking, you need to change the locking scheme of the data control. You do so by adding a LockEdits statement, as shown in Listing 31.3, to the Activate event of the form containing the data control.

CAUTION

You must be careful when using transactions in a multi-user environment. Any record locks that are set by the Edit or Update method are not released until the transaction is committed or rolled back. Therefore, keeping transactions as short as possible is best so that you can avoid having a large number of records locked for a long period of time. In addition, you should be careful when using cascaded updates or deletes because they create more transactions and, therefore, more locks.

Exploring Jet Security Features

Another consideration of multi-user database programming is database security. Because a network environment can allow other people access to your database file, you might want to use methods to prevent them from viewing specific information in your database or possibly prevent them from viewing any of the information.

The Jet engine provides a database security model based on user IDs and passwords. In this model, you can assign to individual users or groups of users permissions to the entire database or any parts of the database. As each user is added to the security file, you must assign him or her to one or more user groups. That user then inherits the permissions of that group. In addition, you can assign other permissions to the user.

If you're working with a secured database, you must perform the following three steps to gain access to the database from your VB program:

- Determine the location of the system database. (The system database is a separate file that stores your security settings.) The default install sets it up as SYSTEM.MDW in the \Windows\System directory.

- Set the IniPath or SystemDB property of the database engine to tell the program where the system database is located. (Note that for 32-bit operating systems, the location of the system database is in the Registry, not an INI file.)

- Use the CreateWorkspace method with the workspace name, user ID, and user password specified to create a workspace to contain the database.

The syntax for each of these statements is shown in Listing 31.4.

Listing 31.4   Gaining Access to a Secured Database

```
Dim wsTemp As Workspace

    DBEngine.SystemDB = "C:\Windows\System\System.mdw"
```

```
Set wsTemp = DBEngine.CreateWorkspace("MYWSPACE", "MyName", "MyPassword", _
    dbUseJet)
```

For the preceding code to work, the user name and password must be set in the system database first. To do this, read the section "Setting Up the Security System" later in this chapter. By default, the SYSTEM.MDW contains an administrator account whose username is admin with no password.

Database Permissions

Within the Jet security system, you can set two database-level permissions: Run/Open and Open Exclusive. The Run/Open permission is required for anyone who needs access to the database. Without this permission, a user cannot open a database for any function. The Open Exclusive permission allows users to open a database exclusively, as described previously. You should give this permission only to administrative users. Otherwise, another user of an application might inadvertently lock everyone else out of the database until he closes it.

Table Permissions

Although database permissions affect the entire database (and every table in it), you often need finer control over access to individual tables. Using the Jet engine, you can set table-level permissions for any table in a database. As with the database permissions, the table permissions can be assigned to individual users or groups of users. The following seven table-level permissions are available with the Jet engine:

- **Read Design**—Enables the user to view the structure of the table
- **Modify Design**—Enables the user to change the structure of the table
- **Administer**—Gives the user full control over the table
- **Read Data**—Enables the user to read information from the table but not to make any changes
- **Modify Data**—Enables the user to modify existing data but not to add or delete data
- **Insert Data**—Enables the user to add new data to the table
- **Delete Data**—Enables the user to remove data from the table

With the Read and Modify Design permissions, the user can work with the structure of the table. The Administer permission gives a user full access to a table, including table-deletion capabilities. The four Data permissions control the type of access a user has to the actual data in the table. You can assign these permissions by table, and you can grant different users different access rights to each table. For the constants used to set permissions, see "Permissions Property" in the help file.

Setting Up the Security System

Visual Basic has no means of creating the system database file needed for the security system. You can create this file using only Microsoft Access. Access also provides the easiest means of establishing and modifying user IDs and setting database and table permissions. However, after the file exists, you can use VB code to create new user IDs, assign users to existing groups, and delete users as described in the following list:

- To add a new user, you create the user object by specifying the user name, user ID, and password. You then append the new user to the workspace. This procedure adds the new user to the system database that was in use when the workspace was created.

- To add a user to an existing user group, you create the user object and then add the user to the Groups collection.

- To delete a user, you use the delete method for the Users collection of the workspace.

Each of these activities is shown in Listing 31.5.

Listing 31.5   Performing Security System Maintenance from Visual Basic

```
Dim wsTemp As Workspace
Dim NewUser As User
Dim NewGrp As Group

'Add a new user to the system database
DBEngine.SystemDB = "C:\Windows\System\System.mdw"
Set wsTemp = DBEngine.Workspaces(0)
Set NewUser = wsTemp.CreateUser("BSILER", "12345", "PASSWORD")

'Add the user to the "Users" group
wsTemp.Groups("Users").Users.Append NewUser

'Delete the user from the system database
wsTemp.Users.Delete "BSILER"
```

Encryption

In addition to the security system, the Jet engine provides a means of encrypting a database that you create. *Encryption* is a method of disguising the data in a database so that someone using a disk-editing program cannot view the contents of the database. You can specify encryption when first creating the database by using the options portion of the CreateDatabase function. After a database has been created, you can add or remove encryption by using the CompactDatabase function. The use of these functions for encrypting data is shown in Listing 31.6.

Listing 31.6   Adding Encryption to Your Database

```
'Create an encrypted database
    Dim dbNew As Database
    Set dbNew = DBEngine.Workspaces(0).CreateDatabase("D:\TEST.MDB",_
        dbLangGeneral, dbEncrypt)
```

```
'Encrypt an existing database
DBEngine.CompactDatabase "D:\TEST.MDB", "D:\TEST2.MDB", , dbEncrypt

'Remove encryption from a database
DBEngine.CompactDatabase "D:\TEST2.MDB", "D:\TEST3.MDB", , dbDecrypt
```

The encryption method used by the Jet engine encrypts the entire database, including table definitions and queries. Also, the encryption results in a performance degradation of about 10 to 15 percent.

For some applications, you might want to encrypt only a portion of the data. For instance, in a payroll system, you might need to encrypt only the actual pay rates, not the entire database. Although no built-in method is available for this type of encryption, you can create your own encryption schemes for these situations.

As an example, a simple encryption scheme for numeric data is to convert each digit (including leading and trailing zeroes) to a character, invert the character string, and then store the data as text. In this way, the number 2534.75 can be stored as EGDCEB. Although this type of encryption is by no means foolproof, it does provide some data security from casual lookers.

Application Passwords

In addition to, or in place of, the security built into the database, you also can choose to put a user ID and password system into your application. With an application-level system, you control the type of access people have to the functions of your application. The drawback to this approach is that someone could access your database by using another program. However, this type of security is fairly easy to implement. Visual Basic even includes a form template for a login box.

Using Network Security

Finally, most network operating systems have their own security system built in. Many of these systems are quite good and can prevent unauthorized users from even knowing that the database exists. For example, the path on the file server containing the database could simply be restricted from unauthorized users. This might be the easiest way to secure your database, because it would involve no programming. To determine the capabilities of your network's security system, refer to your network program manuals or contact your network administrator.

Maintaining Data Currency

Currency of the data is a big issue in multi-user applications, especially those that handle a high volume of data entry and modification. Maintaining currency refers to making sure that the data at which you are looking is the most up-to-date information available. The data you're working with becomes noncurrent if another user changes or deletes the records since you retrieved them. Additionally, your recordset might be noncurrent if other users have added records since you retrieved data.

Part
VI

Ch

31

Using Only Tables

The only way to be sure that your data is always the most current is to work exclusively with tables. Only a table immediately reflects changes, additions, or deletions made by other users. If your application or function works with only one table, using the table instead of a dynaset is probably the best way to go. If your application must work with multiple tables, the drawback to using just the tables is that you have to maintain the table relationships instead of using a dynaset to do it. To decide whether to use tables or dynasets, you must determine the probability that your data will not be current, the consequences of having noncurrent data, and the effort involved in maintaining the table relationships. Weighing these three factors will help you decide which access method is best.

Requerying a Dynaset

If you need to work with a dynaset-type recordset in a multi-user application, you can use the `Requery` method to make it current with the database. The `Requery` method, shown here, basically re-executes the SQL query:

```
rsTemp.Requery
```

You can requery a dynaset only a limited number of times. Therefore, after several requeries, you should close the dynaset and re-create it completely.

N O T E   Depending on how the recordset was created, the `Requery` method might or might not be available. You should check the `Restartable` property of the recordset to verify that it supports the `Requery` operation. ▇

Probing Performance Considerations

The performance of your multi-user application is dependent on, among other things, the type of network, the number of users, and the size of the databases with which you're working. At best, with you as the only user attached to a server, the data-transfer rates across a network are a lot slower than from your local hard drive. This means that you have to work harder in a network environment to keep the performance of your application crisp. In the following sections, I list some ideas for helping the performance of your application.

Keep Recordsets Small

The trick to keeping your recordsets small is to make your queries as specific as possible. This way, you can avoid repeatedly reading data across the network as you move through the records. For example, consider the "Titles" table in the BIBLIO.MDB sample database. Suppose you wanted to print a list of all the titles in the table. One way to do this would be to open a recordset as follows:

```
sSQL = "Select * From Titles"
Set rs = db.OpenRecordset(sSQL, dbOpenDynaset)
rs.MoveFirst
```

```
While Not rs.EOF
    Print rs.Fields("Title")
    rs.MoveNext
Wend
```

However, note that the SQL statement brings back all the fields for each record. Because you only care about the Title field, a better SQL statement would be

```
sSQL = "Select Title From Titles"
```

Copy a Database or Table to a Local Drive

If you have a database that is used for lookup purposes, such as a ZIP Code database, you can make a copy of the database on your local drive. This approach improves the speed of access during searches and queries. For example, the following code copies a database to your drive if the network copy is newer:

```
Dim sLocalMDB As String
Dim sNetMDB As String

sLocalMDB = "C:\ZIPCODES.MDB"
sNetMDB = "\\MYSERVER\MYPATH\ZIPCODES.MDB"

'Make sure your copy of the database
'is closed before attempting this.
If FileDateTime(sNetMDB) > FileDateTime(sLocalMDB) Then
    FileCopy sNetMDB, sLocalMDB
End If
```

Part
VI

Ch
31

For other databases that might change only occasionally (such as a price database), you might consider making the changes at a time when no one else is using the database. That way, the data is always static to the users of the system. In other words, do your data maintenance at night.

Use Snapshot-Type Recordsets Where Possible

Because snapshots are read-only copies of the data stored in memory, they access the network only when the snapshots are created. Therefore, if you don't need to make changes to the data, use a snapshot—but only if the recordset is small. A large snapshot can choke your memory and resources in a hurry.

Use Transactions for Processing Updates

Each time an update is issued, data is written to the database, requiring a disk write—that is, unless transaction processing is used. All the updates between a BeginTrans and a CommitTrans are stored in memory until the transaction is committed. At that time, all the updates are processed at once. This approach cuts down on the amount of writes being performed across the network. However, you should be careful not to allow too many updates to stack up at one time because of the record-locking concerns described earlier.

Using Database Replication to Handle Multiple Users

Although database replication might not be multi-user in the strictest sense of the concept (multiple users accessing the same database at the same time), you can use this process to handle a number of situations in which multiple users need to work with a database. The most easily visualized of these situations is one in which a sales force in different locations works with a common database and then sends information back to a central site where summary reports are developed.

With database replication, each person can work with a copy of the data in a database. Then, at certain times, the individual databases are recombined with the master database. At the same time that the data from the replica databases is passed back to the master database, any structure changes made to the master can be passed to the replicas.

You also can use database replication to create a read-only copy of a database for a user. You do so to make a complete copy of a network database on a user's local machine. You can use this approach to speed up processing of large reports or queries when the user has no need to modify the base information.

Managing database replication involves four basic steps:

1. Making a database replicable (that is, capable of being replicated)
2. Making copies (replicas) of the database
3. Periodically synchronizing the copies of the database
4. Handling synchronization conflicts

N O T E   Database replication features are available only for Jet version 3.0 or later databases. ▓

Making a Replicable Database

To create a database that can be replicated, you must use a user-special, user-defined property of the database—the `Replicable` property.

N O T E   User-defined properties were first introduced in Visual Basic 4. Using these properties, you
can add properties to a database, `Querydef`, table, index, or field object of your
database. User-defined data objects are described in detail in Chapter 28, "Improving Data Access
with the Data Access Objects." ▓

Making a database replicable requires only a few lines of code and a single user-defined property, as shown in the following code example. This property is a text property with the name `Replicable` and a value of `T`:

```
Dim RepProp As Property
Set OldDb = OldWs.OpenDatabase(DataName, True)
```

```
Set RepProp = OldDb.CreateProperty()
RepProp.Name = "Replicable"
RepProp.Type = dbText
RepProp.Value = "T"
OldDb.Properties.Append RepProp
OldDb.Close
```

N O T E   A database must be opened exclusively in order to make it replicable. ▣

Making Copies of the Database

After you change your database so that it can be replicated, you should make copies of the
database to give to the various users. You do so by using the MakeReplica method of the database object, which is shown in the following code:

```
'(dbMaster is a database that has been opened previously)
dbMaster.MakeReplica "E:\REPLTEST\REPLICA2.MDB", "Copy Number 2"
```

With the MakeReplica method, you supply a name and description for the database copy. There
also is a third optional parameter that indicates whether the copy should be read-only. If you
want the copy to be read-only, use the constant dbRepMakeReadOnly as the third argument.
Another constant, dbRepMakePartial, is used to copy only some of the data to the replica. In
the sales force example, this would be useful to provide each mobile person with the information for their region only, which would then be synchronized back into the "master" database.
The help file has details on how to determine which information goes into a partial replica.

Putting the Database Back Together

Finally, after making changes to the master database or one or more of the replicas, you should
make the data and structure consistent between all the databases by using the Synchronize
method. This method synchronizes the data between two databases. You define one of the
databases as the database object, which is running the Synchronize method. You specify the
other database (defined by its path and file name) as an argument of the method. The data
exchange between the files can be one of the following three types as defined by the constants
shown in parentheses:

- **Export**—Changes are passed from the current database object to the target file
  (dbRepExportChanges).
- **Import**—Changes are received by the current database object from the target database
  (dbRepImportChanges).
- **Bidirectional**—Changes are made in both directions (dbRepImExpChanges).

N O T E   A fourth option, dbRepSyncInternet, is available in the Office 97 developer edition. ▣

Part
VI

Ch
31

The `Synchronize` method is shown in the following code:

```
Set OldDb = OldWs.OpenDatabase(DataName)
OldDb.Synchronize "E:\REPLTEST\REPLICA2.MDB", dbRepImportChanges
OldDb.Close
```

Handling Errors and Conflicts

In a multi-user application, errors are triggered when you attempt to open a table or update a record that is locked by another user. These errors can be trapped by your code, and appropriate steps can be taken to either retry the operation or exit the application gracefully. In the following sections, you look at these errors in three major groups:

- Database- and table-locking errors
- Record-locking errors
- Permission errors
- Synchronization conflicts

The way to handle most errors that occur when trying to lock a table, database, or record is to wait for a few seconds and then try the operation again. Unless the other user who has the record locked maintains the lock for a long time, this method will work. In an interactive environment, I usually give the user the choice of retrying or aborting the operation.

Database- and Table-Locking Errors   Database- or table-locking errors occur when you try to access information that is currently locked or in use by another user. These errors occur either when you try to open the database or table, or when you try to lock them. When the errors occur, you need to wait until the other user has released the lock or quit using the recordset. Table 31.1 lists the error numbers and when they occur.

Table 31.1   Locking Errors that Apply to Tables and Databases

Error Number	Error Occurs When
3008	You attempt to open a table that is exclusively opened by another user.
3009	You attempt to lock a table that is in use by another user.
3211	Same as 3009
3212	Same as 3009, except that this error provides information about the user and machine using the table.

Each of these errors can be handled as described previously, with a choice by the user to abort or retry the operation.

Record-Locking Errors   Record-locking errors occur when you try to add, update, or delete records on a page locked by another user. Depending on the type of locking you use, the error can occur either when you use the `Edit` method (pessimistic locking) or when you use the `Update` method (optimistic locking). To determine which locking method is in effect when the error occurs, you can check the LockEdits property of the recordset you are attempting to lock by using the routine shown in Listing 31.7. Then, if you choose to retry the operation, you can re-execute the correct method.

Listing 31.7 Determine Which Locking Method Is in Effect When an Error Occurs

```
'*****************************************
'Determine the type of locking being used
'*****************************************
If NewDyn.LockEdits Then
'*********************************
'If pessimistic locking, retry Edit
'*********************************
    NewDyn.Edit
Else
'*********************************
'If optimistic locking, retry Update
'*********************************
    NewDyn.Update
End If
```

Part
VI

Ch
31

Most of the record errors pertain to problems encountered while locking the record. However, one error requires special handling. This error (3197) occurs when a user attempts to update a record that has already been changed by another user. This error occurs only when optimistic locking is in effect. When it occurs, you need to present your user with the choices of "Make the new changes anyway" or "Keep the changes made by the other user." Showing the other user's changes also is beneficial. If the user decides to make the changes anyway, he or she can execute the Update method a second time to make the changes.

Several other errors might occur when you attempt to lock a record. Table 31.2 lists the error numbers for these errors and when they occur.

Table 31.2 Other Record-Locking Errors

Error Number	Cause
3046	You attempt to save a record locked by another user.
3158	You attempt to save a record locked by another user.
3186	You attempt to save a record locked by another user. The message gives the name of the user who placed the lock.
3187	You attempt to read a record locked by another user.
3188	You attempt to update a record that another program on your machine already has locked.
3189	You attempt to access a table that another user has exclusively locked.

continues

Table 31.2   Continued

Error Number	Cause
3218	You attempt to update a locked record.
3260	You attempt to save a record locked by another user. The message gives the name of the user who placed the lock.

Permission Errors   The other major group of errors is permission errors. These errors occur when the Jet security is in operation and the current user does not have the appropriate permission to perform the operation. The only way to handle these errors is to inform the user of the error and abort the operation. Table 31.3 summarizes the permission errors.

Table 31.3   Permission Errors that Occur When a User Does Not Have the Appropriate Rights for an Operation

Error Number	Permission Required
3107	Insert
3108	Update
3109	Delete
3110	Read Definitions
3111	Create
3112	Read

Handling Synchronization Conflicts   One type of error occurs when you attempt to synchronize incompatible databases. When you use Jet's replication and synchronization features, you are essentially working with a set of databases—a master database and a bunch of replicas. When a replica is created with the MakeReplica method, it is given a unique ID. This ID is stored in the ReplicaID property of the database. Similarly, there is a property called DesignMasterID which identifies one of the databases as having the database design upon which all replicas are based. Together these IDs identify a *replica set*. If you attempt to synchronize across different sets, an error will occur.

Other types of errors that occur are due more to data conflicts than errors in the synchronization process. In the sales force example, suppose there are only two salespeople, each with his own database replica. Let's say the database includes a table that lists customers along with a field called LastVisitDate, which represents the last time any salesperson visited the customer. If synchronization is performed after each visit, conflicts won't occur and the LastVisitDate field will be the same in both replicas. However, suppose our entire sales force visits the same customer and then attempts to synchronize their databases. Which salesman's LastVisitDate field will be propagated to both databases?

The answer is neither. Resolving conflicts like this must be handled by your program code. This makes sense, because Visual Basic cannot be expected to know that the later of the two dates is the logical choice for this database. What Jet does do, however, is give you all the information necessary to resolve a conflict. It does this by creating a new table, the *conflict table*, and placing the conflicting record(s) in it. Your program can then look at the records and make a decision to overwrite the existing one. In our fictional situation, we would simply take the later of the two dates.

Both types of synchronization errors discussed in the preceding can be avoided with better database design. For example, if our sales force of two had a third database located at the sales company, each salesperson could synchronize with that database rather than with each other.

From Here...

Part
VI
Ch
31

As you can see, many more design considerations are involved in creating a multi-user application than in a single-user application. This process is made even more difficult by the fact that each multi-user situation is different, in terms of hardware and network software used, the number of users of the system, and the functional requirements of the individual application. The intent of this chapter was not to provide specific solutions but to make you aware of the challenges involved in multi-user programming and some of the tools available in Visual Basic to help you meet the challenges. Refer to the following chapters for more information:

- See Chapter 24, "Database Design and Normalization," to learn about general database design considerations.

PART VII

Object-Oriented Programming

CHAPTER 32

Using Classes in Visual Basic

The controls that you use in your Visual Basic programs are actually *classes* from which you create *instances* on a form. These classes are very useful because they are reusable and relatively self-contained. Starting with Visual Basic version 4, you can create your own classes in code to help make your programs more efficient and maintainable. Visual Basic version 5 has enhanced the use of classes even further. ■

What is a class?

Classes are used to define reusable objects in your programs. A class contains data and procedures for manipulating the data.

How classes relate to controls

The Visual Basic controls that you use are classes with a visual interface. These classes contain properties, methods, and events.

How classes implement object-oriented programming

Although the classes in Visual Basic are not 100 percent object-oriented, they do provide for encapsulation of data and methods and make it easier to create reusable code.

How to build a class

You will see how to create a class from scratch, and how to use the Class Builder to create new classes from existing ones.

How to access properties, methods, and events of a class

After a class has been defined, you still have to create an instance of the class to be able to use it. You will see how this is done.

Introduction to Classes

Programmers have always been concerned with efficiency in their programs. A programmer wants the program to run as quickly as possible, create the smallest possible executable file, and be as easy as possible to create and maintain. This last aspect of efficiency leads to using *reusable components*—pieces of code that can be used over and over in multiple projects. Most veteran programmers have a library of subroutines and functions that have been developed over time to handle various tasks. These components are then added to a new project as needed.

Since its inception, Visual Basic has supported the notion of reusable components. The controls you use to build the user interface of your programs are components that perform specific functions, such as getting a piece of text input or displaying a picture. These controls contain all the functions necessary to accomplish their tasks. This means that you do not have to add the code for these tasks to each of your programs. The controls are one form of object that can be used in your code. Visual Basic also has supported the use of *object linking and embedding* (OLE), which lets you access other programs to perform specific tasks.

Use of controls and OLE has greatly benefited programmers, but until version 4, one thing was missing: the ability to create your own objects. Visual Basic now lets you create your own objects through the use of *class modules*. A class module is a very similar to a standard code module in your project. The difference is that instead of just containing a bunch of code, a class module consists of the code that defines a particular class. After the class is defined, you can create objects that are instances of the class, similar to the way you create instances of a TextBox control. In this chapter, you learn about what is in a class module and how to use them in your programs.

Understanding Object-Oriented Programming Fundamentals

You have probably heard the term *object-oriented programming* (OOP) or read about it in programming books and magazines. Even with the addition of the capability to create classes, Visual Basic is not a fully object-oriented programming language. To understand what Visual Basic can and can't do, you need to start with a review of some OOP basics.

OOP's key element is its use of reusable objects to build programs. These objects must be capable of supporting the following:

- **Encapsulation**   The information about an object and the manner in which the information is manipulated are all stored within the object definition. This concept is also sometimes referred to as *information hiding*, because the details about how the object works are invisible outside of it.

- **Inheritance**   A new object can be created from an existing object and contains all the properties and methods of the *parent* object. This makes it easier to define new objects for specific needs.

- **Polymorphism**   Although many objects can have the same methods, the method can perform differently for each of the objects. Through polymorphism, the program runs the method appropriate for the current object. For example, the + operator can be used with both strings and integers. Even though the same symbol is used for both data types, VB knows to perform different operations.

Visual Basic, strictly speaking, does not support the concept of inheritance. That is, you can't create a new class based on the definition of another class. However, there are ways around this limitation, such as just copying your class definition from one module to another.

Implementing OOP with Classes in Visual Basic

The classes that you can build in Visual Basic let you encapsulate the data and functions of an object. The classes let you define *properties* (the information or data in the object) and *methods* (what the object does with the information). But, as with the controls in Visual Basic, you can't use inheritance to create a new class from an existing one.

Even with this limitation, Visual Basic classes are powerful programming tools, as you will see in the rest of this chapter.

Using Classes in Your Programs

You can use classes in your Visual Basic programs in several ways. Each way provides you with programming capabilities that did not exist in Visual Basic prior to version 4. Visual Basic 5 has further enhanced the programmer's ability to work with classes.

Part

VII

Ch

32

First, you can use classes to encapsulate program segments to make them more easily reusable. The classes you create define objects that can be created anywhere in your program. The advantage of using the objects to handle certain program functions is that it reduces the need for global variables and procedures in your programs. This is helpful because global variables are one of the most frequent causes of program errors, as well as one of the more difficult errors to trace. The classes that you define also can be added to other program projects to handle the same functions. Used this way, you can build up a library of useful classes for your development work. You can also create multiple instances of a class, with each object (instance) having its own set of property values. This modularity is something that can't be accomplished with global variables or routines.

The second use of classes is in building ActiveX DLLs and EXEs. Used in this way, the objects of a class provide functions to any of your programs, as well as to other programs that can serve as an ActiveX client. You can, for example, put all of your business financial rules in an object and compile it as an ActiveX DLL. By referencing the DLL, other programmers can easily incorporate the rules into their own programs. You can also separate the database-access functions into a separate class. This separation of tasks is the foundation of the three-tier client/server model.

Finally, you can use classes to build Visual Basic *add-ins*. These programs actually let you enhance the Visual Basic development environment itself. Add-ins can be used to build program wizards, such as the Data Form Designer; provide supplemental programs, such as the Visual Data Manager; or provide tools for making your programming easier, such as a routine to automatically reset the tab order of all the controls on a form.

Building a Class in Visual Basic

Classes in Visual Basic are developed using the Class Module. This module contains only variable declarations and procedure code. There is no user-interface component of a class module. However, a class can take action using a form that is in the program. In the case of an ActiveX DLL or EXE, the forms can be included with the project.

> **N O T E** You can add properties to forms and code modules using the same principles as those for adding classes. ▪

A class module is a fairly simple program object. A class module has only three built-in properties and two native events. It has no methods of its own. After a class module is created, you can add properties, methods, and events to the class by declaring variables and by programming procedures and functions in the class module.

Creating a New Class Module

You start the process of creating a new class module by selecting Add Class Module from Visual Basic's Project menu. This starts a new class module with the default name of Class1 and opens the Code window for the class, as shown in Figure 32.1.

FIG. 32.1

When creating a new class module, you use the Code window the same way you did when creating a standard module.

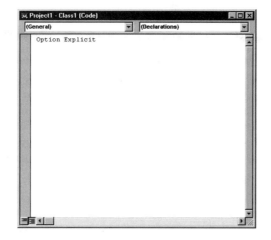

After the new class is created for your project, you need to set the values of some key properties that define the class. These properties are Instancing and Name.

Choosing a Name   You want to give each of your classes a unique name that is descriptive of the function it will perform. In addition, many developers like to preface the class name with the letter *c* to indicate in the programs that this is the name of a class. Using this convention, a class that provided improved printer functionality might be named cPrinter.

Creating a Public Class   When you add a class module to a Standard EXE project, your class module can be used from other modules or forms in the current project only. It cannot be seen from another program. In other words, it is a *private class*.

To create a *public class* that can be made available to other programs, you need to use either an ActiveX EXE or an ActiveX DLL project. After it is created, you then register your DLL (or EXE) with Windows. Your ActiveX project then shows up in the References dialog box of Visual Basic. To use the class, you simply add a reference to it in another project.

The way instances of your class are created depends on whether you created a DLL or EXE, as well as the setting of the `Instancing` property, described in the next section. An ActiveX EXE can be executed like a standard program, but in general is less efficient than a DLL.

N O T E   In Visual Basic version 5.0, ActiveX EXEs and DLLs replace the concept of OLE Automation servers. These new types of projects can still be thought of as servers, because they "serve" up objects to client programs.

Setting the *Instancing* Property   The final property of the class module is the `Instancing` property. The `Instancing` property defines the way instances of your class are created. The valid property values vary depending on what type of VB project you are working with. The `Instancing` property should only concern you if you plan on creating a public class module. If you are working in a Standard EXE project, the `Instancing` property is not even available. While learning the basics of classes and OOP, you can just forget about this property and use a Standard EXE project. However, this property is usually set during the creation of a class, so I mention the property values here. Table 32.1 describes the possible settings for the `Instancing` property.

Table 32.1   Controlling Access to Your Class with *Instancing* Property

Value	Name	Description
1	Private	The class cannot be accessed outside the current project.
2	Public Not Creatable	Instances of the class can be created only within the project that defines the class. However, other applications can control the class after it is created.
3	SingleUse	Other applications can create instances of the class. However, each time another instance of the class is created, a new copy of the program containing the class is started. (This setting is not available for an ActiveX DLL project.)
4	Global SingleUse	Like SingleUse, but makes the class act like a global variable in the client program.

continues

Table 32.1 Continued

Value	Name	Description
5	MultiUse	Other applications can create any number of instances of the class, and only one copy of the program containing the class is started. ActiveX DLL projects generally use this setting.
6	Global MultiUse	Like MultiUse, but makes the class act like a global variable in the client program.

The *Initialize* and *Terminate* Events   In addition to the internal properties of a class module, there are two built-in events: Initialize and Terminate. When you create your class, you might want to include code in these events to cause your programs to take specific actions when an instance of the class is created and destroyed.

For example, if your class needs to know the current system date, you can include a code line in the Initialize event to set an internal variable to the system date. An example of use of the Terminate event would be to close an open database that was being used by the class.

Adding Properties to the Class

After the class module has been created, you can start adding your own properties. The properties you add are the properties of the objects created from your class. Think of the class like a template for objects. Each object you create from the class can have a unique set of property values. These properties provide the way for the user of the object to get information into the object. (You can also supply information to the object when you call a method, as you will see shortly.)

There are two ways to add a property to a class:

- Define a Public variable (you're probably familiar with this).
- Use a Property procedure.

Creating a Public Variable   You create a public variable using a declaration statement with the Public keyword, as shown in the following line of code:

```
Public str1 As String
```

The declaration statements can appear in the Declarations section of the class module or in any Sub procedure in the class.

> **N O T E**   You must explicitly declare public variables, but it is also a good practice to declare all variables. Therefore, you should require variable declaration by placing the Option Explicit statement as the first statement in the Declarations section of the class. You can require variable declaration throughout your program by checking the Require Variable Declaration check box on the Environment tab of the Options dialog box. This dialog box is accessible by choosing Options from the Tools menu. ▪

You can create properties for your class in this manner, but it is not the method recommended by most programmers. A public variable is visible to your application as soon as the object is created. Any part of your program can change the value of the variable without performing any checks on the data. Bad data passed to the object can then cause problems with operations done by the object.

Property Procedures   A better way to create properties in a class is to use the property procedures. These procedures provide the interface to the properties of the object, but they let you write code to verify that the proper data is passed to the class and perform other processing of the data. This protects the functions of your class from crashing as a result of bad data. Property procedures also provide you with the ability to create read-only properties, something that is not possible when using public variables.

There are three types of property procedures available: Property Let, Property Get, and Property Set. These procedures are defined in Table 32.2.

Table 32.2   Three Property Procedures Set and Retrieve the Values of Properties

Procedure Type	What It Does
Property Let	Accepts the value of a property from the calling program. Used to set the value of the property.
Property Get	Sends the value of the property to the calling program. Used to retrieve the value of the property.
Property Set	Special case of the Let procedure, used if the type of variable being set is an object.

To create a property procedure, you need to be in the Code window for the class with which you are working. Then choose Add Procedure from the Tools menu. This displays the Add Procedure dialog box, as shown in Figure 32.2.

FIG. 32.2

Create a property procedure by using the Add Procedure dialog box.

In the Add Procedure dialog box, enter a name for the procedure. (This name will be the name of the property for your object.) Next, choose the Property Option button on the dialog box and then click OK. This creates a Property Let and a Property Get procedure in your class module, as shown in Figure 32.3.

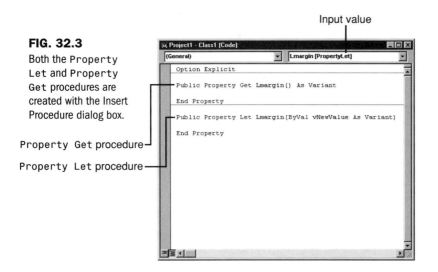

FIG. 32.3

Both the Property Let and Property Get procedures are created with the Insert Procedure dialog box.

Property Get procedure ─┘

Property Let procedure ──

Setting a Property's Value   Notice that in Figure 32.3, the Property Let procedure automatically adds an argument to the procedure. This argument is the value that is passed from the calling program by the property-assignment statement. You can change the name of this argument to any valid variable name. You also can—and should—define the type of the variable by using the As VarType clause of the argument.

The code you place in the Property Let procedure typically takes the argument's value, performs data validation if necessary, and assigns the value to a private variable in the class module. When you use the private variable for any tasks in the class module, the information is protected from being inadvertently changed by other parts of the program. An example of a Property Let procedure follows:

```
Private m_lmarg As Integer

Public Property Let LMargin(LMarg As Integer)
    If LMarg < 0 Then
        m_lmarg = 0
    Else
        m_lmarg = LMarg
    End If
End Property
```

The preceding property procedure simply makes sure the LMargin property of a class is never less than 0. For example, consider the following incorrect use of the property:

```
Myobj.Lmargin = -1234
```

The property procedure would store a 0 in the private variable, instead of the negative value in this line of code. If you defined the property with a public variable, this type of data validation would be much harder to accomplish.

Retrieving a Property's Value   The `Property Get` procedure lets your program retrieve the value of the property. This is done by assigning the value to be returned to the name of the property, as shown here:

```
Public Property Get LMargin() As Integer
    LMargin = m_lmarg
End Property
```

You can also place other code in the procedure when a value for the property needs to be calculated or other actions need to be taken in returning the property's value. Notice that the `Property Get` procedure just shown includes the `As Integer` clause in the first line. This is optional, but if it is included, the type should be the same as that used for the argument passed to the `Property Let` procedure.

You can create a read-only property for a class by including only the `Property Get` procedure for the property. If the `Property Let` procedure is excluded, there is no way for the property value to be set other than by code within the class module.

Objects Are a Special Case   For some of your properties, you will want to be able to pass a database object, a control, or some other object to the class module. In this case, you must use the `Property Set` procedure instead of the `Property Let` procedure to give the property a value. When passing an object, the private variable you're using in the class module must be of the object type. This and the `Property Set` procedure are shown in the following code:

```
Private OutputTo As Object

Public Property Set OutputDev(inDev As Object)
    Set OutputTo = inDev
End Property
```

Notice in the code that the `Set` statement is used to assign the value of the object to the private variable. The `Set` statement is required any time you are setting the value of an object.

Methods Let the Class Take Actions

Because a class that could not perform actions would be practically useless, you need a way to create methods for your class. This is done by writing *public procedures* for the class. These procedures are just like the ones you write for other parts of your program. The procedures in a class can even have arguments passed to the procedures by the calling routines, just like other procedures. Passing arguments provides the final way to get information into the class. (Remember, public variables and property procedures were the other ways.)

▶ **See** "Using Procedures and Functions," **p. 246**

Like all other procedures, the procedure in a class module starts with the declaration statement. If this statement uses the `Public` keyword, then the procedure becomes a method of the class and is accessible to any program that creates an object based on the class. If the procedure is prefaced by the `Private` keyword, the procedure can be called only from within the class itself. The following code shows a simple procedure in a class that prints a line of text to the printer in bold font. Because the procedure is public, it becomes a method of the class module:

```
Public Sub PrintBold(InText As String)
    curBold = Printer.Font.Bold
    Printer.Font.Bold = True
    Printer.Print InText
    Printer.Font.Bold = curBold
End Sub
```

Adding Events to Your Class

In Chapter 4, "Working with Forms and Controls," you learned what events were and how to handle them in your code. An event is triggered when the user takes an action, such as a keystroke, or when a change has taken place, such as having a specific amount of time elapsing. Your classes can also initiate events as they are running. This is a new feature of Visual Basic 5 that enhances the capability of your classes.

▶ **See** "Exploring Properties," **p. 68**

To create an event in your class, you need to do two things:

1. Declare the event in the class.

2. Use the RaiseEvent statement to trigger the event.

To declare an event, you simply supply the name of the event and the variable passed by the event in a statement like the following:

```
Public Event QueryStatus(ByVal Completion As Single, _
ByRef Cancel As Boolean)
```

This statement is placed in the declarations section of the class in which you want the event. The Public keyword is necessary to allow programs using the objects created from the class to respond to the event. The variables allow the event to pass information to the program using the class and to receive information back from the program. The event declared in the preceding code could be used to keep the user informed of the status of a long query and to allow the user to cancel the query prior to completion.

After the event is declared, you can use the RaiseEvent statement to trigger the event anywhere in the code of your class. For the QueryStatus event, you might want to trigger the event after every 100 records that have been processed as shown in Listing 32.1.

Listing 32.1   Triggering an Event in Your Class

```
Public Sub ProcessData()
Dim MaxRecords As Long, RecordsProcessed As Long
Dim blnCancel As Boolean
If ClsRset.RecordCount = 0 Then Exit Sub
ClsRset.MoveLast
MaxRecords = ClsRset.RecordCount
RecordsProcessed = 0
blnCancel = False
ClsRset.MoveFirst
Do While Not ClsRset.EOF
```

```
        If RecordsProcessed Mod 100 = 0 Then
            RaiseEvent QueryStatus(RecordsProcessed / MaxRecords, blnCancel)
            If blnCancel Then Exit Sub
        End If
        ClsRset.MoveNext
        RecordsProcessed = RecordsProcessed + 1
    Loop
End Sub
```

To write code for an object event in your program, see the section titled "Handling an Object's Events" later in this chapter.

Creating Public Constants as Enumerations

You can't declare public constants in a public class module, so how do you make constants available to other applications through a class? You use an *enumeration,* or, in Visual Basic, Enum.

Public enumerations in a public class are available to other applications and viewable through the Object Browser. In the following code, which shows the definition for an enumeration, you need only assign the actual value of the first member (in this case, One). The remaining members are automatically assigned their values sequentially.

```
Public Enum Numbers
    One = 1
    Two
    Three
    Four
    Five
End Enum
```

Part
VII

Ch
32

After including this declaration in your program, you can refer to the constants One, Two, Three, Four, and Five, which will return the values 1, 2, 3, 4, and 5, respectively. Figure 32.4 shows how Enum looks in the Object Browser from another application.

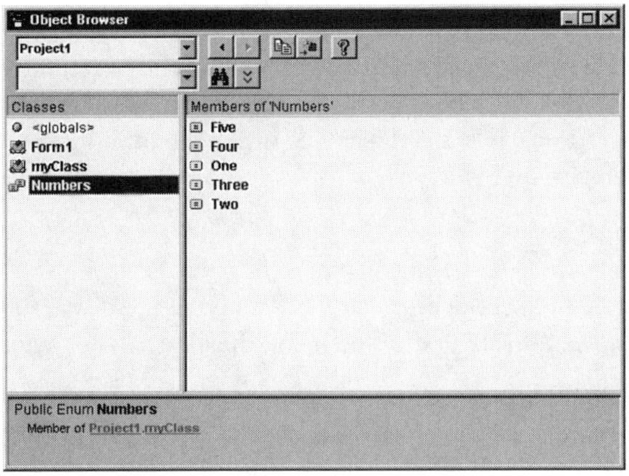

FIG. 32.4

The Enum name appears in the Classes list, and the items appear in the Members list of the Object Browser.

Accessing a Class from a Program

After creating a class, you will, of course, want to use it in your program. In fact, you will probably want to use it in several programs. After all, this is why programmers create reusable components in the first place.

Using a class is relatively easy, but it's a little different than using other program pieces with which you might be familiar. The main thing to remember is that a class cannot be used by itself. You must create an object from the class and then manipulate the object by setting its properties and using its methods. The creation of the object is the key part using the object, because you are already familiar with setting properties and using methods of other objects such as controls.

Creating the Object   There are two ways to create an object from a class that you have developed—using a declaration statement or using a Set statement. After the object is created using either of these ways, you have access to its properties and methods and can use the object in your program. When the object is created using either method, the code in the Initialize event of the class module is run for the object.

Using a Declaration Statement   The first way to create an object from a class is to do it directly, with a declaration statement such as the following:

```
Dim EhnPrint As New cPrint
```

The declaration defines an object variable as being a new instance of the class (in this case, the cPrint class, shown in earlier code segments). Notice the use of the New keyword in the declaration. This keyword is required when you create an instance of an object.

Using the Set Statement   The second way to create an object from a class is by using the Set statement. In this case, an object variable is declared, and then the Set statement is later used to create the instance of the object. The following code illustrates this method of creating an object:

```
Dim EhnPrint As Object
Set EhnPrint = New cPrint
```

Again, after the Set statement is used to create the object variable, the object's properties and methods are available to your program. The only difference from the previous method is that with this method, the object is not actually created until the Set statement is used. This is known as *late binding*, because the object type is not set until the Set statement executes. The preceding code can also be written as follows:

```
Dim EhnPrint As cPrint
Set EhnPrint = New cPrint
```

In this case, the type of object to be created is defined in the declaration statement, but because the New keyword is not present in the statement, the object is not actually created until the Set statement is issued.

If the object you are creating has events associated with it, you need to use the Set method to create the object. You also need to add one more keyword to the variable declaration statement. This is the `WithEvents` keyword. This keyword tells your code that the object will contain custom events that are available to be handled by your program. The use of the `WithEvents` keyword is shown in the following statement:

```
Private WithEvents mDataProc As DataProc
```

Setting and Retrieving the Property Values   After the object has been created, you have access to its properties. You can set and retrieve values of the properties in your code using assignment statements, just as you would for the properties of a control. For example, the following code sets the left margin of the `EhnPrint` object:

```
EhnPrint.LMargin = 500
```

Because I previously defined `LMargin` in the class using a property procedure, this assignment statement causes the `Property Let` procedure of the class to be run. Similarly, to retrieve the value of the left-margin property, you use a statement like the following:

```
curmarg = EhnPrint.LMargin
```

As with properties of controls, you need to make sure that variables and literal values used in accessing the object's properties are of the same type as was defined for the property. Also, if you are going to be retrieving values of the property, it is a good idea to set a default value in the `Initialize` event of the class module.

When the property of an object is itself an object, you cannot use a standard assignment statement to set or retrieve the value. In this case, you must use the `Set` statement. The following code shows how the value of the `OutputDev` property of the `EhnPrint` object is set and retrieved:

```
'Setting the value of the property
Set EhnPrint.OutputDev = Printer

'Retrieving the value of the property
Set objvar = EhnPrint.OutputDev
```

As with any other properties, the variable or literal used in assigning or retrieving a property value must be of the same type as the property. In this case, the `objvar` variable must be defined as an object variable.

Using the Methods   Using the methods of the objects you create is like using the methods of Visual Basic's internal objects and controls. To execute a method, you supply the name of the object and the name of the method and provide any values that are required by the method as arguments. For the methods of your class, these arguments are defined in the argument list of the class module's procedure. The following line of code runs the `Output` method of the `EhnPrint` object:

```
EhnPrint.Output "This is a test."
```

Handling an Object's Events   Handling the events of an object you create is the same as handling the events of a form, control, or other object in your program. Basically, you write code for the events you want to handle and don't write code for the events you want to ignore. After you have declared an object using the `WithEvents` keyword, the object is added to the list

Part
VII

Ch
32

of objects in the Code window of your program. To handle an object's events, you select the object from the left drop-down list, select its event from the right drop-down list, and then write code for the event.

Getting Rid of an Object After you've finished using an object in your program, you want to get rid of it to recover the resources that it was using. You accomplish this by literally setting the object to nothing, as shown in the following code:

```
Set EhnPrint = Nothing
```

Note that an object created within a form or a procedure is usually released when the procedure terminates or when the form is unloaded. However, it's good practice to release the object when you're finished with it. When the object is released, any code that was in the Terminate event of the class is run.

Using the Class Builder

When you create a new class, Visual Basic presents the option of creating an empty class or starting the Class Builder (Figure 32.5).

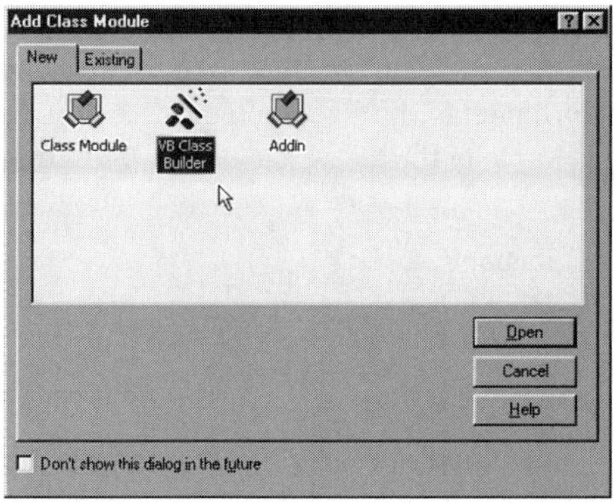

FIG. 32.5
Double-clicking Class Builder starts a tool to help you organize classes in your application.

The Class Builder can be used to generate outlines for new classes or modify and reorganize existing classes. Figure 32.6 shows the Class Builder with the Math class loaded.

To add an item to your project, click one of the toolbar buttons; the Class Builder displays a dialog box where you can enter all the attributes of the new item. Figure 32.7 shows the dialog box presented for a new method.

When you close the Class Builder, it updates your project with any changes or additions that you entered. You still have to fill in the working code, but the Class Builder generates the appropriate declarations and supporting code.

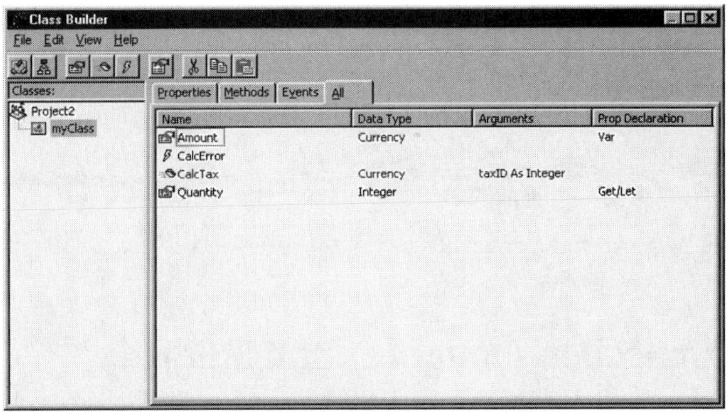

FIG. 32.6
The Class Builder provides a graphic interface to the classes, properties, methods, constants, and events in your application.

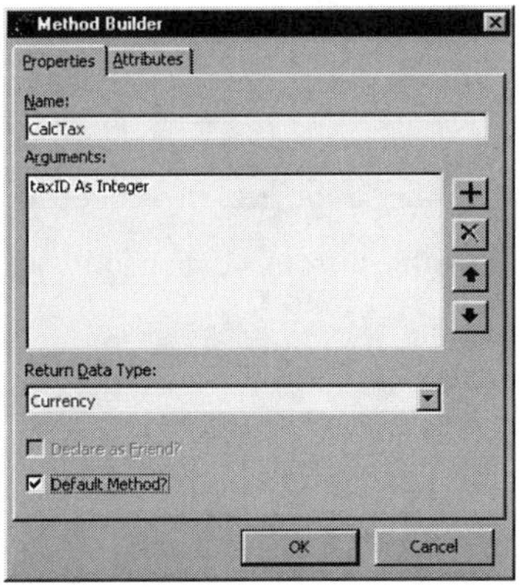

FIG. 32.7
The Method Builder dialog box presents all options available for a method.

Creating Classes that Contain Collections

A *collection* is a group of objects that is itself a type of object. Visual Basic has two built-in collection objects: the Forms collection and the Controls collection. You can use collections with the For Each...Next statement to perform actions on all the objects they contain. The MinimizeAll procedure, shown in Listing 32.2, minimizes each loaded form in an application.

Listing 32.2 MINIMIZE.TXT—Using the *For Each* Structure to Handle All the Objects in a Collection

```
' Minimizes all loaded forms.
Sub MinimizeAll()
    Dim frmElement As Form
    ' For each loaded form.
    For Each frmElement In Forms
        ' Minimize the form.
        frmElement.WindowState = vbMinimized
    Next frmElement
End Sub
```

Collections solve three problems faced by most programmers when working with objects:

- They provide a standardized way to create and track multiple instances of an object.
- They group similar objects for fixed tasks, such as changing color properties or dragging to a new location.
- They organize large systems of objects into a hierarchy.

The following sections describe each of these aspects of using collections when creating object-oriented applications in Visual Basic.

Standard Collection Properties and Methods

Collections share a common set of properties and methods. Some collections might have additional properties and methods, but all collections have at least the set described in Table 32.3.

Table 32.3   Properties and Methods Common to All Collections

Item	Purpose
Count property	Finds the number of objects in a collection
Item method	Gets a single object from a collection

In addition to the items in Table 32.3, collections usually provide two more methods. The methods in Table 32.4 are common to *most* collections.

Table 32.4   Methods Common to Most Collections

Method	Purpose
Add	Adds an object to a collection
Remove	Deletes an object from a collection

The Add and Remove methods provide programmers a standard way to create and delete items in a collection. The Visual Basic Forms and Controls collections are maintained by Visual Basic, so they don't support these methods. Add and Remove are very common in object libraries, such as those provided by Microsoft Excel and Project.

Creating a New Collection for Grouped Actions

You can create new collections to contain forms, controls, and ActiveX objects. Use the Collection object data type when creating a new collection. The following declaration creates a new collection named colSelected:

```
Dim colSelected As New Collection
```

Declaring a variable as a Collection object gives you four built-in properties and methods, as shown in Table 32.5.

Table 32.5 *Collection* **Object Built-In Properties and Methods**

Item	Purpose
Count property	Returns the number of objects in the collection
Add method	Adds an object to the collection
Item method	Gets a single object from the collection
Remove method	Deletes an object from the collection

The code in Listing 32.3 creates a new collection named colTextBoxes and adds all the text boxes on a form to the new collection.

Listing 32.3   CREATECOL.TXT—Creating the *colTextBoxes* Collection

```
Option Explicit

' Create a new collection to contain all the
' text boxes on a form
Dim colTextBoxes As New Collection

Private Sub Form_Initialize()
    ' Variable used in For Each to get controls.
    Dim cntrlItem As Control
    ' Loop through the controls on the form.
    For Each cntrlItem In Me.Controls
        ' If the control is a text box, add it to the
        ' collection of text boxes.
        If TypeName(cntrlItem) = "TextBox" Then
            colTextBoxes.Add cntrlItem
        End If
    Next cntrlItem
End Sub
```

The code in Listing 32.4 uses the collection colTextBoxes to clear all the text entered on the form:

Listing 32.4   Using *For Each* to Handle the Collection

```
Sub cmdClear_Click()
    ' Variable used in For Each to get controls.
    Dim cntrlItem As Control
    ' Clear each of the text boxes in the collection.
    For Each cntrlItem In colTextBoxes
        cntrlItem.Text = ""
    Next cntrlItem
End Sub
```

Using Collections to Organize Objects

Object hierarchies are necessary when an application defines a large number of classes that relate to one another. The hierarchy defines an understandable way for users to choose from among the many objects. You use collections to create a hierarchical organization of classes. The Excel object library is a good example of a large class hierarchy. You can use Excel collections to find individual objects. For example, the following line makes a cell in a worksheet boldfaced:

```
Application.Workbooks("stock.xls").Sheets("Portfolio).Range(1,1).Font = xlBold
```

Table 32.6 describes the action taken by each method or property in the preceding line of code.

Table 32.6   Description of Items in the Excel Boldface Object Example

Item	Purpose
Application	Returns the top-level object in Excel.
Workbooks	The `Application` object's `Workbooks` method returns the collection of all loaded workbooks in Excel.
("stock.xls")	The default method for the `Workbooks` collection is the `Item` method, so `"stock.xls"` returns the STOCK.XLS `Workbook` object within the `Workbooks` collection. An index number would also work here.
Sheets	The `Workbook` object's `Sheets` method returns a collection of all the sheets in a workbook. This includes worksheets, dialog sheets, chart sheets, and so on.
("Portfolio")	Again, the implicit `Item` method returns a single `Sheet` object from within the `Sheets` collection.
Range	The `Worksheet` object's `Range` method returns the collection of cells on a worksheet.
(1,1)	The `Range` object's `Item` method returns a single cell from the Range collection.
Font = xlBold	The `Range` object's `Font` property sets the cell's font to appear bold.

N O T E   Before you can use Excel's objects from Visual Basic, you need to add a reference to Excel's object library. ■

There are a few important points to notice about the example shown in the preceding Excel object code sample and Table 32.6:

■ Each object defines a method that returns the collection of objects the next level down in the hierarchy. This is the mechanism used to navigate downward from the top-level object to the individual cell.

■ Not all collections are homogeneous. For example, the Sheets collection can contain objects of these different types: Worksheet, Chart, Module, and DialogSheet.

■ The bottom-level object (Range) is a collection of items, not a collection of objects. There is no Cell object in the Excel object library.

N O T E For more information about collections, refer to Chapter 16, "Using the Windows Common Controls."

▶ **See** "Creating a Toolbar with Code," **p. 427** ■

Classes in Your Programs

Now that I've covered the basics of developing and using a class module, take a look at a couple of examples of using class modules in actual programs. These examples are relatively simple, but they demonstrate the power of classes. You can enhance these examples to provide powerful tools for your own programs.

A Better Printer

One of the biggest problems with sending data to the printer is that you don't know how long the line of print will be when you send it, and the printer itself isn't smart enough to perform word wrapping. The cPrint class shows a way to handle this problem by providing you with an object that does word wrapping. The object also provides properties that let you set the desired margins for the output. As an added bonus, the object lets you choose where to print the output of the code—to the printer, a form, or a picture box. Figure 32.8 shows the form used to run the example program.

Part
VII

Ch
32

FIG. 32.8
The form pictured here is an interface used to test our sample print class.

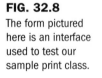
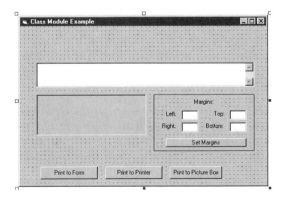

The form has a text box for you to enter the string to be printed, as well as a picture box that is one of the output choices. In addition, three command buttons are placed on the form to let you determine where to direct the output. Also, text boxes and a command button are used to set new margin values for the output device. The code for this program is located in the CLASSEX.VBP file.

The CLASSEX.VBP project shows you how to create and use a class to print information to a variety of objects. Download this project from **www.mcp.com/info/0-7897/0-7897-1288-1**.

Setting Up the Class   The first step in setting up the class for the enhanced printer object is to create the class module. You can do this by choosing Class Module from the Insert menu. You then give the class module the name cPrint by setting the Name property. The Public property of the class module is set to False, because this class is used only inside the current program. At this point, all the properties of the class module have been set, and you're ready to input code for the class.

Defining the Internal Variables   The next step is to define the internal variables that will be used by the class module to store the values of the module's properties. These variables are declared as private, so that they cannot be directly manipulated by the calling program. The code in Listing 32.5 shows the variable declaration for the cPrint class.

Listing 32.5   Declaring the Private Variables of the Class

```
Option Explicit

Private OutputTo As Object
Private m_lmarg As Integer, m_rmarg As Integer
Private m_tmarg As Integer, m_bmarg As Integer
Private objwid As Integer, objhit As Integer
Private txtht As Integer, endpos As Integer, txtlen As Integer
Private strtpos As Integer, endps2 As Integer
Private prntln As String
```

The first line of the code, the Option Explicit statement, indicates that all variables must be declared prior to their use in the code. The next three lines declare the variables that will be used with the object's properties. The OutputTo variable contains the object that is the destination of the printout. This variable is set to another object, such as the printer or the name of a form or picture box. The four variables ending in marg will contain the values of the page margins input by the user. The other declaration statements set up the other variables that are used in the processing of the printout.

Creating the Properties   The cPrint class has an interface that lets the user set the desired output device and the page margins for the printout. This interface consists of the properties defined for the class. These properties are defined by the Property Let, Property Get, and Property Set procedures of the class. Listing 32.6 shows the procedures for the four margin properties and the output-device property.

Listing 32.6   Properties of a Class Are Defined by Property Procedures

```
Public Property Get LMargin() As Integer
    LMargin = m_lmarg
End Property
```

```
Public Property Let LMargin(LMarg As Integer)
    If LMarg < 0 Then
        m_lmarg = 0
    Else
        m_lmarg = LMarg
    End If
    objwid = OutputTo.Width - m_lmarg - m_rmarg
End Property
Public Property Get RMargin() As Integer
    RMargin = m_rmarg
End Property

Public Property Let RMargin(RMarg As Integer)
    If RMarg < 0 Then
        m_rmarg = 0
    Else
        m_rmarg = RMarg
    End If
    objwid = OutputTo.Width - m_lmarg - m_rmarg
End Property
Public Property Get TMargin() As Integer
    TMargin = m_tmarg
End Property

Public Property Let TMargin(TMarg As Integer)
    If TMarg < 0 Then
        m_tmarg = 0
    Else
        m_tmarg = TMarg
    End If
    objhit = OutputTo.Height - m_tmarg - m_bmarg
End Property

Public Property Get BMargin() As Integer
    BMargin = m_bmarg
End Property

Public Property Let BMargin(BMarg As Integer)
    If BMarg < 0 Then
        m_bmarg = 0
    Else
        m_bmarg = BMarg
    End If
    objhit = OutputTo.Height - m_tmarg - m_bmarg
End Property


Public Property Set OutputDev(inDev As Object)
    Set OutputTo = inDev
    objhit = OutputTo.Height - m_tmarg - m_bmarg
    objwid = OutputTo.Width - m_lmarg - m_rmarg
End Property
```

Part

VII

Ch

32

Notice that to set the output-device property, a `Property Set` procedure must be used. This is because the output device is an object.

Supplying an Output Method Next, because the object needs to be able to perform some function, a method must be created for the class. You can do this by creating a `Public` procedure in the class module. The method for the `cPrint` class performs the word-wrapping of the input text. This method is defined by the code in Listing 32.7.

Listing 32.7 A *Public* Procedure Defines the *Output* Method of the cPrint Class

```
Public Sub Output(prntvar As String)
txtht = OutputTo.TextHeight("AbgWq")
    Do
        endpos = 0
        txtlen = 0
        prntln = ""
        Do
            strtpos = endpos + 1
            endpos = InStr(strtpos, prntvar, " ")
            prntln = Left$(prntvar, endpos)
            txtlen = OutputTo.TextWidth(prntln)
        Loop Until txtlen > objwid Or endpos = 0
        If endpos = 0 Then
            prntln = prntvar
            endps2 = InStr(1, prntln, vbCrLf)
            If endps2 > 0 Then
                prntln = Left$(prntvar, endps2 - 1)
                prntvar = LTrim$(Mid$(prntvar, endps2 + 2))
            Else
                prntvar = ""
            End If
        Else
            prntln = Left$(prntvar, strtpos - 1)
            endps2 = InStr(1, prntln, vbCrLf)
            If endps2 > 0 Then
                prntln = Left$(prntvar, endps2 - 1)
                prntvar = LTrim$(Mid$(prntvar, endps2 + 2))
            Else
                prntvar = LTrim$(Mid$(prntvar, strtpos))
            End If
        End If
        OutputTo.CurrentX = m_lmarg
        OutputTo.Print prntln
    Loop While Len(prntvar) > 0
End Sub
```

Initializing the Class Finally, because the user might call the method without first setting the properties of the class, it's a good idea to set initial values for the internal variables. This is done in the `Initialize` event of the class, as shown in Listing 32.8.

Listing 32.8   Setting the Initial Value of Variables

```
Private Sub Class_Initialize()
    m_lmarg = 0
    m_rmarg = 0
    m_tmarg = 0
    m_bmarg = 0
    Set OutputTo = Printer
End Sub
```

Using the Class   As said earlier, to use a class in a program, you must create an instance of the object defined by the class and then set the properties of the object and use its methods. For the cPrint class example, this is all done in the form that supplies the user interface for the example code.

First, the object is defined in the Declarations section of the form using a declaration statement, as shown here:

```
Dim EhnPrint As New cPrint
```

If the user chooses to set page margins for the output, values can be entered in the text boxes for the appropriate margins. The text-box values are then assigned to the properties of the object, using the code in the Click event of the Set Margins command button. This code is shown in Listing 32.9.

Listing 32.9   Setting the Margins of the Output Device

```
Private Sub cmdSetMargin_Click()
  EhnPrint.LMargin = Val(txtMargin(0).Text)
  EhnPrint.RMargin = Val(txtMargin(1).Text)
  EhnPrint.TMargin = Val(txtMargin(2).Text)
  EhnPrint.BMargin = Val(txtMargin(3).Text)
End Sub
```

As you can see, the properties are set using simple assignment statements. The Val function is used in the event that the user accidentally enters a text string instead of a number in the text box.

Finally, after the user has entered some text to be printed, the Output method of the object can be used to print the text. The following code shows how this is done to print the text to the picture box:

```
Private Sub cmdPicture_Click()
  Set EhnPrint.OutputDev = picPrint
  PrntStr = txtInput.Text
  EhnPrint.Output (PrntStr)
End Sub
```

The code first uses the Set statement to tell the EhnPrint object to direct the output to the picPrint picture box. Next, the text to be printed is retrieved from the text box. Finally, the text string is passed to the object's Output method. The results of this operation are shown in Figure 32.9.

FIG. 32.9
The *cPrint* class can be used to output text to different output devices.

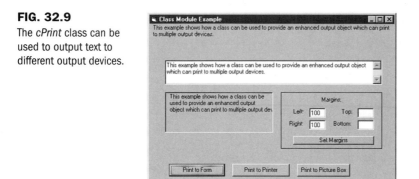

Database Access

Another use of classes is in database access. The sample class shown in this section is used to simply open a database and return the database object to the calling program. You're probably wondering why you wouldn't just use the database objects directly to perform this operation. The answer is that using a class lets you encapsulate the OpenDatabase method and all the associated error-handling code that is required for it.

By using a class, you don't have to repeat this code multiple places in your program or in multiple programs. You simply create it once in a class module and then create an instance of the class any time that you need to open the database in your program. You can also easily create an ActiveX DLL from the class module, which keeps you from having to add the class module to other programs. The final advantage is that if you find additional things that you need your open database routine to handle, you have to change the code in only one place—the class module. Then all your programs have the benefit of the changes. The example case is contained in the file CLSDBEX.VBP.

The CLSDBEX.VBP project shows you how to create and use a class to open databases. You can download the project file from **www.mcp.com/info/0-7897/0-7897-1288-1**.

The *cDataAccess* Class   The cDataAccess class is fairly simple. The class consists of one method and one read-only property. To use the class, the name of a database is passed to the OpenDb method, and then the database object is retrieved using the OpenData property. The code for the class is shown in Listing 32.10.

Listing 32.10   The *cDataAccess* Class Property and Method

```
Private m_ClsDb As Database

Public Property Get OpenData() As Database
Set OpenData = m_ClsDb
End Property
Public Sub OpenDb(dbName As String)
On Error GoTo DBErrHandle
```

```
    Set m_ClsDb = DBEngine.Workspaces(0).OpenDatabase(dbName, _
    False, False)
    On Error GoTo 0
    Exit Sub

DBErrHandle:

    errnum = Err
    Select Case errnum
        Case 3049
            'Corrupt database, attempt to repair
            msgstr = "Your database has been damaged.  Do you wish the "
            msgstr = msgstr & "program to attempt to repair it?"
            msgrtn = MsgBox(msgstr, vbYesNo + vbExclamation, "Database Problem")
            If msgrtn = vbNo Then Exit Sub
            RepairDatabase (dbName)
            Resume
        Case 3056
            'Couldn't repair database
            msgstr = "Your database could not be repaired.  You will "
            msgstr = msgstr & "need to restore the database from your "
            msgstr = msgstr & " latest backup!"
            MsgBox msgstr, vbExclamation, "Database Problem"
            Exit Sub
        Case Else
            'Show any other messages
            msgstr = "The following error occurred while trying to open "
            msgstr = msgstr & "the database: "
            msgstr = msgstr & Error$(errnum)
            MsgBox msgstr, vbExclamation, "Database Problem"
            Exit Sub
    End Select
End Sub
```

Part

VII

Ch

32

Notice that in the `Property Get` procedure, the property is defined as a `Database` object. This is to match the object that will receive the value of the property.

Using *cDataAccess* The case I'll use as a sample calls the object to open the BIBLIO.MDB database that comes with Visual Basic. The code then opens the Authors table of the database and displays a list of authors in a list box. The code for the example is shown in Listing 32.11.

Listing 32.11 Accessing the *cDataAccess* Object

```
Dim db As Database
Dim rs As Recordset
Dim objData As Object

Private Sub cmdAuthors_Click()
    Set objData = New cDataAccess
objData.OpenDb "C:\VB5\BIBLIO.MDB"
    Set db = objData.OpenData
    Set objData = Nothing
```

continues

Listing 32.11   Continued

```
    Set rs = db.OpenRecordset("Authors", dbOpenDynaset)
    Do Until OldRc.EOF
        lstAuthors.AddItem rs("Author")
        rs.MoveNext
    Loop
    Db.Close
End Sub
```

Figure 32.10 shows the results of the sample program.

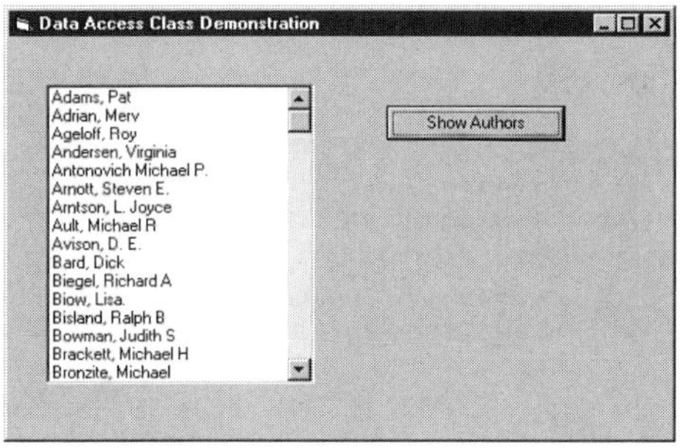

FIG. 32.10

The cDataAccess object is used to handle the opening of the database.

Documenting Objects, Properties, and Methods

One great advantage of using classes is that you can easily distribute them to other programmers. However, unless there is some type of documentation included, understanding how to use your objects could be a major challenge. For example, the programmer needs to know the purpose of each parameter in a function. Fortunately, you can document your objects, properties, and methods at two levels:

- In the Description line of the Object Browser
- In a help file that accompanies your application

To document the object's properties and methods in a project, follow these steps:

1. From the Project menu, choose Project Properties. Visual Basic displays the Project Properties dialog box.

2. Enter the name of the project's help file in the Help File Name text box. The user interface items in your project share the same help file with the project's more technical aspects, such as programming with objects, properties, and methods.

3. From the Tools menu, choose Procedure Attributes. Visual Basic displays the Procedure Attributes dialog box.

4. Select the method or property that you want to document. Type the description that you want to appear in the Object Browser in the Description text box. Type the help context ID for the method or property in the Help Context ID text box.

5. Repeat Step 4 for each item that you want to document.

Help for a project's objects, properties, and methods resides in the same help file as for the rest of the project. When designing your help file, be careful not to confuse users by including highly technical programming topics in the same table of contents used by people seeking help on your application's user interface.

TROUBLESHOOTING

If you have the Professional Edition of Visual Basic but get an error message when you try to create a `Public` class module, your installation might be corrupt. Try reinstalling the Visual Basic development environment.

If your ActiveX object doesn't recognize methods and properties that you've just defined, check to make sure that you are running the correct version of the object. When debugging, it is easy to accidentally load the compiled DLL or EXE rather than the new version that hasn't yet been compiled. To avoid this, be sure to start the ActiveX application in the other instance of Visual Basic *before* calling it from the client application. Also, make sure the client application's reference points to the correct class in the References dialog box.

If you encounter a `Duplicate Definition` error when trying to add an object to a collection, make sure that the key argument is unique within the collection.

From Here...

This chapter provided you with an introduction to the creation of class modules, which allow you to implement the principles of object-oriented programming. Class modules, when compiled into a separate ActiveX DLL or EXE, provide a powerful tool for encapsulating program functions. In this chapter, we created a sample class and used objects from it in a program. To learn more about some of the topics covered in this chapter, see the following chapters:

- To learn more about writing functions and procedures for use in a class module or other modules, see Chapter 10, "Managing Your Project."

- You can learn how the techniques applied to classes can be used in creating your own ActiveX controls by referring to Chapter 20, "Creating ActiveX Controls," Chapter 21, "Extending ActiveX Controls," and Chapter 22, "Creating a User-Drawn Control."

Part
VII

Ch
32

CHAPTER 33

Visual Basic versus VBScript versus VBA

On May 20, 1991, Microsoft announced Visual Basic at Windows World '91 in Atlanta, and the programming world hasn't been the same since. Windows programmers finally had a powerful programming language that was simple to use and intuitive. Microsoft has capitalized on the success of Visual Basic by incorporating it into several of its other products, including Office and Internet Explorer. These other "flavors" of Visual Basic, known as VBA and VBScript, differ slightly from standard Visual Basic. However, because they are based on Visual Basic, you can apply what you already know to either of them. In this chapter, you will learn how to use each of these products to help make your job as a programmer much easier. ■

Learn about differences and similarities of VB, VBA, and VBScript

Find out why there are three versions of Visual Basic and where you can use each one.

Write functions that will work with VB, VBA, and VBScript

Explore the language differences and learn how to write functions for a specific version of Visual Basic.

Program Outlook 97 and learn how to use VBScript to create Web pages

Discover how you can add a VBScript procedure to both a Web page and Microsoft Outlook.

Use the appropriate "flavor" of VB for a specific task

Learn when to use standard VB and when to use another variety.

Understanding the Differences Between VB and VBA

VBA, which stands for *Visual Basic for Applications*, is Microsoft's attempt to create a common macro language for Windows products. VBA is most prevalent in the Microsoft Office family of products. It allows you to place Visual Basic code within an Office document. This enables you to write intelligent documents that work like applications. For example, with a little code, an Excel sheet can read information from a database, perform calculations and formatting, and then send itself to someone via e-mail. Although not as powerful as standard Visual Basic, VBA is as easy to use as Visual Basic and shares most of its core features, such as these:

- Close integration with OLE (including enhanced OLE Automation support)
- A VBA-type library with a fundamental subset of the Visual Basic language
- The capability to use ActiveX controls developed for VB 4.0 or later
- Consistency across different implementations in the form of a common user interface called VBE (Visual Basic Editor). The VBE was introduced with Office 97. Previously, code was stored in a separate page (or sheet) of the document.

In spite of all this, VB and VBA are different. Compared to standard Visual Basic, there are limitations both in language capabilities and the development environment. However, VBA is still a robust language for shared code across multiple applications. VBA's ties to VB make it a mature language, even though it was first released in 1993.

N O T E   For the first time ever, Microsoft has made it possible for any company to purchase the rights to include VBA (and the VBE environment) in that company's own applications. This means your current VB/VBA code can be ported to other applications in addition to those developed by Microsoft, such as Visio Professional. In the future, look for more non-Microsoft applications that use VBA/VBE.

Although VB and VBA are similar, they differ in some important ways. Perhaps the most important difference is the definition of the two languages. Table 33.1 provides these definitions.

Table 33.1   Distinguishing Between VB and VBA

Language	Definition
Visual Basic	Since the advent of Visual Basic 5.0, that version actually contains the shared version of VBA 97. The major difference is that it enables you to create a stand-alone executable or Automation server that you can distribute to users who do not own a Microsoft application.
Visual Basic for Applications	Introduced in the fall of 1993 as a replacement for Microsoft Excel's XLM macro language, VBA 97 is now included in Access, Excel, PowerPoint, and Word. Additional products will also be released with VBA. The most significant difference is that VBA applications

Language	Definition
	require the product they were created in. In addition, its form and control support is significantly different from the enhanced version you'll find in Visual Basic 5.0.

All of this might be rather confusing, but there's a simple way to differentiate between VB and VBA: VB is a separate programming product that enables you to make executables, and VBA is a macro language for applications. As of VB 4.0, both products can share elements (type libraries) through the Object Browser.

Using Visual Basic for Applications

Starting with Visual Basic 5.0, VB has included all the features of VBA (in the form of a shared type library); code written in pure VBA can be shared across all products that use the VBA 97 type library. For example, the code in Listing 33.1 could appear in either VB or VBA.

Listing 33.1   GREETINGS.TXT—The Greetings Routine Is Compatible with Both VB and VBA

```
Sub Greetings(YourName As String)
Dim Reply As Integer

    Reply = MsgBox("Hello " & YourName & _
        ", are you ready to compute?", vbQuestion + vbYesNo)

    If Reply = vbYes Then
        MsgBox "Well then, let's get busy!", vbInformation
    Else
        MsgBox "I'm sorry to hear that, but you must.", _
                vbInformation
    End If

End Sub
```

From looking at the code in Listing 33.1, it is difficult to determine which language was used. Figure 33.1 shows an example of VBA in Microsoft Excel, and Figure 33.2 shows an example of Visual Basic 5.0. Note the differences in the Project window. In both languages, you can have code modules and forms. However, VBA handles forms (or UserForms, as they're called in VBA) a bit differently. This is because when you are working with VBA everything is based on a document.

Part

VII

Ch

33

FIG. 33.1
VBA in Microsoft Excel 97 is very similar to standard Visual Basic.

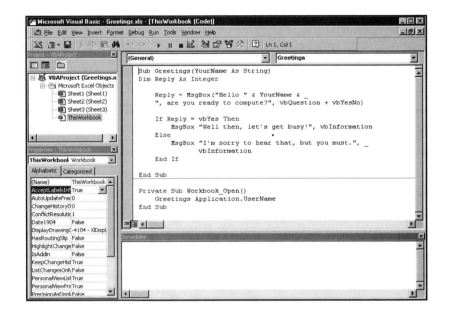

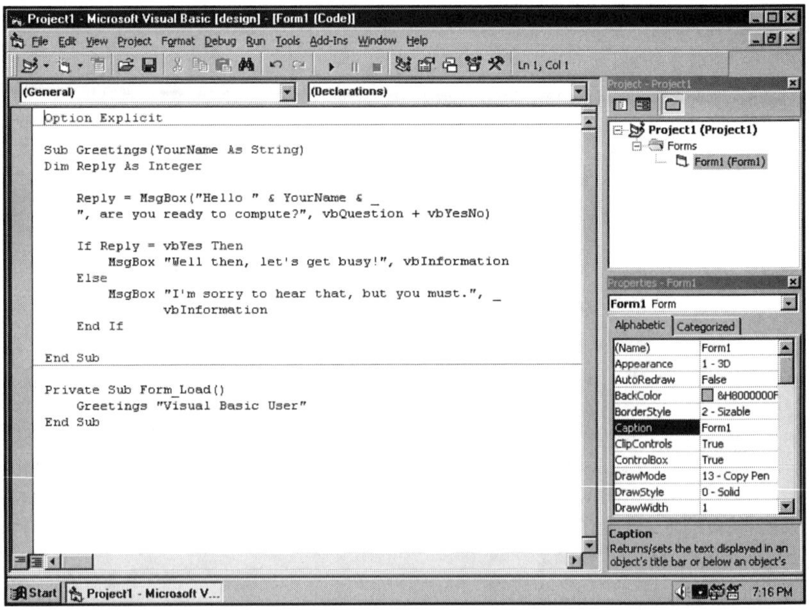

FIG. 33.2
The Visual Basic 5.0 development environment (pictured here) and the Excel VBA development have only minor differences.

The Que Web site contains an implemented sample of Greetings that will work with Access, Excel, PowerPoint, Word, and Visual Basic 5.0. Download *[this sample]* from **www.mcp.com/ info/0-7897/0-7897-1288-1**.

Type Libraries and the Object Browser

How can one language meet all the needs of all these different products? That's where *type libraries* enter the picture. A type library is a file that each variation of Visual Basic provides to add product-specific features (for example, accessing a range of cells in Excel). In fact, all products with VBA share a common VBA type library called VBA. What's more, any variation of VBA can use type libraries from other applications to perform OLE Automation. For example, you could add a reference to the Office 97 type library in a standard Visual Basic project. This would allow you to access all the objects from Word or Excel in your program.

> **N O T E** While most people use the terms *type library* and *object library* interchangeably, there is an arguable difference. A type library (.tlb) is a library that typically describes a single object. An object library (.olb) is a library that contains two or more type libraries within a single file. However, this definition is subject to criticism, because there are type libraries with .olb extensions and object libraries with .tlb extensions. What's worse is that there are even object and type libraries with a .dll extension (such as VBA). Ultimately, the distinction is unimportant so long as you know what these libraries are used for. For simplicity's sake, I use these terms interchangeably. ■

Type libraries can be viewed in a program called the Object Browser, which is built into VBE. Object Browser (see Figure 33.3) provides the user with a list of the available libraries and their elements.

FIG. 33.3
The Object Browser in VBE provides a view of the features of each object.

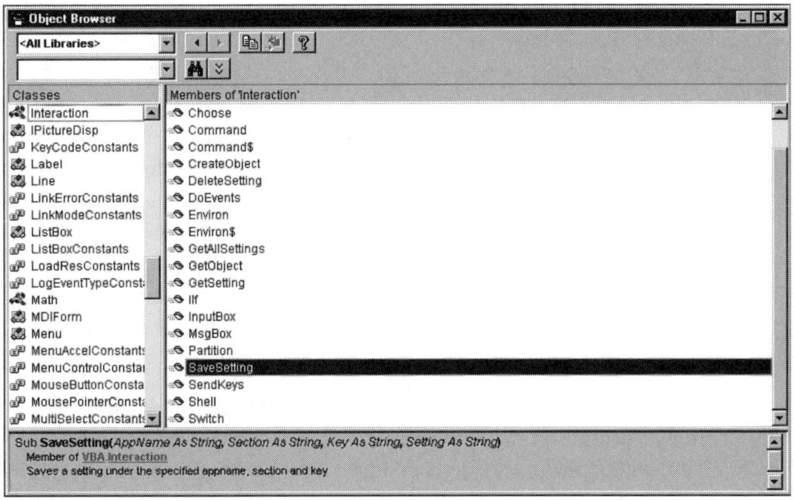

Part
VII

Ch
33

> **N O T E** Visual Basic 5.0 also has the Object Browser. It can be accessed by choosing <u>V</u>iew, <u>O</u>bject Browser, or by pressing the F2 key. ■

▶ **See** "Creating Public Constants as Enumerations," **p. 839**

Although type libraries are a bit more than just aids to make programming easy in VB, as a VB programmer, that's all you need to know about them. More information on type libraries (including developing type libraries for .dlls written in C) can be found on the Microsoft Developers Network.

Introducing the Newest Visual Basic: VBScript

Currently, Microsoft has three shipping versions of BASIC for Windows: Visual Basic, Visual Basic for Applications, and VBScript. You've already seen the two Visual Basic forms, and you've probably heard of VBScript.

VBScript is a scaled-down version of Visual Basic that uses fundamental VB syntax. *Script* refers to the fact that it is intended as a scripting language, similar to a DOS batch file. VBScript code is typically found embedded directly in a Web page, as is JavaScript, but it doesn't have to be. For example, Outlook 97 uses VBScript as its macro language. This section provides a brief overview of VBScript, as well as comments on how it differs from the other varieties of Visual Basic.

An Overview of VBScript

VBScript is a small subset of the features you'll find in the VBA type library. If you have seen VBScript code, you know that it is very limited compared to VB and VBA. However, these language limitations are by design. VBScript is designed to be lightweight because its code is interpreted on-the-fly, but there are also security reasons. This section briefly discusses each of these issues. VBScript was designed for use on Web pages. As you might be aware, the HTML behind a Web page can also include script language code. Scripts are used to enhance Web pages, in the same way VBA can make an Excel document more than just a static spreadsheet. Prior to the introduction of VBScript, JavaScript was established as the industry standard for Web page scripting, but JavaScript's similarity to C++ made it difficult for VB programmers to use. The main purpose for Microsoft's developing VBScript was to provide a Web scripting language compatible with Microsoft's industry standard for Windows development, Visual Basic. However, this new language was going to be embedded into Web pages, so it needed to be simple enough that it could be interpreted as quickly as JavaScript. To accomplish this, the Visual Basic language needed to be simplified.

Since the introduction of VB 1.0, many features have been added to Visual Basic to simplify common programming tasks, but many of these new features could have been accomplished in VB 1.0 with a few extra lines of code. Therefore, the goal of VBScript was to give the VB programmer a small set of fundamental features that could be used together to accomplish more complex tasks. This means that programming in VBScript requires a little more effort and ingenuity than required by VB, but the end result can be just as powerful.

Another reason why VBScript was scaled down from its VB/VBA siblings was for security concerns. If Microsoft let VBScript programmers call the Windows API or perform file I/O, then a hacker easily could write a virus in VBScript to crash every system that executed his or her VBScript Web page. To reduce the chances of someone writing malicious scripts, all the features of VB that potentially could be abused were removed.

Perhaps the biggest difference (and source of frustration) between VBScript and standard VB is that VBScript supports only the `Variant` data type. This means that a statement like `Dim x As Integer` would trigger an error in VBScript, because the `Integer` data type is not supported. This change was made because it simplifies the code for the interpreter, thus making execution much faster. However, this change really isn't a limitation for VB programmers, because the `Variant` data type is flexible enough to support all the data types used by VB.

On the Web

To learn more about VBScript or download the latest version, visit **www.microsoft.com/ vbscript/** on the Internet.

Now let's look at our simple Greetings routine again. Listing 33.1 demonstrated how the code looks in VB or VBA (refer to "Using Visual Basic for Applications" earlier in the chapter); Listing 33.2 shows how the Greetings routine would look in VBScript.

Listing 33.2   GREETINGS.VBS—VB Code Works in VBScript, but Not Without Minor Modifications

```
Sub Greetings(YourName)
    Dim Reply

    Reply = MsgBox("Hello " & YourName & _
        ", are you ready to compute?", vbQuestion + vbYesNo)

    If Reply = vbYes Then
        MsgBox "Well then, let's get busy!", vbInformation
    Else
        MsgBox "I'm sorry to hear that, but you must.",vbInformation
    End If

End Sub
```

Part

VII

Ch

33

Notice in the preceding code that the variable `Reply` is not declared as an `Integer`. Instead, it becomes a `Variant`. Another difference is in `For` loops, as seen in Listing 33.3. Although this might be a little different from what you are used to, you can see that your knowledge of VB goes a long way in creating great VBScript code.

Perhaps the most striking difference is not in the language itself but in how you create applications with it. Chances are you will be working with a text editor and Internet Explorer. In addition, your VBScript code will be mixed in with HTML, as shown in Listing 33.3.

Listing 33.3   GREETINGS2.VBS—A Web Page with Embedded VBScript Code

```
<HTML>
<HEAD>
<TITLE> Sample Page </TITLE>
</HEAD>
<BODY>

<SCRIPT LANGUAGE="VBScript">
<!--

    Dim nValue
    Dim nCounter

    nValue = InputBox("Please Enter a number between 1 and 10")

    For nCounter = 1 to nValue
        Document.Write "You Entered " & nValue & "<BR>"
    Next
-->
</SCRIPT>

</BODY>
</HTML>
```

As you can see, a VBScript For...Next loop just uses the word Next without a variable name. Table 33.2 lists all VBA language elements missing from VBScript.

On the Web

This information was taken directly from the VBScript documentation available at **www.microsoft.com/vbscript/**.

Table 33.2   VBA Features Not in VBScript 2.0

Category	Omitted Feature/Keyword
Array Handling	Option Base Declaring arrays with lower-bound <> 0
Collection	Add, Count, Item, Remove Access to collections using ! character (for example, MyCollection!Foo)
Conditional Compilation	#Const #If...Then...#Else
Control Flow	DoEvents GoSub...Return, GoTo On Error GoTo On...GoSub, On...GoTo Line numbers, Line labels With...End With

Category	Omitted Feature/Keyword
Conversion	CVar, CVDate Str, Val
Data Types	All intrinsic data types except Variant Type…End Type
Date/Time	Date statement, Time statement Timer
DDE	LinkExecute, LinkPoke, LinkRequest, LinkSend
Debugging	Debug.Print End, Stop
Declaration	Declare (for declaring .DLLs) Property Get, Property Let, Property Set Public, Private, Static ParamArray, Optional New
Error Handling	Erl Error On Error…Resume Resume, Resume Next
File Input/Output	All
Financial	All financial functions
Object Manipulation	TypeOf
Objects	Clipboard Collection
Operators	Like
Options	Def*type* Option Base Option Compare Option Private Module
Strings	Fixed-length strings LSet, Rset Mid Statement StrConv
Using Objects	Collection access using !

At first, this long list of omissions might be intimidating, but don't give up. The most important features of VB are included in VBScript, so you still can write powerful scripts. The only difference is that now you have to be more creative doing so. You might find that some of the tricks you invent to overcome these limitations are so good that you want to port them back to your VB applications. VBScript is a new challenge, but it can be a lot of fun.

Using VBScript on a Web Page

The information in the previous section focused on using the VBScript language. VBScript code can be used in any host that supports it, but using VBScript in a Web page is a little more complex. To use VBScript in your Web page, you must add some HTML code that tells the browser that your Web page contains script code. In addition, VBScript doesn't support the forms that you are accustomed to using in VB or VBA. This means that your code also must include information about which controls to use and where to place them. This section discusses how to use VBScript in a Web page and how to simplify the processing of VBScript development.

T I P To make viewing and editing your VBScript HTM files easier, I suggest placing a shortcut to Notepad (or your favorite text editor) in your \Windows\SendTo directory. After doing this, you can right-click a file in Explorer and easily open it for editing.

To begin using VBScript in your Web page, you must first tell your Web browser which scripting language you plan to use. This is easily accomplished by adding a line that reads `<SCRIPT LANGUAGE="VBScript">` in your Web page. Immediately after the `SCRIPT` statement, write your VBScript code in an HTML comment block. Your code must appear inside a comment block, so browsers that do not support VBScript do not display your code in the Web page. At the end of your comment block, inform your browser that there is no more code by closing the script block using the `</SCRIPT>` tag. Listing 33.4 demonstrates a minimal Web page that displays a message box every time the page is accessed.

Listing 33.4   SIMPLE.HTM—Simple.htm Demonstrates a Minimal VBScript Web Page

```
<HTML>
<HEAD>
<SCRIPT LANGUAGE="VBScript">
<!--
    MsgBox "Hello World!"
-->
</SCRIPT>
</HEAD>
</HTML>
```

There are some cases where you want your code executed as soon as the page is loaded, but typically you'll want to execute your code in response to an event (as you do in VB). To do this, you need both a control on the page that the user can interact with and an event handler for that control. In VB, this is done for you when you place a command button on the form, and a `Click` event is created when you double-click the control. In VBScript, you must do this yourself, but it isn't too difficult. For example, Listing 33.5 shows how to create a command button on the form and display a message box in response to the `Click` event.

Listing 33.5 VBSCRIPT.HTM—VBScript.htm Demonstrates How to Interact with the User

```
<HTML>
<HEAD>
<SCRIPT LANGUAGE="VBScript">
<!--
Sub Command1_OnClick()
    MsgBox "Hello World!"
End Sub
-->
</SCRIPT>
<FORM>
    <INPUT NAME="Command1" TYPE="BUTTON" VALUE="Click Me">
</FORM>
</HEAD>
</HTML>
```

Now that you've seen how to work with simple VBScript Web pages, take another look at the Greetings sample. As you learned from Listing 33.4, you can define a subroutine in the comment block in the HEAD section of a Web page. You also learned how to create an event procedure for a command button. Now you can apply these techniques to create a program where the user enters his or her name into a text box, clicks a button, and is greeted with the Greetings routine (see Listing 33.6).

Listing 33.6 GREETINGS.HTM—Greetings.htm Is a Complete VBScript Application in a Web Page

```
<HTML>
<HEAD>
<TITLE>VBScript Demonstration Page</TITLE>
<SCRIPT LANGUAGE="VBScript">
<!--
Option Explicit

Sub Greetings(YourName)
    Dim Reply

    Reply = MsgBox("Hello " & YourName & _
    ", are you ready to compute?", vbQuestion + vbYesNo)

    If Reply = vbYes Then
        MsgBox "Well then, let's get busy!", vbInformation
    Else
        MsgBox "I'm sorry to hear that, but you must.", _
                vbInformation
    End If

End Sub
```

Part
VII

Ch
33

continues

Listing 33.6   Continued

```
Sub Command1_OnClick()
    Greetings Form1.Text1.Value
End Sub
-->
</SCRIPT>
</HEAD>


<!--********************************************************-->
<!-- Display some HTML text to tell the user what to do  -->
<!-- and call the Greetings function from a HTML form.   -->
<!--********************************************************-->

<BODY>
<BR>
<H3>Enter your name:</H3>
<P>
<HR>
<FORM NAME="Form1">
    <INPUT NAME="Text1" TYPE="TEXT" VALUE="">
    <INPUT NAME="Command1" TYPE="BUTTON" VALUE="Click Me">
</FORM>

</BODY>
</HTML>
```

The only major difference between the sample in Listing 33.6 and previous samples is that we included a text box on the form and used its contents as the argument for Greetings. At this point, you have a VBScript application similar to one created in VB (shown in Figure 33.4). The source code looks a little different, and it was a little more difficult to write, but the same result was achieved. This is an important concept to remember when planning VBScript projects. These projects require a little more thought and time than you might be used to, so allow yourself that extra time when setting your client's expectations.

A Quick Look at VBScript Programming in Outlook

Although Internet Explorer is technically the first application to use VBScript as its macro language, Outlook is the first non-Web-based application to use VBScript. This means that you can write simple VBScript code to add interesting features to Outlook. Although a complete discussion of programming Outlook using VBScript is beyond the scope of this book, this section walks you through a simple demonstration upon which you can build.

Programs written in Outlook using VBScript are designed to be executed in response to an event, such as opening an e-mail message. The way you assign code to these events is a little tricky, but the following steps make it easy:

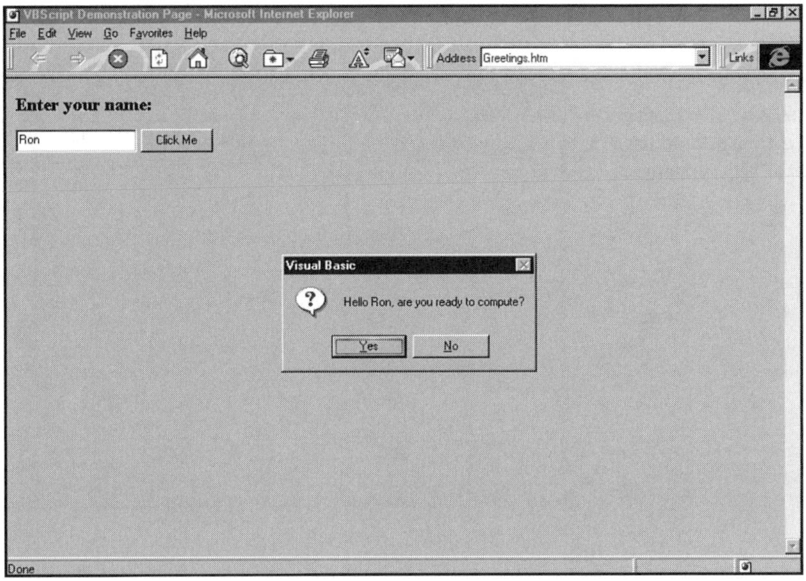

FIG. 33.4

The main purpose of VBScript is creating interactive Web pages for Internet Explorer and Internet Information Server.

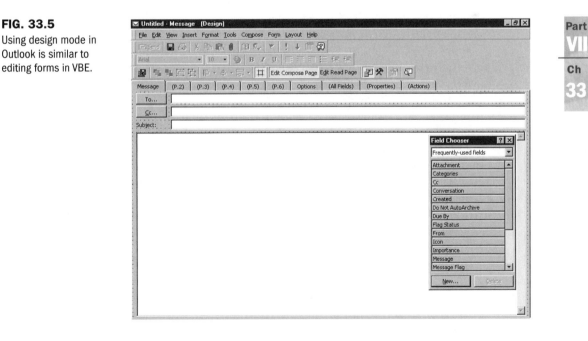

1. Choose File, New. Select any type of Outlook form (for example, a Mail Message).

2. Choose Tools, Design Outlook Form. Your form should now be in design mode, as shown in Figure 33.5.

FIG. 33.5

Using design mode in Outlook is similar to editing forms in VBE.

3. Choose Form, View Code. You should now see the Script Editor (see Figure 33.6).

FIG. 33.6

Outlook's Script Editor allows you to create and edit VBScript commands.

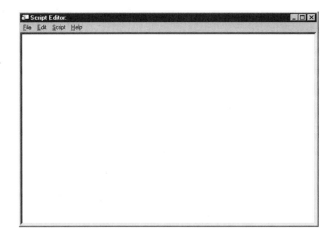

4. Choose Script, Event. Select an event (for example, Open), and then click Add.

5. Type in some VBScript code (for example, **MsgBox "Hello World!"**) and then close the Script Editor. (You are not prompted to save your changes, but that's okay.)

6. Return to the form that you put into design mode in Step 2, and then choose File, Publish Form As.

7. Enter a name and then click Publish.

8. Close the form, and when prompted, save the changes.

9. To test your new form, choose File, New, Choose Form. Select your form and then click OK. (If you chose the Open event in Step 4, your code is executed now.)

10. Execute your form. For example, if you chose Mail Message in Step 1, then send an e-mail message to yourself by using the custom form that you opened in Step 8.

    If you followed our examples, when you try to open your e-mail message you will get a message box that displays "Hello World!" Don't be alarmed when you see the macro virus protection warning message shown in Figure 33.7.

Now return to the familiar Greetings example. Using the 10 steps just listed, replace the code in Step 5 with the code in Listing 33.7. This code is the same VBScript code that we put in our Web page, plus a new line in the Item_Open event. Figure 33.8 shows a message box that results from this code.

FIG. 33.7
Outlook warns you if it senses possible macro virus activity.

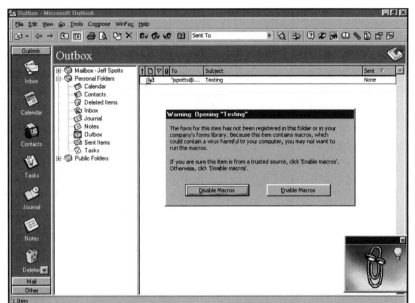

FIG. 33.8
The message generated by the sample VBScript code.

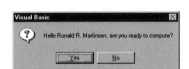

Listing 33.7 OUTLOOK.VBS—The VBScript Version of Greetings Can Be Ported with No Modifications

```vbscript
Sub Greetings(YourName)
    Dim Reply

    Reply = MsgBox("Hello " & YourName & _
        ", are you ready to compute?", vbQuestion + vbYesNo)

    If Reply = vbYes Then
        MsgBox "Well then, let's get busy!", vbInformation
    Else
        MsgBox "I'm sorry to hear that, but you must.", _
                vbInformation
    End If

End Sub

Function Item_Open()
    Greetings Item.Recipients(1).Name
End Function
```

The code in the Item_Open event calls Greetings using the name of the first recipient in your e-mail message as the name passed to Greetings. Easy, right?

Well, you're probably wondering how we knew about the Recipients collection and the Name property. After all, that's the only real Outlook programming in this example. The answer is easy: Outlook uses an object library, the same as VBA. The problem is that VBScript editors have no way of displaying this object library, so it doesn't do you much good if you can't use it.

To view the Outlook object library, launch your favorite version of VBE (such as VB5) and then add a reference to the Microsoft Outlook 8.0 Object Library. From there, you can view all of the objects (such as the Recipients collection or the MailItem object) in the Object Browser. While we wish we could say there is a great reference book on programming Outlook, we can't. You have to trudge through the object library and learn by trial and error. However, if you stick to the ten steps listed previously, half of your battle is complete.

Knowing When to Use Which Variety of Visual Basic

Many programmers often complain that they are confused by all the "Basics" found in Microsoft products. In this section, we will try to clear up this confusion for you. Each of the different flavors of VB has a specific purpose, so choosing the correct one is important.

When should you use any one of these versions of BASIC? The answer depends on your needs. Use Table 33.3 as a guide to help decide which version is best for you.

Table 33.3   Choosing the Right Language

Language	Usage
Visual Basic	If your application requires the maximum amount of flexibility, or if you need to create a stand-alone executable or shared component, then Visual Basic is right for you.
Visual Basic for Applications	If your application depends on an application that uses VBA as its macro language (for example, Excel or Word), then use VBA. Unless your users do not have one of these products, VBA is probably the right choice for your application. Remember that VBA includes support for OLE Automation, so your possibilities are virtually endless. (For more advice, see the Note that follows this table.)
VBScript	If you're programming a Web page or in Outlook, then you have to use VBScript. Although VBScript isn't as feature-rich as VB or VBA, it still can be used to write sophisticated applications.

N O T E If you're developing a custom application that might include working with Office-type documents, and your customer doesn't have Microsoft Office 97, consider buying him a copy. Even the smallest customized solution can cost several thousand dollars, so including Office (typically, you can purchase a competitive upgrade copy very reasonably) can save weeks or months of development time. ▨

While the choice between VBA and VBScript is clear, knowing when to use VB instead of VBA is a little more complex. The best way to think of VB is as an object factory. VB is best suited for creating objects (for example, custom controls, shared OLE objects, and so on). VB is also the better choice for advanced custom solutions that need to be both fast and stand-alone. VBA, on the other hand, is most useful for automating or adding features to powerful products such as Microsoft Excel or even your Web pages in Internet Explorer.

From Here...

Now you know a bit about the varieties of Visual Basic. Although the focus of this book is on VB 5.0, many of the techniques discussed are applicable to VBA. As far as VBScript is concerned, viewing the source code behind Internet Web pages is a great way to learn more. You can also check out these resources:

- ▨ For more information about VBA programming, consult the Microsoft Developers Network CD or visit the MSDN World Wide Web site at **http://www.microsoft.com/msdn**.

- ▨ For more information on VBScript, visit the Visual Basic Scripting Edition Web site at **http://www.microsoft.com/vbscript**.

Part
VII

Ch
33

CHAPTER 34

Working with Sound and Multimedia

U sing multimedia techniques in your programs allows you to be very creative. You can easily create flashy programs with sound and graphic effects. Applications that use multimedia elements are becoming more and more common as the processor speeds and disk capacities of PCs continue to reach new levels. ■

What is multimedia?

Learn the different elements used in creating multimedia applications.

How to access multimedia files from Visual Basic

See how to use the Multimedia control to open and play a variety of multimedia files.

Using animation in your programs

See how to create simple animations that can be used to enhance your programs.

Using sound in your programs

Learn how to play sounds from within Visual Basic.

Working with Multimedia Elements

When you use the term multimedia, most people probably think of movies played on the computer with an accompanying soundtrack, or of graphics-intensive, interactive computer games. Some people might even think of the virtual reality simulations that are becoming more prevalent. While these are all uses of multimedia applications, multimedia itself has a much simpler definition. Multimedia is the use of different visual and audio techniques to present information or entertainment to the user. These techniques can include various types of audio material, animation, video, simple graphics, and even text. To give you a better understanding of multimedia as a whole, take a look at each of the elements of multimedia: sight, sound, and animation. A multimedia application combines these elements to provide an innovative and interesting user interface. Within each of the three broad categories are several elements. The discussion of these elements is the subject of this section.

Working with Sound

Sound is probably the most familiar of all the multimedia elements. One simple example of working with sound is the humble beep. You often encounter a beep when you hit the end of a data entry field or try to click a window while a modal dialog box is being shown. While you would probably realize that you could not enter any more characters or move to another window after the computer refuses to respond to your request, the beep has become a way of notifying you that you have tried to perform an operation that is not allowed. This illustrates the way that sound is used in many applications, as a way to draw attention to the computer and to the task at hand.

As you might know, you can also configure your computer to play different sounds when different tasks are performed in Windows, and in response to different Windows messages. While the use of sounds in this manner is definitely not essential, the aural cues provide notification to the user even if he or she is not looking at the monitor. In addition, if you have a CD-ROM drive, most computers allow you to play music CDs by using a CD Player application like the one shown in Figure 34.1.

FIG. 34.1

Graphical interfaces to multimedia devices are provided by Windows 95's CD Player and a sound card mixer.

A CD Player application mimics what a real CD player looks like. When you use the software, you are actually controlling a real-world device—your CD-ROM drive. This metaphor is extended to your sound card, which has several devices used to produce various sound effects. These devices are usually manipulated in a mixer application (also shown in Figure 34.1) that comes with your sound card.

The sound that you can typically use with your computer is divided into three key types: MIDI sound effects, WaveForm sounds, and CD Audio. Let's take a closer look at these three types of sound, each of which is controllable from Visual Basic.

MIDI   MIDI is the abbreviation for Musical Instrument Digital Interface. MIDI provides a way to store the notes of an instrument (or instruments) in a digital format. The MIDI file actually contains instructions for use by an internal or external *sequencer*. The sequencer interprets the instructions and synthesizes the notes that are contained in the file. Typically, MIDI files are played through the sound card of your computer and output through the speakers. However, with the proper equipment, MIDI also provides you with a way to control instruments, such as electronic keyboards, and to accept input from MIDI instruments for storage.

N O T E   The sound quality of MIDI files depends on the sound card or device on which they are played. Some sound cards use a table of digitally sampled instruments, whereas others use a cruder sounding FM synthesizer. Keep this in mind when distributing a MIDI file. ▪

The audio files for MIDI sounds are much smaller than similar files for WaveForm audio. This is because the MIDI file only contains instructions on how to create the note as opposed to actual sound samples. (This is similar to the differences between bitmap and raster graphics.) MIDI files are great for providing musical backgrounds for an application or Web page. The disadvantage of MIDI files is that you cannot use them for storing voice information, such as narrations or voice annotations, because they only simulate musical instruments.

WaveForm Audio   WaveForm audio is digitized sound that has been stored in files on your computer. Because WaveForm audio is a sample of the actual sounds, it can contain music, voice, or a variety of other sound effects. WaveForm audio is one of the most common forms of audio used in a computer and one of the easiest to create. While MIDI files typically require specialized instruments to create the music, you can create WaveForm audio with a sound card and a microphone. Most sound cards that you get for your computer have the capability of accepting audio input for storage in WaveForm files. This input can come from a microphone, tape deck, or other audio source.

To record WaveForm audio, you can use the Sound Recorder program that comes with Windows 95 (shown in Figure 34.2), or a sound recorder that comes with your sound card. These programs work in the same manner as a tape recorder or VCR. To record sounds, just press the record button and start sampling the sounds you want to record. When you are finished recording, press the stop button and specify the file name and where you want to store the sounds. WaveForm audio provides an easy way to add narration to a program. You can also store tracks from an audio CD in Wave format before writing them to CD-R (recordable) media. WaveForm files, which usually have the extension WAV, are generally much larger than MIDI files. They can be recorded at a number of different sampling rates, which range from AM-radio to CD-sound quality.

FIG. 34.2
The Windows 95 Sound Recorder and other typical sound recorder programs let you record audio for use in your programs.

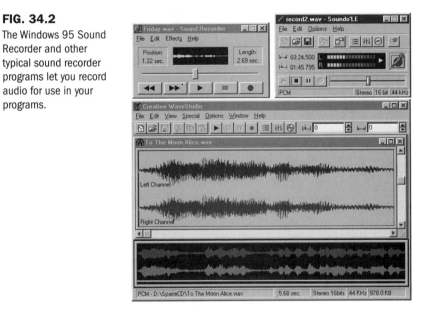

CD Audio   CD audio is the type of audio that you are used to hearing from your home or car stereo. The CD audio capabilities of your computer enable you to play music CDs on your computer. If you do not have a sound card, most CD drives have a headphone jack that lets you listen to the music while the CD Player program controls functions such as Play, Pause, and Skip. If you have a sound card, you can connect the CD to the sound card and play the music through the same speakers that are used for WaveForm files.

CD audio gives you the highest sound quality of any of the audio types. However, it is different from a WAV file in that it is stored on an actual physical CD. You can use VB to play CD tracks in your program. This might be useful in creating a multimedia-enhanced CD-ROM, where you could store both the program and audio tracks on the same CD-ROM. In the past few years, CD-R drives and media have fallen in price, so creating your own CD-ROMS is well within reach. Typically, 176 kilobytes of storage are required for each second of CD audio. This allows about 73 minutes of audio (or 650 megabytes of data) to be stored on a single CD-ROM.

Determining What Your System Will Support   For your computer to work with any of the types of sounds listed in the previous sections, you need to verify that your computer supports the sound type. The easiest way to determine what sounds your system supports is to use the

Windows Media Player application (choose Start, Programs, Accessories, Multimedia, Media Player). After starting the Media Player, click the Device menu. This shows you what types of audio and video devices can be used on your computer (see Figure 34.3).

FIG. 34.3

The Windows 95 Media player (MPLAYER.EXE) lists the multimedia devices installed on your system.

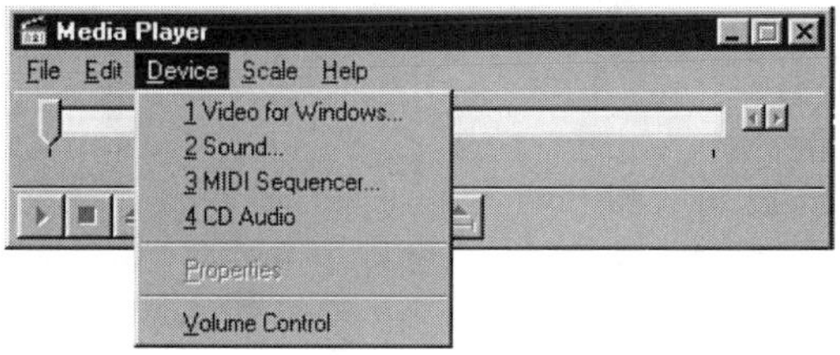

The three sound types discussed earlier in this section are represented by the following menu items in the Device menu:

- *Sound*   WaveForm audio
- *MIDI Sequencer*   MIDI audio
- *CD Audio*   CD music

Working with Graphic Elements

As there were several different types of sound that you could use in your applications, there are also several types of visual elements that can be created or used in your Visual Basic programs. These elements are digital and analog video, animation, and graphics, which includes still pictures, bitmaps, and charts. Which of these elements you use and how you use them depends on the nature of your application. Each element has different capabilities and uses in an application. Let's take a closer look at the major visual elements.

Video   There are two types of video that can be used in your programs: video stored in files and video stored outside your PC. Video files are movies that have been captured by using a video capture board or digital camera and stored in a file on your computer. For motion video, a specified number of frames of information are stored per second of video. Typically, you have from 15 frames per second (fps) to 30 fps, which is considered full motion video. Digital video is the type that you find in most encyclopedia programs or tutorial disks that include video tracks. Some typical video file extensions are AVI, MPEG, and MOV.

Video can also be received from an external device such as a laser disc, camera, or video cassette recorder (VCR). In this case, the computer program might be controlling the device or displaying it on the computer screen. Because of the need for specific external devices, this type of video is more difficult to use and distribute in your programs.

Animation   Animation is simply displaying a series of images to give the user the impression of motion. You have probably seen animation used in Internet Explorer, where the globe spins while you are waiting for a page to load. You might have also seen animation in the Windows Explorer when you are copying a group of files. In this case, letters flying from one folder to another indicate that an operation is occurring (see Figure 34.4).

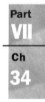

Part
VII

Ch

34

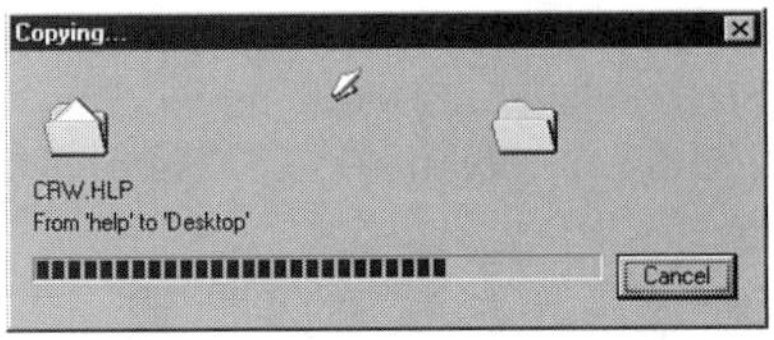

FIG. 34.4
File operations use animation to indicate an ongoing process.

There are two basic types of animation: frame-based animation and object-based animation. Frame-based animation uses a series of frames (usually bitmaps) displayed in rapid succession to give the illusion of motion. Each frame of the animation is a unique picture that displays the entire scene of the animation. Motion is achieved by making subtle changes in the position of objects in each frame of the animation. If you have ever created a flip-book cartoon, you have used frame-based animation. Many animated cartoons use frame-based animation.

In object-based animation, each object of a scene is independent from the others. In object-based animation, an authoring program is used to change the relative placement of each object from scene to scene. This technique is also known as sprite animation. An example would be using a timer control to increment the Left property of a PictureBox, thus making it "move" across the screen.

Graphics   Graphics are static images, in contrast to video or animation. However, graphics comprise a large portion of many multimedia applications. Graphics can include still pictures, bitmap illustrations, business charts, and even dynamic charts that change over time. (For more information about using graphics in your programs, see Chapter 12, "Working with Graphics.")

Working with Text

The final piece of the multimedia puzzle is text. Although text is not as glamorous as video or sound, it is a very important part of almost any program you create. Text still provides you with the most efficient way to present a large amount of information. Text also takes up less space than other media and is easier to use as reference material. Even though text is not fancy, this does not mean that it has to be boring. You can use fonts and color to liven up your text and highlight key information. You can also use specialized text files, like HTML, along with a browser to implement jumps between one document and another. This makes your text interactive to the user.

▶ **See** "Working with Text, Fonts, and Color," **p. 327**

Exploring the Uses of Multimedia

As you have seen, there are a number of elements that can be involved in a multimedia program. Likewise, there are a number of uses for multimedia applications. Some of these uses include:

- ▪ *Games*   Many games include multimedia elements to add to the gaming experience.
- ▪ *Entertainment*   With multimedia applications, you can enjoy music, cartoons, and movies right on your computer screen.

- *Training*   With the use of sound to accompany slide shows or videos, you can create excellent computer-based training programs for a number of training needs. In fact, if you look in your Windows/Media folder, you will find a number of sound-enhanced videos that demonstrate how to perform tasks in Windows.
- *Enhancing business presentations*   Using sound and animation can make dry numbers come alive for your audience.
- *Information Centers*   You can use multimedia elements to build kiosk applications that can direct visitors and display information.

As you begin programming multimedia applications, you will probably find more uses for them than you could have imagined.

Using Animation in Your Programs

Animation is one of the easiest multimedia effects to add to your applications. As you read earlier, animation is simply presenting a series of images in succession. You can use animation to simulate motion of an object, to indicate time passing, or to add transition effect for elements of a presentation. Many parts of the Windows operating system use animation to let the user know that a program is performing a task, such as copying a file or loading a program. Animation is also used in most screen savers to provide a little entertainment. (Some screen savers take this to the extreme by providing a series of animated cartoons. Some of these are so much fun to watch that you forget about doing other work.)

Within Visual Basic, there are two basic ways to handle animation. First, you can write code to present the image series yourself. This method provides you with the most flexibility because you control the images being shown, the timing of the images, and all other aspects of the animation. The second method for adding animation to your program is to use the Animation control.

N O T E   You can also provide some very simple animation for toolbars and command buttons by changing pictures on the buttons as they are pressed. One example is to open a door on the exit button as it is clicked by the user.

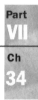

Part

VII

Ch

34

Creating Your Own Animation Effects

To create your own animations, you need three things:

- A control to display the images
- A source for the series of images to be displayed
- A timer routine to determine when to display the next image in the series

To illustrate the concepts involved in creating animation, let's walk through the process of creating a simple animation program that creates a rotating moon on the form.

The source code and bitmaps for this project are located on the Que Web site at **www.mcp.com/info/0-7897/0-7897-1288-1**.

Setting Up the Basic Form   The first step to creating an animation sequence is to set up the basic form for displaying the images of the sequence. The form needs a control to show the images, command buttons to start and stop the animation sequence, and a text box to allow the user to enter the speed of the animation. To create the basic form, follow these steps:

1. Start a new Standard EXE project in Visual Basic.

2. Change the name of the form to `frmAnimate`.

3. Add an Image control to the form and change its name to `imgAnimate`.

4. Add two command buttons to the form and change their names to `cmdStart` and `cmdStop`. Change the `Caption` properties of the command buttons to `Start` and `Stop`, respectively.

5. Add a text box to the form and change its name to `txtSpeed`. Set the `Text` property to `1` to set the default speed of the animation.

6. Add a `Label` control to the form with the caption `Interval:` and place the label next to the text box.

When you have finished these six steps, your form should look like the one in Figure 34.5.

FIG. 34.5
The basic form provides control functions for the animation.

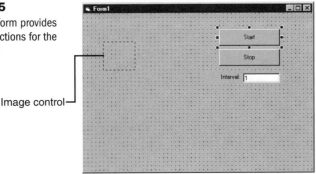

Image control

Setting Up the Image Source   The next step in creating the animation program is to set up the source of the images for the series. For the demonstration, you use an array of image controls. This array is named imgSource and consists of eight image controls with the `Index` properties ranging from `0` to `7`. After you have created the control array, you need to set the picture property of each of the controls. In our example, there are eight bitmaps that display a moon in various phases. These images can be created in the Windows Paint program fairly easily.

After setting the `Picture` property of the Image controls to a different bitmap, you need to set the `Visible` property of the controls of the array to `False`. This keeps the source images from being displayed when the program is run. When you have finished setting up the source images, your form will look like the one in Figure 34.6.

FIG. 34.6

A control array holds the source images.

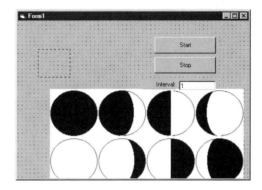

N O T E You could also use an `ImageList` control to store the images for the animation sequence.

Handling the Changing of Images The final step to creating the animation program is to set up the code to show the images in sequence. This involves setting the initial picture of the sequence and displaying subsequent pictures at a specified time interval. The first thing you need to do in the code is to set up module level variables to determine the interval for changing images, the current image sequence number, and a flag to determine whether the animation is running or stopped. These variables are declared in the Declarations section of the frmAnimate form. The declarations are shown in Listing 34.1.

Listing 34.1   FRMANIMATE.FRM—Declaring and Initializing Variables to Control the Animation Sequence

```
Dim PicNum As Integer, RunAnimate As Boolean
Dim RotInterval As Single

Private Sub Form_Load()
  imgAnimate.Picture = imgSource(0).Picture
  PicNum = 0
End Sub
```

Part
VII

Ch
34

After the variables are declared, the `Load` event of the form initializes the variables and places the first image of the sequence in the image control used for display. This is also shown in Listing 34.1.

Next, you need to write the code for the two command buttons that start and stop the animation. In the Click event for the cmdStart button, you retrieve the time interval between image changes from the text box and then set the run flag to indicate that the animation is running. Finally, you call the routine that actually runs the animation. The cmdStop button performs a single function: it sets the RunAnimate flag to False to terminate the animation run. The code for these two command buttons is shown in Listing 34.2.

Listing 34.2   FRMANIMATE.FRM—Command Button Code

```
Private Sub Command1_Click()
  RotInterval = Val(txtSpeed.Text)
  RunAnimate = True
  RotateMoon
End Sub

Private Sub Command2_Click()
  RunAnimate = False
End Sub
```

The final routine is the one that changes the image displayed to the next one in the sequence. The code for this routine is shown in Listing 34.3.

Listing 34.3   FRMANIMATE.FRM—Changing the Image in the Display Control to the Next One in the Animation Sequence

```
Private Sub RotateMoon()
Dim StTime As Single, CurTime As Single
Do While RunAnimate
    imgAnimate.Picture = imgSource(PicNum).Picture
    DoEvents
    StTime = Timer
    Do
        CurTime = Timer
    Loop Until CurTime > StTime + RotInterval
    PicNum = PicNum + 1
    If PicNum > 7 Then PicNum = 0
Loop
End Sub
```

As you can see in Listing 34.3, the code runs as long as the variable RunAnimate is set to True. With each pass through the loop, the Picture property of the imgAnimate control is set to the Picture property of one of the source image controls. The index of the control is determined by the PicNum variable. This variable gets incremented each time you pass through the loop. Because the Index property of the control array only ranges from 0 to 7, the PicNum variable gets reset to 0 each time it goes past 7. This causes the sequence to start over and avoids any errors associated with an index out of range. The interior loop is the one that delays the execution of the next pass of the loop until the specified interval has passed. Timer is a VB function that returns the number of seconds that have elapsed since midnight. The returned value is a

Single data type and can handle fractional seconds. The inner loop repeatedly calls the Timer function until the interval has elapsed.

One final line of note is the DoEvents statement. This statement serves two purposes. First, it gives your program a chance to update the image so the new picture is displayed. Without this, you would see a single image displayed on the form. The second purpose is to allow the user to click the Stop button to terminate the animation.

N O T E Instead of using the Timer function, you could place the code to change the images in the Timer event of a Timer control. You would then set the Interval property of the timer control to the value specified by the text box. ■

Running the Program After saving your program, press F5 or click the Start button to run the program. Set a value for the image interval and click the Start button. If you leave the interval set at 1 second, you see the images change in a discrete manner. If you set the interval to 0.1 seconds, the image changes quickly enough that the rotation of the moon appears to be continuous. Try several settings of the interval and see how it affects the behavior of the animation.

N O T E Because of executing the DoEvents statement, continuing to reduce the interval beyond a certain point produces no appreciable speed increase. For the test machine I was using, this interval was 0.05 seconds. If you require extremely fast graphics, you might want to look into using a graphics API, such as DirectX. ■

Using the Animation Control

The other method of displaying animation sequences in your programs is to use the Animation control. This control displays silent digital video files (.AVI). The control allows you to start and stop the animation process as well as determine whether the animation sequence stops at the end of the file or loops back to repeat the sequence. AVI files can be created by using a video capture card with a video camera or VCR.

▶ **See** "Using Video in Your Programs," **p. 489**

Part
VII

Ch
34

Exploring the Multimedia Control

In the previous sections, you learned about what multimedia is and what types of elements can be used in a multimedia application. You also learned a little bit about creating your own animation effects with code. Although the animation is important, the bulk of your multimedia work will involve accessing different types of multimedia files and playing them through the various multimedia devices on your system. For this, you need a method to open the files, access the appropriate device, and then play the files. In most cases, you also need a method to control the playback of information. For example, most people would not be too happy with a CD player that played all tracks straight through. Your users will want the ability to skip tracks, replay certain tracks, and pause the playback. All these things can be handled with your multimedia programs.

In Windows, multimedia devices are handled through the Media Control Interface (MCI). MCI is a set of Windows functions that can be used to control all aspects of working with multimedia files, from setting up the devices, to pausing playback, to providing information about the current position within the playback (for example, elapsed time). These functions can be accessed directly by declaring the appropriate functions in your Visual Basic program and making the proper function calls to handle your needs. Using the API functions provides you with the most flexibility in programming multimedia applications.

N O T E The API functions used to control multimedia devices are not covered extensively in this book. However, there are some examples of this in Chapter 35, "Accessing the Windows 32 API." ▓

▶ **See** "Calling Basic API and DLLs," **p. 904**

Fortunately, Microsoft has also provided you with an easier way to handle controlling multimedia devices. The Multimedia control (MCI32.OCX) provides you with easy access to most of the functions of the API. The control does this through properties that can be set at design time and changed at runtime. The Multimedia control also uses events to notify you of things taking place in your program, such as the end of playback. Using the Multimedia control will handle a large portion of your multimedia programming needs.

Going Through the Basics

The first step to working with the Multimedia control is to add it to your toolbox. You do this by choosing the Components item from the Project menu, checking the box next to the Microsoft Multimedia Control 5.0 item, and then clicking OK. The next step is to add the control to your form. You do this by clicking the control in the Toolbox and drawing it on the form just like any other control. Figure 34.7 shows a form with two Multimedia controls.

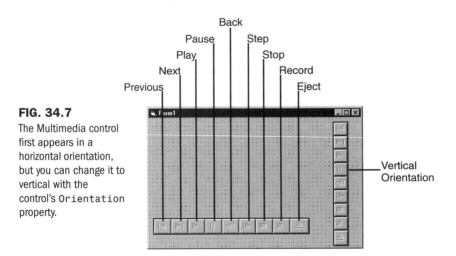

FIG. 34.7
The Multimedia control first appears in a horizontal orientation, but you can change it to vertical with the control's Orientation property.

There are two properties that control the basic appearance of the control. The Orientation property determines whether the control is drawn horizontally or vertically. The BorderStyle property determines whether a single line border is drawn around the buttons of the control.

As you can see in Figure 34.7, all the buttons of the control are displayed when you draw the control and all the buttons are shown as disabled. When you run a program with the Multimedia control, it automatically enables the buttons that are applicable for the type of media you are accessing. As you examine using the Multimedia control to access different types of multimedia elements, you will see which buttons are enabled for each element. For now, let's look at what each button does:

- *Previous* For devices that use tracks, such as CD Audio, moves to the beginning of the current track. If clicked a second time within three seconds, goes to the beginning of the previous track.
- *Next* For devices that use tracks, such as CD Audio, moves to the beginning of the next track.
- *Play* Begins playing the currently open device and file.
- *Pause* Pauses the playing or recording of the current device. When playing or recording is resumed (by clicking the appropriate button), resumption occurs at the point where the program was paused, not at the beginning.
- *Back* Steps backward through the file or track being played. This is the equivalent of a rewind button on a tape recorder.
- *Step* Steps forward through the file or track being played. This is the equivalent of a fast-forward button on a tape recorder.
- *Stop* Halts execution of the current playback or recording and returns the file or track pointer to the starting position.
- *Record* Begins recording sounds from an appropriate input device.
- *Eject* Issues the eject command to remove a CD from the drive.

N O T E Buttons on the control are handled automatically only if the AutoEnable property is set to True (its default setting). If you set the AutoEnable property to False, your program has to handle enabling and disabling the appropriate buttons in the control.

By default, all of the buttons are shown while the Multimedia control is in use and only the appropriate buttons are enabled. If you want to manually enable and disable buttons, or hide the buttons that are not in use, you can do so through the Enabled and Visible properties of each button. These properties are set to either True or False and work just like the Enabled and Visible properties of a regular control. Table 34.1 lists the property names for the different buttons.

Part

VII

Ch

34

Table 34.1 Using Properties to Configure the Multimedia Control Buttons

Button Name	*Enable* Property	*Visible* Property
Previous	PrevEnabled	PrevVisible
Next	NextEnabled	NextVisible
Play	PlayEnabled	PlayVisible
Pause	PauseEnabled	PauseVisible
Back	BackEnabled	BackVisible
Step	StepEnabled	StepVisible
Stop	StopEnabled	StopVisible
Record	RecordEnabled	RecordVisible
Eject	EjectEnabled	EjectVisible

Setting Up the Control

After you have drawn the Multimedia control on your form, you are ready to start working with multimedia devices. To work with any multimedia device, you need to set the DeviceType property of the control. You can set this property at design time or at runtime. The DeviceType property tells the control the type of information that it will be processing, such as a WAV file or CD Audio. Then, depending on the type of device that you are using, you might also need to specify the FileName property. For the devices that use files, the FileName property specifies the file to use for playback or recording. As with the DeviceType property, you can set the FileName property either at design time or runtime. Typically, your applications will include the capability to set the FileName at runtime so that multiple files can be played. Table 34.2 provides a list of the DeviceType settings for the Multimedia control and tells you whether a FileName is required for the device.

Table 34.2 Devices Supported by the Multimedia Control

Device	*DeviceType* Setting	*FileName* Required
AVI videos	AVIVideo	Yes
Music CDs	CDAudio	No
Digital Audio Tape	DAT	No
MIDI	Sequencer	Yes
Wave sounds	WaveAudio	Yes

Working with the Devices in Code

Setting the `DeviceType` and `FileName` properties are the only parts of the Multimedia control setup that can be done in the design environment. To complete the setup of the control, you must open the device and file that you want to use. This function, as well as control of the recording or playback, can be accomplished only by using code while your program is running. You control the multimedia devices through the use of the `Command` property of the Multimedia control. To open a device for use, you need to set the `Command` property, as shown in the following line of code:

```
mmcAudio.Command = "Open"
```

After this command is issued, the device is opened and the appropriate buttons of the Multimedia control are enabled (assuming you left the `AutoEnable` property set to `True`). If you want to use just the Multimedia control for playing sounds and movies, the `Open` command is the only one that you need to use. The control itself handles running the other commands necessary to play or otherwise control the multimedia device. If you want to use your own buttons or other code to control the multimedia device, you need to use other settings of the `Command` property. Table 34.3 lists the settings of the `Command` property and the corresponding button of the Multimedia control.

Table 34.3   Command Property Settings

Command	Button	Command	Button
Open	N/A	Play	Play
Close	N/A	Stop	Stop
Pause	Pause	Back	Back
Prev	Prev	Next	Next
Eject	Eject	Sound	N/A
Save	N/A	Record	Record
Step	Step	Seek	N/A

You might notice that several of the commands do not have corresponding buttons. These commands have special purposes, such as saving a recording to a file or closing the multimedia device. You see how some of these commands are used in the section "Creating Programs to Play Multimedia Files."

Handling the Control's Events

In addition to the property settings of the Multimedia control, it has several events that you will utilize in creating your programs. These events are in addition to the standard events that are applicable to most controls. Let's start the discussion with the button events.

Button Events   For each button of the Multimedia control, there are four events: `Click`, `Completed`, `GotFocus`, and `LostFocus`. These events are identified by the button name and the event name—for example, PlayClick for the Click event of the Play button. The GotFocus and LostFocus events for each button work just like the similar events for any other control. Therefore, focus on the Click and Completed events.

The Click event of each button automatically invokes the command associated with the button. For example, when you click the Play button, play of the device automatically starts; you do not have to write code to make it happen. Therefore, you use the Click event to handle any other tasks that are required when the button is pressed. One other difference between the Click event of the buttons and that of any other control is the Cancel parameter that is passed to the event. By setting this parameter to True, you prevent the button from performing its default command.

N O T E The default command of a button is performed after all the other code in the Click event. ▨

The Completed event of a button occurs when the MCI command issued by the button has finished. This allows you to write code to perform a task at the end of a command. The Completed event also passes an Errorcode parameter. This parameter tells you whether the command completed successfully. If so, the Errorcode parameter is 0; otherwise, the Errorcode is set to a value that indicates the problem that occurred.

Other Events In addition to the button events, there are two other key events for the Multimedia control: the Done event and the StatusUpdate event. The Done event does for the control as a whole what the Completed event does for a button. The Done event is fired when a command has completed. The Done event passes the NotifyCode parameter to tell you the completion status of the command. The values of the NotifyCode parameter are shown in Table 34.4.

Table 34.4 Notification Codes for the *Done* Event

Value	Description
1	The command completed successfully.
2	The command was stopped and superseded by another command.
4	The command was aborted by the user.
8	The command failed.

The StatusUpdate event occurs automatically at specified intervals. This event updates the properties of the Multimedia control that will inform you of the status of the multimedia device. For example, when playing a CD, the Multimedia control keeps track of which CD track is being played and how much of the CD has been played. This information is updated when the StatusUpdate event is fired. You can use the event to display this information in your program. The interval used to fire the StatusUpdate is controlled by the UpdateInterval property. This property sets the number of milliseconds between events. The default value is 1000 milliseconds, which causes the StatusUpdate event to be fired once every second.

Creating Programs to Play Multimedia Files

The best way to demonstrate the capabilities of the Multimedia control is to write some sample programs that use the control and its commands. This section shows you the basics of creating applications to play CD Audio, AVI videos, MIDI files, and WaveForm sounds. In each section, you see how to set up the control and how to get status information from the control. You also see which buttons of the control are enabled for each type of multimedia element.

Playing CD Audio

The first multimedia element you will work with is CD Audio. Beause the CD Audio does not require a file name, it is quite easy to set up. You only have to specify the DeviceType for the Multimedia control and issue the Open command to open the device. The control takes care of the rest of the task. When there is an Audio CD in your CD drive, the following buttons of the Multimedia control are enabled:

- Prev
- Next
- Play
- Pause
- Stop
- Eject

N O T E   The Pause and Stop buttons are only enabled while the CD is playing, and the Play button is only enabled while the CD is stopped. ■

The sample project for this section is located on the Que Web site as CDPLAYER.VBP at **www.mcp.com/info/0-7897/0-7897-1288-1**.

Setting Up the Basic Program   To begin creating a CD player with the Multimedia control, you need to start a new project and then follow these steps:

1. Add the Multimedia control to your Toolbox.
2. Set the Name property of the form to frmCDPlayer and the Caption property to VB CD Player.
3. Draw the Multimedia control on your form and then set the Name property to mmcCDPlayer.
4. Set the DeviceType property of the control to CDAudio.
5. Place the following statement in the Load event of the form:
   ```
   mmcCDPlayer.Command = "Open"
   ```
6. Because several buttons are not used when playing CDs, set the following properties to False: BackVisible, StepVisible, and RecordVisible.

Part
VII

Ch
34

When you have completed these steps, your form should look like the one in Figure 34.8.

FIG. 34.8
A simple CD Player can easily be created with the Multimedia control.

To play a CD, run the program. If you already have an audio CD in the drive, the Play button of the Multimedia control will be enabled and you can start the playback. If there is a data disk or no disk in the drive, only the Eject button will be enabled. The control keeps polling the CD drive to determine when it contains an audio CD. As soon as you place an audio CD in the drive, the appropriate buttons will be enabled.

Determining the Track Number and Total Tracks   While you can now play CDs with your program, the program is not very informative to the user. There is no information about the number of tracks on the CD or which track is being played. You can remedy this situation with a couple of additional controls and a little bit of code. You first need to add controls to keep up with the number of tracks and the current track. You can do this with labels, text boxes, or with a slider control. For the sample project, labels were used.

A   You need to add four Label controls to your form—two to identify the information and two to hold the actual information. The sample application uses two control arrays—lblCDPlayer and lblTracks—to identify and hold the information, respectively. The updated form is shown in Figure 34.9.

▶ **See** "Creating a Control Array," **p. 497**

FIG. 34.9
Keep up with the currently playing track of a CD.

To handle placing the information in the labels, you need to add code to the StatusUpdate event of the Multimedia control. The code accesses the Track and Tracks properties of the control. The Track property tells you the current track that is playing, and the Tracks property tells you the total number of tracks on the CD. The following code handles displaying the current track and total tracks:

```
lblTracks(0).Caption = mmcCDPlayer.Track
lblTracks(1).Caption = mmcCDPlayer.Tracks
```

Determining Track Times   In addition to determining the track information, you probably want your program to show the length of the current track and of the CD. You also probably want to show the elapsed time on the CD and the elapsed or remaining time for the track. Displaying this information is also handled by using code in the StatusUpdate event to access properties of the Multimedia control. To handle time information, there are four properties that you need to access:

- *Length*   Returns the total length of the CD
- *Position*   Returns the current position of the CD
- *TrackLength*   Returns the length of the current track
- *TrackPosition*   Returns the starting position of the current track

Each of these properties return a time value based on the format specified in the TimeFormat property of the Multimedia control. Although there are a variety of formats that can be used, the simplest time format to work with returns the time values in milliseconds. You need to specify this format by setting the TimeFormat property to 0 in the Load event of your form. You also need a routine that converts the times to an hours:minutes:seconds format to display to the users. This function is shown in Listing 34.4.

N O T E   Not all TimeFormat settings are supported by all multimedia devices. ▨

Listing 34.4   FRMCDPLAYER.FRM—Using a Function to Convert Milliseconds into a Readable Format

```
Private Function ConvTime(ByVal TimeIn As Long) As String
  Dim ConvHrs As Integer, ConvMns As Integer, ConvSec As Integer
  Dim RemTime As Long, RetTime As String
  RemTime = TimeIn / 1000
  ConvHrs = Int(RemTime / 3600)
  RemTime = RemTime Mod 3600
  ConvMns = Int(RemTime / 60)
  RemTime = RemTime Mod 60
  ConvSec = RemTime
  If ConvHrs > 0 Then
     RetTime = Trim(Str(ConvHrs)) & ":"
  Else
     RetTime = ""
  End If
  If ConvMns >= 10 Then
     RetTime = RetTime & Trim(Str(ConvMns))
  ElseIf ConvMns > 0 Then
     RetTime = RetTime & "0" & Trim(Str(ConvMns))
  Else
     RetTime = RetTime & "00"
  End If
```

Part

VII

Ch

34

continues

Listing 34.4   Continued

```
    RetTime = RetTime & ":"
    If ConvSec >= 10 Then
        RetTime = RetTime & Trim(Str(ConvSec))
    ElseIf ConvSec > 0 Then
        RetTime = RetTime & "0" & Trim(Str(ConvSec))
    Else
        RetTime = RetTime & "00"
    End If
    ConvTime = RetTime

End Function
```

To display the desired times, you need to add a few more Label controls to your form. You need four more controls to identify the numbers and then two controls for the track times and two for the CD times. The final appearance of the form is shown in Figure 34.10.

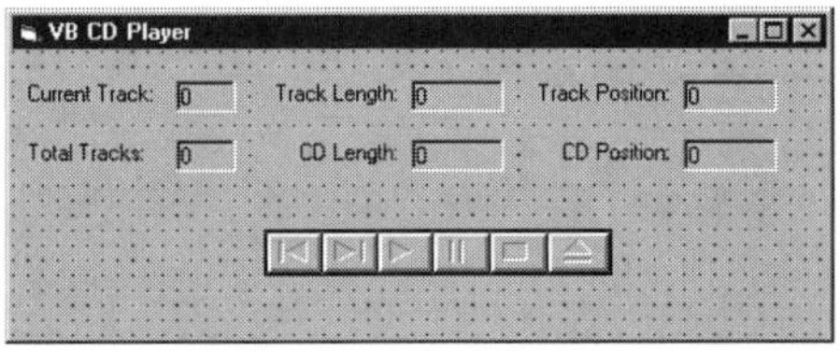

FIG. 34.10
CD Player with track times shown.

Retrieving the track length, CD length, and CD position are quite easy; you simply retrieve the values of the `TrackLength`, `Length`, and `Position` properties respectively and convert the values to the desired time format. To get the position within the track, you have to subtract the starting position of the track (specified by the `TrackPosition` property) from the current CD position (`Position` property). This value is then converted to the appropriate time format. All of this code is placed in the `StatusUpdate` event so that the information gets updated on a regular basis. Listing 34.5 shows the final code for the `StatusUpdate` event.

Listing 34.5   FRMCDPLAYER.FRM—Updating Times from the
***StatusUpdate* Event**

```
Private Sub mmcCDPlayer_StatusUpdate()
    lblTracks(0).Caption = mmcCDPlayer.Track
    lblTracks(1).Caption = mmcCDPlayer.Tracks
    lblTrackTime(0).Caption = ConvTime(mmcCDPlayer.TrackLength)
    lblTrackTime(1).Caption = ConvTime(mmcCDPlayer.Position_
        - mmcCDPlayer.TrackPosition)
    lblCDTime(0).Caption = ConvTime(mmcCDPlayer.Length)
    lblCDTime(1).Caption = ConvTime(mmcCDPlayer.Position)
End Sub
```

Running Movies

The Multimedia control also makes it easy for you to run AVI movies from your applications. These movies are stored in AVI files on your computer. The basic setup for running movies is very similar to that which was used for setting up the CD application. The only additional setup required is that the name of a file containing an AVI clip must be entered into the `FileName` property. After a valid file is opened, the Multimedia control sets the enabled properties of the buttons for the movie. All buttons except the Record and Eject buttons will be enabled.

The sample project for playing AVI movies is downloadable as AVIPLAYER.VBP from the Que Web site at **www.mcp.com/info/0-7897/0-7897-1288-1**.

To create a sample AVIPlayer program, perform the following steps:

1. Start a new project and make sure the `Multimedia` control is part of your Toolbox. Then set the Name of your form to `frmAVIPlayer` and the Caption to `AVI Movie Player`.

2. Place a `Multimedia` control on your form and name it `mmcAVIPlayer`. Set the `RecordVisible` and `EjectVisible` properties of the control to `False` to hide the unused buttons.

3. Add a CommonDialog control to the form to facilitate retrieving file names. (The CommonDialog control is a custom control that can be added from the Project Components menu.) Change the name of the control to `cdlGetFile`.

   ▶ **See** "Using Built-In Dialog Boxes," **p. 135**

4. Add a command button to the form to allow the user to start the process of selecting and opening an AVI file. Name the command button `cmdAVI` and set its Caption to `Get and Play AVI Movie`.

5. Place `Label` controls on the form to identify and hold the Length and Position information for the movie. At this point, your form should look like the one in Figure 34.11.

6. Place the code in Listing 34.6 in the `Click` event of the command button. This code uses the common dialog to retrieve the file and then sets up the `Multimedia` control.

FIG. 34.11
The basic setup for playing AVI movies.

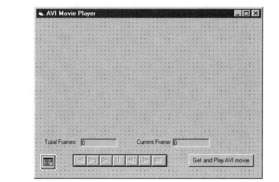

Listing 34.6 FRMAVIPLAYER.FRM—Retrieving and Opening an AVI File

```
Private Sub cmdAvi_Click()
  cdlGetFile.Filter = "AVI Movie Files (*.avi)¦*.avi"
  cdlGetFile.ShowOpen

  mmcAVIPlayer.DeviceType = "AVIVideo"
  mmcAVIPlayer.filename = cdlGetFile.filename
  mmcAVIPlayer.Command = "Open"
  lblStatus(0).Caption = mmcAVIPlayer.Length
End Sub
```

One final piece of code that you need is a line to update the current position of the movie. The following line of code should be placed in the StatusUpdate event of the Multimedia control:

```
lblStatus(1).Caption = mmcAVIPlayer.Position
```

N O T E   The length and position of an AVI movie is specified in frames instead of a time.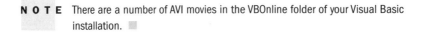

You can now run your program and start playing movies. After the program has started, you can click the command button to bring up the dialog box to open a file. After you have specified a valid file name and opened the file, the Multimedia control enables the appropriate buttons. You can press the Play button to start the movie. When the movie starts playing, it is shown in a separate window from the one that contains your Multimedia control. Figure 34.12 shows an AVI movie from a Windows help video being run in a separate window.

N O T E   There are a number of AVI movies in the VBOnline folder of your Visual Basic installation.

FIG. 34.12

Movies typically run in their own window.

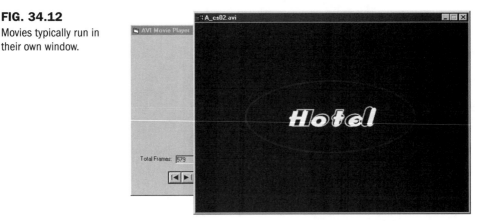

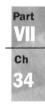

If you want the movie to run on the same form as your control, you can set the hWndDisplay property of the Multimedia control to the hWnd property of the form. This causes the movie to run in the background of the form. However, running the movie this way can cause problems with the display of controls such as labels. A better solution is to place a PictureBox control on the form and use it to display the movie. The following line of code causes a movie to be run inside a picture box on the form:

```
mmcAVIPlayer.hWndDisplay = picMovie.hWnd
```

Figure 34.13 shows the movie running inside the PictureBox control.

FIG. 34.13

Run movies in a picture box to better control their location.

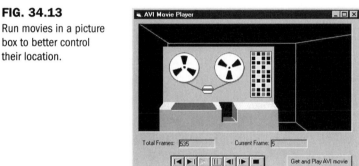

Working with MIDI Files

The setup for a MIDI file player is almost identical to that of the AVI movie player. Your program needs a way to specify and retrieve a file, and then to open the file and start playing the MIDI music. When a valid MIDI file has been opened, the Prev, Next, Play, Pause, and Stop buttons of the Multimedia control are enabled.

The key difference between the player for MIDI files and the player for AVI files is the setting of the DeviceType property of the Multimedia control and the Filter property of the CommonDialog control. For MIDI files, you need to set the DeviceType property to Sequencer. This defines the MIDI device to the Multimedia control. Figure 34.14 shows the MIDI player application and Listing 34.7 shows the code to make it run.

Part
VII

Ch
34

FIG. 34.14

A MIDI player created with the Multimedia control.

Listing 34.7   MIDIPLAYER.FRM—Setting the *DeviceType* to *Sequencer* for MIDI Files

```
Private Sub cmdMIDI_Click()
  cdlGetFile.Filter = "MIDI Files (*.mid)¦*.mid"
  cdlGetFile.ShowOpen

  mmcMIDIPlayer.DeviceType = "Sequencer"
  mmcMIDIPlayer.filename = cdlGetFile.filename
  mmcMIDIPlayer.Command = "Open"
  lblStatus(0).Caption = mmcMIDIPlayer.Length
End Sub
```

N O T E   A couple of MIDI files come with Windows 95 and are located in the \Windows\Media directory. ▪

Playing WaveForm Audio

You can use WaveForm Audio (WAV files) in your programs for sound effects and alerts. For example, I have a VB program that reads caller identification information from the phone company and then plays a WAV file depending on who the caller is. The easiest way to play WAV files from a VB application is to use the Windows API function sndPlaySound. The Windows API, which is covered in detail in Appendix B, "Visual Basic Script Quick Reference," is a group of Windows functions that you can call from Visual Basic.

To use sndPlaySound, do the following:

1. Start a new Standard EXE project.

2. Add a new code module to the project.

3. In the General Declarations section of the code module, add the following lines:

   ```
   Declare Function sndPlaySound Lib "winmm.dll" Alias "sndPlaySoundA"
       (ByVal lpszSoundName As String, ByVal uFlags As Long) As Long
   Public Const SND_ASYNC = &H1
   Public Const SND_SYNC = &H0
   Public Const SND_LOOP = &H8
   ```

   The first line of code is the *API declaration* for sndPlaySound. It is similar to the first line of a user-defined function in that it lists the function name and required parameters, but the actual function code is in a separate DLL file. The next few lines are constant values used with the function.

4. Call the sndPlaySound function from your program.

   ```
   Private Sub cmdPlaySound_Click()
       Dim lRetVal As Long
       lRetVal = sndPlaySound("C:\WAV\MySound.WAV", SND_ASYNC)
       MsgBox "Done"
   End Sub
   ```

As you can see from the code example, the sndPlaySound function is fairly simple. It takes two parameters, the name of the WAV file and a constant, and returns a value of type long.

The Flags parameter is used to modify the behavior of sndPlaySound. In the preceding code example, the SND_ASYNC constant indicates that the sound is played *asynchronously* from the rest of the program. In other words, the MsgBox statement is immediately executed. If the SND_SYNC constant is used, the message box does not appear until after the sound finishes playing. The SND_LOOP constant can be combined with SND_ASYNC to create a continuous background sound, as in the following line of code.

```
lRetVal = sndPlaySound("C:\WAV\MySound.WAV", SND_ASYNC + SND_LOOP)
```

The sound continues playing until the program executes another sndPlaySound call.

From Here...

This chapter has provided you with an introduction to the world of multimedia programming. You have seen how you can add animation effects to your programs and how you can use the multimedia devices of your computer to play music, show movies, play audio CDs, and add sound effects or narrations to your programs. This chapter also touched on a number of other topics that are covered elsewhere in this book. For more information about these topics, refer to the following chapters:

- To learn more about using the CommonDialog control in your programs, see Chapter 6, "Using Dialogs to Get Information."

- To learn more about handling graphics images, including the creation of dynamic charts, see Chapter 12, "Working with Graphics."

- To learn more about text effects for enhancing your applications, see Chapter 13, "Working with Text, Fonts, and Colors."

- To learn more about accessing the API functions of Windows, see Chapter 35, "Accessing the Windows 32 API."

Part
VII

Ch
34

Advanced Visual Basic Programming

Accessing the Windows 32 API

As the structure of Windows evolved, Microsoft intentionally made a great number of programming functions available to all Windows-based programs. This strategy serves the dual purpose of giving Windows applications a consistent look and feel, as well as keeping programmers from having to duplicate programming effort for functions that have already been coded and debugged. These functions are stored in a series of Dynamic Link Libraries (DLLs) and are known collectively as the *Application Programming Interface* (API). Since the evolution to the 32-bit operating systems Windows 95 and Windows NT, the newer version is known as the *Win32 API*. Some of the functions in the Win32 API are available as Visual Basic commands, but the vast majority are accessible only by "calling" the API.

Understand the Windows API

Learn how to use several Win32 API calls and understand the declaration statements for them.

Create API wrappers

Write reusable objects that wrap groups of API functions, that is, provide an interface to the API.

The GDI API

Make the most of the Windows Graphics Device Interface (GDI) in your application in a `TransparentPaint` example.

Master the Registry APIs

Use the Windows API to read information from the Windows Registry or store values in it.

Although Microsoft has added what seems like thousands of great new features to Visual Basic's most recent releases, there are still many features in the Win32 API that the VB language is missing. This omission is intentional, because VB includes the capability to call the API, so not every API function needs to be part of VB. The reason why it doesn't is that each Win32 API that VB "wraps" (duplicates) causes the VB runtime DLL to get larger. The larger the runtime, the slower your applications will be; it will take longer to load the runtime when your application boots. Therefore, Microsoft's exclusion of a large number of the Win32 APIs is really a good thing because the precious space in the VB runtime is being saved for cool new features.

This chapter explains how to use some of the more useful APIs, but it is far from a complete resource. No single chapter could do this subject justice, but there should be enough information here to get you started. Instead, the goal of this chapter is to turn you on to some of neat things you can do with the Win32 API. By using the API, you can write more advanced applications that are not possible with pure VB programming. Read on, and have fun playing with the examples. ■

Calling Basic API and DLLs

Although this chapter is not intended to teach you everything there is to know about accessing the API or writing declarations statements for use with DLLs, I will spend a little time in this section covering some fundamental basics. However, I will assume that you have already read the "Calling Procedures in DLLs" chapter in the *Visual Basic Programmer's Guide*. This information is designed to complement the *Programmer's Guide* by demonstrating how to implement a variety of helpful API calls.

GetVersionEx

The best way to learn how to use (or call) DLLs is to learn by example. The code in Listing 35.1 demonstrates how to use one of the most common Win32 API calls, GetVersionEx. When you call this API, it fills a user-defined type (UDT) called OSVERSIONINFO with information about the Windows version. Closely examine the code in this listing to see how we make this API call and use the return values.

Listing 35.1 WINVER.BAS—*GetWindowsVersion* Returns a Usable String Based on the Values Returned from *GetVersionEx*

```
'*********************************************************************
' Types, constants and declarations required to get the Win version
'*********************************************************************
Private Type OSVERSIONINFO
        dwOSVersionInfoSize As Long
        dwMajorVersion As Long
        dwMinorVersion As Long
        dwBuildNumber As Long
        dwPlatformId As Long
        szCSDVersion As String * 128 'Maintenance string for PSS usage
```

```
End Type

Private Const VER_PLATFORM_WIN32_NT = 2
Private Const VER_PLATFORM_WIN32_WINDOWS = 1

Private Declare Function GetVersionEx Lib "kernel32" Alias _
    "GetVersionExA" (lpVersionInformation As OSVERSIONINFO) As Long
'**********************************************************************
' Returns a string suitable for displaying in a dialog box
'**********************************************************************
Public Function GetWindowsVersion() As String
    Dim strOS As String
    Dim osvVersion As OSVERSIONINFO
    Dim strMaintBuildInfo As String
    '**********************************************************************
    ' Many Win32 APIs have a first parameter that indicates the size
    ' of the structure (in bytes) so these structures will be portable
    ' to future OS versions or different systems (such as 64 bit
    ' systems or OS's). It is your responsibility to set this field
    ' prior to making the API call, and the Len function helps you
    ' to do that.
    '**********************************************************************
    osvVersion.dwOSVersionInfoSize = Len(osvVersion)
    '**********************************************************************
    ' Get the version (exit if the GetVersionEx failed)
    '**********************************************************************
    If GetVersionEx(osvVersion) = 0 Then Exit Function
    '**********************************************************************
    ' Get a string that represents the installed Operating System
    '**********************************************************************
    Select Case osvVersion.dwPlatformId
        Case VER_PLATFORM_WIN32_WINDOWS
            strOS = "Windows "
        Case VER_PLATFORM_WIN32_NT
            strOS = "Windows NT "
        Case Else ' Impossible because VB doesn't run under Win32s
            strOS = "Win32s "
    End Select
    '**********************************************************************
    ' Get the major, minor, and build numbers and concatenate them
    ' to the OS name
    '**********************************************************************
    With osvVersion
        strOS = strOS & CStr(.dwMajorVersion) & "." & _
            CStr(.dwMinorVersion) & "." & _
            CStr(.dwBuildNumber And &HFFFF&)

        strMaintBuildInfo = Left(.szCSDVersion, _
            InStr(.szCSDVersion, Chr(0)))
    End With
    '**********************************************************************
    ' If this isn't a maintenance build (i.e., 4.xx.xxxx A)...
    '**********************************************************************
    If strMaintBuildInfo = Chr(0) Then
```

continues

Listing 35.1 Continued

```
        GetWindowsVersion = strOS
'*****************************************************************
' Otherwise include the maintenance build info
'*****************************************************************
    Else
        GetWindowsVersion = strOS & " " & _
            Left(strMaintBuildInfo, Len(strMaintBuildInfo) - 1)
    End If
End Function
```

This API call exhibits a common trait among many Win32 API calls in that it requires you to set the first member of the structure (dwOSVersionInfoSize) *before* calling the API. This is something new for Win32 that was not required in earlier versions of Windows. This is done so the Win32 API can be ported to future processors without requiring a new set of APIs. This means (in theory) that the Win32 code in this chapter should work unchanged in the future when the desktop computer world moves to 64-bits.

Declaring APIs

Now that you have seen how to use the GetVersionEx API call in VB, let's take a look at how you make this API available to VB. To make a function call from an external source (such as a DLL or the Win32 API), you need to write a declaration for this API in the General Declarations section. Here is what the declaration for GetVersionEx looks like:

```
Private Declare Function GetVersionEx Lib "kernel32" Alias _
"GetVersionExA" (lpVersionInformation As OSVERSIONINFO) As Long
```

Let's dissect this call to understand what it really means. The first three words, Private Declare Function, mean that we are declaring an external function for use only within the current module. The next word, GetVersionEx, when used with the Alias label means that you would like to refer to this function by using the word GetVersionEx in your VB code. When using Alias, this value could be anything. If you wanted, you could have called this MyGetWinVer.

The next two words, Lib "kernel32", tell VB which "library" (DLL—the extension is optional) contains this function. The next two words, Alias "GetVersionExA," tell VB that anytime you call "GetVersionEx" in your program, it should call the function "GetVersionExA" in Kernel32.dll. Until now, the format of this API call is typical. The function, library, and alias names will differ, but all of these items appear in most API calls.

The next part of this call contains the argument list for the function GetVersionExA. It only has one parameter of type OSVERSION info that must be passed by reference (the default). Finally, the last two words, As Long, indicate that the function GetVersionExA returns a long integer.

Calling Functions in Other DLLs

Almost every document you will ever read about using DLLs in Visual Basic is going to use the API DLLs as an example. At the end of these documents, the writer explains how you can also grab these declarations out of the API Text Viewer program. This gives you a false sense of security because you depend heavily on the API Text Viewer for your API declarations. As soon as most programmers get a DLL (or new API) that doesn't appear in the API Text Viewer, they realize that they never really learned how to write a declaration themselves. Therefore, I've created an exercise where you look at the code for a small program and try to guess the API declarations.

Listing 35.2 uses two functions from a DLL that I wrote which creates and resolves shortcuts. The function names are CreateShortcut and ResolveShortcut; they are located in a DLL called Shortcut.dll, and they both return a long value. I have retained all of the comments and source code for this program, but I've relocated the declaration statements to Listing 35.3. Your mission, should you choose to accept it, is to examine the code and figure out what the declaration statement should be. Write your declaration on a sheet of paper and compare it with the actual declarations in Listing 35.3. Good luck!

Listing 35.2 SHORTCUT.FRM—Shortcut.frm Uses a Helper DLL to Manipulate Windows Shortcuts

```
'*********************************************************************
' Shortcut.frm - Uses Ronald R. Martinsen's shortcut.dll file to
'    create and resolve Windows 95 shortcuts.
'*********************************************************************
Option Explicit
'*********************************************************************
' Constant for the path of the shortcut file used for simplicity sake.
' This isn't required.
'*********************************************************************
Private Const SHORTCUTPATH As String = "c:\Shortcut to Notepad.lnk"
'*********************************************************************
' CreateShortcut - Required function declaration to create a shortcut
' with the helper DLL.
'-------------------------------------------------------------------
' strSourceFile - Filename of the target of the shortcut (can be a
'                 file, directory, or object)
' strLinkFile   - Name of the shortcut file on the disk (always use
'                 the LNK extension!!!!)
' strInitDir    - The current directory when the application starts*
' strArgs       - Command Line Arguments (i.e., filename)*
' intCmdShow    - Determines how to display the window (use Shell
'                 function constants)
' strIconPath   - The location of the DLL or EXE with the icon you
'                 wish to use.*
' intIconIndex  - The index of the icon you wish to use (only used if
'                 strIconPath was supplied)
' * = use vbNullString for the default
' RETURNS       - Zero if the call worked, otherwise a SCODE HRESULT.
'*********************************************************************
<< DECLARATION GOES HERE >>
'*********************************************************************
```

Part

VIII

Ch

35

continues

Listing 35.2 Continued

```
' ResolveShortcut - Required function declaration to get the target
' path to a shortcut file.
'-------------------------------------------------------------------
' hWndOfYourForm       - The handle (hWnd property) of the calling
'                        window
' strShortcutFile      - Filename of the shortcut
' strShortcutLocation - Return buffer for the path of the object the
'                        shortcut points to
' RETURNS              - Zero if the call worked, otherwise a SCODE
'                        HRESULT.
'*******************************************************************
<< DECLARATION GOES HERE >>
'*******************************************************************
' Create the Shortcut in c:\
'*******************************************************************
Private Sub cmdCreateShortcut_Click()
    Dim strMessage As String
    '*************************************************************
    ' Get the the path to the windows directory
    '*************************************************************
    Dim strWinDir As String
    strWinDir = Environ("windir")
    '*************************************************************
    ' Try to create a shortcut to notepad.exe. Build the err string
    ' if the call failed.
    '*************************************************************
    If CreateShortcut(strWinDir & "\notepad.exe", SHORTCUTPATH, _
        "c:\", vbNullString, vbMaximizedFocus, vbNullString, 1) Then
        ' Non-zero result, so notify the user that the call failed
        strMessage = "Unable to create a shortcut to Notepad. Check "
        strMessage = strMessage & "the source code parameters and try"
        strMessage = strMessage & "again."
    '*************************************************************
    ' Otherwise, the call worked so tell the user
    '*************************************************************
    Else
        strMessage = "A shortcut to Notepad was created in c:\"
        '*********************************************************
        ' Enable the resolve button now, since the file exists
        '*********************************************************
        cmdResolveShortcut.Enabled = True
    End If
    '*************************************************************
    ' Display the success or failed message
    '*************************************************************
    MsgBox strMessage
End Sub
'*******************************************************************
' Resolve the Shortcut in c:\ (created in Command1_Click)
'*******************************************************************
Private Sub cmdResolveShortcut_Click()
    Dim strShortcutTargetPath As String, strTemp As String
    '*************************************************************
```

```
' Build a buffer for the return string
'*******************************************************************
strShortcutTargetPath = Space(260)
'*******************************************************************
' Make the call
'-------------------------------------------------------------------
' NOTE: If the TARGET (the return value) can't be found,
'        then Win95 will display search dialog while it
'        attempts to find it
'*******************************************************************
If ResolveShortcut(hWnd, SHORTCUTPATH, strShortcutTargetPath) Then
    '*******************************************************************
    ' Non-zero result, so notify the user that the call failed
    '*******************************************************************
    MsgBox "Unable to resolve your shortcut", vbCritical
Else
    '*******************************************************************
    ' Trim the null terminator and display the results
    '*******************************************************************
    strShortcutTargetPath = Left(strShortcutTargetPath, _
        InStr(strShortcutTargetPath, Chr(0)) - 1)
    MsgBox "Your shortcut points to " & strShortcutTargetPath, _
        vbInformation
End If
End Sub
```

Listing 35.2 appears a bit long mainly because I've included a large number of comments. In reality, this program is rather trivial. The essential function, CreateShortcut, simply takes the same values that you would normally see in a property page when creating a shortcut. ResolveShortcut is even easier because you provide it with the path to a shortcut file, and it simply loads the strShortcutLocation with the path to the file to which the shortcut references. This code features some common techniques for working with APIs that use strings, so be sure to pay close attention to the comments.

As promised, Listing 35.3 contains the function declarations to the CreateShortcut and ResolveShortcut functions. Were your declarations the same? If so, congratulations! If not, then don't feel bad. Writing declarations can be a little tricky, especially if you've never programmed Windows in C.

Listing 35.3   SHORTCUT.FRM—Create and Resolve Shortcut Function Declarations

```
Private Declare Function CreateShortcut Lib "shortcut.dll" _
    (ByVal strSourceFile$, ByVal strLinkFile$, ByVal strInitDir$, _
    ByVal strArgs$, ByVal intCmdShow%, ByVal strIconPath$, _
    ByVal lngIconIndex As Long) As Long

Private Declare Function ResolveShortcut Lib "shortcut.dll" _
    (ByVal hWndOfYourForm As Long, ByVal strShortcutFile As String, _
    ByVal strShortcutLocation As String) As Long
```

Part

VIII

Ch

35

This concludes my crash course on writing declarations. If you are interested in learning more, then there is a fantastic reference book called *The Visual Basic Programmer's Guide to the Windows API*, by Daniel Appleman, that covers this topic extensively. I encourage every VB programmer to purchase a copy of this book, as it is the only resource I know of that translates the Windows API into a form usable by Visual Basic programmers.

Using the Windows API

As with most things, learning by doing is a good way to gain some knowledge about the Windows API. I will be discussing API examples that I classify as *cool*. None of these APIs are especially difficult to use, but they all are extremely helpful to have in your sample code library. I'll start off easy and graduate up to a more complex use of the API in combination with advanced VB code techniques. Finally, I'll finish by writing the TransparentPaint function, which is almost pure API programming in VB. All of the listings in this section are rather large due to the complexity of the samples, but do not let that discourage you. Each sample is commented very well, so any intermediate programmer should be able to follow along.

Warming Up with the Memory Class

Rather than diving right in to a complicated example, I thought I'd begin by explaining the memory class. Most programmers like to include basic memory information in their About boxes, but Visual Basic does not provide any method for doing this. If you want to know how much RAM is installed on a machine, then you have to call the Windows API. Although this isn't a bad thing, it does mean that many of us have written duplicate code many different ways to accomplish the same thing. Frustrated by this, I decided to write what I believe to be a useful (and reusable) class for getting memory information.

Listing 35.4 is my interpretation of the ultimate memory class that will prevent you from having to mess with the API. This class is also structured so that you can easily add features that I omitted, should your application require them.

Listing 35.4   MEMORY.CLS—Memory.cls Demonstrates How to Wrap an API into a Reusable Class Object

```
'*********************************************************************
' Memory.cls - This class takes a snapshot of the memory status and
'    provides the user with a simple interface to get common
'    information about the current memory status.
'*********************************************************************
Option Explicit
'*********************************************************************
' Win32 required user-defined type (or struct) and declaration
'*********************************************************************
Private Type MEMORYSTATUS
        dwLength As Long
        dwMemoryLoad As Long
        dwTotalPhys As Long
```

```
            dwAvailPhys As Long
            dwTotalPageFile As Long
            dwAvailPageFile As Long
            dwTotalVirtual As Long
            dwAvailVirtual As Long
End Type

Private Declare Sub GlobalMemoryStatus Lib "kernel32" _
        (lpBuffer As MEMORYSTATUS)
'*************************************************************************
' Private member variable which holds the current memory status
'*************************************************************************
Private mmemMemoryStatus As MEMORYSTATUS
'*************************************************************************
' Returns the number of bytes of available physical RAM (OK if zero)
'*************************************************************************
Public Property Get FreeMemory() As Long
        FreeMemory = mmemMemoryStatus.dwAvailPhys
End Property
'*************************************************************************
' Returns the number of bytes of RAM installed in the computer
'*************************************************************************
Public Property Get TotalMemory() As Long
        TotalMemory = mmemMemoryStatus.dwTotalPhys
End Property
'*************************************************************************
' Returns the number of bytes of virtual memory allocated by the
' operating system
'*************************************************************************
Public Property Get TotalVirtualMemory() As Long
        TotalVirtualMemory = mmemMemoryStatus.dwTotalVirtual
End Property
'*************************************************************************
' Returns the number of bytes of virtual memory available to this
' process
'*************************************************************************
Public Property Get AvailableVirtualMemory() As Long
        AvailableVirtualMemory = mmemMemoryStatus.dwAvailVirtual
End Property
'*************************************************************************
' Calls the operating system to find out the memory status at the
' time this object is created
'*************************************************************************
Private Sub Class_Initialize()
        mmemMemoryStatus.dwLength = Len(mmemMemoryStatus)
        GlobalMemoryStatus mmemMemoryStatus
End Sub
'*************************************************************************
' Updates this object with current memory status
'*************************************************************************
Public Sub Refresh()
        GlobalMemoryStatus mmemMemoryStatus
End Sub
```

This class simply wraps the `GlobalMemoryStatus` API. When the class is created, the API call is made in the `Initialize` event, so this class is ready to use with no additional initialization. Your application needs only to create a new variable of this class and access the properties that satisfy your program's needs. I reluctantly included a public method called `Refresh` that updates `mmemMemoryStatus`, but I couldn't think of any good application of this method. However, it is there for the one person who will claim that he really needs this method.

Listing 35.5 uses `clsMemorySnapshot` the way it is designed to be used. An application should only define a variable of this class in the local sub or function where it is being used. By doing this, every time your sub or function is called, you get the current memory information. Memdemo.frm displays some of the properties from the `clsMem` object and includes a special note about the return value from the `FreeMemory` property.

Listing 35.5   MEMDEMO.FRM—Memdemo.frm Demonstrates How to Use *clsMemorySnapshot*

```
'*********************************************************************
' MemDemo.frm - Demonstrates how to use clsMemorySnapshot
'*********************************************************************
Option Explicit
'*********************************************************************
' Creates a clsMemorySnapshot object and displays the results
'*********************************************************************
Private Sub cmdGetMemoryStatus_Click()
    '*****************************************************************
    ' The efficient way to use clsMemorySnapshot is to create a new
    ' clsMemorySnapshot object every time you need to get the memory
    ' status, so that is what we will do.
    '*****************************************************************
    Dim clsMem As New clsMemorySnapshot
    '*****************************************************************
    ' Holds the current ForeColor of the form since we'll need to
    ' change it temporarily.
    '*****************************************************************
    Dim lngForeColor As Long
    '*****************************************************************
    ' Always clear the form before displaying new information
    '*****************************************************************
    Cls
    With clsMem
        '*************************************************************
        ' Print Physical Memory Information
        '*************************************************************
        Print "Total Installed RAM", Format(.TotalMemory \ 1024, _
            "###,###,###,###,##0") & " KB"
        Print "Free Physical RAM", Format(.FreeMemory \ 1024, _
            "###,###,###,###,##0") & " KB";
        '*************************************************************
        ' Print a asterisk that stands out in bold red
        '*************************************************************
        Font.Bold = True
        lngForeColor = ForeColor
```

```
        ForeColor = RGB(255, 0, 0)
        Print "*"
        '****************************************************************
        ' Restore to the default settings
        '****************************************************************
        ForeColor = lngForeColor
        Font.Bold = False
        '****************************************************************
        ' Print Virtual Memory Information
        '****************************************************************
        Print "Total Virtual Memory", Format(.TotalVirtualMemory \ 1024, _
            "###,###,###,###,##0") & " KB"
        Print "Available Virtual Memory", Format(.AvailableVirtualMemory _
            \ 1024, "###,###,###,###,##0") & " KB"
    End With
    '****************************************************************
    ' Print a blank space, the print a comment in bold
    '****************************************************************
    Print
    Font.Bold = True
    Print "* = It's okay (and common) for this number to be zero."
    '****************************************************************
    ' Restore the form bold value back to false
    '****************************************************************
    Font.Bold = False
End Sub
```

By wrapping the API call in a class, I have made it as easy to use as a standard VB object in our `cmdGetMemoryStatus_Click` event. This is a great way to simplify the use of many API calls, as well as ensure the proper use of them. Not only does it make the API call easy enough to use by new VB programmers, it also promotes building an API object library that is shared among an entire programming team. I encourage you to use this technique as much as possible and try to keep your classes as simple as possible. After all, to have the best performance, you need to remember that "less is more."

Creating Your Own API Interface

Visual Basic is great because it is simple enough for an intermediate Windows user to learn how to write a Windows application. This simplicity is what attracts everyone to it, and it is what allows people to write applications in weeks that would take months (or even years) in C. However, this simplicity comes at a price. The price is that many functions in VB were written during VB 1.0 when Microsoft only envisioned VB as being a hobbyist programming language or a Windows batch language. No one really saw VB as becoming the most common programming language for Windows that it is today, so many of the 1.0 functions contain limited functionality. One such function is `Dir`.

While `Dir` is great for your fundamental needs, it falls short when you try to do something like "search for all the files with the extension BAK on your hard drive." The reason why it falls short is simple—it doesn't support nested calls. Someone at Microsoft realized this shortcoming and wrote the `WinSeek` sample, which uses a file and directory list box control to overcome this limitation, but this workaround is unacceptable. The spaghetti code in WinSeek is hard to follow, poorly commented, and too slow for even the most trivial tasks.

I have written the FindFile class, shown in Listing 35.6, to overcome the shortcomings of Dir and WinSeek. This class uses the previous concept of encapsulating an API into a reusable object that makes it as easy to use as a built-in VB function. FindFile also adheres to the concept of "keep it simple," by including only a minimal amount of core functionality. This allows individual users of this class to write their own algorithms for special tasks such as searching an entire drive for a specific type of file. I encourage you to review the source code and comments for this class in the following listing.

Listing 35.6   FINDFILE.CLS—FindFile.cls Provides an Interface to the Windows API Used for Finding Files

```
'*********************************************************************
' FindFile.cls - Encapsulates the Win32 FindFile functions
'*********************************************************************
Option Explicit
'*********************************************************************
' Attribute constants which differ from VB
'*********************************************************************
Private Const FILE_ATTRIBUTE_COMPRESSED = &H800
Private Const FILE_ATTRIBUTE_NORMAL = &H80
'*********************************************************************
' Win32 API constants required by FindFile
'*********************************************************************
Private Const MAX_PATH = 260
Private Const INVALID_HANDLE_VALUE = -1
'*********************************************************************
' Win32 data types (or structs) required by FindFile
'*********************************************************************
Private Type FILETIME
        dwLowDateTime As Long
        dwHighDateTime As Long
End Type

Private Type WIN32_FIND_DATA
        dwFileAttributes As Long
        ftCreationTime As FILETIME
        ftLastAccessTime As FILETIME
        ftLastWriteTime As FILETIME
        nFileSizeHigh As Long
        nFileSizeLow As Long
        dwReserved0 As Long
        dwReserved1 As Long
        cFileName As String * MAX_PATH
        cAlternate As String * 14
End Type

Private Type SYSTEMTIME
        wYear As Integer
        wMonth As Integer
```

```
            wDayOfWeek As Integer
            wDay As Integer
            wHour As Integer
            wMinute As Integer
            wSecond As Integer
            wMilliseconds As Integer
End Type
'*********************************************************************
' Win32 API calls required by this class
'*********************************************************************
Private Declare Function FileTimeToLocalFileTime Lib "kernel32" _
    (lpFileTime As FILETIME, lpLocalFileTime As FILETIME) As Long
Private Declare Function FileTimeToSystemTime Lib "kernel32" _
    (lpFileTime As FILETIME, lpSystemTime As SYSTEMTIME) As Long
Private Declare Function FindFirstFile Lib "kernel32" Alias _
    "FindFirstFileA" (ByVal lpFileName As String, _
    lpFindFileData As WIN32_FIND_DATA) As Long
Private Declare Function FindNextFile Lib "kernel32" Alias _
    "FindNextFileA" (ByVal hFindFile As Long, lpFindFileData As _
    WIN32_FIND_DATA) As Long
Private Declare Function FindClose& Lib "kernel32" (ByVal hFindFile&)
'*********************************************************************
' clsFindFiles private member variables
'*********************************************************************
Private mlngFile As Long
Private mstrDateFormat As String
Private mstrUnknownDateText As String
Private mwfdFindData As WIN32_FIND_DATA
'*********************************************************************
' Public interface for setting the format string used for dates
'*********************************************************************
Public Property Let DateFormat(strDateFormat As String)
    mstrDateFormat = strDateFormat
End Property
'*********************************************************************
' Public interface for setting the string used when the date for a
' file is unknown
'*********************************************************************
Public Property Let UnknownDateText(strUnknownDateText As String)
    mstrUnknownDateText = strUnknownDateText
End Property
'*********************************************************************
' Returns the file attributes for the current file
'*********************************************************************
Public Property Get FileAttributes() As Long
    If mlngFile Then FileAttributes = mwfdFindData.dwFileAttributes
End Property
'*********************************************************************
' Returns true if the compress bit is set for the current file
'*********************************************************************
Public Property Get IsCompressed() As Boolean
    If mlngFile Then IsCompressed = mwfdFindData.dwFileAttributes _
                            And FILE_ATTRIBUTE_COMPRESSED
End Property
```

Part
VIII

Ch
35

continues

Listing 35.6   Continued

```
'*********************************************************************
' Returns the value of the Normal attribute bit for dwFileAttributes
'*********************************************************************
Public Property Get NormalAttribute() As Long
    NormalAttribute = FILE_ATTRIBUTE_NORMAL
End Property
'*********************************************************************
' Primary method in this class for finding the FIRST matching file in
' a directory that matches the path &¦or pattern in strFile
'*********************************************************************
Public Function Find(strFile As String, Optional blnShowError _
    As Boolean) As String
    '*****************************************************************
    ' If you already searching, then end the current search
    '*****************************************************************
    If mlngFile Then
        If blnShowError Then
            If MsgBox("Cancel the current search?", vbYesNo Or _
                vbQuestion) = vbNo Then Exit Function
        End If
        '*************************************************************
        ' Call cleanup routines before beginning new search
        '*************************************************************
        EndFind
    End If
    '*****************************************************************
    ' Find the first file matching the search pattern in strFile
    '*****************************************************************
    mlngFile = FindFirstFile(strFile, mwfdFindData)
    '*****************************************************************
    ' Check to see if FindFirstFile failed
    '*****************************************************************
    If mlngFile = INVALID_HANDLE_VALUE Then
        mlngFile = 0
        '*************************************************************
        ' If blnShowError, then display a default error message
        '*************************************************************
        If blnShowError Then
            MsgBox strFile & " could not be found!", vbExclamation
        '*************************************************************
        ' Otherwise raise a user-define error with a default err msg
        '*************************************************************
        Else
            Err.Raise vbObjectError + 5000, "clsFindFile_Find", _
                strFile & " could not be found!"
        End If
        Exit Function
    End If
    '*****************************************************************
    ' Return the found filename without any nulls
    '*****************************************************************
    Find = Left(mwfdFindData.cFileName, _
        InStr(mwfdFindData.cFileName, Chr(0)) - 1)
```

```
End Function
'**********************************************************************
' Call this function until it returns "" to get the remaining files
'**********************************************************************
Public Function FindNext() As String
    '******************************************************************
    ' Exit if no files have been found
    '******************************************************************
    If mlngFile = 0 Then Exit Function
    '******************************************************************
    ' Be sure to clear the contents of cFileName before each call to
    ' avoid garbage characters from being returned in your string.
    '******************************************************************
    mwfdFindData.cFileName = Space(MAX_PATH)
    '******************************************************************
    ' If another file is found, then return it. Otherwise EndFind.
    '******************************************************************
    If FindNextFile(mlngFile, mwfdFindData) Then
        FindNext = Left(mwfdFindData.cFileName, _
            InStr(mwfdFindData.cFileName, Chr(0)) - 1)
    Else
        EndFind
    End If
End Function
'**********************************************************************
' A private helper method which is called internally to close the
' FindFile handle and clear mlngFile to end a FindFile operation.
'**********************************************************************
Private Sub EndFind()
    FindClose mlngFile
    mlngFile = 0
End Sub
'**********************************************************************
' Return the short name of a found file (default = long filename)
'**********************************************************************
Public Function GetShortName() As String
    Dim strShortFileName As String
    '******************************************************************
    ' If no current file, then exit
    '******************************************************************
    If mlngFile = 0 Then Exit Function
    '******************************************************************
    ' Get the short filename (without trailing nulls)
    '******************************************************************
    strShortFileName = Left(mwfdFindData.cAlternate, _
        InStr(mwfdFindData.cAlternate, Chr(0)) - 1)
    '******************************************************************
    ' If there is no short filename info, then strShortFilename will
    ' equal null (because of the (- 1) above
    '******************************************************************
    If Len(strShortFileName) = 0 Then
        '**************************************************************
        ' If no short filename, then its already a short filename so
        ' set strShortFileName = .cFileName.
```

Part

VIII

Ch

35

continues

Listing 35.6   Continued

```
        '*************************************************************
        strShortFileName = Left(mwfdFindData.cFileName, _
            InStr(mwfdFindData.cFileName, Chr(0)) - 1)
    End If
    '*************************************************************
    ' Return the short filename
    '*************************************************************
    GetShortName = strShortFileName
End Function
'*************************************************************
' Return the date the current file was created. If the optional args
' are provied, then they will be set = to date and time values.
'*************************************************************
Public Function GetCreationDate(Optional datDate As Date, _
    Optional datTime As Date) As String

    If mlngFile = 0 Then Exit Function
    '*************************************************************
    ' If dwHighDateTime, then Win32 couldn't determine the date so
    ' return the unknown string. "Unknown" is the default.  Set this
    ' value to something else by using the UnknownDateText property.
    '*************************************************************
    If mwfdFindData.ftCreationTime.dwHighDateTime = 0 Then
        GetCreationDate = mstrUnknownDateText
        Exit Function
    End If
    '*************************************************************
    ' Get the time (in the current local/time zone)
    '*************************************************************
    With GetSystemTime(mwfdFindData.ftCreationTime)
        '*************************************************************
        ' If datDate was provided, then set it to a date serial
        '*************************************************************
        datDate = DateSerial(.wYear, .wMonth, .wDay)
        '*************************************************************
        ' If datTime was provided, then set it to a time serial
        '*************************************************************
        datTime = TimeSerial(.wHour, .wMinute, .wSecond)
        '*************************************************************
        ' Use datDate and datTime as local variables (even if they
        ' weren't passed ByRef in the optional args) to create a
        ' a valid date/time value.  Return the date/time formatted
        ' using the default format of "m/d/yy h:nn:ss AM/PM" or
        ' the user-defined value which was set using the DateFormat
        ' property.
        '*************************************************************
        GetCreationDate = Format(datDate + datTime, mstrDateFormat)
    End With
End Function
'*************************************************************
' Similar to GetCreationDate.  See GetCreationDate for comments.
'*************************************************************
Public Function GetLastAccessDate(Optional datDate As Date, _
```

```
        Optional datTime As Date) As String

        If mlngFile = 0 Then Exit Function

        If mwfdFindData.ftLastAccessTime.dwHighDateTime = 0 Then
            GetLastAccessDate = mstrUnknownDateText
            Exit Function
        End If

        With GetSystemTime(mwfdFindData.ftLastAccessTime)
            datDate = DateSerial(.wYear, .wMonth, .wDay)
            datTime = TimeSerial(.wHour, .wMinute, .wSecond)
            GetLastAccessDate = Format(datDate + datTime, mstrDateFormat)
        End With

End Function
'***********************************************************************
' Similar to GetCreationDate.  See GetCreationDate for comments.
'***********************************************************************
Public Function GetLastWriteDate(Optional datDate As Date, _
    Optional datTime As Date) As String

        If mlngFile = 0 Then Exit Function

        If mwfdFindData.ftLastWriteTime.dwHighDateTime = 0 Then
            GetLastWriteDate = mstrUnknownDateText
            Exit Function
        End If

        With GetSystemTime(mwfdFindData.ftLastWriteTime)
            datDate = DateSerial(.wYear, .wMonth, .wDay)
            datTime = TimeSerial(.wHour, .wMinute, .wSecond)
            GetLastWriteDate = Format(datDate + datTime, mstrDateFormat)
        End With

End Function
'***********************************************************************
' Takes a FILETIME and converts it into the local system time
'***********************************************************************
Private Function GetSystemTime(ftmFileTime As FILETIME) As SYSTEMTIME
    Dim ftmLocalTime As FILETIME
    Dim stmSystemTime As SYSTEMTIME
    FileTimeToLocalFileTime ftmFileTime, ftmLocalTime
    FileTimeToSystemTime ftmLocalTime, stmSystemTime
    GetSystemTime = stmSystemTime
End Function
'***********************************************************************
' Sets the default values for private members when this object is
' created
'***********************************************************************
Private Sub Class_Initialize()
    mstrUnknownDateText = "Unknown"
    mstrDateFormat = "m/d/yy h:nn:ss AM/PM"
End Sub
```

Part

VIII

Ch

35

continues

Listing 35.6   Continued

```
'*******************************************************************
' Ends any open finds, if necessary
'*******************************************************************
Private Sub Class_Terminate()
    If mlngFile Then EndFind
End Sub
```

The `FindFile` class contains private declarations for everything it needs to be both an independent and complete object. What's more, it is about 60 percent faster than `WinSeek`. However, performance is not the only reason to use the `FindFile` class. It provides a wealth of information about each found file and supports searching unmapped networked drives using UNC paths.

Now that you have seen `FindFile`, let's use it. `FindFile` is similar to `Dir` in that your first call specifies the search criteria and subsequent calls retrieve the files that correspond to that search criteria. However, `FindFile` is different in that your first call is to the `Find` method, and subsequent calls are to the `FindNext` method. Your application should keep looping as long as strings are being returned from `FindNext`, or until you are ready to begin the next search by calling `Find` again.

Listing 35.7 demonstrates a simple use of the `FindFile` class. In this function, the purpose is to retrieve all of the files in the current directory that satisfy a given search criteria. All of the items found are loaded into a collection provided by the caller. Finally, this function returns the number of files that were added to the `colFiles` collection.

Listing 35.7   FINDFILE.FRM—Searching for Files in a Single Directory

```
'*******************************************************************
' A simple routine that finds all of the files in a directory that
' match the given pattern, loads the results in a collection, then
' returns the number of files that are being returned.
'*******************************************************************
Private Function FindFilesInSingleDir(ByVal strDir As String, _
    strPattern$, colFiles As Collection) As Integer
    '*******************************************************************
    ' Create a new FindFile object every time this function is called
    '*******************************************************************
    Dim clsFind As New clsFindFile
    Dim strFile As String
    '*******************************************************************
    ' Make sure strSearchPath always has a trailing backslash
    '*******************************************************************
    If Right(strDir, 1) <> "\" Then _
        strDir = strDir & "\"
    '*******************************************************************
    ' Get the first file
    '*******************************************************************
    strFile = clsFind.Find(strDir & strPattern)
```

```
'******************************************************************
' Loop while files are being returned
'******************************************************************
Do While Len(strFile)
    '**************************************************************
    ' If the current file found is not a directory...
    '**************************************************************
    If (clsFind.FileAttributes And vbDirectory) = 0 Then
        colFiles.Add strFile ' don't include the path
    End If
    '**************************************************************
    ' Find the next file or directory
    '**************************************************************
    strFile = clsFind.FindNext()
Loop
'******************************************************************
' Return the number of files found
'******************************************************************
FindFilesInSingleDir = colFiles.Count
End Function
```

This function begins by creating a new `clsFindFile` object and building the search string. The first file is then retrieved by a call to the `Find` method, and subsequent files are retrieved by looping until `FindNext` no longer returns a value. If no files are found, `FindFilesInSingleDir` returns zero, and no changes are made to the `colFiles` collection. This function is sufficient for your basic needs, but isn't much better than `Dir` because it does not support searching subdirectories. However, this limitation is due to the implementation of the `FindFile` class and not a limitation of the class itself.

Listing 35.8 goes one step further by including support for searching subdirectories. The `FindAllFiles` function overcomes the limitations of `Dir` and `FindFilesInSingleDir`, but it is slightly slower than the previous function. Your application determines if it really needs to search subdirectories and call the appropriate function. This way, the results can be obtained by using the fastest method possible.

Listing 35.8   FINDFILE.FRM—*FindAllFiles* Includes Subdirectories in Its Search but It Pays a Small Performance Price

```
'******************************************************************
' A complex routine that finds all of the files in a directory (and its
' subdirectories), loads the results in a collection, and returns the
' number of subdirectories that were searched.
'******************************************************************
Private Function FindAllFiles(ByVal strSearchPath$, strPattern As _
    String, Optional colFiles As Collection, Optional colDirs As _
    Collection, Optional blnDirsOnly As Boolean, Optional blnBoth _
    As Boolean) As Integer
    '**************************************************************
    ' Create a new FindFile object every time this function is called
    '**************************************************************
```

Part

VIII

Ch

35

continues

Listing 35.8 Continued

```
Dim clsFind As New clsFindFile
Dim strFile As String
Dim intDirsFound As Integer
'****************************************************************
' Make sure strSearchPath always has a trailing backslash
'****************************************************************
If Right(strSearchPath, 1) <> "\" Then _
    strSearchPath = strSearchPath & "\"
'****************************************************************
' Get the first file
'****************************************************************
strFile = clsFind.Find(strSearchPath & strPattern)
'****************************************************************
' Loop while files are being returned
'****************************************************************
Do While Len(strFile)
    '************************************************************
    ' If the current file found is a directory...
    '************************************************************
    If clsFind.FileAttributes And vbDirectory Then
        '********************************************************
        ' Ignore . and ..
        '********************************************************
        If Left(strFile, 1) <> "." Then
            '****************************************************
            ' If either bln optional arg is true, then add this
            ' directory to the optional colDirs collection
            '****************************************************
            If blnDirsOnly Or blnBoth Then
                colDirs.Add strSearchPath & strFile & "\"
            End If
            '****************************************************
            ' Increment the number of directories found by one
            '****************************************************
            intDirsFound = intDirsFound + 1
            '****************************************************
            ' Recursively call this function to search for matches
            ' in subdirectories.  When the recursed function
            ' completes, intDirsFound must be incremented.
            '****************************************************
            intDirsFound = intDirsFound + FindAllFiles( _
                strSearchPath & strFile & "\", strPattern, _
                colFiles, colDirs, blnDirsOnly)
        End If
        '********************************************************
        ' Find the next file or directory
        '********************************************************
        strFile = clsFind.FindNext()
    '************************************************************
    ' ... otherwise it must be a file.
    '************************************************************
    Else
        '********************************************************
```

```
                ' If the caller wants files, then add them to the colFiles
                ' collection
                '*********************************************************
                If Not blnDirsOnly Or blnBoth Then
                    colFiles.Add strSearchPath & strFile
                End If
                '*********************************************************
                ' Find the next file or directory
                '*********************************************************
                strFile = clsFind.FindNext()
            End If
        Loop
        '*************************************************************
        ' Return the number of directories found
        '*************************************************************
        FindAllFiles = intDirsFound
    End Function
```

The main feature that allows `FindAllFiles` to search subdirectories is the fact that it recursively calls itself. It does this by checking to see if the current file is a directory. If it is, then it makes another call to `FindAllFiles` using all of the same parameters passed in by the original caller with one exception. The `strSearchPath` parameter is modified to point to the next subdirectory to search.

Now that we have our search routines written, let's look at some of the code in FindFile.frm (shown in Figure 35.1) that use this code based on requests from the user of our search dialog box. In Listing 35.9, we perform our search based on the values the user set in our search dialog box. We also play a `FindFile` video during our search, so the user has something to look at during long searches.

FIG. 35.1
FindFile.frm is our VB version of the Windows FindFile dialog box.

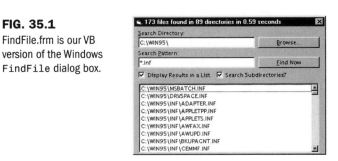

N O T E   When using this sample, the caption displays the number of files and directories found when your search is completed. This value is the correct value, but it might be different from the values returned by the MS-DOS `Dir` command and the Windows Find dialog box. Both `Dir` and the Find dialog box use a different mechanism for counting the number of "files" returned, neither of which is completely accurate. The method I use correlates to the value returned when you view the properties of a directory in the Windows Explorer. ∎

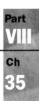

Part
VIII

Ch
35

Listing 35.9   FINDFILE.FRM—Choosing the Right Search Technique

```
'********************************************************************
' Find matching files based on the contents of the text boxes
'********************************************************************
Private Sub cmdFind_Click()
    '****************************************************************
    ' Prevent the user from clicking the find button twice, and
    ' hide the browse button so the AVI can be seen
    '****************************************************************
    cmdFind.Enabled = False
    cmdBrowse.Visible = False
    '****************************************************************
    ' Give the user a video to watch (wasteful, but cool)
    '****************************************************************
    With aniFindFile
        .Open App.Path & "\findfile.avi"
        .Visible = True
        Refresh
        .Play
    End With
    '****************************************************************
    ' Tell the user what you are doing and display an hourglass pointer
    '****************************************************************
    Caption = "Searching..."
    Screen.MousePointer = vbHourglass
    '****************************************************************
    ' Always clear before performing the operation (in case the list
    ' is already visible to the user)
    '****************************************************************
    lstFound.Clear
    '****************************************************************
    ' Perform the appropriate search
    '****************************************************************
    If chkSearchSubs Then
        SearchSubDirs
    Else
        SearchCurDirOnly
    End If
    '****************************************************************
    ' End the video, then restore the buttons and pointer
    '****************************************************************
    aniFindFile.Stop: aniFindFile.Visible = False
    cmdFind.Enabled = True
    cmdBrowse.Visible = True
    Screen.MousePointer = vbDefault
End Sub
```

This code simply controls the user interface, but doesn't actually do any searching. Instead, it determines which helper function to call based on the default value property of the chkSearchSubs control. I chose this technique because the helper search functions are rather complex, so including it in the Click event would make this code difficult to read.

Listing 35.10 starts with the simple `SearchCurDirOnly` helper routine. This routine simply calls `FindFilesInSingleDir` and loads the results from the `colFiles` collection into a list box (if necessary). That is simple enough, but the next routine, `SearchSubDirs`, is a little more complicated. The reason is because, if the user wants to search for all the files with the extension TMP, then we must first get a list of all of the directories by calling `FindAllFiles`. After we have our list of directories, then we can search each of them for TMP files.

Listing 35.10   FINDFILE.FRM—Using the Results from Our *Find* Functions

```
'****************************************************************
' Performs a simple search in a single directory (like dir *.*)
'****************************************************************
Private Sub SearchCurDirOnly()
    Dim dblStart As Long
    Dim colFiles As New Collection
    '****************************************************************
    ' Begin timing then search
    '****************************************************************
    dblStart = Timer
    FindFilesInSingleDir txtSearchDir, txtSearchPattern, colFiles
    '****************************************************************
    ' Adding items to the list is slow, so only do it if you have to
    '****************************************************************
    If chkDisplayInList Then LoadCollectionInList colFiles
    '****************************************************************
    ' Tell the user how many files were found and how long it took _
    ' to find (and load) the files
    '****************************************************************
    Caption = CStr(colFiles.Count) & " files found in" & _
        Str(Timer - dblStart) & " seconds"
End Sub
'****************************************************************
' Performs a complex search in multiple directories (like dir *.* /s)
'****************************************************************
Private Sub SearchSubDirs()
    Dim dblStart As Long
    Dim colFiles As New Collection
    Dim colDirs As New Collection
    Dim intDirsFound As Integer
    Dim vntItem As Variant
    '****************************************************************
    ' Don't forget to add the search directory to your collection
    '****************************************************************
    colDirs.Add txtSearchDir.Text
    '****************************************************************
    ' If the user searches for *.*, then the search is simple (and
    ' much faster)
    '****************************************************************
    If Trim(txtSearchPattern) = "*.*" Then
        dblStart = Timer
        intDirsFound = FindAllFiles(txtSearchDir, "*.*", colFiles, _
            colDirs, , True)
```

Part
VIII

Ch
35

continues

Listing 35.10   Continued

```
'******************************************************************
' Otherwise things get sorta complicated
'******************************************************************
Else
    '**************************************************************
    ' First search to get a collection of all the directories
    '**************************************************************
    intDirsFound = FindAllFiles(txtSearchDir, "*.*", , colDirs, True)
    '**************************************************************
    ' Start timing now, since the last search was just prep work
    '**************************************************************
    dblStart = Timer
    '**************************************************************
    ' Search for the file pattern in each directory in the list
    '**************************************************************
    For Each vntItem In colDirs
        '**********************************************************
        ' Display the current search directory in the caption
        '**********************************************************
        Caption = vntItem
        FindAllFiles CStr(vntItem), txtSearchPattern, colFiles
    Next vntItem
End If
'******************************************************************
' Adding items to the list is slow, so only do it if you have to
'******************************************************************
If chkDisplayInList Then LoadCollectionInList colFiles
'******************************************************************
' Tell the user how many files were found in how many dirs and
' how long it took to find (and load) the files
'******************************************************************
Caption = CStr(colFiles.Count) & " files found in" & _
    Str(intDirsFound) & " directories in" & Str(Timer - dblStart) _
    & " seconds"
End Sub
```

You might notice that, when each of the two routines listed previously complete, they display some basic results in the caption. This is done so that you can experiment with the FindFile program to see that FindFile itself is very fast, but loading the items into a list can be very slow. When using the FindFile.vbp demo program, experiment with different types of searches such as searching a networked drive by using a UNC path. Try improving it to support all of the features that the Windows Find dialog box supports.

Going Graphical with the GDI API

One of the most complex features in the Win32 API are the Graphics Device Interface (GDI) APIs. Because these APIs are very complicated, tedious, and GPF-prone, Microsoft played it safe and excluded most of them from VB. While this shelters you from the complexity and makes your programs more robust, it severely limits your ability to do the cool things that many users expect. VB4 helped to relieve this problem to some extent by providing new features such as `PaintPicture` and the ImageList control, but it still fell short. This means that sometime in the near future, you are going to find yourself calling the GDI APIs from your application. This section demonstrates some of the more common GDI APIs by writing a cool function called `TransparentPaint`.

N O T E   Although I would like to take complete credit for the `TransparentPaint` routine, I cannot. The version you see in this chapter is my Win32 version of the `TransparentBlt` code (written by Mike Bond) that originally appeared in the Microsoft Knowledge Base KB article number Q94961. However, I have made many modifications to this code and included a wealth of new comments. ▓

`TransparentPaint`, shown in Listing 35.11, is designed to treat a bitmap like an icon when you paint it on a surface. Icons allow you to designate a part of them to be transparent, but bitmaps don't. `TransparentPaint` overcomes this limitation by allowing you to make all of a single color on a bitmap transparent. To accomplish this difficult feat, it is necessary to create a series of temporary bitmaps and do some painting in memory only. Although this abstract concept can be very complicated, the comments in `TransparentPaint` try to explain what is happening at each step.

Listing 35.11   TRANSPARENT.BAS—Transparent.bas Allows You to Display Transparent Bitmaps

```
'*****************************************************************
' Paints a bitmap on a given surface using the surface backcolor
' everywhere lngMaskColor appears on the picSource bitmap
'*****************************************************************
Sub TransparentPaint(objDest As Object, picSource As StdPicture, _
    lngX As Long, lngY As Long, ByVal lngMaskColor As Long)
    '*************************************************************
    ' This sub uses a bunch of variables, so let's declare and explain
    ' them in advance...
    '*************************************************************
    Dim lngSrcDC As Long       'Source bitmap
    Dim lngSaveDC As Long      'Copy of Source bitmap
    Dim lngMaskDC As Long      'Monochrome Mask bitmap
    Dim lngInvDC As Long       'Monochrome Inverse of Mask bitmap
    Dim lngNewPicDC As Long    'Combination of Source & Background bmps

    Dim bmpSource As BITMAP    'Description of the Source bitmap

    Dim hResultBmp As Long     'Combination of source & background
    Dim hSaveBmp As Long       'Copy of Source bitmap
    Dim hMaskBmp As Long       'Monochrome Mask bitmap
    Dim hInvBmp As Long        'Monochrome Inverse of Mask bitmap

    Dim hSrcPrevBmp As Long    'Holds prev bitmap in source DC
    Dim hSavePrevBmp As Long   'Holds prev bitmap in saved DC
```

continues

Part
VIII

Ch
35

Listing 35.11 Continued

```
Dim hDestPrevBmp As Long  'Holds prev bitmap in destination DC
Dim hMaskPrevBmp As Long  'Holds prev bitmap in the mask DC
Dim hInvPrevBmp As Long   'Holds prev bitmap in inverted mask DC

Dim lngOrigScaleMode&     'Holds the original ScaleMode
Dim lngOrigColor&         'Holds original backcolor from source DC
'****************************************************************
' Set ScaleMode to pixels for Windows GDI
'****************************************************************
lngOrigScaleMode = objDest.ScaleMode
objDest.ScaleMode = vbPixels
'****************************************************************
' Load the source bitmap to get its width (bmpSource.bmWidth)
' and height (bmpSource.bmHeight)
'****************************************************************
GetObject picSource, Len(bmpSource), bmpSource
'****************************************************************
' Create compatible device contexts (DC's) to hold the temporary
' bitmaps used by this sub
'****************************************************************
lngSrcDC = CreateCompatibleDC(objDest.hdc)
lngSaveDC = CreateCompatibleDC(objDest.hdc)
lngMaskDC = CreateCompatibleDC(objDest.hdc)
lngInvDC = CreateCompatibleDC(objDest.hdc)
lngNewPicDC = CreateCompatibleDC(objDest.hdc)
'****************************************************************
' Create monochrome bitmaps for the mask-related bitmaps
'****************************************************************
hMaskBmp = CreateBitmap(bmpSource.bmWidth, bmpSource.bmHeight, _
    1, 1, ByVal 0&)
hInvBmp = CreateBitmap(bmpSource.bmWidth, bmpSource.bmHeight, _
    1, 1, ByVal 0&)
'****************************************************************
' Create color bitmaps for the final result and the backup copy
' of the source bitmap
'****************************************************************
hResultBmp = CreateCompatibleBitmap(objDest.hdc, _
    bmpSource.bmWidth, bmpSource.bmHeight)
hSaveBmp = CreateCompatibleBitmap(objDest.hdc, _
    bmpSource.bmWidth, bmpSource.bmHeight)
'****************************************************************
' Select bitmap into the device context (DC)
'****************************************************************
hSrcPrevBmp = SelectObject(lngSrcDC, picSource)
hSavePrevBmp = SelectObject(lngSaveDC, hSaveBmp)
hMaskPrevBmp = SelectObject(lngMaskDC, hMaskBmp)
hInvPrevBmp = SelectObject(lngInvDC, hInvBmp)
hDestPrevBmp = SelectObject(lngNewPicDC, hResultBmp)
'****************************************************************
' Make a backup of source bitmap to restore later
'****************************************************************
BitBlt lngSaveDC, 0, 0, bmpSource.bmWidth, bmpSource.bmHeight, _
    lngSrcDC, 0, 0, vbSrcCopy
```

```
'****************************************************************
' Create the mask by setting the background color of source to
' transparent color, then BitBlt'ing that bitmap into the mask
' device context
'****************************************************************
lngOrigColor = SetBkColor(lngSrcDC, lngMaskColor)
BitBlt lngMaskDC, 0, 0, bmpSource.bmWidth, bmpSource.bmHeight, _
    lngSrcDC, 0, 0, vbSrcCopy
'****************************************************************
' Restore the original backcolor in the device context
'****************************************************************
SetBkColor lngSrcDC, lngOrigColor
'****************************************************************
' Create an inverse of the mask to AND with the source and combine
' it with the background
'****************************************************************
BitBlt lngInvDC, 0, 0, bmpSource.bmWidth, bmpSource.bmHeight, _
    lngMaskDC, 0, 0, vbNotSrcCopy
'****************************************************************
' Copy the background bitmap to the new picture device context
' to begin creating the final transparent bitmap
'****************************************************************
BitBlt lngNewPicDC, 0, 0, bmpSource.bmWidth, bmpSource.bmHeight, _
    objDest.hdc, lngX, lngY, vbSrcCopy
'****************************************************************
' AND the mask bitmap with the result device context to create
' a cookie cutter effect in the background by painting the black
' area for the non-transparent portion of the source bitmap
'****************************************************************
BitBlt lngNewPicDC, 0, 0, bmpSource.bmWidth, bmpSource.bmHeight, _
    lngMaskDC, 0, 0, vbSrcAnd
'****************************************************************
' AND the inverse mask with the source bitmap to turn off the bits
' associated with transparent area of source bitmap by making it
' black
'****************************************************************
BitBlt lngSrcDC, 0, 0, bmpSource.bmWidth, bmpSource.bmHeight, _
    lngInvDC, 0, 0, vbSrcAnd
'****************************************************************
' XOR the result with the source bitmap to replace the mask color
' with the background color
'****************************************************************
BitBlt lngNewPicDC, 0, 0, bmpSource.bmWidth, bmpSource.bmHeight, _
    lngSrcDC, 0, 0, vbSrcPaint
'****************************************************************
' Paint the transparent bitmap on source surface
'****************************************************************
BitBlt objDest.hdc, lngX, lngY, bmpSource.bmWidth, _
    bmpSource.bmHeight, lngNewPicDC, 0, 0, vbSrcCopy
'****************************************************************
' Restore backup of bitmap
'****************************************************************
BitBlt lngSrcDC, 0, 0, bmpSource.bmWidth, bmpSource.bmHeight, _
    lngSaveDC, 0, 0, vbSrcCopy
```

Part
VIII

Ch

35

continues

Listing 35.11 Continued

```
'****************************************************************
' Restore the original objects by selecting their original values
'****************************************************************
SelectObject lngSrcDC, hSrcPrevBmp
SelectObject lngSaveDC, hSavePrevBmp
SelectObject lngNewPicDC, hDestPrevBmp
SelectObject lngMaskDC, hMaskPrevBmp
SelectObject lngInvDC, hInvPrevBmp
'****************************************************************
' Free system resources created by this sub
'****************************************************************
DeleteObject hSaveBmp
DeleteObject hMaskBmp
DeleteObject hInvBmp
DeleteObject hResultBmp
DeleteDC lngSrcDC
DeleteDC lngSaveDC
DeleteDC lngInvDC
DeleteDC lngMaskDC
DeleteDC lngNewPicDC
'****************************************************************
' Restores the ScaleMode to its original value
'****************************************************************
objDest.ScaleMode = lngOrigScaleMode
End Sub
```

On the Web

For simplicity's sake, I have omitted the API declarations from Listing 35.11. I could go on for pages explaining exactly what is happening during each step of `TransparentPaint`, but I won't because this sub contains the same comments I've made in this listing. It also would be more difficult to follow this listing if it were broken into several smaller blocks. After reading the comments for this sub, I encourage you to single-step through the TRANSPARENT.VBP project, which you can get from Que's Web site at **www.mcp.com/info/0-7897/0-7897-1288-1**. This will help you to visualize what is happening at each step.

Although `TransparentPaint` is a difficult procedure to follow, using it is easy. Listing 35.12 loads a bitmap from a resource and paints it on the upper-left corner of the form using `TransparentPaint`. Next, it paints it using `PaintPicture`. The last parameter, `vbGreen`, tells `TransparentPaint` to replace any bits in the bitmap that are green with the background color of the form. The result is shown in Figure 35.2.

Listing 35.12 TRANSPARENT.FRM—Transparent.frm Demonstrates the _TransparentPaint_ Procedure

```
'****************************************************************
' Transparent.frm - Demonstrates how to use basTransparent's
'    TransparentPaint using a bitmap from a resource file.
'****************************************************************
```

```
Option Explicit
'***********************************************************************
' Gets a StdPicture handle by loading a bitmap from a resource file
' and paints it transparently on the form by using Gray as the mask
' color.
'***********************************************************************
Private Sub cmdPaintTransBmp_Click()
    TransparentPaint Me, LoadResPicture(103, 0), 0, 0, QBColor(7)
End Sub
```

FIG. 35.2
TransparentPaint
is a must for your
multimedia applica-
tions.

Try replacing the resource file in this project with your own resource file to see how `TransparentPaint` works. Also, try using different mask colors as well as the images from picture boxes. Now you never again have to write an application that appears to be of inferior quality because it doesn't use transparent bitmaps.

Registry Revisited

In Chapter 19, "Advanced Control Techniques," I demonstrated how to use the TreeView and ListView controls in a mini Registry program called Registry.vbp. The code in this section is from a module in that project called Registry.bas. It was that code that was responsible for retrieving the values from the Registry that were subsequently loaded into the TreeView and ListView controls. The listing in this section, like most sections in this chapter, is long because I have included the discussion of the code in line with the code in the form of comments. Before and after each listing, I make some additional comments on the code, but the most important comments are in the listing itself. Given the sheer size of Registry.bas, I have elected to include only some of the functions from that module.

The most common interaction between VB programs and the Registry is writing and reading strings to and from a specific key. Listing 35.13 contains two functions, `GetRegString` and `SetRegString`, that accomplish this task. In addition to setting Registry strings, `SetRegString` also creates new keys in the Registry. If either of these functions fails, it raises a user-defined error. This way, your application can handle this error without notifying your user.

Part
VIII

Ch
35

Listing 35.13 REGISTRY.BAS—*GetRegSetting* and *SetRegSetting* Read and Write Registry Strings

```
'***********************************************************************
' REGISTRY.BAS - Contains the code necessary to access the Windows
'                registration database.
'
```

continues

Listing 35.13   Continued

```
'*********************************************************************
' GetRegString takes three arguments. A HKEY constant (listed above),
' a subkey, and a value in that subkey. This function returns the
' string stored in the strValueName value in the registry.
'*********************************************************************
Public Function GetRegString(HKEY As Long, strSubKey As String, _
                                    strValueName As String) As String
    Dim strSetting As String
    Dim lngDataLen As Long
    Dim hSubKey As Long
    '*****************************************************************
    ' Open the key. If success, then get the data from the key.
    '*****************************************************************
    If RegOpenKeyEx(HKEY, strSubKey, 0, KEY_ALL_ACCESS, hSubKey) = _
        ERROR_SUCCESS Then
        strSetting = Space(255)
        lngDataLen = Len(strSetting)
        '*************************************************************
        ' Query the key for the current setting. If this call
        ' succeeds, then return the string.
        '*************************************************************
        If RegQueryValueEx(hSubKey, strValueName, ByVal 0, _
            REG_SZ, ByVal strSetting, lngDataLen) = _
            ERROR_SUCCESS Then
            If lngDataLen > 1 Then
                GetRegString = Left(strSetting, lngDataLen - 1)
            End If
        Else
            Err.Raise ERRBASE + 1, "GetRegString", _
                "RegQueryValueEx failed!"
        End If
        '*************************************************************
        ' ALWAYS close any keys that you open.
        '*************************************************************
        RegCloseKey hSubKey
    End If
End Function
'*********************************************************************
' SetRegString takes four arguments. A HKEY constant (listed above),
' a subkey, a value in that subkey, and a setting for the key.
'*********************************************************************
Public Sub SetRegString(HKEY As Long, strSubKey As String, _
                                strValueName As String, strSetting _
                                As String)
    Dim hNewHandle As Long
    Dim lpdwDisposition As Long
    '*****************************************************************
    ' Create & open the key. If success, then get then write the data
    ' to the key.
    '*****************************************************************
```

```
    If RegCreateKeyEx(HKEY, strSubKey, 0, strValueName, 0, _
        KEY_ALL_ACCESS, 0&, hNewHandle, lpdwDisposition) = _
        ERROR_SUCCESS Then
        If RegSetValueEx(hNewHandle, strValueName, 0, REG_SZ, _
            ByVal strSetting, Len(strSetting)) <> ERROR_SUCCESS Then
            Err.Raise ERRBASE + 2, "SetRegString", _
                "RegSetValueEx failed!"
        End If
    Else
        Err.Raise ERRBASE + 3, "SetRegString", "RegCreateKeyEx failed!"
    End If
    '****************************************************************
    ' ALWAYS close any keys that you open.
    '****************************************************************
    RegCloseKey hNewHandle
End Sub
```

Although these two functions accomplish different tasks, the method they use to accomplish their task is virtually identical. The user provides a predefined long constant HKEY value (such as HKEY_CURRENT_USER), a subkey (such as "Software\Microsoft" with no leading backslash), and a value to read from or write to. Both functions (using different Registry functions) begin by opening the subkey and then reading or writing to or from it. Finally, they both end by closing the key they opened.

Listing 35.13 demonstrates a fundamental technique required during all coding with the Registry. Subkeys must be opened and closed before any values can be retrieved. The HKEY values are opened and closed by Windows, so you never have to worry about opening or closing them. This concept is repeated during every function in Registry.bas, so keep this in mind should you decide to write your own Registry functions.

Listing 35.14 demonstrates this fundamental technique again using DWORD (or Long) values. The GetRegDWord and SetRegDWord functions allow you to read and write long values to and from the Registry. Because most Registry values you'll ever use will be strings, I have included a conditional compilation argument in Registry.bas called LEAN_AND_MEAN. Because this conditional compilation constant is undefined by default, its value will be 0. This means that all of the code in the LEAN_AND_MEAN section will be included in your application by default. However, if you wanted to write an application that did not take advantage of any of the functions in the LEAN_AND_MEAN section, then you could edit your project properties and set the LEAN_AND_MEAN conditional compilation constant equal to 1. This would prevent this code from being included in your executable, thus reducing its size and memory requirements. All of the remaining code in Registry.bas that appears in this section is part of the LEAN_AND_MEAN section that may be excluded from your application.

Part
VIII

Ch
35

Listing 35.14   REGISTRY.BAS—Extended Registry Functions Using Conditional Compilation

```
'*********************************************************************
' Extended registry functions begin here
'*********************************************************************
#If LEAN_AND_MEAN = 0 Then
'*********************************************************************
' Returns a DWORD value from a given registry key
'*********************************************************************
Public Function GetRegDWord(HKEY&, strSubKey$, strValueName$) As Long
    Dim lngDataLen As Long
    Dim hSubKey As Long
    Dim lngRetVal As Long
    '*****************************************************************
    ' Open the key. If success, then get the data from the key.
    '*****************************************************************
    If RegOpenKeyEx(HKEY, strSubKey, 0, KEY_ALL_ACCESS, hSubKey) = _
        ERROR_SUCCESS Then
        '*************************************************************
        ' Query the key for the current setting. If this call
        ' succeeds, then return the string.
        '*************************************************************
        lngDataLen = 4 'Bytes
        If RegQueryValueEx(hSubKey, strValueName, ByVal 0, _
            REG_DWORD, lngRetVal, lngDataLen) = ERROR_SUCCESS Then
            GetRegDWord = lngRetVal
        Else
            Err.Raise ERRBASE + 1, "GetRegDWord", _
                "RegQueryValueEx failed!"
        End If
        '*************************************************************
        ' ALWAYS close any keys that you open.
        '*************************************************************
        RegCloseKey hSubKey
    End If
End Function
'*********************************************************************
' Sets a registry key to a DWORD value
'*********************************************************************
Public Sub SetRegDWord(HKEY&, strSubKey$, strValueName$, lngSetting&)
    Dim hNewHandle As Long
    Dim lpdwDisposition As Long
    '*****************************************************************
    ' Create & open the key. If success, then get then write the data
    ' to the key.
    '*****************************************************************
    If RegCreateKeyEx(HKEY, strSubKey, 0, strValueName, 0, _
        KEY_ALL_ACCESS, 0&, hNewHandle, lpdwDisposition) = _
        ERROR_SUCCESS Then
        If RegSetValueEx(hNewHandle, strValueName, 0, REG_DWORD, _
            lngSetting, 4) <> ERROR_SUCCESS Then
            Err.Raise ERRBASE + 2, "SetRegDWord", _
                "RegSetValueEx failed!"
        End If
```

```
        Else
            Err.Raise ERRBASE + 3, "SetRegString", "RegCreateKeyEx failed!"
        End If
        '*****************************************************************
        ' ALWAYS close any keys that you open.
        '*****************************************************************
        RegCloseKey hNewHandle
End Sub
```

The way you read and write DWORD (or Long) values to and from the Registry are almost identical to the method you use for strings. The only difference is that, instead of passing the length of your string or buffer to `RegQueryValueEx` and `RegSetValueEx`, you pass the number of bytes of memory occupied by a Long. Because a Long holds 4 bytes, we pass in the number 4.

The last function I'm going to discuss in Registry.bas is the `GetRegKeyValues` function, shown in Listing 35.15. This function enumerates through a given subkey in the Registry and returns all of its values and settings. This function was used to load our ListView control with all of the values of the subkey selected in the TreeView control in Registry.frm. Although this function isn't extraordinarily difficult, it is long and complex given the nature of enumeration and multi-dimensional arrays.

This function is unique to most functions you've ever used or written because it returns a multi-dimensional array that contains the values in the first dimension and the settings in the second dimension. This gives the calling function the flexibility to use the values returned from this function in any manner it chooses. However, it is the responsibility of the caller to both check to make sure an array was returned (in case there were no keys) *and* to treat the results from this function as a two-dimensional array.

`GetRegKeyValues` begins like every function in Registry.bas by opening the subkey, but then it does something unique. It calls a helper function (not shown) called `QueryRegInfoKey` which returns some helpful information about the subkey. `QueryRegInfoKey` simply wraps a Registry function called `RegQueryInfoKey` that provides us with information about subkey like how many values it contains, and the length of the longest value and setting. This information helps to determine if we should begin the enumeration, the size array we will need, and how large our string buffer needs to be. After we have this information, we are ready to begin the enumeration.

Listing 35.15   REGISTRY.BAS—*GetRegKeyValues* Demonstrates Registry Enumeration

```
'*****************************************************************
' Returns a multi dimensional variant array of all the values and
' settings in a given registry subkey.
'*****************************************************************
Public Function GetRegKeyValues(HKEY&, strSubKey$) As Variant
    Dim lngNumValues As Long      ' Number values in this key
```

continues

Listing 35.15   Continued

```
Dim strValues() As String     ' Value and return array
Dim lngMaxValSize  As Long     ' Size of longest value
Dim lngValRetBytes As Long     ' Size of current value

Dim lngMaxSettingSize As Long  ' Size of longest REG_SZ in this key
Dim lngSetRetBytes As Long     ' Size of current REG_SZ

Dim lngSetting As Long         ' Used for DWORD

Dim lngType As Long            ' Type of value returned from
                               ' RegEnumValue

Dim hChildKey As Long          ' The handle of strSubKey
Dim i As Integer               ' Loop counter
'*******************************************************************
' Exit if you did not successfully open the child key
'*******************************************************************
If RegOpenKeyEx(HKEY, strSubKey, 0, KEY_ALL_ACCESS, hChildKey) _
    <> ERROR_SUCCESS Then
    Err.Raise ERRBASE + 4, "GetRegKeyValues", _
        "RegOpenKeyEx failed!"
    Exit Function
End If
'*******************************************************************
' Find out the array and value sizes in advance
'*******************************************************************
If QueryRegInfoKey(hChildKey, , , lngNumValues, lngMaxValSize, _
    lngMaxSettingSize) <> ERROR_SUCCESS Or lngNumValues = 0 Then
    Err.Raise ERRBASE + 5, "GetRegKeyValues", _
        "RegQueryInfoKey failed!"
    RegCloseKey hChildKey
    Exit Function
End If
'*******************************************************************
' Resize the array to fit the return values
'*******************************************************************
lngNumValues = lngNumValues - 1 ' Adjust to zero based
ReDim strValues(0 To lngNumValues, 0 To 1) As String
'*******************************************************************
' Get all of the values and settings for the key
'*******************************************************************
For i = 0 To lngNumValues
    '*******************************************************************
    ' Make the return buffers large enough to hold the results
    '*******************************************************************
    strValues(i, 0) = Space(lngMaxValSize)
    lngValRetBytes = lngMaxValSize

    strValues(i, 1) = Space(lngMaxSettingSize)
    lngSetRetBytes = lngMaxSettingSize
    '*******************************************************************
    ' Get a single value and setting from the registry
```

```
'*******************************************************************
RegEnumValue hChildKey, i, strValues(i, 0), lngValRetBytes, _
    0, lngType, ByVal strValues(i, 1), lngSetRetBytes
'*******************************************************************
' If the return value was a string, then trim trailing nulls
'*******************************************************************
If lngType = REG_SZ Then
    strValues(i, 1) = Left(strValues(i, 1), lngSetRetBytes - 1)
'*******************************************************************
' Else if it was a DWord, call RegEnumValue again to store
' the return setting in a long variable
'*******************************************************************
ElseIf lngType = REG_DWORD Then
    '*******************************************************************
    ' We already know the return size of the value because
    ' we got it in the last call to RegEnumValue, so we
    ' can tell RegEnumValue that its buffer size is the
    ' length of the string already returned, plus one (for
    ' the trailing null terminator)
    '*******************************************************************
    lngValRetBytes = lngValRetBytes + 1
    '*******************************************************************
    ' Make the call again using a long instead of string
    '*******************************************************************
    RegEnumValue hChildKey, i, strValues(i, 0), _
        lngValRetBytes, 0, lngType, lngSetting, lngSetRetBytes
    '*******************************************************************
    ' Return the long as a string
    '*******************************************************************
    strValues(i, 1) = CStr(lngSetting)
'*******************************************************************
' Otherwise let the user know that this code doesn't support
' the format returned (such as REG_BINARY)
'*******************************************************************
Else
    strValues(i, 1) = REG_UNSUPPORTED
End If
'*******************************************************************
' Store the return value and setting in a multi dimensional
' array with the value in the 0 index and the setting in
' the 1 index of the second dimension.
'*******************************************************************
strValues(i, 0) = RTrim(Left(strValues(i, 0), lngValRetBytes))
strValues(i, 1) = RTrim(strValues(i, 1))
Next i
'*******************************************************************
' ALWAYS close any keys you open
'*******************************************************************
RegCloseKey hChildKey
'*******************************************************************
' Return the result as an array of strings
'*******************************************************************
GetRegKeyValues = strValues
End Function
```

During the enumeration, we set all of our string buffers in advance. Next, we attempt to re-trieve the value and setting as strings. If the setting was a string, then we trim off any trailing nulls. If the setting was a DWORD, then we make the call again this time passing in a long value and 4 bytes as the buffer size. After the DWORD has been retrieved, we convert it into a string and load it into the array. If the setting was neither a string nor a DWORD, then we load the array with a special string that tells the caller the return value was in an unsupported format.

We repeat the enumeration for all of the values and settings. When completed, we close the key we opened and return the two-dimensional array by its name. The caller will get a variant re-turn value that contains this two-dimensional array.

The remaining functions are described in detail in Registry.bas. I encourage you to read these comments and experiment with each of them. I've also included some examples that demon-strate how to use each of the functions in Registry.bas in the Form_Load event of Registry.frm. These functions are at the end of the Form_Load event and are commented out. Feel free to use them in Registry.frm, the immediate pane in VB, or in a separate application to see how each of the Registry.bas functions works.

Callbacks Revisited

By using the Windows API, you can create *callbacks* in Visual Basic. This feature allows the operating system to call a procedure in your Visual Basic program. For example, you can have Windows call a procedure in response to a Windows event. Windows knows how to call your procedure because you pass the address of it to Windows when using the API. Before version 5.0, callbacks of this type were not available in VB.

Listing 35.16 demonstrates how to use the EnumWindows API call. EnumWindows takes a function pointer and a pointer to a value that you would like passed to your function pointer. In turn, it iterates through the Windows task list, calling your callback function during each iteration. Callback.bas contains our callback function and some helper routines that allow us to print a list of visible windows on a form.

Listing 35.16   CALLBACK.BAS—Callback.bas Shows a Sample Callback Function

```
'******************************************************************
' Callback.bas - Demonstrates how to do callbacks in VB
'******************************************************************
Option Explicit
'******************************************************************
' EnumWindows takes a function pointer (AddressOf your callback
' function) and a lParam argument (can be a pointer to anything you
' would like sent to your callback function)
'******************************************************************
Private Declare Function EnumWindows Lib "user32" _
    (ByVal lpfn As Long, lParam As Any) As Boolean
'******************************************************************
```

```
' There are a lot of windows loaded that are never visible, so
' I usually use the IsWindowVisible API call to filter out only the
' top-level windows the user sees
'******************************************************************
Private Declare Function IsWindowVisible Lib "user32" _
    (ByVal hWnd As Long) As Long
'******************************************************************
' I use the following APIs to get the captions and classnames of the
' visible windows
'******************************************************************
Private Declare Function GetWindowText Lib "user32" Alias _
    "GetWindowTextA" (ByVal hWnd As Long, ByVal lpString As String, _
    ByVal cch As Long) As Long

Private Declare Function GetWindowTextLength Lib "user32" Alias _
    "GetWindowTextLengthA" (ByVal hWnd As Long) As Long

Private Declare Function GetClassName Lib "user32" Alias _
    "GetClassNameA" (ByVal hWnd As Long, ByVal lpClassName$, _
    ByVal nMaxCount As Long) As Long
'******************************************************************
' This is a callback function. Notice how the function is declared
' as Private. This private flag only applies to VB, not to Windows,
' so it is okay to declare your callback functions as Private if you
' don't want them to be accessible in external modules. Also notice
' how we used the lParam pointer to pass as a form to our callback
'******************************************************************
Private Function CallBackFunc(ByVal hWnd As Long, _
    lParam As Form) As Long
    Dim strhWnd As String * 8
    Dim strClass As String * 20
    '******************************************************************
    ' If the window is visible, then print some information about it
    ' on the lParam form
    '******************************************************************
    If IsWindowVisible(hWnd) Then
        strhWnd = "&H" & Hex(hWnd)
        strClass = GetWindowClassName(hWnd)
        lParam.Print strhWnd & strClass & GetWindowCaption(hWnd)
    End If
    '******************************************************************
    ' Only return false if you want to stop EnumWindows from calling
    ' this callback again
    '******************************************************************
    CallBackFunc = True
End Function
'******************************************************************
' Returns the caption of a window
'******************************************************************
Private Function GetWindowCaption(hWnd As Long) As String
    Dim lngCaptionLen As Long
    Dim strCaption As String
    '******************************************************************
    ' Get the length of the caption and add 1 to account for the
```

Part
VIII

Ch
35

continues

Listing 35.16   Continued

```
    ' null terminator
    '*********************************************************************
    lngCaptionLen = GetWindowTextLength(hWnd) + 1
    '*********************************************************************
    ' Allocate your buffer to hold the caption
    '*********************************************************************
    strCaption = Space(lngCaptionLen)
    '*********************************************************************
    ' Get the caption, and return the characters up to (but not
    ' including) the null terminator
    '*********************************************************************
    lngCaptionLen = GetWindowText(hWnd, strCaption, lngCaptionLen)
    GetWindowCaption = Left(strCaption, lngCaptionLen)
End Function
'*********************************************************************
' Get the class name using the same techniques described above
'*********************************************************************
Private Function GetWindowClassName(hWnd As Long) As String
    Dim strClassName As String
    Dim lngClassLen As Integer
    lngClassLen = 50
    strClassName = Space(lngClassLen)
    lngClassLen = GetClassName(hWnd, strClassName, lngClassLen)
    GetWindowClassName = Left(strClassName, lngClassLen)
End Function
'*********************************************************************
' Print some headers and call EnumWindows to print the window info
'*********************************************************************
Public Sub CallbackDemo(frmName As Form)
    frmName.Cls
    frmName.Print "Handle" & "  Class Name", "Window Caption"
    frmName.Print "------" & "  ----------", "--------------"
    EnumWindows AddressOf CallBackFunc, frmName
End Sub
```

CallBackFunc begins with our callback function that is declared as private. It is private, because we won't be calling this code anywhere in our VB application. However, the private qualifier has no effect on Windows capability to call this function. Each time this function is called, we check to see if the current window is visible. If it is, then we print its hwnd, class name, and window caption on the form passed in as the lParam of EnumWindows. Finally, we always return True. If, for some reason, we wanted to end the enumeration, we would return False from our callback function. You might do this if you used EnumWindows to find a specific window. After you find the window you are searching for, you can stop the enumeration.

GetWindowCaption and GetWindowClassName simply wrap a couple of APIs, so your callback routine is as simple as possible. Because both of these functions are retrieving strings from an API, they both build string buffers before the API call and trim off the null terminator after the API call.

The last, but perhaps the most important, function in Listing 35.16 is the public `CallbackDemo` method. This method is the public interface to your application that is responsible for calling `EnumWindows` and printing the results on the form you provide when you call `CallbackDemo`.

Figure 35.3 shows our callback function at work in Callback.frm. Listing 35.17 demonstrates how to build this task list. We pass in a reference to the form where we make the call by using the `Me` keyword.

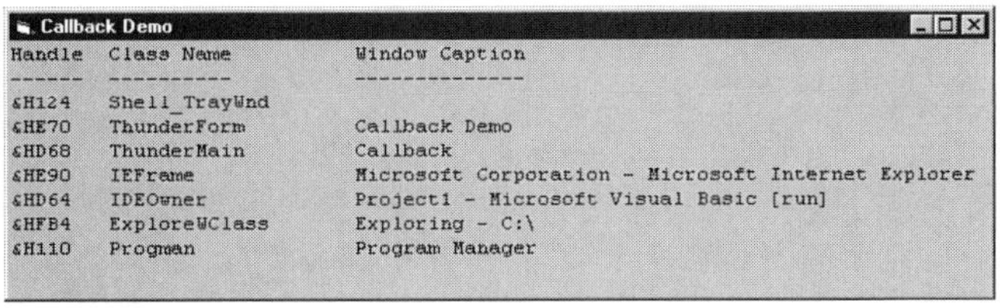

FIG. 35.3

EnumWindows is great for creating a task list.

Handle	Class Name	Window Caption
&H124	Shell_TrayWnd	
&HE70	ThunderForm	Callback Demo
&HD68	ThunderMain	Callback
&HE90	IEFrame	Microsoft Corporation - Microsoft Internet Explorer
&HD64	IDEOwner	Project1 - Microsoft Visual Basic [run]
&HFB4	ExploreWClass	Exploring - C:\
&H110	Progman	Program Manager

Listing 35.17   CALLBACK.FRM—Callback.frm Uses Our Sample Callback Function

```
'********************************************************************
' Callback.frm - Demonstrates how to use basCallback
'********************************************************************
Option Explicit
'********************************************************************
' Updates the form with the current window list every time it gets
' a paint event
'********************************************************************
Private Sub Form_Paint()
    CallbackDemo Me
End Sub
```

Because windows are always being added and removed, I elected to put our call to `CallbackDemo` in the `Form_Paint` event. Because creating or removing windows usually causes our form to be repainted, this technique allows our form to contain the latest visible window list.

From Here...

Now that you've had a small taste of what the Win32 API can do for you, it's time to experiment on your own. Take the samples in this chapter apart and use them in your own applications. Experiment, extend, and optimize them for your own code library. You'll find that, after you get the hang of writing VB programs that leverage the power of Win32, your dependency on third-party controls will be much less. Can you think of any controls you have now that could be replaced by the code in this chapter? If so, begin reworking your program right away.

Part
VIII

Ch
35

■ To learn more about some of the techniques of working with forms mentioned in this chapter, see Chapter 36, "Advanced Form Techniques."

■ For more samples of applications that use the Win32 API, browse the Que Web page for this book at **www.mcp.com/info/0-7897/0-7897-1288-1**.

Advanced Form Techniques

By now, you probably think that you have mastered everything there is to know about forms. However, there are a couple tips and tricks you might not have discovered yet. The purpose of this chapter is to demonstrate some of these techniques. Upon completing this chapter, you should be able to apply new form techniques that make your programs more robust. ■

Adding properties and methods to a form

You already know about the properties and methods that are built into a form, but did you know you can add your own? This chapter will show you how.

Users like to have their programs set up for them

You will see how to save the size and position of a form that the user has changed. You will also see how to restore the settings when the form is loaded.

Custom forms for multimedia applications

You will see how to create a form customized to the needs of a multimedia application.

Creating Properties and Methods

Back in Chapter 4, "Working with Forms and Controls," you saw how the appearance and behavior of forms could be controlled through the setting of properties. You found that the values of properties could be set and retrieved in code just like the values of variables. You also saw that the methods of a form or control were used to take an action such as moving the form or printing text. In other words, you could do a lot with methods and properties.

What you did not know at the time was that you could create your own properties and methods for use on a form. The properties and methods you create can be accessed from your program just like the ones that are native to the form. Creating your own properties and methods allows you to extend the functionality of a form by being able to pass data to the form and to define customized tasks that the form can do.

Creating a Property

Prior to version 4 of Visual Basic, there was no easy way to pass information to a form. About the only thing you could do was to declare a Global variable, set its value before loading the form, and then access the variable in the form. Although this worked, it was not an elegant solution to the problem. One of the key problems of this method was that the value of your Global variable could be reset by other parts of the program, thereby causing problems with the routines in your form that depended on the variable.

Then, in Visual Basic 4, Microsoft introduced the ability to *create a property of a form*. This allows you to specify a value of the property for a particular form without affecting other forms. It works much like the internal properties of the form. For example, each form in your program has a Top, Left, Height, Width, WindowState, and other properties. And, as you know, changing the value of the property for one form has no effect on any of the other forms. The same is true of created properties. Each form in your program can have a property called NeatStuff (or anything else). Changing this property on one form does not affect the property in other forms. In essence, the property maintains a value local to the form, but is accessible from any part of your program.

There are two ways that you can create a property on a form: declaring a Public variable in the form or using a Property procedure. We will look at each of these methods and discuss the advantages of using each.

Using the *Public* Keyword   The simplest way to create a property in a form is to declare a Public variable. You do this by using the Public keyword in the declaration statement for the variable as shown in the following line:

```
Public FormType As Integer
```

As with all variable declarations, you must specify the name of the variable, and you should specify the type of data that the variable will contain.

▶ **See** "Variable Declarations," **p. 168**

This `Public` variable's declaration statement must appear in the General Declarations section of the form's code. This section is at the beginning of the Code window, prior to any procedure definitions. A typical set of declarations is shown in Figure 36.1.

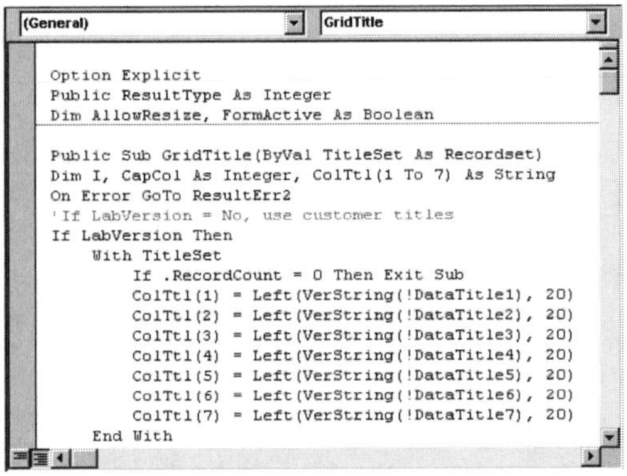

FIG. 36.1

The Declarations section sets up user-defined properties of the form and any private variables.

```
(General)                    ▼  GridTitle                        ▼

    Option Explicit
    Public ResultType As Integer
    Dim AllowResize, FormActive As Boolean

    Public Sub GridTitle(ByVal TitleSet As Recordset)
    Dim I, CapCol As Integer, ColTtl(1 To 7) As String
    On Error GoTo ResultErr2
    'If LabVersion = No, use customer titles
    If LabVersion Then
        With TitleSet
            If .RecordCount = 0 Then Exit Sub
            ColTtl(1) = Left(VerString(!DataTitle1), 20)
            ColTtl(2) = Left(VerString(!DataTitle2), 20)
            ColTtl(3) = Left(VerString(!DataTitle3), 20)
            ColTtl(4) = Left(VerString(!DataTitle4), 20)
            ColTtl(5) = Left(VerString(!DataTitle5), 20)
            ColTtl(6) = Left(VerString(!DataTitle6), 20)
            ColTtl(7) = Left(VerString(!DataTitle7), 20)
        End With
```

After the property has been defined by the `Public` declaration, it can be accessed by any part of your program. This means that you can set or retrieve the value of the property from anywhere. An advantage of using this method of creating a property is its simplicity. A disadvantage is that it provides no protection against undesirable values of the property.

Using a *Property* Procedure   The second way to create a property is to use a `Property` procedure. A `Property` procedure is actually a piece of code that uses the name of the desired property as the procedure name. The procedure then becomes the public interface to the form. By using a procedure, you allow your program to check for proper values of the property being passed to the form. Listing 36.1 shows a typical set of `Property` procedures.

▶ **See** "Adding Properties to the Class," **p. 834**

Listing 36.1   METHODS.FRM—Use a *Property* Procedure to Provide Data Checking When the Property Is Set

```
Dim m_frmType As Integer

Public Property Get FormType() As Integer
FormType = m_frmType
End Property

Public Property Let FormType(inptForm As Integer)
If inptForm < 0 Then
    m_frmType = 0
ElseIf inptForm > 10 Then
    m_frmType = 10
Else
    m_frmType = inptForm
End If
End Property
```

As you can see from the listing, you typically create a private variable in the form's General Declarations section. This is the variable that is actually used throughout the form code. The property procedure is then used to set the value of this variable when the property is set or to retrieve the value of the variable.

There are actually two parts to a property procedure. First is the `Property Let`. This is the procedure that sets the value of an internal variable and allows a value to be passed to the form. Notice in Listing 36.1 that the `Let` procedure contains an argument. This is the actual value that is passed to the procedure from other parts of your program. If you do not include a `Let` procedure, your form's property cannot be set by other code.

N O T E   If you are passing an object to your form, you need to use a Set procedure. This is identical to the `Let` procedure except that the keyword `Set` is used and the input argument must be an object. ▮

The second procedure is the `Get` procedure. This procedure is the one that allows the value of the property to be retrieved by other parts of your program.

CAUTION

If you specify a data type for the argument passed to the `Let` procedure, you must specify the same data type as the return type for the `Get` procedure.

Accessing the Property   As stated previously, you can access a user-defined property the same way you access native properties of the form. This is true no matter which method you used to create the property. If you want to set the value of a property, simply specify the form name, the property name, and the value in an assignment statement as shown in the following:

```
frmTest.FormType = 1
```

To retrieve the value of the property, simply place it on the right side of an assignment statement as shown in the following line:

```
PropValue = frmTest.FormType
```

If you have specified a data type for the property, you must make sure that any values or variables that you use are of the same data type.

Creating a Method

Creating a method for a form can be very useful in that it lets other parts of your program run code that is in your form. You can do this, for example, to set the captions of labels on your form or to reposition the form after some other task has been completed. Creating methods simply allows you to extend the capabilities of your form.

As an example, consider a form that is used to display control data for a manufacturing process. This data is constantly being fed into a database by another part of your program, by another program, or even by another computer. This routine also updates an array of the last 50 data points taken by the program. Now, suppose that you want to update the graph every 2 minutes. One way to handle this would be to create a method to refresh the graph in the form's code. This method could be called by a Timer control's `Timer` event, for example, from anywhere in your program. You could also give the user the capability to update the graph on demand by clicking a command button. In any case, your program would simply call the `Refresh` method of your form, and the rest is done. Although you can do this with procedures elsewhere in your code, the real power of this technique is that you can use the same form in multiple programs and all you ever have to worry about is calling the form's method.

Setting Up the Method   So, if this is such a great thing, it must be hard to implement, right? No way! Creating a method is as easy as creating any other procedure you might use in your program. The only thing you have to do is place the procedure in the form and specify the `Public` keyword in the procedure declaration. Listing 36.2 shows a method that was created to set up the titles of grid columns on a form.

Listing 36.2   METHODS.FRM—Use a *Public* Subroutine to Create a Method for the Form

```
Public Sub GridTitle(ByVal TitleSet As Recordset)
Dim I, CapCol As Integer, ColTtl(1 To 7) As String
On Error GoTo ResultErr2
'If LabVersion = No, use customer titles
If LabVersion Then
    With TitleSet
        If .RecordCount = 0 Then Exit Sub
        ColTtl(1) = Left(VerString(!DataTitle1), 20)
        ColTtl(2) = Left(VerString(!DataTitle2), 20)
        ColTtl(3) = Left(VerString(!DataTitle3), 20)
        ColTtl(4) = Left(VerString(!DataTitle4), 20)
        ColTtl(5) = Left(VerString(!DataTitle5), 20)
        ColTtl(6) = Left(VerString(!DataTitle6), 20)
        ColTtl(7) = Left(VerString(!DataTitle7), 20)
    End With
Else
    With TitleSet
        If .RecordCount = 0 Then Exit Sub
        ColTtl(1) = Left(VerString(!LocalDataTitle1), 20)
        ColTtl(2) = Left(VerString(!LocalDataTitle2), 20)
        ColTtl(3) = Left(VerString(!LocalDataTitle3), 20)
        ColTtl(4) = Left(VerString(!LocalDataTitle4), 20)
        ColTtl(5) = Left(VerString(!LocalDataTitle5), 20)
        ColTtl(6) = Left(VerString(!LocalDataTitle6), 20)
        ColTtl(7) = Left(VerString(!LocalDataTitle7), 20)
    End With
End If
For I = 1 To 7
    CapCol = 4 + I
    If Len(Trim(ColTtl(I))) > 0 Then
```

continues

Listing 36.2 Continued

```
        dbgResults.Columns(CapCol).Caption = ColTtl(I)
        dbgResults.Columns(CapCol).Visible = True
    Else
        dbgResults.Columns(CapCol).Visible = False
    End If
Next I

Exit Sub
ResultErr2:
LogError "List Results", "GridTitle", Err.Number, Err.Description
Resume Next
End Sub
```

You might be wondering why this code is not part of the Load event of the form. The reason is that the form might have already been loaded when the titles need to be changed. Therefore, if the code was in the Load event, it would not be triggered a second time. Also, it is not placed in the Activate event of the form because the code does not need to be run if the user moves to another window and then moves back. The code only needs to be run when different parts of the program display the form. Using a procedure that acts as a method is the best solution. The results of this method are shown in Figure 36.2.

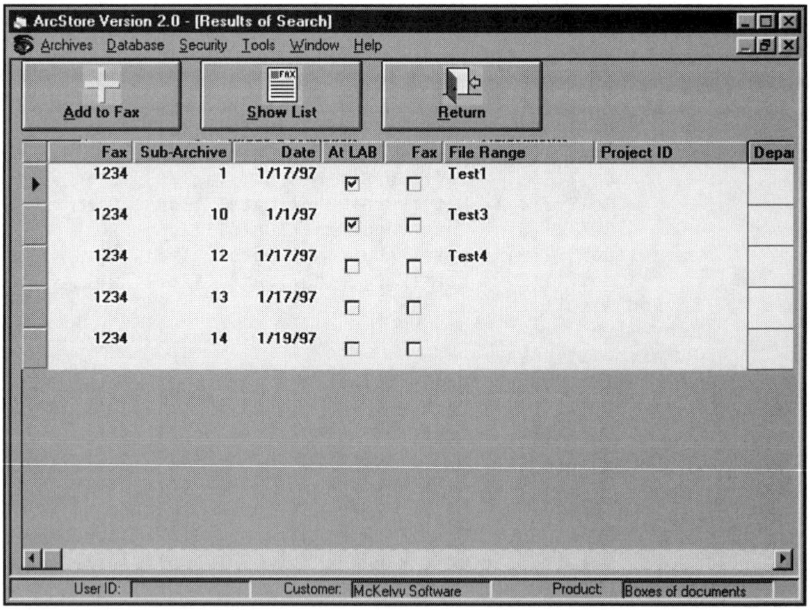

FIG. 36.2
Using a method makes setting titles of a form easy.

To further illustrate the point, Listing 36.3 shows another method of the same form. This method is used to update data that is displayed on the form. Because the data can be updated any number of times while the form is shown, a method again offers the best solution.

Listing 36.3   METHODS.FRM—Updating Data on a Form by Using a Method

```
Public Sub UpdateSearch(ByVal ListTbl As String)
On Error GoTo ResultErr4
datResults.DatabaseName = TempPath & "LabTemp.Mdb"
datResults.RecordSource = ListTbl
datResults.Refresh

Exit Sub
ResultErr4:
LogError "List Results", "UpdateSearch", Err.Number, Err.Description
Resume Next
End Sub
```

Running the Method   Running a method you create is the same as running any other method. Simply specify the form name, the method name, and pass any required arguments to the method. Listing 36.4 illustrates the call to the method defined in Listing 36.2.

Listing 36.4   METHODS.FRM—Calling a User-Defined Method by Using the Familiar Dot Notation

```
'Open customer products recordset for this customer and product
DatSelSQL = "Select * From CustomerProducts Where CustomerID = "
DatSelSQL = DatSelSQL & CustSrch & " And ProductID = " & ProdSrch
Set CustPrSet = OpenRSet(LabDB, DatSelSQL, 2)
'Set the titles for the results form
FormResults.GridTitle CustPrSet
```

Saving Window Positions

Many people have asked me, "How do I save the position of forms at runtime, so I can restore them to their previous state the next time the program is run?" After hearing this question a couple hundred times, I finally got the hint and decided that I had better write a reusable module that would work with any form. The result of this effort is the WindowPosition routine, shown in Listing 36.5.

WindowPosition takes as parameters a pointer to the form and a save/restore flag (called blnSavePosition). The calling form simply passes to the procedure a pointer to the form as the first argument, and a Boolean value as the second argument. If this second argument is True, then the current form position is saved in the Registry. If it is False, then the last (or default) values are retrieved from the Registry, and the form is repositioned.

Listing 36.5   WINPOS.BAS—Saving and Restoring Window Positions

```
'*********************************************************************
' Saves or restores the window position for a form
```

continues

Listing 36.5   Continued

```
'*********************************************************************
Public Sub WindowPosition(frmName As Form, blnSavePostion As Boolean)
    Dim strWinPosKey As String
    Dim strAppName As String
    '*****************************************************************
    ' Use the product name if it exists, otherwise use the exe name
    '*****************************************************************
    strAppName = IIf(Len(App.ProductName), App.ProductName, App.EXEName)

    With frmName
        '*************************************************************
        ' This function is only designed for "normal" windows, so
        ' exit when the form is minimized or maximized.
        '*************************************************************
        If .WindowState <> vbNormal Then Exit Sub
        '*************************************************************
        ' Use the form name and a descriptive string to make it easy
        ' for the user to find these values in the registry
        '*************************************************************
        strWinPosKey = .Name & " Startup Position"
        '*************************************************************
        ' Save the current settings,...
        '*************************************************************
        If blnSavePostion Then
            SaveSetting strAppName, strWinPosKey, "Height", .Height
            SaveSetting strAppName, strWinPosKey, "Width", .Width
            SaveSetting strAppName, strWinPosKey, "Left", .Left
            SaveSetting strAppName, strWinPosKey, "Top", .Top
        '*************************************************************
        ' ...or restore the settings (center the form if not found)
        '*************************************************************
        Else
            .Height = CSng(GetSetting(strAppName, strWinPosKey, _
                "Height", .Height))
            .Width = CSng(GetSetting(strAppName, strWinPosKey, _
                "Width", .Width))
            .Left = CSng(GetSetting(strAppName, strWinPosKey, _
                "Left", (Screen.Width - .Width) / 2))
            .Top = CSng(GetSetting(strAppName, strWinPosKey, _
                "Top", (Screen.Height - .Height) / 2))
        End If
    End With
End Sub
```

You might notice that the WindowPosition routine uses the product name (if available) as the parent Registry key to store the values for the window position. Next, I use the form name along with the string "Startup Position" to create an easy-to-recognize key to hold the window settings. Because two forms can't have the same name in the same project, this approach ensures that users will never have a name conflict in the Registry. The only other important part of this code is the line that reads

```
If .WindowState <> vbNormal Then Exit Sub
```

This line is important because if your resizable form is minimized or maximized, you don't want to save its size or move it. If you do, you will encounter one of two possible problems:

- If you save the size of a minimized form and apply its size parameters to a form whose WindowState property is vbNormal, you would size this form to an unusable size.

- If you try to move a form that is maximized, you will get an error.

To avoid these problems, we simply ignore the minimized and maximized cases. However, you could modify WindowPosition to include a WindowState key in the Registry. This would allow your version of WindowPosition to support restoring windows to their minimized and maximized window states. I elected not to include this code, because it is my opinion that you should only load windows in the vbNormal state.

While writing WinPos.bas, I thought it might be a good idea to also include code that would center a form to the screen or to a parent (or owner) form. At first, I thought that this might not make much sense, because Visual Basic now includes the StartupPosition property, but this property is limited. StartupPosition only works when a form is loaded, so if you want to center a form after it is loaded, you have to do it yourself. Because it is common to hide forms instead of unloading them, I can think of several cases where you would have to center a form yourself. The code in Listing 36.6 demonstrates how to do this.

Listing 36.6 WINPOS.BAS—Centering Your Form with a Simple Routine

```
'*************************************************************
' Centers a form to the screen (default) or to a parent form (optional)
'*************************************************************
Public Sub CenterForm(frmName As Form, Optional frmCenterTo As Form)
    With frmName
        '*************************************************************
        ' If frmCenterTo wasn't provided, then center to screen
        '*************************************************************
        If frmCenterTo Is Nothing Then
            .Move (Screen.Width - .Width) / 2, _
                (Screen.Height - .Height) / 2
        '*************************************************************
        ' Otherwise center to frmCenterTo (useful for dialogs)
        '*************************************************************
        Else
            '*************************************************************
            ' If the child is larger than the parent, then center
            ' to the screen.
            '*************************************************************
            If frmCenterTo.Width < .Width Or _
                frmCenterTo.Height < .Height Then
                CenterForm frmName
            Else
                .Move frmCenterTo.Left + (frmCenterTo.Width - .Width) / 2, _
                    frmCenterTo.Top + (frmCenterTo.Height - .Height) / 2
            End If
        End If
    End With
End Sub
```

The code in `CenterForm` is fairly straightforward because if the optional argument isn't provided, it centers the form to the screen. If it is provided, then a quick check is made to make sure the child is smaller than the parent. If `frmCenterTo` *is* smaller than `frmName`, it is centered to `frmName`. If it is not, then it is centered to the screen. Figure 36.3 shows a child form that has been centered to its parent window by using `CenterForm`.

FIG. 36.3

CenterForm also
supports centering a
form in its parent.

LastPos.vbp, which you can download from **www.mcp.com/info/0-7897/0-7897-1288-1**, demonstrates how to use the code in WindowPos.bas by using several different types of forms. However, I thought it might be useful to discuss one application of this code. LastPos.frm, shown in Listing 36.7, contains code that you can copy and paste into any project that includes WinPos.bas.

Listing 36.7 LASTPOS.FRM—Loading and Unloading Events of the Form Call the Appropriate Procedure

```
'*****************************************************************
' Sets the initial window position and size (centered on the first
' start).
'*****************************************************************
Private Sub Form_Load()
    WindowPosition Me, False
End Sub
'*****************************************************************
' Saves the current window position before the form is destroyed
'*****************************************************************
Private Sub Form_Unload(Cancel As Integer)
    WindowPosition Me, True
End Sub
```

The concept is simple. If your form is loading, restore your previous position by passing False to `WindowPosition`. If your form is unloading, then save your window position by passing True.

Creating Multimedia Forms

Ask 10 people to define the term *multimedia forms* (or windows), and you'll probably get 10 different responses. For our purposes, a multimedia form is a form that has a nonconventional user interface that uses high-resolution graphics, rich text, sound, or video. Examples of Microsoft programs that use multimedia forms are Encarta, Bookshelf, and Money. Although the real success of a multimedia form is great graphic design, there are still some technical challenges that only the programmer can resolve. Items such as nonconventional menus, playback of video and sound, clickable hotspots, and tips are all challenges that you, the programmer, must address. The purpose of this section is to explain some of these techniques so you can create great multimedia applications.

The Multimedia Form

The multimedia form, shown in Figure 36.4, is a simple demo that demonstrates several popular features found in most multimedia applications. It contains the following multimedia elements:

- Transparent GIFs (see "Ski World" in Figure 36.4)
- Activate an Internet Explorer hyperlink to Yahoo! by clicking a form hotspot (on the skier's face)
- Background wave file sound playing in an infinite loop using a timer
- High-resolution form wallpaper using the form's `Picture` property
- ToolTips and a "rich text" description window
- A nonconventional menu that supports playing an AVI file on a picture box

FIG. 36.4
Multimedia forms are easy in Visual Basic.

Listing 36.8 begins with some form level declarations, then continues with the `Form_Load` and `SetupMenu` procedures. These two subs are responsible for setting up our initial hotspots. In addition, the `Form_Load` event procedure starts our background sound if the current machine has a wave-playing device installed.

Listing 36.8   MULTIMEDIA.FRM—Creating Hotspots on a Multimedia Form

```
'*******************************************************************
' MultiMedia.frm - Demonstrates some basic techniques typically found
'   in multimedia applications.
'*******************************************************************
Option Explicit
'*******************************************************************
' PtInRect is a great API to use for "hit testing"
'*******************************************************************
Private Declare Function PtInRect Lib "user32" (lpRect As RECT, _
    ByVal X As Long, ByVal Y As Long) As Long
'*******************************************************************
' Our form changes its caption depending on the location of the mouse,
' so we'll define the default caption in advance
'*******************************************************************
Private Const CAPTION_DEFAULT = "Ski World Rocks!"
'*******************************************************************
' Set a URL for the hotspot hyperlink, and create a IE object
'*******************************************************************
Private Const URL_YAHOO_SKIING = _
                    "http://search.yahoo.com/bin/search?p=Skiing"
Private mclsIExplore As New clsInternetExplorer
'*******************************************************************
' Our app as a hot spot and a non-standard menu, so we need to define
' form-level rects that describe their location for hit tests that
' will be done in the Form_Mouse* events.
'*******************************************************************
Private mrctHotSpot As RECT
Private mrctMenu As RECT
'*******************************************************************
' Prepares the form for initial display
'*******************************************************************
Private Sub Form_Load()
    '*******************************************************************
    ' Most of our code assumes pixels, so set the default scalemode
    ' up front
    '*******************************************************************
    ScaleMode = vbPixels
    '*******************************************************************
    ' We positioned the picAVI control where we want our hotspot to
    ' be at design-time, so we should load its position into the
    ' hotspot rectangle. When complete, we need to move our picAVI
    ' control where it really needs to be to display our AVI.
    '*******************************************************************
    With picAVI
        mrctHotSpot.Left = .Left
        mrctHotSpot.Top = .Top
        mrctHotSpot.Right = .Left + .Width
        mrctHotSpot.Bottom = .Top + .Height
        .Move 180, 7
    End With
    '*******************************************************************
    ' Defines and paints our demo menu
    '*******************************************************************
```

```
        SetupMenu
        '*******************************************************************
        ' Loads the RTF control with some mock data
        '*******************************************************************
        rtfDescription.LoadFile App.Path & "\multimedia.rtf"
        '*******************************************************************
        ' If this machine can play wave files, then begin the background
        ' sound on an infinite loop by using a timer
        '*******************************************************************
        If CanPlayWaves() Then
            tmrBackgroundSound.Enabled = True
            mnuHiddenItems(2).Enabled = True
        End If
End Sub
'***********************************************************************
' Sets the hotspot boundary for the menu and prints it in dark blue
'***********************************************************************
Private Sub SetupMenu()
        Dim sngTextWidth As Single
        Dim sngTextHeight As Single
        '*******************************************************************
        ' Define our menu caption as a constant, since we will only
        ' support one static menu
        '*******************************************************************
        Const MENU_CAPTION As String = "Menu Demo"
        '*******************************************************************
        ' Get the size of the menu caption
        '*******************************************************************
        sngTextWidth = TextWidth(MENU_CAPTION)
        sngTextHeight = TextHeight(MENU_CAPTION)
        '*******************************************************************
        ' Right align the menu to the form (5 pixels from the right edge)
        '*******************************************************************
        CurrentX = ScaleWidth - (sngTextWidth + 5)
        '*******************************************************************
        ' Define the position of the menu for later hit testing
        '*******************************************************************
        With mrctMenu
            .Left = CurrentX
            .Top = CurrentY
            .Right = .Left + sngTextWidth
            .Bottom = .Top + sngTextHeight
        End With
        '*******************************************************************
        ' Turn AutoRedraw on so we don't have to put this code in the
        ' Paint event
        '*******************************************************************
        AutoRedraw = True
        '*******************************************************************
        ' Print the menu caption in dark blue
        '*******************************************************************
        ForeColor = QBColor(1) 'Dark Blue
        Print MENU_CAPTION
End Sub
```

After our initial hotspots are set up, and our controls are loaded and positioned, we are ready to display the form. The form should be displayed quickly enough that our wave file begins at the same time our form appears. This provides a high impact introduction to your multimedia application, because both cool graphics and sound are the first things the user sees and hears. If, for some reason, your form is very large and takes a while to start, you might consider a small multimedia splash screen. This splash screen could start your background music and display a spiffy logo or graphic.

The way hit testing works is by checking to see if the mouse pointer is within our rectangle in the Mouse events using the PtInRect API. Our Form_MouseDown event displays a menu if the user clicks in the menu hotspot. The Form_MouseMove event changes the caption and cursor if the user moves into our hyperlink hotspot. If the user clicks the skier's face, our Form_MouseUp event opens the skiing search page from Yahoo! in Internet Explorer. All of this is accomplished very easily, by just using the PtInRect API. The code in Listing 36.9 demonstrates these hit-testing techniques.

Listing 36.9   MULTIMEDIA.FRM—Hotspot Testing and Event Handling

```
'*********************************************************************
' If the user clicks within our menu with the left button, then
' display it
'*********************************************************************
Private Sub Form_MouseDown(Button%, Shift%, X As Single, Y As Single)
    If Button <> vbLeftButton Then Exit Sub
    If PtInRect(mrctMenu, X, Y) Then
        PopupMenu mnuHidden, , mrctMenu.Left, mrctMenu.Bottom
    End If
End Sub
'*********************************************************************
' If the user moves over our hot spot, then change the caption
' (if necessary)
'*********************************************************************
Private Sub Form_MouseMove(Button%, Shift%, X As Single, Y As Single)
    If PtInRect(mrctHotSpot, X, Y) Then
      If Caption <> URL_YAHOO_SKIING Then Caption = URL_YAHOO_SKIING
      MousePointer = 99
    Else
      If Caption <> CAPTION_DEFAULT Then Caption = CAPTION_DEFAULT
      MousePointer = 0
    End If
End Sub
'*********************************************************************
' If the user clicks our hotspot, then open the URL
'*********************************************************************
Private Sub Form_MouseUp(Button%, Shift%, X As Single, Y As Single)
    If PtInRect(mrctHotSpot, X, Y) Then
        mclsIExplore.OpenURL URL_YAHOO_SKIING
    End If
End Sub
'*********************************************************************
' Our sample menu plays a video or stops playing the background sound
```

```
'***********************************************************************
Private Sub mnuHiddenItems_Click(Index As Integer)
    Select Case Index
        Case 1 ' Play Video
            PlayVideo
        Case 2 ' Stop backround sound
            StopPlayingWave
            tmrBackgroundSound.Enabled = False
    End Select
End Sub
```

One other item included in this listing is our event handler for our menu. This menu was created at design time on our form and the top-level menu item (mnuHidden) was hidden. This way, we can take advantage of the menu, but not see it on our main form. When the user clicks the left button on our form within our hotspot, this menu is displayed using the PopupMenu method shown in the Form_MouseDown event. After the menu is displayed, it works just like an ordinary menu, so our menu handling code is no different.

In Listing 36.10, we have kept our code that handles our audio and video media to a minimum. Both of the subprocedures listed depend on other reusable modules for the act of playing the media, but our form actually selects the media to be played.

Listing 36.10   MULTIMEDIA.FRM—Media Handling Code in Forms Should Be as Simple as Possible

```
'***********************************************************************
' We play our background continously by playing the wave file
' asynchronously from a timer event. This allows the user to perform
' other operations while the sound is playing.
'***********************************************************************
Private Sub tmrBackgroundSound_Timer()
    '*******************************************************************
    ' You MUST set the interval to the number of millseconds it takes
    ' to play the wave file. You can find out how long a wave file is
    ' in seconds by using the sound recorder utility that comes with
    ' windows. Convert the seconds to milliseconds and set that value
    ' here.
    '*******************************************************************
    If tmrBackgroundSound.Interval < 17320 Then
        tmrBackgroundSound.Interval = 17320
    End If
    '*******************************************************************
    ' Play the sound ASYNCHRONOUSLY
    '*******************************************************************
    PlayWaveFile App.Path & "\multimedia.wav", True
End Sub
'***********************************************************************
' Stops playing the background sound (failure is ignored)
'***********************************************************************
Private Sub Form_Unload(Cancel As Integer)
```

continues

Listing 36.10 Continued

```
    StopPlayingWave
End Sub
'*********************************************************************
' Plays an AVI file in a picture box, then hides the box when its done
'*********************************************************************
Private Sub PlayVideo()
    Dim blnPlayingWave As Boolean
    '*****************************************************************
    ' See if the background sound is playing
    '*****************************************************************
    blnPlayingWave = tmrBackgroundSound.Enabled
    '*****************************************************************
    ' Stop playing the wave before displaying the video
    '*****************************************************************
    If blnPlayingWave Then
        tmrBackgroundSound.Enabled = False
        StopPlayingWave
    End If
    '*****************************************************************
    ' Display the window, play the AVI, then hide it again
    '*****************************************************************
    With picAVI
        .Visible = True
        PlayAVI picAVI, App.Path & "\multimedia.avi"
        .Visible = False
    End With
    '*****************************************************************
    ' Restore the background sound immediately by setting its interval
    ' to one and enabling the timer again
    '*****************************************************************
    If blnPlayingWave Then
        tmrBackgroundSound.Interval = 1
        tmrBackgroundSound.Enabled = True
    End If
End Sub
```

You might notice that in the PlayVideo function we are careful to interrupt our background audio (if it is playing) while we play the video, and then we restore it when the video is complete. This is important, because it gives a more professional appeal when there is a smooth continuity between different media being played. Most of the code in the listing is basic Visual Basic programming with the help of some media helper functions. The one exception is the Form_Unload event. Although this event contains only one line of code, its purpose is very important. It ensures that our wave file is stopped before our program is terminated. Without this line, our wave file would play until the end of the file because we chose to play it asynchronously. It is always important to stop a media file from playing before you terminate your application.

Playing AVIs in a Picture Box

Many Visual Basic programmers have already learned how to play AVI in a picture box using the MCI control that comes with VB, but why use this 140K-plus OCX when you can do it with the API? Using the mciSendString API, you can play virtually any media supported by Windows. This section explains the code required to play an AVI in your multimedia form as shown in Figure 36.5.

FIG. 36.5

Why use controls when you can use the API to play videos?

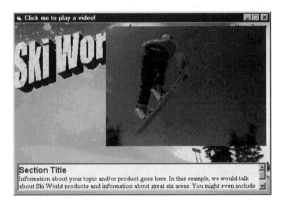

PlayAVI.bas, shown in Listing 36.11, begins with some declarations required by the PlayAVI function. The remaining code for this module has been intentionally omitted from this listing, but is available on the Que Web site at **www.mcp.com/info/0-7897/0-7897-1288-1**. PlayAVI begins by doing a simple check to make sure a valid AVI file was passed. If so, then the AVI file is opened. After each of our mciSendString calls, a check is made to see if mciSendString failed. If it fails anywhere along the way, we exit the function and return the error string.

Listing 36.11 PLAYAVI.BAS—Playing AVIs by Using the API Is Easy

```
'****************************************************************
' PlayAVI.bas - Plays an AVI in a picturebox using the multimedia API
'****************************************************************
Option Explicit
'****************************************************************
' Declare types and API's required by this module
'****************************************************************
Public Type RECT
        Left As Long
        Top As Long
        Right As Long
        Bottom As Long
End Type

Private Declare Function mciSendString Lib "winmm.dll" Alias _
    "mciSendStringA" (ByVal lpstrCommand$, ByVal lpstrRetStr$, _
    ByVal uRetLen As Long, ByVal hwndCallback As Long) As Long
```

continues

Listing 36.11   Continued

```
Private Declare Function mciGetErrorString Lib "winmm.dll" Alias _
    "mciGetErrorStringA" (ByVal dwError As Long, ByVal lpstrBuffer$, _
    ByVal uLength As Long) As Long
'******************************************************************
' Plays an AVI file in a picture box
'******************************************************************
Public Function PlayAVI(picTarget As PictureBox, _
    ByVal strAVIName As String) As String

    Dim strAlias As String
    Dim strRect As String
    Dim rctResize As RECT
    Dim lngError As Long
    '**************************************************************
    ' If the AVI file is not provided or found, the exit
    '**************************************************************
    If strAVIName = "" Or Len(Dir(strAVIName)) = 0 Then
        PlayAVI = strAVIName & " was not found!"
        Exit Function
    End If
    '**************************************************************
    ' Put the AVI file name in quotes (required for long filenames)
    '**************************************************************
    strAVIName = """" & strAVIName & """"
    '**************************************************************
    ' Open the AVI and give it an alias called strAlias
    '**************************************************************
    lngError = mciSendString("open " & strAVIName & " alias strAlias", _
        vbNullString, 0, 0)
    If lngError Then PlayAVI = GetMCIError(lngError): Exit Function
    '**************************************************************
    ' Set the target window using the alias and the window hWnd
    '**************************************************************
    strAlias = "window strAlias handle " & picTarget.hWnd
    lngError = mciSendString(strAlias, vbNullString, 0, 0)
    If lngError Then PlayAVI = GetMCIError(lngError): Exit Function
    '**************************************************************
    ' Force the target window to realize the palette of its background
    ' window. If you don't do this, then you'll see ugly palette
    ' flashes in 256 color mode.
    '**************************************************************
    lngError = mciSendString("realize strAlias background", "", 0, 0)
    If lngError Then PlayAVI = GetMCIError(lngError): Exit Function
    '**************************************************************
    ' Get the size (in pixels) of the AVI in the form of a string
    '**************************************************************
    strRect = Space$(128)
    lngError = mciSendString("where strAlias destination", strRect, _
        Len(strRect), 0)
    If lngError Then PlayAVI = GetMCIError(lngError): Exit Function
    '**************************************************************
    ' Convert the AVI size string into a rect value
    '**************************************************************
    rctResize = ParseStrToRect(RTrim(strRect))
```

```
'*****************************************************************
' Since we are using pixels, set the parent's scalemode to pixels
'*****************************************************************
picTarget.Container.ScaleMode = vbPixels
'*****************************************************************
' If rctResize contains valid data, then resize picTarget
'*****************************************************************
If rctResize.Right > 0 Then
    picTarget.Width = rctResize.Right - rctResize.Left
    picTarget.Height = rctResize.Bottom - rctResize.Top
End If
'*****************************************************************
' Refresh the container to avoid ugly painting problems
'*****************************************************************
picTarget.Container.Refresh
'*****************************************************************
' Play the AVI file synchronously
'*****************************************************************
lngError = mciSendString("play strAlias wait", vbNullString, 0, 0)
If lngError Then PlayAVI = GetMCIError(lngError): Exit Function
'*****************************************************************
' Close the AVI file
'*****************************************************************
lngError = mciSendString("close strAlias", vbNullString, 0, 0)
If lngError Then PlayAVI = GetMCIError(lngError): Exit Function
End Function
```

After the AVI is open, we assign the hWnd property of our picture box to the window, so Windows will know that we want to play our AVI in the picture box. Next, we set our picture box palette to match the palette of our container so there aren't any palette conflicts that might cause our form display to look ugly while we play the AVI. After that, we get the size of the AVI and resize our picture box to hold the AVI. Finally, we refresh the form (to show the resized picture box properly) and play the AVI synchronously. After the AVI is finished playing, PlayAVI closes it.

Playing Wave Files

No great multimedia application is complete without sound. While sound can be played by using MIDI, CD Audio, and other formats, the most popular format still used today is wave files. No sample on multimedia would be complete without mentioning how to play wave files in your application, so this section discusses a small sub called PlayWave.bas.

The basPlayWave module, shown in Listing 36.12, contains one method to determine if the current machine has a wave playback device installed, and the second function plays a wave file. The CanPlayWaves function simply calls waveOutGetNumDevs to find out how many wave device drivers are installed. If one or more is installed, then the current machine can play wave files (even if the user can't hear them because his speakers are off).

Listing 36.12   PLAYWAVE.BAS—Playing a Wave File Is Easy with *PlayWaveFile*

```
'*********************************************************************
' PLAYWAVE.BAS - Plays a wave file.
'*********************************************************************
Option Explicit
Private Declare Function PlaySound Lib "winmm.dll" Alias _
    "PlaySoundA" (ByVal lpszName As String, ByVal hModule As Long, _
    ByVal dwFlags As Long) As Long
Private Declare Function waveOutGetNumDevs Lib "winmm.dll" () As Long
'*********************************************************************
' Returns True if wave files can be played on the current machine
'*********************************************************************
Public Function CanPlayWaves() As Boolean
    CanPlayWaves = waveOutGetNumDevs()
End Function
'*********************************************************************
' Plays a wave file
'*********************************************************************
Public Function PlayWaveFile(strFileName As String, _
    Optional blnAsync As Boolean) As Boolean
    Dim lngFlags As Long
    '*****************************************************************
    ' Flag values for dwFlags parameter
    '*****************************************************************
    Const SND_SYNC = &H0            ' Play synchronously
    Const SND_ASYNC = &H1           ' Play asynchronously
    Const SND_NODEFAULT = &H2       ' No default sound event is used
    Const SND_FILENAME = &H20000    ' Name is a file name
    '*****************************************************************
    ' Set the flags for PlaySound
    '*****************************************************************
    lngFlags = SND_NODEFAULT Or SND_FILENAME Or SND_SYNC
    If blnAsync Then lngFlags = lngFlags Or SND_ASYNC
    '*****************************************************************
    ' Call PlaySound to play the wave file.
    '*****************************************************************
    PlayWaveFile = PlaySound(strFileName, 0&, lngFlags)
End Function
'*********************************************************************
' Stops playing the current wave file
'*********************************************************************
Public Function StopPlayingWave() As Boolean
    Const SND_PURGE = &H40
    PlaySound vbNullString, 0&, SND_PURGE
End Function
```

The PlayWaveFile function plays a wave file from file in either synchronous or asynchronous mode. If you're like me, you get those two terms confused; so just remember that synchronous means that your code stops executing until the file has finished playing. In our example, we needed to play the file asynchronously because we want the user to be able to use our application while the wave file plays in the background.

The final function in this module is the StopPlayingWave function that stops playing an asynchronous wave file immediately. You'll want to use this function when you unload your form to prevent the wave file from playing after your application has terminated.

From Here...

Now that you have learned some new techniques to apply to your forms, you ought to review your current applications to see if you can find places to apply them. Form techniques are something that can be easily overlooked, but that is a big mistake. Forms are the most important part of your application because that is your application's connection to the user. Your form is the package your code is being presented in. Your program can be the best application on the planet, but if it is plagued by poor form design, your users will be less likely to use it. Don't let poor forms ruin your masterpiece. Apply the techniques listed here and elsewhere in this book to improve the robustness of your application.

- To learn more about creating property procedures, see Chapter 32, "Using Classes in Visual Basic."
- To learn how to use calls to procedures in the Windows API to enhance your programs, see Chapter 35, "Accessing the Windows 32 API."

CHAPTER 37

Advanced Code Techniques

This chapter contains a collection of programming samples that demonstrate some advanced features that only a few Visual Basic programmers ever discover. These techniques and features aren't anything new, but are frequently ignored. In fact, some of the techniques shown in this chapter, such as sorting, haven't been done in Visual Basic because its executables couldn't be compiled into native code. Now that VB has overcome this limitation, there is virtually no reason to use any other language to write your entire application. ■

Variants and ParamArrays

Make the most of Variants and ParamArrays in your code for maximum flexibility and with less duplicate code

Computer Science techniques

Apply advanced computer science techniques such as searching and sorting

Doubly-linked lists

Write and use an advanced doubly-linked list in pure VB code

Graphically map values

Manipulate bits, nibbles, and bytes in a sample application that graphically maps these values

Starting Simple

Although this chapter is called "Advanced Code Techniques," there are a couple of techniques discussed in this section that aren't very advanced. Instead, they are very useful code techniques that most VB programmers never really take advantage of in their own programs. By applying the techniques discussed in this section, you can save yourself from writing a lot of duplicate or unnecessary code. If you already are familiar with the techniques described here, then I would encourage you to skip this section and move on to the "Applying Computer Science Techniques in VB" section.

Taking Advantage of Variants

Variants were first introduced in Visual Basic in version 2.0 as a "one size fits all" data type. Variants can hold any of the data types used in Visual Basic, plus any array of these data types. This makes them extremely flexible and powerful. However, this flexibility comes at a price—performance. Behind the scenes, a Variant is really a user-defined type with a member for each data type supported by VB. This structure consumes a minimum of 16 bytes for Variants with numbers, and 22 bytes (plus the length of the string) for Variants with strings. This means that a lot of memory is being wasted when you put a 2-byte integer in a 16-byte Variant, or a 1-byte string in a 23-byte Variant.

The moral to this story is *don't use Variants out of laziness.* Anytime you use a variant, it should be for a good reason. One such reason is in cases where you have a function where you need to return an array. Another case would be in a simple function that needs to support all data types. The latter case is the true purpose for Variants—flexibility. This means that you usually don't want to use Variants as global or static variables, nor do you want to use them in loops. However, a good knowledge of how to use Variants can add some great features to your applications and shared modules.

The code in this section comes from Variant.frm (shown in Figure 37.1), which is a simple demonstration of some cool variant tricks. It begins with Listing 37.1, the `PrintVariant` function, which is designed to print the contents of almost any Variant data type (excluding multidimensional variant arrays) on Variant.frm.

FIG. 37.1

Variant.frm shows `PrintVariant` at work.

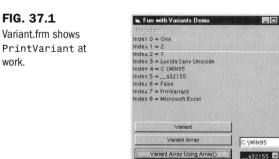

Listing 37.1   VARIANT.FRM—*PrintVariant* Function Prints Variants of Almost Any Data Type

```
'*********************************************************************
' Prints the contents of variant to the form, even if it's a single
' dimension variant array
'*********************************************************************
Private Sub PrintVariant(vntInput As Variant)
    '*************************************************************
    ' If vntInput is an array...
    '*************************************************************
    If VarType(vntInput) And vbArray Then
        Dim i As Integer
        Dim intUBound As Integer
        '*********************************************************
        ' Always cache your upper bounds
        '*********************************************************
        intUBound = UBound(vntInput)
        '*********************************************************
        ' Loop through the array and print the value of each element
        '*********************************************************
        For i = LBound(vntInput) To intUBound
            Print "Index" & Str(i) & " = " & vntInput(i)
        Next i
    '*************************************************************
    ' Otherwise, it must be a single value...
    '*************************************************************
    Else
        Print vntInput
    End If
End Sub
```

The key to this code is that it first checks to see if vntInput contains an array. If it does not, then it is passed to the Print method. If it is an array, then our code prints the array by looping from the lower boundary of the array to the upper boundary of the array. Notice that we did not assume that the array started with 0 or 1, because this assumption would certainly cause our function to fail. However, we do assume that the user won't pass in a multidimensional array, so PrintVariant is certainly not foolproof.

In Listing 37.2, I've demonstrated a simple case of how to handle multidimensional arrays. It, too, is not perfect, but it does work for any two-dimensional array. The major limiting factor that prevents us from writing a function that prints a multidimensional array with any number of dimensions is that there is no easy way to determine the number of dimensions in an array. In addition, we would need to dynamically create a loop for each dimension, which is impossible to do at runtime.

Part VIII

Ch 37

Listing 37.2   VARIANT.FRM—Printing Multidimensional Variants

```
'*****************************************************************
' Demonstrates how to use a multidimensional array returned as a
' variant from a function
'*****************************************************************
Private Sub cmdPrintMultiDim_Click()
    Dim vntArray As Variant
    Dim intRow As Integer
    Dim intCol As Integer
    Dim intMaxRow As Integer
    Dim intMaxCol As Integer
    Cls
    '*************************************************************
    ' Retrieve the multidimensional array...
    '*************************************************************
    vntArray = CreateMultiArray(3, 3)
    '*************************************************************
    ' Cache the upper bounds of each dimension of the array
    '*************************************************************
    intMaxRow = UBound(vntArray, 1)
    intMaxCol = UBound(vntArray, 2)
    '*************************************************************
    ' Loop through the first dimension
    '*************************************************************
    For intRow = LBound(vntArray, 1) To intMaxRow
        '*********************************************************
        ' Loop through the second dimension and print the contents
        '*********************************************************
        For intCol = LBound(vntArray, 2) To intMaxCol
            Print vntArray(intRow, intCol)
        Next intCol
    Next intRow
End Sub
'*****************************************************************
' Shows the results of using the plus operator with the a string and
' a numeric value when using variants
'*****************************************************************
Private Sub cmdVariant_Click()
    Cls
    '*************************************************************
    ' Prints a numeric value using PrintVariant (notice how the string
    ' 1 was added to 100 instead of being concatenated)
    '*************************************************************
    PrintVariant "1" + 100  ' = 101, not 1100
End Sub
'*****************************************************************
' Demonstrates how to return a multidimensional array from a function
'*****************************************************************
Private Function CreateMultiArray(intRows%, intCols%) As Variant
    Dim strReturn() As String
    Dim i As Integer, j As Integer
    '*************************************************************
    ' Build the array based on the sizes provided by the caller
    '*************************************************************
```

```
        ReDim strReturn(0 To intRows, 1 To intCols) As String
        '*********************************************************************
        ' Iterate through the rows
        '*********************************************************************
        For i = 0 To intRows
            '*****************************************************************
            ' Load each element of the array with some default values
            '*****************************************************************
            For j = 1 To intCols
                strReturn(i, j) = "Row" & Str(i) & " Col" & Str(j)
            Next j
        Next i
        '*********************************************************************
        ' Return the array
        '*********************************************************************
        CreateMultiArray = strReturn
End Function
```

The `CreateMultiArray` function is a simple function that creates a two-dimensional array based on the size requested by the caller. It loads the array with bogus data and returns it to the caller.

The two command button `Click` event procedures shown in Listing 37.3 demonstrate how flexible Variants can be. These `Click` events pass a variety of different data types to the `PrintVariant` function to show how flexible it really is.

Listing 37.3   VARIANT.FRM—Using *PrintArray* with Different Types of Variants

```
'*************************************************************************
' Builds a variant array with non-conventional lower and upper
' boundaries and sends this array to PrintVariant to print it to the
' form.
'*************************************************************************
Private Sub cmdVntArray_Click()
    Dim strArray(92 To 104) As String
    Dim i As Integer
    Cls
    '*********************************************************************
    ' Build an array with an unusual lower bounds
    '*********************************************************************
    For i = 92 To 104
        strArray(i) = "Item " & CStr(i - 91)
    Next i
    '*********************************************************************
    ' Notice how PrintVariant can print this array without failing
    '*********************************************************************
    PrintVariant strArray
End Sub
'*************************************************************************
' Demonstrates the flexibility of the Array function and variants by
```

continues

Listing 37.3 Continued

```
' passing in a variety of objects to PrintVariant for further
' processing.
'*****************************************************************
Private Sub cmdVntArray2_Click()
    Dim Excel As Object
    Cls
    '*****************************************************************
    ' Put the path to the windows directory in the text box
    '*****************************************************************
    Text1 = Environ("windir")
    '*****************************************************************
    ' Set the path of the file list box to the windows directory, and
    ' select its first item
    '*****************************************************************
    File1.Path = Text1
    File1.ListIndex = 0
    '*****************************************************************
    ' Don't stop for errors (in case Excel isn't installed)
    '*****************************************************************
    On Error Resume Next
    '*****************************************************************
    ' Create an Excel application object
    '*****************************************************************
    Set Excel = CreateObject("Excel.Application")
    '*****************************************************************
    ' If CreateObject failed, then print everything except Excel
    '*****************************************************************
    If Err.Number Then
        PrintVariant Array("One", 2, vbNull, Font, Text1, File1, _
            Menu1, Name)
    '*****************************************************************
    ' Print everything, including the default property of the Excel
    ' object.  Also be sure to close Excel before the End Sub
    '*****************************************************************
    Else
        '*****************************************************************
        ' Notice the wide variety of objects that will print using
        ' the PrintVariant command! Notice how the default values of
        ' all of the objects (Font, Text1, File1, etc...) are printed.
        '*****************************************************************
        PrintVariant Array("One", 2, vbNull, Font, Text1, File1, _
            Menu1, Name, Excel)
        Excel.Quit
    End If
End Sub
```

In this listing, we use one of my personal favorite functions in VB—the Array function. This function takes a variable number of arguments (by using ParamArray) and returns a variant array of the results. In this example, I passed a string, an integer, a null, a Font object (the Font property of Variant.frm), the Text property of Text1, the first item in the File1 list, the Value property of a menu item, the form name, and (if possible) the Caption property of an Excel

OLE Automation object. Whew, talk about flexible! When you need flexibility, always keep Variants in mind. However, when you need optimal performance (such as loops), always try to use the smallest data type possible.

ParamArray—The King of Flexibility

If you've already used `ParamArray`, feel free to skip this section. If you haven't, this is going to be a real treat for you. `ParamArray` is perhaps one of the best features that was added to Visual Basic in version 4.0, because it finally gave you the ability to write a function that could take an unknown number of arguments (from zero to infinity). This is a language feature that programmers in many other languages have long enjoyed, but it is still rather new to VB. What's more, because `ParamArray` simply converts the arguments passed to your function into a variant array, it is simple to use. Listing 37.4 demonstrates how `ParamArray` can be used to determine what, if any, parameters were passed to a procedure.

Part
VIII

Ch
37

Listing 37.4 PARAMARRAY.BAS—Using *ParamArray* to Allow a Variable Number of Parameters

```
'*******************************************************************
' Demonstrates how to use ParamArray
'*******************************************************************
Public Sub ParamArrayDemo(ParamArray vntArray() As Variant)
    Dim intMax As Integer
    Dim i As Integer
    '***************************************************************
    ' If no arguments were passed, then exit
    '***************************************************************
    If IsMissing(vntArray) Then Exit Sub
    '***************************************************************
    ' Cache the upper boundary of the array
    '***************************************************************
    intMax = UBound(vntArray)
    '***************************************************************
    ' Init i with the lower boundary, and loop through all elements
    '***************************************************************
    For i = LBound(vntArray) To intMax
        '***********************************************************
        ' Display some information about the values passed in
        '***********************************************************
        MsgBox CStr("Input: " & vntArray(i)) & vbLf & _
            "VarType: " & CStr(VarType(vntArray(i))) & vbLf & _
            "TypeName: " & TypeName(vntArray(i)), vbInformation
    Next i
End Sub
```

The `ParamArrayDemo` sub takes an unknown number of arguments. If no arguments are passed to it, it does nothing. Otherwise, it iterates through the array displaying a message box for every argument passed in. Each message displays the item passed in, as well as some information about it. This application doesn't use any forms, so the starting point for it is `Sub Main`.

Sub Main, shown in the following code example, simply passes in five different data types:

```
'*********************************************************************
' Entry point for this windowless application
'*********************************************************************
Private Sub Main()
    '*****************************************************************
    ' Call the demo sub using values of different data types.
    ' Feel free to try some of your own!
    '*****************************************************************
    ParamArrayDemo 1, "2", 3&, 4!, 5#
End Sub
```

The call to ParamArrayDemo causes five message boxes to be displayed that tell the user what types of values were passed. Feel free to experiment with this code to see what happens when you use different data types and numbers of arguments.

Applying Computer Science Techniques in VB

While this chapter is far from being a Computer Science (CS) textbook, I thought it would be useful to apply some common CS principles to VB. The ability to write algorithms that search and sort, creating and using linked lists, and manipulating bits are all fundamental concepts of every good CS curriculum. However, most CS textbooks apply these techniques using languages like C or Pascal. What's more is that most books written for VB ignore this subject completely. Although this section isn't designed to teach you these fundamental concepts, it does show you how to apply them in VB.

Getting Started with Searching and Sorting

Although it has been possible to write searching and sorting algorithms in VB since version 1.0, the fact that VB code was interpreted instead of native code led most people to programming the algorithms in other languages. The reason is that searching and sorting requires a large number of operations that simply bog down even the best of interpreters. However, the ability to compile to native code (introduced in VB 5.0) allows you to write these algorithms in VB without paying a significant performance penalty. In fact, the performance of these algorithms in VB is now comparable with other languages such as C, C++, and Pascal. This section is dedicated to two of the most popular algorithms for searching and sorting: the binary search and QuickSort.

N O T E I wish I could take credit for the algorithms in this section, but I cannot. The code you see in this section is derived from samples found in both other Microsoft languages and *Hardcore Visual Basic* by Bruce McKinney (MSPress, 1995). I have taken the best features from all of these samples and formulated them into a more reusable set of code. ■

Writing Generic Helper Functions   In almost every code module you will ever write, you are certain to code a few private helper functions that make your core functions more readable. In the case of our Searching and Sorting module, Sortsearch.bas, we must have two helper functions to avoid hundreds of lines of additional or duplicate code.

The `Compare` and `Swap` functions shown in Listing 37.5 were written to allow us to have a data-type independent mechanism for comparing and swapping variables. Neither of these functions is very complex, but their roles in the success of `BinarySearch` and `QuickSort` are essential. Even the smallest bug in either function causes our algorithms to fail, so it is important for us to code them carefully.

Part
VIII

Ch

37

Listing 37.5 SORTSEARCH.BAS—Searching and Sorting Helpers

```
'*******************************************************************
' SortSearch.bas - Routines to allow you to search and sort through
'   variant arrays
'*******************************************************************
Option Explicit
'*******************************************************************
' Option Compare Text makes the searches and sorts ignore case. Comment
' out this line if you wish to have case-sensitive searches and sorts.
'*******************************************************************
Option Compare Text
'*******************************************************************
' Same as StrComp, but applies to Variants
'*******************************************************************
Private Function Compare(vntItem1 As Variant, _
                        vntItem2 As Variant) As Integer
    '*******************************************************************
    ' Initialize the return value to 0
    Compare = 0
    '*******************************************************************
    ' If less than, then return -1
    '*******************************************************************
    If vntItem1 < vntItem2 Then
        Compare = -1
    '*******************************************************************
    ' If greater than, then return 1
    '*******************************************************************
    ElseIf vntItem1 > vntItem2 Then
        Compare = 1
    End If
    '*******************************************************************
    ' Otherwise do nothing, which returns zero (indicating that they
    ' are equal)
    '*******************************************************************
End Function
'*******************************************************************
' Swaps two variants -- in place (since we are passing ByRef)
'*******************************************************************
Private Sub Swap(ByRef vntItem1 As Variant, ByRef vntItem2 As Variant)
    '*******************************************************************
    ' Dim a temp value to hold the original value of vntItem1
    '*******************************************************************
    Dim vntTemp As Variant
    '*******************************************************************
```

continues

Listing 37.5   Continued

```
   ' Store vntItem1 in a temporary variable
   '********************************************************************
   vntTemp = vntItem1
   '********************************************************************
   ' Set vntItem2 equal to vntItem1
   '********************************************************************
   vntItem1 = vntItem2
   '********************************************************************
   ' Set vntItem2 equal to the temporary variable
   '********************************************************************
   vntItem2 = vntTemp
End Sub
```

Compare is a *data type independent* version of Visual Basic's StrComp function. It compares two Variants. If the first item is less than the second item, it returns -1. If the first is greater than the second, it returns 1. Otherwise, 0 is returned to indicate that the two Variants are equal. Swap simply takes a reference to two variables and swaps them in place. Nothing fancy is going on here, but as you'll see, these functions are the core of our searching and sorting routines.

You'll also notice that Listing 37.5 begins with some definitions in the General Declarations section of the SortSearch.bas module. The most significant one is Option Compare Text. This tells Visual Basic that we want to ignore the case of strings in our Compare function. Should you decide that you want your searches *and* sorts to be case sensitive, you should comment this line of code out. In addition, you could rewrite your Compare function to support both case-sensitive and case-insensitive comparisons.

Searching with *BinarySearch*   The concept of a binary search is to take a sorted array and find a specific value by a divide-and-conquer mechanism. Because the array is sorted, you begin by checking the middle value with the item you are searching for. If the search item is less than the middle item, you reapply this algorithm to the lower half of the array and so forth. However, the key concept is that your array must be sorted in order for this function to work.

Listing 37.6 begins by making sure the user really passed an array to our function. When working with Variant arrays, it is always important to double-check this in case the caller tries to pass a simple Variant. Next, we make the all-important check of the blnIsSorted optional argument. This flag is optionally set by the caller to tell us that vntArray is already sorted, so we shouldn't try sorting it again. If the caller doesn't set this value or if it is False, then we sort the array using our QuickSort algorithm.

Listing 37.6   SORTSEARCH.BAS—Binary Searching

```
'********************************************************************
' Performs a binary search for vntFind on a variant array, and
' sorts the array if the call doesn't set blnIsSorted = True
'********************************************************************
Public Function BinarySearch(vntArray As Variant, _
    vntFind As Variant, Optional blnIsSorted As Boolean) As Integer
    '********************************************************************
```

```vb
' Dim integers for the high, low and mid points of the array
'****************************************************************
Dim intHigh As Integer
Dim intLow As Integer
Dim intMid As Integer
'****************************************************************
' Make sure vntArray really is an array
'****************************************************************
If VarType(vntArray) And vbArray Then
    intLow = LBound(vntArray)
    intHigh = UBound(vntArray)
'****************************************************************
' If it is not, then exit (returning a not found result)
'****************************************************************
Else
    BinarySearch = -1
    Exit Function
End If
'****************************************************************
' If the array isn't sorted, then sort it (otherwise your binary
' search will likely fail)
'****************************************************************
If Not blnIsSorted Then QuickSort vntArray
'****************************************************************
' Enter into an infinite loop (because we'll exit the loop within
' our case statement)
'****************************************************************
Do
    '****************************************************************
    ' Set the mid point of the half you are currently searching
    '****************************************************************
    intMid = intLow + ((intHigh - intLow) \ 2)
    '****************************************************************
    ' Compare the mid point element with the element you are
    ' searching for, and act accordingly based on the return
    ' value from Compare
    '****************************************************************
    Select Case Compare(vntFind, vntArray(intMid))
        '****************************************************************
        ' vntFind was found, so return the index and exit
        '****************************************************************
        Case 0
            BinarySearch = intMid
            Exit Function
        '****************************************************************
        ' vntFind is in the lower half, so set intHigh to the
        ' mid point and repeat the search
        '****************************************************************
        Case Is < 0
            intHigh = intMid
            '****************************************************************
            ' If intLow is equal to intHigh, then the item was
            ' not found so exit
            '****************************************************************
```

continues

Listing 37.6 Continued

```
            If intLow = intHigh Then Exit Do
        '***********************************************************
        ' vntFind is in the upper half, so set intLow to the
        ' mid point plus one and repeat the search
        '***********************************************************
        Case Is > 0
            intLow = intMid + 1
            '*******************************************************
            ' If intLow is greater than intHigh, then the item
            ' was not found so exit
            '*******************************************************
            If intLow > intHigh Then Exit Do
    End Select
Loop
'***************************************************************
' Item not found, then return a value less than the LBound
'***************************************************************
BinarySearch = LBound(vntArray) - 1
End Function
```

The remaining code applies the concepts of the binary search algorithm by using our Compare function to compare two items against each other. If the item is found, its index is returned. If not, then we return a value that is one less than the lower boundary of the given array to indicate that the item was not found. This is a simple, yet efficient algorithm for finding a given element in an array. Later in this section, we'll see a demonstration of this function using an array provided to us by the user.

Sorting with QuickSort   There are many sorting algorithms developed by many great computer scientists, but perhaps the most popular algorithm ever written is QuickSort. In its simplest form, QuickSort is a sorting algorithm that accomplishes a relatively fast sort by using the CS concept of *recursion*, which occurs when a procedure calls itself. Although there are versions of QuickSort that don't rely on recursion, the form shown in this section is the most common. The downside to using recursion in a sorting algorithm is that each recursive call consumes space on the stack, which limits the number of elements that can be sorted to the available space on the stack. While testing this code, I sorted an array of 10,000 strings without running out of stack space. This would indicate that this function is sufficient for most of your sorting needs.

As in our BinarySearch function, QuickSort (shown in Listing 37.7) begins by making sure that vntArray really is an array. After this determination is made, we check to make sure that the given array contains more than two elements. If vntArray contains only two elements, then we do a simple compare, swap (if necessary), and exit.

Listing 37.7 SORTSEARCH.BAS—Sorting with QuickSort

```
'***************************************************************
' Sorts a Variant array using the QuickSort algorithm
'***************************************************************
```

```
Public Sub QuickSort(vntArray As Variant, _
    Optional intLBound As Integer, Optional intUBound As Integer)
    '****************************************************************
    ' Holds the pivot point
    '****************************************************************

    Dim vntMid As Variant
    '****************************************************************
    ' Make sure vntArray really is an array
    '****************************************************************

    If (VarType(vntArray) And vbArray) = 0 Then Exit Sub
    '****************************************************************
    ' If Optional args weren't provided, then get the default values
    '****************************************************************

    If intLBound = 0 And intUBound = 0 Then
        intLBound = LBound(vntArray)
        intUBound = UBound(vntArray)
    End If
    '****************************************************************
    ' If the LBound is greater than the UBound then there is nothing
    ' to do, so exit
    '****************************************************************

    If intLBound > intUBound Then Exit Sub
    '****************************************************************
    ' If there are only two elements in this array, then swap them
    ' (if necessary) and exit
    '****************************************************************

    If (intUBound - intLBound) = 1 Then
        If Compare(vntArray(intLBound), vntArray(intUBound)) > 0 Then
            Swap vntArray(intLBound), vntArray(intUBound)
        End If
        Exit Sub
    End If
    '****************************************************************
    ' Dim the indices
    '****************************************************************

    Dim i As Integer, j As Integer
    '****************************************************************
    ' Set your pivot point
    '****************************************************************

    vntMid = vntArray(intUBound)
    '****************************************************************
    ' Loop while lower bound is less than the upper bound
    '****************************************************************

    Do
        '************************************************************
        ' Init i and j to the array boundary
        '************************************************************

        i = intLBound
        j = intUBound
        '************************************************************
        ' Compare each element with vntMid (the pivot) until the
        ' current element is the less than or equal to the midpoint
        '************************************************************
```

continues

Listing 37.7 Continued

```
            Do While (i < j) And Compare(vntArray(i), vntMid) <= 0
                i = i + 1
            Loop
            '**************************************************************
            ' Compare each element with vntMid (the pivot) until the
            ' current element is the greater than or equal to the mid
            ' point
            '**************************************************************
            Do While (j > i) And Compare(vntArray(j), vntMid) >= 0
                j = j - 1
            Loop
            '**************************************************************
            ' If you never reached the pivot point then the two elements
            ' are out of order, so swap them
            '**************************************************************
            If i < j Then Swap vntArray(i), vntArray(j)
        Loop While i < j
        '**************************************************************
        ' Now that i has been adjusted it the above loop, we should swap
        ' element i with element at intUBound
        '**************************************************************
        Swap vntArray(i), vntArray(intUBound)
        '**************************************************************
        ' If index i minus the index of intLBound is less than the index
        ' of intUBound minus index i then...
        '**************************************************************
        If (i - intLBound) < (intUBound - i) Then
            '**************************************************************
            ' Recursively sort with adjusted values for upper and lower
            ' bounds
            '**************************************************************
            QuickSort vntArray, intLBound, i - 1
            QuickSort vntArray, i + 1, intUBound
        '**************************************************************
        ' Otherwise...
        '**************************************************************
        Else
            '**************************************************************
            ' Recursively sort with adjusted values for upper and lower
            ' bounds
            '**************************************************************
            QuickSort vntArray, i + 1, intUBound
            QuickSort vntArray, intLBound, i - 1
        End If
End Sub
```

If after all of our initial tests we still determine that the array needs to be sorted, then we apply our sorting algorithm. Examine the code in Listing 37.7 for details on each step of this algorithm.

Using *BinarySearch* and *QuickSort*   Now that our algorithms are written, it's time to put them to use in a sample. The way our sample works is we have a text box with a default list of strings. When the user clicks the search or sort command buttons, we apply the appropriate algorithm and display the results in a read-only rich text box. Figure 37.2 shows the result of doing a search for the word *Texas*.

FIG. 37.2

The SortSearchDemo. vbp project demonstrates flexible searching techniques.

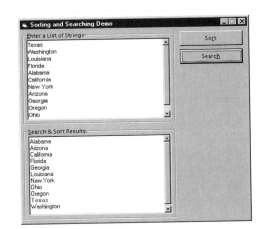

For simplicity's sake, I have omitted some of the helper code from Listing 37.8. However, this code is available on the Que Web site at **www.mcp.com/info/0-7897/0-7897-1288-1**, so feel free to view this code along with the entire sample in the SortSearchDemo.vbp project.

Both the cmdSearch_Click and cmdSort_Click events are similar in that they extract their arrays from input provided by the user in a text box. After they have applied their algorithm, the results are displayed in the rtfResults control. The cmdSearch_Click event procedure is slightly different in that it does a special check to see if the array has already been sorted. If the array were sorted, then the sorted elements are in the rtfResults control. If not, then the unsorted elements are gathered from the txtInput control. This information is used later when the call is made to the BinarySearch function to tell it if the array being passed is already sorted or not.

Listing 37.8 SORTSEARCH.FRM

```
'*************************************************************************
' SortSearch.frm - Demonstrates how to use basSortSearch
'*************************************************************************

Option Explicit
'*************************************************************************
' Prompts the user for a string to search for, and searches for that
' string based on the list in txtInput
'*************************************************************************
```

continues

Listing 37.8   Continued

```
Private Sub cmdSearch_Click()
    Dim vntArray As Variant
    Dim strFind As String
    Dim intFoundIndex As Integer
    Dim blnSorted As Boolean
    '******************************************************************
    ' If any text is in rtfResults, then the list has already been
    ' sorted
    '******************************************************************
    blnSorted = Len(rtfResults.Text)
    '******************************************************************
    ' Load the sorted list if it is available
    '******************************************************************
    If blnSorted Then
        vntArray = LoadStringsIntoArray(rtfResults.Text)
    Else
        vntArray = LoadStringsIntoArray(txtInput)
    End If
    '******************************************************************
    ' Prompt the user for a search string
    '******************************************************************
    strFind = _
        InputBox("Enter the item to search for:", "Search", vntArray(0))
    '******************************************************************
    ' If no input was provided, then exit
    '******************************************************************
    If Len(strFind) = 0 Then Exit Sub
    '******************************************************************
    ' Search for strFind in the array of strings (and only sort if
    ' the array is not already sorted)
    '******************************************************************
    intFoundIndex = BinarySearch(vntArray, strFind, blnSorted)
    '******************************************************************
    ' If not found, then tell the user
    '******************************************************************
    If intFoundIndex < LBound(vntArray) Then
        MsgBox "Item not found!", vbExclamation
    End If
    '******************************************************************
    ' Update the RTF control with the sorted array. If the search
    ' item was found, it will be highlighted in bold red.
    '******************************************************************
    LoadArrayIntoRTF rtfResults, vntArray, intFoundIndex
End Sub
'******************************************************************
' QuickSort the list in txtInput and put the results in rtfResults
'******************************************************************
Private Sub cmdSort_Click()
    Dim vntArray As Variant
    '******************************************************************
    ' If rtfResults is not empty, then the list is sorted so exit
    '******************************************************************
    If Len(rtfResults.Text) Then
        MsgBox "The input values are already sorted.", vbInformation
        Exit Sub
```

```
      End If
      '****************************************************************
      ' Load the list in txtInput into an array
      '****************************************************************
      vntArray = LoadStringsIntoArray(txtInput)
      '****************************************************************
      ' Sort the array
      '****************************************************************
      QuickSort vntArray
      '****************************************************************
      ' Display the sorted array in rtfResults
      '****************************************************************
      LoadArrayIntoRTF rtfResults, vntArray
   End Sub
```

The cmdSort_Click event procedure simply sorts the values in the text box and puts the results in the rtfInput control. The cmdSearch_Click event also puts a sorted array into the rtfInput control, but it also highlights the element you were searching for if it was found. This is done by a special series of code in the LoadArrayIntoRTF method not shown in this chapter.

Going a Step Further with Linked Lists

The example in this section demonstrates the CS concept of a doubly-linked list using Visual Basic classes. This concept already exists in Visual Basic in the form of collections, but this code should help you better understand how collections work. In addition, this implementation allows you to extend the concept of collections by writing your own doubly-linked list which supports features not found in standard collections.

Creating the *Item* Object and Helper Functions   Let's begin by discussing our class object called Item. Item, shown in Listing 37.9, is a simple class that only contains the members for our object and our pointers to the next and previous items in the list.

Listing 37.9   ITEM.CLS—A Class Used to Set Up the Data Structure for a Doubly-Linked List

```
'****************************************************************
' Item.cls - This class is simply the data structure for a doubly-
' linked list.
'****************************************************************
Option Explicit
'****************************************************************
' Data members
'****************************************************************
Public strData As String
Public intData As Integer
'****************************************************************
' Doubly-Linked List Pointers
'****************************************************************
Public clsItemNext As clsItem
Public clsItemPrev As clsItem
```

By creating our object using a class module, we have the flexibility to create as many data members as we choose. The only implication is that our helper functions need to be modified to support any additions or removal of data members from this class.

Now that we have our `Item` object, we need to write helper routines that allow us to build and navigate our linked list. Listing 37.10 includes the `InsertAfter` and `RemoveItem` functions that are designed to add new and remove elements from the list. ListHelpers.bas also includes an `InsertBefore` function, but it is not shown because it is virtually identical to the `InsertAfter` function.

Listing 37.10   LISTHELPERS.BAS—Adding and Removing Elements

```
'*********************************************************************
' Inserts a new item in the your linked list after an existing item
'*********************************************************************
Public Function InsertAfter(clsPrevious As clsItem, _
    Optional strData$, Optional intData As Integer) As clsItem
    '*************************************************************
    ' If clsPrevious hasn't been initialzed, then bail...
    '*************************************************************
    If clsPrevious Is Nothing Then
        MsgBox "InsertAfter failed: Previous item was invalid", _
            vbExclamation
        Exit Function
    End If
    '*************************************************************
    ' Create the new item
    '*************************************************************
    Dim clsNewItem As New clsItem
    '*************************************************************
    ' The clsPrevious is the not the tail item, then the item after
    ' clsPrevious needs its clsItemPrev pointer set to the new item.
    '*************************************************************
    If Not (clsPrevious.clsItemNext Is Nothing) Then
        Set clsPrevious.clsItemNext.clsItemPrev = clsNewItem
    End If
    '*************************************************************
    ' Set the values for the newly created item
    '*************************************************************
    With clsNewItem
        .strData = strData
        .intData = intData
        Set .clsItemPrev = clsPrevious
        Set .clsItemNext = clsPrevious.clsItemNext
    End With
    '*************************************************************
    ' Point the previous item to the newly created item
    '*************************************************************
    Set clsPrevious.clsItemNext = clsNewItem
    '*************************************************************
    ' Increment the item count
    '*************************************************************
    mintCount = mintCount + 1
```

```
'******************************************************************
' Return a pointer to the newly inserted item
'******************************************************************
    Set InsertAfter = clsNewItem
End Function
'******************************************************************
' Remove an item in the doubly-linked list
'******************************************************************
Public Function RemoveItem(clsItemToRemove As clsItem) As clsItem
    '**************************************************************
    ' If a valid item was not passed, then bail...
    '**************************************************************
    If clsItemToRemove Is Nothing Then
        MsgBox "You can't remove an uninitialized item!", vbExclamation
    End If
    '**************************************************************
    ' If the item to remove is the tail...
    '**************************************************************
    If clsItemToRemove.clsItemNext Is Nothing Then
        '**********************************************************
        ' If Next = Nothing & Prev = Nothing, the last item in list!
        '**********************************************************
        If clsItemToRemove.clsItemPrev Is Nothing Then
            MsgBox "Can not remove the last item in the list!", _
                vbExclamation
            '******************************************************
            ' Return a pointer to clsItemToRemove
            '******************************************************
            Set RemoveItem = clsItemToRemove
            Exit Function
        '**********************************************************
        ' Otherwise, remove the item and return a pointer to the
        ' previous item
        '**********************************************************
        Else
            Set clsItemToRemove.clsItemPrev.clsItemNext = _
                clsItemToRemove.clsItemNext
            Set RemoveItem = clsItemToRemove.clsItemPrev
        End If
    '**************************************************************
    ' Otherwise, something must be after the item to remove...
    '**************************************************************
    Else
        '**********************************************************
        ' If clsItemToRemove is the head, so remove the head and
        ' set a new head of the list.
        ' OPTIONAL: You may want to raise an error here
        '**********************************************************
        If clsItemToRemove.clsItemPrev Is Nothing Then
            Set clsItemToRemove.clsItemNext.clsItemPrev = _
                clsItemToRemove.clsItemPrev
            Set RemoveItem = clsItemToRemove.clsItemNext
        '**********************************************************
        ' Otherwise clsItemToRemove is in the middle of the list...
```

Part
VIII

Ch
37

continues

Listing 37.10 Continued

```
        '*****************************************************************
        Else
            Set clsItemToRemove.clsItemPrev.clsItemNext =
clsItemToRemove.clsItemNext
            Set clsItemToRemove.clsItemNext.clsItemPrev =
clsItemToRemove.clsItemPrev
            Set RemoveItem = clsItemToRemove.clsItemPrev
        End If
    End If
    '*****************************************************************
    ' Decrement the linked list item count
    '*****************************************************************
    mintCount = mintCount - 1
    '*****************************************************************
    ' Destroy the item to be removed
    '*****************************************************************
    Set clsItemToRemove = Nothing
End Function
```

Although the purposes of these two functions are entirely different, the methodology used to accomplish their result is similar. When an item is added or removed from the list, the clsItemPrev and clsItemNext member variables of the list must be manipulated. The AddItem function points these members to the newly created item, whereas the RemoveItem points these members to the objects before and after the item being removed. When the operation is complete, both functions return a pointer to a valid object in the list. Closely examine each of these functions to see how various situations influence the code path of these functions.

The GetIndex function is useful for retrieving a specific element of the collection. The index can be retrieved using any of the data members of Item as the index or key. The element is retrieved by doing a linear search through the linked list until the requested element is found. If no match was found, then the function returns Nothing.

Listing 37.11 presents ListHelpers.bas, a module whose Name property has been set to basListHelpers. Note in later listings the use of basListHelpers.Count, which allows us to determine the number of instances of this module that have been created.

Listing 37.11 ListHelpers.bas—Retrieving a Specific Element

```
'*****************************************************************
' Returns a pointer to a specific item in the list
'*****************************************************************
Public Function GetIndex(clsStart As clsItem, Optional strData$, _
    Optional intData As Integer) As clsItem
    '*****************************************************************
    ' If the user didn't tell us where to start, then bail...
    '*****************************************************************
    If clsStart Is Nothing Then Exit Function
    '*****************************************************************
    ' If the user didn't tell us which item to select, then bail...
    '*****************************************************************
```

```
If intData = 0 And strData = "" Then Exit Function
'*****************************************************************
' Dim a pointer for iterating through the linked list
'*****************************************************************
Dim clsCurItem As clsItem
'*****************************************************************
' Set the pointer to the item the user told us to begin with
'*****************************************************************
Set clsCurItem = clsStart
'*****************************************************************
' Linear search through all items in the list
'*****************************************************************
Do While Not (clsCurItem.clsItemNext Is Nothing)
    With clsCurItem
        If .intData = intData Or .strData = strData Then
            '*****************************************************
            ' Return a pointer to the found item and exit
            '*****************************************************
            Set GetIndex = clsCurItem
            Exit Function
        End If
        Set clsCurItem = .clsItemNext
    End With
Loop
'*****************************************************************
' Check the data members of the last item in the list
'*****************************************************************
With clsCurItem
    If .intData = intData Or .strData = strData Then
        '*********************************************************
        ' Return a pointer to the found item
        '*********************************************************
        Set GetIndex = clsCurItem
    End If
End With
'*****************************************************************
' If not found, then return Nothing (by not doing anything)
'*****************************************************************
End Function
```

The key to this function working is being able to iterate through the linked list. We do this by creating a pointer to the given start item and walking the list. We walk the list by setting the clsCurItem pointer to the clsNextItem member of clsCurItem until we reach the tail.

Using the Doubly-Linked List   Now that our Item object has been defined and our helper functions are in place, we are ready to use our linked list. I encourage you to experiment with this sample to discover advantages and disadvantages of this linked list compared to arrays and VB collections.

Listing 37.12 shows one way to populate and destroy the linked list. Although our example is rather simple, it does highlight some of the challenges involved with using linked lists. Our list initially begins with a head element and three additional objects. After our initial list is built, the mclsCurItem pointer points to the last item added to the list.

Listing 37.12 LISTDEMO.FRM—Building and Destroying the List

```
'******************************************************************
' ListDemo - Demonstrates one way to build and use a linked list
'******************************************************************
Option Explicit
'******************************************************************
' Form level pointers to the head and current item in the linked list
'******************************************************************
Private mclsHead As New clsItem
Private mclsCurItem As clsItem
'******************************************************************
' Builds the initial list, sets the head, and does some prep work
'******************************************************************
Private Sub Form_Load()
    Dim i As Integer
    '******************************************************************
    ' Optional - label the head (helpful during debugging)
    '******************************************************************
    mclsHead.strData = "Head"
    '******************************************************************
    ' Set the current item to the head
    '******************************************************************
    Set mclsCurItem = mclsHead
    '******************************************************************
    ' Create three items to give the user something to play with
    '******************************************************************
    For i = 1 To 3
        Set mclsCurItem = _
                    InsertAfter(mclsCurItem, "Item " & CStr(i), i)
    Next i
    ... ' Code has been intentionally omitted from this listing
End Sub
'******************************************************************
' Although VB is supposed to do cleanup, I feel better freeing the
' list myself.  This is not a required element of this program.
'******************************************************************
Private Sub Form_Unload(Cancel As Integer)
    '******************************************************************
    ' Let's be good citizens and free the list ourselves
    '******************************************************************
    Dim clsCurItem As clsItem
    Set clsCurItem = mclsHead.clsItemNext
    '******************************************************************
    ' Remove all of the items in the list (printing the count in the
    ' Immediate window)
    '******************************************************************
    Do While Not (clsCurItem.clsItemNext Is Nothing)
        Set clsCurItem = RemoveItem(clsCurItem)
        Debug.Print basListHelpers.Count
    Loop
End Sub
```

In the `Form_Unload` event procedure, I demonstrate the concept of "walking" the list to destroy all of its elements. I specifically unload this list because I can't rely on VB doing the proper cleanup of these objects itself. Someone out there might be able to prove that this is unnecessary, but until they do, I'll continue to include this code in my sample.

After our initial list has been created and our form is loaded, the user is in control of our linked list. Items can be added or removed at the user's discretion using the `cmdInsertBefore` and `cmdRemoveItem` command buttons. The `Click` event procedures for each of these controls is described in detail in Listing 37.13

Part VIII

Ch

37

Listing 37.13 LISTDEMO.FRM—Adding and Removing Items

```
'***************************************************************
' Inserts an item in the list before the item specified by the user
'***************************************************************
Private Sub cmdInsertBefore_Click()
    '***********************************************************
    ' Get a pointer to the item that will be after the newly inserted
    ' item.
    '***********************************************************
    Set mclsCurItem = GetIndex(mclsHead, , Val(InputBox( _
        "Enter a integer index:", "InsertBefore", _
        CStr(mclsCurItem.intData))))
    '***********************************************************
    ' Insert the item in the list (using some generated default data)
    '***********************************************************
    Set mclsCurItem = InsertBefore(mclsCurItem, "Item " & _
        CStr(basListHelpers.Count + 1), basListHelpers.Count + 1)
    '***********************************************************
    ' If InsertBefore worked, then update the listbox and labels
    '***********************************************************
    If Not (mclsCurItem Is Nothing) Then UpdateFormItems
End Sub
'***************************************************************
' Removes the currently selected item
'***************************************************************
Private Sub cmdRemoveItem_Click()
    '***********************************************************
    ' Remove item returns a pointer to another item in the list, so
    ' keep that value for further processing.
    '***********************************************************
    Dim clsReturn As clsItem
    '***********************************************************
    ' Don't let the user remove the head (optional)
    '***********************************************************
    If mclsCurItem.strData = mclsHead.strData Then
        MsgBox "You can't remove the head. Please select another item."
        Exit Sub
    End If
    '***********************************************************
    ' If there is more than one item in the list...
    '***********************************************************
    If basListHelpers.Count > 1 Then
```

continues

Listing 37.13 Continued

```
        '****************************************************************
        ' Remove the current item and catch the pointer to the item
        ' returned by RemoveItem.
        '****************************************************************
        Set clsReturn = RemoveItem(mclsCurItem)
        '****************************************************************
        ' If clsReturn doesn't have an item in front of it, then it
        ' is the tail.
        '****************************************************************
        If clsReturn.clsItemNext Is Nothing Then
            '****************************************************************
            ' If nothing is before the item returned, then clsReturn
            ' is the last item in the list (which is the head)
            '****************************************************************
            If clsReturn.clsItemPrev Is Nothing Then
                Set mclsCurItem = Nothing
            '****************************************************************
            ' Otherwise set the current item to the 2nd to last item
            '****************************************************************
            Else
                Set mclsCurItem = clsReturn.clsItemPrev
            End If
        '****************************************************************
        ' Otherwise, set the current item to whatever is in front of
        ' clsReturn (because clsReturn could be the head)
        '****************************************************************
        Else
            Set mclsCurItem = clsReturn.clsItemNext
        End If
        '****************************************************************
        ' Update the listbox and labels to reflect this change
        '****************************************************************
        UpdateFormItems
    End If
End Sub
```

Adding items is rather simple. We ask the user where to add the item, then let `InsertBefore` do the dirty work. Adding the new item updates our form level pointer, `mclsCurItem`, to the current item in the list. If the item was added successfully, then we update our display.

Removing items is a little more tedious because we have to test for special cases such as deleting the head or tail. After the item is removed, we check to make sure there was a valid pointer returned. If there was, then we set our `mclsCurItem` variable to a valid object. Finally, we update our display to reflect the contents of the modified list.

Twiddling Bits in VB

This section demonstrates some fundamental concepts of bit manipulation. Figure 37.3 shows our bit-twiddling program. This program provides a graphical display of the effects of setting bits and extracting words and bytes for larger values.

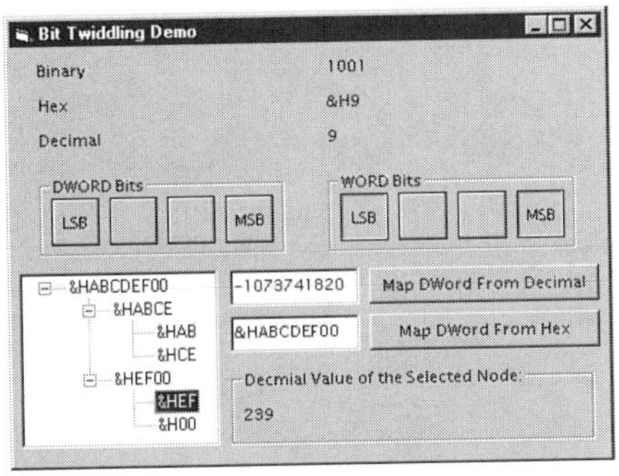

FIG. 37.3

HexToBin.vbp demonstrates basic bit manipulation techniques.

To break double words into words and words into bytes, we need a module that performs these operations for us. The basConvert module shown in Listing 37.14 accomplishes this by defining four of the most common bit conversion functions used in the Win32 API. These functions might look familiar to you because just about everyone has had to write these at some time in their VB programming career. The ones you see here are my interpretation of how they should be written. You might have already written your own version, but if you haven't, then you'll want to include these as a basic part of your code library.

Listing 37.14   BITCONVERT.BAS—Adding Easy-to-Use Calls to Bit Conversion APIs

```
'**************************************************************
' BitConvert.bas - Extracts high and low bits from values
'**************************************************************
Option Explicit
'**************************************************************
' Get the low byte of a Word
'**************************************************************
Public Function LoByte(intWord As Integer) As Integer
    Dim intResult As Integer
    intResult = intWord And &HFF
    LoByte = intResult
End Function
'**************************************************************
' Get the high byte of a Word
'**************************************************************
Public Function HiByte(intWord As Integer) As Integer
    Dim intResult As Integer
    intResult = (intWord And &HFF00&) \ &HFF&
    HiByte = intResult
End Function
'**************************************************************
' Returns the lower 4 bytes of a DWORD
'**************************************************************
Public Function LoWord(lngDWord As Long) As Integer
    If lngDWord And &H8000& Then
        LoWord = &H8000 Or (lngDWord And &H7FFF&)
```

continues

Listing 37.14   Continued

```
    Else
        LoWord = lngDWord And &HFFFF&
    End If
End Function
'**********************************************************************
' Returns the upper 4 bytes of a DWORD
'**********************************************************************
Public Function HiWord(lngDWord As Long) As Integer
    HiWord = lngDWord \ &H10000
End Function
```

These functions all apply the same concept of taking a larger value and returning one half of the original bits. Examine the code to see how this extraction is done and experiment with them using our sample program. Because we only use signed values in VB, the return values for some of these might surprise you.

Listing 37.15 contains the code for the `picWord_Click` event. `picWord` is a control array of picture boxes that act like buttons for the purpose of setting and clearing bits. Figure 37.3 shows this control array in the WORD Bits frame on the right side of the form.

When one of these controls is clicked, the bit is either set or cleared using the `Xor` operator. The control is then displayed as either up or down to indicate its current setting. After the bit has been set and the button has been drawn, the labels are populated with a graphical representation of the current bit pattern.

Listing 37.15   HEXTOBIN.FRM—Toggling Specific Bits

```
'**********************************************************************
' Toggles bits on and off (PictureBox acting as button)
'**********************************************************************
Private Sub picWord_Click(Index As Integer)
    '**********************************************************************
    ' A persistent variable to hold the WORD
    '**********************************************************************
    Static sintBits As Integer
    '**********************************************************************
    ' Maintain the state of the PictureBox in its tag
    '**********************************************************************
    picWord(Index).Tag = Not CBool(picWord(Index).Tag)
    '**********************************************************************
    ' Declare an integer to mask with sintBits
    '**********************************************************************
    Dim intMask As Integer
    '**********************************************************************
    ' Get the mask for the bit button that was clicked
    '**********************************************************************
    Select Case Index
        Case 0 ' LSB
            intMask = &H1 '1
```

```
        Case 1
            intMask = &H2 '2
        Case 2
            intMask = &H4 '4
        Case 3 ' MSB
            intMask = &H8 '8
    End Select
    '****************************************************************
    ' You toggle bits by Xor'ing them with their mask value
    '****************************************************************
    sintBits = sintBits Xor intMask
    '****************************************************************
    ' Draw raised or depressed depending on the setting of the bits
    '****************************************************************
    Draw3DBorder picWord(Index), sintBits And intMask
    '****************************************************************
    ' Update the labels to show the different views of sintBits
    '****************************************************************
    UpdateLabels sintBits
End Sub
```

To set a specific bit, your code needs to apply the Xor operator to a bit mask. To put it simply, you mask with the "on" bit of the bit you are trying to set. For example, if you want to toggle the first bit, your mask would be 1. If you want to toggle the third bit, your mask would be 4. Our code sample demonstrates this with a 2-byte integer value (also called a WORD). HexToBin.frm also includes the source code for applying this same concept to a 4-byte long value (also called a DWORD). Rarely in your VB programming life will you need to see the actual binary representation of a value. However, the whole purpose of the HexToBin example is to present data in its hex, decimal, and binary equivalents. To convert a value into its binary equivalent, you need to divide a quotient by 2 until it can't be divided anymore and use the remainder of each iteration as the value of the bit. Listing 37.16 performs this operation in a loop and sets the value of each bit in a string that is returned to the caller.

Listing 37.16 HEXTOBIN.FRM—*ConvertToBinary* Displays a Value as Its Binary Equivalent

```
'******************************************************************
' Converts a long into its binary equivalent and returns a string
' with spaces between every four bits
'******************************************************************
Private Function ConvertToBinary(ByVal lngQuotient As Long, _
    Optional intBits As Integer) As String

    Dim strBinary As String
    Dim strReturn As String
    Dim i As Integer
    '**************************************************************
    ' If intBits isn't provided, then use the default of 4
    '**************************************************************
```

continues

Listing 37.16   Continued

```
    i = IIf(intBits, intBits, 4)
    '****************************************************************
    ' Create a string that is large enough to hold the bits so we can
    ' use the Mid statement to replace the zeroes with the real bit
    ' values.
    '****************************************************************
    strBinary = String(i, "0")
    '****************************************************************
    ' Loop while the quotient is not zero
    '****************************************************************
    Do While lngQuotient
        '****************************************************************
        ' The remainder is the bit value, so set this value in the str
        '****************************************************************
        Mid(strBinary, i, 1) = CStr(lngQuotient Mod 2)
        '****************************************************************
        ' Divide the quotient by 2 again
        '****************************************************************
        lngQuotient = lngQuotient \ 2
        '****************************************************************
        ' Decrement i, so we'll know which bit to set in strBinary
        '****************************************************************
        i = i - 1
    Loop
    '****************************************************************
    ' DWords can be hard to read, so add space between every four bits
    '****************************************************************
    For i = 1 To (intBits \ 4)
        strReturn = strReturn & Left(strBinary, 4) & " "
        strBinary = Mid(strBinary, 5)
    Next i
    '****************************************************************
    ' Return the neatly spaced binary representation of lngQuotient
    '****************************************************************
    ConvertToBinary = strReturn
End Function
```

Our code begins by building a default zero bit string. After we enter the loop, each bit is set in place using the Mid statement. After our loop, we check to see if the bit string was a DWORD. If it was, then we add spaces after each nibble so it is easier to read.

Listing 37.17 is similar to ConvertToBinary, except that it is a little easier because VB already includes the Hex function to convert a value to its hex equivalent. This code simply takes a value, converts it to its hex equivalent, and pads it with leading zeroes if it needs them.

Listing 37.17   HEXTOBIN.FRM—Displaying a Fixed Length Hex Value

```
'****************************************************************
' Returns a hex string with leading zeroes (if necessary)
```

```
'******************************************************************
Private Function GetFixedHex(vntBits As Variant, Optional intNibbles _
    As Integer) As String

    Dim strResult As String
    Dim strHex As String
    '******************************************************************
    ' If intNibbles wasn't provided, then assume 4 nibbles
    '******************************************************************
    intNibbles = IIf(intNibbles, intNibbles, 4)
    '******************************************************************
    ' Get the Hex representation of the bits
    '******************************************************************
    strHex = Hex(vntBits)
    '******************************************************************
    ' If negative, then check to see if we need to remove leading F's
    '******************************************************************
    If vntBits < 0 And Len(strHex) > intNibbles Then
        strHex = Mid(strHex, intNibbles + 1)
    '******************************************************************
    ' Otherwise, add leading zeroes (if necessary)
    '******************************************************************
    Else
        strHex = String(intNibbles - Len(strHex), "0") & strHex
    End If
    '******************************************************************
    ' Return the result with the VB hex prefix (&H)
    '******************************************************************
    GetFixedHex = "&H" & strHex
End Function
```

This code allows our program to always display our hex value in an easy-to-read format. Because each hex value represents a nibble, we ask the user how many nibbles should be represented by the result string. This allows us to determine how many leading zeroes might be needed to pad the string.

From Here...

This chapter's topic is broad, and we've only scratched the surface. You've seen a few techniques that you can adapt to your program; however, as your applications grow more complex, you'll discover many opportunities to develop advanced techniques specifically for a given situation. The best way to learn advanced code techniques is to study other programmers' work. Whenever you get a chance, look through program code to determine how the programmer is trying to accomplish a specific task. Microsoft also encourages the sharing of code among Visual Basic programmers by publishing articles that contain interesting (as well as problem-solving) techniques.

- Hundreds of great samples are available on the Microsoft Knowledge Base. You can browse the Knowledge Base on the Microsoft Web site at **http://www.microsoft. com/kb/**.

Appendix

Visual Basic Resources

This book has covered a lot of material about programming in Visual Basic. You have seen how to create the interface of your programs with forms and controls, how to perform tasks using the BASIC programming language, how to handle databases, and a host of other things. Although this book provides you with a great beginning in the world of Visual Basic programming, it should not be the end of your learning experience. As a programmer in a rapidly changing world, you should be constantly learning new skills and refining old ones.

To help you in this continuous learning process, this appendix provides you with a look at some of the additional controls you might want to explore, as well as some other materials that will help you learn more about programming in Visual Basic. ■

Using Other Controls

As you have seen through the course of the book, the bulk of your Visual Basic programs are made up of controls. These controls are used to build your program the same way ignition systems, radios, and transmissions are used to build a car. And, just like a car, you can add optional equipment to your development environment. This is done in the form of custom controls and add-ins. You have probably already seen how a few of these are used, as you learned about the Masked Edit control, Tabbed Dialog control, RichTextBox control, and others in earlier chapters.

Some of these controls provide an enhanced version of a standard control. This is akin to replacing the basic radio in a car with the radio/cassette/CD combination. It still handles the basic functions, but also provides you with more capabilities. Other controls provide completely new capabilities. This is like adding a sunroof to your car.

Using Other Controls You Already Have

Although we have already touched on a few of the custom controls and add-ins that are included with Visual Basic, there are a number of others that you might want to look at. The following controls and add-ins provide additional capabilities to Visual Basic that allow you to build better and more complex programs:

- **PicClip control**—Helps you manage picture images. This control is especially useful in helping with animation or toolbar applications.
- **MSComm control**—Is used to create applications that communicate directly through the serial or parallel ports of your computer.
- **MAPI controls**—Are used with e-mail applications.

You can find out more about these controls and others in Visual Basic's Custom Controls Help file. The Help file provides you with descriptions of the controls and their properties and methods. You will also find some usage examples.

Using Third-Party Controls

Third-party controls are one of the great benefits of using Visual Basic. Like other custom controls, these controls can allow your application to perform a variety of tasks. Typically vendors create both "enhanced" versions of the standard controls as well as controls that give you entirely new capabilities. Two of my favorite controls are VSView by VideoSoft and Calendar Widgets by Sheridan.

VSView provides a replacement for the Printer object in Visual Basic. With VSView, you can easily create multi-column tables and handle word wrapping on the page. You also don't have to worry about keeping track of when page breaks should occur. This is handled for you. Also, one of the best features of the product is that you can easily include print preview capabilities in your code (see Figure A.1). This requires some simple code that you can obtain from the samples included with the product.

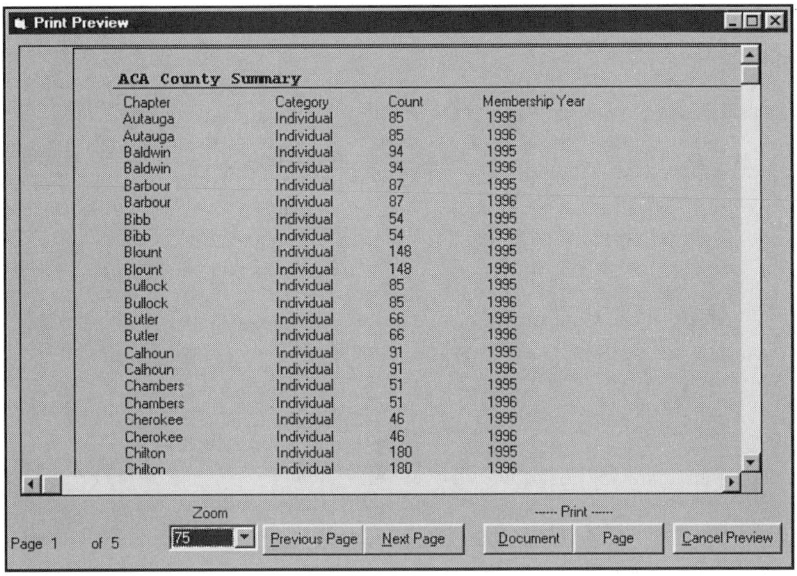

FIG. A.1

Print preview is made easy with one third-party control.

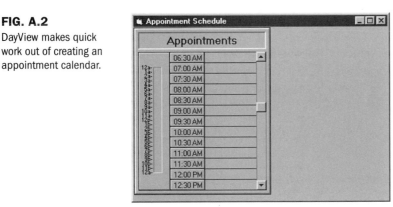

The other control, Calendar Widgets, provides you with a series of controls for handling dates. These controls make it easier for you to create programs such as appointment schedulers, to do lists, and other date dependent programs (see Figure A.2). One of the best controls in the group is the Date Combo. This control uses a drop-down calendar that allows the user to pick a date with ease (see Figure A.3). It also makes your programming job easier because you know that the dates are valid and are the correct data type. (Handling dates can be one of the greatest pains in programming.)

FIG. A.2

DayView makes quick work out of creating an appointment calendar.

There are a number of vendors that make third-party controls for a variety of tasks. Table A.1 provides a list of some of these vendors, as well as contact information.

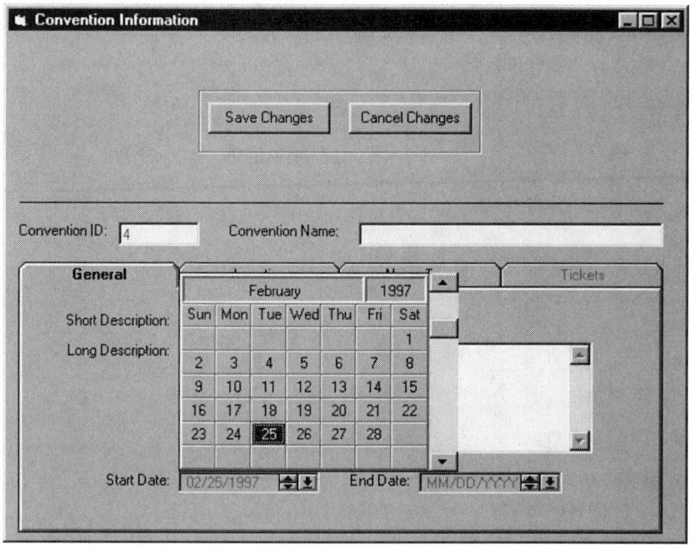

FIG. A.3
DateCombo makes selecting dates as simple as a mouse click.

Table A.1   Vendors of Custom Controls

Vendor	Web Site	Products
Apex Software Corporation	www.apexsc.com	MyData Control, True DBGrid, VBA Companion
Crescent Division of Progress Software	www.progress.com/ crescent	DBPak, PowerPak Pro, Internet Toolpak
Desaware, Inc.	www.desaware.com	SpyWorks, VersionStamper
FarPoint Technologies, Inc.	www.fpoint.com	ButtonMaker, Tab Pro, Spread
Sax Software	www.saxsoft.com	Basic Engine Pro, Setup Wizard, Webster Control
Sheridan Software Systems	www.shersoft.com	ClassAssist, Sheridan Components Suite, VBAssist
VideoSoft	www.videosoft.com	VSFlex/OCX, VS-OCX, VSView
Visual Components, Inc.	www.visualcomp.com	CodeBank, Formula One, First Impression, Visual Developers Suite Deal OCX

Finding More Information About Visual Basic

This book has provided you with a lot of the information you need to develop programs using Visual Basic. Obviously, though, there is a lot of information that could not be squeezed into this book. Fortunately for you, there are a number of other sources available to teach you about advanced programming topics.

The first source of additional information is part of the Visual Basic package itself. Visual Basic comes with an extensive set of help files that provide all the details about each control and programming command. If this is not enough for you, VB Books Online also comes with the Visual Basic package. This product provides you with additional in-depth help on a variety of programming topics. Books Online also has a good search engine that helps you find what you are looking for (see Figure A.4).

FIG. A.4
VB Books Online is a useful database of programming help and sample code.

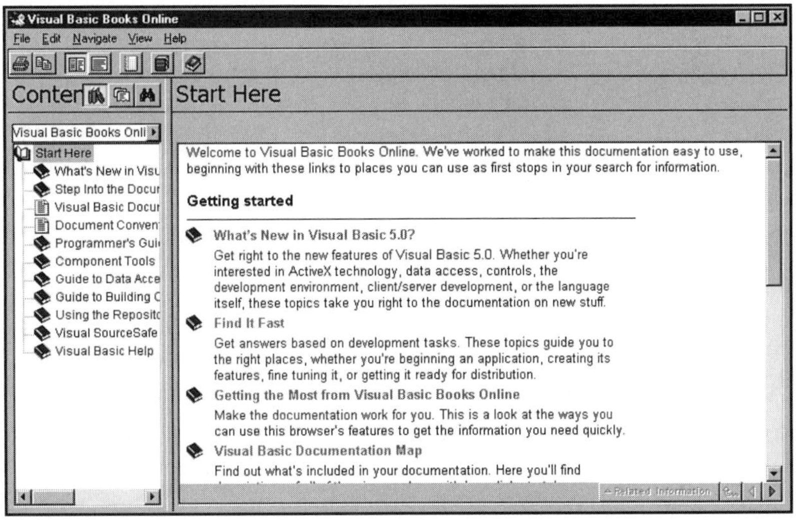

Using Microsoft Sources

As you might expect, Microsoft is a great source of additional information on Visual Basic. There are two really good sources of information available from Microsoft. One is free, and the other is available at a reasonable price.

The free resource is, of course, Microsoft's Visual Basic Web site. You can access this site at **http://www.microsoft.com/vbasic**. This site, shown in Figure A.5, provides some great information, including the following:

- Information about the latest developments in Visual Basic
- Access to the knowledge base of bug fixes and coding techniques
- Free downloads of sample programs and occasionally some product betas
- Descriptions of what some companies are doing with Visual Basic programs

FIG. A.5

Microsoft's Visual Basic Web site provides samples, Visual Basic technical articles, and access to MSDN information.

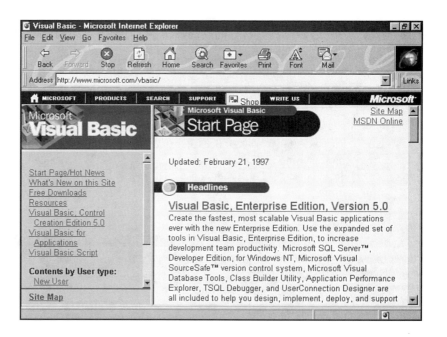

The other source available from Microsoft is the Microsoft Developer's Network (MSDN). This product is a subscription to a set of CDs. These CDs come about once per quarter and provide you with the latest information on bugs, Microsoft reports about Visual Basic topics, papers from technical conferences, and a bunch of other information. In addition to the CDs, Microsoft sends out the MSDN newsletter to its subscribers. The newsletter also provides timely information about Visual Basic and other Microsoft developer products.

Reading Other Books About Visual Basic

The first source of additional information are books that cover advanced topics such as OLE automation and client/server programming. Other books delve deeply into building multimedia applications, the Windows API, and programming with objects.

Some additional books available from Macmillan include the following:

- *Building Windows 95 Applications with Visual Basic*
- *Building Multimedia Applications with Visual Basic*
- *Database Developer's Guide with Visual Basic*
- *Doing Objects in Microsoft Visual Basic*

You will also find some good books published by Que on related topics such as the following:

- *Special Edition Using Microsoft Access 97*
- *Access 97 Expert Solutions*
- *Special Edition Using VBA for Excel*

Using Other Print Materials

In addition to books, there are a number of magazines that are dedicated to Visual Basic. These magazines provide descriptions of programming techniques, reviews of custom controls, and informative columns by noted authors. Table A.2 lists several of these magazines along with their publishers and contact numbers.

Table A.2   Magazines Covering Visual Basic

Magazine	Publisher	Phone
Visual Basic Programmer's Journal	Fawcette Technical Publications	(800) 848-5523
VB Tech Journal	Oakley Publishing Co.	(800) 234-0386
Inside Visual Basic	The Cobb Group	(800) 223-8720
Access/Visual Basic Advisor	Advisor Publications, Inc.	(619) 483-6400

Using Online Resources

Finally, your best source of the most up-to-date information is the Web. There are a number of Web sites out there that are devoted exclusively to Visual Basic, as well as sites that include Visual Basic among their topics.

Using Web Sites   The first site is Que's Visual Basic Resource Center. This site, shown in Figure A.6, contains information relating to the following:

- The latest books on Visual Basic
- Downloadable files containing Visual Basic tools
- Online Books, which are full text online copies of some of Que's books about Visual Basic
- Links to other Visual Basic sites

The Visual Basic Resource center can be found at **http://www.mcp.com/que/vb4/**.

Another great site is the WINDX site maintained by the publishers of Visual Basic Programmer's Journal. This site contains, among other things, the latest news about Visual Basic products and source code for the articles from the VBPJ Magazine. The WINDX site can be found at **http://www.windx.com** (see Figure A.7).

One final site to mention is Carl and Gary's Visual Basic Homepage. This is one of the oldest and best known Web sites devoted to Visual Basic. As with other sites, this one contains the latest news about VB, reviews of third-party controls, technical papers about in-depth VB topics, and links to other Web sites. Visit Carl & Gary's, shown in Figure A.8, at **http://www.apexwsc.com/vb/**.

FIG. A.6
Que's Visual Basic
Resource Center.

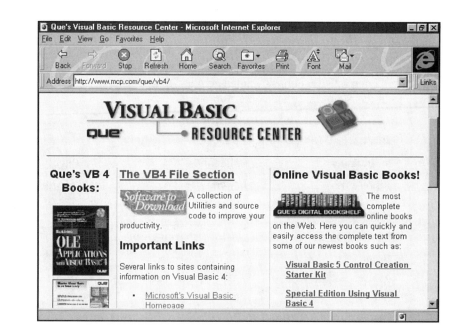

FIG. A.7
*Visual Basic
Programmer's Journal*
maintains the Windows
Development Exchange
(WINDX) site.

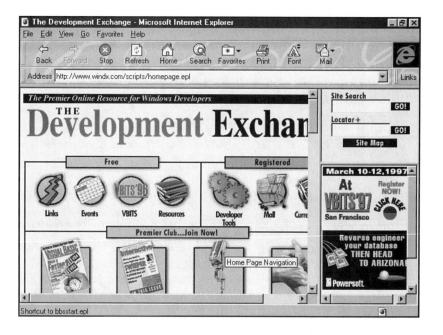

FIG. A.8
Carl & Gary's is one of the best known Visual Basic Web sites.

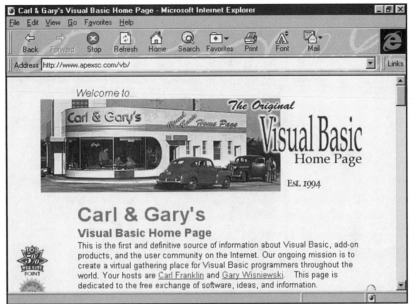

App

A

Using Other Online Resources In addition to the Web sites mentioned earlier, there are newsgroups on the Web that are devoted to Visual Basic. There are also two major forums on CompuServe that are devoted to Visual Basic—MSBASIC and VBPJFORUM.

The following is a partial list of Visual Basic newsgroups:

- **comp.lang.basic.visual**
- **comp.lang.basic.visual.database**
- **microsoft.public.vb.3rdparty** (information about third-party controls)
- **microsoft.public.vb.internet** (Internet controls)
- **microsoft.public.vb.database** (general database issues)
- **microsoft.public.vb.database.dao** (Data Access Object issues)
- **microsoft.public.vb.database.rdo** (Remote Data Objects issues)
- **microsoft.public.vb.installation** (setup issues)
- **microsoft.public.vb.winapi** (Windows API topics)

Index

C

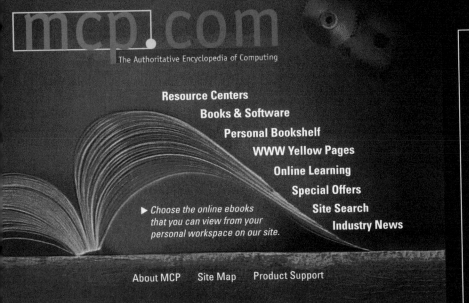

Complete and Return This Card
for a *FREE* Computer Book Catalog

Thank you for purchasing this book! You have purchased a superior computer book written expressly for your needs. To continue to provide the kind of up-to-date, pertinent coverage you've come to expect from us, we need to hear from you. Please take a minute to complete and return this self-addressed, postage-paid form. In return, we'll send you a free catalog of all our computer books on topics ranging from word processing to programming and the Internet.

Mr. ☐   Mrs. ☐   Ms. ☐   Dr. ☐

Name (first) [ ] (M.I.) ☐ (last) [ ]

Address [ ]
[ ]

City [ ]   State [ ]   Zip [ ]

Phone [ ]   Fax [ ]

Company Name [ ]

E-mail address [ ]

1. Please check at least three (3) influencing factors for purchasing this book.

Front or back cover information on book .... ☐
Special approach to the content .... ☐
Completeness of content .... ☐
Author's reputation .... ☐
Publisher's reputation .... ☐
Book cover design or layout .... ☐
Index or table of contents of book .... ☐
Price of book .... ☐
Special effects, graphics, illustrations .... ☐
Other (Please specify): _____ ☐

2. How did you first learn about this book?

Saw in Macmillan Computer Publishing catalog .... ☐
Recommended by store personnel .... ☐
Saw the book on bookshelf at store .... ☐
Recommended by a friend .... ☐
Received advertisement in the mail .... ☐
Saw an advertisement in: _____ ☐
Read book review in: _____ ☐
Other (Please specify): _____ ☐

3. How many computer books have you purchased in the last six months?

This book only .... ☐   3 to 5 books .... ☐
2 books .... ☐   More than 5 .... ☐

4. Where did you purchase this book?

Bookstore .... ☐
Computer Store .... ☐
Consumer Electronics Store .... ☐
Department Store .... ☐
Office Club .... ☐
Warehouse Club .... ☐
Mail Order .... ☐
Direct from Publisher .... ☐
Internet site .... ☐
Other (Please specify): _____ ☐

5. How long have you been using a computer?

☐ Less than 6 months   ☐ 6 months to a year
☐ 1 to 3 years   ☐ More than 3 years

6. What is your level of experience with personal computers and with the subject of this book?

	With PCs	With subject of book
New	☐	☐
Casual	☐	☐
Accomplished	☐	☐
Expert	☐	☐

Source Code ISBN: 0-7897-1288-1

7. Which of the following best describes your job title?

- Administrative Assistant ☐
- Coordinator ☐
- Manager/Supervisor ☐
- Director ☐
- Vice President ☐
- President/CEO/COO ☐
- Lawyer/Doctor/Medical Professional ☐
- Teacher/Educator/Trainer ☐
- Engineer/Technician ☐
- Consultant ☐
- Not employed/Student/Retired ☐
- Other (Please specify): _____ ☐

8. Which of the following best describes the area of the company your job title falls under?

- Accounting ☐
- Engineering ☐
- Manufacturing ☐
- Operations ☐
- Marketing ☐
- Sales ☐
- Other (Please specify): _____ ☐

9. What is your age?

- Under 20 ☐
- 21-29 ☐
- 30-39 ☐
- 40-49 ☐
- 50-59 ☐
- 60-over ☐

10. Are you:

- Male ☐
- Female ☐

11. Which computer publications do you read regularly? (Please list)

_____
_____
_____
_____
_____
_____
_____
_____
_____

Comments: _____
_____
_____

Fold here and scotch-tape to mail

Sams Teach Yourself ActiveX Control Programming with Visual Basic 5 in 21 Days

Keith Brophy & Tim Koets

Visual Basic is a programming language that lets users add interactivity and multimedia to their Web sites by working with Microsoft's ActiveX technologies. This book shows users how to maximize Visual Basic to create ActiveX applications that can be used with Microsoft's Internet Explorer Web browser. Covers Visual Basic and ActiveX.

CD-ROM contains all the source code from the book, powerful utilities, and third party software.

Price: $39.99 USA/$56.95 CAN   *User Level: Casual–Expert*
ISBN: 1-57521-245-5   *600 pages*

Sams Teach Yourself Visual Café 2 in 21 Days

Mike Cohn

Symantec has finally released the first true visual programming language based on Java, Visual Café—shipping with very little documentation.

Teach Yourself Visual Café 2 in 21 Days will teach you how to use the Symantec Visual Café development environment to do Java programming. This book assumes that you already knows some Java, still the hottest programming language for the Web.

Price: $39.99 US/$56.95 CAN   *User Level: New–Casual*
ISBN: 1-57521-303-6   *888 pages*

Sams Teach Yourself Microsoft Visual InterDev in 21 Days

Michael Van Hoozer

Using the familiar, day-by-day format of the best-selling *Teach Yourself* series, this easy-to-follow tutorial provides users with a solid understanding of Visual InterDev, Microsoft's new Web application development environment. In no time, users will learn how to perform a variety of tasks, including front-end scripting, database and query design, content creation, server-side scripting, and more.

Price: $39.99 USA/$56.95 CAN   *User Level: New–Casual–Accomplished*
ISBN: 1-57521-093-2   *816 pages*

Sams Teach Yourself Visual Basic for Applications 5 in 21 Days, Third Edition

Matthew Harris

This book covers the fundamental aspects of this programming language and teaches novice programmers how to design, create, and debug macro programs written in VBA. Through its coverage of 32-bit Microsoft Office applications running on Windows 95, you learn techniques to add functionality to existing applications such as Microsoft Excel and Microsoft Access.

Price: $39.99 USA/$56.95 CAN   *User Level: New–Casual*
ISBN: 0-672-31016-3   *1,214 pages*

Add to Your Sams Library Today with the Best Books for Programming, Operating Systems, and New Technologies

To order, visit our Web site at www.mcp.com or fax us at

1-800-835-3202

ISBN	Quantity	Description of Item	Unit Cost	Total Cost
1-57521-245-5		Sams Teach Yourself ActiveX Control Programming with Visual Basic 5 in 21 Days	$39.99	
1-57521-303-6		Sams Teach Yourself Visual Café 2 in 21 Days	$39.99	
1-57521-093-2		Sams Teach Yourself Microsoft Visual InterDev in 21 Days	$39.99	
0-672-31016-3		Sams Teach Yourself Visual Basic for Applications 5 in 21 Days, Third Edition	$39.99	
		Shipping and Handling: See information below.		
		TOTAL		

Shipping and Handling

Standard	$ 5.00
2nd Day	$10.00
Next Day	$17.50
International	$40.00

201 W. 103rd Street, Indianapolis, Indiana 46290   1-800-835-3202—Fax

Book ISBN 0-7897-1288-1